CIVIL AIRCRAFT MARKINGS 2021

The first edition of ABC Civil Aircraft Markings published over seventy years ago in 1950 comprised just 72 pages. Just as today CAM listed British civil aircraft registrations in alphabetical order with the type and owner or operator. The information was correct to June 1950 and the latest entry was G-AMCG an ex-RAF Halifax. That first edition also included a listing of overseas airlines likely to operate into the UK with entries beginning with Trans Canada Air Lines North Star CF-TFA and ending with EI AI DC-4 4X-ACD. Throughout its history Civil Aircraft Markings has maintained the same basic format but is of course now a much larger book with the 2020 edition stretching to 464 pages.

The familiar 'G' prefixed four-letter registration system was adopted in 1919 after a short-lived spell with serial numbers commencing at K-100. Until July 1928 the UK allocations were issued in the G-Exxx range but, as a result of further international agreements, this series ended at G-EBZZ, the replacement being G-Axxx. From this point registrations were issued in a reasonably orderly manner through to G-AZZZ, the position reached in July 1972. There were, however, two exceptions. In order to prevent possible confusion with signal codes, the G-AQxx sequence was omitted, while G-AUxx was reserved for Australian use originally. In recent years however, individual requests for a mark in the latter range have been granted by the Authorities.

Although the next logical sequence was started at G-Bxxx, it was not long before the strictly applied rules relating to aircraft registration began to be relaxed. Permission was readily given for personalised marks to be issued, incorporating virtually any four-letter combination, while re-registration also became a common feature – a practice almost unheard of in the past. In this book, where this has taken place at some time, all previous UK identities carried appear in parenthesis after the operator's/owner's name. For example, during its career Cherokee Six G-PECK has also carried the identities G-AYWK, G-LADA, G-MCAR and G-ETAV.

Some aircraft have also been allowed to wear military markings without displaying their civil identity. In this case the serial number actually carried is shown in parenthesis after the type's name. For example Auster 6A G-ARRX flies in military colours as VF512, its genuine previous identity. As an aid to the identification of such machines, a conversion list is provided.

Various factors caused an acceleration in the number of registrations allocated by the Civil Aviation Authority in the early 1980s. The first surge followed the discovery that it was possible to register plastic bags, and other items even less likely to fly, on payment of the standard fee. This erosion of the main register was checked in early 1982 by the issue of a special sequence for such devices commencing with G-FYAA. Powered hang-gliders provided the second glut of allocations as a result of the decision that these types should be officially registered. Although a few of the early examples penetrated the current in-sequence register, in due course all new applicants were given marks in special ranges, this time G-MBxx, G-MGxx, G-MJxx, G-MMxx, G-MNxx, G-MTxx, G-MVxx, G-MWxx, G-MYxx and G-MZxx. It took some time before all microlights displayed an official mark but gradually the registration was carried, the size and position depending on the dimensions of the component to which it was applied.

There was news of a further change in mid-1998 when the CAA announced that with immediate effect microlights would be issued with registrations in the normal sequence alongside aircraft in other classes. In addition, it meant that owners could also apply for a personalised identity upon payment of the then current fee of £170 from April 1999, a low price for those wishing to display their status symbol. These various changes played their part in exhausting the current G-Bxxx range after some 26 years, with G-BZxx coming into use before the end of 1999. As this batch approached completion the next series to be used began at G-CBxx instead of the anticipated G-CAxx. The reason for this step was to avoid the re-use of marks issued in Canada during the 1920s, although a few have appeared more recently as personalised UK registrations.

Another large increase in the number of aircraft registered resulted from the EU-inspired changes in glider registration. After many years of self-regulation by the British Gliding Association, new gliders must now comply with EASA regulations and hence receive registrations in the main G-Cxxx sequence. The phasing-in of EASA registration for the then existing glider fleet was a fairly lengthy process but came to an end by the beginning of 2012.

September 2007 saw the issue of the 50,000th UK aircraft registration with G-MITC being allocated to a Robinson R44 Raven. The total number of aircraft on the Register has risen over the past 25 years from just under 10,000 at the beginning of 1985 to a figure which now exceeds 21,000. Each year there are changes made to about 35% of the total, whether by new allocations, cancellations, changes of ownership or changes of type.

The Isle of Man launched its own aircraft register in May 2007 aimed mainly at private and corporate business jets and helicopters and the first to be allocated was Cessna 525B Citation M-ELON. This has now been followed by the Channel Islands Aircraft Registry which was launched by the States of Guernsey on 9 December 2013 and the Jersey Aircraft Registry in November 2015. The M- (Isle of Man), 2- (Guernsey) and TJ- (Jersey) registers can be found at the end of the British Civil Aircraft Registrations section of this book. Also included are some non-airworthy and preserved aircraft which are shown with a star (★) after the type.

Included in this book are details of those overseas airliners most likely to be seen at UK airports on scheduled or charter passenger or cargo flights. It is always difficult knowing what to include as at the time of writing the airlines' summer programmes have not been finalised. However, the full fleets of the big European 'national' carriers such as Air France, Lufthansa, SAS and others are listed although it is unlikely that many of their long haul aircraft will visit the UK in any given year.

The three-letter codes used by airlines to prefix flight numbers are included for those carriers most likely to appear in the UK. Radio frequencies for the many UK airfields and airports are also listed.

A book of this nature is already out of date before it is published as changes to aircraft registers and airline fleets take place on a daily basis. The 2021 edition includes new allocations to the UK Register up to early February 2021.

ASW

ACKNOWLEDGEMENTS: Once again thanks are extended to the Registration Department of the Civil Aviation Authority for its assistance and allowing access to its files, thanks ara also given to all those who have contributed items for possible use in this edition.

AJ Aviation's shop and retail counter **IS OPEN** at 4 |Horton Parade, Horton Road, West Drayton, Middlesex, UB7 8EP. Monday thru Saturday 10.00 – 16.00 hours. LAAS International & Air Britain members prices are available on over the counter purchases, on production of a current membership card. We also offer a 10% discount on selected items in our shop to laas International & Air Britain Members. We carry a varied range of aviation related books from other publishers, a large selection of Black & White photographs and a large range of plastic kits & accessories.

We attend numerous aviation Fly-ins, conventions and model shows. We look forward to seeing you soon.

We accept major credit & debit cards, cheques and postal order made payable to AJ Aviaion. POST FREE IN THE UK, OVERSEAS AT COST.

You can now follow us on Twitter & Facebook. Our website is **www.ajaviation.co.uk**

BOOKS FROM AJ AVIATION PUBLISHING
Blackbushe – London's lost airport 1942-1960   £14.99p.

AIRLINES 2021
Soft back in card cover with comb binding   £17.95p.
Square bound with wrap around cover   £17.95p.
Refill Pages for those who already have a binder   £17.95p.
Loose-leaf Binder edition   £22.95p.

WORLD AIRLINE FLEETS 2021 (Back to Basics)
Soft back in card cover with comb binding   £11.95p.
Soft back in card cover square bound with wrap around cover   £11.95p.
AIRLINES TO EUROPE 2021   £ 7.50p.

JET AIRLINER PRODUCTION LIST – VOLUME 3 (Oct.2019)
Covers RJ.100/200/700/900/1000, Comac ARJ.21, Convair CV 880/990, Douglas DC-8/9/10 & MD 80,
Embraer 135/145/170/190, Lockheed L-1011, McDonnell-Douglas MD-11 & Mitsubishi Spacejet.
Soft back in card cover with comb binding   £21.95p.
Square bound with wrap around cover   £21.95p.
Refill pages for those who already have a binder   £21.95p.
Loose-leaf Binder Edition   £27.95p.

TURBOPROP AIRLINER PRODUCTION LIST – VOLUME 1 (2016)
Soft back in card cover with comb binding   £14.95p.
Square bound with wrap around cover   £14.95p.
Refill pages for those who already have a binder   £14.95p.
Loose-leaf Binder Edition   £19.95p.

JET AIRLINER PRODUCTION LIST – VOLUME 2 (2014)
Covers Airbus A318/319/320/321/330/340/380/Caravelle
Soft back in card cover with comb binding   £19.95p.
Square bound with wrap around cover   £19.95p.
Refill pages for those who already have a binder   £19.95p.
Loose-leaf Binder Edition   £25.95p.

BOOKS FROM THE AVIATION HOBBY SHOP
JET AIRLINER PRODUCTION LIST – VOLUME 1 BOEING PART 2 (2012)
Covers 737 NG/747/757/767/777 & 787
Soft back in card cover with comb binding   £17.95p.
Square bound with wrap around cover   £17.95p.
Refill pages for those who already have a binder   £17.95p.
Loose-leaf Binder Edition   £23.95p.

JET AIRLINER PRODUCTION LIST – VOLUME 1 BOEING PART 1 (2011)
Covers 717/707/720/727 & 737 Classic
(2) Square bound with wrap around cover   £17.95p.
Refill pages for those who already have a binder   £17.95p.
(4) Loose-leaf Binder Edition   £23.95p.

PISTON ENGINED AIRLINER PRODUCTION LIST
Covers Ambassador, Carvair, Tudor, York, Trislander, Stratocruiser,
Bristol 170, Canadair C-4, Convair 240/330/440, Curtiss C-46, DH.114
Halifax/Halton, Hermes, DC-4/6/7 L-049/649/749/1049/1649,
Martin 2-0-2/4-0-4, Marathon, SAAB Scandia, Twin Pioneer, Viking
Soft back in card cover with comb binding   £16.95p.
Square bound with wrap around cover   £16.95p.
Refill pages for those who already have a binder   £16.95p.
Loose-leaf Binder Edition   £21.95p.

AJ AVIATION AIRLINER NEWS

Published Approximately every four weeks, with details of new and secondhand delivery dates, first flight dates, constructors numbers and line numbers. Done in country order, and by registration. We also list all we know about future orders, airliner demises, airlines going into store. Aso photographs from our readers home countries and their travels around the globe. As well as readers in the UK, we are read in the following countries. United States, Canada, Ireland, France, Germany, Austria, The Netherlands, Belgium, Cyprus and the Seychelles. **It is only available by email attachment, there is no paper version and best of all IT'S FREE.** CONTACT:-ajnewsletter@outlook.com

PROPLINER AVIATION MAGAZINE
2018 EDITION   £12.00p.
2019 EDITION   £12.00p.
2020 EDITION   £12.00p.
2021 EDITION April   £TBA

AJ AVIATION (CAM 2021), 4 Horton Parade, Horton Road, West Drayton, Middlesex, UB7 8EP.
Phone: 01895 442123 Email:ajaviation@outlook.com

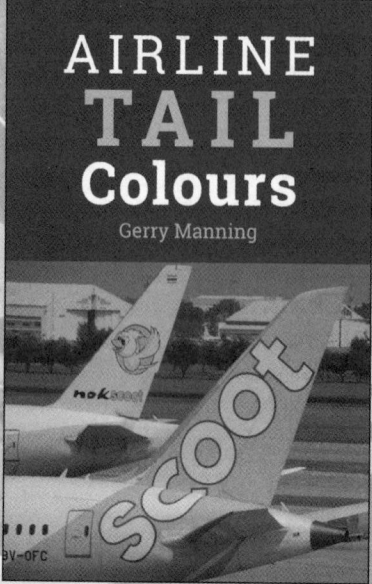

A2-	Botswana	JY-	Jordan
A3-	Tonga	LN-	Norway
A5-	Bhutan	LV-	Argentina
A6-	United Arab Emirates	LX-	Luxembourg
A7-	Qatar	LY-	Lithuania
A8-	Liberia	LZ-	Bulgaria
A9C-	Bahrain	M-	Isle of Man
A40-	Oman	N-	United States of America
AP-	Pakistan	OB-	Peru
B-	China/Taiwan/Hong Kong/Macao	OD-	Lebanon
C-	Canada	OE-	Austria
C2-	Nauru	OH-	Finland
C3-	Andorra	OK-	Czech Republic
C5-	Gambia	OM-	Slovakia
C6-	Bahamas	OO-	Belgium
C9-	Mozambique	OY-	Denmark
CC-	Chile	P-	North Korea
CN-	Morocco	P2-	Papua New Guinea
CP-	Bolivia	P4-	Aruba
CS-	Portugal	PH-	Netherlands
CU-	Cuba	PJ-	Netherlands Antilles
CX-	Uruguay	PK-	Indonesia
D-	Germany	PP-	Brazil
D2-	Angola	PR-	Brazil
D4-	Cape Verde Islands	PT-	Brazil
D6-	Comores Islands	PU-	Brazil
DQ-	Fiji	PZ-	Surinam
E3-	Eritrea	RA-	Russia
E5-	Cook Islands	RDPL-	Laos
E7-	Bosnia and Herzegovina	RP-	Philippines
EC-	Spain	S2-	Bangladesh
EI-	Republic of Ireland	S5-	Slovenia
EK-	Armenia	S7-	Seychelles
EP-	Iran	S9-	Säo Tomé
ER-	Moldova	SE-	Sweden
ES-	Estonia	SP-	Poland
ET-	Ethiopia	ST-	Sudan
EW-	Belarus	SU-	Egypt
EX-	Kyrgyzstan	SX-	Greece
EY-	Tajikistan	T2-	Tuvalu
EZ-	Turkmenistan	T3-	Kiribati
F-	France, inc Colonies and Protectorates	T7-	San Marino
G-	United Kingdom	T8-	Palau
H4-	Solomon Islands	T9-	Bosnia and Herzegovina
HA-	Hungary	TC-	Turkey
HB-	Switzerland and Liechtenstein	TF-	Iceland
HC-	Ecuador	TG-	Guatemala
HH-	Haiti	TI-	Costa Rica
HI-	Dominican Republic	TJ-	Cameroon
HK-	Colombia	TL-	Central African Republic
HL-	South Korea	TN-	Republic of Congo
HP-	Panama	TR-	Gabon
HR-	Honduras	TS-	Tunisia
HS-	Thailand	TT-	Tchad
HZ-	Saudi Arabia	TU-	Ivory Coast
I-	Italy	TY-	Benin
J2-	Djibouti	TZ-	Mali
J3-	Grenada	UK-	Uzbekistan
J5-	Guinea Bissau	UN-	Kazakhstan
J6-	St. Lucia	UR-	Ukraine
J7-	Dominica	V2-	Antigua
J8-	St. Vincent	V3-	Belize
JA-	Japan	V4	St. Kitts & Nevis
JU-	Mongolia	V5-	Namibia

Notes	Reg	Type	Owner or Operator
	G-AAAH	DH.60G Moth (replica) (BAPC 168) ★	Yorkshire Air Museum/Elvington
	G-AAAH	DH.60G Moth ★	Science Museum/South Kensington
	G-AACA	Avro 504K (BAPC 177) ★	Brooklands Museum of Aviation/Weybridge
	G-AACN	HP.39 Gugnunc★	Science Museum/South Kensington
	G-AADR	DH.60GM Moth	E. V. Moffatt
	G-AAEG	DH.60G Gipsy Moth	I. B. Grace
	G-AAHI	DH.60G Moth	Nigel John Western Reid Discretionary Settlement 2008
	G-AAHY	DH.60M Moth	D. J. Elliott
	G-AAIN	Parnall Elf II	The Shuttleworth Collection/Old Warden
	G-AAJT	DH.60G Moth	M. R. Paul
	G-AALY	DH.60G Moth	K. M. Fresson
	G-AAMX	DH.60GM Moth ★	RAF Museum/Hendon
	G-AANG	Blériot XI	The Shuttleworth Collection/Old Warden
	G-AANH	Deperdussin Monoplane	The Shuttleworth Collection/Old Warden
	G-AANI	Blackburn Monoplane	The Shuttleworth Collection/Old Warden
	G-AANJ	L.V.G. C VI (7198/18)	Aerospace Museum/Cosford
	G-AANL	DH.60M Moth	R. A. Palmer
	G-AANO	DH.60GMW Gipsy Moth	K. F. Crumplin
	G-AAOK	Curtiss Wright Travel Air 12Q	Just Plane Trading Ltd
	G-AAPZ	Desoutter I (mod.)	The Shuttleworth Collection
	G-AATC	DH.80A Puss Moth	R. A. Palmer
	G-AAUP	Klemm L.25-1A	Oldstead Aero LLP
	G-AAWO	DH.60G Moth	Iain Charles Reid Discretionary Settlement 2009
	G-AAXG	DH 60M Moth	S. H. Kidston
	G-AAXK	Klemm L.25-1A ★	C. C. Russell-Vick (stored)
	G-AAYT	DH.60G Moth	P. Groves
	G-AAYX	Southern Martlet	The Shuttleworth Collection
	G-AAZG	DH.60G Moth	E. G. & N. S. C. English
	G-AAZP	DH.80A Puss Moth	R. P. Williams
	G-ABAA	Avro 504K ★	Manchester Museum of Science & Industry
	G-ABAG	DH.60G Moth	A. & P. A. Wood
	G-ABBB	B.105A Bulldog IIA (K2227) ★	RAF Museum/Hendon
	G-ABDA	DH.60G Moth	T. A. Bechtolsheimer
	G-ABDW	DH.80A Puss Moth (VH-UQB) ★	Museum of Flight/East Fortune
	G-ABDX	DH.60G Moth	M. D. Souch
	G-ABEV	DH.60G Moth	S. L. G. Darch
	G-ABHE	Aeronca C.2	N. S. Chittenden
	G-ABIH	DH.80A Puss Moth	M. D. Souch
	G-ABJJ	DH.60G Moth	B. R. Cox
	G-ABLM	Cierva C.24 ★	De Havilland Heritage Museum/London Colney
	G-ABLS	DH.80A Puss Moth	T. W. Harris
	G-ABMR	Hawker Hart 2 (J9941) ★	RAF Museum/Hendon
	G-ABNT	Civilian C.A.C.1 Coupe	Shipping & Airlines Ltd
	G-ABNX	Redwing 2	Redwing Syndicate
	G-ABOI	Wheeler Slymph ★	Midland Air Museum/Coventry
	G-ABOX	Sopwith Pup (N5195)	C. M. D. & A. P. St. Cyrien
	G-ABSD	DH.60G Moth	M. E. Vaisey
	G-ABUL†	DH.82A Tiger Moth ★	F.A.A. Museum/Yeovilton (G-AOXG)
	G-ABUS	Comper CLA.7 Swift	R. C. F. Bailey
	G-ABVE	Arrow Active 2	B. R. Cox
	G-ABWD	DH.83 Fox Moth	M. D. Souch
	G-ABWP	Spartan Arrow	R. T. Blain
	G-ABXL	Granger Archaeopteryx ★	J. R. Granger
	G-ABYA	DH.60G Gipsy Moth	M. J. Luck
	G-ABZB	DH.60G-III Moth Major	G. M. Turner
	G-ACBH	Blackburn B.2 ★	South Yorkshire Aircraft Museum/Doncaster
	G-ACCB	DH.83 Fox Moth	E. A. Gautrey
	G-ACDA	DH.82A Tiger Moth	J. Turnbull
	G-ACDC	DH.82A Tiger Moth	Tiger Club Ltd
	G-ACDI	DH.82A Tiger Moth	Doublecube Aviation LLP
	G-ACDJ	DH.82A Tiger Moth	R. H. & J. A. Cooper
	G-ACEJ	DH.83 Fox Moth	K. F. Grimminger
	G-ACET	DH.84 Dragon	G. Cormack
	G-ACGL	Comper Swift ★	RAF Museum/Cosford
	G-ACGS	DH.85 Leopard Moth	M. J. Miller (G-APKH)
	G-ACGT	Avro 594 Avian IIIA	B. R. Cox

Reg	Type	Owner or Operator	Notes
G-ACGZ	DH.60G-III Moth Major	N. H. Lemon	
G-ACIT	DH.84 Dragon ★	Science Museum/Wroughton	
G-ACLL	DH.85 Leopard Moth	V. M & D. C. M. Stiles	
G-ACMA	DH.85 Leopard Moth	C. A. Hawkins	
G-ACMD	DH.82A Tiger Moth	M. J. Bonnick	
G-ACMN	DH.85 Leopard Moth	M. R. & K. E. Slack	
G-ACNS	DH.60G-III Moth Major	D. Shew	
G-ACOJ	DH.85 Leopard Moth	Norman Aeroplane Trust	
G-ACOL	DH.85 Leopard Moth	J. Cresswell	
G-ACSP	DH.88 Comet ★	T. M., M. L., D. A. & P. M. Jones	
G-ACSS	DH.88 Comet ★	The Shuttleworth Collection Grosvenor House/Old Warden	
G-ACSS†	DH.88 Comet (replica) ★	G. Gayward (BAPC216)	
G-ACSS†	DH.88 Comet (replica) ★	The Galleria Hatfield (BAPC257)	
G-ACTF	Comper CLA.7 Swift ★	The Shuttleworth Collection/Old Warden	
G-ACUS	DH.85 Leopard Moth	R. A. & V. A. Gammons	
G-ACUU	Cierva C.30A (HM580) ★	Imperial War Museum/Duxford	
G-ACUX	S.16 Scion (VH-UUP) ★	Ulster Folk & Transport Museum	
G-ACVA	Kay Gyroplane ★	National Museum of Scotland/Edinburgh	
G-ACWM	Cierva C.30A (AP506) ★	The Helicopter Museum/Weston-super-Mare	
G-ACWP	Cierva C.30A (AP507) ★	Science Museum/South Kensington	
G-ACXB	DH.60G-III Moth Major	D. F. Hodgkinson	
G-ACXE	B.K. L-25C Swallow	J. F. Copeman	
G-ACYK	Spartan Cruiser III ★	Museum of Flight (front fuselage)/East Fortune	
G-ACYZ	Miles M.2H Hawk Major	M. R. Paul	
G-ADAH	DH.89A Dragon Rapide ★	Manchester Museum of Science & Industry Pioneer	
G-ADEV	Avro 504K (E3273)	The Shuttleworth Collection/Old Warden (G-ACNB)	
G-ADGP	M.2L Hawk Speed Six	The Richard Ormonde Shuttleworth Remembrance Trust	
G-ADGT	DH.82A Tiger Moth (BB697)	The London Aerobatic Company Ltd	
G-ADGV	DH.82A Tiger Moth	M. van Dijk & M. R. Van der Straaten (G-BACW)	
G-ADHD	DH.60G-III Moth Major	M. E. Vaisey	
G-ADIA	DH.82A Tiger Moth	S. J. Beaty	
G-ADJJ	DH.82A Tiger Moth	J. M. Preston	
G-ADKC	DH.87B Hornet Moth	C. G. & S. Winch	
G-ADKK	DH.87B Hornet Moth	S. W. Barratt & A. J. Herbert	
G-ADKL	DH.87B Hornet Moth	J. S. & P. R. Johnson	
G-ADKM	DH.87B Hornet Moth	J. M. O. Miller	
G-ADLY	DH.87B Hornet Moth	Treetops Aircraft LLP	
G-ADMF	BA L.25C Swallow II	D. A. Edwards	
G-ADMT	DH.87B Hornet Moth	J. A. Jennings	
G-ADMW	M.2H Hawk Major (DG590) ★	RAF Museum Storage & Restoration Centre/RAF Stafford	
G-ADND	DH.87B Hornet Moth (W9385)	D. M. & S. M. Weston	
G-ADNE	DH.87B Hornet Moth	G-ADNE Group	
G-ADNL	M.5 Sparrowhawk	D. Shew	
G-ADNZ	DH.82A Tiger Moth (DE673)	D. C. Wall	
G-ADOT	DH.87B Hornet Moth ★	De Havilland Heritage Museum/London Colney	
G-ADPC	DH.82A Tiger Moth	P. D. & S. E. Ford	
G-ADPJ	B.A.C. Drone	M. J. Aubrey	
G-ADPS	B.A. Swallow 2	J. F. Hopkins	
G-ADRA	Pietenpol Air Camper	A. J. Mason	
G-ADRG†	Mignet HM.14 (replica) ★	Lower Stondon Transport Museum (BAPC77)	
G-ADRR	Aeronca C.3	C. J. & M. A. Essex	
G-ADRX†	Mignet HM.14 (replica) ★	S. Copeland Aviation Group (BAPC231)	
G-ADRY†	Mignet HM.14 (replica) (BAPC29) ★	Brooklands Museum of Aviation/Weybridge	
G-ADUR	DJ.87B Hornet Moth	C. J. & P. R. Harvey	
G-ADVU†	Mignet HM.14 (replica) ★	North East Aircraft Museum/Usworth (BAPC211)	
G-ADWJ	DH.82A Tiger Moth (BB803)	K. F. Crumplin	
G-ADWO	DH.82A Tiger Moth (BB807) ★	Solent Sky, Southampton	
G-ADWT	M.2W Hawk Trainer	K-F Grimminger	
G-ADXS	Mignet HM.14 ★	Thameside Aviation Museum/Shoreham	
G-ADYS	Aeronca C.3	E. P. & P. A. Gliddon	
G-ADYV†	Mignet HM.14 (replica) ★	P. Ward (BAPC243)	
G-ADZW†	Mignet HM.14 (replica) ★	Solent Sky/Southampton (BAPC253)	
G-AEBB	Mignet HM.14 ★	The Shuttleworth Collection/Old Warden	

BRITISH CIVIL AIRCRAFT MARKINGS

Notes	Reg	Type	Owner or Operator
	G-AEBJ	Blackburn B-2	BAe Systems (Operations) Ltd
	G-AEDB	B.A.C. Drone 2	M. J. & S. Honeychurch
	G-AEDU	DH.90 Dragonfly	GAEDU Ltd
	G-AEEG	M.3A Falcon Skysport	Shipping & Airlines Ltd
	G-AEEH	Mignet HM.14 ★	RAF Museum/Cosford
	G-AEFG	Mignet HM.14 (BAPC75) ★	N. H. Ponsford/Breighton
	G-AEFT	Aeronca C.3	N. S. Chittenden
	G-AEGV	Mignet HM.14 ★	Midland Air Museum/Coventry
	G-AEHM	Mignet HM.14 ★	Science Museum/Wroughton
	G-AEJZ	Mignet HM.14 (BAPC120) ★	Aero Venture
	G-AEKR	Mignet HM.14 (BAPC121) ★	Doncaster Museum & Art Gallery
	G-AEKV	Kronfeld Drone ★	Brooklands Museum of Aviation/Weybridge
	G-AEKW	M.12 Mohawk ★	RAF Museum
	G-AELO	DH.87B Hornet Moth	M. J. Miller
	G-AENP	Hawker Hind (K5414) (BAPC78)	The Shuttleworth Collection
	G-AEOA	DH.80A Puss Moth	P. & A. Wood/Old Warden
	G-AEOF†	Mignet HM.14 (BAPC22) ★	Aviodrome/Lelystad, Netherlands
	G-AEOF	Rearwin 8500	Just Plane Trading Ltd
	G-AEPH	Bristol F.2B (D8096)	The Shuttleworth Collection
	G-AERV	M.11A Whitney Straight	P. W. Bishop
	G-AESB	Aeronca C.3	R. J. M. Turnbull
	G-AESE	DH.87B Hornet Moth	B. R. Cox
	G-AESZ	Chilton D.W.1	R. A. Fleming
	G-AETA	Caudron G.3 (3066) ★	RAF Museum/Hendon
	G-AETG	Aeronca 100	J. Teagle and Partners
	G-AEUJ	M.11A Whitney Straight	R. E. Mitchell
	G-AEVS	Aeronca 100	R. A. Fleming
	G-AEXD	Aeronca 100	M. A. & N. Mills
	G-AEXF	P.6 Mew Gull	Richard Shuttleworth Trustees
	G-AEXT	Dart Kitten II	R. A. Fleming
	G-AEXZ	Piper J-2 Cub	M. J. Honeychurch
	G-AEZF	S.16 Scion 2 ★	Acebell Aviation/Redhill
	G-AEZJ	P.10 Vega Gull	Comanche Warbirds Ltd
	G-AEZX	Bucker Bu.133C Jungmeister	S. P. Reeve (G-PTDP)
	G-AFAP†	CASA C.352L ★	RAF Museum/Cosford
	G-AFBS	M.14A Hawk Trainer 3 ★	Imperial War Museum/Duxford (G-AKKU)
	G-AFCL	B. A. Swallow 2	D. & J. Cresswell
	G-AFDO	Piper J-3F-60 Cub	R. Wald
	G-AFDX	Hanriot HD.1 (HD-75) ★	RAF Museum/Hendon
	G-AFEL	Monocoupe 90A	M. Rieser
	G-AFFD	Percival Type Q Six	The London Aerobatic Company Ltd
	G-AFFH	Piper J-2 Cub	M. J. Honeychurch
	G-AFFI†	Mignet HM.14 (replica) (BAPC76) ★	Yorkshire Air Museum/Elvington
	G-AFGD	B. A. Swallow 2	South Wales Swallow Group
	G-AFGE	B. A. Swallow 2	A. A. M. & C. W. N. Huke
	G-AFGH	Chilton D.W.1.	M. L. & G. L. Joseph
	G-AFGI	Chilton D.W.1.	K. A. A. McDonald
	G-AFGM	Piper J-4A Cub Coupé	M. Ward
	G-AFGZ	DH.82A Tiger Moth	M. R. Paul (G-AMHI)
	G-AFHA	Mosscraft MA.1.	K. Miller
	G-AFIN	Chrislea LC.1 Airguard (BAPC203) ★	T. W. J. Carnall
	G-AFIR	Luton LA-4 Minor	Parasol Aircraft Company Ltd
	G-AFIU	Parker CA-4 Parasol ★	The Aeroplane Collection/Hooton Park
	G-AFJB	Foster-Wikner G.M.1. Wicko	J. Dible
	G-AFJR	Tipsy Trainer 1 ★	Royal Museum of the Armed Forces and Military History/Brussels
	G-AFJU	M.17 Monarch	Museum of Flight/East Fortune
	G-AFJV	Mosscraft MA.2	K. Miller
	G-AFNI	DH.94 Moth Minor	J. Jennings
	G-AFOB	DH.94 Moth Minor	K. Cantwell
	G-AFOJ	DH.94 Moth Minor	S. C. Harris, B. Long & F. M. Murray
	G-AFPN	DH.94 Moth Minor	The Moth Minor Group
	G-AFRV	Tipsy Trainer 1★	Royal Museum of the Armed Forces and Military History/Brussels
	G-AFRZ	M.17 Monarch	R. E. Mitchell/Sleap (G-AIDE)
	G-AFSC	Tipsy Trainer 1	D. M. Forshaw
	G-AFSV	Chilton D.W.1A	R. A. Fleming
	G-AFTA	Hawker Tomtit (K1786)	The Shuttleworth Collection
	G-AFTN	Taylorcraft Plus C2 ★	Leicestershire County Council Museums/Snibston

Reg	Type	Owner or Operator	Notes
G-AFUP	Luscombe 8A Silvaire	R. Dispain	
G-AFWH	Piper J-4A Cub Coupé	C. W. Stearn & R. D. W. Norton	
G-AFWI	DH.82A Tiger Moth	J. N. Bailey	
G-AFWN	Auster J/1 Autocrat ★	Danmarks Flymuseum/Stauning	
G-AFWT	Tipsy Trainer 1	N. Parkhouse	
G-AFYD	Luscombe 8F Silvaire	J. D. Iliffe	
G-AFYO	Stinson H.W.75	M. Lodge	
G-AFZA	Piper J-4A Cub Coupe	R. A. Benson	
G-AFZE	Heath Parasol	C. J. Essex	
G-AFZK	Luscombe 8A Silvaire	M. G. Byrnes	
G-AFZL	Porterfield CP.50	P. G. Lucas & S. H. Sharpe	
G-AGAT	Piper J-3F-50 Cub	A. S. Bathgate	
G-AGBN	GAL.42 Cygnet 2 ★	Museum of Flight/East Fortune	
G-AGEG	DH.82A Tiger Moth	H. D. Labouchere	
G-AGHY	DH.82A Tiger Moth	P. Groves	
G-AGIV	Piper J-3C-65 Cub	J-3 Cub Group	
G-AGJG	DH.89A Dragon Rapide	M. J. & D. J. T. Miller	
G-AGLK	Auster 5D	M. A. Farrelly & D. K. Chambers	
G-AGMI	Luscombe 8A Silvaire	Oscar Flying Group	
G-AGNV	Avro 685 York 1 (TS798) ★	Aerospace Museum/Cosford	
G-AGOS	R.S.4 Desford Trainer (VZ728)	Leicestershire County Council	
G-AGOY	Miles M.48 Messenger 3	S. A. Blanchard	
G-AGPG	Avro 19 Srs 2 ★	The Aeroplane Collection/Hooton Park	
G-AGPK	DH.82A Tiger Moth (PG657)	T. K. Butcher	
G-AGRU	V.498 Viking 1A ★	Brooklands Museum of Aviation/Weybridge	
G-AGSH	DH.89A Dragon Rapide 6	P. H. Meeson	
G-AGTM	DH.89A Dragon Rapide 6	B. R. Cox	
G-AGTO	Auster 5 J/1 Autocrat	M. J. Barnett & D. J. T. Miller	
G-AGTT	Auster 5 J/1 Autocrat	Parasol Aircraft Company Ltd	
G-AGVG	Auster 5 J/1 Autocrat (modified)	P. J. & S. J. Benest	
G-AGXN	Auster J/1N Alpha	Gentleman's Aerial Touring Carriage Group	
G-AGXU	Auster J/1N Alpha	L. J. Kingscott	
G-AGXV	Auster J/1 Autocrat	M. J. Barnett	
G-AGYD	Auster J/1N Alpha	P. D. Hodson	
G-AGYH	Auster J/1N Alpha	I. M. Staves	
G-AGYT	Auster J/1N Alpha	P. J. Barrett	
G-AGYU	DH.82A Tiger Moth (DE208)	S. A. Firth	
G-AGYY	Ryan ST3KR (27)	H. de Vries/Holland	
G-AGZZ	DH.82A Tiger Moth	C. R. Davies	
G-AHAA	Miles M.28 Mercury 6	S. A. Blanchard	
G-AHAG	DH.89A Rapide	Scillonia Airways Ltd	
G-AHAL	Auster J/1N Alpha	Wickenby Aviation	
G-AHAM	Auster J/1 Autocrat	Interna Engineering BVBA/Belgium	
G-AHAN	DH.82A Tiger Moth	G-AHAN Flying Group	
G-AHAO	Auster 5 J/1 Autocrat	R. Callaway-Lewis	
G-AHAP	Auster J/1 Autocrat	W. D. Hill	
G-AHAT	Auster J/1N Alpha ★	Dumfries & Galloway Aviation Museum	
G-AHAU	Auster 5 J/1 Autocrat	Andreas Auster Group	
G-AHBL	DH.87B Hornet Moth	Shipping and Airlines Ltd	
G-AHBM	DH.87B Hornet Moth	P. A. & E. P. Gliddon	
G-AHCL	Auster J/1N Alpha (modified)	N. Musgrave	
G-AHCR	Gould-Taylorcraft Plus D Special	M. J. Laundy	
G-AHEC	Luscombe 8A Silvaire	A. F. Wankowski	
G-AHED	DH.89A Dragon Rapide (RL962) ★	RAF Museum Storage & Restoration Centre/RAF Stafford	
G-AHGW	Taylorcraft Plus D (LB375)	D. A. Gathercole	
G-AHGZ	Taylorcraft Plus D (LB367)	A. D. Pearce	
G-AHHH	Auster J/1 Autocrat	A. L. Hall-Carpenter	
G-AHHY	Taylorcraft Plus D	G. W. & M. G. Maddams	
G-AHHT	Auster J/1N Alpha	South Downs Auster Group	
G-AHIP	Piper J-3C-65 Cub (479712:8-R)	A. D. Pearce	
G-AHIZ	DH.82A Tiger Moth	C.F.G. Flying Ltd	
G-AHKX	Avro 19 Srs 2 (TX176)	The Shuttleworth Collection	
G-AHKY	Miles M.18 Series 2 ★	Museum of Flight/East Fortune	
G-AHLK	Auster 3 (NJ889)	J. H. Powell-Tuck	
G-AHLT	DH.82A Tiger Moth	M. P. Waring	
G-AHMN	DH.82A Tiger Moth	A. D. Barton	
G-AHOO	DH.82A Tiger Moth	J. T. Milsom	
G-AHPZ	DH.82A Tiger Moth	N. J. Wareing	
G-AHRI	DH.104 Dove 1 ★	Newark Air Museum/Newark	

15

Notes	Reg	Type	Owner or Operator
	G-AHSA	Avro 621 Tutor (K3241)	The Shuttleworth Collection
	G-AHSD	Taylorcraft Plus D (LB323)	A. L. Hall-Carpenter
	G-AHSP	Auster J/1 Autocrat	R. M. Weeks
	G-AHSS	Auster J/1N Alpha	C. W. Tomkins
	G-AHST	Auster J/1N Alpha	A. C. Frost
	G-AHTE	P.44 Proctor V	D. K. Tregilgas
	G-AHTW	A.S.40 Oxford (V3388) ★	Skyfame Collection/Duxford
	G-AHUF	DH.Tiger Moth (T7997)	Eaglescott Tiger Moth Group
	G-AHUG	Taylorcraft Plus D	N. C. Dickinson
	G-AHUI	M.38 Messenger 2A ★	The Aeroplane Collection/Hooton Park
	G-AHUJ	M.14A Hawk Trainer 3 (R1914)	F. Baldanza
	G-AHUN	Globe GC-1B Swift	R. J. Hamlett
	G-AHUV	DH.82A Tiger Moth	A. D. Gordon
	G-AHVU	DH.82A Tiger Moth	Vintage Aircraft Factory Ltd
	G-AHVV	DH.82A Tiger Moth	M. Arter
	G-AHXE	Taylorcraft Plus D	Historic Aircraft Flight Trust
	G-AIBE	Fulmar II (N1854) ★	F.A.A. Museum/Yeovilton
	G-AIBH	Auster J/1N Alpha	M. J. Bonnick
	G-AIBM	Auster J/1 Autocrat	R. Greatrex
	G-AIBR	Auster J/1 Autocrat	P. R. Hodson
	G-AIBW	Auster J/1N Alpha	C. R. Sunter
	G-AIBX	Auster J/1 Autocrat	Wasp Flying Group
	G-AIBY	Auster J/1 Autocrat	D. Morris
	G-AICX	Luscombe 8A Silvaire	C. C. & J. M. Lovell
	G-AIDL	DH.89A Dragon Rapide 6 (TX310)	Avalon Ventures Ltd
	G-AIDN	VS.502 Spitfire Tr.VII (MT818)	Biggin Hill Heritage Hangar Ltd
	G-AIDS	DH.82A Tiger Moth	K. D. Pogmore & T. Dann
	G-AIEK	M.38 Messenger 2A (RG333)	M. Hales
	G-AIFZ	Auster J/1N Alpha	M. D. Ansley
	G-AIGD	Auster V J/1 Autocrat	R. M. D. Saw
	G-AIGF	Auster J/1N Alpha	D. W. Mathie
	G-AIGT	Auster J/1N Alpha	M. J. Miller & J. G. Langley
	G-AIIH	Piper J-3C-65 Cub	N. G. Busschau & M. S. Pettit
	G-AIJM	Auster J/4	N. Huxtable
	G-AIJS	Auster J/4	R. J. Lane
	G-AIJT	Auster J/4 Srs 100	Aberdeen Auster Flying Group
	G-AIKE	Auster 5 (NJ728)	J. D. C. Pritchard
	G-AIPR	Auster J/4	M. A. & N. Mills
	G-AIPV	Auster J/1 Autocrat	S. P. Miller
	G-AIRC	Auster J/1 Autocrat	K. & C. Jones & C. Morris
	G-AIRK	DH.82A Tiger Moth	J. S. & P. R. Johnson
	G-AISA	Tipsy B Srs 1	J. Pollard
	G-AISC	Tipsy B Srs 1	Wagtail Flying Group
	G-AISS	Piper J-3C-65 Cub	K. W. Wood & F. Watson
	G-AIST	VS.300 Spitfire 1A (P7308/XR-D)	Spitfire The One Ltd
	G-AISX	Piper J-3C-65 Cub (330372)	Cubfly
	G-AITB	A.S.10 Oxford (MP425) ★	RAF Museum/Hendon
	G-AIUA	M.14A Hawk Trainer 3 (T9768)	D. S. Hunt
	G-AIUL	DH.89A Dragon Rapide 6	I. Jones
	G-AIXA	Taylorcraft Plus D (LB264) ★	RAF Museum/Hendon
	G-AIXJ	DH.82A Tiger Moth	D. Green
	G-AIXN	Benes-Mraz M.1C Sokol	Sokol Flying Group Ltd
	G-AIYG	SNCAN Stampe SV.4B	J. E. Henny/Belgium
	G-AIYR	DH.89A Dragon Rapide (HG691)	Avalon Ventures Ltd
	G-AIYS	DH.85 Leopard Moth	M. R. Paul
	G-AIZE	Fairchild F.24W Argus 2 (FS628) ★	RAF Museum/Cosford
	G-AIZG	VS.236 Walrus 1 (L2301) ★	F.A.A. Museum/Yeovilton
	G-AIZU	Auster J/1 Autocrat	C. J. & J. G. B. Morley
	G-AJAD	Piper J-3C-65 Cub	C. R. Shipley
	G-AJAJ	Auster J/1N Alpha	N. K. Geddes
	G-AJAM	Auster J/2 Arrow	D. A. Porter
	G-AJAP	Luscombe 8A Silvaire	M. Flint
	G-AJAS	Auster J/1N Alpha	T. C. Garner & C. Briggs
	G-AJCP	D.31 Turbulent	B. R. Pearson
	G-AJDW	Auster J/1 Autocrat	D. R. Hunt
	G-AJDY	Auster J/1N Alpha (MT182)	W. Bayman
	G-AJEB	Auster J/1N Alpha ★	The Aeroplane Collection/Hooton Park
	G-AJEE	Auster J/1 Autocrat	A. C. Whitehead
	G-AJEH	Auster J/1N Alpha	P. & T. J. Harrison

Reg	Type	Owner or Operator	Notes
G-AJEI	Auster J/1N Alpha	G. J. Siddall	
G-AJEM	Auster J/1 Autocrat	A. L. Aish	
G-AJES	Piper J-3C-65 Cub (330485:C-44)	D. E. Jarvis	
G-AJGJ	Auster 5 (RT486) ★	RAF History Museum	
G-AJHS	DH.82A Tiger Moth	Flying Wires/Netherlands	
G-AJIH	Auster J/1 Autocrat (TJ518)	S. Alexander	
G-AJIS	Auster J/1N Alpha	J. J. Hill	
G-AJIT	Auster J/1 Kingsland Autocrat	S. J. Farrant	
G-AJIU	Auster J/1 Autocrat	M. D. Greenhalgh	
G-AJIW	Auster J/1N Alpha	R. J. Guess	
G-AJIX	Auster J/1 Autocrat	S. G. Rule	
G-AJJP	Fairey Jet Gyrodyne (XJ389) ★	Museum of Berkshire Aviation/Woodley	
G-AJJS	Cessna 120	G. A. Robson	
G-AJJT	Cessna 120	Juliet Tango Group	
G-AJJU	Luscombe 8E Silvaire	M. F. A. Hudson	
G-AJKB	Luscombe 8E Silvaire	T. Carter	
G-AJOA	DH.82A Tiger Moth	K. A. Nutley	
G-AJOC	M.38 Messenger 2A ★	Ulster Folk & Transport Museum	
G-AJOE	M.38 Messenger 2A	P. W. Bishop	
G-AJON	Aeronca 7AC Champion (	Mudsville Flyers	
G-AJOV†	Westland WS-51 Dragonfly ★	RAF Museum/Cosford	
G-AJOZ	Fairchild F.24W Argus 2 ★ (FK338)	Yorkshire Air Museum/Elvington	
G-AJPI	Fairchild F.24R-41a Argus 3 (314887)	R. Sijben/Netherlands	
G-AJRB	Auster J/1 Autocrat	Southern Alps Ltd	
G-AJRH	Auster J/1N Alpha ★	Charnwood Museum/Loughborough	
G-AJRS	M.14A Hawk Trainer 3 (P6382:C)	The Shuttleworth Collection	
G-AJSN	Fairchild 24W-41A Argus ★ (HB612)	Ulster Aviation Society/Long Kesh	
G-AJTW	DH.82A Tiger Moth (N6965:FL-J)	J. A. Barker	
G-AJUE	Auster J/1 Autocrat	P. H. B. Cole	
G-AJUL	Auster J/1N Alpha	A. J. Martin	
G-AJVE	DH.82A Tiger Moth	R. A. Gammons	
G-AJWB	M.38 Messenger 2A	P. W. Bishop	
G-AJXC	Auster 5 (TJ343)	R. D. Helliar-Symonds, K. A. & S. E. W. Williams	
G-AJXV	Auster 4 (NJ695)	M. D. Roberts	
G-AJXY	Auster 4	X-Ray Yankee Group	
G-AJYB	Auster J/1N Alpha	P. J. Shotbolt	
G-AKAT	M.14A Hawk Trainer 3 (T9738)	R. A. Fleming	
G-AKBO	M.38 Messenger 2A	N. P. Lee	
G-AKDF	M.38 Messenger 2A	C. W. P. Turner	
G-AKDK	M.65 Gemini 1A	C. W. P. Turner	
G-AKDN	DHC.1A-1 Chipmunk	K. A. Large & J. Morley	
G-AKDW	DH.89A Dragon Rapide ★	De Havilland Heritage Museum/London Colney	
G-AKEL	M.65 Gemini 1A ★	Ulster Folk & Transport Museum	
G-AKEN	M.65 Gemini 1A	C. W. P. Turner	
G-AKEX	Percival Proctor III	M. Biddulph (G-AKIU)	
G-AKGE	M.65 Gemini 3C ★	Ulster Folk & Transport Museum	
G-AKHP	M.65 Gemini 1A	S. A. Blanchard	
G-AKHU	M.65 Gemini 1A	C. W. P. Turner	
G-AKHZ	M.65 Gemini 7 ★	The Aeroplane Collection/Hooton Park	
G-AKIB	Piper J-3C-90 Cub (480015:M-44)	R. Horner	
G-AKIF	DH.89A Dragon Rapide	Airborne Taxi Services Ltd	
G-AKIN	M.38 Messenger 2A	Sywell Messenger Trust	
G-AKIU	P.44 Proctor V	G. G. L. James	
G-AKKB	M.65 Gemini 1A	C. Gray	
G-AKKH	M.65 Gemini 1A	P. J. Hebdon	
G-AKKR	M.14A Magister (T9707) ★	Museum of Army Flying/Middle Wallop	
G-AKKY	M.14A Hawk Trainer 3 (L6906) ★ (BAPC44)	Museum of Berkshire Aviation/Woodley	
G-AKLW	Short SA.6 Sealand 1 ★	Ulster Folk & Transport Museum	
G-AKNV	DH.89A Rapide	Royal Museum of the Armed Forces and Military History/Brussels	
G-AKOW	Auster 5 (TJ569) ★	Museum of Army Flying/Middle Wallop	
G-AKPF	M.14A Hawk Trainer 3 (N3788)	D. S. Bramwell	
G-AKPI	Auster 5 (NJ703)	M. D. Grinstead	
G-AKRP	DH.89A Dragon Rapide 4	Eaglescott Dominie Group	
G-AKSY	Auster 5 (TJ534)	A. Brier	
G-AKSZ	Auster 5D (modified)	M. A. Farrelly & D. K. Chambers	
G-AKTH	Piper J-3C-65 Cub	G. W. S. Turner	
G-AKTI	Luscombe 8A Silvaire	C. Chambers	

17

Notes	Reg	Type	Owner or Operator
	G-AKTK	Aeronca 11BC Chief	A. C. Batchelar
	G-AKTP	PA-17 Vagabond	Golf Tango Papa Group
	G-AKTR	Aeronca 7AC Champion	E. Gordon
	G-AKTS	Cessna 120	M. Isterling
	G-AKTT	Luscombe 8A Silvaire	S. J. Charters
	G-AKUE	DH.82A Tiger Moth	D. F. Hodgkinson
	G-AKUF	Luscombe 8E Silvaire	M. O. Loxton
	G-AKUH	Luscombe 8E Silvaire	A. G. Palmer (G-GIST)
	G-AKUJ	Luscombe 8E Silvaire	P. R. Bentley
	G-AKUK	Luscombe 8A Silvaire	O. R. Watts
	G-AKUL	Luscombe 8A Silvaire	G. E. Clegg
	G-AKUM	Luscombe 8F Silvaire	D. A. Young
	G-AKUN	Piper J-3F-65 Cub	W. R. Savin
	G-AKUO	Aeronca 11AC Chief	C. V. Dadswell & A. G. Collicot
	G-AKUP	Luscombe 8E Silvaire	D. A. Young
	G-AKUR	Cessna 140	C. G. Applegate
	G-AKUW	Chrislea CH.3 Super Ace 2	R. J. S. G. Clark
	G-AKVM	Cessna 120	P. A. Espin
	G-AKVN	Aeronca 11AC Chief	P. A. Jackson
	G-AKVO	Taylorcraft BC-12D	G. Taylor
	G-AKVR	Chrislea CH.3 Skyjeep 4	R. B. Webber
	G-AKVZ	M.38 Messenger 4B	Shipping & Airlines Ltd
	G-AKWS	Auster 5A-160 (RT610)	M. C. Hayes
	G-AKWT	Auster 5 ★	C. Baker
	G-AKXP	Auster 5 (NJ633)	M. J. Nicholson
	G-AKXS	DH.82A Tiger Moth	J. & G. J. Eagles
	G-AKZN	P.34A Proctor 3 (Z7197) ★	RAF Museum/Hendon
	G-ALAH	Miles M.38 Messenger 4A	C. W. P. Turner
	G-ALAR	Miles M.38 Messenger 4A	C. W. P. Turner
	G-ALAX	DH.89A Dragon Rapide ★	Durney Aeronautical Collection/Andover
	G-ALBD	DH.82A Tiger Moth	K. Redfearn
	G-ALBJ	Auster 5 (TW501)	B. M. Vigor
	G-ALBK	Auster 5	J. S. & J. S. Allison
	G-ALBN	Bristol 173 (XF785) ★	RAF Museum Storage & Restoration Centre/Cardington
	G-ALCK	P.34A Proctor 3 (LZ766) ★	Imperial War Museum/Duxford
	G-ALCU	DH.104 Dove 2 (G-ALVD)★	Midland Air Museum/Coventry
	G-ALDG	HP.81 Hermes 4 ★	Imperial War Museum/Duxford
	G-ALEH	PA-17 Vagabond	A. J. Coker
	G-ALFA	Auster 5	A. E. Jones
	G-ALFU	DH.104 Dove 6 ★	Imperial War Museum/Duxford
	G-ALGA	PA-15 Vagabond	S. T. Gilbert
	G-ALGT	VS.379 Spitfire F.XIVH (RM689)	Rolls-Royce PLC
	G-ALIJ	PA-17 Vagabond	D. J. Jack
	G-ALIW	DH.82A Tiger Moth	F. R. Curry
	G-ALJF	P.34A Proctor 3	J. F. Moore
	G-ALJL	DH.82A Tiger Moth	T. A. Kinnaird
	G-ALJR	Abbott-Baynes Scud III	The Gliding Heritage Centre
	G-ALLF	Slingsby T.30A Prefect (ARK)	The Gliding Heritage Centre
	G-ALMA	Piper J3C-65 Cub	M. J. Butler (G-BBXS)
	G-ALNA	DH.82A Tiger Moth (EM973)	S. E. Ford
	G-ALND	DH.82A Tiger Moth (N9191)	K. J. Fraser
	G-ALSP	Bristol 171 Sycamore (WV783) ★	RAF Museum/Hendon
	G-ALSS	Bristol 171 Sycamore (WA576) ★	Dumfries & Galloway Aviation Museum
	G-ALST	Bristol 171 Sycamore (WA577) ★	North East Aircraft Museum/Usworth
	G-ALSW	Bristol 171 Sycamore (WT933) ★	Newark Air Museum
	G-ALSX	Bristol 171 Sycamore (G-48-1) ★	The Helicopter Museum/Weston-super-Mare
	G-ALTO	Cessna 140	T. M. Jones & ptnrs
	G-ALUC	DH.82A Tiger Moth	Tiger Moth Experience Ltd
	G-ALWB	DHC.1 Chipmunk 22A	D. M. Neville
	G-ALWF	V.701 Viscount ★	Imperial War Museum/Duxford
	G-ALWS	DH.82A Tiger Moth (N9328)	J. G. Norris
	G-ALWW	DH.82A Tiger Moth	D. E. Findon
	G-ALXT	DH.89A Dragon Rapide ★	Science Museum/Wroughton
	G-ALXZ	Auster 5-150 (NJ689)	P. J. Tyler
	G-ALYB	Auster 5 (RT520) ★	South Yorkshire Aviation Museum/Doncaster
	G-ALYW	DH.106 Comet 1 ★	RAF Exhibition Flight (fuselage converted to 'Nimrod')
	G-ALZE	BN-1F ★	Solent Sky Museum/Southampton
	G-ALZO	A.S.57 Ambassador ★	Imperial War Museum/Duxford

Reg	Type	Owner or Operator	Notes
G-AMAW	Luton LA-4 Minor	The Real Aeroplane Co.Ltd	
G-AMBB	DH.82A Tiger Moth	J. Eagles	
G-AMCK	DH.82A Tiger Moth	M. R. Masters	
G-AMCM	DH.82A Tiger Moth	A. K. & K. J. O'Brien	
G-AMDA	Avro 652A Anson 1 (N4877:MK-V) ★	Imperial War Museum/Duxford	
G-AMEN	PA-18 Super Cub 95	The G-AMEN Flying Group	
G-AMHF	DH.82A Tiger Moth	A. J. West	
G-AMHJ	Douglas C-47A Dakota 6 (KG651) ★	Assault Glider Association/Shawbury	
G-AMIV	DH.82A Tiger Moth (R5246)	RAF Station Czechoslovakia SRO	
G-AMJM	Auster 5	J. R. Davison	
G-AMKU	Auster J/1B Aiglet	P. G. Lipman	
G-AMLZ	P.50 Prince 6E ★	The Jetstream Club	
G-AMMS	Auster J/5K Aiglet Trainer	G. P. J. Rowden	
G-AMNN	DH.82A Tiger Moth	I. J. Perry	
G-AMOG	V.701 Viscount ★	Museum of Flight/East Fortune	
G-AMPG	PA-12 Super Cruiser	D. J. Harrison	
G-AMPI	SNCAN Stampe SV.4C	Ardmore Aviation Services Ltd	
G-AMPO	Douglas C-47B (FZ626/YS-DH) ★	(gate guardian)/RAF Lyneham	
G-AMPY	Douglas C-47B (KK116)	C. Keane	
G-AMRF	Auster J/5F Aiglet Trainer	D. A. Hill	
G-AMRK	G.37 Gladiator I (K7985)	The Shuttleworth Collection	
G-AMSG	SIPA 903	S. W. Markham	
G-AMSN	Douglas C-47B ★	Aceball Aviation/Redhill	
G-AMTA	Auster J/5F Aiglet Trainer	J. D. Manson	
G-AMTF	DH.82A Tiger Moth (T7842)	H. A. D. Monro	
G-AMTK	DH.82A Tiger Moth	S. W. McKay & M. E. Vaisey	
G-AMTM	Auster J/1 Autocrat	R. J. Stobo (G-AJUJ)	
G-AMTV	DH.82A Tiger Moth	E. Scurr	
G-AMUF	DHC.1 Chipmunk 21	C. L. S. von Altishofen	
G-AMUI	Auster J/5F Aiglet Trainer	R. B. Webber	
G-AMVD	Auster 5 (TJ565)	M.Hammond	
G-AMVP	Tipsy Junior	R. A. Fleming	
G-AMVS	DH.82A Tiger Moth	D. Shew	
G-AMYD	Auster J/5L Aiglet Trainer	R. D. Thomasson	
G-AMYJ	Douglas C-47B (KN353) ★	Yorkshire Air Museum/Elvington	
G-AMZI	Auster J/5F Aiglet Trainer	J. F. Moore	
G-AMZT	Auster J/5F Aiglet Trainer	C. D. Butters	
G-ANAF	Douglas C-47B (KP220)	Aero Legends Leasing Ltd	
G-ANAP	DH.104 Dove 6 ★	Brunel Technical College/Lulsgate	
G-ANBZ	DH.82A Tiger Moth	D. Shew	
G-ANCF	B.175 Britannia 308 ★	Bristol Aero Collection (stored)/Kemble	
G-ANCS	DH.82A Tiger Moth	C. E. Edwards & E. A. Higgins	
G-ANDE	DH.82A Tiger Moth (EM726)	K. M. Perkins	
G-ANDM	DH.82A Tiger Moth	N. J. Stagg	
G-ANDP	DH.82A Tiger Moth	J. McCullough	
G-ANEH	DH.82A Tiger Moth (N6797)	G. J. Wells	
G-ANEL	DH.82A Tiger Moth	Totalsure Ltd	
G-ANEM	DH.82A Tiger Moth	P. J. Benest	
G-ANEN	DH.82A Tiger Moth	G-ANEN Group	
G-ANEW	DH.82A Tiger Moth (NM138)	K. F. Crumplin	
G-ANEZ	DH.82A Tiger Moth	C. D. J. Bland	
G-ANFC	DH.82A Tiger Moth	G. Pierce	
G-ANFH	Westland WS-55 Whirlwind ★	The Helicopter Museum/Weston-super-Mare	
G-ANFI	DH.82A Tiger Moth (DE623)	G. P. Graham	
G-ANFL	DH.82A Tiger Moth	Felthorpe Tiger Group Ltd	
G-ANFM	DH.82A Tiger Moth	Reading Flying Group	
G-ANFP	DH.82A Tiger Moth (N9503)	R. Santus	
G-ANFU	Auster 5 (NJ719) ★	North East Aircraft Museum/Usworth	
G-ANFV	DH.82A Tiger Moth	Avalon Ventures Ltd	
G-ANHI	DH.82A Tiger Moth	A. D. Barton	
G-ANHK	DH.82A Tiger Moth	T. A. Jackson	
G-ANHR	Auster 5	H. L. Swallow	
G-ANHS	Auster 4 (MT197)	R. Ellingworth & C. Tyers	
G-ANHX	Auster 5D (TW519)	T. Taylor	
G-ANIE	Auster 5 (TW467)	R. T. Ingram	
G-ANIJ	Auster 5D (TJ672)	G. M. Rundle	
G-ANIS	Auster 5	J. Clarke-Cockburn	
G-ANJA	DH.82A Tiger Moth (N9389)	A. D. Hodgkinson	
G-ANJD	DH.82A Tiger Moth	D. O. Lewis	
G-ANJI	DH.82A Tiger Moth (T6830)	A. Watt	

Notes	Reg	Type	Owner or Operator
	G-ANJK	DH.82A Tiger Moth	H. M. M. Haines
	G-ANJV	Westland Whirlwind Series 3 ★	The Helicopter Museum/Weston-super-Mare
	G-ANKK	DH.82A Tiger Moth (T5854)	Halfpenny Green Tiger Group
	G-ANKT	DH.82A Tiger Moth (K2585)	The Shuttleworth Collection
	G-ANKV	DH.82A Tiger Moth (T7793)	J. A. Cooper
	G-ANKZ	DH.82A Tiger Moth (N6466)	T. D. Le Mesurier
	G-ANLD	DH.82A Tiger Moth	M. Groves
	G-ANLS	DH.82A Tiger Moth	P. A. Gliddon
	G-ANLW	Westland WS-51/2 Widgeon ★	Norfolk & Suffolk Museum/Flixton
	G-ANMO	DH.82A Tiger Moth (K4259:71)	K. M. Perkins
	G-ANMY	DH.82A Tiger Moth (DE470)	A. R. & M. A. Baxter
	G-ANNG	DH.82A Tiger Moth	Parachuting Aircraft Ltd
	G-ANNI	DH.82A Tiger Moth (T6953)	C. E. Ponsford & ptnrs
	G-ANNK	DH.82A Tiger Moth (T7290)	J. Y. Kaye
	G-ANNN	DH.82A Tiger Moth ★	Thorpe Park Visitor Centre/Tattershall Thorpe
	G-ANOA	Hiller UH-12A ★	Redhill Technical College
	G-ANOD	DH.82A Tiger Moth	M. D. Souch
	G-ANOH	DH.82A Tiger Moth	N. Parkhouse
	G-ANOK	SAAB S.91C Safir	N. C. Stone
	G-ANOM	DH.82A Tiger Moth	W. J. Pitts
	G-ANON	DH.82A Tiger Moth (T7909)	M. Kelly
	G-ANOO	DH.82A Tiger Moth	R. K. Packman
	G-ANOV	DH.104 Dove 6 ★	Museum of Flight/East Fortune
	G-ANPE	DH.82A Tiger Moth	T. K. Butcher (G-IESH)
	G-ANPK	DH.82A Tiger Moth	A. D. Hodgkinson
	G-ANPP	P.34A Proctor 3	C. P. A. & J. Jeffrey
	G-ANRF	DH.82A Tiger Moth	C. D. Cyster
	G-ANRM	DH.82A Tiger Moth (DF112)	Avalon Ventures Ltd
	G-ANRN	DH.82A Tiger Moth	J. J. V. Elwes
	G-ANRP	Auster 5 (TW439)	C. L. Petty
	G-ANRX	DH.82A Tiger Moth ★	De Havilland Heritage Museum/London Colney
	G-ANSM	DH.82A Tiger Moth	Douglas Aviation
	G-ANTE	DH.82A Tiger Moth (T6562)	I. L. Cheese
	G-ANTK	Avro 685 York ★	Imperial War Museum/Duxford
	G-ANUO	DH.114 Heron 2D (G-AOXL) ★	Westmead Business Group/Croydon Airport
	G-ANUW	DH.104 Dove 6 ★	Aeropark/East Midlands
	G-ANVY	P.31 Proctor 4	G. E. J. Spooner
	G-ANWB	DHC-1 Chipmunk 21	G. Briggs
	G-ANXB	DH.114 Heron 1B ★	Newark Air Museum/Newark
	G-ANXC	Auster J/5R Alpine	Alpine Group
	G-ANXR	P.31C Proctor 4 (RM221)	N. H. T. Cottrell
	G-ANZT	Thruxton Jackaroo (T7798)	D. J. Neville & P. A. Dear
	G-ANZU	DH.82A Tiger Moth	M. I. Lodge
	G-ANZZ	DH.82A Tiger Moth (DE974)	T. K. Butcher
	G-AOAA	DH.82A Tiger Moth	R. C. P. Brookhouse
	G-AOBG	Somers-Kendall SK.1	P. W. Bishop
	G-AOBH	DH.82A Tiger Moth (NL750)	P. Nutley
	G-AOBJ	DH.82A Tiger Moth	A. D. Hodgkinson
	G-AOBU	P.84 Jet Provost T.1 (XD693)	T. J. Manna
	G-AOBX	DH.82A Tiger Moth	David Ross Flying Group
	G-AOCP	Auster 5 ★	C. J. Baker (stored)
	G-AOCR	Auster 5D (NJ673)	D. A. Hill
	G-AOCU	Auster 5	S. J. Ball
	G-AODA	Westland S-55 Srs 3 ★	The Helicopter Museum/Weston-super-Mare
	G-AODR	DH.82A Tiger Moth	G-AODR Group (G-ISIS)
	G-AODT	DH.82A Tiger Moth (R5250)	R. A. Harrowven
	G-AOEH	Aeronca 7AC Champion	A. Gregori
	G-AOEI	DH.82A Tiger Moth	C.F.G. Flying Ltd
	G-AOEL	DH.82A Tiger Moth ★	National Museum of Scotland/Edinburgh
	G-AOES	DH.82A Tiger Moth	P. D. & S. E. Ford
	G-AOET	DH.82A Tiger Moth	P. H. Meeson
	G-AOEX	Thruxton Jackaroo	A. T. Christian
	G-AOFE	DHC.1 Chipmunk 22A (WB702)	W. J. Quinn
	G-AOFS	Auster J/5L Aiglet Trainer	P. N. A. Whitehead
	G-AOGA	M.75 Aries ★	Irish Aviation Museum (stored)
	G-AOGI	DH.82A Tiger Moth	A. E. Taylor
	G-AOGR	DH.82A Tiger Moth (XL714)	R. J. S. G. Clark
	G-AOGV	Auster J/5R Alpine	R. E. Heading
	G-AOHY	DH.82A Tiger Moth (N6537)	S. W. Turley & G. Cooper

Reg	Type	Owner or Operator	Notes
G-AOHZ	Auster J/5P Autocar	A. J. Kay & R. W. Eaton	
G-AOIM	DH.82A Tiger Moth (T7109)	R. C. P. Brookhouse	
G-AOIR	Thruxton Jackaroo	K. M. Perkins	
G-AOIS	DH.82A Tiger Moth (R5172)	R. J. Moore & B. S. Floodgate	
G-AOJH	DH.83C Fox Moth	Connect Properties Ltd	
G-AOJJ	DH.82A Tiger Moth (DF128)	JJ Flying Group	
G-AOJK	DH.82A Tiger Moth	P. L. Green	
G-AOJT	DH.106 Comet 1 (F-BGNX) ★	De Havilland Heritage Museum (fuselage only)	
G-AOKH	P.40 Prentice 1	J. F. Moore	
G-AOKL	P.40 Prentice 1 (VS610)	N. J. Butler	
G-AOKO	P.40 Prentice 1 ★	Aero Venture	
G-AOKZ	P.40 Prentice 1 (VS623) ★	Midland Air Museum/Coventry	
G-AOLK	P.40 Prentice 1 ★	RAF Museum	
G-AOLU	P.40 Prentice 1 (VS356)	N. J. Butler	
G-AORG	DH.114 Heron 2	Duchess of Brittany (Jersey) Ltd	
G-AORW	DHC.1 Chipmunk 22A	S. Maric	
G-AOSK	DHC.1 Chipmunk 22 (WB726)	P. McMillan	
G-AOSY	DHC.1 Chipmunk 22 (WB585:M)	Chippy Sierra Yankee Group	
G-AOTD	DHC.1 Chipmunk 22 (WB588)	S. Piech	
G-AOTF	DHC.1 Chipmunk 23 (Lycoming)	Northants Aerial Advertising Ltd	
G-AOTI	DH.114 Heron 2D ★	De Havilland Heritage Museum/London Colney	
G-AOTK	D.53 Turbi	J. S. & P. R. Johnson	
G-AOTR	DHC.1 Chipmunk 22	S. J. Sykes	
G-AOTY	DHC.1 Chipmunk 22A (WG472)	Retro Track & Air (UK) Ltd	
G-AOUJ	Fairey Ultra-Light ★	IHM/Weston-super-Mare	
G-AOUP	DHC.1 Chipmunk 22	A. R. Harding	
G-AOUR	DH.82A Tiger Moth ★	Ulster Folk & Transport Museum	
G-AOVF	B.175 Britannia 312F (XM497) ★	RAF Museum/Cosford	
G-AOVT	B.175 Britannia 312F ★	Imperial War Museum/Duxford	
G-AOVW	Auster 5	B. Marriott	
G-AOXL	DHC.114 Heron 2D ★	Croydon Airport Visitor Centre	
G-AOXN	DH.82A Tiger Moth	S. L. G. Darch	
G-AOZE	Westland Widgeon 2 ★	The Helicopter Museum/Weston-super-Mare	
G-AOZH	DH.82A Tiger Moth (K2572)	The Frensham Tiger Company Ltd	
G-AOZL	Auster J/5Q Alpine	R. M. Weeks	
G-AOZP	DHC.1 Chipmunk 22	S. J. Davies	
G-APAF	Auster 5 (TW511)	J. J. J. Mostyn (G-CMAL)	
G-APAH	Auster 5	T. J. Goodwin	
G-APAJ	Thruxton Jackaroo	A. J. Perry	
G-APAL	DH.82A Tiger Moth (N6847)	P. J. Shotbolt	
G-APAM	DH.82A Tiger Moth	R. P. Williams	
G-APAO	DH.82A Tiger Moth (R4922)	H. J. Maguire	
G-APAP	DH.82A Tiger Moth (R5136)	S. E. Ford	
G-APAS	DH.106 Comet 1XB ★	RAF Museum/Cosford	
G-APBE	Auster 5	E. G. & G. R. Woods	
G-APBI	DH.82A Tiger Moth	C. J. Zeal	
G-APBO	D.53 Turbi	R. C. Hibberd	
G-APBW	Auster 5	N. Huxtable	
G-APCB	Auster J/5Q Alpine	A. A. Beswick	
G-APCC	DH.82A Tiger Moth	L. J. Rice/Henstridge	
G-APDB	DH.106 Comet 4 ★	Imperial War Museum/Duxford	
G-APEP	V.953C Merchantman ★	Brooklands Museum of Aviation/Weybridge	
G-APFA	D.54 Turbi	T. W. J. Carnall	
G-APFJ	Boeing 707-436 ★	Museum of Flight/East Fortune	
G-APFU	DH.82A Tiger Moth	C. L. Griffiths	
G-APFV	PA-23-160 Apache	J. L. Thorogood (G-MOLY)	
G-APHV	Avro 19 Srs 2 (VM360) ★	Museum of Flight/East Fortune	
G-APIE	Tipsy Belfair B	D. Beale	
G-APIK	Auster J/1N Alpha	Deadwood Flying Group	
G-APIM	V.806 Viscount ★	Brooklands Museum of Aviation/Weybridge	
G-APIT	P.40 Prentice 1 (VR192) ★	WWII Aircraft Preservation Society/Lasham	
G-APIY	P.40 Prentice 1 (VR249) ★	Newark Air Museum	
G-APIZ	D.31 Turbulent	R. G. Meredith	
G-APJB	P.40 Prentice 1 (VR259)	K. M. Perkins	
G-APJJ	Fairey Ultra-light ★	Midland Air Museum/Coventry	
G-APJZ	Auster J/1N Alpha	P. G. Lipman	
G-APLG	Auster J/5L Aiglet Trainer ★	Solway Aviation Museum/Carlisle	
G-APLK	Miles M.100 Student ★	Museum of Berkshire Aviation/Woodley	
G-APLO	DHC.1 Chipmunk 22A (WD379)	P. M. Luijken/Netherlands	

BRITISH CIVIL AIRCRAFT MARKINGS

Notes	Reg	Type	Owner or Operator
	G-APLU	DH.82A Tiger Moth	M. E. Vaisey
	G-APMB	DH.106 Comet 4B ★	Gatwick Handling Ltd (ground trainer)
	G-APMH	Auster J/1U Workmaster	M. R. P. Thorogood
	G-APMX	DH.82A Tiger Moth	Foley Farm Flying Group
	G-APMY	PA-23 Apache 160 ★	South Yorkshire Aircraft Museum/Doncaster
	G-APNJ	Cessna 310 ★	Newark Air Museum/Newark
	G-APNT	Currie Wot	S. Slater
	G-APNZ	D.31 Turbulent	Turbulent G-APNZ Preservation Society
	G-APOI	Westland Skeeter 8 ★	Solent Sky Museum/Southampton
	G-APPA	DHC.1 Chipmunk 22	H G Flight Training
	G-APPL	P.40 Prentice 1	S. J. Saggers
	G-APPM	DHC.1 Chipmunk 22 (WB711)	E. H. W. Moore
	G-APRL	AW.650 Argosy 101 ★	Midland Air Museum/Coventry
	G-APRO	Auster 6A	A. F. & H. Wankowski
	G-APRT	Taylor JT.1 Monoplane ★	Newark Air Museum/Newark
	G-APSA	Douglas DC-6A	G-APSA Ltd
	G-APSR	Auster J/1U Workmaster	D. & K. Aero Services Ltd
	G-APTR	Auster J/1N Alpha	C. R. Shipley
	G-APTU	Auster 5	G-APTU Flying Group
	G-APTW	Westland WS-51/2 Widgeon ★	North East Land Sea and Air Museum/Sunderland
	G-APTY	Beech G.35 Bonanza	G. E. Brennand
	G-APTZ	D.31 Turbulent	R. A. H. Vary
	G-APUD	Bensen B.7M (modified) ★	Manchester Museum of Science & Industry
	G-APUE	L.40 Meta Sokol	I. Tvrdik
	G-APUG	Luton LA-5 Minor ★	Norfolk and Suffolk Aviation Museum/Flixton
	G-APUP	Sopwith Pup (replica) (N5182) ★	RAF Museum/Hendon
	G-APUR	PA-22 Tri-Pacer 160	S. T. A. Hutchinson
	G-APUW	Auster J/5V-160 Autocar	E. S. E. & P. B. Hibbard
	G-APUY	D.31 Turbulent	A. Parnell
	G-APVG	Auster J/5L Aiglet Trainer	R. E. Tyers
	G-APVN	D.31 Turbulent	R. Sherwin
	G-APVS	Cessna 170B	N. Simpson Stormin' Norman
	G-APVT	DH.82A Tiger Moth	M. C. Boddington
	G-APVU	L.40 Meta Sokol	S. E. & M. J. Aherne
	G-APVV	Mooney M.20A ★	Newark Air Museum/Newark
	G-APVZ	D.31 Turbulent	The Tiger Club (1990) Ltd
	G-APWA	HPR.7 Herald 101 ★	Museum of Berkshire Aviation/Woodley
	G-APWJ	HPR.7 Herald 201 ★	Imperial War Museum/Duxford
	G-APWN	Westland WS-55 Whirlwind 3 ★	Midland Air Museum/Coventry
	G-APWY	Piaggio P.166 ★	Science Museum/Wroughton
	G-APXJ	PA-24 Comanche 250	T. Wildsmith
	G-APXR	PA-22 Tri-Pacer 160	A. Troughton
	G-APXT	PA-22 Tri-Pacer 150 (modified)	A. D. A. Smith
	G-APXU	PA-22 Tri-Pacer 125 (modified)	M. Dilkes & S. D. Barnard
	G-APXW	EP.9 Prospector (XM819) ★	Museum of Army Flying/Middle Wallop
	G-APXX	DHA.3 Drover 2 (VH-FDT) ★	WWII Aircraft Preservation Society/Lasham
	G-APYB	Tipsy T.66 Nipper 3	B. O. Smith
	G-APYD	DH.106 Comet 4B ★	Science Museum/Wroughton
	G-APYG	DHC.1 Chipmunk 22	P. A. & J. M. Doyle
	G-APYT	Champion 7FC Tri-Traveller	N. F. O'Neill
	G-APZJ	PA-18 Super Cub 150	S. G. Jones
	G-APZL	PA-22 Tri-Pacer 160	B. Robins
	G-ARAD	Luton LA-5 Major ★	North East Land Sea and Air Museum/Sunderland
	G-ARAM	PA-18 Super Cub 150	Skymax (Aviation) Ltd
	G-ARAN	PA-18 Super Cub 150	G-ARAN Group
	G-ARAP	Champion 7EC	J. J. McGonagle
	G-ARAS	Champion 7FC Tri-Traveller	Alpha Sierra Flying Group
	G-ARAW	Cessna 182C Skylane	R. L. McLean & A. J. Homes
	G-ARAX	PA-22-150 Tri-Pacer	C. W. Carnall
	G-ARAZ	DH.82A Tiger Moth (R4959:59)	Avalon Adventures Ltd
	G-ARBE	DH.104 Dove 8	M. Whale
	G-ARBG	Tipsy T.66 Nipper 2	D. Shrimpton
	G-ARBM	Auster V J1B Aiglet	A. D. Hodgkinson
	G-ARBS	PA-22 Tri-Pacer 160 (tailwheel)	S. D. Rowell
	G-ARBZ	D.31 Turbulent	G-ARBZ Group
	G-ARCF	PA-22 Tri-Pacer 150	M. J. Speakman
	G-ARCS	Auster D6/180	L. I. Bailey
	G-ARCV	Cessna 175A	R. Francis & C. Campbell

Reg	Type	Owner or Operator	Notes
G-ARCW	PA-23 Apache 160	F. W. Ellis	
G-ARCX	A.W. Meteor 14 ★	Museum of Flight/East Fortune	
G-ARDB	PA-24 Comanche 250	P. Crook	
G-ARDD	CP.301C1 Emeraude	P. J. Huxley & D. Hurst	
G-ARDE	DH.104 Dove 6 ★	T. E. Evans	
G-ARDJ	Auster D.6/180	P. N. A. Whitehead	
G-ARDO	Jodel D.112	W. R. Prescott	
G-ARDS	PA-22 Caribbean 150	N. J. Szkiler	
G-ARDY	Tipsy T.66 Nipper 2	J. K. Davies	
G-ARDZ	Jodel D.140A	G-ARDZ Flying Group	
G-AREA	DH.104 Dove 8 ★	De Havilland Heritage Museum/London Colney	
G-AREH	DH.82A Tiger Moth	A. J. Hastings & A. Mustard	
G-AREI	Auster 3 (MT438)	R. B. Webber	
G-AREL	PA-22 Caribbean 150	The Caribbean Flying Club	
G-AREO	PA-18 Super Cub 150	E. P. Parkin	
G-ARET	PA-22 Tri-Pacer 160	L. A. Runnalls	
G-AREX	Aeronca 15AC Sedan	R. J. M. Turnbull	
G-AREZ	D.31 Turbulent	Turbulent Flying Group	
G-ARFB	PA-22 Caribbean 150	Airspeed Aviation Ltd	
G-ARFD	PA-22 Tri-Pacer 160	T. J. Alderdice	
G-ARFI	Cessna 150A	N. M. G. Pearson	
G-ARFO	Cessna 150A	P. M. Fawley	
G-ARFT	Jodel DR.1050	R. Shaw	
G-ARFV	Tipsy T.66 Nipper 2	J. J. Austin	
G-ARGO	PA-22 Colt 108	M. Magrabi	
G-ARGV	PA-18 Super Cub 180	Wolds Gliding Club Ltd	
G-ARGZ	D.31 Turbulent	The Tiger Club (1990) Ltd	
G-ARHB	Forney F-1A Aircoupe	R. E. Dagless	
G-ARHC	Forney F-1A Aircoupe	E. G. Girardey	
G-ARHL	PA-23 Aztec 250	C. J. Freeman	
G-ARHM	Auster 6A (VF557:H)	R. C. P. Brookhouse	
G-ARHR	PA-22 Caribbean 150	A. R. Wyatt	
G-ARHX	DH.104 Dove 8 ★	South Yorkshire Aircraft Museum/Doncaster	
G-ARHZ	D.62 Condor	B. R. Hunter	
G-ARIF	Ord-Hume O-H.7 Minor Coupé ★	M. J. Aubrey	
G-ARIK	PA-22 Caribbean 150	A. Taylor	
G-ARIL	PA-22 Caribbean 150	S. Eustathiou	
G-ARIM	D.31 Turbulent	S. R. P. Harper	
G-ARJB	DH.104 Dove 8	M. Whale	
G-ARJR	PA-23 Apache 160G ★	Instructional airframe/Kidlington	
G-ARJS	PA-23 Apache 160G	Bencray Ltd	
G-ARJU	PA-23 Apache 160G	I. C. Marshall	
G-ARKD	CAC CA-18 Mk.22 Mustang P-51D	Classic Flying Machine Collection Ltd	
G-ARKG	Auster J/5G Autocar (A11-301/931)	A. G. Boon & C. L. Towell	
G-ARKJ	Beech N35 Bonanza	G. D. E. Macdonald	
G-ARKK	PA-22 Colt 108	R. D. Welfare	
G-ARKM	PA-22 Colt 108	R. L. Northover	
G-ARKP	PA-22 Colt 108	D. S. White & I. J. Mitchell	
G-ARKS	PA-22 Colt 108	A. J. Silvester	
G-ARLG	Auster D.4/108	S. P. Bowers & A. R. Allan	
G-ARLK	PA-24 Comanche 250	R. P. Jackson	
G-ARLR	Beagle A.61 Terrier 2	M. Palfreman	
G-ARLU	Cessna 172B Skyhawk ★	Instructional airframe/Irish Air Corps	
G-ARLZ	D.31A Turbulent	A. D. Wilson	
G-ARMC	DHC.1 Chipmunk 22 (WB703)	John Henderson Children's Trust	
G-ARMF	DHC.1 Chipmunk 22A (WZ868:H)	M. Harvey	
G-ARMG	DHC.1 Chipmunk 22A (WK558:DH)	L. J. Irvine	
G-ARMN	Cessna 175B Skylark	Brimpton Aviation Group Ltd	
G-ARMO	Cessna 172B Skyhawk	R. D. Leigh	
G-ARMR	Cessna 172B Skyhawk	M. J. Flint	
G-ARMZ	D.31 Turbulent	The Tiger Club (1990) Ltd	
G-ARNB	Auster J/5G Autocar	K. B. Owen	
G-ARNE	PA-22 Colt 108	The Shiny Colt Group	
G-ARNG	PA-22 Colt 108	D. Lamb	
G-ARNJ	PA-22 Colt 108	R. A. Keech	
G-ARNK	PA-22 Colt 108 (tailwheel)	S. J. Smith	
G-ARNL	PA-22 Colt 108	M. R. Harrison	
G-ARNO	Beagle A.61 Terrier 1 (VX113)	M. C. R. Wills	
G-ARNP	Beagle A.109 Airedale	S. W. & M. Isbister	
G-ARNY	Jodel D.117	G-ARNY Flying Group	
G-ARNZ	D.31 Turbulent	The Tiger Club (1990) Ltd	

Notes	Reg	Type	Owner or Operator
	G-AROA	Cessna 172B Skyhawk	Vu JV18 Ltd
	G-AROJ	Beagle A.109 Airedale ★	D. J. Shaw (stored)
	G-ARON	PA-22 Colt 108	G. X. P. C. Wouters
	G-AROW	Jodel D.140B	J. P. M. & P. M. White
	G-AROY	Boeing Stearman A75N.1	J. S. Mann
	G-ARPH	HS.121 Trident 1C ★	Museum of Flight/East Fortune
	G-ARPK	HS.121 Trident 1C ★	Manchester Airport Authority
	G-ARPO	HS.121 Trident 1C ★	North East Land Sea and Air Museum/Sunderland
	G-ARRD	Jodel DR.1050	R. J. Arnold
	G-ARRE	Jodel DR.1050	R. Weininger
	G-ARRI	Cessna 175B	R. J. Bentley
	G-ARRL	Auster J/1N Alpha	A. C. Ladd
	G-ARRM	Beagle B.206-X ★	Farnborough Air Sciences Trust
	G-ARRO	Beagle A.109 Airedale	M. & S. W. Isbister
	G-ARRS	CP.301A Emeraude	J. F. Sully
	G-ARRU	D.31 Turbulent	D. G. Huck
	G-ARRX	Auster 6A (VF512)	J. E. D. Mackie
	G-ARRY	Jodel D.140B	C. Thomas
	G-ARRZ	D.31 Turbulent	T. A. Stambach
	G-ARSG	Roe Triplane Type IV (replica)	The Shuttleworth Collection/Old Warden
	G-ARTH	PA-12 Super Cruiser	G. R. Trotter
	G-ARTJ	Bensen B.8M ★	Museum of Flight/East Fortune
	G-ARTL	DH.82A Tiger Moth (T7281)	J. J. Hill
	G-ARTT	MS.880B Rallye Club	R. N. Scott
	G-ARTZ	McCandless M.4 gyroplane	W. R. Partridge
	G-ARUG	Auster J/5G Autocar	D. P. H. Hulme
	G-ARUI	Beagle A.61 Terrier	T. W. J. Dann
	G-ARUL	LeVier Cosmic Wind	P. G. Kynsey
	G-ARUY	Auster J/1N Alpha	D. K. Tregilgas
	G-ARVM	V.1101 VC10 ★	Brooklands Museum of Aviation/Weybridge
	G-ARVN	Servotec Grasshopper ★	The Helicopter Museum/Weston-super-Mare
	G-ARVO	PA-18 Super Cub 95	M. P. & S. T. Barnard
	G-ARVT	PA-28 Cherokee 160	S. Hynd
	G-ARVU	PA-28 Cherokee 160	VU JV2 Ltd
	G-ARVV	PA-28 Cherokee 160	G. E. Hopkins
	G-ARVZ	D.62B Condor	A. A. M. Huke
	G-ARWB	DHC.1 Chipmunk 22 (WK611)	Thruxton Chipmunk Flying Club
	G-ARWR	Cessna 172C	Devanha Flying Group
	G-ARWS	Cessna 175C	M. D. Fage
	G-ARXB	Beagle A.109 Airedale	S. W. & M. Isbister
	G-ARXD	Beagle A.109 Airedale	D. Howden
	G-ARXG	PA-24 Comanche 250	H. T.& I. A. Robinson
	G-ARXH	Bell 47G	T. B. Searle
	G-ARXN	Tipsy Nipper T.66 Srs.2	V. Asquith
	G-ARXP	Luton LA-4 Minor	R. M. Weeks
	G-ARXT	Jodel DR.1050	CJM Flying Group
	G-ARXU	Auster 6A (VF526)	S. D. & S. P. Allen
	G-ARYB	HS.125 Srs 1 ★	Midland Air Museum/Coventry
	G-ARYC	HS.125 Srs 1 ★	De Havilland Heritage Museum/London Colney
	G-ARYD	Auster AOP.6 (WJ358) ★	Museum of Army Flying/Middle Wallop
	G-ARYK	Cessna 172C	G-ARYK Owners Group
	G-ARYR	PA-28 Cherokee 180	G-ARYR Flying Group
	G-ARYS	Cessna 172C	G-ARYS Group
	G-ARYV	PA-24 Comanche 250	D. C. Hanss
	G-ARYZ	Beagle A.109 Airedale ★	South Yorkshire Aircraft Museum/Doncaster
	G-ARZS	Beagle A.109 Airedale	M. & S. W. Isbister
	G-ARZW	Currie Wot	B. R. Pearson
	G-ASAA	Luton LA-4 Minor	M. J. Aubrey (stored)
	G-ASAI	Beagle A.109 Airedale	K. R. Howden
	G-ASAJ	Beagle A.61 Terrier 2 (WE569)	T. Bailey
	G-ASAL	SA Bulldog Srs 120/124	Pioneer Flying Co Ltd
	G-ASAT	MS.880B Rallye Club ★	City of Norwich Aviation Museum/Norwich
	G-ASAU	MS.880B Rallye Club	Juliet Tango Group
	G-ASAX	Beagle A.61 Terrier 2	A. D. Hodgkinson
	G-ASBA	Phoenix Currie Wot	K. Higbee
	G-ASBH	Beagle A.109 Airedale	D. T. Smollett
	G-ASCC	Beagle E3 Mk 11 (XP254)	R. Warner
	G-ASCD	Beagle A.61 Terrier 2 (TJ704) ★	Yorkshire Air Museum/Elvington
	G-ASCH	Beagle A.61 Terrier 2	D. S. Wilkinson

Reg	Type	Owner or Operator	Notes
G-ASCM	Isaacs Fury II (K2050)	P. J. Shenton	
G-ASCT	Bensen B.7M ★	The Helicopter Museum/Weston-super-Mare	
G-ASCZ	CP.301A Emeraude	I. Denham-Brown	
G-ASDF	Edwards Gyrocopter ★	B. King	
G-ASDK	Beagle A.61 Terrier 2	J. Swallow (G-ARLM)	
G-ASEA	Luton LA-4A Minor	B. W. Faulkner	
G-ASEB	Luton LA-4A Minor	S. R. P. Harper	
G-ASEJ	PA-28-180 Cherokee B	Perranporth Pilots Group	
G-ASEO	PA-24 Comanche 250	M. Scott	
G-ASEP	PA-23 Apache 235	J. R. & R. J. Sharpe	
G-ASEU	D.62A Condor	R. A. S. Sutherland	
G-ASFA	Cessna 172D	D. Austin	
G-ASFD	L-200A Morava	M. Emery	
G-ASFL	PA-28 Cherokee 180	G-ASFL Group	
G-ASFR	Bölkow Bö.208A1 Junior	S. T. Dauncey	
G-ASFX	D.31 Turbulent	E. F. Clapham & T. A. Wilcox	
G-ASGC	V.1151 Super VC-10 ★	Imperial War Museum/Duxford	
G-ASHD	Brantly B.2A ★	The Helicopter Museum/Weston-super-Mare	
G-ASHS	SNCAN Stampe SV.4C	J. W. Beaty	
G-ASHT	D.31 Turbulent	C. W. N. Huke	
G-ASHU	PA-15 Vagabond (modified)	The Calybe Flying Group	
G-ASHX	PA-28 Cherokee 180	Powertheme Ltd	
G-ASII	PA-28 Cherokee 180	T. N. & T. R. Hart & R. W. S. Matthews	
G-ASIJ	PA-28 Cherokee 180	A. Wilson	
G-ASIL	PA-28 Cherokee 180	M. J. Pink	
G-ASIS	Jodel D.112	W. R. Prescott	
G-ASIT	Cessna 180	A. P. Rouse	
G-ASIY	PA-25 Pawnee 235	Kent Gliding Club Ltd	
G-ASJL	Beech H.35 Bonanza	Chem Tools GmbH	
G-ASJV	VS.361 Spitfire IX (MH434/PK-K)	Merlin Aviation Ltd	
G-ASJZ	Jodel D.117A	B. Russel	
G-ASKC	DH.98 Mosquito 35 (TA719) ★	Skyfame Collection/Duxford	
G-ASKK	HPR.7 Herald 211 ★	City of Norwich Aviation Museum/Norwich	
G-ASKL	Jodel D.150	J. M. Graty	
G-ASKP	DH.82A Tiger Moth	Tiger Club (1990) Ltd	
G-ASKT	PA-28 Cherokee 180	T. J. Herbert	
G-ASLV	PA-28 Cherokee 235	S. W. Goodswen	
G-ASMA	PA-30 Twin Comanche 160 C/R	K. Cooper	
G-ASMJ	Cessna F.172E	Aeroscene Ltd	
G-ASML	Luton LA-4A Minor	O. D. Lewis	
G-ASMM	D.31 Tubulent	K. J. Butler	
G-ASMS	Cessna 150A	M. & W. Long	
G-ASMT	Fairtravel Linnet 2	P. Harrison	
G-ASMV	CP.1310-C3 Super Emeraude	D. G. Hammersley	
G-ASMW	Cessna 150D	Dukeries Aviation	
G-ASMY	PA-23 Apache 160 ★	R. D. Forster	
G-ASMZ	Beagle A.61 Terrier 2 (VF516)	J. & R. Pike & S. Woodgate	
G-ASNC	Beagle D.5/180 Husky	Peterborough & Spalding Gliding Club Ltd	
G-ASNK	Cessna 205	Justgold Ltd	
G-ASNW	Cessna F.172E	G-ASNW Group	
G-ASNY	Campbell-Bensen B.8M gyroplane ★	Newark Air Museum/Newark	
G-ASOH	Beech 95-B55A Baron	G. Davis & C. Middlemiss	
G-ASOI	Beagle A.61 Terrier 2 (WJ404)	G.D.B. Delmege	
G-ASOK	Cessna F.172E	D. W. Disney	
G-ASOL	Bell 47D ★	North East Land Sea and Air Museum/Sunderland	
G-ASOM	Beagle A.61 Terrier 2	GASOM.org (G-JETS)	
G-ASPF	Jodel D.120	B. J. Rawlings	
G-ASPP	Bristol Boxkite (replica)	The Shuttleworth Collection/Old Warden	
G-ASPS	Piper J-3C-90 Cub	S. Slater	
G-ASPV	DH.82A Tiger Moth (T7794)	Oldstead Aero LLP	
G-ASRC	D.62C Condor	T. Garnham	
G-ASRF	Gowland Jenny Wren ★	Norfolk and Suffolk Aviation Museum/Flixton	
G-ASRK	Beagle A.109 Airedale	M. Wilson	
G-ASRO	PA-30 Twin Comanche 160	D. W. Blake	
G-ASRT	Jodel 150	P. Turton	
G-ASRW	PA-28 Cherokee 180	R. M. Davies	
G-ASSM	HS.125 Srs 1/522 ★	Science Museum/South Kensington	
G-ASSP	PA-30 Twin Comanche 160	P. H. Tavener	
G-ASSS	Cessna 172E	P. R. & A. P. March t/a Triple Sierra Flying Group	

25

Notes	Reg	Type	Owner or Operator
	G-ASSV	Kensinger KF	C. I. Jefferson
	G-ASSW	PA-28 Cherokee 140	Juliet Tango Group
	G-ASSY	D.31 Turbulent	C. M. Bracewell
	G-ASTG	Nord 1002 Pingouin II (BG + KM)	R. J. Fray
	G-ASTI	Auster 6A	S. J. Partridge
	G-ASTL	Fairey Firefly I (Z2033) ★	F.A. A. Museum/Yeovilton
	G-ASTP	Hiller UH-12C ★	The Helicopter Museum/Weston-super-Mare
	G-ASUB	Mooney M.20E Super 21	S. C. Coulbeck
	G-ASUD	PA-28 Cherokee 180	G-ASUD Group
	G-ASUE	Cessna 150D	D. Huckle
	G-ASUG	Beech E18S ★	Museum of Flight/East Fortune
	G-ASUP	Cessna F.172E	S. A. Williams
	G-ASUS	Jurca MJ.2B Tempete	D. J. Millin & R. E. Hughes
	G-ASVG	CP.301B Emeraude	R. B. McKenzie
	G-ASVM	Cessna F.172E	M. Tobutt
	G-ASVO	HPR.7 Herald 214 ★	Highland Aircraft Museum/Inverness (cockpit section)
	G-ASVZ	PA-28 Cherokee 140	Scillonian Marine Consultants Ltd
	G-ASWJ	Beagle 206 Srs 1 (8449M) ★	Brunel Technical College/Bristol
	G-ASWX	PA-28 Cherokee 180	Gasworks Flying Group Ltd
	G-ASXC	SIPA 903	T. M. Buick (G-DWEL)
	G-ASXD	Brantly B.2B	G-ASXD Group
	G-ASXS	Jodel DR.1050	C. P. Wilkinson
	G-ASXU	Jodel D.120A	G-ASXU Group
	G-ASXX	Avro 683 Lancaster 7 (NX611) ★	Panton Family Trust/East Kirkby
	G-ASYD	BAC One-Eleven 475 ★	Brooklands Museum of Aviation/Weybridge
	G-ASYG	Beagle A.61 Terrier 2 (VX927)	D. & R. L. McDonald
	G-ASYP	Cessna 150E	Henlow Flying Group
	G-ASZB	Cessna 150E	Akki Aviation Services Ltd
	G-ASZD	Bölkow Bö.208A2 Junior	S. L. Wilkes
	G-ASZR	Fairtravel Linnet 2	R. Hodgson
	G-ASZU	Cessna 150E	IAE Ltd
	G-ASZV	Tipsy T.66 Nipper 2	A. M. E. Vervaeke/Belgium
	G-ASZX	Beagle A.61 Terrier 1 (WJ368)	R. B. Webber
	G-ATAG	Jodel DR.1050	T. M. Gamble
	G-ATAS	PA-28 Cherokee 180	G-ATAS Group
	G-ATAU	D.62B Condor	M. C. Burlock
	G-ATAV	D.62C Condor	C. D. Swift
	G-ATBG	Nord 1002 (NJ+C11)	Ardmore Aviation Service
	G-ATBH	Aero 145	P. D. Aberbach
	G-ATBL	DH.60G Moth	Comanche Warbirds Ltd
	G-ATBP	Fournier RF-3	D. McNicholl
	G-ATBS	D.31 Turbulent	C. J. L. Wolf
	G-ATBU	Beagle A.61 Terrier 2	T. Jarvis
	G-ATBX	PA-20 Pacer 135	G. D. & P. M. Thomson
	G-ATBZ	Westland WS-58 Wessex 60 ★	The Helicopter Museum/Weston-super-Mare
	G-ATCC	Beagle A.109 Airedale	North East Flight Training Ltd
	G-ATCD	Beagle D.5/180 Husky	M. Stewart
	G-ATCJ	Luton LA-4A Minor	A. R. Hutton
	G-ATCL	Victa Airtourer 100	A. D. Goodall
	G-ATCN	Luton LA-4A Minor	The Real Aeroplane Co.Ltd
	G-ATCX	Cessna 182H	K. Sheppard
	G-ATDA	PA-28 Cherokee 160	Henstridge Airfield Ltd
	G-ATDN	Beagle A.61 Terrier 2 (TW641)	S. J. Saggers
	G-ATDO	Bölkow Bö.208C1 Junior	P. Thompson
	G-ATEF	Cessna 150E	Swans Aviation
	G-ATEM	PA-28 Cherokee 180	G. D. Wyles
	G-ATEP	EAA Biplane ★	E. L. Martin (red)/Guernsey
	G-ATEV	Jodel DR.1050	J. C. Carter & J. L. Altrip
	G-ATEW	PA-30 Twin Comanche 160	J. M. Charlton
	G-ATEX	Victor Airtourer 100	S. Turner
	G-ATEZ	PA-28 Cherokee 140	EFI Aviation Ltd
	G-ATFD	Jodel DR.1050	K. D. Hills
	G-ATFG	Brantly B.2B ★	The Helicopter Museum/Weston-super-Mare
	G-ATFM	Sikorsky S-61N	British International Helicopter Services Ltd
	G-ATFV	Agusta-Bell 47J-2A ★	Caernarfon Air World
	G-ATFY	Cessna F.172G	J. M. Vinall
	G-ATGN	Thorn Coal Gas Balloon	British Balloon Museum/Newbury
	G-ATGP	Jodel DR.1050	Madley Flying Group
	G-ATGY	Gardan GY-80 Horizon	D. H. Mackay

Reg	Type	Owner or Operator	Notes
G-ATHA	PA-23 Apache 235 ★	Brunel Technical College/Bristol	
G-ATHD	DHC.1 Chipmunk 22 (WP971)	O. L. Cubitt	
G-ATHK	Aeronca 7AC Champion	T. C. Barron	
G-ATHR	PA-28 Cherokee 180	Azure Flying Club Ltd	
G-ATHT	Victa Airtourer 115	Cotswold Flying Group	
G-ATHU	Beagle A.61 Terrier 1	J. A. L. Irwin	
G-ATHV	Cessna 150F	Air Navgation & Trading Co.Ltd	
G-ATHZ	Cessna 150F	R. D. Forster	
G-ATIC	Jodel DR.1050	T. A. Major	
G-ATIG	HPR.7 Herald 214 ★	Norwich Airport towing trainer	
G-ATIN	Jodel D.117	C. E. C. & C. M. Hives	
G-ATIR	AIA Stampe SV.4C	A. Trueman	
G-ATIS	PA-28 Cherokee 160	VU JV3 Ltd	
G-ATIZ	Jodel D.117	R. A. Smith	
G-ATJA	Jodel DR.1050	Bicester Flying Group	
G-ATJC	Victa Airtourer 100 (modfied)	Aviation West Ltd	
G-ATJG	PA-28 Cherokee 140	D. & J. Albon	
G-ATJL	PA-24 Comanche 260	M. P. Blokland	
G-ATJN	Jodel D.119	Real Hart Flying Group	
G-ATJV	PA-32 Cherokee Six 260	Wingglider Ltd	
G-ATKH	Luton LA-4A Minor	H. E. Jenner	
G-ATKI	Piper J-3C-65 Cub	M. B. Blackmore	
G-ATKT	Cessna F.172G	R. J. D. Blois	
G-ATKX	Jodel D.140C	Kilo Xray Syndicate	
G-ATLA	Cessna 182J Skylane	G. R. Read	
G-ATLB	Jodel DR.1050/M1	Le Syndicate du Petit Oiseau	
G-ATLM	Cessna F.172G	M. Wilson	
G-ATLP	Bensen B.8M	R. F. G. Moyle	
G-ATLT	Cessna U.206A	Skydive Jersey Ltd	
G-ATLV	Jodel D.120	G. Cameron	
G-ATMC	Cessna F.150F	M. Biddulph	
G-ATMH	Beagle D.5/180 Husky	J. L. Thorogood	
G-ATMM	Cessna F.150F	R. D. Forster	
G-ATNE	Cessna F.150F	Cirrus Aircraft UK Ltd & T. & T. Wright	
G-ATNL	Cessna F.150F	Wicklow Wings	
G-ATNV	PA-24-260 Comanche	K. Powell	
G-ATOH	D.62B Condor	Three Spires Flying Group	
G-ATOI	PA-28-140 Cherokee	Rayham Ltd	
G-ATOJ	PA-28-140 Cherokee	British North West Airlines Ltd	
G-ATOK	PA-28-140 Cherokee	Airways Aero Associations Ltd	
G-ATON	PA-28-140 Cherokee	Stirling Flying Syndicate	
G-ATOO	PA-28-140 Cherokee	Caralair Aviation	
G-ATOP	PA-28-140 Cherokee	P. R. Coombs	
G-ATOR	PA-28-140 Cherokee	S. J. McBride	
G-ATOT	PA-28-180 Cherokee	Sirius Aviation Ltd	
G-ATOU	Mooney M.20E Super 21	DbProf Doo	
G-ATOY	PA-24 Comanche 260 ★	Museum of Flight/East Fortune	
G-ATPT	Cessna 182J Skylane	C. Beer t/a Papa Tango Group	
G-ATPV	JB.01 Minicab	P. T. Stephenson	
G-ATRG	PA-18 Super Cub 150	Dorset Gliding Club Ltd	
G-ATRK	Cessna F.150F	Falcon Aviation Ltd	
G-ATRL	Cessna F.150F	A. A. W. Stevens	
G-ATRM	Cessna F.150F	North East Aviation Ltd	
G-ATRW	PA-32-260 Cherokee Six	WF Aviation	
G-ATRX	PA-32-260 Cherokee Six	S. P. Vincent	
G-ATSL	Bölkow Bö.208C1 Junior	GATSI Bolkow Group	
G-ATSL	Cessna F.172G	Aircraft Engineers Ltd	
G-ATSR	Beech M.35 Bonanza	V. S. E. Norman	
G-ATSZ	PA-30 Twin Comanche 160B	Sierra Zulu Aviation Ltd	
G-ATTB	Wallis WA-116-1 (XR944)	Aerial Media Ltd	
G-ATTI	PA-28 Cherokee 140	A. I. Wilson	
G-ATTK	PA-28 Cherokee 140	G-ATTK Flying Group	
G-ATTN	Piccard HA Balloon ★	Science Museum/South Kensington	
G-ATTR	Bölkow Bö.208C1 Junior	S. Luck	
G-ATTV	PA-28 Cherokee 140	G-ATTV Group	
G-ATTX	PA-28 Cherokee 180	G-ATTX Flying Group	
G-ATUB	PA-28 Cherokee 140	Wicklow Wings	
G-ATUG	D.62B Condor	S. K. Teasdale	
G-ATUH	Tipsy T.66 Nipper 1	H. Abraham	
G-ATUI	Bölkow Bö.208C1 Junior	G. J. Ball	
G-ATVF	DHC.1 Chipmunk 22 (WD327)	ATVF Syndicate	

Notes	Reg	Type	Owner or Operator
	G-ATVK	PA-28 Cherokee 140	J. Turner
	G-ATVO	PA-28 Cherokee 140	Perryair Ltd
	G-ATVP	Vickers FB.5 Gunbus replica (2345) ★	RAF Museum/Hendon
	G-ATVW	D.62B Condor	A. G. & B. N. Stevens
	G-ATVX	Bölkow Bö.208C1 Junior	The Moray Firth Flying Group
	G-ATWA	Jodel DR.1050	One Twenty Group
	G-ATWB	Jodel D.117	Andrewsfield Whisky Bravo Group
	G-ATWJ	Cessna F.172F	J. P. A. Freeman
	G-ATXA	PA-22 Tri-Pacer 150	S. C. J. Hall
	G-ATXD	PA-30 Twin Comanche 160B	M. Bagshaw
	G-ATXJ	HP.137 Jetstream 300 ★	Fire Service training airframe/Cardiff
	G-ATXN	Mitchell-Proctor Kittiwake 1	R. G. Day
	G-ATXO	SIPA 903	C. H. Morris
	G-ATXX	McCandless M.4 gyroplane ★	Ulster Folk & Transport Museum
	G-ATXZ	Bölkow Bö.208C1 Junior	M. J. Beardmore
	G-ATYM	Cessna F.150G	Gym Group
	G-ATYN	Cessna F.150G	J. S. Grant
	G-ATYS	PA-28 Cherokee 180	Cherokee Challenge Syndicate
	G-ATZM	Piper J-3C-90 Cub	N. D. Marshall
	G-ATZS	Wassmer Wa.41 Super Baladou IV	I. R. Siddell
	G-ATZZ	Cessna F.150G	J. P. Nugent
	G-AVAA	Cessna F.150G ★	South Yorkshire Aircraft Museum/Doncaster
	G-AVAV	VS Spitfire IXT (MJ772:GW-A)	Warbird Experiences Ltd
	G-AVAW	D.62B Condor	Condor Aircraft Group
	G-AVBG	PA-28-180 Cherokee	T. W. & W. S. Gilbert
	G-AVBH	PA-28-180 Cherokee	Tenterfield (Holdings) Ltd
	G-AVBR	PA-28-180 Cherokee	G. Cormack
	G-AVBS	PA-28-180 Cherokee	Bravo Sierra Flying Group
	G-AVBT	PA-28-180 Cherokee	Gear-up Aviation Ltd
	G-AVCM	PA-24 Comanche 260	R. F. Smith
	G-AVCN	BN-26A-8 Islander ★	Britten-Norman Aircraft Preservation Society
	G-AVCV	Cessna 182J	K. Hendry
	G-AVDA	Cessna 182K Skylane	F. W. & I. F. Ellis
	G-AVDF	Beagle B.121 Pup 1	D. I. Collings
	G-AVDJ	Supermarine 361 Spitfire LF.IXb	Air Leasing Ltd
	G-AVDS	Beech 65-B80 Queen Air ★	Airport Fire Service/Filton
	G-AVDT	Aeronca 7AC Champion	D. & N. Cheney
	G-AVDV	PA-22-150 Tri-Pacer	L. Beardmore & R. W. Taberner
	G-AVEF	Jodel 150	C. A. Bulman
	G-AVEH	SIAI-Marchetti S.205	S. W. Brown
	G-AVEM	Cessna F.150G	N. J. A. Rutherford
	G-AVEN	Cessna F.150G	M. I. Metcalfe
	G-AVEO	Cessna F.150G	T. W. Gilbert (G-DENA)
	G-AVER	Cessna F.150G	LAC Flying School
	G-AVEU	Wassmer Wa.41 Baladou IV	The Baladou Flying Group
	G-AVEX	D.62B Condor	G. W. Hilferty
	G-AVEY	Currie Super Wot	F. R. Donaldson
	G-AVEZ	HPR.7 Herald 210 ★	Rescue trainer/Norwich
	G-AVFB	HS.121 Trident 2E ★	Imperial War Museum/Duxford
	G-AVFE	HS.121 Trident 2E ★	Belfast Airport Authority
	G-AVFH	HS.121 Trident 2E ★	De Havilland Heritage Museum (fuselage only)/ London Colney
	G-AVFM	HS.121 Trident 2E ★	Brunel Technical College/Bristol
	G-AVFR	PA-28 Cherokee 140	C. Holden & S. Powell
	G-AVFU	PA-32 Cherokee Six 300	Tertium Treuboden Immobilien GmbH/Germany
	G-AVFX	PA-28 Cherokee 140	A. E. Fielding
	G-AVFZ	PA-28 Cherokee 140	G-AVFZ Flying Group
	G-AVGA	PA-24 Comanche 260	G. McD. Moir
	G-AVGC	PA-28 Cherokee 140	L. McIlwain
	G-AVGE	PA-28 Cherokee 140	D. Dunn
	G-AVGJ	Jodel DR.1050	I. B. Melville
	G-AVGZ	Jodel DR.1050	A. F. & S. Williams
	G-AVHH	Cessna F.172	Alpha Victor Ltd
	G-AVHL	Jodel DR.105A	Seething Jodel Group
	G-AVHM	Cessna F.150G	R. D. Forster
	G-AVHY	Fournier RF.4D	I. G. K. Mitchell
	G-AVIB	Cessna F.150G	K. W. Wood
	G-AVIC	Cessna F.172H ★	Leeside Flying Ltd
	G-AVIL	Alon A.2 Aircoupe (VX147)	G. D. J. Wilson
	G-AVIN	MS.880B Rallye Club	R. A. C. Stephens

Reg	Type	Owner or Operator	Notes
G-AVIP	Brantly B.2B	Eaglescott Brantly Group	
G-AVIS	Cessna F.172 ★	J. P. A. Freeman	
G-AVIT	Cessna F.150G	P. Cottrell	
G-AVJF	Cessna F.172H	J. A. & D. T. A. Rees	
G-AVJJ	PA-30 Twin Comanche 160B	The Little Jet Co.Ltd	
G-AVJK	Jodel DR.1050/M1	Juliet Kilo Syndicate	
G-AVJO	Fokker E.III (replica) (422/15)	Flying Aces Movie Aircraft Collection	
G-AVKB	Brochet MB.50 Pipistrelle	R. E. Garforth	
G-AVKD	Fournier RF-4D	Lasham RF4 Group	
G-AVKE	Gadfly HDW.1 ★	The Helicopter Museum/Weston-super-Mare	
G-AVKI	Slingsby T.66 Nipper 3	T. C. R. Trudgill	
G-AVKK	Slingsby T.66 Nipper 3	C. F. O'Neill	
G-AVKP	Beagle A.109 Airedale	R. Callaway-Lewis	
G-AVKR	Bölkow Bö.208C1 Junior	L. Hawkins	
G-AVLB	PA-28 Cherokee 140	M. Wilson	
G-AVLC	PA-28 Cherokee 140	P. G. Evans & R. G. Allgood	
G-AVLE	PA-28 Cherokee 140	S. Doherty	
G-AVLF	PA-28 Cherokee 140	Woodbine Group	
G-AVLG	PA-28 Cherokee 140	R. J. Everett	
G-AVLI	PA-28 Cherokee 140	Lima India Aviation Group	
G-AVLJ	PA-28 Cherokee 140	Cherokee Aviation Holdings Jersey Ltd	
G-AVLM	Beagle B.121 Pup 3	T. M. & D. A. Jones	
G-AVLN	Beagle B.121 Pup 2	Dogs Flying Group	
G-AVLO	Bölkow Bö.208C1 Junior	A. J. Tobias	
G-AVLT	PA-28-140 Cherokee	R. F. Redknap (G-KELC)	
G-AVLW	Fournier RF-4D	J. C. A. C. da Silva	
G-AVLY	Jodel D.120A	S. M. S. Smith	
G-AVMB	D.62B Condor	F. Baldanza	
G-AVMD	Cessna 150G	LAC Flying School	
G-AVMF	Cessna F. 150G	J. F. Marsh	
G-AVMJ	BAC One-Eleven 510ED ★	European Aviation Ltd (cabin trainer)	
G-AVMK	BAC One-Eleven 510ED ★	Gravesend College (fuselage only)	
G-AVMO	BAC One-Eleven 510ED ★	Museum of Flight/East Fortune	
G-AVMU	BAC One-Eleven 510ED ★	Imperial War Museum/Duxford	
G-AVNC	Cessna F.150G	J. Turner	
G-AVNE	Westland WS-58 Wessex Mk 60 Srs 1 ★	The Helicopter Museum/Weston-super-Mare	
G-AVNN	PA-28 Cherokee 180	G-AVNN Flying Group	
G-AVNO	PA-28 Cherokee 180	November Oscar Flying Group	
G-AVNS	PA-28 Cherokee 180	Fly (Fu Lai) Aviation Ltd	
G-AVNU	PA-28 Cherokee 180	D. Durrant	
G-AVNW	PA-28 Cherokee 180	Len Smith's (Aviation) Ltd	
G-AVNY	Fournier RF-4D	J. B. Giddins (G-IVEL)	
G-AVNZ	Fournier RF-4D	C. D. Pidler	
G-AVOA	Jodel DR.1050	D. A. Willies	
G-AVOD	Beagle D.5/180 Husky	PAW Flying Services Ltd	
G-AVOH	D.62B Condor	Condor Group	
G-AVOM	CEA Jodel DR.221	Avon Flying Group	
G-AVOO	PA-18 Super Cub 150	Dublin Gliding Club Ltd	
G-AVOU	Slingsby T.56 S.E.5A Replica	Sywell SE5 Group	
G-AVOZ	PA-28 Cherokee 180	Oscar Zulu Flying Group	
G-AVPC	D.31 Turbulent ★	Museum of Flight/East Fortune	
G-AVPD	Jodel D.9 Bébé ★	S. W. McKay (stored)	
G-AVPI	Cessna F.172H	D. R. Larder	
G-AVPJ	DH.82A Tiger Moth	C. C. Silk	
G-AVPM	Jodel D.117	L. B. Clark	
G-AVPN	HPR.7 Herald 213 ★	Yorkshire Air Museum/Elvington	
G-AVPO	Hindustan HAL-26 Pushpak	B. Johns	
G-AVPV	PA-18 Cherokee 180	K. A. Passmore	
G-AVPY	PA-25 Pawnee 235C	Southdown Gliding Club Ltd	
G-AVRK	PA-28 Cherokee 180	Scenic Air Tours North East Ltd	
G-AVRS	Gardan GY-80 Horizon 180	N. M. Robbins	
G-AVRW	Gardan GY-20 Minicab	Kestrel Flying Group	
G-AVRZ	PA-28 Cherokee 180	RZ Group	
G-AVSA	PA-28 Cherokee 180	Easter Flying Group	
G-AVSB	PA-28 Cherokee 180	G. Cormack	
G-AVSC	PA-28 Cherokee 180	G-AVSC Group	
G-AVSD	PA-28 Cherokee 180	C. B. D. Owen	
G-AVSE	PA-28 Cherokee 180	F. Glendon/Ireland	
G-AVSF	PA-28 Cherokee 180	Monday Club	
G-AVSI	PA-28 Cherokee 140	G-AVSI Flying Group	
G-AVSP	PA-28 Cherokee 180	C. & J. Willis	

Notes	Reg	Type	Owner or Operator
	G-AVSR	Beagle D.5/180 Husky	S. D. J. Holwill
	G-AVTC	Slingsby Nipper T.66 RA.45 Srs 3	J. Crawford
	G-AVTP	Cessna F.172H	Cessna Ltd
	G-AVTT	Ercoupe 415D ★	South Yorkshire Aircraft Museum/Doncaster
	G-AVUG	Cessna F.150H	Skyways Flying Group
	G-AVUH	Cessna F.150H	A. G. McLaren
	G-AVUO	Luton LA4 Minor	M. E. Vaisey
	G-AVUS	PA-28 Cherokee 140	P. K. Pemberton
	G-AVUT	PA-28 Cherokee 140	Bencray Ltd
	G-AVUZ	PA-32 Cherokee Six 300	Ceesix Ltd
	G-AVVC	Cessna F.172H	Aerohire Ltd
	G-AVVO	Avro 652A Anson 19 (VL348) ★	Newark Air Museum
	G-AVWA	PA-28 Cherokee 140	SFG Ltd
	G-AVWD	PA-28 Cherokee 140	M. Howells
	G-AVWI	PA-28 Cherokee 140	L. M. Veitch
	G-AVWL	PA-28 Cherokee 140	G-AVWL Group
	G-AVWM	PA-28 Cherokee 140	G-AVWM Group
	G-AVWO	PA-28R Cherokee Arrow 180	S. S. Bamrah
	G-AVWR	PA-28R Cherokee Arrow 180	G-AVWR Flying Group
	G-AVWT	PA-28R Cherokee Arrow 180	A. C. Brett
	G-AVWU	PA-28R Cherokee Arrow 180	M. Ali & S. Din
	G-AVWV	PA-28R Cherokee Arrow 180	R. V. Thornton
	G-AVWY	Fournier RF-4D	S. A. W. Becker
	G-AVXA	PA-25 Pawnee 235	S. Wales Gliding Club Ltd
	G-AVXD	Slingsby T.66 Nipper 3	J. A. Brompton
	G-AVXF	PA-28R Cherokee Arrow 180	G-AVXF Group
	G-AVXW	D.62B Condor	C. W. A. Holliday
	G-AVXY	Auster AOP.9	G. J. Siddall
	G-AVXZ	PA-28 Cherokee 140 ★	ATC Hayle (instructional airframe)
	G-AVYB	HS.121 Trident 1E-140 ★	SAS training airframe/Hereford
	G-AVYK	Beagle A.61 Terrier 3	R. Burgun
	G-AVYL	PA-28 Cherokee 180	Cotswold Aero Maintenance Ltd
	G-AVYM	PA-28 Cherokee 180	R. A. Danby
	G-AVYS	PA-28R Cherokee Arrow 180	A. N. Harris
	G-AVYT	PA-28R Cherokee Arrow 180	M. Bonsall
	G-AVZB	Aero Z-37 Cmelak ★	Science Museum/Wroughton
	G-AVZP	Beagle B.121 Pup 1	T. A. White
	G-AVZU	Cessna F.150H	R. D. Forster
	G-AVZV	Cessna F.172H	G. Farrar
	G-AVZW	EAA Biplane Model P	C. Edmondson
	G-AWAC	Gardan GY-80 Horizon 180	P. B. Hodgson
	G-AWAJ	Beech 95-D55 Baron	B. F. Whitworth
	G-AWAU	Vickers FB.27A Vimy (replica) (F8614) ★	RAF Museum/Hendon
	G-AWAW	Cessna F.150F ★	Science Museum/South Kensington
	G-AWAX	Cessna 150D	Flying Support SRL
	G-AWAZ	PA-28R Cherokee Arrow 180	R. A. Mailer & D. A. C. Clissett
	G-AWBB	PA-28R Cherokee Arrow 180	P. J. Young
	G-AWBC	PA-28R Cherokee Arrow 180	Anglo Property Services Ltd
	G-AWBG	PA-28 Cherokee 140	I. Herdis
	G-AWBM	D.31 Turbulent	J. J. B. Leasor
	G-AWBS	PA-28 Cherokee 140	Full Sutton Flying Centre Ltd
	G-AWBT	PA-30 Twin Comanche 160B ★	Instructional airframe/Cranfield
	G-AWBU	Morane-Saulnier N (replica) (MS824)	Flying Aces Movie Aircraft Collection
	G-AWBX	Cessna F.150H	R. Nightingale
	G-AWCM	Cessna F.150H	R. Garbett
	G-AWCN	Cessna FR.172E	J. J. N. Carpenter
	G-AWCP	Cessna F.150H (tailwheel)	C. E. Mason
	G-AWDA	Slingsby T.66 Nipper 3	H. Abraham
	G-AWDO	D.31 Turbulent	R. N. Crosland
	G-AWDU	Brantly B.2B	N. J. M. Freeman
	G-AWEA	Beagle B.121 Pup Srs.1	T. S. Walker
	G-AWEF	SNCAN Stampe SV.4B	RAF Buchanan
	G-AWEI	D.62B Condor	P. A. Gange
	G-AWEK	Fournier RF-4D	A. F. & M. P. J. Hill
	G-AWEL	Fournier RF-4D	Hallam Aviation Services Ltd
	G-AWEP	Barritault JB-01 Minicab	R. K. Thomas
	G-AWES	Cessna 150H	R. J. Willis
	G-AWEV	PA-28 Cherokee 140	A. A. Raymond
	G-AWEX	PA-28 Cherokee 140	CBM Associates Consulting Ltd
	G-AWFB	PA-28R Cherokee Arrow 180	P. R. Holloway

Reg	Type	Owner or Operator	Notes
G-AWFC	PA-28R Cherokee Arrow 180	A. Simpson	
G-AWFD	PA-28R Cherokee Arrow 180	C. G. Sims	
G-AWFF	Cessna F.150H	R. A. Marven	
G-AWFJ	PA-28R Cherokee Arrow 180	Airways Aero Associations Ltd	
G-AWFN	D.62B Condor	C. C. Bland	
G-AWFO	D.62B Condor	T. A. & R. E. Major	
G-AWFP	D.62B Condor	S. J. Westley	
G-AWFT	Jodel D.9 Bébé	W. H. Cole	
G-AWFW	Jodel D.117	J. Pool	
G-AWFZ	Beech A23 Musketeer	R. E. Crowe	
G-AWGB	Supermarine Spitfire T.IX (A58-606/ZP-W)	Warbird Experiences Ltd	
G-AWGK	Cessna F.150H	G. E. Allen	
G-AWGM	Mitchell Kittiwake II	P. J. Tanulak	
G-AWGN	Fournier RF-4D	R. J. Grimstead	
G-AWGZ	Taylor JT.1 Monoplane	A. D. Szymanski	
G-AWHB	CASA 2-111D (6J+PR) ★	Aces High Ltd/North Weald	
G-AWHC	Hispano HA.1112 M4L (11)	Air Leasing Ltd	
G-AWHH	Hispano HA.1112 M1L (9)	Anglia Aircraft Restorations Ltd	
G-AWHK	Hispano HA.1112 M1L (10)	Propshop Ltd (G-BWUE)	
G-AWHM	Hispano HA.1112 M1L (7)	K. Seidel	
G-AWHR	Hispano HA.1112 M1L	Air Leasing Ltd	
G-AWHX	Rollason Beta B.2	T. Jarvis	
G-AWHY	Falconar F.11-3	E. L. Watts (G-BDPB)	
G-AWII	VS.349 Spitfire VC (AR501:DU-E))	The Shuttleworth Collection	
G-AWIV	Airmark TSR.3	J. A. Wardlow	
G-AWIW	SNCAN Stampe SV.4B	R. E. Mitchell	
G-AWJE	Slingsby T.66 Nipper 3	K G. G. Howe	
G-AWJV	DH.98 Mosquito TT Mk 35 (TA634) ★	De Havilland Heritage Museum/London Colney	
G-AWJX	Zlin Z.526 Trener Master	M. Baer	
G-AWKD	PA-17 Vagabond	Kilo Delta Flying Group	
G-AWKO	Beagle B.121 Pup 1	Osprey Group	
G-AWKP	Jodel DR.253	G-AWKP Group	
G-AWKX	Beech A65 Queen Air ★	(Instructional airframe)/Shoreham	
G-AWLF	Cessna F.172H	C. Robb	
G-AWLG	SIPA 903	S. W. Markham	
G-AWLI	PA-22 Tri-Pacer 150	North Hangar Group	
G-AWLO	Boeing Stearman E75	N. D. Pickard	
G-AWLP	Mooney M.20F	I. C. Lomax	
G-AWLR	Slingsby T.66 Nipper 3	T. D. Reid	
G-AWLS	Slingsby T.66 Nipper 3	G. A. Dunster & B. Gallagher	
G-AWLX	Auster 5 J/2 Arrow	A. E..Taylor	
G-AWLZ	Fournier RF-4D	Nympsfield RF-4 Group	
G-AWMD	Jodel D.11	J. R. Cooper	
G-AWMF	PA-18 Super Cub 150 (modified)	Booker Gliding Club Ltd	
G-AWMR	D.31 Turbulent	B. E. Holz	
G-AWMT	Cessna F.150H	M. Paisley	
G-AWNT	BN-2A Islander	Precision Terrain Surveys Ltd	
G-AWOH	PA-17 Vagabond	A. Lovejoy & K. Downes	
G-AWOT	Cessna F.150H	North East Aviation Ltd	
G-AWOU	Cessna 170B	S. Billington	
G-AWOX	Westland WS-58 Wessex 60 (150225) ★	Paintball Adventure West/Bristol	
G-AWPH	P.56 Provost T.1	J. A. D. Bradshaw	
G-AWPJ	Cessna F.150H	Global Aviation Ltd	
G-AWPN	Shield Xyla	J. P. Gilbert	
G-AWPU	Cessna F.150J	Westair Flying Services Ltd	
G-AWPW	PA-12 Super Cruiser	AK Leasing (Jersey) Ltd	
G-AWPZ	Andreasson BA-4B	J. M. Vening	
G-AWRP	Cierva Rotorcraft ★	The Helicopter Museum/Weston-super-Mare	
G-AWRS	Avro 19 Srs. 2 (TX213) ★	North East Land Sea and Air Museum/Sunderland	
G-AWRY	P.56 Provost T.1 (XF836)	A. J. House	
G-AWSA	Avro 652A Anson 19 (VL349) ★	Norfolk & Suffolk Aviation Museum/Flixton	
G-AWSH	Zlin Z.526 Trener Master	P. A. Colman	
G-AWSL	PA-28 Cherokee 180D	A. H. & A. H. Brown	
G-AWSM	PA-28 Cherokee 235	Aviation Projects Ltd	
G-AWSN	D.62B Condor	The Condor Club	
G-AWSP	D.62B Condor	A. Waters	
G-AWSS	D.62A Condor	N. J. Butler	
G-AWST	D.62B Condor	J. E. Hobbs	
G-AWSV	Skeeter 12 (XM553)	Maj. M. Somerton-Rayner	
G-AWSW	Beagle D.5/180 Husky (XW635)	Windmill Aviation	

31

Notes	Reg	Type	Owner or Operator
	G-AWTL	PA-28 Cherokee 180D	Ravenair Aircraft Ltd
	G-AWTP	Schleicher Ka 6E	S. A. Smith
	G-AWTS	Beech A.23 Musketeer	Golf Tango Sierra Ltd
	G-AWTV	Beech 19A Musketeer Sport	J. Whittaker
	G-AWTX	Cessna F.150J	R. D. Forster
	G-AWUB	Gardan GY-201 Minicab	R. A. Hand
	G-AWUE	Jodel DR.1050	K. W. Wood & F. M. Watson
	G-AWUJ	Cessna F.150H	Hardman Aviation Ltd
	G-AWUL	Cessna F.150H	A. J. Baron
	G-AWUN	Cessna F.150H	G-AWUN Group
	G-AWUT	Cessna F.150J	Aerospace Resources Ltd
	G-AWUU	Cessna F.150J	D. P. Jones
	G-AWUZ	Cessna F.172H	Five Percent Flying Group
	G-AWVA	Cessna F.172H	Barton Air Ltd
	G-AWVC	Beagle B.121 Pup 1	Beagle Victor Charlie Group
	G-AWVE	Jodel DR.1050/M1	J. Owen
	G-AWVG	AESL Airtourer T.2	C. J. Schofield
	G-AWVN	Aeronca 7AC Champion	Champ Flying Group
	G-AWVZ	Jodel D.112	D. C. Stokes
	G-AWWE	Beagle B.121 Pup 2	Pup Flyers
	G-AWWI	Jodel D.117	W. Richens
	G-AWWN	Jodel DR.1050	M. A. Baker
	G-AWWO	Jodel DR.1050	W. G. Brooks
	G-AWWP	Aerosport Woody Pusher III	M. S. Bird & R. D. Bird
	G-AWWU	Cessna FR.172F	V. A. Aldea & S. Sabau
	G-AWXS	PA-28 Cherokee 180D	J. E. Rowley
	G-AWXY	MS.885 Super Rallye	K. Henderson
	G-AWXZ	SNCAN Stampe SV.4C	Bianchi Aviation Film Services Ltd
	G-AWYI	BE.2c replica (687)	M. C. Boddington & S. Slater
	G-AWYJ	Beagle B.121 Pup 2	H. C. Taylor
	G-AWYL	Jodel DR.253B	T. C. Van Lonkhuyzen
	G-AWYO	Beagle B.121 Pup 1	B. R. C. Wild
	G-AWYY	Slingsby T.57 Camel replica (B6401) ★	F.A.A. Museum/Yeovilton
	G-AWZI	HS.121 Trident 3B ★	A. Lee/FAST Museum (nose only)/Farnborough
	G-AWZJ	HS.121 Trident 3B ★	Dumfries & Galloway Museum
	G-AWZK	HS.121 Trident 3B ★	Runway Visitor Park/Manchester
	G-AWZM	HS.121 Trident 3B ★	Science Museum/Wroughton
	G-AWZP	HS.121 Trident 3B ★	Manchester Museum of Science & Industry (nose only)
	G-AWZX	HS.121 Trident 3B ★	BAA Airport Fire Services/Gatwick
	G-AXAB	PA-28 Cherokee 140	Bencray Ltd
	G-AXAN	DH.82A Tiger Moth (EM720)	A. J. Harrison
	G-AXAT	Jodel D.117A	R. A. Stocks
	G-AXBJ	Cessna F.172H	Central Horizon Partnership LLP
	G-AXBW	DH.82A Tiger Moth (T5879:RUC-W)	WJE Associates Ltd
	G-AXBZ	DH.82A Tiger Moth	W. J. de Jong Cleyndert
	G-AXCA	PA-28R Cherokee Arrow 200	A. J. Bale
	G-AXCG	Jodel D.117	D. J. Millin
	G-AXCY	Jodel D.117A	R. S. Marom
	G-AXDI	Cessna F.172H	M. F. & J. R. Leusby
	G-AXDK	Jodel DR.315	D. W. Wiseman
	G-AXDN	BAC-Sud Concorde 01 ★	Imperial War Museum/Duxford
	G-AXDV	Beagle B.121 Pup 1	S. R. Hopkins
	G-AXDZ	Cassutt Racer IIIM	A. Chadwick
	G-AXED	PA-25 Pawnee 235	Wolds Gliding Club Ltd
	G-AXEH	B.125 Bulldog 1 ★	Museum of Flight/East Fortune
	G-AXEI	Ward Gnome ★	Real Aeroplane Club/Breighton
	G-AXEO	Scheibe SF.25B Falke	P. F. Moffatt
	G-AXEV	Beagle B.121 Pup 2	D. S. Russell & D. G. Benson
	G-AXFG	Cessna 337D	County Garage (Cheltenham) Ltd
	G-AXFM	Servotec Grasshopper III ★	The Helicopter Museum/Weston-super-Mare
	G-AXFN	Jodel D.119	D. W. Garbe
	G-AXGE	MS.880B Rallye Club	T. R. Scorer
	G-AXGG	Cessna F.150J	A. J. Simpson
	G-AXGP	Piper J-3C-90 Cub (3681)	A. P. Acres
	G-AXGR	Luton LA-4A Minor	B. A. Schlussler
	G-AXGS	D.62B Condor	SAS Flying Group
	G-AXGV	D.62B Condor	AXGV Group
	G-AXGZ	D.62B Condor	G. E. Horder

Reg	Type	Owner or Operator	Notes
G-AXHO	Beagle B.121 Pup 2	L. W. Grundy	
G-AXHP	Piper J-3C-65 Cub (480636:A-58)	Witham (Specialist) Vehicles Ltd	
G-AXHR	Piper J-3C-65 Cub (329601:D-44)	D. J. Dash	
G-AXHV	Jodel D.117A	Derwent Flying Group	
G-AXIA	Beagle B.121 Pup 1	C. K. Parsons	
G-AXIE	Beagle B.121 Pup 2	M. Cowan	
G-AXIG	Scottish Aviation B.125 Bulldog 104 ★	National Museum of Scotland/Edinburgh	
G-AXIO	PA-28 Cherokee 140B	R. Wallace	
G-AXIR	PA-28 Cherokee 140B	J. L. Sparks	
G-AXIX	Glos-Airtourer 150	K. R. Wilson	
G-AXJB	Omega 84 balloon	Southern Balloon Group	
G-AXJH	Beagle B.121 Pup 2	The Henry Flying Group	
G-AXJI	Beagle B.121 Pup 2	P. L. Parsons	
G-AXJJ	Beagle B.121 Pup 2	M. L. Jones & ptnrs	
G-AXJO	Beagle B.121 Pup 2	J. A. D. Bradshaw	
G-AXJR	Scheibe SF.25B Falke	Falke Syndicate	
G-AXJV	PA-28 Cherokee 140B	AT Aviation Sales Ltd	
G-AXJX	PA-28 Cherokee 140B	T. W. Gilbert	
G-AXKH	Luton LA-4A Minor	M. E. Vaisey	
G-AXKJ	Jodel D.9	K. D. Boyle	
G-AXKO	Westland-Bell 47G-4A	M. Gallagher	
G-AXKS	Westland Bell 47G-4A ★	Museum of Army Flying/Middle Wallop	
G-AXKX	Westland Bell 47G-4A	R. A. Dale	
G-AXLI	Slingsby T.66 Nipper 3	P. R. Howson	
G-AXLJ	Slingsby T.66 Nipper 3	R. J. Hodder	
G-AXLS	Jodel DR.105A	Axle Flying Club	
G-AXLZ	PA-18 Super Cub 95	Perryair Ltd	
G-AXMA	PA-24 Comanche 180	C. Martin	
G-AXMD	Omega O-56 balloon ★	British Balloon Museum/Newbury	
G-AXMT	Bucker Bu.133 Jungmeister	A. J. E. Smith & R. A. Fleming	
G-AXMW	Beagle B.121 Pup 1	DJP Engineering (Knebworth) Ltd	
G-AXMX	Beagle B.121 Pup 2	Bob The Beagle Group	
G-AXNJ	Wassmer Jodel D.120	J. Pool	
G-AXNN	Beagle B.121 Pup 2	November November Flying Group	
G-AXNP	Beagle B.121 Pup 2	J. W. Ellis & R. J. Hemmings	
G-AXNR	Beagle B.121 Pup 2	AXNR Group	
G-AXNS	Beagle B.121 Pup 2	Derwent Aero Group	
G-AXNW	SNCAN Stampe SV.4C	R. S. Grace	
G-AXNZ	Pitts S.1C Special	November Zulu Group	
G-AXOG	PA-E23 Aztec 250D	G. H. Nolan	
G-AXOH	MS.894 Rallye Minerva	L. C. Clark	
G-AXOJ	Beagle B.121 Pup 2	Pup Flying Group	
G-AXOM	Penn-Smith Gyroplane ★	Stondon Motor Museum/Lower Stondon	
G-AXOR	PA-28 Cherokee 180D	Oscar Romeo Aviation Ltd	
G-AXOT	MS.893 Rallye Commodore 180	P. Evans	
G-AXOZ	Beagle B.121 Pup 1	E. G. Williams	
G-AXPA	Beagle B.121 Pup 1	C. B. Copsey	
G-AXPC	Beagle B.121 Pup 2	T. A. White	
G-AXPF	Cessna F.150K	T. W. Gilbert	
G-AXPG	Mignet HM.293	W. H. Cole (stored)	
G-AXPN	Beagle B.121 Pup 2	P. Wood & R. J. Burgess	
G-AXPZ	Campbell Cricket	W. R. Partridge	
G-AXRC	Campbell Cricket	L. R. Morris	
G-AXRP	SNCAN Stampe SV.4C	C. C. & C. D. Manning (G-BLOL)	
G-AXRR	Auster AOP.9 (XR241)	R. B. Webber	
G-AXSC	Beagle B.121 Pup 1	M. P. Whitley	
G-AXSG	PA-28 Cherokee 180	Seagull Aviation Ltd	
G-AXSM	Jodel DR.1051	T. R. G. & M. S. Barnby	
G-AXSW	Cessna FA.150K	R. J. Whyham	
G-AXSZ	PA-28 Cherokee 140B	White Wings Flying Group	
G-AXTA	PA-28 Cherokee 140B	G-AXTA Aircraft Group	
G-AXTC	PA-28 Cherokee 140B	G-AXTC Group	
G-AXTJ	PA-28 Cherokee 140B	J. P. Nugent	
G-AXTL	PA-28 Cherokee 140B	Bristol and West Aeroplane Club Ltd	
G-AXTO	PA-24 Comanche 260	D. L. Edwards	
G-AXTX	Jodel D.112	C. Sawford	
G-AXUA	Beagle B.121 Pup 1	P. Wood	
G-AXUB	BN-2A Islander	Britten-Norman Ltd	
G-AXUC	PA-12 Super Cruiser	Weald Air Services Ltd	
G-AXUF	Cessna FA.150K	K. A. O'Connor	
G-AXUJ	Auster J/1 Autocrat	S. Seale-Finch (G-OSTA)	

33

Notes	Reg	Type	Owner or Operator
	G-AXUK	Jodel DR.1050	Downland Flying Group
	G-AXUM	HP.137 Jetstream 1 ★	Sodeteg Formation/France
	G-AXVB	Cessna F.172H	M. Lazar
	G-AXVM	Campbell Cricket	D. M. Organ
	G-AXVN	McCandless M.4	W. R. Partridge
	G-AXWA	Auster AOP.9 (XN437)	C. M. Edwards
	G-AXWT	Jodel D.11	C. S. Jackson
	G-AXWV	Jodel DR.253	R. Friedlander & D. C. Ray
	G-AXWZ	PA-28R Cherokee Arrow 200	Whisky Zulu Group
	G-AXXV	DH.82A Tiger Moth (DE992)	Fly Tiger Moth Ltd
	G-AXXW	Jodel D.117	R. K. G. Delve
	G-AXYK	Taylor JT.1 Monoplane	D. E. Findoin
	G-AXYU	Jodel D.9 Bébé	P. Turton
	G-AXZD	PA-28 Cherokee 180E	M. Watson & M. A. Lee
	G-AXZH	Glasflugel H201B Standard Libelle	M. C. Gregorie
	G-AXZM	Slingsby T.66 Nipper 3	G. R. Harlow
	G-AXZO	Cessna 180	M. D. Pryce & D. A. Hunt
	G-AXZP	PA-E23 Aztec 250D	D. M. Harbottle
	G-AXZT	Jodel D.117	P. Guest
	G-AXZU	Cessna 182N	W. Gollan
	G-AYAB	PA-28 Cherokee 180E	L. Kretschmann
	G-AYAC	PA-28R Cherokee Arrow 200	Fersfield Flying Group
	G-AYAJ	Cameron O-84 balloon	E. T. Hall
	G-AYAL	Omega 56 balloon ★	British Balloon Museum/Newbury
	G-AYAN	Slingsby Motor Cadet III	R. Moyse
	G-AYAR	PA-28 Cherokee 180E	North East Flight Academy Ltd
	G-AYAT	PA-28 Cherokee 180E	G-AYAT Flying Group
	G-AYAW	PA-28 Cherokee 180E	North East Flyers Group
	G-AYBG	Scheibe SF.25B Falke	Anglia Sailplanes
	G-AYBP	Jodel D.112	A. C. Oliver
	G-AYBR	Jodel D.112	I. S. Parker
	G-AYCC	Campbell Cricket	G. W. Auld
	G-AYCE	Scintex CP.301-C1 Emeraude	A. C. Beech
	G-AYCG	SNCAN Stampe SV.4C	A. Page
	G-AYCK	AIA Stampe SV.4C	A. A. M. & C. W. M. Huke (G-BUNT)
	G-AYCN	Piper J-3C-65 Cub	W. R. & B. M. Young
	G-AYCO	CEA DR.360	P. G. Hayward
	G-AYCP	Jodel D.112	J. D. Bradley
	G-AYCT	Cessna F.172H	J. R. Benson
	G-AYDI	DH.82A Tiger Moth	E. G. & G. R. Woods
	G-AYDR	SNCAN Stampe SV.4C	D. J. Ashley
	G-AYDV	Coates Swalesong SA11	The Real Aeroplane Co.Ltd
	G-AYDW	Beagle A.61 Terrier 2	A. S. Topen
	G-AYDX	Beagle A.61 Terrier 2	T. S. Lee
	G-AYDY	Luton LA-4A Minor	J. Dible/Ireland
	G-AYDZ	Jodel DR.200	Zero One Group
	G-AYEB	Jodel D.112	Echo Bravo Partnership
	G-AYEF	PA-28 Cherokee 180E	Pegasus Flying Group
	G-AYEG	Falconar F-9	J. P. Taylor
	G-AYEH	Jodel DR.1050	T. J. N. H. Palmer
	G-AYEJ	Jodel DR.1050	The Bluebird Flying Group
	G-AYEN	Piper J-3C-65 Cub	P. Warde & C. F. Morris
	G-AYET	MS.892A Rallye Commodore 150	A. T. R. Bingley
	G-AYEW	Jodel DR.1051	J. R. Hope
	G-AYFC	D.62B Condor	A. R. Chadwick
	G-AYFD	D.62B Condor	B. G. Manning
	G-AYFE	D.62C Condor	M. Soulsby
	G-AYFF	D.62B Condor	H. Stuart
	G-AYFJ	MS.880B Rallye Club	Rallye FJ Group
	G-AYFV	Crosby BA-4B	N. J. W. Reid
	G-AYGA	Jodel D.117	J. W. Bowes
	G-AYGB	Cessna 310Q ★	Instructional airframe/Perth
	G-AYGC	Cessna F.150K	Alpha Aviation Group
	G-AYGD	Jodel DR.1051	J. F. M. Barlett & J. P. Liber
	G-AYGE	SNCAN Stampe SV.4C	P. Anderson
	G-AYGG	Jodel D.120	J. M. Dean
	G-AYGX	Cessna FR.172G	AW Aviation Consultancy Services Ltd
	G-AYHA	AA-1 Yankee	N. T. Oakman & G. J. Fricker
	G-AYHX	Jodel D.117A	L. E. Cowling
	G-AYIA	Hughes 369HS	G. D. E. Bilton/Sywell

Reg	Type	Owner or Operator	Notes
G-AYIG	PA-28 Cherokee 140C	J. L. Sparks	
G-AYII	PA-28R Cherokee Arrow 200	N. P. Wilson	
G-AYIJ	SNCAN Stampe SV.4B	India Juliet Stampe Group	
G-AYJA	Jodel DR.1050	D. M. Blair	
G-AYJB	SNCAN Stampe SV.4C	F. J. M. & J. P. Esson	
G-AYJD	Alpavia-Fournier RF-3	Juliet Delta Group	
G-AYJP	PA-28 Cherokee 140C	Demero Ltd & LV Skies Ltd	
G-AYJR	PA-28 Cherokee 140C	T. W. Gilbert	
G-AYJY	Isaacs Fury II (K2065)	G. E. Croft	
G-AYKD	Jodel DR.1050	A. James	
G-AYKJ	Jodel D.117A	R. J. Hughes	
G-AYKK	Jodel D.117	J. M. Whitham	
G-AYKS	Leopoldoff L.7 Colibri	W. B. Cooper	
G-AYKT	Jodel D.117	D. I. Walker	
G-AYKW	PA-28 Cherokee 140C	Kilo Whiskey Group	
G-AYKZ	SAI KZ-8	R. E. Mitchell	
G-AYLA	Glos-Airtourer 115	C. P. L. Jenkins	
G-AYLC	Jodel DR.1051	G-AYLC Flying Group	
G-AYLF	Jodel DR.1051 (modified)	R. Twigg	
G-AYLL	Jodel DR.1050	G. Bell	
G-AYLP	AA-1 Yankee	D. Nairn	
G-AYME	Fournier RF-5	Romeo Foxtrot Group	
G-AYMK	PA-28 Cherokee 140C	R. Quinn & B. Hutchinson	
G-AYMP	Currie Wot	R. C. Hibberd	
G-AYMR	Lederlin 380L	P. J. Brayshaw	
G-AYMU	Jodel D.112	M. R. Baker	
G-AYMV	Western 20 balloon	R. G. Turnbull	
G-AYNA	Phoenix Currie Wot	S-J. Niles	
G-AYNF	PA-28 Cherokee 140C	BW Aviation Ltd	
G-AYNJ	PA-28 Cherokee 140C	S. Doherty	
G-AYNN	Cessna 185B	Bencray Ltd	
G-AYNP	Westland WS-55 Whirlwind Srs 3 ★	IHM/Weston-super-Mare	
G-AYOW	Cessna 182N	M. Elsey	
G-AYOZ	Cessna FA.150L	P. J. Worrall	
G-AYPE	MBB Bö.209 Monsun	Papa Echo Ltd	
G-AYPG	Cessna F.177RG	N. R. Burton	
G-AYPH	Cessna F.177RG	M. L. & T. M. Jones	
G-AYPJ	PA-28 Cherokee 180	R. B. Petrie	
G-AYPM	PA-18 Super Cub 95 (115373)	R. C. Piper	
G-AYPO	PA-18 Super Cub 95	A. W. Knowles	
G-AYPS	PA-18 Super Cub 95	D. Racionzer & P. Wayman	
G-AYPU	PA-28R Cherokee Arrow 200	Monalto Investments Ltd	
G-AYPV	PA-28 Cherokee 140D	Ashley Gardner Flying Club Ltd	
G-AYPZ	Campbell Cricket	A. Melody	
G-AYRC	Campbell Cricket	B. L. Johnson	
G-AYRG	Cessna F.172K	I. G. Harrison	
G-AYRI	PA-28R Cherokee Arrow 200	J. C. Houdret	
G-AYRL	Sportavia-Putzer SFS31 Milan	A.Hoskins & K. M. Fresson	
G-AYRM	PA-28 Cherokee 140D	M. J. Luck	
G-AYRO	Cessna FA.150L Aerobat	AJW Construction Ltd	
G-AYRS	Jodel D.120A	L. R. H. D'Eath	
G-AYRT	Cessna F.172K	R. F. Tuff	
G-AYSB	PA-30 Twin Comanche 160C	Charles Lock (1963) Ltd	
G-AYSH	Taylor JT.1 Monoplane	C. J. Lodge	
G-AYSK	Luton LA-4A Minor	P. A. Gasson	
G-AYSX	Cessna F.177RG	AT Aviation Sales Ltd	
G-AYSY	Cessna F.177RG	G. C. W. Davies	
G-AYTA	SOCATA MS.880B Rallye Club ★	Manchester Museum of Science & Industry	
G-AYTR	CP.301A Emeraude	M. A. Smith	
G-AYTT	Phoenix PM-3 Duet	C. M. Bracewell	
G-AYTV	Jurca Tempete	C. W. Kirk	
G-AYUB	CEA DR.253B	P. J. Coward, EES Aviation Services Ltd & Forbes Insurance Ltd	
G-AYUH	PA-28 Cherokee 180F	Broadland Flying Group Ltd	
G-AYUJ	Evans VP-1	T. N. Howard	
G-AYUM	Slingsby T.61A Falke	M. H. Simms	
G-AYUN	Slingsby T.61A Falke	G-AYUN Group	
G-AYUP	Slingsby T.61A Falke	P. R. Williams	
G-AYUR	Slingsby T.61A Falke	C. O'Mahoney	
G-AYUS	Taylor JT.1 Monoplane	J. G. W. Newton	
G-AYUT	Jodel DR.1050	G. Bell & S. P. Garton	

35

Notes	Reg	Type	Owner or Operator
	G-AYUV	Cessna F.172H	Justgold Ltd
	G-AYVP	Woody Pusher	J. R. Wraight
	G-AYWD	Cessna 182N	Wild Dreams Group
	G-AYWH	Jodel D.117A	D. Kynaston
	G-AYWM	Glos-Airtourer Super 150	Star Flying Group
	G-AYWT	AIA Stampe SV.4C	S. T. Carrel
	G-AYXP	Jodel D.117A	G. N. Davies
	G-AYXT	WS-55 Whirlwind Srs 2 (XK940:911) ★	IHM/Weston-super-Mare
	G-AYYO	Jodel DR.1050/M1	Bustard Jodel Group
	G-AYYT	Jodel DR.1050/M1	O. Prince
	G-AYYU	Beech C23 Musketeer	M. R. Harness
	G-AYZH	Taylor JT.2 Titch	T. Jarvis
	G-AYZI	SNCAN Stampe SV.4C	R. J. & R. J. Anderson
	G-AYZJ	Westland WS-55 Whirlwind HAS.7 ★	Newark Air Museum (XM685)
	G-AYZK	Jodel DR.1050/M1	G. J. McDill
	G-AYZS	D.62B Condor	P. S. Bates
	G-AYZU	Slingsby T.61A Falke	J. Pool
	G-AYZW	Slingsby T.61A Falke	Y-ZW Group
	G-AZAB	PA-30 Twin Comanche 160B	D. T. Cairns
	G-AZAJ	PA-28R Cherokee Arrow 200B	P. Woulfe
	G-AZAU	Servotec Grasshopper III ★	The Helicopter Museum/Weston-super-Mare
	G-AZAZ	Bensen B.8M ★	F.A.A. Museum/Yeovilton
	G-AZBB	MBB Bö.209 Monsun 160FV	J. A. Webb
	G-AZBI	Jodel 150	R. J. Wald
	G-AZBL	Jodel D.9 Bébé	P. A. Gasson
	G-AZBN	Noorduyn AT-16 Harvard IIB (FT391)	Swaygate Ltd
	G-AZBU	Auster AOP.9 (XR246)	Auster Nine Group
	G-AZCB	SNCAN Stampe SV.4C	M. Coward
	G-AZCK	Beagle B.121 Pup 2	P. Crone
	G-AZCL	Beagle B.121 Pup 2	Flew LLP & J. M. Henry
	G-AZCN	Beagle B.121 Pup 2	Snoopy Flying Group
	G-AZCP	Beagle B.121 Pup 1	K. N. St.Aubyn
	G-AZCT	Beagle B.121 Pup 1	J. C. Metcalf
	G-AZCU	Beagle B.121 Pup 1	D. W. Locke
	G-AZCV	Beagle B.121 Pup 2	N. R. W. Long
	G-AZCZ	Beagle B.121 Pup 2	L. Northover
	G-AZDD	MBB Bö.209 Monsun 150FF	Double Delta Flying Group
	G-AZDE	PA-28R Cherokee Arrow 200B	Insight Aviation Group Ltd
	G-AZDG	Beagle B.121 Pup 2	P. J. Beeson
	G-AZDJ	PA-32 Cherokee Six 300	K. J. Mansbridge & D. C. Gibbs
	G-AZDK	Beech 95-B55 Baron	T. W. Harris (G-SWEE)
	G-AZDY	DH.82A Tiger Moth	B. A. Mills
	G-AZEF	Jodel D.120	G-AZEF Group
	G-AZEG	PA-28 Cherokee 140D	M. Drijfhout & P. C. Baker
	G-AZEU	Beagle B.121 Pup 2	G. M. Moir
	G-AZEV	Beagle B.121 Pup 2	A. P. Amor
	G-AZEW	Beagle B.121 Pup 2	D. G. Russell
	G-AZEY	Beagle B.121 Pup 2	A. H. Cameron
	G-AZFA	Beagle B.121 Pup 2	A. Lonsdale
	G-AZFC	PA-28 Cherokee 140D	WLS Flying Group
	G-AZFI	PA-28R Cherokee Arrow 200B	G-AZFI Ltd
	G-AZFM	PA-28R Cherokee Arrow 200B	PL Photography Ltd
	G-AZGA	Jodel D.120	P. Turton & N. J. Owen
	G-AZGC	SNCAN Stampe SV.4C	D. J. Ashley
	G-AZGE	SNCAN Stampe SV.4C	D. Capon & M. Flint
	G-AZGF	Beagle B.121 Pup 2	J. W. Ellis & G. Van Aston
	G-AZGL	MS.894A Rallye Minerva	N. Parkhouse
	G-AZGY	CP.301B Emeraude	R. H. Braithwaite
	G-AZGZ	DH.82A Tiger Moth (NM181)	R. J. King
	G-AZHC	Jodel D.112	Aerodel Flying Group
	G-AZHD	Slingsby T.61A Falke	R. J. Shallcrass
	G-AZHH	SA 102.5 Cavalier	M. W. Place
	G-AZHI	Glos-Airtourer Super 150	Flying Grasshoppers Ltd
	G-AZHK	Robin HR.100/200B	The Bield Flying Group (G-ILEG)
	G-AZHT	AESL Airtourer (modified)	Aviation West Ltd
	G-AZHU	Luton LA-4A Minor	J. Owen
	G-AZHX	SA Bulldog Srs 100/101	K. J. Fraser (G-DOGE)
	G-AZIB	ST-10 Diplomate	W. B. Bateson
	G-AZII	Jodel D.117A	D. H. G. Cotter
	G-AZIJ	Jodel DR.360	Fenland Flying School Ltd

Reg	Type	Owner or Operator	Notes
G-AZIL	Slingsby T.61A Falke	M. A. Savage	
G-AZIP	Cameron O-65 balloon	Dante Balloon Group	
G-AZJC	Fournier RF-5	Seighford RF5 Group	
G-AZJE	Ord-Hume JB-01 Minicab	J. Evans	
G-AZJN	Robin DR.300/140	B. J. Atkins	
G-AZJV	Cessna F.172L	G-AZJV Flying Group	
G-AZKE	MS.880B Rallye Club	Profit Invest Sp.Z.O.O./Poland	
G-AZKP	Jodel D.117	J. Pool	
G-AZKR	PA-24 Comanche	S. J. McGovern	
G-AZKS	AA-1A Trainer	I. R. Matterface	
G-AZKW	Cessna F.172L	D. N. Emery	
G-AZKZ	Cessna F.172L	R. D. & E. Forster	
G-AZLE	Boeing N2S-5 Kaydet (1102:102)	DH Heritage Flights Ltd	
G-AZLF	Jodel D.120	D. C. O'Dwyer	
G-AZLN	PA-28 Cherokee 180F	Enstone Sales & Services Ltd and J. Logan	
G-AZLV	Cessna 172K	G-AZLV Flying Group	
G-AZLY	Cessna F.150L	H. Mackintosh	
G-AZMC	Slingsby T.61A Falke	P. J. R. White	
G-AZMD	Slingsby T.61C Falke	H. Abraham	
G-AZMJ	AA-5 Traveler	W. R. Partridge	
G-AZMX	PA-28 Cherokee 140 ★	NE Wales Institute of Higher Education (Instructional airframe)/Flintshire	
G-AZMZ	MS.893A Rallye Commodore 150	J. Palethorpe	
G-AZNK	SNCAN Stampe SV.4A	I. Noakes	
G-AZNL	PA-28R Cherokee Arrow 200D	B. P. Liversidge	
G-AZNO	Cessna 182P	N. A. Baxter	
G-AZNT	Cameron O-84 balloon	P. Glydon	
G-AZOA	MBB Bö.209 Monsun 150FF	M. W. Hurst	
G-AZOB	MBB Bö.209 Monsun 150FF	J. A. Webb	
G-AZOE	Glos-Airtourer 115	R. Smith	
G-AZOF	Glos-Airtourer Super 150	C. Goldsmith	
G-AZOG	PA-28R Cherokee Arrow 200D	S. J. Lowe	
G-AZOL	PA-34-200 Seneca II	Stapleford Flying Club Ltd	
G-AZOS	Jurca MJ.5-H1 Sirocco	P. J. Tanulak	
G-AZOU	Jodel DR.1050	Horsham Flying Group	
G-AZOZ	Cessna FRA.150L	A. Mitchell	
G-AZPA	PA-25 Pawnee 235	Black Mountains Gliding Club Ltd	
G-AZPC	Slingsby T.61C Falke	D. Heslop & J. R. Kimberley	
G-AZPF	Fournier RF-5	E. C. Mort	
G-AZPH	Craft-Pitts S-1S Special ★	Science Museum/South Kensington	
G-AZPX	Western O-31 balloon	Zebedee Balloon Service Ltd	
G-AZRA	MBB Bö.209 Monsun 150FF	Alpha Flying Ltd	
G-AZRH	PA-28 Cherokee 140D	Trust Flying Group	
G-AZRI	Payne Free Balloon	C. A. Butter & J. J. T. Cooke	
G-AZRK	Fournier RF-5	J. F. Rogers & S. C. Clyno	
G-AZRL	PA-18 Super Cub 95	I. Laws, P. Cooper & R. D. Potter	
G-AZRM	Fournier RF-5	Romeo Mike Group	
G-AZRN	Cameron O-84 balloon	C. J. Desmet/Belgium	
G-AZRS	PA-22 Tri-Pacer 150	R. H. Hulls	
G-AZRZ	Cessna U.206F	Cornish Parachute Club Ltd	
G-AZSA	Stampe et Renard SV.4B	M. R. Dolman	
G-AZSC	Noorduyn AT-16 Harvard IIB (43:SC)	Goodwood Road Racing Co Ltd	
G-AZSF	PA-28R Cherokee Arrow 200D	Aeros Leasing Ltd	
G-AZTA	MBB Bö.209 Monsun 150FF	E. C. Dugard	
G-AZTF	Cessna F.177RG	R. Burgun	
G-AZTM	AESL Airtourer T2	Victa Restoration Group	
G-AZTR	SNCAN Stampe SV-4C	G. W. Lynch	
G-AZTS	Cessna F.172L	Eastern Air Executive Ltd	
G-AZTV	Stolp SA.500 Starlet	G. R. Rowland	
G-AZUM	Cessna F.172L	Fowlmere Flyers	
G-AZUY	Cessna E.310L	W. B. Bateson	
G-AZUZ	Cessna FRA.150L	D. J. Parker & J. T. Bonsall	
G-AZVA	MBB Bö.209 Monsun 150FF	M. P. Brinkmann	
G-AZVB	MBB Bö.209 Monsun 150FF	R. K. Galbally & E. W. Russell	
G-AZVG	AA-5 Traveler	BSI Aviation Trust	
G-AZVI	MS.892A Rallye Commodore	G. C. Jarvis	
G-AZVL	Jodel D.119	D. & J. M. R. Royle	
G-AZWB	PA-28 Cherokee 140	G-AZWB Flying Group	
G-AZWF	SAN Jodel DR.1050	D. Silsbury	
G-AZWS	PA-28R Cherokee Arrow 180	K. M. Turner	
G-AZWT	Westland Lysander IIIA (V9367)	The Shuttleworth Collection	

Notes	Reg	Type	Owner or Operator
	G-AZWY	PA-24 Comanche 260	H. M. Donnan
	G-AZXG	PA-23 Aztec 250D ★	Instructional airframe/Cranfield
	G-AZYA	Gardan GY-80 Horizon 160	F. M. L. S. Godhino
	G-AZYB	Bell 47H-1 ★	The Helicopter Museum/Weston-super-Mare
	G-AZYD	MS.893A Rallye Commodore	Staffordshire Gliding Club Ltd
	G-AZYF	PA-28-180 Cherokee D	SI Aviation Services Ltd
	G-AZYS	CP.301C-1 Emeraude	C. G. Ferguson & D. Drew
	G-AZYU	PA-23 Aztec 250E	M. E. & M. H. Cromati
	G-AZYY	Slingsby T.61A Falke	T. A. Smith
	G-AZYZ	Wassmer Wa.51A Pacific	W. A. Stewart
	G-AZZR	Cessna F.150L	Blue Cloud Industries Ltd
	G-AZZV	Cessna F.172L	ZV Flying Group
	G-AZZZ	DH.82A Tiger Moth	S. W. McKay
	G-BAAD	Evans Super VP-1	The Breighton VP-1 Group
	G-BAAF	Manning-Flanders MF1 (replica)	Aviation Film Services Ltd
	G-BAAI	MS.893A Rallye Commodore	R. D. Taylor
	G-BAAW	Jodel D.119	Alpha Whiskey Flying Group
	G-BABC	Cessna F.150L	P. Tribble
	G-BABD	Cessna FRA.150L (modified)	G. G. Chandler
	G-BABG	PA-28 Cherokee 180	R. Nightingale
	G-BABY	Taylor JT.2 Titch ★	Norfolk and Suffolk Aviation Museum/Flixton
	G-BACB	PA-34-200 Seneca II	Milbrooke Motors Ltd
	G-BACE	Fournier RF-5	G-BACE Fournier Group
	G-BACJ	Jodel D.120	Wearside Flying Association
	G-BACL	Jodel 150	P. I. Morgans
	G-BACN	Cessna FRA.150L	F. Bundy
	G-BACO	Cessna FRA.150L	Limora Oldtimer GmbH & Co KG/Germany
	G-BADC	Rollason Beta B.2A	A. P. Grimley
	G-BADH	Slingsby T.61A Falke	I. P. Sumeghi
	G-BADJ	PA-E23 Aztec 250E	K. A. W. Ashcroft
	G-BADM	D.62B Condor	Delta Mike Condor Group
	G-BADV	Brochet MB50	W. B. Cooper
	G-BADW	Pitts S-2A Special	R. E. Mitchell
	G-BADZ	Aerotek Pitts S-2A Special	R. F. Warner
	G-BAEE	Jodel DR.1050/M1	R. Little
	G-BAEM	Robin DR.400/125	M. A. Webb
	G-BAEN	Robin DR.400/180	C. R. Brown
	G-BAEO	Cessna F.172M	Fairbank Investments Ltd
	G-BAEP	Cessna FRA.150L (modified)	Peterborough Flying School Ltd
	G-BAER	Cosmic Wind	A. G. Truman
	G-BAET	Piper J-3C-65 Cub (330314)	C. J. Rees
	G-BAEW	Cessna F.172M	London Denham Aviation Ltd
	G-BAEY	Cessna F.172M	GHP Air Service LP
	G-BAEZ	Cessna FRA.150L	Donair Flying Club Ltd
	G-BAFA	AA-5 Traveler	C. F. Mackley
	G-BAFG	DH.82A Tiger Moth	Tiger Moth Experience Ltd
	G-BAFL	Cessna 182P	R. B. Hopkinson & A. S. Pike
	G-BAFT	PA-18 Super Cub 150	J. F. Hammond
	G-BAFU	PA-28 Cherokee 140	C. E. Taylor
	G-BAFV	PA-18 Super Cub 95	T. F. & S. J. Thorpe
	G-BAFW	PA-28 Cherokee 140	A. J. Peters
	G-BAFX	Robin DR.400/140	High Flight Training Solutions Ltd
	G-BAGB	SIAI Marchetti SF.260	V. Balzer
	G-BAGC	Robin DR.400/140	J. R. Roberts
	G-BAGF	Jodel D.92 Bébé	J. Hoskins
	G-BAGG	PA-32 Cherokee Six 300E	Aero Rentals Ltd
	G-BAGJ	Westland SA.341G Gazelle ★	North East Land Sea and Air Museum/Sunderland
	G-BAGN	Cessna F.177RG	F. T. Marty
	G-BAGR	Robin DR.400/140	Aeroclub du Bassin D'Arcachon/France
	G-BAGS	Robin DR.400/180 2+2	M. Whale
	G-BAGT	Helio H.295 Courier (66-374:EO)	D. C. Hanss
	G-BAGX	PA-28 Cherokee 140	I. Lwanga
	G-BAGY	Cameron O-84 balloon	P. G. Dunnington
	G-BAHF	PA-28 Cherokee 140	Warwickshire Leasing Ltd
	G-BAHJ	PA-24 Comanche 250	K. Cooper
	G-BAHL	Robin DR.400/160	J. B. McVeighty
	G-BAHP	Volmer VJ.22 Sportsman	Seaplane Group
	G-BAHS	PA-28R Cherokee Arrow 200-II	J. L. Sparks
	G-BAHX	Cessna 182P	M. D. J. Moore

Reg	Type	Owner or Operator	Notes
G-BAIG	PA-34-200-2 Seneca	Mid-Anglia School of Flying	
G-BAIH	PA-28R Cherokee Arrow 200-II	M. G. West	
G-BAIK	Cessna F.150L	D. A. & T. M. Jones	
G-BAIS	Cessna F.177RG	Cardinal Syndicate	
G-BAIW	Cessna F.172M	Jindalee Ltd	
G-BAIZ	Slingsby T.61A Falke	Falke Syndicate	
G-BAJB	Cessna F.177RG	J. D. Loveridge	
G-BAJE	Cessna 177	C. Quist	
G-BAJN	AA-5 Traveler	Turweston Flying Club Ltd	
G-BAJO	AA-5 Traveler	Montgomery Aviation Ltd	
G-BAJR	PA-28 Cherokee 180	A. C. Sturgeon	
G-BAJZ	Robin DR.400/125	Prestwick Flying Club Ltd	
G-BAKJ	PA-30 Twin Comanche 160B	E. R. & P. M. Jones	
G-BAKM	Robin DR.400/140	D. V. Pieri	
G-BAKN	SNCAN Stampe SV.4C	M. Holloway	
G-BAKR	Jodel D.117	J. Jennings	
G-BAKV	PA-18 Super Cub 150	W. J. Murray	
G-BAKW	Beagle B.121 Pup 2	Cunning Stunts Flying Group	
G-BALD	Cameron O-84 balloon	C. A. Gould	
G-BALF	Robin DR.400/140	G. & D. A. Wasey	
G-BALG	Robin DR.400/180	S. G. Jones	
G-BALH	Robin DR.400/140B	SARL HM MAT Import/France	
G-BALJ	Robin DR.400/180	D. R. Godfrey	
G-BALN	Cessna T.310Q	O'Brien Properties Ltd	
G-BALS	Tipsy Nipper T.66 Srs.3	N. C. Spooner	
G-BAMB	Slingsby T.61C Falke	H. J. Bradley	
G-BAMC	Cessna F.150L	K. Meredith & R. W. Marchant	
G-BAML	Bell 206B Jet Ranger II ★	Aero Venture	
G-BAMR	PA-16 Clipper	R. H. Royce	
G-BAMU	Robin DR.400/160	The Alternative Flying Group	
G-BAMV	Robin DR.400/180	K. Jones	
G-BAMY	PA-28R Cherokee Arrow 200-II	Flying Pig UK Ltd	
G-BANA	Robin DR.221	G. T. Pryor	
G-BANB	Robin DR.400/180	M. Ingvardsen	
G-BANC	Gardan GY-201 Minicab	C. R. Shipley	
G-BANF	Luton LA-4A Minor	N. F. O'Neill	
G-BANU	Wassmer Jodel D.120	C. H. Kilner	
G-BANV	Phoenix Currie Wot	A. A. M. & C. W. N. Huke	
G-BANW	CP.1330 Super Emeraude	A. Berry	
G-BANX	Cessna F.172M	Oakfleet 2000 Ltd	
G-BAOM	MS.880B Rallye Club	P. J. D. Feehan	
G-BAOU	AA-5 Traveler	R. C. Mark	
G-BAPB	DHC.1 Chipmunk 22 (WB549:7)	R. C. P. Brookhouse	
G-BAPI	Cessna FRA.150L	M. Bonsall	
G-BAPJ	Cessna FRA.150L	T. White	
G-BAPL	PA-23 Turbo Aztec 250E	Donington Aviation Ltd	
G-BAPR	Jodel D.11	D. J. Bobka	
G-BAPS	Campbell Cougar ★	The Helicopter Museum/Weston-super-Mare	
G-BAPV	Robin DR.400/160	J. D. & M. Millne	
G-BAPW	PA-28R Cherokee Arrow 180	J. L. Shields	
G-BAPX	Robin DR.400/160	White Rose Aviators	
G-BAPY	Robin HR.100/210	D. G. Doyle	
G-BARC	Cessna FR.172J	Severn Valley Aviation Group	
G-BARF	Jodel D.112 Club	R. N. Jones	
G-BARH	Beech C.23 Sundowner	R. McPherson	
G-BARN	Taylor JT.2 Titch	R. G. W. Newton	
G-BARS	DHC.1 Chipmunk 22 (1377)	J. Beattie & R. M. Scarre	
G-BARZ	Scheibe SF.28A Tandem Falke	K. Kiely	
G-BASH	AA-5 Traveler	BASH Flying Group	
G-BASJ	PA-28-180 Cherokee	Bristol Aero Club	
G-BASN	Beech C.23 Sundowner	Beech G-BASN Group Syndicate	
G-BASO	Lake LA-4 Amphibian	Uulster Seaplane Association Ltd	
G-BASP	Beagle B.121 Pup 1	B. J. Coutts	
G-BATV	PA-28-180D Cherokee	Scoreby Flying Group	
G-BAUC	PA-25 Pawnee 235	Southdown Gliding Club Ltd	
G-BAUH	Jodel D.112	D. Nutt	
G-BAVB	Cessna F.172M	D. G. Smith	
G-BAVH	DHC.1 Chipmunk 22	G-BAVH Syndicate	
G-BAVL	PA-23 Aztec 250E	S. P. & A. V. Chillott	
G-BAVO	Boeing Stearman N2S (26)	R. C. McCarthy	
G-BAWG	PA-28R Cherokee Arrow 200-II	Solent Air Ltd	

39

Notes	Reg	Type	Owner or Operator
	G-BAWK	PA-28 Cherokee 140	J. P. Nugent
	G-BAXS	Bell 47G-5	C. R. Johnson
	G-BAXU	Cessna F.150L	Peterborough Flying School Ltd
	G-BAXV	Cessna F.150L	H. Quinn
	G-BAXY	Cessna F.172M	Peterborough Flying School Ltd
	G-BAXZ	PA-28 Cherokee 140	G-BAXZ (87) Syndicate
	G-BAYL	SNCAN Nord 1101 Norecrin ★	(stored)/Chirk
	G-BAYO	Cessna 150L	J. A. & D. T. A. Rees
	G-BAYP	Cessna 150L	Yankee Papa Flying Group
	G-BAYR	Robin HR.100/210	D. G. Doyle
	G-BAZC	Robin DR.400/160	S. G. Jones
	G-BAZM	Jodel D.11	Watchford Jodel Group
	G-BAZS	Cessna F.150L	Full Sutton Flying Centre Ltd
	G-BBAW	Robin HR.100/210	F. A. Purvis
	G-BBAX	Robin DR.400/140	G. J. Bissex & P. H. Garbutt
	G-BBAY	Robin DR.400/140	S. R. Evans
	G-BBBB	Taylor JT.1 Monoplane	M. C. Arnold
	G-BBBC	Cessna F.150L	S. Collins & C. A. Widdowson
	G-BBBI	AA-5 Traveler	R. Madden
	G-BBBN	PA-28 Cherokee 180	Estuary Aviation Ltd
	G-BBBW	FRED Srs 2	M. Palfreman
	G-BBBY	PA-28 Cherokee 140	Ledbury Flying Group
	G-BBCH	Robin DR.400/2+2	A. V. Harmer
	G-BBCN	Robin HR.100/210	J. C. King
	G-BBCS	Robin DR.400/140	M. J. Medland
	G-BBCY	Luton LA-4A Minor	A. W. McBlain
	G-BBDC	PA-28-140 Cherokee	N. Wright
	G-BBDE	PA-28R Cherokee Arrow 200-II	R. L. Coleman, P. Knott & J. Kemp
	G-BBDG	BAC-Aérospatiale Concorde 100 ★	Brooklands Museum of Aviation/Weybridge
	G-BBDH	Cessna F.172M	J. D. Woodward
	G-BBDL	AA-5 Traveler	M. Kadir
	G-BBDM	AA-5 Traveler	Jackeroo Aviation Group
	G-BBDO	PA-23 Turbo Aztec 250E	J. W. Anstee
	G-BBDP	Robin DR.400-160	High Aviation Ltd
	G-BBDT	Cessna 150H	Delta Tango Group
	G-BBDV	SIPA S.903	J. Owen
	G-BBEA	Luton LA-4 Minor	D. S. Evans
	G-BBEB	PA-28R Cherokee Arrow 200-II	March Flying Group
	G-BBED	MS.894A Rallye Minerva ★	Aeropark/East Midlands
	G-BBEN	Bellanca 7GCBC Citabria	C. A. G. Schofield
	G-BBEO	Cessna FRA.150L	Dukeries Aviation (G-PNIX)
	G-BBFD	PA-28R Cherokee Arrow 200-II	G-BBFD Flying Group
	G-BBFL	Gardan GY-201 Minicab	R. Smith
	G-BBFV	PA-32 Cherokee Six 260	A. M. W. Driskell
	G-BBGI	Fuji FA.200-160	A and P West
	G-BBHF	PA-23-250 Aztec E	Eastern Air Executive Ltd
	G-BBHJ	Piper J-3C-65 Cub	Wellcross Flying Group
	G-BBHK	Noorduyn AT-16 Harvard IIB (FH153)	M. Kubrak
	G-BBHY	PA-28 Cherokee 180	G. K. Clarkson
	G-BBIF	PA-23 Aztec 250E	Marshall of Cambridge Aerospace Ltd
	G-BBIL	PA-28 Cherokee 140	Saxondale Group
	G-BBIO	Robin HR.100/210	R. P. Caley
	G-BBIX	PA-28 Cherokee 140	Sterling Aviation
	G-BBJI	Isaacs Spitfire (RN218)	S. Vince
	G-BBJU	Robin DR.400/140	P. F. Moderate
	G-BBJX	Cessna F.150L	York Aircraft Leasing Ltd
	G-BBJY	Cessna F.172M	D. G. Wright
	G-BBJZ	Cessna F.172M	Peter Monk Ltd
	G-BBKA	Cessna F.150L	Aviolease Ltd
	G-BBKB	Cessna F.150L	Justgold Ltd
	G-BBKG	Cessna FR.172J	R. Wright
	G-BBKI	Cessna F.172M	R. E. Dagless
	G-BBKL	CP.301A Emeraude	K. R. Nestor
	G-BBKX	PA-28 Cherokee 180	DRA Flying Club Ltd
	G-BBKY	Cessna F.150L	F. W. Astbury
	G-BBKZ	Cessna 172M	KZ Flying Group
	G-BBLH	Piper J-3C-65 Cub (31145:G-26)	Shipping & Airlines Ltd
	G-BBLM	SOCATA Rallye 100S ★	Aeropark/East Midlands
	G-BBLS	AA-5 Traveler	A. Grant
	G-BBLU	PA-34-200 Seneca II	R. H. R. Rue

Reg	Type	Owner or Operator	Notes
G-BBMB	Robin DR.400/180	K. Wade & N. Clark	
G-BBMH	EAA. Sports Biplane Model P.1	G-BBMH Flying Group	
G-BBMN	DHC.1 Chipmunk 22	S. Baker	
G-BBMO	DHC.1 Chipmunk 22 (WK514)	Mike Oscar Group	
G-BBMR	DHC.1 Chipmunk 22 (WB763:14)	G-BBMR Syndicate	
G-BBMT	DHC.1 Chipmunk 22 (WP831)	MT Group	
G-BBMV	DHC.1 Chipmunk 22 (WG348)	Boultbee Classic LLP	
G-BBMW	DHC.1 Chipmunk 22 (WK628)	G. Fielder & A. Wilson	
G-BBMZ	DHC.1 Chipmunk 22	G-BBMZ Chipmunk Syndicate	
G-BBNA	DHC.1 Chipmunk 22 (Lycoming)	Coventry Gliding Club Ltd	
G-BBNC	DHC.1 Chipmunk T.10 (WP790) ★	De Havilland Heritage Museum/London Colney	
G-BBND	DHC.1 Chipmunk 22 (WD286)	Bernoulli Syndicate	
G-BBNI	PA-34-200 Seneca II	D. H. G. Penney	
G-BBNT	PA-31-350 Navajo Chieftain	Atlantic Bridge Aviation Ltd	
G-BBNZ	Cessna F.172M	NAL Engineering Ltd	
G-BBOA	Cessna F.172M	Avalon Ventures Ltd	
G-BBOH	Pitts S-1S Special	P. H. Meeson	
G-BBOL	PA-18 Super Cub 150	N. Moore	
G-BBOR	Bell 206B JetRanger 2	G. D. B. Budworth	
G-BBPP	PA-28-180 Cherokee	A. D. R. Northeast (G-WACP)	
G-BBPS	Jodel D.117	V. F. Flett	
G-BBRA	PA-23 Aztec 250D	Sulafat OU/Estonia	
G-BBRB	DH.82A Tiger Moth (DF198)	R. Barham	
G-BBRC	Fuji FA.200-180	BBRC Ltd	
G-BBRI	Bell 47G-5A	Alan Mann Aviation Group Ltd	
G-BBRN	Procter Kittiwake 1 (XW784/VL)	H. M. Price	
G-BBRZ	AA-5 Traveler	B. McIntyre	
G-BBSA	AA-5 Traveler	Usworth 84 Flying Associates Ltd	
G-BBSS	DHC.1A Chipmunk 22	Coventry Gliding Club Ltd	
G-BBTB	Cessna FRA.150L	A. D. Taylor	
G-BBTG	Cessna F.172M	Jetstream Aero	
G-BBTK	Cessna FRA.150L	Cleveland Flying School Ltd	
G-BBTY	Beech C23 Sundowner	G-BBTY Group	
G-BBUJ	Cessna 421B	Aero VIP Companhia de Transportes & Servicios Aereos SA/Portugal	
G-BBUT	Western O-65 balloon	R. G. Turnbull	
G-BBUU	Piper J-3C-65 Cub	C. Stokes	
G-BBVF	SA Twin Pioneer Srs 3 ★	Museum of Flight/East Fortune	
G-BBVO	Isaacs Fury II (K5682)	S. Vince	
G-BBXB	Cessna FRA.150L	D. C. Somerville	
G-BBXK	PA-34-200 Seneca	A. Elliott (G-FBPL)	
G-BBXW	PA-28-151 Cherokee Warrior	Bristol Aero Club	
G-BBXY	Bellanca 7GCBC Citabria	S. A. Windus	
G-BBYB	PA-18 Super Cub 95	Perryair Ltd	
G-BBYH	Cessna 182P	Ramco (UK) Ltd	
G-BBYM	HP.137 Jetstream 200 ★	Aerospace Museum/Cosford (G-AYWR)	
G-BBYP	PA-28 Cherokee 140	Blue Angel Air Ltd	
G-BBYU	Cameron O-56 balloon ★	British Balloon Museum	
G-BBZH	PA-28R-200 Cherokee Arrow II	S. I. Tugwell	
G-BBZN	Fuji FA.200-180	D. Kynaston & ptnrs	
G-BBZV	PA-28R Cherokee Arrow 200-II	P. B. Mellor	
G-BCAH	DHC.1 Chipmunk 22 (WG316)	Century Aviation Ltd	
G-BCAP	Cameron O-56 balloon ★	Balloon Preservation Group/Lancing	
G-BCAR	Thunder Ax7-77 balloon ★	British Balloon Museum/Newbury	
G-BCAZ	PA-12 Super Cruiser	J. Forshaw	
G-BCBH	Fairchild 24R-46A Argus III (HB737)	H. Mackintosh	
G-BCBJ	PA-25 Pawnee 235	Deeside Gliding Club (Aberdeenshire) Ltd	
G-BCBL	Fairchild 24R-46A Argus III (HB751)	F. J. Cox	
G-BCBR	AJEP/Wittman W.8 Tailwind	D. P. Jones	
G-BCBX	Cessna F.150L	P. Lodge & J. G. McVey	
G-BCCE	PA-23 Aztec 250E	Golf Charlie Echo Ltd	
G-BCCF	PA-28 Cherokee 180	Charlie Foxtrot Aviation	
G-BCCK	AA-5 Traveler	N. M. Gonzalez	
G-BCCR	CP.301A Emeraude (modified)	I. Taberer	
G-BCCX	DHC.1 Chipmunk 22 (Lycoming)	Charlie X-Ray Syndicate Ltd	
G-BCCY	Robin HR.200/100	B. A. Mills	
G-BCDK	Partenavia P.68B	Amazon Air Services	
G-BCDL	Cameron O-42 balloon	D. P. & Mrs B. O. Turner Chums	
G-BCDN	F.27 Friendship Mk 200 ★	Instructional airframe/Norwich	

41

BRITISH CIVIL AIRCRAFT MARKINGS

Notes	Reg	Type	Owner or Operator
	G-BCDY	Cessna FRA.150L	Leased Flight Ltd
	G-BCEE	AA-5 Traveler	D. Joy
	G-BCEN	BN-2A-26 Islander	Britten-Norman Ltd
	G-BCEP	AA-5 Traveler	Sandown Aircraft Group G-BCEP
	G-BCER	Gardan GY-201 Minicab	J. A. & A. Stewart
	G-BCEU	Cameron O-42 balloon	P. Glydon
	G-BCEY	DHC.1 Chipmunk 22 (WG465)	Gopher Flying Group
	G-BCFO	PA-18-150 Super Cub	D. J. Ashley (G-MUDI)
	G-BCFR	Cessna FRA.150L	Foxtrot Romeo Group
	G-BCFW	SAAB 91D Safir	R. Callaway-Lewis
	G-BCGB	Bensen B.8	A. Melody
	G-BCGC	DHC.1 Chipmunk 22 (WP903)	Henlow Chipmunk Group
	G-BCGH	SNCAN NC.854S	P. L. Lovegrove
	G-BCGI	PA-28 Cherokee 140	D. H. G. Penny
	G-BCGJ	PA-28 Cherokee 140	Demero Ltd & LV Skies Ltd
	G-BCGM	Jodel D.120	S. E. Wilks
	G-BCGN	PA-28 Cherokee 140	C. F. Hessey
	G-BCGS	PA-28R Cherokee Arrow 200	Leased Flight Ltd
	G-BCGW	Jodel D.11	G. H. Chittenden
	G-BCHL	DHC.1 Chipmunk 22A (WP788)	Shropshire Soaring Ltd
	G-BCHP	CP.1310-C3 Super Emeraude	P. Purdey (G-JOSI)
	G-BCHT	Schleicher ASK.16	Dunstable K16 Group
	G-BCIH	DHC.1 Chipmunk 22 (WD363)	P. J. Richie
	G-BCIR	PA-28-151 Warrior	Aerobility
	G-BCJM	PA-28 Cherokee 140	J. G. McVey & P. Lodge
	G-BCJN	PA-28 Cherokee 140	Bristol and Wessex Aeroplane Club Ltd
	G-BCJO	PA-28R Cherokee Arrow 200	G-BCJO Group
	G-BCJP	PA-28 Cherokee 140	S. Turton
	G-BCKN	DHC.1A Chipmunk 22 (Lycoming) (WP811)	M. D. Cowburn
	G-BCKS	Fuji FA.200-180AO	G. J. Ward
	G-BCKT	Fuji FA.200-180	A. G. Dobson
	G-BCKV	Cessna FRA.150L	M. Bonsall
	G-BCLI	AA-5 Traveler	A. Vaicvenas
	G-BCLS	Cessna 170B	M. J. Whiteman-Haywood
	G-BCLU	Jodel D.117	D. H. G. Cotter
	G-BCMD	PA-18 Super Cub 95	P. Stephenson
	G-BCMJ	Squarecraft Cavalier SA.102-5	N. F. Andrews
	G-BCMT	Isaacs Fury II	R.W. Burrows
	G-BCNC	Gardan GY-201 Minicab	J. R. Wraight
	G-BCNP	Cameron O-77 balloon	P. Spellward
	G-BCNX	Piper J-3C-65 Cub (540)	C. M. L. Edwards
	G-BCOB	Piper J-3C-65 Cub (329405:A-23)	C. Marklew-Brown
	G-BCOI	DHC.1 Chipmunk 22 (WP870:12)	M. J. Diggins
	G-BCOM	Piper J-3C-65 Cub	BCOM Flying Group
	G-BCOO	DHC.1 Chipmunk 22	Double Oscar Chipmunk Group
	G-BCOU	DHC.1 Chipmunk 22 (WK522)	Loweth Flying Group
	G-BCOY	DHC.1 Chipmunk 22	Coventry Gliding Club Ltd
	G-BCPD	Gardan GY-201 Minicab	P. R. Cozens
	G-BCPG	PA-28R Cherokee Arrow 200-II	A. J. B. Borak & E. J. Burgham
	G-BCPH	Piper J-3C-65 Cub (329934:B-72)	G. Earl
	G-BCPJ	Piper J-3C-65 Cub	J. C. Tempest
	G-BCPN	AA-5 Traveler	G-BCPN Group
	G-BCPU	DHC.1 Chipmunk 22 (WP973)	P. Green
	G-BCRB	Cessna F.172M	Wingtask 1995Ltd
	G-BCRE	Cameron O-77 balloon ★	Balloon Preservation Group/Lancing
	G-BCRL	PA-28-151 Warrior	Romeo Lima Flying Club
	G-BCRR	AA-5B Tiger	S. Waite
	G-BCRX	DHC.1 Chipmunk 22 (WD292)	P. J. Tuplin & M. I. Robinson
	G-BCSA	DHC.1 Chipmunk 22 (Lycoming)	Shenington Gliding Club Ltd
	G-BCSL	DHC.1 Chipmunk 22	de Havilland & Partners Ltd
	G-BCTF	PA-28-151 Warrior	I. J. Hiatt
	G-BCTI	Schleicher ASK.16	Tango India Syndicate
	G-BCTK	Cessna FR.172J	M. G. E. Morton
	G-BCUB	Piper J-3C-65 Cub	S. L. Goldspink
	G-BCUF	Cessna F.172M	Howell Plant Hire & Construction
	G-BCUH	Cessna F.150M	G-BCUH Group
	G-BCUJ	Cessna F.150M	C. G. Dodds
	G-BCUL	SOCATA Rallye 100ST	C. A. Ussher & Fountain Estates Ltd
	G-BCUO	SA Bulldog Srs 120/122	Cranfield University
	G-BCUS	SA Bulldog Srs 120/122	Falcon Group
	G-BCUV	SA Bulldog Srs 120/122 (XX704)	Flew LLP

Reg	Type	Owner or Operator	Notes
G-BCUW	Cessna F.177RG	S. J. Westley	
G-BCUY	Cessna FRA.150M	Dunmall Construction Ltd	
G-BCVB	PA-17 Vagabond	A. T. Nowak	
G-BCVC	SOCATA Rallye 100ST	W. Haddow	
G-BCVE	Evans VP-2	D. Masterson & D. B. Winstanley	
G-BCVF	Practavia Pilot Sprite	A. C. Barber	
G-BCVG	Cessna FRA.150L	G-BCVG Flying Group	
G-BCVH	Cessna FRA.150L	C. Quist	
G-BCVJ	Cessna F.172M	Rothland Ltd	
G-BCVY	PA-34-200T Seneca II	Topex Ltd	
G-BCWB	Cessna 182P	D. Sluman	
G-BCWH	Practavia Pilot Sprite	A. T. Fines	
G-BCWK	Alpavia Fournier RF-3	P. Andrews	
G-BCXE	Robin DR.400/2+2	Weald Air Services Ltd	
G-BCXJ	Piper L-4J Cub (480752:E-39)	A. J. Blackford	
G-BCXN	DHC.1 Chipmunk 22 (WP800)	J. A. Moolenschot	
G-BCYH	DAW Privateer Mk. 3	G-BCYH Group	
G-BCYK	Avro CF.100 Mk 4 Canuck (18393) ★	Imperial War Museum/Duxford	
G-BCYM	DHC.1 Chipmunk 22 (WK577)	G-BCYM Group	
G-BCYR	Cessna F.172M	D. M. Lockley	
G-BDAD	Taylor JT.1 Monoplane	S. Woodgate & R. Pike	
G-BDAG	Taylor JT.1 Monoplane	S. Woodgate & R. Pike	
G-BDAH	Evans VP-1	G. H. J. Geurts	
G-BDAI	Cessna FRA.150M	D. J. M. Randall	
G-BDAK	Rockwell Commander 112	M. C. Wilson	
G-BDAM	RT-16 Harvard IIB (FE992:ER-992)	Avalon Ventures Ltd	
G-BDAO	SIPA S.91	S. B. Churchill	
G-BDAP	AJEP Tailwind	D. G. Kelly	
G-BDAR	Evans VP-1	A. J. Gillson & P. W. Cooper	
G-BDAY	Thunder Ax5-42S1 balloon	J. F. Till	
G-BDBD	Wittman W.8 Tailwind	P. A. Hall	
G-BDBF	FRED Srs 2	G. E. & R. E. Collins	
G-BDBI	Cameron O-77 balloon	C. Jones	
G-BDBS	Short SD3-30 ★	Ulster Aviation Society/Long Kesh	
G-BDBU	Cessna F.150M	G. E. Fox	
G-BDBV	Jodel D.11A	Seething Jodel Group	
G-BDBZ	Westland WS-55 Whirlwind (XJ398) ★	Aeroventure/Doncaster	
G-BDCD	Piper J-3C-85 Cub (480133:B-44)	Cubby Cub Group	
G-BDCI	CP.301A Emeraude	M. T. Slater	
G-BDCO	Beagle B.121 Pup Series 1	M. R. Badminton	
G-BDDF	Jodel D.120	J. V. Thompson	
G-BDDG	Jodel D.112	J. Pool & D. G. Palmer	
G-BDDS	PA-25 Pawnee 235	Black Mountains Gliding Club	
G-BDDX	Whittaker MW2B Excalibur ★	Cornwall Aero Park/Helston	
G-BDEH	Jodel D.120A	N. J. Cronin	
G-BDEI	Jodel D.9 Bébé	The Noddy Flying Group	
G-BDEX	Cessna FRA.150M	A. P. F. Tucker	
G-BDEY	Piper J-3C-65 Cub	A. V. Williams	
G-BDFB	Currie Wot	J. Jennings	
G-BDFH	Auster AOP.9 (XR240)	R. B. Webber	
G-BDFR	Fuji FA.200-160	C. B. Mellor	
G-BDFU	Dragonfly MPA Mk 1 ★	Museum of Flight/East Fortune	
G-BDFX	Taylorcraft Auster 5	A. D. Pearce	
G-BDFY	AA-5 Traveler	Grumman Group	
G-BDGB	Gardan GY-20 Minicab	T. W. Slater	
G-BDGM	PA-28-151 Cherokee Warrior	W. Ali	
G-BDGY	PA-28-140 Cherokee	J. Eagles	
G-BDHK	Piper J-3C-65 Cub (329417)	Knight Flying Group	
G-BDIE	Rockwell Commander 112	J. McAleer & R. J. Adams	
G-BDIG	Cessna 182P	J. A. Lee	
G-BDIH	Jodel D.117	T. A. S. Rayner	
G-BDIX	DH.106 Comet 4C ★	Museum of Flight/East Fortune	
G-BDJD	Jodel D.112	The Real Aeroplane Company Ltd	
G-BDJG	Luton LA-4A Minor	Luton Minor Group	
G-BDJP	Piper J-3C-90 Cub	S. T. Gilbert	
G-BDJR	SNCAN Nord NC.858	P. L. Lovegrove	
G-BDKC	Cessna A185F	Lude & Invergarry Farm Partnership	
G-BDKD	Enstrom F-28A	P. J. Price	
G-BDKH	CP.301A Emeraude	R. K. Griggs	
G-BDKM	SIPA 903	S. W. Markham	

43

Notes	Reg	Type	Owner or Operator
	G-BDKW	Rockwell Commander 112A	S. D. Cansdale
	G-BDLO	AA-5A Cheetah	D. Kryl
	G-BDLT	Rockwell Commander 112	I. Parkinson
	G-BDLY	K & S SA.102.5 Cavalier	P. R. Stevens
	G-BDMS	Piper J-3C-65 Cub (FR886)	A. J. Blackford
	G-BDMW	Jodel DR.100A	Mike Whiskey Group
	G-BDNC	Taylor JT.1 Monoplane	R. Pike & S. Woodgate
	G-BDNG	Taylor JT.1 Monoplane	C. E. A. J. Pearce
	G-BDNR	Cessna FRA.150M	M. Bonsall
	G-BDNT	Jodel D.92 Bébé	R. J. Stobo
	G-BDNU	Cessna F.172M	Greenbaum Training & Consultancy Ltd
	G-BDNW	AA-1B Trainer	N. A. Baxter
	G-BDNX	AA-1B Trainer	N. C, W. R. & T. J. Stone
	G-BDOD	Cessna F.150M	OD Group
	G-BDOG	SA Bulldog Srs 200	D. C. Bonsall
	G-BDOL	Piper J-3C-65 Cub (454630)	L. R. Balthazor
	G-BDPA	PA-28-151 Warrior	J. H. Sandham Aviation
	G-BDPJ	PA-25 Pawnee 235B	Glider FX
	G-BDRD	Cessna FRA.150M	CBM Associates Consulting Ltd
	G-BDRG	Taylor JT.2 Titch	C. Gray
	G-BDSB	PA-28-181 Archer II	Testair Ltd
	G-BDSF	Cameron O-56 balloon	J. H. Greensides
	G-BDSH	PA-28 Cherokee 140 (modified)	The Wright Brothers Flying Group
	G-BDSK	Cameron O-65 balloon	Southern Balloon Group Carousel II
	G-BDSM	Slingsby T.31B Cadet III	F. C. J. Wevers/Netherlands
	G-BDTB	Evans VP-1	C. J. Riley
	G-BDTL	Evans VP-1 series 2	S. A. Daniels
	G-BDTU	Omega III gas balloon	R. G. Turnbull
	G-BDTX	Cessna F.150M	F. W. & I. F. Ellis
	G-BDUI	Cameron V-56 balloon	D. J. W. Johnson
	G-BDUL	Evans VP-1 Srs.2	G-BDUL Flying Group
	G-BDUO	Cessna F.150M	Z. S. Khan
	G-BDUY	Robin DR.400/140B	I. A. Anderson
	G-BDUZ	Cameron V-56 balloon	Zebedee Balloon Service
	G-BDVA	PA-17 Vagabond	I. M. Callier
	G-BDVB	PA-15 (PA-17) Vagabond	B. P. Gardner
	G-BDVC	PA-17 Vagabond	C. R. & R. J. Whitcombe
	G-BDWE	Flaglor Scooter	P. King
	G-BDWJ	SE-5A (replica) (F8010:Z)	D. W. Linney
	G-BDWM	Mustang scale replica (414673:LH-I))	D. C. Bonsall
	G-BDXX	SNCAN NC.858S	K. M. Davis
	G-BDYG	P.56 Provost T.1 (WV493) ★	Museum of Flight/East Fortune
	G-BDZA	Scheibe SF.25E Super Falke	Hereward Flying Group
	G-BDZD	Cessna F.172M	M. Watkinson
	G-BDZG	Slingsby T.59H Kestrel	R. E. Gretton
	G-BEAB	Jodel DR.1051	R. C. Hibberd
	G-BEAC	PA-28 Cherokee 140	R. Murray & A. Bagley-Murray
	G-BEAD	WG.13 Lynx ★	Instructional airframe/Middle Wallop
	G-BEAH	Auster J/2 Arrow	Bedwell Hey Flying Group
	G-BEBC	Westland WS-55 Whirlwind 3 (XP355) ★	Norwich Aviation Museum
	G-BEBN	Cessna 177B	S. K. Gheyi
	G-BEBR	GY-201 Minicab	R. L. Northover
	G-BEBS	Andreasson BA-4B	T. D. Wood
	G-BEBU	Rockwell Commander 112A	I. Hunt
	G-BEBZ	PA-28-151 Warrior	P. E. Taylor
	G-BECB	SOCATA Rallye 100ST	D. H. Tonkin
	G-BECK	Cameron V-56 balloon	N. H. & A. M. Ponsford
	G-BECN	Piper J-3C-65 Cub (480480:E-44)	CN Cub Group
	G-BECT	CASA 1.131E Jungmann 2000 (A-57)	I. R. Hannah
	G-BECW	CASA 1.131E Jungmann 2000 (A-10)	C. M. Rampton
	G-BECZ	CAARP CAP-10B	The London Aerobatic Company Ltd
	G-BEDA	CASA 1-131E Jungmann Srs.2000	T. Callier
	G-BEDB	Nord 1203 Norecrin ★	B. F. G. Lister (stored)/Chirk
	G-BEDF	Boeing B-17G-105-VE (124485:DF-A)	B-17 Preservation Ltd
	G-BEDG	Rockwell Commander 112	G-BEDG Group
	G-BEDJ	Piper J-3C-65 Cub (44-80594)	I. S. L. Rutland
	G-BEDV	V.668 Varsity T.1 (WJ945) ★	Duxford Aviation Society
	G-BEEE	Thunder Ax6-56A balloon ★	British Balloon Museum/Newbury
	G-BEEI	Cameron N-77 balloon	G. C. N. van der Pluijm
	G-BEER	Isaacs Fury II (K2075)	C. E. Styles

Reg	Type	Owner or Operator	Notes
G-BEFA	PA-28-151 Warrior	M. Lawrynowicz	
G-BEGG	Scheibe SF.25E Super Falke	G-BEGG Motorfalke	
G-BEHH	PA-32R Cherokee Lance 300	K. Swallow	
G-BEHU	PA-34-200T Seneca II	Heli Air Ltd	
G-BEHV	Cessna F.172N	Leading Edge Flight Training Ltd	
G-BEIF	Cameron O-65 balloon	C. Vening	
G-BEIG	Cessna F.150M	R. D. Forster	
G-BEII	PA-25 Pawnee 235D	Burn Gliding Club Ltd	
G-BEIS	Evans VP-1	D. L. Haines	
G-BEJK	Cameron S-31 balloon	Rango Balloon and Kite Company	
G-BEKN	Cessna FRA.150M	Peterborough Flying School Ltd	
G-BEKO	Cessna F.182Q	G. J. & F. J. Leese	
G-BELF	BN-2A-26 Islander ★	Museum of Flight/East Fortune	
G-BELT	Cessna F.150J	R. J. Whyham (G-AWUV)	
G-BEMB	Cessna F.172M	Stocklaunch Ltd	
G-BEMW	PA-28-181 Archer II	Touch & Go Ltd	
G-BEMY	Cessna FRA.150M	J. R. Power	
G-BEND	Cameron V-56 balloon	Dante Balloon Group	
G-BENJ	Rockwell Commander 112B	BENJ Flying Group	
G-BEOE	Cessna FRA.150M	W. J. Henderson	
G-BEOH	PA-28R-201T Turbo Arrow III	Gloucestershire Flying Club	
G-BEOI	PA-18 Super Cub 150	Southdown Gliding Club Ltd	
G-BEOX	Lockheed 414 Hudson IV (A16-199) ★	RAF Museum/Hendon	
G-BEOY	Cessna FRA.150L	J. N. Ponsford	
G-BEOZ	A.W.650 Argosy 101 ★	Aeropark/East Midlands	
G-BEPV	Fokker S.11-1 Instructor (174)	S. W. & M. Isbister & C. Tyers	
G-BEPY	Rockwell Commander 112B	T. L. Rippon	
G-BERA	SOCATA Rallye 150ST	A. C. Stamp	
G-BERI	Rockwell Commander 114	G-BERI Group	
G-BERN	Saffrey S-330 balloon	B. Martin	
G-BERT	Cameron V-56 balloon	E. C. Barker	
G-BERY	AA-1B Trainer	P. B. Anderson	
G-BETD	Robin HR.200/100	J. P. Kistner	
G-BETE	Rollason B.2A Beta	T. M. Jones	
G-BETF	Cameron 'Champion' SS balloon ★	British Balloon Museum/Newbury	
G-BETM	PA-25 Pawnee 235D	Yorkshire Gliding Club (Pty) Ltd	
G-BEUA	PA-18 Super Cub 150	London Gliding Club (Pty) Ltd	
G-BEUD	Robin HR.100/285R	A. J. Verlander	
G-BEUI	Piper J-3C-65 Cub (479878)	Lytham St. Annes Spitfire Display Team Ltd	
G-BEUP	Robin DR.400/180	MCRS Aviation	
G-BEUU	PA-18 Super Cub 95	C. Gartland	
G-BEUX	Cessna F.172N	Aerohire Ltd	
G-BEUY	Cameron N-31 balloon	J. J. Daly	
G-BEVB	SOCATA Rallye 150ST	L. Clarke	
G-BEVC	SOCATA Rallye 150ST	Wolds Flyers Syndicate	
G-BEVG	PA-34-200T Seneca II	AWA Aeronautical Web Academy LDA	
G-BEVO	Sportavia-Pützer RF-5	M. Hill	
G-BEVP	Evans VP-2	G. Moscrop & R. C. Crowley	
G-BEVS	Taylor JT.1 Monoplane	N. D. Hunter	
G-BEVT	BN-2A Mk II-2 Trislander ★	Imperial War Museum/Duxford	
G-BEWN	DH.82A Tiger Moth	H. D. Labouchere	
G-BEWO	Zlin Z.326 Trener Master	T. Cooper	
G-BEWR	Cessna F.172N	Bliss Aviation Ltd	
G-BEWX	PA-28R-201 Arrow III	Three Greens Arrow Group	
G-BEWY	Bell 206B JetRanger 3	Polo Aviation Ltd (G-CULL)	
G-BEXN	AA-1C Lynx	G. S. Page	
G-BEXW	PA-28-181 Cherokee Archer II	Jet World	
G-BEYA	Enstrom 280C	D. Brown	
G-BEYB	Fairey Flycatcher (replica) (S1287) ★	F.A.A. Museum/Yeovilton	
G-BEYF	HPR.7 Herald 401 ★	Jet Heritage Museum/Bournemouth	
G-BEYL	PA-28 Cherokee 180	Yankee Lima Group	
G-BEYT	PA-28 Cherokee 140	J. N. Plange	
G-BEYV	Cessna T.210M	P. Middleton	
G-BEYZ	Jodel DR.1051/M1	W. H. Bliss	
G-BEZC	AA-5 Traveler	Easter Flying Group	
G-BEZE	Rutan Vari-Eze	S. K. Cockburn	
G-BEZF	AA-5 Traveler	Phoenix Flying Group	
G-BEZG	AA-5 Traveler	M. D. R. Harling	
G-BEZI	AA-5 Traveler	C. J. & L. Campbell	
G-BEZK	Cessna F.172H	Alpha Victor Ltd	
G-BEZL	PA-31-310 Turbo Navajo C	2 Excel Aviation Ltd	

Notes	Reg	Type	Owner or Operator
	G-BEZO	Cessna F.172M	Staverton Flying School @ Skypark Ltd
	G-BEZP	PA-32 Cherokee Six 300D	T. P. McCormack & J. K. Zealley
	G-BEZV	Cessna F.172M	Alexander Air Ltd
	G-BEZY	Rutan Vari-Eze	J. P. Kynaston
	G-BEZZ	Jodel D.112	G-BEZZ Jodel Group
	G-BFAF	Aeronca 7BCM Champion (7797)	D. A. Crompton
	G-BFAP	SIAI-Marchetti S.205-20R	N. C. du Piesanie
	G-BFAS	Evans VP-1	A. I. Sutherland
	G-BFAW	DHC.1 Chipmunk 22 (WP848)	M. L. J. Goff
	G-BFAX	DHC.1 Chipmunk 22 (WG422)	Symonds Aviation UK Ltd
	G-BFBA	Jodel DR.100A	R. E. Nicholson
	G-BFBE	Robin HR.200/100	A. C. Pearson
	G-BFBM	Saffery S.330 balloon	B. Martin
	G-BFBY	PA-28-161 Warrior II	Phoenix Aviation
	G-BFBY	Piper J-3C-65 Cub (329707:S-44)	M. Shaw
	G-BFCT	Cessna Tu.206F	K. A. Stewart
	G-BFCZ	Sopwith Camel F.1 Replica (B7270) ★	Brooklands Museum of Aviation/Weybridge
	G-BFDC	DHC.1 Chipmunk 22 (WG475)	N. F. O'Neill
	G-BFDE	Sopwith Tabloid (replica) (168) ★	RAF Museum/Hendon
	G-BFDI	PA-28-181 Archer II	Truman Aviation Ltd
	G-BFDK	PA-28-161 Warrior II	S. T. Gilbert
	G-BFDL	Piper J-3C-65 Cub (454537:J-04)	B. A. Nicholson
	G-BFDO	PA-28R-201T Turbo Arrow III	B. Simon
	G-BFEB	Jodel 150	G-BFEB Syndicate
	G-BFEF	Agusta-Bell 47G-3B1	I. F. Vaughan
	G-BFEH	Jodel D.117A	M. D. Mold
	G-BFEK	Cessna F.152	Staverton Flying School @ Skypark Ltd
	G-BFEV	PA-25 Pawnee 235	Yorkshire Gliding Club (Proprietary) Ltd
	G-BFFE	Cessna F.152-II	A. J. Hastings
	G-BFFP	PA-18 Super Cub 150 (modified)	East Sussex Gliding Club Ltd
	G-BFFW	Cessna F.152	Stapleford Flying Club Ltd
	G-BFGD	Cessna F.172N-II	Wannabe Flyers
	G-BFGG	Cessna FRA.150M	G. Oliver
	G-BFGH	Cessna F.337G	S. Findlay
	G-BFGK	Jodel D.117	A. D. Eastwood
	G-BFGL	Cessna FA.152	D. H. G. Penney
	G-BFGS	MS.893E Rallye 180GT	Chiltern Flyers Ltd
	G-BFGZ	Cessna FRA.150M	India Victor Flying Group
	G-BFHH	DH.82A Tiger Moth	P. & T. J. Harrison
	G-BFHI	Piper J-3C-65 Cub	J. Glass & A. J. Richardson
	G-BFHP	Champion 7GCAA Citabria	M. Walker & M. R. Keen
	G-BFHR	Jodel DR.220/2+2	G-BFHR Group
	G-BFHU	Cessna F.152-II	M. Bonsall
	G-BFHX	Evans VP-1	D. A. Milstead
	G-BFIB	PA-31 Turbo Navajo	2 Excel Aviation Ltd
	G-BFID	Taylor JT.2 Titch Mk III	R. L. Soutar & R. C. Bunce
	G-BFIE	Cessna FRA.150M	J. P. A. Freeman
	G-BFIG	Cessna FR.172K XPII	K. Rogan
	G-BFIN	AA-5A Cheetah	Aircraft Engineers Ltd
	G-BFIP	Wallbro Monoplane 1909 (replica) ★	Norfolk & Suffolk Aviation Museum/Flixton
	G-BFIT	Thunder Ax6-56Z balloon	J. A. G. Tyson
	G-BFIU	Cessna FR.172K XP	A. R. Greenly
	G-BFIV	Cessna F.177RG	C. Fisher & M. L. Miller
	G-BFIX	Thunder Ax7-77A balloon	S. J. Owen
	G-BFIY	Cessna F.150M	UK Flying Clubs Ltd
	G-BFJR	Cessna F.337G	City North Ltd
	G-BFJZ	Robin DR.400/140B	Weald Air Services Ltd
	G-BFKB	Cessna F.172N	Shropshire Flying Group
	G-BFLU	Cessna F.152	Swiftair Maintenance Ltd
	G-BFLX	AA-5A Cheetah	A. M. Verdon
	G-BFLZ	Beech 95-A55 Baron	D. Pye
	G-BFMF	Cassutt Racer IIIM	T. D. Gardner
	G-BFMG	PA-28-161 Warrior II	Andrewsfield Aviation Ltd
	G-BFMH	Cessna 177B	Aerofoil Aviation Ltd
	G-BFMK	Cessna FA.152	The Leicestershire Aero Club Ltd
	G-BFMR	PA-20 Pacer 125	J. Knight
	G-BFMX	Cessna F.172N	M. Rowe
	G-BFNG	Jodel D.112	NG Group
	G-BFNI	PA-28-161 Warrior II	Surrey Aero LLP
	G-BFNK	PA-28-161 Warrior II	Parachuting Aircraft Ltd
	G-BFNM	Globe GC-1B Swift	M. J. Butler

Reg	Type	Owner or Operator	Notes
G-BFOE	Cessna F.152	Redhill Air Services Ltd	
G-BFOG	Cessna 150M	Wicklow Wings	
G-BFOJ	AA-1 Yankee	J. Batey	
G-BFOU	Taylor JT.1 Monoplane	G. Bee	
G-BFOV	Cessna F.172N	M. C. Walker	
G-BFPA	Scheibe SF.25B Falke	W. J. Grieve	
G-BFPH	Cessna F.172K	Linc-Air Flying Group	
G-BFPP	Bell 47J-2 Ranger	M. R. Masters	
G-BFPR	PA-25 Pawnee 235D	The Windrushers Gliding Club Ltd	
G-BFPS	PA-25 Pawnee 235D	C. A. M. M. Neidt	
G-BFPZ	Cessna F.177RG	G. E. Thompson	
G-BFRI	Sikorsky S-61N	British International	
G-BFRR	Cessna FRA.150M	Romeo Romeo Flying Group	
G-BFRS	Cessna F.172N	Aerocomm Ltd	
G-BFRV	Cessna FA.152	Cristal Air Ltd	
G-BFRY	PA-25 Pawnee 260	Yorkshire Gliding Club (Pty) Ltd	
G-BFSA	Cessna F.182Q	Delta Lima Flying Group	
G-BFSC	PA-25 Pawnee 235D	Essex Gliding Club Ltd	
G-BFSD	PA-25 Pawnee 235D	Deeside Gliding Club (Aberdeenshire) Ltd	
G-BFSS	Cessna FR.172G	Albedale Farms Ltd	
G-BFSY	PA-28-181 Archer II	Downland Aviation	
G-BFSZ	PA-28-161 Warrior II	R. J. Whyham (G-KBPI)	
G-BFTC	PA-28R-201T Turbo Arrow III	Top Cat Flying Group	
G-BFTF	AA-5B Tiger	F. C. Burrow Ltd	
G-BFTG	AA-5B Tiger	D. Hepburn & G. R. Montgomery	
G-BFTH	Cessna F.172N	T. W. Oakley	
G-BFTZ	MS.880B Rallye Club ★	Newark Air Museum/Newark	
G-BFUB	PA-32RT-300 Lance II	J. Lowndes	
G-BFUD	Scheibe SF.25E Super Falke	SF25E Syndicate	
G-BFVH	DH.2 (replica) (5964)	S. W. Turley	
G-BFVS	AA-5B Tiger	G-BFVS Flying Group	
G-BFVU	Cessna 150L	A. N. Mole	
G-BFWB	PA-28-161 Warrior II	Mid-Anglia School of Flying	
G-BFWD	Currie Wot (C3009)	P. D. Ford	
G-BFXF	Andreasson BA.4B	P. N. Birch	
G-BFXG	D.31 Turbulent	XG Group	
G-BFXK	PA-28 Cherokee 140	G-BFXK Owners Ltd	
G-BFXL	Albatros D.5a replica (D5397/17) ★	F.A.A. Museum/Yeovilton	
G-BFXR	Jodel D.112	R. G. Marshall	
G-BFXW	AA-5B Tiger	A. M. & J. D. Arnold	
G-BFXX	AA-5B Tiger	W. R. Gibson	
G-BFYA	MBB Bö.105DB	Wessex Aviation Ltd	
G-BFYI	Westland-Bell 47G-3B1	K. P. Mayes	
G-BFYK	Cameron V-77 balloon	L. E. Jones	
G-BFYL	Evans VP-2	F. C. Handy	
G-BFYO	SPAD XIII (replica) (4513:1) ★	American Air Museum/Duxford	
G-BFYW	Slingsby T.65A Vega	D. J. Blackman	
G-BFZB	Piper J-3C-85 Cub (480723:E5-J)	M. S. Pettit	
G-BFZD	Cessna FR.182RG	Skylane Group	
G-BFZH	PA-28R Cherokee Arrow 200	CG Aviation Ltd	
G-BFZM	Rockwell Commander 112TC	J. A. Hart & R. J. Lamplough	
G-BGAA	Cessna 152 II	PJC Leasing Ltd	
G-BGAB	Cessna F.152 II	TG Aviation Ltd	
G-BGAE	Cessna F.152 II	Aerolease Ltd	
G-BGAJ	Cessna F.182Q II	B. & C. Blumberg	
G-BGAZ	Cameron V-77 balloon	C. J. Madigan & D. H. McGibbon	
G-BGBE	Jodel DR.1050	J. A. & B. Mawby	
G-BGBF	Druine D.31 Turbulent	T. A. Stambach	
G-BGBG	PA-28-181 Archer II	North East Flight Academy Ltd	
G-BGBI	Cessna F.150L	Modern Air (UK) Ltd	
G-BGBK	PA-38-112 Tomahawk	Aeros Leasing Ltd	
G-BGBV	Slingsby T65A Vega	J. P. W. Roche-Kelly	
G-BGBW	PA-38-112 Tomahawk	D. H. G. Penney	
G-BGCB	Slingsby T.65A Vega	F. J. Bradley & E. P. Lambert	
G-BGCM	AA-5A Cheetah	R. W. Walker	
G-BGCO	PA-44-180 Seminole	BAE Systems (Operations) Ltd	
G-BGCU	Slingsby T.65A Vega	P. Hadfield	
G-BGCY	Taylor JT.1 Monoplane	G. W. Hancox	
G-BGEF	Jodel D.112	G. G. Johnson	
G-BGEI	Baby Great Lakes	D. H. Greenwood	

Notes	Reg	Type	Owner or Operator
	G-BGES	Phoenix Currie Super Wot	ZE Shadow Team Ltd
	G-BGFG	AA-5A Cheetah	A. J. Williams
	G-BGFX	Cessna F.152	Redhill Air Services Ltd
	G-BGGA	Bellanca 7GCBC Citabria	R. N. R. Bellamy
	G-BGGB	Bellanca 7GCBC Citabria	D. A. Payne
	G-BGGC	Bellanca 7GCBC Citabria	BGGC Flying Group
	G-BGGD	Bellanca 8GCBC Scout	Bidford Gliding & Flying Club Ltd
	G-BGGE	PA-38-112 Tomahawk	Aeros Leasing Ltd
	G-BGGI	PA-38-112 Tomahawk	Aeros Leasing Ltd
	G-BGGM	PA-38-112 Tomahawk	G. E. Fox
	G-BGGO	Cessna F.152	East Midlands Flying School Ltd
	G-BGGP	Cessna F.152	East Midlands Flying School Ltd
	G-BGHF	Westland WG.30 ★	The Helicopter Museum/Weston-super-Mare
	G-BGHJ	Cessna F.172N	Air Plane Ltd
	G-BGHM	Robin R.1180T	P. Price
	G-BGHS	Cameron N-31 balloon	G. Gray
	G-BGHT	Falconar F-12	C. R. Coates
	G-BGHU	NA T-6G Texan (115042:TA-042)	Aero Legends Leasing Ltd
	G-BGHY	Taylor JT.1 Monoplane	J. H. Mangan
	G-BGIB	Cessna 152 II	Redhill Air Services Ltd
	G-BGIG	PA-38-112 Tomahawk	Leading Edge Fliying Club Ltd
	G-BGIU	Cessna F.172H	S. J. Windle
	G-BGIY	Cessna F.172N	Leading Edge Flying Club Ltd
	G-BGKO	Gardan GY-20 Minicab	Condor Aviation International Ltd
	G-BGKS	PA-28-161 Warrior II	Fly with the Best Ltd
	G-BGKT	Auster AOP.9 (XN441)	Kilo Tango Group
	G-BGKU	PA-28R-201 Arrow III	Aerolease Ltd
	G-BGKV	PA-28R-201 Arrow III	R. N. Mayle
	G-BGKY	PA-38-112 Tomahawk	APB Leasing Ltd
	G-BGKZ	Auster J/5F Aiglet Trainer	R. B. Webber
	G-BGLA	PA-38-112 Tomahawk	E. J. Partridge
	G-BGLB	Bede BD-5B ★	Science Museum/Wroughton
	G-BGLF	Evans VP-1 Srs 2	B. A. Schlussler
	G-BGLG	Cessna 152	Cloud Global Ltd
	G-BGLO	Cessna F.172N	D. K. Fung
	G-BGLZ	Stits SA-3A Playboy	W. Hinchcliffe
	G-BGME	SIPA 903	M. Emery (G-BCML)
	G-BGMJ	Gardan GY-201 Minicab	G-BGMJ Group
	G-BGMP	Cessna F.172G	H. Wall
	G-BGMR	Gardan GY-20 Minicab	M. P. M. Clements
	G-BGMS	Taylor JT.2 Titch	M. A. J. Spice
	G-BGMT	SOCATA Rallye 235E	C. G. Wheeler & M. Faulkner
	G-BGND	Cessna F.172N	A. J. M. Freeman
	G-BGNT	Cessna F.152	Aerolease Ltd
	G-BGNV	GA-7 Cougar	D. D. Saint
	G-BGOG	PA-28-161 Warrior II	W. D. Moore & F. J. Morris
	G-BGOL	PA-28R-201T Turbo Arrow III	R. G. Jackson
	G-BGON	GA-7 Cougar	R. Ellingworth, D. A. Gathercole & H. Mackintosh
	G-BGOR	AT-6D Harvard III (14863)	A. P. Wilson & M. B. Levy
	G-BGPB	CCF T-6J Texan (1747)	Aircraft Spares & Materials Ltd
	G-BGPD	Piper J-3C-65 Cub (479744:M-49)	P. R. Whiteman
	G-BGPH	AA-5B Tiger	Shipping & Airlines Ltd
	G-BGPI	Plumb BGP-1	B. G. Plumb
	G-BGPJ	PA-28-161 Warrior II	W. Lancs Warrior Co Ltd
	G-BGPL	PA-28-161 Warrior II	JABM Ltd
	G-BGPM	Evans VP-2	Condor Aviation International Ltd
	G-BGPN	PA-18 Super Cub 150	A. R. Darke
	G-BGRE	Beech A200 Super King Air	Killinchy Aerospace Holdings Ltd
	G-BGRI	Jodel DR.1051	R. G. Hallam
	G-BGRO	Cessna F.172M	Cammo Aviation
	G-BGRR	PA-38-112 Tomahawk	C. L. Webb & R. J. Kirk
	G-BGRT	Steen Skybolt	F. Ager
	G-BGRX	PA-38-112 Tomahawk	Sky Solution Ltd
	G-BGSA	Morane MS.892A-150	B. Huda & P. W. Osborne
	G-BGSJ	Piper J-3C-65 Cub (236657)	M. A. V. Gatehouse
	G-BGSW	Beech F33 Debonair	J. J. Noakes
	G-BGTC	Auster AOP.9 (XP282)	J. R. Davison
	G-BGTF	PA-44-180 Seminole	N. A. Baxter (G-OPTC)
	G-BGTI	Piper J-3C-65 Cub	A. P. Broad
	G-BGUB	PA-32 Cherokee Six 300E	D. P. & E. A. Morris

Reg	Type	Owner or Operator	Notes
G-BGVB	Robin DR.315	K. Hartmann	
G-BGVE	CP.1310-C3 Super Emeraude	R. Whitwell	
G-BGVH	Beech 76 Duchess	M. D. Darragh	
G-BGVN	PA-28RT-201 Arrow IV	John Wailing Ltd	
G-BGVS	Cessna F.172M	Enterprise Purchasing Ltd	
G-BGVV	AA-5A Cheetah	J. M. Currie	
G-BGVY	AA-5B Tiger	G-BGVY Co-Ownership	
G-BGVZ	PA-28-181 Archer II	M. & W. Walsh	
G-BGWC	Robin DR.400/180	G. C. Bremner & R. J. Guess	
G-BGWM	PA-28-181 Archer II	Thames Valley Flying Club Ltd	
G-BGWO	Jodel D.112	G-BGWO Group	
G-BGWZ	Eclipse Super Eagle ★	F.A.A. Museum/Yeovilton	
G-BGXA	Piper J-3C-65 Cub (329471:F-44)	P. King	
G-BGXC	SOCATA TB10 Tobago	M. H. & S. H. Cundey	
G-BGXD	SNCATA TB10 Tobago	Whitewest Ltd	
G-BGXO	PA-38-112 Tomahawk	Goodwood Terrena Ltd	
G-BGXR	Robin HR.200/100	J. R. Cross	
G-BGXS	PA-28-236 Dakota	G-BGXS Group	
G-BGXT	SOCATA TB10 Tobago	P. G. Leonard & T. Jackson	
G-BGYH	PA-28-161 Warrior II	Tayside Aviation Ltd	
G-BGYN	PA-18 Super Cub 150	D. B. & J. R. Dunford	
G-BHAA	Cessna 152 II	Herefordshire Aero Club Ltd	
G-BHAD	Cessna A.152	Touchdown Engineering Ltd	
G-BHAI	Cessna F.152	ACS Aviation Ltd	
G-BHAJ	Robin DR.400/160	Rowantask Ltd	
G-BHAV	Cessna F.152	T. M. & M. L. Jones	
G-BHBA	Campbell Cricket	S. N. McGovern	
G-BHBB	Colt 77C balloon	R. H. A. Hall	
G-BHBE	Westland-Bell 47G-3B1 (Soloy)	T. R. Smith (Agricultural Machinery) Ltd	
G-BHBG	PA-32R Cherokee Lance 300	D. Moorman	
G-BHBT	Marquart MA.5 Charger	Bravo Tango Group	
G-BHCC	Cessna 172M	Staverton Flying School @ Skypark	
G-BHCE	Jodel D.112	Charles Echo Group	
G-BHCM	Cessna F.172H	E. P. White & A. P. Headland	
G-BHCP	Cessna F.152	Eastern Air Executive Ltd	
G-BHCZ	PA-38-112 Tomahawk	J. E. Abbott	
G-BHDD	V.668 Varsity T.1 (WL626:P) ★	Aeropark/East Midlands	
G-BHDE	SOCATA TB10 Tobago	J. C. Parker	
G-BHDK	Boeing B-29A-BN (461748:Y) ★	Imperial War Museum/Duxford	
G-BHDM	Cessna F.152 II	A. D. R. Northeast	
G-BHDP	Cessna F.182Q II	Zone Travel Ltd	
G-BHDS	Cessna F.152 II	Redmosaic Formacao de Technicos de Aeronaves Unipessoal	
G-BHDV	Cameron V-77 balloon	P. Glydon	
G-BHDX	Cessna F.172N	P. C. & P. T. Appleton	
G-BHDZ	Cessna F.172N	H. Mackintosh	
G-BHEG	Jodel 150	M. Kolev	
G-BHEK	CP.1315-C3 Super Emeraude	D. B. Winstanley	
G-BHEL	Jodel D.117	J. C. Metcalf	
G-BHEN	Cessna FA.152	Leicestershire Aero Club Ltd	
G-BHEU	Thunder Ax7-65 balloon	L. J. Wigfield	
G-BHEV	PA-28R Cherokee Arrow 200	Seven-Up Group	
G-BHFC	Cessna F.152	JH Sandham Aviation	
G-BHFE	PA-44-180 Seminole	Transport Command Ltd	
G-BHFG	SNCAN Stampe SV.4C	G. W. Lynch	
G-BHFH	PA-34-200T Seneca II	Andrews Professional Colour Laboratories Ltd	
G-BHFI	Cessna F.152	BAe (Warton) Flying Club	
G-BHFJ	PA-28RT-201T Turbo Arrow IV	S. A. Cook & D. R. Northeast	
G-BHFK	PA-28-151 Warrior	G-BHFK Flying Group	
G-BHGC	PA-18 Super Cub 150	C. R. Dacey	
G-BHGF	Cameron V-56 balloon	P. Smallwood	
G-BHGJ	Jodel D.120	M. Devlin	
G-BHGO	PA-32 Cherokee Six 260	R. Cranborne & Aviation Global Services Ltd	
G-BHGY	PA-28R Cherokee Arrow 200	Truman Aviation Ltd	
G-BHHE	Jodel DR.1051/M1	M. Hales	
G-BHHG	Cessna F.152 II	TG Aviation Ltd	
G-BHHH	Thunder Ax7-65 balloon	J. M. J. Roberts	
G-BHHK	Cameron N-77 balloon ★	British Balloon Museum	
G-BHHN	Cameron V-77 balloon	Itchen Valley Balloon Group	
G-BHIB	Cessna F.182Q	M. S. Williams	

49

Notes	Reg	Type	Owner or Operator
	G-BHII	Cameron V-77 balloon	R. V. Brown
	G-BHIJ	Eiri PIK-20E-1 (898)	P. J. Shout & I. P. Freestone
	G-BHIN	Cessna F.152	Sussex Flying Club Ltd
	G-BHIR	PA-28R Cherokee Arrow 200	Factorcore Ltd
	G-BHIS	Thunder Ax7-65 balloon	Hedgehoppers Balloon Group
	G-BHIY	Cessna F.150K	N. J. Butler
	G-BHJF	SOCATA TB10 Tobago	J. L. Sparks
	G-BHJI	Mooney M.20J	Otomed APS/Denmark
	G-BHJK	Maule M5-235C Lunar Rocket	M. K. H. Bell
	G-BHJN	Fournier RF-4D	RF-4 Group
	G-BHJO	PA-28-161 Warrior II	S C Airlease Ltd
	G-BHJS	Partenavia P.68B	Flew LLP
	G-BHJU	Robin DR.400/2+2	Ageless Aeronautics
	G-BHKE	Bensen B.8MS	A. R. Hawes
	G-BHKR	Colt 12A balloon ★	British Balloon Museum/Newbury
	G-BHKT	Jodel D.112	G. Dawes
	G-BHLE	Robin DR.400/180	A. V. Harmer
	G-BHLH	Robin DR.400/180	G-BHLH Group
	G-BHLJ	Saffery-Rigg S.200 balloon	I. A. Rigg
	G-BHLU	Alpavia Fournier RF-3	Lima Zulu Services Ltd
	G-BHLW	Cessna 120	Moray Flying Group
	G-BHLX	AA-5B Tiger	M. D. McPherson
	G-BHMA	SIPA 903	H. J. Taggart
	G-BHMG	Cessna FA.152	North Weald Flying Group Ltd
	G-BHMJ	Avenger T.200-2112 balloon	R. Light *Lord Anthony 1*
	G-BHMK	Avenger T.200-2112 balloon	P. Kinder *Lord Anthony 2*
	G-BHMT	Evans VP-1	D. W. Curtis
	G-BHMY	F.27 Friendship Mk.200 ★	City of Norwich Aviation Museum/Norwich
	G-BHNC	Cameron O-65 balloon	D. & C. Bareford
	G-BHNK	Jodel D.120A	G. J. Prisk
	G-BHNO	PA-28-181 Archer II	HJK Asset Management Ltd
	G-BHNP	Eiri PIK-20E-1	D. A. Sutton
	G-BHNV	Westland-Bell 47G-3B1	S. W. Hutchinson
	G-BHNX	Jodel D.117	C. P. Davey
	G-BHOA	Robin DR.400/160	T. L. Trott
	G-BHOL	Jodel DR.1050	S. J. Pearson
	G-BHOM	PA-18 Super Cub 95	D. R. & R. M. Lee
	G-BHOR	PA-28-161 Warrior II	Oscar Romeo Flying Group
	G-BHOT	Cameron V-65 balloon	Dante Balloon Group
	G-BHOZ	SOCATA TB9 Tampico	A. W. Hill
	G-BHPK	Piper J-3C-65 Cub (238410:A-44)	L-4 Group
	G-BHPL	CASA 1.131E Jungmann 1000 (E3B-350:05-97)	A. Burroughes
	G-BHPS	Jodel D.120A	M. C. Hayes
	G-BHPZ	Cessna 172N	O'Brien Properties Ltd
	G-BHRC	PA-28-161 Warrior II	Sherwood Flying Club Ltd
	G-BHRH	Cessna FA.150K	Merlin Flying Club Ltd
	G-BHRK	Colt Saucepan 56 SS balloon	D. P. Busby
	G-BHRO	Rockwell Commander 112	M. G. Cookson
	G-BHRR	CP.301A Emeraude	B. Mills
	G-BHSB	Cessna 172N	J. W. Cope & M. P. Wimsey
	G-BHSD	Scheibe SF.25E Super Falke	K. E. Ballington
	G-BHSL	CASA 1-131E Jungmann	A. F. Kutz
	G-BHSY	Jodel DR.1050	T. R. Allebone
	G-BHTA	PA-28-236 Dakota	Dakota Ltd
	G-BHTG	Thunder Ax6-56 Bolt balloon	The British Balloon Museum & Library Ltd
	G-BHUB	Douglas C-47A (315509:W7-S) ★	Imperial War Museum/Duxford
	G-BHUE	Jodel DR.1050	M. J. Harris
	G-BHUG	Cessna 172N	A. Humphreys & R. Wainwright
	G-BHUI	Cessna 152	South Warwickshire School of Flying Ltd
	G-BHUM	DH.82A Tiger Moth	S. G. Towers
	G-BHUU	PA-25 Pawnee 235	Booker Gliding Club Ltd
	G-BHVB	PA-28-161 Warrior II	Falcon Flying Services
	G-BHVF	Jodel 150A	Groupe Ariel
	G-BHVP	Cessna 182Q	The G-BHVP Flying Group
	G-BHVR	Cessna 172N	Victor Romeo Group
	G-BHVV	Piper J-3C-65 Cub (42-38384)	T. Kattinger
	G-BHWA	Cessna F.152	DSFT Ltd
	G-BHWY	PA-28R Cherokee Arrow 200-II	Kilo Foxtrot Flying Group
	G-BHWZ	PA-28-181 Archer II	M. A. Abbott
	G-BHXA	SA Bulldog Srs 120/1210	Air Plan Flight Equipment Ltd

Reg	Type	Owner or Operator	Notes
G-BHXB	SA Bulldog Srs 120/1210	XB Group (G-JWCM)	
G-BHXD	Jodel D.120	R. E. Guscott	
G-BHXS	Jodel D.120	Plymouth Jodel Group	
G-BHXY	Piper J-3C-65 Cub (44-79609:44-S)	F. W. Rogers	
G-BHYA	Cessna R.182RG II	J-P. Jarier	
G-BHYC	Cessna 172RG II	BHM Aviation	
G-BHYI	SNCAN Stampe SV.4A	D. Hicklin	
G-BHYP	Cessna F.172M	Avior Ltd	
G-BHYR	Cessna F.172M	G-BHYR Group	
G-BHZE	PA-28-181 Archer II	Dave Flying Group	
G-BHZH	Cessna F.152	Fly NQY Pilot Training	
G-BHZK	AA-5B Tiger	ZK Group	
G-BHZR	SA Bulldog Srs 120/1210	Archdog Group	
G-BHZT	SA Bulldog Srs 120/1210	D. M. Curties	
G-BHZU	Piper J-3C-65 Cub	P. F. Durnford	
G-BHZV	Jodel D.120A	G-BHZV Group	
G-BIAC	SOCATA Rallye 235E	West India Flying Group	
G-BIAH	Jodel D.112	K. J. Steele	
G-BIAI	WMB.2 Windtracker balloon	I. Chadwick	
G-BIAP	PA-16 Clipper	G-BIAP Flying Group	
G-BIAR	Rigg Skyliner II balloon	I. A. Rigg	
G-BIAU	Sopwith Pup (replica) (N6452) ★	F.A.A. Museum/Yeovilton	
G-BIAX	Taylor JT.2 Titch	P. J. Hebdon & C. S. Hales	
G-BIBA	SOCATA TB9 Tampico	TB Aviation Ltd	
G-BIBO	Cameron V-65 balloon	D. M. Hoddinott	
G-BIBS	Cameron P-20 balloon	Cameron Balloons Ltd	
G-BIBT	AA-5B Tiger	Bravo Tango Ltd	
G-BIBX	WMB.2 Windtracker balloon	I. A. Rigg	
G-BICD	Auster 5 (MT166)	T. R. Parsons	
G-BICE	NA AT-6C Harvard IIA (41-33275:CE)	C. M. L. Edwards	
G-BICG	Cessna F.152 II	M. A. Khan	
G-BICM	Colt 56A balloon	M. R. Stokoe	
G-BICP	Robin DR.360	B. McVeighty	
G-BICR	Jodel D.120A	T. W. J. Carnall & M. B. Blackmore	
G-BICU	Cameron V-56 balloon	S. D. Bather	
G-BICW	PA-28-161 Warrior II	Blueplane Ltd	
G-BIDD	Evans VP-1	J. Hodgkinson	
G-BIDG	Jodel 150A	D. H. Greenwood	
G-BIDH	Cessna 152 II	Hull Aero Club Ltd (G-DONA)	
G-BIDI	PA-28R-201 Arrow III	S. Jameson	
G-BIDJ	PA-18A Super Cub 150	S. M. Hart	
G-BIDK	PA-18 Super Cub 150	Y. Leysen	
G-BIDO	CP.301A Emeraude	A. R. Plumb	
G-BIDV	Colt 14A balloon ★	British Balloon Museum/Newbury	
G-BIDW	Sopwith 1½ Strutter (replica) (A8226) ★	RAF Museum/Cosford	
G-BIDX	Jodel D.112	P. Turton	
G-BIEN	Jodel D.120A	M. J. Sharp	
G-BIEO	Jodel D.112	R. S. & S. C. Solley	
G-BIES	Maule M5-235C Lunar Rocket	William Proctor Ltd	
G-BIET	Cameron O-77 balloon	G. M. Westley	
G-BIEY	PA-28-151 Warrior	M. J. Isaac	
G-BIFB	PA-28-150 Cherokee C	D. H. G. Penney	
G-BIFO	Evans VP-1 Srs.2	E. L. E. Webley	
G-BIFP	Colt 56A balloon	C. J. Freeman	
G-BIFY	Cessna F.150L	North Weald Flying Group Ltd	
G-BIGB	Bell 212	Heli-Lift Services	
G-BIGJ	Cessna F.172M	Cirrus Aviation Ltd	
G-BIGK	Taylorcraft BC12D	M. J. Kirk	
G-BIGL	Cameron O-65 balloon	P. L. Mossman	
G-BIGP	Bensen B.8M ★	The Helicopter Museum/Weston-super-Mare	
G-BIGR	Avenger T.200-2112 balloon	R. Light	
G-BIGX	Bensen B.8M	W. C. Turner	
G-BIHD	Robin DR.400/160	R. C. Boll	
G-BIHF	SE-5A (replica) (F943)	C. J. Zeal	
G-BIHI	Cessna 172M	D. H. G. Penney	
G-BIHO	DHC.6 Twin Otter 310	Isles of Scilly Skybus Ltd	
G-BIHT	PA-17 Vagabond	N. F. Andrews	
G-BIHU	Saffrey S.200 balloon	B. L. King	
G-BIHX	Bensen B.8M	P. P. Willmott	
G-BIIA	Fournier RF-3	C. H. Dennis	

Notes	Reg	Type	Owner or Operator
	G-BIID	PA-18 Super Cub 95	D. A. Lacey
	G-BIIF	Fournier RF-4D	K. M. Fresson (G-BVET)
	G-BIIK	MS.883 Rallye 115	A. C. Bloomberg
	G-BIIO	BN-2T Islander	Gama Aviation (UK) Ltd
	G-BIIT	PA-28-161 Warrior II	Tayside Aviation Ltd
	G-BIIZ	Great Lakes 2T-1A Sport Trainer	Airborne Adventures Ltd
	G-BIJB	PA-18 Super Cub 150	James Aero Ltd
	G-BIJD	Bölkow Bö.208C Junior	J. D. Day
	G-BIJE	Piper J-3C-65 Cub	R. L. Hayward & A. G. Scott
	G-BIJS	Luton LA-4A Minor	B. W. Faulkner
	G-BIJU	CP-301A Emeraude	Eastern Taildraggers Flying Group (G-BHTX)
	G-BIJV	Cessna F.152 II	Falcon Flying Services
	G-BIJW	Cessna F.152 II	Falcon Flying Services
	G-BIJX	Cessna F.152 II	Falcon Flying Services
	G-BIKE	PA-28R Cherokee Arrow 200	R. Taylor
	G-BIKT	Boeing 757-236F	DHL Air Ltd
	G-BILB	WMB.2 Windtracker balloon	B. L. King
	G-BILE	Scruggs BL.2B balloon	P. D. Ridout
	G-BILG	Scruggs BL.2B balloon	P. D. Ridout
	G-BILH	Slingsby T.65C Vega	P. Woodcock
	G-BILI	Piper J-3C-65 Cub (454467:J-44)	Historic & Classic Aircraft Sales
	G-BILR	Cessna 152 II	APB Leasing Ltd
	G-BILS	Cessna 152 II	Mona Flying Club
	G-BILU	Cessna 172RG	Full Sutton Flying Centre Ltd
	G-BILZ	Taylor JT.1 Monoplane	A. Petherbridge
	G-BIMK	Tiger T.200 Srs 1 balloon	M. K. Baron
	G-BIMM	PA-18 Super Cub 150	Avalon Ventures Ltd
	G-BIMN	Steen Skybolt	R. J. Thomas
	G-BIMT	Cessna FA.152	Staverton Flying School @ Skypark Ltd
	G-BIMX	Rutan Vari-Eze	D. G. Crow
	G-BIMZ	Beech 76 Duchess	D. C. S. Gunning
	G-BINL	Scruggs BL.2B balloon	P. D. Ridout
	G-BINM	Scruggs BL.2B balloon	P. D. Ridout
	G-BINR	Unicorn UE.1A balloon	Unicorn Group
	G-BINS	Unicorn UE.2A balloon	Unicorn Group
	G-BINT	Unicorn UE.1A balloon	D. E. Bint
	G-BINX	Scruggs BL.2B balloon	P. D. Ridout
	G-BINY	Oriental balloon	J. L. Morton
	G-BIOA	Hughes 369D	AH Helicopter Services Ltd
	G-BIOB	Cessna F.172P	High Level Photography Ltd
	G-BIOI	Jodel DR.1051/M	A. A. Alderdice
	G-BIOK	Cessna F.152	N. Foster
	G-BIOM	Cessna F.152	J. B. P. E. Fernandes
	G-BIOU	Jodel D.117A	M. R. Routh
	G-BIPH	Scruggs BL.2B balloon	C. M. Dewsnap
	G-BIPI	Everett gyroplane	J. G. Farina
	G-BIPN	Fournier RF-3	G-BIPN Group
	G-BIPT	Jodel D.112	C. R. Davies
	G-BIPV	AA-5B Tiger	Echo Echo Ltd
	G-BIPW	Avenger T.200-2112 balloon	B. L. King
	G-BIRD	Pitts S-1D Special	N. E. Smith
	G-BIRI	CASA 1.131E Jungmann 1000	D. Watt
	G-BIRL	Avenger T.200-2112 balloon	R. Light
	G-BIRP	Arena Mk 17 Skyship balloon	A. S. Viel
	G-BIRT	Robin R.1180TD	W. D'A. Hall
	G-BIRW	MS.505 Criquet (F+IS) ★	Museum of Flight/East Fortune
	G-BISG	FRED Srs 3	T. Littlefair
	G-BISH	Cameron V-65 balloon	P. J. Bish
	G-BISL	Scruggs BL.2B balloon	P. D. Ridout
	G-BISM	Scruggs BL.2B balloon	P. D. Ridout
	G-BISS	Scruggs BL.2C balloon	P. D. Ridout
	G-BIST	Scruggs BL.2C balloon	P. D. Ridout
	G-BISX	Colt 56A balloon	C. D. Steel
	G-BITA	PA-18 Super Cub 150	P. T. Shaw
	G-BITE	SOCATA TB10 Tobago	N. A. Baxter
	G-BITF	Cessna F.152 II	G-BITF Owners Group
	G-BITH	Cessna F.152 II	J. R. Hyde (G-TFSA)
	G-BITO	Jodel D.112D	A. Dunbar
	G-BITY	FD.31T balloon	A. J. Bell
	G-BIUP	SNCAN NC.854S	S. A. Richardson
	G-BIUY	PA-28-181 Archer II	Redhill Air Services Ltd

Reg	Type	Owner or Operator	Notes
G-BIVA	Robin R.2112	Victor Alpha Group	
G-BIVB	Jodel D.112	S. J. Heighway	
G-BIVC	Jodel D.112	T. D. Wood	
G-BIVF	CP.301C-3 Emeraude	Hampshire Flying Group	
G-BIVK	Bensen B.8M	M. J. Atyeo	
G-BIWB	Scruggs RS.5000 balloon	P. D. Ridout	
G-BIWC	Scruggs RS.5000 balloon	P. D. Ridout	
G-BIWF	Warren balloon	P. D. Ridout	
G-BIWG	Zelenski Mk 2 balloon	P. D. Ridout	
G-BIWJ	Unicorn UE.1A balloon	B. L. King	
G-BIWN	Jodel D.112	J. Steele	
G-BIWR	Mooney M.20F	M. Broady	
G-BIWY	Westland WG.30 ★	Instructional airframe/Yeovil	
G-BIXA	SOCATA TB9 Tampico	P. Jones	
G-BIXB	SOCATA TB9 Tampico	B. G. Adams	
G-BIXL	P-51D Mustang (472216:HO-M)	R. W. Tyrrell	
G-BIXN	Boeing Stearman A75N1 (FJ777)	V. S. E. Norman	
G-BIXW	Colt 56B balloon	N. A. P. Bates	
G-BIXX	Pearson Srs 2 balloon	D. Pearson	
G-BIXZ	Grob G-109	C. Beck	
G-BIYI	Cameron V-65 balloon	R. J. Mitchener & P. F. Smart	
G-BIYK	Isaacs Fury II	M. White & D. J. Fry	
G-BIYR	PA-18 Super Cub 150 (R-151)	Delta Foxtrot Flying Group	
G-BIYU	Fokker S.11.1 Instructor (E-15)	Fokker Syndicate	
G-BIYW	Jodel D.112	R. C. Hibberd	
G-BIYX	PA-28 Cherokee 140	W. B. Bateson	
G-BIYY	PA-18 Super Cub 95	A. E. & Taylor	
G-BIZF	Cessna F.172P	R. S. Bentley	
G-BIZG	Cessna F.152	M. A. Judge	
G-BIZK	Nord 3202 (78)	A. I. Milne	
G-BIZM	Nord 3202	Global Aviation Ltd	
G-BIZO	PA-28R Cherokee Arrow 200	Bristol Flying Club Ltd	
G-BIZY	Jodel D.112	T. R. Fray	
G-BJAD	FRED Srs 2 ★	Newark Air Museum/Newark	
G-BJAE	Lavadoux Starck AS.80	D. J. & S. A. E. Phillips/Coventry	
G-BJAF	Piper J-3C-65 Cub	V. Goddard	
G-BJAG	PA-28-181 Archer II	C. R. Chubb	
G-BJAJ	AA-5B Tiger	Draycott Tiger Club	
G-BJAL	CASA 1.131E Jungmann 1000	G-BJAL Group	
G-BJAO	Bensen B.8M	A. P. Lay	
G-BJAP	DH.82A Tiger Moth (K2587)	T. J. Orchard	
G-BJAS	Rango NA.9 balloon	A. Lindsay	
G-BJAY	Piper J-3C-65 Cub (44-79790)	D. W. Finlay	
G-BJBK	PA-18 Super Cub 95	M. S. Bird	
G-BJBO	Jodel DR.250/160	Wiltshire Flying Group	
G-BJBW	PA-28-161 Warrior II	152 Group	
G-BJCA	PA-28-161 Warrior II	Falcon Flying Services Ltd	
G-BJCF	CP.1310-C3 Super Emeraude	A. C. Gunning	
G-BJCI	PA-18 Super Cub 150 (modified)	The Borders (Milfield) Gliding Club Ltd	
G-BJCW	PA-32R-301 Saratoga SP	Golf Charlie Whisky Ltd	
G-BJDE	Cessna F.172M	M. Rowntree & S. Bridgeman	
G-BJDJ	HS.125 Srs 700B	TAG Farnborough Engineering Ltd (G-RCDI)	
G-BJDK	European E.14 balloon	Aeroprint Tours	
G-BJDW	Cessna F.172M	Hardman Aviation Ltd	
G-BJEC	BN-2T Turbine Islander	Gama Aviation (UK) Ltd (G-SELX)	
G-BJED	BN-2T Turbine Islander	Islander Aircraft Ltd (G-MAFF)	
G-BJEI	PA-18 Super Cub 95	E. M. Cox	
G-BJEJ	BN-2T Turbine Islander	Islander Aircraft Ltd	
G-BJEL	SNCAN NC.854	C. A. James	
G-BJEV	Aeronca 11AC Chief (897)	M. B. Blackmore	
G-BJEX	Bölkow Bö.208C Junior	G. D. H. Crawford	
G-BJFC	European E.8 balloon	P. D. Ridout	
G-BJFE	PA-18 Super Cub 95	J. Allistone	
G-BJFM	Jodel D.120	J. V. George	
G-BJGM	Unicorn UE.1A balloon	D. Eaves & P. D. Ridout	
G-BJGY	Cessna F.172P	K. & S. Martin	
G-BJHB	Mooney M.20J	Zitair Flying Club Ltd	
G-BJHK	EAA Acro Sport	M. R. Holden	
G-BJHV	Voisin Replica ★	Brooklands Museum of Aviation/Weybridge	
G-BJIA	Allport balloon	D. J. Allport	

Notes	Reg	Type	Owner or Operator
	G-BKOT	Wassmer WA.81 Piranha	B. J. Griffiths
	G-BKOU	P.84 Jet Provost T.3 (XN637)	G-BKOU/2 Ltd
	G-BKPA	Hoffmann H-36 Dimona	R. S. Skinner
	G-BKPB	Aerosport Scamp	J. M. Brightwell
	G-BKPC	Cessna A.185F	C. Taylor & P. C. Hambilton
	G-BKPD	Viking Dragonfly	E. P. Browne & G. J. Sargent
	G-BKPG	Luscombe Rattler ★	Newark Air Museum/Newark
	G-BKPS	AA-5B Tiger	A. E. T. Clarke
	G-BKPX	Jodel D.120A	S. H. Barr
	G-BKPY	SAAB 91B/2 Safir (56321:U-AB) ★	Newark Air Museum
	G-BKPZ	Pitts S-1T Special	D. A. Slater
	G-BKRA	NA T-6G Texan (51-15227)	First Air Ltd
	G-BKRF	PA-18 Super Cub 95	T. F. F. van Erck
	G-BKRH	Brügger MB.2 Colibri	T. C. Darters
	G-BKRK	SNCAN Stampe SV.4C	Strathgadie Stampe Group
	G-BKRL	Chichester-Miles Leopard ★	Bournemouth Aviation Museum
	G-BKRN	Beechcraft D.18S (43-35943)	A. A. Marshall & P. L. Turland
	G-BKRU	Crossley Racer	S. Alexander
	G-BKSC	Saro Skeeter AOP.12 (XN351) ★	R. A. L. Falconer
	G-BKSE	QAC Quickie Q.1	C. J. Riley
	G-BKST	Rutan Vari-Eze	R. Towle
	G-BKTA	PA-18 Super Cub 95	M. J. Dyson
	G-BKTH	CCF Hawker Sea Hurricane IB (Z7015)	The Shuttleworth Collection
	G-BKTM	PZL SZD-45A Ogar	Hinton Ogar Group
	G-BKTZ	Slingsby T.67M Firefly	Formation Flying Ltd (G-SFTV)
	G-BKUE	SOCATA TB9 Tampico	Fife TB9ers
	G-BKUI	D.31 Turbulent	E. Shouler
	G-BKUR	CP.301A Emeraude	T. Harvey
	G-BKVC	SOCATA TB9 Tampico	Fly-Bro KFT/Hungary
	G-BKVG	Scheibe SF.25E Super Falke	G-BKVG Ltd
	G-BKVK	Auster AOP.9 (WZ662)	J. A. Keen & M. Walker
	G-BKVL	Robin DR.400/160	G-BKVL Group
	G-BKVM	PA-18 Super Cub 150 (115684)	M. C. Curtis
	G-BKVP	Pitts S-1D Special	S. A. Smith
	G-BKVY	Airtour B-31 balloon	Cloud Nine Balloon Group
	G-BKWD	Taylor JT.2 Titch	J. F. Sully
	G-BKWR	Cameron V-65 balloon	Window on the World Ltd
	G-BKXA	Robin R.2100	M. Wilson
	G-BKXF	PA-28R Cherokee Arrow 200	Just Plane Trading Ltd
	G-BKXJ	Rutan VariEze	K. O. Miller (G-TIMB)
	G-BKXM	Colt 17A balloon	R. G. Turnbull
	G-BKXO	Rutan LongEz	R. A. G. M. Jolly & J. G. Cox
	G-BKXP	Auster AOP.6	M. A. Farrelly & D. K. Chambers
	G-BKXR	D.31A Turbulent	G-BKXR Turbulent Group
	G-BKZM	Isaacs Fury	L. C. Wells
	G-BKZT	FRED Srs 2	U. Chakravorty
	G-BLAC	Cessna FA.152	W. Ali
	G-BLAF	Stolp SA.900 V-Star	H. Hawkins & P. D. G. Grist
	G-BLAG	Pitts S-1D Special	Cirrus Aircraft UK Ltd (G-IIIP)
	G-BLAI	Monnett Sonerai 2L	T. Simpon
	G-BLAM	Jodel DR.360	J. S. Dalton
	G-BLAT	Jodel 150	Edghill Aviation Services Ltd
	G-BLCH	Colt 65D balloon	R. S. Breakwell
	G-BLCI	EAA Acro Sport	M. R. Holden
	G-BLCT	Jodel DR.220 2+2	F. N. P. Maurin
	G-BLCU	Scheibe SF.25B Falke	Charlie Uniform Syndicate
	G-BLCY	Thunder Ax7-65Z balloon	M. A. Stelling
	G-BLDB	Taylor JT.1 Monoplane	J. P. J. Hefford
	G-BLDG	PA-25 Pawnee 260C	Ouse Gliding Club Ltd
	G-BLDK	Robinson R22	Flight Academy (Gyrocopters) Ltd
	G-BLDN	Rand-Robinson KR-2	P. R. Diffey
	G-BLDV	BN-2B-26 Islander	Loganair Ltd
	G-BLES	Stolp SA.750 Acroduster Too	I. Annett
	G-BLFI	PA-28-181 Archer II	Fly Elstree Ltd
	G-BLGH	Robin DR.300/180R	Booker Gliding Club Ltd
	G-BLGV	Bell 206B JetRanger 3	Heliflight (UK) Ltd
	G-BLHH	Jodel DR.315	S. J. Luck
	G-BLHJ	Cessna F.172P	J. H. Sandham Aviation
	G-BLHM	PA-18 Super Cub 95	A. G. Edwards
	G-BLHR	GA-7 Cougar	H. Mackintosh & R. Ellingworth

Reg	Type	Owner or Operator	Notes
G-BLHS	Bellanca 7ECA Citabria	Devon & Somerset Flight Training Ltd	
G-BLHW	Varga 2150A Kachina	J. B. Webb	
G-BLID	DH.112 Venom FB.50 (J-1605) ★	P. G. Vallance Ltd	
G-BLIT	Thorp T-18 CW	R. M. Weeks	
G-BLIW	P.56 Provost T.51 (WV514)	A. D. M. & K. B. Edie	
G-BLIX	Saro Skeeter Mk 12 (XL809)	K. M. Scholes	
G-BLJM	Beech 95-B55 Baron	A. H. G. Herbst	
G-BLJO	Cessna F.152	Redhill Air Services Ltd	
G-BLKA	DH.112 Venom FB.54 (J-1790) ★	Fishburn Historic Aviation Centre	
G-BLKM	Jodel DR.1051	Kilo Mike Group	
G-BLLA	Bensen B.8M	K. T. Donaghey	
G-BLLB	Bensen B.8M	D. H. Moss	
G-BLLD	Cameron O-77 balloon	G. Birchall	
G-BLLH	Jodel DR.220A 2+2	J. K. Houlgrave	
G-BLLO	PA-18 Super Cub 95	M. F. Watts	
G-BLLP	Slingsby T.67B	Air Navigation and Trading Co Ltd	
G-BLLR	Slingsby T.67B	R. L. Brinklow	
G-BLLS	Slingsby T.67B	T. Wolfshohl	
G-BLLW	Colt 56B balloon	C. J. Dunkley	
G-BLLZ	Rutan LongEz	R. S. Stoddart-Stones	
G-BLMA	Zlin 326 Trener Master	G. P. Northcott	
G-BLMC	Avro 698 Vulcan B.2A ★	Aeropark/East Midlands	
G-BLMG	Grob G.109B	G-BLMG Group	
G-BLMI	PA-18-95 Super Cub (R-55)	T. F. F. Van Erck	
G-BLMN	Rutan LongEz	K. W. Taylor	
G-BLMP	PA-17 Vagabond	C. W. Thirtle	
G-BLMR	PA-18 Super Cub 150	M. Vickers	
G-BLMT	PA-18 Super Cub 135	I. S. Runnalls	
G-BLMW	T.66 Nipper 3	S. L. Millar	
G-BLNI	BN-2B-26 Islander	Air Alderney Ltd	
G-BLNO	FRED Srs 3	L. W. Smith	
G-BLOR	PA-30 Twin Comanche 160	M. C. Jordan	
G-BLOS	Cessna 185A (also flown with floats)	G. P. Harrington & J. R. Chapman	
G-BLOT	Colt Ax6-56B balloon	M. A. Stelling	
G-BLPB	Turner TSW Hot Two Wot	Papa Bravo Group	
G-BLPE	PA-18 Super Cub 95	A. A. Haig-Thomas	
G-BLPF	Cessna FR.172G	S. Culpin	
G-BLPG	Auster J/1N Alpha (16693:693)	S. J. Heighway (G-AIZH)	
G-BLPP	Cameron V-77 balloon	G. B. Davies	
G-BLRC	PA-18 Super Cub 135	Supercub Group	
G-BLRF	Slingsby T.67C	R. C. Nicholls	
G-BLRL	CP.301C-1 Emeraude	A. M. Smith	
G-BLSD	DH.112 Venom FB.54 (J-1758) ★	R. Lamplough/North Weald	
G-BLSX	Cameron O-105 balloon	B. J. Petteford	
G-BLTC	D.31A Turbulent	S. J. Butler	
G-BLTM	Robin HR.200/100	Troughton Engineering Aircraft Maintenance Ltd	
G-BLTN	Thunder Ax7-65 balloon	V. Michel	
G-BLTR	Scheibe SF.25B Falke	V. Mallon/Germany	
G-BLTS	Rutan LongEz	R. W. Cutler	
G-BLTV	Slingsby T.67B	R. L. Brinklow	
G-BLTW	Slingsby T.67B	Cheshire Air Training Services Ltd	
G-BLTY	Westland WG.30 Srs 160	D. Brem-Wilson	
G-BLUE	Colt 77A balloon	D. P. Busby	
G-BLUJ	Cameron V-56 balloon	F. R. Battersby	
G-BLUV	Grob G.109B	109 Flying Group	
G-BLUX	Slingsby T.67M Firefly 200	R. L. Brinklow	
G-BLUZ	DH.82B Queen Bee (LF858)	The Bee Keepers Group	
G-BLVA	Airtour AH-31 balloon	D. L. Peltan & S. Church	
G-BLVB	Airtour AH-56 balloon	Z. Daly	
G-BLVI	Slingsby T.67M Firefly Mk II	M. L. Scott	
G-BLVK	CAARP CAP-10B	R. W. H. Cole	
G-BLVL	PA-28-161 Warrior II	TG Aviation Ltd	
G-BLVS	Cessna 150M	D. H. G. Penney	
G-BLVW	Cessna F.172H	R. Holloway	
G-BLWD	PA-34-200T Seneca 2	Bencray Ltd	
G-BLWM	Bristol M.1C (replica) (C4994) ★	RAF Museum/Cosford	
G-BLWP	PA-38-112 Tomahawk	APB Leasing Ltd	
G-BLWT	Evans VP-1	M. W. Olliver	
G-BLWW	Taylor Mini-Imp C	D. F. Hurn & M. George	
G-BLWY	Robin R.2160D	Pure Aviation Support Services Ltd	
G-BLXG	Colt 21A balloon	D. P. Busby	

Notes	Reg	Type	Owner or Operator
	G-BLXH	Fournier RF-3	G-BLXH Group
	G-BLXI	CP.1310-C3 Super Emeraude	W. D. Garlick
	G-BLXO	Jodel 150	P. P. Chapman
	G-BLXT	Eberhardt S.E.5E	Flying A Services Ltd
	G-BLYD	SOCATA TB20 Trinidad	S. Picco
	G-BLZA	Scheibe SF.25B Falke	Zulu Alpha Syndicate
	G-BLZH	Cessna F.152 II	P. D'Costa
	G-BLZJ	Aerospatiale AS.332L Super Puma	Airbus Helicopters (G-PUMJ)
	G-BLZP	Cessna F.152	East Midlands Flying School Ltd
	G-BMAD	Cameron V-77 balloon	M. A. Stelling
	G-BMAO	Taylor JT.1 Monoplane	N. D. Plumb
	G-BMAX	FRED Srs 2	J. P. Gilbert
	G-BMAY	PA-18 Super Cub 135	R. W. Davies
	G-BMBB	Cessna F.150L	Ken Hills Ltd
	G-BMBJ	Schempp-Hirth Janus CM	BJ Flying Group
	G-BMCC	Thunder Ax7-77 balloon	D. P. Busby
	G-BMCD	Cameron V-65 balloon	R. Lillyman
	G-BMCG	Grob G.109B	D. K. R. Draper
	G-BMCI	Cessna F.172H	A. B. Davis
	G-BMCN	Cessna F.152	Skytrek Air Services
	G-BMCS	PA-22 Tri-Pacer 135	M. P. Brigden-Gwinnutt
	G-BMCV	Cessna F.152	M. Bonsall
	G-BMCX	AS.332L Super Puma	Airbus Helicopters
	G-BMDB	SE-5A (replica) (F235:B)	D. E. Blaxland
	G-BMDD	Cadet Motor Glider	A. R. Hutton
	G-BMDE	Pietenpol AirCamper	P. B. Childs
	G-BMDJ	Price Ax7-77S balloon	R. A. Benham
	G-BMDP	Partenavia P.64B Oscar 200	J. L. Sparks
	G-BMDS	Jodel D.120	A. James
	G-BMEA	PA-18 Super Cub 95	M. J. Butler
	G-BMEH	Jodel 150 Special Super Mascaret	R. J. & C. J. Lewis
	G-BMET	Taylor JT.1 Monoplane	M. K. A. Blyth
	G-BMEU	Isaacs Fury II	I. G. Harrison
	G-BMEX	Cessna A.150K	Cotswold Flying School Ltd
	G-BMFD	PA-23 Aztec 250F	Giles Aviation Ltd (G-BGYY)
	G-BMFN	QAC Quickie Tri-Q 200	R. F. Thomson
	G-BMFP	PA-28-161 Warrior II	Aerobility
	G-BMFY	Grob G.109B	P. J. Shearer
	G-BMGB	PA-28R Cherokee Arrow 200	G-BMGB Group
	G-BMGC	Fairey Swordfish Mk II (W5856)	Fly Navy Heritage Trust Ltd
	G-BMGG	Cessna 152 II	J. R. Flieger
	G-BMGR	Grob G.109B	G-BMGR Group
	G-BMHA	Rutan LongEz	A. Bloomfield
	G-BMHL	Wittman W.8 Tailwind	S. J. Moody
	G-BMHS	Cessna F.172M	G. Campbell
	G-BMHT	PA-28RT-201T Turbo Arrow	G-BMHT Flying Group
	G-BMID	Jodel D.120	G-BMID Flying Group
	G-BMIG	Cessna 172N	R. B. Singleton-McGuire
	G-BMIM	Rutan LongEz	V. E. Jones
	G-BMIO	Stoddard-Hamilton Glasair RG	G-BMIO Group
	G-BMIP	Jodel D.112	F. J. E. Brownsill
	G-BMIR	Westland Wasp HAS.1 (XT788) ★	Park Aviation Supply/Charlwood
	G-BMIV	PA-28R-201T Turbo Arrow III	Firmbeam Ltd
	G-BMIW	PA-28-181 Archer II	Oldbus Ltd
	G-BMIX	SOCATA TB20 Trinidad	Falcon Flying Group
	G-BMIZ	Robinson R22 Beta	Heli Air Ltd
	G-BMJA	PA-32R-301 Saratoga SP	J. Cottrell
	G-BMJB	Cessna 152	Endrick Aviation LLP
	G-BMJD	Cessna 152 II	Donair Flying Club Ltd
	G-BMJJ	Cameron Watch 75 SS balloon	D. P. Busby
	G-BMJM	Evans VP-1 Series 2	R. M. I. Taylor
	G-BMJN	Cameron O-65 balloon	P. M. Traviss
	G-BMJO	PA-34-220T Seneca III	M. J. Casey
	G-BMJY	Yakovlev C18M (07)	W. A. E. Moore
	G-BMKB	PA-18 Super Cub 135	D. J. & S. N. Taplin
	G-BMKC	Piper J-3C-65 Cub (329854:R-44)	P. R. Monk
	G-BMKF	Jodel DR.221	S. T. & L. A. Gilbert
	G-BMKJ	Cameron V-77 balloon	Zebedee Balloon Service Ltd
	G-BMKK	PA-28R-200 Cherokee Arrow II	P. M. Murray
	G-BMKR	PA-28-161 Warrior II	Steve Batchelor Ltd (G-BGKR)

Reg	Type	Owner or Operator	Notes
G-BMKV	Thunder Ax7-77 balloon	Zebedee Balloon Service Ltd	
G-BMLK	Grob G.109B	Brams Syndicate	
G-BMLL	Grob G.109B	G-BMLL Flying Group	
G-BMLS	PA-28R-201 Arrow III	S. N. Adamson	
G-BMLT	Pietenpol Air Camper	W. E. R. Jenkins	
G-BMLX	Cessna F.150L	J. P. A. Freeman	
G-BMMF	FRED Srs 2	R. C. Thomas	
G-BMMI	Pazmany PL.4A	P. I. Morgans	
G-BMMJ	Siren Pik-30	LRU Group	
G-BMMK	Cessna 182P	Lambley Flying Group	
G-BMMM	Cessna 152 II	AWA Aeronautical Web Academy LDA	
G-BMMP	Grob G.109B	G-BMMP Ltd	
G-BMMV	ICA-Brasov IS-28M2A	C. D. King & C. I. Roberts	
G-BMMW	Thunder Ax7-77 balloon	P. A. George	
G-BMOE	PA-28R Cherokee Arrow 200	S. C. Airlease Ltd	
G-BMOF	Cessna U206G	Wild Geese Parachute Ltd	
G-BMOH	Cameron N-77 balloon	I. M. Taylor	
G-BMOK	ARV Super 2	R. E. Griffiths	
G-BMOL	PA-23 Aztec 250D	LDL Enterprises (G-BBSR)	
G-BMPC	PA-28-181 Archer II	C. J. & R. J. Barnes	
G-BMPL	Optica Industries OA.7 Optica	J. K. Edgley	
G-BMPR	PA-28R-201 Arrow III	Sterling Aviation	
G-BMPY	DH.82A Tiger Moth	S. M. Eisenstein	
G-BMRA	Boeing 757-236F	DHL Air Ltd	
G-BMRB	Boeing 757-236F	DHL Air Ltd	
G-BMRD	Boeing 757-236F	DHL Air Ltd	
G-BMRF	Boeing 757-236F	DHL Air Ltd	
G-BMRI	Boeing 757-236F	DHL Air Ltd	
G-BMRJ	Boeing 757-236F	DHL Air Ltd	
G-BMSA	Stinson HW-75 Voyager	P. Fraser-Bennison (G-MIRM/G-BCUM)	
G-BMSB	VS.509 Spitfire IX (MJ627:9G-Q)	Warbird Experiences Ltd (G-ASOZ)	
G-BMSC	Evans VP-2	R. S. Acreman	
G-BMSD	PA-28-181 Archer II	R. E. Parsons	
G-BMSE	Valentin Taifun 17E	D. O'Donnell	
G-BMSL	Clutton FRED Series 3	G. Smith	
G-BMTB	Cessna 152 II	Stapleford Flying Club Ltd	
G-BMTJ	Cessna 152 II	The Pilot Centre Ltd	
G-BMTU	Pitts S-1E Special	N. A. A. Pogmore	
G-BMTX	Cameron V-77 balloon	J. A. Langley	
G-BMUG	Rutan LongEz	A. G. Sayers	
G-BMUJ	Colt Drachenfisch balloon	Virgin Airship & Balloon Co Ltd	
G-BMUO	Cessna A.152	Redhill Air Services Ltd	
G-BMUT	PA-34-200T Seneca II	M. Iqbal	
G-BMUZ	PA-28-161 Warrior II	Redhill Air Services Ltd	
G-BMVB	Cessna F.152	A. J. Gomes	
G-BMVL	PA-38-112 Tomahawk	Flightpathblackpool Ltd	
G-BMVU	Monnett Moni	T. McKinley	
G-BMWF	ARV1 Super 2	D. L. Aspinall	
G-BMWR	Rockwell Commander 112	T. A. Stoate	
G-BMWU	Cameron N-42 balloon	I. Chadwick	
G-BMXB	Cessna 152 II	Devon & Somerset Flight Training Ltd	
G-BMXC	Cessna 152 II	MK Aero Support Ltd	
G-BMYG	Cessna FA.152	Central Horizon Partnership LLC	
G-BMYI	AA-5 Traveler	W. C. & S. C. Westran	
G-BMYU	Jodel D.120	J. A. Northen	
G-BMZF	WSK-Mielec LiM-2 (MiG-15bis) (01420) ★	F.A.A. Museum/Yeovilton	
G-BMZN	Everett gyroplane	P. A. Gardner	
G-BMZP	Everett gyroplane	P. A. Gardner	
G-BMZS	Everett gyroplane	R. F. G. Moyle	
G-BMZW	Bensen B.8MR	P. D. Widdicombe	
G-BMZX	Wolf W-11 Boredom Fighter	N. Wright	
G-BNAI	Wolf W-II Boredom Fighter (146-11083)	C. M. Bunn	
G-BNAJ	Cessna 152 II	Arion Aviation Ltd	
G-BNAN	Cameron V-65 balloon	Rango Balloon and Kite Company	
G-BNAW	Cameron V-65 balloon	A. Walker	
G-BNBU	Bensen B.8MV	B. A. Lyford	
G-BNCB	Cameron V-77 balloon	E. K. Read	
G-BNCM	Cameron N-77 balloon	C. A. Stone	
G-BNCR	PA-28-161 Warrior II	Airways Aero Associations Ltd	
G-BNCS	Cessna 180	C. Elwell Transport Ltd	

Notes	Reg	Type	Owner or Operator
	G-BNCX	Hawker Hunter T.7 (XL621) ★	Brooklands Museum of Aviation/Weybridge
	G-BNDP	Brügger MB.2 Colibri	P. A. Gasson
	G-BNDR	SOCATA TB10 Tobago	J-M Segonne
	G-BNDT	Brügger MB.2 Colibri	G. D. Gunby & P. Coman
	G-BNEE	PA-28R-201 Arrow III	Britannic Management Aviation
	G-BNEL	PA-28-161 Warrior II	NM Flight ervices Ltd
	G-BNEO	Cameron V-77 balloon	J. G. O'Connell
	G-BNFP	Cameron O-84 balloon	M. Clarke
	G-BNFR	Cessna 152 II	A. Jahanfar
	G-BNFV	Robin DR.400/120	J. P. A. Freeman
	G-BNGE	Auster AOP.6 (TW536)	K. A. Hale
	G-BNGJ	Cameron N-77 balloon	S. W. K. Smeeton
	G-BNGO	Thunder Ax7-77 balloon	J. S. Finlan
	G-BNGT	PA-28-181 Archer II	A. Soojeri
	G-BNGV	ARV Super 2	N. A. Onions
	G-BNGW	ARV Super 2	Southern Gas Turbines Ltd
	G-BNGY	ARV Super 2	J. & P. Morris (G-BMWL)
	G-BNHB	ARV Super 2	N. A. Onions
	G-BNHJ	Cessna 152 II	The Pilot Centre Ltd
	G-BNHK	Cessna 152 II	Wayfarers Flying Group
	G-BNHL	Colt beer glass SS balloon	M. R. Stokoe
	G-BNHN	Colt Ariel Bottle SS balloon ★	British Balloon Museum
	G-BNHT	Fournier RF-3	G-BNHT Group
	G-BNID	Cessna 152 II	MK Aero Support Ltd
	G-BNIK	Robin HR.200/120	J. W. Poynor
	G-BNIN	Cameron V-77 balloon	Cloud Nine Balloon Group
	G-BNIO	Luscombe 8A Silvaire	M. Richardson & R. C. Dyer
	G-BNIP	Luscombe 8A Silvaire	J. P. Coyne-Downhill
	G-BNIU	Cameron O-77 balloon	M. E. Dubois/France
	G-BNIV	Cessna 152 II	Aeros Leasing Ltd
	G-BNIW	Boeing Stearman PT-17	Skymax (Aviation) Ltd
	G-BNJB	Cessna 152 II	Aerolease Ltd
	G-BNJH	Cessna 152 II	ACS Aviation Ltd
	G-BNJT	PA-28-161 Warrior II	Hawarden Flying Group
	G-BNJX	Cameron N-90 balloon	Mars UK Ltd
	G-BNKC	Cessna 152 II	Herefordshire Aero Club Ltd
	G-BNKD	Cessna 172N	R. Nightingale
	G-BNKE	Cessna 172N	Kilo Echo Flying Group
	G-BNKI	Cessna 152 II	RAF Halton Aeroplane Club Ltd
	G-BNKP	Cessna 152 II	Avalon Ventures Ltd
	G-BNKR	Cessna 152 II	Airways Aero Associations Ltd
	G-BNKS	Cessna 152 II	APB Leasing Ltd
	G-BNKT	Cameron O-77 balloon	A. A. Brown
	G-BNKV	Cessna 152 II	North Weald Flight Training Ltd
	G-BNLY	Boeing 747-436 ★	preserved/Dunsfold
	G-BNMB	PA-28-151 Warrior	JABM Ltd
	G-BNMD	Cessna 152 II	T. M. Jones
	G-BNME	Cessna 152 II	M. Bonsall
	G-BNMF	Cessna 152 II	Redhill Air Services Ltd
	G-BNMH	Pietenpol Air Camper	N. M. Hitchman
	G-BNMI	Colt Flying Fantasy SS balloon	Air 2 Air Ltd
	G-BNML	Rand-Robinson KR-2	P. J. Brookman
	G-BNMX	Thunder Ax7-77 balloon	P. Coman
	G-BNNE	Cameron N-77 balloon	R. D. Allen, L. P. Hooper & M. J. Streat
	G-BNNO	PA-28-161 Warrior II	Tor Financial Consulting Ltd
	G-BNNT	PA-28-151 Warrior	S. T. Gilbert
	G-BNNX	PA-28R-201T Turbo Arrow III	Professional Flying Ltd
	G-BNNY	PA-28-161 Warrior II	Falcon Flying Services
	G-BNNZ	PA-28-161 Warrior II	Falcon Flying Services Ltd
	G-BNOB	Wittman W.8 Tailwind	D. G. Hammersley
	G-BNOF	PA-28-161 Warrior II	Tayside Aviation Ltd
	G-BNOH	PA-28-161 Warrior II	Sherburn Aero Club Ltd
	G-BNOJ	PA-28-161 Warrior II	BAE (Warton) Flying Club
	G-BNOM	PA-28-161 Warrior II	J. H. Sandham Aviation
	G-BNON	PA-28-161 Warrior II	Tayside Aviation Ltd
	G-BNOP	PA-28-161 Warrior II	BAE (Warton) Flying Club
	G-BNPE	Cameron N-77 balloon	R. N. Simpkins
	G-BNPF	Slingsby T.31M	S. Luck & ptnrs
	G-BNPH	P.66 Pembroke C.1 (WV740)	M. A. Stott
	G-BNPM	PA-38-112 Tomahawk	Papa Mike Aviation

Reg	Type	Owner or Operator	Notes
G-BNPO	PA-28-181 Archer II	The Shackleton Syndicate 2020 Flying Group Ltd	
G-BNPV	Bowers Fly-Baby 1B (1801/18)	A. Berry	
G-BNPY	Cessna 152 II	Gamston Flying School Ltd	
G-BNRA	SOCATA TB10 Tobago	Double D Airgroup	
G-BNRG	PA-28-161 Warrior II	Glenn Aviation Ltd	
G-BNRL	Cessna 152 II	Andrewsfield Aviation Ltd	
G-BNRP	PA-28-181 Archer II	PA-28 Warrior Ltd	
G-BNRR	Cessna 172P	Wentworth Productions	
G-BNRW	Colt 69A balloon	J. F. Till	
G-BNRX	PA-34-200T Seneca II	AWA Aeronautical Web Academy LDA/Portugal	
G-BNRY	Cessna 182Q	Just Plane Trading Ltd	
G-BNSG	PA-28R-201 Arrow III	Odhams Air Services Ltd	
G-BNSM	Cessna 152 II	Cornwall Flying Club Ltd	
G-BNSN	Cessna 152 II	The Pilot Centre Ltd	
G-BNSR	Slingsby T.67M Firefly Mk II	Slingsby SR Group	
G-BNST	Cessna 172N	J. Revill	
G-BNSU	Cessna 152 II	Sor Air-Sociedade de Aeronautica SA/Portugal	
G-BNSY	PA-28-161 Warrior II	Fasat Aviation Ltd	
G-BNSZ	PA-28-161 Warrior II	O. H. Hogan	
G-BNTD	PA-28-161 Warrior II	DSFT Ltd	
G-BNTP	Cessna 172N	Westnet Ltd	
G-BNUL	Cessna 152 II	A. D. R. Northeast	
G-BNUN	Beech 95-58PA Baron	SMB Aviation Ltd	
G-BNUO	Beech 76 Duchess	Sor Air-Sociedade de Aeronautica SA/Portugal	
G-BNUT	Cessna 152 Turbo	Stapleford Flying Club Ltd	
G-BNUY	PA-38-112 Tomahawk II	D. C. Storey	
G-BNVB	AA-5A Cheetah	M. E. Hicks	
G-BNVE	PA-28-181 Archer II	M. C. Plomer-Roberts	
G-BNVT	PA-28R-201T Turbo Arrow III	Victor Tango Group	
G-BNXE	PA-28-161 Warrior II	Aviation South West Ltd	
G-BNXL	Glaser-Dirks DG.400	J. Mjels	
G-BNXM	PA-18 Super Cub 95	K. A. A. McDonald & N. G. Rhind	
G-BNXU	PA-28-161 Warrior II	Friendly Warrior Group	
G-BNXV	PA-38-112 Tomahawk	W. B. Bateson	
G-BNYD	Bell 206B JetRanger 3	Heli Consultants Ltd	
G-BNYL	Cessna 152 II	V. J. Freeman	
G-BNYM	Cessna 172N	Kestrel Syndicate	
G-BNYP	PA-28-181 Archer II	D. H. Nash	
G-BNYZ	SNCAN Stampe SV.4E	Bianchi Film Aviation Services Ltd	
G-BNZB	PA-28-161 Warrior II	Falcon Flying Services Ltd	
G-BNZC	DHC.1 Chipmunk 22 (671)	The Shuttleworth Collection	
G-BNZK	Thunder Ax7-77 balloon	T. D. Marsden	
G-BNZL	Rotorway Scorpion 133	J. R. Wraight	
G-BNZM	Cessna T.210N	A. J. M. Freeman	
G-BNZN	Cameron N-56 balloon	P. Lesser	
G-BNZO	Rotorway Executive	J. S. David	
G-BNZZ	PA-28-161 Warrior II	S. Magrabi	
G-BOAA	BAC-Aérospatiale Concorde 102 ★	Museum Of Flight East Fortune (G-N94AA)	
G-BOAB	BAC-Aérospatiale Concorde 102 ★	Preserved at Heathrow (G-N94AB)	
G-BOAC	BAC-Aérospatiale Concorde 102 ★	Runway Visitor Park/Manchester International (G-N81AC)	
G-BOAF	BAC-Aérospatiale Concorde 102 ★	Bristol Aero Collection/Filton (G-N94AF)	
G-BOAH	PA-28-161 Warrior II	CG Aviation Ltd	
G-BOAI	Cessna 152 II	Aviation Spirit Ltd	
G-BOAL	Cameron V-65 balloon	N. H. & A. M. Ponsford	
G-BOAU	Cameron V-77 balloon	G. T. Barstow	
G-BOBA	PA-28R-201 Arrow III	Three Greens Flying Group	
G-BOBR	Cameron N-77 balloon	I. R. F. Worsman	
G-BOBT	Stolp SA.300 Starduster Too	G-BOBT Group	
G-BOBV	Cessna F.150M	M. L. Brown & P. L. Hill	
G-BOBY	Monnett Sonerai II	R. G. Hallam	
G-BOCI	Cessna 140A	Charlie India Aviators	
G-BOCK	Sopwith Triplane (replica) (N6290)	The Shuttleworth Collection	
G-BOCL	Slingsby T.67C	Richard Brinklow Aviation Ltd	
G-BOCM	Slingsby T.67C	Richard Brinklow Aviation Ltd	
G-BOCN	Robinson R22 Beta	HQ Aviation Ltd	

Notes	Reg	Type	Owner or Operator
	G-BOCU	PA-34-220T Seneca III	Advanced Aircraft Leasing (Teesside) Ltd
	G-BODB	PA-28-161 Warrior II	Sherburn Aero Club Ltd
	G-BODD	PA-28-161 Warrior II	CG Aviation Ltd
	G-BODE	PA-28-161 Warrior II	Sherburn Aero Club Ltd
	G-BODI	Glasair III Model SH-3R	A. P. Durston
	G-BODO	Cessna 152	Enstone Sales and Services Ltd
	G-BODR	PA-28-161 Warrior II	Airways Aero Associations Ltd
	G-BODS	PA-38-112 Tomahawk	T. W. Gilbert
	G-BODT	Jodel D.18	G-BODT Flying Group
	G-BODU	Scheibe SF.25C Falke	Hertfordshire County Scout Council
	G-BODW	Bell 206B Jet Ranger II ★	The Helicopter Museum/Weston-super-Mare
	G-BODY	Cessna 310R	Reconnaissance Ventures Ltd
	G-BODZ	Robinson R22 Beta	Langley Aviation Ltd
	G-BOEE	PA-28-181 Archer II	J. C. & G. M. Brinkley
	G-BOEH	Jodel DR.340	B. W. Griffiths
	G-BOEK	Cameron V-77 balloon	R. I. M. Kerr & ptnrs
	G-BOEM	Pitts S-2A	M. Murphy
	G-BOEN	Cessna 172M	R. Kolozsi
	G-BOER	PA-28-161 Warrior II	E. L. Fox
	G-BOET	PA-28RT-201 Arrow IV	B. C. Chambers (G-IBEC)
	G-BOFC	Beech 76 Duchess	Odhams Air Services Ltd
	G-BOFE	PA-34-200T Seneca II	Atlantic Flight Training Ltd
	G-BOFL	Cessna 152 II	S. A. Abid
	G-BOFW	Cessna A.150M	Golf Fox Whisky Group
	G-BOFY	PA-28-140 Cherokee	Cherokee Aviation Ltd
	G-BOGI	Robin DR.400/180	T. Davis
	G-BOGK	ARV Super 2	J. D. Winder
	G-BOGM	PA-28RT-201T Turbo Arrow IV	G. Marsango
	G-BOGO	PA-32R-301T Saratoga SP	GIF International Services KFT/Hungary
	G-BOHA	PA-28-161 Warrior II	Phoenix Aviation
	G-BOHD	Colt 77A balloon	D. B. Court
	G-BOHH	Cessna 172N	Staverton Flying School @ Skypark Ltd
	G-BOHI	Cessna 152 II	Modern Air (UK) Ltd
	G-BOHJ	Cessna 152 II	A A Scurei
	G-BOHM	PA-28 Cherokee 180	B. F. Keogh & R. A. Scott
	G-BOHO	PA-28-161 Warrior II	Egressus Flying Group
	G-BOHR	PA-28-151 Warrior	R. M. E. Garforth
	G-BOHV	Wittman W.8 Tailwind	D. H. Greenwood
	G-BOHW	Van's RV-4	E. C. Murgatroyd
	G-BOIB	Wittman W.10 Tailwind	C. R. Nash
	G-BOIC	PA-28R-201T Turbo Arrow III	S. P. Donoghue
	G-BOID	Bellanca 7ECA Citabria	D. Mallinson
	G-BOIG	PA-28-161 Warrior II	GFT Warrior Group
	G-BOIL	Cessna 172N	Upperstack Ltd
	G-BOIO	Cessna 152	Sandham Aviation
	G-BOIR	Cessna 152	APB Leasing Ltd
	G-BOIT	SOCATA TB10 Tobago	Naval Aviation Ltd
	G-BOIV	Cessna 150M	Hangar 1 Ltd
	G-BOIX	Cessna 172N	J. W. N. Sharpe
	G-BOIY	Cessna 172N	S. Smith
	G-BOIZ	PA-34-200T Seneca II	OCTN Trust
	G-BOJB	Cameron V-77 balloon	T. Taylor
	G-BOJI	PA-28RT-201 Arrow IV	Arrow Two Group
	G-BOJM	PA-28-181 Archer II	R. P. Emms
	G-BOJS	Cessna 172P	Paul's Planes Ltd
	G-BOJW	PA-28-161 Warrior II	Phoenix Aviation
	G-BOJZ	PA-28-161 Warrior II	Scenic Air Tours North East Ltd
	G-BOKA	PA-28-201T Turbo Dakota	CBG Aviation Ltd
	G-BOKH	Whittaker MW7	I. Pearson
	G-BOKW	Bolkow Bo.208C Junior	The Bat Group
	G-BOKX	PA-28-161 Warrior II	Turweston Flying Club Ltd
	G-BOKY	Cessna 152 II	D. F. F. & J. E. Poore
	G-BOLB	Taylorcraft BC-12-65	C. E. Tudor
	G-BOLC	Fournier RF-6B-100	Devon & Somerset RF Group
	G-BOLD	PA-38-112 Tomahawk	G-BOLD Group
	G-BOLE	PA-38-112 Tomahawk	Aeros Leasing Ltd
	G-BOLG	Bellanca 7KCAB Citabria	B. R. Pearson
	G-BOLI	Cessna 172P	Boli Flying Club
	G-BOLL	Lake LA-4 Skimmer	M. C. Holmes
	G-BOLN	Colt 21A balloon	G. Everett
	G-BOLO	Bell 206B JetRanger	Time Line International Ltd

Reg	Type	Owner or Operator	Notes
G-BOLR	Colt 21A balloon	C. J. Sanger-Davies	
G-BOLS	FRED Srs 2	I. F. Vaughan	
G-BOLT	Rockwell Commander 114	N. N. Drew	
G-BOLU	Robin R.3000/120	P. J. R. White & J. M. Smith	
G-BOLV	Cessna 152 II	A. J. Gomes	
G-BOLW	Cessna 152 II	G-BOLW Flying Group	
G-BOLY	Cessna 172N	Lima Yankee Flying Group	
G-BOMB	Cassutt Racer IIIM	Air Race CC Ltd	
G-BOMO	PA-38-112 Tomahawk II	APB Leasing Ltd	
G-BOMP	PA-28-181 Archer II	A. Flinn	
G-BOMS	Cessna 172N	Penchant Ltd	
G-BOMU	PA-28-181 Archer II	R. J. Houghton	
G-BOMY	PA-28-161 Warrior II	Sunrise Global Asset Management Ltd	
G-BOMZ	PA-38-112 Tomahawk	G-BOMZ Aviation	
G-BONC	PA-28RT-201 Arrow IV	SC Airlease Ltd	
G-BONG	Enstrom F-28A-UK	G. E. Heritage	
G-BONP	CFM Streak Shadow	G. J. Chater	
G-BONR	Cessna 172N	D. I. Craikl	
G-BONS	Cessna 172N	R. W. Marchant & K. Meredith	
G-BONT	Slingsby T.67M Firefly II	Vigilant Aviation Ltd (G-UCRM)	
G-BONU	Slingsby T.67B	R. L. Brinklow	
G-BONW	Cessna 152 II	LAC Flying School	
G-BONY	Denney Kitfox Model 1	R. Dunn	
G-BONZ	Beech V35B Bonanza	R. H. Townsend	
G-BOOB	Cameron N-65 balloon	P. J. Hooper	
G-BOOC	PA-18 Super Cub 150	S. A. C. Whitcombe	
G-BOOD	Slingsby T.31M Motor Tutor	D. G. Bilcliffe	
G-BOOE	GA-7 Cougar	S. J. Olechnowicz	
G-BOOF	PA-28-181 Archer II	UK Flying Clubs Ltd	
G-BOOG	PA-28RT-201T Turbo Arrow IV	S. J. Brenchley	
G-BOOH	Jodel D.112	T. K. Duffy	
G-BOOL	Cessna 172N	A. van Rooijen/Belgium	
G-BOOW	Aerosport Scamp	D. A. Weldon/Ireland	
G-BOOX	Rutan LongEz	I. R. Wilde	
G-BOPA	PA-28-181 Archer II	Flyco Ltd	
G-BOPC	PA-28-161 Warrior II	Aeros Ltd	
G-BOPD	Bede BD-4	S. T. Dauncey	
G-BOPH	Cessna TR.182RG	J. M. Mitchell	
G-BOPO	Brooklands OA.7 Optica	J. K. Edgley	
G-BOPR	Brooklands OA.7 Optica	Aeroelvira Ltd	
G-BOPU	Grob G.115	J. L. Sparks	
G-BORB	Cameron V-77 balloon	B. M. O'Brien	
G-BORE	Colt 77A balloon	C. J. Medcalf	
G-BORG	Campbell Cricket	R. L. Gilmore	
G-BORK	PA-28-161 Warrior II	Turweston Flying Club Ltd (G-IIIC)	
G-BORL	PA-28-161 Warrior II	Westair Flying Services Ltd	
G-BORM	HS.748 Srs 2B ★	Airport Fire Service/Exeter	
G-BORN	Cameron N-77 balloon	I. Chadwick	
G-BORW	Cessna 172P	Briter Aviation Ltd	
G-BORY	Cessna 150L	D. H. G. Penney	
G-BOSE	PA-28-181 Archer II	G-BOSE Group	
G-BOSJ	Nord 3400 (124)	A. I. Milne	
G-BOSM	Jodel DR.253B	A. G. Stevens	
G-BOSN	AS.355F1 Ecureuill II	Helicopter & Pilot Services Ltd	
G-BOSO	Cessna A.152	Redhill Air Services Ltd	
G-BOTD	Cameron O-105 balloon	J. Taylor	
G-BOTF	PA-28-151 Warrior	G-BOTF Group	
G-BOTG	Cessna 152 II	Donington Aviation Ltd	
G-BOTH	Cessna 182Q	P. G. Guilbert	
G-BOTI	PA-28-151 Warrior	Falcon Flying Services	
G-BOTK	Cameron O-105 balloon	N. Woodham	
G-BOTO	Bellanca 7ECA Citabria	Tango Oscar Group	
G-BOTP	Cessna 150J	R. F. Finnis & C. P. Williams	
G-BOTU	Piper J-3C-65 Cub	T. L. Giles	
G-BOTV	PA-32RT-300 Lance II	High Aviation Ltd	
G-BOTW	Cameron V-77 balloon	M. R. Jeynes	
G-BOUE	Cessna 172N	Swift Group	
G-BOUJ	Cessna 150M	The UJ Flying Group	
G-BOUK	PA-34-200T Seneca II	C. J. & R. J. Barnes	
G-BOUM	PA-34-200T Seneca II	Work Zone LDA	
G-BOUV	Bensen B.8MR	L. R. Phillips	

Notes	Reg	Type	Owner or Operator
	G-BOVB	PA-15 Vagabond	J. R. Kimberley
	G-BOVK	PA-28-161 Warrior II	Tayside Aviation Ltd
	G-BOVU	Stoddard-Hamilton Glasair III	E. Andersen
	G-BOWM	Cameron V-56 balloon	R. S. Breakwell
	G-BOWN	PA-12 Super Cruiser	T. L. Giles
	G-BOWO	Cessna R.182	P. E. Crees (G-BOTR)
	G-BOWP	Jodel D.120A	T. E. Cummins
	G-BOWV	Cameron V-65 balloon	R. A. Harris
	G-BOWY	PA-28RT-201T Turbo Arrow IV	D. R. D. Lassiter, S. G. Moreley & B. Moseley
	G-BOWZ	Bensen B.80V	A. J. Gascoigne
	G-BOXA	PA-28-161 Warrior II	Westwings International Ltd
	G-BOXC	PA-28-161 Warrior II	M. A. Lee
	G-BOXG	Cameron O-77 balloon	Aociazione Sportiva Dilettantistica Experience/Italy
	G-BOXH	Pitts S-1S Special	S. A. Wilson
	G-BOXJ	Piper J-3C-65 Cub (479897)	A. Bendkowski
	G-BOXT	Hughes 269C	Goldenfly Ltd
	G-BOXV	Pitts S-1S Special	C. Waddington
	G-BOXW	Cassutt Racer Srs IIIM	D. I. Johnson
	G-BOYB	Cessna A.152	Fly Elstree Ltd
	G-BOYC	Robinson R22 Beta	Yorkshire Helicopters
	G-BOYF	Sikorsky S-76B	Von Essen Aviation Ltd
	G-BOYH	PA-28-151 Warrior	R. Nightingale
	G-BOYI	PA-28-161 Warrior II	JABM Ltd
	G-BOYL	Cessna 152 II	Redhill Air Services Ltd
	G-BOYM	Cameron O-84 balloon	M. P. Ryan
	G-BOYO	Cameron V-20 balloon	T. Ward
	G-BOYV	PA-28R-201T Turbo Arrow III	P. Lodge
	G-BOYX	Robinson R22 Beta	R. Towle
	G-BOZI	PA-28-161 Warrior II	Aerolease Ltd
	G-BOZO	AA-5B Tiger	Griffin Flight Ltd
	G-BOZR	Cessna 152 II	Adam Russell Ltd
	G-BOZS	Pitts S-1C Special	A. A. Cole
	G-BOZV	CEA DR.340 Major	C. J. Turner & S. D. Kent
	G-BOZW	Bensen B.8M	M. E. Wills
	G-BOZY	Cameron RTW-120 balloon	Magical Adventures Ltd
	G-BPAA	Acro Advanced	B. O. & F. A. Smith
	G-BPAB	Cessna 150M	A. Carter
	G-BPAF	PA-28-161 Warrior II	S. T. & T. W. Gilbert
	G-BPAJ	DH.82A Tiger Moth	J. M. Hodgson & J. D. Smith (G-AOIX)
	G-BPAL	DHC.1 Chipmunk 22 (WG350)	K. F. & P. Tomsett (G-BCYE)
	G-BPAW	Cessna 150M	G-BPAW Group
	G-BPAY	PA-28-181 Archer II	White Waltham Airfield Ltd
	G-BPBJ	Cessna 152 II	W. Shaw
	G-BPBK	Cessna 152 II	Swiftair Maintenance Ltd
	G-BPBM	PA-28-161 Warrior II	Redhill Air Services Ltd
	G-BPBO	PA-28RT-201T Turbo Arrow IV	G. N. Broom & T. R. Lister
	G-BPBP	Brügger MB.2 Colibri	D. A. Preston
	G-BPCA	BN-2B-26 Islander	Loganair Ltd (G-BLNX)
	G-BPCF	Piper J-3C-65 Cub	B. M. O'Brien
	G-BPCI	Cessna R.172K	N. A. Bairstol
	G-BPCK	PA-28-161 Warrior II	Compton Abbas Airfield Ltd
	G-BPCL	SA Bulldog Srs 120/128 (HKG-6)	Isohigh Ltd
	G-BPCR	Mooney M.20K	T. & R. Harris
	G-BPCX	PA-28-236 Dakota	Blue Yonder Aviation Ltd
	G-BPDE	Colt 56A balloon	J. E. Weidema/Netherlands
	G-BPDJ	Christena Mini Coupe	R. B. McCornish
	G-BPDM	CASA 1.131E Jungmann 2000(781-32)	J. D. Haslam
	G-BPDT	PA-28-161 Warrior II	Westwings International Ltd
	G-BPDV	Pitts S-1S Special	G-BPDV Syndicate
	G-BPEM	Cessna 150K	D. Wright
	G-BPEO	Cessna 152 II	Swiftair Maintenance Ltd
	G-BPES	PA-38-112 Tomahawk II	Aeros Leasing Ltd
	G-BPEZ	Colt 77A balloon	J. W. Adkins
	G-BPFD	Jodel D.112	M. & S. Mills
	G-BPFH	PA-28-161 Warrior II	CG Aviation Ltd
	G-BPFI	PA-28-181 Archer II	S. D. Hodgson & S. Pegg
	G-BPFL	Davis DA-2	P. E. Barker
	G-BPFM	Aeronca 7AC Champion	C. C. Burton
	G-BPGD	Cameron V-65 balloon	Gone With The Wind Ltd

Reg	Type	Owner or Operator	Notes
G-BPGE	Cessna U.206C	Scottish Parachute Club	
G-BPGH	EAA Acro Sport II	R. Clark & A. C. May	
G-BPGU	PA-28-181 Archer II	G. Underwood	
G-BPGZ	Cessna 150G	J. B. Scott	
G-BPHG	Robin DR.400/180	A. R. Paul	
G-BPHH	Cameron V-77 balloon	C. D. Aindow	
G-BPHI	PA-38-112 Tomahawk	Flying Fox Aviation	
G-BPHP	Taylorcraft BC-12-65	J. M. Brightwell	
G-BPHR	DH.82A Tiger Moth (A17-48)	N. Parry	
G-BPHU	Thunder Ax7-77 balloon	R. P. Waite	
G-BPHZ	MS.500 Criquet (DM+BK)	Aero Vintage Ltd	
G-BPIF	Bensen-Parsons 2-place gyroplane	B. J. L. P. & W. J. A. L. de Saar	
G-BPII	Denney Kitfox	Dolphin Flying Group	
G-BPIR	Scheibe SF.25E Super Falke	A. P. Askwith	
G-BPIU	PA-28-161 Warrior II	Golf India Uniform Group	
G-BPIV	B.149 Bolingbroke Mk IVT (L6739)	Blenheim (Duxford) Ltd	
G-BPIZ	AA-5B Tiger	D. A. Horsley	
G-BPJB	Schweizer 269C	J. Gasienica	
G-BPJG	PA-18 Super Cub 150	N. P. Shields	
G-BPJS	PA-28-161 Cadet	Redhill Air Services Ltd	
G-BPJZ	Cameron O-160 balloon	M. L. Gabb	
G-BPKF	Grob G.115	Swiftair Maintenance Ltd	
G-BPKK	Denney Kitfox Mk 1	F. McDonagh	
G-BPKM	PA-28-161 Warrior II	Pure Aviation Support Services Ltd	
G-BPKT	Piper J.5A Cub Cruiser	A. J. Greenslade	
G-BPLM	AIA Stampe SV.4C	C. J. Jesson	
G-BPLV	Cameron V-77 balloon	O. Le Clercq/France	
G-BPLZ	Hughes 369HS	M. A. & R. J. Fawcett	
G-BPME	Cessna 152 II	London School of Flying Ltd	
G-BPMF	PA-28-151 Warrior	Mike Foxtrot Group	
G-BPML	Cessna 172M	N. A. Bilton	
G-BPMM	Champion 7ECA Citabria	J. McCullough	
G-BPMW	QAC Quickie Q.2	P. M. Wright (G-OICI/G-OGKN)	
G-BPNI	Robinson R22 Beta	G. J. Collins	
G-BPNO	Zlin Z.326 Trener Master	E. Bunnage-Flavell	
G-BPOA	Gloster Meteor T.7 (WF877) ★	39 Restoration Group	
G-BPOB	Sopwith Camel F.1 (replica) (N6377)	Flying Aces Movie Aircraft Collection	
G-BPOM	PA-28-161 Warrior II	POM Flying Group	
G-BPOS	Cessna 150M	Hull Aero Club Ltd	
G-BPOT	PA-28-181 Archer II	P. S. Simpson	
G-BPOU	Luscombe 8A Silvaire	J. L. Grayer	
G-BPPE	PA-38-112 Tomahawk	First Air Ltd	
G-BPPF	PA-38-112 Tomahawk	Bristol Strut Flying Group	
G-BPPJ	Cameron A-180 balloon	D. J. Farrar	
G-BPPK	PA-28-151 Warrior	Aviation South West Ltd	
G-BPPO	Luscombe 8A Silvaire	P. Dyer	
G-BPPP	Cameron V-77 balloon	The Sarnia Balloon Group	
G-BPPZ	Taylorcraft BC-12D	G. C. Smith	
G-BPRC	Cameron 77 Elephant SS balloon	A. Schneider/Germany	
G-BPRD	Pitts S-1C Special	R. J. Hodder	
G-BPRI	AS.355F1 Twin Squirrel	Excel Charter Ltd (G-TVPA)	
G-BPRJ	AS.355F1 Twin Squirrel	PLM Dollar Group Ltd	
G-BPRL	AS.355F1 Twin Squirrel	Excel Charter Ltd	
G-BPRM	Cessna F.172L	BJ Aviation Ltd (G-AZKG)	
G-BPRX	Aeronca 11AC Chief	A. F. Kutz	
G-BPRY	PA-28-161 Warrior II	White Wings Aviation Ltd	
G-BPSR	Cameron V-77 balloon	K. J. A. Maxwell	
G-BPTA	Stinson 108-2	M. L. Ryan	
G-BPTD	Cameron V-77 balloon	J. Lippett	
G-BPTE	PA-28-181 Archer II	A. J. Gomes	
G-BPTG	Rockwell Commander 112TC	B. Ogunyemi	
G-BPTI	SOCATA TB20 Trinidad	Blueplane Ltd	
G-BPTL	Cessna 172N	M. J. Spittal	
G-BPTS	CASA 1.131E Jungmann 1000 (E3B-153:781-75)	E. P. Parkin	
G-BPTV	Bensen B.8	C. Munro	
G-BPUA	EAA Sport Biplane	T. M. Leitan & N. C. Scanlan	
G-BPUB	Cameron V-31 balloon	M. T. Evans	
G-BPUL	PA-18 Super Cub 150	Vintage Tug Group	
G-BPUM	Cessna R.182RG	R. C. Chapman	
G-BPUR	Piper J-3L-65 Cub (379994 52/J)	G. R. J. Caunter	

Notes	Reg	Type	Owner or Operator
	G-BPUU	Cessna 140	D. R. Speight
	G-BPVA	Cessna 172F	South Lancashire Flyers Group
	G-BPVE	Bleriot IX (replica) (1)	Bianchi Aviation Film Services Ltd
	G-BPVH	Cub Aircraft J-3C-65 Prospector	D. E. Cooper-Maguire
	G-BPVI	PA-32R-301 Saratoga SP	M. T. Coppen
	G-BPVK	Varga 2150A Kachina	B. F. Hill
	G-BPVN	PA-32R-301T Turbo Saratoga SP	O. Green
	G-BPVO	Cassutt Racer IIIM	A. J. Harris
	G-BPVW	CASA 1.131E Jungmann 2000	C. & J-W. Labeij/Netherlands
	G-BPVZ	Luscombe 8E Silvaire	S. M. Thomas & A. P. Wilkie
	G-BPWD	Cessna 120	C. G. Applegarth
	G-BPWE	PA-28-161 Warrior II	Warrior BPWE Ltd
	G-BPWG	Cessna 150M	GB Pilots Wilsford Group
	G-BPWK	Sportavia-Putzer Fournier RF-5B	G-BPWK Group
	G-BPWL	PA-25 Pawnee 235	M. H. Sims
	G-BPWM	Cessna 150L	P. D. Button
	G-BPWN	Cessna 150L	Bristol Flying Club Ltd
	G-BPWR	Cessna R.172K	J. A. & D. T. A. Rees
	G-BPWS	Cessna 172P	Chartstone Ltd
	G-BPXA	PA-28-181 Archer II	Cherokee Flying Group
	G-BPXE	Enstrom 280C Shark	A. Healy
	G-BPXJ	PA-28RT-201T Turbo Arrow IV	E. Swift
	G-BPXX	PA-34-200T Seneca II	M. Magrabi
	G-BPYJ	Wittman W.8 Tailwind	J. P. & Y. Mills
	G-BPYK	Thunder Ax7-77 balloon	P. Spellward
	G-BPYL	Hughes 369D	Morcorp (BVI) Ltd
	G-BPYN	Piper J-3C-65 Cub	The Aquila Group
	G-BPYR	PA-31-310 Turbo Navajo	Excel Aviation Ltd
	G-BPYT	Cameron V-77 balloon	M. H. Redman
	G-BPYY	Cameron A-180 balloon	G. D. Fitzpatrick
	G-BPZB	Cessna 120	Cessna 120 Group
	G-BPZD	SNCAN NC.858S	Zula Delta Syndicate
	G-BPZE	Luscombe 8E Silvaire	M. A. Watts
	G-BPZY	Pitts S-1C Special	J. S. Mitchell
	G-BRAA	Pitts S-1C Special	A. Stiff
	G-BRAK	Cessna 172N	W. Ali
	G-BRAM	Mikoyan MiG-21PF (503) ★	FAST Museum/Farnborough
	G-BRAP	Thermal Aircraft 104 balloon	J. Yarrow
	G-BRAR	Aeronca 7AC Champion	D. Ridley
	G-BRBA	PA-28-161 Warrior II	G-HIRE Ltd
	G-BRBC	NA T-6G Texan	A. P. Murphy
	G-BRBD	PA-28-151 Warrior	Compton Abbas Airfield Ltd
	G-BRBE	PA-28-161 Warrior II	Jesterhoudt Holding BV/Netherlands
	G-BRBG	PA-28 Cherokee 180	P. M. Carter
	G-BRBI	Cessna 172N	Skyhawk Flying Group
	G-BRBJ	Cessna 172M	J. H. Sandham Aviation
	G-BRBK	Robin DR.400/180	A. D. Friday
	G-BRBL	Robin DR.400/180	U. A. Schliessler & R. J. Kelly
	G-BRBM	Robin DR.400/180	R. W. H. Cole
	G-BRBN	Pitts S-1S Special	G-BRBN Flying Group
	G-BRBP	Cessna 152	The Pilot Centre Ltd
	G-BRBV	Piper J-4A Cub Coupe	P. Clarke
	G-BRBW	PA-28 Cherokee 140	Air Navigation and Trading Co Ltd
	G-BRBX	PA-28-181 Archer II	Trent 199 Flying Group
	G-BRCD	Cessna A.152	Cristal Air Ltd
	G-BRCE	Pitts S-1C Special	M. P. & S. T. Barnard
	G-BRCJ	Cameron H-20 balloon	P. A. Sweatman
	G-BRCM	Cessna 172L	Falcon Flying Services Ltd
	G-BRCT	Denney Kitfox Mk 2	J. Shrosbree
	G-BRCV	Aeronca 7AC Champion	J. Davies
	G-BRCW	Aeronca 11AC Chief	R. B. Griffin
	G-BRDD	Avions Mudry CAP-10B	T. A. Smith
	G-BRDF	PA-28-161 Warrior II	White Waltham Airfield Ltd
	G-BRDG	PA-28-161 Warrior II	Falcon Flying Services
	G-BRDJ	Luscombe 8A Silvaire	G-BRDJ Group
	G-BRDM	PA-28-161 Warrior II	White Waltham Airfield Ltd
	G-BRDO	Cessna 177B	Cardinal Aviation
	G-BRDV	Viking Wood Products Spitfire Prototype replica (K5054) ★	Solent Sky, Southampton
	G-BREA	Bensen B.8MR	D. J. Martin

Reg	Type	Owner or Operator	Notes
G-BREB	Piper J-3C-65 Cub	J. R. Wraight	
G-BREL	Cameron O-77 balloon	R. A. Patey	
G-BRER	Aeronca 7AC Champion	M. J. Laundy t/a G-BRER Group	
G-BREU	Montgomerie-Bensen B.8MR	J. S. Firth	
G-BREX	Cameron O-84 balloon	R. T. Gourley	
G-BREY	Taylorcraft BC-12D	BREY Group	
G-BREZ	Cessna 172M	R. G. Rutty	
G-BRFB	Rutan LongEz	N. M. Robbins	
G-BRFC	Percival P.57 Sea Prince T.Mk.1 (WP321) ★	South West Aviation Museum/St.Athan	
G-BRFF	Colt 90A balloon	Amber Valley Aviation	
G-BRFI	Aeronca 7DC Champion	S. J. Ball	
G-BRFJ	Aeronca 11AC Chief	J. M. Mooney	
G-BRFM	PA-28-161 Warrior II	Swiftair Maintenance Ltd	
G-BRFW	Montgomerie-Bensen B.8 2-seat	A. J. Barker	
G-BRFX	Pazmany PL.4A	D. E. Hills	
G-BRGD	Cameron O-84 balloon	P. A. Davies	
G-BRGE	Cameron N-90 balloon	Oakfield Farm Products Ltd	
G-BRGF	Luscombe 8E Silvaire	J. A. Coutts	
G-BRGI	PA-28 Cherokee 180	R. A. Buckfield	
G-BRGT	PA-32 Cherokee Six 260	A. A. Mattacks & T. J. W. Hood	
G-BRGW	Gardan GY-201 Minicab	R. G. White	
G-BRHA	PA-32RT-300 Lance II	Lance G-BRHA Group	
G-BRHP	Aeronca O-58B Grasshopper (31923)	R. B. McComish	
G-BRHR	PA-38-112 Tomahawk	Tango Romeo Aviation Ltd	
G-BRHX	Luscombe 8E Silvaire	N. F. Hemming	
G-BRHY	Luscombe 8E Silvaire	R. A. Keech	
G-BRIH	Taylorcraft BC-12D	M. J. Medland	
G-BRIJ	Taylorcraft F-19	E. N. L. Troffigue	
G-BRIK	T.66 Nipper 3	M. G. Read	
G-BRIL	Piper J-5A Cub Cruiser	D. J. Bone	
G-BRIV	SOCATA TB9 Tampico Club	S. J. Taft	
G-BRIY	Taylorcraft DF-65 (42-58678:IY)	S. R. Potts	
G-BRJA	Luscombe 8A Silvaire	K. R. H. Wingate	
G-BRJC	Cessna 120	J. Hodgson	
G-BRJK	Luscombe 8A Silvaire	M. Richardson & R. C. Dyer	
G-BRJL	PA-15 Vagabond	A. R. Williams	
G-BRJN	Pitts S-1C Special	W. Chapel	
G-BRJV	PA-28-161 Cadet	Redhill Air Services Ltd	
G-BRJX	Rand-Robinson KR-2	B. L. R. J. Keeping	
G-BRJY	Rand-Robinson KR-2	R. E. Taylor	
G-BRKC	Auster J/1 Autocrat	S. James & J. Havers	
G-BRKH	PA-28-236 Dakota	T. A. White	
G-BRKL	Cameron H-34 balloon	M. H. Read	
G-BRKW	Cameron V-77 balloon	T. J. Parker	
G-BRKY	Viking Dragonfly Mk II	Polar Bear Services Ltd	
G-BRLB	Air Command 532 Elite	F. G. Shepherd	
G-BRLF	Campbell Cricket (replica)	J. L. G. McLane	
G-BRLG	PA-28RT-201T Turbo Arrow IV	N. R. Quirk	
G-BRLI	Piper J-5A Cub Cruiser	D. J. M. Eardley	
G-BRLL	Cameron A-105 balloon	P. A. Sweatman	
G-BRLO	PA-38-112 Tomahawk	A. J. Gomes	
G-BRLP	PA-38-112 Tomahawk	Highland Aviation Training Ltd	
G-BRLR	Cessna 150G	Air Northumbria	
G-BRLS	Thunder Ax7-77 balloon	J. R. Palmer	
G-BRMA	WS-51 Dragonfly HR.5 (WG719) ★	IHM/Weston-super-Mare	
G-BRMB	Bristol192 Belvedere HC.1 ★	IHM/Weston-super-Mare	
G-BRME	PA-28-181 Archer II	S. S. Bamrah	
G-BRMT	Cameron V-31 balloon	B. Reed	
G-BRMU	Cameron V-77 balloon	P. Spellward	
G-BRNC	Cessna 150M	G-BRNC Group	
G-BRND	Cessna 152 II	T. M. & M. L. Jones	
G-BRNE	Cessna 152 II	Redhill Air Services Ltd	
G-BRNK	Cessna 152 II	D. C. & M. Bonsall	
G-BRNM	Chichester-Miles Leopard ★	Midland Air Museum/Coventry	
G-BRNN	Cessna 152 II	Eastern Air Executive Ltd	
G-BRNT	Robin DR.400/180	C. E. Ponsford & ptnrs	
G-BRNU	Robin DR.400/180	November Uniform Travel Syndicate Ltd	
G-BRNW	Cameron V-77 balloon	N. Robertson & G. Smith	
G-BRNX	PA-22 Tri-Pacer 150	S. N. Askey	
G-BROE	Cameron N-65 balloon	A. I. Attwood	
G-BROG	Cameron V-65 balloon	R. Kunert	

67

Notes	Reg	Type	Owner or Operator
	G-BROJ	Colt 31A balloon	N. J. Langley
	G-BROO	Luscombe 8E Silvaire	P. R. Bush
	G-BROP	Van's RV-4	M. W. Bodger (G-NADZ)
	G-BROR	Piper J-3C-65 Cub	White Hart Flying Group
	G-BROX	Robinson R22 Beta	Phoenix Helicopter Academy Ltd
	G-BROY	Cameron V-77 balloon	R. Rebosio
	G-BROZ	PA-18 Super Cub 150	P. G. Kynsey
	G-BRPE	Cessna 120	C. G. Applegarth
	G-BRPF	Cessna 120	M. A. Potter
	G-BRPG	Cessna 120	I. C. Lomax
	G-BRPH	Cessna 120	R. B. Webb
	G-BRPK	PA-28 Cherokee 140	G-BRPK Group
	G-BRPL	PA-28-140 Cherokee	British North West Airlines Ltd
	G-BRPM	T.66 Nipper 3	J. H. H. Turner
	G-BRPP	Brookland Hornet (modified)	B. J. L. P. & W. J. A. L. de Saar
	G-BRPR	Aeronca O-58B Grasshopper (31952)	A. F. Kutz
	G-BRPS	Cessna 177B	W. Parent
	G-BRPT	Rans S.10 Sakota	J. A. Harris
	G-BRPV	Cessna 152	Eastern Air Executive Ltd
	G-BRPX	Taylorcraft BC-12D	G-BRPX Group
	G-BRPY	PA-15 Vagabond	C. S. Whitwell
	G-BRPZ	Luscombe 8A Silvaire	C. A. Flint
	G-BRRA	VS.361 Spitfire LF.IX (MK912:SH-L)	Peter Monk Ltd
	G-BRRF	Cameron O-77 balloon	K. P. & G. J. Storey
	G-BRRK	Cessna 182Q	Werewolf Aviation Ltd
	G-BRRP	Pitts S-1S Special	T. Q. Short (G-WAZZ)
	G-BRRR	Cameron V-77 balloon	K. P. & G. J. Storey
	G-BRRU	Colt 90A balloon	Reach For The Sky Ltd
	G-BRSF	VS.361 Spitfire HF.9c (RR232)	M. B. Phillips
	G-BRSL	Cameron N-56 balloon	S. Budd
	G-BRSP	Air Command 532 Elite	G. M. Hobman
	G-BRSV	Pilatus B-N BN-2T Islander	G. Cormack
	G-BRSW	Luscombe 8A Silvaire	Bloody Mary Aviation
	G-BRSX	PA-15 Vagabond	Sierra Xray Group
	G-BRTD	Cessna 152 II	152 Group
	G-BRTJ	Cessna 150F	T. O"Driscoll
	G-BRTP	Cessna 152 II	R. Lee
	G-BRTW	Glaser-Dirks DG.400	I. J. Carruthers
	G-BRTX	PA-28-151 Warrior	W. Ali
	G-BRUB	PA-28-161 Warrior II	Flytrek Ltd
	G-BRUD	PA-28-181 Archer II	Falcon Flying Services
	G-BRUG	Luscombe 8E Silvaire	N. W. Barratt
	G-BRUJ	Boeing Stearman A.75N1 (6136:205)	Tatramarket Poprad SRO
	G-BRUM	Cessna A.152	A. J. Gomes
	G-BRUN	Cessna 120	J. G. D. Diana (G-BRDH)
	G-BRUO	Taylor JT.1 Monoplane	The Mighty Monoplane Group
	G-BRUV	Cameron V-77 balloon	T. W. & R. F. Benbrook
	G-BRUX	PA-44-180 Seminole	M. Ali
	G-BRVE	Beech D.17S	Patina Ltd
	G-BRVF	Colt 77A balloon	J. Adkins
	G-BRVG	NA SNJ-7 Texan (27)	Quattro Plant Ltd
	G-BRVH	Smyth Model S Sidewinder	B. D. Deleporte
	G-BRVI	Robinson R22 Beta	York Helicopters
	G-BRVJ	Slingsby T.31 Motor Cadet III	B. Outhwaite
	G-BRVL	Pitts S-1C Special	S. D. Blakey
	G-BRVO	AS.350B Ecureuil	Steda Ltd
	G-BRVZ	Jodel D.117	L. Holland
	G-BRWA	Aeronca 7AC Champion	P. T. Price
	G-BRWB	NA T-6G Texan (526)	R. Clifford
	G-BRWR	Aeronca 11AC Chief	A. W. Crutcher
	G-BRWT	Scheibe SF.25C Falke	Booker Gliding Club Ltd
	G-BRWU	Luton LA-4A Minor	R. A. Benson
	G-BRWV	Brügger MB.2 Colibri	M. P. Wakem
	G-BRXD	PA-28-181 Archer II	Xraydelta Ltd
	G-BRXE	Taylorcraft BC-12D	B. T. Morgan & W. J. Durrad
	G-BRXF	Aeronca 11AC Chief	Aeronca Flying Group
	G-BRXG	Aeronca 7AC Champion	X-Ray Golf Flying Group
	G-BRXH	Cessna 120	BRXH Group
	G-BRXL	Aeronca 11AC Chief (42-78044)	P. L. Green
	G-BRXP	SNCAN Stampe SV.4C (modified)	T. Brown
	G-BRXS	Howard Special T Minus	F. A. Bakir

Reg	Type	Owner or Operator	Notes
G-BRXU	Aerospatiale AS.332L Super Puma	Airbus Helicopters	
G-BRXY	Pietenpol Air Camper	G. Chisnall	
G-BRZA	Cameron O-77 balloon	S. J. Nichols & N. M. Benjamin	
G-BRZB	Cameron A-105 balloon	Headland Services Ltd	
G-BRZD	HAPI Cygnet SF-2A	P. D. Begley	
G-BRZF	Enstrom 280C Shark	M. Richardson (G-IDUP)	
G-BRZK	Stinson 108-2	D. A. Gathercole	
G-BRZL	Pitts S-1D Special	T. R. G. Barnby	
G-BRZS	Cessna 172P	YP Flying Group	
G-BRZW	Rans S.10 Sakota	D. L. Davies	
G-BRZX	Pitts S-1S Special	Zulu Xray Group	
G-BSAH	BN-2T Turbine Islander	Gama Aviation (UK) Ltd	
G-BSAI	Stoddard-Hamilton Glasair III	K. J. & P. J. Whitehead	
G-BSAJ	CASA 1.131E Jungmann 2000	P. G. Kynsey	
G-BSAK	Colt 21A balloon	M. D. Mitchell	
G-BSAW	PA-28-161 Warrior II	Compton Abbas Airfield Ltd	
G-BSAX	J-3C-65 Cub	A. L. Walker & P. G. Kynsey (G-OLEZ)	
G-BSAZ	Denney Kitfox Mk 2	A. J. Lloyd	
G-BSBA	PA-28-161 Warrior II	Falcon Flying Services Ltd	
G-BSBG	CCF Harvard IV (20310:310)	A. P. St. John	
G-BSBT	Piper J-3C-65 Cub	A. R. Elliott	
G-BSBV	Rans S.10 Sakota	S. Bain	
G-BSCC	Colt 105A balloon	A. F. Selby	
G-BSCG	Denney Kitfox Mk 2	D. J. Couzens	
G-BSCI	Colt 77A balloon	S. C. Kinsey	
G-BSCK	Cameron H-24 balloon	J. D. Shapland	
G-BSCM	Denney Kitfox Mk 2	H. D. Colliver (G-MSCM)	
G-BSCN	SOCATA TB20 Trinidad	D. Norman	
G-BSCO	Thunder Ax7-77 balloon	F. J. Whalley	
G-BSCP	Cessna 152 II	Moray Flying Club (1990) Ltd	
G-BSCS	PA-28-181 Archer II	A. C. Renouf	
G-BSCV	PA-28-161 Warrior II	Southwood Flying Group	
G-BSCW	Taylorcraft BC-65	G. Johnson	
G-BSCY	PA-28-151 Warrior	M. C. Plomer-Roberts	
G-BSCZ	Cessna 152 II	The RAF Halton Aeroplane Club Ltd	
G-BSDA	Taylorcraft BC-12D	A. D. Pearce	
G-BSDD	Denney Kitfox Mk 2	C. Morris	
G-BSDH	Robin DR.400/180	G-BSDH Group	
G-BSDK	Piper J-5A Cub Cruiser	Ballyboughal J5 Flying Group	
G-BSDO	Cessna 152 II	Cloud Global Ltd	
G-BSDP	Cessna 152 II	Paul's Planes Ltd	
G-BSDS	Boeing Stearman E75 (118)	L. W. Scattergood	
G-BSDW	Cessna 182P	Clipper Data Ltd	
G-BSDX	Cameron V-77 balloon	G. P. & S. J. Allen	
G-BSDZ	Enstrom 280FX	One Parking Solution Ltd	
G-BSEA	Thunder Ax7-77 balloon	B. T. Lewis	
G-BSED	PA-22 Tri-Pacer 160 (modified)	P. G. Whitehead	
G-BSEE	Rans S.9	A. R. Hawes	
G-BSEF	PA-28 Cherokee 180	I. D. Wakeling	
G-BSEH	Cameron V-77 balloon	R. M. Rebosio	
G-BSEJ	Cessna 150M	G. Mappledorham	
G-BSEL	Slingsby T.61G Super Falke	D. G. Holley	
G-BSER	PA-28 Cherokee 160	Yorkair Ltd	
G-BSEU	PA-28-181 Archer II	Herefordshire Aero Club Ltd	
G-BSEV	Cameron O-77 balloon	L. J. Whitelock	
G-BSEX	Cameron A-180 balloon	Heart of England Balloons	
G-BSEY	Beech A36 Bonanza	P. Malam-Wilson	
G-BSFA	Aero Designs Pulsar	P. F. Lorriman	
G-BSFD	Piper J-3C-65 Cub (16037)	P. E. S. Latham	
G-BSFE	PA-38-112 Tomahawk II	Leading Edge Flying Club Ltd	
G-BSFF	Robin DR.400/180R	Lasham Gliding Society Ltd	
G-BSFP	Cessna 152T	The Pilot Centre Ltd	
G-BSFR	Cessna 152 II	Galair Ltd	
G-BSFW	PA-15 Vagabond	J. R. Kimberley	
G-BSFX	Denney Kitfox Mk 2	F. Colman	
G-BSGD	PA-28 Cherokee 180	R. J. Cleverley	
G-BSGF	Robinson R22 Beta	Heliyorks Ltd	
G-BSGG	Denney Kitfox Mk 2	S. E. Lyden	
G-BSGJ	Monnett Sonerai 2	J. L. Loweth	
G-BSGS	Rans S.10 Sakota	M. R. Parr	

Notes	Reg	Type	Owner or Operator
	G-BSGT	Cessna T.210N	E. A. T. Brenninkmeyer
	G-BSHA	PA-34-200T Seneca II	Justgold Ltd
	G-BSHC	Colt 69A balloon	Magical Adventures Ltd
	G-BSHH	Luscombe 8E Silvaire	M. Craft & P. R. Bush
	G-BSHO	Cameron V-77 balloon	D. J. Duckworth & J. C. Stewart
	G-BSHP	PA-28-161 Warrior II	Devleminck Air Service
	G-BSHR	Cessna F.172N	Deep Cleavage Ltd (G-BFGE)
	G-BSIC	Cameron V-77 balloon	C. Wilson
	G-BSIF	Denney Kitfox Mk 2	S. M. Dougan
	G-BSIG	Colt 21A Cloudhopper balloon	C. J. Dunkley
	G-BSIH	Rutan Long-Ez	W. S. Allen
	G-BSIJ	Cameron V-77 balloon	G. B. Davies
	G-BSIM	PA-28-181 Archer II	A. S. Bamrah
	G-BSIO	Cameron 80 Shed SS balloon	R. E. Jones
	G-BSIY	Schleicher ASK.14	D. & M. Shrimpton
	G-BSJX	PA-28-161 Warrior II	Andrewsfield Aviation Ltd
	G-BSJZ	Cessna 150J	J. M. Vinall
	G-BSKA	Cessna 150M	Aviolease Ltd
	G-BSKG	Maule MX-7-180	A. J. Lewis
	G-BSKP	Supermarine Spitfire F.XIV E (RN201)	Aerial Speed Icons Ltd
	G-BSKW	PA-28-181 Archer II	R. J. Whyham
	G-BSLA	Robin DR.400/180	A. B. McCoig
	G-BSLH	CASA 1.131E Jungmann 2000	M. A. Warden
	G-BSLK	PA-28-161 Warrior II	T. W. Gilbert
	G-BSLM	PA-28 Cherokee 160	Fly (Fu Lai) Aviation Ltd
	G-BSLT	PA-28-161 Warrior II	CG Aviation Ltd
	G-BSLU	PA-28 Cherokee 140	Merseyflight Air Training School
	G-BSLV	Enstrom 280FX	J. P. C. Alunni
	G-BSLW	Bellanca 7ECA Citabria	Aviation Wingman Ltd
	G-BSLX	WAR Focke-Wulf Fw 190 (replica) (4+)	S. Freeman
	G-BSME	Bölkow Bö.208C1 Junior	D. J. Hampson
	G-BSMM	Colt 31A balloon	P. Spellward
	G-BSMN	CFM Streak Shadow	D. R. C. Pugh
	G-BSMT	Rans S-10 Sakota	T. D. Wood
	G-BSMV	PA-17 Vagabond (modified)	A. Cheriton
	G-BSNE	Luscombe 8E Silvaire	O. R. Watts
	G-BSNF	Piper J-3C-65 Cub	D. A. Hammant
	G-BSNG	Cessna 172N	A. J. & P. C. MacDonald
	G-BSNT	Luscombe 8A Silvaire	H. E. Simons
	G-BSNU	Colt 105A balloon	Gone Ballooning
	G-BSNX	PA-28-181 Archer II	Redhill Air Services Ltd
	G-BSOE	Luscombe 8A Silvaire	R. G. Downhill
	G-BSOF	Colt 25A balloon	J. M. Bailey
	G-BSOG	Cessna 172M	Gloster Aero Group
	G-BSOK	PA-28-161 Warrior II	G. E. Fox
	G-BSOM	Glaser-Dirks DG.400	P. Ryland
	G-BSON	Green S.25 balloon	J. J. Green
	G-BSOO	Cessna 172F	The Oscar Oscar Group
	G-BSOR	CFM Streak Shadow Srs SA	A. Parr
	G-BSOU	PA-38-112 Tomahawk II	Leading Edge Flight Training Ltd
	G-BSOX	Luscombe 8AE Silvaire	R. Dauncey
	G-BSOZ	PA-28-161 Warrior II	Pactum Company Ltd
	G-BSPA	QAC Quickie Q.2	G. V. McKirdy & B. K. Glover
	G-BSPC	Jodel D.140C	B. E. Cotton
	G-BSPE	Cessna F.172P	G. E. Fox
	G-BSPG	PA-34-200T Seneca II	Andrews Professional Colour Laboratories Ltd
	G-BSPK	Cessna 195A	A. G. & D. L. Bompas
	G-BSPL	CFM Streak Shadow Srs SA	G. L. Turner
	G-BSPN	PA-28R-201T Turbo Arrow III	J. A. Crew, J. Gisbourne & E. Syson
	G-BSRH	Pitts S-1C Special	T. L. & T. W. Davis
	G-BSRI	Lancair 235	D. A. Gathercole
	G-BSRK	ARV Super 2	J. Svenson
	G-BSRL	Campbell Cricket Mk.4 gyroplane	M. Brudnicki
	G-BSRP	Rotorway Executive	R. J. Baker
	G-BSRR	Cessna 182Q	C. M. Moore
	G-BSRT	Denney Kitfox Mk 2	S. J. Walker
	G-BSRX	CFM Streak Shadow	I. P. Freestone
	G-BSSA	Luscombe 8E Silvaire	Luscombe Flying Group
	G-BSSB	Cessna 150L	D. T. A. Rees
	G-BSSC	PA-28-161 Warrior II	Tor Financial Consulting Ltd
	G-BSSF	Denney Kitfox Mk 2	F. W. Astbury

Reg	Type	Owner or Operator	Notes
G-BSSI	Rans S.6 Coyote II	D. Brunton (G-MWJA)	
G-BSSK	QAC Quickie Q.2	R. Greatrex	
G-BSSP	Robin DR.400/180R	Soaring (Oxford) Ltd	
G-BSST	BAC-Sud Concorde 002 ★	F.A.A. Museum/Yeovilton	
G-BSSY	Polikarpov Po-2 (28)	Richard Shuttleworth Trustees	
G-BSTC	Aeronca 11AC Chief	J. Armstrong & D. Lamb	
G-BSTE	AS.355F2 Twin Squirrel	Oscar Mayer Ltd	
G-BSTH	PA-25-235 Pawnee C	L. G. Appelbeck	
G-BSTI	Piper J-3C-65 Cub	S. P. Reeve	
G-BSTK	Thunder Ax8-90 balloon	M. Williams	
G-BSTL	Rand-Robinson KR-2	C. S. Hales & N. Brauns	
G-BSTM	Cessna 172L	G-BSTM Group	
G-BSTO	Cessna 152 II	M. A. Stott	
G-BSTP	Cessna 152 II	LAC Aircraft Ltd	
G-BSTR	AA-5 Traveler	J. C. M. Alty	
G-BSTT	Rans S.6 Coyote II	D. G. Palmer	
G-BSTX	Luscombe 8A Silvaire	M. C. Fox	
G-BSTZ	PA-28 Cherokee 140	Air Navigation & Trading Co Ltd	
G-BSUA	Rans S.6 Coyote II	A. J. Todd	
G-BSUD	Luscombe 8A Silvaire	Luscombe Quartet	
G-BSUK	Colt 77A balloon	T. Knight	
G-BSUO	Scheibe SF.25C Falke	Southwest Motorgliders	
G-BSUV	Cameron O-77 balloon	I. R. F. Worsman	
G-BSUX	Carlson Sparrow II	K. Redfearn	
G-BSVB	PA-28-181 Archer II	Veebee Aviation Ltd	
G-BSVE	Binder CP.301S Smaragd	Smaragd Flying Group	
G-BSVG	PA-28-161 Warrior II	Airways Aero Associations Ltd	
G-BSVH	Piper J-3C-65 Cub	G. J. Digby	
G-BSVK	Denney Kitfox Model 2	H. D. Colliver	
G-BSVM	PA-28-161 Warrior II	EFG Flying Services	
G-BSVN	Thorp T-18	M. D. Moaby	
G-BSVP	PA-23-250 Aztec F	S. G. Spier	
G-BSVR	Schweizer 269C	M. K. E. Askham	
G-BSVS	Robin DR.400/100	D. McK. Chalmers	
G-BSWB	Rans S.10 Sakota	F. A. Hewitt	
G-BSWC	Boeing Stearman E75 (112)	D. A. Jack	
G-BSWG	PA-17 Vagabond	P. N. Deighton	
G-BSWH	Cessna 152 II	Airspeed Aviation Ltd	
G-BSWL	Slingsby T.61F Venture T.2	Trent Valley Venture Group	
G-BSWM	Slingsby T.61F Venture T.2	Venture Gliding Group	
G-BSWR	BN-2T-26 Turbine Islander	Police Service of Northern Ireland	
G-BSWV	Cameron N-77 balloon	S. Charlish	
G-BSXA	PA-28-161 Warrior II	Falcon Flying Services	
G-BSXB	PA-28-161 Warrior II	S. R. Mendes	
G-BSXC	PA-28-161 Warrior II	G-EXPO LLP	
G-BSXD	Soko P-2 Kraguj (30146)	Airfield Aviation Ltd	
G-BSXI	Mooney M.20E	D. H. G. Penney	
G-BSXM	Cameron V-77 balloon	C. A. Oxby	
G-BSXT	Piper J-5A Cub Cruiser	J. R. Hodgson	
G-BSYA	Jodel D.18	R. W. Rose & J. T. Houghton	
G-BSYF	Luscombe 8A Silvaire	V. R. Leggott	
G-BSYG	PA-12 Super Cruiser	Fat Cub Group	
G-BSYH	Luscombe 8A Silvaire	N. R. Osborne	
G-BSYJ	Cameron N-77 balloon	Chubb Fire Ltd	
G-BSYO	Piper J-3C-90 Cub	C. R. Reynolds (G-BSMJ/G-BRHE)	
G-BSYU	Robin DR.400/180	P. D. Smoothy	
G-BSYV	Cessna 150M	Aviolease Ltd	
G-BSYY	PA-28-161 Warrior II	Aerobility	
G-BSYZ	PA-28-161 Warrior II	F. C. P. Hood	
G-BSZB	Stolp SA.300 Starduster Too	P. J. B. Lewis	
G-BSZF	Jodel DR.250/160	Cole Aviation Ltd	
G-BSZJ	PA-28-181 Archer II	M. L. A. Pudney & R. D. Fuller	
G-BSZM	Montgomerie-Bensen B.8MR	J. G. Pumford	
G-BSZO	Cessna 152	A. Jahanfar	
G-BSZT	PA-28-161 Warrior II	Golf Charlie Echo Ltd	
G-BSZV	Cessna 150F	M. Hill	
G-BSZW	Cessna 152	S. T. & T. W. Gilbert	
G-BTAK	EAA Acrosport II	S. R. Green	
G-BTAL	Cessna F.152 II	Herefordshire Aero Club Ltd	
G-BTAM	PA-28-181 Archer II	The Ashley Gardner Flying Club Ltd	

BRITISH CIVIL AIRCRAFT MARKINGS

Notes	Reg	Type	Owner or Operator
	G-BTAW	PA-28-161 Warrior II	Piper Flying Group
	G-BTAZ	Evans VP-2 ★	City of Norwich Aviation Museum/Norwich
	G-BTBA	Robinson R22 Beta	EFL Helicopters Ltd
	G-BTBC	PA-28-161 Warrior II	M. A. Khan
	G-BTBG	Denney Kitfox Mk 2	A. S. Cadney
	G-BTBH	Ryan ST3KR (854)	R. C. Piper
	G-BTBJ	Cessna 190	P. W. Moorcroft
	G-BTBL	Montgomerie-Bensen B.8MR	AES Radionic Surveillance Systems
	G-BTBU	PA-18 Super Cub 150	S. D. Edwards
	G-BTBY	PA-17 Vagabond	K. Perratt
	G-BTCB	Air Command 582 Sport	G. Scurrah
	G-BTCE	Cessna 152	S. T. Gilbert
	G-BTCH	Luscombe 8E Silvaire Deluxe	M. W. Orr
	G-BTCI	PA-17 Vagabond	T. R. Whittome
	G-BTCJ	Luscombe 8E Silvaire	D. Snook
	G-BTCZ	Cameron Chateau 84 balloon	Balleroy Developpement SAS
	G-BTDA	Slingsby T.61G Falke	G-BTDA Group
	G-BTDC	Denney Kitfox Mk 2	R. Palmer
	G-BTDD	CFM Streak Shadow	The Adventurous SSDR Group
	G-BTDE	Cessna C-165 Airmaster	R. H. Screen
	G-BTDF	Luscombe 8A Silvaire	G. Johnson
	G-BTDN	Denney Kitfox Mk 2	D. Rudd
	G-BTDR	Aero Designs Pulsar	A. & P. Kingsley-Dobson
	G-BTDT	CASA 1.131E Jungmann 2000	T. J. Alderdice
	G-BTDV	PA-28-161 Warrior II	Falcon Flying Services Ltd
	G-BTDW	Cessna 152 II	J. H. Sandham Aviation
	G-BTDY	PA.18-150 Super Cub	N. J. Butler
	G-BTDZ	CASA 1.131E Jungmann 2000	R. J. & M. Pickin
	G-BTEL	CFM Streak Shadow	J. E. Eatwell
	G-BTES	Cessna 150H	UK Flying Clubs Ltd
	G-BTET	Piper J-3C-65 Cub	City of Oxford Flying Group
	G-BTEW	Cessna 120	A. I. & J. H. Milne
	G-BTFC	Cessna F.152 II	Aircraft Engineers Ltd
	G-BTFE	Bensen-Parsons 2-seat gyroplane	A. Corleanca
	G-BTFG	Boeing Stearman A75N1 (441)	TG Aviation Ltd
	G-BTFJ	PA-15 Vagabond	R. Ellingworth & N. A. Preston
	G-BTFL	Aeronca 11AC Chief	BTFL Group
	G-BTFO	PA-28-161 Warrior II	Flyfar Ltd
	G-BTFP	PA-38-112 Tomahawk	M. Lee
	G-BTFT	Beech 58 Baron	Fastwing Air Charter Ltd
	G-BTFU	Cameron N-90 balloon	J. J. Rudoni & A. C. K. Rawson
	G-BTFV	Whittaker MW7	P. A. Gasson
	G-BTGD	Rand-Robinson KR-2 (modified)	S. R. Winter
	G-BTGI	Rearwin 175 Skyranger	J. M. Fforde
	G-BTGJ	Smith DSA-1 Miniplane	D. J. Howell
	G-BTGL	Light Aero Avid Flyer	J. S. Clair-Quentin
	G-BTGM	Aeronca 7AC Champion	Heligan Champ Group
	G-BTGO	PA-28 Cherokee 140	Demero Ltd & LV Skies Ltd
	G-BTGR	Cessna 152 II	A. J. Gomes
	G-BTGS	Stolp SA.300 Starduster Too	G. N. Elliott & ptnrs (G-AYMA)
	G-BTGT	CFM Streak Shadow	I. Heunis (G-MWPY)
	G-BTGW	Cessna 152 II	Stapleford Flying Club Ltd
	G-BTGY	PA-28-161 Warrior II	Stapleford Flying Club Ltd
	G-BTGZ	PA-28-181 Archer II	Nick Deyong Ltd
	G-BTHE	Cessna 150L	UK Flying Clubs Ltd
	G-BTHF	Cameron V-90 balloon	N. J. & S. J. Langley
	G-BTHK	Thunder Ax7-77 balloon	M. S.Trend
	G-BTHP	Thorp T.211	M. Gardner
	G-BTHX	Colt 105A balloon	I. J. Wadey
	G-BTHY	Bell 206B JetRanger 3	Suffolk Helicopters Ltd
	G-BTIE	SOCATA TB10 Tobago	D. J. & S. N. Taplin
	G-BTIF	Denney Kitfox Mk 3	D. S. Lally
	G-BTIG	Montgomerie-Bensen B.8MR	G. H. Leeming
	G-BTII	AA-5B Tiger	G-BTII Group
	G-BTIJ	Luscombe 8E Silvaire	S. J. Hornsby
	G-BTIL	PA-38-112 Tomahawk	B. J. Pearson
	G-BTIM	PA-28-161 Cadet	White Waltham Airfield Ltd
	G-BTIV	PA-28-161 Warrior II	Warrior Group
	G-BTJA	Luscombe 8E Silvaire	N. C. Wildey
	G-BTJB	Luscombe 8E Silvaire	M. Loxton
	G-BTJC	Luscombe 8F Silvaire	M. Colson

Reg	Type	Owner or Operator	Notes
G-BTJD	Thunder Ax8-90 S2 balloon	L. J. Whitelock	
G-BTJL	PA-38-112 Tomahawk	A5E Ltd	
G-BTJS	Montgomerie-Bensen B.8MR	B. F. Pearson	
G-BTJX	Rans S.10 Sakota	J. A. Harris	
G-BTKA	Piper J-5A Cub Cruiser	Turweston Flying Club Ltd	
G-BTKB	Renegade Spirit 912	P. J. Calvert	
G-BTKD	Denney Kitfox Mk 4	R. A. Hills	
G-BTKL	MBB Bö.105DB-4	Airphot AG/Switzerland	
G-BTKP	CFM Streak Shadow	M. J. Mawle & P. F. Morgan	
G-BTKT	PA-28-161 Warrior II	Falcon Flying Services Ltd	
G-BTKV	PA-22 Tri-Pacer 160	R. A. Moore	
G-BTKW	Cameron O-105 balloon	L. J. Whitelock	
G-BTKX	PA-28-181 Archer II	D. J. Perkins	
G-BTLB	Wassmer Wa.52 Europa	Hampshire Flying Group	
G-BTLG	PA-28R Cherokee Arrow 200	S. A. Thomas	
G-BTLL	Pilatus P.3-03 (A-806)	R. E. Dagless	
G-BTLP	AA-1C Lynx	Partlease Ltd	
G-BTMA	Cessna 172N	R. F. Wondrak	
G-BTMK	Cessna R.172K XPII	K. E. Halford	
G-BTML	Cameron Rupert Bear 90 balloon	S. C. Kinsey	
G-BTMO	Colt 69A balloon	Cameron Balloons Ltd	
G-BTMP	Campbell Cricket replica	P. J. Gardner	
G-BTMR	Cessna 172M	Hull Aero Club Ltd	
G-BTMV	Everett Srs 2 gyroplane	L. Armes	
G-BTNH	PA-28-161 Warrior II	Falcon Flying Services Ltd (G-DENH)	
G-BTNO	Aeronca 7AC Champion	J. M. Farquhar	
G-BTNR	Denney Kitfox Mk 3	High Notions Flying Group	
G-BTNT	PA-28-151 Warrior	Azure Flying Club Ltd	
G-BTNV	PA-28-161 Warrior II	B. Somerville & P. A. Teasdale	
G-BTNW	Rans S.6-ESA Coyote II	P. J. Fahie	
G-BTOG	DH.82A Tiger Moth	TOG Group	
G-BTOI	Cameron N-77 balloon	Zebedee Balloon Service Ltd	
G-BTOL	Denney Kitfox Mk 3	P. J. Gibbs	
G-BTON	PA-28 Cherokee 140	R. Nightingale	
G-BTOO	Pitts S-1C Special	T. L. Davis	
G-BTOP	Cameron V-77 balloon	J. J. Winter	
G-BTOT	PA-15 Vagabond	Vagabond Flying Group	
G-BTOU	Cameron O-120 balloon	J. J. Daly	
G-BTOW	SOCATA Rallye 180GT	M. Jarrett	
G-BTOZ	Thunder Ax9-120 S2 balloon	H. G. Davies	
G-BTPT	Cameron N-77 balloon	H. J. Andrews	
G-BTPV	Colt 90A balloon	C. J. Wootton & J. S. Russon	
G-BTRC	Light Aero Avid Speedwing	H. Bishop	
G-BTRF	Aero Designs Pulsar	P. F. Crosby & C. Smith	
G-BTRG	Aeronca 65C Super Chief	Condor Aviation International Ltd	
G-BTRI	Aeronca 11CC Super Chief	A. F. Wankowski & H. Wankowska	
G-BTRK	PA-28-161 Warrior II	Stapleford Flying Club Ltd	
G-BTRL	Cameron N-105 balloon	J. Lippett	
G-BTRR	Thunder Ax7-77 balloon	P. J. Wentworth	
G-BTRS	PA-28-161 Warrior II	Airwise Flying Group	
G-BTRT	PA-28R Cherokee Arrow 200-II	B. Swain	
G-BTRU	Robin DR.400/180	R. H. Mackay	
G-BTRW	Slingsby T.61F Venture T.2	P. Asbridge	
G-BTRY	PA-28-161 Warrior II	C. S. Jennings	
G-BTRZ	Jodel D.18	A. P. Aspinall	
G-BTSC	Evans VP-2	I. Pearson	
G-BTSJ	PA-28-161 Warrior II	Coastal Air (SW) Ltd	
G-BTSP	Piper J-3C-65 Cub	C. M. Brittlebank	
G-BTSR	Aeronca 11AC Chief	J. M. Miller	
G-BTSV	Denney Kitfox Mk 3	Fox Flyers	
G-BTSX	Thunder Ax7-77 balloon	A. J. Gregory	
G-BTSY	EE Lightning F.6 (XR724) ★	Lightning Association	
G-BTSZ	Cessna 177A	V. Kiminius	
G-BTTD	Montgomerie-Bensen B.8MR	A. J. P. Herculson	
G-BTTR	Aerotek Pitts S-2A Special	Collett Aviation Services Ltd	
G-BTTW	Thunder Ax7-77 balloon	T. D. Gibbs	
G-BTTY	Denney Kitfox Mk 2	B. J. Clews & L. W. Whittington	
G-BTTZ	Slingsby T.61F Venture T.2	Upwood Motorglider Group	
G-BTUA	Slingsby T.61F Venture T.2	Shenington Gliding Club	
G-BTUB	Yakovlev C.11	Fly the Dream Ltd	
G-BTUC	EMB-312 Tucano ★	Ulster Aviation Society/Long Kesh	

Notes	Reg	Type	Owner or Operator
	G-BTUG	SOCATA Rallye 180T	D. Moore & L. C. Clark
	G-BTUH	Cameron N-65 balloon	J. S. Russon
	G-BTUK	Aerotek Pitts S-2A Special	S. H. Elkington
	G-BTUM	Piper J-3C-65 Cub	G-BTUM Syndicate
	G-BTUR	PA-18 Super Cub 95 (modified)	N. J. Butler
	G-BTUS	Whittaker MW7	C. T. Bailey
	G-BTUW	PA-28-151 Warrior	T. S. Kemp
	G-BTUZ	American General AG-5B Tiger	Meadowland Aviation Ltd
	G-BTVA	Thunder Ax7-77 balloon	M. Mansfield
	G-BTVC	Denney Kitfox Mk 2	G. C. Jiggins
	G-BTVE	Hawker Demon I (K8203)	Demon Displays Ltd
	G-BTVW	Cessna 152 II	Madalena Cruel Lda/Portugal
	G-BTVX	Cessna 152 II	S. J. Nicholls
	G-BTWB	Denney Kitfox Mk 3	C. J. Scott (G-BTTM)
	G-BTWC	Slingsby T.61F Venture T.2 (ZA656)	621 Venture Syndicate
	G-BTWD	Slingsby T.61F Venture T.2	York Gliding Centre
	G-BTWE	Slingsby T.61F Venture T.2	Aston Down G-BTWE Syndicate
	G-BTWI	EAA Acro Sport I	J. O'Connell
	G-BTWL	WAG-Aero Acro Sport Trainer	F. E. Tofield
	G-BTWY	Aero Designs Pulsar	R. Bishop
	G-BTWZ	Rans S.10 Sakota	J. T. Phipps
	G-BTXD	Rans S.6-ESA Coyote II	A. I. Sutherland
	G-BTXF	Cameron V-90 balloon	G. Thompson
	G-BTXH	Colt A5-56 Airship	H. Moine
	G-BTXI	Noorduyn AT-16 Harvard IIB (FE695)	Patina Ltd
	G-BTXK	Thunder Ax7-65 balloon	A. F. Selby
	G-BTXM	Colt 21A Cloudhopper balloon	H. J. Andrews
	G-BTXZ	Zenair CH.250	G-BTXZ Group
	G-BTYC	Cessna 150L	Z. Stevens
	G-BTYI	PA-28-181 Archer II	S. W. Hedges
	G-BTYT	Cessna 152 II	Cristal Air Ltd
	G-BTYX	Cessna 140 ★	South Yorkshire Aircraft Museum/Doncaster
	G-BTYY	Curtiss Robertson C-2 Robin	R. W. Hatton
	G-BTZA	Beech F33A Bonanza	G-BTZA Group
	G-BTZB	Yakovlev Yak-50 (10 yellow)	Airborne Services Ltd
	G-BTZD	Yakovlev Yak-1 (1342)	Historic Aircraft Collection Ltd
	G-BTZP	SOCATA TB9 Tampico	M. W. Orr
	G-BTZS	Colt 77A balloon	P. T. R. Ollivere
	G-BTZV	Cameron V-77 balloon	J. W. Tyrell
	G-BTZX	Piper J-3C-65 Cub	ZX Cub Group
	G-BTZY	Colt 56A balloon	M. H. Read
	G-BTZZ	CFM Streak Shadow	B. P. Cater
	G-BUAB	Aeronca 11AC Chief	P. King
	G-BUAC	Slingsby T.31 Motor Cadet III	J. D. Hill
	G-BUAG	Jodel D.18	R. W. Buckley
	G-BUAI	Everett Srs 3 gyroplane	D. Stevenson
	G-BUAO	Luscombe 8E Silvaire	G-BUAO Group
	G-BUAR	Westland Seafire Mk.III (PP972:II-5)	Flying A Services Ltd
	G-BUAV	Cameron O-105 balloon	D. & T. Dorrell
	G-BUBL	Thunder Ax8-105 balloon ★	British Balloon Museum/Newbury
	G-BUBN	BN-2B-26 Islander	Isles of Scilly Skybus Ltd
	G-BUBP	BN-2B-26 Islander	Isles of Scilly Skybus Ltd
	G-BUBS	Lindstrand LBL-77B balloon	M. Saveri
	G-BUBT	Stoddard-Hamilton Glasair II-SRG	Signs Plus Ltd
	G-BUCA	Cessna A.150K	R. J. Whyham
	G-BUCC	CASA 1.131E Jungmann 2000 (BU+CC)	R. N. Crosland (G-BUEM)
	G-BUCH	Stinson V-77 Reliant	Sopwith Court Ltd
	G-BUCK	CASA 1.131E Jungmann 1000 (BU+CK)	Jungmann Flying Group
	G-BUCM	Hawker Sea Fury FB.11 (VX653)	Patina Ltd
	G-BUCO	Pietenpol Air Camper	A. James
	G-BUCT	Cessna 150L	Air Navigation & Trading Co.Ltd
	G-BUDA	Slingsby T.61F Venture T.2	G-BUDA Syndicate
	G-BUDC	Slingsby T.61F Venture T.2 (ZA652)	P. R. Williams
	G-BUDE	PA-22 Tri-Pacer 135 (tailwheel)	P. Robinson
	G-BUDI	Aero Designs Pulsar	R. W. L. Oliver
	G-BUDK	Thunder Ax7-77 balloon	W. Evans
	G-BUDL	Auster 3 (NX534)	L. R. Leek
	G-BUDN	Cameron 90 Shoe SS balloon	Magical Adventures Ltd
	G-BUDO	PZL-110 Koliber 150	A. S. Vine
	G-BUDR	Denney Kitfox Mk 3	J. R. Davis

Reg	Type	Owner or Operator	Notes
G-BUDS	Rand-Robinson KR-2	B. E. Wagenhauser	
G-BUDT	Slingsby T.61F Venture T.2	G-BUDT Group	
G-BUEC	Van's RV-6	A. H. Harper	
G-BUED	Slingsby T.61F Venture T.2	Venture Syndicate	
G-BUEF	Cessna 152 II	Modern Air (UK) Ltd	
G-BUEG	Cessna 152 II	P. Rudd	
G-BUEI	Thunder Ax8-105 balloon	P. J. Hooper	
G-BUEK	Slingsby T.61F Venture T.2	G-BUEK Group	
G-BUEN	VPM M-14 Scout	C. R. Gordon	
G-BUEP	Maule MX-7-180	N. J. B. Bennett	
G-BUEW	Rans S-6 Coyote II	C. Cheeseman (G-MWYE)	
G-BUFG	Slingsby T.61F Venture T.2	G. W. Withers	
G-BUFH	PA-28-161 Warrior II	Bliss Aviation Ltd	
G-BUFR	Slingsby T.61F Venture T.2	Buckminster Gliding Club Ltd	
G-BUFY	PA-28-161 Warrior II	Bickertons Aerodromes Ltd	
G-BUGJ	Robin DR.400/180	W. E. R. Jenkins	
G-BUGL	Slingsby T.61F Venture T.2	S. L. Hoy	
G-BUGP	Cameron V-77 balloon	R. Churcher	
G-BUGS	Cameron V-77 balloon	T. J. Orchard	
G-BUGV	Slingsby T.61F Venture T.2	Venture Flying Group	
G-BUGW	Slingsby T.61F Venture T.2	G. M. Wiseman	
G-BUGY	Cameron V-90 balloon	Dante Balloon Group	
G-BUGZ	Slingsby T.61F Venture T.2	R. W. Spiller	
G-BUHA	Slingsby T.61F Venture T.2 (ZA634:C)	Saltby Flying Group	
G-BUHM	Cameron V-77 balloon	P. T. Lickorish	
G-BUHO	Cessna 140	W. B. Bateson	
G-BUHR	Slingsby T.61F Venture T.2	M. R. Fox	
G-BUHS	Stoddard-Hamilton Glasair SH TD-1	T. F. Horrocks	
G-BUHU	Cameron N-105 balloon	M. Rate	
G-BUHZ	Cessna 120	The Cessna 140 Group	
G-BUIF	PA-28-161 Warrior II	Redhill Air Services Ltd	
G-BUIG	Campbell Cricket (replica)	R. H. Braithwaite	
G-BUIH	Slingsby T.61F Venture T.2	The Falcon Gliding Group	
G-BUIJ	PA-28-161 Warrior II	D. J. Taplin	
G-BUIK	PA-28-161 Warrior II	E. J. Lamb	
G-BUIL	CFM Streak Shadow	A. A. Castleton	
G-BUIN	Thunder Ax7-77 balloon	P. C. Johnson	
G-BUIP	Denney Kitfox Mk 2	R. Line	
G-BUIZ	Cameron N-90 balloon	G. A. Boyle	
G-BUJA	Slingsby T.61F Venture T.2	Wolds Gliding Club Ltd	
G-BUJB	Slingsby T.61F Venture T.2	Falke Syndicate	
G-BUJE	Cessna 177B	FG93 Group	
G-BUJH	Colt 77B balloon	B. Fisher	
G-BUJI	Slingsby T.61F Venture T.2	Solent Venture Syndicate	
G-BUJJ	Avid Speedwing	P. P. Trangmar	
G-BUJM	Cessna 120	K. G. Grayson	
G-BUJN	Cessna 172N	Warwickshire Leasing Ltd	
G-BUJO	PA-28-161 Warrior II	Falcon Flying Services	
G-BUJP	PA-28-161 Warrior II	Phoenix Aviation	
G-BUJV	Light Aero Avid Speedwing Mk 4	C. Thomas	
G-BUJX	Slingsby T.61F Venture T.2	York Gliding Centre Ltd	
G-BUKB	Rans S.10 Sakota	M. K. Blatch	
G-BUKF	Denney Kitfox Mk 4	Kilo Foxtrot Group	
G-BUKH	D.31 Turbulent	G. Haye	
G-BUKI	Thunder Ax7-77 balloon	Virgin Balloon Flights	
G-BUKK	Bücker Bü 133C Jungmeister (U-80)	B. R. Cox	
G-BUKO	Cessna 120	C. J. Varley	
G-BUKP	Denney Kitfox Mk 2	K. C. Smith	
G-BUKR	MS.880B Rallye Club 100T	G-BUKR Flying Group	
G-BUKU	Luscombe 8E Silvaire	Silvaire Flying Group	
G-BUKZ	Evans VP-2	P. R. Farnell	
G-BULC	Light Aero Avid Flyer Mk 4	P. P. Trangmar	
G-BULG	Van's RV-4	V. D. Long	
G-BULJ	CFM Streak Shadow	D. R. Stansfield	
G-BULL	SA Bulldog Srs 120/128 (HKG-5)	Bulldog Aeros Ltd	
G-BULO	Luscombe 8A Silvaire	Ridgway Aviation Ltd	
G-BULR	PA-28-140 Cherokee B	D. H. G. Penny	
G-BULY	Light Aero Avid Flyer	C. Coleman	
G-BULZ	Denney Kitfox Mk 2	T. G. F. Trenchard	
G-BUMP	PA-28-181 Archer II	M. J. Green & D. Major	
G-BUNA	SNCAN Stampe SV-4C	J. P. O'Donnell	

Notes	Reg	Type	Owner or Operator
	G-BUNB	Slingsby T.61F Venture T.2	Wessex Ventures 2016
	G-BUNC	PZL-104 Wilga 35	R. F. Goodman
	G-BUNG	Cameron N-77 balloon	A. Kaye
	G-BUNO	Lancair 320	J. Softley
	G-BUOA	Whittaker MW6-S Fatboy Flyer	H. N. Graham
	G-BUOB	CFM Streak Shadow	J. M. Hunter
	G-BUOD	SE-5A (replica) (B595:W)	M. D. Waldron/Belgium
	G-BUOF	D.62B Condor	J. Cotterill & N. C. du Piesanie
	G-BUOL	Denney Kitfox Mk 3	P. Dennington
	G-BUON	Light Aero Avid Aerobat	T. P. Beare
	G-BUOS	VS.394 Spitfire FR.XVIII (SM845:R)	Fliegerhorst GmbH & Co KG
	G-BUOW	Aero Designs Pulsar XP	T. J. Hartwell
	G-BUPA	Rutan LongEz	N. G. Henry
	G-BUPB	Stolp SA.300 Starduster Too	J. R. Edwards & J. W. Widdows
	G-BUPC	Rollason Beta B.2	C. A. Rolph
	G-BUPF	Bensen B.8R	P. W. Hewitt-Dean
	G-BUPH	Colt 25A balloon	M. E. White
	G-BUPM	VPM M-16 Tandem Trainer	A. Kitson
	G-BUPP	Cameron V-42 balloon	C. L. Schoeman
	G-BUPR	Jodel D.18	R. W. Burrows
	G-BUPU	Thunder Ax7-77 balloon	R. C. Barkworth & D. G. Maguire/USA
	G-BUPV	Great Lakes 2T-1A	R. J. Fray
	G-BUPW	Denney Kitfox Mk 3	S. G. Metcalfe
	G-BURI	Enstrom F-28C	D. W. C. Holmes
	G-BURL	Colt 105A balloon	J. E. Rose
	G-BURP	Rotorway Executive 90	D. H. Baker
	G-BURR	Auster AOP.9 (WZ706)	Annic Aviation
	G-BURZ	Hawker Nimrod II (K3661:362)	Historic Aircraft Collection Ltd
	G-BUSN	Rotorway Executive 90	D. & J. Parke
	G-BUSR	Aero Designs Pulsar	S. S. Bateman & R. A. Watts
	G-BUSS	Cameron 90 Bus SS balloon	Magical Adventures Ltd
	G-BUSV	Colt 105A balloon	H. C. J. Williams
	G-BUSW	Rockwell Commander 114	M. J. P. Lynch
	G-BUTB	CFM Streak Shadow	H. O. Maclean
	G-BUTD	Van's RV-6	B. S. Carpenter
	G-BUTF	Aeronca 11AC Chief	A. W. Crutcher
	G-BUTG	Zenair CH.601HD	A. Brown
	G-BUTH	CEA DR.220 2+2	Phoenix Flying Group
	G-BUTJ	Cameron O-77 balloon	C. & P. Collins
	G-BUTK	Murphy Rebel	A. J. Gibson
	G-BUTM	Rans S.6-116 Coyote II	Coyote Flying Group
	G-BUTT	Cessna FA150K	Fis Ato Europe SL/Spain (G-AXSJ)
	G-BUTX	CASA 1.133C Jungmeister (ES.1-4)	S. R. Stead
	G-BUTY	Brügger MB.2 Colibri	R. M. Lawday
	G-BUTZ	PA-28 Cherokee 180C	R. J. Anderson, N. T. W. Pooley & M. Royal (G-DARL)
	G-BUUA	Slingsby T.67M Firefly Mk II	Heartland Aviation Ltd
	G-BUUC	Slingsby T.67M Firefly Mk II	Swiftair Maintenance Ltd
	G-BUUE	Slingsby T.67M Firefly Mk II	J. R. Bratty
	G-BUUF	Slingsby T.67M Firefly Mk II	Nautx Aviation Ltd
	G-BUUI	Slingsby T.67M Firefly Mk II	Bustard Flying Club Ltd
	G-BUUJ	Slingsby T.67M Firefly Mk II	Blue Skies Group
	G-BUUK	Slingsby T.67M Firefly Mk II	Avalanche Aviation Ltd
	G-BUUL	SlingsbtyT.67M Firefly Mk II	Air Ministry Aviation Ltd
	G-BUUU	Cameron Bottle SS balloon ★	British Balloon Museum/Newbury
	G-BUUX	PA-28 Cherokee 180D	Aero Group 78
	G-BUVA	PA-22-135 Tri-Pacer	Oaksey VA Group
	G-BUVB	Colt 77A balloon	L. B. Humphrey
	G-BUVM	CEA DR.250/160	T. W. Gilbert
	G-BUVO	Cessna F.182P	Romeo Mike Flying Group (G-WTFA)
	G-BUVR	Christen A.1 Husky	E. M. Smiley-Jones
	G-BUVT	Colt 77A balloon	N. A. Carr
	G-BUVW	Cameron N-90 balloon	L. J. Whitelock
	G-BUVX	CFM Streak Shadow	C. W. A. Holliday
	G-BUWE	SE-5A (replica) (C9533:M)	Airpark Flight Centre Ltd
	G-BUWF	Cameron N-105 balloon	R. E. Jones
	G-BUWH	Parsons 2-seat gyroplane	R. V. Brunskill
	G-BUWI	Lindstrand LBL-77A balloon	G. A. Chadwick
	G-BUWK	Rans S.6-116 Coyote II	R. Warriner
	G-BUWL	Piper J-4A	M. L. Ryan
	G-BUWR	CFM Streak Shadow	T. Harvey

Reg	Type	Owner or Operator	Notes
G-BUWT	Rand-Robinson KR-2	G. Bailey-Woods	
G-BUWU	Cameron V-77 balloon	T. R. Dews	
G-BUXC	CFM Streak Shadow SA-M	S. D. J. Harvey	
G-BUXI	Steen Skybolt	Leipzig Aviators Group	
G-BUXK	Pietenpol Air Camper	B. M. D. Nelson	
G-BUXL	Taylor JT.1 Monoplane	P. J. Hebdon	
G-BUXW	Thunder Ax8-90 S2 balloon	N. T. Parry	
G-BUXX	PA-17 Vagabond	G-BUXX Group	
G-BUXY	PA-25 Pawnee 235	Bath, Wilts & North Dorset Gliding Club Ltd	
G-BUYB	Aero Designs Pulsar	A. R. Thorpe	
G-BUYC	Cameron 80 Concept balloon	R. P. Cross	
G-BUYE	Aeronca 7AC Champion	A. A. Gillon	
G-BUYF	Falcon XP	M. J. Hadland	
G-BUYK	Denney Kitfox Mk 4	M. S. Shelton	
G-BUYL	RAF 2000GT gyroplane	M. H. J. Goldring	
G-BUYO	Colt 77A balloon	D. A. B. Ackermann/Germany	
G-BUYS	Robin DR.400/180	G-BUYS Flying Group	
G-BUYU	Bowers Fly-Baby 1A (1803/18)	R. C. Piper	
G-BUYY	PA-28 Cherokee 180	G-BUYY Group	
G-BUZA	Denney Kitfox Mk 3	G. O. Newell	
G-BUZB	Aero Designs Pulsar XP	S. M. Macintyre	
G-BUZG	Zenair CH.601HD	G. Cox	
G-BUZH	Aero Designs Star-Lite SL-1	B. A. Lyford	
G-BUZK	Cameron V-77 balloon	Zebedee Balloon Service Ltd	
G-BUZL	VPM M.16 Tandem Trainer	J. D. Winder	
G-BUZM	Light Aero Avid Flyer Mk 3	J. F. Bakewell	
G-BUZO	Pietenpol Air Camper	D. A. Jones	
G-BUZR	Lindstrand LBL-77A balloon	Lindstrand Technologies Ltd	
G-BUZZ	Agusta-Bell 206B JetRanger 2	Skypark (UK) Ltd	
G-BVAB	Zenair CH.601HDS	B. N. Rides	
G-BVAC	Zenair CH.601HD	J. A. Tyndall	
G-BVAF	Piper J-3C-65 Cub	G-BVAF Group	
G-BVAH	Denney Kitfox Mk.3	G. M. Cruise-Smith	
G-BVAI	PZL-110 Koliber 150	P. Coomber	
G-BVAM	Evans VP-1 Series 2	The Breighton VP-1 Group	
G-BVAW	Staaken Z-1 Flitzer (D-692)	L. R. Williams	
G-BVBF	PA-28-151 Warrior	R. K. Spence	
G-BVBJ	Colt Flying Coffee Jar SS balloon	The British Balloon Museum & Library Ltd	
G-BVBK	Colt Flying Coffee Jar SS balloon	J. V. Edwards	
G-BVBU	Cameron V-77 balloon	J. Ricards	
G-BVCA	Cameron N-105 balloon	J. D. Phillips	
G-BVCG	Van's RV-6	A. W. Shellis	
G-BVCL	Rans S.6-116 Coyote II	A. M. Colman	
G-BVCN	Colt 56A balloon	G. A. & I. Chadwick & S. Richards	
G-BVCO	FRED Srs 2	BCVO Group	
G-BVCP	Piper CP.1 Metisse	B. M. Diggins	
G-BVCS	Aeronca 7BCM Champion	A. C. Lines	
G-BVCT	Denney Kitfox Mk 4	A. F. Reid	
G-BVCY	Cameron H-24 balloon	A. C. K. Rawson & J. J. Rudoni	
G-BVDB	Thunder Ax7-77 balloon	M. K. Bellamy (G-ORDY)	
G-BVDC	Van's RV-3	R. S. Hatwell	
G-BVDF	Cameron Doll 105 SS balloon	A. Kaye & K-H Gruenauer	
G-BVDG	VPM M-15	R. F. G. Moyle	
G-BVDI	Van's RV-4	J. G. Gorman & H. Tallini	
G-BVDJ	Campbell Cricket (replica)	S. Jennings	
G-BVDP	Sequoia F.8L Falco	N. M. Turner	
G-BVDR	Cameron O-77 balloon	T. Duggan	
G-BVDT	CFM Streak Shadow	A. Harner	
G-BVDW	Thunder Ax8-90 balloon	S. C. Vora	
G-BVDX	Cameron V-90 balloon	R. K. Scott	
G-BVDY	Cameron 60 Concept balloon	P. Baker/Ireland	
G-BVDZ	Taylorcraft BC-12D	I. Maddock & A. Sharp	
G-BVEA	Mosler Motors N.3 Pup	M. D. Grinstead (G-MWEA)	
G-BVEH	Jodel D.112	M. L. Copland	
G-BVEL	Evans VP-1 Srs.2	M. J. & S. J. Quinn	
G-BVEN	Cameron 80 Concept balloon	B. J. & M. A. Alford	
G-BVEP	Luscombe 8A Master	B. H. Austen	
G-BVER	DHC.2 Beaver 1 (XV268)	Seaflite Ltd (G-BTDM)	
G-BVEV	PA-34-200 Seneca	M. Ali	
G-BVEY	Denney Kitfox Mk 4-1200	J. H. H. Turner	

Notes	Reg	Type	Owner or Operator
	G-BVEZ	P.84 Jet Provost T.3A (XM479)	Newcastle Jet Provost Group
	G-BVFA	Rans S.10 Sakota	J. C. Longmore & S. M. Hall
	G-BVFB	Cameron N-31 balloon	P. Lawman
	G-BVFF	Cameron V-77 balloon	R. J. Kerr & G. P. Allen
	G-BVFM	Rans S.6-116 Coyote II	J. Fleming
	G-BVFO	Light Aero Avid Speedwing	T. G. Solomon
	G-BVFR	CFM Streak Shadow	S. G. Smith
	G-BVFS	Slingsby T.31M	S. R. Williams
	G-BVFZ	Maule M5-180C Lunar Rocket	R. C. Robinson
	G-BVGA	Bell 206B JetRanger3	Bucklefields Business Developments Ltd
	G-BVGB	Thunder Ax8-105 S2 balloon	E. K. Read
	G-BVGE	WS-55 Whirlwind HAR.10 (XJ729)	A. D. Whitehouse
	G-BVGF	Shaw Europa	T. C. Hyde
	G-BVGH	Hawker Hunter T.7 (XL573)	M. Stott
	G-BVGI	Pereira Osprey II	D. Westoby
	G-BVGK	Lindstrand LBL Newspaper SS balloon	H. Holmqvist
	G-BVGO	Denney Kitfox Mk 4-1200	P. Madden
	G-BVGP	Bücker Bü 133 Jungmeister (U-95)	T. A. Bechtolsheimer
	G-BVGT	Auster J/1 (modified)	M. Flint
	G-BVGW	Luscombe 8A Silvaire	H. E. Simons
	G-BVGY	Luscombe 8E Silvaire	G. H. Matthews
	G-BVGZ	Fokker Dr.1 (replica) (152/17)	R. A. Fleming
	G-BVHC	Grob G.115D-2 Heron	R. A. Gregory
	G-BVHD	Grob G.115D-2 Heron	J. A. Woodcock
	G-BVHE	Grob G.115D-2 Heron	Tayside Aviation Ltd
	G-BVHG	Grob G.115D-2 Heron	KFZ Kogl Alexander EU/Austria
	G-BVHI	Rans S.10 Sakota	J. D. Amos
	G-BVHK	Cameron V-77 balloon	C. M. Duggan & M. J. Axtell
	G-BVHL	Nicollier HN.700 Menestrel II	G. W. Lynch
	G-BVHO	Cameron V-90 balloon	N. W. B. Bews
	G-BVHR	Cameron V-90 balloon	G. P. Walton
	G-BVHS	Murphy Rebel	S. T. Raby
	G-BVHV	Cameron N-105 balloon	K. F. Lowry
	G-BVIE	PA-18 Super Cub 95 (modified)	J. C. Best (G-CLIK/G-BLMB)
	G-BVIK	Maule MXT-7-180 Star Rocket	Graveley Flying Group
	G-BVIS	Brügger MB.2 Colibri	M. Shaw
	G-BVIV	Light Aero Avid Speedwing	S. Styles
	G-BVIW	PA-18-Super Cub 150	I. H. Logan
	G-BVIZ	Shaw Europa	M. Dovey
	G-BVJK	Glaser-Dirks DG.800A	P. S. Birkett
	G-BVJT	Cessna F.406	Nor Leasing
	G-BVJU	Evans VP-1	BVJU Flying Club & Associates
	G-BVJX	Marquart MA.5 Charger	Lancashire Barnstormers Group
	G-BVKK	Slingsby T.61F Venture T.2	Buckminster Gliding Club Ltd
	G-BVKM	Rutan Vari-Eze	J. P. G. Lindquist/Switzerland
	G-BVKU	Slingsby T.61F Venture T.2	G-BVKU Syndicate
	G-BVKV	Cameron N-90 balloon	I. R. Jones
	G-BVLA	Lancair 320	K. W. Scrivens
	G-BVLD	Campbell Cricket (replica)	S. J. Smith
	G-BVLF	CFM Starstreak Shadow SS-D	J. C. Pratelli
	G-BVLG	AS.355F1 Twin Squirrel	PLM Dollar Group PLC
	G-BVLN	Aero Designs Pulsar XP	D. A. Campbell
	G-BVLR	Van's RV-4	RV4 Group
	G-BVLT	Bellanca 7GCBC Citabria	Slade Associates
	G-BVLU	D.31 Turbulent	C. D. Bancroft
	G-BVLV	Shaw Europa	C. R. Stone
	G-BVLX	Slingsby T.61F Venture T.2	Wessex Ventures 2016
	G-BVMA	Beech 200 Super King Air	D. T. A. Rees (G-VPLC)
	G-BVMM	Robin HR.200/100	Gift of Flight Ltd
	G-BVMN	Ken Brock KB-2 gyroplane	G-BVMN Group
	G-BVMR	Cameron V-90 balloon	J. Greatrix
	G-BVNG	DH.60G-III Moth Major	P. & G. Groves
	G-BVNI	Taylor JT-2 Titch	P. M. Jones
	G-BVNS	PA-28-181 Archer II	SAF Prestwick Ltd
	G-BVNU	FLS Aerospace Sprint Club	N. M. Rosser
	G-BVNY	Rans S.7 Courier	S. Hazleden
	G-BVOH	Campbell Cricket (replica)	A. Kitson
	G-BVOI	Rans S.6-116 Coyote II	S. J. Taft
	G-BVOP	Cameron N-90 balloon	M. A. Stelling
	G-BVOR	CFM Streak Shadow	J. M. Chandler
	G-BVOS	Shaw Europa	R. M. Peach

Reg	Type	Owner or Operator	Notes
G-BVOY	Rotorway Executive 90	C. O'Neill	
G-BVOZ	Colt 56A balloon	G. G. Scaife	
G-BVPA	Thunder Ax8-105 S2 balloon	B. J. B. Smith	
G-BVPD	CASA 1-131E Jungmann Series 2000	I. V. Staines	
G-BVPM	Evans VP-2 Coupé	P. Marigold	
G-BVPS	Jodel D.112	P. J. Brookman	
G-BVPV	Lindstrand LBL-77B balloon	I. W. Robertshaw	
G-BVPW	Rans S.6-116 Coyote II	T. B. Woolley	
G-BVPX	Bensen B.8 (modified) Tyro Gyro	A. W. Harvey	
G-BVPY	CFM Streak Shadow	A. J. Grant	
G-BVRA	Shaw Europa	D. F. Keedy	
G-BVRH	Taylorcraft BL-65	M. J. Kirk	
G-BVRV	Van's RV-4	A. Troughton	
G-BVRZ	PA-18 Super Cub 95	R. W. Davison	
G-BVSB	TEAM mini-MAX	D. G. Palmer	
G-BVSF	Aero Designs Pulsar	R. J. & J. A. Freestone	
G-BVSG	BN-2B-20 Islander	Britten-Norman Ltd	
G-BVSK	BN-2T Turbine Islander	G. Cormack	
G-BVSM	RAF2000	A van Rooijen/Belgium	
G-BVSP	P.84 Jet Provost T.3A	Weald Aviation Services Ltd	
G-BVSS	Jodel D.150	M. F. R. B. Collett & M. S. C. Ball	
G-BVST	Jodel D.150	A. Shipp	
G-BVSX	TEAM mini-MAX 91	J. A. Sephton	
G-BVSZ	Pitts S-1E (S) Special	H. J. Morton	
G-BVTC	P.84 Jet Provost T.5A (XW333)	Global Aviation Ltd	
G-BVTL	Colt 31A balloon	A. Lindsay	
G-BVTM	Cessna F.152 II	RAF Halton Aeroplane Club (G-WACS)	
G-BVTV	Rotorway Executive 90	P. M. Scheiwiller	
G-BVTW	Aero Designs Pulsar	R. J. Panther	
G-BVTX	DHC.1 Chipmunk 22A (WP809)	N. P. Woods	
G-BVUA	Cameron O-105 balloon	Wickers World Ltd	
G-BVUG	Betts TB.1 (Stampe SV.4C)	H. F. Fekete (G-BEUS)	
G-BVUH	Thunder Ax6-65B balloon	H. J. M. Lacoste	
G-BVUK	Cameron V-77 balloon	H. G. Griffiths & W. A. Steel	
G-BVUM	Rans S.6-116 Coyote II	M. A. Abbott	
G-BVUN	Van's RV-4	D. J. Harvey	
G-BVUT	Evans VP-1 Srs. 2	M. J. Barnett	
G-BVUV	Shaw Europa	R. J. Mills	
G-BVUZ	Cessna 120	A. Fairfield	
G-BVVB	Carlson Sparrow II	L. M. McCullen	
G-BVVE	Jodel D.112	M. Balls	
G-BVVG	Nanchang CJ-6A (68)	P. C. Woolley	
G-BVVH	Shaw Europa	M. Giudici	
G-BVVI	Hawker Audax I (K5600)	Aero Vintage Ltd	
G-BVVK	DHC.6 Twin Otter 310	Loganair Ltd	
G-BVVL	EAA Acro Sport II	G-BVVL Syndicate	
G-BVVM	Zenair CH.601HD	T. H. Jones	
G-BVVN	Brügger MB.2 Colibri	N. F. Andrews	
G-BVVO	Yakovlev Yak-50	R. Ellingworth	
G-BVVP	Shaw Europa	S. D. R. Dray	
G-BVVR	Stits SA-3A Playboy	J. H. Prendergast	
G-BVVS	Van's RV-4	E. G. & N. S. C. English	
G-BVVU	Lindstrand LBL Four SS balloon	Magical Adventures Ltd/USA	
G-BVVW	Yakovlev Yak-52	M. Blackman	
G-BVVZ	Corby CJ-1 Starlet	P. V. Flack	
G-BVWB	Thunder Ax8-90 S2 balloon	D. W. Torrington	
G-BVWI	Cameron light bulb SS balloon	M. E. White	
G-BVWL	Air & Space 18A Gyroplane ★	The Helicopter Museum/Weston-super-Mare	
G-BVWM	Shaw Europa	A. Head	
G-BVWW	Lindstrand LBL-90A balloon	J. D. A. Shields	
G-BVWZ	PA-32-301 Saratoga	Ambar Kelly Ltd	
G-BVXA	Cameron N-105 balloon	R. E. Jones	
G-BVXC	EE Canberra B.6 (WT333) ★	Classic Aviation Projects Ltd/Bruntingthorpe	
G-BVXD	Cameron O-84 balloon	C. J. Dunkley	
G-BVXK	Yakovlev Yak-52 (26 grey)	A. R. Dent	
G-BVYG	CEA DR.300/180	PA Technologies Ltd	
G-BVYM	CEA DR.300/180	London Gliding Club (Pty) Ltd	
G-BVYO	Robin R.2160 Alpha Sport	Insight Machines	
G-BVYP	PA-25 Pawnee 235B	Bidford Gliding & Flying Club Ltd	
G-BVYX	Light Aero Avid Speedwing Mk 4	B. Howlett & A. J. L. Eves	
G-BVYY	Pietenpol Air Camper	T. F. Harrison	

Notes	Reg	Type	Owner or Operator
	G-BVZJ	Rand-Robinson KR-2	G. M. Rundle
	G-BVZN	Cameron C-80 balloon	S. J. Clarke
	G-BVZO	Rans S.6-116 Coyote II	P. J. Brion
	G-BVZR	Zenair CH.601HD	R. A. Perkins
	G-BVZT	Lindstrand LBL-90A balloon	J. Edwards
	G-BVZY	Mooney M.20R Ovation	DK Mecatronic-Engineering Innovation Ltd
	G-BVZZ	DHC.1 Chipmunk 22 (WP795)	Portsmouth Naval Gliding Centre
	G-BWAB	Jodel D.14	R. G. Fairall
	G-BWAC	Waco YKS-7	D. N. Peters
	G-BWAD	RAF 2000GT gyroplane	B. J. Payne
	G-BWAF	Hawker Hunter F.6A (XG160:U) ★	Bournemouth Aviation Museum/Bournemouth
	G-BWAH	Montgomerie-Bensen B.8MR	S. Broszek
	G-BWAI	CFM Streak Shadow	S. J. Smith
	G-BWAN	Cameron N-77 balloon	I. Chadwick
	G-BWAO	Cameron C-80 balloon	R. D. Allen
	G-BWAP	FRED Srs 3	G. A. Shepherd
	G-BWAR	Denney Kitfox Mk 3	M. J. Downes
	G-BWAT	Pietenpol Air Camper	P. W. Aitchison
	G-BWAU	Cameron V-90 balloon	K. M. & A. M. F. Hall
	G-BWAW	Lindstrand LBL-77A balloon	D. Bareford
	G-BWBI	Taylorcraft F-22A	M. W. Cave
	G-BWBO	Lindstrand LBL-77A balloon	T. J. Orchard
	G-BWBZ	ARV-1 Super 2	M. P. Holdstock
	G-BWCA	CFM Streak Shadow	I. C. Pearson
	G-BWCK	Everett Srs 2 gyroplane	N. M. Gent
	G-BWCT	Tipsy T.66 Nipper 1	M. J. Davis
	G-BWCY	Murphy Rebel	A. J. Glading
	G-BWDH	Cameron N-105 balloon	M. W. Shepherd
	G-BWDO	Sikorsky S-76B	Von Essen Aviation Ltd
	G-BWDP	Shaw Europa	S. Attubato
	G-BWDS	P.84 Jet Provost T.3A (XM424)	AT Aviation Sales Ltd, D. C. Cooper & J. A. Gibson
	G-BWDV	Schweizer 269C	Cirrus UK Training Ltd
	G-BWDX	Shaw Europa	C. J. Sweenie
	G-BWEB	P.84 Jet Provost T.5A (XW422:3)	Flight Test Support
	G-BWEE	Cameron V-42 balloon	J. A. Hibberd/Netherlands
	G-BWEF	SNCAN Stampe SV.4C	Acebell G-BWEF Syndicate (G-BOVL)
	G-BWEG	Shaw Europa	J. W. Kelly
	G-BWEM	VS.358 Seafire L.IIIC (RX168)	Aircraft Spares & Materials Ltd
	G-BWEN	Macair Merlin GT	D. A. Hill
	G-BWEW	Cameron N-105 balloon	Unipart Balloon Club
	G-BWEY	Bensen B.8	F. G. Shepherd
	G-BWEZ	Piper J-3C-65 Cub (436021)	Edenfield Aero
	G-BWFG	Robin HR.200/120B	T. J. Lowe
	G-BWFH	Shaw Europa	G. M. Quinn
	G-BWFJ	Evans VP-1	G. Robson
	G-BWFK	Lindstrand LBL-77A balloon	C. J. Wootton & J. S. Russon
	G-BWFL	Cessna 500 Citation 1	Corbally Group (Aviation) Ltd (G-JTNC/G-OEJA)
	G-BWFM	Yakovlev Yak-50	Fox Mike Group
	G-BWFN	Hapi Cygnet SF-2A	I. P. Manley
	G-BWFO	Colomban MC.15 Cri-Cri	K. D. & C. S. Rhodes
	G-BWFX	Shaw Europa	T. P. R. Pickford
	G-BWFZ	Murphy Rebel	S. Irving (G-SAVS)
	G-BWGF	P.84 Jet Provost T.5A (XW325)	G-JPVA Ltd
	G-BWGJ	Chilton DW.1A	T. J. Harrison
	G-BWGL	Hawker Hunter T.8C (N-321)	Stichting Hawker Hunter Foundation/Netherlands
	G-BWGO	Slingsby T.67M Firefly 200	R. Gray
	G-BWGY	HOAC Katana DV.20	Gemstone Aviation Ltd
	G-BWHA	Hawker Hurricane IIB (Z5252)	Historic Flying Ltd
	G-BWHD	Lindstrand LBL-31A balloon	M. R. Noyce & R. P. E. Phillips
	G-BWHI	DHC.1 Chipmunk 22A (WK624)	E. H. N. M. Clare
	G-BWHK	Rans S.6-116 Coyote II	S. J. Wakeling
	G-BWHP	CASA 1.131E Jungmann (S4+A07)	J. F. Hopkins
	G-BWHR	Tipsy Nipper T.66 Srs 1	L. R. Marnef
	G-BWHS	RAF 2000 gyroplane	V. G. Freke
	G-BWHU	Westland Scout AH.1 (XR595)	Dragonfly Aviation
	G-BWID	D.31 Turbulent	T. W. J. Carnall
	G-BWII	Cessna 150G	S. Sabau & V. A. Aldea (G-BSKB)

Reg	Type	Owner or Operator	Notes
G-BWIJ	Shaw Europa	Condor Aviation International Ltd	
G-BWIL	Rans S-10	G. Forde	
G-BWIP	Cameron N-90 balloon	O. J. Evans	
G-BWIV	Shaw Europa	T. G. Ledbury	
G-BWIX	Sky 120-24 balloon	J. M. Percival	
G-BWIZ	QAC Quickie Tri-Q 200	M. C. Davies	
G-BWJH	Shaw Europa	C. H. Nisbet	
G-BWJM	Bristol M.1C (replica) (C4918)	The Shuttleworth Collection	
G-BWKT	Stephens Akro Laser	T. A. Cleaver	
G-BWKW	Thunder Ax8-90 balloon	Gone With The Wind Ltd	
G-BWKZ	Lindstrand LBL-77A balloon	J. H. Dobson	
G-BWLD	Cameron O-120 balloon	D. Pedri/Italy	
G-BWLF	Cessna 404	Reconnaisance Ventures Ltd (G-BNXS)	
G-BWLJ	Taylorcraft DCO-65 (42-35870/129)	B. J. Robe	
G-BWLL	Murphy Rebel	F. W. Parker & A. F. Ratcliffe	
G-BWLM	Sky 65-24 balloon	W. J. Brogan	
G-BWLW	Avid Speed Wing Mk.4	F. E. Tofield (G-XXRG)	
G-BWLY	Rotorway Executive 90	P. W. & I. P. Bewley	
G-BWMB	Jodel D.119	C. Hughes	
G-BWMC	Cessna 182P	Aeroplane Views	
G-BWMH	Lindstrand LBL-77B balloon	W. C. Wood	
G-BWMI	PA-28RT-201T Turbo Arrow IV	R. W. Pascoe	
G-BWMJ	Nieuport 17/2B (replica) (N1977:8)	J. P. Gilbert	
G-BWMK	DH.82A Tiger Moth (T8191)	K. F. Crumplin	
G-BWMN	Rans S.7 Courier	D. C. Stokes	
G-BWMO	Oldfield Baby Lakes	D. Maddocks (G-CIII)	
G-BWMS	DH.82A Tiger Moth	Stichting Vroege Vogels/Netherlands	
G-BWMU	Cameron 105 Monster Truck SS balloon	Magical Adventures Ltd/Canada	
G-BWMX	DHC.1 Chipmunk 22 (WG407:67)	407th Flying Group	
G-BWMY	Cameron Bradford & Bingley SS balloon	Magical Adventures Ltd/USA	
G-BWNB	Cessna 152 II	South Warwickshire School of Flying Ltd	
G-BWNC	Cessna 152 II	South Warwickshire School of Flying Ltd	
G-BWND	Cessna 152 II	South Warwickshire School of Flying Ltd	
G-BWNI	PA-24 Comanche 180	B. V. & J. B. Haslam	
G-BWNJ	Hughes 269C	L. R. Fenwick	
G-BWNK	D,H,C,1 Chipmunk 22 (WD390)	WD390 Group	
G-BWNM	PA-28R Cherokee Arrow 180	M. & R. C. Ramnial	
G-BWNO	Cameron O-90 balloon	T. Knight	
G-BWNS	Cameron O-90 balloon	I. C. Steward	
G-BWNT	DHC.1 Chipmunk 22 (WP901)	J. W. F. Pijnenburg	
G-BWNU	PA-38-112 Tomahawk	Kemble Aero Club Ltd	
G-BWNY	Aeromot AMT-200 Super Ximango	Forbes Insurance Ltd	
G-BWOF	BAC Jet Provost T.5	P. H. Meeson	
G-BWOH	PA-28-161 Cadet	Redhill Air Services Ltd	
G-BWOI	PA-28-161 Cadet	N. Ludlow	
G-BWOK	Lindstrand LBL-105G balloon	C. J. Sanger-Davies	
G-BWOR	PA-18 Super Cub 135	S. S. & R. D. Houston	
G-BWOT	P.84 Jet Provost T.3A (XN459)	Haye House Aviation Ltd	
G-BWOV	Enstrom F-28A	P. A. Goss	
G-BWOY	Sky 31-24 balloon	C. Wolstenholme	
G-BWPE	Murphy Renegade Spirit UK	J. Hatswell/France	
G-BWPH	PA-28-181 Archer II	D. R. Lewis	
G-BWPJ	Steen Skybolt	A. J. Hurran	
G-BWPP	Sky 105-24 balloon	Sarnia Balloon Group	
G-BWPS	CFM Streak Shadow SA	P. J. Mogg	
G-BWRA	Sopwith LC-1T Triplane (replica) (N500)	J. G. Brander (G-PENY)	
G-BWRC	Light Aero Avid Speedwing	R. A. Stephens	
G-BWRO	Europa	R. A. Darley	
G-BWRR	Cessna 182Q	A. & R. Reid	
G-BWRS	SNCAN Stampe SV.4C	G. P. J. M. Valvekens/Belgium	
G-BWSB	Lindstrand LBL-105A balloon	R. Calvert-Fisher	
G-BWSD	Campbell Cricket	R. F. G. Moyle	
G-BWSG	P.84 Jet Provost T.5 (XW324/K)	J. Bell	
G-BWSH	P.84 Jet Provost T.3A (XN498)	Global Aviation Ltd	
G-BWSI	Squarecraft Cavalier SA.102-5	M. W. Place	
G-BWSJ	Denney Kitfox Mk 3	A. J. Calvert	
G-BWSL	Sky 77-24 balloon	F9 (Holdings) Ltd	
G-BWSN	Denney Kitfox Mk 3	R. J. Mitchell	
G-BWSU	Cameron N-105 balloon	A. M. Marten	
G-BWSV	Yakovlev Yak-52 (43)	M. W. Fitch	
G-BWTE	Cameron O-140 balloon	T. G. Church	

81

Notes	Reg	Type	Owner or Operator
	G-BWTG	DHC.1 Chipmunk 22 (WB671:910)	R. G. T. de Man/Netherlands
	G-BWTJ	Cameron V-77 balloon	A. J. Montgomery
	G-BWTK	RAF 2000 GTX-SE gyroplane	L. P. Rolfe
	G-BWTO	DHC.1 Chipmunk 22 (WP984)	Skycraft Services Ltd
	G-BWTW	Mooney M.20C	T. J. Berry
	G-BWUH	PA-28-181 Archer III	Phoenix Aviation
	G-BWUJ	Rotorway Executive 162F	Southern Helicopters Ltd
	G-BWUN	DHC.1 Chipmunk 22 (WD310)	E. H. W. Moore
	G-BWUP	Shaw Europa	V. Goddard
	G-BWUS	Sky 65-24 balloon	N. A. P. Bates
	G-BWUT	DHC.1 Chipmunk 22 (WZ879)	A. J. Herbert
	G-BWUU	Cameron N-90 balloon	M. T. Evans
	G-BWUV	DHC.1 Chipmunk 22A (WK640)	A. C. Darby
	G-BWVB	Pietenpol Air Camper	G. Oldfield & A. T. Marshall
	G-BWVF	Pietenpol Air Camper	N. Clark
	G-BWVI	Stern ST.80	J. Lynden
	G-BWVR	Yakovlev Yak-52 (52 yellow)	I. Parkinson
	G-BWVS	Shaw Europa	D. R. Bishop
	G-BWVT	DHA.82A Tiger Moth	N. L. MacKaness
	G-BWVU	Cameron O-90 balloon	J. Atkinson
	G-BWVY	DHC.1 Chipmunk 22 (WP896)	N. Gardner
	G-BWVZ	DHC.1 Chipmunk 22A (WK590)	D. Campion/Belgium
	G-BWWA	Ultravia Pelican Club GS	J. S. Aplin
	G-BWWB	Shaw Europa	WB Group
	G-BWWF	Cessna 185A	T. N. Bartlett & S. M. C. Harvey
	G-BWWK	Hawker Nimrod I (S1581)	Patina Ltd
	G-BWWL	Colt Flying Egg SS balloon	Magical Adventures Ltd/USA
	G-BWWN	Isaacs Fury II (K8303:D)	J. S. Marten-Hale
	G-BWWU	PA-22 Tri-Pacer 150	K. M. Bowen
	G-BWWW	BAe Jetstream 3102	British Aerospace PLC
	G-BWWX	Yakovlev Yak-50	D. P. McCoy
	G-BWWY	Lindstrand LBL-105A balloon	MSJ Ballooning
	G-BWXA	Slingsby T.67M Firefly 260	Power Aerobatics Ltd
	G-BWXB	Slingsby T.67M Firefly 260	Power Aerobatics Ltd
	G-BWXF	Slingsby T.67M Firefly 260	L3 CTS Airline and Academy Training Ltd
	G-BWXJ	Slingsby T.67M Firefly 260	D. I. Stanbridge
	G-BWXS	Slingsby T.67M Firefly 260	Power Aerobatics Ltd
	G-BWXT	Slingsby T.67M Firefly 260	Cranfield University
	G-BWXV	Slingsby T.67M Firefly 260	Fastnet Jet Alliance Ltd
	G-BWYB	PA-28 Cherokee 160	A. J. Peters
	G-BWYD	Europa	D. L. Morris
	G-BWYK	Yakovlev Yak-50	A. Marangoni
	G-BWYN	Cameron O-77 balloon	A. M. Daniels (G-ODER)
	G-BWYO	Sequoia F.8L Falco	S. G. Roux
	G-BWYR	Rans S.6-116 Coyote II	D. A. Lord
	G-BWYU	Sky 120-24 balloon	Aerosauras Balloons Ltd
	G-BWZA	Shaw Europa	T. G. Cowlishaw
	G-BWZG	Robin R.2160	Sherburn Aero Club Ltd
	G-BWZY	Hughes 269A	J. A. Maginn (G-FSDT)
	G-BXAB	PA-28-161 Warrior II	TG Aviation Ltd (G-BTGK)
	G-BXAC	RAF 2000 GTX-SE gyroplane	J. A. Robinson
	G-BXAF	Pitts S-1D Special	N. J. Watson
	G-BXAJ	Lindstrand LBL-14A balloon	Oscair Project AB/Sweden
	G-BXAK	Yakovlev Yak-52 (44 black)	A. M. Holman-West
	G-BXAN	Scheibe SF-25C Falke	C. Falke Syndicate
	G-BXAO	Avtech Jabiru SK	P. J. Thompson
	G-BXAU	Pitts S-1 Special	L. Westnage
	G-BXAX	Cameron N-77 balloon ★	Balloon Preservation Group
	G-BXAY	Bell 206B JetRanger 3	Paddy Aviation Ltd
	G-BXBB	PA-20 Pacer 150	M. E. R. Coghlan
	G-BXBK	Avions Mudry CAP-10B	S. Skipworth
	G-BXBL	Lindstrand LBL-240A balloon	J. Fenton
	G-BXBU	Avions Mudry CAP-10B	J. Mann
	G-BXBZ	PZL-104 Wilga 80	J. H. Sandham Aviation
	G-BXCA	Hapi Cygnet SF-2A	J. D. C. Henslow
	G-BXCC	PA-28-201T Turbo Dakota	Greer Aviation Ltd
	G-BXCD	TEAM mini-MAX 91A	A. Maltby
	G-BXCG	Jodel DR.250/160	P.G. Morris
	G-BXCJ	Campbell Cricket (replica)	A. G. Peel
	G-BXCO	Colt 120A balloon	J. R. Lawson

Reg	Type	Owner or Operator	Notes
G-BXCT	DHC.1 Chipmunk 22 (WB697)	Wickenby Aviation	
G-BXCU	Rans S.6-116 Coyote II	T. C. Garner	
G-BXCV	DHC.1 Chipmunk 22 (WP929)	Ardmore Aviation Services Ltd/Hong Kong	
G-BXCW	Denney Kitfox Mk 3	D. R. Piercy	
G-BXDA	DHC.1 Chipmunk 22 (WP860)	D. P. Curtis	
G-BXDB	Cessna U.206F	D. A. Howard (G-BMNZ)	
G-BXDE	RAF 2000GTX-SE gyroplane	V. G. Freke	
G-BXDG	DHC.1 Chipmunk 22 (WK630)	Felthorpe Flying Group	
G-BXDH	DHC.1 Chipmunk 22 (WD331)	Royal Aircraft Establishment Aero Club Ltd	
G-BXDI	DHC.1 Chipmunk 22 (WD373)	A. M. Dinnie	
G-BXDN	DHC.1 Chipmunk 22 (WK609)	W. D. Lowe, G. James & L. A. Edwards	
G-BXDO	Rutan Cozy	Cozy Group	
G-BXDR	Lindstrand LBL-77A balloon	A. J. & A. R. Brown	
G-BXDS	Bell 206B JetRanger III	Aerospeed Limited (G-TAMF/G-OVBJ)	
G-BXDU	Aero Designs Pulsar	A. J. Price	
G-BXDV	Sky 105-24 balloon	N. A. Carr	
G-BXDY	Shaw Europa	S. Attubato & D. G. Watts	
G-BXDZ	Lindstrand LBL-105A balloon	D. J. & A. D. Sutcliffe	
G-BXEC	DHC.1 Chipmunk 22 (WK633)	A. J. Robinson & M. J. Miller	
G-BXEF	Europa	C. Busuttil-Reynard	
G-BXEJ	VPM M-16 Tandem Trainer	AES Radionic Surveillance Systems	
G-BXEN	Cameron N-105 balloon	E. Ghio/Italy	
G-BXES	P.66 Pembroke C.1 (XL954)	C. Keane	
G-BXEX	PA-28-181 Archer II	Nottingham Archer Aviators	
G-BXEZ	Cessna 182P	Forhawk Ltd	
G-BXFB	Pitts S-1 Special	J. F. Dowe	
G-BXFC	Jodel D.18	M. Godbold	
G-BXFE	Avions Mudry CAP-10B	Avion Aerobatic Ltd	
G-BXFG	Shaw Europa	A. Rawicz-Szczerbo	
G-BXFK	CFM Streak Shadow	P. D. Curtis	
G-BXFN	Colt 77A balloon	R. S. McDonald	
G-BXGA	AS.350B2 Ecureuil	PLM Dollar Group Ltd	
G-BXGG	Shaw Europa	D. J. Joyce	
G-BXGL	DHC.1 Chipmunk 22	GL Group	
G-BXGM	DHC.1 Chipmunk 22 (WP928:D)	Skyblue Aero Services Ltd	
G-BXGO	DHC.1 Chipmunk 22 (WB654:U)	B. C. Griffiths & A. J. Gurr	
G-BXGP	DHC.1 Chipmunk 22 (WZ882)	V. Dean	
G-BXGS	RAF 2000 gyroplane	D. W. Howell	
G-BXGT	I.I.I. Sky Arrow 650T	J. S. C. Goodale	
G-BXGV	Cessna 172R	G-BXGV Skyhawk Group	
G-BXGX	DHC.1 Chipmunk 22 (WK586:V)	The Real Flying Co.Ltd	
G-BXGY	Cameron V-65 balloon	Dante Balloon Group	
G-BXGZ	Stemme S.10V	G. S. Craven & A. J. Garner	
G-BXHA	DHC.1 Chipmunk 22 (WP925:C)	Shipping & Airlines Ltd (G-HVII)	
G-BXHF	DHC.1 Chipmunk 22 (WP930:J)	Hotel Fox Syndicate	
G-BXHH	AA-5A Cheetah	K. Ziems & C. Anhalt	
G-BXHJ	Hapi Cygnet SF-2A	I. J. Smith	
G-BXHL	Sky 77-24 balloon	C. Timbrell	
G-BXHO	Lindstrand Telewest Sphere SS balloon	Magical Adventures Ltd	
G-BXHR	Stemme S.10V	J. H. Rutherford	
G-BXHT	Bushby-Long Midget Mustang	K. Manley	
G-BXHU	Campbell Cricket Mk 6	B. F. Pearson	
G-BXHY	Shaw Europa	A. L. Thorne	
G-BXIA	DHC.1 Chipmunk 22 (WB615)	WB615 Group	
G-BXIE	Colt 77B balloon	I. R. Warrington	
G-BXIF	PA-28-161 Warrior II	Piper Flight Ltd	
G-BXIG	Zenair CH.701 STOL	S. Ingram	
G-BXIH	Sky 200-24 balloon	Kent Ballooning	
G-BXII	Shaw Europa	D. A. McFadyean	
G-BXIJ	Shaw Europa	P. N. Birch	
G-BXIM	DHC.1 Chipmunk 22 (WK512)	A. B. Ashcroft & P. R. Joshua	
G-BXIT	Zebedee V-31 balloon	Zebedee Balloon Service Ltd	
G-BXIW	Sky 105-24 balloon	A. G. A. Barclay-Faulkner	
G-BXIX	VPM M-16 Tandem Trainer	P. P. Willmott	
G-BXIY	Blake Bluetit (BAPC37)	M. J. Aubrey	
G-BXIZ	Lindstrand LBL-31A balloon	David P Hopkins	
G-BXJB	Yakovlev Yak-52	Bulldog Aviation Ltd	
G-BXJD	PA-28-180C Cherokee	S. Atherton	
G-BXJH	Cameron N-42 balloon	D. M. Hoddinott	
G-BXJO	Cameron O-90 balloon	Dragon Balloon Co Ltd	
G-BXJT	Sky 90-24 balloon	J. G. O'Connell	

Notes	Reg	Type	Owner or Operator
	G-BXJY	Van's RV-6	J. P. Kynaston
	G-BXJZ	Cameron C-60 balloon	N. J. & S. J. Bettin
	G-BXKF	Hawker Hunter T.7(XL577/V)	R. F. Harvey
	G-BXKL	Bell 206B JetRanger 3	Swattons Aviation Ltd
	G-BXKM	RAF 2000 GTX-SE gyroplane	E. Mangles
	G-BXKU	Colt AS-120 Mk II airship	D. C. Chipping/Portugal
	G-BXKW	Slingsby T.67M Firefly 200 (HKG-13)	J-F Jansen
	G-BXKX	Auster V	J. A. Sephton
	G-BXLF	Lindstrand LBL-90A balloon	S. McMahon & J. Edwards
	G-BXLG	Cameron C-80 balloon	S. M. Anthony
	G-BXLK	Shaw Europa	R. J. Sheridan
	G-BXLN	Fournier RF-4D	P. W. Cooper
	G-BXLO	P.84 Jet Provost T.4 (XR673/L)	Century Aviation Ltd
	G-BXLS	PZL-110 Koliber 160A	P. R. Powell
	G-BXLT	SOCATA TB200 Tobago XL	C., G. & J. Fisher & D. Fitton
	G-BXLW	Enstrom F.28F	N. R. H. Briggs
	G-BXLY	PA-28-151 Warrior	North East Flight Academy Ltd (G-WATZ)
	G-BXMV	Scheibe SF.25C Falke 1700	K. E. Ballington
	G-BXMX	Currie Wot	J. M. Chapman
	G-BXMY	Hughes 269C	K. & M. Pinfold
	G-BXNC	Shaw Europa	J. K. Cantwell
	G-BXNN	DHC.1 Chipmunk 22 (WP983:B)	E. N. Skinner
	G-BXOA	Robinson R22 Beta	Swift Helicopter Services Ltd
	G-BXOC	Evans VP-2	Condor Aviation International Ltd
	G-BXOF	Diamond Katana DA20-A1	Aircraft Engineers Ltd
	G-BXOI	Cessna 172R	E. J. Watts
	G-BXOJ	PA-28-161 Warrior III	Tayside Aviation Ltd
	G-BXOT	Cameron C-70 balloon	Dante Balloon Group
	G-BXOU	CEA DR.360	J. A. Lofthouse
	G-BXOX	AA-5A Cheetah	R. L. Carter & P. J. Large
	G-BXOY	QAC Quickie Q.235	C. C. Clapham
	G-BXOZ	PA-28-181 Archer II	Spritetone Ltd
	G-BXPC	Diamond Katana DA20-A1	D. J. & S. N. Taplin
	G-BXPD	Diamond Katana DA20-A1	Cubair Flight Training Ltd
	G-BXPI	Van's RV-4	B. M. Diggins
	G-BXPP	Sky 90-24 balloon	S. A. Nother
	G-BXPT	Ultramagic H-77 balloon	L. P. Hooper
	G-BXRA	Avions Mudry CAP-10B	Cole Aviation Ltd
	G-BXRB	Avions Mudry CAP-10B	T. T. Duhig
	G-BXRC	Avions Mudry CAP-10B	Group Alpha
	G-BXRF	CP.1310-C3 Super Emeraude	D. T. Gethin
	G-BXRO	Cessna U.206G	Wild Geese Parachute Ltd
	G-BXRS	Westland Scout AH.1 (XW613)	C. J. Marsden
	G-BXRT	Robin DR.400-180	T. P. Usborne
	G-BXRV	Van's RV-4	Cleeve Flying Grouip
	G-BXRY	Bell 206B JetRanger	Twylight Management Ltd
	G-BXRZ	Rans S.6-116 Coyote II	M. P. Hallam
	G-BXSC	Cameron C-80 balloon	V. A. B. Rolland
	G-BXSD	Cessna 172R	Warwickshire Leasing Ltd
	G-BXSE	Cessna 172R	MK Aero Support Ltd
	G-BXSG	Robinson R22 Beta II	F. W. Henderson
	G-BXSH	Glaser-Dirks DG.800B	D. Crimmins
	G-BXSI	Avtech Jabiru SK	P. F. Gandy
	G-BXSP	Grob G.109B	Deeside Grob Group
	G-BXST	PA-25 Pawnee 235C	Staffordshire Gliding Club Ltd
	G-BXSV	SNCAN Stampe SV.4C	M. A. Watts
	G-BXSX	Cameron V-77 balloon	D. R. Medcalf
	G-BXSY	Robinson R22 Beta	N. M. G. Pearson
	G-BXTD	Shaw Europa	P. G. Noonan
	G-BXTF	Cameron N-105 balloon	C. J. Dunkley
	G-BXTG	Cameron N-42 balloon	P. M. Watkins & S. M. M. Carden
	G-BXTI	Pitts S-1S Special	A. Schmer
	G-BXTO	Hindustan HAL-6 Pushpak	P. Q. Benn
	G-BXTS	Diamond DA20-A1 Katana	P. Webb
	G-BXTT	AA-5B Tiger	J. Ducray
	G-BXTW	PA-28-181 Archer III	Davison Plant Hire
	G-BXTY	PA-28-161 Cadet	Flew LLP
	G-BXTZ	PA-28-161 Cadet	Flew LLP
	G-BXUA	Campbell Cricket Mk.5	A. W. Harvey
	G-BXUC	Robinson R22 Beta	Swift Helicopter Services Ltd
	G-BXUF	Agusta-Bell 206B JetRanger 3	SJ Contracting Services Ltd

Reg	Type	Owner or Operator	Notes
G-BXUG	Lindstrand Baby Bel SS balloon	K-H. Gruenauer/Germany	
G-BXUH	Lindstrand LBL-31A balloon	R. A. Lovell	
G-BXUI	Glaser-Dirks DG.800B	J. Le Coyte	
G-BXUO	Lindstrand LBL-105A balloon	Lindstrand Technologies Ltd	
G-BXUU	Cameron V-65 balloon	M. & S. Mitchell	
G-BXUW	Cameron Colt 90A balloon	M. Sampson	
G-BXVA	SOCATA TB200 Tobago XL	M. Goehen	
G-BXVG	Sky 77-24 balloon	M. Wolf	
G-BXVK	Robin HR.200/120B	B. D. & J. Cottrell	
G-BXVO	Van's RV-6A	R. Marsden	
G-BXVP	Sky 31-24 balloon	S. I. Williams & H. G. Griffiths	
G-BXVR	Sky 90-24 balloon	P. Hegarty	
G-BXVS	Brügger MB.2 Colibri	G. T. Snoddon	
G-BXVU	PA-28-161 Warrior II	D. C. & M. Brooks	
G-BXVV	Cameron V-90 balloon	Adeilad Cladding	
G-BXVX	Rutan Cozy	G. E. Murray	
G-BXVY	Cessna 152	Stapleford Flying Club Ltd	
G-BXVZ	PZL TS-11 Iskra ★	RAF Manston History Museum/Manston	
G-BXWB	Robin HR.100/200B	Yorkshire Land Ltd	
G-BXWG	Sky 120-24 balloon	M. E. White	
G-BXWH	Denney Kitfox Mk.4-1200	M. G. Porter	
G-BXWK	Rans S.6-ESA Coyote II	M. Taylor	
G-BXWL	Sky 90-24 balloon	E. J. Briggs	
G-BXWO	PA-28-181 Archer II	A. J. Gomes	
G-BXWP	PA-32 Cherokee Six 300	Main Event Travel.com Ltd	
G-BXWR	CFM Streak Shadow	J. C. Pratelli (G-MZMI)	
G-BXWT	Van's RV-6	R. C. Owen	
G-BXWU	FLS Aerospace Sprint 160	Aeroelvia Ltd	
G-BXWV	FLS Aerospace Sprint 160	Aeroelvia Ltd	
G-BXWX	Sky 25-16 balloon	C. O'N. Davis	
G-BXXG	Cameron N-105 balloon	R. N. Simpkins	
G-BXXH	Hatz CB-1	R. D. Shingler	
G-BXXI	Grob G.109B	Malcolm Martin Flying Group	
G-BXXJ	Colt Flying Yacht SS balloon	Magical Adventures Ltd/USA	
G-BXXK	Cessna FR.172N	Flybai SL/Spain	
G-BXXL	Cameron N-105 balloon	C. J. Dunkley	
G-BXXO	Lindstrand LBL-90B balloon	G. P. Walton	
G-BXXP	Sky 77-24 balloon	T. R. Wood	
G-BXXR	Lovegrove BGL Four-Runner ★	Science Museum/Wroughton	
G-BXXT	Beech 76 Duchess	Air Navigation & Trading Co.Ltd	
G-BXXU	Colt 31A balloon	I. A. Jones	
G-BXXW	Enstrom F-28F	D. A. Marks (G-SCOX)	
G-BXYE	CP.301-C1 Emeraude	D. T. Gethin	
G-BXYF	Colt AS-105 GD airship	Alex Air Media Ltd	
G-BXYI	Cameron H-34 balloon	D. J. Groombridge	
G-BXYJ	Jodel DR.1050	G-BXYJ Group	
G-BXYM	PA-28 Cherokee 235	I. K. Burnett	
G-BXYO	PA-28RT-201 Arrow IV	D. Atherton	
G-BXYP	PA-28RT-201 Arrow IV	G. W. Eves	
G-BXYT	PA-28RT-201 Arrow IV	Wayne Poulter Enterprises Ltd	
G-BXZB	Nanchang CJ-6A (2632019)	R. Davy, J. L. Swallow & P. Lloyd	
G-BXZF	Lindstrand LBL-90A balloon	S. McGuigan	
G-BXZI	Lindstrand LBL-90A balloon	C. M. Morley	
G-BXZO	Pietenpol Air Camper	C. Dray	
G-BXZU	Micro Aviation Bantam B.22-S	M. E. Whapham & R. W. Hollamby	
G-BXZV	CFM Streak Shadow	D. J. S. Maclean	
G-BXZY	CFM Streak Shadow Srs DD	G. L. Turner	
G-BYAV	Taylor JT.1 Monoplane	A. F. S. & T. C. Caldecourt	
G-BYAW	Boeing 757-204ER	ACH Excalibur Ltd	
G-BYAY	Boeing 757-204ER	TUI Airways Ltd	
G-BYAZ	CFM Streak Shadow	A. G. Wright	
G-BYBD	Cessna F.172H	R. Macbeth-Seath (G-OBHX/G-AWMU)	
G-BYBF	Robin R.2160i	D. J. R. Lloyd-Evans	
G-BYBI	Bell 206B JetRanger 3	Castle Air Ltd	
G-BYBK	Murphy Rebel	P. R. Goodwill	
G-BYBL	Gardan GY-80 Horizon 160D	Bluewing Flying Group	
G-BYBM	Avtech Jabiru SK	D. O'Keefe & K. Davies	
G-BYBP	Cessna A.185F	G. M. S. Scott	
G-BYBS	Sky 80-16 balloon	B. K. Rippon	
G-BYBU	Renegade Spirit UK	M. E. Gilman	

Reg	Type	Owner or Operator
G-BYBV	Mainair Rapier	M. W. Robson
G-BYBY	Thorp T.18C Tiger	P. G. Mair
G-BYBZ	Jabiru SK	P. J. Whitehouse
G-BYCA	PA-28-140 Cherokee D	Go Fly Oxford Ltd
G-BYCJ	CFM Shadow Srs DD	P. W. Dunn, C. A. S. Powell & A. R. Vincent
G-BYCL	Raj Hamsa X'Air Jabiru(3)	A. A. Ross
G-BYCM	Rans S.6-ES Coyote II	E. W. McMullan
G-BYCN	Rans S.6-ES Coyote II	T. J. Croskery
G-BYCS	Jodel DR.1051	G. A. Stops
G-BYCT	Aero L-29A Delfin	G-BKOU/2 Ltd
G-BYCW	Mainair Blade 912	P. C. Watson
G-BYCX	Westland Wasp HAS.1	Military Vehicle Solutions Ltd
G-BYCY	Sky Arrow 650T	K. A. Daniels
G-BYCZ	Avtech Jabiru SK	T. Herbert
G-BYDB	Grob G.115B	A. R. Willis & A. P. Shoobert
G-BYDK	SNCAN Stampe SV.4C	Bianchi Aviation Film Services Ltd
G-BYDL	Hawker Hurricane IIB (Z5207)	K-F Grimminger
G-BYDV	Van's RV-6	B. F. Hill
G-BYDY	Beech 58 Baron	Pilot Services Flying Group Ltd
G-BYDZ	Pegasus Quantum 15-912	A. C. Hardiman
G-BYEA	Cessna 172P	M. Thambiah
G-BYEC	Glaser-Dirks DG.800B	P. D. Craven
G-BYEE	Mooney M.20K	G. Mexias
G-BYEH	CEA Jodel DR.250	J. D. Bally
G-BYEJ	Scheibe SF-28A Tandem Falke	D. Shrimpton
G-BYEK	Stoddard Hamilton Glastar	T. A. Reed
G-BYEL	Van's RV-6	D. Millar
G-BYEM	Cessna R.182 RG	Bickertons Aerodromes Ltd
G-BYEO	Zenair CH.601HDS	J. R. Clarke
G-BYER	Cameron C-80 balloon	J. M. Langley
G-BYEW	Pegasus Quantum 15-912	R. S. Matheson
G-BYEY	Lindstrand LBL-21 Silver Dream balloon	Oscair Project Ltd/Sweden
G-BYFA	Cessna F.152 II	Redhill Air Services Ltd (G-WACA)
G-BYFF	Pegasus Quantum 15-912	T. A. Willcox
G-BYFI	CFM Starstreak Shadow SA	J. A. Cook
G-BYFK	Cameron Printer 105 SS balloon	Mobberley Balloon Collection
G-BYFL	Diamond HK.36 TTS	Seahawk Gliding Club
G-BYFR	PA-32R-301 Saratoga II HP	Ebor Air Ltd
G-BYFT	Pietenpol Air Camper	G. Everett
G-BYFV	TEAM mini-MAX 91	W. E. Gillham
G-BYFX	Colt 77A balloon	Wye Valley Aviation Ltd
G-BYFY	Avions Mudry CAP-10B	R. N. Crosland
G-BYGB	Boeing 747-436	British Airways
G-BYGC	Boeing 747-436 ★	preserved
G-BYGE	Boeing 747-436	British Airways
G-BYHC	Cameron Z-90 balloon	T. J. Wilkinson
G-BYHE	Robinson R22 Beta	Helimech Ltd
G-BYHG	Dornier 328-100	Loganair Ltd
G-BYHH	PA-28-161 Warrior III	Stapleford Flying Club Ltd
G-BYHI	PA-28-161 Warrior II	T. W. & W. S. Gilbert
G-BYHJ	PA-28R-201 Arrow	White Waltham Airfield Ltd
G-BYHK	PA-28-181 Archer III	T-Air Services
G-BYHL	DHC.1 Chipmunk 22 (WG308)	I. D. Higgins
G-BYHO	Mainair Blade 912	I. E. Barry
G-BYHP	CEA DR.253B	HP Flying Group
G-BYHR	Pegasus Quantum 15-912	I. D. Chantler
G-BYHS	Mainair Blade 912	J. Flynn
G-BYHT	Robin DR.400/180R	Deeside Robin Group
G-BYHU	Cameron N-105 balloon	Ezmerelda Balloon Syndicate
G-BYHV	Raj Hamsa X'Air 582	C-More Flying School
G-BYHY	Cameron V-77 balloon	P. Spellward
G-BYIA	Avtech Jabiru SK	M. D. Doyle
G-BYID	Rans S.6-ES Coyote II	R. M. Watson
G-BYIE	Robinson R22 Beta II	P. M. Phillips
G-BYIJ	CASA 1.131E Jungmann 2000	R. N. Crosland
G-BYIK	Shaw Europa	D. Allen
G-BYIN	RAF 2000 gyroplane	C. J. Watkinson
G-BYIP	Aerotek Pitts S-2A Special	D. P. Heather-Hayes
G-BYIS	Pegasus Quantum 15-912	M. S. Ahmadu
G-BYIV	Cameron PM-80 balloon	A. Schneider/Germany
G-BYIW	Cameron PM-80 balloon	T. Gleixner/Switzerland

Reg	Type	Owner or Operator	Notes
G-BYIX	Cameron PM-80 balloon	A. Schneider/Germany	
G-BYJA	RAF 2000 GTX-SE	C. R. W. Lyne	
G-BYJB	Mainair Blade 912	R. G. Mason	
G-BYJD	Avtech Jabiru UL	CMR Flying Group	
G-BYJE	TEAM Mini-MAX 91	T. A. Willcox	
G-BYJF	Thorpe T.211	M. J. Newton	
G-BYJH	Grob G.109B	GJH Group	
G-BYJI	Shaw Europa	M. Gibson (G-ODTI)	
G-BYJK	Pegasus Quantum 15-912	S. J. Wilson	
G-BYJL	Aero Designs Pulsar	A. Young	
G-BYJN	Lindstrand LBL-105A balloon	B. Meeson	
G-BYJO	Rans S.6-ES Coyote II	K. Garnett	
G-BYJP	Aerotek Pitts S-1S Special	Eaglescott Pitts Group	
G-BYJR	Lindstrand LBL-77B balloon	B. M. Reed	
G-BYJS	SOCATA TB20 Trinidad	A. P. Bedford	
G-BYJT	Zenair CH.601HD	C. C. Beardmore	
G-BYJW	Cameron Sphere 105 balloon	Balleroy Developpement SAS	
G-BYJX	Cameron C-70 balloon	Mony Pizza SNC	
G-BYKA	Lindstrand LBL-69A balloon	B. Meeson	
G-BYKB	Rockwell Commander 114	D. L. Macdonald	
G-BYKC	Mainair Blade 912	A. Williams	
G-BYKD	Mainair Blade 912	D. C. Boyle	
G-BYKG	Pietenpol Air Camper	K. B. Hodge	
G-BYKL	PA-28-181 Archer II	Transport Command Ltd	
G-BYKP	PA-28R-201T Turbo Arrow IV	J. Cameron & R. Cromar	
G-BYKT	Pegasus Quantum 15-912	T. Lee	
G-BYKU	BFC Challenger II	P. A. Tarplee & L. G. G. Faulkner	
G-BYKX	Cameron N-90 balloon	C. O'N. Davis	
G-BYLB	D. H. 82A Tiger Moth	H. E. Snowling	
G-BYLC	Pegasus Quantum 15-912	G. P. D. Coan	
G-BYLD	Pietenpol Air Camper	S. Bryan	
G-BYLF	Zenair CH.601HDS Zodiac	S. Plater	
G-BYLI	Nova Vertex 22 hang glider	M. Hay	
G-BYLJ	Letov LK-2M Sluka	T. Barnby	
G-BYLO	T.66 Nipper Srs 1	M. J. A. Trudgill	
G-BYLP	Rand-Robinson KR-2	C. S. Hales	
G-BYLS	Bede BD-4	P. J. Greenrod	
G-BYLT	Raj Hamsa X'Air 582	T. W. Phipps	
G-BYLW	Lindstrand LBL-77A balloon	Associazione Gran Premio Italiano	
G-BYLX	Lindstrand LBL-105A balloon	Italiana Aeronavi/Italy	
G-BYLZ	Rutan Cozy	W. S. Allen	
G-BYMB	Diamond Katana DA20-C1	M. Zakaras	
G-BYMD	PA-38-112 Tomahawk II	Merseyflight Ltd	
G-BYMF	Pegasus Quantum 15-912	G. R. Stockdale	
G-BYMI	Pegasus Quantum 15	J. Childs	
G-BYMJ	Cessna 152	PJC (Leasing) Ltd	
G-BYMN	Rans S.6-ESA Coyote II	R. J. P. Herivel	
G-BYMR	Raj Hamsa X'Air R100(3)	W. Drury	
G-BYMW	Boland 52-12 balloon	C. Jones	
G-BYNA	Cessna F.172H	D. M. White (G-AWTH)	
G-BYND	Pegasus Quantum 15	W. J. Upton	
G-BYNF	NA-64 Yale I (3349)	I. D. Jones	
G-BYNK	Robin HR.200/160	Penguin Flight Group	
G-BYNM	Mainair Blade 912	D. E. Ashton	
G-BYNN	Cameron V-90 balloon	Cloud Nine Balloon Group	
G-BYNP	Rans S.6-ES Coyote II	C. J. Lines	
G-BYNS	Avtech Jabiru SK	D. K. Lawry	
G-BYNU	Cameron Thunder Ax7-77 balloon	B. Fisher	
G-BYNW	Cameron H-34 balloon	S. R. Skinner	
G-BYNX	Cameron RX-105 balloon	Cameron Balloons Ltd	
G-BYOB	Slingsby T.67M Firefly 260	Stapleford Flying Club Ltd	
G-BYOD	Slingsby T.67C	D. I. Stanbridge	
G-BYOG	Pegasus Quantum 15-912	A. C. Tyler	
G-BYOH	Raj Hamsa X'Air 582 (5)	G. Lafferty	
G-BYOI	Sky 80-16 balloon	D. Sulcas	
G-BYOJ	Raj Hamsa X'Air 582 (1)	P. J. Hopkins	
G-BYOO	CFM Streak Shadow	D. F. Neill	
G-BYOR	Raj Hamsa X'Air 582(7)	A. J. Sharratt	
G-BYOS	Mainair Blade 912	S. D. Hutchinson	
G-BYOT	Rans S.6-ES Coyote II	G-BYOT Syndicate	
G-BYOV	Pegasus Quantum 15-912	M. Howland	

Notes	Reg	Type	Owner or Operator
	G-BYOW	Mainair Blade	P. Szymanski & P. Gadek
	G-BYOZ	Mainair Rapier	G. P. Hodgson
	G-BYPB	Pegasus Quantum 15-912	D. A. Jaques
	G-BYPF	Thruster T.600N	T. R. Villa
	G-BYPH	Thruster T.600N	D. M. Canham
	G-BYPJ	Pegasus Quantum 15-912	R. J. Coombs
	G-BYPM	Shaw Europa XS	A. Pritchard
	G-BYPN	MS.880B Rallye Club	R. Edwards, D. & S. A. Bell & G. A. Rossington
	G-BYPO	Raj Hamsa X'Air 582 (1)	E. Doyle
	G-BYPR	Zenair CH.601HD Zodiac	N. Surman
	G-BYPU	PA-32R-301 Saratoga SP	GOBOB Flying Group
	G-BYPZ	Rans S.6-116 Super 6	R. A. Blackbourne
	G-BYRC	Westland WS-58 Wessex HC.2 (XT671)	D. Brem-Wilson
	G-BYRG	Rans S.6-ES Coyote II	S. J. Macmillan
	G-BYRJ	Pegasus Quantum 15-912	J. M. & R. W. Thompson
	G-BYRK	Cameron V-42 balloon	R. Kunert
	G-BYRO	Mainair Blade	T. W. Thiele
	G-BYRR	Mainair Blade 912	W. J. Dowty
	G-BYRU	Pegasus Quantum 15-912	J. R. Noble
	G-BYRV	Raj Hamsa X'Air 582 (1)	A. D. Russell
	G-BYRX	Westland Scout AH.1 (XT634)	Edwalton Aviation Ltd
	G-BYSE	Agusta-Bell 206B JetRanger 2	L. Rubner (G-BFND)
	G-BYSF	Avtech Jabiru UL	Jabber 430
	G-BYSG	Robin HR.200/120B	B. M. Gay
	G-BYSI	WSK-PZL Koliber 160A	J. & D. F. Evans
	G-BYSJ	DHC.1 Chipmunk 22 (WB569:R)	S. C. Swire
	G-BYSM	Cameron A-210 balloon	Adventure Balloons Ltd
	G-BYSP	PA-28-181 Archer II	M. C. Plomer-Roberts
	G-BYSV	Cameron N-120 balloon	S. Simmington
	G-BYSX	Pegasus Quantum 15-912	K. A. Landers
	G-BYSY	Raj Hamsa X'Air 582 (1)	A. Cochrane
	G-BYTB	SOCATA TB20 Trinidad	Watchman Aircraft Ltd
	G-BYTC	Pegasus Quantum 15-912	J. C. & J. E. Munro-Hunt
	G-BYTI	PA-24 Comanche 250	M. Carruthers & G. Auchterlonie
	G-BYTJ	Cameron C-80 balloon	J. D. Smallridge
	G-BYTK	Avtech Jabiru UL	G. R. Phillips
	G-BYTL	Mainair Blade 912	D. A. Meek & T.J. Burrow
	G-BYTM	Dyn' Aero MCR-01	I. Lang
	G-BYTN	DH.82A Tiger Moth (N6720:VX)	G. A. Rossington
	G-BYTR	Raj Hamsa X'Air 582 (1)	L. A. Dotchin
	G-BYTS	Montgomerie-Bensen B.8MR gyroplane	B. F. Pearson
	G-BYTV	Avtech Jabiru UL-450	F. McDonagh
	G-BYTW	Cameron O-90 balloon	D. R. King
	G-BYTX	MW6-S Fat Boy Flyer	J. K. Ewing
	G-BYTZ	Raj Hamsa X'Air 582 (1)	J. R. Kinder
	G-BYUB	Grob G.115E Tutor	Babcock Aerospace Ltd
	G-BYUC	Grob G.115E Tutor	Babcock Aerospace Ltd
	G-BYUD	Grob G.115E Tutor	Babcock Aerospace Ltd
	G-BYUE	Grob G.115E Tutor	Babcock Aerospace Ltd
	G-BYUF	Grob G.115E Tutor	Babcock Aerospace Ltd
	G-BYUH	Grob G.115E Tutor	Babcock Aerospace Ltd
	G-BYUI	Grob G.115E Tutor	Babcock Aerospace Ltd
	G-BYUJ	Grob G.115E Tutor	Babcock Aerospace Ltd
	G-BYUK	Grob G.115E Tutor	Babcock Aerospace Ltd
	G-BYUL	Grob G.115E Tutor	Babcock Aerospace Ltd
	G-BYUM	Grob G.115E Tutor	Babcock Aerospace Ltd
	G-BYUN	Grob G.115E Tutor	Babcock Aerospace Ltd
	G-BYUO	Grob G.115E Tutor	Babcock Aerospace Ltd
	G-BYUR	Grob G.115E Tutor	Babcock Aerospace Ltd
	G-BYUS	Grob G.115E Tutor	Babcock Aerospace Ltd
	G-BYUU	Grob G.115E Tutor	Babcock Aerospace Ltd
	G-BYUV	Grob G.115E Tutor	Babcock Aerospace Ltd
	G-BYUW	Grob G.115E Tutor	Babcock Aerospace Ltd
	G-BYUX	Grob G.115E Tutor	Babcock Aerospace Ltd
	G-BYUY	Grob.G.115E Tutor	Babcock Aerospace Ltd
	G-BYUZ	Grob G.115E Tutor	Babcock Aerospace Ltd
	G-BYVA	Grob G.115E Tutor	Babcock Aerospace Ltd
	G-BYVB	Grob G.115E Tutor	Babcock Aerospace Ltd
	G-BYVC	Grob G.115E Tutor	Babcock Aerospace Ltd
	G-BYVD	Grob G.115E Tutor	Babcock Aerospace Ltd

Reg	Type	Owner or Operator	Notes
G-BYVE	Grob G.115E Tutor	Babcock Aerospace Ltd	
G-BYVF	Grob G.115E Tutor	Babcock Aerospace Ltd	
G-BYVG	Grob G.115E Tutor	Babcock Aerospace Ltd	
G-BYVH	Grob G.115E Tutor	Babcock Aerospace Ltd	
G-BYVI	Grob G.115E Tutor	Babcock Aerospace Ltd	
G-BYVK	Grob G.115E Tutor	Babcock Aerospace Ltd	
G-BYVL	Grob G.115E Tutor	Babcock Aerospace Ltd	
G-BYVM	Grob G.115E Tutor	Babcock Aerospace Ltd	
G-BYVO	Grob G.115E Tutor	Babcock Aerospace Ltd	
G-BYVP	Grob G.115E Tutor	Babcock Aerospace Ltd	
G-BYVR	Grob G.115E Tutor	Babcock Aerospace Ltd	
G-BYVU	Grob G.115E Tutor	Babcock Aerospace Ltd	
G-BYVW	Grob G.115E Tutor	Babcock Aerospace Ltd	
G-BYVY	Grob G.115E Tutor	Babcock Aerospace Ltd	
G-BYVZ	Grob G.115E Tutor	Babcock Aerospace Ltd	
G-BYWA	Grob G.115E Tutor	Babcock Aerospace Ltd	
G-BYWB	Grob G.115E Tutor	Babcock Aerospace Ltd	
G-BYWD	Grob G.115E Tutor	Babcock Aerospace Ltd	
G-BYWF	Grob G.115E Tutor	Babcock Aerospace Ltd	
G-BYWG	Grob G.115E Tutor	Babcock Aerospace Ltd	
G-BYWH	Grob G.115E Tutor	Babcock Aerospace Ltd	
G-BYWI	Grob G.115E Tutor	Babcock Aerospace Ltd	
G-BYWK	Grob G.115E Tutor	Babcock Aerospace Ltd	
G-BYWL	Grob G.115E Tutor	Babcock Aerospace Ltd	
G-BYWM	Grob G.115E Tutor	Babcock Aerospace Ltd	
G-BYWO	Grob G.115E Tutor	Babcock Aerospace Ltd	
G-BYWR	Grob G.115E Tutor	Babcock Aerospace Ltd	
G-BYWS	Grob G.115E Tutor	Babcock Aerospace Ltd	
G-BYWU	Grob G.115E Tutor	Babcock Aerospace Ltd	
G-BYWV	Grob G.115E Tutor	Babcock Aerospace Ltd	
G-BYWW	Grob G.115E Tutor	Babcock Aerospace Ltd	
G-BYWX	Grob G.115E Tutor	Babcock Aerospace Ltd	
G-BYWY	Grob G.115E Tutor	Babcock Aerospace Ltd	
G-BYWZ	Grob G.115E Tutor	Babcock Aerospace Ltd	
G-BYXA	Grob G.115E Tutor	Babcock Aerospace Ltd	
G-BYXC	Grob G.115E Tutor	Babcock Aerospace Ltd	
G-BYXD	Grob G.115E Tutor	Babcock Aerospace Ltd	
G-BYXE	Grob G.115E Tutor	Babcock Aerospace Ltd	
G-BYXF	Grob G.115E Tutor	Babcock Aerospace Ltd	
G-BYXG	Grob G.115E Tutor	Babcock Aerospace Ltd	
G-BYXH	Grob G.115E Tutor	Babcock Aerospace Ltd	
G-BYXI	Grob G.115E Tutor	Babcock Aerospace Ltd	
G-BYXJ	Grob G.115E Tutor	Babcock Aerospace Ltd	
G-BYXK	Grob G.115E Tutor	Babcock Aerospace Ltd	
G-BYXL	Grob G.115E Tutor	Babcock Aerospace Ltd	
G-BYXM	Grob G.115E Tutor	Babcock Aerospace Ltd	
G-BYXO	Grob G.115E Tutor	Babcock Aerospace Ltd	
G-BYXP	Grob G.115E Tutor	Babcock Aerospace Ltd	
G-BYXS	Grob G.115E Tutor	Babcock Aerospace Ltd	
G-BYXT	Grob G.115E Tutor	Babcock Aerospace Ltd	
G-BYXW	Medway Eclipser	G. A. Hazell	
G-BYXX	Grob G.115E Tutor	Babcock Aerospace Ltd	
G-BYXZ	Grob G.115E Tutor	Babcock Aerospace Ltd	
G-BYYA	Grob G.115E Tutor	Babcock Aerospace Ltd	
G-BYYB	Grob G.115E Tutor	Babcock Aerospace Ltd	
G-BYYC	Hapi Cygnet SF-2A	G. H. Smith	
G-BYYE	Lindstrand LBL-77A balloon	Virgin Balloon Flights	
G-BYYG	Slingsby T.67C	The Pathfinder Flying Club Ltd	
G-BYYJ	Lindstrand LBL-25A balloon	G-BYYJ Go Hopping	
G-BYYL	Avtech Jabiru SPL-450	Triangulum Flying Group	
G-BYYM	Raj Hamsa X'Air 582 (1)	J. Pozniak	
G-BYYN	Pegasus Quantum 15-912	R. J. Bullock	
G-BYYO	PA-28R -201 Arrow III	Stapleford Flying Club Ltd	
G-BYYP	Pegasus Quantum 15	D. A. Linsey	
G-BYYT	Avtech Jabiru UL 450	A. T. Carter	
G-BYYX	TEAM mini-MAX 91	P. J. Bishop	
G-BYYY	Pegasus Quantum 15-912	Quantum 1 Group	
G-BYZA	AS.355F2 Twin Squirrel	PLM Dollar Group Ltd	
G-BYZB	Mainair Blade	A. M. Thornley	
G-BYZF	Raj Hamsa X'Air 582 (1)	R. P. Davies	
G-BYZO	Rans S.6-ES Coyote II	S. Ganguly	

Notes	Reg	Type	Owner or Operator
	G-BYZR	I.I.I. Sky Arrow 650TC	G-BYZR Flying Group
	G-BYZS	Avtech Jabiru UL-450	G. J. Stafford
	G-BYZT	Nova Vertex 26	M. Hay
	G-BYZU	Pegasus Quantum 15	L. Adams
	G-BYZV	Sky 90-24 balloon	M. A. Stelling
	G-BYZW	Raj Hamsa X'Air 582 (2)	H. C. Lowther
	G-BYZY	Pietenpol Aircamper	D. M. Hanchett
	G-BZAE	Cessna 152	Tatenhill Aviation Ltd
	G-BZAH	Cessna 208B Grand Caravan	Army Parachute Association
	G-BZAI	Pegasus Quantum 15	S. A. Holmes
	G-BZAK	Raj Hamsa X'Air 582 (1)	L. M. Devine
	G-BZAL	Mainair Blade 912	S. G. A. Milburn & S. Hall
	G-BZAM	Europa	N. M. Graham
	G-BZAP	Avtech Jabiru UL-450	I. J. Grindley & D. R. Griffiths
	G-BZAR	Denney Kitfox 4-1200 Speedster	N. J. France (G-LEZJ)
	G-BZAS	Isaacs Fury II (K5673)	N. C. Stone
	G-BZBC	Rans S.6-ES Coyote II	A. J. Baldwin
	G-BZBE	Cameron A-210 balloon	Border Ballooning Ltd
	G-BZBF	Cessna 172M	Aviolease Ltd
	G-BZBH	Thunder Ax6-65 balloon	P. J. Hebdon & A. C. Fraser
	G-BZBJ	Lindstrand LBL-77A balloon	P. T. R. Ollivere
	G-BZBL	Lindstrand LBL-120A balloon	A. G. A. Barclay-Faulkner
	G-BZBO	Stoddard-Hamilton Glasair III	M. B. Hamlett/France
	G-BZBP	Raj Hamsa X'Air 582 (1)	J. L. B. Roy
	G-BZBS	PA-28-161 Warrior III	White Waltham Airfield Ltd
	G-BZBT	Cameron H-34 Hopper balloon	P. Lesser
	G-BZBW	Rotorway Executive 162F	G-BZBW Group
	G-BZBX	Rans S.6-ES Coyote II	C. P. Koke
	G-BZBZ	Jodel D.9	D. C. Unwin
	G-BZDA	PA-28-161 Warrior III	White Waltham Airfield Ltd
	G-BZDC	Mainair Blade	E. J. Wells & P. J. Smith
	G-BZDD	Mainair Blade 912	Buzzing Double-D's Syndicate
	G-BZDE	Lindstrand LBL-210A balloon	Toucan Travel Ltd
	G-BZDF	CFM Streak Shadow SA	A. D. Parsons
	G-BZDH	PA-28R Cherokee Arrow 200-II	R. P. Pearson & A. M. Mumford
	G-BZDK	X'Air 582(2)	J. Bagnall
	G-BZDM	Stoddard-Hamilton Glastar	F. G. Miskelly
	G-BZDN	Cameron N-105 balloon	I. R. Warrington & P. A. Foot
	G-BZDP	SA Bulldog Srs 120/121 (XX551:E)	R. M. Raikes
	G-BZDR	Tri-R Kis	D. F. Sutherland
	G-BZDS	Pegasus Quantum 15-912	J. Ayre
	G-BZDT	Maule MXT-7-180	Strongcrew Ltd
	G-BZDV	Westland Gazelle HT.2	G. R. Harrison
	G-BZEA	Cessna A.152	Blueplane Ltd
	G-BZEB	Cessna 152	Blueplane Ltd
	G-BZEC	Cessna 152	Redhill Air Services Ltd
	G-BZED	Pegasus Quantum 15-912	D. Crozier
	G-BZEG	Mainair Blade 912	S. S. Dawbarn
	G-BZEI	Agusta A.109E Power	Myheli Ltd (G-RCMS)
	G-BZEJ	Raj Hamsa X'Air 582 (7)	H-Flight X'Air Flying Group
	G-BZEN	Avtech Jabiru UL-450	J. R. Hunt
	G-BZEP	SA Bulldog Srs 120/121 (XX561:7)	R. C. Skinner
	G-BZER	Raj Hamsa X'Air 582(2)	N. P. Lloyd & H. Lloyd-Jones
	G-BZEU	Raj Hamsa X'Air 582 (2)	W. J. McCarroll
	G-BZEW	Rans S.6-ES Coyote II	N. P. Gayton
	G-BZEY	Cameron N-90 balloon	G. L. Forde
	G-BZEZ	CFM Streak Shadow	G. J. Pearce
	G-BZFB	Robin R.2112A	O. Bryan
	G-BZFD	Cameron N-90 balloon	C. D. & E. Gingell
	G-BZFG	Sky 105 balloon	Virgin Airship & Balloon Co Ltd
	G-BZFH	Pegasus Quantum 15-912	G. R. Ambrose
	G-BZFI	Avtech Jabiru UL	B. S. Lapthorn
	G-BZFN	SA Bulldog Srs 120/121 (XX667:16)	Risk Logical Ltd
	G-BZFS	Mainair Blade 912	Snowdonia Flyers Group
	G-BZFT	Murphy Rebel	R. M. Pols
	G-BZGA	DHC.1 Chipmunk 22 (WK585)	Compton Abbas Airfield Ltd
	G-BZGF	Rans S.6-ES Coyote II	C. A. Purvis
	G-BZGJ	Thunder Ax10-180 S2 balloon	Spirit Operations Ltd
	G-BZGL	NA OV-10B Bronco (99+26)	Liberty Aviation Ltd
	G-BZGM	Mainair Blade 912	D. Avery

Reg	Type	Owner or Operator	Notes
G-BZGO	Robinson R44	Flight Academy (Gyrocopters) Ltd	
G-BZGS	Mainair Blade 912	M. W. Holmes	
G-BZGT	Avtech Jabiru SPL-450	C. M. Bellas	
G-BZGV	Lindstrand LBL-77A balloon	J. H. Dryden	
G-BZGW	Mainair Blade	M. Liptrot	
G-BZGY	Dyn'Aéro CR.100	B. Appleby	
G-BZGZ	Pegasus Quantum 15-912	D. W. Beech	
G-BZHE	Cessna 152	Andrewsfield Aviation Ltd	
G-BZHF	Cessna 152	Modi Aviation Ltd	
G-BZHG	Tecnam P92 Echo	R. W. F. Boarder	
G-BZHJ	Raj Hamsa X'Air 582 (7)	T. R. Allebone	
G-BZHL	Noorduyn AT-16 Harvard IIB	S. Swallow	
G-BZHN	Pegasus Quantum 15-912	A. M. Sirant	
G-BZHO	Pegasus Quantum 15	G-BZHO Group	
G-BZHR	Avtech Jabiru UL-450	N. Morrison	
G-BZHT	PA-18A Super Cub 150	D. Bennett	
G-BZHU	Wag-Aero Sport Trainer	Teddy Boys Flying Group	
G-BZHV	PA-28-181 Archer III	R. M. & T. A. Limb	
G-BZHX	Thunder Ax11-250 S2 balloon	Wizard Balloons Ltd	
G-BZHY	Mainair Blade 912	M. J. Booth	
G-BZIA	Raj Hamsa X'Air 700 (1)	J. L. Pritchett	
G-BZIC	Lindstrand LBL Sun SS balloon	Life Less Ordinary AB/Sweden	
G-BZID	Montgomerie-Bensen B.8MR	A. Gault	
G-BZIG	Thruster T.600N	K. M. Jones	
G-BZIH	Lindstrand LBL-31A balloon	H. & L. D. Vaughan	
G-BZII	Extra EA.300/1	Airdisplays.com Ltd	
G-BZIJ	Robin DR.400/500	Rob Airways Ltd	
G-BZIL	Colt 120A balloon	Champagne Flights	
G-BZIM	Pegasus Quantum 15-912	M. J. Stalker	
G-BZIO	PA-28-161 Warrior III	White Waltham Airfield Ltd	
G-BZIP	Montgomerie-Bensen B.8MR	V. G. Freke	
G-BZIS	Raj Hamsa X'Air 582 (2)	Let's Fly Right	
G-BZIT	Beech 95-B55 Baron	E. P. Dablin	
G-BZIV	Avtech Jabiru UL-450	A. Parr	
G-BZIW	Pegasus Quantum 15-912	J. M. Hodgson	
G-BZIX	Cameron N-90 balloon	M. Stefanini & P. Marmugi/Italy	
G-BZIY	Raj Hamsa X'Air 582 (2)	K. W. Hogg	
G-BZIZ	Ultramagic H-31 balloon	C. J. Davies	
G-BZJA	Cameron Fire 90 balloon	Chubb Fire and Security Ltd	
G-BZJC	Thruster T.600N	D. Hurst	
G-BZJD	Thruster T.600T	C. C. Belcher	
G-BZJH	Cameron Z-90 balloon	Egroup SRL/Italy	
G-BZJI	Nova X-Large 37 paraplane	M. Hay	
G-BZJM	VPM M-16 Tandem Trainer	A. Phillips & J. K. Padden	
G-BZJN	Mainair Blade 912	K. Roberts	
G-BZJO	Pegasus Quantum 15	D. Minnock	
G-BZJR	Montgomerie-Bensen B.8MR	K. A. O'Neill (G-IPFM)	
G-BZJV	CASA 1-131E Jungmann 1000	R. A. Cumming	
G-BZJW	Cessna 150F	P. Ligertwood	
G-BZJZ	Pegasus Quantum 15	S. Baker	
G-BZKC	Raj Hamsa X'Air 582 (11)	N. R. Beale	
G-BZKD	Stolp Starduster Too	P. & C. Edmunds	
G-BZKF	Rans S.6-ES Coyote II	S. Cartwright & D. G. Stothard	
G-BZKL	PA-28R-201 Arrow III	M. A. & M. H. Cromati	
G-BZKO	Rans S-6-ES Coyote II	B. N. & P. Ringland	
G-BZKU	Cameron Z-105 balloon	N. A. Fishlock	
G-BZKV	Cameron Sky 90-24 balloon	D. P. Busby	
G-BZKW	Ultramagic M-77 balloon	Slowfly Montgolfiere SNC/Italy	
G-BZLC	WSK-PZL Koliber 160A	G. F. Smith	
G-BZLE	Rans S.6-ES Coyote II	G. Spittlehouse	
G-BZLF	CFM Shadow Srs CD	D. W. Stacey	
G-BZLG	Robin HR.200/120B	O. J. O'Reilly	
G-BZLH	PA-28-161 Warrior II	Hields Aviation	
G-BZLK	Slingsby T.31M Motor Tutor	G. Smith	
G-BZLL	Pegasus Quantum 15-912	P. F. Willey	
G-BZLP	Robinson R44	Polar Helicopters Ltd	
G-BZLS	Cameron Sky 77-24 balloon	D. W. Young	
G-BZLU	Lindstrand LBL-90A balloon	A. E. Lusty	
G-BZLV	Avtech Jabiru UL-450	G. Dalton	
G-BZLX	Pegasus Quantum 15-912	G. J. P. Skinner	
G-BZLY	Grob G.109B	G-BZLY Group	

Notes	Reg	Type	Owner or Operator
	G-BZLZ	Pegasus Quantum 15-912	J. Hill
	G-BZMB	PA-28R-201 Arrow III	Thurrock Arrow Group
	G-BZMC	Avtech Jabiru UL	S. Farnworth
	G-BZME	SA Bulldog Srs 120/121 (XX698:9)	XX698 Bulldog Group
	G-BZMF	Rutan LongEz	D. Marshall
	G-BZMH	SA Bulldog Srs 120/121 (XX692:A)	M. E. J. Hingley
	G-BZMJ	Rans S-6-ES Coyote II	R. J. G. Clark
	G-BZML	SA Bulldog Srs 120/121 (XX693:07)	I. D. Anderson
	G-BZMM	Robin DR.400/180R	Cairngorm Gliding Club
	G-BZMS	Mainair Blade	S. Elmazouri
	G-BZMY	SPP Yakovlev Yak C-11 (I)	A. M. Holman-West
	G-BZNA	Lindstrand LBL-90A balloon	M. A. Stelling & A. J. Kinsella
	G-BZNH	Rans S-6-ES Coyote II	B. A. Coombe
	G-BZNI	Bell 206B Jet Ranger II	Shawgrove Aviation Ltd (G-ODIG/G-NEEP)
	G-BZNJ	Rans S-6-ES Coyote II	R. A. McKee
	G-BZNK	Morane Saulnier MS.315-D2 (354)	R. H. Cooper & S. Swallow
	G-BZNM	Pegasus Quantum 15	M. Ward
	G-BZNN	Beech 76 Duchess	Flew LLP
	G-BZNP	Thruster T.600N	P. D. Twissell
	G-BZNS	Mainair Blade 912	J. Grey
	G-BZNV	Lindstrand LBL-31A balloon	G. R. Down
	G-BZNW	Isaacs Fury II (K2048)	S. M. Johnston
	G-BZNY	Shaw Europa XS	T. J. Poulter
	G-BZOB	Slepcev Storch (6G-ED)	A. Bendkowski
	G-BZOE	Pegasus Quantum 15	B. Dale
	G-BZOF	Montgomerie-Bensen B.8MR gyroplane	S. J. M. Ledingham
	G-BZOI	Nicollier HN.700 Menestrel II	S. J. McCollum
	G-BZOL	Robin R.3000/140	M. C. R. Willis
	G-BZOM	Rotorway Executive 162F	I. C. Bedford (G-RALF)
	G-BZON	SA Bulldog Srs 120/121 (XX528:D)	D. J. Critchley
	G-BZOO	Pegasus Quantum 15-912	D. W. Guest
	G-BZOR	TEAM mini-MAX 91	A. W. Gunn
	G-BZOU	Pegasus Quantum 15-912	M. A. Bradford
	G-BZOW	Whittaker MW7	G. W. Peacock
	G-BZOX	Cameron Colt 90B balloon	D. J. Head
	G-BZOZ	Van's RV-6	M. & S. Sheppard
	G-BZPA	Mainair Blade 912S	W. McDowell
	G-BZPD	Cameron V-65 balloon	P. Spellward
	G-BZPF	Scheibe SF-24B Motorspatz	D. & M. Shrimpton
	G-BZPG	Beech C24R Sierra 200	Peter J. Ward Nurseryman Ltd
	G-BZPH	Van's RV-4	G-BZPH RV-4 Group
	G-BZPI	SOCATA TB20 Trinidad	Transair (UK) Ltd
	G-BZPK	Cameron C-80 balloon	D. L. Homer
	G-BZPN	Mainair Blade 912S	J. Kilpatrick
	G-BZPW	Cameron V-77 balloon	J. Vonka
	G-BZPX	Ultramagic S-105 balloon	Scotair Balloons
	G-BZPY	Ultramagic H-31 balloon	Scotair Balloons
	G-BZPZ	Mainair Blade	R. J. Burke
	G-BZRF	Percival P.56 Provost T.Mk.1	P. B. Childs
	G-BZRJ	Pegasus Quantum 15-912	D. A. Hutchinson
	G-BZRO	PA-30 Twin Comanche C	Gloucester Comanche Group
	G-BZRP	Pegasus Quantum 15-912	M. F. Sheerman-Chase
	G-BZRR	Pegasus Quantum 15-912	BZRR Syndicate
	G-BZRS	Eurocopter EC 135T2	Babcock Mission Critical Services Onshore Ltd
	G-BZRV	Van's RV-6	N. M. Hitchman
	G-BZRW	Mainair Blade 912S	G. J. E. Alcorn
	G-BZRY	Rans S.6-ES Coyote II	M. J. Buchanan
	G-BZRZ	Thunder Ax11-250 S2 balloon	A. C. K. Rawson & J. J. Rudoni
	G-BZSB	Pitts S-1S Special	A. D. Ingold
	G-BZSC	Sopwith Camel F.1 (replica) (D1851)	The Shuttleworth Collection
	G-BZSE	Hawker Hunter T.8B (WV322:VL)	Canfield Hunter Ltd
	G-BZSG	Pegasus Quantum 15-912	A. J. Harris
	G-BZSH	Ultramagic H-77 balloon	P. M. G. Vale
	G-BZSI	Pegasus Quantum 15	T. J. Drew
	G-BZSM	Pegasus Quantum 15	G. Jenkinson
	G-BZSP	Stemme S.10	A. Flewelling & L. Bleaken
	G-BZSS	Pegasus Quantum 15-912	RKAT Ltd
	G-BZST	Jabiru SPL-450	M. D. Tulloch
	G-BZSX	Pegasus Quantum 15-912	G. Reid
	G-BZSZ	Avtech Jabiru UL-450	D. W. Allan
	G-BZTA	Robinson R44	Jarretts Motors Ltd

Reg	Type	Owner or Operator	Notes
G-BZTC	TEAM mini-MAX 91	G. G. Clayton	
G-BZTD	Thruster T.600T 450 JAB	A. R. Hughes	
G-BZTH	Shaw Europa	D. J. Shipley	
G-BZTK	Cameron V-90 balloon	E. Appollodorus	
G-BZTM	Mainair Blade	I. Stanulet	
G-BZTN	Europa XS	P. R. Norwood	
G-BZTS	Cameron 90 Bertie Bassett SS balloon	Trebor Bassett Ltd	
G-BZTV	Mainair Blade 912S	R. D. McManus	
G-BZTW	Hunt Wing Avon 582 (1)	T. S. Walker	
G-BZTX	Mainair Blade 912	K. A. Ingham	
G-BZTY	Avtech Jabiru UL	R. P. Lewis	
G-BZUB	Mainair Blade	J. Campbell	
G-BZUC	Pegasus Quantum 15-912	J. J. D. Firmino do Carmo	
G-BZUD	Lindstrand LBL-105A balloon	D. Venegoni/Italy	
G-BZUE	Pegasus Quantum 15-912	D. T. Richardson	
G-BZUF	Mainair Rapier	B. Craig	
G-BZUG	RL.7A XP Sherwood Ranger	J. G. Boxall	
G-BZUH	Rans S.6-ES Coyote II	R. A. Darley	
G-BZUI	Pegasus Quantum 15-912	C. Garton	
G-BZUL	Avtech Jabiru UL	J. G. Campbell	
G-BZUP	Raj Hamsa X'Air Jabiru(3)	M. T. Sheelan	
G-BZUU	Cameron C-90 balloon	D. C. Ball	
G-BZUV	Cameron H-24 balloon	J. N. Race	
G-BZUX	Pegasus Quantum 15	C. Gorvett	
G-BZUY	Van's RV-6	D. J. Butt	
G-BZUZ	Hunt Avon-Blade R.100 (1)	C. F. Janes	
G-BZVA	Zenair CH.701UL	W. K. MacGillivray	
G-BZVB	Cessna FR.172H	Victor Bravo Group Ltd (G-BLMX)	
G-BZVI	Nova Vertex 24 hang glider	M. Hay	
G-BZVJ	Pegasus Quantum 15	R. Blackhall	
G-BZVK	Raj Hamsa X'Air 582 (2)	R. J. Hamilton	
G-BZVM	Rans S.6-ES Coyote II	M. P. Booth	
G-BZVN	Van's RV-6	Syndicate RV6 G-BZVN	
G-BZVR	Raj Hamsa X'Air 582 (4)	R. F. E. Berry	
G-BZVT	I.I.I. Sky Arrow 650T	E. J. Hadley	
G-BZVV	Pegasus Quantum 15-912	S. Smith & J. Giladjian	
G-BZVW	Ilyushin IL-2 Stormovik	S. Swallow	
G-BZVX	Ilyushin IL-2 Stormovik	S. Swallow	
G-BZWB	Mainair Blade 912	O. M. Blythin & L. G. Penson	
G-BZWC	Raj Hamsa X'Air Falcon 912 (1)	J. Webb	
G-BZWJ	CFM Streak Shadow	T. A. Morgan	
G-BZWK	Avtech Jabiru SK	M. Housley	
G-BZWM	Pegasus XL-Q	D. T. Evans	
G-BZWN	Van's RV-8	A. J. Symms	
G-BZWR	Mainair Rapier	M. A. Steele	
G-BZWS	Pegasus Quantum 15-912	G-BZWS Syndicate	
G-BZWT	Technam P.92-EM Echo	R. F. Cooper	
G-BZWU	Pegasus Quantum 15-912	M. D. Evans	
G-BZWV	Steen Skybolt	D. E. Blaxland, P. D. Baisden & J. P. Gilbert	
G-BZWX	Whittaker MW5D Sorcerer	J. Bate	
G-BZWZ	Van's RV-6	Bizzywizzy Group	
G-BZXB	Van's RV-6	R. A. Pritchard & G. W. Cunningham	
G-BZXC	SA Bulldog Srs 120/121 (XX612:A, 03) ★	Carnegie College	
G-BZXI	Nova Philou 26 hang glider	M. Hay	
G-BZXK	Robin HR.200/120B	R. Kellett	
G-BZXM	Mainair Blade 912	S. Dolan	
G-BZXN	Avtech Jabiru SPL-450	A. J. Z. Collins	
G-BZXO	Cameron Z-105 balloon	J. C. M. Greatrix	
G-BZXP	Kiss 400-582 (1)	A. Fairbrother	
G-BZXR	Cameron N-90 balloon	F. R. Battersby	
G-BZXS	SA Bulldog Srs 120/121 (XX631:W)	K. J. Thompson	
G-BZXT	Mainair Blade 912	J. D. Sings & S. C. Stinchcombe	
G-BZXV	Pegasus Quantum 15-912	A. P. & J. M. Cadd	
G-BZXW	VPM M-16 Tandem Trainer	P. J. Troy-Davies (G-NANA)	
G-BZXX	Pegasus Quantum 15-912	D. J. Johnston & D. Ostle	
G-BZXY	Robinson R44	Flight Checks Ltd	
G-BZXZ	SA Bulldog Srs 120/121 (XX629:V)	C. N. Wright	
G-BZYA	Rans S.6-ES Coyote II	P. D. Neilson	
G-BZYD	Westland Gazelle AH.1 (XZ329)	C. D. Meek	
G-BZYG	Glaser-Dirks DG.500MB	R. C. Bromwich	
G-BZYI	Nova Phocus 123 hang glider	M. Hay	

Notes	Reg	Type	Owner or Operator
	G-BZYK	Avtech Jabiru UL	S. J. Carr
	G-BZYN	Pegasus Quantum 15-912	J. Cannon
	G-BZYR	Cameron N-31 balloon	C. J. Sanger-Davies
	G-BZYS	Micro Aviation Bantam B.22-S	D. L. Howell
	G-BZYX	Raj Hamsa X'Air 700 (1A)	A. M. Sutton
	G-BZYY	Cameron N-90 balloon	M. E. Mason
	G-CAHA	PA-34-200T Seneca II	Tayside Aviation Ltd
	G-CALL	PA-23 Aztec 250F	J. D. Moon
	G-CAMM	Hawker Cygnet (replica)	Richard Shuttleworth Trustees
	G-CAMR	BFC Challenger II	P. R. A. Walker
	G-CAPI	Mudry/CAARP CAP-10B	P. F. D. Waltham (G-BEXR)
	G-CAPX	Avions Mudry CAP-10B	H. J. Pessall
	G-CBAD	Mainair Blade 912	J. Stocking
	G-CBAF	Lancair 320	L. H. & M. van Cleeff
	G-CBAK	Robinson R44	Phoenix Building Systems Ltd
	G-CBAL	PA-28-161 Warrior II	CBAL Flying Group
	G-CBAN	SA Bulldog Srs 120/121 (XX668:1)	A. C. S. Reynolds
	G-CBAP	Zenair CH.601ULA	G. D. Summers
	G-CBAR	Stoddard-Hamilton Glastar	Fishburn Flyers
	G-CBAS	Rans S.6-ES Coyote II	S. Stockill
	G-CBAT	Cameron Z-90 balloon	British Telecommunications PLC
	G-CBAU	Rand-Robinson KR-2	C. B. Copsey
	G-CBAW	Cameron A-300 balloon	Bailey Balloons Ltd
	G-CBAX	Tecnam P92-EA Echo	L. Collier
	G-CBAZ	Rans S.6-ES Coyote II	E. S. Wills
	G-CBBB	Pegasus Quantum 15-912	F. A. Dimmock
	G-CBBC	SA Bulldog Srs 120/121 (XX515:4)	Bulldog Support Ltd
	G-CBBF	Beech 76 Duchess	Flew LLP
	G-CBBG	Mainair Blade	B. Donnan
	G-CBBH	Raj Hamsa X'Air 582 (11)	D. A. Norwood
	G-CBBK	Robinson R22	R. J. Everett
	G-CBBL	SA Bulldog Srs 120/121 (XX550:Z)	A. Cunningham
	G-CBBM	Savannah VG Jabiru (1)	J. Pavelin
	G-CBBN	Pegasus Quantum 15-912	G-CBBN Flying Group
	G-CBBO	Whittaker MW5D Sorcerer	P. J. Gripton
	G-CBBP	Pegasus Quantum 15-912	A. C. Richards
	G-CBBS	SA Bulldog Srs 120/121 (XX694:E)	D. R. Keene
	G-CBBT	SA Bulldog Srs 120/121 (XX695:3)	K. A. Johnston
	G-CBBW	SA Bulldog Srs 120/121 (XX619:T)	S. E. Robottom-Scott
	G-CBCB	SA Bulldog Srs 120/121 (XX537:C)	M. W. Minary & M. R. Bromiley
	G-CBCD	Pegasus Quantum 15	I. A. Lumley
	G-CBCF	Pegasus Quantum 15-912	P. A. Bromley
	G-CBCH	Zenair CH.701UL	I. J. McNally
	G-CBCI	Raj Hamsa X'Air 582 (2)	R. McKie
	G-CBCL	Stoddard-Hamilton Glastar	D. W. Parfrey
	G-CBCM	Raj Hamsa X'Air Jabiru(3)	C. Childs
	G-CBCP	Van's RV-6A	G-CBCP Group
	G-CBCR	SA Bulldog Srs 120/121 (XX702:P)	Seven O Two Flying Group
	G-CBCY	Beech C24R Sierra Super	J. Waldie
	G-CBCZ	CFM Streak Shadow SLA	J. O'Malley-Kane
	G-CBDC	Thruster T.600N 450-JAB	T. J. Gallacher
	G-CBDD	Mainair Blade 912	G. Hird
	G-CBDG	Zenair CH.601HD	R. E. Lasnier
	G-CBDH	Flight Design CT2K	S. J. Goate
	G-CBDI	Denney Kitfox Mk.2	M. Barbour & G. Wilson
	G-CBDJ	Flight Design CT2K	P. J. Walker
	G-CBDK	SA Bulldog Srs 120/121 (XX611:7)	J. N. Randle
	G-CBDL	Mainair Blade	T. R. Villa
	G-CBDM	Tecnam P92-EM Echo	J. J. Cozens
	G-CBDN	Mainair Blade	B. C. C. Middleton
	G-CBDO	Raj Hamsa X'Air 582(1)	A. Campbell
	G-CBDP	Mainair Blade 912	S. T. Hayes
	G-CBDS	SA. Bulldog Srs.120/121	J. R. Parry
	G-CBDU	Quad City Challenger II	E. J. Brooks
	G-CBDV	Raj Hamsa X'Air 582	U. J. Anderson
	G-CBDX	Pegasus Quantum 15	P. Sinkler
	G-CBDZ	Pegasus Quantum 15-912	P. Smith
	G-CBEB	Kiss 400-582 (1)	J. C. Ring & S. Bowden
	G-CBEC	Cameron Z-105 balloon	John Aimo Balloons SAS/Italy

94

Reg	Type	Owner or Operator	Notes
G-CBEE	PA-28R Cherokee Arrow 200	J. Stevenson	
G-CBEF	SA Bulldog Srs 120/121 (XX621:H)	A. L. Butcher & F. W. Sandwell	
G-CBEH	SA Bulldog Srs 120/121 (XX521:H)	J. E. Lewis	
G-CBEI	PA-22 Colt 108	D. & S. J. Sharp	
G-CBEJ	Colt 120A balloon	Airxcite Ltd	
G-CBEK	SA Bulldog Srs 120/121 (XX700:17)	J. T. Crump	
G-CBEL	Hawker Fury F.Mk.11 (SR661)	Anglia Aircraft Restorations Ltd	
G-CBEM	Mainair Blade	K. W. Bodley	
G-CBEN	Pegasus Quantum 15-912	A. T. Cook	
G-CBES	Shaw Europa XS	D. J. Shipley	
G-CBEU	Pegasus Quantum 15-912	I. Flack	
G-CBEV	Pegasus Quantum 15-912	A. W. G. Ambler	
G-CBEW	Flight Design CT2K	Cruise Flight Group	
G-CBEX	Flight Design CT2K	A. G. Quinn	
G-CBEY	Cameron C-80 balloon	M. N. Hume	
G-CBEZ	Robin DR.400/180	K. V. Field	
G-CBFA	Diamond DA40 Star	Lyrastar Ltd	
G-CBFE	Raj Hamsa X'Air V.2 (1)	A. R. Rainford	
G-CBFJ	Robinson R44	F. Klinge	
G-CBFK	Murphy Rebel	P. J. Gibbs	
G-CBFN	Robin DR.100/200B	A. F. Gillett	
G-CBFP	SA Bulldog Srs 120/121 (XX636:Y)	Shacklewell Bulldog Group	
G-CBFU	SA Bulldog Srs 120/121 (XX628:9)	J. R. & S. J. Huggins	
G-CBFW	Bensen B.8	A. J. Thomas	
G-CBFX	Rans S.6-ES Coyote II	O. C. Rash	
G-CBGB	Zenair CH.601UL	J. F. Woodham	
G-CBGD	Zenair CH.701UL	I. S. Walsh	
G-CBGE	Tecnam P92-EM Echo	J. P. Spiteri	
G-CBGG	Pegasus Quantum 15	T. E. Davies	
G-CBGH	Teverson Bisport	Phoenix Flyers	
G-CBGJ	Aeroprakt A.22 Foxbat	E. Smyth & T. G. Fitzpatrick	
G-CBGL	MH.1521M Broussard	K. M. Perkins	
G-CBGO	Murphy Maverick 430	K. J. Miles & R. Withall	
G-CBGP	Ikarus C.42 FB UK	C. F. Welby	
G-CBGR	Avtech Jabiru UL-450	M. D. Brown	
G-CBGU	Thruster T.600N 450-JAB	B. R. Cardosi	
G-CBGV	Thruster T.600N 450	West Flight Aviators	
G-CBGW	Thruster T.600N 450-JAB	A. R. Pluck	
G-CBGX	SA Bulldog Srs 120/121 (XX622:B)	Bulldog GX Group	
G-CBGZ	Westland Gazelle HT.2 (ZB646:59/CU)	D. Weatherhead Ltd	
G-CBHA	SOCATA TB10 Tobago	Oscar Romeo Aviation Ltd	
G-CBHC	RAF 2000 GTX-SE gyroplane	R. Barton	
G-CBHE	Slingsby T.67M-200 Firefly	Go 2 Fly SIA	
G-CBHG	Mainair Blade 912S	C. R. Buckle	
G-CBHI	Shaw Europa XS	Alpha Syndicate	
G-CBHJ	Mainair Blade 912	A. W. Leadley	
G-CBHK	Pegasus Quantum 15 (HKS)	I. R. Price	
G-CBHN	Pegasus Quantum 15-912	S. P. D. Hill	
G-CBHO	Gloster Gladiator II (N5719)	Retro Track & Air (UK) Ltd	
G-CBHP	Corby CJ-1 Starlet	K. M. Hodson	
G-CBHR	Lazer Z200	The G-CBHR Group	
G-CBHU	RL.5A Sherwood Ranger	D. J. Seymour	
G-CBHW	Cameron Z-105 balloon	Bristol Chamber of Commerce, Industry & Shipping	
G-CBHX	Cameron V-77 balloon	A. Hook	
G-CBHY	Pegasus Quantum 15-912	D. W. Allen	
G-CBHZ	RAF 2000 GTX-SE gyroplane	M. P. Donnelly	
G-CBIB	Flight Design CT2K	D. Petch	
G-CBIC	Raj Hamsa X'Air V2 (2)	G. A. J. Salter	
G-CBID	SA Bulldog Srs 120/121(XX549:6)	The Red Dog Group	
G-CBIE	Flight Design CT2K	S. Willis	
G-CBIF	Avtech Jabiru SPL-450	A. G. Sindrey	
G-CBII	Raj Hamsa X'Air 582(8)	J. D. H. Robson	
G-CBIL	Cessna 182K	E. Bannister (G-BFZZ)	
G-CBIM	Lindstrand LBL-90A balloon	R. K. Parsons	
G-CBIN	TEAM mini-MAX 91	A. R. Mikolaczyk	
G-CBIP	Thruster T.600N 450-JAB	G. Crossan	
G-CBIR	Thruster T.600N 450-JAB	M. Keenan	
G-CBIS	Raj Hamsa X'Air 582 (2)	P. T. W. T. Derges	
G-CBIT	RAF 2000 GTX-SE gyroplane	Terrafirma Services Ltd	
G-CBIV	Skyranger 912 (1)	R. H. Dennis	

Notes	Reg	Type	Owner or Operator
	G-CBIX	Zenair CH.601UL	R. A. Roberts
	G-CBIY	Aerotechnik EV-97 Eurostar	W. R. Grantham & B. J. Sheppard
	G-CBJD	Stoddard-Hamilton Glastar	K. F. Farey
	G-CBJE	RAF 2000 GTX-SE gyroplane	V. G. Freke
	G-CBJG	DHC.1 Chipmunk 20 (1373)	C. J. Rees
	G-CBJH	Aeroprakt A.22 Foxbat	H. Smith
	G-CBJL	Kiss 400-582 (1)	R. E. Morris
	G-CBJM	Avtech Jabiru SP-470	J. M. P. Elliott
	G-CBJN	RAF 2000 GTX-SE	G. W. Duffill
	G-CBJO	Pegasus Quantum 15-912	A. E. Kemp
	G-CBJP	Zenair CH.601UL	T. J. Heaton
	G-CBJR	Aerotechnik EV-97A Eurostar	Madley Flying Group
	G-CBJS	Cameron C-60 balloon	N. Ivison
	G-CBJT	Mainair Blade	M. A. Hartill
	G-CBJV	Rotorway Executive 162F	P. W. Vaughan
	G-CBJW	Ikarus C.42 Cyclone FB UK	E. Foster & J. H. Peet
	G-CBJX	Raj Hamsa X'Air Falcon J22	R. D. Bateman
	G-CBJY	Jabiru UL-450	M. A. Gould
	G-CBJZ	Westland Gazelle HT.3	K. G. Theurer/Germany
	G-CBKA	Westland Gazelle HT.3 (XZ937:Y)	J. Windmill
	G-CBKB	Bücker Bü 181C Bestmann	G. D. Snadden
	G-CBKD	Westland Gazelle HT.2	Flying Scout Ltd
	G-CBKF	Easy Raider J2.2 (2)	G. A. J. Salter
	G-CBKG	Thruster T.600N 450 JAB	M. J. E. Fogarty
	G-CBKK	Ultramagic S-130 balloon	Hayrick Ltd
	G-CBKL	Raj Hamsa X'Air Jabiru(2)	G. Baxter & G. Ferries
	G-CBKM	Mainair Blade 912	T. E. Robinson
	G-CBKN	Mainair Blade 912	D. S. Clews
	G-CBKO	Mainair Blade 912S	S. J. Taft
	G-CBKR	PA-28-161 Warrior III	Yeovil Auto Tuning
	G-CBKU	Ikarus C.42 Cyclone FB UK	C. Blackburn
	G-CBKW	Pegasus Quantum 15-912	A. Sharma
	G-CBKY	Avtech Jabiru SP-470	I. A.Lavey
	G-CBLA	Aero Designs Pulsar XP	T. J. Searle
	G-CBLB	Technam P.92-EM Echo	R. Lewis-Evans
	G-CBLD	Mainair Blade 912S	N. E. King
	G-CBLF	Raj Hamsa X'Air 582(11)	L. J. Nelson
	G-CBLK	Hawker Hind	Aero Vintage Ltd
	G-CBLL	Pegasus Quantum 15-912	P. D. Alford
	G-CBLM	Mainair Blade 912	A. S. Saunders
	G-CBLN	Cameron Z-31 balloon	J. R. Lawson
	G-CBLO	Lindstrand LBL-42A balloon	D. G. Such
	G-CBLP	Raj Hamsa X'Air Falcon	A. C. Parsons
	G-CBLS	Fiat CR.42	Fighter Collection Ltd
	G-CBLT	Mainair Blade 912	E. D. Locke
	G-CBLW	Raj Hamsa X'Air Falcon 582(3)	R. G. Halliwell
	G-CBLY	Grob G.109B	G-CBLY Syndicate
	G-CBLZ	Rutan LongEz	Agent CEL, SLU
	G-CBMB	Cyclone Ax2000	T. H. Chadwick
	G-CBMC	Cameron Z-105 balloon	D. Jacobus
	G-CBME	Cessna F.172M	Skytrax Aviation Ltd
	G-CBML	DHC.6 Twin Otter 310	Isles of Scilly Skybus Ltd
	G-CBMM	Mainair Blade 912	W. L. Millar
	G-CBMO	PA-28 Cherokee 180	T. Rawlings
	G-CBMP	Cessna R.182	Orman (Carrolls Farm) Ltd
	G-CBMR	Medway Eclipser	D. S. Blofeld
	G-CBMT	Robin DR.400/180	R. J. Williamson
	G-CBMV	Pegasus Quantum 15	A. I. Howes
	G-CBMZ	Aerotechnik EV-97 Eurostar	J. C. O'Donnell
	G-CBNC	Mainair Blade 912	K. L. Smith
	G-CBNF	Rans S.7 Courier	I. M. Ross
	G-CBNG	Robin R.2112	D. Curtin, B. Heath, D. Marrani & P. Ruderham
	G-CBNI	Lindstrand LBL-180A balloon	L. Arias & M. A. Derbyshire
	G-CBNJ	Raj Hamsa X'Air 582 (11)	T. W. Whitty
	G-CBNL	Dyn'Aéro MCR-01 Club	D. H. Wilson
	G-CBNO	CFM Streak Shadow	P. J. Porter
	G-CBNT	Pegasus Quantum 15-912	R. D. Leigh
	G-CBNV	Rans S.6-ES Coyote II	C. Ricketts
	G-CBNW	Cameron N-105 balloon	Bailey Balloons
	G-CBNX	Mongomerie-Bensen B.8MR	J. B. Allan
	G-CBNZ	TEAM hi-MAX 1700R	A. P. S. John

Reg	Type	Owner or Operator	Notes
G-CBOC	Raj Hamsa X'Air 582 (5)	M. Donnelly	
G-CBOE	Hawker Hurricane IIB (AG244)	K. F. Grimminger	
G-CBOF	Shaw Europa XS	P. R. Tunney	
G-CBOG	Mainair Blade 912S	OG Group	
G-CBOM	Mainair Blade 912	G. Suckling	
G-CBOP	Avtech Jabiru UL-450	T. Briton	
G-CBOR	Cessna F.172N	R. P. Rochester	
G-CBOS	Rans S.6-ES Coyote II	J. T. Athulathmudali	
G-CBOW	Cameron Z-120 balloon	Ballooning Network Ltd	
G-CBOY	Pegasus Quantum 15-912	RM Aviation Ltd	
G-CBOZ	IDA Bacau Yakovlev Yak-52	M. J. Babbage	
G-CBPC	Sportavia-Putzer RF-5B	R. J. Woodhams	
G-CBPD	Ikarus C.42 Cyclone FB UK	Waxwing Group	
G-CBPE	SOCATA TB10 Tobago	A. F. Welch	
G-CBPI	PA-28R-201 Arrow III	M. L. Roland	
G-CBPM	Yakovlev Yak-50 (50 black)	P. W. Ansell	
G-CBPR	Avtech Jabiru UL-450	N. R. Andrew	
G-CBPU	Raj Hamsa X'Air R100(3)	R. Power	
G-CBPV	Zenair CH.601UL	C. J. Meadows	
G-CBPW	Lindstrand LBL-105A balloon	P. Donkin	
G-CBRB	Ultramagic S-105 balloon	P. C. Bailey	
G-CBRC	Jodel D.18	P. J.Gripton	
G-CBRD	Jodel D.18	J. D. Haslam	
G-CBRE	Mainair Blade 912	L. M. Marsh	
G-CBRK	Ultramagic M-77 balloon	R. Gower	
G-CBRM	Mainair Blade	M. H. Levy	
G-CBRR	Aerotechnik EV-97A Eurostar	T. O. Powley & M. S. Turner	
G-CBRT	Murphy Elite	T. W. Baylie	
G-CBRV	Cameron C-90 balloon	C. J. Teall	
G-CBRW	Aerostar Yakovlev Yak-52 (50 grey)	Max-Alpha Aviation GmbH/Germany	
G-CBRX	Zenair CH.601UL Zodiac	C. J. Meadows	
G-CBSF	Westland Gazelle HT.2	Falcon Aviation Ltd	
G-CBSI	Westland Gazelle HT.3 (XZ934:U)	P. S. Unwin	
G-CBSK	Westland Gazelle HT.3 (ZB627:A)	Falcon Flying Group	
G-CBSO	PA-28-181 Archer II	Archer One Ltd	
G-CBSU	Avtech Jabiru UL	K. R. Crawley	
G-CBSZ	Mainair Blade 912S	P. J. Nolan	
G-CBTB	I.I.I. Sky Arrow 650TS	S. J. Hatherall	
G-CBTD	Pegasus Quantum 15-912	D. Baillie	
G-CBTE	Mainair Blade 912S	K. R. Hine	
G-CBTK	Raj Hamsa X'Air 582 (5)	J. Dewinter	
G-CBTM	Mainair Blade	K. G. Osborne	
G-CBTN	PA-31 Navajo C	Durban Aviation Services Ltd	
G-CBTO	Rans S.6-ES Coyote II	A. J. Gibson	
G-CBTR	Lindstrand LBL-120A balloon	R. H. Etherington	
G-CBTS	Gloster Gamecock (replica)	Retro Track & Air (UK) Ltd	
G-CBTT	PA-28-181 Archer II	Cedar Aviation Ltd (G-BFMM)	
G-CBTW	Mainair Blade 912	J. R. Davis	
G-CBTX	Denney Kitfox Mk.2	G. I. Doake	
G-CBUC	Raj Hamsa X'Air 582 (5)	G-CBUC Group	
G-CBUD	Pegasus Quantum 15-912	G. N. S. Farrant	
G-CBUF	Flight Design CT2K	D. B. Bluff	
G-CBUG	Technam P.92-EM Echo	S. R. A. Brierley & K. D. Mitchell	
G-CBUI	Westland Wasp HAS.1 (XT420:606)	C. J. Marsden	
G-CBUJ	Raj Hamsa X'Air 582 (10)	R. G. Herrod	
G-CBUK	Van's RV-6A	P. G. Greenslade	
G-CBUN	Barker Charade	T. M. Jones	
G-CBUO	Cameron O-90 balloon	W. J. Treacy & P. M. Smith	
G-CBUP	VPM M-16 Tandem Trainer	J. S. Firth	
G-CBUS	Pegasus Quantum 15	G. Hitchcox	
G-CBUU	Pegasus Quantum 15-912	J. A. Walker	
G-CBUX	Cyclone AX2000	T. J. Wilkinson	
G-CBUY	Rans S.6-ES Coyote II	S. T. Cadywould	
G-CBUZ	Pegasus Quantum 15	D. G. Seymour	
G-CBVA	Thruster T.600N 450	J. H. Brady	
G-CBVC	Raj Hamsa X'Air 582 (5)	J. Waring	
G-CBVD	Cameron C-60 balloon	Phoenix Balloons Ltd	
G-CBVF	Murphy Maverick 430	D. S. Evans	
G-CBVH	Lindstrand LBL-120A balloon	Alba Ballooning Ltd	
G-CBVM	Aerotechnik EV-97 Eurostar	M. Sharpe	
G-CBVN	Pegasus Quik	RIKI Group	

Notes	Reg	Type	Owner or Operator
	G-CBVP	Bell 412EP	FB Leasing Ltd
	G-CBVR	Best Off Skyranger 912 (2)	S. H. Lunney
	G-CBVS	Best Off Skyranger 912 (1)	S. C. Cornock
	G-CBVU	PA-28R Cherokee Arrow 200-II	M. P. Laing
	G-CBVV	Cameron N-120 balloon	John Aimo Balloons SAS/Italy
	G-CBVX	Cessna 182P	S. J. Brenchley
	G-CBVY	Ikarus C.42 Cyclone FB UK	Grandpa's Flying Group
	G-CBVZ	Flight Design CT2K	O. W. Achurch
	G-CBWA	Flight Design CT2K	J. Paterson
	G-CBWD	PA-28-161 Warrior III	J. Wright
	G-CBWE	Aerotechnik EV-97 Eurostar	J. & C. W. Hood
	G-CBWG	Aerotechnik EV-97 Eurostar	W. J. Upton
	G-CBWJ	Thruster T. 600N 450	J. K. Clayton & K. D. Smith
	G-CBWK	Ultramagic H-77 balloon	S. J. Stevens
	G-CBWN	Campbell Cricket Mk.6	R. S. Sanby
	G-CBWO	Rotorway Executive 162F	N. T. Oakman
	G-CBWP	Shaw Europa	T. W. Greaves
	G-CBWS	Whittaker MW6 Merlin	K. R. Emery
	G-CBWW	Skyranger Swift 912 (1)	A. Gilruth
	G-CBWY	Raj Hamsa X'Air 582 (6)	J. C. Rose
	G-CBWZ	Robinson R22 Beta	J. Fleming
	G-CBXB	Lindstrand LBL-150A balloon	M. A. Webb
	G-CBXC	Ikarus C.42 Cyclone FB UK	M. & P. L. Eardley
	G-CBXE	Easy Raider J2.2 (3)	A. K. Day
	G-CBXF	Easy Raider J2.2 (2)	M. R. Grunwell
	G-CBXG	Thruster T.600N 450	A. Campbell
	G-CBXM	Mainair Blade	A. R. Young
	G-CBXN	Robinson R22 Beta	N. M. G. Pearson
	G-CBXR	Raj Hamsa X-Air Falcon 582 (1)	J. F. Heath
	G-CBXS	Skyranger 912 (2)	The Ince Skyranger Group
	G-CBXU	TEAM miniMAX 91A	D. Crowhurst
	G-CBXW	Shaw Europa XS	R. G. Fairall
	G-CBXZ	Rans S.6-ES Coyote II	A. Faehndrich
	G-CBYB	Rotorway Executive 162F	Clark Contracting
	G-CBYD	Rans S.6-ES Coyote II	R. Burland
	G-CBYF	Mainair Blade	R. Watton
	G-CBYH	Aeroprakt A.22 Foxbat	G. C. Moore
	G-CBYI	Pegasus Quantum 15-503	The G-BCYI Group
	G-CBYM	Mainair Blade	D. Reid
	G-CBYN	Shaw Europa XS	G. M. Tagg
	G-CBYO	Pegasus Quik	G-CBYO Syndicate
	G-CBYP	Whittaker MW6-S Fat Boy Flyer	W. G. Reynolds
	G-CBYR	Bell 412EP	FB Heliservices Ltd
	G-CBYS	Lindstrand LBL-21 balloon France	B. M. Reed/France
	G-CBYT	Thruster T.600N 450	P. McAteer
	G-CBYU	PA-28-161 Warrior II	Stapleford Flying Club Ltd
	G-CBYV	Pegasus Quantum 15-912	G-CBYV Syndicate
	G-CBYW	Hatz CB-1	T. A. Hinton
	G-CBYZ	Tecnam P92-EM Echo-Super	B. Weaver
	G-CBZA	Mainair Blade	M. Lowe
	G-CBZD	Mainair Blade	G. P. J. Davies
	G-CBZE	Robinson R44	Alps (Scotland) Ltd
	G-CBZH	Pegasus Quik	M. P. Chew
	G-CBZJ	Lindstrand LBL-25A balloon	Pegasus Ballooning
	G-CBZM	Avtech Jabiru UL-450	A. R. Vincent & C. A. S. Powell
	G-CBZN	Rans S.6-ES Coyote II	K. Stevens
	G-CBZP	Hawker Fury 1 (K5674)	Historic Aircraft Collection
	G-CBZR	PA-28R-201 Arrow III	Folada Aero & Technical Services Ltd
	G-CBZS	Aurora	J. Lynden
	G-CBZT	Pegasus Quik	H. M. Roberts
	G-CBZW	Zenair CH.701 STOL	S. Richens
	G-CBZX	Dyn' Aero MCR-01 ULC	A. C. N. Freeman & M. P. Wilson
	G-CBZZ	Cameron Z-275 balloon	A. C. K. Rawson & J. J. Rudoni
	G-CCAB	Mainair Blade	L. Friend
	G-CCAC	Aerotech EV-97 Eurostar	K. W. Eskins
	G-CCAD	Mainair Pegasus Quik	M. Richardson
	G-CCAE	Avtech Jabiru UL-450	D. Logan
	G-CCAF	Best Off Skyranger 912 (1)	G. Everett & D. N. Smith
	G-CCAG	Mainair Blade 912	A. Robinson
	G-CCAK	Zenair CN.601HD	G and J E Trading Ltd

Reg	Type	Owner or Operator	Notes
G-CCAL	Technam P.92-EA Echo	G. Hawkins	
G-CCAP	Robinson R22 Beta II	D. Baker, M. Healer & H. Price	
G-CCAS	Pegasus Quik	Caunton Alpha Syndicate	
G-CCAT	AA-5A Cheetah	Rate 1 Aero Ltd (G-OAJH/G-KILT/G-BJFA)	
G-CCAV	PA-28-181 Archer II	Archer II Ltd	
G-CCAW	Mainair Blade 912	I. G. Molesworth	
G-CCAY	Cameron Z-42 balloon	P. Stern	
G-CCAZ	Mainair Pegasus Quik	J. P. Floyd	
G-CCBA	Skyranger R.100	Fourstrokes Group	
G-CCBB	Cameron N-90 balloon	D. M. Turley & L. M. Franks	
G-CCBC	Thruster T.600N 450	M. K. Boydle	
G-CCBG	Skyranger Swift 912(1)	K. Wileman	
G-CCBH	PA-28 Cherokee 236	B. C. Faulkner	
G-CCBI	Raj Hamsa X'Air 582(11)	N. Byrne	
G-CCBJ	Skyranger 912 (2)	S. D. J. Harvey	
G-CCBK	Aerotechnik EV-97 Eurostar	B. S. Waycott	
G-CCBM	Aerotechnik EV-97 Eurostar	P. W. Nestor & B. Hunter	
G-CCBN	Scale Replica SE-5a (80105/19)	S. P. Rollason	
G-CCBR	Jodel D.120	A. & S. Dunne	
G-CCBT	Cameron Z-90 balloon	I. J. Sharpe	
G-CCBW	Sherwood Ranger	A. L. Virgoe	
G-CCBX	Raj Hamsa X'Air 133 (2)	S. Hunt	
G-CCBZ	Aero Designs Pulsar	J. M. Keane	
G-CCCA	VS.509 Spitfire Tr.IX (PV202)	Propshop Ltd (G-TRIX)	
G-CCCB	Thruster T.600N 450	J. Hartland	
G-CCCD	Mainair Pegasus Quantum 15	R. N. Gamble	
G-CCCE	Aeroprakt A.22 Foxbat	P. Sykes	
G-CCCF	Thruster T.600N 450	P. R. Norman	
G-CCCG	Mainair Pegasus Quik	J. W. Sandars	
G-CCCH	Thruster T600N 450	G. Scullion	
G-CCCJ	Nicollier HN.700 Menestrel II	G. A. Rodmell	
G-CCCK	Skyranger 912 (2)	Hilltop Flying Club	
G-CCCM	Skyranger 912 (2)	Connel Gliding Group	
G-CCCO	Aerotechnik EV-97A Eurostar	D. R. G. Whitelaw	
G-CCCR	Sky Ranger 912(2)	M. Norman	
G-CCCT	Ikarus C42 FB UK	N. Armstrong	
G-CCCV	Raj Hamsa X'Air Falcon 133 (1)	G. J. Boyer	
G-CCCW	Pereira Osprey 2	D. J. Southward	
G-CCCY	Skyranger 912 (2)	A. Watson	
G-CCDB	Mainair Pegasus Quik	P. K. Dale	
G-CCDC	Rans S-6-ES Coyote II	D. W. Bayliss	
G-CCDD	Mainair Pegasus Quik	G. Clark	
G-CCDF	Mainair Pegasus Quik	R. P. McGann	
G-CCDG	Skyranger 912 (1)	Freebird Group	
G-CCDH	Skyranger 912 (2)	C. F. Rogers	
G-CCDJ	Raj Hamsa X'Air Falcon 582 (2)	A. L. Lyons	
G-CCDK	Pegasus Quantum 15-912	D. Bishop	
G-CCDL	Raj Hamsa X'Air Falcon 582 (2)	J. Cropper	
G-CCDO	Mainair Pegasus Quik	S. T. Welsh	
G-CCDP	Raj Hamsa X'Air R.100 (3)	B. Moore & M. V. Daly	
G-CCDS	Nicollier HN.700 Menestrel II	J. J. Mason	
G-CCDU	Tecnam P92-EM Echo	G. P. & P. T. Willcox	
G-CCDV	Thruster T.600N 450	G. C. Hobson	
G-CCDX	Aerotechnik EV-97 Eurostar	G-CCDX Syndicate 2013	
G-CCDY	Skyranger 912 (2)	I. Brumpton	
G-CCDZ	Pegasus Quantum 15-912	C. Dawes	
G-CCEA	Mainair Pegasus Quik	G. D. Ritchie	
G-CCEB	Thruster T600N 450	M. Young	
G-CCED	Zenair CH.601UL	J. Donaldson	
G-CCEF	Shaw Europa	C. P. Garner	
G-CCEH	Skyranger 912 (2)	ZC Owners	
G-CCEJ	Aerotechnik EV-97 Eurostar	J. R. Iveson	
G-CCEK	Kiss 400-582 (1)	J. L. Stone	
G-CCEL	Avtech Jabiru UL	F. McMullan	
G-CCEM	Aerotechnik EV-97 Eurostar	Oxenhope Flying Group	
G-CCEN	Cameron Z-120 balloon	T. Hook	
G-CCES	Raj Hamsa X'Air 3203(1)	G. V. McCloskey	
G-CCET	Nova Vertex 28 hang glider	M. Hay	
G-CCEU	RAF 2000 GTX-SE gyroplane	J. G. Roberts	
G-CCEW	Mainair Pegasus Quik	A. B. Mackinnon	
G-CCEY	Raj Hamsa X'582 (11)	I. B. Lavelle	

Notes	Reg	Type	Owner or Operator
	G-CCEZ	Easy Raider J2.2	A. N. George
	G-CCFA	Air Creation 581(1)/Kiss 400	A. E. Barron
	G-CCFC	Robinson R44 II	Quinn Construction Ltd
	G-CCFD	BFC Challenger II	T. H. Knapton
	G-CCFE	Tipsy Nipper T.66 Srs 2	N. S. Dell
	G-CCFG	Dyn'Aéro MCR-01 Club	P. H. Milward
	G-CCFI	PA-32 Cherokee Six 260	P. McManus & N. Whelan
	G-CCFJ	Kolb Twinstar Mk.3	M. P. Wiseman
	G-CCFK	Shaw Europa	C. R. Knapton
	G-CCFL	Mainair Pegasus Quik	T. E. Thomas
	G-CCFO	Pitts S-1S Special	A. D. Hoy
	G-CCFS	Diamond DA40D Star	A. Tullie
	G-CCFT	Mainair Pegasus Quantum 15-912	D. P. Gawlowski
	G-CCFU	Diamond DA40D Star	Jetstream Aviation Training & Services SA/Greece
	G-CCFV	Lindstrand LBL-77A balloon	Lindstrand Media Ltd
	G-CCFW	WAR Focke-Wulf Fw.190	K. S. Thomas
	G-CCFX	EAA Acrosport 2	G. Cameron
	G-CCFY	Rotorway Executive 162F	A. & A. Thomas
	G-CCFZ	Ikarus C.42 FB UK	B. W. Drake
	G-CCGA	Medway EclipseR	N. Brigginshaw
	G-CCGB	TEAM mini-MAX	A. D, Pentland
	G-CCGC	Mainair Pegasus Quik	C. A. McLean & D. T. McAfee
	G-CCGF	Robinson R22 Beta	Road & Air Vehicle Sales Ltd
	G-CCGG	Jabiru Aircraft Jabiru J430	A. Simmers
	G-CCGH	Supermarine Aircraft Spitfire Mk.26 (AB196)	Cokebusters Ltd
	G-CCGK	Mainair Blade	C. M. Babiy & M. Hurn
	G-CCGM	Kiss 450-582 (1)	J. Howarth
	G-CCGO	Medway EclipseR	D. A. Coupland
	G-CCGS	Dornier 328-100	Loganair Ltd
	G-CCGU	Van's RV-9A	B. J. Main & A. Strachan
	G-CCGW	Shaw Europa	D. Buckley
	G-CCGY	Cameron Z-105 balloon	Atlantic Ballooning BVBA/Belgium
	G-CCHH	Pegasus Quik	J. Viner & W. Barton
	G-CCHI	Mainair Pegasus Quik	M. R. Starling
	G-CCHL	PA-28-181 Archer iii	Archer Three Ltd
	G-CCHM	Kiss 450-582(1)	M. J. Jessup
	G-CCHN	Corby CJ.1 Starlet	M. F. Pocock
	G-CCHP	Cameron Z-31 balloon	M. H. Redman
	G-CCHR	Easy Raider 583 (1)	S. Wilkes
	G-CCHS	Raj Hamsa X'Air 582	M. Law
	G-CCHT	Cessna 152	A. J. Gomes
	G-CCHV	Mainair Rapier	B. J. Wesley
	G-CCHX	Scheibe SF.25C Falke	Lasham Gliding Society Ltd
	G-CCID	Jabiru Aircraft Jabiru J430	B. J. Robe & F. Patterson
	G-CCIF	Mainair Blade	A. R. Vincent & P. W. Dunn
	G-CCII	ICP Savannah Jabiru (3)	D. C. Crawley
	G-CCIJ	PA-28R Cherokee Arrow 180	S. A. Hughes
	G-CCIK	Skyranger 912 (2)	M. D. Kirby
	G-CCIR	Van's RV-8	G-CCIR Group
	G-CCIU	Cameron N-105 balloon	P. Wiemann
	G-CCIW	Raj Hamsa X'Air 582 (2)	A. Evans
	G-CCIY	Skyranger 912 (2)	L. F. Tanner
	G-CCIZ	PZL-110 Koliber 160A	M. Whelehan
	G-CCJA	Skyranger 912 (2)	I. F. Bastin
	G-CCJD	Pegasus Quantum 15	P. Clark
	G-CCJH	Lindstrand LBL-90A balloon	J. R. Hoare
	G-CCJI	Van's RV-6	R. N. Bennison
	G-CCJJ	Medway Pirana	J. K. Sargent
	G-CCJK	Aerostar Yakovlev Yak-52	G-CCJK Group
	G-CCJL	Supermarine Spitfire XXVI (PV303)	P. M. Whitaker
	G-CCJM	Mainair Pegasus Quik	S. R. Smyth
	G-CCJN	Rans S.6ES Coyote II	W. A. Ritchie
	G-CCJO	ICP-740 Savannah Jabiru 4	R. & I. Fletcher
	G-CCJT	Skyranger 912 (2)	Juliet Tango Group
	G-CCJU	ICP MXP-740 Savannah Jabiru (4)	G. Carr
	G-CCJV	Aeroprakt A.22 Foxbat	J. Keats
	G-CCJW	Skyranger 912 (2)	J. R. Walter
	G-CCJX	Shaw Europa XS	J. S. Baranski
	G-CCKF	Best Off Skyranger 912 (1)	M. Johnson
	G-CCKG	Best Off Skyranger 912 (2)	R. J. Ripley

Reg	Type	Owner or Operator	Notes
G-CCKH	Diamond DA40D Star	Flying Time Ltd	
G-CCKJ	Raj Hamsa X'Air 133 (3)	G. A. Davidson	
G-CCKL	Aerotechnik EV-97A Eurostar	G-CCKL Group	
G-CCKM	Mainair Pegasus Quik	J. P. Quinlan	
G-CCKN	Nicollier HN.700 Menestrel II	C. R. Partington	
G-CCKO	Mainair Pegasus Quik	L. A. Harper	
G-CCKR	Pietenpol Air Camper	N. L. Parker & E. S. E. Hibbard	
G-CCKT	Hapi Cygnet SF-2	P. W. Abraham	
G-CCKV	Isaacs Fury II (K7271)	M. J. Laundy	
G-CCKZ	Customcraft A-25 balloon	P. A. George	
G-CCLF	Best Off Skyranger 912 (2)	C. R. Stevens & S. S. Uzochukwu	
G-CCLG	Lindstrand LBL-105A balloon	M. A. Derbyshire	
G-CCLH	Rans S.6-ES Coyote II	N. D. Townend	
G-CCLJ	PA-28-140 Cherokee Cruiser	A. M. George	
G-CCLM	Mainair Pegasus Quik	G. Cole	
G-CCLO	Ultramagic H-77 balloon-	S. J. M. Hornsby	
G-CCLP	ICP MXP-740 Savannah	C. J. Powell & A. H. Watkins	
G-CCLR	Schleicher Ash 26E	A. Darby & R. N. John	
G-CCLS	Comco Ikarus C.42 FB UK	B. D. Wykes	
G-CCLT	Powerchute Kestrel ★	Newark Air Museum/Newark	
G-CCLU	Best Off Skyranger 912	K. Wensley	
G-CCLW	Diamond DA40D Star	Shacklewell Diamond Group	
G-CCLX	Mainair Pegasus Quik	T. D. Welburn	
G-CCMC	Jabiru Aircraft Jabiru UL 450	K. J. Simpson	
G-CCMD	Mainair Pegasus Quik	J. T. McCormack	
G-CCME	Mainair Pegasus Quik	A. R. Hughes	
G-CCMH	M.2H Hawk Major	M. C. Ochoa	
G-CCMJ	Easy Raider J2.2 (1)	G. F. Clews	
G-CCMK	Raj Hamsa X'Air Falcon	M. J. J. Clutterbuck	
G-CCML	Mainair Pegasus Quik	G-CCML Syndicate	
G-CCMM	Dyn'Aéro MCR-01 ULC Banbi	J. D. Harris	
G-CCMN	Cameron C-90 balloon	C. Butler	
G-CCMO	Aerotechnik EV-97 Eurostar	IBFC EV97 Group	
G-CCMP	Aerotechnik EV-97 Eurostar	M. Dunlop	
G-CCMR	Robinson R22 Beta	G. F. Smith	
G-CCMT	Thruster T.600N 450	E. J. Studdert-Kennedy	
G-CCMU	Rotorway Executive 162F	Southern Helicopters Ltd	
G-CCMW	CFM Shadow Srs.DD	K. H. Creed	
G-CCMZ	Best Off Skyranger 912 (2)	D. D. Appleford	
G-CCNA	Jodel DR.100A (Replica)	R. Everitt	
G-CCND	Van's RV-9A	R. Stalker	
G-CCNE	Mainair Pegasus Quantum 15	G. D. Barker	
G-CCNF	Raj Hamsa X'Air Falcon 912(2)	B. P. & L. A. Perkins	
G-CCNG	Flight Design CT2K	Atheys Moor CT2K Group	
G-CCNH	Rans S.6ES Coyote II	J. E. Howard & R. S. Noremberg	
G-CCNJ	Skyranger 912 (2)	J. D. Buchanan	
G-CCNL	Raj Hamsa X'Air Falcon 133(1)	S. E. Vallance	
G-CCNM	Mainair Pegasus Quik	F. J. Thorne & K. D. Adams	
G-CCNP	Flight Design CT2K	North East Flying Club Ltd	
G-CCNR	Skyranger 912 (2)	P. Horsley	
G-CCNS	Skyranger 912 (2)	D. Murdoch, P. V. Griffiths & F. Gallacher	
G-CCNT	Ikarus C.42 FB80	November Tango Group	
G-CCNW	Mainair Pegasus Quantum Lite	T. D. Cacutt	
G-CCNX	CAB CAP-10B	Arc Input Ltd	
G-CCOB	Aero C.104 Jungmann	H. C. Tomkins	
G-CCOC	Mainair Pegasus Quantum 15	C. M. Ayres	
G-CCOF	Rans S.6-ESA Coyote II	G. J. Jones	
G-CCOG	Mainair Pegasus Quik	D. P. Clarke	
G-CCOH	Raj Hamsa X'Air Falcon Jabiru(3)	D. R. Sutton	
G-CCOK	Mainair Pegasus Quik	C. Curtin	
G-CCOM	Westland Lysander IIIA (V9312)	Propshop Ltd	
G-CCOP	Ultramagic M-105 balloon	M. E. J. Whitewood	
G-CCOR	Sequoia F.8L Falco	D. J. Thoma	
G-CCOT	Cameron Z-105 balloon	A. D. McCutcheon	
G-CCOU	Mainair Pegasus Quik	D. E. J. McVicker	
G-CCOV	Shaw Europa XS	B. C. Barton	
G-CCOW	Mainair Pegasus Quik	S. Gibson	
G-CCOY	NA AT-6D Harvard II	Classic Flying Machine Collection Ltd	
G-CCOZ	Monnett Sonerai II	W. H. Cole	
G-CCPC	Mainair Pegasus Quik	S. M. Oliver	
G-CCPD	Campbell Cricket Mk.4	T. H. Geake	

Notes	Reg	Type	Owner or Operator
	G-CCPE	Steen Skybolt	C. Moore
	G-CCPF	Skyranger 912 (2)	J. R. M. Macpherson
	G-CCPG	Mainair Pegasus Quik	A.W. Lowrie
	G-CCPH	EV-97 TeamEurostar UK	A. H. Woolley
	G-CCPJ	EV-97 TeamEurostar UK	J. S. Webb
	G-CCPL	Skyranger 912 (2)	B. Drinkwater
	G-CCPM	Mainair Blade 912	P. S. Davies
	G-CCPN	Dyn'Aéro MCR-01 Club	J. C. Thompson
	G-CCPP	Cameron 70 Concept balloon	Sarnia Balloon Group
	G-CCPS	Ikarus C.42 FB100 VLA	H. Cullens
	G-CCPT	Cameron Z-90 balloon	A. Hall
	G-CCPV	Jabiru J400	J. R. Lawrence
	G-CCRB	Kolb Twinstar Mk.3 (modified)	D. H. Lewis
	G-CCRC	Cessna Tu.206G	D. M. Penny
	G-CCRF	Mainair Pegasus Quantum 15	C. J. Middleton
	G-CCRG	Ultramagic M-77 balloon	M. Cowling
	G-CCRI	Raj Hamsa X'Air 582 (5)	D. K. Beaumont
	G-CCRJ	Shaw Europa	F. M. Ward
	G-CCRK	Luscombe 8A Silvaire	J. R. Kimberley
	G-CCRN	Thruster T.600N 450	S. J. Evans
	G-CCRP	Thruster T.600N 450	W. R. Grantham & R. J. Edgell (G-ULLY)
	G-CCRT	Mainair Pegasus Quantum 15	N. Mitchell
	G-CCRV	Skyranger 912 (1)	D. Matthews
	G-CCRW	Mainair Pegasus Quik	M. L. Cade
	G-CCRX	Jabiru UL-450	M. Everest
	G-CCSD	Mainair Pegasus Quik	A. D. Dias
	G-CCSF	Mainair Pegasus Quik	D. G. Barnes & A. Sorah
	G-CCSG	Cameron Z-275 balloon	Wickers World Ltd
	G-CCSH	Mainair Pegasus Quik	G. Carr
	G-CCSL	Mainair Pegasus Quik	A. J. Harper
	G-CCSP	Cameron N-77 balloon	D. Berg
	G-CCSR	Aerotechnik EV-97A Eurostar	I. & S. Sharpe
	G-CCST	PA-32R-301 Saratoga	A. R. Whibley
	G-CCSX	Best Off Skyranger 912(1)	T. Jackson
	G-CCSY	Mainair Pegasus Quik	G. J. Gibson
	G-CCTA	Zenair CH.601UL Zodiac	J. R. Hunt
	G-CCTC	Mainair Pegasus Quik	D. R. Purslow
	G-CCTD	Mainair Pegasus Quik	R. N. S. Taylor
	G-CCTE	Dyn'Aéro MCR-01 Banbi	C. J. McInnes
	G-CCTF	Aerotek Pitts S-2A Special	Stampe and Pitts Flying Group
	G-CCTG	Van's RV-3B	E. R. J. Hicks
	G-CCTH	EV-97 TeamEurostar UK	T. C. Hilder
	G-CCTI	EV-97 TeamEurostar UK	TI Group
	G-CCTM	Mainair Blade	J. N. Hanso
	G-CCTO	EV-97 Eurostar	H. Cooke& B. Robertson
	G-CCTP	EV-97 Eurostar	P. E. Rose
	G-CCTR	Skyranger 912	K. Mallin
	G-CCTT	Cessna 172S	Highland Aviation Training Ltd
	G-CCTU	Mainair Pegasus Quik	N. J. Lindsay
	G-CCTV	Rans S.6ESA Coyote II	B. Swindon
	G-CCTZ	Mainair Pegasus Quik 912S	S. Baker
	G-CCUA	Mainair Pegasus Quik	J. B. Crawford
	G-CCUB	Piper J-3C-65 Cub	G. Cormack
	G-CCUC	Best Off Skyranger J2.2(1)	R. Marrs
	G-CCUE	Ultramagic T-180 balloon	N. J. Dunnington
	G-CCUF	Skyranger 912(2)	R. E. Parker
	G-CCUH	RAF 2000 GTX-SE	V. G. Freke
	G-CCUI	Dyn'Aéro MCR-01 Banbi	J. T. Morgan
	G-CCUL	Shaw Europa XS	Europa 6
	G-CCUR	Mainair Pegasus Quantum 15-912	B. J. Fallows
	G-CCUT	Aerotechnik EV-97 Eurostar	Doctor & the Medics
	G-CCUY	Shaw Europa	N. Evans
	G-CCVA	Aerotechnik EV-97 Eurostar	K. J. Scott
	G-CCVE	Raj Hamsa X'Air Jabiru (3)	G. J. Slater
	G-CCVF	Lindstrand LBL-105 balloon	Alan Patterson Design
	G-CCVH	Curtiss H-75A-1 (82:8)	The Fighter Collection
	G-CCVI	Zenair CH.701 SP	P. J. Bunce
	G-CCVJ	Raj Hamsa X'Air Falcon Jabiru (3)	M. Pritchard
	G-CCVK	Aerotechnik EV-97 TeamEurostar UK	J. Holditch
	G-CCVL	Zenair CH.601XL Zodiac	A. Y.-T. Leung & G. Constantine
	G-CCVM	Van's RV-7	M. J. Mothershaw

Reg	Type	Owner or Operator	Notes
G-CCVN	Jabiru SP-470	Midlands Flying Group	
G-CCVP	Beech 58	Richard Nash Cars Ltd	
G-CCVR	Skyranger 912(2)	M. J. Batchelor	
G-CCVS	Van's RV-6A	L. Jensen (G-CCVC)	
G-CCVU	Robinson R22 Beta II	J. H. P. S. Sargent	
G-CCVW	Nicollier HN.700 Menestrel II	B. F. Enock	
G-CCVX	Mainair Tri Flyer 330	J. A. Shufflebotham	
G-CCVZ	Cameron O-120 balloon	T. M. C. McCoy	
G-CCWC	Skyranger 912	E. S. Jones	
G-CCWL	Mainair Blade	M. S. Eglin	
G-CCWM	Robin DR.400/180	D. M. Scorer	
G-CCWO	Mainair Pegasus Quantum 15-912	R. Fitzgerald	
G-CCWP	Aerotechnik EV-97 TeamEurostar UK	Airsports	
G-CCWU	Skyranger 912(1)	A. R. Young	
G-CCWV	Mainair Pegasus Quik	C. Buttery	
G-CCWW	Mainair Pegasus Quantum 15-912	T. Hudson	
G-CCWZ	Raj Hamsa X'Air Falcon Jabiru(3)	A. P. Love	
G-CCXA	Boeing Stearman A75N-1 Kaydet (669)	Skymax (Aviation) Ltd	
G-CCXB	Boeing Stearman B75N1 (699)	C. D. Walker	
G-CCXC	Avion Mudry CAP-10B	J. E. Keighley	
G-CCXF	Cameron Z-90 balloon	A. J. M. Pollock	
G-CCXG	SE-5A (replica) (C5430)	C. Morris	
G-CCXH	Skyranger J2.2	M. J. O'Connor	
G-CCXK	Pitts S-1S Special	P. G. Bond	
G-CCXM	Skyranger 912(1)	P. Batchelor	
G-CCXN	Skyranger 912(1)	G. D. P. Clouting	
G-CCXO	Corgy CJ-1 Starlet	S. C. Ord	
G-CCXP	ICP Savannah Jabiru	D. Ballard	
G-CCXS	Montgomerie-Bensen B.8MR	A. Morgan	
G-CCXT	Mainair Pegasus Quik	C. F. Yaxley	
G-CCXU	Diamond DA40D Star	R. J. & L. Hole	
G-CCXV	Thruster T.600N 450	R. J. Humphries	
G-CCXW	Thruster T.600N 450	D. J. Atkinson	
G-CCXX	AG-5B Tiger	P. D. Lock	
G-CCXZ	Mainair Pegasus Quik	M. Innes	
G-CCYB	Escapade 912(1)	B. E. & S. M. Renehan	
G-CCYC	Robinson R44 II	J. Butler	
G-CCYE	Mainair Pegasus Quik	P. M. Scrivener	
G-CCYG	Robinson R44 II	Mosswood Carsavan Park	
G-CCYI	Cameron O-105 balloon	S. Bitti/Italy	
G-CCYJ	Mainair Pegasus Quik	G. M. Cruise-Smith	
G-CCYL	MainairPegasus Quantum 15	D. Pattenden & S. Haines	
G-CCYM	Skyranger 912	I. Pilton	
G-CCYO	Christen Eagle II	P. C. Woolley	
G-CCYP	Colt 56A balloon	Magical Adventures Ltd	
G-CCYS	Ikarus C.42 FB80	Airbourne Aviation Ltd	
G-CCYS	Cessna F.182Q	C. J. Griffiths	
G-CCYU	Ultramagic S-90 balloon	J. Francis	
G-CCYY	PA-28-161 Warrior II	Flightcontrol Ltd	
G-CCYZ	Dornier EKW C3605	CW Tomkins Ltd	
G-CCZB	Mainair Pegasus Quantum 15	J. A. Crofts	
G-CCZD	Van's RV-7	A. P. Hatton & E. A. Stokes	
G-CCZJ	Raj Hamsa X' Air Falcon 582	J. Walker	
G-CCZL	Ikarus C-42 FB80	Shadow Aviation Ltd	
G-CCZM	Skyranger 912S	M. Smith & S. Holsey	
G-CCZN	Rans S.6-ES Coyote II	R. D. Proctor	
G-CCZO	Mainair Pegasus Quik	P. G. Penhaligon	
G-CCZR	Medway EclipseR	G. A. Hazell	
G-CCZS	Raj Hamsa X'Air Falcon 582	S. Siddiqui	
G-CCZT	Van's RV-9A	Zulu Tango Flying Group	
G-CCZV	PA-28-151 Warrior	London School of Flying Ltd	
G-CCZW	Mainair Pegasus Blade	D. Sisson	
G-CCZX	Robin DR.400/180	Robin Flying Club Ltd	
G-CCZY	Van's RV-9A	A. Hutchinson	
G-CCZZ	Aerotechnik EV-97 Eurostar	B. M Starck & J. P. Aitken	
G-CDAA	Mainair Pegasus Quantum 15-912	G. E. Parker	
G-CDAB	Glasair Super IISRG	D. A. Payne	
G-GDAC	Aerotechnik EV-97 TeamEurostar	C. R. Cousins	
G-CDAD	Lindstrand LBL-25A balloon	G. J. Madelin	
G-CDAE	Van's RV-6A	The Alpha Echo Group	

Notes	Reg	Type	Owner or Operator
	G-CDAI	Robin DR.400/140B	D. Hardy & J. Sambrook
	G-CDAL	Zenair CH.601UL Zodiac	D. S. T. Harris
	G-CDAO	Mainair Pegasus Quantum 15 -912	J. C. Duncan
	G-CDAP	Aerotechnik EV-97 TeamEurostar UK	L. N. Givens
	G-CDAR	Mainair Pegasus Quik	Caunton Graphites Syndicate
	G-CDAT	ICP MXP-740 Savannah Jabiru	G. M. Railson
	G-CDAX	Mainair Pegasus Quik	L. Hurman
	G-CDAY	Skyranger 912	Redlands Skyranger Group
	G-CDAZ	Aerotechnik EV-97 Eurostar	K. M. Howell
	G-CDBA	Skyranger 912(1)	G-CDBA Group
	G-CDBB	Mainair Pegasus Quik	J. McLaughlin
	G-CDBC	Aviation Enterprises Magnum	A. M. Fleming
	G-CDBD	Jabiru J400	I. D. Rutherford
	G-CDBE	Montgomerie-Bensen B.8M	P. Harwood
	G-CDBG	Robinson R22 Beta	Jepar Rotorcraft
	G-CDBJ	Yakovlev Yak-3	C. E. Bellhouse
	G-CDBK	Rotorway Executive 162F	R. S. Snell
	G-CDBM	Robin DR.400/180	C. M. Simmonds
	G-CDBO	Skyranger 912	G-CDBO Flying Group
	G-CDBR	Stolp SA.300 Starduster Too	R. J. Warren
	G-CDBU	Ikarus C.42 FB100	S. E. Meehan
	G-CDBV	Skyranger 912S	T. Smith & K. Hall
	G-CDBX	Shaw Europa XS	R. J. Bastin
	G-CDBY	Dyn'Aero MCR-01 ULC	A. Thornton
	G-CDBZ	Thruster T.600N 450	BZ Flying Group
	G-CDCC	Aerotechnik EV-97 Eurostar	J. R. Tomlin
	G-CDCD	Van's RVF-9A	RV9ers
	G-CDCE	Avions Mudry CAP-10B	The Tiger Club (1990) Ltd
	G-CDCF	Mainair Pegasus Quik	P. Thaxter
	G-CDCG	Ikarus C.42 FB UK	N. E. Ashton
	G-CDCH	Skyranger 912(1)	M. D. Protheroe
	G-CDCI	Pegasus Quik	R. J. Allarton
	G-CDCK	Pegasus Quik	P. W. Turrell
	G-CDCM	Ikarus C.42 FB UK	S. T. Allen
	G-CDCO	Ikarus C.42 FB UK	R. Urquhart
	G-CDCP	Avtech Jabiru J400	G. G. Johnstone
	G-CDCR	Savannah Jabiru(1)	T. Davidson
	G-CDCS	PA-12 Super Cruiser	P. Westerby-Jones
	G-CDCT	Aerotechnik EV-97 TeamEurostar UK	G. R. Nicholson
	G-CDCV	Robinson R44 II	3GR Comm Ltd
	G-CDCW	Escapade 912 (1)	S. G. Brown
	G-CDDA	SOCATA TB20 Trinidad	Z. Clean
	G-CDDB	Grob/Schempp-Hirth CS-11	R. Robins
	G-CDDF	Mainair Pegasus Quantum 15-912	Jarvy Enterprises Ltd
	G-CDDG	PA-26-161 Warrior II	JABM Ltd
	G-CDDH	Raj Hamsa X'Air Falcon	M. Roberts
	G-CDDI	Thruster T.600N 450	R. Nayak
	G-CDDK	Cessna 172M	B. K. & W. G. Ranger
	G-CDDL	Cameron Z-350 balloon	Adventure Balloons Ltd
	G-CDDN	Lindstrand LBL 90A balloon	Flying Enterprises
	G-CDDO	Raj Hamsa X'Air 133(2)	S. Bain
	G-CDDP	Lazer Z.230	G-CDDP Flying Group
	G-CDDR	Skyranger 582(1)	A. Greenwell & A. Carver
	G-CDDS	Zenair CH.601HD	P. R. Dalton
	G-CDDU	Skyranger 912(2)	R. Newton & P. A. Burton
	G-CDDW	Aeroprakt A.22 Foxbat	A. Assiaian
	G-CDDX	Thruster T.600N 450	B. S. P. Finch
	G-CDDY	Van's RV-8	J. F. D. Hallam
	G-CDEB	Saab 2000	Eastern Airways
	G-CDEF	PA-28-161 Cadet	Falcon Flying Services Ltd
	G-CDEH	ICP MXP-740 Savannah VG LS(1)	D. C. Crawley
	G-CDEM	Raj Hamsa X' Air 133	R. J. Froud
	G-CDEN	Mainair Pegasus Quantum 15 912	J. D. J. Spragg
	G-CDEO	PA-28 Cherokee 180	Perranporth Flying Club Ltd
	G-CDEP	Aerotechnik EV-97 TeamEurostar	Echo Papa Group
	G-CDET	Culver LCA Cadet	J. Gregson
	G-CDEU	Lindstrand LBL-90B balloon	N. Florence & P. J. Marshall
	G-CDEV	Escapade 912 (1)	Echo Victor Group
	G-CDEW	Pegasus Quik	S. D. Sparrow
	G-CDEX	Shaw Europa	K. Martindale

Reg	Type	Owner or Operator	Notes
G-CDFD	Scheibe SF.25C Falke	The Royal Air Force Gliding and Soaring Association	
G-CDFG	Mainair Pegasus Quik	D. Seiler	
G-CDFJ	Skyranger 912(1)	K. S. Reardon	
G-CDFK	Jabiru UL-450	J. C. Eagle	
G-CDFM	Raj Hamsa X'Air 582 (5)	W. A. Keel-Stocker	
G-CDFN	Thunder Ax7-77 balloon	E. Rullo/Italy	
G-CDFO	Pegasus Quik	The Foxtrot Oscars	
G-CDFR	Mainair Pegasus Quantum 15	P. D. J. Davies	
G-CDFU	Rans S.6-ES Coyote II	G. Mudd	
G-CDFW	Lovegrove Sheffy Gyroplane ★	Norfolk and Suffolk Aviation Museum/Flixton	
G-CDGA	Taylor JT.1 Monoplane	R. M. Larimore	
G-CDGB	Rans S.6-116 Coyote	S. Penoyre	
G-CDGC	Pegasus Quik	A. T. K. Crozier	
G-CDGD	Pegasus Quik	I. D. & V. A. Milne	
G-CDGE	Edge XT912-IIIB	M & G Flight	
G-CDGF	Ultramagic S-105 balloon	D. & K. Bareford	
G-CDGH	Rans S.6-ES Coyote	R. W. Keene & R. P. Carroll	
G-CDGI	Thruster T600N 450	P. A. Pilkington	
G-CDGN	Cameron C-90 balloon	M. C. Gibbons	
G-CDGO	Pegasus Quik	J. C. Townsend	
G-CDGP	Zenair CH 601XL	B. & P. J. Chandler	
G-CDGR	Zenair CH 701UL	I. A. R. Sim	
G-CDGS	AG-5B Tiger	R. K. Hyatt	
G-CDGT	Montgomerie-Parsons Two Place g/p	J. B. Allan	
G-CDGU	VS.300 Spitfire I (X4276)	Peter Monk Ltd	
G-CDGV	Bell 206B Jet Ranger III	1212BB LLP (G-GBRU)	
G-CDGW	PA-28-181 Archer III	Rutland Flying Group	
G-CDGX	Pegasus Quantum 15-912	S. R. Green	
G-CDGY	VS.349 Spitfire Mk VC	Aero Vintage Ltd	
G-CDHA	Best Off Skyranger 912S(1)	A. T. Cameron	
G-CDHC	Slingsby T67C	Brimpton Flying Group	
G-CDHE	Skyranger 912(2)	T. Collins	
G-CDHF	PA-30 Twin Comanche B	Green Go Aircraft KFT	
G-CDHG	Mainair Pegasus Quik	T. W. Pelan	
G-CDHJ	Lindstrand LBL-90B balloon	Lindstrand Hot Air Balloons Ltd	
G-CDHM	Pegasus Quantum 15	M. R. Smith	
G-CDHO	Raj Hamsa X'Air 133 (1)	S. Warburton	
G-CDHR	Ikarus C.42 FB80	Progress Vehicle Management Ltd	
G-CDHU	Best Off Skyranger Swift 912 (1)	G-CDHU Group	
G-CDHX	Aeroprakt A.22 Foxbat	N. E. Stokes	
G-CDHY	Cameron Z-90 balloon	S. F. Caie	
G-CDHZ	Nicollier HN.700 Menestrel II	G. E. Whittaker	
G-CDIA	Thruster T.600N 450	IA Flying Group	
G-CDIB	Cameron Z-350Z balloon	Ballooning Network Ltd	
G-CDIF	Mudry CAP-10B	J. D. Gordon	
G-CDIG	Aerotechnik EV-97 Eurostar	R. D. Masters	
G-CDIH	Cameron Z-275 balloon	Bailey Balloons Ltd	
G-CDIJ	Best Off Skyranger 912 (2)	K. C. Yeates	
G-CDIL	Pegasus Quantum 15-912	P. J. Doherty	
G-CDIO	Cameron Z-90 balloon	Slowfly Montgolfiere SNC/Italy	
G-CDIR	Mainair Pegasus Quantum 15-912	M. Crane	
G-CDIT	Cameron Z-105 balloon	Bailey Balloons Ltd	
G-CDIU	Skyranger 912S(1)	A. C. McAllister	
G-CDIX	Ikarus C.42 FB.100	T. G. Greenhill & J. G. Spinks	
G-CDIY	Aerotechnik EV-97A Eurostar	R. E. Woolsey	
G-CDIZ	Escapade 912(3)	E. G. Bishop & E. N. Dunn	
G-CDJB	Van's RV-4	J. K. Cook	
G-CDJD	ICP MXP-740 Savannah Jabiru (4)	D. W. Mullin	
G-CDJE	Thruster T.600N 450	R. J. Stamp	
G-CDJF	Flight Design CT2K	P. A. James	
G-CDJG	Zenair 601UL Zodiac	G-CDJG Group	
G-CDJI	UltraMagic M-120 balloon	Ascension Cider Co.Ltd	
G-CDJJ	IAV Yakovlev Yak-52	Digitakumi Ltd	
G-CDJK	Ikarus C.42 FB 80	R. C. Best	
G-CDJL	Avtech Jabiru J400	J. Gardiner	
G-CDJN	RAF 2000 GTX-SE gyroplane	C. J. Watkinson	
G-CDJP	Best Off Skyranger 912(2)	I. A. Cunningham	
G-CDJR	Aerotechnik EV-97 TeamEurostar	M. Smith	
G-CDJU	CASA 1.131E Jungmann Srs.1000	P. Gaskell	
G-CDJV	Beech A.36 Bonanza	D. A. Gathercole	

Notes	Reg	Type	Owner or Operator
	G-CDJY	Cameron C-80 balloon	British Airways PLC
	G-CDKA	SAAB 2000	Eastern Airways
	G-CDKB	SAAB 2000	Eastern Airways
	G-CDKE	Rans S6-ES Coyote II	J. E. Holloway
	G-CDKF	Escapade 912 (1)	K. R. Butcher
	G-CDKH	Skyranger 912S (1)	C. Lenaghan
	G-CDKI	Skyranger 912S (1)	J. M. Hucker
	G-CDKK	Mainair Pegasus Quik	P. M. Knight
	G-CDKL	Escapade 912 (2)	G-CDKL Group
	G-CDKM	Pegasus Quik	P. Lister
	G-CDKN	ICP MXP-740 Savannah Jabiru (4)	T. Wicks
	G-CDKO	ICP MXP-740 Savannah Jabiru (4)	A. L. Robey
	G-CDKP	Avtech Jabiru UL-D Calypso	C. Bruce & P. Brown
	G-CDKX	Skyranger J.2 .2 (1)	E. Lewis
	G-CDLA	Mainair Pegasus Quik	S. M. Smith
	G-CDLC	CASA 1.131E Jungmann 2000	R. D. Loder
	G-CDLD	Mainair Pegasus Quik 912S	W. Williams
	G-CDLG	Skyranger 912 (2)	CDLG Skyranger Group
	G-CDLI	Airco DH.9 (E8894)	Aero Vintage Ltd
	G-CDLJ	Mainair Pegasus Quik	J. S. James & R. S. Keyser
	G-CDLK	Skyranger 912S (1)	C. T. Graham
	G-CDLL	Dyn'Aéro MCR-01 ULC	R. F. Connell
	G-CDLR	ICP MXP / 740 Savannah Jabiru (4)	G-CDLR Syndicate
	G-CDLS	Jabiru Aircrraft Jabiru J400	Teesside Aviators Group
	G-CDLW	Zenair ZH.601UL Zodiac	W. A. Stphen
	G-CDLY	Cirrus SR20	Talama/France
	G-CDMA	PA-28-151 Warrior	Falcon Flying Services Ltd
	G-CDMC	Cameron Z-105 balloon	F. M. H. Audenaert
	G-CDMD	Robin DR.400/500	P. R. Liddle
	G-CDME	Van's RV-7	W. H. Greenwood
	G-CDMF	Van's RV-9A	J. R. Bowden
	G-CDMH	Cessna P.210N	A. M. Holman-West
	G-CDMJ	Mainair Pegasus Quik	M. J. R. Dean
	G-CDMK	Montgomerie-Bensen B8MR	P. Rentell
	G-CDML	Mainair Pegasus Quik	Flyingscool
	G-CDMN	Van's RV-9	G. J. Smith
	G-CDMO	Cameron S Can-100 balloon	T. Gleixner
	G-CDMP	Best Off Skyranger 912(1)	J. A. Charlton
	G-CDMS	Ikarus C.42 FB 80	Airbourne Aviation Ltd
	G-CDMT	Zenair CH.601XL Zodiac	H. Drever
	G-CDMV	Best Off Skyranger 912S(1)	D. O'Keeffe & K. E. Rutter
	G-CDMX	PA-28-161 Warrior II	C. Sher
	G-CDMY	PA-28-161 Warrior II	Redhill Air Services Ltd
	G-CDNA	Grob G.109A	Army Gliding Association
	G-CDND	GA-7 Cougar	IFA Instituto de Formacao Aeronautica LDA/Portugal
	G-CDNE	Best Off Skyranger Swift 912S(1)	St. Michael's Skyranger Syndicate
	G-CDNF	Aero Design Pulsar 3	D. Ringer
	G-CDNG	Aerotechnik EV-97 TeamEurostar UK	A. C. Thomson
	G-CDNH	Mainair Pegasus Quik	T. P. R. Wright
	G-CDNM	Aerotechnik EV-97 TeamEurostar UK	H. C. Lowther
	G-CDNO	Westland Gazelle AH.1 (XX432)	S. Atherton
	G-CDNP	Aerotechnik EV-97 TeamEurostar UK	Eaglescott Eurostar Group
	G-CDNS	Westland Gazelle AH.1 (XZ321)	Falcon Aviation Ltd
	G-CDNT	Zenair CH.601XL Zodiac	W. McCormack
	G-CDNW	Ikarus C.42 FB UK	W. Gabbott
	G-CDNY	Jabiru SP-470	G. Lucey
	G-CDOA	EV-97 TeamEurostar UK	Mainair Microlight School Ltd
	G-CDOB	Cameron C-90 balloon	G. T. Holmes
	G-CDOC	Mainair Quik GT450	R. J. Carver
	G-CDOK	Ikarus C.42 FB 100	M Aviation Ltd
	G-CDON	PA-28-161 Warrior II	G-CDON Group
	G-CDOO	Mainair Pegasus Quantum 15-912	O. C. Harding
	G-CDOP	Mainair Pegasus Quik	G-CDOP Syndicate
	G-CDOT	Ikarus C.42 FB 100	A. C. Anderson
	G-CDOY	Skyranger 912(2)	N. Grugan
	G-CDOY	Robin DR.400/180R	Lasham Gliding Society Ltd
	G-CDOZ	EV-97 TeamEurostar UK	Wizards of Oz
	G-CDPA	Alpi Pioneer 300	N. D. White
	G-CDPB	Skyranger 982(1)	A. W. Collett
	G-CDPD	Mainair Pegasus Quik	T. N. Jerry

Reg	Type	Owner or Operator	Notes
G-CDPE	Skyranger 912(2)	I. M. Hull	
G-CDPG	Crofton Auster J1-A	G-CDPG Group	
G-CDPH	Tiger Cub RL5A LW Sherwood Ranger ST	L. Challinger	
G-CDPL	EV-97 TeamEurostar UK	C. I. D. H Garrison	
G-CDPP	Ikarus C42 FB UK	H. M. Owen	
G-CDPS	Raj Hamsa X'Air 133	C. G., M. & N. Chambers	
G-CDPV	PA-34-200T Seneca II	Globebrow Ltd	
G-CDPW	Mainair Pegasus Quantum 15-912	Hadair Flexwing Flyers	
G-CDPY	Shaw Europa	A. Burrill	
G-CDPZ	Flight Design CT2K	M. E. Henwick	
G-CDRC	Cessna 182Q	P. D. Meakin	
G-CDRD	AirBorne XT912-B Edge/Streak III-B	V. D. Carmichael	
G-CDRF	Cameron Z-90 balloon	Chalmers Ballong Corps	
G-CDRG	Mainair Pegasus Quik	S. P. Adams	
G-CDRH	Thruster T.600N	Carlisle Thruster Group	
G-CDRI	Cameron O-105 balloon	Snapdragon Balloon Group	
G-CDRJ	Tanarg/Ixess 15 912S(1)	G. F. Frend	
G-CDRN	Cameron Z-225 balloon	Pearl Balloons SPRL/Belgium	
G-CDRO	Ikarus C42 F880	Airbourne Aviation Ltd	
G-CDRP	Ikarus C42 FB80	D. S. Parker	
G-CDRR	Mainair Pegasus Quantum 15-912	S. D. Moran	
G-CDRS	Rotorway Executive 162F	R. C. Swann	
G-CDRT	Mainair Pegasus Quik	R. Tetlow	
G-CDRU	CASA 1.131E Jungmann 2000	P. Cunniff	
G-CDRV	Van's RV-9A	R. J. Woodford	
G-CDRW	Mainair Pegasus Quik	C. J. Meadows	
G-CDRY	Ikarus C42 FB100 VLA	R. J. Mitchell	
G-CDSA	Mainair Pegasus Quik	F. R. Simpson	
G-CDSB	Alpi Pioneer 200	F. M. Ward	
G-CDSC	Scheibe SF.25C Rotax-Falke	Devon & Somerset Motorglider Group	
G-CDSF	Diamond DA40D Star	Flying Time Ltd	
G-CDSH	ICP MXP-740 Savannah Jabiru (5)	G. Miller	
G-CDSK	Reality Escapade Jabiru(3)	R. H. Sear	
G-CDSM	P & M Aviation Quik GT450	S. L. Cogger	
G-CDSS	Mainair Pegasus Quik	R. N. S. Taylor	
G-CDST	Ultramagic N-250 balloon	Adventure Balloons Ltd	
G-CDSX	EE Canberra T.Mk.4 (VN799) ★	Classic Air Force/Newquay	
G-CDTA	EV-97 TeamEurostar UK	R. D. Stein	
G-CDTB	Mainair Pegasus Quantum 15-912	D. W. Corbett	
G-CDTG	Diamond DA.42 Twin Star	CTC Aviation Group Ltd	
G-CDTH	Schempp-Hirth Nimbus 4DM	S. J. Clark	
G-CDTI	Messerschmitt Bf.109E (4034)	Rare Aero Ltd	
G-CDTJ	Escapade Jabiru(5)	M. E. Gilbert	
G-CDTL	Avtech Jabiru J-400	M. I. Sistern	
G-CDTO	P & M Quik GT450	A. R. Watt	
G-CDTP	Skyranger 912S (1)	P. M. Whitaker	
G-CDTR	P & M Quik GT450	S. M. Furner	
G-CDTT	Savannah Jabiru(4)	M. J. Day	
G-CDTU	EV-97 TeamEurostar UK	G-CDTU Group	
G-CDTV	Tecnam P2002 EA Sierra	S. A. Noble	
G-CDTX	Cessna F.152	Blueplane Ltd	
G-CDTY	Savannah Jabiru (5)	D. A. Cook	
G-CDTZ	Aeroprakt A.22 Foxbat	Colditz Group	
G-CDUE	Robinson R44 1	Southport Golf Complex Ltd	
G-CDUH	P & M Quik GT450	N. F. Taylor	
G-CDUJ	Lindstrand LBL 31A balloon	R. G. Griffin	
G-CDUK	Ikarus C.42 FB UK	G-CDUK C42 Group	
G-CDUL	Skyranger 912S (2)	M. B. Wallbutton & M. P. D. Cook	
G-CDUS	Skyranger 912S (1)	D. Coppin	
G-CDUT	Jabiru J400	T. W. & A. Pullin.	
G-CDUU	P & M Quik GT450	K. D. & N. J. Perrell	
G-CDUV	Savannah Jabiru(5)	D. M. Blackman	
G-CDUW	Aeronca C3	N. K. Geddes	
G-CDUY	Thunder & Colt 77A balloon	G. Birchall	
G-CDVA	Skyranger 912 (1)	R. Dilkes	
G-CDVD	EV-97 Eurostar	The Northern Flying Group	
G-CDVG	Pegasus Quik	C. M. Lewis	
G-CDVH	Pegasus Quantum 15-912	F. Godfrey	
G-CDVI	Ikarus C42 FB80	Airbourne Aviation Ltd	
G-CDVJ	Montgomerie-Bensen B8MR	J. A. McGill	
G-CDVK	Savannah Jabiru (5)	M. Peters	

Notes	Reg	Type	Owner or Operator
	G-CDVL	Alpi Pioneer 300	J. D. Clabon
	G-CDVN	P & M Quik GT450	P. Warrener
	G-CDVO	P & M Quik	D. A. Eastough
	G-CDVR	P & M Quik GT450	M. J. King
	G-CDVS	Europa XS	J. F. Lawn
	G-CDVT	Van's RV-6	P. J. Wood
	G-CDVU	Aerotechnik EV-97 TeamEurostar	M. R. Smith
	G-CDVV	SA Bulldog Srs. 120/121 (XX626:02, W)	W. H. M. Mott
	G-CDVZ	P & M Quik GT450	S. M. Green & M. D. Peacock
	G-CDWB	Skyranger 912(2)	C. Booth
	G-CDWD	Cameron Z-105 balloon	Bristol University Ballooning Society
	G-CDWE	Nord NC.856 Norvigie (N856)	J. R. Davison
	G-CDWG	Dyn'Aéro MCR-01 Club	A. W. Lowrie
	G-CDWI	Ikarus C42 FB80	CDWI Syndicate
	G-CDWJ	Flight Design CTSW	G. P. Rood
	G-CDWK	Robinson R44	B. Morgan
	G-CDWM	Skyranger 912S (1)	S. P. McVeigh & P. Fox
	G-CDWO	P & M Quik GT450	G. W. Carwardine
	G-CDWR	P & M Quik GT450	I. C. Macbeth
	G-CDWT	Flight Design CTSW	R. Scammell
	G-CDWU	Zenair CH.601UL Zodiac	J. White
	G-CDWZ	P & M Quik GT450	D. Higton
	G-CDXD	Medway SLA100 Executive	A. J. Baker & G. Withers
	G-CDXF	Lindstrand LBL 31A balloon	R. K. Worsman
	G-CDXG	P & M Pegasus Quantum 15-912	I. C. Braybrook
	G-CDXI	Cessna 182P	B. G. McBeath
	G-CDXJ	Jabiru J400	J. C. Collingwood
	G-CDXK	Diamond DA42 Twin Star	A. M. Healy
	G-CDXL	Flight Design CTSW	A. K. Paterson
	G-CDXN	P & M Quik GT450	M. A. Elliott
	G-CDXP	Aerotechnik EV-97 Eurostar	R. J. Crockett
	G-CDXR	Replica Fokker DR.1 (403/17)	P. B. Dickinson
	G-CDXS	Aerotechnik EV-97 Eurostar	T. R. James
	G-CDXT	Van's RV-9	T. M. Storey
	G-CDXU	Chilton DW.1A	M. Gibbs & J. Pollard
	G-CDXV	Campbell Cricket Mk.6A	T. L. Morley
	G-CDXW	Cameron Orange 120 SS balloon	You've Been Tangoed
	G-CDXY	Skystar Kitfox Mk.7	D. E. Steade
	G-CDYB	Rans S.6-ES Coyote II	J. A. Matthews
	G-CDYD	Ikarus C42 FB80	C42 Group
	G-CDYG	Cameron Z-105 balloon	N-E Kjellen
	G-CDYL	Lindstrand LBL-77A balloon	J. S. Morge
	G-CDYM	Murphy Maverick 430	D. J. Marchand
	G-CDYO	Ikarus C42 FB80	Progress Vehicle Management Ltd
	G-CDYP	Aerotechnik EV-97 TeamEurostar UK	R. V. Buxton & R. Cranborne
	G-CDYR	Bell 206L-3 LongRanger III	Yorkshire Helicopters
	G-CDYT	Ikarus C42 FB80	P. Bayliss
	G-CDYU	Zenair CH.701UL	A. Gannon
	G-CDYX	Lindstrand LBL-77B balloon	H. M. Savage
	G-CDYY	Alpi Pioneer 300	B. Williams
	G-CDYZ	Van's RV-7	Holden Group Ltd
	G-CDZA	Alpi Pioneer 300	J. F. Dowe
	G-CDZB	Zenair CH.601UL Zodiac	L. J. Dutch
	G-CDZG	Ikarus C42-FB80	Mainair Microlight School Ltd
	G-CDZO	Lindstrand LBL-60X balloon	R. D. Parry
	G-CDZR	Nicollier HN.700 Menestrel II	S. J. Bowles & C. Antrobus
	G-CDZS	Kolb Twinstar Mk.3 Extra	P. J. Nolan & K. V. Hill
	G-CDZT	Beech B200 Super King Air	RVL Aviation Ltd
	G-CDZU	ICP MXP-740 Savannah Jabiru (5)	P. J. Cheyney & A. H. McBreen
	G-CDZW	Cameron N-105 balloon	Backetorp Byggconsult AB
	G-CDZY	Medway SLA 80 Executive	G-CDZY Group
	G-CDZZ	Rotorsport UK MT-03	D. J. Bell
	G-CEAK	Ikarus C42 FB80	Barton Heritage Flying Group
	G-CEAM	Aerotechnik EV-97 TeamEurostar UK	Flylight Airsports Ltd
	G-CEAN	Ikarus C42 FB80	G-CEAN Syndicate
	G-CEAO	Jurca MJ.5 Sirocco	P. S. Watts
	G-CEAR	Alpi Pioneer 300	R. E. Rayner
	G-CEAT	Zenair CH.601HDS Zodiac	T. B. Smith
	G-CEAU	Robinson R44	Mullahead Property Co Ltd
	G-CEAY	Ultramagic H-42 balloon	J. D. A. Shields

Reg	Type	Owner or Operator	Notes
G-CEBA	Zenair CH.601XL Zodiac	Lamb Holm Flyers	
G-CEBC	ICP MXP-740 Savannah Jabiru (5)	H. C. Lowther	
G-CEBE	Schweizer 269C-1	Millburn World Travel Services Ltd	
G-CEBF	Aerotechnik EV-97A Eurostar	M. Lang	
G-CEBG	Balóny Kubíček BB26 balloon	P. M. Smith	
G-CEBH	Tanarg 912S/Bionix 15	G. McAnelly	
G-CEBI	Kolb Twinstar Mk.3	R. W. Livingstone	
G-CEBL	Balóny Kubíček BB20GP balloon	Associazione Sportiva Aerostatica Lombada/Italy	
G-CEBM	P & M Quik GT450	R. L. Davies	
G-CEBO	Ultramagic M-65C balloon	M. G. Howard	
G-CEBP	EV-97 TeamEurostar UK	M. J. Morson	
G-CEBT	P & M Quik GT450	N. J. Paine	
G-CEBW	P-51D Mustang	Iceni International Ltd	
G-CEBZ	Zenair CH.601UL Zodiac	W. J. Miazek	
G-CECA	P & M Quik GT450	A. Weatherall	
G-CECC	Ikarus C42 FB80	G. P. Burns	
G-CECD	Cameron C-90 balloon	J. de Flou & M. de Keyzer	
G-CECE	Jabiru UL-D	ST Aviation Ltd	
G-CECF	Just/Reality Escapade Jabiru (3)	M. M. Hamer	
G-CECG	Jabiru UL-D	A. N. C. P. Lester	
G-CECH	Jodel D.150	W. R. Prescott	
G-CECJ	Aeromot AMT-200S Super Ximango	G-CECJ Syndicate	
G-CECK	ICP MXP-740 Savannah Jabiru (5)	J. F. Boyce	
G-CECL	Ikarus C42 FB80	C. Lee	
G-CECP	Best Off Skyranger 912(2)	Woobugly Flying Group	
G-CECS	Lindstrand LBL-105A balloon	R. P. Ashfo	
G-CECV	Van's RV-7	D. M. Stevens	
G-CECY	EV-97 Eurostar	M. R. M. Welch	
G-CECZ	Zenair CH.601XL Zodiac	M. D. White	
G-CEDB	Reality Escapade Jabiru (5)	G. T. M. Beale	
G-CEDC	Ikarus C42 FB100	L. M. Call	
G-CEDE	Flight Design CTSW	M. B. Hayter	
G-CEDF	Cameron N-105 balloon	Bailey Balloons Ltd	
G-CEDI	Best Off Skyranger 912(2)	G-CEDI Group	
G-CEDJ	Aero Designs Pulsar XP	P. F. Lorriman	
G-CEDL	TEAM Minimax 91	A. J. Weir	
G-CEDN	Pegasus Quik	Sheffield Aero Club Ltd	
G-CEDO	Raj Hamsa X'Air Falcon 133(2)	OCTN Trust	
G-CEDT	Tanarg/Ixess 15 912S (2)	N. S. Brayn	
G-CEDV	Evektor EV-97 TeamEurostar UK	G-CEDV Flying Group	
G-CEDX	Evektor EV-97 TeamEurostar UK	Delta X-Ray Group	
G-CEEC	Raj Hamsa X'Air Hawk	G-CEEC Group	
G-CEED	ICP MXP-740 Savannah Jabiru(5)	A. C. Thompson	
G-CEEG	Alpi Pioneer 300	D. McCormack	
G-CEEI	P & M Quik GT450	G. J. Eaton	
G-CEEJ	Rans S-7S Courier	R. Dunn	
G-CEEK	Cameron Z-105 balloon	T. R. Wood & J. Campbell	
G-CEEL	Ultramagic S-90 balloon	Anga Company SRO	
G-CEEN	PA-28-161 Cadet	North Weald Flight Training Ltd	
G-CEEO	Flight Design CTSW	Airmasters (UK) Ltd	
G-CEEP	Van's RV-9A	B. M. Jones	
G-CEER	ELA 07R	F. G. Shepherd	
G-CEEU	PA-28-161 Cadet	White Waltham Airfield Ltd	
G-CEEW	Ikarus C42 FB100	C-More Flying School Ltd	
G-CEEX	ICP MXP-740 Savannah Jabiru(5)	R. G. Whyte	
G-CEFA	Ikarus C42 FB100 VLA	Ikarus Group	
G-CEFB	Ultramagic H-31 balloon	M. Ekeroos	
G-CEFC	Super Marine Spitfire 26 (RB142)	D. R. Bishop	
G-CEFJ	Sonex	R. W. Chatterton	
G-CEFK	Evektor EV-97 TeamEurostar UK	P. Morgan	
G-CEFM	Cessna 152	Westair Flying Services Ltd	
G-CEFP	Jabiru J430	R. W. Brown	
G-CEFS	Cameron C-100 balloon	Gone With The Wind Ltd	
G-CEFT	Whittaker MW5-D Sorcerer	A. M. R. Bruce	
G-CEFV	Cessna 182T Skylane	G. H. Smith & Son Ltd	
G-CEFZ	EV-97 TeamEurostar uk	Robo Flying Group	
G-CEGG	Lindstrand LBL-25A Cloudhopper balloon	M. W. A. Shemitt	
G-CEGH	Van's RV-9A	M. E. Creasey	
G-CEGI	Van's RV-8	D. R. Fraser & R. Tye	
G-CEGJ	P & M Quik GT450	C. A. Mason	
G-CEGK	ICP MXP-740 Savannah VG Jabiru(1)	A. & C. Kimpton	

Notes	Reg	Type	Owner or Operator
	G-CEGL	Ikarus C42 FB80	G-CEGL Flying Group
	G-CEGO	Evektor EV-97A Eurostar	D. W. Allen, R. F. McLachlan & J. A. Charlton
	G-CEGP	Beech 200 Super King Air	Alto Aerospace Ltd
	G-CEGS	PA-28-161 Warrior II	Parachuting Aircraft Ltd
	G-CEGT	P & M Quik GT450	S. J. Fisher
	G-CEGU	PA-28-151 Warrior	White Waltham Airfield Ltd
	G-CEGV	P & M Quik GT450	S. P. A. Morris
	G-CEGW	P & M Quik GT450	D. Moore
	G-CEGZ	Ikarus C42 FB80	C42 Swift Instruction Group
	G-CEHC	P & M Quik GT450	G-CEHC Syndicate
	G-CEHD	Best Off Skyranger 912(2)	R. Higton
	G-CEHE	Medway SLA 100 Executive	R. P. Stoner
	G-CEHG	Ikarus C42 FB100	C. J. Hayward & C. Walters
	G-CEHL	EV-97 TeamEurostar UK	A. C. Richards
	G-CEHM	Rotorsport UK MT-03	1013 Aviation Ltd
	G-CEHN	Rotorsport UK MT-03	B. N. Trowbridge
	G-CEHR	Auster AOP.9 (XP241)	C. R. Wheeldon & M. H. Bichan
	G-CEHS	CAP.10B	M. D. Wynne
	G-CEHT	Rand KR-2	P. P. Geoghegan
	G-CEHV	Ikarus C42 FB80	Pickup & Son Ltd
	G-CEHW	P & M Quik GT450	G-CEHW Group
	G-CEHX	Lindstrand LBL-9A balloon	P. Baker
	G-CEHZ	Edge XT912-B/Streak III-B	J. Daly
	G-CEIA	Rotorsport UK MT-03	T. J. Willis
	G-CEIB	Yakovlev Yak-18A (03)	R. A. Fleming
	G-CEID	Van's RV-7	A. Moyce
	G-CEIE	Flight Design CTSW	R. D. Jordan
	G-CEIG	Van's RV-7	W. K. Wilkie
	G-CEII	Medway SLA80 Executive	G. P. Burns
	G-CEIL	Reality Escapade 912(2)	T. N. Crawley
	G-CEIS	Jodel DR.1050	Prestwick Tailwheel Group
	G-CEIT	Van's RV-7	W. Jones & I. R. Court
	G-CEIV	Tanarg/Ixess 15 912S(2)	W. O. Fogden
	G-CEIW	Europa	R. Scanlan
	G-CEIX	Alpi Pioneer 300	I. M. Walton
	G-CEIY	Ultramagic M-120 balloon	N. Banducci/Italy
	G-CEIZ	PA-28-161 Warrior II	IZ Aviation
	G-CEJA	Cameron V-77 balloon	G. Gray (G-BTOF)
	G-CEJC	Cameron N-77 balloon	M. Cooper
	G-CEJD	PA-28-161 Warrior III	Western Air (Thruxton) Ltd
	G-CEJE	Wittman W.10 Tailwind	R. A. Povall
	G-CEJG	Ultramagic M-56 balloon	Dragon Balloon Co.Ltd
	G-CEJI	Lindstrand LBL-105A balloon	Richard Nash Cars Ltd
	G-CEJJ	P & M Quik GT450	G. McLaughlin
	G-CEJN	Mooney M.20F	Social Infrastructure Ltd
	G-CEJW	Ikarus C42 FB80	A. Mauldsley
	G-CEJX	P & M Quik GT450	A. J. Huntly
	G-CEJY	Aerospool Dynamic WT9 UK	E. Kaplan
	G-CEJZ	Cameron C-90 balloon	M. J. Woodcock
	G-CEKC	Medway SLA100 Executive	J. A. Robinson
	G-CEKD	Flight Design CTSW	S. Best
	G-CEKG	P & M Quik GT450	C. R. Whitton
	G-CEKI	Cessna 172P	N. Houghton
	G-CEKJ	Evektor EV-97A Eurostar	D. K. Short & G. Thompson
	G-CEKK	Best Off Sky Ranger Swift 912S(1)	M. S. Schofield
	G-CEKO	Robin DR400/100	Exavia Ltd
	G-CEKS	Cameron Z-105 balloon	Phoenix Balloons Ltd
	G-CEKT	Flight Design CTSW	Charlie Tango Group
	G-CEKV	Europa	K. Atkinson
	G-CEKW	Jabiru J430	J430 Syndicate
	G-CELM	Cameron C-80 balloon	L. Greaves
	G-CEMA	Alpi Pioneer 200	R. W. Skelton
	G-CEMB	P & M Quik GT450	D. W. Logue
	G-CEMC	Robinson R44 Raven II	Express Charters Ltd
	G-CEME	Evektor EV-97 Eurostar	D. Godman & S. S. Aujla
	G-CEMF	Cameron C-80 balloon	Linear Communications Consultants Ltd
	G-CEMI	Europa XS	B. D. A. Morris
	G-CEMM	P & M Quik GT450	M. A. Rhodes
	G-CEMO	P & M Quik GT450	T. D. Stock
	G-CEMR	Mainair Blade 912	P. J. Kirkpatrick
	G-CEMT	P & M Quik GT450	A. Brier

Reg	Type	Owner or Operator	Notes
G-CEMU	Cameron C-80 balloon	J. G. O'Connell	
G-CEMV	Lindstrand LBL-105A balloon	R. G. Turnbull	
G-CEMX	P & M Pegasus Quik	S. J. Meehan	
G-CEMY	Alpi Pioneer 300	J. C. A. Garland & P. F. Salter	
G-CENA	Dyn'Aero MCR-01 ULC Banbi	I. N. Drury	
G-CENB	Evektor EV-97 TeamEurostar UK	A. C. Bell	
G-CEND	Evektor EV-97 TeamEurostar UK	York Aircraft Leasing Ltd	
G-CENE	Flight Design CTSW	The CT Flying Group	
G-CENG	SkyRanger 912(2)	R. A. Knight	
G-CENH	Tecnam P2002-EA Sierra	M. W. Taylor	
G-CENJ	Medway SLA 951	M. Ingleton	
G-CENL	P & M Quik GT450	P. Von Sydow & S. Baker	
G-CENM	Evektor EV-97 Eurostar	N. D. Meer	
G-CENN	Cameron C-60 balloon	C. J. Y. Holvoet	
G-CENO	Aerospool Dynamic WT9 UK	J. H. Sands & M. D. S. Williams	
G-CENP	Ace Magic Laser	A. G. Curtis	
G-CENS	SkyRanger Swift 912S(1)	J. Spence	
G-CENW	Evektor EV-97A Eurostar	Southside Flyers	
G-CENX	Lindstrand LBL-360A	Wickers World Ltd	
G-CENZ	Aeros Discus/Alize	A. M. Singhvi	
G-CEOB	Pitts S-1 Special	N. J. Radford	
G-CEOC	Tecnam P2002-EA Sierra	M. Nicholas	
G-CEOG	PA-28R-201 Arrow	A. J. Gardiner	
G-CEOH	Raj Hamsa X'Air Falcon ULP(1)	J. C. Miles	
G-CEOL	Flylight Lightfly/Aeros Discus 15T	J. M. Pearce	
G-CEOM	Jabiru UL-450	J. R. Caylow	
G-CEON	Raj Hamsa X'Air Hawk	K. S. Campbell	
G-CEOP	Aeroprakt A22-L Foxbat	G. F. Elvis	
G-CEOS	Cameron C-90 balloon	G. G. Scaife	
G-CEOU	Lindstrand LBL-31A balloon	R. D. Allen	
G-CEOW	Europa XS	Europa OW Group	
G-CEOX	Rotorsport UK MT-03	A. J. Saunders	
G-CEOZ	Paramania Action GT26/PAP Chariot Z	A. M. Shepherd	
G-CEPL	Super Marine Spitfire Mk.26 (P9398)	S. R. Marsh	
G-CEPM	Jabiru J430	T. R. Sinclair	
G-CEPP	P & M Quik GT450	W. M. Studley	
G-CEPR	Cameron Z-90 balloon	Sport Promotion SRL/Italy	
G-CEPU	Cameron Z-77 balloon	G. Forgione/Italy	
G-CEPV	Cameron Z-77 balloon	P. Boetti & O. Lombardo/Italy	
G-CEPW	Alpi Pioneer 300	N. K. Spedding	
G-CEPX	Cessna 152	Devon & Somerset Flight Training Ltd	
G-CEPY	Ikarus C42 FB80	L. A. Hosegood	
G-CERB	SkyRanger Swift 912S(1)	J. J. Littler	
G-CERC	Cameron Z-350 balloon	Ballooning Network Ltd	
G-CERD	D.H.C.1 Chipmunk 22	A. C. Darby	
G-CERE	Evektor EV-97 TeamEurostar UK	A. G. & G. I. Doake	
G-CERF	Rotorsport UK MT-03	P. J. Robinson	
G-CERH	Cameron C-90 balloon	A. Walker	
G-CERI	Shaw Europa XS	S. J. M. Shepherd	
G-CERK	Van's RV-9A	P. E. Brown	
G-CERL	Ultramagic M-77 balloon	A. P. Jay	
G-CERN	P & M Quik GT450	P. M. Jackson	
G-CERP	P & M Quik GT450	RP Syndicate	
G-CERV	P & M Quik GT450	C. J. R. Hardman	
G-CERW	P & M Pegasus Quik	D. J. Cornelius	
G-CERX	Hawker 850XP	Hangar 8 Management Ltd	
G-CERZ	SAAB 2000	Eastern Airways	
G-CESA	Replica Jodel DR.1050	T. J. Bates	
G-CESD	SkyRanger Swift 912S(1)	B. R. Trotman	
G-CESH	Cameron Z-90 balloon	A. P. Jay	
G-CESI	Aeroprakt A22-L Foxbat	D. N. L. Howell	
G-CESJ	Raj Hamsa X'Air Hawk	G-CESJ Group	
G-CESM	TL2000UK Sting Carbon	Deanland Flight Training Ltd	
G-CESR	P & M Quik GT450	G-CESR Syndicate	
G-CEST	Robinson R44	Startrade Heli Gmbh & Co KG/Germany	
G-CESV	EV-97 TeamEurostar UK	W. D. Kyle & T. J. Dowling	
G-CESW	Flight Design CTSW	J. Whiting	
G-CESZ	CZAW Sportcruiser	G. P. D. Glover	
G-CETB	Robin DR.400/180	QR Flying Club	
G-CETF	Flight Design CTSW	M. Cackett	
G-CETK	Cameron Z-145 balloon	J. C. M. Greatrix	

Notes	Reg	Type	Owner or Operator
	G-CETL	P & M Quik GT450	J. Urrutia
	G-CETM	P & M Quik GT450	G-CETM Flying Group
	G-CETN	Hummel Bird	A. A. Haseldine
	G-CETO	Best Off Sky Ranger Swift 912S(1)	S. C. Stoodley
	G-CETP	Van's RV-9A	D. Boxall & S. Hill
	G-CETR	Ikarus C42 FB80	Cloudbase Paragliding Ltd
	G-CETS	Van's RV-7	TS Group
	G-CETU	Best Off Sky Ranger Swift 912S(1)	A. Raithby & N. McCusker
	G-CETV	Best Off Sky Ranger Swift 912S(1)	C. J. Johnson
	G-CETX	Alpi Pioneer 300	J. M. P. Ree
	G-CETY	Rans S-6-ES Coyote II	V. Asquith
	G-CETZ	Ikarus C42 FB100	Micro Aviation Ltd
	G-CEUF	P & M Quik GT450	G. T. Snoddon
	G-CEUH	P & M Quik GT450	J. A. Currie
	G-CEUJ	SkyRanger Swift 912S(1)	The CUEJ Group
	G-CEUL	Ultramagic M-105 balloon	R. A. Vale
	G-CEUM	Ultramagic M-120 balloon	Skydive Chatteris Club Ltd
	G-CEUN	Orlican Discus CS	The Royal Air Force Gliding and Soaring Association
	G-CEUU	Robinson R44 II	D. K. Richardson
	G-CEUV	Cameron C-90 balloon	M. S. Stevens & M. L. Cooper
	G-CEUW	Zenair CH.601XL Zodiac	P. Connolly
	G-CEUZ	P & M Quik GT450	P. M. Williamson
	G-CEVA	Ikarus C42 FB80	The Scottish Flying Group
	G-CEVB	P & M Quik GT450	C. Traher
	G-CEVC	Van's RV-4	P. A. Brook
	G-CEVD	Rolladen-Schneider LS3	P. G. Warner
	G-CEVE	Centrair 101A	T. P. Newham
	G-CEVH	Cameron V-65 balloon	J. A. Atkinson
	G-CEVJ	Alpi Pioneer 200-M	K. Worthington
	G-CEVK	Schleicher Ka 6CR	K. E. & O. J. Wilson
	G-CEVM	Tecnam P2002-EA Sierra	J. A. Ellis
	G-CEVN	Rolladen-Schneider LS7	N. Gaunt & B. C. Toon
	G-CEVO	Grob G.109B	BR Aviation Ltd
	G-CEVP	P & M Quik GT450	P. J. Lowe
	G-CEVS	EV-97 TeamEurostar UK	Golf Victor Sierra Flying Group
	G-CEVU	Savannah VG Jabiru(4)	I. C. May
	G-CEVV	Rolladen-Schneider LS3	LS3 307 Syndicate
	G-CEVW	P & M Quik GT450	J. M. Mooney
	G-CEVX	Aeriane Swift Light PAS	P. Trueman
	G-CEVY	Rotorsport UK MT-03	Silver Birch Pet Jets Ltd
	G-CEVZ	Centrair ASW-20FL	B. Watkins
	G-CEWC	Schleicher ASK-21	London Gliding Club Proprietary Ltd
	G-CEWD	P & M Quik GT450	S. C. Key
	G-CEWE	Schempp-Hirth Nimbus 2	T. Clark
	G-CEWF	Jacobs V35 Airchair balloon	G. F. & I. Chadwick & M. G. Roberts
	G-CEWH	P & M Quik GT450	G-CEWH Syndicate
	G-CEWI	Schleicher ASW-19B	S. R. Edwards
	G-CEWL	Alpi Pioneer 200	E. A. Wilson
	G-CEWM	DHC.6 Twin Otter 300	Isles of Scilly Skybus Ltd
	G-CEWO	Schleicher Ka 6CR	D. P. Westcott
	G-CEWP	Grob G.102 Astir CS	G-CEWP Flying Group
	G-CEWR	Aeroprakt A22-L Foxbat	C. S. Bourne & G. P. Wiley
	G-CEWS	Zenair CH.701SP	A. I. Sutherland
	G-CEWT	Flight Design CTSW	K. Tuck
	G-CEWU	Ultramagic H-77 balloon	P. C. Waterhouse
	G-CEWW	Grob G.102 Astir CS	The South Wales Gliding Club Ltd
	G-CEWX	Cameron Z-350 balloon	Celador Radio (South West) Ltd
	G-CEWY	Quicksilver GT500	N. Andrews
	G-CEWZ	Schempp-Hirth Discus bT	J. F. Goudie
	G-CEXL	Ikarus C42 FB80	Syndicate C42-1
	G-CEXM	Best Off Sky Ranger Swift 912S(1)	A. F. Batchelor
	G-CEXN	Cameron A-120 balloon	Dragon Balloon Company Ltd
	G-CEXP	HPR.7 Herald 209 ★	Towing and rescue trainer/Gatwick
	G-CEXX	Rotorsport UK MT-03	D. Goh
	G-CEYC	DG Flugzeugbau DG-505 Elan Orion	Scottish Gliding Union Ltd
	G-CEYE	PA-32R-300 Cherokee Lance	D. C. McH. Wilson
	G-CEYG	Cessna 152	H. E. da Costa Alburquerque/Portugal
	G-CEYH	Cessna 152	Stapleford Flying Club Ltd
	G-CEYK	Europa XS	A. B. Milne
	G-CEYL	Bombardier BD-700-1A10 Global Express	Voluxis Ltd

Reg	Type	Owner or Operator	Notes
G-CEYM	Van's RV-6	R. B. Skinner	
G-CEYN	Grob G.109B	G-CEYN Flying Group	
G-CEYP	North Wing Design Stratus/ATF	J. S. James	
G-CEYR	Rotorsport UK MT-03	S. R. Voller	
G-CEYY	EV-97 TeamEurostar UK	N. J. James	
G-CEZA	Ikarus C42 FB80	P. J. Morton & D. E. Bassett	
G-CEZB	Savannah VG Jabiru(1)	W. E. Dudley	
G-CEZD	EV-97 TeamEurostar	N. A. Janes	
G-CEZE	Best Off Sky Ranger Swift 912S	Newtownards Microlight Group	
G-CEZF	EV-97 TeamEurostar UK	D. J. Dick	
G-CEZH	Aerochute Dual	S. T. P. Askew	
G-CEZI	PA-28-161 Cadet	Redhill Air Services Ltd	
G-CEZK	Stolp S.750 Acroduster Too	R. I. M. Hague	
G-CEZL	PA-28-161 Cadet	Chalrey Ltd	
G-CEZM	Cessna 152	Modern Air (UK) Ltd	
G-CEZO	PA-28-161 Cadet	Redhill Air Services Ltd	
G-CEZR	Diamond DA.40D Star	Flying Time Ltd	
G-CEZS	Zenair CH.601HDS Zodiac	V. D. Asque	
G-CEZT	P & M Aviation Quik GT450	A. A. Greig	
G-CEZU	CFM Streak Shadow SA	A. W. Hodder	
G-CEZW	Jodel D.150 Mascaret	J. C. Carter	
G-CEZX	P & M Aviation Quik GT450	Zulu Xray Group	
G-CEZZ	Flight Design CTSW	J. A. Lynch	
G-CFAJ	Glaser-Dirks DG-300 Elan	J. P. Borland & R. S. Rand	
G-CFAK	Rotorsport UK MT-03	R. M. Savage	
G-CFAM	Schempp-Hirth Nimbus 3/24.5	T. M. Mitchell	
G-CFAO	Rolladen-Schneider LS4	V. R. Roberts	
G-CFAP	Interplane ZJ-Viera	P. I. Passmore	
G-CFAR	Rotorsport UK MT-03	P. M. Twose	
G-CFAS	Escapade Jabiru(3)	C. G. N. Boyd	
G-CFAT	P & M Aviation Quik GT450	A. H. C. Morris	
G-CFAV	Ikarus C42 FB80	D. Crouch	
G-CFAW	Lindstrand LBL-35A Cloudhopper balloon	A. Walker	
G-CFAX	Ikarus C42 FB80	R. E. Parker & B. Cook	
G-CFAY	Sky 120-24 balloon	G. B. Lescott	
G-CFBA	Schleicher ASW-20BL	D. A. Close	
G-CFBB	Schempp-Hirth Standard Cirrus	C. A. J. Allen	
G-CFBC	Schleicher ASW-15B	C. C. Pike & P. Morgan	
G-CFBE	Ikarus C42 FB80	K. H. Denham	
G-CFBH	Glaser-Dirks DG-100G Elan	IBM Gliding Club	
G-CFBJ	Rotorsport UK MT-03	P. S. Ball	
G-CFBL	Best Off Sky Ranger Swift 912S(1)	D. Hennings & M. A. Azeem	
G-CFBM	P & M Quantum 15-912	B. J. Youngs	
G-CFBN	Glasflugel Mosquito B	S. R. & J. Nash	
G-CFBT	Schempp-Hirth Ventus bT	P. R. Stafford-Allen	
G-CFBV	Schleicher ASK-21	London Gliding Club Proprietary Ltd	
G-CFBW	DG-100G Elan	G-CFBW Syndicate	
G-CFBY	Best Off Sky Ranger Swift 912S(1)	K. Washbourne	
G-CFCA	Schempp-Hirth Discus b	O. Rzhondkovskyi	
G-CFCB	Centrair 101	M. Phillimore & K. Kinnon	
G-CFCC	Cameron Z-275 balloon	Ballooning Network Ltd	
G-CFCD	SkyRanger Swift 912S(1)	D. & L. Payn	
G-CFCE	Raj Hamsa X'Air Hawk	B. M. Tibenham	
G-CFCF	Aerochute Dual	C. J. Kendal & S. G. Smith	
G-CFCI	Cessna F.172N	P. A. Spurrs	
G-CFCJ	Grob G.102 Astir CS	P. Hardwick & P. J. Howarth	
G-CFCK	Best Off Sky Ranger 912S(1)	J. Smith	
G-CFCL	Rotorsport UK MT-03	D. D. Taylor	
G-CFCM	Robinson R44	Newmarket Plant Hire Ltd	
G-CFCN	Schempp-Hirth Standard Cirrus	P. C. Bunniss	
G-CFCP	Rolladen-Schneider LS6-a	M. A. Hall	
G-CFCR	Schleicher Ka-6E	R. F. Whittaker	
G-CFCS	Schempp-Hirth Nimbus 2	G-CFCS Group	
G-CFCT	EV-97 TeamEurostar UK	Sutton Eurostar Group	
G-CFCV	Schleicher ASW-20	I. R. Gallacher	
G-CFCW	Rotorsport UK MT-03	C. M. Jones	
G-CFCX	Rans S-6-ES Coyote II	D. & S. Morrison	
G-CFCY	Best Off Sky Ranger Swift 912S(1)	M. E. & T. E. Simpson	
G-CFCZ	P & M Quik GT450	P. K. Dale	
G-CFDA	Schleicher ASW-15	N. B. Coggins	

Notes	Reg	Type	Owner or Operator
	G-CFDE	Schempp-Hirth Ventus bT	K. W. Clarke
	G-CFDF	Ultramagic S-90 balloon	Edinburgh University Hot Air Balloon Club
	G-CFDG	Schleicher Ka 6CR	Delta-Golf Group
	G-CFDI	Van's RV-6	M. D. Challoner
	G-CFDJ	EV-97 TeamEurostar UK	J. D. J. Spragg & M. Jones
	G-CFDK	Rans S-6-ES Coyote II	J. Fleming
	G-CFDL	P & M QuikR	N. A. Higgins
	G-CFDM	Schempp-Hirth Discus b	J. L. & T. G. M. Whiting
	G-CFDN	Best Off Sky Ranger Swift 912S(1)	Hadair Fixed Wing Flyers
	G-CFDO	Flight Design CTSW	M. Harris
	G-CFDP	Flight Design CTSW	N. Fielding
	G-CFDS	TL2000UK Sting Carbon	A. G. Cummings
	G-CFDT	Aerola Alatus-M	M. J. Reader-Hoer & G. Rainey
	G-CFDX	PZL-Bielsko SZD-48-1 Jantar Standard 2	A. Phillips
	G-CFDY	P &M Quik GT450	C. N. Thornton
	G-CFEA	Cameron C-90 balloon	A. M. Holly
	G-CFEB	Cameron C-80 balloon	N. Edmunds
	G-CFED	Van's RV-9	E. W. Taylor
	G-CFEE	Evektor EV-97 Eurostar	G-CFEE Flying Group
	G-CFEF	Grob G.102 Astir CS	Oxford University Gliding Club
	G-CFEG	Schempp-Hirth Ventus b/16.6	D. K. McCarthy
	G-CFEH	Centrair 101 Pegase	Booker Gliding Club Ltd
	G-CFEI	RAF 2000 GTX-SE	C. J. Watkinson
	G-CFEJ	Schempp-Hirth Discus b	Lima Charlie Syndicate
	G-CFEK	Cameron Z-105 balloon	R. M. Penny (Plant Hire and Demolition) Ltd
	G-CFEL	EV-97A Eurostar	J. A. Crook
	G-CFEI	RAF 2000 GTX-SE	A. M. Wells
	G-CFEM	P & M Aviation Quik GT450	A. M. King
	G-CFEN	PZL-Bielsko SZD-50-3 Puchacz	The Northumbria Gliding Club Ltd
	G-CFEO	EV-97 Eurostar	J. B. Binks
	G-CFER	Schempp-Hirth Discus b	S. R. Westlake
	G-CFES	Schempp-Hirth Discus b	D. C. & K. J. Mockford
	G-CFET	Van's RV-7	J. Astor
	G-CFEV	P & M Pegasus Quik	V. C. Bull & W. T. Davis
	G-CFEX	P & M Quik GT450	H. Wilson
	G-CFEY	Aerola Alatus-M	M. S. Hayman
	G-CFEZ	CZAW Sportcruiser	J. F. Barber & J. R. Large
	G-CFFA	Ultramagic M-90 balloon	Proxim SPA/Italy
	G-CFFB	Grob G.102 Astir CS	R. Millins
	G-CFFC	Centrair 101A	M. J. Perman & M. P. Capps
	G-CFFE	EV-97 TeamEurostar UK	R. W. Osborne
	G-CFFF	Pitts S-1S Special	P. J. Roy
	G-CFFG	Aerochute Dual	G. J. Pemberton
	G-CFFJ	Flight Design CTSW	R. Germany
	G-CFFN	P & M Quik GT450	S. D. Cox
	G-CFFO	P & M Quik GT450	D. Ben-Lamri & R. Wade
	G-CFFS	Centrair 101A	R. C. Verdier
	G-CFFT	Schempp-Hirth Discus b	Goalrace Ltd
	G-CFFU	Glaser-Dirks DG-101G Elan	FFU Group
	G-CFFV	PZL-Bielsko SZD-51-1 Junior	Herefordshire Gliding Club Ltd
	G-CFFX	Schempp-Hirth Discus b	P. J. Richards
	G-CFFY	PZL-Bielsko SZD-51-1 Junior	Scottish Gliding Union Ltd
	G-CFGA	VS Spitfire VIII	TSIB Ltd
	G-CFGC	Aeros Discus 15T	S. M. Smith & G. Cousins
	G-CFGD	P & M Quik GT450	J. Featherstone
	G-CFGE	Stinson 108-1 Voyager (108-1601:H)	Windmill Aviation
	G-CFGF	Schempp-Hirth Nimbus 3T	R. E. Cross
	G-CFGG	Rotorsport UK MT-03	G-CFGG Flying Group
	G-CFGH	Jabiru J160	P. J. Watson
	G-CFGJ	VS.300 Spitfire I (N3200)	Imperial War Museum
	G-CFGK	Grob G.102 Astir CS	P. Allingham
	G-CFGM	Ikarus C42 FB80	G. P. Burns
	G-CFGO	Best Off Sky Ranger Swift 912S	R. G. Hearsey
	G-CFGP	Schleicher ASW-19	A. E. Prime
	G-CFGR	Schleicher ASK-13	Edensoaring Ltd
	G-CFGT	P & M Aviation Quik GT450	G. P. Preston
	G-CFGU	Schempp-Hirth Standard Cirrus	P. K. Zochling & W. R. R. Carter
	G-CFGV	P & M Quik GT450	R. Bennett
	G-CFGX	EV-97 TeamEurostar UK	Golf XRay Group
	G-CFGY	Rotorsport UK MT-03	A. R. Hawes
	G-CFGW	Centrair 101A	L. A. Lawes

Reg	Type	Owner or Operator	Notes
G-CFGZ	Flight Design CTSW	G. R. Cassie	
G-CFHB	Micro Aviation B.22J Bantam	P. Rayson	
G-CFHC	Micro Aviation B.22J Bantam	M. Russell	
G-CFHD	Schleicher ASW-20 BL	P. J. Joslin	
G-CFHF	PZL-Bielsko SZD-51-1	Black Mountains Gliding Club	
G-CFHG	Schempp-Hirth Mini Nimbus C	187 Syndicate	
G-CFHI	Van's RV-9	J. R. Dawe	
G-CFHK	Aeroprakt A22-L Foxbat	R. Bellew	
G-CFHL	Rolladen-Schneider LS4	G-CFHL Syndicate	
G-CFHM	Schleicher ASK-13	Lasham Gliding Society Ltd	
G-CFHN	Schleicher K 8B	The Nene Valley Gliding Club Ltd	
G-CFHO	Grob G.103 Twin Astir II	The Surrey Hills Gliding Club Ltd	
G-CFHP	Ikarus C42 FB80	Perranporth Flying Club Ltd	
G-CFHR	Schempp-Hirth Discus b	Q5 Syndicate	
G-CFHS	Tchemma T01/77 balloon	J. Dyer	
G-CFHU	Robinson R22 Beta	Cameron and Brown Partnership	
G-CFHW	Grob G.102 Astir CS	D. J. Wedlock & D. Brown	
G-CFHX	Schroeder Fire Balloons G22/24 balloon	T. J. Ellenrieder	
G-CFHY	Fokker Dr.1 Triplane replica (556/17)	P. G. Bond	
G-CFIA	Best Off Sky Ranger Swift 912S(1)	I. D. Worthington	
G-CFIC	Jodel DR.1050/M1	J. H. & P. I. Kempton	
G-CFID	Tanarg/Ixess 15 912S	D. Smith	
G-CFIE	Rotorsport UK MT-03	The India Echo Flyers	
G-CFIF	Christen Eagle II	Eagle Group FGP	
G-CFIG	P & M Aviation Quik GT450	J. Whitfield	
G-CFIH	Piel CP.1320	A. R. Wade	
G-CFII	DH.82A Tiger Moth	Avalon Ventures Ltd	
G-CFIJ	Christen Eagle II	V. Kiminius	
G-CFIK	Lindstrand LBL-60X balloon	L. Sambrook	
G-CFIL	P & M Aviation Quik GT450	S. N. Catchpole	
G-CFIM	P & M Aviation Quik GT450	G-CFIM Flying Group	
G-CFIO	Cessna 172S	Skytrek Air Services	
G-CFIT	Ikarus C42 FB100	G-CFIT Group	
G-CFIU	CZAW Sportcruiser	G. Everett & D. Smith	
G-CFIW	Balony Kubicek BB20XR balloon	I. S. Bridge	
G-CFIZ	Best Off Sky Ranger 912(2)	J. A. Hartshorne	
G-CFJB	Rotorsport UK MT-03	N. J. Hargreaves	
G-CFJF	Schempp-Hirth SHK-1	D. W. McCormick	
G-CFJG	Best Off Sky Ranger Swift 912S(1)	A. P. Finn	
G-CFJH	Grob G.102 Astir CS77	D. B. Harrison	
G-CFJI	Ultramagic M-105 balloon	Res Ballooning/Italy	
G-CFJJ	Best Off Sky Ranger Swift 912S(1)	J. J. Ewing	
G-CFJK	Centrair 101A	G-CFJK Flying Group	
G-CFJL	Raj Hamsa X'Air Hawk	I. S. Doig	
G-CFJM	Rolladen-Schneider LS4-a	I. G. Sullivan	
G-CFJR	Glaser-Dirks DG-300 Club Elan	W. Palmer & H. Inigo-Jones	
G-CFJS	Glaser-Dirks DG-300 Club Elan	K. L. Goldsmith	
G-CFJU	Raj Hamsa X'Air Hawk	J. Beattie	
G-CFJV	Schleicher ASW-15	D. J. Price	
G-CFJW	Schleicher K7	K7 Group	
G-CFJX	DG-300 Elan	Crown Service Gliding Club	
G-CFJZ	Schempp-Hirth SHK-1	C. I. Knowles	
G-CFKA	Rotorsport UK MT-03	M. J. L. Carter	
G-CFKB	CZAW Sportcruiser	KB Flying Group	
G-CFKD	Raj Hamsa X'Air Falcon Jabiru(2)	J. C. Dawson	
G-CFKE	Raj Hamsa X'Air Hawk	J. F. Northey & S. P. Read	
G-CFKG	Rolladen-Schneider LS4-a	R. J. Purdie	
G-CFKH	Zenair CH.601XL Zodiac	C. Long	
G-CFKJ	P & M Aviation Quik GT450	E. Avery & J. Witcombe	
G-CFKL	Schleicher ASW-20 BL	J. Ley	
G-CFKM	Schempp-Hirth Discus b	Lasham Gliding Society Ltd	
G-CFKN	Lindstrand GA22 Mk.II airship	Lindstrand Technologies Ltd	
G-CFKO	P & M Quik GT450	A. Maudsley	
G-CFKP	Performance Designs Barnstormer/Voyager	G. P. Foyle	
G-CFKR	P & M Pegasus Quik	R. D. Ballard	
G-CFKS	Flight Design CTSW	L. I. Bailey	
G-CFKT	Schleicher K 8B	FKT Group	
G-CFKU	P & M Aviation Quik GT450	P. W. Frost	
G-CFKW	Alpi Pioneer 200	J. M. Watts	
G-CFKX	Cameron Z-160 balloon	Ballooning in Tuscany SRL	
G-CFKY	Schleicher Ka 6CR	J. A. Timmis	

Notes	Reg	Type	Owner or Operator
	G-CFKZ	Europa XS	G-CFKZ Group
	G-CFLA	P & M Aviation Quik GT450	P. H. Woodward
	G-CFLC	Glaser-Dirks DG-300 Club Elan	J. L.Hey
	G-CFLD	Ikarus C42 FB80	M. R. Badminton
	G-CFLE	Schempp-Hirth Discus b	D. A. Humphreys
	G-CFLF	Rolladen-Schneider LS4-a	D. Lamb
	G-CFLG	CZAW Sportcruiser	G. R. Greensall
	G-CFLH	Schleicher K8B	The Windrushers Gliding Club Ltd
	G-CFLI	Europa Aviation Europa	A. & E. Bennett
	G-CFLK	Cameron C-90 balloon	D. S. Tree
	G-CFLL	EV-97A Eurostar	I. Galea
	G-CFLM	P & M Pegasus Quik	The JAG Flyers
	G-CFLN	Best Off Sky Ranger Swift 912S(1)	D. Bletcher
	G-CFLO	Rotorsport UK MT-03	The Flo Rider Group
	G-CFLP	D.31 Turbulent	Eaglescott Turbulent Group
	G-CFLR	P & M Aviation Quik GT450	S. J. Baker
	G-CFLS	Schleicher Ka 6CR	University College London Union
	G-CFLW	Schempp-Hirth Standard Cirrus 75	S. M. & S. Law
	G-CFLX	DG-300 Club Elan	Felix Flying Group
	G-CFLZ	Scheibe SF-27A Zugvogel V	Dartmoor Gliding Society
	G-CFMA	BB03 Trya/BB103	S. Uzochukwu
	G-CFMC	Van's RV-9A	G-CFMC Flying Group
	G-CFMD	P & M Aviation Quik GT450	M. J. C. & S. A. C. Curtis
	G-CFMI	Best Off Sky Ranger 912(1)	P. Shelton
	G-CFMM	Cessna 172S	Atlantic Flight Training Ltd
	G-CFMN	Schempp-Hirth Ventus cT	FMN Glider Syndicate
	G-CFMO	Schempp-Hirth Discus b	P. D. Bagnall
	G-CFMP	Europa XS	A. T. Cross & I. R. Caesar
	G-CFMR	Ultramagic V-14 balloon	P. Baker
	G-CFMS	Schleicher ASW-15	D. A. Logan
	G-CFMT	Schempp-Hirth Standard Cirrus	P. D. Whitters
	G-CFMU	Schempp-Hirth Standard Cirrus	T. J. Williamson
	G-CFMV	Aerola Alatus-M	P. J. Wood
	G-CFMW	Scheibe SF-25C	The Mike Whisky Flying Group
	G-CFMX	PA-28-161 Warrior II	Stapleford Flying Club Ltd
	G-CFNB	Cameron TR-70 balloon	P. Bals
	G-CFNC	Flylight Dragonfly	W. G. Minns
	G-CFND	Schleicher Ka 6E	C. Scutt
	G-CFNE	PZL-Bielsko SZD-38A Jantar 1	T. Robson, J. Murray & I. Gordon
	G-CFNF	Robinson R44 II	Kuki Helicopter Sales Ltd
	G-CFNH	Schleicher ASW-19	Rattlesden Gliding Club Ltd
	G-CFNI	Airborne Edge XT912-B/Streak III-B	V. D. Carmichael
	G-CFNK	Slingsby T.65A Vega	I. P. Goldstraw
	G-CFNL	Schempp-Hirth Discus b	A. S. Ramsay & P. P. Musto
	G-CFNM	Centrair 101B Pegase	D. T. Hartley
	G-CFNO	Best Off Sky Ranger Swift 912S(1)	P. R. Hanman
	G-CFNP	Schleicher Ka 6CR	P. Pollard-Wilkins
	G-CFNR	Schempp-Hirth Discus b	C. Martin-Pitt
	G-CFNS	Glaser-Dirks DG-300 Club Elan	FNS Syndicate
	G-CFNT	Glaser-Dirks DG-600	G-CFNT Group
	G-CFNU	Rolladen Schneider LS4-a	R. J. Simpson
	G-CFNW	EV-97 TeamEurostar UK	The Scottish Aero Club Ltd
	G-CFNX	ixess 13 modified Tanarg 912 Trike	D. A. Eastough
	G-CFNZ	Airborne Edge XT912-B/Streak III-B	N. C. Grayson
	G-CFOB	Schleicher ASW-15B	S. Whybrow
	G-CFOC	Glaser-Dirks DG200/17	R. J. Robinson & K. R. Snell
	G-CFOF	Scheibe SF-27A Zugvogel V	Essex & Suffolk Gliding Club Ltd
	G-CFOG	Ikarus C42 FB UK	P. D. Coppin
	G-CFOJ	Eurocopter EC.155 B1	Starspeed Ltd
	G-CFOM	Scheibe SF27A	A. Ruddle & P. DrakeK. A. Ford
	G-CFON	Wittman W8 Tailwind	G-CFON Group
	G-CFOO	P & M Aviation Quik R	S. Dixon
	G-CFOP	Cameron Hopping Bag 120 SS balloon	J. Ravibalan
	G-CFOR	Schleicher K 8B	Dorset Gliding Club Ltd
	G-CFOS	Flylight Dragonfly	A. Westmoreland
	G-CFOT	PZL-Bielsko SZD-48-3 Jantar Standard 3	T. Greenwood
	G-CFOU	Schleicher K7	Eaglescott ASK7 Group
	G-CFOV	CZAW Sportcruiser	J. G. Murphy
	G-CFOW	Best Off Sky Ranger Swift 912S(1)	Oscar Whiskey Syndicate
	G-CFOX	Marganski MDM-1	M. Makari
	G-CFOY	Schempp-Hirth Discus b	J. W. Slater, R. F. Dowty & G. Myerson

Reg	Type	Owner or Operator	Notes
G-CFOZ	Rolladen-Schneider LS1-f	C. Booker	
G-CFPA	CZAW Sportcruiser	M. Cooper	
G-CFPB	Schleicher ASW-15B	G-CFPB Syndicate	
G-CFPD	Rolladen-Schneider LS7	LS7 Group	
G-CFPE	Schempp-Hirth Ventus cT	R. Palmer	
G-CFPH	Centrair ASW-20F	J. Hunt	
G-CFPI	P & M Aviation Quik GT450	E. J. Douglas	
G-CFPJ	CZAW Sportcruiser	S. R. Winter	
G-CFPL	Schempp-Hirth Ventus c	R. V. Barrett	
G-CFPM	PZL-Bielsko SZD-51-1 Junior	Kent Gliding Club Ltd	
G-CFPN	Schleicher ASW-20	J. C. M. Docherty	
G-CFPP	Schempp-Hirth Nimbus 2B	D. W. North	
G-CFPR	P & M Quik R	J. A. Horn	
G-CFPS	Sky 25-16 balloon	G. B. Lescott	
G-CFPT	Schleicher ASW-20	L. Hornsey and L. Weeks Syndicate	
G-CFPW	Glaser-Dirks DG-600	P. B. Gray	
G-CFRC	Schempp-Hirth Nimbus 2B	P. A. I. Guthrie	
G-CFRE	Schleicher Ka 6E	R. A. Foreshew	
G-CFRF	Lindstrand LBL-31A	RAF Halton Hot Air Balloon Club	
G-CFRH	Schleicher ASW-20CL	J. N. Wilton	
G-CFRI	Ultramagic N-355 balloon	Kent Ballooning	
G-CFRJ	Schempp-Hirth Standard Cirrus	A. N. Mayer	
G-CFRK	Schleicher ASW-15B	P. R. Boet	
G-CFRM	SkyRanger Swift 912S(1)	R. K. & T. A. Willcox	
G-CFRN	Rotorsport UK MTO Sport	R. Marks	
G-CFRP	Centrair 101A Pegase	L. Bourne	
G-CFRR	Centrair 101A	G-CFRR Syndicate	
G-CFRS	Scheibe Zugvogel IIIB	G-CFRS Flying Group	
G-CFRT	EV-97 TeamEurostar UK	K. A. O'Neill	
G-CFRV	Centrair 101A	J. D. Hubberstey	
G-CFRW	Schleicher ASW-20L	R. M. Green	
G-CFRX	Centrair 101A	S. Woolrich & M. A. Lithgow	
G-CFRY	Zenair CH 601UL	C. K. Fry	
G-CFRZ	Schempp-Hirth Standard Cirrus	S. G. Lapworth	
G-CFSB	Tecnam P2002-RG Sierra	W. J. Gale and Son	
G-CFSD	Schleicher ASK-13	Edensoaring Ltd	
G-CFSF	P & M Aviation QuikR	C. J. Gordon	
G-CFSG	Van's RV-9	Foley Farm Flying Group	
G-CFSH	Grob G.102 Astir CS Jeans	Buckminster Gliding Club Ltd	
G-CFSJ	Jabiru J160	S. Langley	
G-CFSL	Kubicek BB-26Z balloon	M. R. Jeynes	
G-CFSR	DG-300 Elan	A. P. Montague	
G-CFSS	Schleicher Ka 6E	FSS Syndicate	
G-CFST	Schleicher ASH-25E	D. Tucker & K. H. Lloyd	
G-CFSW	Skyranger Swift 912S(1)	C. T. Hanbury-Tenison	
G-CFSX	Savannah VG Jabiru(1)	M. E. Caton	
G-CFTB	Schleicher Ka 6CR	B. T. Green & M. W. Bennett	
G-CFTC	PZL-Bielsko SZD-51-1 Junior	Seahawk Gliding Club	
G-CFTD	Schleicher ASW-15B	A. A. Thornburn	
G-CFTG	P & M Aviation Quik R	G-CFTG Group	
G-CFTH	PZL-Bielsko SZD-50-3 Puchacz	Buckminster Gliding Club Ltd	
G-CFTI	Evektor EV-97A Eurostar	R. J. Dance	
G-CFTJ	Aerotechnik EV-97A Eurostar	C. B. Flood	
G-CFTK	Grob G.102 Astir CS Jeans	Ulster Gliding Club Ltd	
G-CFTL	Schleicher ASW-20CL	Carow Developments Ltd	
G-CFTM	Cameron C-80 balloon	P. A. Meecham	
G-CFTN	Schleicher K 8B	Mendip Gliding Club Ltd	
G-CFTO	Ikarus C42 FB80	Fly Hire Ltd	
G-CFTP	Schleicher ASW-20CL	D. J. Pengilley	
G-CFTR	Grob G.102 Astir CS77	The University of Nottingham Students Union	
G-CFTS	Glaser-Dirks DG-300 Club Elan	FTS Syndicate	
G-CFTT	Van's RV-7	J. A. Paley	
C-CFTU	Flylight Dragonfly	R. J. Cook	
G-CFTV	Rolladen-Schneider LS7-WL	D. Hilton	
G-CFTW	Schempp-Hirth Discus b	230 Syndicate	
G-CFTX	Jabiru J160	J. Williamson & J. King	
G-CFTY	Rolladen-Schneider LS7-WL	M. Nowak	
G-CFTZ	Evektor EV-97 Eurostar	TZ Flyers	
G-CFUA	Van's RV-9A	I. M. Macleod	
G-CFUB	Schleicher Ka 6CR	H. Gascoyne & M. W. Bennett	
G-CFUD	Skyranger Swift 912S(1)	G-CFUD Group	

BRITISH CIVIL AIRCRAFT MARKINGS

Notes	Reg	Type	Owner or Operator
	G-CFUE	Alpi Pioneer 300 Hawk	A. Dayani
	G-CFUG	Grob G.109B	Portsmouth Naval Gliding Centre
	G-CFUH	Schempp-Hirth Ventus c	C. G. T. Huck & S. E. Lucas
	G-CFUI	Hunt Wing/Avon 503(4)	R. F. G. Moyle
	G-CFUJ	Glaser-Dirks DG-300 Elan	T. J. Rusin & K. Z. Handzlik
	G-CFUL	Schempp-Hirth Discus b	Discus 803 Syndicate
	G-CFUN	Schleicher ASW-20CL	G-CFUN Group
	G-CFUP	Schempp-Hirth Discus b	Lasham Gliding Society Ltd
	G-CFUR	Schempp-Hirth Ventus cT	A. P. Carpenter
	G-CFUS	PZL-Bielsko SZD-51-1 Junior	Scottish Gliding Union Ltd
	G-CFUT	Glaser-Dirks DG-300 Club Elan	P. E. Newman
	G-CFUU	DG-300 Club Elan	G. Cooksey
	G-CFUV	Rolladen-Schneider LS7-WL	C. H. Braithwaite
	G-CFUW	Rotorsport UK MTO Sport	D. A. Robertson
	G-CFUX	Cameron C-80 balloon	A. E. Still
	G-CFUY	PZL-Bielsko SZD-50-3 Puchacz	The Bath, Wilts and North Dorset Gliding Club
	G-CFUZ	CZAW Sportcruiser	M. Gislam
	G-CFVC	Schleicher ASK-13	Mendip Gliding Club Ltd
	G-CFVE	Schempp-Hirth Nimbus 2	L. Mitchell
	G-CFVF	Air Creation 582(1)/Kiss 400	G. R. Wilson
	G-CFVH	Rolladen-Schneider LS7	C. C. & J. C. Marshall
	G-CFVJ	Cvjetkovic CA-65 Skyfly	N. D. Hunter
	G-CFVK	Best Off Skyranger 912(2)	K. Perryman & C. S. Wilson
	G-CFVL	Scheibe Zugvogel IIIB	D. Cobham
	G-CFVM	Centrair 101A Pegase	S. H. North
	G-CFVN	Centrair 101A Pegase	K. Samuels
	G-CFVP	Centrair 101A Pegase	Pegasus FVP Syndicate
	G-CFVR	Europa XS	G-CFVR Group
	G-CFVU	Schleicher ASK-13	Edensoaring Ltd
	G-CFVV	Centrair 101A Pegase	Cambridge Gliding Club Ltd
	G-CFVW	Schempp-Hirth Ventus bT	J. F. de Hollander
	G-CFVX	Cameron C-80 balloon	A. Hornshaw
	G-CFVY	Cameron A-120 balloon	C. A. Petre
	G-CFVZ	Schleicher Ka 6E	N. R. Bowers
	G-CFWA	Schleicher Ka 6CR	C. C. Walley
	G-CFWB	Schleicher ASK-13	Cotswold Gliding Club
	G-CFWC	Grob G.103C Twin III Acro	The South Wales Gliding Club Ltd
	G-CFWD	Rotorsport UK MTO Sport	Gower Gyronautics
	G-CFWF	Rolladen-Schneider LS7	G. B. Hibberd
	G-CFWH	Scheibe SF27A	A. S. Carter
	G-CFWJ	P & M Quik GT450	T. Porter & D. Whiteley
	G-CFWK	Schempp-Hirth Nimbus-3DT	29 Syndicate
	G-CFWL	Schleicher K8B	D. S. Downton
	G-CFWM	Glaser-Dirks DG-300 Club Elan	FWM Group
	G-CFWN	P & M Quik GT450	G-CFWN Group
	G-CFWP	Schleicher ASW-19B	A. Zuchora
	G-CFWR	Best Off Sky Ranger 912(2)	D. Squire
	G-CFWS	Schleicher ASW-20C	B. N. M. House
	G-CFWT	PZL-Bielsko SZD-50-3 Puchacz	Goalrace Ltd
	G-CFWU	Rolladen-Schneider LS7-WL	T. W. Arscott
	G-CFWV	Van's RV-7	D. K. Sington
	G-CFWW	Schleicher ASH-25E	N. A. C. Norman
	G-CFWY	Centrair 101A Pegase	G. M. Dodwell & J. Randall
	G-CFXA	Grob G.104 Speed Astir IIB	Ringmer Speedy Syndicate
	G-CFXB	Schleicher K 8B	Dartmoor Gliding Society
	G-CFXC	Schleicher Ka 6E	D. J. Pike
	G-CFXF	Magni M-16C Tandem Trainer	P. I. Jordan
	G-CFXG	Flylight Dragonfly	C. A. Mason
	G-CFXK	Flylight Dragonfly	N. R. Pettigrew
	G-CFXM	Schempp-Hirth Discus bT	G. R. E. Bottomley
	G-CFXN	CZAW Sportcruiser	H. Bishop
	G-CFXO	PZL-Bielsko SZD-50-3 Puchacz	Derbyshire & Lancashire Gliding Club Ltd
	G-CFXP	Lindstrand LBL-105A balloon	Shaun Bradley Project Services Ltd
	G-CFXR	Lindstrand LBL-105A balloon	Lindstrand Media Ltd
	G-CFXS	Schleicher Ka 6E	D. P. Aherne
	G-CFXT	Naval Aircraft Factory N3N-3	R. H. & J. A. Cooper
	G-CFXU	Schleicher Ka-6E	Xray Uniform Group
	G-CFXW	Schleicher K8B	The South Wales Gliding Club Ltd
	G-CFXX	P & M Quik R	G. Bates
	G-CFXY	Schleicher ASW-15B	P. W. Armstrong
	G-CFXZ	P & M Quik R	M. Naylor

Reg	Type	Owner or Operator	Notes
G-CFYA	PZL-Bielsko SZD-50-3 Puchacz	Cairngorm Gliding Club	
G-CFYB	Rolladen-Schneider LS7	A. T. Macdonald & V. P. Haley	
G-CFYC	Schempp-Hirth Ventus b	J. M. Brooke	
G-CFYD	Aeroprakt A22-L Foxbat	A. P. Fenn	
G-CFYE	Scheibe Zugvogel IIIB	The Gliding Heritage Centre	
G-CFYF	Schleicher ASK-21	London Gliding Club Proprietary Ltd	
G-CFYG	Glasflugel Club Libelle 205	FYG Syndicate	
G-CFYH	Rolladen-Schneider LS4-a	G. W. & C. A. Craig	
G-CFYI	Grob G.102 Astir CS	S. R. Hill, A. H. Kay & W. E. Roper	
G-CFYJ	Schempp-Hirth Standard Cirrus	W. Blackburn	
G-CFYK	Rolladen-Schneider LS7-WL	S. D. S. Smith & S. K. Haigh	
G-CFYM	Schempp-Hirth Discus bT	T. Wright	
G-CFYN	Schempp-Hirth Discus b	N. White & P. R. Foulger	
G-CFYO	P & M Quik R	M. A. Sandwith	
G-CFYP	FBM & W Silex M/Flyke/Monster	A. J. R. Carver	
G-CFYR	LET L-23 Super Blanik	G-CFYR Group	
G-CFYS	Dynamic WT9 UK	E. M. Middleton	
G-CFYU	Glaser-Dirks DG-100 Elan	C. A. Chappell, H. S. Stewart & W. J. Prince	
G-CFYV	Schleicher ASK-21	The Bristol Gliding Club Proprietary Ltd	
G-CFYW	Rolladen-Schneider LS7	J. Douglass	
G-CFYX	Schempp-Hirth Discus b	D. A. Salmon	
G-CFYY	Schleicher ASK-13	Lasham Gliding Society Ltd	
G-CFYZ	Schleicher ASH-25	171 Syndicate	
G-CFZB	Glasflugel H201B Standard Libelle	J. C. Meyer	
G-CFZD	Jabiru J430	C. J. Judd & A. Macknish	
G-CFZF	PZL-Bielsko SZD-51-1 Junior	Devon and Somerset Gliding Club Ltd	
G-CFZH	Schempp-Hirth Ventus c	FZH Group	
G-CFZI	Savannah Jabiru (5)	J. T., A. L. & O. D. Lewis	
G-CFZJ	VS.388 Seafire F.46	C. T. Charleston	
G-CFZK	Schempp-Hirth Standard Cirrus	S. Lucas & R. Burgoyne	
G-CFZL	Schleicher ASW-20 CL	A. L. & R. M. Housden	
G-CFZO	Schempp-Hirth Nimbus 3	954 Syndicate	
G-CFZP	PZL-Bielsko SZD-51-1 Junior	Midland Gliding Club Ltd	
G-CFZR	Schleicher Ka 6CR	T. K. Gooch	
G-CFZT	Ace Magic Laser	G. Cousins	
G-CFZW	Glaser-Dirks DG-300 Club Elan	D. O'Flanagan & G. Stilgoe	
G-CFZX	Rotorsport UK MTO Sport	Gyro-I Ltd	
G-CFZZ	LET L-33 Solo	The Andreas L33 Group	
G-CGAA	Flylight Dragonfly	G. Adkins	
G-CGAB	AB Sportine LAK-12 Lietuva	W. T. Emery	
G-CGAC	P & M Quik GT450	G. Brockhurst	
G-CGAD	Rolladen-Schneider LS3	J. D. Brister	
G-CGAF	Schleicher ASK-21	Lasham Gliding Society Ltd	
G-CGAG	Scleicher ASK-21	Stratford on Avon Gliding Club Ltd	
G-CGAH	Schempp-Hirth Standard Cirrus	J. W. Williams	
G-CGAI	Raj Hamsa X'Air Hawk	R. G. Cheshire	
G-CGAJ	Alpi Pioneer 400	V. T. Betts	
G-CGAK	Acrosport II	P. D. Sibbons	
G-CGAL	P & M Quik R	R. A. Keene	
G-CGAM	Schleicher ASK-21	T. R. Dews	
G-CGAN	Glasflugel H301 Libelle	M. D. Butcher	
G-CGAO	DHC.1 Chipmunk 22 (1350)	G-CGAO Group	
G-CGAP	Schempp-Hirth Ventus bT	J. R. Greenwell	
G-CGAR	Rolladen-Schneider LS6-c	A. Warbrick	
G-CGAS	Schempp-Hirth Ventus cT	R. A. Davenport	
G-CGAT	Grob G.102 Astir CS	N. J. Hooper	
G-CGAU	Glasflugel H201B Standard Libelle	G-CGAU Group	
G-CGAV	Scheibe SF-27A Zugvogel V	Golf Alpha Victor Group	
G-CGAX	PZL-Bielsko SZD-55-1 Promyk	Golf Alpha Xray Group	
G-CGAZ	P & M Quik R	I. Tulkan	
G-CGBB	Schleicher ASK-21	University of Edinburgh Sports Union	
G-CGBD	PZL-Bielsko SZD-50-3	The Northumbria Gliding Club Ltd	
G-CGBF	Schleicher ASK-21	London Gliding Club Pty Ltd	
G-CGBG	Rolladen-Schneider LS6-18w	J. Bayford	
G-CGBH	Raj Hamsa X'Air Hawk	S. E. McEwen	
G-CGBJ	Grob G.102 Astir CS	Banbury Gliding Club Ltd	
G-CGBL	Rolladen-Schneider LS7-WL	P. A. Roche	
G-CGBM	Flight Design CTSW	P. P. Duffy	
G-CGBN	Schleicher ASK-21	Essex and Suffolk Gliding Club Ltd	
G-CGBO	Rolladen-Schneider LS6	G-CGBO Syndicate	

BRITISH CIVIL AIRCRAFT MARKINGS

Notes	Reg	Type	Owner or Operator
	G-CGBR	Rolladen-Schneider LS6-c	V. L. Brown
	G-CGBS	Glaser-Dirks DG-300 Club Elan	B. Fulton & J. Thomas
	G-CGBU	Centrair 101A Pegase	D. J. Arblaster
	G-CGBV	Schleicher ASK-21	Wolds Gliding Club Ltd
	G-CGBY	Rolladen-Schneider LS7-WL	B. N. Searle
	G-CGBZ	Glaser-Dirks DG-500 Elan Trainer	G. N. Turner
	G-CGCA	Schleicher ASW-19B	P. Armstrong
	G-CGCC	PZL-Bielsko SZD-51-1 Junior	Coventry Gliding Club Ltd
	G-CGCD	Schempp-Hirth Standard Cirrus	Cirrus Syndicate
	G-CGCE	Magni M16C Tandem Trainer	A. J. A. Fowler
	G-CGCF	Schleicher ASK-23	Cotswold Gliding Club
	G-CGCH	CZAW Sportcruiser	J. E. Preston
	G-CGCI	Sikorsky S-92A	Bristow Helicopters Ltd
	G-CGCK	PZL-Bielsko SZD-50-3 Puchacz	Kent Gliding Club Ltd (G-BTJV)
	G-CGCL	Grob G.102 Astir CS	Southdown Gliding Club Ltd
	G-CGCM	Rolladen-Schneider LS6-c	G. R. Glazebrook
	G-CGCN	MCR-01 Club	D. J. Smith
	G-CGCO	Schempp-Hirth Cirrus VTC	I. D. Symon
	G-CGCP	Schleicher Ka-6CR	Burn K8 G-CGCP Group
	G-CGCR	Schleicher ASW-15B	N. J. Khan
	G-CGCS	Glasflugel Club Libelle 205	D. G. Coats
	G-CGCT	Schempp-Hirth Discus b	Banbury Gliding Club Ltd
	G-CGCU	PZL-Bielsko SZD-50-3 Puchacz	Peterbourgh & Spalding Gliding Club Ltd
	G-CGCV	Raj Hamsa X'Air Hawk	K. Buckley & B. L. Prime
	G-CGCX	Schleicher ASW-15	R. L. Horsnell
	G-CGDA	Rolladen-Schneider LS3-17	J. S. Romanes
	G-CGDB	Schleicher K 8B	T. A. Odom
	G-CGDC	Rotorsport UK MTO Sport	R. E. Derham & T. R. Kingsley
	G-CGDD	Bolkow Phoebus C	G. C. Kench
	G-CGDE	Schleicher Ka 6CR	K6 Syndicate
	G-CGDF	Schleicher Ka 6BR	G-CGDF Group
	G-CGDG	Cameron C-80 balloon	J. Braeckman/Belgium
	G-CGDH	Europa XS	G-CGDH Group
	G-CGDI	EV-97A Eurostar	Delta India Group
	G-CGDK	Schleicher K 8B	Dartmoor Gliding Society
	G-CGDL	P & M Quik R	S. C. Reeve
	G-CGDM	Sonex Sonex	P. Johnson
	G-CGDN	Rolladen-Schneider LS3-17	I. B. Kennedy
	G-CGDO	Grob G.102 Astir CS	P. Lowe & R. Bostock
	G-CGDR	Schempp-Hirth Discus CS	D. Daniels
	G-CGDS	Schleicher ASW-15B	B. Birk & P. A. Crouch
	G-CGDT	Schleicher ASW-24	Tango 54 Syndicate
	G-CGDV	CSA Sportcruiser	G. J. Richardson
	G-CGDW	CSA PS-28 Sportcruiser	Onega Ltd
	G-CGDX	Orlican Discus CS	D. Bieniasz
	G-CGDY	Schleicher ASW-15B	L. White & P. Bannister
	G-CGDZ	Schleicher ASW-24	J. M. Norman
	G-CGEA	Schleicher Ka 6CR	Scottish Gliding Union Ltd
	G-CGEB	Grob G.102 Astir CS77	T. R. Dews
	G-CGEC	Flight Design CTLS	S. Munday
	G-CGEE	Glasflugel H201B Standard Libelle	D. Plumb
	G-CGEG	Schleicher K 8B	The Windrushers Gliding Club Ltd
	G-CGEH	Schleicher ASW-15B	Syndicate 219
	G-CGEJ	Alpi Pioneer 200-M	D. E. Foster
	G-CGEK	Ace Magic Laser	T. Smith
	G-CGEL	PZL-Bielsko SZD-50-3	The Northumbria Gliding Club Ltd
	G-CGEM	Schleicher Ka 6CR	GEM Syndicate
	G-CGEO	CSA Sportcruiser	The Jester Flying Group
	G-CGEP	Schempp-Hirth Standard Cirrus	A. Ratcliffe
	G-CGER	Cameron Z-105 balloon	M. Casaburo/Italy
	G-CGEU	Flylight Dragonfly	I. Hesling-Gibson
	G-CGEW	Rotorsport UK MTO Sport	J. L. V. Lowry-Corry
	G-CGEX	P & M Quik GT450	A. C. Hayward
	G-CGEY	Julian CD Dingbat	A. H. H. Mole
	G-CGEZ	Raj Hamsa X'Air Hawk	Coyote Ugly Group
	G-CGFB	BB03 Trya/BB103	B. J. Fallows
	G-CGFG	Cessna 152	LAC Flying School
	G-CGFH	Cessna T182T Turbo Skylane	Tatlock & Thomson Ltd
	G-CGFK	Ace Magic Laser	B. B. Adams
	G-CGFN	Cameron C-60 balloon	G. J. Madelin
	G-CGFO	Ultramagic H-42 balloon	D. G. SuchJ

Reg	Type	Owner or Operator	Notes
G-CGFP	Pietenpol Aircamper	M. D. Waldron	
G-CGFR	Lindstranbd LBL HS-120 airship	D. Duke	
G-CGFS	Nanchang CJ-6A	Red Star Squadron	
G-CGFU	Schempp-Hirth Mini-Nimbus C	S. Foster	
G-CGFY	Lindstrand LBL-105A balloon	Gone Ballooning	
G-CGFZ	Thruster T.600N 450	K. J. Crompton	
G-CGGC	P & M QuikR	Oakley Flyers	
G-CGGD	Eurocopter AS365N2 Dauphin 2	Multiflight Ltd	
G-CGGG	Robinson R44	Flying Pig & Elstree Helicopters (G-SJDI)	
G-CGGK	Westland Wasp HAS Mk.1	The Real Aeroplane Co.Ltd	
G-CGGM	EV-97 TeamEurostar UK	Golf Mike Group	
G-CGGO	Robin DR.400-180 Regent	G. I. J. Thomson & R. A. Hawkins	
G-CGGP	Autogyro MTOSport	J. Taylforth & G. P. Gibson	
G-CGGS	Robinson R44 II	Oakfield Investments Ltd	
G-CGGT	P & M Quik GT450	A. H. Beveridge	
G-CGGV	Rotorsport UK MTO Sport	S. Morris	
G-CGGW	Rotorsport UK MTO Sport	P. Adams	
G-CGGY	UltraMagic N-425 balloon	Adventure Balloons Ltd	
G-CGGZ	UltraMagic S-90 balloon	P. Lawman	
G-CGHA	P & M Quik R	C. A. Green	
G-CGHB	NAMC CJ-6A (61367)	M. J. Harvey	
G-CGHG	P & M Quik GT450	J. & K. D. McAlpine	
G-CGHH	P & M Quik R	C. Pyle & N. Richardson	
G-CGHJ	Staaken Z-21A Flitzer	D. J. Ashley	
G-CGHK	Alpi Pioneer 300 Hawk	D. J. Ashley	
G-CGHL	Rotorsport UK MTOSport	P. K. Hinault	
G-CGHN	Aeros Discus/Alize	R. Simpson & N. Sutton	
G-CGHR	Magic Laser	N. P. Power	
G-CGHT	Dyn'Aero MCR-01 Banbi	R. P. Trives (G-POOP)	
G-CGHU	Hawker Hunter T.Mk.8C	Hawker Hunter Aviation Ltd	
G-CGHV	Raj Hamsa X'Air Hawk	H. Adams	
G-CGHW	Czech Sport Aircraft Sportcruiser	Sportcruiser 290 Ltd	
G-CGHZ	P & M Quik R	J. Rockey	
G-CGIA	Paramania Action/Adventure	A. E. C. Phillips	
G-CGIB	Magic Cyclone	S. B. Walters	
G-CGIC	Rotorsport MTO Sport	D. J. Kenyon	
G-CGID	PA-31-350 Navajo Chieftain	T. Michaels	
G-CGIE	Flylight Dragonfly	N. S. Brayn	
G-CGIF	Flylight Dragonfly	R. D. Leigh	
G-CGIG	Lindstrand LBL-90A balloon	M. R. Stokoe	
G-CGIH	Cameron C-90 balloon	A. & P. Gunning-Stevenson	
G-CGIK	Isaacs Spitfire (EN961 SD-X)	S. J. Cowley	
G-CGIL	CZAW Sportcruiser	G-CGIL Group	
G-CGIM	Ace Aviation Magic Laser	C. Royle	
G-CGIN	Paramania Action GT/Adventure	A. E. C. Phillips	
G-CGIO	Medway SLA100 Executive	G-CGIO Syndicate	
G-CGIP	CZAW Sportcruiser	G-CGIP Flying Group	
G-CGIR	Remos GX	L. R. Marks & J. A. Pereira	
G-CGIV	Kolb Firefly	W. A. Emmerson	
G-CGIX	Rotorsport UK MTO Sport	J. W. G. Andrews	
G-CGIY	Piper J3C-65 (330244:C-46)	R. D. Myles	
G-CGIZ	Flight Design CTSW	J. Hilton	
G-CGJB	Schempp-Hirth Duo Discus T	G. J. Basey	
G-CGJC	Rotorsport UK MTO Sport	J. C. Collingwood	
G-CGJE	VS.361 Spitfire IX	Propshop Ltd	
G-CGJF	Fokker E.111 Replica	E. Paterson	
G-CGJJ	P & M Quik R	Juliet Juliet Group	
G-CGJL	CZAW Sportcruiser	S. Catalano	
G-CGJM	Skyranger Swift 912S(1)	J. Pye	
G-CGJN	Van's RV-7	T. Stavrou	
G-CGJP	Van's RV-10	G-CGIP Group	
G-CGJS	CZAW Sportcruiser	J. M. Tiley	
G-CGJT	CZAW Sportcruiser	D. F. Toller	
G-CGJW	RAF 2000 GTX-SE	J. J. Wollen	
G-CGJX	SA.341B Gazelle AH Mk.1	The Gazelle Squadron Display Team	
G-CGJZ	SA.341D Gazelle HT Mk.3 (XZ933)	The Gazelle Squadron Display Team	
G-CGKD	Grob G115E Tutor	Babcock Aerospace Ltd	
G-CGKE	Grob G115E Tutor	Babcock Aerospace Ltd	
G-CGKG	Grob G115E Tutor	Babcock Aerospace Ltd	
G-CGKH	Grob G115E Tutor	Babcock Aerospace Ltd	
G-CGKK	Grob G115E Tutor	Babcock Aerospace Ltd	

BRITISH CIVIL AIRCRAFT MARKINGS

Notes	Reg	Type	Owner or Operator
	G-CGKL	Grob G115E Tutor	Babcock Aerospace Ltd
	G-CGKN	Grob G115E Tutor	Babcock Aerospace Ltd
	G-CGKP	Grob G115E Tutor	Babcock Aerospace Ltd
	G-CGKR	Grob G115E Tutor	Babcock Aerospace Ltd
	G-CGKS	Grob G115E Tutor	Babcock Aerospace Ltd
	G-CGKU	Grob G115E Tutor	Babcock Aerospace Ltd
	G-CGKW	Grob G115E Tutor	Babcock Aerospace Ltd
	G-CGKY	Cessna 182T	T. A. E. Dobell
	G-CGKZ	Best Off Sky Ranger Swift 912S(1)	M. Hilton
	G-CGLB	Airdrome Dream Classic	R. D. Leigh
	G-CGLC	Czech Sport Aircraft Sportcruiser	M. A. Ulrick
	G-CGLE	Flylight Dragonfly	B. Skelding
	G-CGLF	Magni M-16C Tandem Trainer	J. S. Walton
	G-CGLG	P & M Quik GT450	P. H. Evans
	G-CGLI	Alpi Pioneer 200M	B. A. Lyford
	G-CGLJ	TL 2000UK Sting Carbon	L. A. James
	G-CGLK	Magni M-16C Tandem Trainer	R. M. Savage
	G-CGLM	Rotorsport UK MTO Sport	M. P. Rainford
	G-CGLN	Jabiru J430	A. J. Thomas
	G-CGLO	P & M Quik R	R. H. Lowndes
	G-CGLP	CZAW Sportcruiser	P. S. Tanner
	G-CGLR	Czech Sport Aircraft Sportcruiser	J. S. Fogel
	G-CGLT	Czech Sport Aircraft Sportcruiser	I. Jalowiecki
	G-CGLY	Rotorsport UK Calidus	R. J. Steel
	G-CGLZ	TL 2000UK Sting Carbon	Newtownards Microlight Group
	G-CGMA	Ace Magic Laser	J. N. Hanson
	G-CGMC	Embraer EMB-135ER	Eastern Airways International Ltd
	G-CGMD	Rotorsport UK Calidus	W. H. Morgan
	G-CGMG	Van's RV-9	D. J. Bone
	G-CGMH	Jodel D150A Mascaret	C. H. Hamp
	G-CGMI	P & M Quik GT450	W. G. Reynolds
	G-CGML	TL 2000UK Sting Carbon	G. T. Leedham
	G-CGMM	CZAW Sportcruiser	TAF and Co
	G-CGMN	Best Off Sky Ranger Swift 912S	G-CGMN Flying Group
	G-CGMO	Ace Magic Laser	G. J. Latham
	G-CGMP	CZAW Sportcruiser	R. Hasler
	G-CGMR	Colt Bibendum-110 balloon	Mobberley Balloon Collection (G-GRIP)
	G-CGMV	Roko Aero NG 4HD	Roko NG4
	G-CGMW	Alpi Pioneer 200M	M. S. McCrudden
	G-CGMZ	P & M Quik R	T. J. Heaton
	G-CGNA	Cameron Super FMG-100 balloon	Cameron Balloons Ltd
	G-CGNC	Rotorsport UK MTO Sport	Bath Leasing & Supplies Ltd
	G-CGNE	Robinson R44 II	Heli Air Ltd
	G-CGNG	CZAW Sportcruiser	H. M. Wooldridge
	G-CGNH	Reality Escapade Jabiru(3)	J. M. Ingram
	G-CGNI	Ikarus C42 FB80	S. Conion
	G-CGNJ	Cameron Z-105 balloon	Loughborough Students Union Hot Air Balloon Club
	G-CGNM	Magni M-16C Tandem Trainer	The Ruffians Gyro Syndicate
	G-CGNO	P & M Quik GT450	Mid Anglia Microlights Ltd
	G-CGNS	Sky 65-24 balloon	R. L. Bovell
	G-CGNV	Reality Escapade	P. M. Noonan
	G-CGNW	Scheibe SF-25C Falke	Army Gliding Association
	G-CGNX	Rotorsport UK MTO Sport	L. McCallum
	G-CGNZ	Europa XS	R. Vianello
	G-CGOA	Cessna 550 Citation II	XJC Jets Ltd (G-JMDW)
	G-CGOG	Evektor EV-97 Eurostar	D. C. & S. G. Emmons
	G-CGOH	Cameron C-80 balloon	Cameron Balloons Ltd
	G-CGOJ	Jodel D.11	J. Laszio
	G-CGOK	Ace Magic Cyclone	C. R. Dunford
	G-CGOL	Jabiru J430	J. F. Woodham
	G-CGOM	Flight Design MC	A. Vaicvenas
	G-CGOR	Jodel D.18	R. D. Cook
	G-CGOS	PA-28-161 Warrior III	S. H. B. Smith
	G-CGOT	Rotorsport UK Calidus	P. Slater
	G-CGOV	Raj Hamsa X'Air Falcon 582(2)	L. Fee
	G-CGOW	Cameron Z-77 balloon	V. Daley
	G-CGOX	Raj Hamsa X'Air Hawk	W. B. Russell
	G-CGPA	Ace Magic Cyclone	A. Williams
	G-CGPB	Magni M-24C	D. Beevers
	G-CGPC	P & M Pegasus Quik	D. W. Watson & E. McCallum

Reg	Type	Owner or Operator	Notes
G-CGPD	Ultramagic S-90 balloon	S. J. Farrant	
G-CGPE	P & M Quik GT450	E. H. Gatehouse	
G-CGPF	Flylight Dragonfly	C. G. Langham	
G-CGPG	Rotosport UK MTO Sport	E. Barnes	
G-CGPH	Ultramagic S-50 balloon	O. G. V. Smallwood	
G-CGPJ	Robin DR.400-140	W. H. Cole & P. Dass	
G-CGPK	Rotorsport UK MT-03	Ellis Flying Group (G-RIFS)	
G-CGPL	Sonex Sonex	P. C. Askew	
G-CGPO	TL2000UK Sting Carbon	N. A. Quintin	
G-CGPR	Czech Sport Aircraft Pipersport	J. T. Langford	
G-CGPS	EV-97 Eurostar SL	P. R. Jenson & R. A. Morris	
G-CGPW	Raj Hamsa X'Air Hawk	G. J. Langston	
G-CGPX	Zenair CH.601XL Zodiac	A. James	
G-CGPY	Boeing A75L 300 Stearman (671)	Mike Papa Delta Ltd	
G-CGPZ	Rans S-4 Coyote	G. J. Jones	
G-CGRB	Flight Design CTLS	Heathcliff Associates Ltd	
G-CGRC	P & M Quik R	R. J. Cook	
G-CGRJ	Carnet Paramotor	M. Carnet	
G-CGRM	VS.329 Spitfire Mk.IIA	M. R. Oliver	
G-CGRN	Pazmany PL-4A	G. Hudson	
G-CGRR	P & M Quik	C. R. Chapman	
G-CGRS	P & M Quik	J. Crosby	
G-CGRV	DG Flugzeugbau DG-1000M	BR Aviation Ltd	
G-CGRW	P & M Quik	P. M. Coppola	
G-CGRX	Cessna F.172N	Ormand Flying Club Ltd	
G-CGRY	Magni M-24C	Pollards Wholesale Ltd	
G-CGRZ	Magni M-24C	C-More Flying School Ltd	
G-CGSA	Flylight Dragonfly	G. Sykes	
G-CGSC	Quad City Challenger II	L. Gregory	
G-CGSD	Magni M-16C	The Gyrocopter Company UK Ltd	
G-CGSG	Cessna 421C	J. R. Shannon	
G-CGSH	Evektor EV-97 TeamEurostar UK	D. B. Medland	
G-CGSI	Zenair CH.601HDS Zodiac	E. McHugh	
G-CGSO	P & M Quik GT450	Light Vending Ltd	
G-CGSP	Cessna 152	H. E. da Costa Alburquerque	
G-CGSW	Flylight Motorfloater	R. D. Leigh	
G-CGSX	Aeroprakt A22-L Foxbat	M. W. Luke	
G-CGSZ	Schempp-Hirth Ventus 2CM	D. B. Smith	
G-CGTC	BN-2T-4S Islander	Police Service of Northern Ireland	
G-CGTD	EV-97 TeamEurostar UK	R. J. Butler	
G-CGTE	Cherry BX-2	D.Roberts	
G-CGTF	AutoGyro MT-03	N. R. Osborne	
G-CGTJ	AS.332L2 Super Puma	Airbus Helicopters	
G-CGTK	Magni M-24C	S. Brogden	
G-CGTL	Alpi Pioneer 300	G. A. Forbes	
G-CGTM	Cessna 172S	Skytrek Air Services	
G-CGTR	Best Off Sky Ranger Nynja 912S(1)	G-CGTR Syndicate	
G-CGTS	Cameron A-140 balloon	A. A. Brown	
G-CGTT	EV-97 Eurostar SL	D. L. Walker	
G-CGTU	P & M Quik GT450	I. G. R. Christie	
G-CGTV	MXP-740 Savannah VG Jabiru(1)	R. Thompson	
G-CGTW	Flylight MotorFloater	S. J. Varden	
G-CGTX	CASA 1-131E Jungmann Srs 2000	G. Hunter & T. A. S. Rayner	
G-CGUD	Lindstrand LBL-77A balloon	I. J. Sharpe	
G-CGUE	Aroprakt A-22-L Foxbat	A. T. Hayward	
G-CGUG	P & M Quik R	G. Bennett	
G-CGUI	Clutton FRED Srs.II	I. Pearson	
G-CGUK	VS.300 Spitfire 1A (X4650)	Comanche Warbirds Ltd	
G-CGUO	DH.83C Fox Moth	Airtime Aerobatics Ltd	
G-CGUP	P & M Quik GT450	D. J. Allen	
G-CGUR	P & M QuikR	M. J. Williams	
G-CGUU	Sky Ranger Nynja 912S(1)	K. Kiernan	
G-CGUW	Tecnam P2002-EA Sierra	D. J. Burton	
G-CGUY	Rotorsport UK Calidus	R. F. Harrison	
G-CGVA	Aeroprakt A-22-L Foxbat	M. E. Gilman	
G-CGVC	PA-28-181 Archer III	Western Air (Thruxton) Ltd	
G-CGVD	Van's RV-12	A. D. Heath	
G-CGVE	Raj Hamsa X'Air Hawk	D. J. Baird	
G-CGVG	Flight Design CTSW	B. Cook	
G-CGVH	Flylight Motorfloater	P. F. Mayes	
G-CGVJ	Europa XS	D. Glowa	

Notes	Reg	Type	Owner or Operator
	G-CGVK	Autogyro UK Calidus	B & H Mouldings Ltd
	G-CGVP	EV-97 Eurstar	G. R. Pritchard
	G-CGVS	Raj Hamsa X'Air Hawk	D. Matthews
	G-CGVT	EV-97 TeamEurostar UK	Mainair Microlight School Ltd
	G-CGVV	Cameron Z-90 Balloon	John Aimo Balloons SAS/Italy
	G-CGVX	Europa	M. P. Sambrook
	G-CGVY	Cameron Z-77 balloon	M. P. Hill
	G-CGVZ	Zenair CH.601XL Zodiac	K. A. Dilks
	G-CGWA	Ikarus C42 FB80	C. Williams
	G-CGWC	Ultramagic H-31 balloon	K. Dodman
	G-CGWE	EV-97A Eurostar	W. S. Long
	G-CGWF	Van's RV-7	M. S. Hill
	G-CGWG	Van's RV-7	G. Waters
	G-CGWH	CZAW Sportcruiser	G-CGWH Group
	G-CGWI	Spitfire Mk.26 (BL927:JH-I)	Bertha Property LLP
	G-CGWK	Ikarus C42 FB80	B. H. Goldsmith
	G-CGWM	Dragonfly Lite	P. A. Gardner
	G-CGWN	Dragonfly Lite	R. Stalker
	G-CGWO	Tecnam P2002-JF Sierra	Academy Aviation Ltd
	G-CGWP	Aeroprakt A22-L Foxbat	P. K. Goff
	G-CGWR	Nord NC.856A Norvigie (54)	R. Ellingworth
	G-CGWS	Raj Hamsa X'Air Hawk	I. S. McNulty
	G-CGWT	Best Off Sky Ranger Swift 912(1)	D. Hamilton
	G-CGWU	UltraMagic S-90 balloon	P. Pruchnickj & R. P. Allan
	G-CGWX	Cameron C-90 balloon	J. D. A. Shields
	G-CGWZ	P & M QuikR	RP Syndicate
	G-CGXB	Glasair Super IIS RG	P. J. Brion
	G-CGXE	P & M Quik GT450	N. G. Nikolov
	G-CGXF	North Wing Stratus/Skycycle	I. D. Smith
	G-CGXI	Ikarus C42 FB80	G. V. Aggett
	G-CGXL	Robin DR.400/180	M. F. Ashton (G-GLKE)
	G-CGXN	American Legend Cub	P. L. Gaze
	G-CGXO	Lindstrand LBL-105A balloon	Aerosaurus Balloons Ltd
	G-CGXP	Grob G.109B	S. M. Rathband
	G-CGXR	Van's RV-9A	Solway Flyers 2010 Ltd
	G-CGXT	Kowacs Midgie	J. P. Kovacs
	G-CGXV	P & M Quik R	A. Nikulin
	G-CGXW	Grob G.109B	I. B. Kennedy
	G-CGXY	Flylight Dragonfly	A. I. Lea
	G-CGXZ	AutoGyro MTO Sport	G-CGXZ Flying Group
	G-CGYA	Stoddard-Hamilton Glasair III	Aerocars Ltd
	G-CGYB	EV-97 TeamEurostar UK	J. Waite
	G-CGYC	Aeropro Eurofox 912(S)	J. C. Taylor
	G-CGYD	Fairey Firefly TT.1	Propshop Ltd
	G-CGYF	Gloster Gamecock II	Retro Track & Air (UK) Ltd
	G-CGYG	Aeropro Eurofox 912(S)	Highland Gliding Club Ltd
	G-CGYH	Magni M-24C	J. L. Ward
	G-CGYI	Van's RV-12	M. J. Poole
	G-CGYJ	VS.361 Spitfire HF.IX (TD314)	Aero Legends Leasing Ltd
	G-CGYO	Van's RV-6A	M. Paterson, M. Sutherland & R. J. Kennedy
	G-CGYP	Best Off Sky Ranger 912(2)	Yankee Papa Group
	G-CGYR	Avro RJ-85	Trident Turboprop (Dublin) Ltd
	G-CGYT	Flylight Dragonfly	S. J. Varden
	G-CGYW	Sikorsky S-92A	Wilmington Trust SP Services (Dublin) Ltd
	G-CGYX	AutoGyro Cavalon	K. Hall
	G-CGYY	MXP-740 Savannah VG Jabiru(1)	Carlisle Skyrangers
	G-CGYZ	P & M Quik GT450	M. Florence
	G-CGZE	Rotorsport UK MTO Sport	Rufforth No.1 Gyro Syndicate
	G-CGZF	EV-97 TeamEurostar UK	B. P. Keating
	G-CGZG	AutoGyro MTO Sport	W. S. Roomes
	G-CGZI	SOCATA TB-21 Trinidad TC	Keith Hallam & Partners
	G-CGZJ	ITV Dakota XL	C. J. Lines
	G-CGZM	AutoGyro MTO Sport	J. W. Cope
	G-CGZN	Dudek Synthesis 31/Nirvana Carbon	P. M. Jones
	G-CGZP	Curtiss P-40F Kittyhawk (41-19841 X-17)	The Fighter Collection
	G-CGZR	Cameron Z-350 balloon	Ballooning Network Ltd
	G-CGZT	Aeroprakt A22-L Foxbat	D. Jessop
	G-CGZU	VS.361 Spitfire F.IXc (LZ842:EF-F)	M. A. Bennett
	G-CGZV	Europa XS	I. M. Moxon
	G-CGZW	Scheibe SF-25C Falke	Airborne Services International
	G-CGZY	EV-97 TeamEurostar UK	D. C. & P. R. Smith

Reg	Type	Owner or Operator	Notes
G-CGZZ	Kubicek BB22E balloon	T. Taylor	
G-CHAB	Schleicher Ka 6CR	J. March	
G-CHAC	PZL-Bielsko SZD-50-3 Puchacz	Peterborough and Spalding Gliding Club Ltd	
G-CHAD	Aeroprakt A.22 Foxbat	DJB Foxbat	
G-CHAE	Glasflugel H205 Club Libelle	E. A. & S. R. Scothern	
G-CHAF	PZL-Bielsko SZD-50-3 Puchacz	Seahawk Gliding Club	
G-CHAG	Guimbal Cabri G2	Heligroup Operations Ltd	
G-CHAH	Shaw Europa	T. Higgins	
G-CHAJ	Cirrus SR22	R. J. Garbutt	
G-CHAN	Robinson R22 Beta	J. S. Everett	
G-CHAO	Rolladen-Schneider LS6-b	Cloud Nine Syndicate	
G-CHAR	Grob G.109B	The Royal Air Force Gliding and Soaring Association	
G-CHAS	PA-28-181 Archer II	G-CHAS Flying Group	
G-CHAU	Cameron C-80 balloon	G. G. Cannon & P. Haworth	
G-CHAW	Replica Fokker EIII	P. A. Harvie	
G-CHAX	Schempp-Hirth Standard Cirrus	J. Hunneman	
G-CHAY	Rolladen-Schneider LS7	N. J. Leaton	
G-CHBA	Rolladen-Schneider LS7	LS7 Crew	
G-CHBB	Schleicher ASW-24	London Gliding Club Propietary Ltd	
G-CHBC	Rolladen-Schneider LS6-c	A. Crowden	
G-CHBD	Glaser-Dirks DG-200	HBD Syndicate	
G-CHBE	Glaser-Dirks DG-300 Club Elan	DG 356 Group	
G-CHBF	Schempp-Hirth Nimbus 2C	J. A. Clark	
G-CHBG	Schleicher ASW-24	Imperial College of Science, Technology and Medicine	
G-CHBH	Grob G.103C Twin III Acro	Imperial College of Science, Technology and Medicine	
G-CHBK	Grob G.103 Twin Astir II	S. Naylor	
G-CHBL	Grob G.102 Astir CS77	Bidford Gliding & Flying Club Ltd	
G-CHBM	Grob G.102 Astir CS77	T. S. de Oliveira	
G-CHBO	Schleicher Ka 6CR	C, McCallin & M. Selby	
G-CHBS	PZL-Bielsko SZD-41A Jantar Standard 1	P. J. Chaisty & D. Hendry	
G-CHBT	Grob G.102 Astir CS Jeans	Darlton Gliding Club Ltd	
G-CHBV	Schempp-Hirth Nimbus 2B	G. J. Evison & R. Beezer	
G-CHBW	Jurca Spitfire (AD370:PJ-C)	T. A. Major	
G-CHBX	Lindstrand LBL-77A balloon	K. Hull	
G-CHBY	Agusta AW.139	Bristow Helicopters Ltd	
G-CHBZ	TL2000UK Sting Carbon	C. R. Ashley	
G-CHCF	AS.332L-2 Super Puma	Questral Helicopters Ltd	
G-CHCG	AS.332L-2 Super Puma	Airbus Helicopters Ltd	
G-CHCH	AS.332L-2 Super Puma	Airbus Helicopters Ltd	
G-CHCI	AS.332L-2 Super Puma	Questral Helicopters Ltd	
G-CHCM	EC.225LP Super Puma	CHC Scotia Ltd	
G-CHCU	AS.332L2 Super Puma II	Airbus Helicopters Ltd	
G-CHCY	EC.225LP Super Puma	Airbus Helicopters Ltd	
G-CHDA	Pilatus B4-PC11AF	HDA Syndicate	
G-CHDB	PZL-Bielsko SZD-51-1 Junior	Stratford on Avon Gliding Club Ltd	
G-CHDD	Centrair 101B Pegase 90	591 Glider Syndicate	
G-CHDH	Lindstrand LBL-77A balloon	R. D. Allen	
G-CHDJ	Schleicher ASW-20CL	G. E. G. Lambert & L. M. M. Sebreights	
G-CHDK	Magni M-16C Tandem Trainer	J. Gledhill	
G-CHDL	Schleicher ASW-20	D. Reeves & B. D. Allen	
G-CHDM	P & M QuikR	A. Sheveleu	
G-CHDN	Schleicher K 8B	Cotswold Gliding Club	
G-CHDP	PZL-Bielsko SZD-50-3 Puchacz	Heron Gliding Club	
G-CHDR	DG-300 Elan	G-CHDR Syndicate	
G-CHDU	PZL-Bielsko SZD-51-1 Junior	Cambridge Gliding Club Ltd	
G-CHDV	Schleicher ASW-19B	S. D. Anthony	
G-CHDX	Rolladen-Schneider LS7-WL	D. Holborn & R. T. Halliburton	
G-CHDY	Schleicher K 8B	V. Mallon	
G-CHDZ	Cameron O-120 balloon	W. D. MacKinnon	
G-CHEB	Shaw Europa	I. C. Smit & P. Whittingham	
G-CHEC	PZL-Bielsko SZD-55-1	D. Pye	
G-CHED	Flylight Dragonfly	G. W. Cameron	
G-CHEE	Schempp-Hirth Discus b	A. Henderson	
G-CHEF	Glaser-Dirks DG-500 Elan Trainer	Yorkshire Gliding Club (Proprietary) Ltd	
G-CHEG	AB Sportine Aviacija LAK-12	J. M. Caldwell, D. Cockburn, Z. Kmita & R. G. Parker	
G-CHEH	Rolladen-Schneider LS7-WL	S. Brown	

Notes	Reg	Type	Owner or Operator
	G-CHEJ	Schleicher ASW-15B	W. E. Lozowski
	G-CHEL	Colt 77B balloon	Chelsea Financial Services PLC
	G-CHEN	Schempp-Hirth Discus b	G-CHEN Group
	G-CHEO	Schleicher ASW-20	P. A. Woodcock
	G-CHEP	PZL-Bielsko SZD-50-3 Puchacz	Peterborough and Spalding Gliding Club Ltd
	G-CHER	PA-38-112 Tomahawk II	G. E. Fox
	G-CHEW	Rolladen-Schneider LS6-c18	A. C. Pledger
	G-CHEX	Aero Designs Pulsar	I. Izcue
	G-CHFA	Schempp-Hirth Ventus b/16.6	A. K. Lincoln
	G-CHFB	Schleicher Ka-6CR	R. K. T. Stevens
	G-CHFC	P & M Quik GTR	A. Niarchos
	G-CHFD	Agusta AW.109SP	Flight Charter Services Pty Ltd
	G-CHFF	Schempp-Hirth Standard Cirrus	Foxtrot 2 Group
	G-CHFG	Van's RV-6	RV Flying Group
	G-CHFH	PZL-Bielsko SZD-50-3	Trent Valley Gliding Club Ltd
	G-CHFL	Scheibe SF-25C Falke	Staffordshire Gliding Club Ltd
	G-CHFM	Cameron Z-120 balloon	David Hathaway Transport Ltd
	G-CHFO	P & M Quik GTR	T. A. Dobbins
	G-CHFT	Tanarg Bionix 15 912S(1)	N. C. Stubbs
	G-CHFU	P & M Quik GTR	P. H. J. Fenn
	G-CHFV	Schempp-Hirth Ventus B/16.6	A. Cliffe & B. Pearson
	G-CHFW	Schleicher K 8B	Oxford Gliding Co.Ltd
	G-CHFX	Schempp-Hirth Nimbus 4T	R. F. Barber
	G-CHFZ	Best Off Sky Ranger Nynja 912S(1)	Skyview Systems Ltd
	G-CHGA	P & M Quik GTR	Flying for Freedom Ltd
	G-CHGB	Grob G.102 Astir CS	D. R. D. Murray
	G-CHGE	EV-97 TeamEurostar UK	J. R. Mackay
	G-CHGF	Schleicher ASW-15B	HGF Flying Group
	G-CHGG	Schempp-Hirth Standard Cirrus	HGG Flying Group
	G-CHGJ	Flylight MotorFloater Fox 16T	A. Brooks
	G-CHGK	Schempp-Hirth Discus bT	P. W. Berridge
	G-CHGL	Bell 206B JetRanger II	Vantage Aviation Ltd (G-BPNG/G-ORTC)
	G-CHGM	Groppo Trail	J. Walker
	G-CHGN	Ace Aviation Easy Riser Spirit	Tideswell Trading Ltd
	G-CHGP	Rolladen-Schneider LS6-c	D. J. Miller
	G-CHGR	AB Sportline Aviacija LAK-12	M. R. Garwood
	G-CHGS	Schempp-Hirth Discus b	G-CHGS Syndicate
	G-CHGT	FFA Diamant 16.5	T. E. Lynch
	G-CHGU	Ace Aviation Easy Riser Touch	T. A. Dobbins
	G-CHGV	Glaser-Dirks DG500/22 Elan	Hotel Golf Victor Syndicate
	G-CHGW	Centrair ASW-20F	P. J. Coward
	G-CHGX	AB Sportine LAK-12 Lietuva	M. Jenks
	G-CHGY	Schleicher ASW-27-18	D. Breeze, V. Derrick & M. Oliver
	G-CHGZ	Schempp-Hirth Discus bT	G. C. Bell
	G-CHHB	Aeroprakt A22-LS Foxbat	R. A. Pugh
	G-CHHC	Cameron A-300 balloon	Wickers World Ltd
	G-CHHD	RL7A XP Sherwood Ranger	R. Simpson
	G-CHHF	Sikorsky S-92A	MUFG Americas Capital Leasing & Finance LLC
	G-CHHH	Rolladen-Schneider LS6-c	D. H. Smith
	G-CHHI	Van's RV-7	M. G. Jefferies
	G-CHHJ	Aeropro Eurofox 912(1)	S. R. Kirkham
	G-CHHK	Schleicher ASW-19B	P. Lysak & R. Hubrecht
	G-CHHL	Cameron C-80 balloon	H. G. Griffiths & W. A. Steel
	G-CHHN	Schempp-Hirth Ventus b/16.6	Ventus 979 Syndicate
	G-CHHO	Schempp-Hirth Discus bT	S. G. Jones
	G-CHHP	Schempp-Hirth Discus b	F. R. Knowles
	G-CHHR	PZL-Bielsko SZD-55-1 Promyk	J. & S. R. Nash
	G-CHHS	Schleicher ASW-20	P.J. Rocks & D. Britt
	G-CHHT	Rolladen-Schneider LS6-c	L. J. Kaye
	G-CHHU	Rolladen-Schneider LS6-c	445 Syndicate
	G-CHHV	Junqua Ibis RJ.03	J. J. R. Joubert
	G-CHHW	AB Sportine LAK-12	A. J. Dibdin
	G-CHHY	Ace Magic Laser	B. J. Harrison
	G-CHHZ	Schempp-Hirth Cirrus	B. J. Dawson & S. E. Richardson
	G-CHIA	North American SNJ-5 Texan (85061:7F 061)	The Warplane Flying Company Ltd
	G-CHID	Eurofox 912(1)	A. P. Scott & P. David
	G-CHIG	Grob G.109B	Southdown Gliding Club Ltd
	G-CHIH	Aeropro Eurofox 912(S)	Banbury Gliding Club Ltd
	G-CHII	CASA 1-131E Jungmann Srs 1000	R. J. Allan, A. J. Maxwell & N. Jones
	G-CHIJ	Ikarus C42 FB80	R. G. Herrod

Reg	Type	Owner or Operator	Notes
G-CHIM	Ultramagic H-31 balloon	G. B. Lescott	
G-CHIP	PA-28-181 Archer II	Golden Lion Aviation Ltd	
G-CHIS	Robinson R22	A. R. Collett	
G-CHIT	AutoGyro MTO Sport	N. G. H. Staunton	
G-CHIV	P & M Quik R	G-CHIV Syndicate	
G-CHIW	Raj Hamsa X'Air Hawk	M. D. Boley	
G-CHIX	Robin DR.400/500	P. A. & R. Stephens	
G-CHIY	Flylight MotorFloater	S. Polley	
G-CHIZ	Flylight Dragonfly	J. Paterson	
G-CHJB	Flylight Dragonfly	S. J. Robson	
G-CHJD	Schleicher Ka 6E	The Ruby Syndicate	
G-CHJE	Schleicher K 8B	Staffordshire Gliding Club Ltd	
G-CHJF	Rolladen-Schneider LS6-c	J. L. Bridge	
G-CHJG	Evektor EV-97 TeamEurostar UK	P. A. Bass	
G-CHJJ	Medway Clipper-100	J. Bulpin	
G-CHJK	Cessna T.206H Turbo Stationair	G. G. Weston	
G-CHJL	Schempp-Hirth Discus bT	Discus JL Group	
G-CHJM	Cameron C-80 balloon	C. L. Smith	
G-CHJN	Schempp-Hirth Standard Cirrus	P. M. Hardingham	
G-CHJO	Bushby-Long Midget Mustang M-1	R. J. Hodder	
G-CHJP	Schleicher Ka-6CR	D. M. Cornelius	
G-CHJR	Glasflugel H201B Standard Libelle	R. P. G. Hayhoe	
G-CHJS	Schleicher ASW-27-18E	J. D. Spencer	
G-CHJT	Centrair ASW-20F	A. F. Irwin	
G-CHJV	Grob G.102 Astir CS	LX Avionics Ltd	
G-CHJW	P & M Quik GTR	A. C. Rowlands	
G-CHJX	Rolladen-Schneider LS6-c	M. R. Haynes	
G-CHJY	Schempp-Hirth Standard Cirrus	Cirrus-459 Group	
G-CHKA	Orlican Discus CS	M. E. S. Thomas	
G-CHKB	Grob G.102 Astir CS77	C. D. Woodward	
G-CHKC	Schempp-Hirth Standard Cirrus	J. M. Hilll	
G-CHKD	Schempp-Hirth Standard Cirrus	B. Hudson	
G-CHKF	Grob G.109B	CHKF Group	
G-CHKG	Best Off Skyranger Nynja 912S(1)	D. L. Turner	
G-CHKH	Schleicher ASW-28	D. F. McKinney	
G-CHKI	Sikorsky S-92A	Wilmington Trust SP Services (Dublin) Ltd	
G-CHKK	Schleicher K8B	Tweeetie Bird	
G-CHKM	Grob G.102 Astir CS Jeans	Essex and Suffolk Gliding Club Ltd	
G-CHKN	Kiss 400-582(1)	P. J. Higgins	
G-CHKO	Best Off Skyranger Swift 912S(1)	J. R. Hoole	
G-CHKR	Jastreb Standard Cirrus G/81	N. A. White	
G-CHKS	Jastreb Standard Cirrus G/81	G-CHKS Flying Group	
G-CHKT	Balony Kubicek BB22E balloon	D. L. Beckwith	
G-CHKU	Schempp-Hirth Standard Cirrus	T. J. Wheeler	
G-CHKX	Rolladen-Schneider LS4-B	G-CHKX Flying Group	
G-CHKY	Schempp-Hirth Discus b	M. T. Davis	
G-CHKZ	CARMAM JP 15-36AR Aiglon	T. A. & A. J. Hollings	
G-CHLB	Rolladen-Schneider LS4-b	E. G. Leach & K. F. Rogers	
G-CHLC	Pilatus B4-PC11AF	E. Lockhart	
G-CHLD	AutoGyro MTO Sport	D. L. Sivyer	
G-CHLH	Schleicher K 8B	Shenington Gliding Club	
G-CHLI	Cosmik Aviation Superchaser	Cosmik Aviation Ltd	
G-CHLK	Glasflugel H.301 Libelle	D. T. Bray	
G-CHLM	Schleicher ASW-19B	G-CHLM Group	
G-CHLN	Schempp-Hirth Discus CS	Portsmouth Naval Gliding Centre	
G-CHLP	Schleicher ASK-21	Southdown Gliding Club Ltd	
G-CHLS	Schempp-Hirth Discus b	R. Roberts	
G-CHLV	Schleicher ASW-19B	P. M. Shelton	
G-CHLY	Schempp-Hirth Discus CS	S. J. Pearce	
G-CHLZ	Best Off Skyranger LS 912(1)	S. K. Ridge	
G-CHMA	PZL-Bielsko SZD-51-1 Junior	The Welland Gliding Club Ltd	
G-CHMB	Glaser-Dirks DG-300 Elan	A. D. & P. Langlands	
G-CHMD	DG Flugzeugbau LS8-T	G. B. Monslow & A. P. Balkwill	
G-CHME	Glaser-Dirks DG-300 Elan	A. G. Gibbs	
G-CHMG	ICA IS-28B2	Edensoaring Ltd	
G-CHMH	Schleicher K8B	Shenington Gliding Club	
G-CHMI	Lindstrand LBL-105A balloon	J. A. Lawton	
G-CHMK	Rolladen-Schneider LS6-18W	R. C. Hodge	
G-CHML	Schempp-Hirth Discus CS	I. D. Bateman	
G-CHMM	Glasflugel 304B	A. F. Greenhalgh	
G-CHMN	Raj Hamsa X'Air Falcon Jabiru(1)	F. C. Claydon	

Notes	Reg	Type	Owner or Operator
	G-CIMB	Cessna 177RG	A. R. Willis
	G-CIMC	Hoffmann H.36 Dimona	East Sussex Gliding Club Ltd
	G-CIMD	Alpi Pioneer 400	Hardwick Flying Group
	G-CIME	Balony Kubicek BB30Z balloon	Loogo SRLS/Italy
	G-CIMG	Aerochute Dual	M. R. Gaylor
	G-CIMH	P & M Quik Lite	C. Clarkson
	G-CIMI	Grob G.115	M. Kostiuk
	G-CIMK	P & M Quik Lite	N. R. Beale
	G-CIML	Eurofox 912(S)	G-CIML Eurofox Flying Group
	G-CIMM	Cessna T.182 Turbo Skylane II	A. W. Oliver (G-PDHJ)
	G-CIMN	Zenair CH.750	D. A. G. Johnson
	G-CIMP	Scheibe SF.25C Falke	Southwest Motorgliders
	G-CIMS	Aeropro Eurofox 912(1)	C. M. Sperring
	G-CIMT	Autogyro Cavalon	M. L. Watson
	G-CIMU	AgustaWestland AW139	Bristow Helicopters Ltd
	G-CIMV	Groppo Trail	Atomite Ltd
	G-CIMW	Cameron O-31 balloon	B. Geeraerts
	G-CIMX	Westland Scout AH.Mk.1 (XW283)	G. P. Hinkley
	G-CIMY	Sadler Vampire SV2	I. P. Freestone
	G-CIMZ	Robinson R44 II	JMR Aviation LLP
	G-CINA	Cessna 152	Swiftair Maintenance Ltd
	G-CINC	Magnaghi Sky Arrow 650 TCNS	Spectrum Aviation Ltd
	G-CIND	Cameron C-70 balloon	Gone with the Wind Ltd
	G-CING	Sherwood Ranger ST	S. J. Westley
	G-CINH	P & M Quik R	P. Martin
	G-CINI	Rans S7S	D. R. P. Mole
	G-CINJ	Milholland Legal Eagle	N. S. Jeffrey
	G-CINK	Grob G.109	The Lyveden Motor Gliding Syndicate
	G-CINL	Skyranger Swift 912(S)1	B. Richardson
	G-CINM	Grob G.109B	Grob 109B Motorglider Syndicate G-CINM
	G-CINN	Cameron Z-31 balloon	Turner Balloons Ltd
	G-CINO	Grob G.109B	T. R. Dews
	G-CINU	Eurocopter EC225LP Super Puma	Airbus Helicopters
	G-CINV	Aeroprakt A22-LS Foxbat	J. P. Mimnagh
	G-CINZ	Ace Aviation Magic/Cyclone	R. Lewis-Evans
	G-CIOA	Murphy Rebel	O. P. Sparrow
	G-CIOD	P &M Quik Lite	D. D'Arcy-Ewing
	G-CIOF	Aeropro Eurofox 912(S)	Yorkshire Gliding Club (Proprietary) Ltd
	G-CIOG	Fresh Breeze Bullix Trike/Relax	D. Burton
	G-CIOJ	Aeropro Eurofox 912(IS)	A. C. S. Paterson
	G-CIOK	Skyranger Swift 912(S)(1)	J. de Pree & B. Janson
	G-CIOL	P &M Quik GTR	D. L. Clark
	G-CIOM	Magni M24C Orion	P. H. J. Fenn
	G-CIOO	Van's RV-7	M. Albert-Recht
	G-CIOP	Aerospatiale AS.355F Ecureuil 2	RCR Aviation Ltd
	G-CIOR	Nicollier HN.700 Menestrel II	R. C. & R. P. C. Teverson
	G-CIOS	MD Helicopters MD.900 Explorer	Specialist Aviation Services Ltd (G-SASO)
	G-CIOU	Cameron Z-70 balloon	P. K. Durgam
	G-CIOV	Ultramagic H-31 balloon	J. A. Lawton
	G-CIOW	Westland SA.341C Gazelle HT Mk.2	S. Atherton
	G-CIOX	Flylight Foxcub	P. J. Cheyney
	G-CIOY	Beech G.36 Bonanza	Bonanzair Ltd
	G-CIOZ	Ikarus C42 FB100	C. L. G. Innocent
	G-CIPA	P & M Pegasus Quik	D. W. C. Beer
	G-CIPB	Messerschmitt Bf109E-4	Biggin Hill Heritage Hangar Ltd
	G-CIPD	Cameron O-31 balloon	Gone with the Wind Ltd
	G-CIPE	Boeing Stearman A75L300	Retro Track and Air (UK) Ltd
	G-CIPF	Alisport Silent 2 Electro	A. & M. Truelove
	G-CIPG	BRM Aero Bristell NG5 Speed Wing	G-CIPG Syndicate
	G-CIPJ	DH.83 Fox Moth	B. K. Broady
	G-CIPL	Van's RV-9	R. Manning
	G-CIPM	P & M Quik R	M. R. Niznik
	G-CIPO	Ikarus C42 FB80	J. Richards
	G-CIPP	AutoGyro Calidus	Dragon Gyrocopters
	G-CIPR	Skyranger Nynja 912(1)	J. M. Ross
	G-CIPS	Eurofox 912(1)	P. Stretton
	G-CIPT	BRM Aero Bristell NG5 Speed Wing	A. J. Radford
	G-CIPU	Cessna F.172F	G. Hinz/Germany
	G-CIPW	Agusta Westland AW.139	Bristow Helicopters Ltd
	G-CIPX	Agusta Westland AW.139	Bristow Helicopters Ltd
	G-CIPY	Cessna F.172 II	Swiftair Maintenance Ltd

Reg	Type	Owner or Operator	Notes
G-CIPZ	Pazmany PL-4A	J. J. Hill	
G-CIRB	EV-97 Eurostar SL	R. J. Garbutt	
G-CIRC	Such BM60-20 balloon	D. G. Such	
G-CIRE	Corby CJ-1 Starlet	J. Evans	
G-CIRG	Airbus Helicopters AS350B3 Ecureuil	Airbus Helicopters UK Ltd	
G-CIRH	Magni M16C Tandem Trainer	Willy Rose Technology Ltd	
G-CIRI	Cirrus SR20	Cirrus Flyers Group	
G-CIRK	Alisport Silent 2 Electro	S. V. Jones	
G-CIRL	Ultramagic S-90 balloon	M. A. Scholes & D. J. Day	
G-CIRM	Van's RV-12	P. J. Hynes	
G-CIRO	Cessna F.172H	H. G. Stroemer	
G-CIRP	Aeropro Eurofox 912(S)	M. Petrie & S. D. Kellner	
G-CIRT	AutoGyro MTOSport	M. Pugh & J. Gleeson	
G-CIRU	Cirrus SR20	Cirrent BV/Netherlands	
G-CIRV	Van's RV-7	R. J. Fray	
G-CIRW	Cessna FA.150K	Air Navigation and Trading Company Ltd	
G-CIRX	Cameron Z-150 balloon	Phoenix Balloons Ltd	
G-CIRY	EV-97 Eurostar SL	Hotel Victor Flying Group	
G-CIRZ	Ikarus C42 FB80	Mainair Microlight School Ltd	
G-CISA	Sprite Stinger	Sprite Aviation Services Ltd	
G-CISB	Sackville AH56 balloon	T. J. Wilkinson	
G-CISC	Sackville AH77 balloon	T. I. Laws	
G-CISD	Sackville AH31 balloon	L. S. Crossland-Clarke	
G-CISE	Aero Designs Pulsar XP	S. C. Goozee	
G-CISF	Quad City Challenger II	S. A. Beddus	
G-CISG	Ikarus C42 FB80	C. Williams	
G-CISH	Thatcher CX4	M. A. Sims	
G-CISI	P & M Quik GTR	Kent County Scout Council	
G-CISJ	Ultramagic H-31 balloon	R. P. Wade	
G-CISK	Embraer EMB-145LR	Eastern Airways	
G-CISL	Cameron C-70 balloon	S. Lundin	
G-CISN	Flylight Foxcub	G. Nicholas	
G-CISO	Cessna 150G	Enterprise Purchasing Ltd	
G-CISR	Flying K Sky Raider 1	J. A. Harris	
G-CISS	Ikarus C42 FB80	C-More Flying School	
G-CIST	P & M Quik GT450	G. J. Prisk	
G-CISU	CM Sunbird	C. W. Mitchinson	
G-CISW	La Mouette Samson 12	N. Pain	
G-CISX	Cessna 172M	D. Sluman	
G-CISZ	Van's RV-7	D. C. Hanss	
G-CITC	Apollo Delta Jet 2	P. Broome	
G-CITD	Sportavia-Putzer Fournier RF-5	G-CITD Group	
G-CITE	Grob G.102 Astir CS Jeans	The Bath, Wilts & North Dorset Gliding Club Ltd	
G-CITF	EV-97 Eurostar SL	J. C. Rose	
G-CITG	Skyranger Nynja 912S(1)	A. C. Aiken & J. Attard	
G-CITH	Eans S-6-ES Coyote II	D. P. Molloy	
G-CITK	Alisport Silent 2 Targa	B. T. Green	
G-CITL	Ace Magic Cyclone	S. F. Beardsell	
G-CITM	Magni M16C Tandem Trainer	Lambdatek Ltd	
G-CITN	P-51D-25-NA Mustang	P. Earthey	
G-CITO	P & M Quik	M. P. Jackson	
G-CITP	Grumman AA-1B Trainer	J-C. Vanderstricht/Belgium	
G-CITR	Cameron Z-105 balloon	A. Kaye	
G-CITS	Groppo Trail	D. A. Buttress	
G-CITT	Mooney M.20J Model 201	J. M. Tiley	
G-CITV	AutoGyro Cavalon	N. R. W. Whitling	
G-CITW	Extra EA.400	LAC Marine Ltd	
G-CITX	AutoGyro MTOSport	D. Brooksbank	
G-CITY	PA-31-350 Navajo Chieftain	Blue Sky Investments Ltd	
G-CIUA	Ultramagic B-70 balloon	K. W. Graham	
G-CIUB	Cameron Z-90 balloon	G. Forster	
G-CIUD	ACLA Sirocco SW FT	S. Siddiqui (G-ROCO)	
G-CIUE	CASA 1-131E Jungmann Srs 2000	R. A. Fleming	
G-CIUF	Aviad Zigolo MG12	J. D. C. Henslow & C. B. Jones	
G-CIUG	Aeropro Eurofox 3K	J. V. Clewer	
G-CIUH	Cessna 152	J. M. Perfettini	
G-CIUM	PA-12 Super Cruiser	J. Havers & S. James	
G-CIUN	Flylight Foxcub	C. I. Chegwen	
G-CIUO	Ekolot KR-010 ELF	P. V. Griffiths	
G-CIUP	Europa XS	P. C. Matthews & P. Bridges	
G-CIUU	Cessna F.152	DSFT Ltd	

135

Notes	Reg	Type	Owner or Operator
	G-CJDG	Rolladen-Schneider LS6B	R. H. & A. Moss
	G-CJDJ	Rolladen-Schneider LS3	S. Wilkinson & B. J. R. Moate
	G-CJDL	Pipistrel Apis 15M M FES	M. E. Hughes
	G-CJDM	Schleicher ASW-15B	J. D. Morris
	G-CJDN	Cameron C-90 balloon	N. Ivison
	G-CJDP	Glaser-Dirks DG-200/17	G. K. Hutchinson
	G-CJDR	Schleicher ASW-15	S. Mudaliar
	G-CJDS	Schempp-Hirth Standard Cirrus 75	P. Nicholls
	G-CJDV	DG Flugzeugbau DG-300 Elan Acro	M. K. Lavender
	G-CJDW	Magni M-16C Tandem Trainer	R. W. D. Noon
	G-CJDX	Wassmer WA-28	G. B. Marshall
	G-CJEA	Rolladen-Schneider LS8-18	M. W. Durham
	G-CJEB	Schleicher ASW-24	P. C. Scholz
	G-CJEC	PZL-Bielsko SZD-50-3 Puchasz	Cambridge Gliding Club Ltd
	G-CJED	Schempp-Hirth Nimbus 3/24.5	J. Edyvean
	G-CJEE	Schleicher ASW-20L	P. Woodcock
	G-CJEH	Glasflugel Mosquito B	M. J. Vickery
	G-CJEI	UltraMagic M-77 balloon	British Telecommunications PLC
	G-CJEJ	Best Off Skyranger Nynja 912(1)	G-CJEJ Rossall Skyranger
	G-CJEK	Guimbai Cabri G2	I. C. Macdonald
	G-CJEL	Schleicher ASW-24	C. W. Lewis
	G-CJEP	Rolladen-Schneider LS4-b	C. F. Carter & N. Backes
	G-CJER	Schempp-Hirth Standard Cirrus 75	C. Parvin
	G-CJES	Cameron TR-77 balloon	International Merchandising, Promotion and Services
	G-CJEU	Glasflugel Standard Libelle	D. B. Johns
	G-CJEW	Schleicher Ka 6CR	W. J. Prince
	G-CJEX	Schempp-Hirth Ventus 2a	D. S. Watt
	G-CJEY	Flylight Dragon Combat 12T	A. E. Barron
	G-CJEZ	Glaser-Dirks DG-100	D. P. Spragg
	G-CJFA	Schempp-Hirth Standard Cirrus	P. M. Sheahan
	G-CJFC	Schempp-Hirth Discus CS	C. J. Tooze
	G-CJFG	Aeriane Swift Light PAS	M. Jackson
	G-CJFH	Schempp-Hirth Duo Discus	The Royal Air Force Gliding and Soaring Association
	G-CJFJ	Schleicher ASW-20CL	Selby Flyers
	G-CJFN	DHC.8-402Q Dash Eight	NAC Aviation 23 Ltd
	G-CJFP	Dudek Synthesis LT29	P. A. Sadowski
	G-CJFS	Pulse SSDR	D. Stephens
	G-CJFT	Schleicher K-8B	The Surrey Hills Gliding Club Ltd
	G-CJFU	Schleicher ASW-19B	M. T. Stanley
	G-CJFW	Ace As-tec 15	S. E. Dancaster
	G-CJFX	Rolladen-Schneider LS8-a	J. E. Gatfield
	G-CJFZ	Fedorov ME7 Mechta	R. J. Colbourne
	G-CJGA	Cameron Z-90 balloon	Spoon Service Multimedia SAS/Italy
	G-CJGB	Schleicher K 8B	L. R. Merritt
	G-CJGC	Cameron Z-105 balloon	GSM Aeropanorami SRL/Italy
	G-CJGD	Scleicher K 8B	R. E. Pettifer & C. A. McLay
	G-CJGE	Schleicher ASK-21	M. R. Wall
	G-CJGF	Schempp-Hirth Ventus c	R. D. Slater
	G-CJGG	P & M Quik GT450	J. M. Pearce
	G-CJGH	Schempp-Hirth Nimbus 2C	G-CJGH Syndicate
	G-CJGJ	Schleicher ASK-21	Midland Gliding Club Ltd
	G-CJGK	Eiri PIL-200	The Four Aces
	G-CJGL	Schempp-Hirth Discus CS	The Royal Air Force Gliding and Soaring Association
	G-CJGM	Schempp-Hirth Discus CS	The Royal Air Force Gliding and Soaring Association
	G-CJGN	Schempp-Hirth Standard Cirrus	P. A. Shuttleworth
	G-CJGP	Breezer M400	B. S. Keene
	G-CJGR	Schempp-Hirth Discus bT	G. W. Kemp
	G-CJGS	Rolladen-Schneider LS8-18	T. Stupnik
	G-CJGT	AMS-Flight Apis M	R. G. Parker & A. Spencer
	G-CJGU	Schempp-Hirth Mini-Nimbus B	N. D. Ashton
	G-CJGV	Flylight Foxcub	S. J. E. Smith
	G-CJGW	Schleicher ASK-13	Darlton Gliding Club Ltd
	G-CJGX	Schleicher K 8B	Andreas K8 Group
	G-CJGY	Schempp-Hirth Standard Cirrus	P. J. Shout
	G-CJGZ	Glasflugel Standard Libelle 201B	D. A. Joosten
	G-CJHC	Kolb Firefly	D. J. Pilkington
	G-CJHF	Aeroprpo Eurofox 912(iS)	BGC Eurofox Group

Reg	Type	Owner or Operator	Notes
G-CIPZ	Pazmany PL-4A	J. J. Hill	
G-CIRB	EV-97 Eurostar SL	R. J. Garbutt	
G-CIRC	Such BM60-20 balloon	D. G. Such	
G-CIRE	Corby CJ-1 Starlet	J. Evans	
G-CIRG	Airbus Helicopters AS350B3 Ecureuil	Airbus Helicopters UK Ltd	
G-CIRH	Magni M16C Tandem Trainer	Willy Rose Technology Ltd	
G-CIRI	Cirrus SR20	Cirrus Flyers Group	
G-CIRK	Alisport Silent 2 Electro	S. V. Jones	
G-CIRL	Ultramagic S-90 balloon	M. A. Scholes & D. J. Day	
G-CIRM	Van's RV-12	P. J. Hynes	
G-CIRO	Cessna F.172H	H. G. Stroemer	
G-CIRP	Aeropro Eurofox 912(S)	M. Petrie & S. D. Kellner	
G-CIRT	AutoGyro MTOSport	M. Pugh & J. Gleeson	
G-CIRU	Cirrus SR20	Cirrent BV/Netherlands	
G-CIRV	Van's RV-7	R. J. Fray	
G-CIRW	Cessna FA.150K	Air Navigation and Trading Company Ltd	
G-CIRX	Cameron Z-150 balloon	Phoenix Balloons Ltd	
G-CIRY	EV-97 Eurostar SL	Hotel Victor Flying Group	
G-CIRZ	Ikarus C42 FB80	Mainair Microlight School Ltd	
G-CISA	Sprite Stinger	Sprite Aviation Services Ltd	
G-CISB	Sackville AH56 balloon	T. J. Wilkinson	
G-CISC	Sackville AH77 balloon	T. I. Laws	
G-CISD	Sackville AH31 balloon	L. S. Crossland-Clarke	
G-CISE	Aero Designs Pulsar XP	S. C. Goozee	
G-CISF	Quad City Challenger II	S. A. Beddus	
G-CISG	Ikarus C42 FB80	C. Williams	
G-CISH	Thatcher CX4	M. A. Sims	
G-CISI	P & M Quik GTR	Kent County Scout Council	
G-CISJ	Ultramagic H-31 balloon	R. P. Wade	
G-CISK	Embraer EMB-145LR	Eastern Airways	
G-CISL	Cameron C-70 balloon	S. Lundin	
G-CISN	Flylight Foxcub	G. Nicholas	
G-CISO	Cessna 150G	Enterprise Purchasing Ltd	
G-CISR	Flying K Sky Raider 1	J. A. Harris	
G-CISS	Ikarus C42 FB80	C-More Flying School	
G-CIST	P & M Quik GT450	G. J. Prisk	
G-CISU	CM Sunbird	C. W. Mitchinson	
G-CISW	La Mouette Samson 12	N. Pain	
G-CISX	Cessna 172M	D. Sluman	
G-CISZ	Van's RV-7	D. C. Hanss	
G-CITC	Apollo Delta Jet 2	P. Broome	
G-CITD	Sportavia-Putzer Fournier RF-5	G-CITD Group	
G-CITE	Grob G.102 Astir CS Jeans	The Bath, Wilts & North Dorset Gliding Club Ltd	
G-CITF	EV-97 Eurostar SL	J. C. Rose	
G-CITG	Skyranger Nynja 912S(1)	A. C. Aiken & J. Attard	
G-CITH	Eans S-6-ES Coyote II	D. P. Molloy	
G-CITK	Alisport Silent 2 Targa	B. T. Green	
G-CITL	Ace Magic Cyclone	S. F. Beardsell	
G-CITM	Magni M16C Tandem Trainer	Lambdatek Ltd	
G-CITN	P-51D-25-NA Mustang	P. Earthey	
G-CITO	P & M Quik	M. P. Jackson	
G-CITP	Grumman AA-1B Trainer	J-C. Vanderstricht/Belgium	
G-CITR	Cameron Z-105 balloon	A. Kaye	
G-CITS	Groppo Trail	D. A. Buttress	
G-CITT	Mooney M.20J Model 201	J. M. Tiley	
G-CITV	AutoGyro Cavalon	N. R. W. Whitling	
G-CITW	Extra EA.400	LAC Marine Ltd	
G-CITX	AutoGyro MTOSport	D. Brooksbank	
G-CITY	PA-31-350 Navajo Chieftain	Blue Sky Investments Ltd	
G-CIUA	Ultramagic B-70 balloon	K. W. Graham	
G-CIUB	Cameron Z-90 balloon	G. Forster	
G-CIUD	ACLA Sirocco SW FT	S. Siddiqui (G-ROCO)	
G-CIUE	CASA 1-131E Jungmann Srs 2000	R. A. Fleming	
G-CIUF	Aviad Zigolo MG12	J. D. C. Henslow & C. B. Jones	
G-CIUG	Aeropro Eurofox 3K	J. V. Clewer	
G-CIUH	Cessna 152	J. M. Perfettini	
G-CIUM	PA-12 Super Cruiser	J. Havers & S. James	
G-CIUN	Flylight Foxcub	C. I. Chegwen	
G-CIUO	Ekolot KR-010 ELF	P. V. Griffiths	
G-CIUP	Europa XS	P. C. Matthews & P. Bridges	
G-CIUU	Cessna F.152	DSFT Ltd	

135

Notes	Reg	Type	Owner or Operator
	G-CIUW	AT-16 Harvard IIB (FE511)	J. Brown
	G-CIUX	Auster AOP.Mk.9 (WZ679)	R. Warner
	G-CIUZ	P & M Quik GTR	S. Spyrou
	G-CIVA	Boeing 747-436	British Airways
	G-CIVB	Boeing 747-436 ★	preserved Cotswold Airport
	G-CIVJ	Boeing 747-436	British Airways
	G-CIVR	Boeing 747-436	British Airways
	G-CIVS	Boeing 747-436	British Airways
	G-CIVT	Boeing 747-436	British Airways
	G-CIVW	Boeing 747-436 ★	preserved Cotswold Airport
	G-CIVX	Boeing 747-436	British Airways
	G-CIWA	Skyranger Swift 912(1)	S. D. Lilley
	G-CIWB	Van's RV-6	G. D. Price
	G-CIWC	Raj Hamsa X'Air Hawk	G. A. J. Salter
	G-CIWD	TLAC Sherwood Ranger ST	A. R. Pitcher
	G-CIWF	EC.225LP Super Puma	Babcock Mission Critical Services Offshore Ltd
	G-CIWG	Aeropro Eurofox (IS)	A. Hegner
	G-CIWH	Agusta-Bell 206B-3 Jet Ranger III	P. Rosati
	G-CIWI	EV-97 Eurostar SL	Mademoiselle CIWI Group
	G-CIWL	Techpro Merlin 100UL	Sprite Aviation Services Ltd
	G-CIWN	Such BM42-16 balloon	D. G. Such
	G-CIWO	AS.350B3 Ecureuil	R & J Helicopters LLP
	G-CIWP	Ikarus C42 FB100	G-CIWP Syndicate
	G-CIWT	Ikarus C42 FB80	J. W. Lorains
	G-CIWU	McDonnell Douglas MD.369E	Century Aviation (Training) Ltd
	G-CIWV	Van's RV-7	J. W. Baker
	G-CIWW	Sackville BM-56 balloon	T. J. Wilkinson
	G-CIWX	Sackville 65 balloon	A. E. Austin
	G-CIWY	Sackville 90 balloon	T. J. Wilkinson
	G-CIWZ	Sackville 6BM-34 balloon	T. J. Wilkinson
	G-CIXA	Dudek Nucleon 31	P. Sinkler
	G-CIXB	Grob G.109B	G-CIXB Syndicate
	G-CIXD	Cameron A-105 balloon	Ballooning in Tuscany SRL/Italy
	G-CIXE	Moravan Zlin Z-326 Trener Master	J. P. Armitage
	G-CIXG	Phantom X1	K. B. Woods
	G-CIXH	Schempp-Hirth Ventus 2a	P. M. Shelton
	G-CIXJ	Curtiss P-36C Hawk	Patina Ltd
	G-CIXL	Air Creation Ifun 13 Pixel 250XC	S. C. Reeve
	G-CIXM	Supermarine Spitfire Mk.26 (PL793)	S. W. Markham
	G-CIXN	CFM Shadow Series E	U. J. Anderson
	G-CIXP	Cessna 152	H. E. da Costa Alburquerque
	G-CIXR	Cameron Z-77 balloon	Airship and Balloon Company Ltd
	G-CIXS	Zenair CH.701SP	S. Foreman
	G-CIXT	Flylight Foxcub	A. G. Cummings
	G-CIXU	Cameron Z-77 balloon	Airship and Balloon Company Ltd
	G-CIXW	Embraer ERJ170-100LR	Eastern Airways
	G-CIXX	AutoGyro Cavalon	M. J. Taylor
	G-CIXY	Ikarus C42 FB80	T. H. Brown
	G-CIXZ	P & M Quik R	N. H. N. Douglas
	G-CIYB	CEA Jodel DR.1051M1	A. G. & G. I. Doake
	G-CIYC	Flylight Foxcub	B. Plunkett
	G-CIYG	Airbike Light Sport	N. Allen
	G-CIYH	Eurocopter EC.225LP Super Puma	Leonardo SpA/Norway
	G-CIYJ	MD Helicopter Inc Hughes 369E	Studwelders Holdings Ltd
	G-CIYK	Free Spirit Biplane	J. C. Greenslade
	G-CIYL	Aeropro Eurofox 912iS(1)	G. E. Rattray
	G-CIYN	Skyranger Nynja 912S(1)	R. W. Sutherland
	G-CIYO	Groppo Trail	M. A. McLoughlin
	G-CIYP	Aeropro Eurofox 912(1)	J. Andrews
	G-CIYR	Lindstrand LTL-177T Skyflyer gas balloon	Lindstrand Technologies Ltd
	G-CIYT	Flugastol	F. B. Rich
	G-CIYV	Van's RV-9A	M. S. Ashby
	G-CIYY	TLAC Sherwood Ranger XP	M. R. M. Welch
	G-CIYZ	P & M Quik R	R. Keene & Sons
	G-CIZA	Spacek SD-1 Minisport	M. Drake-Knight
	G-CIZB	Magni M-24C Orion	J. E. Fallis
	G-CIZD	P & M Quik GT450	D. Orton
	G-CIZE	Cameron O-56 balloon	P. Spellward
	G-CIZF	Ozone Indy/Paramotor Flyer Trike	M. R. Gaylor
	G-CIZG	Robinson R66	Buildrandom Ltd
	G-CIZL	P & M Quik R	East Fortune Flyers

Reg	Type	Owner or Operator	Notes
G-CIZM	Cameron Z-210 balloon	The Balloon Company Ltd	
G-CIZN	J-5B Cub Cruiser	M. Howells	
G-CIZO	PA-28-161 Cadet	Falcon Flying Services Ltd	
G-CIZP	AutoGyro Cavalon Pro	C. Coffield	
G-CIZR	Van's RV-9	M. L. Martin	
G-CIZS	Tipsy Nipper T.66 Series 2	S. R. Green	
G-CIZT	Ace Magic Cyclone	T. Robinson	
G-CIZU	EV-97 Eurostar SL	E. K. McAlinden	
G-CIZV	P & M Quik R	G-CIZV Syndicate	
G-CIZW	Alisport Silent 2 Electro	P. C. Jarvis & C. C. Redrup	
G-CIZY	PA-34-200T Seneca II	Fenix Aero Services SA/Greece	
G-CJAF	Cessna 182T	F. M. Kleinau & S. F. Alsabah	
G-CJAI	P & M Quik GT450	J. C. Kitchen	
G-CJAJ	P & M Quik GT450	D. Al-Bassam	
G-CJAK	Skyranger Nynja 912S(1)	A. K. Birt	
G-CJAL	Schleicher Ka 6E	JAL Syndicate	
G-CJAM	Ikarus C42 FB80	G. C. Linley	
G-CJAO	Schempp-Hirth Discus b	R. W. Coombs	
G-CJAP	Ikarus C42 FB80	M. A. McLoughlin	
G-CJAR	Schempp-Hirth Discus bT	C. J. H. Donnelly	
G-CJAS	Glasflugel Standard Libelle 201B	M. J. Collett	
G-CJAT	Schleicher K8B	Wolds Gliding Club Ltd	
G-CJAU	White Sports Monoplane	J. Aubert	
G-CJAV	Schleicher ASK-21	Wolds Gliding Club Ltd	
G-CJAW	Glaser-Dirks DG-200/17	F. Friend	
G-CJAX	Schleicher ASK-21	Wolds Gliding Club Ltd	
G-CJAY	Mainair Pegasus Quik GT450	J. C. Kitchen	
G-CJAZ	Grob G.102 Astir CS Jeans	M. R. Dews	
G-CJBA	Alisport Silent 2 Electro	B. A. Fairston & A. Stotter	
G-CJBC	PA-28 Cherokee 180	J. B. Cave	
G-CJBD	Spacek SD-1 Minisport	D. Cox	
G-CJBE	Ikarus C42 FB80	J. H. Bradbury	
G-CJBH	Eiriavion PIK-20D	G. A. Darby	
G-CJBI	Aeropro Eurofox 912(iS)	M. B. Z. de Ferranti	
G-CJBJ	Schempp-Hirth Standard Cirrus	S. T. Dutton	
G-CJBK	Schleicher ASW-19B	D. Caielli & P. Deane	
G-CJBL	Flylight Foxtug	R. W. Twamley	
G-CJBM	Schleicher ASK-21	The Burn Gliding Club Ltd	
G-CJBN	Sackville BM-65 balloon	B. J. Newman	
G-CJBO	Rolladen-Schneider LS8-18	A. & M. Truelove	
G-CJBP	Flylight Foxcub	G. Evans	
G-CJBR	Schempp-Hirth Discus b	G-CJBR Group	
G-CJBT	Schleicher ASW-19B	Black Mountains Gliding Club	
G-CJBU	BRM Aero Bristell NG5 Speed Wing	H. R. Pearson	
G-CJBV	IAV Bacau Yak-52	R. J. Harper	
G-CJBW	Schempp-Hirth Discus bT	G-CJBW Syndicate	
G-CJBX	Rolladen-Schneider LS4-a	P. W. Lee	
G-CJBZ	Grob G.102 Astir CS	The Royal Air Force Gliding Association	
G-CJCD	Schleicher ASW-24	G. G. Dale & A. K. Laylee	
G-CJCE	Ultramagic M-77C	G. A. Chadwick & J. W. Adams	
G-CJCF	Grob G.102 Astir CS77	The Northumbria Gliding Club Ltd	
G-CJCG	PZL-Swidnik PW-5 Smyk	K. Cullen, S. Kinnear & M. Walsh	
G-CJCH	AB Sportine Aviacija LAK-19T	LAK 19T Syndicate	
G-CJCJ	Schempp-Hirth Standard Cirrus	G-CJCJ Syndicate	
G-CJCK	Schempp-Hirth Discus bT	G. A. Friedrich	
G-CJCL	EV-97B Eurostar SL	M. Dunlop	
G-CJCM	Schleicher ASW-27	Zulu Glasstek Ltd	
G-CJCN	Schempp-Hirth Standard Cirrus 75	G. D. E. Macdonald	
G-CJCO	Ikarus C42 FB80	GS Aviation (Europe) Ltd	
G-CJCR	Grob G.102 Astir CS	B. J. Harrison	
G-CJCS	Balony Kubicek BB-60Z balloon	Ballooning in Tuscany SRL/Italy	
G-CJCT	Schempp-Hirth Nimbus 4T	E. W. Richards	
G-CJCU	Schempp-Hirth Standard Cirrus B	G-GJCU Group	
G-CJCW	Grob G.102 Astir CS77	Essex Gliding Club Ltd	
G-CJCX	Schempp-Hirth Discus bT	A. D. Johnson	
G-CJDA	Ikarus C42 FB80	Mainair Microlight School Ltd	
G-CJDB	Cessna 525 Citationjet	Breed Aircraft Ltd	
G-CJDC	Schleicher ASW-27	T. A. Sage	
G-CJDD	Glaser-Dirks DG-200/17	N. P. Harrison	
G-CJDE	Rolladen-Schneider LS8-18	Army Gliding Association	

Notes	Reg	Type	Owner or Operator
	G-CJDG	Rolladen-Schneider LS6B	R. H. & A. Moss
	G-CJDJ	Rolladen-Schneider LS3	S. Wilkinson & B. J. R. Moate
	G-CJDL	Pipistrel Apis 15M M FES	M. E. Hughes
	G-CJDM	Schleicher ASW-15B	J. D. Morris
	G-CJDN	Cameron C-90 balloon	N. Ivison
	G-CJDP	Glaser-Dirks DG-200/17	G. K. Hutchinson
	G-CJDR	Schleicher ASW-15	S. Mudaliar
	G-CJDS	Schempp-Hirth Standard Cirrus 75	P. Nicholls
	G-CJDV	DG Flugzeugbau DG-300 Elan Acro	M. K. Lavender
	G-CJDW	Magni M-16C Tandem Trainer	R. W. D. Noon
	G-CJDX	Wassmer WA-28	G. B. Marshall
	G-CJEA	Rolladen-Schneider LS8-18	M. W. Durham
	G-CJEB	Schleicher ASW-24	P. C. Scholz
	G-CJEC	PZL-Bielsko SZD-50-3 Puchasz	Cambridge Gliding Club Ltd
	G-CJED	Schempp-Hirth Nimbus 3/24.5	J. Edyvean
	G-CJEE	Schleicher ASW-20L	P. Woodcock
	G-CJEH	Glasflugel Mosquito B	M. J. Vickery
	G-CJEI	UltraMagic M-77 balloon	British Telecommunications PLC
	G-CJEJ	Best Off Skyranger Nynja 912(1)	G-CJEJ Rossall Skyranger
	G-CJEK	Guimbai Cabri G2	I. C. Macdonald
	G-CJEL	Schleicher ASW-24	C. W. Lewis
	G-CJEP	Rolladen-Schneider LS4-b	C. F. Carter & N. Backes
	G-CJER	Schempp-Hirth Standard Cirrus 75	C. Parvin
	G-CJES	Cameron TR-77 balloon	International Merchandising, Promotion and Services
	G-CJEU	Glasflugel Standard Libelle	D. B. Johns
	G-CJEW	Schleicher Ka 6CR	W. J. Prince
	G-CJEX	Schempp-Hirth Ventus 2a	D. S. Watt
	G-CJEY	Flylight Dragon Combat 12T	A. E. Barron
	G-CJEZ	Glaser-Dirks DG-100	D. P. Spragg
	G-CJFA	Schempp-Hirth Standard Cirrus	P. M. Sheahan
	G-CJFC	Schempp-Hirth Discus CS	C. J. Tooze
	G-CJFG	Aeriane Swift Light PAS	M. Jackson
	G-CJFH	Schempp-Hirth Duo Discus	The Royal Air Force Gliding and Soaring Association
	G-CJFJ	Schleicher ASW-20CL	Selby Flyers
	G-CJFN	DHC.8-402Q Dash Eight	NAC Aviation 23 Ltd
	G-CJFP	Dudek Synthesis LT29	P. A. Sadowski
	G-CJFS	Pulse SSDR	D. Stephens
	G-CJFT	Schleicher K-8B	The Surrey Hills Gliding Club Ltd
	G-CJFU	Schleicher ASW-19B	M. T. Stanley
	G-CJFW	Ace As-tec 15	S. E. Dancaster
	G-CJFX	Rolladen-Schneider LS8-a	J. E. Gatfield
	G-CJFZ	Fedorov ME7 Mechta	R. J. Colbourne
	G-CJGA	Cameron Z-90 balloon	Spoon Service Multimedia SAS/Italy
	G-CJGB	Schleicher K 8B	L. R. Merritt
	G-CJGC	Cameron Z-105 balloon	GSM Aeropanorami SRL/Italy
	G-CJGD	Scleicher K 8B	R. E. Pettifer & C. A. McLay
	G-CJGE	Schleicher ASK-21	M. R. Wall
	G-CJGF	Schempp-Hirth Ventus c	R. D. Slater
	G-CJGG	P & M Quik GT450	J. M. Pearce
	G-CJGH	Schempp-Hirth Nimbus 2C	G-CJGH Syndicate
	G-CJGJ	Schleicher ASK-21	Midland Gliding Club Ltd
	G-CJGK	Eiri PIL-200	The Four Aces
	G-CJGL	Schempp-Hirth Discus CS	The Royal Air Force Gliding and Soaring Association
	G-CJGM	Schempp-Hirth Discus CS	The Royal Air Force Gliding and Soaring Association
	G-CJGN	Schempp-Hirth Standard Cirrus	P. A. Shuttleworth
	G-CJGP	Breezer M400	B. S. Keene
	G-CJGR	Schempp-Hirth Discus bT	G. W. Kemp
	G-CJGS	Rolladen-Schneider LS8-18	T. Stupnik
	G-CJGT	AMS-Flight Apis M	R. G. Parker & A. Spencer
	G-CJGU	Schempp-Hirth Mini-Nimbus B	N. D. Ashton
	G-CJGV	Flylight Foxcub	S. J. E. Smith
	G-CJGW	Schleicher ASK-13	Darlton Gliding Club Ltd
	G-CJGX	Schleicher K 8B	Andreas K8 Group
	G-CJGY	Schempp-Hirth Standard Cirrus	P. J. Shout
	G-CJGZ	Glasflugel Standard Libelle 201B	D. A. Joosten
	G-CJHC	Kolb Firefly	D. J. Pilkington
	G-CJHF	Aeroprpo Eurofox 912(iS)	BGC Eurofox Group

Reg	Type	Owner or Operator	Notes
G-CJHG	Grob G.102 Astir CS	P. L. E. Zelazowski	
G-CJHJ	Glasflugel Standard Libelle 201B	N. P. Marriott	
G-CJHK	Schleicher K8B	East Sussex Gliding Club Ltd	
G-CJHL	Schleicher Ka 6E	J. R. Gilbert	
G-CJHM	Schempp-Hirth Discus b	E. N. Hellawell	
G-CJHN	Grob G.102 Astir CS Jeans	A. J. Morgan	
G-CJHO	Schleicher ASK-18	RAF Gliding and Soaring Association	
G-CJHP	Flight Design CTSW	S. J. Reader	
G-CJHR	Centrair SNC34C Alliance	The Borders (Milfield) Gliding Club Ltd	
G-CJHS	Schleicher ASW-19B	JHS Syndicate	
G-CJHT	Aeropro Eurofox 3K	GS Aviation (Europe) Ltd	
G-CJHV	Lindstrand LTL Series 1-31 balloon	N. Rowan & J. L. Hilditch	
G-CJHW	Glaser-Dirks DG-200	I. A. Rudy	
G-CJHY	Rolladen-Schneider LS8-18	S. J. Eyles	
G-CJHZ	Schleicher ASW-20	T. J. Stanley	
G-CJIA	Lindstrand LTL Series 2-70 balloon	Lindstrand Technologies Ltd	
G-CJIB	Alisport Silent 2 Electro	G-CJIB Gransden Group	
G-CJIC	Van's RV-12	Kernow RV Ltd	
G-CJID	Alisport Silent 2	A. K. Carver	
G-CJIE	Flylight Foxcub	M. J. Pollard	
G-CJIG	Lindstrand LTL Series 1-70 balloon	A. M. Holly	
G-CJIH	Lindstrand LTL Series 1-105 balloon	R. M. Theil	
G-CJII	TLAC Sherwood Ranger ST	M. M. A. Darcy	
G-CJIK	Cameron Z-77 balloon	P. Greaves	
G-CJIL	Sackville BM-90 balloon	B. Mead	
G-CJIN	Boeing Stearman A75L300	R. D. Leigh	
G-CJIO	Rans S-6S Sport	D. Bedford	
G-CJIP	Aero 31 AM9 balloon	C. J. Sanger-Davies	
G-CJIR	Rotorway Executive 162F	Scothouse Quarries Ltd	
G-CJIT	Ikarus C42 FB100	SARM Group	
G-CJIX	Cameron O-31 balloon	D. J. Head	
G-CJJA	EV-97 Eurostar SL	G-CJJA Group	
G-CJJB	Rolladen-Schneider LS4	M. Tomlinson	
G-CJJC	Lindstrand LTL Series 1-105 balloon	A. M. Holly	
G-CJJD	Schempp-Hirth Discus bT	G-CJJD Syndicate	
G-CJJE	Schempp-Hirth Discus-a	A. Soffici	
G-CJJH	DG Flugzeugbau DG-800S	J. S. Weston	
G-CJJJ	Schempp-Hirth Standard Cirrus	Cirrus JJJ Syndicate	
G-CJJK	Rolladen-Schneider LS8-18	A. D. Roch	
G-CJJL	Schleicher ASW-19B	G-CJJL Group	
G-CJJN	Robin HR.100/210 Safari II	The Saffari JJN Syndicate	
G-CJJP	Schempp-Hirth Duo Discus	494 Syndicate	
G-CJJS	PA-28-151 Cherokee Warrior	Phil Short Electrical Ltd (G-VIVS)	
G-CJJT	Schleicher ASW-27	Portsmouth Naval Gliding Centre	
G-CJJV	Van's RV-12	K. Handley	
G-CJJW	Lambert Mission M108	D. S. James	
G-CJJX	Schleicher ASW-15B	A. Snell	
G-CJJY	Aerochute SSDR	G. R. Britton	
G-CJJZ	Schempp-Hirth Discus bT	S. J. C. Parker	
G-CJKA	Schleicher ASK-21	East Sussex Gliding Club Ltd	
G-CJKB	PZL-Swidnik PW-5 Smyk	B. Parry	
G-CJKE	PZL-Swidnik PW-5 Smyk	D. Hertzberg	
G-CJKF	Glaser-Dirks DG-200	D. O. Sandells	
G-CJKG	Schleicher ASK-18	The Royal Air Force Gliding and Soaring Association	
G-CJKH	Ultramagic M-120 balloon	Cold Climate Expeditions Ltd	
G-CJKI	Ultramagic S-90 balloon	M. P. Rowley	
G-CJKJ	Schleicher ASK-21	The Royal Air Force Gliding and Soaring Association	
G-CJKK	Schleicher ASK-21	Army Gliding Association	
G-CJKM	Glaser-Dirks DG200/17	G. F. Coles & E. W. Russell	
G-CJKN	Rolladen-Schneider LS8-18	790 Syndicate	
G-CJKO	Schleicher ASK-21	The Royal Air Force Gliding and Soaring Association	
G-CJKP	Rolladen-Schneider LS4-b	D. A. Spencer	
G-CJKS	Schleicher ASW-19B	R. J. P. Lancaster	
G-CJKT	Schleicher ASK-13	The Royal Air Force Gliding and Soaring Association	
G-CJKU	Schleicher ASK-18	Derbyshire & Lancashire Gliding Club Ltd	
G-CJKV	Grob G.103A Twin II Acro	The Welland Gliding Club Ltd	

Notes	Reg	Type	Owner or Operator
	G-CJKW	Grob G.102 Astir CS77	The Bath, Wilts and North Dorset Gliding Club Ltd
	G-CJKY	Schempp-Hirth Ventus cT	G. V. Matthews & M. P. Osborn
	G-CJKZ	Schleicher ASK-21	The Royal Air Force Gliding and Soaring Association
	G-CJLA	Schempp-Hirth Ventus 2cT	S. G. Jones
	G-CJLC	Schempp-Hirth Discus CS	S. M. Stannard & M. A. Stephens
	G-CJLD	Lambert Mission M108	P. R. Mailer
	G-CJLF	Schleicher ASK-13	V. Mallon
	G-CJLH	Rolladen-Schneider LS4	JLH Syndicate
	G-CJLI	PA-28-161 Warrior II	Aeros Leasing Ltd
	G-CJLJ	Rolladen-Schneider LS4-b	Army Gliding Association
	G-CJLK	Rolladen-Schneider LS7	D. N. Munro & S. Urry
	G-CJLL	Robinson R44 II	R. D. J. Alexander
	G-CJLM	Denney Kitfox 4-1050 Speedster	C. Kinder & T. Neale
	G-CJLN	Rolladen-Schneider LS8-18	The Royal Air Force Gliding and Soaring Association
	G-CJLO	Schleicher ASK-13	Bowland Forest Gliding Club Ltd
	G-CJLP	Schempp-Hirth Discus CS	The Royal Air Force Gliding and Soaring Association
	G-CJLS	Schleicher K-8B	E. Ustenler
	G-CJLT	Cameron O-84 balloon	T. M. Lee
	G-CJLV	Schleicher Ka 6E	J. C. Cooper
	G-CJLW	Schempp-Hirth Discus CS	The Royal Air Force Gliding and Soaring Association
	G-CJLX	Schempp-Hirth Standard Cirrus	J. Hunneman
	G-CJLY	Schleicher ASW-27	L. M. Astle & P. C. Piggott
	G-CJLZ	Grob G.103A Twin II Acro	21 Syndicate
	G-CJMA	Schleicher ASK-18	S. D. Codd
	G-CJMF	BRM Aero Bristell NG5 Speed Wing	G. E. Collard
	G-CJMG	PZL-Bielsko SZD-51-1 Junior	Kent Gliding Club Ltd
	G-CJMJ	Schleicher ASK-13	The Royal Air Force Gliding and Soaring Association
	G-CJMK	Schleicher ASK-18	The Royal Air Force Gliding and Soaring Association
	G-CJML	Grob G.102 Astir CS77	The Royal Air Force Gliding and Soaring Association
	G-CJMN	Schempp-Hirth Nimbus 2	R. A. Holroyd
	G-CJMO	Rolladen-Schneider LS8-18	J. M. Hood
	G-CJMP	Schleicher ASK-13	East Sussex Gliding Club Ltd
	G-CJMS	Schleicher ASK-21	The Royal Air Force Gliding and Soaring Association
	G-CJMU	Rolladen-Schneider LS8-18	R. Lorenz
	G-CJMV	Schempp-Hirth Nimbus-2C	G. Tucker & K. R. Walton
	G-CJMW	Schleicher ASK-13	The Royal Air Force Gliding and Soaring Association
	G-CJMX	Schleicher ASK-13	The Nene Valley Gliding Club Ltd
	G-CJMY	PZL-Bielsko SZD-51-1 Junior	Highland Gliding Club Ltd
	G-CJMZ	Schleicher ASK-13	Mendip Gliding Club Ltd
	G-CJNA	Grob G.102 Astir CS Jeans	PA Technologies Ltd
	G-CJNB	Rolladen-Schneider LS8-18	A. P. & A. R. Wheeler
	G-CJND	Eurocopter MBB-BK117 C-2	The Milestone Aviation Asset Holding Group No.8 Ltd
	G-CJNF	Schempp-Hirth Discus 2a	T. Pavis
	G-CJNG	Glasflugel Standard Libelle 201B	Navboys Ltd
	G-CJNH	P & M Quik R	N. Hammerton
	G-CJNI	Agusta Westland AW139	Bristow Helicopters Ltd
	G-CJNJ	Rolladen-Schneider LS8-18	A. B. Laws
	G-CJNK	Rolladen-Schneider LS8-18	Army Gliding Association
	G-CJNL	Jodel DR.1050M Replica	M. G. Dolphin
	G-CJNN	Schleicher K 8B	Buckminster Gliding Club Ltd
	G-CJNO	Glaser-Dirks DG-300 Elan	Yankee Kilo Group
	G-CJNP	Rolladen-Schneider LS6-b	E. & P. S. Fink
	G-CJNR	Glasflugel Mosquito B	L. S. Hitchins & R. A. Markham
	G-CJNU	Techpro Merlin 100UL	B. S. Carpenter
	G-CJNZ	Glaser-Dirks DG-100	G. Syndedrcombe
	G-CJOA	Schempp-Hirth Discus b	K. A. Jarrett
	G-CJOB	Schleicher K 8B	JQB Syndicate
	G-CJOC	Schempp-Hirth Discus bT	S. G. Jones
	G-CJOD	Rolladen-Schneider LS8-18	The Royal Air Force Gliding and Soaring Association

Reg	Type	Owner or Operator	Notes
G-CJOE	Schempp-Hirth Standard Cirrus	A. B. Cresswell	
G-CJOJ	Schleicher K 8B	M. P. Webb	
G-CJOK	HpH Glasflugel 304 MS Shark	JOK Syndicate	
G-CJOL	Eurofox 3K	C. D. Waldron	
G-CJOM	Eurofox 3K	G. R. Postans	
G-CJON	Grob G.102 Astir CS77	The Royal Air Force Gliding and Soaring Association	
G-CJOO	Schempp-Hirth Duo Discus	185 Syndicate	
G-CJOR	Schempp-Hirth Ventus 2cT	A. M. George & N. A. Maclean	
G-CJOS	Schempp-Hirth Standard Cirrus	G-CJOS Group	
G-CJOT	Ikarus C42 FB80	Cumulus International Services Ltd	
G-CJOV	Schleicher ASW-27	J. W. White	
G-CJOW	Schempp-Hirth Cirrus VTC	North Wales Gliding Club Ltd	
G-CJOX	Schleicher ASK-21	Southdown Gliding Club Ltd	
G-CJOY	Zenair CH.601HDS Zodiac	G. M. Johnson	
G-CJOZ	Schleicher K 8B	Derbyshire and Lancashire Gliding Club Ltd	
G-CJPA	Schempp-Hirth Duo Discus	Coventry Gliding Club Ltd	
G-CJPB	Skyranger Swift 582(1)	T. W. Thiele	
G-CJPC	Schleicher ASK-13	Shalbourne Soaring Society Ltd	
G-CJPD	Cameron O-56 balloon	Cameron Balloons Ltd	
G-CJPE	Skyranger Nynja 912S(1)	R. J. Sutherland & M. J. Stolworthy	
G-CJPG	Cameron C-80 balloon	Atlantic Ballooning BVBA/Belgium	
G-CJPI	HPH Glasflugel 304MS Shark	J. Whelan-C. Davison Syndicate	
G-CJPJ	Grob G.104 Speed Astir IIB	M. A. Jones	
G-CJPK	Sgian Dubh	Sgian Dubh Flying Group	
G-CJPL	Rolladen-Schneider LS8-18	I. A. Reekie	
G-CJPM	Grob G.102 Astir CS Jeans	G-CJPM Syndicate	
G-CJPN	Cessna 152	M. Pirrie	
G-CJPO	Schleicher ASK-18	The Royal Air Force Gliding and Soaring Association	
G-CJPP	Schempp-Hirth Discus b	A. K. Rose	
G-CJPR	Rolladen-Schneider LS8-18	D. M. Byass & J. A. McCoshim	
G-CJPT	Schleicher ASW-27	M. A. Stephens & S. M. Stannard	
G-CJPV	Schleicher ASK-13	Cyprus Gliding Group/Cyprus	
G-CJPW	Glaser-Dirks DG-200	A. Kitchen & R. Truchan	
G-CJPX	Schleicher ASW-15	P. Johnstone & S. J. Naisby	
G-CJPY	Schleicher ASK-13	The Royal Air Force Gliding and Soaring Association	
G-CJPZ	Schleicher ASK-18	Cotswold Gliding Club	
G-CJRA	Rolladen-Schneider LS8-18	J. Williams	
G-CJRB	Schleicher ASW-19B	J. W. Baxter	
G-CJRC	Glaser-Dirks DG-300 Elan	P. J. Sillett	
G-CJRD	Grob G.102 Astir CS	The Vale of The White Horse Gliding Centre Ltd	
G-CJRE	Scleicher ASW-15	R. A. Starling	
G-CJRF	PZL-Bielsko SZD-50-3 Puchacz	Wolds Gliding Club Ltd	
G-CJRG	Schempp-Hirth Standard Cirrus	N. J. Laux	
G-CJRJ	PZL-Bielsko SZD-50-3 Puchacz	Derbyshire & Lancashire Gliding Club Ltd	
G-CJRK	Cameron Z-31 balloon	BWS Standfast Fire and Security Systems	
G-CJRL	Glaser-Dirks DG-100G Elan	Southampton University Gliding Club	
G-CJRM	Grob G.102 Astir CS	A. R. Moore	
G-CJRN	Glaser-Dirks DG-200/17	T. G. Roberts	
G-CJRO	Cameron Z-105 balloon	BWS Standfast Fire and Security Systems	
G-CJRR	Schempp-Hirth Discus bT	N. A. Hays	
G-CJRS	BRM Aero Bristell NG5 Speed Wing	A. Watt	
G-CJRU	Schleicher ASW-24	I. G. Walker & D. Tait	
G-CJRV	Schleicher ASW-19B	R. E. Corner	
G-CJRX	Schleicher ASK-13	The Royal Air Force Gliding and Soaring Association	
G-CJRZ	Ikarus C42 FB80	D. W. Cross	
G-CJSA	Nanchang NAMC CJ-6A	J. N. Ware & M. Elmes	
G-CJSB	Republic RC-3 Seabee	J. A. & R. H. Cooper	
G-CJSC	Schempp-Hirth Nimbus-3DT	S. G. Jones	
G-CJSD	Grob G.102 Astir CS	The Royal Air Force Gliding and Soaring Association	
G-CJSE	Schempp-Hirth Discus b	Imperial College of Science, Technology and Medicine	
G-CJSF	PA-28R-180 Cherokee Arrow	Y. N. Dimitrov & V. I. Genchev (G-SBMM/G-BBEL)	
G-CJSG	Schleicher Ka 6E	A. J. Emck	
G-CJSH	Grob G.102 Club Astir IIIB	Lasham Gliding Society Ltd	
G-CJSK	Grob G.102 Astir CS	Sierra Kilo Group	

Notes	Reg	Type	Owner or Operator
	G-CJSL	Schempp-Hirth Ventus cT	D. J. Wilson
	G-CJSM	Van's RV-8	S. T. G. Lloyd
	G-CJSN	Schleicher K 8B	Cotswold Gliding Club
	G-CJSP	PA-28-180 Cherokee Archer	J. R. Wright
	G-CJSR	Steen Skybolt	S. L. Millar
	G-CJSS	Schleicher ASW-27	G. K. & S. R. Drury
	G-CJST	Rolladen-Schneider LS1-c	A. M. Walker
	G-CJSU	Rolladen-Schneider LS8-18	J. G. Bell
	G-CJSV	Schleicher ASK-13	The Royal Air Force Gliding and Soaring Association
	G-CJSX	AMS-Flight DG-500	Oxford Gliding Company Ltd
	G-CJSY	Sackville BM-34 balloon	B. J. Newman
	G-CJSZ	Schleicher ASK-18	C. Weston
	G-CJTA	Autogyro MTOSport	R. Brain
	G-CJTB	Schleicher ASW-24	T. Davies
	G-CJTC	AutoGyro Calidus	C. J. Rose
	G-CJTD	Techpro Aviation Merlin 100UL	J. Murphy
	G-CJTE	Aeropro Eurofox 3K	C. M. Theakstone
	G-CJTG	Hoffman H36 Dimona II	Dimona Syndicate
	G-CJTH	Schleicher ASW-24	R. J. & J. E. Lodge
	G-CJTI	Aerochute Industries Hummerchute	S. T. P. Askew
	G-CJTJ	Schempp-Hirth Mini-Nimbus B	W. H. Stockings
	G-CJTK	DG Flugzeugbau DG-300 Elan Acro	A. Drury
	G-CJTM	Rolladen-Schneider LS8-18	A. D. Holmes
	G-CJTN	Glaser-Dirks DG-300 Elan	P. R. Gardner & S. F. Ducker
	G-CJTO	Glasflugel H303A Mosquito	P. J. Gilli
	G-CJTP	Schleicher ASW-20L	C. A. Sheldon & R. Abercrombie
	G-CJTS	Schempp-Hirth Cirrus VTC	G-CJTS Cirrus Group
	G-CJTT	Aerochute Industries Hummerchute	D. Townsend
	G-CJTU	Schempp-Hirth Duo Discus T	G-CJTU Syndicate
	G-CJTW	Glasflugel Mosquito B	B. L. C. Gordon
	G-CJTX	EV-97 Eurostar SL	G-TX Group
	G-CJTY	Rolladen-Schneider LS8-a	JTY Syndicate
	G-CJUB	Schempp-Hirth Discus CS	Coventry Gliding Club Ltd
	G-CJUD	Denney Kitfox Mk 3	S. Nixon & J. E. Jeffrey
	G-CJUF	Schempp-Hirth Ventus 2cT	A. L. Farr
	G-CJUJ	Schleicher ASW-27	T. K. Gooch
	G-CJUK	Grob G.102 Astir CS	P. Freer & S. J. Calvert
	G-CJUN	Schleicher ASW-19B	M. P. S. Roberts
	G-CJUO	Cameron Z-42 balloon	MC Cornick van Haarne & Co/Belgium
	G-CJUR	Valentin Mistral C	East Sussex Gliding Club Ltd
	G-CJUT	Skyranger Nynja 912S(1)	A. Jackson
	G-CJUU	Schempp-Hirth Standard Cirrus	A. R. Jones
	G-CJUV	Schempp-Hirth Discus b	Lasham Gliding Society Ltd
	G-CJUX	Aviastroitel AC-4C	J. R. Stiles & A. Jarvis
	G-CJUY	SNS-8 Hiperlight	R. H. Cooper
	G-CJUZ	Schleicher ASW-19B	J. M. Hough
	G-CJVA	Schempp-Hirth Ventus 2cT	M. S. Armstrong
	G-CJVB	Schempp-Hirth Discus bT	C. J. Edwards
	G-CJVC	PZL-Bielsko SZD-51-1 Junior	York Gliding Centre (Operations) Ltd
	G-CJVD	Team Minimax 1600	D. R. Thompson
	G-CJVE	Eiriavion PIK-20D	S. R. Wilkinson
	G-CJVG	Schempp-Hirth Discus bT	P. M. Holland & M. J. Beaumont
	G-CJVH	Lindstrand LTL Series 1-105 balloon	Lindstrand Balloons Ltd
	G-CJVI	Techpro Merlin 100UL	P. A. Tarplee
	G-CJVK	Skyranger Nynja 912S(1)	R. J. Speight
	G-CJVL	DG-300 Elan	A. T. Vidion & M. S. Hoy
	G-CJVM	Schleicher ASW-27	G. K. Payne
	G-CJVN	Lindstrand Racer 65 balloon	Slowfly Montgolfiere SNC/Italy
	G-CJVO	Lindstrand Racer 56 balloon	Lindstrand Technologies Ltd
	G-CJVP	Glaser-Dirks DG-200	L. M. Wilkinson & R. W. Iddon
	G-CJVS	Schleicher ASW-28	W. J. Veitch
	G-CJVU	Standard Cirrus CS-11-75L	J. B. Chapman
	G-CJVV	Schempp-Hirth Janus C	G. Johnson
	G-CJVW	Schleicher ASW-15	Channel Gliding Club
	G-CJVX	Schempp-Hirth Discus CS	G-CJVX Syndicate
	G-CJVZ	Schleicher ASK-21	Yorkshire Gliding Club (Proprietary) Ltd
	G-CJWA	Schleicher ASW-28	R. Jones & J. R. Martindale
	G-CJWB	Schleicher ASK-13	East Sussex Gliding Club Ltd
	G-CJWD	Schleicher ASK-21	London Gliding Club Proprietary Ltd
	G-CJWE	Harvard 4	Cirrus Aircraft UK Ltd

Reg	Type	Owner or Operator	Notes
G-CJWG	Schempp-Hirth Nimbus 3	880 Syndicate	
G-CJWH	Lindstrans LTL series 1-90 balloon	Flintnine Fasteners Ltd	
G-CJWI	Streak Shadow (modified)	C. Johnson	
G-CJWJ	Schleicher ASK-13	The Royal Air Force Gliding and Soaring Association	
G-CJWK	Schempp-Hirth Discus bT	722 Syndicate	
G-CJWL	Hawker Hunter Mk.58A	Hawker Hunter Aviation Ltd	
G-CJWM	Grob G.103 Twin Astir II	The South Wales Gliding Club Ltd	
G-CJWO	VS Spitfire LFVB	R. M. B. Parnall	
G-CJWP	Bolkow Phoebus B1	A. Fidler	
G-CJWR	Grob G.102 Astir CS	Cairngorm Gliding Club	
G-CJWT	Glaser-Dirks DG-200	K. R. Nash	
G-CJWU	Schempp-Hirth Ventus bT	B. C. P. & C. Crook	
G-CJWW	Spitfire Mk.26 (MH526:LO-D)	M. R. Overall	
G-CJWY	Cameron O-31 balloon	Cameron Balloons Ltd	
G-CJXA	Schempp-Hirth Nimbus 3	A. Rieder, P. T. Johnson & S. L. Barnes	
G-CJXB	Centrair 201B Marianne	A. C. Cherry	
G-CJXC	Wassmer WA28	A. P. Montague	
G-CJXD	Ultramagic H-77 balloon	C. G. Dobson	
G-CJXE	Lindstrand LTL series 1-120 balloon	N. R. Beckwith	
G-CJXF	Skyranger Swift 912(1)	I. F. Bastin	
G-CJXG	Eiriavion PIK-20D	G-CJXG Group	
G-CJXI	Cameron A-300 balloon	Bailey Balloons Ltd	
G-CJXJ	Cameron Z-105 balloon	Bristol University Hot Air Ballooning Society	
G-CJXK	Cameron O-31 balloon	A. P. Jay	
G-CJXL	Schempp-Hirth Discus CS	J. Hall	
G-CJXM	Schleicher ASK-13	J. A. Inglis	
G-CJXN	Centrair 201B	C. E. Metcalfe & G. R. Davey	
G-CJXO	Flylight Dragonfly	P. C. Knowles	
G-CJXP	Glaser-Dirks DG-100	N. L. Morris	
G-CJXR	Schempp-Hirth Discus b	Cambridge Gliding Club Ltd	
G-CJXT	Schleicher ASW-24B	JXT Syndicate	
G-CJXW	Schempp-Hirth Duo Discus T	R. A. Beatty & R. R. Bryan	
G-CJXX	Pilatus B4-PC11AF	C. B. Shepperd	
G-CJXY	Neukom Elfe S4A	Rufforth Elfe S4A Syndicate	
G-CJYC	Grob G.102 Astir CS	R. A. Christie	
G-CJYE	Schleicher ASK-13	North Wales Gliding Club Ltd	
G-CJYF	Schempp Hirth Discus CS	C. D. Sword	
G-CJYI	PA-28-140 Cherokee	N. Butler	
G-CJYJ	Cameron O-31 balloon	P. Spellward	
G-CJYL	AB Sportine Aviacija LAK-12	A. Camerotto	
G-CJYM	Ultramagic S-90 balloon	M. A. Wrigglesworth	
G-CJYO	Glaser-Dirks DG-100G Elan	D. W. Wilde	
G-CJYP	Grob G.102 Club Astir II	Norfolk Gliding Club Ltd	
G-CJYR	Schempp-Hirth Duo Discus T	CJYR Flying Group	
G-CJYS	Schempp-Hirth Mini Nimbus C	A. Jenkins	
G-CJYU	Schempp-Hirth Ventus 2cT	P. Brown & M. T. Davis	
G-CJYY	Spitfire Mk.26 (X4496)	D. A. Whitmore	
G-CJYZ	Cameron Z-120 balloon	MSJ Ballooning Ltd	
G-CJZB	Glaser-Dirks DG-500 Elan Orion	The Borders (Milfield) Gliding Club Ltd	
G-CJZD	Aeropro Eurofox 912(S)	R. Maddocks-Born	
G-CJZE	Schleicher ASK-13	Bowland Forest Gliding Club Ltd	
G-CJZG	Schempp-Hirth Discus bT	I. K. G. Mitchell	
G-CJZH	Schleicher ASW-20 CL	R. A. Robertson	
G-CJZK	Glaser-Dirks DG-505 Elan Orion	Devon and Somerset Gliding Club Ltd	
G-CJZL	Schempp-Hirth Mini Nimbus B	J. F. Wells	
G-CJZM	Schempp-Hirth Ventus 2a	S. Crabb	
G-CJZN	Schleicher ASW-28	D. M. Rushton	
G-CJZO	RAF BE2e replica (A2943)	O. Wulff	
G-CJZP	RAF BE.2e replica (A2767)	D. A. Whitmore	
G-CJZU	Rogers Sky Prince	M. C. R. Sims & S. R. Kendall	
G-CJZV	PA-28RT-201T Turbo Arrow IV	L. Tomatis/Italy	
G-CJZW	Van's RV-12	H. M. & M. A. Child	
G-CJZZ	Rolladen-Schneider LS7	C. L. Rogers	
G-CKAA	Whittaker MW9 Plank	M. W. J. Whittaker	
G-CKAB	Eurofox 912(S)	Trent Valley Gliding Club Ltd	
G-CKAC	Glaser-Dirks DG-200	N. Frost	
G-CKAD	Cameron O-56 balloon	Gone with the Wind Ltd (G-DKGM)	
G-CKAE	Centrair 101A Pegase	J. P. Gilbert	
G-CKAI	Griffin RG28 balloon	R. G. Griffin	

143

Notes	Reg	Type	Owner or Operator
	G-CKAM	Glasflugel Club Libelle 205	P. A. Cronk & R. C. Tallowin
	G-CKAN	PZL-Bielsko SZD-50-3 Puchacz	The Bath Wilts and North Dorset Gliding Club Ltd
	G-CKAO	Lindstrand LTL Series 1-17 balloon	Lindstrand Technologies Ltd
	G-CKAP	Schempp-Hirth Discus CS	H. A. Johnston & R. Gollings
	G-CKAR	Schempp-Hirth Duo Discus T	977 Syndicate
	G-CKAS	Schempp-Hirth Ventus 2cT	KAS Club
	G-CKAT	Cessna F.152	A. S. Bamrah
	G-CKAU	DG Flugzeugbau DG-303 Elan Acro	G. Earle
	G-CKAX	AMS-Flight DG-500 Elan Orion	York Gliding Centre (Operations) Ltd
	G-CKAY	Grob G.102 Astir CS	P. Fowler & R. G. Skerry
	G-CKAZ	Embraer EMB-505 Phenom 300	Trustflight (Jersey) Ltd
	G-CKBA	Centrair 101A Pegase	KBA Pegase 101A Syndicate
	G-CKBB	Sopwith 7F1 Snipe replica (F2367)	The Vintage Aviator Ltd
	G-CKBC	Rolladen-Schneider LS6-c18	A. W. Lyth
	G-CKBD	Grob G.102 Astir CS	Peterborough & Spalding Gliding Club Ltd
	G-CKBE	Van's RV-8	B. E. Smith
	G-CKBF	AMS-Flight DG-303 Elan	G. A. Burtenshaw
	G-CKBG	Schempp-Hirth Ventus 2cT	R. Fielding
	G-CKBH	Rolladen-Schneider LS6	M. P. Day
	G-CKBJ	Ultramagic H-31 balloon	R. D. Parry
	G-CKBL	Grob G.102 Astir CS	Norfolk Gliding Club Ltd
	G-CKBM	Schleicher ASW-28	P. J. Brown
	G-CKBN	PZL-Bielsko SZD-55-1 Promyk	G-CKBN Group
	G-CKBP	Smudger 77 balloon	C. E. Smith
	G-CKBT	Schempp-Hirth Standard Cirrus	K. R. Kay
	G-CKBU	Schleicher ASW-28	G. C. Metcalfe
	G-CKBV	Schleicher ASW-28	G. Johnson
	G-CKBW	Cessna 150M	D. Avramidis
	G-CKBX	Schleicher ASW-27	M. Wright
	G-CKCB	Rolladen-Schneider LS4-a	The Bristol Gliding Club Proprietary Ltd
	G-CKCC	Cameron Z-105 balloon	First Flight
	G-CKCD	Schempp-Hirth Ventus 2cT	R. S. Jobar & S. G. Jones
	G-CKCE	Schempp-Hirth Ventus 2cT	Ventus 24 Group
	G-CKCF	Scintex CP.301C-1 Emeraude	N. C. Scanlan
	G-CKCH	Schempp-Hirth Ventus 2cT	J. J. Pridal
	G-CKCI	Guimbal Cabri G2	Meadowland Aviation LLP
	G-CKCJ	Schleicher ASW-28	M. McHugo
	G-CKCL	Cessna 182T	P. D. Stonham Ltd
	G-CKCM	Glasflugel Standard Libelle 201B	A. Davey
	G-CKCP	Grob G.102 Astir CS	Norfolk Gliding Club Ltd
	G-CKCR	AB Sportine Aviacija LAK-17A	M. Kessler/Italy
	G-CKCT	Schleicher ASK-21	Kent Gliding Club
	G-CKCV	Schempp-Hirth Duo Discus T	WE4 Group
	G-CKCY	Schleicher ASW-20	R. S. Hood
	G-CKCZ	Schleicher ASK-21	Booker Gliding Club Ltd
	G-CKDA	Schempp-Hirth Ventus 2B	D. T. Bray
	G-CKDD	Aeropro Eurofox 2K	W. M. Holmes
	G-CKDE	Grob G.109B	Navboys Ltd
	G-CKDF	Schleicher ASK-21	Portsmouth Naval Gliding Centre
	G-CKDG	BB03 Tyra/BB103	Z. G. Nagygyorgy
	G-CKDJ	Sonex	S. Rance
	G-CKDK	Rolladen-Schneider LS4-a	M. C. & P. A. Ridger
	G-CKDL	Robinson R.22 Beta II	Elicast SRL/Italy
	G-CKDM	Zenair CH.750	M. R. Cleveley
	G-CKDN	Schleicher ASW-27B	A. F. W. Watson
	G-CKDO	Schempp-Hirth Ventus 2cT	M. W. Edwards
	G-CKDP	Schleicher ASK-21	Kent Gliding Club
	G-CKDS	Schleicher ASW-27	G. D. Morris
	G-CKDT	Cameron C-80 balloon	W. Thijs
	G-CKDU	Glaser-Dirks DG-200/17	Prestige Worldwide
	G-CKDV	Schempp-Hirth Ventus B/16.6	M. A. Codd
	G-CKDW	Schleicher ASW-27	C. Colton
	G-CKDX	Glaser-Dirks DG-200	Delta X Ray Group
	G-CKDY	Glaser-Dirks DG-100	503 Syndicate
	G-CKEA	Schempp-Hirth Cirrus 18	S. G. Jessup
	G-CKEB	Schempp-Hirth Standard Cirrus	R. H. Buzza
	G-CKED	Schleicher ASW-27B	A. & R. Maskell
	G-CKEE	Grob G.102 Astir CS	Essex and Suffolk Gliding Club Ltd
	G-CKEG	Cameron Z-105 balloon	First Flight
	G-CKEH	Kolb Twister Mk.III Xtra	The Darley Tail Draggers

Reg	Type	Owner or Operator	Notes
G-CKEI	Diamond DA.40NG Star	D. B. Smith	
G-CKEJ	Schleicher ASK-21	London Gliding Club Proprietary Ltd	
G-CKEK	Schleicher ASK-21	Devon and Somerset Gliding Club Ltd	
G-CKER	Schleicher ASW-19B	W. A. Bowness & E. Richards	
G-CKES	Schempp-Hirth Cirrus 18	D. Judd & N. Hawley	
G-CKET	Rolladen-Schneider LS8-t	M. B. Jefferyes & J. C. Taylor	
G-CKEV	Schempp-Hirth Duo Discus	The Royal Air Force Gliding and Soaring Association	
G-CKEY	PA-28-161 Warrior II	Warwickshire Leasing Ltd	
G-CKEZ	DG Flugzeugbau LS8	D. A. Jesty	
G-CKFA	Schempp-Hirth Standard Cirrus 75	University of the West of England	
G-CKFB	Schempp-Hirth Discus-2T	P. L. & P. A. G. Holland	
G-CKFD	Schleicher ASW-27B	W. T. Craig	
G-CKFE	Eiriavion PIK-20D	G. E. Rabe	
G-CKFF	Zenair CH.701SP	J. C. Woolard	
G-CKFG	Grob G.103A Twin II Acro	The Surrey Hills Gliding Club Ltd	
G-CKFH	Schempp-Hirth Mini Nimbus	C. J. Friar	
G-CKFI	Cameron Drop-95 balloon	Belvoir Fruit Farms Ltd	
G-CKFJ	Schleicher ASK-13	York Gliding Centre (Operations) Ltd	
G-CKFK	Schempp-Hirth Standard Cirrus 75	G-CKFK Syndicate	
G-CKFL	Rolladen-Schneider LS4	D. O'Brien & D. R. Taylor	
G-CKFN	DG Flugzeugbau DG1000	Yorkshire Gliding Club (Proprietary) Ltd	
G-CKFP	Schempp-Hirth Ventus 2cxT	D. A. Smith	
G-CKFS	Schleicher ASK-14	G. K. Stanford	
G-CKFT	Schempp-Hirth Duo Discus T	Duo Discus Syndicate	
G-CKFV	DG Flugzeugbau LS8-t	G. A. Rowden & K. I. Arkley	
G-CKFW	Mauchline Quaich	Quaich Flying Group	
G-CKFY	Schleicher ASK.21	Cambridge Gliding Club	
G-CKFZ	Ultramagic M-77 balloon	E. C. Meek	
G-CKGA	Schempp-Hirth Ventus 2cxT	D. R. Campbell	
G-CKGC	Schempp-Hirth Ventus 2cxT	J. McLaughlin	
G-CKGD	Schempp-Hirth Ventus 2cxT	C. Morris	
G-CKGF	Schempp-Hirth Duo Discus T	Duo 233 Group	
G-CKGG	Grob G.109B	R. Banks	
G-CKGH	Grob G.102 Club Astir II	K. Bennett, R. Grady & M. Spalding	
G-CKGI	Ultramagic M-77C balloon	D. J. L. Gillespie	
G-CKGJ	Nicollier HN.700 Menestrel II	J. R., S. J. & T. M. Rickett	
G-CKGK	Schleicher ASK-21	The Royal Air Force Gliding & Soaring Association	
G-CKGL	Schempp-Hirth Ventus 2cT	T. R. Dews	
G-CKGM	Centrair 101A Pegase	S. France	
G-CKGS	Ikarus C42 FB80	GS Aviation (Europe) Ltd	
G-CKGV	Schleicher ASW-20	A. H. Reynolds	
G-CKGX	Schleicher ASK-21	Coventry Gliding Club Ltd	
G-CKGY	Scheibe Bergfalke IV	B. R. Pearson	
G-CKHB	Rolladen-Schneider LS3	T. J. Milner	
G-CKHC	DG Flugzeugbau DG.505	C. A. Boyle	
G-CKHD	Schleicher ASW-27B	R. L. Smith	
G-CKHE	AB Sportine Aviacija LAK-17AT	V. S. Bettle	
G-CKHH	Schleicher ASK-13	The South Wales Gliding Club Ltd	
G-CKHI	P & M Quik R	G-CKHI Syndicate	
G-CKHJ	Ultramagic H-31 balloon	G. A. Board	
G-CKHK	Schempp-Hirth Duo Discus T	Duo Discus Syndicate	
G-CKHM	Centrair 101A Pegase 90	J. A. Tipler	
G-CKHN	PZL SZD-51-1 Junior	The Nene Valley Gliding Club Ltd	
G-CKHO	Flight Design CT-Supralight	J. A. Horn	
G-CKHR	PZL-Bielsko SZD-51-1 Junior	Wolds Gliding Club Ltd	
G-CKHS	Rolladen-Schneider LS7-WL	M. Lawson & D. Wallis	
G-CKHU	Balony Kubicek BB17XR balloon	Balloon Flight	
G-CKHV	Glaser-Dirks DG-100	The Assets G-CKHV Trust	
G-CKHW	PZL SZD-50-3 Puchacz	Derbyshire and Lancashire Gliding Club Ltd	
G-CKHY	P &M Hyper GTR	E. J. Douglas	
G-CKHZ	Aeriane Swift Light PAS	M. J. Pollard	
G-CKIE	Cessna 172S	Western Air (Thruxton) Ltd	
G-CKIF	Cessna 172S	Western Air (Thruxton) Ltd	
G-CKIG	Flylight Fox Tug	Malvern Aerotow Club	
G-CKIH	Agusta A.109S Grand	Heli Delta BV/Netherlands	
G-CKIN	Lindstrand LTL Series 1-105 balloon	A. M. Holly	
G-CKIO	PA-28-151 Cherokee Warrior	W. Ali	
G-CKIP	Cessna 172N	Aero Club de Leiria/Portugal	
G-CKIS	Aero Designs Pulsar XP	D. R. Piercy	

Notes	Reg	Type	Owner or Operator
	G-CKIT	Cameron C-60 balloon	Turner Balloons Ltd
	G-CKIU	Scheibe SF-25C Rotax-Falke	The Burn Gliding Club Ltd
	G-CKIX	Aeropro Eurofox 3K	T. W. Pawson & A. J. Ferguson
	G-CKIY	Best Off Skyranger Nynja 912S(1)	D. Lamb & N. Elahi
	G-CKIZ	Eurofly Minifox	R. M. Patwardhan
	G-CKJB	Schempp-Hirth Ventus bT	KJB Group
	G-CKJC	Schempp-Hirth Nimbus 3T	A. C. Wright
	G-CKJE	DG Flugzeugbau LS8-18	M. D. Wells
	G-CKJF	Schempp-Hirth Standard Cirrus	R. W. Skuse
	G-CKJG	Schempp-Hirth Cirrus VTC	C. Nobbs & A. R. Blanchard
	G-CKJH	Glaser-Dirks DG.300 Elan	Yorkshire Gliding Club
	G-CKJI	Best Off Skyranger Nynja 912S(1)	A. Sawdon
	G-CKJJ	DG Flugzeugbau DG-500 Elan Orion	Ulster Gliding Club Ltd
	G-CKJL	Scleicher ASK-13	Lincolnshire Gliding Club Ltd
	G-CKJM	Schempp-Hirth Ventus cT	G-CKJM Group
	G-CKJN	Schleicher ASW-20	R. Logan
	G-CKJP	Schleicher ASK-21	The Royal Air Force Gliding and Soaring Association
	G-CKJS	Schleicher ASW-28-18E	J. J. Schets
	G-CKJT	Ultramagic H-42 balloon	J. Taylor
	G-CKJV	Schleicher ASW-28-18E	A. C. Price
	G-CKJZ	Schempp-Hirth Discus bT	D. Lowe
	G-CKKB	Centrair 101A Pegase	W. B. Wood & G. C. Taffs
	G-CKKC	DG Flugzeugbau DG-300 Elan Acro	Charlie Kilo Kilo Charlie Syndicate
	G-CKKE	Schempp-Hirth Duo Discus T	R. A. Vaughan
	G-CKKF	Schempp-Hirth Ventus 2cT	M. S. Davidson
	G-CKKH	Schleicher ASW-27	P. L. Hurd
	G-CKKO	Ultramagic H-77 balloon	I. C. Steward
	G-CKKP	Schleicher ASK-21	Bowland Forest Gliding Club Ltd
	G-CKKR	Schleicher ASK-13	The Windrushers Gliding Club Ltd
	G-CKKX	Rolladen-Schneider LS4-A	Lleweni Parc Ltd
	G-CKKY	Schempp-Hirth Duo Discus T	P. D. Duffin
	G-CKLA	Schleicher ASK-13	Booker Gliding Club Ltd
	G-CKLC	Glasflugel H206 Hornet	W. Ellis
	G-CKLD	Schempp-Hirth Discus 2cT	797 Syndicate
	G-CKLE	Autogyro MTOsport 2017	J. R. Wilkinson
	G-CKLG	Rolladen-Schneider LS4	P. M. Scheiwiller
	G-CKLI	PA-28R-180 Cherokee Arrow	J. R. S. Benson
	G-CKLK	Autogyro MTOsport 2017	R. Peach
	G-CKLL	Waco YKS-7	K. D. Pearce
	G-CKLN	Rolladen-Schneider LS4-A	Army Gliding Association
	G-CKLP	Scleicher ASW-28-18	P. E. Baker
	G-CKLS	Rolladen-Schneider LS4	Wolds Gliding Club Ltd
	G-CKLT	Schempp-Hirth Nimbus 3/24.5	G. N. Thomas
	G-CKLV	Schempp-Hirth Discus 2cT	KLV Syndicate
	G-CKLW	Schleicher ASK-21	Yorkshire Gliding Club
	G-CKLY	DG Flugzeugbau DG-1000T	G-CKLY Flying Group
	G-CKMB	AB Sportline Aviacija LAK-19T	D. J. McKenzie
	G-CKMD	Schempp-Hirth Standard Cirrus	S. A. Crabb
	G-CKME	DG Flugzeugbau LS8-T	S. M. Smith
	G-CKMF	Centrair 101A Pegase	D. L. M. Jamin
	G-CKMG	Glaser-Dirks DG-101G Elan	R. A. Johnson
	G-CKMH	Kavanagh Balloons EX-65 balloon	L. J. M. Muir
	G-CKMI	Schleicher K8C	V. Mallon
	G-CKMJ	Schleicher Ka 6CR	V. Mallon
	G-CKMK	Sportine Aviacija LAK-17AT	B. N. Searle & P. M. Yeoman
	G-CKML	Schempp-Hirth Duo Discus T	G-CKML Group
	G-CKMM	Schleicher ASW-28-18E	R. G. Munro
	G-CKMO	Rolladen-Schneider LS7-WL	J. C. Brattle
	G-CKMP	AB Sportine Aviacija LAK-17A	J. L. McIver
	G-CKMT	Grob G103C	Essex & Suffolk Gliding Club Ltd
	G-CKMV	Rolladen-Schneider LS3-17	S. Procter & M. P. Woolmer
	G-CKMW	Schleicher ASK-21	The Royal Air Force Gliding & Soaring Association
	G-CKMX	Van's RV-7	S. J. Cummins
	G-CKMZ	Schleicher ASW-28-18E	Deesside ASW28 Group
	G-CKNB	Schempp-Hirth Standard Cirrus	S. Potter
	G-CKNC	Caproni Calif A21S	Calif 240 Syndicate
	G-CKND	DG Flugzeugbau DG-1000T	KND Group
	G-CKNE	Schempp-Hirth Standard Cirrus 75-VTC	G. D. E. Macdonald
	G-CKNF	DG Flugzeugbau DG-1000T	DG 1000 Syndicate

Reg	Type	Owner or Operator	Notes
G-CKNG	Schleicher ASW-28-18E	NG209 Group	
G-CKNK	Glaser-Dirks DG.500	Cotswold Gliding Club	
G-CKNL	Schleicher ASK-21	Buckminster Gliding Club Ltd	
G-CKNM	Sleicher ASK-18	Derbyshire & Lancashire Gliding Club Ltd	
G-CKNO	Schempp-Hirth Ventus 2cxT	R. T. Starling	
G-CKNR	Schempp-Hirth Ventus 2cxT	R. Kalin	
G-CKNS	Rolladen-Schneider LS4-A	I. R. Willows	
G-CKNV	Schleicher ASW-28-18E	The KNV Group	
G-CKNX	Ozone Buzz Z4 ML/Parajet VI Macro Trike	I. T. Callaghan	
G-CKOD	Schempp-Hirth Discus BT	M. W. Talbot & D. Ascroft	
G-CKOE	Schleicher ASW-27-18	R. C. Bromwich	
G-CKOF	Boeing 787-9	Norwegian Air UK Ltd	
G-CKOG	Boeing 787-9	Norwegian Air UK Ltd	
G-CKOH	DG Flugzeugbau DG-1000T	A. D. & P. Langlands	
G-CKOI	AB Sportine Aviacija LAK-17AT	C. G. Corbett	
G-CKOK	Schempp-Hirth Discus 2cT	P. Topping	
G-CKOL	Schempp-Hirth Duo Discus T	Oscar Lima Syndicate	
G-CKOM	Schleicher ASW-27-18	P. G. Whipp	
G-CKON	Schleicher ASW-27-18E	J. P. Gorringe	
G-CKOO	Schleicher ASW-27-18E	G-CKOO Flying Group	
G-CKOR	Glaser-Dirks DG-300 Elan	D. Jokinen & W. Xu	
G-CKOT	Schleicher ASK-21	Ulster Gliding Club Ltd	
G-CKOU	AB Sportine Aviacija LAK-19T	P. Allingham & R. M. Wootten	
G-CKOW	DG-505 Elan Orion	Southdown Gliding Club Ltd	
G-CKOX	AMS-Flight DG-505 Elan Orion	Seahawk Gliding Club	
G-CKOY	Schleicher ASW-27-18E	G-CKOY Group	
G-CKOZ	Schleicher ASW-27-18E	E. W. Johnston	
G-CKPA	AB Sportline Aviacija LAK-19T	M. J. Hargreaves	
G-CKPC	Cameron Z-77 balloon	A. A. Osman	
G-CKPE	Schempp-Hirth Duo Discus	Portsmouth Naval Gliding Centre	
G-CKPF	Champion 7GCBC Citabria	C. F. Dukes	
G-CKPG	Schempp-Hirth Discus 2cT	KPG Syndicate	
G-CKPJ	Neukom S-4D Elfe	W. B. Hartnett	
G-CKPK	Schempp-Hirth Ventus 2cxT	I. C. Lees	
G-CKPM	DG Flugzeugbau LS8-T	S. P. Woolcock	
G-CKPN	PZL-Bielsko SZD-51-1 Junior	Rattlesden Gliding Club Ltd	
G-CKPO	Schempp-Hirth Duo Discus xT	KPO Syndicate	
G-CKPP	Schleicher ASK-21	Zulu Glasstek Ltd	
G-CKPR	Cameron TR-65 balloon	Cameron Balloons Ltd	
G-CKPS	Aerospatiale AS.350B2 Ecureuil	Helitrain Ltd	
G-CKPU	Schleicher ASW-27-18E	C. S. & M. E. Newland-Smith	
G-CKPV	Schempp-Hirth HS.7 Mini-Nimbus B	N. McLaughlin	
G-CKPX	ZS Jezow PW-6U	North Wales Gliding Club Ltd	
G-CKPY	Schempp-Hirth Duo Discus xT	Duo-Discus Syndicate	
G-CKPZ	Schleicher ASW-20	T. C. J. Hogarth	
G-CKRB	Schleicher ASK-13	Derbyshire and Lancashire Gliding Club Ltd	
G-CKRC	Schleicher ASW-28-18E	G-CKRC Flying Group	
G-CKRD	Schleicher ASW-27-18E	R. F. Thirkell	
G-CKRE	La Mouette Samson/Atos-VR	J. S. Prosser	
G-CKRF	DG-300 Elan	G. A. King	
G-CKRH	Grob G.103 Twin Astir II	Staffordshire Gliding Club Ltd	
G-CKRI	Schleicher ASK-21	Kent Gliding Club	
G-CKRJ	Schleicher ASW-27-18E	J. J. Marshall	
G-CKRK	Guimbal Cabri G2	Lyza Aviation Ltd	
G-CKRL	Europa XS	D. M. Cope	
G-CKRR	Schleicher ASW-15B	D. T. Edwards	
G-CKRU	ZS Jezow PW-6U	Essex Gliding Club Ltd	
G-CKRV	Schleicher ASW-27-18E	W. J. Head	
G-CKRW	Schleicher ASK-21	The Royal Air Force Gliding and Soaring Association	
G-CKRX	Jezow PW-6U	Essex Gliding Club Ltd	
G-CKRZ	Skyranger Nynja 912S(1)	R. J. Clarke	
G-CKSC	Czech Sport Aircraft Sportcruiser	Czechmate Syndicate	
G-CKSD	Rolladen-Schneider LS8-a	J. H. Cox	
G-CKSE	Cessna 208B Grand Caravan	Wingglider Ltd	
G-CKSK	Pilatus B4-PC11	K. Steinmair	
G-CKSL	Schleicher ASW-15B	Sierra Lima Group	
G-CKSM	Schempp-Hirth Duo Discus T	J. M. Herman & N. J. Hoare	
G-CKSP	PA-28-180 Cherokee Archer	Italian Wings ASD/Italy	
G-CKSR	Boeing Stearman D75N	C. R. Maher	
G-CKST	Boeing Stearman B75N1	T. W. Gilbert	

Notes	Reg	Type	Owner or Operator
	G-CKSU	Boeing Stearman A75N1	R. N. Lamb
	G-CKSV	Boeing Stearman A75	T. W. Gilbert
	G-CKSW	Cameron O-26 balloon	S. G. Whatley
	G-CKSX	Schleicher ASW-27-18E	E. Sparrow & S. Pozerskis
	G-CKSY	Rolladen-Schneider LS-7-WL	ICKSY Syndicate
	G-CKTA	Aerochute Hummerchute	G. Stokes
	G-CKTB	Schempp-Hirth Ventus 2cT	M. H. Player
	G-CKTC	Schleicher Ka 6CR	B. Brannigan
	G-CKTD	Colomban MC-30 Luciole	D. K. Lawry
	G-CKTE	Aeropro Eurofox 3K	R. J. Bird
	G-CKTF	Van's RV-6A	D. Bennett
	G-CKTG	Balony Kubicek BB26E balloon	Nova Balloon Service Ltd
	G-CKTJ	Lindstrand LTL Racer 65 balloon	A. M. Holly
	G-CKTK	Denney Kitfox Model 4-1200	Scotflight Aviation Ltd
	G-CKTL	Aerochute Hummerchute	R. D. Knight
	G-CKTM	Pitts S-1 Special	R. Farrer
	G-CKTN	BRM Aero Bristell NG5 Speed Wing	E. O. Ridley & T. H. Crow
	G-CKTP	Ultramagic M-90 balloon	Proximm SPA/Italy
	G-CKTS	Jodel D.9 Bebe	P. R. Harvey
	G-CKTT	P & M Quik GTR	M. K. Ashmore
	G-CKTU	Ultramagic M-90 balloon	Proximm SPA/Italy
	G-CKTV	Lindstrand LTL Series 1-105 balloon	A. M. Holly
	G-CKTW	Cameron O-31 balloon	M. & S. Mitchell
	G-CKTX	Van's RV-7	M. M. McElrea
	G-CKUB	Cessna 560XL Citation XLS+	Air Charter Scotland Ltd
	G-CKUH	CZAW Sportcruiser	I. C. Waddell
	G-CKUJ	ATEC 212 Solo	Mission Capital Ltd
	G-CKUK	Ultramagic Shemilt Eco 50 balloon	Thames Valley Balloons Ltd
	G-CKUL	Ace As-Tec 13	G. L. Logan
	G-CKUM	Swing XWing/Xcitor paratrike	D. Burton
	G-CKUN	Bareford DB-6R balloon	D. Bareford
	G-CKUO	Aeroprakt A22-LS Foxbat	P. Gosney
	G-CKUP	Cameron Z-77 balloon	Airship and Balloon Company Ltd
	G-CKUR	Skyranger Swift 912(1)	R. F. Pearce
	G-CKUS	Conway Viper	D. B. Conway
	G-CKUU	PA-23-250 Aztec	G. Scillieri
	G-CKUV	PA-34-220T Seneca V	Craigard Property Trading Ltd (G-VYND)
	G-CKUW	Colt 21A balloon	Airship and Balloon Company Ltd
	G-CKUX	Magic Laser	S. C. Stinchcombe
	G-CKUZ	Boeing 737-46J	West Atlantic UK Ltd
	G-CKVC	Rotorsport UK Cavalon	Blue Thunder Ltd
	G-CKVD	Rolladen-Schneider LS-1f	G. M. Spreckley
	G-CKVE	Aero 31 AM9 balloon	A. Marshall
	G-CKVF	Aeroprakt A22-LS Foxbat	R. J. Davey
	G-CKVG	Ikarus C42 FB80	GS Aviation (Europe) Ltd
	G-CKVI	Cameron A-120 balloon	B. J. Davies
	G-CKVJ	Titan T-51 Mustang	C. Firth
	G-CKVP	Rotorsport UK Calidus	P. M. Bidston
	G-CKVT	Schempp-Hirth Ventus 3T	S. G. Jones
	G-CKVV	PA-28-181 Cherokee Archer II	London Transport Flying Club Ltd
	G-CKVX	Breezer M400	M. W. Houghton
	G-CKVY	Aeropro Eurofox 2K	P. D. Sibbons
	G-CKVZ	Rotorsport UK Cavalon Pro	Autogyro GmbH
	G-CKWA	Boeing 787-9	Norwegian Air UK Ltd
	G-CKWB	Boeing 787-9	Norwegian Air UK Ltd
	G-CKWC	Boeing 787-9	Norwegian Air UK Ltd
	G-CKWD	Boeing 787-9	Norwegian Air UK Ltd
	G-CKWE	Boeing 787-9	Norwegian Air UK Ltd
	G-CKWF	Boeing 787-9	Norwegian Air UK Ltd
	G-CKWG	Spacek SD-1 Minisport	R. Y. Kendal
	G-CKWH	Cameron Ronald 105 balloon	L. Bingley & D. Bovington
	G-CKWI	Tecnam P92-JS Echo	Associazione Sportiva Aeronautica/Italy
	G-CKWJ	Lindstrand LBL-77A balloon	C. J. Sanger-Davies
	G-CKWL	Lindstrand LTL-130G gas balloon	Aeronauts Productions Ltd
	G-CKWM	Van's RV-8	C. A. G. Schofield
	G-CKWN	Boeing 787-9	Norwegian Air UK Ltd
	G-CKWO	Aeropro Eurofox 912(S)	G. J. Slater
	G-CKWP	Boeing 787-9	Norwegian Air UK Ltd
	G-CKWS	Boeing 787-9	Norwegian Air UK Ltd
	G-CKWT	Boeing 787-9	Norwegian Air UK Ltd
	G-CKWU	Boeing 787-9	Norwegian Air UK Ltd

Reg	Type	Owner or Operator	Notes
G-CKWW	Cameron Sport 50 balloon	Cameron Balloons Ltd	
G-CKWX	Ikarus C42 FB100	M. J. Slack	
G-CKWY	Cameron Z-90 balloon	Balloon Team Jos Seghler	
G-CKWZ	Grob G.109B	J. I. Staton	
G-CKXA	Cameron Sprt 90 balloon	S. Church	
G-CKXC	Best Off Skyranger Swift 912(1)	M. T. Dawson	
G-CKXD	PZL-Bielsko SZD-22C Mucha Standard	Eaglescott Mucha Group	
G-CKXE	Cameron Sport 90 balloon	K. D. Peirce	
G-CKXF	Auster J/5G Cirrus Autocar	R. B. Webber	
G-CKXG	Cameron C-70 balloon	J. T. Wilkinson	
G-CKXH	Ultramagic M-65C balloon	D. Bareford	
G-CKXI	Mooney M20E	G. C. Rogers	
G-CKXJ	Cessna F.172M	J. A. Kroger	
G-CKXK	Cameron C-90 balloon	P. Michiels	
G-CKXL	Sikorsky S-92A	Bristow Helicopters Ltd	
G-CKXM	Aeropro Eurofox 3K	J. A. Walker	
G-CKXP	Aerochute Hummerchute	G. Stokes	
G-CKXR	Lindstrand LTL Series 1-105 balloon	B. T. Harris	
G-CKXT	Balony Kubicek BB22 balloon	S. Venegoni	
G-CKXU	PA-28-181 Archer II	S. P. Adshead	
G-CKXV	PA-28-181 Archer III	S. P. Adshead	
G-CKXY	Boeing Stearman A75N1	T. W. Gilbert	
G-CKXZ	Team Himax 1700R	S. Richens	
G-CKYA	Autogyro MTOsport 2017	Rotorsport Sales & Service Ltd	
G-CKYB	Autogyro MTOsport 2017	Rotorsport Sales & Service Ltd	
G-CKYD	Autogyro MTOsport 2017	Rotorsport Sales & Service Ltd	
G-CKYF	Aeropro Eurofox 912(S)	Wolds Gliding Club Ltd	
G-CKYG	Aeropro Eurofox 3K	F. S. Ogden	
G-CKYI	DAR Solo 120	Aeroplanes DAR (Bulgaria) Group	
G-CKYJ	PA-28RT-201 Arrow IV	Altus Flying Group	
G-CKYL	Ikarus C42 FB80	L. M. Cox	
G-CKYM	VS.361 Spitfire LF.IX	M. A. Bennett	
G-CKYN	Colomban MC-15 Cri-Cri	M. Hajdukiewicz	
G-CKYO	Schempp-Hirth Ventus 3T	C. P. A. Jeffery	
G-CKYP	AgustaWestland AW139	Bristow Helicopters Ltd	
G-CKYS	P & M Quik GT450	P. G. Eastlake	
G-CKYT	Autogyro Davalon	A. Sinclair	
G-CKYU	Lindstrand LBL-31A balloon	G. B. Dey	
G-CKYX	Cameron O-31 balloon	W. Rousell & J. Tyrrell	
G-CKYZ	Eurofly Minifox	F. Kratky	
G-CKZA	TAF Sling 4	J. Smith	
G-CKZB	Spacek SD-1 Minisport	C. J. Lines	
G-CKZD	Aeropro Eurofox 3K	Breeze Aviation Services Ltd	
G-CKZE	Medway SLA80 Executive	The Light Aircraft Co.Ltd	
G-CKZF	P & M Quik GTR	J. M. & R. W. Thompson	
G-CKZG	Apco Cruiser 550/Parajet Explorer	G. B. N. Cardozo	
G-CKZH	Van's RV-12	M. Dutton	
G-CKZI	Techpro Merlin 100UK	F. Sayyah	
G-CKZJ	Kubicek BB26E balloon	M. R. Crossley	
G-CKZL	PA-28RT-201 Arrow IV	Magna Carta Aviation Ltd	
G-CKZM	Aerochute Hummerchute	G. J. Pemberton	
G-CKZP	TL2000UK Sting Carbon S4	F. Pilkington	
G-CKZR	Steen Skybolt	N. Musgrave	
G-CKZS	Lindstrand LTL TGB197T Gas balloon	Lindstrand Technologies Ltd	
G-CKZT	PA-28-235 Cherokee Pathfinder	Quickprinter Ltd	
G-CKZU	Air Creation Tanarg/Bionix 13	C. R. Buckle	
G-CKZX	Stoddard-Hamilton GlaStar	P. M. Harrison	
G-CKZY	HpH Glasflugel 304 ES Shark	M. M. Heslop	
G-CKZZ	Magni M.16C Tandem Trainer	O. L. B. Brooking	
G-CLAA	Boeing 747-446F	Cargologicair Ltd	
G-CLAC	PA-28-161 Warrior II	G-CLAC Group	
G-CLAD	Cameron V-90 balloon	Adeilad Cladding	
G-CLAI	Ikarus C42 FB100	R. S. O'Carroll	
G-CLAJ	Robin DR400-180R	Kent Gliding Club Ltd	
G-CLAK	TLAC Sherwood Scout	The Light Aircraft Company Ltd	
G-CLAL	Ikarus C42 FB100	C. I. Law	
G-CLAM	DAR Solo 120	Ferrari Flying Group	
G-CLAO	Van'sa RV-7	M. A. Carter	
G-CLAP	Cessna 152	Swiftair Maintenance Ltd	
G-CLAT	P & M Quik R	G-CLAT Syndicate	

Notes	Reg	Type	Owner or Operator
	G-CLAV	Shaw Europa	J. S. Russell & R. A. Gardiner
	G-CLAY	Bell 206B JetRanger 3	Tiger Properties (Kent) Ltd (G-DENN)
	G-CLAZ	Autogyro Cavalon	Detoney Ltd
	G-CLBA	Boeing 747-428ERF	Cargologicair Ltd
	G-CLBD	Cameron Z-120 balloon	M. E. Dunstan
	G-CLBG	Van's RV-7	T. Groves
	G-CLBH	Lindstrand LTL Series SS balloon	A. M. Holly
	G-CLBI	Extra EA.300/S	Airdisplays.com Ltd
	G-CLBJ	Cessna 172S	Atlantic Flight Training Ltd
	G-CLBK	Ultramagic H-77 balloon	M. A. Wrigglesworth
	G-CLBN	P & M QuikR	N. J. Lister
	G-CLBP	Lindstrand LTL Series 1-180 balloon	Spirit Operations Ltd
	G-CLBR	Parajet Explorer/Apco Cruiser 500	G. B. N. Cardozo
	G-CLBS	Flylight Foxtug	Cambridge Aerotow Club
	G-CLBT	BRM Bristell NG5 Speed Wing	C. W. Thompson
	G-CLBV	Aeriane P Swift	A. Nelson
	G-CLBX	Messerschmitt Bf.109E-4/7	C. T. Charleston
	G-CLBY	Robinson R44 II	Q. Griffiths
	G-CLBZ	Cessna FR.172J	E. Marinoni
	G-CLCA	Extra EA.300/LC	N. J. Wakefield
	G-CLCC	Cameron Sport-90 balloon	Cameron Balloons Ltd
	G-CLCD	Advance Iota Mk.4	S. Siddiqui
	G-CLCJ	T-6 Harvard 4M (EX490)	T. W. Gilbert
	G-CLCK	PA-28RT-201T Turbo Arrow IV	M. Ali
	G-CLCL	Van's RV-7	R. M. Powell
	G-CLCM	Lambert Mission M108	K. L. Shern, L. D. L. & V. Soutter
	G-CLCO	Groppo Trail Mk.2	C. M. Barnes
	G-CLCP	Bell 505 Jet Ranger X	D. M. Hunter
	G-CLCR	Cameron Z-90 balloon	A2Z Projects BVBA/Belgium
	G-CLCS	VS Spitfire HF.IX	Propshop Ltd
	G-CLCT	VS Spitfire F.Mk.XIVE	Propshop Ltd
	G-CLCU	Robinson R44 II	D. M. McGarrity
	G-CLCW	Zenair CH.701SP	C. W. Wilkins
	G-CLCZ	Ultramagic M-105 balloon	Kent Ballooning
	G-CLDA	Mission M108	D. R. & C.A. Ho
	G-CLDB	EV-97 Eurostar SL 912(1)	R. W. Thorpe
	G-CLDC	EV-97 Eurostar	P. Weston
	G-CLDD	PA-32R-300 Cherokee Lance	J. L. Mossman
	G-CLDE	Jabiru UL-450	E. Bentley
	G-CLDH	Pietenpol Air Camper	S. Eustace
	G-CLDI	Just SuperSTOL	Whitearrow Associates Ltd
	G-CLDJ	Lindstrand LTL Racer 60	R. D. Parry
	G-CLDK	PA-28-161 Warrior II	G-HIRE Ltd
	G-CLDL	Robin DR.400-180R	Lasham Gliding Society Ltd
	G-CLDM	Skyranger Swift 912(1)	Skyranger One LTD
	G-CLDN	Best Off Skyranger Swift 912(1)	A. R. Pluck
	G-CLDR	Raj Hamsa X'Air Hawk	D. R. Western & J. E. Merriman
	G-CLDT	Aeropro Eurofox 3K	J. R. Elcocks
	G-CLDV	Autogyro Cavalon	J. Harmon
	G-CLDW	Autogyro Calidus	I. Ingram
	G-CLDX	Boeing Stearman B75N1 Kaydet	T. W. Gilbert
	G-CLDY	Spacek SD-1 Minisport	J. R. Grundy
	G-CLDZ	Autogyro Calidus	Gyro Partnership
	G-CLEA	PA-28-161 Warrior II	Freedom Aviation Ltd
	G-CLEB	Cameron A-315 balloon	Attacama Holdings Pty Ltd
	G-CLEC	Cameron A-450LW balloon	Attacama Holdings Pty Ltd
	G-CLED	Cameron A-450LW balloon	Attacama Holdings Pty Ltd
	G-CLEH	Aeroprakt A-32 Vixxen	C. A. Pollard
	G-CLEE	Rans S.6-ES Coyote II	P. S. Chapman
	G-CLEI	Eurofox 2K	R. M. Cornwell
	G-CLEL	Raj Hamsa X'Air 582(11)	D. A. Karniewicz
	G-CLEM	Bölkow Bö.208A2 Junior	G-CLEM Group (G-ASWE)
	G-CLEN	Boeing Stearman A.75N1 Kaydet	T. W. Gilbert
	G-CLEO	Zenair CH.601HD	K. M. Bowen
	G-CLER	Flylight Foxcub	M. P. Wimsey
	G-CLES	Scheicher ASW-27-18E	A. P. Brown
	G-CLEU	Glaser-Dirks DG-200	D. T. Freeman
	G-CLEV	Ikarus C42 FB80	A. R. Hughes
	G-CLEW	P & M QuikR	A. Atkin
	G-CLEX	Flylight Dragon/Grif HX11	C. J. Johnson
	G-CLEY	Skyranger Nynja 912S(1)	Exodus Airsports Ltd

Reg	Type	Owner or Operator	Notes
G-CLEZ	Robinson R44 I	V. Nash	
G-CLFA	TL200UK Sting Carbon S4	D. Durrans	
G-CLFB	Rolladen-Schneider LS4-A	K2 Syndicate	
G-CLFC	Mainair Blade	T. L. Aydon	
G-CLFD	Brandli BX-2 Cherry	R. H. Rawles	
G-CLFE	Murphy Renegade Spirit UK	K. Thomas	
G-CLFF	Cameron Z-42	P. Lesser	
G-CLFG	TL3000 Sirius	R. E. Scott	
G-CLFH	Schleicher ASW-20C	P. Armstrong	
G-CLFI	Messerschmitt Bf.109G-2	Fighter Aviation Engineering Ltd	
G-CLFJ	P & M Quik GTR	Flying for Freedom Ltd	
G-CLFK	Aeropro Eurofox 912(S)	D. W. , A. & J. Murcott	
G-CLFL	Kubicek BB-S/Mascot	M. J. Axtell	
G-CLFM	Glasair GlaStar Sportsman	J. Edgeworth	
G-CLFN	Messerschmitt Bf.109F-4	Fighter Aviation Engineering Ltd	
G-CLFO	Eurofly Snake/Grif 3DC	J. E. Orbell	
G-CLFU	Messerschmitt Bf.109F-4/Z	Fighter Aviation Engineering Ltd	
G-CLFX	Schempp-Hirth Duo Discus T	M. G. Lynes & S. Holland	
G-CLFY	PA-28-181 Archer II	G-CLFY Group	
G-CLFZ	Schleicher ASW-18E	C. F. Cownden & J. P. Davies	
G-CLGB	Ultramagic M-77 balloon	British Telecommunications PLC	
G-CLGC	Schempp-Hirth Duo Discus	London Gliding Club Proprietary Ltd	
G-CLGD	Aeroprakt A-32 Vixxen	M. A. Lomas	
G-CLGE	Tri-R KIS	A. E. F. Bryant (G-MANW)	
G-CLGF	Sikorsky S-92A	Bristow Helicopters Ltd	
G-CLGG	AutoGyro Cavalon	Clifton Cruisers Ltd	
G-CLGI	Stoddard-Hamilton Glastar	J. L. Bone	
G-CLGJ	Cameron O-120 balloon	D. van Avermaet/Belgium	
G-CLGK	Ultramagic M-105 balloon	S. J. Thomas	
G-CLGL	Schempp-Hirth Ventus 2c	S. C. Williams	
G-CLGO	Westland SA.341C Gazelle HT.Mk.2	The Gazelle Squadron Display Team Ltd	
G-CLGP	Ultramagic B-70 balloon	D. Baker	
G-CLGR	Glasflugel Club Libelle 205	LGR Libelle Group	
G-CLGS	Supermarine 361 Spitfire LF.IX (MJ755)	The Icarus Foundation	
G-CLGT	Rolladen-Schneider LS4	N. M. Hill & L. Laks	
G-CLGU	Schleicher ASW-27-18	T. J. Scott	
G-CLGV	Cameron Z-160 balloon	Atlantic Ballooning BVBA/Belgium	
G-CLGW	Centrair 101A Pegase	M. White	
G-CLGX	Sackville BM-56 balloon	N. A. Carr	
G-CLGY	Ultramagic H-31 balloon	D. K. Hempleman-Adams	
G-CLGZ	Schempp-Hirth Duo Discus T	P. Dolan	
G-CLHF	Scheibe Bergfalke IV	Andreas Gliding Club Ltd	
G-CLHG	Schempp-Hirth Discus b	S. J. Edinborough	
G-CLHH	Kavanagh EX-60 balloon	Balloon Aloft	
G-CLHI	Aeropro Eurofox 3K	T. R. Southall	
G-CLHJ	Supermarine Spitfire Mk.26B	Molly Rose Group	
G-CLHK	Fokker DVI replica	A. J. Gibson	
G-CLHL	Boeing Stearman B75N1 Kaydet	T. W. Gilbert	
G-CLHM	Flylight Fox Cub	W. D. Foster	
G-CLHN	Cessna F.150M	Henlow Aviation Ltd	
G-CLHO	Westland SA.341D Gazelle HT.Mk.3	The Gazelle Squadron Display Team Ltd	
G-CLHP	Flylight Peabee	A. J. Morrell	
G-CLHR	BN-2B-26 Islander	Britten-Norman Aircraft Ltd	
G-CLHS	Ultramagic M-65C balloon	D. Bareford	
G-CLHT	Flylight Peabee Red Line	G. W. Cameron	
G-CLHU	Alisport Silent IN	P. M. Yeoman	
G-CLHV	Cameron Z-105 balloon	The Belmont Estate (Farm) Ltd	
G-CLHW	Sikorsky S-92A	Bristow Helicopters Ltd	
G-CLHY	Miles M.14A Hawk Trainer 3	RAF Station Czechoslovakia SRO/Czech Republic	
G-CLHZ	Europa XS	M. E. Henwick	
G-CLIA	Grob G.109	J. Callaghan & A. Fontwell	
G-CLIB	Cameron O-31 balloon	J. D. Smith	
G-CLIC	Cameron A-105 balloon	M. Arno	
G-CLID	Best Off Skyranger Nynja LS 912S(1)	D. Street	
G-CLIE	Lindstrand LTL Series 1-450	Lindstrand Technologies Ltd	
G-CLIF	Ikarus C42 FB UK	E. R. Sims	
G-CLIG	Cameron Z-105 balloon	M. Cintio	
G-CLIH	Supermarine 300 Spitfire 1	G. F. T. Van Eerd	
G-CLIJ	Schleicher Ka 6E	G. N. Smith	
G-CLIL	Lindstrand LTL Series 1-120 balloon	Spirit Operations Ltd	

Notes	Reg	Type	Owner or Operator
	G-CLIM	Hoffman H.36 Dimona	The Northumbria Gliding Club Ltd
	G-CLIN	Ikarus C42 FB100	J. O'Halloran
	G-CLIO	Robinson R44	ECU Flash Ltd
	G-CLIR	Aero Adventure Aventura UL	Ulster Seaplane Association Ltd
	G-CLIS	Medway Rumour	M. Ingleton
	G-CLIW	Cessna 208B Grand Caravan	Windglider Ltd
	G-CLIX	Aviat A-1B Husky	C. H. M. Brown
	G-CLIZ	Van's RV-8	M. S. Pettit & R. D. Morcom
	G-CLJA	Ikarus C42 FB80	Skyranger One Ltd
	G-CLJB	Eurofly Snake/Grif HX11	A. Brown
	G-CLJC	Scottish Aviation Bulldog Srs.120/121	Excelis Ltd
	G-CLJD	Scottish Aviation Bulldog Srs.120/121	Excelis Ltd
	G-CLJE	Schleicher ASH-25M	Juliet Echo Syndicate
	G-CLJI	Super Marine Spitfire Mk.26	M. R. Love & P. Wilding
	G-CLJL	Kubicek BB22Z	A. G. A. Barclay-Faulkner
	G-CLJM	Cessna F.172G	G. Buso
	G-CLJN	Boeing 787-9	Norwegian Air UK
	G-CLJO	Cameron O-105 balloon	L. Dalberto
	G-CLJP	Cessna F.172G	C. Marti
	G-CLJR	Robinson R44 II	HQ Aviation Ltd
	G-CLJS	PA-32R-301T Turbo Sarastoga SP	Paul's Planes Ltd
	G-CLJT	Sackville BM-56 LW balloon	T. J. Wilkinson
	G-CLJU	Wassmer WA.40 Super IV	A. P. Sellars
	G-CLJV	Balony Kubicek BB30Z	Loogo SRLS/Italy
	G-CLJW	BAC Jet Provost T.Mk.5A	M. F. Edwards
	G-CLJX	UTVA U-66	Blackstone Aviation
	G-CLJY	Tecnam P2002-JF Sierra	E. J. Lamb
	G-CLJZ	Schleicher ASH-31Mi	J. C. Thompson
	G-CLKA	Diamond DA.42 Twin Star	Atlantic Flight Training Ltd
	G-CLKB	Cessna 172N	S. P. Vincent
	G-CLKC	Cameron O-31 balloon	S. J. Roake
	G-CLKD	Cameron Z-105 balloon	M. Lokeren
	G-CLKF	Schempp-Hirth Cirrus VTC	G. D. Ackroyd
	G-CLKG	Schempp-Hirth Janus CM	Lakes Janus Group
	G-CLKH	Pietenpol Air Camper	K. Redfearn
	G-CLKJ	Aurore MB.02 Souricette	A. R. Hawes
	G-CLKK	Schleicher ASH-31 Mi	Zulu Glasstek Ltd
	G-CLKL	Robinson R44	Whitearrow Associates Ltd
	G-CLKM	Taylor JT.2 Titch	A. S. Wyatt
	G-CLKN	Super Marine Spitfire Mk.26	I. V. Staines
	G-CLKR	ICA-Brasov IS-28M2A	M. J. Lane
	G-CLKT	Mead BM-77 balloon	C. Timbrell
	G-CLKU	Schleicher Ka 6E	K. Richards
	G-CLKV	Bucker Bu.131 Jungmann	N. Barnard
	G-CLKW	Sikorsky S-92A	Macquarie Rotorcraft Leasing Holding Ltd
	G-CLKX	DHC-1 Chipmunk 22	M. Harvey
	G-CLKY	Lambert Mission M108	M. A. Wood
	G-CLLA	Best Off Skyranger Swift 912(1)	P. M. Dewhurst
	G-CLLB	Schempp-Hirth Discus 2cT	R. A.Vaughan
	G-CLLC	HpH Glasflugel 304 Shark	F16 Group
	G-CLLD	Robin DR.400RP	C. J. O. Fox
	G-CLLE	Schleicher ASG 32 Mi	O. J. Walters
	G-CLLF	Flylight Peabee Red Line	D. S. Walsh
	G-CLLG	Spacek SD-1 Minisport	G. A. Squires
	G-CLLH	HpH Glasflugel 304 Shark	J. Haigh
	G-CLLI	DHC.1 Chipmunk 22	J. & R. Pike & S. Woodgate
	G-CLLJ	Enstrom 480B	D. J. Golding
	G-CLLK	Avions Max Holste MH 1521	J. M. B. Prior
	G-CLLL	Schleicher ASW-27-18E	I. P. Hick
	G-CLLM	Cameron Sport-90 balloon	P. Detemmerman
	G-CLLN	Pietenpol Air Camper	D. Scott
	G-CLLO	Bristell NG5 Speed Wing	O. D. Horvath
	G-CLLP	Agusta Westland AW.139	Wilmington Trust SP Services (Dublin) Ltd
	G-CLLR	PA-28-140 Cherokee	G-HIRE Ltd
	G-CLLS	Sackville BM-56 balloon	T. J. Wilkinson
	G-CLLT	Grob G.102 Standard Astir II	Staffordshire Gliding Club Ltd
	G-CLLU	Ultra-UAS	University of Southampton
	G-CLLV	Schleicher ASW-28-18E	R. D. Payne
	G-CLLW	Boeing A75N1 Stearman	T. W. Gilbert
	G-CLLX	Schempp-Hirth Duo Discus T	J. F. Paterson
	G-CLLY	Rolladen-Schneider LS6-C18	P. W. Brown

Reg	Type	Owner or Operator	Notes
G-CLMA	Van's RV-12	M. Wilkinson	
G-CLMB	Schempp-Hirth Discus-2c FES	A. E. & G. J. Hoile	
G-CLMC	Isaacs Spitfire	R. C. Teverson	
G-CLMD	AB Sportine Aviacija LAK-17B FES	R. C. Bromwich	
G-CLME	Schempp-Hirth Ventus 2cT	J. H. May	
G-CLMF	Glaser-Dirks DG-200	I. Godding	
G-CLMG	Alisport Silent-IN	O. J. Anderson	
G-CLMH	Pipistrel Alpha BCAR-S 164	Micro Leasing Ltd	
G-CLMI	Pipistrel Alpha BCAR-S 164	Golden Wings Aviation Ltd	
G-CLMK	Cessna 172S	Atlantic Flight Training Ltd	
G-CLMM	Cameron Sport-70 balloon	Cameron Balloons Ltd	
G-CLMN	Griffin RG56	R. G. Griffin	
G-CLMO	Schleicher ASW-28-18E	B. Bobrovnikov	
G-CLMR	EV-97 Eurostar	C. M. James	
G-CLMS	Sackville BM-56 balloon	T. J. Wilkinson	
G-CLMT	DHC.8-402Q Dash Eight	EIC Aircraft Leasing Ltd	
G-CLMU	Schleicher Ka.6BR	N. J. Pusey	
G-CLMV	Glasflugel 304 SJ Shark	G. J. Bowser	
G-CLMW	Lambert Mission M108	D. W. Collins	
G-CLMX	Cessna 172S	Atlantic Flight Training Ltd	
G-CLMY	Glaser-Dirks DG-300	LMY Glider Syndicate	
G-CLMZ	Fairchild 24W-41A	A. C. Whitehead	
G-CLNA	Cessna 152	Brinkley Aviation Ltd	
G-CLNB	Cessna 152	Brinkley Aviation Ltd	
G-CLNC	Cessna 152	Brinkley Aviation Ltd	
G-CLND	Airdrome Dream Classic	G. F. M. Garner	
G-CLNF	Airbus EC135 T3	Vertical Aviation No.2 Ltd	
G-CLNG	Schleicher ASW-27-18	G-CLNG Flying Group	
G-CLNH	Sikorsky S-92A	Wilmington Trust SP Services (Dublin) Ltd	
G-CLNI	DHC.1 Chipmunk 22A (WK608)	Fly Navy Heritage Trust Ltd	
G-CLNJ	Hawker Sea Fury FB.Mk.11 (VR930)	Fly Navy Heritage Trust Ltd	
G-CLNK	Avions Transport ATR-72-211F	West Atlantic UK Ltd	
G-CLNN	Best Off Skyranger Swift 912(1)	C. J. Tomlin	
G-CLNO	KFA Safari	Sprite Aviation Services Ltd	
G-CLNP	Stolp SA.500 Starlet	B. J. Towers	
G-CLNS	Sackville BM-56 balloon	T. J. Wilkinson	
G-CLNU	Bucker Bu181 Bestmann	P. S. Watts	
G-CLNV	North American P-51D Mustang	Fighter Aviation Engineering Ltd (G-MSTG)	
G-CLNW	Best Off Skyranger Swift 912S(1)	G-CLNW Group	
G-CLNX	Balony Kubicek BB18E balloon	Nova Balloon Services Ltd	
G-CLNY	Balony Kubicek BB26Z balloon	Yorkshire Balloon Flights Ltd	
G-CLNZ	Sherwood Ranger ST	P. Nicholls	
G-CLOA	Best BlueTwo	A. J. Best	
G-CLOB	Pietenpol Air Camper	J. A. Northen	
G-CLOC	Schleicher ASK-13	J. V. Edge	
G-CLOF	Kubicek BB22	P. Salomone	
G-CLOG	Schleicher ASW-27-18E	R. E. D. Bailey	
G-CLOH	Greatrix O-56 balloon	J. C. M. Greatrx	
G-CLOI	Best Off Skyranger Nynja	D. M. Lonnen	
G-CLOJ	Greatrix O-90 balloon	J. C. M. Greatrx	
G-CLOK	Ultramagic B-60 balloon	E. C. Meek	
G-CLOL	Schleicher ASK-21	Lasham Gliding Society Ltd	
G-CLOM	Greatrix O-105 balloon	J. C. M. Greatrx	
G-CLON	HPH Glasflugel 304S Shark	P. D. Ruskin	
G-CLOO	Grob G.103 Twin Astir	R. G. J. Tait	
G-CLOR	Gyro-Lite Micro-Gyrocopter	Condor Aviation International Ltd	
G-CLOS	PA-34-200 Seneca II	R. A. Doherty	
G-CLOU	Best Off Skyranger Nynja	Flylight Airsports Ltd	
G-CLOV	Schleicher ASK-21	Scottish Gliding Union Ltd	
G-CLOX	Ultramagic B-26 balloon	E. C. Meek	
G-CLOY	Squadron SE5 (F5621/K)	J. M. Blackiston	
G-CLOZ	KFA Explorer	P. Marsden	
G-CLPA	Flylight BivvyBee	P. Batterton	
G-CLPB	Rolladen-Schneider LS6c-18W	C. J. Harrison	
G-CLPC	Cameron Sport-70 balloon	M. J. Woodcock	
G-CLPD	Cameron Sport-50 balloon	Gone with the Wind Ltd	
G-CLPE	Schempp-Hirth Discus bT	R. A. Braithwaite	
G-CLPG	Agusta Westland AW139	Sloane Helicopters Ltd	
G-CLPI	Sikorsky S-92A	Wilmington Trust SP Services (Dublin) Ltd	
G-CLPJ	Sikorsky S-92A	Wilmington Trust SP Services (Dublin) Ltd	
G-CLPK	Cessna 172S	Atlantic Flight Training Ltd	

Notes	Reg	Type	Owner or Operator
	G-CLPL	Rolladen-Schneider LS7-WL	W. M. Davies
	G-CLPM	Robin DR400/180S	M. A. Pettican & D. M. Hook
	G-CLPN	Replica Nieuport 11	R. A. H. Vary
	G-CLPP	Van's RV-7	J. P. Chaplin
	G-CLPS	Best Off Skyranger Nynja	Wanafly Airsports Ltd
	G-CLPT	Ikarus C42 FB100	The Light Aircraft Company Ltd
	G-CLPU	Schleicher ASW-27-18E	A. R. J. Hughes
	G-CLPV	Schleicher ASK-21	Portsmouth Naval Gliding Centre
	G-CLPW	Camewron O-31 balloon	C. R. Rawson
	G-CLPX	Grob G.103C Twin III Acro	The Windrushers Gliding Club Ltd
	G-CLPY	Van's RV-7	A. Spencer
	G-CLPZ	Jonker JS-MD Single	Bailey Aviation
	G-CLRA	Schleicher ASW-27-18E	C. A. Hunt & C. P. J. Gibson
	G-CLRB	Sonex Onex	Condor Aviation International Ltd
	G-CLRC	Schleicher ASW-27-18E	W. R. Tandy
	G-CLRD	PZL-Bielsko SZD-51-1 Junior	Devon & Somerset Gliding Club Ltd
	G-CLRF	Schleicher ASW-27-18E	C. G. Starkey
	G-CLRG	North American P-51D-5-NA Mustang	Air Leasing Ltd
	G-CLRH	HPH Glasflugel 304S Shark	The Shark Group
	G-CLRI	Zenair CH.750 Cruzer	J. Evans
	G-CLRJ	Schempp-Hirth Discus bT	M. S. Smith
	G-CLRK	Sky 77-24 balloon	William Clark & Son (Parkgate) Ltd
	G-CLRM	Best Off Skyranger Swift 912S(1)	R. A., R. S. & S. Mott
	G-CLRN	Glaser-Dirks DG-100G Elan	DG100 Group
	G-CLRO	Glaser-Dirks DG-300 Elan	P. E. Kerman
	G-CLRP	Schempp-Hirth Janus B	S. M. Grant & W. I. H. Hall
	G-CLRR	Zenair CH.750 Cruzer	Nuncats CIC
	G-CLRS	Schleicher ASW-27-18E	G-CLRS Flying Group
	G-CLRT	Schleicher ASK-21	Cotswold Gliding Club
	G-CLRU	Aeriane Swift Light E	W. True
	G-CLRW	PA-28R-201 Arrow III	Midlands Aviation Ltd
	G-CLRX	Sikorsky S-92A	CHC Scotia Ltd
	G-CLRY	Rolladen Schneider LS4	S. O. Boye
	G-CLRZ	Rolladen-Schneider LS-1f	C. B. Hill
	G-CLSA	Westland SA.341B Gazellew AH.Mk.1	S. Atherton
	G-CLSC	EV-97 Sportstar SLM	Sportstar Aviation
	G-CLSF	Van's RV-12	R. J. Dawson
	G-CLSG	Rolladen-Schneider LS4-b	C. Marriott & C. Taunton
	G-CLSH	Schleicher ASK-21	Lasham Gliding Society Ltd
	G-CLSJ	HPH Glasflugel 304S Shark	C. M. Lewis
	G-CLSK	Flylight BivvyBee	M. Warren
	G-CLSL	Glaser-Dirks DG-500 Elan Trainer	Needwood Forest Soaring Gliding Ltd
	G-CLSM	DH.85 Leopard Moth ('G-AUSM')	D. C. Reid
	G-CLSO	Schempp-Hirth Nimbus 3T	R. S. Rose
	G-CLSP	SAAB 91B Safir	N. C. Stone
	G-CLSR	Grob G103 Twin Astir	The Nene Valley Gliding Club Ltd
	G-CLSS	Schempp-Hirth Arcus T	Sixty-Six Group
	G-CLST	Cessna U.206F Stationair	CG Aviation Ltd
	G-CLSV	Flylight Dragon/Aeros Fox 13T	J. R. Kendall
	G-CLSW	Schleicher ASW-20BL	A. Docherty
	G-CLSY	Schempp-Hirth SHK-1	J. R. Stiles
	G-CLSZ	DG Flugzeugbau DG-800B	M. Roberts
	G-CLTA	HpH Glasflugel 304ES	R. R. Bryan
	G-CLTC	Schempp-Hirth Janus CE	C. A. Willson & P. J. D. Smith
	G-CLTD	Schleicher K.8B	G. D. Western
	G-CLTE	Magni M24C Plus	C. Wakerley & D. Bevan
	G-CLTF	Schempp-Hirth Discus a	L. Runhaar
	G-CLTG	Glaser-Dirks DG-100	T. Pearson
	G-CLTJ	Sportine Aviacija LAK-17B FES	J. T. Newbery
	G-CLTL	Schleicher ASW-19B	J. P. Salt
	G-CLTO	Schleicher ASW-27-18E	J. Pack
	G-CLTP	Rolladen-Schneider LS3-17	D. J. Blackman
	G-CLTS	Schempp-Hirth Arcus T	A. & G. S. J. Bambrook
	G-CLTW	Glasflugel 304ES	S. Murdoch & A. Holswilder
	G-CLTX	Sportine Aviacija LAK-17B FES Mini	D. R. Bennett
	G-CLTY	Fisher 404XP	Balbert's Flying Circus
	G-CLTZ	Textron 3000 Texan II	Ministry of Defence
	G-CLUA	Textron 3000 Texan II	Ministry of Defence
	G-CLUC	Textron 3000 Texan II	Ministry of Defence
	G-CLUD	Grob G.102 Club Astir IIIB	Lasham Gliding Society Ltd
	G-CLUE	PA-34-200T Seneca II	P. Wilkinson

Reg	Type	Owner or Operator	Notes
G-CLUF	Textron 3000 Texan II	Ministry of Defence	
G-CLUG	Schleicher K.8B	The Nene Valley Gliding Club Ltd	
G-CLUH	PA-28-180 Cherokee Archer	G. Y. Phillips	
G-CLUI	Bristell NG5 Classic HD	J. C. Simpson	
G-CLUJ	Sportine Aviacija LAK-17B FES Mini	R. Emms & J. I. B. Bennett	
G-CLUK	Schleicher ASK-23B	London Gliding Club Proprietary Ltd	
G-CLUL	Airbus MBB BK117 D-2	Airbus Helicopters UK Ltd	
G-CLUM	Sackville BM-56 balloon	A. E. Austin	
G-CLUN	Vans RV-3B	J. A. Harris	
G-CLUP	Schleicher ASH-25	A. K. Laylee & G. G. Dale	
G-CLUU	Ultramagic H-65 balloon	A. G. A. Barclay-Faulkner	
G-CLUV	Schleicher ASK-23B	Midland Gliding Club Ltd	
G-CLUX	Cessna F.172N	E. J. O'Rafferty	
G-CLUY	Ultramagic M-145 balloon	C. W. Wood	
G-CLUZ	Schempp-Hirth Discus 2c FES	G-CLUZ Group	
G-CLVA	Rolladen-Scneider LS3-a	J. Franke	
G-CLVB	Cessna 172R	Chalrey Ltd	
G-CLVD	Schempp-Hirth Discus 2c FES	C. K. Davis, M. B. Margetson & P. R. Wilson	
G-CLVF	Flylight BivvyBee	Flylight Airsports Ltd	
G-CLVH	Embraer ERJ170-200 STD	Drake Jet Leasing 3 DAC	
G-CLVI	Glasair Sportsman	Amanda Investments Ltd	
G-CLVJ	DG Flugzeugbau DG-505 Elan Orion	Coventry Gliding Club Ltd	
G-CLVK	Embraer ERJ170-200 STD	Drake Jet Leasing 3 DAC	
G-CLVL	Schempp-Hirth Arcus T	G-CLVL Syndicate	
G-CLVM	Schleicher ASK-21	York Gliding Centre (Operations) Ltd	
G-CLVN	Embraer ERJ170-200 STD	Drake Jet Leasing 3 DAC	
G-CLVO	SZD-54-2 Perkoz	Deesside Gliding Club (Aberdeenshire) Ltd	
G-CLVP	PZL-Bielsko SZD-42-2 Jantar 2B	J2B Flying Group	
G-CLVR	Best Off Skyranger Nynja LS 912S(1)	M. D. Wheeler	
G-CLVS	HpH Glasflugel 304 ES Shark	R. G. Corbin & S. E. Buckley	
G-CLVT	Embraer ERJ170-200 STD	Drake Jet Leasing 3 DAC	
G-CLVU	Schleicher ASK-21	Stratford on Avon Gliding Club Ltd	
G-CLVW	Rolladen-Schneider LS4-a	C. Edkins	
G-CLWA	Schleicher LS8-a	M. D. A. Brown	
G-CLWB	PA-28-161 Cherokee Warrior III	Brighton Aviation Ltd	
G-CLWC	PZL SZD-54-2 Perkoz	Essex and Suffolk Gliding Club Ltd	
G-CLWG	Albatross QuikR	G-CLWG Syndicate	
G-CLWH	Zlin Z.381	P. S. Watts	
G-CLWI	Welsh W-1	F. P. Welsh	
G-CLWJ	Schleicher ASW-27-18E	P. Johnson	
G-CLWK	DHC-1 Chipmunk 22	Historic Aircraft Flight Trust	
G-CLWK	DHC-1 Chipmunk 22	Historic Aircraft Flight Trust	
G-CLWL	Schempp-Hirth Discus BT	N. H. Wal	
G-CLWM	Schempp-Hirth Ventus 3T	W. J. Murray	
G-CLWN	Cameron Clown SS balloon	Magical Adventures Ltd (G-UBBE)	
G-CLWO	Pipistrel Virus SW 121	Fly About Aviation Ltd	
G-CLWP	Sportine Aviacija LAK-17B FES	J. A. Thomson	
G-CLWR	Rolladen-Schneider LS8-a	M. D. A. Brown	
G-CLWS	Airbus EC130 T2	Airbus Helicopters	
G-CLWT	TLAC Sherwood Scout	Kingsmuir Group	
G-CLWU	Boeing D75N1 Stearman	T. W. Gilbert	
G-CLWV	Boeing E75N1 Stearman	T. W. Gilbert	
G-CLWW	Pipistrel Virus AW 121	Fly About Aviation Ltd	
G-CLWX	Robinson R66	Eastern Atlantic Helicopters Ltd	
G-CLWZ	Schempp-Hirth Ventus-2c	M. J. & T. J. Webb	
G-CLXA	Agusta Westland AW119 Mk.II	Helicom SRL	
G-CLXC	DHC.8-402 Dash Eight	Thyme Opco Ltd	
G-CLXD	DHC.1 Chipmunk 22	M. Harvey	
G-CLXF	Flylight Foxcub	B. Skelding	
G-CLXG	Lange E1 Antares	J. A. Inglis	
G-CLXH	Grob G.103C Twin III Acro	The Windrushers Gliding Club Ltd	
G-CLXI	Airbus Helicopters EC130 T2	Airbus Helicopters	
G-CLXJ	Ace Aviation AS-TEC 13	D. J. T. Reckitt	
G-CLXK	Hoffmann H36 Dimona	Suffolk Soaring Group	
G-CLXL	Shawtrike Paramotor	G. B. Shaw	
G-CLXN	Schempp-Hirth Ventus-3T	R. J. Nicholls	
G-CLXO	Schempp-Hirth Ventus-3M	J. P. Galloway	
G-CLXV	PZL-Bielsko SZD-51-1	East Sussex Gliding Club Ltd	
G-CLXW	Schempp-Hirth Ventus-3T	J. S. McCullagh	
G-CLYC	M & D Flugzeugbau JS-MD Single	R. A. Cheetham	
G-CLYE	Rolladen-Schneider LS4A	Deesside Gliding Club (Aberdeenshire) Ltd	

Notes	Reg	Type	Owner or Operator
	G-CLYF	Schleicher ASW-27-18E	P. L. Turner
	G-CLYG	Van's RV-14A	J. C. & E. Woolard
	G-CLYH	Van's RV-12	M. L. Thorne
	G-CLYL	PZL SZD-51-1	Cambridge Gliding Club Ltd
	G-CLYM	Schleicher AS-33 Es	P. J. O'Connell & M. C. Foreman
	G-CLYO	Schleicher AS-33 Es	J. E. Gatfield
	G-CLYT	Pipistrel Alpha BCAR-S 164	Fly About Aviation Ltd
	G-CLYX	Rotorsport UK MTOSport 2017	Autogyro GmbH/Germany
	G-CLYY	Dyn'Aero MCR-01 VLA Sportster	P. G. Leonard
	G-CLZA	Zenair CH.601HDS Zodiac	S. Foreman
	G-CLZB	Schleicher ASK-21B	Coventry Gliding Club Ltd
	G-CLZD	Offpiste Discovery Tandem 210	J. Soper
	G-CLZF	Centrair 101D Pegase	T. Skorzewski
	G-CLZG	Schempp-Hirth Ventus 3T	G. R. Glazebrook
	G-CLZH	Schempp-Hirth Discus bT	A. H. Brown
	G-CLZK	Schempp-Hirth Ventus 3M	D. Latimer
	G-CLZM	Eurofly Snake/Grif Zip	M. A. Fay
	G-CLZO	Evektor Sportstar	Lukesfield Aero Services Ltd
	G-CLZT	Aero 31 AM9 balloon	R. J. Clements
	G-CLZV	Rotorsport UK Cavalon	C. G. Gilbert
	G-CLZZ	Magni M24C Plus	C. R. Lear
	G-CMAP	Van's RV-7	N. G. Goodacre
	G-CMAX	Eurofox 2K	Ascent Industries Ltd
	G-CMBC	Cessna 550 Citation Bravo	Bond Business Services Ltd (G-CGEI0
	G-CMCL	Agusta Westland AW169	Bradbury Estates LLP
	G-CMDG	P & M Quik R	C. Fender
	G-CMDM	Van's RV-9	D. S. Murrell
	G-CMDO	Westland Sea King HC.Mk.4	A. D, Whitehouse
	G-CMEW	Aerospool Dynamic WT9 UK	M. W. Frost
	G-CMGD	Grob G109B	Aerobility Holdings CIC
	G-CMGE	Grob G109B	Aerobility Holdings CIC
	G-CGMF	Grob G109B	Aerobility Holdings CIC
	G-CMGG	Grob G109B	Aerobility Holdings CIC
	G-CMGH	Grob G109B	Aerobility Holdings CIC
	G-CMGI	Grob G109B	Aerobility Holdings CIC
	G-CMGJ	Grob G109B	Aerobility Holdings CIC
	G-CMGK	Grob G109B	Aerobility Holdings CIC
	G-CMGL	Grob G109B	Aerobility Holdings CIC
	G-CMGM	Grob G109B	Aerobility Holdings CIC
	G-CMGN	Grob G109B	Aerobility Holdings CIC
	G-CMGO	Grob G109B	Aerobility Holdings CIC
	G-CMGP	Grob G109B	Aerobility Holdings CIC
	G-CMGR	Grob G109B	Aerobility Holdings CIC
	G-CMGS	Grob G109B	Aerobility Holdings CIC
	G-CMGT	Grob G109B	Aerobility Holdings CIC
	G-CMGU	Grob G109B	Aerobility Holdings CIC
	G-CMGV	Grob G109B	Aerobility Holdings CIC
	G-CMGW	Grob G109B	Aerobility Holdings CIC
	G-CMGX	Grob G109B	Aerobility Holdings CIC
	G-CMGY	Grob G109B	Aerobility Holdings CIC
	G-CMGZ	Grob G109B	Aerobility Holdings CIC
	G-CMHA	Grob G109B	Aerobility Holdings CIC
	G-CMHB	Grob G109B	Aerobility Holdings CIC
	G-CMHC	Grob G109B	Aerobility Holdings CIC
	G-CMHD	Grob G109B	Aerobility Holdings CIC
	G-CMHE	Grob G109B	Aerobility Holdings CIC
	G-CMHF	Grob G109B	Aerobility Holdings CIC
	G-CMHG	Grob G109B	Aerobility Holdings CIC
	G-CMHH	Grob G109B	Aerobility Holdings CIC
	G-CMHI	Grob G109B	Aerobility Holdings CIC
	G-CMHJ	Grob G109B	Aerobility Holdings CIC
	G-CMHK	Grob G109B	Aerobility Holdings CIC
	G-CMHL	Grob G109B	Aerobility Holdings CIC
	G-CMHM	Grob G109B	Aerobility Holdings CIC
	G-CMHN	Grob G109B	Aerobility Holdings CIC
	G-CMHO	Grob G109B	Aerobility Holdings CIC
	G-CMHP	Grob G109B	Aerobility Holdings CIC
	G-CMHR	Grob G109B	Aerobility Holdings CIC
	G-CMHS	Grob G109B	Aerobility Holdings CIC
	G-CMHT	Grob G109B	Aerobility Holdings CIC

Reg	Type	Owner or Operator	Notes
G-CMHU	Grob G109B	Aerobility Holdings CIC	
G-CMHV	Grob G109B	Aerobility Holdings CIC	
G-CMHW	Grob G109B	Aerobility Holdings CIC	
G-CMHX	Grob G109B	Aerobility Holdings CIC	
G-CMHY	Grob G109B	Aerobility Holdings CIC	
G-CMHZ	Grob G109B	Aerobility Holdings CIC	
G-CMIA	Grob G109B	Aerobility Holdings CIC	
G-CMIB	Grob G109B	Aerobility Holdings CIC	
G-CMIC	Grob G109B	Aerobility Holdings CIC	
G-CMID	Grob G109B	Aerobility Holdings CIC	
G-CMIE	Grob G109B	Aerobility Holdings CIC	
G-CMIF	Grob G109B	Aerobility Holdings CIC	
G-CMIG	Grob G109B	Aerobility Holdings CIC	
G-CMIH	Grob G109B	Aerobility Holdings CIC	
G-CMII	Grob G109B	Aerobility Holdings CIC	
G-CMIJ	Grob G109B	Aerobility Holdings CIC	
G-CMIK	Grob G109B	Aerobility Holdings CIC	
G-CMIL	Grob G109B	Aerobility Holdings CIC	
G-CMIM	Grob G109B	Aerobility Holdings CIC	
G-CMIN	Grob G109B	Aerobility Holdings CIC	
G-CMKL	Van's RV-12	K. L. Sangster	
G-CMNK	DHC.1 Chipmunk 22	Vintage Aircraft Factory Ltd	
G-CMON	Van's RV-7	F. McMullan	
G-CMOR	Skyranger 912(2)	C. A. W. Harvey	
G-CMOS	Cessna T.303 Crusader	Stenball Holdings Ltd	
G-CMPA	PA-28RT-201Arrow IV	G. J. Melen (G-BREP)	
G-CMPC	Titan T-51 Mustang	J. A. Carey	
G-CMRA	Eurocopter AS.355N Ecureuil 2	Cheshire Helicopters Ltd	
G-CMTO	Cessna 525 Citation M2	Zepiar LLP	
G-CMWK	Grob G.102 Astir CS	J. Schaper	
G-CNAB	Avtech Jabiru UL	G-CNAB Group	
G-CNCN	Rockwell Commander 112CA	112 Group Ltd	
G-CNHB	Van's RV-7	T. G. Llloyd	
G-CNWL	MD.900 Explorer	Specialist Aviation Services Ltd (G-CIGX)	
G-COBS	Diamond DA.42 M-NG	Thales UK Ltd	
G-COCG	Aeropro Eurofox 3K	G. A. Cockrell	
G-COCO	Cessna F.172M	R. C. Larder	
G-CODA	Hughes 369E	Studwelders Holdings Ltd (G-CIYJ)	
G-COGS	Bell 407	R. B. Matthews	
G-COIN	Bell 206B JetRanger 2	J. P. Niehorster	
G-COLA	Beech F33C Bonanza	Airport Direction Ltd (G-BUAZ)	
G-COLF	BRM Bristell NG-5 Speed Wing	C. Firth	
G-COLI	Rotorsport UK MT-03	G. D. Smith	
G-COLR	Colt 69A balloon ★	British School of Ballooning/Lancing	
G-COLS	Van's RV-7A	C. Terry	
G-COLY	Aeropro Eurofox 912(S)	D. H. Nash	
G-COMB	PA-30 Twin Comanche 160B	M. Bonsall (G-AVBL)	
G-COMP	Cameron N-90 balloon	Computacenter Ltd	
G-CONA	Flight Design CTLS	R. A. Eve (G-CGED)	
G-CONB	Robin DR.400/180	Flight Software Services Ltd & LX Avionics Ltd (G-BUPX)	
G-CONC	Cameron N-90 balloon	A. A. Brown	
G-CONL	SOCATA TB10 Tobago	J. M. Huntington	
G-CONN	Eurocopter EC.120B Colibri	M. J. Connors (G-BZMK)	
G-CONR	Champion 7GCBC Scout	Aerofoyle Group	
G-CONS	Groppo Trail	G. Constantine	
G-CONV	Convair CV-440-54 ★	Reynard Nursery/Carluke	
G-COOT	Taylor Coot A	P. M. Napp	
G-COPP	Schleicher ASW-27-18E	J. B. Giddins	
G-COPR	Robinson R44 II	HQ Aviation Ltd	
G-COPS	Piper J-3C-65 Cub	R. W. Sproat	
G-CORA	Shaw Europa XS	A. P. Gardner (G-ILUM)	
G-CORB	SOCATA TB20 Trinidad	Corvid Aviation Ltd	
G-CORD	Slingsby T.66 Nipper 3	P. S. Gilmour (G-AVTB)	
G-CORS	Noorduyn AT-16-ND Harvard IIB (KF183)	Propshop Ltd	
G-CORW	PA-28-180 Cherokee C	R. P. Osborne & C. A. Wilson (G-AVRY)	
G-CORY	Guimbal Cabri G2	CJS Helicopters Ltd (G-PERU)	
G-COSF	PA-28-161 Warrior II	PA-28 Warrior Ltd	
G-COSY	Lindstrand LBL-56A balloon	M. H. Read & J. E. Wetters	

Notes	Reg	Type	Owner or Operator
	G-COTH	MD-900 Explorer	Specialist Aviation Services Ltd
	G-COTT	Cameron 60 Cottage SS balloon	Dragon Balloon Co Ltd
	G-COUZ	Raj Hamsa X'Air 582(2)	D. J. Tully
	G-COVA	PA-26-161 Warrior III	Coventry (Civil) Aviation Ltd (G-CDCL)
	G-COVC	PA-28-161 Warrior II	Coventry (Civil) Aviation Ltd
	G-COVZ	Cessna F.150M	S. J. Brenchley (G-BCRT)
	G-COXI	Xtremeair XA42	ABD Networks LLP
	G-COXS	Aeroprakt A.22 Foxbat	S. Cox
	G-COZI	Rutan Cozy III	R. Machin
	G-CPAO	Eurocopter EC.135P2+	Police & Crime Commissioner for West Yorkshire
	G-CPAS	Eurocopter EC.135P2+	Police & Crime Commissioner for West Yorkshire
	G-CPCD	CEA DR.221	P. J. Taylor
	G-CPDA	DH.106 Comet 4C (XS235) ★	C. Walton Ltd/Bruntingthorpe
	G-CPDW	Avions Mudry CAP.10B	Hilfa Ltd
	G-CPFC	Cessna F.152 II	Falcon Flying Services Ltd
	G-CPLG	AutoGyro Cavalon Pro	Commotion Aviation Ltd
	G-CPLH	Guimbal Cabri G2	Helicentre Aviation Ltd
	G-CPMK	DHC.1 Chipmunk 22 (WZ847)	P. A. Walley
	G-CPMS	SOCATA TB20 Trinidad	N. G. P. White & N. Cavalier-Smith
	G-CPMW	PA-32R-301 Saratoga II HP	P. D. Wheelen
	G-CPOL	AS.355F1 Twin Squirrel	Excel Charter Ltd
	G-CPPG	Alpi Pioneer 400	P. B. Godfrey
	G-CPPM	North American Harvard II (3091)	S. D. Wilch
	G-CPSS	Cessna 208B Grand Caravan	Army Parachute Association
	G-CPTM	PA-28-151 Warrior	T. J. & C. Mackay (G-BTOE)
	G-CPXC	Avions Mudry CAP-10C	JRW Aerobatics Ltd
	G-CRAB	Skyranger 912 (2)	S. W. Plume
	G-CRAR	CZAW Sportcruiser	J. S. Kinsey
	G-CRBV	Balóny Kubíček BB26 balloon	A. Hall
	G-CRES	Denney Kitfox Mk 3	Silver Fox Group
	G-CREY	SeaRey Amphibian	K. M. & M. Gallagher & A. F. Reid
	G-CRIC	Colomban MC.15 Cri-Cri	R. S. Stoddart-Stones
	G-CRIK	Colomban MC.15 Cri-Cri	N. Huxtable
	G-CRIL	Rockwell Commander 112B	Rockwell Aviation Group
	G-CRIS	Taylor JT.1 Monoplane	C. R. Steer
	G-CRJW	Schleicher ASW-27-18	R. J. Welford
	G-CRNL	Fairchild M62A-4 Cornell	CRNL Aviation Ltd (G-CEVL)
	G-CRNS	Dassault Falcon 7X	Execujet Europe
	G-CROE	Robin HR200/120B	R. J. Williamson (G-MFLA/G-HHUK)
	G-CROI	Robin HR200/120B	R. J. Williamson (G-MFLE/G-BYLH)
	G-CROL	Maule MXT-7-180	J. R. Pratt
	G-CROW	Robinson R44	Hover Helicopters Ltd
	G-CROY	Shaw Europa	M. T. Austin
	G-CRSR	Czech Sport Aircraft Sportcruiser	G-CRSR Flying Group
	G-CRSS	Guimbal Cabri G2	MTC Helicopters Ltd
	G-CRUE	Van's RV-7	C. Arnold
	G-CRUI	CZAW Sportcruiser	J. Massey
	G-CRUM	Westland Scout AH.1 (XV137)	G-CRUM Group
	G-CRUZ	Cessna T.303	S. J. & J. J. Ollier
	G-CRVC	Van's RV-14	I. A. Sweetland
	G-CRWL	Leonardo AW.169	Cornwall Air Ambulance Trust
	G-CRWZ	CZAW Sportcruiser	T. J. Gayton-Polley
	G-CRZA	CZAW Sportcruiser	I. M. Mackay
	G-CRZE	Ultramagic M-105 balloon	Fresh Air Ltd
	G-CRZR	Czech Sport PS-28 Cruiser	Fife Cruiser Group (G-EGHA)
	G-CSAM	Van's RV-9A	N. J. L. Heald
	G-CSAV	Thruster T.600N 450	S. Gennery
	G-CSAW	CZAW Sportcruiser	B. C. Fitzgerald-O'Connor
	G-CSBD	PA-28-236 Dakota	WF Aviation (G-CSBO)
	G-CSCS	Cessna F.172N	L. E. Winstanley & J. M. Grainger
	G-CSDJ	Avtech Jabiru UL	K. A. McDonnell
	G-CSDR	Corvus CA22	Crusader Syndicate
	G-CSEE	Balony Kubicek BB20ED balloon	Fairfax Aviation Ltd
	G-CSFT	PA-23 Aztec 250D ★	Aces High Ltd (G-AYKU)
	G-CSGT	PA-28-161 Warrior II	W. Ali (G-BPHB)
	G-CSHB	Czech Sport PS-28 Cruiser	P. Moodie & D. Gilham

Reg	Type	Owner or Operator	Notes
G-CSIX	PA-32 Cherokee Six 300	T. W. Gilbert	
G-CSKW	Van's RV-7	G-CSKW Group (G-CDJW)	
G-CSMK	Aerotechnik EV-97 Eurostar	R. Frey	
G-CSPR	Van's RV-6A	Casper Group	
G-CSPT	Gippsaero GA8 Airvan	Downlock Ltd	
G-CSUE	Savannah VG Jabiru (5)	J. R. Stratton & R. K. Stephens	
G-CSZM	Zenair CH.601XL Zodiac	C. Budd	
G-CTAB	Bellanca 7GCAA Citabria	V. Boddy (G-BFHP)	
G-CTAV	Aerotechnik EV-97 Eurostar	P. Simpson	
G-CTCB	Diamond DA42 Twin Star	L3 CTS Airline and Academy Training Ltd (G-CDTG)	
G-CTCC	Diamond DA42 Twin Star	L3 CTS Airline and Academy Training Ltd (G-OCCZ)	
G-CTCD	Diamond DA42 Twin Star	L3 CTS Airline and Academy Training Ltd	
G-CTCE	Diamond DA42 Twin Star	L3 CTS Airline and Academy Training Ltd	
G-CTCF	Diamond DA42 Twin Star	L3 CTS Airline and Academy Training Ltd	
G-CTCG	Diamond DA42 Twin Star	AJW Construction Ltd	
G-CTCH	Diamond DA42 Twin Star	L3 CTS Airline and Academy Training Ltd	
G-CTCL	SOCATA TB10 Tobago	Double S Group (G-BSIV)	
G-CTDH	Flight Design CT2K	A. D. Thelwall	
G-CTDW	Flight Design CTSW	H. D. Colliver	
G-CTED	Van's RV-7A	J. J. Nicholson	
G-CTEE	Flight Design CTSW	P. J. Clegg (G-CLEG)	
G-CTEL	Cameron N-90 balloon	M. R. Noyce	
G-CTFL	Robinson R44	Heli Air Scotland Ltd (G-CLOT)	
G-CTFS	Westland SA.341C Gazelle HT2	Beverley Polo Club Ltd (G-OJCO/G-LEDR/ G-CBSB)	
G-CTIO	SOCATA TB20 Trinidad	I. R. Hunt	
G-CTIX	VS.509 Spitfire T.IX (PT462)	Propshop Ltd	
G-CTKL	Noorduyn AT-16 Harvard IIB (54137)	M. R. Simpson	
G-CTLS	Flight Design CTLS	D. J. Haygreen	
G-CTNG	Cirrus SR20	J. Crackett	
G-CTOY	Denney Kitfox Mk 3	J. I. V. Hill	
G-CTSA	Diamond DA.40NG Star	L3 CTS Airline and Academy Training Ltd	
G-CTSB	Diamond DA.40NG Star	L3 CTS Airline and Academy Training Ltd	
G-CTSC	Diamond DA.40NG Star	Escola de Aviacao Aerocondor SA/Portugal	
G-CTSD	Diamond DA.40NG Star	Escola de Aviacao Aerocondor SA/Portugal	
G-CTSE	Diamond DA.40NG Star	Escola de Aviacao Aerocondor SA/Portugal	
G-CTSF	Diamond DA.40NG Star	Escola de Aviacao Aerocondor SA/Portugal	
G-CTSG	Diamond DA.40NG Star	Escola de Aviacao Aerocondor SA/Portugal	
C-CTSH	Diamond DA.40NG Star	Escola de Aviacao Aerocondor SA/Portugal	
G-CTSJ	Diamond DA.40NG Star	Escola de Aviacao Aerocondor SA/Portugal	
G-CTSK	Diamond DA.40NG Star	Escola de Aviacao Aerocondor SA/Portugal	
G-CTSL	Flight Design CT-Supralight	J. E. Lander	
G-CTSM	Diamond DA.40NG Star	Escola de Aviacao Aerocondor SA/Portugal	
G-CTSN	Diamond DA.40NG Star	Escola de Aviacao Aerocondor SA/Portugal	
G-CTSO	Diamond DA.40NG Star	Escola de Aviacao Aerocondor SA/Portugal	
G-CTSP	Diamond DA.40NG Star	Escola de Aviacao Aerocondor SA/Portugal	
G-CTSR	Diamond DA.40NG Star	Escola de Aviacao Aerocondor SA/Portugal	
G-CTSS	Diamond DA.40NG Star	Escola de Aviacao Aerocondor SA/Portugal	
G-CTST	Diamond DA.40NG Star	Escola de Aviacao Aerocondor SA/Portugal	
G-CTSU	Diamond DA.42 Twin Star	L3 CTS Airline and Academy Training Ltd	
G-CTSV	Diamond DA.42 Twin Star	L3 CTS Airline and Academy Training Ltd	
G-CTSX	Diamond DA.40NG Star	Escola de Aviacao Aerocondor SA/Portugal	
G-CTSY	Diamond DA.42 Twin Star	Escola de Aviacao Aerocondor SA/Portugal	
G-CTSZ	Diamond DA.42 Twin Star	Escola de Aviacao Aerocondor SA/Portugal	
G-CTTS	English Electric Canberra B.Mk.2	Vulcan to the Sky Trust (G-BVWC)	
G-CTUK	Cirrus SR20	Cirrus Aircraft UK Ltd	
G-CTWO	Schempp-Hirth Standard Cirrus	R. J. Griffin	
G-CTZO	SOCATA TB20 Trinidad GT	G-CTZO Group	
G-CUBA	PA-32R-301T Turbo Saratoge	M. Atlass	
G-CUBB	PA-18 Super Cub 180	EP. A. Colman	
G-CUBI	PA-18 Super Cub 125	G. T. Fisher	
G-CUBJ	PA-18 Super Cub 150 (18-5395:CDG)	Zweefvliegclub Flevo/Netherlands	
G-CUBN	PA-18 Super Cub 150	N. J. R. Minchin	
G-CUBS	Piper J-3C-65 Cub	S. M. Rolfe (G-BHPT)	
G-CUBW	WAG-Aero Acro Trainer	B. G. Plumb & A. G. Bourne	
G-CUCU	Colt 180A balloon	Spoon Services Multimedia SAS	
G-CUGC	Schleicher ASW-19B	Cambridge University Gliding Club (G-CKEX)	

Notes	Reg	Type	Owner or Operator
	G-CUMU	Schempp-Hirth Discus b	C. E. Fernando
	G-CUPP	Pitts S-2A	Avmarine Ltd
	G-CURV	Avid Speedwing	K. S. Kelso
	G-CUSS	Van's RV-7	J. W. Beaty
	G-CUTE	Dyn'Aéro MCR-01	J. M. Keane
	G-CUTH	P & M Quik R	A. R. & S. Cuthbertson
	G-CVAL	Ikarus C42 FB100	J. C. Nudd
	G-CVBA	Rolladen-Schneider LS6-18W	J. S. Moore
	G-CVBF	Cameron A-210 balloon	Virgin Balloon Flights Ltd
	G-CVET	Flight Design CTLS	S. J. Sykes (G-CGVR)
	G-CVII	Dan Rihn DR.107 One Design	One Design Group
	G-CVIX	DH.110 Sea Vixen D.3 (XP924)	Naval Aviation Ltd
	G-CVLN	Autogyro Cavalon	M. Groom (G-CIAT)
	G-CVMI	PA-18-150 Super Cub	J. S. Peplow & E. V. Moffatt
	G-CVST	Jodel D.140E	Forge Consulting Ltd
	G-CVXN	Cessna F.406 Caravan	Directflight Ltd (G-SFPA)
	G-CVZT	Schempp-Hirth Ventus 2cT	A. & M. C. Conboy
	G-CWAG	Sequoia F. 8L Falco	D. R. Austin
	G-CWAL	Raj Hamsa X'Air 133	L. R. Morris
	G-CWAY	Ikarus C42 FB100	M. Conway
	G-CWBM	Phoenix Currie Wot	R. S. Acton (G-BTVP)
	G-CWCD	Beech B.200GT Super King Air	Clowes Estates Ltd
	G-CWDW	Cessna 182T	R. A. S. White (G-PCBC)
	G-CWEB	P & M Quik GT450	G-CWEB Syndicate
	G-CWFC	PA-38-112 Tomahawk ★	Cardiff-Wales Flying Club Ltd (G-BRTA)
	G-CWFS	Tecnam P2002-JF Sierra	S. Adey
	G-CWFT	Cessna 172N	Avalon Ventures Ltd
	G-CWIC	Mainair Pegasus Quik	G-CWIC Group
	G-CWLC	Schleicher ASH-25	G-CWLC Group
	G-CWMC	P & M Quik GT450	A. R. Hughes
	G-CWOW	Balony Kubicek BB45Z balloon	Skybus Ballooning
	G-CWTD	Aeroprakt A22 Foxbat	Newtownards Microlight Group
	G-CWTT	Cessna 182T	C. W. Ivill
	G-CWVY	P & M Pegasus Quik	D. A. Eastough
	G-CXCX	Cameron N-90 balloon	Cathay Pacific Airways (London) Ltd
	G-CXDZ	Cassutt Speed Two	J. A. H. Chadwick
	G-CXIP	Thruster T.600N	R. J. Howells
	G-CXIV	Thatcher CX4	I. B. Melville
	G-CXLS	Cessna 560 XL Citation XLS	Aviation Beauport (G-PKRG)
	G-CXSM	Cessna 172R	S. Eustathiou (G-BXSM)
	G-CXTE	BRM Aero Bristell NG5 Speed Wing	M. Langmead
	G-CYGI	HAPI Cygnet SF-2A	P. J. Kember
	G-CYLL	Sequoia F.8L Falco	N. J. Langrick & A. J. Newall
	G-CYMA	GA-7 Cougar	Cyma Petroleum (UK) Ltd (G-BKOM)
	G-CYPC	Cessna 208B Grand Caravan	The Cyprus Combined Services Parachute Club
	G-CYPM	Cirrus SR22	M. J. Matthews
	G-CYRA	Kolb Twinstar Mk. 3 (Modified)	S. J. Fox (G-MYRA)
	G-CYRL	Cessna 182T	S. R. Wilson
	G-CZAC	Zenair CH.601XL	J. P. Pullin
	G-CZAG	Sky 90-24 balloon	D. S. Tree
	G-CZAW	CZAW Sportcruiser	G. N. Smith
	G-CZCZ	Avions Mudry CAP-10B	M. Farmer
	G-CZMI	Best Off Skyranger Swift 912(1)	D. G. Baker
	G-CZNE	BN-2B-20 Islander	Skyhopper LLP (G-BWZF)
	G-CZOS	Cirrus SR20	W. R. M. Beesley
	G-CZSC	CZAW Sportcruiser	F. J. Wadia
	G-DAAN	Eurocopter EC 135P2+	Devon Air Ambulance Trading Co.Ltd
	G-DAAS	Airbus Helicopters MBBBK 117 D-2	Devon Air Ambulance Trading Co.Ltd
	G-DAAY	Ultramagic B-70 balloon	A. M. Holly
	G-DAAZ	PA-28RT-201T Turbo Arrow IV	G. Sheddon
	G-DACA	P.57 Sea Prince T.1 (WF118) ★	P. G. Vallance Ltd/Charlwood
	G-DACE	Corben Baby Ace D	P. King (G-BTSB)
	G-DACF	Cessna 152 II	T. M. & M. L. Jones (G-BURY)
	G-DADA	Rotorsport UK MT-03	J. C. Hilton-Johnson

Reg	Type	Owner or Operator	Notes
G-DADD	Reality Escapade 912(2)	P. S. Balmer	
G-DADG	PA-18-150 Super Cub	F. J. Cox	
G-DADJ	Glaser-Dirks DG-200	M. A. Hunton	
G-DADZ	CZAW Sportcruiser	Meon Flying Group	
G-DAGF	EAA Acrosport II	M. G. Pahle	
G-DAGJ	Zenair CH.601HD Zodiac	D. A. G. Johnson	
G-DAGN	Ikarus C42 FB80	N. L. James	
G-DAIR	Luscombe 8A Silvaire	D. F. Soul (G-BURK)	
G-DAKA	PA-28-236 Dakota	M. M. Zienkiewicz	
G-DAKK	Douglas C-47A	R. G. T. de Man	
G-DAKM	Diamond DA.40D Star	AJW Construction Ltd	
G-DAKO	PA-28-236 Dakota	M. H. D. Smith	
G-DAMB	Sequoia F.8L Falco	S. O. Foxlee (G-OGKB)	
G-DAME	Vans RV-7	S. James	
G-DAMS	Best Off Skyranger Nynja 912S(1)	Dambusters Ltd	
G-DAMY	Shaw Europa	U. A. Schliessler & R. J. Kelly	
G-DANA	Jodel DR.200 (replica)	Cheshire Eagles (G-DAST)	
G-DANB	Sherwood Ranger ST	W. A. Douthwaite	
G-DAND	SOCATA TB10 Tobago	Coventry Aviators Flying Group	
G-DANJ	Cameron TR-65 balloon	D. J. Gregory	
G-DANL	Beech 76 Duchess	Folada Aero & Technical Services Ltd & UK Flying Clubs Ltd (G-GPAT)	
G-DANP	Van's RV-7	D. T. Pangbourne	
G-DANY	Avtech Jabiru UL	D. A. Crosbie	
G-DASG	Schleicher ASW-27-18E	E. Alston	
G-DASH	Rockwell Commander 112	M. J. P. Lynch (G-BDAJ)	
G-DASS	Ikarus C.42 FB100	Fly 365	
G-DATR	Agusta-Bell 206B-3 JetRanger 3	P. J. Spinks (G-JLEE/G-JOKE/G-CSKY/G-TALY)	
G-DAVB	Aerosport Scamp	D. R. Burns	
G-DAVD	Cessna FR.172K	M. Klies	
G-DAVE	Jodel D.112	I. D. Worthington	
G-DAVH	Cessna 150H	J. M. Harbottle (G-BRBH)	
G-DAVM	Akrotech Europe CAP.10B	D. Moorman	
G-DAVS	AB Sportine Aviacija LAK-17AT	G-DAVS Syndicate	
G-DAWG	SA Bulldog Srs 120/121 (XX522)	High G Bulldog Ltd	
G-DAYA	Bombardier CL600-2B16 Challenger 604	Gama Aviation (UK) Ltd (G-RCAV)	
G-DAYD	Agusta A109S Grand	Sky Border Logistics Ltd (G-SKBL/G-PDAY/G-CDWY)	
G-DAYF	Agusta AW109SP Grand New	Sky Border Logistics Ltd (G-SKBH)	
G-DAYI	Europa	R. S. Cullum	
G-DAYO	Beech A36 Bonanza	Exeter Aviation Ltd	
G-DAYP	Beech B.300C Super King Air	Gama Aviation (Asset 2) Ltd	
G-DAYR	Bombardier CL600-2B16 Challenger 605	Gama Aviation (UK) Ltd	
G-DAYS	Europa	R. M. F. Pereira	
G-DAYZ	Pietenpol Air Camper	T. W. J. Carnall & M. B. Blackmore	
G-DAZO	Diamond DA.20-A1 Katana	Cubair Flight Training Ltd	
G-DAZW	Zenair CH.750 Cruzer	D. Weston	
G-DAZZ	Van's RV-8	Wishangar RV8	
G-DBCA	Airbus A.319-131	British Airways plc	
G-DBCB	Airbus A.319-131	British Airways plc	
G-DBCC	Airbus A.319-131	British Airways plc	
G-DBCD	Airbus A.319-131	British Airways plc	
G-DBCE	Airbus A.319-131	British Airways plc	
G-DBCF	Airbus A.319-131	British Airways plc	
G-DBCG	Airbus A.319-131	British Airways plc	
G-DBCH	Airbus A.319-131	British Airways plc	
G-DBCJ	Airbus A.319-131	British Airways plc	
G-DBCK	Airbus A.319-131	British Airways plc	
G-DBDM	Aeropro Eurofox 3K	D. Murphy & D. W. Buggins	
G-DBEE	Jabiru J430	A. G. Bridger	
G-DBEN	Schleicher ASW-15	Oscar 8 Syndicate	
G-DBIN	Medway SLA 80 Executive	P. M. Alty	
G-DBIT	Cameron A-210 balloon	Ballooning in Tuscany SRL	
G-DBJD	PZL-Bielsko SZD-9BIS Bocian 1D	Bertie the Bocian Glider Syndicate	
G-DBKL	VS.379 Spitfire F.Mk.XIV	P. M. Andrews	
G-DBND	Schleicher Ka 6CR	A. L. R. Roth	
G-DBNH	Schleicher Ka 6CR	The Bath, Wilts and North Dorset Gliding Club Ltd	
G-DBNK	Eurocopter EC.120B Colibri	De Banke Aviation LLP (G-PERF)	

BRITISH CIVIL AIRCRAFT MARKINGS

Notes	Reg	Type	Owner or Operator
	G-DBOD	Cessna 172S	Goodwood Road Racing Co Ltd
	G-DBOL	Schleicher Ka 6CR	G-DBOL Group
	G-DBRT	Slingsby T.51 Dart	C. W. Logue
	G-DBRU	Slingsby T.51 Dart	P. S. Whitehead
	G-DBRY	Slingsby T.51 Dart	G. B. Marshall
	G-DBSA	Slingsby T.51 Dart	The Gliding Heritage Centre
	G-DBSB	TL2000UK Sting Carbon S4	G-DBSB Group
	G-DBSL	Slingsby T.51 Dart	W. R. Davis
	G-DBSW	Slingsby T.51 Dart 15	G-DBSW Syndicate
	G-DBTJ	Schleicher Ka 6CR	I. R. Duncan
	G-DBUZ	Schleicher Ka 6CR	J. J. Hartwell
	G-DBVB	Schleicher K7	Dartmoor Gliding Society Ltd
	G-DBVH	Slingsby T.51 Dart 17R	R. D. Brister
	G-DBVR	Schleicher Ka 6CR	A. L. Hoskin
	G-DBVX	Schleicher Ka 6CR	Y. Marom
	G-DBVZ	Schleicher Ka 6CR	G-DBVZ Group
	G-DBWC	Schleicher Ka 6CR	T. W. Humphrey
	G-DBWJ	Slingsby T.51 Dart 17R	M. F. Defendi
	G-DBWM	Slingsby T.51 Dart 17R	L. Bennett-Poole
	G-DBWO	Slingsby T.51 Dart	C. R. Stacey
	G-DBWP	Slingsby T.51 Dart 17R	S. P. Withey & A. J. Whiteman
	G-DBWS	Slingsby T.51 Dart 17R	R. D. Broome
	G-DBXG	Slingsby T.51 Dart 17R	J. M. Whelan
	G-DBXT	Schleicher Ka 6CR	C. I. Knowles
	G-DBYC	Slingsby T.51 Dart 17R	R. L. Horsnell & N. A. Jaffray
	G-DBYG	Slingsby T.51 Dart 17R	J. R. G. Furnell
	G-DBYL	Schleicher Ka 6CR	The Surrey Hills Gliding Club Ltd
	G-DBYM	Schleicher Ka 6CR	S. F. Smith
	G-DBYU	Schleicher Ka-6CR	K. D. Walker
	G-DBYX	Schleicher Ka-6E	I. Bannister
	G-DBZF	Slingsby T.51 Dart 17R	S. Rhenius
	G-DBZJ	Slingsby T.51 Dart 17R	L. Ingram
	G-DBZX	Schleicher Ka 6CR	B. Brockwell
	G-DCAE	Schleicher Ka 6E	J. R. & P. R. Larner
	G-DCAG	Schleicher Ka 6E	715 Syndicate
	G-DCAM	Eurocopter AS.355NP Ecureuil 2	Cameron Charters LLP
	G-DCAO	Schempp-Hirth SHK-1	P. B.Hibbard
	G-DCAR	Magni M24C Plus	R. Carey
	G-DCAS	Schleicher Ka 6E	R. F. Tindall
	G-DCAZ	Slingsby T-51 Dart 17R	D. A. Bullock & Man L. C.
	G-DCBA	Slingsby T.51 Dart 17R	K. T. Kreis
	G-DCBI	Schweizer 269C-1	P. T. Shaw
	G-DCBM	Schleicher Ka 6CR	R. J. Shepherd
	G-DCBP	SZD-24C Foka	The Gliding Heritage Centre
	G-DCBW	Schleicher ASK-13	Stratford on Avon Gliding Club Ltd
	G-DCBY	Schleicher Ka 6CR	R. G. Appleboom
	G-DCCA	Schleicher Ka 6E	R. W. Iddon
	G-DCCB	Schempp-Hirth SHK-1	CCB Syndicate
	G-DCCD	Schleicher Ka 6E	Charlie Charlie Delta Group
	G-DCCE	Schleicher ASK-13	The Welland Gliding Club Ltd
	G-DCCG	Schleicher Ka 6E	R. J. Playle
	G-DCCL	Schleicher Ka 6E	A. Sanders
	G-DCCM	Schleicher ASK-13	The Burn Gliding Club Ltd
	G-DCCP	Schleicher ASK-13	Lima 99 Syndicate
	G-DCCR	Schleicher Ka 6E	G-DCCR Syndicate
	G-DCCT	Schleicher ASK-13	East Sussex Gliding Club Ltd
	G-DCCU	Schleicher Ka 6E	J. L. Hasker
	G-DCCV	Schleicher Ka 6E	B. J. Darton
	G-DCCW	Schleicher ASK-13	Midland Gliding Club Ltd
	G-DCCX	Schleicher ASK-13	Trent Valley Gliding Club Ltd
	G-DCCY	Schleicher ASK-13	Dartmoor Gliding Society
	G-DCCZ	Schleicher ASK-13	The Windrushers Gliding Club Ltd
	G-DCDA	Schleicher Ka 6E	R. E. Musselwhite & D. C. Kirby-Smith
	G-DCDC	Lange E1 Antares	J. D. Williams
	G-DCDF	Schleicher Ka 6E	CDF Syndicate
	G-DCDG	FFA Diamant 18	J. Cashin & D. McCarty
	G-DCDI	Robin DR400/140B	N. W. Charles
	G-DCDO	Ikarus C42 FB80	M. Cheetham
	G-DCDW	Diamant 18	D. R. Chapman
	G-DCDZ	Schleicher Ka 6E	J. R. J. Minns

Reg	Type	Owner or Operator	Notes
G-DCEB	PZL-Bielsko SZD-9BIS Bocian 1E	G-DCEB Syndicate	
G-DCEC	Schempp-Hirth Cirrus	CEC Group	
G-DCEM	Schleicher Ka 6E	S. G. Jessup	
G-DCEO	Schleicher Ka 6E	C. L. Lagden & J. C. Green	
G-DCEW	Schleicher Ka 6E	J. W. Richardson and Partners Group	
G-DCFA	Schleicher ASK-13	Dorset Gliding Club Ltd	
G-DCFF	Schleicher K 8B	Derbyshire and Lancashire Gliding Club Ltd	
G-DCFG	Schleicher ASK-13	The Nene Valley Gliding Club Ltd	
G-DCFK	Schempp-Hirth Cirrus	P. D. Whitters	
G-DCFL	Schleicher Ka 6E	D. M. Cornelius	
G-DCFS	Glasflugel Standard Libelle 201B	J. E. Hoy	
G-DCFW	Glasflugel Standard Libelle 201B	A. P. Bulmer	
G-DCFX	Glasflugel Standard Libelle 201B	A. S. Burton	
G-DCFY	Glasflugel Standard Libelle 201B	C. W. Stevens	
G-DCGB	Schleicher Ka 6E	P. M. Turner & S. C. Male	
G-DCGD	Schleicher Ka 6E	Charlie Golf Delta Group	
G-DCGE	Schleicher Ka 6E	O. J. Anderson & B. Silke	
G-DCGH	Schleicher K 8B	M. F. Jenkins	
G-DCGM	FFA Diamant 18	J. G. Batch	
G-DCGO	Schleicher ASK-13	Oxford Gliding Company Ltd	
G-DCGT	Schempp-Hirth SHK-1	T. Callier	
G-DCGY	Schempp-Hirth Cirrus	S. H. Fletcher	
G-DCHB	Schleicher Ka 6E	577 Syndicate	
G-DCHG	PZL-Bielsko SZD-30 Pirat	Pirat Syndicate	
G-DCHJ	Bolkow Phoebus C	Edensoaring Ltd	
G-DCHL	PZL-Bielsko SZD-30	A. M. Bennett & P. M. Green	
G-DCHT	Schleicher ASW-15	D. Edwards	
G-DCHU	Schleicher K 8B	G-DCHU Syndicate	
G-DCHW	Schleicher ASK-13	Dorset Gliding Club Ltd	
G-DCHZ	Schleicher Ka 6E	S. Sullivan & P. K. Bunnage	
G-DCII	Agusta Westland AW139	Executive Jet Charter Ltd	
G-DCJB	Bolkow Phoebus C	R. Idle	
G-DCJF	Schleicher K-8B	G. Smith	
G-DCJJ	Bolkow Phoebus C	P. N. Maddocks	
G-DCJK	Schempp-Hirth SHK-1	R. H. Short	
G-DCJM	Schleicher K-8B	Midland Gliding Club Ltd	
G-DCJN	Schempp-Hirth SHK-1	J. J. Sconce & S. Marlor	
G-DCJR	Schempp-Hirth Cirrus	C. Thirkell	
G-DCJY	Schleicher Ka 6CR	CJY Syndicate	
G-DCKD	PZL-Bielsko SZD-30	Pirat Flying Group	
G-DCKK	Cessna F.172N	DCKK Group	
G-DCKL	Schleicher Ka 6E	C. J. Sturdy	
G-DCKP	Schleicher ASW-15	M. W. Black	
G-DCKR	Schleicher ASK-13	Midland Gliding Club Ltd	
G-DCKY	Glasflugel Standard Libelle 201B	M. N. K. Willcox	
G-DCKZ	Schempp-Hirth Standard Cirrus	G. I. Bustin	
G-DCLM	Glasflugel Standard Libelle 201B	R. L. Smith	
G-DCLO	Schempp-Hirth Cirrus	Bravo Delta Group	
G-DCLP	Glasflugel Standard Libelle 201B	K. Stokes	
G-DCLT	Schleicher K7	Dartmoor Gliding Society	
G-DCLZ	Schleicher Ka 6E	G-DCLZ Flying Group	
G-DCMI	Mainair Pegasus Quik	F. Omaraie-Hamdanie	
G-DCMK	Schleicher ASK-13	Black Mountains Gliding Club	
G-DCMN	Schleicher K 8B	The Bristol Gliding Club Proprietary Ltd	
G-DCMO	Glasflugel Standard Libelle 201B	M. Oliver	
G-DCMR	Glasflugel Standard Libelle 201B	J. M. Oatridge & A. Elliott	
G-DCMS	Glasflugel Standard Libelle 201B	Libelle 602 Syndicate	
G-DCMT	Embraer EMB505 Phenom 300	Voluxis Ltd	
G-DCMW	Glasflugel Standard Libelle 201B	D. Williams	
G-DCNC	Schempp-Hirth Standard Cirrus	M. D. Cobham	
G-DCNE	Glasflugel Standard Libelle 201B	S. J. Cooksey	
G-DCNG	Glasflugel Standard Libelle 201B	M. C. J. Gardner	
G-DCNJ	Glasflugel Standard Libelle 201B	P. I. Jameson	
G-DCNM	PZL-Bielsko SZD-9bis Bocian 1E	Bocian Syndicate	
G-DCNP	Glasflugel Standard Libelle 201B	I. G. Carrick & D. J. Shepherd	
G-DCNS	Slingsby T.59A Kestrel	J. R. Greenwell	
G-DCNW	Slingsby T.59F Kestrel	S. R. Watson	
G-DCNX	Slingsby T.59F Kestrel	M. Boxall	
G-DCOC	PZL-Bielsko SZD-30 Pirat	B. M. Sutherland & N. A. Betteridge	
G-DCOE	Van's RV-6	R. E. Welch	
G-DCOJ	Slingsby T.59A Kestrel	J. Mills	

Notes	Reg	Type	Owner or Operator
	G-DCOR	Schempp-Hirth Standard Cirrus	H. R. Ford
	G-DCOY	Schempp-Hirth Standard Cirrus	RPG
	G-DCPB	Eurocopter MBB-BK 117C-1	Police & Crime Commissioner for West Yorkshire
	G-DCPD	Schleicher ASW-17	A. J. Hewitt
	G-DCPF	Glasflugel Standard Libelle 201B	S. D. Hepburn
	G-DCPJ	Schleicher KA6E	The K6 Group
	G-DCPM	Glasflugel Standard Libelle 201B	P. E. Jessop & A. M. Carpenter
	G-DCPU	Schempp-Hirth Standard Cirrus	P. J. Ketelaar
	G-DCRB	Glasflugel Standard Libelle 201B	C. J. Riley
	G-DCRH	Schempp-Hirth Standard Cirrus	P. E. Thelwall
	G-DCRN	Schempp-Hirth Standard Cirrus	D. J. van der Werf
	G-DCRO	Glasflugel Standard Libelle 201B	G-DCRO Group
	G-DCRS	Glasflugel standard Libelle 201B	C. J. Davison
	G-DCRV	Glasflugel Standard Libelle 201B	A. J. Harris
	G-DCRW	Glasflugel Standard Libelle 201B	T. Fletcher
	G-DCSB	Slingsby T.59F Kestrel	W. Fischer
	G-DCSD	Slingsby T.59D Kestrel	L. P. Davidson
	G-DCSF	Slingsby T.59F Kestrel 19	R. Birch
	G-DCSI	Robinson R44 II	Cotswold Ventures Ltd (G-TGDL)
	G-DCSJ	Glasflugel Standard Libelle 201B	P. J. Gill
	G-DCSK	Slingsby T.59D Kestrel	Kestrel CSK Group
	G-DCSN	Pilatus B4-PC11AF	J. S. Firth
	G-DCSP	Pilatus B4-PC11	G-DCSP Group
	G-DCSR	Glasflugel Standard Libelle 201B	Glasgow and West of Scotland Gliding Club
	G-DCTB	Schempp-Hirth Standard Cirrus	S. E. McCurdy
	G-DCTJ	Slingsby T.59D Kestrel	J. Young & R. J. Aylesbury
	G-DCTL	Slingsby T.59D Kestrel	E. S. E. Hibbard
	G-DCTM	Slingsby T.59D Kestrel	C. Swain
	G-DCTO	Slingsby T.59D Kestrel	G-DCTO Gliding Syndicate
	G-DCTP	Slingsby T.59D Kestrel	D. C. Austin
	G-DCTR	Slingsby T.59D Kestrel	K. M. Charlton
	G-DCTT	Schempp-Hirth Standard Cirrus	N. I. van Genugten
	G-DCTU	Glasflugel Standard Libelle 201B	P. M. Davies & R. Cobb
	G-DCTV	PZL-Bielsko SZD-30	M. Cudmore & R. Walters
	G-DCTX	PZL-Bielsko SZD-30	A. M. Bennett & P. M. Green
	G-DCUB	Pilatus B4-PC11	G-DCUB Group
	G-DCUC	Pilatus B4-PC11	G. M. Cumner
	G-DCUD	Yorkshire Sailplanes YS53 Sovereign	T. J. Wilkinson
	G-DCUJ	Glasflugel Standard Libelle 201B	C. I. Knowles
	G-DCUS	Schempp-Hirth Cirrus VTC	R. C. Graham
	G-DCUT	Pilatus B4 PC11AF	A. L. Walker
	G-DCVE	Schempp-Hirth Cirrus VTC	S. Hardy
	G-DCVK	Pilatus B4-PC11AF	J. P. Marriott
	G-DCVL	Glasflugel Standard Libelle 201B	J. Williams
	G-DCVR	PZL-Bielsko SZD-30 Pirat	M. T. Pitorak
	G-DCVV	Pilatus B4-PC11AF	D. W. Poll
	G-DCVW	Slingsby T.59D Kestrel	J. J. Green & J. A. Tonkin
	G-DCVY	Slingsby T.59D Kestrel	N. Dickenson
	G-DCWB	Slingsby T.59D Kestrel	I. J. Ashdown
	G-DCWD	Slingsby T.59D Kestrel	G. J. Palmer
	G-DCWE	Glasflugel Standard Libelle 201B	L. J. Maksymowicz
	G-DCWF	Slingsby T.59D Kestrel	P. F. Nicholson
	G-DCWG	Glasflugel Standard Libelle 201B	T. D. Farquhar
	G-DCWH	Schleicher ASK-13	York Gliding Centre (Operations) Ltd
	G-DCWJ	Schleicher K7	M. P. Webb
	G-DCWP	PZL-Bielsko SZD-36A Cobra 15	P. Kalcher
	G-DCWR	Schempp-Hirth Cirrus VTC	CWR Group
	G-DCWS	Schempp-Hirth Cirrus VTC	Cirrus G-DCWS Syndicate
	G-DCWT	Glasflugel Standard Libelle 201B	A. A. Tills
	G-DCWX	Glasflugel Standard Libelle	A. Coatsworth
	G-DCWY	Glasflugel Standard Libelle 201B	S. J. Taylor
	G-DCXH	PZL-Bielsko SZD-36A Cobra 15	J. Dudzik
	G-DCXI	Slingsby T.61F Venture T.2	611 Vintage Flight (G-BUDB)
	G-DCXK	Glasflugel Standard Libelle 201B	J. C. Richards
	G-DCXV	Yorkshire Sailplanes YS-53 Sovereign	The Gliding Heritage Centre
	G-DCYA	Pilatus B4 PC-11	B4-072 Group
	G-DCYC	Pilatus B4 PC-11	D. P. Aherne
	G-DCYG	Glasflugel H201B Standard Libelle	R. J. Barsby & G. Wheldon
	G-DCYM	Schempp-Hirth Standard Cirrus	K. M. Fisher
	G-DCYO	Schempp-Hirth Standard Cirrus	M. J. Layton

Reg	Type	Owner or Operator	Notes
G-DCYP	Schempp-Hirth Standard Cirrus	A. F. Scott	
G-DCYT	Schempp-Hirth Standard Cirrus	W. A. L. Leader	
G-DCYZ	Schleicher K 8B	UWE Students Union	
G-DCZD	Pilatus B4 PC-11AF	T. Dale	
G-DCZE	PZL-Bielsko SZD-30	L. A. Bean	
G-DCZG	PZL-Bielsko SZD-30	J. T. Pajdak	
G-DCZJ	PZL-Bielsko SZD-30	Lincolnshire Gliding Club Ltd	
G-DCZN	Schleicher ASW-15B	J. R. Walters	
G-DCZR	Slingsby T.59D Kestrel	G. I. Corbett	
G-DCZU	Slingsby T.59D Kestrel	R. A. Morris	
G-DDAC	PZL-Bielsko SZD-36A	R. J. A. Colenso	
G-DDAJ	Shempp-Hirth Nimbus 2	North Devon Gliding Club Nimbus Group	
G-DDAN	PZL-Bielsko SZD-30	J. M. A. Shannon	
G-DDAP	SZL-Bielsko SZD-30	Delta Alpha Papa Group	
G-DDAS	Schempp-Hirth Standard Cirrus	G. Goodenough	
G-DDBB	Slingsby T.51 Dart 17R	A. J. A. Forrest	
G-DDBC	Pilatus B4-PC11	J. H. France & G. R. Harris	
G-DDBD	Shaw Europa XS	B. Davies	
G-DDBG	ICA IS-29D	P. S. Whitehead	
G-DDBK	Slingsby T.59D Kestrel	523 Syndicate	
G-DDBN	Slingsby T.59D Kestrel	Navboys Ltd	
G-DDBP	Glasflugel Club Libelle 205	K. Fuks	
G-DDBS	Slingsby T.59D Kestrel	K. Millar	
G-DDBV	PZL-Bielsko SZD-30	G-DDBV Syndicate	
G-DDCA	PZL-Bielsko SZD-36A Cobra 15	J. Young & J. R. Aylesbury	
G-DDCC	Glasflugel Standard Libelle 201B	G-DDCC Syndicate	
G-DDCW	Schleicher Ka 6CR	B. W. Rendall	
G-DDDA	Schempp-Hirth Standard Cirrus	G-DDDA Group	
G-DDDB	Schleicher ASK-13	Shenington Gliding Club	
G-DDDE	PZL-Bielsko SZD-38A Jantar 1	Jantar One Syndicate	
G-DDDK	PZL-Bielsko SZD-30 Pirat	Buckminster Gliding Club Ltd	
G-DDDL	Schleicher K8B	The Windrushers Gliding Club Ltd	
G-DDDM	Schempp-Hirth Cirrus	H. D. Maddams	
G-DDDR	Schempp-Hirth Standard Cirrus	A. J. Davis	
G-DDDY	P & M Quik GT450	J. W. Dodson	
G-DDEB	Slingsby T.59D Kestrel	J. L. Smoker	
G-DDEG	ICA IS-28B2	P. S. Whitehead	
G-DDEO	Glasflugel H205 Club Libelle	716 Group	
G-DDEV	Schleicher Ka-6CR	DEV Group	
G-DDEW	ICA-Brasov IS-29D	P. S. Whitehead	
G-DDFC	Schempp-Hirth Standard Cirrus	C. E. Hooper	
G-DDFE	Molino PIK-20B	M. A. Roff-Jarrett	
G-DDFK	Molino PIK-20B	B. H. & M. J. Fairclough	
G-DDFL	PZL-Bielsko SZD-38A Jantar 1	G-DDFL Group	
G-DDFR	Grob G.102 Astir CS	The Windrushers Gliding Club Ltd	
G-DDFU	PZL-Bielsko SZD-38A Jantar 1	Jantar 38A Group	
G-DDGA	Schleicher K-8B	The Welland Gliding Club Ltd	
G-DDGE	Schempp-Hirth Standard Cirrus	T. P. Brown	
G-DDGG	Schleicher Ka 6E	N. F. Holmes & F. D. Platt	
G-DDGJ	Champion 8KCAB	Western Air (Thruxton) Ltd	
G-DDGK	Schleicher Ka 6CR	K. J. Butler	
G-DDGV	Breguet 905S Fauvette	J. N. Lee	
G-DDGY	Schempp-Hirth Nimbus 2	Nimbus 195 Group	
G-DDHA	Schleicher K 8B	Shalborne Soaring Society Ltd	
G-DDHE	Slingsby T.53B	L. H. Hart	
G-DDHG	Schleicher Ka 6CR	M. W. Roberts	
G-DDHJ	Glaser-Dirks DG-100	G. E. McLaughlin	
G-DDHK	Glaser-Dirks DG-100	K. Dillon & R. Allcoat	
G-DDHL	Glaser-Dirks DG-100	DHL Syndicate	
G-DDHT	Schleicher Ka 6E	P. J. Flack	
G-DDHW	Schempp-Hirth Nimbus 2	M. J. Carruthers & D. Thompson	
G-DDHX	Schempp-Hirth Standard Cirrus B	J. Franke	
G-DDHZ	PZL-Bielsko SZD-30	A. M. Bennett & P. M. Green	
G-DDJB	Schleicher K-8B	Portsmouth Naval Gliding Centre	
G-DDJD	Grob G.102 Astir CS	T. Harrod & J. Andrewartha	
G-DDJF	Schempp-Hirth Duo Discus T	R. J. H. Fack	
G-DDJK	Schleicher ASK-18	Dorset Gliding Club Ltd	
G-DDJN	Eiriavion PIK-20B	M. Ireland & S. Lambourne	
G-DDJR	Schleicher Ka 6CR	K6CR Syndicate	
G-DDJX	Grob G.102 Astir CS	Trent Valley Gliding Club Ltd	

Notes	Reg	Type	Owner or Operator
	G-DDKD	Glasflugel Hornet	Hornet Syndicate
	G-DDKE	Schleicher ASK-13	The South Wales Gliding Club Ltd
	G-DDKG	Schleicher Ka 6CR	C. B. Woolf
	G-DDKL	Schempp-Hirth Nimbus 2	G. J. Croll
	G-DDKM	Glasflugel Hornet	R. S. Lee
	G-DDKR	Grob G.102 Astir CS	Oxford Gliding Co.Ltd
	G-DDKS	Grob G.102 Astir CS	Oxford Gliding Co.Ltd
	G-DDKU	Grob G.102 Astir CS	R. H. Lee
	G-DDKV	Grob G.102 Astir CS	T. J. Ireson
	G-DDKW	Grob G.102 Astir CS	M. Rudnicki, A. H. Mair & N. T. Bale
	G-DDKX	Grob G.102 Astir CS	The South Wales Gliding Club Ltd
	G-DDLA	Pilatus B4 PC-11	P. R. Seddon
	G-DDLB	Schleicher ASK-18	B. A. Fairston & A. Stotter
	G-DDLC	Schleicher ASK-13	Lasham Gliding Society Ltd
	G-DDLE	Schleicher Ka 6E	P. J. Abbott & J. Banks
	G-DDLG	Schempp-Hirth Standard Cirrus 75	S. Naylor
	G-DDLH	Grob G.102 Astir CS77	M. D. & M. E. Saunders
	G-DDLJ	Eiriavion PIK-20B	R. J. Pye
	G-DDLM	Grob G.102 Astir CS	Astir Syndicate
	G-DDLP	Schleicher Ka 6CR	J. R. Crosse
	G-DDLS	Schleicher K 8B	North Devon Gliding Club
	G-DDMB	Schleicher K 8B	Crown Service Gliding Club
	G-DDMG	Schleicher K 8B	Dorset Gliding Club Ltd
	G-DDMH	Grob G.102 Astir CS	C. K. Lewis
	G-DDMK	Schempp-Hirth SHK-1	D. Breeze
	G-DDML	Schleicher K-7	Z. A. Mallam
	G-DDMM	Schempp-Hirth Nimbus 2	T. Linee
	G-DDMN	Glasflugel Mosquito	DMN Group
	G-DDMO	Schleicher Ka 6E	R. C. Sharman
	G-DDMP	Grob G.102 Astir CS	Kingswood Syndicate
	G-DDMR	Grob G.102 Astir CS	Mendip Gliding Club Ltd
	G-DDMS	Glasflugel Standard Libelle 201B	G-DDMS Group
	G-DDMU	Eiriavion PIK-20D	P. Goodchild
	G-DDMV	NA T-6G Texan (493209)	K. M. Perkins
	G-DDMX	Schleicher ASK-13	Dartmoor Gliding Society Ltd
	G-DDNC	Grob G.102 Astir CS	J. B. Marchant
	G-DDND	Pilatus B4-PC11AF	DND Group
	G-DDNE	Grob G.102 Astir CS77	621 Astir Syndicate
	G-DDNG	Schempp-Hirth Nimbus 2	P. D. Wright
	G-DDNK	Grob G.102 Astir CS	G-DDNK Group
	G-DDNU	PZL-Bielsko SZD-42-1 Jantar 2	D. Mattano
	G-DDNV	Schleicher ASK-13	Channel Gliding Club
	G-DDNW	Schleicher Ks 6CR	G-DDNW Group
	G-DDNX	Schleicher Ka 6CR	Black Mountains Gliding Club
	G-DDNZ	Schleicher K 8B	G. Brind
	G-DDOA	Schleicher ASK-13	Essex and Suffolk Gliding Club Ltd
	G-DDOC	Schleicher Ka 6CR	W. St. G. V. Stoney
	G-DDOE	Grob G.102 Astir CS77	Heron Gliding Club
	G-DDOF	Schleicher Ka 6CR	G-DDOF Group
	G-DDOG	SA Bulldog Srs 120/121 (XX524:04)	Deltaero Ltd
	G-DDOK	Schleicher Ka 6E	R. S. Hawley & S. Y. Duxbury
	G-DDOU	Eiriavion PIK-20D	J. M. A. Shannon
	G-DDOX	Schleicher K-7	The Nene Valley Gliding Club Ltd
	G-DDPA	Schleicher ASK-18	M. J. Huddart
	G-DDPH	Schempp-Hirth Mini-Nimbus B	J. W. Murdoch
	G-DDPJ	Grob G.102 Astir CS77	DPJ Syndicate
	G-DDPK	Glasflugel H303A Mosquito	H. Nolz
	G-DDPL	Eiriavion PIK-20D	437 Syndicate
	G-DDPO	Grob G.102 Astir CS77	Yorkshire Gliding Club (Proprietary) Ltd
	G-DDPY	Grob G.102 Astir CS77	C. A. Bailey
	G-DDRA	Schleicher Ka 6CR	K6CR Group Shobdon
	G-DDRB	Glaser-Dirks DG-100	M. C. Bailey
	G-DDRD	Schleicher Ka 6CR	Essex & Suffolk Gliding Club Ltd
	G-DDRE	Schleicher Ka 6CR	DRE Syndicate
	G-DDRJ	Schleicher ASK-13	Lasham Gliding Society Ltd
	G-DDRL	Scheibe SF26A	T. A. Lipinski
	G-DDRM	Schleicher K 7	K7 DRM Syndicate
	G-DDRN	Glasflugel H303A Mosquito	K. J. King
	G-DDRO	Grob G.103 Twin Astir	Twin Astir 258 Syndicate
	G-DDRP	Pilatus B4-PC11	DRP Syndicate
	G-DDRT	Eiriavion PIK-20D	N. Braithwaite

Reg	Type	Owner or Operator	Notes
G-DDRV	Schleicher K 8B	DRV Syndicate	
G-DDRW	Grob G.102 Astir CS	The Royal Air Force Gliding & Soaring Associationl	
G-DDRY	Schleicher Ka 6CR	M. K. Bradford	
G-DDRZ	Schleicher K-8B	East Sussex Gliding Club Ltd	
G-DDSG	Schleicher Ka 6CR	S. McGuirk	
G-DDSH	Grob G.102 Astir CS77	Astir 648 Syndicate	
G-DDSJ	Grob G.103 Twin Astir II	Herefordshire Gliding Club Ltd	
G-DDSL	Grob G.103 Twin Astir	DSL Group	
G-DDSP	Schempp-Hirth Mini Nimbus B	DDSP Group	
G-DDST	Schleicher ASW-20L	H. A. Bloxham	
G-DDSU	Grob G.102 Astir CS77	Bowland Forest Gliding Club Ltd	
G-DDSV	Pilatus B4-PC11AF	G. M. Drinkell	
G-DDSX	Schleicher ASW-19B	G-DDSX Group '877'	
G-DDSY	Schleicher Ka-6CR	D. J. Shepherd	
G-DDTA	Glaser-Dirks DG-200	M. Rose	
G-DDTC	Schempp-Hirth Janus B	Darlton Gliding Club Ltd	
G-DDTE	Schleicher ASW-19B	G. R. Purcell	
G-DDTG	Schempp-Hirth SHK-1	M. W. Roberts	
G-DDTK	Glasflugel Mosquito B	M. G. Entwisle	
G-DDTM	Glaser-Dirks DG-200	M. C. Bailey	
G-DDTN	Schleicher K 8B	C. G. & G. N. Thomas	
G-DDTP	Schleicher ASW-20	T. S. & S. M. Hills	
G-DDTS	CARMAM M-100S	J. P. Dyne	
G-DDTU	Schempp-Hirth Nimbus 2B	M. D. Miskimmin	
G-DDTV	Glasflugel Mosquito B	D. R. Allan	
G-DDTW	PZL-Bielsko SZD-30 Pirat	NDGC Pirat Syndicate	
G-DDTX	Glasflugel Mosquito B	P. T. S. Nash	
G-DDTY	Glasflugel H303 Mosquito B	W. H. L. Bullimore	
G-DDUB	Glasflugel H303 Mosquito B	Mosquito G-DDUB Syndicate	
G-DDUE	Schleicher ASK-13	J. P. Gilbert	
G-DDUH	Scheibe L-Spatz 55	R. J. Aylesbury & J. Young	
G-DDUK	Schleicher K-8B	The Bristol Gliding Club Propietary Ltd	
G-DDUL	Grob G.102 Astir CS77	M. G. Dodd & K. Nattrass	
G-DDUR	Schleicher Ka 6CR	B. N. Bromley	
G-DDUS	Schleicher Ka 6E	D.E. Findon	
G-DDUT	Schleicher ASW-20	M. E. Doig & E. T. J. Murphy	
G-DDUY	Glaser-Dirks DG-100	R. L. & K. P. McLean	
G-DDVA	Schempp-Hirth Nimbus 2B	L. W. Bishop	
G-DDVB	Schleicher ASK-13	Essex and Suffolk Gliding Club Ltd	
G-DDVC	Schleicher ASK-13	Staffordshire Gliding Club Ltd	
G-DDVG	Schleicher Ka-6CR	G-DDVG Banana Group	
G-DDVH	Schleicher Ka 6E	M. A. K. Cropper	
G-DDVK	PZL-Bielsko SZD-48 Jantar Standard 2	R. Goodchild	
G-DDVL	Schleicher ASW-19	J. Gavin, P. K. Newman & G. Prophet	
G-DDVM	Glasflugel H205 Club Libelle	M. A. Field	
G-DDVN	Eiriavion PIL-20D-78	P. A. & T. P. Bassett	
G-DDVP	Schleicher ASW-19	VP Syndicate	
G-DDVS	Schempp-Hirth Standard Cirrus	W. T. J. Wilson	
G-DDVV	Schleicher ASW-20L	D. M. Hurst & C. J. Bishop	
G-DDVX	Schleicher ASK-13	Shenington Gliding Club	
G-DDVY	Schempp-Hirth Cirrus	M. G. Ashton & G. Martin	
G-DDVZ	Glasflugel H303 Mosquito B	R. M. Spreckley	
G-DDWB	Glasflugel H303 Mosquito B	D. T. Edwards	
G-DDWC	Schleicher Ka 6E	C. Hitchings	
G-DDWJ	Glaser-Dirks DG-200	A. P. Kamp & P. R. Desmond	
G-DDWL	Glasflugel Mosquito B	H. A. Stanford	
G-DDWN	Schleicher K7 Rhonadler	L. R. & J. E. Merritt	
G-DDWP	Glasflugel Mosquito B	I. H. Murdoch	
G-DDWR	Glasflugel Mosquito B	C. D. Lovell	
G-DDWS	Eiriavion PIK-20D	D. G. Slocombe	
G-DDWT	Slingsby T.65C Vega	A. P. Grimley	
G-DDWU	Grob G.102 Astir CS	Astir G-DDWU Syndicate	
G-DDWW	Slingsby T.65A Vega	M. Finnie & B. Grice	
G-DDWZ	Schleicher ASW-19B	P. Woodcock	
G-DDXB	Schleicher ASW-20	81 Syndicate	
G-DDXD	Slingsby T.65A Vega	G-DDXD Flying Group	
G-DDXE	Slingsby T.65A Vega	M. C. Hayes	
G-DDXF	Slingsby T.65A Vega	B. A. Walker	
G-DDXG	Slingsby T.65A Vega	P. J. Smith	
G-DDXH	Schleicher Ka 6E	G. C. Grainger & C. D. Bingham	

Notes	Reg	Type	Owner or Operator
	G-DDXJ	Grob G.102 Astir CS77	DXJ Syndicate
	G-DDXK	Centrair ASW-20F	E. & A. Townsend
	G-DDXL	Schempp-Hirth Standard Cirrus	A. C. Bridges
	G-DDXN	Glaser-Dirks DG-200	J. A. Johnston
	G-DDXT	Schempp-Hirth Mini-Nimbus C	M. J. Love
	G-DDXW	Glasflugel Mosquito B	B. L. C. Gordon
	G-DDXX	Schleicher ASW-19B	D. Neave
	G-DDYC	Schleicher Ka 6CR	C. M. Tunnicliffe
	G-DDYE	Schleicher ASW-20L	G. Cook & D. F. Adams
	G-DDYF	Grob G.102 Astir CS77	York Gliding Centre (Operations) Ltd
	G-DDYH	Glaser-Dirks DG-200	W. A. B. Roberts
	G-DDYJ	Schleicher Ka 6CR	T. J. Wilkinson
	G-DDYL	CARMAM JP 15-36AR	J. M. Caldwell
	G-DDYU	Schempp-Hirth Nimbus -2C	C. B. Shepperd
	G-DDZA	Slingsby T.65A Vega	A. W. Roberts
	G-DDZB	Slingsby T.65A Vega	A. L. Maitland
	G-DDZF	Schempp-Hirth Standard Cirrus	J. D. E. Macdonald
	G-DDZM	Slingsby T.65A Vega	A. Mattano
	G-DDZN	Slingsby T.65A Vega	D. A. White
	G-DDZP	Slingsby T.65A Vega	M. T. Crews
	G-DDZR	IS-28B2	Lakes Gliding Club Ltd
	G-DDZT	Eiriavion PIK-20D	PIK-20D 106 Group
	G-DDZU	Grob G.102 Astir CS	P. Clarke
	G-DDZV	Scheibe SF-27A	N. Newham
	G-DDZW	Schleicher Ka 6CR	S. W. Naylor
	G-DDZY	Schleicher ASW-19B	M. C. Fairman
	G-DEAE	Schleicher ASW-20L	R. Burghall
	G-DEAF	Grob G.102 Astir CS77	The Borders (Milfield) Gliding Club Ltd
	G-DEAG	Slingsby T.65A Vega	P. Hadfield
	G-DEAH	Schleicher Ka 6E	R. J. King
	G-DEAJ	Schempp-Hirth Nimbus 2	A. O'Keefe
	G-DEAK	Glasflugel H303 Mosquito B	T. A. L. Barnes
	G-DEAM	Schempp-Hirth Nimbus 2B	Alpha Mike Syndicate
	G-DEAN	Solar Wings Pegasus XL-Q	IM. G. J. Bridges (G-MVJV)
	G-DEAR	Eiriavion PIK-20D	G-DEAR Group
	G-DEAT	Eiriavion PIK-20D	D. J. Knights
	G-DEAU	Schleicher K7	The Welland Gliding Club Ltd
	G-DEAV	Schempp-Hirth Mini-Nimbus C	G. D. H. Crawford
	G-DEAW	Grob G.102 Astir CS77	EAW Group
	G-DEBT	Pioneer 300	N. J. T. Tonks & A. J. Lloyd
	G-DEBX	Schleicher ASW-20	S. M. Economou & R. M Harris
	G-DECC	Schleicher Ka 6CR	P. Weaver
	G-DECF	Schleicher Ka 6CR	E. L. Burns
	G-DECJ	Slingsby T.65A Vega	J. E. B. Hart
	G-DECL	Slingsby T.65A Vega	J. M. Sherman
	G-DECM	Slingsby T.65A Vega	F. Wilson
	G-DECO	Dyn'Aéro MCR-01 Club	A. P. Wheelwright & A. W. Bishop
	G-DECP	Rolladen-Schneider LS3-17	LS3-17 ECP Syndicate
	G-DECR	P & M Quik R	D. J. Lawrence
	G-DECS	Glasflugel H303 Mosquito B	G. Richardson
	G-DECW	Schleicher ASK-21	Norfolk Gliding Club Ltd
	G-DECZ	Schleicher ASK-21	Booker Gliding Club Ltd
	G-DEDG	Schleicher Ka 6CR	M. Wood
	G-DEDH	Glasflugel H303 Mosquito B	B. L. Liddiard
	G-DEDJ	Glasflugel H303 Mosquito B	D. M. Ward
	G-DEDK	Schleicher K7 Rhonadler	Cyprus Gliding Group
	G-DEDM	Glaser-Dirks DG-200	D. Watson
	G-DEDN	Glaser-Dirks DG-100G	DG 280 Syndicate
	G-DEDU	Schleicher ASK-13	Channel Gliding Club
	G-DEDX	Slingsby T.65D Vega	G. Kirkham
	G-DEDY	Slingsby T.65D Vega	G. Spelman & J. Shaw
	G-DEDZ	Slingsby T.65C Vega	R. C. R. Copley
	G-DEEA	Slingsby T.65C Vega	S. J. Harrison
	G-DEEC	Schleicher ASW-20L	D. Beams
	G-DEED	Schleicher K-8B	The Windrushers Gliding Club Ltd
	G-DEEF	Rolladen-Schneider LS3-17	Echo Echo Foxtrot Group
	G-DEEG	Slingsby T.65C Vega	Vega Syndicate
	G-DEEO	Schleicher ASW-19	K. Kiely
	G-DEEJ	Schleicher ASW-20L	T. R. Dews
	G-DEEK	Schempp-Hirth Nimbus 2C	G. D. Palmer

Reg	Type	Owner or Operator	Notes
G-DEEM	Schleicher K-8	The South Wales Gliding Club Ltd	
G-DEEN	Schempp-Hirth Standard Cirrus 75	G-DEEN Flying Group	
G-DEEO	Grob G.102 Club Astir II	G-DEEO Group	
G-DEEP	Wassmer WA.26P Squale	Wassmer G-DEEP Group	
G-DEES	Rolladen-Schneider LS3-17	J. B. Illidge	
G-DEEX	Rolladen-Schneider LS3-17	G-DEEX Group	
G-DEEZ	Denney Kitfox Mk.3	J. D. & D. Cheesman	
G-DEFA	Schleicher ASW-20L	Eight Eighties Syndicate	
G-DEFB	Schempp-Hirth Nimbus 2C	G. D. Palmer	
G-DEFE	Centrair ASW-20F	W. A. Horne & D. A. Mackenzie	
G-DEFF	Schempp-Hirth Nimbus 2C	J. W. L. Clarke and P. J. D. Smith	
G-DEFS	Rolladen-Schneider LS3	A. Twigg	
G-DEFV	Schleicher ASW-20	A. R. McKillen	
G-DEFW	Slingsby T.65C Sport Vega	H. Yildiz	
G-DEFZ	Rolladen-Schneider LS3-a	EFZ Syndicate	
G-DEGE	Rolladen-Schneider LS3-a	S. J. Kohnstamm	
G-DEGF	Slingsby T.65D Vega	Shalbourne Soaring Society Ltd	
G-DEGH	Slingsby T.65C Vega	P. Thomas	
G-DEGJ	Slingsby T.65C Vega	Sport Vega Syndicate	
G-DEGK	Schempp-Hirth Standard Cirrus	D. A. Parker	
G-DEGN	Grob G.103 Twin Astir II	Staffordshire Gliding Club Ltd	
G-DEGP	Schleicher ASW-20L	D. Hoolahan & J. R. Paine	
G-DEGS	Schempp-Hirth Nimbus 2CS	A. Klapa	
G-DEGT	Slingsby T.65D Vega	G-DEGT Group	
G-DEGW	Schempp-Hirth Mini-Nimbus C	I. F. Barnes and Partners	
G-DEGX	Slingsby T.65C Vega	Haddenham Vega Syndicate	
G-DEGZ	Schleicher ASK-21	Oxford Gliding Co.Ltd	
G-DEHC	Akaflieg Braunschweig SB-5B	D. J. Hopgood	
G-DEHG	Slingsby T.65C Vega	S. R. Hopkins	
G-DEHH	Schempp-Hirth Ventus a	L. B. Roberts	
G-DEHK	Rolladen-Schneider LS4	R. P. M. Symons	
G-DEHM	Schleicher Ka 6E	J. B. Symonds	
G-DEHO	Schleicher ASK-21	Lasham Gliding Society Ltd	
G-DEHP	Schempp-Hirth Nimbus 2C	D. J. King	
G-DEHT	Schempp-Hirth Nimbus 2C	M. V. Boydon	
G-DEHU	Glasflugel 304	F. Townsend	
G-DEHY	Slingsby T.65D Vega	C. J. A. Rosales	
G-DEHZ	Schleicher ASW-20L	G-DEHZ Syndicate	
G-DEJA	ICA IS-28B2	M. H. Simms	
G-DEJB	Slingsby T.65C Vega	DEV Group	
G-DEJC	Slingsby T.65C Vega	I. Powis	
G-DEJD	Slingsby T.65D Vega	R. L. & K. P. McLean	
G-DEJE	Slingsby T.65C Vega	Crown Service Gliding Club	
G-DEJF	Schleicher K 8B	Cotswold Gliding Club	
G-DEJR	Schleicher ASW-19B	M. C. Woerner	
G-DEJY	PZL-Bielsko SZD-9bis Bocian 1D	G-DEJY Group	
G-DEKA	Cameron Z-90 balloon	P. G. Bogliaccino	
G-DEKC	Schleicher Ka 6E	M. N. K. Willcox	
G-DEKF	Grob G.102 Club Astir III	The Bristol Gliding Club Proprietary Ltd	
G-DEKG	Schleicher ASK-21	Army Gliding Association	
G-DEKJ	Schempp-Hirth Ventus b	I. J. Metcalfe	
G-DEKS	Scheibe SF27A Zugvogel V	T. Emms	
G-DEKU	Schleicher ASW-20L	A. J. Gillson	
G-DEKV	Rolladen-Schneider LS4	S. L. Helstrip	
G-DEKW	Schempp-Hirth Nimbus 2B	V. Luscombe-Mahoney	
G-DEKX	Schleicher Ka 6E	D. S. Downton	
G-DELA	Schleicher ASW-19B	S. G. Jones	
G-DELB	Robinson R-22 Beta ★	South Yorkshire Aircraft Museum/Doncaster	
G-DELD	Slingsby T65C Vega	The Surrey Hills Gliding Club Ltd	
G-DELG	Schempp-Hirth Ventus b/16.6	A. Jelden	
G-DELN	Grob G.102 Astir CS Jeans	Bowland Forest Gliding Club Ltd	
G-DELO	Slingsby T.65D Vega	I. Sim & I. Surley	
G-DELR	Schempp-Hirth Ventus b	I. D. Smith	
G-DELU	Schleicher ASW-20L	P. G. Roberts	
G-DELZ	Schleicher ASW-20L	D. A. Fogden	
G-DEME	Glaser-Dirks DG-200/17	E. D. Casagrande	
G-DEMF	Rolladen-Schneider LS4	R. N. Johnston	
G-DEMG	Rolladen-Schneider LS4	Stratford on Avon Gliding Club	
G-DEMH	Cessna F.172M (modified)	M. Hammond (G-BFLO)	
G-DEMN	Slingsby T.65D Vega	J. C. Jenks	
G-DEMP	Slingsby T.65C Vega	I. P. Stork	

Notes	Reg	Type	Owner or Operator
	G-DEMR	Slingsby T.65C Vega	Llantysilio Team
	G-DEMT	Rolladen-Schneider LS4	M. R. Fox
	G-DEMU	Glaser-Dirks DG-202/17	A. Butterfield & N. Swinton
	G-DEMZ	Slingsby T65A Vega	K. Western (G-BGCA)
	G-DENC	Cessna F.150G	G-DENC Cessna Group (G-AVAP)
	G-DEND	Cessna F.150M	Wicklow Wings (G-WAFC/G-BDFI)
	G-DENI	PA-32-300 Cherokee Six	A. Bendkowski (G-BAIA)
	G-DENJ	Schempp-Hirth Ventus b/16.6	S. Boyden
	G-DENM	BB03 Trya	D. A. Morgan
	G-DENO	Glasflugel Standard Libelle 201B	D. M. Bland
	G-DENS	Binder CP.301S Smaragd	Garston Smaragd Group
	G-DENU	Glaser-Dirks DG-100G	N. M. C. Robinson
	G-DENV	Schleicher ASW-20L	J. H. B. Jones
	G-DENX	PZL-Bielsko SZD-48 Jantar Standard 2	J. M. Hire
	G-DENY	Robinson R44 II	P. D. Sanders & M. A. Copley
	G-DEOB	PZL-Bielsko SZD-30	R. M. Golding
	G-DEOD	Grob G.102 Astir CS77	South Wales Gliding Club Ltd
	G-DEOE	Schleicher ASK-13	Essex Gliding Club Ltd
	G-DEOF	Schleicher ASK-13	K13-DEOF Syndicate
	G-DEOJ	Centrair ASW-20FL	C. J. Bowden
	G-DEOK	Centrair 101A Pegase	C. M. Scott
	G-DEOM	Carman M100S	S. W. Hutchinson
	G-DEON	Schempp-Hirth Nimbus 3	117 Syndicate
	G-DEOT	Grob G.103A Twin II Acro	R. Tyrrell
	G-DEOU	Pilatus B4-PC11AF	J. E. Lambert
	G-DEOV	Schempp-Hirth Janus C	Burn Gliding Club Ltd
	G-DEOW	Schempp-Hirth Janus C	383 Syndicate
	G-DEOX	Carmam M-200 Foehn	B. S. Goodspeed
	G-DEOZ	Schleicher K 8B	Cotswold Gliding Club
	G-DEPD	Schleicher ASK-21	London Gliding Club Proprietary Ltd
	G-DEPF	Centrair ASW-20FL	S. G. Lapworth
	G-DEPG	CARMAM M100S	J. Kohlmetz
	G-DEPP	Schleicher ASK-13	Mendip Gliding Club Ltd
	G-DEPS	Schleicher ASW-20L	C. Beveridge
	G-DEPT	Schleicher K-8B	R. McEvoy
	G-DEPU	Glaser-Dirks DG-101G Elan	J. F. Rogers
	G-DEPX	Schempp-Hirth Ventus b/16.6	M. E. S. Thomas
	G-DERA	Centrair ASW-20FL	R. J. Lockett
	G-DERH	Schleicher ASK-21	The Burn Gliding Club Ltd
	G-DERJ	Schleicher ASK-21	The Royal Air Force Gliding and Soaring Association
	G-DERO	Van's RV-10	D. Atkinson
	G-DERR	Schleicher ASW-19B	University of Edinburgh Sports Union
	G-DERS	Schleicher ASW-19B	Booker Gliding Club Ltd
	G-DERV	Cameron Truck SS balloon	J. M. Percival
	G-DERX	Centrair 101A Pegase	I. P. Freestone
	G-DESB	Schleicher ASK-21	Oxford University Gliding Club
	G-DESC	Rolladen-Schneider LS4	J. Crawford & J. M. Staley
	G-DESH	Centrair 101A	J. E. Moore
	G-DESO	Glaser-Dirks DG-300 Elan	G. R. P. Brown
	G-DESU	Schleicher ASK-21	Banbury Gliding Club Ltd
	G-DETA	Schleicher ASK-21	P. Hawkins
	G-DETG	Rolladen-Schneider LS4	K. J. Woods
	G-DETJ	Centrair 101A	S. C. Phillips
	G-DETM	Centrair 101A	J. E. Masheder & A. Carden
	G-DETV	Rolladen-Schneider LS4	P. Fabian
	G-DETY	Rolladen-Schneider LS4	D. T. Staff
	G-DETZ	Schleicher ASW-20CL	The 20 Syndicate
	G-DEUC	Schleicher ASK-13	North Wales Gliding Club Ltd
	G-DEUD	Schleicher ASW-20C	R. Tietema
	G-DEUF	PZL-Bielsko SZD-50-3	Shalbourne Soaring Society Ltd
	G-DEUH	Rolladen-Schneider LS4	F. J. Parkinson
	G-DEUJ	Schempp-Hirth Ventus b/16.6	C. Bessent
	G-DEUK	Centrair ASW-20FL	P. A. Clark
	G-DEUS	Schempp-Hirth Ventus b/16.6	R. J. Whitaker
	G-DEUV	PZL-Bielsko SZD-42-2 Jantar 2B	G. V. McKirdy
	G-DEUY	Schleicher ASW-20BL	ASW20BL-G-DUEY Group
	G-DEVF	Schempp-Hirth Nimbus 3T	A. G. Leach
	G-DEVH	Schleicher Ka 10	C. W. & K. T. Matten
	G-DEVJ	Schleicher ASK-13	Lasham Gliding Society Ltd
	G-DEVK	Grob G.102 Astir CS	Peterborough and Spalding Gliding Club Ltd

Reg	Type	Owner or Operator	Notes
G-DEVM	Centrair 101A	Seahawk Gliding Club	
G-DEVO	Centrair 101A	G-DEVO Pegase Glider	
G-DEVP	Schleicher ASK-13	R. Maksowicz, A. J. Palfreyman & A. Sutton	
G-DEVS	PA-28 Cherokee 180	180 Group (G-BGVJ)	
G-DEVV	Schleicher ASK-23	Midland Gliding Club Ltd	
G-DEVW	Schleicher ASK-23	London Gliding Club Proprietary Ltd	
G-DEVX	Schleicher ASK-23	London Gliding Club Proprietary Ltd	
G-DEWE	P & M Flight Design CTSW	A. R. Hughes	
G-DEWG	Grob G.103A Twin II Acro	Herefordshire Gliding Club Ltd	
G-DEWI	Rotorsport UK MTO Sport	D. V. Nockels	
G-DEWP	Grob G.103A Twin II Acro	Bowland Forest Gliding Club Ltd	
G-DEWR	Grob G.103A Twin II Acro	The Bristol Gliding Club Proprietary Ltd	
G-DEWS	Grob G.109B	Aerobility Holdings CIC	
G-DEWZ	Grob G.103A Twin II Acro	T. R. Dews	
G-DEXA	Grob G.103A Twin II Acro	Trent Valley Gliding Club Ltd	
G-DEXP	ARV Super 2	R. W. Clarke	
G-DEXT	Robinson R44 II	Berkley Properties Ltd	
G-DFAF	Schleicher ASW-20L	G-DFAF Group	
G-DFAR	Glasflugel H205 Club Libelle	R. G. Appleboom	
G-DFAT	Schleicher ASK-13	Dorset Gliding Club Ltd	
G-DFAW	Schempp-Hirth Ventus b/16.6	J. Hanlon	
G-DFBD	Schleicher ASW-15B	J. J. Mion	
G-DFBE	Rolladen-Schneider LS6	T. Pavis	
G-DFBJ	Schleicher K 8B	Bidford Gliding & Flying Club Ltd	
G-DFBO	Schleicher ASW-20BL	A. M. Cridge	
G-DFBR	Grob G.102 Astir CS77	C. N. Enmarch	
G-DFBY	Schempp-Hirth Discus b	D. Latimer	
G-DFCD	Centrair 101A	G. J. Bass	
G-DFCK	Schempp-Hirth Ventus b	S. A. Adlard	
G-DFCM	Glaser-Dirks DG-300	A. Davis & I. D. Roberts	
G-DFCW	Schleicher ASK-13	Black Mountains Gliding Club	
G-DFCY	Schleicher ASW-15	M. R. Shaw	
G-DFDF	Grob G.102 Astir CS	W. D. Harrop	
G-DFDO	Evektor EV-97 Eurostar SL	C. D. Taylor	
G-DFDW	Glaser-Dirks DG-300	C. M. Hadley	
G-DFEB	Grob G.102 Club Astir III	Lasham Gliding Society Ltd	
G-DFES	Schempp-Hirth Discus 2c FES	C. J. Short	
G-DFEX	Grob G.102 Astir CS77	Loughborough Students Union	
G-DFFP	Schleicher ASW-19B	Foxtrot Papa Group	
G-DFGJ	Schleicher Ka 6CR	G. D. S. Caldwell	
G-DFGT	Glaser-Dirks DG-300 Elan	L. Clarke & M. J. Love	
G-DFHS	Schempp-Hirth Ventus cT	154 Group	
G-DFHY	Scheibe SF-27A	J. M. Pursey	
G-DFJO	Schempp-Hirth Ventus cT	FJO Syndicate	
G-DFKI	Westland Gazelle HT.2	D. J. Fravigar (G-BZOT)	
G-DFKX	Schleicher Ka 6CR	Dorset Gliding Club Ltd	
G-DFOG	Rolladen-Schneider LS7	R. B. Porteous	
G-DFOV	CARMAM JP 15-36AR Aiglon	M. Howley	
G-DFRA	Rolladen-Schneider LS6-b	79 Syndicate	
G-DFSA	Grob G.102 Astir CS	Astir 498 Syndicate	
G-DFTF	Schleicher Ka-6CR	J. Preller	
G-DFTJ	PZL-Bielsko SZD-48-1 Jantar Standard 2	P. Nock	
G-DFUF	Scheibe SF-27A Zugvogel V	R. J. Savage	
G-DFUN	Van's RV-6	G-DFUN Flying Group	
G-DFXE	Rolladen-Schneider LS7	V. J. R. Day	
G-DFXR	Sportine Aviacija LAK-12	I. P. Freestone	
G-DGAJ	Glaser-Dirks DG-300 Club Elan	S. Lewis	
G-DGAL	Ikarus C42 FB80 Bravo	D. Crozier	
G-DGAV	P & M Quik R	M. D. Howe	
G-DGAW	Schleicher Ka 6CR	D. Searle	
G-DGDJ	Rolladen-Schneider LS4-a	W. H. Greenwood	
G-DGDW	Scheibe SF-27A Zugvogel V	G. Wardle	
G-DGEF	Schleicher Ka 6CR	Lee K6CR Group	
G-DGFD	Robinson R44 II	Macrae Aviation Ltd (G-CGNF)	
G-DGFY	Flylight Dragonfly	M. R. Sands	
G-DGHI	Dyn'Aéro MCR-01 Club	J. M. Keane	
G-DGIO	Glaser-Dirks DG-100G Elan	DG1 Group	
G-DGKB	Centrair ASW-20F	F. W. Wiltshire	
G-DGMT	III Sky Arrow 650 T	D. C. Lewin	

Notes	Reg	Type	Owner or Operator
	G-DGON	Taylor JT.2 Titch	E. D. Rogerson & S. Eason (G-RKET/G-BIBK)
	G-DGPS	Diamond DA-42 Twin Star	AJW Construction Ltd
	G-DGRE	Guimbal Cabri G2	Helicentre Aviation Ltd
	G-DGSC	CZAW Sportcruiser	Sierra Charlie Group
	G-DGST	Beech 95-B55 Baron	P. R. Ross (G-BXDF)
	G-DGUN	Agusta AW109SP Grand New	Orchard Holdings Ltd
	G-DHAA	Glasflugel H201B Standard Libelle	D. J. Jones & R. N. Turner
	G-DHAD	Glasflugel H201B Standard Libelle	R. Hines
	G-DHAH	Aeronca 7BCM Champion	Alpha Hotel Group (G-JTYE)
	G-DHAL	Schleicher ASK-13	Dumfries & District Gliding Club
	G-DHAM	Robinson R44 II	D. B. Hamilton
	G-DHAP	Schleicher Ka 6E	T. Turner & R. King
	G-DHAT	Glaser-Dirks DG-200/17	G-DHAT Group
	G-DHBZ	DH.82A Tiger Moth (NL985)	H. M. M. Haines (G-BWIK)
	G-DHCA	Grob G.103 Twin Astir	G-DHCA Group
	G-DHCC	DHC.1 Chipmunk 22 (WG321:G)	Liberty Aviation Ltd
	G-DHCE	Schleicher ASW-19B	A. M. Wilmot
	G-DHCF	PZL-Bielsko SZD-50-3	Shalbourne Soaring Society Ltd
	G-DHCJ	Grob G.103A Twin II Acro	Peterborough and Spalding Gliding Club Ltd
	G-DHCL	Schempp-Hirth Discus b	A. I. Lambe
	G-DHCO	Glasflugel Standard Libelle 201B	M. J. Birch
	G-DHCR	PZL-Bielsko SZD-51-1	East Sussex Gliding Club Ltd
	G-DHCU	DG-300 Club Elan	R. B. Hankey & J. B. Symonds
	G-DHCV	Schleicher ASW-19B	R. C. May
	G-DHCW	PZL-Bielsko SZD-51-1	Deeside Gliding Club (Aberdeenshire) Ltd
	G-DHCX	Schleicher ASK-21	Devon and Somerset Gliding Club Ltd
	G-DHCY	Glaser-Dirks DG-300 Club Elan	R. M. Wootten
	G-DHCZ	DHC.2 Beaver 1	Propshop Ltd (G-BUCJ)
	G-DHDH	Glaser-Dirks DG-200	Delta Hotel Syndicate
	G-DHDV	DH.104 Dove 8 (VP981)	K. M. Perkins
	G-DHEB	Schleicher Ka 6CR	J. Burrow
	G-DHEM	Schempp-Hirth Discus CS	473 Syndicate
	G-DHER	Schleicher ASW-19B	J. E. & F. C. Roberts
	G-DHES	Centrair 101A	G. H. Lawrence & G. S. Sanderson
	G-DHET	Rolladen-Schneider LS6-c18	A. Lake & M. D. Langford
	G-DHEV	Schempp-Hirth Cirrus	L. K. Nazar
	G-DHGL	Schempp-Hirth Discus b	E. A. Martin
	G-DHGS	Robinson R22 Beta	Helimech Ltd
	G-DHHD	PZL-Bielsko SZD-51-1	Scottish Gliding Union Ltd
	G-DHHF	North American AT-6 Harvard II	DH Heritage Flights Ltd
	G-DHJH	Airbus A.321-211	Titan Airways Ltd
	G-DHKB	Boeing 757-256	DHL Air Ltd
	G-DHKC	Boeing 757-256	DHL Air Ltd
	G-DHKD	Boeing 757-23N	DHL Air Ltd
	G-DHKE	Boeing 757-23N	DHL Air Ltd
	G-DHKF	Boeing 757-236	DHL Air Ltd (G-TCBB)
	G-DHKG	Boeing 757-236	DHL Air Ltd (G-TCBC)
	G-DHKH	Boeing 757-28A	DHL Air Ltd (G-FCLI)
	G-DHKK	Boeing 757-28A	DHL Air Ltd
	G-DHKL	Schempp-Hirth Discus bT	M. A. Thorne
	G-DHKM	Boeing 757-223	DHL Air Ltd
	G-DHKN	Boeing 757-223	DHL Air Ltd
	G-DHKO	Boeing 757-223	DHL Air Ltd
	G-DHKP	Boeing 757-223	DHL Air Ltd
	G-DHKR	Boeing 757-223	DHL Air Ltd
	G-DHKS	Boeing 757-223	DHL Air Ltd
	G-DHKT	Boeing 757-223	DHL Air Ltd
	G-DHKU	Boeing 757-223	DHL Air Ltd
	G-DHKX	Boeing 757-23APF	DHL Air Ltd
	G-DHKZ	Boeing 757-236	DHL Air Ltd (G-CSVS/G-IEAC)
	G-DHLE	Boeing 767-3JHF	DHL Air Ltd
	G-DHLF	Boeing 767-3JHF	DHL Air Ltd
	G-DHLG	Boeing 767-3JHF	DHL Air Ltd
	G-DHMP	Schempp-Hirth Discus b	S. Harding
	G-DHNX	Rolladen-Schneider LS4-b	J. Brand
	G-DHOC	Scheibe Bergfalke II-55	The Gliding Heritage Centre
	G-DHOK	Schleicher ASW-20CL	S. D. Minson
	G-DHOP	Van's RV-9A	C. Partington
	G-DHPA	Issoire E-78 Silene	P. Woodcock
	G-DHPM	OGMA DHC.1 Chipmunk 20 (1365)	P. G. Winterbottom

Reg	Type	Owner or Operator	Notes
G-DHPR	Schempp-Hirth Discus b	Knibbs Johnson Syndicate	
G-DHRR	Schleicher ASK-21	Lakes Gliding Club Ltd	
G-DHSJ	Schempp-Hirth Discus b	D. Byrne	
G-DHSR	AB Sportine LAK-12 Lietuva	A. G. A. Parker	
G-DHTG	Grob G.102 Astir CS	North Wales Gliding Club Ltd	
G-DHYL	Schempp-Hirth Ventus 2a	M. J. Cook	
G-DHYS	Titan T-51 Mustang (414907:CY-S)	D. Houghton	
G-DHZF	DH.82A Tiger Moth (N9192)	S. S. Johnson (G-BSTJ)	
G-DHZP	Rolladen-Schneider LS8-18	A. D. May & D. J. Bennett	
G-DICA	SIAI Marchetti S.208	P. di Carlo/Italy	
G-DICK	Thunder Ax6-56Z balloon	S. Dyer	
G-DIDG	Van's RV-7	B. R. Alexander	
G-DIDO	Agusta A109E Power	A. D. Whitehouse	
G-DIDY	Thruster T600T 450	M. M. P. Evans	
G-DIGA	Robinson R66	Helicopter & Pilot Services Ltd	
G-DIGI	PA-32 Cherokee Six 300	Security Unlimited Group	
G-DIGS	Hughes 369HE	W Aircollection (G-DIZZ)	
G-DIGZ	Hughes 369D	Mackinnon Construction Ltd (G-MCDD)	
G-DIII	Pitts S-2B Special	J. A. Coutts (G-STUB)	
G-DIKY	Murphy Rebel	Stoke Golding Flyers	
G-DIME	Rockwell Commander 114	H. B. Richardson	
G-DINA	AA-5B Tiger	Portway Aviation Ltd	
G-DINO	Pegasus Quantum 15	R. D. J. Buchanan (G-MGMT)	
G-DIPI	Cameron 80 Tub SS balloon	C. G. Dobson	
G-DIPM	PA-46-350P Malibu Mirage	MAS Mix Ltd	
G-DIPZ	Colt 17A Cloudhopper balloon	C. G. Dobson	
G-DIRK	Glaser-Dirks DG.400	Romeo-Kilo Gliding Club	
G-DISA	SA Bulldog Srs 120/125	I. W. Whiting	
G-DISO	Jodel 150	P. K. Morley & C. R. Coates	
G-DISP	AutoGyro Calidus	P. J. Troy-Davies	
G-DIYA	TAF Sling 4 TSI	Inditu Air Services Ltd	
G-DIZI	Reality Escapade 912(2)	J. C. Carter	
G-DIZO	Jodel D.120A	N. M. Harwood (G-EMKM)	
G-DIZY	PA-28R-201T Turbo Arrow III	Dizy Aviation Ltd	
G-DJAA	Schempp-Hirth Janus B	Bidford Gliding & Flying Club Ltd	
G-DJAC	Schempp-Hirth Duo Discus	G-DJAC Group	
G-DJAD	Schleicher ASK-21	The Borders (Milfield) Gliding Club Ltd	
G-DJAH	Schempp-Hirth Discus b	S. C. Moss	
G-DJAN	Schempp-Hirth Discus b	N. F. Perren	
G-DJAY	Avtech Jabiru UL-450	M. A. Grant	
G-DJBC	Ikarus C42 FB100	Bluecool Water Dispensers	
G-DJBX	Aeropro Eurofox 912(IS)	D. J. Barrott	
G-DJCR	Varga 2150A Kachina	M. Robertson (G-BLWG)	
G-DJEB	HpH Glasflugel 304 ES Shark	P. D. Candler	
G-DJET	Diamond DA42 Twin Star	DEA Aviation Ltd	
G-DJGG	Schleicher ASW-15B	R. E. Perry	
G-DJHP	Valentin Mistral C	P. B. Higgs	
G-DJJA	PA-28-181 Archer II	Interactive Aviation Ltd	
G-DJLL	Schleicher ASK-13	Bidford Gliding & Flying Club Ltd	
G-DJMC	Schleicher ASK-21	The Royal Air Force Gliding and Soaring Association	
G-DJMD	Schempp-Hirth Discus b	G-DJMD Syndicate	
G-DJNC	ICA-Brasov IS-28B2	Delta Juliet November Group	
G-DJNE	DG Flugzeugbau DG-808C	J. N. Ellis (G-DGRA)	
G-DJNH	Denney Kitfox Mk 3	Titan Airways Ltd	
G-DJSM	Eurocopter AS.350B3 Ecureuil	Meoble Estate (G-CICZ)	
G-DJST	Ixess 912(1)	G-DJST Flying Group	
G-DJVY	Scintex CP.1315-C3 Super Emeraude	A. P. Goodwin	
G-DJWS	Schleicher ASW-15B	A. J. Grant	
G-DKBA	DKBA AT 0301-0 balloon	I. Chadwick	
G-DKDP	Grob G.109	P. Wardell	
G-DKEN	Rolladen-Schneider LS4-a	K. L. Sangster & B. Lytollis	
G-DKEY	PA-28-161 Warrior II	PA-28 Warrior Ltd	
G-DKFU	Schempp-Hirth Ventus 2cxT	R. L. Watson (G-CKFU)	
G-DKGF	Viking Dragonfly ★	(stored)/Enstone	
G-DKNY	Robinson R44 II	R. R. Orr	
G-DKTA	PA-28-236 Dakota	Dakota Flying Group	

Notes	Reg	Type	Owner or Operator
	G-DLAD	Cessna 208 Caravan I	Avonvale Ltd
	G-DLAF	Bristell NG5 Speed Wing	A. French & G. Dangerfield
	G-DLAK	Cessna 208 Caravan 1	Eggesford Ltd
	G-DLAL	Beech E90 King Air	Penylan Ltd
	G-DLBR	Airbus EC.175B	Crystal Sky Ltd
	G-DLCB	Shaw Europa	G. F. Perry
	G-DLDL	Robinson R22 Beta	Helimech Ltd
	G-DLEE	SOCATA TB9 Tampico Club	D. A. Lee (G-BPGX)
	G-DLFN	Aero L-29 Delfin	AMP Aviation Ltd
	G-DLMH	Tecnam P2010	P. J. Harle
	G-DLOE	Schleicher ASW-27-18E	R. E. Robertson
	G-DLOM	SOCATA TB20 Trinidad	P. A Rieck
	G-DLOT	Glasflugel 304S	Shark G-DLOT Syndicate
	G-DLOW	Grob G.103 Twin II	The Vale of the White Horse Gliding Centre Ltd
	G-DLRA	BN-2T Islander	Britten-Norman Ltd (G-BJYU)
	G-DLRL	Glasflugel 304S Shark	M. P. Brooks
	G-DLTY	HpH Glasflugel 304 ES	B. D. Michael & J. M. Gilbey
	G-DLUT	HpH Glasflugel 304 ES	A. R. Fish
	G-DLUX	Eurocopter EC.120B Colibri	EBG (Helicopters) Ltd (G-IGPW/G-CBRI)
	G-DMAC	Avtech Jabiru SP-430	C. J. Pratt
	G-DMAH	SOCATA TB20 Trinidad	S. D. Pike
	G-DMAZ	Bombardier BD700-1A10 Global Express	TAG Aviation (UK) Ltd (G-IRAP/G-CJME)
	G-DMBO	Van's RV-7	C. J. Goodwin
	G-DMCA	Douglas DC-10-30 ★	Forward fuselage/Manchester Airport Viewing Park
	G-DMCI	Ikarus C42 FB100	C-More Flying School Ltd
	G-DMCP	Tecnam P2008-JC	R. J. Alderson
	G-DMCS	PA-28R Cherokee Arrow 200-II	Arrow Associates (G-CPAC)
	G-DMCT	Flight Design CT2K	A. M. Sirant
	G-DMCW	Magni M-24C	B. A. Carnegie (G-CGVF)
	G-DMEE	Cameron Z-105 balloon	Airship & Balloon Company Ltd
	G-DMES	Cameron Minion 105 SS balloon	Airship & Balloon Company Ltd
	G-DMEZ	Cameron Minion 105 SS balloon	Airship & Balloon Company Ltd
	G-DMND	Diamond DA42 Twin Star	Flying Time Ltd
	G-DMNG	Diamond DA.42M-NG Twin Star	DEA Aviation Ltd (G-PEEK)
	G-DMON	Xtremeair XA-42 Sbach 342	R. M. Hockey
	G-DMPI	Agusta A.109E Power	D E & M C Pipe Partnership (G-FVIP/G-HCFC)
	G-DMPL	Van's RV-7A	P. J. & W. M. Hodgkins
	G-DMPP	Diamond DA42M-NG Twin Star	DEA Aviation Ltd
	G-DMSS	Westland Gazelle HT.3 (XW858:C)	G. Wood
	G-DMWW	CFM Shadow Srs DD	M. Whittle
	G-DNBH	Raj Hamsa X'Air Hawk	D. N. B. Hearn
	G-DNGR	Colt 31A balloon	M. J. & T. J. Turner
	G-DNKS	Ikarus C42 FB80	D. N. K. & M. A. Symon
	G-DNOP	PA-46-350P Malibu Mirage	Campbell Aviation Ltd
	G-DOBS	Van's RV-8	BS Flying Group
	G-DOCB	Boeing 737-436 ★	Cranfield University instructional airframe
	G-DODD	Cessna F.172P-II	M. D. Darragh
	G-DODG	Aerotechnik EV-97A Eurostar	J. Jones
	G-DOFY	Bell 206B JetRanger 3	Adventure 001 Ltd
	G-DOGG	SA Bulldog Srs 120/121 (XX638)	P. Sengupta
	G-DOGI	Robinson R22 Beta	Phoenix Helicopter Academy Ltd (G-BVGS)
	G-DOGZ	Horizon 1	M. J. Nolan
	G-DOIG	CZAW Sportcruiser	C. J. May
	G-DOIN	Skyranger 912(S)1	M. Geczy
	G-DOLI	Cirrus SR20	Chiltern Cirrus Ltd
	G-DOLY	Cessna T.303	KW Aviation Ltd (G-BJZK)
	G-DOMS	Aerotechnik EV-97A Eurostar	R. K. & C. A. Stewart
	G-DONE	Bell 505 Jet Ranger X	Simpson Heli Charters Ltd
	G-DONK	Ultramagic M-77 balloon	K. R. Holzer
	G-DONT	Xenair CH.601XL Zodiac	J. A. Kentzer
	G-DORN	EKW C-3605	Yak UK Ltd
	G-DORO	Robin DR.400-140B	R. D. W. Evans
	G-DORS	Eurocopter EC 135T3	Babcock Mission Critical Services Onshore Ltd
	G-DOSB	Diamond DA42 Twin Star	Acrobat Ltd
	G-DOSC	Diamond DA42 Twin Star	Acrobat Ltd

Reg	Type	Owner or Operator	Notes
G-DOTS	Dornier Do.27A-4	lLiberty Aviation Ltd	
G-DOTT	CFM Streak Shadow	R. J. Bell	
G-DOTY	Van's RV-7	J. K. Zgorzynska-Scott & J. W. Scott	
G-DOUZ	Van's RV-12	J and G Aerospace Ltd	
G-DOVE	Cessna 182Q	P. Puri	
G-DOVS	Robinson R44 II	J. Watt	
G-DOZI	Ikarus C.42 FB100	G-DOZI Group	
G-DOZZ	Best Off Sky Ranger Swift 912S(1)	H. G. Reid	
G-DPAI	Diamond DA.62	DPAero Ltd	
G-DPAZ	Diamond DA.40NG	DPAero Ltd	
G-DPER	M & D Flugzeugbau JS-MD	M. P. Clark	
G-DPRV	Van's RV-7A	D. H. Pattison	
G-DRAM	Cessna FR.172F (floatplane)	H. R. Mitchell	
G-DRAT	Slingsby T.51 Dart 17R	W. R. Longstaff	
G-DRAW	Colt 77A balloon	A. G. Odell	
G-DRCC	EV-97 TeamEurostar UK	Sanctuary Medical Ltd (G-SLNM)	
G-DRCS	Schleicher ASH-25E	C. R. Smithers	
G-DREG	Superchaser	N. R. Beale	
G-DREI	Fokker DR.1 Triplane Replica	P. M. Brueggemann	
G-DREW	Aeroprakt A-32 Vixxen	A. L. Virgoe	
G-DRGC	P & M Quik GT450	D. R. G. Cornwell	
G-DRGL	PA-18-135 Super Cub	Goodwood Road Racing Company Ltd (G-BLIH)	
G-DRGS	Cessna 182S	Walter Scott & Partners Ltd	
G-DRIO	Jodel DR.1050M	B. N. Stevens (G-BXIO)	
G-DRJH	Hill Helicopters HX50	Dynamiq Engineering Ltd	
G-DRLA	Leonardo AW109SP Grand New	Sloane Helicopters Ltd	
G-DRMM	Shaw Europa	T. J. Harrison	
G-DROP	Cessna U.206C	K. Brady (G-UKNO/G-BAMN)	
G-DRPK	Reality Escapade	P. A. Kirkham	
G-DRPO	Cameron Z-105 balloon	D. R. di Dio	
G-DRRT	Slingsby T.51 Dart 17R	M. G. Lynes & S. Holland (G-DBXH)	
G-DRSV	CEA DR.315 (modified)	R. S. Voice	
G-DRTA	Boeing 737-85P	Jet 2.com	
G-DRTB	Boeing 737-85N	Jet 2.com	
G-DRTC	Boeing 737-808	Jet 2.com	
G-DRTD	Boeing 737-808	Jet 2.com	
G-DRTE	Boeing 737-8K5	Jet 2.com	
G-DRTF	Boeing 737-85P	Jet 2.com	
G-DRTG	Boeing 737-8BK	Jet 2.com	
G-DRTH	Boeing 737-8BK	Jet 2.com	
G-DRTI	Boeing 737-8FH	Jet 2.com	
G-DRTL	Boeing 737-8AL	Jet 2.com	
G-DRTM	Boeing 737-85P	Jet 2.com	
G-DRTN	Boeing 737-86N	Jet 2.com	
G-DRTO	Boeing 737-8JP	Jet 2.com	
G-DRTP	Boeing 737-8AL	Jet 2.com	
G-DRTR	Boeing 737-86N	Jet 2.com	
G-DRTT	Boeing 737-8Q8	Jet 2.com	
G-DRTU	Boeing 737-86N	Jet 2.com	
G-DRTW	Boeing 737-86N	Jet 2.com	
G-DRTY	Boeing 737-8AS	Jet 2.com	
G-DRTZ	Boeing 737-8AS	Jet 2.com	
G-DRYS	Cameron N-90 balloon	C. A. Butter	
G-DRZF	CEA DR.360	P. K. Kaufeler	
G-DSAA	Leonardo AW169	SAS (Dorset and Somerset) Ltd	
G-DSFT	PA-28R Cherokee Arrow 200-II	J. Jones (G-LFSE/G-BAXT)	
G-DSGC	PA-25 Pawnee 235C	Devon & Somerset Gliding Club Ltd	
G-DSID	PA-34-220T Seneca III	I. M. Worthington	
G-DSJT	Cessna 182T	D. S. J. Tait	
G-DSKI	Aerotechnik EV-97 Eurostar	G-DSKI Group	
G-DSKY	Diamond DA.42 Twin Star	Aeros Global Ltd (G-CDSZ)	
G-DSLL	Pegasus Quantum 15-912	D. T. Evans	
G-DSMA	P & M Aviation Quik R	DSMA Flying Group	
G-DSMR	Gulfstream 650	TAG Aviation (UK) Ltd	
G-DSOO	Glaser-Dirks DG-500M	Twin Astir Syndicate	
G-DSPK	Cameron Z-140	Bailey Balloons Ltd	
G-DSPZ	Robinson R44 II	Focal Point Communications Ltd	

Notes	Reg	Type	Owner or Operator
	G-DSRV	Van's RV-7	S. J. Boynett
	G-DSUE	Aeropro Eurofox 912(S)	D. M. Garrett
	G-DSVN	Rolladen-Schneider LS8-18	A. R. Paul
	G-DTAR	P & M Aviation Quik GT450	The Scottish Aero Club Ltd
	G-DTCP	PA-32R-300 Cherokee Lance	R. S. Cook (G-TEEM)
	G-DTFF	Cessna T.182T Turbo Skylane	Ridgway Aviation Ltd
	G-DTOF	Schempp-Hirth Discus 2c FES	K. Neave & C. F. M. Smith
	G-DTOY	Ikarus C.42.FB100	C. W. Laske
	G-DTPC	Van's RV-9A	P. M. Clayton & D. Turner
	G-DTSM	EV-97 TeamEurostar UK	J. R. Stothart
	G-DTUG	Wag-Aero Super Sport	D. A. Bullock
	G-DUBI	Lindstrand LBL-120A balloon	M. B. Vennard
	G-DUDE	Van's RV-8	J. P. Marriott
	G-DUDI	Rotorsport UK MTO Sport	M. B. & R. J. Trickey
	G-DUDP	KFA Safari	D. H. Pattison
	G-DUDZ	Robin DR.400/180	W. J. Lee (G-BXNK)
	G-DUFF	Rand Robinson KR-2	J. I. B. Duff
	G-DUGE	Ikarus C42 FB UK	D. Stevenson
	G-DUMA	Ultramagic B-70 balloon	A. M. Holly & R. T. Brown
	G-DUMP	Customcraft A25	Department of Doing Ltd
	G-DUNK	Cessna F172M Skyhawk	Devon and Somerset Flight Training Ltd
	G-DUNS	Lindstrand LBL-90A balloon	W. Rousell & J. Tyrrell
	G-DUOT	Schempp-Hirth Duo Discus T	G-DUOT Soaring Group
	G-DURO	Shaw Europa	M. Yeend & M. J. W. Harris
	G-DURX	Thunder 77A balloon	P. Coman & D. J. Stagg
	G-DUSK	DH.115 Vampire T.11 (XE856) ★	Bournemouth Aviation Museum
	G-DUST	Stolp SA.300 Starduster Too	A. R. R. Holden
	G-DUVL	Cessna F.172N	G-DUVL Flying Group
	G-DVAA	Eurocopter EC135 T2+	Devon Air Ambulance Trading Co.Ltd
	G-DVBF	Lindstrand LBL-210A balloon	Virgin Balloon Flights
	G-DVCI	Ultramagic H-31 balloon	Davinci Associates Ltd
	G-DVIO	Leonardo AW139	Executive Jet Charter Ltd
	G-DVIP	Agusta A.109E Power	Castle Air Ltd
	G-DVMI	Van's RV-7	North West RV Flyers
	G-DVON	DH.104 Devon C.2 (VP955)	C. L. Thatcher
	G-DVOR	Diamond DA.62	Flight Calibration Services Ltd
	G-DVOY	CZAW Sportcruiser	J. Devoy (G-TDKI)
	G-DVTA	Cessna T.206H	C. S. Ringer
	G-DWCB	Chilton DW.1A	C. M. Barnes
	G-DWCE	Robinson R44 II	3CR Comm Ltd
	G-DWIA	Chilton D.W.1A	D. Elliott
	G-DWIB	Chilton D.W.1B (replica)	J. Jennings
	G-DWMS	Avtech Jabiru UL-450	S. McLatchie
	G-DWRU	Chilton DW.1A	K. J. Steele
	G-DXLT	Schempp-Hirth Duo Discus xLT	G-DXLT Group
	G-DXTR	Beech B.200 Super King Air	Synergy Aviation Ltd (G-RIOO)
	G-DYKE	Dyke JD.2 Delta	M. S. Bird
	G-DYNA	Dynamic WT9 UK	J. C. Stubbs
	G-DYNM	Aerospool Dynamic WT9 UK	November Mike Group
	G-DYUP	Europa	A. Hunter
	G-DZDZ	Rolladen-Schneider LS4	I. MacArthur
	G-DZKY	Diamond DA.40D Star	Go 2 Aviation Ltd (G-CEZP)
	G-DZZY	Champion 8KCAB	Paul's Planes Ltd
	G-EAGA	Sopwith Dove (replica)	A. Wood
	G-EAOU†	Vickers Vimy (replica)(NX71MY)	Greenco (UK) Ltd
	G-EASD	Avro 504L	G. M. New
	G-EASQ†	Bristol Babe (replica) (BAPC87) ★	Bristol Aero Collection (stored)/Kemble
	G-EAVX	Sopwith Pup (B1807)	K. A. M. Baker
	G-EBED†	Vickers 60 Viking (replica) (BAPC114)★	Brooklands Museum of Aviation/Weybridge
	G-EBHB	Avro 504K (E2977)	T. W. Harris
	G-EBHX	DH.53 Humming Bird	The Shuttleworth Collection
	G-EBIA	RAF SE-5A (F904)	The Shuttleworth Collection

Reg	Type	Owner or Operator	Notes
G-EBIB	RAF SE-5A ★	Science Museum/South Kensington	
G-EBIC	RAF SE-5A (F938) ★	RAF Museum/Hendon	
G-EBIR	DH.51	The Shuttleworth Collection	
G-EBJE	Avro 504K (E449) ★	RAF Museum/Hendon	
G-EBJG	Parnall Pixie IIIH	Midland Aircraft Preservation Society	
G-EBJI	Hawker Cygnet (replica)	C. J. Essex	
G-EBJO	ANEC IIH	The Shuttleworth Collection	
G-EBKY	Sopwith Pup (9917)	The Shuttleworth Collection	
G-EBLV	DH.60 Cirrus Moth	British Aerospace PLC	
G-EBMB	Hawker Cygnet I ★	RAF Museum/Cosford	
G-EBNV	English Electric Wren	The Shuttleworth Collection	
G-EBQP	DH.53 Humming Bird (J7326) ★	P. L. Kirk & T. G. Pankhurst	
G-EBWD	DH.60X Hermes Moth	The Shuttleworth Collection	
G-EBZM	Avro 594 Avian IIIA ★	Manchester Museum of Science & Industry	
G-EBZN	DH.60X Moth	J. Hodgkinson (G-UAAP)	
G-ECAC	Alpha R21620U	Bulldog Aviation Ltd	
G-ECAD	Cessna FA.152	Andrewsfield Aviation Ltd & Corvalis Aircraft Leasing Ltd (G-JEET/G-BHMF)	
G-ECAE	Royal Aircraft Factory SE.5A	West Flyg AB/Sweden	
G-ECAF	Robin HR.200-120B	Bulldog Aviation Ltd (G-BZET)	
G-ECAG	Robin HR.200-120B	Bulldog Aviation Ltd (G-MFLD/G-BXDT)	
G-ECAK	Cessna F.172M	Bulldog Aviation Ltd (G-BENK)	
G-ECAM	EAA Acrosport II	C. England	
G-ECAN	DH.84 Dragon	Norman Aeroplane Trust	
G-ECAP	Robin HR.200-120B	Bulldog Aviation Ltd (G-NSOF)	
G-ECAR	Robin HR.200-120B	Bulldog Aviation Ltd (G-MFLB/G-BXOR)	
G-ECBI	Schweizer 269C-1	JBS-Helicopters Ltd	
G-ECDB	Schleicher Ka 6E	C. W. R. Neve	
G-ECDS	DH.82A Tiger Moth	S. D. Wilch	
G-ECDX	DH.71 Tiger Moth (replica)	Airtime Aerobatics Ltd	
G-ECEA	Schempp-Hirth Cirrus	CEA Group	
G-ECET	Cessna T.182T	W. J. Forrest	
G-ECGC	Cessna F.172N	D. H. G. Penney	
G-ECGO	Bölkow Bö.208C1 Junior	P. Norman	
G-ECHB	Dassault Falcon 900DX	Concierge U Ltd	
G-ECJM	PA-28R-201T Turbo Arrow III	Regishire Ltd (G-FESL/G-BNRN)	
G-ECKB	Escapade 912(2)	C. M. & C. P. Bradford	
G-ECLA	Airbus A.340-642	European Aviation Ltd	
G-ECLB	Airbus A.340-642	European Aviation Ltd (G-VFIT)	
G-ECLW	Glasflugel Standard Libelle 201B	R. Harkness & S. Leach	
G-ECMK	PA-18-150 Super Cub	Shacklewell Super Cub Group	
G-ECOA	DHC.8-402 Dash Eight	Nordeutsche Landesbank Girozentrale	
G-ECOB	DHC.8-402 Dash Eight	Nordeutsche Landesbank Girozentrale	
G-ECOC	DHC.8-402 Dash Eight	HEH Aviation Hamburg Beteiligungsgesellschaft MBH & Co KG	
G-ECOD	DHC.8-402 Dash Eight	HEH Aviation Manchester Beteiligungsgesellschaft MBH & Co KG	
G-ECOE	DHC.8-402 Dash Eight	Nordeutsche Landesbank Girozentrale	
G-ECOF	DHC.8-402 Dash Eight	Wilmington Trust SP Services (Dublin) Ltd	
G-ECOG	DHC.8-402 Dash Eight	HEH Aviation Newcastle Beteiligungsgesellschaft MBH & Co KG	
G-ECOH	DHC.8-402 Dash Eight	Wilmington Trust SP Services (Dublin) Ltd	
G-ECOI	DHC.8-402 Dash Eight	Donegal Q400 Leasing Ltd	
G-ECOJ	DHC.8-402 Dash Eight	HEH Aviation Birmingham Beteiligungsgesellschaft MBH & Co KG	
G-ECOK	DHC.8-402 Dash Eight	Donegal Q400 Leasing Ltd	
G-ECOL	Schempp-Hirth Nimbus 2	M. Upex & L. I. Rigby	
G-ECOM	DHC.8-402 Dash Eight	HEH Aviation Bristol Beteiligungsgesellschaft MBH & Co KG	
G-ECOO	DHC.8-402 Dash Eight	Wilmington Trust SP Services (Dublin) Ltd	
G-ECOP	DHC.8-402 Dash Eight	NAC Aviation 2 Ltd	
G-ECOR	DHC.8-402 Dash Eight	NAC Aviation 2 Ltd	
G-ECOT	DHC.8-402 Dash Eight	HEH Aviation Cologne Beteiligungsgesellschaft MBH & Co KG	
G-ECPA	Glasflugel H201B Standard Libelle	M. J. Witton	
G-ECRM	Slingsby T.67M Firefly Mk II	CRM Aviation Europe Ltd (G-BNSP)	
G-ECTF	Comper CLA.7 Swift Replica	P. R. Cozens	
G-ECUB	PA-18 Super Cub 150	G-ECUB Flying Group (G-CBFI)	
G-ECVZ	Staaken Z-1S Flitzer	J. Cresswell	
G-ECXL	PZL-Bielsko SZD-30 Pirat	Charlie X-Ray Lima Group	

Notes	Reg	Type	Owner or Operator
	G-EDAM	Ultramagic M-77C balloon	A. M. Holly
	G-EDAV	SA Bulldog Srs 120/121 (XX534:B)	Edwalton Aviation Ltd
	G-EDBD	PZL-Bielsko SZD-30 Pirat	S. P. Burgess
	G-EDDD	Schempp-Hirth Nimbus 2	C. A. Mansfield (G-BKPM)
	G-EDDS	CZAW Sportcruiser	C. P. Davis
	G-EDDV	PZL-Bielsko SZD-38A Jantar 1	S. R. Bruce
	G-EDEE	Comco Ikarus C.42 FB100	C. L. & D. Godfrey
	G-EDEL	PA-32-300 Cherokee Six D	J. Francis
	G-EDFS	Pietenpol Air Camper	J. V. Comfort
	G-EDGA	PA-28-161 Warrior II	The RAF Halton Aeroplane Club Ltd
	G-EDGE	Jodel 150	A. D. Edge
	G-EDGI	PA-28-161 Warrior II	H. K. & T. W. Gilbert
	G-EDGY	Flight Test Edge 540	C. R. A. Scrope & P. C. Massetti
	G-EDLY	Airborne Edge 912/Streak IIIB	M. & P. L. Eardley
	G-EDMC	Pegasus Quantum 15-912	R. Frost
	G-EDMK	Boeing A75 N1 Stearman	T. W. Harris
	G-EDRE	Lindstrand LBL 90A balloon	Edren Homes Ltd
	G-EDRV	Van's RV-6A	P. R. Sears
	G-EDTO	Cessna FR.172F	N. G. Hopkinson
	G-EDVK	RH78 Tiger Light	M. Peters (G-MZGT)
	G-EDVL	PA-28R Cherokee Arrow 200-II	Redhill Air Services Ltd (G-BXIN)
	G-EDWA	Agusta A.109E Power	C. J. Edwards
	G-EDYO	PA-32-260 Cherokee Six	Japa Aviation & D. M. Mendoza
	G-EDZZ	Ikarus C42 FB100 Bravo	Microavionics UK Ltd
	G-EEAA	Pietenpol Air Camper	P. G. Humphrey
	G-EEAD	Slingsby T.65A Vega	G-EEAD Group
	G-EEBA	Slingsby T.65A Vega	D. A. Johnstone
	G-EEBF	Schempp-Hirth Mini Nimbus C	M. Pingel
	G-EEBK	Schempp-Hirth Mini Nimbus C	J. R. Elkington & R. A. Davis
	G-EEBL	Schleicher ASK-13	Lincolnshire Gliding Club Ltd
	G-EEBN	Centrair ASW-20FL	S. MacArthur & R. Carlisle
	G-EEBR	Glaser-Dirks DG200/17	EBR Glider Syndicate
	G-EEBS	Scheibe Zugvogel IIIA	G-EEBS Syndicate
	G-EEBZ	Schleicher ASK-13	Buckminster Gliding Club Ltd
	G-EECC	Aerospool Dynamic WT9 UK	C. V. Ellingworth
	G-EECK	Slingsby T65A Vega	Vega G-EECK 2014
	G-EECO	Lindstrand LBL-25A balloon	A. Jay
	G-EECY	PA-28-140 Cherokee Cruiser	J. L. Sparks (G-OLPH/G-BELR)
	G-EEDE	Centrair ASW-20F	G. M. Cumner
	G-EEEK	Extra EA.300/200	A. R. Willis
	G-EEER	Schempp-Hirth Mini Nimbus C	D. J. Uren
	G-EEEZ	Champion 8KCAB	P. J. Webb
	G-EEFK	Centrair ASW-20FL	N. Dickenson
	G-EEFT	Schempp-Hirth Nimbus 2B	S. A. Adlard
	G-EEGL	Christen Eagle II	M. P. Swoboda & S. L. Nicholson
	G-EEGU	PA-28-161 Warrior II	Tor Financial Consulting Ltd
	G-EEHA	Sonex	T. J. Fane de Salis
	G-EEKA	Glaser-Dirks DG-202/17	D. M. Betts
	G-EEKE	Best Off Skyranger Swift 912(1)	A. J. Harding
	G-EEKI	Sportine Aviacija LAK-17B FES	F. Stinat & L. Doniselli
	G-EEKK	Cessna 152	A. D. R. Northeast (G-BNSW)
	G-EEKY	PA-28-140 Cherokee B	J. L. Sparks
	G-EEKZ	P & M Quik GTR	A. P. Douglas-Dixon
	G-EELS	Cessna 208B Caravan 1	Glass Eels Ltd
	G-EELT	Rolladen-Schneider LS4	ELT Syndicate
	G-EELY	Schleicher Ka 6CR	K6 ELY Syndicate
	G-EEMX	PA-25-235 Pawnee B	Associazione Volovelistica Scaligera/Italy
	G-EENI	Shaw Europa	M. P. Grimshaw
	G-EENK	Schleicher ASK-21	Cotswold Gliding Club
	G-EENT	Glasflugel 304	M. Hastings & P. D. Morrison
	G-EENW	Schleicher ASW-20L	M. Newburn
	G-EENZ	Schleicher ASW-19B	C. J. & G. J. Walker
	G-EEPJ	Pitts S-1S Special	R. J. Porter
	G-EERV	Van's RV-6	J. M. Pipping
	G-EERY	Robinson R22	EGB (Helicopters) Ltd
	G-EESA	Shaw Europa	E. J. Wallington (G-HIIL)
	G-EESY	Rolladen-Schneider LS4	S. G. D. Gaze
	G-EETG	Cessna 172Q Cutlass	A. Kiernan
	G-EETH	Schleicher K.8B	Bowland Forest Gliding Club Ltd
	G-EEUP	SNCAN Stampe SV.4C	A. M. Wajih

Reg	Type	Owner or Operator	Notes
G-EEVL	Grob G.102 Astir CS77	L. F. Escartin/Spain	
G-EEVY	Cessna 170A	Fly by Wire Flying Group	
G-EEWA	Beech F.33A Bonanza	P. Osborne	
G-EEWZ	Mainair Pegasus Quik	G. K. Smith	
G-EEXW	Beech 95-B55 Baron	W. M. Burnett	
G-EEYE	Mainair Blade 912	B. J. Egerton	
G-EEZR	Robinson R44	Geezer Aviation LLP	
G-EEZS	Cessna 182P	F. T. M. Tarczykowski	
G-EEZZ	Zenair CH.601XL Zodiac	S. Michaelson	
G-EFAO	Scintex CP.301-C1 Emeraude	T. A. S. Rayner	
G-EFBP	Cessna FR.172K	Sierra Mike Juliet Flying Group	
G-EFCG	Aeropro Eurofox 912(S)	C. A. White	
G-EFCM	PA-28-180 Cherokee D	Charlie Mike Syndicate	
G-EFER	PA-18-150 Super Cub	J. Tayler	
G-EFFH	Cessna T.210L Turbo Centurion	R. Paletar	
G-EFIZ	Pitts S-2B Special	R. S. Goodwin & G. V. Paino	
G-EFJD	MBB Bo.209 Monsun	A. H. & F. A. Macaskill	
G-EFLT	Glasflugel Standard Libelle 201B	P. A. Tietema	
G-EFLY	Centrair ASW-20FL	S. A. Whitaker	
G-EFNH	Cessna FR.182	C. J. & V. J. Crawford	
G-EFOF	Robinson R22 Beta	Helicopter & Pilot Services Ltd	
G-EFON	Robinson R22 II	Burton Aviation Ltd (G-SCHO)	
G-EFOX	Eurofox 912(2)	H. J. Parker	
G-EFRP	Bower Fly Baby 1A	R. A. Phillips (G-BFRD)	
G-EFSD	Eurofox 912(IS)	S. E. Dancaster	
G-EFSF	Cessna FR.172K	A. Vaughan	
G-EFSM	Slingsby T.67M Firefly 260	Anglo Europe Aviation Ltd (G-BPLK)	
G-EFTE	Bölkow Bö.207	B. Morris & R. L. Earl	
G-EFTF	AS.350B Ecureuil	T French & Son (G-CWIZ/G-DJEM/G-ZBAC/G-SEBI/G-BMCU)	
G-EFUN	Bishop & Castelli E-Go	Giocas Ltd	
G-EGAG	SOCATA TB20 Trinidad	J. J. Sinnott	
G-EGAL	Christen Eagle II	Sky 4 G-EGAL Ltd	
G-EGBJ	PA-28-161 Warrior II	JABM Ltd (G-CPFM/G-BNNS)	
G-EGBP	American Champion 7ECA Citabria Aurora	Freedom Aviation Ltd (G-IRGJ)	
G-EGBS	Van's RV-9A	Shobdon RV-9A Group	
G-EGBW	PA-28-161 Cherokee Warrior II	Social Infrastructures Ltd	
G-EGCA	Rans S-6-ES Coyote II	P. A. Linford	
G-EGCD	Cessna 172S	Avro Flying Group (G-PFCL)	
G-EGEG	Cessna 172R	Echo Golf Flying Ltd	
G-EGES	Lindstrand LBL Triangle balloon	Lighter Than Air Ltds	
G-EGEN	Piel CP301A Emeraude	Croft Aviators Flying Group	
G-EGGI	Ikarus C.42FB UK	J. S. D. Llewellyn	
G-EGGS	Robin DR.400/180	G-EGGS Syndicate	
G-EGGZ	Best Off Sky Ranger Swift 912S(1)	J. C. Sheardown	
G-EGHP	Ikarus C42 FB80	Airbourne Aviation Ltd (G-CFHP)	
G-EGIA	UltraMagic M-65C balloon	A. Dizioli/Italy	
G-EGIB	PA-28-181 Archer II	P. A. Venton	
G-EGIL	Christen Eagle II	Smoke On Go Ltd	
G-EGJA	SOCATA TB20 Trinidad	Kraydon Services Ltd	
G-EGJJ	P & M Quik GTR	A. W. O'Connor	
G-EGLA	Cessna 172M	Cornwall Flying Club Ltd (G-CGFJ)	
G-EGLE	Christen Eagle II	D. Thorpe	
G-EGLK	CSA PS-28 Cruiser	D. J. & L. Medcraft & Yonder Plains Ltd	
G-EGLL	PA-28-161 Warrior II	Airways Aero Associations Ltd (G-BLEJ)	
G-EGLS	PA-28-181 Archer III	M. Wallace	
G-EGLT	Cessna 310R	RVL Aviation Ltd (G-BHTV)	
G-EGPF	PA-28R-201 Arrow III	Abbotsinch Aviation Ltd	
G-EGPG	PA-18-135 Super Cub	G. Cormack (G-BWUC)	
G-EGRV	Van's RV-8	B. M. Gwynnett (G-PHMG)	
G-EGSJ	Jabiru J400	C. N. & K. J. Stephen (G-MGRK)	
G-EGSL	Cessna F.152	Andrewsfield Aviation Ltd	
G-EGSR	Van's RV-7A	S. J. Carr & C. A. Acland	
G-EGTB	PA-28-161 Warrior II	Tayside Aviation Ltd (G-BPWA)	
G-EGTF	EV-97 Eurostar SL	J. R. C. Wark	
G-EGTU	Cessna F.152 II	Devon and Somerset Flight Training Ltd (G-BGLR/G-HFCL)	
G-EGUR	Jodel D.140B	S. H. Williams	
G-EGVA	PA-28R-200 Cherokee Arrow	Social Infrastructure Ltd	
G-EGVO	Dassault Falcon 900EX	Concierge U Ltd	

Notes	Reg	Type	Owner or Operator
	G-EGWN	American Champion 7ECA	Freedom Aviation Ltd
	G-EGZM	Cessna FR.172K	P. A. Edwards
	G-EHAA	MDH MD-900 Explorer	Specialist Aviation Services Ltd (G-GNAA)
	G-EHAV	Glasflugel Standard Libelle 201B	G-EHAV Syndicate
	G-EHAZ	PA-28-161 Warrior III	Freedom Aviation Ltd (G-CEEY)
	G-EHBJ	CASA 1.131E Jungmann 2000	E. P. Howard
	G-EHCB	Schempp-Hirth Nimbus 3DT	G-EHCB Group
	G-EHCC	PZL-Bielsko SZD-50-3 Puchacz	Heron Gliding Club
	G-EHDS	CASA 1.131E Jungmann 2000	I. C. Underwood (G-DUDS)
	G-EHEH	Lindstrand LTL Series 1 balloon	M. A. Webb & J. Pierson
	G-EHEM	MDH MD-900 Explorer	Specialist Aviation Services Ltd (G-LNCT)
	G-EHGF	PA-28-181 Archer II	S. J. Colson
	G-EHIC	Jodel D.140B	G-EHIC Group
	G-EHIL	EH Industries EH101 ★	The Helicopter Museum/Weston-super-Mare
	G-EHLT	DH.82A Tiger Moth	R. C. P. Brookhouse (G-BHLT)
	G-EHLX	PA-28-181 Archer II	ASG Leasing Ltd
	G-EHMF	Isaacs Fury II	G. Haye
	G-EHMJ	Beech S35 Bonanza	A. J. Daley
	G-EHMM	Robin DR.400/180R	London Gliding Club Proprietary Ltd
	G-EHMS	MD Helicopters MD-900	London's Air Ambulance Ltd
	G-EHTT	Schleicher ASW-20CL	HTT Syndicate
	G-EHZT	Zlin Z.526F Trener Master	E. P. Howard
	G-EIAP	Jodel DR.1050	P. M. Irvine
	G-EIAR	Jodel DR250/160	D. G. Holman
	G-EICK	Cessna 172S	Centenary Flying Group
	G-EIGT	Van's RV-8	M. J. Benham
	G-EIKY	Shaw Europa	J. D. Milbank
	G-EIMS	Bell 505 Jet Ranger X	N. V. Cook
	G-EINI	Europa XS	K. J. Burns (G-KDCC)
	G-EISG	Beech A36 Bonanza	R. J. & B. Howard
	G-EISO	SOCATA MS.892A Rallye Commodore 150★	Sammy Miller Motorcycle Museum/Nrew Milton
	G-EITE	Luscombe 8F Silvaire	C. P. Davey
	G-EIWT	Cessna FR.182RG	Avitrata Sociedad de Tratamentos Fitossanitarios Aeros Lda/Portugal
	G-EIZO	Eurocopter EC 120B	Blok (UK) Ltd
	G-EJAC	Mudry CAP.232	G. C. J. Cooper, P. Varinot & E. Vazeille (G-OGBR)
	G-EJAE	GlaserDirks DG-200	D. L. P. H. Waller
	G-EJAS	Skystar Kitfox Model 7	D. A. Holl
	G-EJBI	Bolkow Bo.207	A. A. R. Moore
	G-EJEL	Cessna 550 Citation II	HMPR SA
	G-EJGO	Z.226HE Trener	S. K. T. & C. M. Neofytou
	G-EJHH	Schempp-Hirth Standard Cirrus	I. S. Simmonds
	G-EJIM	Schempp-Hirth Discus 2cT	N. A. L. Stuart
	G-EJOC	AS.350B Ecureuil	CK's Supermarket Ltd (G-GEDS/G-HMAN/ G-SKIM/G-BIVP)
	G-EJRS	PA-28-161 Cadet	Carlisle Flight Traing Ltd
	G-EJTC	Robinson R44	N. Parkhouse
	G-EJWI	Flight Design CTLS	D. D. J. Rossdale
	G-EKBA	SOCATA TB-200 Tobago XL	Aviametro LLP
	G-EKEY	Schleicher ASW-20 CL	A. P. Nisbet
	G-EKHW	PA-28R-201T Turbo Arrow IV	D. V. Shaw
	G-EKIM	Alpi Pioneer 300	R. J. Raven
	G-EKIR	PA-28-262 Cadet	Aeros Global Ltd
	G-EKKL	PA-28-161 Warrior II	Perryair Ltd
	G-EKOS	Cessna FR.182 RG	S. Charlton
	G-ELAK	Sportine Aviacija LAK-17B FES	G. N. Frasere & G. A. Marshall
	G-ELAM	PA-30 Twin Comanche160B	Hangar 39 Ltd (G-BAWU/G-BAWV)
	G-ELBE	Pipistrel Alpha BCAR-S 164	Fly About Aviation Ltd
	G-ELBE	Van's RV-7	E. G. Jones & I. E. Blackburn
	G-ELCH	Commandeer 114B	L. Ormsby
	G-ELDR	PA-32 Cherokee Six 260	AT Aviation Sales Ltd
	G-ELEC	Westland WG.30 ★	The Helicopter Museum/Weston-super-Mare (G-BKNV)
	G-ELEE	Cameron Z-105 balloon	M. A. Stelling
	G-ELEN	Robin DR.400/180	Foster ELEN Group

Reg	Type	Owner or Operator	Notes
G-ELIS	PA-34-200T Seneca II	A. Gougas (G-BOPV)	
G-ELKA	Christen Eagle II	J. T. Matthews	
G-ELKE	Cirrus SR-20	S. Auer/Germany	
G-ELKI	Diamond DA.40 NG Star	Euro Aircraft Leasing Ltd	
G-ELKO	Diamond DA.42 NG Twin Star	Euro Aircraft Leasing Ltd	
G-ELLA	PA-32R-301 Saratoga IIHP	A. I. Freeman	
G-ELLI	Bell 206B JetRanger 3	A. Chatham	
G-ELMH	NA AT-6D Harvard III (42-84555:EP-H)	M. Hammond	
G-ELRT	Sopwith Pup (N6161)	T. A. Bechtolsheimer	
G-ELSB	Robin DR.400-180R	Cambridge Gliding Club Ltd	
G-ELSE	Diamond DA.42 Twin Star	A. M. Clark	
G-ELSI	Tanarg/Ixess 15 912S(1)	S. J. Tennant	
G-ELSR	Robin DR400/180R	Viscount Cobham	
G-ELUE	PA-28-161 Warrior II	Freedom Aviation Ltd	
G-ELUN	Robin DR.400/180R	Cotswold DR.400 Syndicate	
G-ELVN	Van's RV-7	M. Rothwell	
G-ELWK	Van's RV-12	J. Devlin	
G-ELWM	Robin DR400/180 Regent	Aeroclub Renault	
G-ELXE	Cessna 182T	O. Petrov	
G-ELYS	Cessna FA.150K	Skyworthy Hire (G-BIBN)	
G-ELZN	PA-28-161 Warrior II	ZN Flying Group	
G-ELZY	PA-28-161 Warrior II	Redhill Air Services Ltd	
G-EMAA	Eurocopter EC 135T2+	Babcock Mission Critical Services Onshore Ltd	
G-EMAC	Robinson R22 Beta	Rotorspan Helicopters Ltd (G-CBDB)	
G-EMAT	Diamond DA.62	Galaxy Flair Ltd	
G-EMCA	Commander Aircraft 114B	S. Roberts	
G-EMDM	Diamond DA40-P9 Star	D. J. Munson	
G-EMEB	Airbus EC175B	CHC Scotia Ltd	
G-EMEC	Airbus EC175B	CHC Scotia Ltd	
G-EMED	Airbus EC175B	CHC Scotia Ltd	
G-EMET	Supermarine 300 Spitfire I	G. P. Jones	
G-EMHE	Agusta A109S Grand	East Midlands Helicopters	
G-EMHK	MBB Bö.209 Monsun 150FV	C. Elder (G-BLRD)	
G-EMHN	Agusta A109S Grand	Burton Aviation Ltd	
G-EMID	Eurocopter EC 135P2	Police & Crime Commissioner for West Yorkshire	
G-EMIN	Shaw Europa	S. A. Lamb	
G-EMJA	CASA 1.131E Jungmann 2000	T. A. Fulcher	
G-EMKT	Cameron Z-105 balloon	Webster Adventures Ltd	
G-EMLE	Aerotechnik EV-97 Eurostar	A. R. White	
G-EMLS	Cessna T210L Turbo Centurion	I. K. F. Simcock	
G-EMLY	Pegasus Quantum 15	S. J. Reid	
G-EMMX	P & M Quik GT450	Airmasters (UK) Ltd	
G-EMMY	Rutan Vari-Eze	M. J. Tooze	
G-EMOL	Schweizer 269C-1	Bliss Aviation Ltd	
G-EMPP	Diamond DA.42M-NG Twin Star	DEA Aviation Ltd (G-DSPY)	
G-EMSA	Czech Sport Aircraft Sportcruiser	A. C. & M. A. Naylor	
G-EMSI	Shaw Europa	P. W. L. Thomas	
G-EMSS	Airbus MBB-BK 117 D-2	Babcock Mission Critical Services Onshore Ltd	
G-EMSY	DH.82A Tiger Moth	G-EMSY Group (G-ASPZ)	
G-ENAA	Supermarine Spitfire Mk.26B (EN130:FN-A)	G-ENAA Syndicate	
G-ENBA	Embraer EMB—505 Phenom 300	ENB Aviation Ltd	
G-ENBW	Robin DR.400-180R	P. S. Carder & B. Elliott	
G-ENCE	Partenavia P.68B	Exeter Flights Ltd (G-OROY/G-BFSU)	
G-ENEA	Cessna 182P	Air Ads Ltd	
G-ENEE	CFM Streak Shadow SA	A. L. & S. Roberts	
G-ENGO	Steen Skybolt	R. G. Fulton	
G-ENGR	Head AX8-105 balloon	S. Dyer	
G-ENHP	Enstrom 480B	Transair (UK) Ltd	
G-ENIA	Staaken Z-21 Flitzer	A. F. Wankowski	
G-ENID	Reality Escapade ULP(1)	Q. Irving	
G-ENIE	Tipsy T.66 Nipper 3	M. J. Freeman	
G-ENIO	Pitts S-2C Special	Advanced Flying (London) Ltd	
G-ENKH	Cirrus SR22T	M. Greve	
G-ENKO	Yakovlev Yak-18T	D. Ischenko	
G-ENKY	Skyranger Swift 912S(1)	P. A. Jenkins	
G-ENNA	PA-28-161 Warrior II	Falcon Flying Serices Ltd (G-ESFT)	
G-ENOA	Cessna F.172F	M. K. Acors (G-ASZW)	
G-ENRE	Avtech Jabiru UL	P. R. Turton	

Notes	Reg	Type	Owner or Operator
	G-ENRI	Lindstrand LBL-105A balloon	P. G. Hall
	G-ENST	CZAW Sportcruiser	Enstone Flyers
	G-ENSX	Robinson R44 II	HQ Aviation Ltd (G-CLII)
	G-ENTL	P & M QuikR	D. A. Hopkinson
	G-ENTO	American General AG-5B Tiger	G-ENTO Group
	G-ENTT	Cessna F.152 II	C. & A. R. Hyett (G-BHHI)
	G-ENTW	Cessna F.152 II	London School of Flying Ltd (G-BFLK)
	G-ENVO	MBB Bo.105CBS-4	F. C. Owen
	G-ENVV	Aeroprakt A-32 Vixxen	P. A. Murdock & P. Sloan
	G-ENZO	Cameron Z-105 balloon	Garelli VI SPA
	G-EOFW	Pegasus Quantum 15-912	G-EOFW Microlight Group
	G-EOGE	Gefa-Flug AS105GD airship (hot air)	George Brazil 2015 Ltd
	G-EOHL	Cessna 182L	Branton Knight Ltd
	G-EOID	Aeroprakt A22-L Foxbat	J. Pearce
	G-EOIN	Zenair CH.701UL	G-EOIN Group
	G-EOJB	Robinson R44 II	Difuria Contractors Ltd (G-EDES)
	G-EOLD	PA-28-161 Warrior II	Phoenix Aviation Ltd
	G-EOLE	Cameron O-84 balloon	McCornick, Van Haarne and Co
	G-EOPH	Cameron C-90 balloon	A. J. Cherrett
	G-EORG	PA-38-112 Tomahawk	G. W. & T. W. Gilbert
	G-EORJ	Shaw Europa	P. E. George
	G-EPAR	Robinson R22 Beta II	Jepar Rotorcraft
	G-EPIC	Jabiru UL-450	T. Chadwick
	G-EPIM	Cessna R172K	A. H. Creaser
	G-EPOC	Jabiru UL-450	S. Cope
	G-EPSN	Ultramagic M-105 balloon	G. Everett
	G-EPTR	PA-28R Cherokee Arrow 200-II	ACS Aviation Ltd
	G-EPYW	PA-28-181 Archer II	LAC Aircraft Ltd
	G-ERAS	Cameron O-31 balloon	A. A. Laing
	G-ERBA	Leonardo AW189	CHC Scotia Ltd
	G-ERBE	Cessna P.210N	J. Luschnig
	G-ERCO	Ercoupe 415D	E. G. Girardey
	G-ERDA	Staaken Z-21A Flitzer	J. Cresswell
	G-ERDS	DH.82A Tiger Moth	W. A. Gerdes
	G-ERDW	Enstrom F-28F Falcon	G. Wolfshohl/Germany
	G-ERFC	S.E.5A replica (C1096)	R. A. Palmer
	G-ERFS	PA-28-161 Warrior II	Steptoe and Son Properties Ltd
	G-ERFX	Embraer EMB-135BJ Legacy 600	Flexjet Ltd
	G-ERGP	Pilatus PC-12/47E	Solid Rock Aviation GP Ltd
	G-ERIC	Rockwell Commander 112TC	D. P. Williams
	G-ERIW	Staaken Z-21 Flitzer	R. I. Wasey
	G-ERJR	Agusta A109C	3GRCOMM Ltd (G-DBOY)
	G-ERMN	Staaken Z-21 Flitzer	T. G. Lloyd (G-WIDZ)
	G-ERMO	ARV Super 2	M. J. Slack (G-BMWK)
	G-ERMY	Utramagic N-210	A. M. Holly
	G-ERNI	PA-28-181 Archer II	J. Gardener & N. F. P. Hopwood (G-OSSY)
	G-EROB	Europa XS	R. J. Bull (G-RBJW)
	G-EROE	Avro 504K Replica	British Aviation 100
	G-EROS	Cameron H-34 balloon	Evening Standard Co Ltd
	G-ERRI	Lindstrand LBL-77A balloon	S. M. Jones
	G-ERRY	AA-5B Tiger	M. Reischi
	G-ERTE	Skyranger 912S (1)	A. P. Trumper
	G-ERTI	Staaken Z-21A Flitzer	T. D. Gardner
	G-ERYN	Ikarus C42 FB100	R. & W. Bell
	G-ERYR	P & M Aviation Quik GT450	R. D. Ellis
	G-ESAA	Caudron C68	AREC 68 Group
	G-ESCA	Escapade Jabiru (1)	G. W. E. & R. H. May
	G-ESCC	Escapade 912	G. & S. Simons
	G-ESCP	Escapade 912(1)	A. Palmer
	G-ESET	Eurocopter EC.130B4 Ecureuil	Hogs Head Transportation Ltd
	G-ESGA	Reality Escapade	I. Bamford
	G-ESKA	Escapade 912 (2)	C. G. Thompson
	G-ESME	Cessna R.182 II (15211)	G. C. Cherrington (G-BNOX)
	G-ESNA	Embraer EMB-500 Legacy 500	Air Charter Scotland Ltd
	G-ESSL	Cessna R.182	J. W. F. Russell
	G-ESTR	Van's RV-6	J. P. M. & P. M. White

Reg	Type	Owner or Operator	Notes
G-ETAC	Dornier 228-212	Aurigny Air Services Ltd	
G-ETAT	Cessna 172S	I. R. Malby	
G-ETBT	PA-38-112 Tomahawk	Highland Aviation Training Ltd	
G-ETBY	PA-32 Cherokee Six 260	G-ETBY Group (G-AWCY)	
G-ETDC	Cessna 172P	The Moray Flying Club	
G-ETET	PA-46-600TP Meridian M600	British European Aviation Ltd	
G-ETGO	Groppo Trail Mk.2	S. Taylor & S. E. Gribble	
G-ETIM	Eurocopter EC 120B	Tenterfield (Holdings) Ltd	
G-ETIN	Robinson R22 Beta	R. F. McLachlan	
G-ETIV	Robin DR.400/180	C. A. Prior	
G-ETKT	Robinson R44 II	Heli-Sphere Helicopters Ltd	
G-ETLX	PA-28R-200 Cherokee Arrow II	Blue Skys Aviation Ltd	
G-ETME	Nord 1002 Pingouin (KG+EM)	S. H. O'Connell	
G-ETNT	Robinson R44	Irwin Plant Hire	
G-ETOY	CASA 1-131E Jungmann Series 2000	L. B. Clark	
G-ETPA	Pilatus PC-21	QinetiQ Ltd	
G-ETPB	Pilatus PC-21	QinetiQ Ltd	
G-ETPE	Airbus AS.350B3 Ecureuil	QinetiQ Ltd	
G-ETPF	Airbus AS.350B3 Ecureuil	QinetiQ Ltd	
G-ETPG	Airbus AS.350B3 Ecureuil	QinetiQ Ltd	
G-ETPH	Airbus AS.350B3 Ecureuil	QinetiQ Ltd	
G-ETPI	Agusta A.109E Power	QinetiQ Ltd	
G-ETPJ	Agusta A.109E Power	QinetiQ Ltd (G-ESLH)	
G-ETPK	Avro RJ70	QinetiQ Ltd (G-BVRJ)	
G-ETPL	Avro RJ100	QinetiQ Ltd (G-BZAY)	
G-ETPM	Diamond DA.42M-NG Twin Star	QinetiQ Ltd (G-LTPA)	
G-ETUG	Aeropro Eurofox 912(S)	The Nortumbria Gliding Club Ltd	
G-ETVS	Alpi Pioneer 300 Hawk	V. Serazzi	
G-ETWO	Guimbal Cabri G2	Heligroup Operations Ltd	
G-EUAB	Europa XS	A. D. Stephens	
G-EUAN	Jabiru UL-D	M. S. Lusted	
G-EUEL	Europa Elite	Europa Aircraft (2004) Ltd	
G-EUFO	Rolladen-Schneider LS7-WL	G. D. Alcock & M. J. Mingay	
G-EUFX	Aeropro Eurofox 912(IS)	P. S. Harvey	
G-EUJG	Avro 594 Avian IIIA	D. Shew	
G-EUKS	Westland Widgeon III	D. Shew	
G-EUNA	Airbus A.318-112	British Airways	
G-EUNB	Airbus A.318-112	Titan Airways Ltd	
G-EUNG	Europa NG	D. I. Stanbridge	
G-EUNI	Beech B200 Super King Air	Universita Telematica E-Campus (G-TAGH)	
G-EUOA	Airbus A.319-131	British Airways	
G-EUOB	Airbus A.319-131	British Airways	
G-EUOC	Airbus A.319-131	British Airways	
G-EUOD	Airbus A.319-131	British Airways	
G-EUOE	Airbus A.319-131	British Airways	
G-EUOF	Airbus A.319-131	British Airways	
G-EUOG	Airbus A.319-131	British Airways	
G-EUPA	Airbus A.319-131	British Airways	
G-EUPB	Airbus A.319-131	British Airways	
G-EUPC	Airbus A.319-131	British Airways	
G-EUPD	Airbus A.319-131	British Airways	
G-EUPE	Airbus A.319-131	British Airways	
G-EUPF	Airbus A.319-131	British Airways	
G-EUPG	Airbus A.319-131	British Airways	
G-EUPH	Airbus A.319-131	British Airways	
G-EUPJ	Airbus A.319-131	British Airways	
G-EUPK	Airbus A.319-131	British Airways	
G-EUPL	Airbus A.319-131	British Airways	
G-EUPM	Airbus A.319-131	British Airways	
G-EUPN	Airbus A.319-131	British Airways	
G-EUPO	Airbus A.319-131	British Airways	
G-EUPP	Airbus A.319-131	British Airways	
G-EUPR	Airbus A.319-131	British Airways	
G-EUPS	Airbus A.319-131	British Airways	
G-EUPT	Airbus A.319-131	British Airways	
G-EUPU	Airbus A.319-131	British Airways	
G-EUPW	Airbus A.319-131	British Airways	
G-EUPY	Airbus A.319-131	British Airways	
G-EUPZ	Airbus A.319-131	British Airways	
G-EUSO	Robin DR.400/140 Major	Weald Air Services Ltd	

Notes	Reg	Type	Owner or Operator
	G-EUUA	Airbus A.320-232	British Airways
	G-EUUB	Airbus A.320-232	British Airways
	G-EUUC	Airbus A.320-232	British Airways
	G-EUUD	Airbus A.320-232	British Airways
	G-EUUE	Airbus A.320-232	British Airways
	G-EUUF	Airbus A.320-232	British Airways
	G-EUUG	Airbus A.320-232	British Airways
	G-EUUH	Airbus A.320-232	British Airways
	G-EUUI	Airbus A.320-232	British Airways
	G-EUUJ	Airbus A.320-232	British Airways
	G-EUUK	Airbus A.320-232	British Airways
	G-EUUL	Airbus A.320-232	British Airways
	G-EUUM	Airbus A.320-232	British Airways
	G-EUUN	Airbus A.320-232	British Airways
	G-EUUO	Airbus A.320-232	British Airways
	G-EUUP	Airbus A.320-232	British Airways
	G-EUUR	Airbus A.320-232	British Airways
	G-EUUS	Airbus A.320-232	British Airways
	G-EUUT	Airbus A.320-232	British Airways
	G-EUUU	Airbus A.320-232	British Airways
	G-EUUV	Airbus A.320-232	British Airways
	G-EUUW	Airbus A.320-232	British Airways
	G-EUUX	Airbus A.320-232	British Airways
	G-EUUY	Airbus A.320-232	British Airways
	G-EUUZ	Airbus A.320-232	British Airways
	G-EUXC	Airbus A.321-231	British Airways
	G-EUXD	Airbus A.321-231	British Airways
	G-EUXE	Airbus A.321-231	British Airways
	G-EUXF	Airbus A.321-231	British Airways
	G-EUXG	Airbus A.321-231	British Airways
	G-EUXH	Airbus A.321-231	British Airways
	G-EUXI	Airbus A.321-231	British Airways
	G-EUXJ	Airbus A.321-231	British Airways
	G-EUXK	Airbus A.321-231	British Airways
	G-EUXL	Airbus A.321-231	British Airways
	G-EUXM	Airbus A.321-231	British Airways
	G-EUYA	Airbus A.320-232	British Airways
	G-EUYB	Airbus A.320-232	British Airways
	G-EUYC	Airbus A.320-232	British Airways
	G-EUYD	Airbus A.320-232	British Airways
	G-EUYE	Airbus A.320-232	British Airways
	G-EUYF	Airbus A.320-232	British Airways
	G-EUYG	Airbus A.320-232	British Airways
	G-EUYH	Airbus A.320-232	British Airways
	G-EUYI	Airbus A.320-232	British Airways
	G-EUYJ	Airbus A.320-232	British Airways
	G-EUYK	Airbus A.320-232	British Airways
	G-EUYL	Airbus A.320-232	British Airways
	G-EUYM	Airbus A.320-232	British Airways
	G-EUYN	Airbus A.320-232	British Airways
	G-EUYO	Airbus A.320-232	British Airways
	G-EUYP	Airbus A.320-232	British Airways
	G-EUYR	Airbus A.320-232	British Airways
	G-EUYS	Airbus A.320-232	British Airways
	G-EUYT	Airbus A.320-232	British Airways
	G-EUYU	Airbus A.320-232	British Airways
	G-EUYV	Airbus A.320-232	British Airways
	G-EUYW	Airbus A.320-232	British Airways
	G-EUYX	Airbus A.320-232	British Airways
	G-EUYY	Airbus A.320-232	British Airways
	G-EVAA	Autogyro Cavalon	G-EVAA Syndicate
	G-EVAJ	Best Off Skyranger 912S(1)	A. B. Gridley
	G-EVBF	Cameron Z-350 balloon	Virgin Balloon Flights
	G-EVEE	Robinson R44	EFL Helicopters Ltd (G-REGE)
	G-EVEN	Cirrus SR22	Glemmestad Invest AS (G-CGRD)
	G-EVET	Cameron 80 Concept balloon	M. D. J. Walker
	G-EVEY	Thruster T.600N 450-JAB	The G-EVEY Flying Group
	G-EVIB	Cirrus SR22	S. D. Paver
	G-EVIE	PA-28-181 Warrior II	Tayside Aviation Ltd (G-ZULU)
	G-EVIG	Evektor EV-97 TeamEurostar UK	A. S. Mitchell

Reg	Type	Owner or Operator	Notes
G-EVII	Schempp-Hirth Ventus 2cT	Ventus G-EVII Syndicate	
G-EVLE	Rearwin 8125 Cloudster	W. D. Gray (G-BVLK)	
G-EVMK	deHavilland DHC-2 Beaver 1	T. W. Harris	
G-EVPI	Evans VP-1 Srs 2	C. P. Martyr	
G-EVRO	Aerotechnik EV-97 Eurostar	J. E. Rourke	
G-EVSL	Aerotechnik EV-97 Eurostar SL	P. E. Thompson	
G-EVSW	Evektor EV-97 Sportstar	I. Shulver	
G-EVTO	PA-28-161 Warrior II	Redhill Air Services Ltd	
G-EWAD	Robinson R44 II	MG Helicopters Ltd	
G-EWAN	Prostar PT-2C	C. G. Shaw	
G-EWBC	Avtec Jabiru SK	E. W. B. Comber	
G-EWEN	Aeropro Eurofox 912(S)	M. H. Talbot	
G-EWES	Alpi Pioneer 300	G. E. MacCuish	
G-EWEW	AB Sportine Aviacija LAK-19T	J. B. Strzebrakowski	
G-EWIZ	Pitts S-2E Special	R. S. Goodwin	
G-EWME	PA-28 Cherokee 235	Y. Remacle	
G-EXAM	PA-28RT-201T Turbo Arrow IV	RR. S. Urquhart & A. Cameron	
G-EXCC	Carbon Cub EX-2	M. S. Colebrook	
G-EXEC	PA-34-200 Seneca	Sky Air Travel Ltd	
G-EXES	Shaw Europa XS	M. W. Olliver	
G-EXGC	Extra EA.300/200	P. J. Bull	
G-EXHL	Cameron C-70 balloon	K. C. Tanner	
G-EXII	Extra EA.300	Z. Lidzius	
G-EXIL	Extra EA.300/S	G-Force Aerobatics LLP	
G-EXIT	MS.893E Rallye 180GT	G-EXIT Group	
G-EXLL	Zenair CH.601	M. R. Brumby	
G-EXLT	Extra EA.300/LT	J. W. Marshall	
G-EXNG	Extra NG	J. W. Marshall	
G-EXPO	PA-46R-350T Malibu Matrix	G-EXPO LLP	
G-EXTC	Experimental Aviation Berkut	P. Wyckaert	
G-EXTR	Extra EA.260	Principia Aerobatics LLP	
G-EXXL	Zenair CH.601XL Zodiac	J. H. Ellwood	
G-EYAK	Yakovlev Yak-50 (50 yellow)	P. N. A. Whitehead	
G-EYCO	Robin DR.400/180	M. J. Hanlon	
G-EYOR	Van's RV-6	S. I. Fraser	
G-EZAB	Airbus A.319-111	easyJet Airline Co.Ltd	
G-EZAC	Airbus A.319-111	easyJet Airline Co.Ltd	
G-EZAF	Airbus A.319-111	easyJet Airline Co.Ltd	
G-EZAG	Airbus A.319-111	easyJet Airline Co.Ltd	
G-EZAI	Airbus A.319-111	easyJet Airline Co.Ltd	
G-EZAJ	Airbus A.319-111	easyJet Airline Co.Ltd	
G-EZAK	Airbus A.319-111	easyJet Airline Co.Ltd	
G-EZAN	Airbus A.319-111	easyJet Airline Co.Ltd	
G-EZAO	Airbus A.319-111	easyJet Airline Co.Ltd	
G-EZAP	Airbus A.319-111	easyJet Airline Co.Ltd	
G-EZAR	Pegasus Quik	D. McCormack	
G-EZAS	Airbus A.319-111	easyJet Airline Co.Ltd	
G-EZAT	Airbus A.319-111	easyJet Airline Co.Ltd	
G-EZAU	Airbus A.319-111	easyJet Airline Co.Ltd	
G-EZAV	Airbus A.319-111	easyJet Airline Co.Ltd	
G-EZAW	Airbus A.319-111	easyJet Airline Co.Ltd	
G-EZAX	Airbus A.319-111	easyJet Airline Co.Ltd	
G-EZAY	Airbus A.319-111	easyJet Airline Co.Ltd	
G-EZBA	Airbus A.319-111	easyJet Airline Co.Ltd	
G-EZBB	Airbus A.319-111	easyJet Airline Co.Ltd	
G-EZBC	Airbus A.319-111	easyJet Airline Co.Ltd	
G-EZBD	Airbus A.319-111	easyJet Airline Co.Ltd	
G-EZBE	Airbus A.319-111	easyJet Airline Co.Ltd	
G-EZBF	Airbus A.319-111	easyJet Airline Co.Ltd	
G-EZBH	Airbus A.319-111	easyJet Airline Co.Ltd	
G-EZBI	Airbus A.319-111	easyJet Airline Co.Ltd	
G-EZBJ	Airbus A.319-111	easyJet Airline Co.Ltd	
G-EZBK	Airbus A.319-111	easyJet Airline Co.Ltd	
G-EZBO	Airbus A.319-111	easyJet Airline Co.Ltd	
G-EZBR	Airbus A.319-111	easyJet Airline Co.Ltd	
G-EZBT	Airbus A.319-111	easyJet Airline Co.Ltd	
G-EZBU	Airbus A.319-111	easyJet Airline Co.Ltd	

Notes	Reg	Type	Owner or Operator
	G-EZBV	Airbus A.319-111	easyJet Airline Co.Ltd
	G-EZBW	Airbus A.319-111	easyJet Airline.Co.Ltd
	G-EZBX	Airbus A.319-111	easyJet Airline Co.Ltd
	G-EZBY	Airbus A.319-111	easyJet Airline Co.Ltd
	G-EZBZ	Airbus A.319-111	easyJet Airline Co.Ltd
	G-EZDA	Airbus A.319-111	easyJet Airline Co.Ltd
	G-EZDD	Airbus A.319-111	easyJet Airline Co.Ltd
	G-EZDF	Airbus A.319-111	easyJet Airline Co.Ltd
	G-EZDG	Rutan Vari-Eze	Varieze Flying Group (G-EZOS)
	G-EZDH	Airbus A.319-111	easyJet Airline Co.Ltd
	G-EZDI	Airbus A.319-111	easyJet Airline Co.Ltd
	G-EZDJ	Airbus A.319-111	easyJet Airline Co.Ltd
	G-EZDK	Airbus A.319-111	easyJet Airline Co.Ltd
	G-EZDL	Airbus A.319-111	easyJet Airline Co.Ltd
	G-EZDM	Airbus A.319-111	easyJet Airline Co.Ltd
	G-EZDN	Airbus A.319-111	easyJet Airline Co.Ltd
	G-EZDR	Airbus A.319-111	easyJet Airline Co.Ltd
	G-EZDV	Airbus A.319-111	easyJet Airline Co.Ltd
	G-EZDX	Airbus A.319-111	easyJet Airline Co.Ltd
	G-EZEH	Airbus A.319-111	easyJet Airline Co.Ltd
	G-EZES	Airbus A.319-111	easyJet Airline Co
	G-EZEV	Airbus A.319-111	easyJet Airline Co.Ltd
	G-EZEY	Airbus A.319-111	easyJet Airline Co.Ltd
	G-EZFI	Airbus A.319-111	easyJet Airline Co.Ltd
	G-EZFR	Airbus A.319-111	easyJet Airline Co.Ltd
	G-EZFT	Airbus A.319-111	easyJet Airline Co.Ltd
	G-EZFU	Airbus A.319-111	easyJet Airline Co.Ltd
	G-EZFV	Airbus A.319-111	easyJet Airline Co.Ltd
	G-EZFW	Airbus A.319-111	easyJet Airline Co.Ltd
	G-EZFX	Airbus A.319-111	easyJet Airline Co.Ltd
	G-EZFY	Airbus A.319-111	easyJet Airline Co.Ltd
	G-EZFZ	Airbus A.319-111	easyJet Airline Co.Ltd
	G-EZGA	Airbus A.319-111	easyJet Airline Co.Ltd
	G-EZGB	Airbus A.319-111	easyJet Airline Co.Ltd
	G-EZGC	Airbus A.319-111	easyJet Airline Co.Ltd
	G-EZGE	Airbus A.319-111	easyJet Airline Co.Ltd
	G-EZGF	Airbus A.319-111	easyJet Airline Co.Ltd
	G-EZGG	Airbus A.319-111	easyJet Airline Co.Ltd
	G-EZGH	Airbus A.319-111	easyJet Airline Co.Ltd
	G-EZGI	Airbus A.319-111	easyJet Airline Co.Ltd
	G-EZGN	Airbus A.319-111	easyJet Airline Co.Ltd
	G-EZGO	Airbus A.319-111	easyJet Airline Co.Ltd
	G-EZGR	Airbus A.319-111	easyJet Airline Co.Ltd
	G-EZGX	Airbus A.320-214	easyJet Airline Co.Ltd
	G-EZGY	Airbus A.320-214	easyJet Airline Co.Ltd
	G-EZIH	Airbus A.319-111	easyJet Airline Co.Ltd
	G-EZIW	Airbus A.319-111	easyJet Airline Co.Ltd
	G-EZIX	Airbus A.319-111	easyJet Airline Co.Ltd
	G-EZIY	Airbus A.319-111	easyJet Airline Co.Ltd
	G-EZIZ	Airbus A.319-111	easyJet Airline Co.Ltd
	G-EZMA	Robinson R22 II	Mercia Property Developments Ltd (G-WRWR)
	G-EZMK	Airbus A.319-111	easyJet Airline.Co.Ltd
	G-EZMT	Extra EA.300/200	Joff Ltd
	G-EZNM	Airbus A.319-111	easyJet Airline Co.Ltd
	G-EZOA	Airbus A.320-214	easyJet Airline Co.Ltd
	G-EZOF	Airbus A.320-214	easyJet Airline Co.Ltd
	G-EZOI	Airbus A.320-214	easyJet Airline Co.Ltd
	G-EZOK	Airbus A.320-214	easyJet Airline Co.Ltd
	G-EZOM	Airbus A.320-214	easyJet Airline Co.Ltd
	G-EZOP	Airbus A.320-214	easyJet Airline Co.Ltd
	G-EZOT	Airbus A.320-214	easyJet Airline Co.Ltd
	G-EZOU	Airbus A.320-214	easyJet Airline Co.Ltd
	G-EZOX	Airbus A.320-214	easyJet Airline Co.Ltd
	G-EZPB	Airbus A.320-214	easyJet Airline Co.Ltd
	G-EZPD	Airbus A.320-214	easyJet Airline Co.Ltd
	G-EZPE	Airbus A.320-214	easyJet Airline Co.Ltd
	G-EZPG	Airbus A.319-111	easyJet Airline Co.Ltd
	G-EZRT	Airbus A.320-214	easyJet Airline Co.Ltd
	G-EZRX	Airbus A.320-214	easyJet Airline Co.Ltd
	G-EZRY	Airbus A.320-214	easyJet Airline Co.Ltd
	G-EZRZ	Airbus A.320-214	easyJet Airline Co.Ltd

Reg	Type	Owner or Operator	Notes
G-EZTA	Airbus A.320-214	easyJet Airline Co.Ltd	
G-EZTB	Airbus A.320-214	easyJet Airline Co.Ltd	
G-EZTC	Airbus A.320-214	easyJet Airline Co.Ltd	
G-EZTD	Airbus A.320-214	easyJet Airline Co.Ltd	
G-EZTG	Airbus A.320-214	easyJet Airline Co.Ltd	
G-EZTH	Airbus A.320-214	easyJet Airline Co.Ltd	
G-EZTJ	Airbus A.320-214	easyJet Airline Co.Ltd	
G-EZTK	Airbus A.320-214	easyJet Airline Co.Ltd	
G-EZTL	Airbus A.320-214	easyJet Airline Co.Ltd	
G-EZTM	Airbus A.320-214	easyJet Airline Co.Ltd	
G-EZTN	Airbus A.320-214	easyJet Airline Co.Ltd	
G-EZTR	Airbus A.320-214	easyJet Airline Co.Ltd	
G-EZTT	Airbus A.320-214	easyJet Airline Co.Ltd	
G-EZTV	Airbus A.320-214	easyJet Airline Co.Ltd	
G-EZTX	Airbus A.320-214	easyJet Airline Co.Ltd	
G-EZTY	Airbus A.320-214	easyJet Airline Co.Ltd	
G-EZTZ	Airbus A.320-214	easyJet Airline Co.Ltd	
G-EZUA	Airbus A.320-214	easyJet Airline Co.Ltd	
G-EZUB	Zenair CH.601HD Zodiac	J. R. Davis	
G-EZUC	Airbus A.320-214	easyJet Airline Co.Ltd	
G-EZUF	Airbus A.320-214	easyJet Airline Co.Ltd	
G-EZUK	Airbus A.320-214	easyJet Airline Co.Ltd	
G-EZUL	Airbus A.320-214	easyJet Airline Co.Ltd	
G-EZUN	Airbus A.320-214	easyJet Airline Co.Ltd	
G-EZUO	Airbus A.320-214	easyJet Airline Co.Ltd	
G-EZUP	Airbus A.320-214	easyJet Airline Co.Ltd	
G-EZUR	Airbus A.320-214	easyJet Airline Co.Ltd	
G-EZUS	Airbus A.320-214	easyJet Airline Co.Ltd	
G-EZUT	Airbus A.320-214	easyJet Airline Co.Ltd	
G-EZUW	Airbus A.320-214	easyJet Airline Co.Ltd	
G-EZUZ	Airbus A.320-214	easyJet Airline Co.Ltd	
G-EZVS	Colt 77B balloon	A. J. Lovell	
G-EZWA	Airbus A.320-214	easyJet Airline Co.Ltd	
G-EZWB	Airbus A.320-214	easyJet Airline Co.Ltd	
G-EZWC	Airbus A.320-214	easyJet Airline Co.Ltd	
G-EZWD	Airbus A.320-214	easyJet Airline Co.Ltd	
G-EZWE	Airbus A.320-214	easyJet Airline Co.Ltd	
G-EZWF	Airbus A.320-214	easyJet Airline Co.Ltd	
G-EZWG	Airbus A.320-214	easyJet Airline Co.Ltd	
G-EZWH	Airbus A.320-214	easyJet Airline Co.Ltd	
G-EZWI	Airbus A.320-214	easyJet Airline Co.Ltd	
G-EZWJ	Airbus A.320-214	easyJet Airline Co.Ltd	
G-EZWL	Airbus A.320-214	easyJet Airline Co.Ltd	
G-EZWP	Airbus A.320-214	easyJet Airline Co.Ltd	
G-EZWU	Airbus A.320-214	easyJet Airline Co.Ltd	
G-EZWX	Airbus A.320-214	easyJet Airline Co.Ltd	
G-EZWY	Airbus A.320-214	easyJet Airline Co.Ltd	
G-EZWZ	Airbus A.320-214	easyJet Airline Co.Ltd	
G-EZXO	Colt 56A balloon	K. Jakobsson/Sweden	
G-EZZA	Shaw Europa XS	J. C. R. Davey	
G-EZZE	CZAW Sportcruiser	P. Hade	
G-EZZL	Westland Gazelle HT.3	Regal Group UK (G-CBKC)	
G-EZZY	Evektor EV-97A Eurostar	D. P. Creedy	
G-FABA	PA-31-350 Navajo Chieftain	Atlantic Bridge Aviation Ltd (G-OJIL)	
G-FABO	Bombardier CL600-2B16 Challenger 604	Hangar 8 Management Ltd	
G-FABS	Thunder Ax9-120 S2 balloon	R. Corrall & A. B. Court	
G-FACE	Cessna 172S	Oxford Aviation Services Ltd	
G-FADF	PA-18-150 Super Cub	J. Neale	
G-FAEJ	Cessna 182A	C. Keller, S. Koch & B. Schmiedel/Germany	
G-FAGK	DH.60M Moth	G. Cormack	
G-FAIR	SOCATA TB10 Tobago	A. J. Gomes	
G-FAIT	Airbus Helicopters AS.350B3 Ecureuil	A. S. Fitzgibbons	
G-FAJC	Alpi Pioneer 300 Hawk	M. Clare	
G-FALC	Aeromere F.8L Falco	D. M. Burbridge (G-AROT)	
G-FAME	Starstreak Shadow SA-II	P. R. Cooke	
G-FAMG	Bombardier BD700-1A11	Concierge U Ltd	
G-FANL	Cessna FR.172K XP-II	J. A. Rees	
G-FARE	Robinson R44 II	Toriamos Ltd/Ireland	
G-FARL	Pitts S-1E Special	J. P. Barrenechea	
G-FARO	Aero Designs Star-Lite SL.1	S. C. Goozee	

Notes	Reg	Type	Owner or Operator
	G-FARR	Jodel 150	S. J. Farr
	G-FARY	QAC Quickie Tri-Q	A. Bloomfield
	G-FATB	Rockwell Commander 114B	James D. Pearce & Co
	G-FATE	Falco F8L	G-FATE Flying Group
	G-FAZT	Stoddard-Hamilton Glasair II-SRG	C. Bruce
	G-FBAR	Diamond DA.40 Star	Exceedingly Ltd
	G-FBAT	Aeroprakt A.22 Foxbat	J. Jordan
	G-FBCY	Skystar Kitfox Mk 7	A. Bray (G-FBOY)
	G-FBEF	Embraer ERJ190-200LR	Ravelin Jet Leasing 1 DAC
	G-FBEG	Embraer ERJ190-200LR	Ravelin Jet Leasing 2 DAC
	G-FBEH	Embraer ERJ190-200LR	Ravelin Jet Leasing 2 DAC
	G-FBEI	Embraer ERJ190-200LR	Ravelin Jet Leasing 2 DAC
	G-FBEJ	Embraer ERJ190-200LR	Ravelin Jet Leasing 1 DAC
	G-FBEK	Embraer ERJ190-200LR	Ravelin Jet Leasing 1 DAC
	G-FBFB	PA-32R-301 Saratoga SP	Flying Fox Aviation (G-ROLF)
	G-FBHA	Agusta AW.139	FB Heliservices Ltd
	G-FBII	Ikarus C.42 FB100	F. Beeson
	G-FBJI	Embraer ERJ170-200STD	HEH Aviation Southampton Beteiligungsgesellschaft MBH & Co KG
	G-FBJJ	Embraer ERJ170-200STD	HEH Aviation Dublin Beteiligungsgesellschaft MBH & Co KG
	G-FBKF	Cessna 510 Citation Mustang	Jetcom SRL/Italy
	G-FBKG	Cessna 510 Citation Mustang	Jetcom SRL/Italy
	G-FBRN	PA-28-181 Archer II	G. E. Fox
	G-FBSS	Aeroprakt A22-LS Foxbat	S. R. V. McNeill
	G-FBTT	Aeroprakt A22-L Foxbat	J. Toner & J. Coyle
	G-FBWH	PA-28R-180 Cherokee Arrow	P3 Engineering Ltd
	G-FBXA	Aerospatiale ATR-72-212A	Loganair Ltd
	G-FBXB	Aerospatiale ATR-72-212A	Loganair Ltd
	G-FCAC	Diamond DA.42 Twin Star	ACS Aviation Ltd (G-ORZA)
	G-FCAV	Schleicher ASK-13	M. F. Cuming
	G-FCCC	Schleicher ASK-13	Shenington Gliding Club
	G-FCKD	Eurocopter EC 120B	Red Dragon Management LLP
	G-FCOM	Slingsby T.59F Kestrel	P. A. C. Wheatcroft & A. G. Truman
	G-FCSL	PA-32-350 Navajo Chieftain	Flight Calibration Services Ltd (G-CLAN)
	G-FCSP	Robin DR.400/180	J. D. McCarthy
	G-FCTK	DH.82C Tiger Moth (5084)	A. J. Palmer
	G-FCTY	DHC.1B-2-S5 Chipmunk	Rayburn Properties Ltd
	G-FCUK	Pitts S-1C Special	H. C. & M. J. Luck
	G-FCUM	Robinson R44 II	Hummingbird Helicopters Ltd
	G-FDDB	PA-32RT-300 Lance II	B. Nedjati-Gilani (G-NROY/G-LYNN/G-BGNY)
	G-FDHB	Bristol Scout Model C Replica (1264)	Bristol Scout Group
	G-FDHS	Leonardo AW109SP Grand New	Knaresborough Aviation LLP
	G-FDPS	Aviat Pitts S-2C Special	Dreamz Concepts BV/Belgium
	G-FDZB	Boeing 737-8K5	TUI Airways Ltd
	G-FDZD	Boeing 737-8K5	TUI Airways Ltd
	G-FDZF	Boeing 737-8K5	TUI Airways Ltd
	G-FDZS	Boeing 737-8K5	TUI Airways Ltd
	G-FDZT	Boeing 737-8K5	TUI Airways Ltd
	G-FDZU	Boeing 737-8K5	TUI Airways Ltd
	G-FDZX	Boeing 737-8K5	TUI Airways Ltd
	G-FDZY	Boeing 737-8K5	TUI Airways Ltd
	G-FDZZ	Boeing 737-8K5	TUI Airways Ltd
	G-FEAB	PA-28-181 Archer III	Feabrex Ltd
	G-FEBB	Grob G.104 Speed Astir IIB	C. P. A. Jones
	G-FEBJ	Schleicher ASW-19B	N. C. Day
	G-FEBU	DG Flugzeugbau DG-1000S	University of Bristol
	G-FECK	Raj Hamsa X'Air Jabiru(3)	R. J. Spence (G-CDSN)
	G-FECO	Grob G.102 Astir CS77	Stratford on Avon Gliding Club
	G-FEED	Cameron Z-90 balloon	O. Rosellino/Italy
	G-FEET	Mainair Pegasus Quik	G. Burns
	G-FEGN	PA-28-236 Dakota	G-FEGN Group Ltd
	G-FELD	Rotorsport UK MTO Sport	S. Pearce
	G-FELL	Shaw Europa	M. C. Costin & J. A. Inglis
	G-FELT	Cameron N-77 balloon	R. P. Allan
	G-FELX	CZAW Sportcruiser	T. F. Smith
	G-FERN	Mainair Blade 912	C. R. Buckle

Reg	Type	Owner or Operator	Notes
G-FERV	Rolladen-Schneider LS4	S. Walker	
G-FESB	Pipistrel Apis 15M M FES	P. C. Piggott	
G-FESS	Pegasus Quantum 15-912	P. M. Fessi (G-CBBZ)	
G-FEST	AS.350B Ecureuil	Wavendon Social Housing Ltd	
G-FESX	Schempp-Hirth Discus 2C FES	P. K. Carpenter	
G-FEVS	PZL-Bielsko SZD-50-3 Puchacz	Norfolk Gliding Club Ltd	
G-FEWG	Fuji FA.200-160	Cirrus UK Training Ltd (G-BBNV)	
G-FEZZ	Bell 206B JetRanger II	R. J. Myram	
G-FFAB	Cameron N-105 balloon	G. A. Boyle	
G-FFAF	Cessna F.150L	R. J. Fletcher	
G-FFBG	Cessna F.182Q	Synnova Aviation Ltd	
G-FFEN	Cessna F.150M	Wicklow Wings	
G-FFFA	P & M PulsR	I. A. Macadam	
G-FFFB	P & M Quik GTR	Flying for Freedom Ltd	
G-FFFC	Cessna 510 Citation Mustang	Synergy Aircraft Leasing Ltd	
G-FFFF	Zenair CH.750	J. Bate	
G-FFFT	Lindstrand LBL-31A balloon	G. B. Dey	
G-FFIT	Pegasus Quik	M. J. Hyde	
G-FFMV	Diamond DA.42 M-NG Twin Star	Cobham Leasing Ltd	
G-FFRA	Dassault Falcon 20DC	FR Aviation Ltd	
G-FFRV	Van's RV-10	Fairoaks Flyers	
G-FFUN	Pegasus Quantum 15	M. D. & R. M. Jarvis	
G-FFWD	Cessna 310R	T. S. Courtman (G-TVKE/G-EURO)	
G-FGAZ	Schleicher Ka 6E	P. W. Graves	
G-FGID	Vought FG-1D Corsair (KD345:130-A)	Patina Ltd	
G-FGSI	Montgomerie-Bensen B8MR	F. G. Shepherd	
G-FHAS	Scheibe SF.25E Super Falke	Upwood Motorglider Group	
G-FHFX	Wmbraer EMB-550 Praetor 600	Flexjet Ltd	
G-FIAT	PA-28 Cherokee 140	Demero Ltd & LV Skies Ltd (G-BBYW)	
G-FIBS	AS.350BA Ecureuil	Helicopter Services International Ltd	
G-FIBT	Robinson R44 II	G. Mazza & A. Curnis/Italy	
G-FICH	Guimbal Cabri G2	Helicentre Aviation Ltd	
G-FICS	Flight Design CTSW	N. Harris	
G-FIDL	Thruster T.600T 450 Jab	P. H. Thomas & G. R. Jones (G-CBIO)	
G-FIDO	Best Off Skyranger Nynja 912S(1)	P. D. Hollands	
G-FIFA	Cessna 404 Titan	RVL Aviation Ltd (G-TVIP/G-KIWI/G-BHNI)	
G-FIFE	Cessna FA.152	The Moray Flying Club (1990) (G-BFYN)	
G-FIFI	SOCATA TB20 Trinidad	The Foxtrot India Group (G-BMWS)	
G-FIFT	Ikarus C.42 FB 100	A. R. Jones	
G-FIFY	Colomban MC-30 Luciole	I. J. M. Donnelly	
G-FIGB	Cessna 152	A. J. Gomes	
G-FIII	Extra EA.300/L	M. & R. M. Nagel (G-RGEE)	
G-FIJJ	Cessna F.177RG	Fly 177 SARL/France (G-AZFP)	
G-FILE	PA-34-200T Seneca	G-FILE Group	
G-FINA	Cessna F.150L	K. M. Rigby (G-BIFT)	
G-FIND	Cessna F.406	Reconnaissance Ventures Ltd	
G-FINT	Piper L-4B Grasshopper (43583)	G. & H. M. Picarella	
G-FINZ	I.I.I Sky Arrow 650T	C. A. Bloom	
G-FION	Titan T-51 Mustang	A. A. Wordsworth	
G-FITC	Pilatus PC-12/47E	Elstree Ink Ltd	
G-FITY	Europa XS	Lios Cathain Group	
G-FIXX	Van's RV-7	P. C. Hambilton	
G-FIZY	Shaw Europa XS	C. Callicott (G-DDSC)	
G-FIZZ	PA-28-161 Warrior II	G-FIZZ Group	
G-FJET	Cessna 550 Citation II	London Executive Aviation Ltd (G-DCFR/ G-WYLX/G-JETD)	
G-FJMS	Partenavia P.68B	J. B. Randle (G-SVHA)	
G-FJTH	Aeroprakt A.22 Foxbat	A. J. Tuson	
G-FKKR	Fokker D.VII replica	P. D. & S. E. Ford	
G-FKNH	PA-15 Vagabond	M. J. Mothershaw	
G-FKOS	PA-28-181 Archer II	SVM Glasgow	
G-FLAG	Colt 77A balloon	B. A. Williams	
G-FLAV	PA-28-161 Warrior II	G. E. Fox	
G-FLAX	Aeropro Eurofox 914	Lleweni Parc Ltd	

Notes	Reg	Type	Owner or Operator
	G-FLBA	DHC.8-402 Dash Eight	NAC Aviation 2 Ltd
	G-FLBB	DHC.8-402 Dash Eight	NAC Aviation 2 Ltd
	G-FLBC	DHC.8-402 Dash Eight	HEH Aviation Leeds Beteiligungsgesellschaft MBH & Co KG
	G-FLBD	DHC.8-402 Dash Eight	HEH Aviation Liverpool Beteiligungsgesellschaft MBH & Co KG
	G-FLBE	DHC.8-402 Dash Eight	HEH Aviation Edinburgh Beteiligungsgesellschaft MBH & Co KG
	G-FLBX	Eurofox 914	Lleweni Parc Ltd
	G-FLBY	Ikarus C42 FB100 Bravo	Fly by Light
	G-FLCA	Fleet Model 80 Canuck	S. P. Evans
	G-FLCT	Hallam Fleche	R. G. Hallam
	G-FLDG	Skyranger 912	D. James & D. W. Power
	G-FLEA	SOCATA TB10 Tobago	N. J. Thomas
	G-FLEE	ZJ-Viera	P. C. Piggott
	G-FLEW	Lindstrand LBL-90A balloon	H. C. Loveday
	G-FLFX	Embraer EMB-550 Praetor 600	Flexjet Ltd
	G-FLIA	AutoGyro Calidus	P. Davies
	G-FLIK	Pitts S-1S Special	R. P. Millinship
	G-FLIP	Cessna FA.152	South East Area Flying Section (G-BOES)
	G-FLIS	Magni M.16C	M. L. L. Temple
	G-FLKE	Scheibe SF.25C Falke	The Royal Air Force Gliding & Soaring Association
	G-FLKI	Sikorsky S-61N Mk.II	British International Helicopter Services Ltd (G-BZSN)
	G-FLKS	Scheibe SF.25C Falke	London Gliding Club Propietary Ltd
	G-FLKY	Cessna 172S	Hields Aviation
	G-FLNT	Van's RV-8	Southern Alps Ltd
	G-FLOE	Robinson R66	Countyclean Holdings Ltd
	G-FLOR	Shaw Europa	A. T. Cross & I. R. Caesar
	G-FLOW	Cessna 172N	P. H. Archard
	G-FLOX	Shaw Europa	N. T. Read
	G-FLPI	Rockwell Commander 112	J. B. Thompson
	G-FLUZ	Rolladen-Schneider LS8-18	D. M. King
	G-FLXI	Pilatus PC-12/47E	Flexifly Aircraft Hire Ltd
	G-FLXY	PA-28-181 Archer TX	Flexifly Aircraft Hire Ltd
	G-FLYA	Mooney M.20J	B. Willis
	G-FLYB	Ikarus C.42 FB100	M. D. Stewart
	G-FLYC	Ikarus C.42 FB100	Solent Flight Ltd
	G-FLYG	Slingsby T.67C	G. Laden
	G-FLYJ	EV-97 Eurostar SL	The Scottish Aero Club Ltd
	G-FLYK	Beech B.200 Super King Air	D. T. A. Rees
	G-FLYO	EV-97 Eurostar SL	N. A. & P. A. Allwood
	G-FLYP	Beagle B.206 Srs 2	R. H. Ford & A. T. J. Darrah (G-AVHO)
	G-FLYT	Shaw Europa	K. F. & R. Richardson
	G-FLYW	Beech B.200 Super King Air	J. A. Rees (G-LIVY/G-PSTR)
	G-FLYY	BAC.167 Strikemaster 80A	High G Jets Ltd
	G-FLZR	Staaken Z-21 Flitzer	I. V. Staines
	G-FMAM	PA-28-151 Warrior (modified)	Air Training Club Aviation Ltd (G-BBXV)
	G-FMBS	Inverted US 12	W. P. Wright
	G-FMGB	Cameron Z-90 balloon	A. M. Holly
	G-FMGG	Maule M5-235C Lunar Rocket	S. Bierbaum (G-RAGG)
	G-FMLY	Commander 114B	PNG Air Ltd (G-VICS)
	G-FNAV	PA-31-350 Navajo Chieftain	Airpart Supply Ltd (G-BFFR)
	G-FNEY	Cessna F.177RG	F. Ney
	G-FNLD	Cessna 172N	Papa Hotel Flying Group
	G-FOCX	Aeropro Eurofox 2K	P. R. Simmonds-Short
	G-FOEW	M + R BM-77	Fields of Every When Flying Group
	G-FOFO	Robinson R44 II	Pickup & Son Ltd
	G-FOGG	Cameron N-90 balloon	J. P. E. Money-Kyrle
	G-FOGI	Shaw Europa XS	B. Fogg
	G-FOKK	Fokker DR1 (replica) (477/17)	P. D. & S. E. Ford
	G-FOKR	Fokker E.III (replica) (422/15)	R. D. Myles
	G-FOKS	Aeropro Eurofox 912(S)	E. R. Scougall
	G-FOKX	Eurofox 912(S)	Trent Valley Eurofox Group
	G-FOKZ	Aeropro Eurofox 912(IS)	R. J. Evans
	G-FOLI	Robinson R22 Beta II	Elstree Helicopters Ltd
	G-FOLY	Aerotek Pitts S-2A Modified	C. T. Charleston

Reg	Type	Owner or Operator	Notes
G-FOMO	Bombardier BD700-1A10 Global 6000	London Executive Aviation Ltd	
G-FOOT	Robinson R44 I	J. Pratt	
G-FOPP	Lancair 320	Great Circle Design Ltd	
G-FORA	Schempp-Hirth Ventus cT	W. H. Greenwood	
G-FORD	SNCAN Stampe SV.4C	P. H. Meeson	
G-FORZ	Pitts S-1S Special	N. W. Parkinson	
G-FOSY	MS.880B Rallye Club	A. G. Foster (G-AXAK)	
G-FOTN	Van's RV-7	M. T. Manwaring	
G-FOWL	Colt 90A balloon	M. R. Stokoe	
G-FOXA	PA-28-161 Cadet	Leicestershire Aero Club Ltd	
G-FOXB	Aeroprakt A.22 Foxbat	G. D. McCullough	
G-FOXC	Denney Kitfox Mk 3	T. Willford & R. M. Bremner	
G-FOXD	Denney Kitfox Mk 2	C. G. Langham	
G-FOXF	Denney Kitfox Mk 4	M. S. Goodwin	
G-FOXG	Denney Kitfox Mk 2	M. V. Hearns	
G-FOXH	Schempp-Hirth Ventus-2a	O. M. McCormack	
G-FOXI	Denney Kitfox	I. M. Walton	
G-FOXL	Zenair CH.601XL Zodiac	R. W. Taylor	
G-FOXM	Bell 206B JetRanger 2	Hessle Dock Company Ltd (G-STAK/G-BNIS)	
G-FOXO	Aeropro Eurofox 912(S)	J. C. Holland	
G-FOXS	Denney Kitfox Mk 2	Darley Taildraggers	
G-FOXT	Aeros Ant/Fox 13TL	R. Bower	
G-FOXU	Aeropro Eurofox 912S(1)	K. P. I. Kent & Simply Signs Ltd	
G-FOXV	Aeroprakt A22-LS Foxbat	M. W. Meynell (G-CHSY)	
G-FOXW	Aeropro Eurofox 912(1)	A. P. Whitmarsh	
G-FOXX	Denney Kitfox	J. Skelson	
G-FOXZ	Denney Kitfox	S. C. Goozee	
G-FOZY	Van's RV-7	M. G. Forrest (G-COPZ)	
G-FPEH	Guimbal Cabri G2	Elstree Helicopters Ltd	
G-FPIG	PA-28-151 Warrior	G. F. Strain (G-BSSR)	
G-FPLD	Beech 200 Super King Air	Thales UK Ltd	
G-FPRD	Cirrus SR22	F. Pearson & R. G. Drury	
G-FPSA	PA-28-161 Warrior II	Falcon Flying Services (G-RSFT/G-WARI)	
G-FRAD	Dassault Falcon 20E	Cobham Leasing Ltd (G-BCYF)	
G-FRAF	Dassault Falcon 20E	FR Aviation Ltd	
G-FRAG	PA-32 Cherokee Six 300E	T. A. Houghton	
G-FRAH	Dassault Falcon 20DC	FR Aviation Ltd	
G-FRAI	Dassault Falcon 20E	FR Aviation Ltd	
G-FRAJ	Dassault Falcon 20E	FR Aviation Ltd	
G-FRAK	Dassault Falcon 20DC	FR Aviation Ltd	
G-FRAL	Dassault Falcon 20DC	FR Aviation Ltd	
G-FRAN	Piper J-3C-90 Cub (480321:H-44)	Essex L-4 Group (G-BIXY)	
G-FRAP	Dassault Falcon 20DC	FR Aviation Ltd	
G-FRAR	Dassault Falcon 20DC	FR Aviation Ltd	
G-FRAS	Dassault Falcon 20C	FR Aviation Ltd	
G-FRAT	Dassault Falcon 20C	FR Aviation Ltd	
G-FRAU	Dassault Falcon 20C	FR Aviation Ltd	
G-FRAW	Dassault Falcon 20ECM	FR Aviation Ltd	
G-FRCE	Folland Gnat T.Mk.1 (XS104)	Red Gnat Ltd	
G-FRCX	P & M Quik GTR	G-FRCX Syndicate	
G-FRDM	Boeing Stearman B75N1	G. A. Bliss	
G-FRDY	Dynamic WT9 UK	J. A. Lockert	
G-FREY	Cirrus SR20	MAJ Aviation Ltd	
G-FRGT	P & M Quik GT450	G-FRGT Group	
G-FRJB	Britten Sheriff SA-1 ★	Aeropark/East Midlands	
G-FRNK	Skyranger 912(2)	D. L. Foxley & G. Lace	
G-FRNS	Bell 407GX	Ferns Surfacing Ltd	
G-FROM	Ikarus C.42 FB100	G-FROM Group	
G-FRRN	Leonardo AW109SP Grand New	Harrier Enterprises Ltd	
G-FRSB	Dassault Falcon 20F-5	Cobham Aviation Services UK	
G-FRSX	VS.388 Seafire F.46 (LA564)	Seafire Displays Ltd	
G-FRYA	Robinson R44 II	Pickup & Son Ltd (G-EJRC)	
G-FRYL	Beech 390 Premier 1	Hawk Air Ltd	
G-FSAR	Agusta Westland AW189	British International Helicopter Services Ltd	
G-FSBW	Aeropro Eurofox 912S(1)	N. G. Heywood	
G-FSEU	Beech 200 Super King Air	Nimbus Air Ltd	
G-FSZY	TB-10 Tobago	R. Arquier	

Notes	Reg	Type	Owner or Operator
	G-FTAB	PA-28-161 Warrior II	Flying Time Ltd (G-OZAM/G-LACA)
	G-FTAC	PA-28-161 Warrior II	Flying Time Ltd
	G-FTAD	PA-28-161 Warrior II	Flying Time Ltd
	G-FTAF	PA-28-161 Cherokee Warrior II	Flying Time Ltd (G-BOKB)
	G-FTAG	PA-28-161 Cherokee Warrior II	Flying Time Ltd (G-BOTN)
	G-FTAX	Cessna 421C	Gold Air International Ltd (G-BFFM)
	G-FTIL	Robin DR.400/180R	RAF Wyton Flying Club Ltd
	G-FTUS	Ultramagic F-12 Paquete balloon	A. M. Holly
	G-FUEL	Robin DR.400/180	S. L. G. Darch
	G-FUKM	Westland Gazelle AH.1 (ZA730)	Falcon Aviation Ltd
	G-FULL	PA-28R Cherokee Arrow 200-II	Stapleford Flying Club Ltd (G-HWAY/G-JULI)
	G-FUND	Thunder Ax7-65Z balloon	G. B. Davies
	G-FUNN	Plumb BGP-1A	J. Riley
	G-FURI	Isaacs Fury II	S. M. Johnston
	G-FURO	Furio	Falcotec Ltd
	G-FURZ	Best Off Sky Ranger Nynja 912S(1)	D. J. Tomlin
	G-FUSE	Cameron N-105 balloon	S. A. Lacey
	G-FUUN	Silence SA.180 Twister	A. W. McKee
	G-FUZZ	PA-18 Super Cub 95 (51-15319)	G. W. Cline
	G-FVEE	Monnett Sonerai 1	J. S. Baldwin
	G-FVEL	Cameron Z-90 balloon	Fort Vale Engineering Ltd
	G-FWJR	Ultramagic M-56 balloon	Harding and Sons Ltd
	G-FWKS	Tanarg/Ixess 15 912S(1)	M. A. Coffin (G-SYUT)
	G-FWLR	Flylight PeaBee Yellow Line	G. M. Fowler
	G-FWPW	PA-28-236 Dakota	P. A. & F. C. Winters
	G-FXBA	Aeroprakt A22-LS Foxbat	R. G. G. Pinder
	G-FXBT	Aeroprakt A.22 Foxbat	R. H. Jago
	G-FXER	Raytheon 400A	Flexjet Ltd
	G-FXFX	Embraer EMB-550 Legacy 500	Flexjet Ltd
	G-FXII	VS.366 Spitfire F.XII (EN224)	Air Leasing Ltd
	G-FYAN	Williams Westwind MLB	M. D. Williams
	G-FYAO	Williams Westwind MLB	M. D. Williams
	G-FYAU	Williams Westwind Mk 2 MLB	M. D. Williams
	G-FYAV	Osprey Mk 4E2 MLB	C. D. Egan & C. Stiles
	G-FYBX	Portswood Mk XVI MLB	I. Chadwick
	G-FYCL	Osprey Mk 4G MLB	P. J. Rogers
	G-FYCV	Osprey Mk 4D MLB	M. Thomson
	G-FYDF	Osprey Mk 4DV	K. A. Jones
	G-FYDI	Williams Westwind Two MLB	M. D. Williams
	G-FYDN	European 8C MLB	P. D. Ridout
	G-FYDO	Osprey Mk 4D MLB	N. L. Scallan
	G-FYDP	Williams Westwind Three MLB	M. D. Williams
	G-FYDS	Osprey Mk 4D MLB	N. L. Scallan
	G-FYEK	Unicorn UE.1C MLB	D. & D. Eaves
	G-FYEO	Eagle Mk 1 MLB	M. E. Scallan
	G-FYEV	Osprey Mk 1C MLB	M. E. Scallan
	G-FYEZ	Firefly Mk 1 MLB	M. E. & N. L. Scallan
	G-FYFI	European E.84DS MLB	M. Stelling
	G-FYFJ	Williams Westland 2 MLB	M. D. Williams
	G-FYFN	Osprey Saturn 2 MLB	J. & M. Woods
	G-FYFW	Rango NA-55 MLB	Rango Balloon and Kite Company
	G-FYFY	Rango NA-55RC MLB	Rango Balloon and Kite Company
	G-FYGC	Rango NA-42B MLB	L. J. Wardle
	G-FYGJ	Airspeed 300 MLB	N. Wells
	G-FYGM	Saffrey/Smith Princess MLB	A. Smith
	G-FZZA	General Avia F22-A	W. A. Stewart
	G-FZZI	Cameron H-34 balloon	Magical Adventures Ltd
	G-GAAL	Cessna 560XL Citation XLS	London Executive Aviation Ltd (G-DEIA)
	G-GAAZ	Cessna F.172N	M. Baumeister
	G-GABI	Lindstrand LBL-35A Cloudhopper balloon	R. D. Sargeant
	G-GABS	Cameron TR-70 balloon	N. M. Gabriel
	G-GABY	Bombardier BD-700-1A10 Global Express	Blue Square Aviation Group Malta Ltd
	G-GACA	P.57 Sea Prince T.1 (WP308:572CU) ★	P. G. Vallance Ltd/Charlwood
	G-GACB	Robinson R44 II	East Midlands Helicopters Engineering Ltd

Reg	Type	Owner or Operator	Notes
G-GAGE	Cameron Z-105 balloon	A. J. Thompson	
G-GAII	Hawker Hunter GA.11 (XE685)	Hawker Hunter Aviation Ltd	
G-GAJB	AA-5B Tiger	G-GAJB Group (G-BHZN)	
G-GALA	PA-28 Cherokee 180E	T. W. Gilbert	
G-GALB	PA-28-161 Warrior II	Gamston Flying School Ltd	
G-GALI	Agusta Westland AW.109SP Grand New	Gall Air LLP (G-HLSA/G-HCOM)	
G-GAMA	Beech 58 Baron	Gama Aviation (UK) Ltd (G-WWIZ/G-BBSD)	
G-GAME	Cessna T.303	P. Wadsley	
G-GAND	Agusta-Bell 206B Jet Ranger	R. Henderson (G-AWMK)	
G-GAOH	Robin DR.400 / 2 +2	M. A. Stott	
G-GAOM	Robin DR.400 / 2+2	Marine & Aviation Ltd	
G-GARE	Cessna 560XL Citation XLS	Virtus Aviation Ltd	
G-GARI	Ace Aviation Touch/Buzz	G. B. Shaw	
G-GASP	PA-28-181 Archer II	G-GASP Flying Group	
G-GAST	Van's RV-8	G. M. R. Abrey	
G-GATH	Airbus A.320-232	British Airways	
G-GATJ	Airbus A.320-232	British Airways	
G-GATK	Airbus A.320-232	British Airways	
G-GATL	Airbus A.320-232	British Airways	
G-GATM	Airbus A.320-232	British Airways	
G-GATN	Airbus A.320-232	British Airways	
G-GATP	Airbus A.320-232	British Airways	
G-GATR	Airbus A.320-232	British Airways	
G-GATS	Airbus A.320-232	British Airways	
G-GATT	Robinson R44 II	B. W. Faulkner	
G-GATU	Airbus A.320-232	British Airways	
G-GAVH	P & M Quik	I. J. Richardson	
G-GAVV	Flight Design CTSL	G. Hardman	
G-GAWA	Cessna 140	C140 Group (G-BRSM)	
G-GAXC	Robin R2160 Alpha Sport	D. D. McMaster	
G-GAZA	Aérospatiale SA.341G Gazelle 1	The Auster Aircraft Co Ltd (G-RALE/G-SFTG)	
G-GAZN	P & M Quik GT450	C. Hughes	
G-GAZO	Ace Magic Cyclone	G. J. Pearce	
G-GAZZ	Aérospatiale SA.341G Gazelle 1	Cheqair Ltd	
G-GBAO	Robin R1180TD	E. R. Hall	
G-GBAS	Diamond DA.62	Flight Calibration Services Ltd	
G-GBBB	Schleicher ASH-25	ASH25 BB Glider Syndicate	
G-GBBT	Ultramagic M-90 balloon	S. J. Chatfield	
G-GBCC	Ikarus C42 FB100	I. R. Westrope	
G-GBEE	Mainair Pegasus Quik	G. S. Bulpitt	
G-GBET	Ikarus C42 FB UL	P. K. Meech (G-BDBMK/G-MROY)	
G-GBFI	Kreimendahl K-10 Shoestring	T. Jarvis	
G-GBFR	Cessna F.177RG	Airspeed Aviation Ltd	
G-GBGA	Scheibe SF.25C Falke	The Royal Air Force Gliding and Soaring Association	
G-GBGB	Ultramagic M.105 balloon	S. A. Nother	
G-GBGF	Cameron Dragon SS balloon	Magical Adventures Ltd (G-BUVH)	
G-GBHB	SOCATA TB-10 Tobago	B. A. Mills	
G-GBHI	SOCATA TB-10 Tobago	P. T. Osbourne	
G-GBLP	Cessna F.172M	Leading Edge Flight Training Ltd (G-GWEN)	
G-GBMM	Agusta A109S Grand	Orchard Holdings Ltd (G-GRND)	
G-GBNZ	Eurofox 912(iS)	C. F. Pote	
G-GBOB	Alpi Pioneer 300 Hawk	R. E. Burgess	
G-GBPP	Rolladen-Schneider LS6-c18	G. J. Lyons & R. Sinden	
G-GBRB	PA-28 Cherokee 180C	Bravo Romeo Group	
G-CBRI	Best Off Skyranger Nynja LS 912S(1)	B. Greenwood	
G-GBRV	Van's RV-9A	J. S. Chaggar (G-THMB)	
G-GBSL	Beech 76 Duchess	M. H. Cundey & R. D. A. Berliand (G-BGVG)	
G-GBTV	Eurocopter AS.355N Ecureuil II	Cheshire Helicopters Ltd	
G-GBUE	Robin DR.400/120A	J. A. Kane (G-BPXD)	
G-GBUN	Cessna 182T	G. M. Bunn	
G-GBVN	Robin DR400/180	Bicester Robin Crew	
G-GBVX	Robin DR400/120A	N. Foster	
G-GCAC	Europa XS T-G	W. G. Miller	
G-GCAT	PA-28 Cherokee 140B	Group Cat (G-BFRH)	
G-GCCC	Cameron Z-105 balloon	Gloucestershire County Cricket Club Ltd	
G-GCCM	Bombardier CL600-2B16 Challenger 650	Gama Aviation (UK) Ltd	
G-GCDA	Cirrus SR20	M. R. Munn	
G-GCDB	Cirrus SR20	S. James	

BRITISH CIVIL AIRCRAFT MARKINGS

Notes	Reg	Type	Owner or Operator
	G-GCEA	Pegasus Quik	K. & P. Bailey
	G-GCFM	Diamond DA.40D Star	V. Babaca
	G-GCIY	Robin DR.400-140B	M. S. Lonsdale
	G-GCJA	Rolladen-Schneider LS8-18	N. T. Mallender
	G-GCKI	Mooney M.20K	P. J. Gamble
	G-GCMW	Grob G.102 Astir CS	M. S. F. Wood
	G-GCUF	Robin DR400/160	Bolter's Dowry Ltd
	G-GCVV	Cirrus SR22	Daedalus Aviation (Services) Ltd
	G-GCYC	Cessna F.182Q	The Cessna 180 Group
	G-GDAC	AA-5A Cheetah	D. S. Tarmey
	G-GDAV	Robinson R44 II	G. H. Weston
	G-GDEF	Robin DR.400/120	J. M. Shackleton
	G-GDEJ	Raytheon Hawker 800XP	Caribou Holdings Ltd (G-VOLA?G-XCSP)
	G-GDER	Robin R.1180TD	Berkshire Aviation Services Ltd
	G-GDFC	Boeing 737-8K2	Jet 2
	G-GDFD	Boeing 737-8K5	Jet 2
	G-GDFF	Boeing 737-85P	Jet 2
	G-GDFG	Boeing 737-36Q	Jet 2
	G-GDFJ	Boeing 737-804	Jet 2 (G-CDZI)
	G-GDFK	Boeing 737-36N	Jet 2 (G-STRE/G-XBHX)
	G-GDFL	Boeing 737-36N	Jet 2
	G-GDFM	Boeing 737-36N	Jet 2
	G-GDFN	Boeing 737-33V	Jet 2 (G-EZYH)
	G-GDFO	Boeing 737-3U3	Jet 2 (G-THOP)
	G-GDFP	Boeing 737-8Z9	Jet 2
	G-GDFR	Boeing 737-8Z9	Jet 2
	G-GDFS	Boeing 737-86N	Jet 2
	G-GDFT	Boeing 737-36Q	Jet 2 (G-TOYM/G-OHAJ)
	G-GDFU	Boeing 737-8K5	Jet 2
	G-GDFV	Boeing 737-85F	Jet 2
	G-GDFW	Boeing 737-8K5	Jet 2
	G-GDFX	Boeing 737-8K5	Jet 2
	G-GDFY	Boeing 737-86Q	Jet 2
	G-GDFZ	Boeing 737-86Q	Jet 2
	G-GDHI	Boeing 737-8K5	Jet 2
	G-GDIA	Cessna F.152	Skytrek Flying School Ltd
	G-GDKJ	Robin DR400/120	W. H. Cole
	G-GDKR	Robin DR400/140B	Hampshire Flying Group
	G-GDMW	Beech 76 Duchess	Flew LLP
	G-GDOG	PA-28R Cherokee Arrow 200-II	The Mutley Crew Group (G-BDXW)
	G-GDRV	Van's RV-6	J. R. S. Heaton & R. Feather
	G-GDSG	Agusta A109E Power	Palmhall Ltd
	G-GDSO	Autogyro Cavalon	P. Setterfield
	G-GDTU	Avions Mudry CAP-10B	R. W. H. Cole
	G-GECO	Hughes 369HS	N. Duggan (G-ATVEE/G-GCXK)
	G-GEEP	Robin R.1180TD	The Aiglon Flying Group
	G-GEFF	Pilatus PC-12/47E	GT Aviation (Elwick) LLP
	G-GEHL	Cessna 172S	K. A. & M. Whittaker
	G-GEHP	PA-28RT-201 Arrow IV	J. D. C. Lea
	G-GEJS	Extra EA300/LT	G. Sealey
	G-GELI	Colt 31A balloon	M. Rowlands (G-CDFI)
	G-GEMM	Cirrus SR20	Schmolke Grosskuechensysteme GmbH
	G-GEMS	Thunder Ax8-90 Srs 2 balloon	Kraft Bauprojekt GmbH/Germany
	G-GEMX	P & M Quik GT450	A. R. Oliver
	G-GEOF	Pereira Osprey 2	G. Crossley
	G-GEOS	Diamond HK.36 TTC-ECO	University Court (School of Geosciences) of the Super Dimona University of Edinburgh
	G-GERI	Robinson R44 1	Robraven Ltd
	G-GERT	Van's RV-7	C. R. A. Scrope
	G-GETU	Leonardo AW169	Jetheli Ltd
	G-GEZZ	Bell 206B JetRanger II	Lakeside Helicopters Ltd
	G-GFCA	PA-28-161 Cadet	JABM Ltd
	G-GFCB	PA-28-161 Cadet	Bristol and Wessex Aeroplane Club Ltd
	G-GFCE	PA-28-161 Warrior II	Falcon Flying Services Ltd (G-BVIH/G-BNJP)
	G-GFIB	Cessna F.152 II	Westair Flying Services Ltd (G-BPIO)
	G-GFID	Cessna 152 II	Pure Aviation Support Services Ltd (G-BORJ)
	G-GFIG	Cessna 152	The Pilot Centre Ltd (G-BNOZ)
	G-GFKY	Zenair CH.250	R. G. Kelsall

Reg	Type	Owner or Operator	Notes
G-GFLY	Cessna F.150L	Hangar 1 Ltd	
G-GFNO	Robin ATL	M. J. Pink	
G-GFOA	PA-28-161 Warrior II	Go Fly Oxford Ltd	
G-GFRA	PA-28RT-201T Turbo Arrow IV	Ravenair Aircraft Ltd (G-LROY/G-BNTS)	
G-GFSA	Cessna 172R Skyhawk	Atlantic Flight Training Ltd	
G-GFTA	PA-28-161 Warrior III	Guernsey Flying Training Ltd	
G-GFZG	PA-28-140 Cherokee E	B. A. Mills	
G-GGBD	PA-32-301T Turbo Saratoga	M. R. Crossley	
G-GGDV	Schleicher Ka 6E	East Sussex Gliding Club Ltd	
G-GGEM	PA-28-161 Warrior III	Hull Aero Club Ltd	
G-GGGR	Eurocopter AS.350B3 Ecureuil	AH Helicopter Services Ltd	
G-GGHZ	Robin ATL	M. J. Pink	
G-GGJK	Robin DR.400/140B	Headcorn Jodelers	
G-GGRH	Robinson R44	Heli Air Ltd	
G-GGRN	PA-28R-201 Cherokee Arrow III	J. P. Durnford	
G-GGRR	SA Bulldog Srs 120/121 (XX614:V)	D. J. Sharp (G-CBAM)	
G-GGRV	Van's RV-8	C. F. O'Neill	
G-GGTT	Agusta-Bell 47G-4A	P. R. Smith	
G-GGZZ	Aviat A-1B Husky	Honesdale Ltd	
G-GHEE	Aerotechnik EV-97 Eurostar	P. R. Howson	
G-GHER	AS.355N Ecureuil II	Gallagher Air LLP	
G-GHOP	Cameron Z-77 balloon	David P Hopkins	
G-GHOW	Cessna F.182Q	UK Flying Clubs Ltd, A. L. Handley & R. Kruit	
G-GHRW	PA-28RT-201 Arrow IV	P. Cowley (G-ONAB/G-BHAK)	
G-GHSV	Beech 200 Super King Air	Atlantic Bridge Aviation Lt	
G-GHZJ	SOCATA TB9 Tampico	P. K. Hayward	
G-GIAN	Ikarus C42 FB100	I. Newman & P. Read	
G-GIAS	Ikarus C42 FB80	R. D. Wilson	
G-GIBP	Moravan Zlin Z.526 Trener Master	D. G. Cowden	
G-GIGZ	Van's RV-8	N. G. Rhind & K. A. A. McDonald	
G-GIPC	PA-32R-301 Saratoga SP	GIPC Flying Group	
G-GIRY	AG-5B Tiger	Romeo Yankee Flying Group	
G-GIWT	Shaw Europa XS	A. Twigg	
G-GJCD	Robinson R22 Beta	J. C. Lane	
G-GKAT	Enstrom 280C	D. G. Allsop & A. J. Clark	
G-GKFC	RL-5A LW Sherwood Ranger	G. L. Davies (G-MYZI)	
G-GKKI	Avions Mudry CAP 231EX	D. R. Farley	
G-GKRC	Cessna 180K	W. J. Pitts	
G-GKUE	SOCATA TB-9 Tampico Club	R. S. McMaster	
G-GLAA	Eurocopter EC135 T2	PDG Helicopters	
G-GLAB	Eurocopter EC135 T2+	PLM Dollar Group Ltd (G-CFFR)	
G-GLAD	Gloster G.37 Gladiator II (N5903:H)	Patina Ltd	
G-GLAK	AB Sportine LAK-12	C. Roney	
G-GLAW	Cameron N-90 balloon	N. D. Humphries	
G-GLED	Cessna 150M	Westminster Academies Ltd	
G-GLHI	Skyranger 912	S. F. Winter	
G-GLID	Schleicher ASW-28-18E	S. Bovin	
G-GLII	Great Lakes 2T-1A-2	T. J. Richardson	
G-GLLY	Bell 505 Jet Ranger X	Twylight Management Ltd	
G-GLOB	Bombardier BD700-1A10 Global Express	Execujet (UK) Ltd	
G-GLOC	Extra EA.300/200	The Cambridge Aero Club Ltd	
G-GLSA	EV-97 Eurostar SL	LSA1 Group	
G-GLST	Great Lakes Sport Trainer	T. Boehmerle & A. Hofmann	
G-GLUC	Van's RV-6	A. K. Rostant	
G-GLUE	Cameron N-65 balloon	L. J. M. Muir & G. D. Hallett	
G-GMAD	Beech B.300C Super King Air 350C	Gama Aviation (Asset 2) Ltd	
G-GMAE	Beech B.200 Super King Air	Gama Aviation (UK) Ltd	
G-GMAF	Beech B.200 Super King Air	Gama Aviation (UK) Ltd	
G-GMAH	Airbus MBB BK117 D-2	Gama Aviation (UK) Ltd	
G-GMAX	SNCAN Stampe SV.4C	S. T. Carrel (G-BXNW)	
G-GMCM	AS.350B3 Ecureuil	T. J. Morris Ltd	
G-GMGH	Robinson R66	M. G. Holland	
G-GMIB	Robin DR400/500	D.A. & A. L. Sadler	
G-GMKA	PA-28-140 Cherokee F	GMK Aviation Services Ltd (G-KALI/G-BASL)	

Notes	Reg	Type	Owner or Operator
	G-GMKB	PA-28RT-201T Turbo Arrow IV	GMK Aviation Services Ltd (G-OPEP)
	G-GMOX	Cessna 152	Staverton Flying School @ Skypark Ltd
	G-GMSI	SOCATA TB9 Tampico	M. L. Rhodes
	G-GNJW	Ikarus C.42	N. C. Pearse
	G-GNMM	Agusta AW109SP Grand New	Hadleigh Partners LLP
	G-GNRV	Van's RV-9A	N. K. Beavins
	G-GNSS	Diamond DA.62	Flight Calibration Services Ltd
	G-GNTB	SAAB SF.340A	Loganair Ltd
	G-GNTF	SAAB SF.340A	Loganair Ltd
	G-GOAC	PA-34-200T Seneca II	J. P. de C. P. Calhamar/Portugal
	G-GOAL	Lindstrand LBL-105A balloon	I. Chadwick
	G-GODV	CAP Aviation CAP232	G-GODV Group
	G-GOER	Bushby-Long Midget Mustang	C. Antrobus
	G-GOES	Robinson R44-II	Helicentre Ltd
	G-GOFF	Extra EA.300/LC	George J. Goff Ltd
	G-GOFR	Ultramagic M-105 balloon	Associazione Vivere Paestum/Italy
	G-GOGB	Lindstrand LBL ,90A	J. Dyer (G-CDFX)
	G-GOGW	Cameron N-90 balloon	B. O'Rourke
	G-GOHI	Cessna 208 Caravan 1 amphibian	Headcorn Parachute Club Ltd
	G-GOLF	SOCATA TB10 Tobago	B. Lee
	G-GOLX	Europa XS	D. M. Hook (G-CROB)
	G-GOMS	Robinson R66	Bri-Stor Systems Ltd
	G-GOOF	Flylight Dragonfly	M. G. Preston
	G-GOPR	Cameron Z-90 balloon	Flying Enterprises
	G-GORD	Robin DR.401	J. G. Bellerby (G-JSMH)
	G-GORE	CFM Streak Shadow	P. F. Stares
	G-GORV	Van's RV-8	G-GORV Group
	G-GOSL	Robin DR.400/180	R. M. Gosling (G-BSDG)
	G-GOSP	Agusta Westland AW109SP Grand New	Castle Air Ltd
	G-GOSS	Jodel DR.221	Avon Flying Group
	G-GOTC	GA-7 Cougar	D. Hart
	G-GOTH	PA-28-161 Warrior III	Guernsey Flying Training Ltd
	G-GOUP	Robinson R22 Beta	AKP Aviation Ltd (G-DIRE)
	G-GOXC	HpH Glasflugel 304S Shark	S. M. Tilling
	G-GOXL	AS.355F2 Ecureuil II	Excel Charter Ltd (G-KHCG/G-SDAY/G-SYPA/ G-BPRE)
	G-GPAG	Van's RV-6	J. & N. Salmon
	G-GPEG	Sky 90-24 balloon	R. Cains-Collinson
	G-GPIG	Lindstrand LTL Series 1-80 balloon	A. M. Holly, K. W. Scott & R. J. Shortall
	G-GPMW	PA-28RT-201T Turbo Arrow IV	Calverton Flying Group Ltd
	G-GPSI	Grob G.115	Swiftair Maintenance Ltd
	G-GPSR	Grob G.115	Swiftair Maintenance Ltd (G-BOCD)
	G-GPSX	Grob G.115	Swiftair Maintenance Ltd
	G-GPWE	Ikarus C42 FB100	P. W. Ellis
	G-GREC	Sequoia F.8L Falco	D. O'Donnell
	G-GREM	MD Helicopters MD.600N	Gremlin Air LLP
	G-GRIN	Van's RV-6	E. Andersen
	G-GRIZ	PA-18-135 Super Cub (modified)	P. N. Elkington (G-BSHV)
	G-GRLS	Skyranger Swift 912S(1)	GRLS Flying Group
	G-GRLW	Jabiru J400	S. Rickard & J. Boniface (G-NMBG)
	G-GRMN	Aerospool Dynamic WT9 UK	I. D. Worthington
	G-GROE	Grob G.115A	B. Baylis & P. B. Readings
	G-GROW	Cameron N-77 balloon	Derbyshire Building Society
	G-GRPA	Ikarus C.42 FB100	G-GRPA Group
	G-GRRR	SA Bulldog Srs 120/122	Horizons Europe Ltd (G-BXGU)
	G-GRVE	Van's RV-6	G-GRVE Group
	G-GRVY	Van's RV-8	A. Page
	G-GRWL	Lilliput Type 4 balloon	A. E. & D. E. Thomas
	G-GRYN	Rotorsport UK Calidus	G. A. Speich
	G-GRYZ	Beech F33A Bonanza	J. Kawadri & M. Kaveh
	G-GRZZ	Robinson R44 II	Model Farm Shop Ltd
	G-GSAL	Fokker E.III Reolica (416/15)	Grass Strip Aviation Ltd
	G-GSAS	Airbus MBB BK117 D-2	Gama Aviation Ltd
	G-GSCV	Ikarus C42 FB UK	C. Parkinson & S. Coulton
	G-GSFS	Cessna 152	Staverton Flying School @ Skypark Ltd
	G-GSGS	HpH Glasflugel 304 ES	G. E. Smith

Reg	Type	Owner or Operator	Notes
G-GSIX	PA-32-300 Cherokee Six	I. Blamire	
G-GSMR	Bell 206B Jet Ranger III	SNM Holdings Ltd (G-BXNS)	
G-GSPY	Robinson R44 II	HQ Aviation Ltd	
G-GSST	Grob G.102 Astir CS77	A. J. M. Anderson	
G-GSVI	Gulfstream 650	Executive Jet Charter Ltd	
G-GSYL	PA-28RT-201T Turbo Arrow IV	S. J. Sylvester (G-DAAH)	
G-GSYS	PA-34-220T Seneca V	Cloudbase Aero Services Ltd	
G-GTAX	PA-31-350 Navajo Chieftain	Hadagain Investments Ltd (G-OIAS)	
G-GTFB	Magni M-24C	Rotormurf Ltd	
G-GTFC	P & M Quik	A. J. Fell	
G-GTGT	P & M Quik GT.450	T. J. Lewis	
G-GTHM	PA-38-112 Tomahawk	D. R. Clyde	
G-GTJD	P & M Quik GT450	A. J. Bacon	
G-GTOM	Alpi Pioneer 300	S. C. Oliphant & J. Watkins	
G-GTRE	P & M Quik GTR	M. J. Austin	
G-GTRR	P & M Quik GTR	M. R. Wallis	
G-GTRX	P & M Quik GTR	N. Matthews	
G-GTSD	P & M Quik GT450	P. Bayliss	
G-GTSO	P & M Quik GT450	D. Jones	
G-GTTP	P & M Quik GT450	L. M. Westwood	
G-GTWL	Aeropro Eurofox 912 (iS)	G. W. Brown	
G-GTWO	Schleicher ASW-15	J. M. G. Carlton & R. Jackson	
G-GUAR	PA-28-161 Warrior II	B. A. Mills	
G-GUIN	Ultramagic B-70 balloon	A. M. Holly	
G-GULP	I.I.I. Sky Arrow 650T	L. J. Betts	
G-GULY	Beech C.90A King Air	Victoria Group Holdings Ltd	
G-GULZ	Christen Eagle II	T. N. Jinks	
G-GUMM	Aviat A-1B	R. F. Pooler (G-LTMM)	
G-GUNS	Cameron V-77 balloon	O. Le Clercq/France	
G-GUNZ	Van's RV-8	Cirrus Aircraft UK Ltd	
G-GURU	PA-28-161 Warrior II	Avro-Marine Ltd	
G-GUSS	PA-28-151 Warrior	The Sierra Flying Group (G-BJRY)	
G-GVOE	Dassault Falcon 8X	Concierge U Ltd	
G-GVPI	Evans VP-1 srs.2	G. Martin	
G-GVSL	Evektor EV-97 Eurostar SL	G. Verity	
G-GWAC	Eurocopter EC.135 T2+	Babcock Mission Critical Services Onshore Ltd (G-WASN)	
G-GWFT	Rans S-6-ES Coyote II	The Georgia Williams Trust	
G-GWIZ	Colt Clown SS balloon	Magical Adventures Ltd	
G-GWMB	Pacific Aerospace PAC 750XL	Hinton Skydiving Centre Ltd	
G-GWYN	Cessna F.172M	G. Dunne	
G-GYAK	Yakovlev Yak-50	O. Luehring	
G-GYAV	Cessna 172N	Southport & Merseyside Aero Club (1979) Ltd	
G-GYRA	AutoGyro Calidus	W. C. Walters & D. B. Roberts	
G-GYRO	Campbell Cricket	J. W. Pavitt	
G-GYTO	PA-28-161 Warrior III	White Waltham Airfield Ltd	
G-GZDO	Cessna 172N	Eagle Flying Ltd	
G-GZIP	Rolladen-Schneider LS8-18	D. S. S. Haughton	
G-HAAH	Schempp-Hirth Ventus 2cT	V66 Syndicate	
G-HAAR	Eurofox 912(S)	Longside Flying Group	
G-HAAT	MDH MD.900 Explorer	Specialist Aviation Services Ltd (G-GMPS)	
G-HABI	Best Off SkyRanger 912S(1)	J. Habicht	
G-HABT	Supermarine Aircraft Spitfire Mk.26 (BL735:BT-A)	Wright Grumman Aviation Ltd	
G-HACE	Van's RV-6A	S. Woolmington	
G-HACK	PA-18 Super Cub 150	Intrepid Aviation Co	
G-HACS	Tecnam P2002-JF	The RAF Halton Aeroplane Club Ltd	
G-HADD	P & M Quik R	L. A. Wood	
G-HAEF	EV-97 TeamEurostar UK	RAF Microlight Flying Association	
G-HAFG	Cessna 340A	BH Aviation Flight Services Ltd	
G-HAGL	Robinson R44 II	HQ Aviation Ltd	
G-HAHU	Yakovlev Yak-18T	A. Leftwich	
G-HAIG	Rutan LongEz	P. R. Dalton	
G-HAIR	Robin DR.400/180	S. P. Copson	

Notes	Reg	Type	Owner or Operator
	G-HAJJ	Glaser-Dirks DG.400	W. G. Upton & J. G. Kosak
	G-HAKA	Diamond DA.42NG Twin Star	Directflight Ltd
	G-HALC	PA-28R Cherokee Arrow 200	Halcyon Aviation Ltd
	G-HALJ	Cessna 140	A. R. Wills
	G-HALL	PA-22 Tri-Pacer 160	F. P. Hall (G-ARAH)
	G-HALS	Robinson R44 II	Adventure 001 Ltd (G-CEKA)
	G-HALT	Mainair Pegasus Quik	J. McGrath
	G-HAMD	Aeropro Eurofox 3K	D. R. Hammond
	G-HAMI	Fuji FA.200-180	HAMI Group (G-OISF/G-BAPT)
	G-HAMP	Bellanca 7ACA Champ	R. J. Grimstead
	G-HAMR	PA-28-161 Warrior II	CG Aviation Ltd
	G-HAMS	Pegasus Quik	D. R. Morton
	G-HAMW	Aeropro Eurofox 3K	M. D. Hamwee
	G-HANC	Robinson R22	Pickup & Son Ltd (G-CHIS)
	G-HANS	Robin DR.400 2+2	The Cotswold Aero Club Ltd
	G-HANY	Agusta-Bell 206B JetRanger 3	Heliflight (UK) Ltd (G-ESAL/G-BHXW/G-JEKP)
	G-HAPE	Pietenpol Aircamper	J. P. Chape
	G-HAPI	Lindstrand LBL-105A balloon	Adventure Balloons Ltd
	G-HAPY	DHC.1 Chipmunk 22A (WP803)	Astrojet Ltd
	G-HARE	Cameron N-77 balloon	D. H. Sheryn & C. A. Buck
	G-HARG	Embraer EMB-550 Legacy 500	Centreline AV Ltd
	G-HARI	Raj Hamsa X'Air V2 (2)	XAir Group
	G-HARN	PA-28-181 Archer II	Dennis Flying Group (G-DENK/G-BXRJ)
	G-HARR	Robinson R22 Beta	L. G. Milne
	G-HART	Cessna 152 (tailwheel)	Taildraggers Flying Group (G-BPBF)
	G-HARY	Alon A-2 Aircoupe	M. B. Willis & A. D. Wilson (G-ATWP)
	G-HASS	Raytheon Hawker 850XP	Bookajet Aircraft Management Ltd
	G-HATH	Techpro Merlin 100UL	N. R. Hathaway
	G-HATZ	Hatz CB-1	S. P. Rollason
	G-HAUL	Westland WG.30 Srs 300 ★	The Helicopter Museum/Weston-super-Mare
	G-HAUT	Schempp-Hirth Mini Nimbus C	A. D. Peacock
	G-HAWC	BAe. Hawk T.Mk.1	L39 Aviation Ltd
	G-HAYE	Mudry CAP 232	G. Haye (G-SKEW)
	G-HAYS	Skyranger Swift 912S(1)	F. J. M. & S. F. Blatchford (G-CFBS)
	G-HAYY	Czech Sport Aircraft Sportcruiser	Sportcrew YY
	G-HAZA	Diamond DA.42NG Twin Star	R. W. F. Jackson
	G-HAZD	Cameron Z-56 balloon	L. S. Crossland-Clarke
	G-HAZL	Best Off Skyranger Nynja 912S(1)	J. A. Walker
	G-HAZZ	Eurocopter AS.350B3 Ecureuil	Milford Aviation Services Ltd (G-IANW)
	G-HBBC	DH.104 Dove 8	Roger Gawn 2007 Family Trust (G-ALFM)
	G-HBBH	Ikarus C42 FB100	Golf Bravo Hotel Group
	G-HBEE	Lindstrand LTL Series 2-80 balloon	R. P. Waite
	G-HBEK	Agusta A109C	HPM Investments Ltd (G-RNLD/G-DATE)
	G-HBJT	Eurocopter EC.155B1	Starspeed Ltd
	G-HBOS	Scheibe SF-25C Rotax-Falke	Coventry Gliding Club Ltd
	G-HBRB	Ikarus C42 FB100 Bravo	H. K. & R. M. Bilbe
	G-HCAC	Schleicher Ka 6E	Ka 6E 994 Group
	G-HCAT	Sindlinger Hawker Hurricane	G. S. Jones
	G-HCBW	Sequoia Falco F.8L	R. A. F. Buchanan
	G-HCCF	Vans RV-8A	M. R. Overall
	G-HCEN	Guimbal Cabri G2	Helicentre Aviation Ltd
	G-HCNX	Eurocopter EC.155B1	Silvercrest Aviation LP Inc
	G-HCPD	Cameron C-80 balloon	H. Crawley& P. Dopson
	G-HCSA	Cessna 525A CJ2	Bookajet Aircraft Management Ltd
	G-HCUB	J-5B Cub Cruiser	R. L. Northover (G-CIZN)
	G-HCUP	Magni M-22C Voyager	A. Harcup
	G-HCUS	Lindstrand LTL Series 2-80	D. G. Such & M. Tomlin
	G-HDAE	DHC.1 Chipmunk 22 (WP964)	Airborne Classics Ltd
	G-HDBV	MD MD-900 Explorer	Heli Delta BV/Netherlands (G-SASH)
	G-HDEW	PA-32R-301 Saratoga SP	G. Kirk
	G-HDTV	Agusta A109A-II	Castle Air Ltd (G-BXWD)
	G-HDUO	Ultramagic M-56 balloon	S. J. Colin
	G-HEAD	Colt Flying Head SS balloon	Ikeair
	G-HEAL	Lindstrand LTL Series 1-31 balloon	A. G. A. Barclay-Faulkner
	G-HEAN	AS.355NP Ecureuil 2	Brookview Developments Ltd
	G-HEBO	BN-2B-20 Islander	G. Cormack (G-BUBK)

Reg	Type	Owner or Operator	Notes
G-HEBS	BN-2B-26 Islander	Hebridean Air Services Ltd (G-BUBJ)	
G-HECB	Fuji FA.200-160	H. E. W. E. Bailey (G-BBZO)	
G-HECK	Robinson R44 II	Helivation Aviation Ltd (G-ILLG)	
G-HECT	Flight Design CTLS	R. C. Kelly	
G-HEDL	Extra EA.300/LC	H. J. R. Aylott	
G-HEHE	Eurocopter EC.120B Colibri	HE Group Ltd	
G-HEKL	Percival Mew Gull Replica	D. Beale	
G-HELA	SOCATA TB10 Tobago	Future Flight	
G-HELE	Bell 206B JetRanger 3	B. E. E. Smith (G-OJFR)	
G-HELL	Sonex	T. J. Shaw	
G-HELN	Piper PA-18-95 Super Cub (MM-52 2392:EI-69)	Helen Group	
G-HEMC	Airbus Helicopters MBB BK-117D-2	Babcock Mission Critical Services Onshore Ltd	
G-HEMN	Eurocopter EC135 T2+	Babcock Mission Critical Services Onshore Ltd	
G-HEMZ	Agusta A109S Grand	Sloane Helicopters Ltd	
G-HENT	SOCATA Rallye 110ST	G. Dolan	
G-HENY	Cameron V-77 balloon	Zebedee Balloon Service Ltd	
G-HENZ	Autogyro Cavalon	A. Henson	
G-HEOI	Eurocopter EC135 P2+	Police & Crime Commisioner for West Yorkshire	
G-HERC	Cessna 172S	Cambridge Aero Club Ltd	
G-HERD	Lindstrand LBL-77B balloon	S. W. Herd	
G-HETY	Aeropro Eurofox 912	Yorkshire Gliding Club (Proprietary) Ltd	
G-HEVI	Boeing 737-3M8	TAG Aviation (Stansted) Ltd (G-EZYB)	
G-HEVR	Ikarus C42 FB80	Deanland Flight Training Ltd	
G-HEWI	Piper J-3C-90 Cub	Denham Grasshopper Group (G-BLEN)	
G-HEWZ	Hughes 369HS	A. S. Mackenzie (G-LEEJ)	
G-HEXE	Colt 17A balloon	A. Dunnington	
G-HEYY	Cameron 72 Bear SS balloon	Magical Adventures Ltd	
G-HFBM	Curtiss Robin C-2	D. M. Forshaw	
G-HFCB	Cessna F.150L	J. H. Francis	
G-HFCF	SOCATA TB-20 Trinidad	A. P. Shoobert	
G-HFCT	Cessna F.152	Stapleford Flying Club Ltd	
G-HFRH	DHC-1 Chipmunk 22 (WK635)	NWMAS Leasing Ltd	
G-HGPI	SOCATA TB20 Trinidad	M. J. Jackson	
G-HGRB	Robinson R44	Nick Cook Plant Hire Ltd (G-BZIN)	
G-HHAA	HS. Buccaneer S.2B (XX885)	Hawker Hunter Aviation Ltd	
G-HHAC	Hawker Hunter F.58 (J-4021)	Hawker Hunter Aviation Ltd (G-BWIU)	
G-HHDR	Cessna 182T	I. D. Brierley	
G-HHEM	Leonardo AW169	Essex & Herts Air Ambulance Trust	
G-HHII	Hawker Hurricane IIB (BE505: XP-L)	Hawker Restorations Ltd (G-HRLO)	
G-HHPM	Cameron Z-105 balloon	J. Armstrong	
G-HIAL	Viking DHC-6-400 Twin Otter	Loganair Ltd	
G-HIBB	Avtech Jabiru J430	C. M. Hibbert	
G-HIBM	Cameron N-145 balloon	Alba Ballooning Ltd	
G-HICU	Schleicher ASW-27-18E	N. Hoare	
G-HIDE	Airbus AS.350B3 Ecureuil	Loxwood Holdings Ltd (G-CLBE)	
G-HIGA	Cessna 172P	High-G Flight Training (G-BRZS)	
G-HIGB	Robin R2120U	High-G Flight Training (G-CBVB)	
G-HIGC	Robin R2120U	High-G Flight Training (G-CBLE)	
G-HIJK	Cessna 421C	Acrobat Ltd (G-OSAL)	
G-HIJN	Ikarus C.42 FB80	G. P. Burns	
G-HILI	Van's RV-3B	A. G. & E. A. Hill	
G-HILO	Rockwell Commander 114	Alpha Golf Flying Group	
G-HILS	Cessna F.172H	A. S. C. Rathwell-Davey (G-AWCH)	
G-HILT	SOCATA TB10 Tobago	L. Windle	
G-HILY	Zenair CH.600 Zodiac	K. V. Hill (G-BRII)	
G-HILZ	Van's RV-8	A. G. & E. A. Hill	
G-HIMM	Cameron Z-105 balloon	C. M. D. Haynes	
G-HIND	Maule MT-7-235	A. & S. Gregori	
G-HINZ	Avtec Jabiru SK	P. J. Jackson	
G-HIOW	Airbus Helicopters EC.135T3	Babcock Mission Critical Services Onshore Ltd	
G-HIPE	Sorrell SNS-7 Hiperbipe	Aerosprite Informatics LtdD. G. Curran (G-ISMS)	
G-HIRE	GA-7 Cougar	Cristal Air Ltd (G-BGSZ)	
G-HISP	Hispano HA-1112 M1L Buchon	Air Leasing Ltd	
G-HITA	Airbus Helicopters AS.350B3 Ecureuil	Elstree Ink Ltd (G-CLBW)	
G-HITI	Airbus Helicopters AS.350B3 Ecureuil	Elstree Ink Ltd	
G-HITL	Airbus AS.350B3 Ecureuil	Elstree Ink Ltd (G-CKPH)	

Notes	Reg	Type	Owner or Operator
	G-HITM	Raj Hamsa X'Air 582 (1)	J. Hennegan
	G-HITT	Hawker Hurricane 1 (P3717:SW-P)	H. Taylor
	G-HITX	Leonardo A109S Trekker	Elstree Ink Ltd
	G-HIVE	Cessna F.150M	Peterborough Flying School Ltd (G-BCXT)
	G-HIYA	Best Off Skyranger 912(2)	R. D. & C. M. Parkinson
	G-HIZZ	Robinson R22 II	Flyfare (G-CNDY/G-BXEW)
	G-HJSM	Schempp-Hirth Nimbus 4DM	60 Syndicate (G-ROAM)
	G-HJSS	AIA Stampe SV.4C (modified)	R. S. Ward (G-AZNF)
	G-HKAA	Schempp-Hirth Duo Discus T	J. Randall
	G-HKCC	Robinson R66	HQ Aviation Ltd
	G-HKCF	Enstrom 280C-UK	HKC Helicopter Services (G-MHCF/G-GSML/
			G-BNNV)
	G-HKHK	Robinson R66	HQ Aviation Ltd
	G-HKHM	Hughes 369B	HQ Aviation Ltd
	G-HKPC	Robinson R66	HQ Aviation Ltd
	G-HLAM	Baloney Kubicek BB-S/Phare balloon	Lighter Than Air Ltd
	G-HLCF	Starstreak Shadow SA-II	F. E. Tofield
	G-HLCM	Leonardo AW109SP Grand New	Helicom
	G-HLEE	Best Off Sky Ranger J2.2(1)	P. G. Hill
	G-HLOB	Cessna 172S	Goodwood Road Racing Co.Ltd
	G-HLYF	Airbus A.321-211	Jet 2.com
	G-HMCA	EV-97 TeamEurostar UK	RAF Microlight Flying Association
	G-HMCB	Skyranger Swift 912S(1)	R. W. Goddin
	G-HMCD	Ikarus C42 FB80	B. Murkin
	G-HMCE	Ikarus C42 FB80	RAF Microlight Flying Association
	G-HMCF	EV-97 Eurostar SL mictolight	RAF Microlight Flying Association
	G-HMCH	EV-97 Eurostar SL	RAF Microlight Flying Association
	G-HMDX	MDH MD-900 Explorer	Specialist Aviation Services Ltd
	G-HMEC	Robinson R22	Helimech Ltd (G-BWTH)
	G-HMED	PA-28-161 Warrior III	Eglinton Flying Club Ltd
	G-HMEK	Robinson R22	Helimech Ltd (G-HIEL)
	G-HMGA	Beech 200 Super King Air	ACH London Ltd
	G-HMGB	Beech 200 Super King Air	ACH London Ltd
	G-HMHM	Rotorsport UK MTO Sport	R. M. Kimbell
	G-HMJB	PA-34-220T Seneca III	W. B. Bateson
	G-HMPS	CZAW Sportcruiser	A. Nicholson
	G-HMPT	Agusta-Bell 206B JetRanger 2	Yorkshire Helicopters
	G-HNGE	Ikarus C42 FB80	Compton Abbas Airfield Ltd
	G-HNPN	Embraer EMB-505 Phenom 300	Centreline
	G-HNTR	Hawker Hunter T.7 (XL571:V) ★	Yorkshire Air Museum/Elvington
	G-HODD	Schleicher ASW-27-18E	A. K. Eckton & K. Tipples
	G-HODR	Skyranger Swift 912S(1)	A. W. Hodder
	G-HOFF	P & M Aviation Quik GT450	L. Mazurek
	G-HOFM	Cameron N-56 balloon	Magical Adventures Ltd
	G-HOGB	Airbus EC130 T2	Hogs Head Transportation Ltd
	G-HOGC	Airbus EC130 T2	Hogs Head Transportation Ltd
	G-HOGS	Cameron 90 Pig SS balloon	Magical Adventures Ltd
	G-HOJO	Schempp-Hirth Discus 2a	S. G. Jones
	G-HOLA	PA-28-201T Turbo Dakota	D. A. Abel (G-BNYB)
	G-HOLE	P & M Quik GT450	B. Birtle (G-CEBD)
	G-HOLM	Eurocopter EC.120B Colibri	Oxford Air Services Ltd
	G-HONK	Cameron O-105 balloon	M. A. Green
	G-HONY	Lilliput Type 1 Srs A balloon	A. E. & D. E. Thomas
	G-HOON	Pitts S-1S Special	R. J. Allan, N. Jones & M. Furniss
	G-HOOZ	Kettley N-77 balloon	H. D. Jones
	G-HOPA	Lindstrand LBL-35A balloon	J. A. Hibberd
	G-HOPE	Beech F33A Bonanza	Hope Aviation Ltd
	G-HOPR	Lindstrand LBL-25A balloon	K. C. Tanner
	G-HOPY	Van's RV-6A	R. C. Hopkinson
	G-HORK	Pioneer 300 Hawk	R. Y. Kendal
	G-HOSS	Beech F33A	T. D. Broadhurst
	G-HOTA	EV-97 TeamEurostar UK	W. Chang
	G-HOTB	Eurocopter EC155 B1	Multiflight Ltd (G-CEXZ)
	G-HOTC	AutoGyro MTOSport	G. Hotchen (G-CINW)
	G-HOTM	Cameron C-80 balloon	M. G. Howard

Reg	Type	Owner or Operator	Notes
G-HOTR	P & M Quik GTR	M. E. Fowler	
G-HOTY	Bombardier CL600-2B16 Challenger 604	Jet Exchange Ltd	
G-HOTZ	Colt 77B balloon	C. J. & S. M. Davies	
G-HOUR	Max Holste MH.1521 C1 Broussard	Bremont Watch Company Ltd	
G-HOUS	Colt 31A balloon ★	The British Balloon Museum and Library	
G-HOWD	Magni M-24C Orion	M. G. Howard	
G-HOWI	Cessna F.182Q	N. Halsall	
G-HOWL	RAF 2000 GTX-SE gyroplane	C. J. Watkinson	
G-HOXN	Van's RV-9	XRay November Flying Club	
G-HPCB	Ultramagic S-90 balloon	D. A. Rawlings	
G-HPDM	Agusta A.109E Power	Adonby International Ltd (G-DPPF)	
G-HPIN	Bell 429	Harpin Ltd	
G-HPSF	Rockwell Commander 114B	R. W. Scandrett	
G-HPSL	Rockwell Commander 114B	M. B. Endean	
G-HPUX	Hawker Hunter T.7 (XL587)	Hawker Hunter Aviation Ltd	
G-HPWA	Van's RV-8	M. de Ferranti	
G-HRAF	Schleicher ASK-13	K13 – HRAF Syndicate (G-DETS)	
G-HRDB	Agusta A.109S Grand	Helicentre Aviation Ltd	
G-HRDY	Cameron Z-105 balloon	Flying Enterprises	
G-HRLI	Hawker Hurricane 1 (V7497)	Hawker Restorations Ltd & Hurricane Restoration Ltd	
G-HRND	Cessna 182T	R. H. Wicks	
G-HROI	Rockwell Commander RC.112	Intereuropean Aviation Ltd	
G-HRVD	CCF Harvard IV	P. Earthy (G-BSBC)	
G-HRVS	Van's RV-8	D. J. Harvey	
G-HRYZ	PA-28-180 Cherokee Archer	Gama Engineering Ltd (G-WACR/G-BCZF)	
G-HSDL	Westland Gazelle AH. Mk 1	Howard Stott Demolition Ltd	
G-HSEB	Pegasus Quantum 15-912	D. Gwyther (G-BYNO)	
G-HSKE	Aviat A-18 Husky	R. B. Armitage & S. L. Davis	
G-HSKI	Aviat A-1B	C. J. R. Flint	
G-HSOO	Hughes 369HE	Century Aviation Ltd (G-BFYJ)	
G-HSTH	Lindstrand LBL. HS-110 balloon	C. J. Sanger-Davies	
G-HSTI	Robinson R44 II	H S Thirsk & Son (G-SHAF)	
G-HSVI	Cessna FR.172J	S. J. Sylvester	
G-HTAX	PA-31-350 Navajo Chieftain	Hadagain Investments Ltd	
G-HTEK	Ultramagic M-77 balloon	A. D. McCutcheon	
G-HTFU	Gippsland GA8-TC 320 Airvan	Skydiving Aircraft Ltd	
G-HTML	P & M Aviation Quik R	FlyingsCool	
G-HTRL	PA-34-220T Seneca III	Techtest Ltd (G-BXXY)	
G-HTWE	Rans S6-116	G. R. Hill	
G-HUBB	Partenavia P.68B	Ravenair Aircraft Ltd	
G-HUCH	Cameron 80 Carrots SS balloon	Magical Adventures Ltd (G-BYPS)	
G-HUDS	P & M Quik GTR	S. J. M. Morling	
G-HUEW	Shaw Europa XS	C. R. Wright	
G-HUEY	Bell UH-1H	MX Jets Ltd	
G-HUEZ	Hughes 369E	Falcon Helicopters Ltd (G-WEBI)	
G-HUFF	Cessna 182P	Cousins Holdings Ltd	
G-HUGO	Colt 260A balloon	Thames Valley Balloons Ltd	
G-HUKA	MDH Hughes 369E	Muskany Ltd (G-OSOO)	
G-HUKS	Balony Kubicek BB22XR balloon	Wharf Farm Ltd	
G-HULK	Skyranger 912(2)	L. C. Stockman	
G-HULL	Cessna F.150M	Wicklow Wings	
G-HUME	EAA Acrosport 2	G. Home	
G-HUMH	Van's RV-9A	D. F. Daines	
G-HUMM	Bell 407	Century Aviation Ltd	
G-HUNI	Bellanca 7GCBC Scout	Paul's Planes Ltd	
G-HUPW	Hawker Hurricane 1 (R4118:UP-W)	J. Brown	
G-HURI	CCF Hawker Hurricane XIIA (P3700:RF-E)	Historic Aircraft Collection Ltd	
G-HUSH	Hughes 269C	Cirrus UK Training Ltd	
G-HUTY	Van's RV-7	S. A. Hutt	
G-HUXY	Cessna 152	Iris Aviation Ltd	
G-HVBF	Lindstrand LBL-210A balloon	Virgin Balloon Flights	
G-HVER	Robinson R44 II	Equation Associates Ltd	
G-HVRZ	Eurocopter EC 120B	J. S. Tobias	

Notes	Reg	Type	Owner or Operator
	G-HWAA	Eurocopter EC135T2	Babcock Mission Critical Services Onshore Ltd
	G-HWKS	Robinson R44	Rapid International (Holdings) Ltd (G-ETFF/G-HSLJ)
	G-HWKW	Hughes 369E	Flitwick Helicopters Ltd
	G-HWOW	Robinson R44	J. Pratt
	G-HXJT	Glasflugel 304 S Shark	H. Hingley
	G-HXTD	Robin DR.400/180	S. R. Evans
	G-HYBD	Gramex Song	University of Cambridge
	G-HYBR	TAF Sling 4	Boeing United Kingdom Ltd
	G-HYLA	Balony Kubicek BB26E balloon	J. A. Viner
	G-HYND	Robinson R44	Heli Air Scotland Ltd
	G-HYZA	PA-46-350P Malibu Mirage	Zeroavia Ltd
	G-HZRD	AgustaWestland AW.119 Mk.II	SaxonAir Helicopters
	G-IACA	Sikorsky S-92A	Bristow Helicopters Ltd
	G-IACB	Sikorsky S-92A	Bristow Helicopters Ltd
	G-IACC	Sikorsky S-92A	Bristow Helicopters Ltd
	G-IACD	Sikorsky S-92A	Bristow Helicopters Ltd
	G-IACE	Sikorsky S-92A	Bristow Helicopters Ltd
	G-IACF	Sikorsky S-92A	Bristow Helicopters Ltd
	G-IACY	Avions Transport ATR-72-212A	Eastern Airways
	G-IACZ	Avions Transport ATR-72-212A	Eastern Airways
	G-IAGL	Eurocopter EC.120B Colibri	AGL Helicopters (G-UYFI)
	G-IAGO	Groppo Trail Mk.2	J. Jones & J. W. Armstrong
	G-IAHS	EV-97 TeamEurostar UK	I. A. Holden
	G-IAJJ	Robinson R44 II	HH-Aviation (Manchester) Ltd
	G-IAJS	Ikarus C.42 FB UK	A. J. Slater
	G-IALC	AS.355F2 Ecureuil II	Alcaline UK Ltd (G-VVBA/G-DBOK)
	G-IAMP	Cameron H-34 balloon	W. D. Mackinnon
	G-IANB	Glaser-Dirks DG-800B	I. S. Bullous
	G-IANC	SOCATA TB10 Tobago	Kemble Flyers Ltd (G-BIAK)
	G-IANH	SOCATA TB10 Tobago	Severn Valley Aero Group
	G-IANI	Shaw Europa XS T-G	G. Hayes
	G-IANJ	Cessna F.150K	J. A. & D. T. A. Rees (G-AXVW)
	G-IANM	AB Sportine LAK-17AT	I. H. Molesworth
	G-IANZ	P & M Quik GT450	I. W. Harriman
	G-IARC	Stoddard-Hamilton Glastar	A. A. Craig
	G-IART	Cessna 182F	Aeroclub of Attica/Greece
	G-IASA	Beech B.200 Super King Air	IAS Medical Ltd
	G-IASB	Beech B.200GT Super King Air	IAS Medical Ltd
	G-IASC	Beech B.200 Super King Air	IAS Medical Ltd (G-CLOW)
	G-IASM	Beech B.200 Super King Air	2Excel Aviation Ltd (G-OEAS)
	G-IBAZ	Ikarus C.42 FB100	B. R. Underwood
	G-IBBJ	Rotorsport UK Cavalon	J. W. Payne
	G-IBBS	Shaw Europa	R. H. Gibbs
	G-IBCF	Cameron Z-105 balloon	Cash 4 Cars
	G-IBEA	PA-28-181 Archer LX	J. Dobson
	G-IBED	Robinson R22A	Swift Helicopter Services Ltd (G-BMHN)
	G-IBEE	Pipistrel Apis	Fly About Aviation Ltd
	G-IBEN	Van's RV-7	B. A. Fawke (G-CHIR)
	G-IBFC	BFC Challenger II	S. D. Puddle
	G-IBFF	Beech A23-24 Musketeer Super	D. H. G. Penney (G-AXCJ)
	G-IBFP	VPM .M.16 Tandem Trainer	B. F. Pearson
	G-IBFW	PA-28R-201 Arrow III	Archer Four Ltd
	G-IBIG	Bell 206B JetRanger 3	D. W. Bevan (G-BORV)
	G-IBII	Pitts S-2A Special	First Light Aviation Ltd (G-XATS)
	G-IBLP	P & M Quik GT450	P. G. Evans
	G-IBMS	Robinson R44	S. Rimmer
	G-IBNH	Westland Gazelle HT Mk.2 (XW853)	Buckland Newton Hire Ltd (G-SWWM)
	G-IBSY	VS.349 Spitfire Mk.VC (EE602/DV-V)	Anglia Aircraft Restorations Ltd (G-VMIJ)
	G-IBUZ	CZAW Sportcruiser	G. L. Fearon
	G-ICAN	Zenair CH.750	Aerobility
	G-ICAS	Pitts S-2B Special	J. C. Smith
	G-ICBM	Stoddard-Hamilton Glasair III Turbine	G. V. Walters & D. N. Brown
	G-ICDM	Jabiru UL-450	L. E. & N. P. Douch (G-CEKM)
	G-ICDP	Cessna F.150L	P. Morton

Reg	Type	Owner or Operator	Notes
G-ICEI	Leonardo AW169	Iceland International Ltd	
G-ICEJ	Guimbal Cabri G2	Ice Helicopters Ltd (G-VVBZ)	
G-ICEL	Robinson R66	Ice Helicopters Ltd	
G-ICES	Thunder Ax6-56 balloon ★	British Balloon Museum & Library Ltd	
G-ICEZ	Robinson R44	Ice London Aviation	
G-ICGA	PA-28-140 Cherokee E	M. Lalik/Poland	
G-ICLC	Cessna 150L	Devleminck Air Service/Belgium	
G-ICMT	Evektor EV-97 Eurostar	R. Haslam	
G-ICOM	Cessna F.172M	Stuart Taylor Aviation Ltd (G-BFXI)	
G-ICON	Rutan LongEz	S. J. & M. A. Carradice	
G-ICOR	Lindstrand LTL Series 2-60 balloon	R. G. Griffin	
G-ICRM	Slingsby T.67M-200 Firefly	CRM Aviation Europe Ltd (G-HONG)	
G-ICRR	Aeronca 11AC Chief	The Chieftains Flying Group	
G-ICRS	Ikarus C.42 FB UK Cyclone	Ikarus Flying Group Ltd	
G-ICRV	Van's RV-7	I. A. Coates	
G-ICUT	Maule MX-7-180A Super Rocket	R. A. Smith	
G-ICWT	Pegasus Quantum 15-912	Whisky Tango Group	
G-IDAY	Skyfox CA-25N Gazelle	G. G. Johnstone	
G-IDEB	AS.355F1 Ecureuil 2	Hideroute Ltd (G-ORMA/G-SITE/G-BPHC)	
G-IDFE	Bell 505 Jet Ranger X	Pwersense LLP	
G-IDID	SA. Bulldog Srs.120/121 (XX699/F)	N. J. Tucker (G-CBCV)	
G-IDII	Dan Rihn DR.107 One Design	C. Darlow	
G-IDMG	Robinson R44	B. Davis	
G-IDOL	Evektor EV-97 Eurostar	IDOL Group	
G-IDOO	Grob G.109B	Aerobility Holdings CIC	
G-IDRS	Van's RV-8	T. I. Williams	
G-IDTO	PA-28RT-201 Turbo Arrow IV	G. Cresdee	
G-IDYL	AutoGyro Cavalon	M. J. Newman	
G-IEEF	Raj Hamsa X'Air Hawk	P. J. Sheehy	
G-IEJH	Jodel 150A	A. Turner & D. Worth (G-BPAM)	
G-IENN	Cirrus SR20	Transcirrus BV/Netherlands (G-TSGE)	
G-IEZI	Rutan LongEz	K. H. McConnell & B. K. Ashworth (G-RAEM)	
G-IFAB	Cessna F.182Q	H. E. Thomas & A. Bruce	
G-IFBP	AS.350B2 Ecureuil	Frank Bird Aviation	
G-IFDA	Van's RV-6A	D. McKendrick	
G-IFES	Schempp-Hirth Discus 2c FES	J. M. Bevan	
G-IFFR	PA-32 Cherokee Six 300	Brendair (G-BWVO)	
G-IFFY	Flylight Dragonfly	R. D. Leigh	
G-IFIF	Cameron TR-60 balloon	M. G. Howard	
G-IFIK	Cessna 421C	N. Neumann/Germany	
G-IFIT	PA-31-350 Navajo Chieftain	Dart Group PLC (G-NABI/G-MARG)	
G-IFLE	Aerotechnik EV-97 TeamEurostar UK	Team Eurostar G-ILFE	
G-IFLI	AA-5A Cheetah	M. Sinkovec	
G-IFLP	PA-34-200T Seneca II	JABM Ltd	
G-IFOS	Ultramagic M-90 balloon	I. J. Sharpe	
G-IFWD	Schempp-Hirth Ventus cT	C. J. Hamilton	
G-IGEL	Cameron N-90 balloon	Computacenter Ltd	
G-IGET	Best Off Skyranger Nynja 912S(1)	D. C. Maybury	
G-IGGI	Bell 505 Jet Ranger X	Pristheath Ltd	
G-IGGL	SOCATA TB10 Tobago	Cavendish Aviation UK Ltd (G-BYDC)	
G-IGHT	Van's RV-8	E. A. Yates	
G-IGIA	AS.350B3 Ecureuil	Faloria Ltd	
G-IGIE	SIAI Marchetti SF.260	Flew LLP	
G-IGIS	Bell 206B JetRanger II	AT Aviation Sales Ltd (G-CHGL/G-BPNG/ G-ORTC)	
G-IGLE	Cameron V-90 balloon	G-IGLE Group	
G-IGLI	Schempp-Hirth Duo Discus T	C. Fox	
G-IGLL	AutoGyro MTO Sport	I. M. Donnellan	
G-IGLY	P & M Aviation Quik GT450	R. Davies	
G-IGLZ	Champion 8KCAB	C. A. Parsons	
G-IHAR	Cessna 172P	CG Aviation Ltd	
G-IHCI	Europa	I. H. Clarke (G-VKIT)	
G-IHHI	Extra EA.300/SC	Airdisplays.com Ltd	
G-IHOP	Cameron Z-31 balloon	N. W. Roberts	
G-IHOT	Aerotechnik EV-97 Eurostar UK	Exodus Airsports Ltd	
G-IHXD	Cessna F.150M	Air Navigation & Trading Co.Ltd	

Notes	Reg	Type	Owner or Operator
	G-IIAC	Aeronca 11AC Chief	N. Jamieson (G-BTPY)
	G-IIAI	Mudry CAP.232	DEP Promotions Ltd
	G-IIAL	Aerospool Dynamic WT9 UK	A. Howell (G-GCJH)
	G-IIAN	Aero Designs Pulsar	I. G. Harrison
	G-IIBB	Bell 505 Jet Ranger X	MJL Plant Hire (Cornwall) Ltd
	G-IICC	Van's RV-4	P. R. Fabish & J. C. Carter (G-MARX)
	G-IICP	Hughes 369E	Eastern Atlantic Helicopters Ltd (G-OGJP)
	G-IICT	Schempp-Hirth Ventus 2Ct	P. McLean
	G-IICX	Schempp-Hirth Ventus 2cxT	M. J. M. Turnbull
	G-IIDC	Midget Mustang	D. Cooke (G-IIMT/G-BDGA)
	G-IIDD	Van's RV-8	A. D. Friday
	G-IIDI	Extra EA.300/L	Power Aerobatics Ltd (G-XTRS)
	G-IIDR	Ikarus C42 FB100	I. A. Harper & S. G. Penk
	G-IIDW	Flylight Dragon Combat 12T	J. S. Prosser
	G-IIDY	Aerotek Pitts S-2B Special	The S-2B Group (G-BPVP)
	G-IIEX	Extra EA.300/L	S. G. Jones
	G-IIFI	Xtremair XA41	Attitude Aerobatics Ltd
	G-IIFM	Edge 360	F. L. McGee
	G-IIFX	Marganski MDM-1	Glider FX
	G-IIGI	Van's RV-4	C. J. L. Wolf
	G-IIGL	Christen Eagle II	C. Butler & G. G. Ferriman (G-RIFY)
	G-IIHL	Extra EA.300/SC	Aerobatic Show SP ZOO
	G-IIHX	Bushby-Long Midget Mustang	M. C. Huxtable
	G-IIHZ	Avions Murdy CAP 231	J. Taylor & R. Bates (G-OZZO)
	G-IIID	Dan Rihn DR.107 One Design	D. A. Kean
	G-IIIE	Aerotek Pitts S-2B Special	R. M. C. R. de Aguiar/Portugal
	G-IIIF	Xtremeair XA-41	Airtime Aerobatics Ltd
	G-IIIG	Boeing Stearman A75N1 (309)	Stearman G-IIIG Group /Belgium (G-BSDR)
	G-IIII	Aerotek Pitts S-2B Special	K. M. Balla
	G-IIIJ	American Champion 8GCBC	J. D. May
	G-IIIK	Extra EA.300/SC	Extra 300SC LLP
	G-IIIL	Pitts S-1T Special	I. F. Thompson
	G-IIIM	Stolp SA.100 Starduster	R. O. Johnson
	G-IIIN	Pitts S-1C Special	R. P. Evans
	G-IIIR	Pitts S-1S Special	P. J. & W. M. Hodgkins
	G-IIIV	Pitts Super Stinker 11-260	S. D. Barnard & A. N. R. Houghton
	G-IIIX	Pitts S-1S Special	D. F. Friel (G-LBAT/G-UCCI/G-BIYN)
	G-IIIY	Boeing A75N1 Stearman	Aero-Super-Batics Ltd
	G-IIJC	Midget Mustang	D. M. Casey (G-CEKU)
	G-IIJI	Xtremeair XA-42 Sbach 342	G. H. Willson
	G-IILL	Vans RV-7	C. P. Wilkinson
	G-IILX	Extra EA.300/LC	Collett Aviation Services Ltd
	G-IILY	Robinson R44 I	Whizzard Helicopters (G-DCSG/G-TRYG)
	G-IIMI	Extra EA.300/L	Firebird Aerobatics Ltd
	G-IINI	Van's RV-9A	N. W. Thomas
	G-IINK	Cirrus SR22	N. P. Kingdon
	G-IIOO	Schleicher ASW-27-18E	N. A. Taylor
	G-IIPI	Steen Skybolt	J. Burglass (G-BVXE/G-LISA)
	G-IIPT	Robinson R22 Beta	Swift Helicopter Services Ltd (G-FUSI)
	G-IIRG	Stoddard-Hamilton Glasair IIS RG	Ayeaye Group
	G-IIRI	Xtreme Air Sbach 300	L. Love & One Sky Aviation LLP
	G-IIRP	Mudry CAP.232	R. J. Pickin
	G-IIRV	Van's RV-7	D. J. Lee
	G-IIRW	Van's RV-8	G. G. Ferriman
	G-IISC	Extra EA.300/SC	G-IISC Group
	G-IITC	Mudry CAP.232	Skyboard Aerobatics Ltd
	G-IIXF	Van's RV-7	C. A. & S. Noujaim
	G-IIXI	Extra EA.300/L	B. Nielsen
	G-IIXX	Parsons 2-seat gyroplane	J. M. Montgomerie
	G-IIXZ	Schleicher ASG-32 Mi	Zulu Glasstek Ltd
	G-IIYI	Boeing Stearman A75N1	V. S. EW. Norman
	G-IIYK	Yakovlev Yak-50	Eaglescott Yak 50 Group
	G-IIYY	Cessna 421C	H-J Simon
	G-IIZI	Extra EA.300	M. G. Jefferies
	G-IJAC	Light Aero Avid Speedwing Mk 4	I. J. A. Charlton
	G-IJAG	Cessna 182T Skylane	N. J. Ratcliffe
	G-IJBB	Enstrom 480	Transair (UK) Ltd (G-LIVA/G-PBTT)
	G-IJMC	Magni M-16 Tandem Trainer	R. F. G. Moyle (G-POSA/G-BVJM)
	G-IJOE	PA-28RT-201T Turbo Arrow IV	J. Stella

Reg	Type	Owner or Operator	Notes
G-IKAH	Slingsby T.51 Dart 17R	K. A. Hale	
G-IKBP	PA-28-161 Warrior II	NWMAS Leasing Ltd	
G-IKES	Stoddard-Hamilton GlaStar	M. Stow	
G-IKEV	Jabiru UL-450	S. A. Wilson & P. J. Findlay	
G-IKON	Van's RV-4	N. C. Spooner	
G-IKOS	Cessna 550 Citation Bravo	Medox Enterprises Ltd	
G-IKRK	Shaw Europa	K. R. Kesterton	
G-IKRS	Ikarus C42 FB UK	K. J. Warburton	
G-IKUS	Ikarus C42 FB UK	R. Wilkinson	
G-ILBG	Cessna 525A Citationjet CJ2	Catreus AOC Ltd	
G-ILBO	Rolladen-Schneider LS3-A	J. P. Gilbert	
G-ILBT	Cessna 182T	G. E. Gilbert	
G-ILDA	VS.361 Spitfire HF.IX (SM520 : KJ-1)	Boultbee Classic LLP (G-BXHZ)	
G-ILEE	Colt 56A balloon	B. W. Smith	
G-ILES	Cameron O-90 balloon	G. N. Lantos	
G-ILEW	Schempp Hirth Arcus M	Lleweni Parc Ltd	
G-ILHR	Cirrus SR22	R. R. Tyler	
G-ILIB	PZL-Bielsko SZD-36A	D. Poll	
G-ILLD	Robinson R44 II	SJH-ALL Plant Group Ltd	
G-ILLE	Boeing Stearman A75L3 (379)	M. Minkler	
G-ILLY	PA-28-181 Archer II	R. A. & G. M. Spiers	
G-ILLZ	Europa XS	R. S. Palmer	
G-ILRS	Ikarus C.42 FB UK Cyclone	J. J. Oliver	
G-ILSE	Corby CJ-1 Starlet	S. Stride	
G-ILUA	Alpha R2160I	A. R. Haynes	
G-ILYA	Agusta-Bell 206B Jet Ranger II	Aerospeed Ltd (G-MHMH/G-HOLZ/G-CDBT)	
G-ILZZ	PA-31 Navajo	T. D. Nathan & I. Kazi	
G-IMAB	Europa XS	N. J. France	
G-IMAG	Colt 77A balloon ★	Balloon Preservation Group	
G-IMBI	QAC Quickie 1	P. Churcher (G-BWIT)	
G-IMBJ	QAC Quickie	P. Churcher (G-WAHL)	
G-IMBO	CEA Jodel DR.250/160	Training & Leisure Consultants Ltd	
G-IMCD	Van's RV-7	I. G. McDowell	
G-IMCH	Lindstrand LTL Series SS Cube balloon	A. M. Holly	
G-IMEA	Beech 200 Super King Air	2 Excel Aviation Ltd (G-OWAX)	
G-IMEL	Rotary Air Force RAF 2000 GTX-SE	N. A. Smith	
G-IMGP	Raytheon Hawker 850XP	Voluxis Ltd	
G-IMIK	PA-28-180 Cherokee C	M. K. Kent (G-ATNB)	
G-IMME	Zenair CH.701SP	T. R. Sinclair	
G-IMMI	Escapade Kid	C. Summerfield & R. K. W. Moss	
G-IMMY	Robinson R44	F. Vitali/Italy	
G-IMNY	Escapade 912	D. S. Bremner	
G-IMOK	Hoffmann HK-36R Super Dimona	G-IMOK Syndicate	
G-IMPS	Skyranger Nynja 912S	B. J. Killick	
G-IMPX	Rockwell Commander 112B	G. Valluzzi/Italy	
G-IMUP	Tanarg/Ixess 15 912S (1)	C. R. Buckle	
G-INAS	PA-28-181 Archer II	D. N. F. & R. Barrington-Bullock (G-BRNV)	
G-INCA	Glaser-Dirks DG.400	C. Rau	
G-INDC	Cessna T.303	Valco Marketing	
G-INDX	Robinson R44	Ice London Aviation	
G-INDY	Robinson R44	Lincoln Aviation	
G-INES	Zenair CH.650B	P. W. Day & N. J. Brownlow	
G-INGA	Thunder Ax8-84 balloon	M. L. J. Ritchie	
G-INGS	American Champion 8KCAB	The Leicestershire Aero Club Ltd	
G-INII	Pitts S-1 Special	C. Davidson (G-BTEF)	
G-INJA	Ikarus C42 FB UK	G. Sloan	
G-INNI	Jodel D.112	K. Dermott	
G-INNY	SE-5A (replica) (F5459:Y)	J. M. Gammidge	
G-INSR	Cameron N-90 balloon	P. J. Waller	
G-INTS	Van's RV-4	H. R. Carey	
G-INTV	AS.355F2 Ecureuil 2	Arena Aviation Ltd (G-JETU)	
G-INVN	Hawker Sea Fury T.Mk.20 (WG655)	S. Patrick (G-CHFP)	
G-INYS	TLAC Sherwood Scout	S. D. Pain	
G-IOCJ	PA-28R-200 Cherokee Arrow II	M. J. Jewers (G-RONG)	
G-IOFR	Lindstrand LBL-105A balloon	RAF Halton Hot Air Balloon Club	
G-IOIA	I.I.I. Sky Arrow 650T	G-IOIA Group	
G-IOOI	Robin DR.400-160	N. B. Mason, R. P. Jones & D. J. Goodman	

Notes	Reg	Type	Owner or Operator
	G-IOOK	Agusta A.109E	Hundred Percent Aviation Ltd (G-VIPE)
	G-IOOP	Christen Eagle II	A. P. S. Maynard
	G-IOOZ	Agusta A109S Grand	Castle Air Ltd
	G-IORV	Van's RV-10	J. E. Howe
	G-IOSI	Jodel DR.1051	G-IOSI Group
	G-IOSL	Van's RV-9	S. Leach (G-CFIX)
	G-IOSO	Jodel DR.1050	A. J. Roxburgh
	G-IOVE	BRM Bristell NG5 Speedwing	S. D. Austen
	G-IOWE	Shaw Europa XS	P. G. & S. J. Jeffers
	G-IPAT	Jabiru SP	Fly Jabiru Scotland
	G-IPAV	PA-32R-301T Saratoga IITC	Tofana Aviation Ltd
	G-IPAX	Cessna 560XL Citation Excel	Pacific Aviation Ltd
	G-IPCE	Guimbal Cabri G2	T. Gallop & J. Cook
	G-IPEN	UltraMagic M-90 balloon	R. A. Benham
	G-IPEP	Beech 95-B55 Baron	M. W. Fitch (G-FABM)
	G-IPGL	AgustaWestland AW109SP Grand New	IPGL No.7 Ltd
	G-IPIG	Elan 550/Pegasus Cosmos Fly Away 01	R. Frankham
	G-IPII	Steen Skybolt	J. Burglass
	G-IPJF	Robinson R44 II	Specialist Group International Ltd (G-RGNT/ G-DMCG)
	G-IPKA	Alpi Pioneer 300	M. E. Hughes
	G-IPLY	Cessna 550 Citation Bravo	International Plywood (Aviation) Ltd (G-OPEM)
	G-IPOD	Europa XS	J. Wighton (G-CEBV)
	G-IPSE	Airbus EC.130 T2	Best Holdings (UK) Ltd (G-CKYH)
	G-IPSI	Grob G.109B	G-IPSI Flying Group (G-BMLO)
	G-IPSY	Rutan Vari-Eze ★	Science Museum/Wroughton
	G-IPUP	Beagle B.121 Pup 2	T. S. Walker
	G-IRAF	RAF 2000 GTX-SE gyroplane	Condor Aviation International Ltd
	G-IRAK	SOCATA TB-10 Tobago	Flying Feather Ltd
	G-IRAL	Thruster T600N 450	J. Giraldez
	G-IRAY	Best Off Skyranger 912S(1)	G. R. Breadon
	G-IRED	Ikarus C42 FB80	Deanland Flight Training Ltd
	G-IRIS	AA-5B Tiger	H. de Libouton (G-BIXU)
	G-IRJE	Diamond DA.62	Sere Ltd
	G-IRJX	Avro RJX-100 ★	Runway Visitor Park/Manchester
	G-IRLE	Schempp-Hirth Ventus cT	D. J. Scholey
	G-IRLI	P & M Quik GTR	N. Griffin
	G-IRLY	Colt 90A balloon	J. A. Viner
	G-IROB	SOCATA TB-10 Tobago	R. Forman
	G-IROD	Rotorsport UK MTO Sport	R. A. R. Stringer (G-FELD)
	G-IROJ	Magni M-16 Tandem Trainer	A. G. Jones
	G-IRON	Shaw Europa XS	J. R. Gardiner
	G-IROS	Rotorsport UK Calidus	SSN Hampshire Ltd
	G-IROW	Magni VPM M16 Tandem Trainer	Danelander Ltd (G-DBDB)
	G-IROX	Magni M-24C Orion	A. J. Roxburgh
	G-IRPC	Cessna 182Q	A. T. Jeans (G-BSKM)
	G-IRPW	Europa XS	R. P. Wheelwright
	G-IRTY	VS.361 Spitfire LF.IX	Boultbee Flight Academy LLP
	G-IRYC	Schweizer 269-1	Virage Helicopter Academy LLP
	G-ISAC	Isaacs Spitfire (TZ164:OI-A)	A. James
	G-ISAR	Cessna 421C	Skycab Ltd (G-BHKJ)
	G-ISAS	Airbus MBB BK117 D-2	Gama Aviation (UK) Ltd
	G-ISAX	PA-28-181 Archer III	Spectrum Flying Group
	G-ISAY	BAe Jetstream 4102	Airtime AB/Sweden (G-MAJN)
	G-ISBD	Alpi Pioneer 300 Hawk	GMK Aviation Services Ltd
	G-ISCD	Czech Sport Aircraft Sportcruiser	P. W. Shepherd
	G-ISDB	PA-28-161 Warrior II	K. Bartholomew (G-BWET)
	G-ISDN	Boeing Stearman A75N1 (14)	D. R. L. Jones
	G-ISEH	Cessna 182R	D. Jaffa (G-BIWS)
	G-ISEL	Best Off Skyranger 912 (2)	P. A. Robertson
	G-ISEW	P & M Quik GT450	R. & T. Raffle
	G-ISHA	PA-28-161 Warrior III	LAC Flying School
	G-ISLC	BAe Jetstream 3202	Oberbank Leasing GmbH/Austria
	G-ISLF	Aerospatiale ATR-42-500	Elix Assets 12 Ltd
	G-ISLH	Aerospatiale ATR-42-320	Blue Islands Ltd
	G-ISLK	Aerospatiale ATR-72-212A	Blue Islands Ltd
	G-ISLL	Aerospatiale ATR-72-212A	Blue Islands Ltd
	G-ISLM	Aerospatiale ATR-72-212A	Blue Islands Ltd

Reg	Type	Owner or Operator	Notes
G-ISLN	Aerospatiale ATR-72-212A	Blue Islands Ltd	
G-ISLY	Cessna 172S	RMACF Aviation (G-IZZS)	
G-ISMA	Van's RV-7	D. King (G-STAF)	
G-ISMC	Cessna F.152	Stapleford Flying Club Ltd	
G-ISMO	Robinson R22 Beta	Kuki Helicopter Sales Ltd	
G-ISOB	Cameron O-31 balloon	A. C. Booth	
G-ISPH	Bell 206B JetRanger 2	Blades Aviation (UK) LLP (G-OPJM)	
G-ISRV	Van's RV-7	I. A. Sweetland	
G-ISSG	DHC.6-310 Twin Otter	Isles of Scilly Skybus Ltd	
G-ISSW	Eurocopter EC.155 B1	Wilmington Trust SP Services (Dublin) Ltd	
G-ISZA	Aerotek Pitts S-2A Special	T. J. B. Dugan (G-HISS/G-BLVU)	
G-ITAF	SIAI-Marchetti SF.260AM	N. A. Whatling	
G-ITAR	Magni M-16C Tandem Trainer	Hartis Autogyro Syndicate	
G-ITII	Aerotech Pitts S-2A Special	Hurricane Restoration Ltd	
G-ITOI	Cameron N-90 balloon	Flying Pictures Ltd	
G-ITOR	Robinson R44 II	Tubrid Ltd	
G-ITPH	Robinson R44 II	Helicopter Services Europe Ltd	
G-ITST	Europa	I. Tucker	
G-ITVM	Lindstrand LBL-105A balloon	Elmer Balloon Team	
G-ITWB	DHC.1 Chipmunk 22	I. T. Whitaker-Bethe	
G-IUII	Aerostar Yakovlev Yak-52	Cosmos Technology Ltd	
G-IUMB	Schleicher ASW-20L	M. S. Szymkowicz	
G-IVAL	CAB CAP-10B	H. Thomas	
G-IVAR	Yakovlev Yak-50	A. H. Soper	
G-IVEN	Robinson R44 II	OKR Group/Ireland	
G-IVER	Shaw Europa XS	I. Phillips	
G-IVES	Shaw Europa	I. Wyatt (G-JOST)	
G-IVET	Shaw Europa	K. J. Fraser	
G-IVII	Van's RV-7	M. A. N. Newall	
G-IVIP	Agusta A109E Power	Castle Air Ltd (G-VIRU)	
G-IVOR	Aeronca 11AC Chief	South Western Aeronca Group	
G-IWIN	Raj Hamsa X'Air Hawk	C. G. & M. G. Chambers	
G-IWON	Cameron V-90 balloon	D. P. P. Jenkinson (G-BTCV)	
G-IWPI	Agusta AW109SP Grand New	GB Helicopters	
G-IXII	Christen Eagle II	S. J. Perkins & D. Dobson (G-BPZI)	
G-IXXI	Schleicher ASW-27-18E	D. J. Langrick	
G-IXXY	Magic Cyclone	L. Hogan	
G-IYII	Boeing B75N1 Stearman	Mike Papa Delta Ltd	
G-IYRO	RAF2000 GTX-SE	G. Golding (G-BXDD)	
G-IZIT	Rans S.6-116 Coyote II	D. J. Flower	
G-IZOB	Eurocopter EC.120B Colibri	Beechview Developments Ltd	
G-IZRV	Van's RV-12	D. J. Mountain & H. W. Hall	
G-IZZI	Cessna T.182T	A. I. Freenan	
G-IZZT	Cirrus SR22T	H. G. Dilloway	
G-IZZZ	Champion 8KCAB	P. J. Randell	
G-JAAB	Avtech Jabiru UL	I. A. Smith	
G-JAAP	Aeroprakt A-32 Vixxen	J. Rademaker	
G-JABE	Jabiru Aircraft Jabiru UL-D	K. J. Reynolds	
G-JABI	Jabiru Aircraft Jabiru J400	K. & M. A. Payne	
G-JABJ	Jabiru Aircraft Jabiru J400	South Essex Flying Group	
G-JABS	Avtech Jabiru UL-450	Jabiru Flying Group	
G-JABU	Jabiru J430	S. D. Miller	
G-JABY	Avtech Jabiru UL-450	D. R. Watson	
G-JABZ	Avtech Jabiru UL-450	G-JABZ Group	
G-JACA	PA-28-161 Warrior II	The Pilot Centre Ltd	
G-JACB	PA-28-181 Archer III	P. R. Coe (G-PNNI)	
G-JACH	PA-28-181 Archer III	Alderney Flight Training Ltd (G-IDPH)	
G-JACL	Tecnam P2010	Jersey Jet Centre Ltd	
G-JACM	Tecnam P2008-JC	Jersey Jet Centre Ltd	
G-JACN	Tecnam P2008-JC	Jersey Jet Centre Ltd	
G-JACO	Avtech Jabiru UL	J. R. Morrison	
G-JACS	PA-28-181 Archer III	Modern Air (UK) Ltd	
G-JADJ	PA-28-181 Archer III	G-Hire Ltd	
G-JADW	Ikarus C42 FB80	G-JADW Group	

Notes	Reg	Type	Owner or Operator
	G-JAEE	Van's RV-6A	J. A. E. Edser
	G-JAES	Bell 206B JetRanger 3	Associazione Croce Italia Area Flegreal/Italy (G-STOX/G-BNIR)
	G-JAFS	PA-32R-301 Saratoga II HP	Hambleton Aviation Ltd (G-VMFC)
	G-JAFT	Diamond DA.42 Twin Star	Atlantic Flight Training Ltd
	G-JAGA	Embraer EMB-505 Phenom 300	London Executive Aviation Ltd
	G-JAGS	Cessna FRA.150L	RAF Marham Aero Club (G-BAUY)
	G-JAIR	Mainair Blade	G. Spittlehouse
	G-JAJA	Robinson R44 II	J. D. Richardson
	G-JAJB	AA-5A Cheetah	D. Hadlow & Partners Flying Group
	G-JAJK	PA-31-350 Navajo Chieftain	Blue Sky Investments Ltd (G-OLDB/G-DIXI)
	G-JAJP	Avtech Jabiru UL	J. Anderson
	G-JAKF	Robinson R44 Raven II	J. G. Froggatt
	G-JAKS	PA-28 Cherokee 160	J. L. & M. Harper (G-ARVS)
	G-JAKX	Cameron Z-69 balloon	J. A. Hibberd
	G-JAME	Zenair CH 601UL	J. J. Damp (G-CDFZ)
	G-JAMP	PA-28-151 Warrior	Lapwing Flying Group Ltd (G-BRJU)
	G-JAMY	Shaw Europa XS	J. P. Sharp
	G-JAMZ	P & M QuikR	S. Cuthbertson
	G-JANA	PA-28-181 Archer II	J. Majeethia
	G-JANB	Colt Flying Bottle SS balloon	Justerini & Brooks Ltd
	G-JANF	BRM Aero Bristell NG5 Speed Wing	G-JANF Group
	G-JANI	Robinson R44	JT Helicopters Ltd
	G-JANN	PA-34-220T Seneca III	D. J. Whitcombe
	G-JANS	Cessna FR.172J	R. G. & S. F. Scott
	G-JANT	PA-28-181 Archer II	Janair Aviation Ltd
	G-JAOC	Best Off Sky Ranger Swift 912S(1)	R. L. Domiczew
	G-JAPK	Grob G.130A Twin II Acro	Cairngorm Gliding Club
	G-JARM	Robinson R44	J. Armstrong
	G-JARY	PA-24-260 Comanche	C. Roberts-York (G-BRXW)
	G-JASE	PA-28-161 Warrior II	Mid-Anglia School of Flying
	G-JASS	Beech B200 Super King Air	ACH (Witham) Ltd
	G-JAVO	PA-28-161 Warrior II	Victor Oscar Ltd (G-BSXW)
	G-JAWC	Pegasus Quantum 15-912	E. Simkus
	G-JAWZ	Pitts S-1S Special	A. R. Harding
	G-JAYI	Auster J/1 Autocrat	A. L. Hall-Carpenter
	G-JAYK	Robinson R44 II	AMH Heli LLP (G-MACU/G-SEFI)
	G-JAYS	Skyranger 912S(1)	K. O'Connor & T. L. Whitcombe
	G-JAYZ	CZAW Sportcruiser	J. Williams
	G-JBAN	P & M Quik GT450	A. Nourse
	G-JBAS	Neico Lancair 200	A. Slater
	G-JBAV	EV-97 Eurostar SL	K. J. Gay
	G-JBBB	Eurocopter EC120B Colibri	Bartram Land Ltd
	G-JBBZ	AS.350B3 Ecureuil	D. Donnelly
	G-JBCB	Agusta A.109E Power	SDP Developers (G-PLPL/G-TMWC)
	G-JBDH	Robin DR.400/180	W. A. Clark
	G-JBEE	Robinson R44	Beeston Manor Ltd (G-CGWD)
	G-JBEN	Mainair Blade 912	G. J. Bentley
	G-JBHL	Bell 505 Jet Ranger X	Jones Brothers (Henllan) Ltd
	G-JBIB	Diamond DA.62	Diamond Aviation Training Ltd
	G-JBKA	Robinson R44	J. G. Harrison
	G-JBLL	BAe.125 series 800B	Sovereign Business Jets Ltd (G-VIPI)
	G-JBOB	Schempp-Hirth Discus 2c FES	O. J. Bosanko & J. M. Robson
	G-JBRD	Mooney M.20K	R. J. Doughton
	G-JBRE	Rotorsport UK MT-03	P. A. Remfry
	G-JBRS	Van's RV-8	C. Jobling
	G-JBSP	Avtech Jabiru SP-470	M. D. Beeby and C. K. & C. R. James
	G-JBUZ	Robin DR400/180R Remorqueur	D. A. Saywell
	G-JBVP	Aeropro Eurofox 3K	J. A. Valentine & B. J. Partridge
	G-JCBS	Piper J-3C-65 Cub	J. Slade (G-CUBY/G-BTZW)
	G-JCIH	Van's RV-7A	M. A. Hughes & D. F. Chamberlain
	G-JCJC	Colt Flying Jeans SS balloon	Magical Adventures Ltd
	G-JCKT	Stemme S.10VT	M. B. Jefferyes & J. C. Taylor
	G-JCOP	Eurocopter AS.350B3 Ecureuil	Optimum Ltd
	G-JCWM	Robinson R44 II	M. L. J. Goff
	G-JCWS	Reality Escapade 912(2)	D. W. Allen
	G-JDBC	PA-34-200T Seneca II	Bristol Flying Club Ltd (G-BDEF)
	G-JDEL	Jodel 150	K. F. & R. Richardson (G-JDLI)

Reg	Type	Owner or Operator	Notes
G-JDHN	Rotorway Executive 162F	J. N. Price (G-FLIT)	
G-JDOG	Cessna 305C Bird Dog (24541/BMG)	BC Arrow Ltd	
G-JDPB	PA-28R-201T Turbo Arrow III	BC Arrow Ltd (G-DNCS)	
G-JDRD	Alpi Pioneer 300	RD Pioneer Flying Group	
G-JDUN	Robinson R66	Nationwide Pathology Ltd	
G-JEAO	BAe.146-100 ★	deHavilland Aircraft Heritage Centre/London Colney	
G-JEBS	Cessna 172S	Integrated Hi-Tech Ltd	
G-JECK	DHC.8-402 Dash Eight	NAC Aviation 19 Ltd	
G-JECL	DHC.8-402 Dash Eight	NAC Aviation 19 Ltd	
G-JECM	DHC.8-402 Dash Eight	NAC Aviation 19 Ltd	
G-JECN	DHC.8-402 Dash Eight	NAC Aviation 19 Ltd	
G-JECO	DHC.8-402 Dash Eight	NAC Aviation 19 Ltd	
G-JECP	DHC.8-402 Dash Eight	NAC Aviation 19 Ltd	
G-JECR	DHC.8-402 Dash Eight	NAC Aviation 19 Ltd	
G-JECX	DHC.8-402 Dash Eight	NAC Aviation 19 Ltd	
G-JECY	DHC.8-402 Dash Eight	NAC Aviation 19 Ltd	
G-JECZ	DHC.8-402 Dash Eight	HEH Aviation London Beteiligungsgesellschaft MBH & Co KG	
G-JEDH	Robin DR.400/180	Regent Aero Group	
G-JEDM	DHC.8-402 Dash Eight	Nordeutsche Landesbank Girozentrale	
G-JEDP	DHC.8-402 Dash Eight	Nordeutsche Landesbank Girozentrale	
G-JEDR	DHC.8-402 Dash Eight	Nordeutsche Landesbank Girozentrale	
G-JEDS	Andreasson BA-4B	S. B. Jedburgh (G-BEBT)	
G-JEDT	DHC.8-402 Dash Eight	Nordeutsche Landesbank Girozentrale	
G-JEDU	DHC.8-402 Dash Eight	Nordeutsche Landesbank Girozentrale	
G-JEDV	DHC.8-402 Dash Eight	Nordeutsche Landesbank Girozentrale	
G-JEDW	DHC.8-402 Dash Eight	Nordeutsche Landesbank Girozentrale	
G-JEEP	Evektor EV-97 Eurostar	G-JEEP Group (G-CBNK)	
G-JEFA	Robinson R44	Simlot Ltd	
G-JEJE	RAF 2000 GTX-SE gyroplane	A. F. Smallacombe	
G-JEJH	Jodel DR.1050 Ambassadeur	Bredon Hill Flying Group	
G-JEMI	Lindstrand LBL-90A balloon	S. W. K. Smeeton	
G-JEMM	Jodel DR.1050	D. W. Garbe	
G-JEMP	BRM Aero Bristell NG5 Speed Wing	W. Precious	
G-JEMS	Ultramagic S-90 balloon	D. J. , J. E. & L. V. McDonald	
G-JEMZ	Ultramagic H-31 balloon	J. A. Atkinson	
G-JENA	Mooney M.20K	K. I. Zahariev	
G-JENK	Ikarus C42 FB80	G-JENK Chatteris 2015	
G-JEOL	Slingsby T67C Firefly	London Transport Flying Training Ltd	
G-JERO	Shaw Europa XS	P. Jenkinson & N. Robshaw	
G-JERR	Aeropro Eurofox 3K	J. Robertson	
G-JESS	PA-28R-201T Turbo Arrow III	R. E. Trawicki (G-REIS)	
G-JETH	Hawker Sea Hawk FGA.6 (XE489) ★	P. G. Vallance Ltd/Charlwood	
G-JETM	Gloster Meteor T.7 (VZ638) ★	P. G. Vallance Ltd/Charlwood	
G-JETV	HPH Glasflugel 304S Shark	Sierra Hotel Shark Group	
G-JEWL	Van's RV-7	H. A. & J. S. Jewell	
G-JEZZ	Skyranger 912S(1)	C. Callicott & I. Harvey	
G-JFAN	P & M Quik R	P. R. Brooker & G. R. Hall	
G-JFDI	Dynamic WT9 UK	S. Turnbull	
G-JFER	Rockwell Commander 114B	D. T. Woodward (G-HPSE)	
G-JFLO	Aerospool Dynamic WT9 UK	J. Flood	
G-JFLY	Schleicher ASW-24	G. Cardillo-Zallo	
G-JFMK	Zenair CH.701SP	J. D. Pearson	
G-JFRV	Van's RV-7A	J. H. Fisher	
G-JFWI	Cessna F.172N	R. P. van der Hoorn	
G-JGAR	Robinson R44 II	Garratt Aviation Ltd (G-DMRS)	
G-JGBI	Bell 206L-4 LongRanger	Dorbcrest Homes Ltd	
G-JGCA	VS.361 Spitfire LF.IXe (TE517)	P. R. Monk (G-CCIX/G-BIXP)	
G-JGMN	CASA 1.131E Jungmann 2000	P. D. Scandrett	
G-JGRV	Van's RV-14A	J. Greenhalgh	
G-JGSI	Pegasus Quantum 15-912	G-JGSI Group	
G-JHAA	Csameron Z-90 balloon	B. T. Lewis	
G-JHAC	Cessna FRA.150L	A. A. Whitewick (G-BACM)	
G-JHDD	Czech Sport Aircraft Sportcruiser	G-JHDD Syndicate	
G-JHEW	Robinson R22 Beta	Heli Air Ltd	
G-JHKP	Shaw Europa XS	N. I. Claughton	

Notes	Reg	Type	Owner or Operator
	G-JHLE	P & M Quik GTR	A. D. Carr
	G-JHLP	Flylight Dragon Chaser	N. L. Stammers
	G-JHMP	SOCATA TB-20 Trinidad	M. R. Lea
	G-JHNY	Cameron A.210 balloon	Bailey Balloons Ltd
	G-JHPC	Cessna 182T	G-JHPC Group
	G-JHYS	Shaw Europa	G-JHYS Group
	G-JIBO	BAe Jetstream 3102	KB Leasing Ltd (G-OJSA/G-BTYG)
	G-JIFI	Schempp-Hirth Duo Discus T	620 Syndicate
	G-JIII	Stolp SA.300 Starduster Too	VT10 Aero Company
	G-JIIL	Pitts S-2AE Special	A. M. Southwell
	G-JIMA	Cameron Z-105 balloon	Bristol and Avon Transport and Recycling Ltd
	G-JIMB	Beagle B.121 Pup 1	K. D. H. Gray & P. G. Fowler (G-AWWF)
	G-JIMC	Van's RV-7	J. Chapman
	G-JIMH	Cessna F.152 II	D. J. Howell (G-SHAH)
	G-JIMM	Shaw Europa XS	J. Cherry
	G-JIMP	Messerschmitt Bf 109G-2	M. R. Oliver
	G-JIMZ	Van's RV-4	P. S. Waghorne
	G-JINI	Cameron V-77 balloon	I. R. Warrington
	G-JINX	Silence SA.180 Twister	P. M. Wells
	G-JJAB	Jabiru J400	K. Ingebrigsten
	G-JJAN	PA-28-181 Archer II	Blueplane Ltd
	G-JJEN	PA-28-181 Archer III	K. M. R. Jenkins
	G-JJGI	SNCAN Stampe SV.4A	S. L. Goldspink
	G-JJIL	Extra EA.300/L	M. M. Choim
	G-JJMM	Magni M24C Plus	International Road Safety Training Ltd
	G-JKAT	Robinson R22	J. N. Kenwright (G-WIZY/G-BMWX)
	G-JKAY	Robinson R44	Dydb Marketing Ltd
	G-JKBN	Starstreak Shadow SA-II	J. A. Cook
	G-JKEE	Diamond DA.42NG Twin Star	Morgan Land and Sea Ltd
	G-JKEL	Van's RV-7	S. J. Birt (G-LNNE)
	G-JKHT	Robinson R22	J K Helicopter Training Ltd (G-OTUA/G-LHCA)
	G-JKKK	Cessna 172S	P. Eaton
	G-JKMH	Diamond DA42 Twin Star	Flying Time Ltd
	G-JKMI	Diamond DA42 Twin Star	Flying Time Ltd (G-KELV)
	G-JKPF	Cessna 172S	G-JKPF Group (G-CEWK)
	G-JKRV	Schempp-Hirth Arcus T	Syndicate 291
	G-JKSN	Best Off Skyranger Nynja 912S(1)	G-JKSN Group
	G-JLAT	Aerotechnik EV-97 Eurostar	N. E. Watts
	G-JLCA	PA-34-200T Seneca II	Premier Flight Training Ltd (G-BOKE)
	G-JLHS	Beech A36 Bonanza	S. Parisse
	G-JLIA	Cameron O-90 balloon	M. Thompson
	G-JLIN	PA-28-161 Cadet	JH Sandham Aviation
	G-JLRW	Beech 76 Duchess	Aviation South West Asset Leasing Ltd
	G-JMAC	BAe Jetstream 4100 ★	Jetstream Club, Liverpool Marriott Hotel South, Speke (G-JAMD/G-JXLI)
	G-JMAL	Jabiru UL-D	K. Lewis
	G-JMAN	Mainair Blade 912S	S. T. Cain
	G-JMAW	Beech B200GT King Air	Martin-Baker Aircraft Company Ltd
	G-JMBJ	Magni M24C Orion	B. Lesslie
	G-JMBO	Embraer EMB-505 Phenom 300	Catreus AOC Ltd
	G-JMBS	Agusta A109S Grand	Avery Charter Services Ltd
	G-JMCH	Boeing 737-476	Atlantic Airlines Ltd (G-RAJG)
	G-JMCK	Boeing 737-4D7	Atlantic Airlines Ltd
	G-JMCL	Boeing 737-322	Atlantic Airlines Ltd
	G-JMCM	Boeing 737-3YO	Atlantic Airlines Ltd
	G-JMCO	Boeing 737-3TOF	Atlantic Airlines Ltd
	G-JMCP	Boeing 737-3TO	Atlantic Airlines Ltd
	G-JMCS	Boeing 737-4YO	Atlantic Airlines Ltd
	G-JMCT	Boeing 737-3YO	Atlantic Airlines Ltd (G-ZAPV/G-IGOC)
	G-JMCU	Boeing 737-301SF	Atlantic Airlines Ltd
	G-JMCV	Boeing 737-4K5	Atlantic Airlines Ltd
	G-JMCY	Boeing 737-4Q8	Atlantic Airlines Ltd
	G-JMCZ	Boeing 737-4K5	Atlantic Airlines Ltd
	G-JMDI	Schweizer 269C	Welch Holdings Ltd (G-FLAT)
	G-JMIA	PA-28-180 Cherokee E	JMI Aviation Group Ltd (G-AYEE)
	G-JMKE	Cessna 172S	M. C. Plomer-Roberts & H. White

Reg	Type	Owner or Operator	Notes
G-JMNN	CASA 1-131E Jungmann	B. S. Charters	
G-JMON	Agusta A109A-II	Falcon Aviation Ltd (G-RFDS/G-BOLA)	
G-JMOS	PA-34-220T Seneca V	Moss Aviation LLP	
G-JMRT	Ikarus C42 FB80	Kennedy Tuck Air Ltd	
G-JMRV	Van's RV-7	J. W. Marshall	
G-JNAP	Ace Aviation Magic/As-Tec 13	C. D. Willis	
G-JNET	Robinson R22 Beta	R. L. Hartshorn	
G-JNMA	VS.379 Spitfire FR.Mk.XIVe	P. M. Andrews	
G-JNNB	Colt 90A balloon	N. A. P. Godfrey	
G-JNRE	Cessna 525A Citationjet CJ2	Synergy Aviation Ltd	
G-JNSC	Schempp-Hirth Janus CT	R. C. Tatlow	
G-JNSH	Robinson R22	Hawes Bates LLP	
G-JNUS	Schempp-Hirth Janus C	N. A. Peatfield	
G-JOBA	P & M Quik GT450	S. P. Durnall	
G-JODB	Jodel D.9 Bebe	M. R. Routh	
G-JODE	Jodel D.150	B. R. Vickers	
G-JODL	Jodel D.1050/M	D. Silsbury	
G-JOED	Lindstrand LBL-77A balloon	G. R. Down	
G-JOET	Aeropro Eurofox 912(S)	J. A. Thomas	
G-JOHA	Cirrus SR20	N. Harris	
G-JOID	Cirrus SR20	I. F. Doubtfire	
G-JOJO	Cameron A-210 balloon	A. C. Rawson & J. J. Rudoni	
G-JOKR	Extra EA.300/L	C. Jefferies	
G-JOLY	Cessna 120	B. V. Meade	
G-JONG	Rotorway Executive 162F	S. D. Barnard	
G-JONL	CZAW Sportcruiser	J. R. Linford	
G-JONM	PA-28-181 Archer III	C. C. Wilson-Hart	
G-JONO	Colt 77A balloon★	British Balloon Museum and Library	
G-JONT	Cirrus SR22	J. A. Green	
G-JONX	Aeropro Eurofox 912(1)	A. J. South	
G-JONY	Cyclone AX2000	S and A Logistics Ltd	
G-JONZ	Cessna 172P	21st Century Flyers CLG	
G-JOOL	Mainair Blade 912	P. C. Collins	
G-JORD	Robinson R44 II	G. Riddell	
G-JOTC	BAe.146-300QT	Jota Aircraft Leasing Ltd (G-TNTM/G-BSLZ)	
G-JOTD	BAe.146-300QT	Jota Aircraft Leasing Ltd (G-TNTL/G-BSGI)	
G-JOTE	BAe.146-300QT	Jota Aircraft Leasing Ltd (G-TNTG/G-BSUY)	
G-JOTF	BAe.146-300QT	Jota Aircraft Leasing Ltd (G-TNTK/G-BSXK)	
G-JOTR	Avro RJ-85	Jota Aircraft Leasing Ltd (G-CHFE)	
G-JOTS	Avro RJ-100	Jota Aviation Ltd	
G-JOYT	PA-28-181 Archer II	Alan Cathcart Ltd (G-BOVO)	
G-JOYZ	PA-28-181 Archer III	Zulu Group	
G-JOZI	AS.350BA Ecureuil	C & L Fairburn Property Developments Ltd	
G-JPBA	Van's RV-6	S. B. Austin	
G-JPIT	Pitts S-2SE Special	R. S. Goodwin	
G-JPJR	Robinson R44 II	Longstop Investments Ltd	
G-JPMA	Avtech Jabiru UL	S. Southan	
G-JPOT	PA-32R-301 Saratoga SP	The Big 6 Flyers Ltd (G-BIYM)	
G-JPRO	P.84 Jet Provost T.5A (XW433)	J. A. Campbell	
G-JPTV	P.84 Jet Provost T.5A (XW354)	Callegari SRL/Italy	
G-JPWM	Skyranger 912 (2)	R. S. Waters & M. Pittock	
G-JRBC	PA-28-140 Cherokee	N. Livni	
G-JRCR	Bell 206L-1 LongRanger II	RSCP Management Ltd (G-EYRE/G-STVI)	
G-JREE	Maule MX-7-180	C. R. P. Briand	
G-JRER	Tecnam P2006T	3GRCOMM Ltd	
G-JRHH	Diamond DA.42NG Twin Star	J. Hale	
G-JRLR	Sackville BM-65 balloon	J. S. Russon	
G-JRME	Jodel D.140E	J. L. Mellor	
G-JROO	Agusta-Bell 206B JetRanger II	GH Byproducts (Derby) Ltd (G-VJMJ/G-PEAK/ G-BLJE)	
G-JRSH	Cirrus SR22T	Lismore Instruments Ltd	
G-JRVB	Van's RV-8	J. W. Salter	
G-JRXV	Bell 505 Jet Ranger X	Scotbeef Ltd	
G-JRZE	Best Off Skyranger Nynja	J. R. A. Russell	
G-JSAK	Robinson R22 Beta II	Thurston Helicopters Ltd	
G-JSAT	BN-2T Turbine Islander	Chewton Glen Aviation (G-BVFK)	

Notes	Reg	Type	Owner or Operator
	G-JSAW	Robinson R66	GT40 Aviation Ltd
	G-JSCA	PA-28RT-201 Arrow IV	G-JSCA Flying Group (G-ICSA)
	G-JSCB	Eurocopter EC.120B Colibri	S. J. B. Brooks (G-OLDO/G-HIGI)
	G-JSEY	Bollonbau Worner NL-STU/1000	M. Leblanc
	G-JSFC	Tecnam P2008-JC	Stapleford Flying Club Ltd
	G-JSIC	M & D Flugzeugbau JS-MD Single	A. G. W. Hall & K. Barker
	G-JSKY	Ikarus C42 FB80	M. S. Westman
	G-JSLE	M & D Flugzeugbau JS-MD 3	L. M. P. Wells
	G-JSMA	Gloster Meteor T.Mk.7.5 (WL419)	Martin-Baker Aircraft Company Ltd
	G-JSMD	M&D Flugzeugbau JS-MD 3	A. J. Davis
	G-JSPL	Avtech Jabiru UL-450	R. S. Cochrane
	G-JSPR	Glaser-Dirks DG400	I. P. Freestone
	G-JSRK	HpH Glasflugel 304S Shark	Great White Syndicate
	G-JSRV	Van's RV-6	J. Stringer
	G-JSSD	HP.137 Jetstream 3001 ★	Museum of Flight/East Fortune
	G-JSTS	Van's RV-7	S. T. Starkie
	G-JSUE	Van's RV-7A	A. Jenkins
	G-JTBP	PA-46-350P Malibu Mirage	J. R. Turner
	G-JTBX	Bell 206B Jet Ranger III	G. Reidy (G-EWAW/G-DORB)
	G-JTII	Pitts S-1S Special	J. C. Tempest
	G-JTPC	Aeromot AMT-200 Super Ximango	J. T. Potter & G. C. Alexander
	G-JTSA	Robinson R44 II	D. Gregor
	G-JUDD	Avtech Jabiru UL-450	R. E. Cotterrell
	G-JUDE	Robin DR.400/180	Bravo India Flying Group Ltd
	G-JUDY	AA-5A Cheetah	The Bield Flying Group
	G-JUFS	SOCATA TB-9 Tampico	N. J. Richardson
	G-JUGE	Aerotechnik EV-97 TeamEurostar UK	I. A. Baker
	G-JUGS	Autogyro MTOSport	S. J. M. Hornsby
	G-JUJU	Chilton DW1A	D. C. Reid
	G-JULE	P & M Quik GT450	G. Almond
	G-JULL	Stemme S.10VT	J. P. C. Fuchs
	G-JULU	Cameron V-90 balloon	J. M. Searle
	G-JULZ	Shaw Europa XS	J. S. Firth
	G-JUNG	CASA 1.131E Jungmann 1000 (E3B-143)	I. V. Staines
	G-JUNO	Fokker D.VII Replica	S. J. Green
	G-JUNR	Bolkow BO.208C Junior	The 3 Amigos
	G-JURG	Rockwell Commander 114A	M. G. Wright
	G-JUST	Beech F33A Bonanza	N. M. R. Richards
	G-JVBF	Lindstrand LBL-210A balloon	Virgin Balloon Flights
	G-JVBP	Aerotechnik EV-97 Team Eurostar UK	Otherton Blue Skies Syndicate
	G-JVET	Aeropro Eurofox 912(IS)	B. J. Finch
	G-JWBI	Agusta-Bell 206B JetRanger 2	The Cloudy Bay Trading Company (G-RODS/ G-NOEL/G-BCWN)
	G-JWDB	Ikarus C.42 FB80	A. R. Hughes
	G-JWDS	Cessna F.150G	G. Sayer (G-AVNB)
	G-JWDW	Ikarus C42 FB80	D. A. & J. W. Wilding
	G-JWIV	Jodel DR.1051	C. M. Fitton
	G-JWJW	CASA 1-131E Jungmann Srs.2000	J. W. & J. T. Whicher
	G-JWMA	Gloster Meteor T.Mk.7 (WA638)	Martin-Baker Aircraft Co.Ltd
	G-JWNI	Just Super STOL	J. D. Williams
	G-JWNW	Magni M-16C Tandem Trainer	J. A. Ingram
	G-JWPP	Aeropro Eurofox 912(S)	J. Padley
	G-JWRN	Robinson R44 II	Heritage Automotive Holdings LTD (G-JSCH)
	G-JWXS	Shaw Europa XS T-G	J. Wishart
	G-JXTC	BAe Jetstream 3108★	University of Glamorgan instructional airframe (G-LOGT/G-BSFH)
	G-JYRO	Rotorsport UK MT-03	A. Richards
	G-JZBA	Boeing 737-800	Jet 2.com
	G-JZBB	Boeing 737-800	Jet 2.com
	G-JZBC	Boeing 737-800	Jet 2.com
	G-JZBD	Boeing 737-800	Jet 2.com
	G-JZBE	Boeing 737-800	Jet 2.com
	G-JZBF	Boeing 737-800	Jet 2.com
	G-JZBG	Boeing 737-800	Jet 2.com

Reg	Type	Owner or Operator	Notes
G-JZBH	Boeing 737-800	Jet 2.com	
G-JZBI	Boeing 737-800	Jet 2.com	
G-JZBJ	Boeing 737-800	Jet 2.com	
G-JZBK	Boeing 737-800	Jet 2.com	
G-JZBL	Boeing 737-800	Jet 2.com	
G-JZBM	Boeing 737-800	Jet 2.com	
G-JZBN	Boeing 737-800	Jet 2.com	
G-JZBO	Boeing 737-800	Jet 2.com	
G-JZBP	Boeing 737-800	Jet 2.com	
G-JZBR	Boeing 737-800	Jet 2.com	
G-JZBS	Boeing 737-800	Jet 2.com	
G-JZHA	Boeing 737-8K5	Jet 2.com	
G-JZHB	Boeing 737-8K5	Jet 2.com	
G-JZHC	Boeing 737-8K5	Jet 2.com	
G-JZHD	Boeing 737-808	Jet 2.com	
G-JZHE	Boeing 737-8K2	Jet 2.com	
G-JZHF	Boeing 737-8K2	Jet 2.com	
G-JZHG	Boeing 737-85P	Jet 2.com	
G-JZHH	Boeing 737-85P	Jet 2.com	
G-JZHJ	Boeing 737-8MG	Jet 2.com	
G-JZHK	Boeing 737-8MG	Jet 2.com	
G-JZHL	Boeing 737-8MG	Jet 2.com	
G-JZHM	Boeing 737-8MG	Jet 2.com	
G-JZHN	Boeing 737-8MG	Jet 2.com	
G-JZHO	Boeing 737-8MG	Jet 2.com	
G-JZHP	Boeing 737-8MG	Jet 2.com	
G-JZHR	Boeing 737-8MG	Jet 2.com	
G-JZHS	Boeing 737-8MG	Jet 2.com	
G-JZHT	Boeing 737-8MG	Jet 2.com	
G-JZHU	Boeing 737-8MG	Jet 2.com	
G-JZHV	Boeing 737-8MG	Jet 2.com	
G-JZHW	Boeing 737-8MG	Jet 2.com	
G-JZHX	Boeing 737-8MG	Jet 2.com	
G-JZHY	Boeing 737-8MG	Jet 2.com	
G-JZHZ	Boeing 737-8MG	Jet 2.com	
G-KAAT	MDH MD-902 Explorer	Specialist Aviation Services Ltd (G-PASS)	
G-KADS	Schempp-Hirth Ventus 2cT	P. Dolan	
G-KAEW	Fairey Gannet AEW Mk.3	M. Stott	
G-KAIR	PA-28-181 Archer II	Wingtask 1995 Ltd	
G-KALM	Aeroprakt A22-LS Foxbat	G. Roberts (G-CLNM)	
G-KALS	Bombardier BD-100-1A10	Volar Ltd	
G-KAMY	AT-6D Harvard III (8084)	Orion Enterprises Ltd	
G-KAOM	Scheibe SF.25C Falke	Falke G-KAOM Syndicate	
G-KAOS	Van's RV-7	I. A. Harding	
G-KAPW	P.56 Provost T.1 (XF603)	The Shuttleworth Collection	
G-KARA	Brügger MB.2 Colibri	C. L. Hill (G-BMUI)	
G-KARE	Pilatus PC-12/47E	Flexifly Aircraft Hire Ltd	
G-KARK	Dyn'Aéro MCR-01 Club	M. J. Dawson	
G-KARL	Guimbal Cabri G2	Helicentre Aviation Ltd	
G-KARN	Rotorway Executive 90	U. G. P. Nimz (G-VART/G-BSUR)	
G-KART	PA-28-161 Warrior II	Romeo Tango Aviation Ltd	
G-KASW	Rotorsport UK Calidus	R. A. Clarkson	
G-KASX	VS.384 Seafire Mk.XVII (SX336)	T. J. Manna (G-BRMG)	
G-KATI	Rans S.7 Courier	H. A. C. Morrison	
G-KATO	Sonex	J. M. Greenway	
G-KATT	Cessna 152 II	C. M. de C. C. Cabral/Portugal (G-BMTK)	
G-KATZ	Flight Design CT2K	A. N. D. Arthur	
G-KAWA	Denney Kitfox Mk 2	J. K. Ewing	
G-KAXF	Hawker Hunter F.6A (N-294)	Stichting Dutch Hawker Hunter Foundation/Netherlands	
G-KAXT	Westland Wasp HAS.1 (XT787)	T. E. Martin	
G-KAXW	Westland Scout AH.1 (XW612)	Military Vehicle Solutions Ltd (G-BXRR)	
G-KAYD	Boeing Stearman A75N1	R. H. Butterfield	
G-KAYI	Cameron Z-90 balloon	R. Bayly	
G-KAYX	Best Off Skyranger Nynja 912(1)	R. N. J. Hughes	
G-KBEB	Cessna 182P	K. S. & E. B. Bowlt	
G-KBOJ	Autogyro MTOSport	K. M. G. Barnett	
G-KBOS	Flight Design CTSW	G. N. S. Farrant (G-KBOX)	
G-KBWP	Schempp-Hirth Arcus T	G-KBWP Gliding Group	

Notes	Reg	Type	Owner or Operator
	G-KCHG	Schempp-Hirth Ventus Ct	J. Burrow
	G-KCIG	Sportavia RF-5B	Deeside Fournier Group
	G-KCIN	PA-28-161 Cadet	The Pilot Centre Ltd (G-CDOX)
	G-KCMI	PA-46-600TP Meridian M600	British European Aviation Ltd
	G-KCWJ	Schempp-Hirth Duo Discus T	G-KCWJ Group
	G-KDCD	Thruster T.600N 450	M. N. Watson
	G-KDEN	Ikarus C42 FB80	K. H. Denham
	G-KDHI	PA-28-181 Archer III	Air-Unlimited Sweden AB/Sweden
	G-KDIX	Jodel D.9 Bébé	S. J. Johns
	G-KDOG	SA Bulldog Srs 120/121 (XX624:E)	S. R. Tilling
	G-KDRZ	PA-28-181 Archer LX	Pringle Commercial Estates Ltd
	G-KEAM	Schleicher ASH 26E	J. W. Paterson
	G-KEAY	AutoGyro MTO Sport	R. Keay
	G-KEDK	Schempp-Hirth Discus bT	S. G. Vardigans
	G-KEEF	Commander Aircraft 112A	K. D. Pearse
	G-KEEN	Stolp SA.300 Starduster Too	Sharp Aerobatics Ltd/Netherlands
	G-KEES	PA-28 Cherokee 180	C. N. Ellerbrook
	G-KEJY	Aerotechnik EV-97 TeamEurostar UK	M. Dagg & M. Hall
	G-KELL	Van's RV-6	P. R. Watkins
	G-KELP	Aeroprakt A22-LS Foxbat	J. F. Macknay
	G-KELS	Van's RV-7	F. W. Hardiman & G. J. Collins
	G-KELT	Airbus A.320-251N	Acropolis Aviation Ltd
	G-KELX	Van's RV-6	P. J. McMahon (G-HAMY)
	G-KELZ	Van's RV-8	B. F. Hill (G-DJRV)
	G-KEMC	Grob G.109	Norfolk Gliding Club Ltd
	G-KEMD	Westland SA.341B Gazelle AH.Mk.1	Excel Charter Ltd (G-CHBR)
	G-KEMH	Westland SA.341B Gazelle AH.Mk.1	T. Manning
	G-KEMI	PA-28-181 Archer III	Modern Air (UK) Ltd
	G-KEMJ	Schempp-Hirth Duo Discus T	H. Anderson
	G-KENA	Cameron A-300 balloon	Ballooning in Tuscany SRL/Italy
	G-KENC	Ikarus C42 FB100	K. Clark
	G-KENG	Rotorsport UK MT-03	K. A. Graham
	G-KENK	Cameron TR-70 balloon	K. R. Karlstrom
	G-KENL	Sackville BM-65 balloon	K. F. Lowry
	G-KENM	Luscombe 8EF Silvaire	M. G. Waters
	G-KENR	Balony Kubicek BB20XR balloon	K. R. Karlstrom
	G-KENW	Robin DR400/500	K. J. White
	G-KENX	Cameron Sport-90 balloon	K. R. Karlstrom
	G-KENZ	Rutan Vari-Eze	K. M. McConnel I (G-BNUI)
	G-KEPE	Schempp-Hirth Nimbus 3DT	Nimbus Syndicate PE
	G-KEPP	Rans S.6-ES Coyote II	R. G. Johnston
	G-KESS	Glaser-Dirks DG-400	M. T. Collins & T. Flude
	G-KEST	Steen Skybolt	G-KEST Syndicate
	G-KESY	Slingsby T.59D Kestrel	C. J., K. A. & P. J. Teagle
	G-KETH	Agusta-Bell 206B JetRanger 2	DAC Leasing Ltd
	G-KEVA	Ace Magic Cyclone	K. A. Armstrong
	G-KEVB	PA-28-181 Archer III	Victor Bravo Flying Ltd
	G-KEVG	Rotorsport UK MT-03	C. J. Morton
	G-KEVH	Avtech Jabiru UL-450	K. L. Harris (G-CBPP)
	G-KEVI	Jabiru J400	The Jabo Club
	G-KEVL	Rotorway Executive 162F	K. D. Longhurst (G-CBIK)
	G-KEVS	P 7 M Quik GT450	J. Durber
	G-KEVZ	P & M Quik R	K. Mallin
	G-KEWT	Ultramagic M.90 balloon	R. D. Parry
	G-KEYS	PA-23 Aztec 250F	Giles Aviation Ltd
	G-KEYY	Cameron N-77 balloon	L. J. Whitelock (G-BORZ)
	G-KFBA	Valentin Taifun 17E	M. T. Collins
	G-KFCA	Ikarus C42 FB80	D. Young
	G-KFFD	Schempp-Hirth Arcus M	Gemstone Aviation Ltd
	G-KFLY	Flight Design CTSW	G. WF. Morton & J. J. Brutnell (G-LFLY)
	G-KFOG	Van's RV-7	K. Fogarty
	G-KFOX	Denney Kitfox	R. A. Hampshire
	G-KFTI	Pilatus PC-12/47E	Daki Aviation Ltd
	G-KFVG	Schempp-Hirth Arcus M	M. T. Burton
	G-KGAO	Scheibe SF.25C Falke 1700	Midland Gliding Club Ltd
	G-KGAW	Scheibe SF.25C	Rattlesden Gliding Club Ltd
	G-KGKG	Embraer EMB-135BJ Legacy 600	London Executive Aviation Ltd

Reg	Type	Owner or Operator	Notes
G-KGMM	Schempp-Hirth Ventus 2cT	G. Smith	
G-KGRP	Agusta A109E Power Elite	CE Aviation UK Ltd (G-ZIPE)	
G-KHCC	Schempp-Hirth Ventus Bt	S. R. Thompson	
G-KHEA	Scheibe SF.25B Falke	R. J. Hale	
G-KHOP	Zenair CH.601HDS Zodiac	P. M. Porter	
G-KHPI	Schleicher ASW-28-18E	J. C. Ferguson	
G-KHRE	MS.893E Rallye 150SV	C. Judd & S. Bemment	
G-KIAB	Scheibe SF-25C Falke 2000	L. Ingram	
G-KIAN	PA-28R-201 Arrow III	Flightco Ltd	
G-KIAU	Scheibe SF.25C Falke 2000	L. Ingram	
G-KICK	Pegasus Quantum 15-912	G. D. Hall	
G-KIDD	Jabiru J430	R. L. Lidd (G-CEBB)	
G-KIEV	DKBA AT 0300-0 balloon	The Volga Balloon Team	
G-KIII	Extra EA.300/L	Extra 200 Ltd	
G-KIKI	PA-28-181 Archer II	Flight Training London (G-BSIZ)	
G-KIMA	Zenair CH.601XL Zodiac	J. R. Powell	
G-KIMB	Robin DR.300/140	A. D. Hoy	
G-KIMH	Rotorsport UK MTO Sport	P. B. Harrison	
G-KIMI	PA-46-500TP Malibu Meridian	S. N. Mitchell & M. Konstantinovic	
G-KIMK	Partenavia P.68B	R. Turrell & P. Mason (G-BCPO)	
G-KIMM	Shaw Europa XS	R. A. Collins	
G-KIMS	Ikarus C42 FB100	J. W. D. Blythe	
G-KIMY	Robin DR.400/140B	J. H. Wood	
G-KIMZ	PA-28-160 Cherokee D	Ravenair Aircraft Ltd (G-AWDP)	
G-KIND	Cirrus SR20	Europe Enterprise Innovation	
G-KINL	Grumman FM-2 Wildcat	T. W. Harris (G-CHPN)	
G-KINT	Scheibe SF.25C Falke 2000	G-KINT Syndicate	
G-KION	Cessna 525 Citationjet	Apex Global Investments Ltd	
G-KIRB	Europa XS	M. H. Wylde (G-OIZI)	
G-KIRC	Pietenpol/Challis Chaffinch	M. J. Kirk (G-BSVZ)	
G-KIRT	Stoddard-Hamilton GlaStar	P. J. Clegg	
G-KISP	Rolladen-Schneider LS10-st	D. G. Pask & C. Thirkell	
G-KISS	Rand-Robinson KR-2	B. L. R. J. Keeping	
G-KITH	Alpi Pioneer 300	K. G. Atkinson	
G-KITI	Pitts S-2E Special	J. C. W. Seward	
G-KITO	PA-24-260 Comanche B	A. Costi	
G-KITS	Europa XS	C. I. Randle	
G-KIZZ	Kiss 450-582	D. L. Price	
G-KJBS	Czech Sport Sportcruiser	S. Styles	
G-KJJR	Schempp-Hirth Ventus 2cT	R. J. L. Maisonpierre	
G-KJTT	Cessna 182A	Associazione Sportiva Dilettantistica Alisei/Italy	
G-KKAM	Schleicher ASW-22BLE	D. P. Taylor	
G-KKCT	Flight Design CTSL	K. Kirby	
G-KKER	Avtech Jabiru UL-450	M. A. Coffin	
G-KKEV	DHC.8-402 Dash Eight	HEH Aviation Exeter Beteiligungsgesellschaft MBH & Co KG	
G-KKKK	SA Bulldog Srs 120/121 (XX513:10)	M. Cowan (G-CCMI)	
G-KKRN	Robinson R22	Kilkern Ltd (G-WFWS/G-LINS/G-DMCD/G-OOLI)	
G-KKTG	Cessna 182R	T. Knight & S. Thomas	
G-KLAW	Christen Eagle II	The Eagle Group	
G-KLLY	Airbus AS.350B2 Ecureuil	Performance Focus Ltd	
G-KLNH	Leonardo AW109SP Grand New	Saxonair Charter Ltd	
G-KLNM	Aibus AS.350B3 Ecureuil	Klyne Air Ltd (G-OGLE/G-CIEU)	
G-KLNW	Cessna 510 Citation Mustang	Saxonair Charter Ltd	
G-KLUB	Scheibe SF.25C Rotax-Falke	L. Ingram	
G-KLYE	Best Off Sky Ranger Swift 912S(1)	D. R. Devlin	
G-KMAK	P & M Quik GT450	K. I. Making	
G-KMBB	Scheibe SF-25D Falke	K. P. & R. L. McLean	
G-KMIR	Schleicher ASH-31 Mi	M. Woodcock	
G-KMJK	DG Flugzeugbau DG-808C	N. Burke, L. Rayment & D. W. Smith	
G-KMKM	AutoGyro MTO Sport	J. M. Boddy	
G-KMLA	Cirrus SR20	KML Aviation OY/Finland	

Notes	Reg	Type	Owner or Operator
	G-KMOS	Robinson R44 II	Aikmo Aviation and Marine Ltd
	G-KMRV	Van-s RV-9A	G. K. Mutch
	G-KNCG	PA-32-301FT 6X	M. C. Plomer-Roberts & T. Moore
	G-KNEE	Ultramagic M-77C balloon	M. A.Green
	G-KNEK	Grob G.109B	Syndicate 109
	G-KNIB	Robinson R22 Beta II	Glenntrade Ltd
	G-KNOW	PA-32 Cherokee Six 300	M. & W. M. Wilkins
	G-KNYT	Robinson R44	Brosters Environmental Ltd
	G-KOBH	Schempp-Hirth Discus bT	C. F. M. Smith & K. Neave
	G-KOCO	Cirrus SR22	I. S. L. Rutland
	G-KOFM	Glaser-Dirks DG.600/18M	A. Mossman
	G-KOKO	Cirrus SR22T	R. K. Fitzgerald
	G-KOLB	Kolb Twinstar Mk 3A	Condor Aviation International Ltd
	G-KOLI	WSK PZL-110 Koliber 150	G-KOLI Group
	G-KOLO	Dassault Falcon 8X	Centreline AV Ltd
	G-KONG	Slingsby T.67M Firefly 200	N. A. & O. O'Sullivan
	G-KOOL	DH.104 Devon C2 (VP967) ★	Yorkshire Air Museum/Elvington
	G-KORE	Sportavia SFS31 Milan	J. R. Edyvean
	G-KOSC	Supermarine 329 Spitfire IIB (P8331/RF-M)	Spitfire P8331 Restoration Ltd
	G-KOTA	PA-28-236 Dakota	M. D. Rush
	G-KOVU	Cessna FA.150K	European Aviation School of Barcelona SL/Spain (G-FMSG/G-POTS/ G-AYUY)
	G-KOYY	Schempp-Hirth Nimbus 4T	D. Pitman
	G-KPEM	Schempp-Hirth Ventus 3T	O. J. Walters
	G-KRAN	Scheibe SF25C Rotax-Falke	Morgan Land Sea and Air LLP
	G-KRBN	Embraer EMB-505 Phenom 300	Saxonair Charter Ltd
	G-KRBY	Van's RV-8	P. Kirby
	G-KRES	Stoddard-Hamilton Glasair IIS RG	A. D. Murray
	G-KRFX	Embraer EMB-135BJ Legacy 600	Flexjet Ltd
	G-KRIB	Robinson R44 II	Jim Davies Civil Engineering Ltd
	G-KRTO	Rand KR-2	Condor Aviation International Ltd
	G-KRUZ	CZAW Sportcruiser	A. W. Shellis & P. Whittingham
	G-KRWR	Glaser-Dirks DG-600/18M	A. D. W. Hislop
	G-KSHI	Beech A36 Bonanza	Hangar 11 Collection
	G-KSIR	Stoddard-Hamilton Glasair IIS RG	K. M. Bowen
	G-KSKS	Cameron N-105 balloon	Kiss the Sky Ballooning
	G-KSKY	Sky 77-24 balloon	M. W. Durham
	G-KSOH	Cessna 525 Citation M2	Air Charter Scotland Ltd
	G-KSSA	MDH MD-900 Explorer	Specialist Aviation Services Ltd
	G-KSSC	Leonardo AW169	Specialist Aviation Services Ltd
	G-KSSH	MDH MD-900 Explorer	Specialist Aviation Services Ltd (G-WMID)
	G-KSST	Agusta AW.169	Specialist Aviation Services Ltd
	G-KSSX	Schleicher ASW-27-18E	L. M. Brady
	G-KSVB	PA-24 Comanche 260	Knockin Flying Club Ltd
	G-KTCH	Magni M16C Tandem Trainer	L. H. J. Spiller
	G-KTEA	Robin DR.400-140B	A. B. English
	G-KTOW	Ikarus C42 FB100	Mayfly G-KTOW Ltd
	G-KTTY	Denney Kitfox Model 3	T. Pennington (G-LESJ)
	G-KTWO	Cessna 182T	S. J. G. Mole
	G-KUBE	Robinson R44 II	Pentacle Ltd (G-VEIT)
	G-KUBY	PA-18-150 Super Cub	Propshop Ltd
	G-KUGG	Schleicher ASW-27-18E	J. W. L. Otty
	G-KUIK	Mainair Pegasus Quik	P. Nugent
	G-KUIP	CZAW Sportcruiser	A. J. Kuipers
	G-KULA	Best Off Skyranger 912S(1)	G. S. Cridland
	G-KUPP	Flight Design CTSW	Cloudbase Group
	G-KURK	J-3C-65 Cub	M. J. Kirk (G-BJTO)
	G-KURT	Jurca MJ.8 Fw190	S. D. Howes
	G-KUTI	Flight Design CTSW	D. F. & S. M. Kenny
	G-KUTU	Quickie Q.2	R. Nash
	G-KUUI	J-3C-65 Cub	V. S. E. Norman
	G-KVAN	Flight Design CTSW	K. Brown (G-IROE)
	G-KVBF	Cameron A-340HL balloon	Virgin Balloon Flights

Reg	Type	Owner or Operator	Notes
G-KVIP	Beech 200 Super King Air	Centreline AV Ltd	
G-KWAK	Scheibe SF.25C	Mendip Gliding Club Ltd	
G-KWET	Cessna 150L	M. Ali (G-CSFC)	
G-KWFL	EV-97 Eurostar SL	Aqueous 1st Kwikflow Ltd	
G-KWIC	Mainair Sports Pegasus Quik	M. Gibson	
G-KWKI	QAC Quickie Q.200	R. Greatrex	
G-KWKR	P and M Aviation QuikR	L. G. White	
G-KWKX	P & M Quik R	M. G. Evans	
G-KXMS	Schempp-Hirth Ventus cT	A. J. McNamara	
G-KXXI	Schleicher ASK-21	Shenington Gliding Club	
G-KYLA	Cirrus SR22	J. Bannister	
G-KYLE	Thruster T600N 450	RM Aviation Ltd	
G-KYTE	Piper PA-28-161 Warrior II	G. Whitlow (G-BRRN)	
G-KYTT	PA-18-150 Super Cub	F. Actis	
G-KZEN	Lange E1 Antares	I. C. Baker	
G-LAAC	Cameron C-90 balloon	S. Dyer	
G-LAAI	Druine D.5 Turbi	D. Silsbury	
G-LABS	Shaw Europa	P. J. Tyler	
G-LACB	PA-28-161 Warrior II	LAC Flying School	
G-LACR	Denney Kitfox	C. M. Rose	
G-LADD	Enstrom 480	Davad Partnership	
G-LADS	Rockwell Commander 114	D. F. Soul	
G-LAIR	Stoddard-Hamilton Glasair IIS FT	S. T. Raby	
G-LAKE	Lake LA-250 Renegade	Lake Aviation Ltd	
G-LAKI	Jodel DR.1050	D. Evans (G-JWBB)	
G-LALA	Cessna FA.150K	L. J. Liveras	
G-LAMM	Shaw Europa	S. A. Lamb	
G-LAMO	Bombardier BD700-1A11 Global 5000	Concierge U Ltd	
G-LAMP	Cameron 110 Lampbulb SS balloon	D. M. Hoddinott	
G-LAMS	Cessna F.152 II	APB Leasing Ltd	
G-LANC	Avro 683 Lancaster X (KB889) ★	Imperial War Museum/Duxford	
G-LANE	Cessna F.172N	M. J. Hadley	
G-LAOL	PA-28RT-201 Arrow IV	Arrow Flying Group	
G-LAPL	Scheibe SF25C Rotax-Falke	L. Ingram	
G-LAPW	PA-46-350P Malibu Mirage	D. P. Wood (G-PTEA)	
G-LARA	Robin DR.400/180	K. D. & C. A. Brackwell	
G-LARD	Robinson R66	Perry Farming Company	
G-LARE	PA-39 Twin Comanche 160 C/R	Glareways (Neasden) Ltd	
G-LARK	Helton Lark 95	Lark Group	
G-LARR	AS.350B3 Squirrel	TSL Contractors Ltd	
G-LASN	Skyranger J2.2(1)	A. J. Coote	
G-LASR	Stoddard-Hamilton Glasair II	G. Lewis	
G-LASS	Rutan Vari-Eze	J. Mellor	
G-LATE	Falcon 2000EX	Executive Jet Charter Ltd	
G-LATO	Cessna 680A Citation Latitude	Zenith Aviation Ltd	
G-LAUD	Cessna 208 Caravan 1	Laudale Estate LLP	
G-LAVE	Cessna 172R	Trim Flying Club Ltd (G-BYEV)	
G-LAVN	Guimbal Cabri G2	Heligroup Operations Ltd	
G-LAWA	Agusta Westland AW139	Castle Air Ltd (G-VIPG)	
G-LAWX	Sikorsky S-92A	Starspeed Ltd	
G-LAZL	PA-28-161 Warrior II	Highland Aviation Training Ltd	
G-LAZR	Cameron O-77 balloon	Wickers World Ltd	
G-LAZZ	Stoddard-Hamilton Glastar	D. F. P. Finan & P. W. Carlton	
G-LBAC	Evektor EV-97 TeamEurostar UK	G. Burder & A. Cox	
G-LBDC	Bell 206B JetRanger III	Heli Logistics Ltd	
G-LBMM	PA-28-161 Warrior II	M. R. & P. M. Shelton	
G-LBRC	PA-28RT-201 Arrow IV	D. J. V. Morgan	
G-LBRR	Eurocopter AS.350B3 Ecureuil	Skyhook Helicopters	
G-LBRT	Beech D17S	T. W. Gilbert	
G-LBUK	Lindstrand LBL-77A balloon	D. E. Hartland	
G-LBUZ	Aerotechnick EV-97A Eurostar	D. P. Tassart	
G-LCAA	Embraer ERJ190-100SR	BA Cityflyer Ltd	
G-LCAB	Embraer ERJ190-100SR	BA Cityflyer Ltd	
G-LCAC	Embraer ERJ190-100SR	BA Cityflyer Ltd	

Notes	Reg	Type	Owner or Operator
	G-LCAD	Embraer ERJ190-100SR	BA Cityflyer Ltd
	G-LCAE	Embraer ERJ190-100SR	BA Cityflyer Ltd
	G-LCAF	Embraer ERJ190-100SR	BA Cityflyer Ltd
	G-LCGL	Comper CLA.7 Swift (replica)	R. A. Fleming
	G-LCKY	Flight Design CTSW	D. Subhani
	G-LCLE	Colomban MC-30 Luciole	J. A. Harris
	G-LCMW	TL 2000UK Sting Carbon	B. J. Tyre
	G-LCPL	AS.365N-2 Dauphin 2	AS Aerospace Ltd
	G-LCPX	Eurocopter EC155 B1	Charterstyle Ltd (G-WINV/G-WJCJ)
	G-LCTA	PA-28-181 Archer III	L3 CTS Airline and Academy Training Ltd
	G-LCTB	PA-28-181 Archer III	L3 CTS Airline and Academy Training Ltd
	G-LCTC	PA-28-181 Archer III	L3 CTS Airline and Academy Training Ltd
	G-LCTD	PA-28-181 Archer III	L3 CTS Airline and Academy Training Ltd
	G-LCTE	PA-28-181 Archer III	L3 CTS Airline and Academy Training Ltd
	G-LCTF	PA-28-181 Archer III	Escola de Aviacao Aerocondor SA/Portugal
	G-LCTG	PA-28-181 Archer III	Escola de Aviacao Aerocondor SA/Portugal
	G-LCTH	PA-28-181 Archer III	Escola de Aviacao Aerocondor SA/Portugal
	G-LCTI	PA-28-181 Archer III	Escola de Aviacao Aerocondor SA/Portugal
	G-LCTJ	PA-28-181 Archer III	Escola de Aviacao Aerocondor SA/Portugal
	G-LCTK	PA-28-181 Archer III	Escola de Aviacao Aerocondor SA/Portugal
	G-LCTL	PA-28-181 Archer III	Escola de Aviacao Aerocondor SA/Portugal
	G-LCTM	PA-28-181 Archer III	Escola de Aviacao Aerocondor SA/Portugal
	G-LCTN	PA-28-181 Archer III	Escola de Aviacao Aerocondor SA/Portugal
	G-LCTO	PA-28-181 Archer III	Escola de Aviacao Aerocondor SA/Portugal
	G-LCTP	PA-28-181 Archer III	Escola de Aviacao Aerocondor SA/Portugal
	G-LCTR	PA-28-181 Archer III	Escola de Aviacao Aerocondor SA/Portugal
	G-LCTS	PA-28-181 Archer III	Escola de Aviacao Aerocondor SA/Portugal
	G-LCUB	PA-18 Super Cub 95	The Tiger Club 1990 Ltd (G-AYPR)
	G-LCYD	Embraer ERJ170-100STD	BA Cityflyer Ltd
	G-LCYE	Embraer ERJ170-100STD	BA Cityflyer Ltd
	G-LCYF	Embraer ERJ170-100STD	BA Cityflyer Ltd
	G-LCYG	Embraer ERJ170-100STD	BA Cityflyer Ltd
	G-LCYH	Embraer ERJ170-100STD	BA Cityflyer Ltd
	G-LCYI	Embraer ERJ170-100STD	BA Cityflyer Ltd
	G-LCYJ	Embraer ERJ190-100SR	BA Cityflyer Ltd
	G-LCYK	Embraer ERJ190-100SR	BA Cityflyer Ltd
	G-LCYL	Embraer ERJ190-100SR	BA Cityflyer Ltd
	G-LCYM	Embraer ERJ190-100SR	BA Cityflyer Ltd
	G-LCYN	Embraer ERJ190-100SR	BA Cityflyer Ltd
	G-LCYO	Embraer ERJ190-100SR	BA Cityflyer Ltd
	G-LCYP	Embraer ERJ190-100SR	BA Cityflyer Ltd
	G-LCYR	Embraer ERJ190-100SR	BA Cityflyer Ltd
	G-LCYS	Embraer ERJ190-100SR	BA Cityflyer Ltd
	G-LCYT	Embraer ERJ190-100SR	BA Cityflyer Ltd
	G-LCYU	Embraer ERJ190-100SR	BA Cityflyer Ltd
	G-LCYV	Embraer ERJ190-100SR	BA Cityflyer Ltd
	G-LCYW	Embraer ERJ190-100SR	BA Cityflyer Ltd
	G-LCYX	Embraer ERJ190-100SR	BA Cityflyer Ltd
	G-LCYY	Embraer ERJ190-100SR	BA Cityflyer Ltd
	G-LCYZ	Embraer ERJ190-100SR	BA Cityflyer Ltd
	G-LDAH	Skyranger 912 (2)	S. Davies
	G-LDER	Schleicher ASW-22	P. Shrosbree & D. Starer
	G-LDGA	Diamond DA.42NG Twin Star	Twinstar4hire Ltd
	G-LDGB	Diamond DA.42NG Twin Star	Twinstar4hire Ltd
	G-LDGC	Diamond DA.40D Star	Twinstar4hire Ltd (G-OCCU)
	G-LDGD	Diamond DA.40D Star	Leading Edge Aviation Ltd (G-TULA)
	G-LDGF	Diamond DA.42NG YTwin Star	Twinstar4hire Ltd
	G-LDGU	Slingsby T67M-200 Firefly	Leading Edge Aviation Ltd (G-BYRY)
	G-LDSA	TAF Sting 4	L. J. d'Sa
	G-LDVO	Europa Aviation Europa XS	D. J. Park
	G-LDWS	Jodel D.150	A. L. Hall-Carpenter (G-BKSS)
	G-LDYS	Colt 56A balloon	M. J. Myddelton
	G-LEAC	Cessna 510 Citation Mustang	Leacop SAS
	G-LEAF	Cessna F.406	Reconnaisance Ventures Ltd
	G-LEAH	Alpi Pioneer 300	B. W. Russell
	G-LEAM	PA-28-236 Dakota	G-LEAM Group (G-BHLS)
	G-LEAS	Sky 90-24 balloon	C. I. Humphrey
	G-LEAT	Ultramagic B-70 balloon	A. M. Holly
	G-LEAX	Cessna 560XL Citation XLS	London Executive Aviation Ltd

Reg	Type	Owner or Operator	Notes
G-LEBE	Europa	P. G. Noonan	
G-LEDE	Zenair CH.601UL Zodiac	R. Vicary	
G-LEED	Denney Kitfox Mk 2	O. C. Rash	
G-LEEE	Avtech Jabiru UL-450	T. Bailey	
G-LEEH	Ultramagic M-90 balloon	Sport Promotion SRL/Italy	
G-LEEK	Reality Escapade	G-LEEK Phoenix Flying Group	
G-LEEN	Aero Designs Pulsar XP	R. B. Hemsworth (G-BZMP/G-DESI)	
G-LEEZ	Bell 206L-1 LongRanger 2	Heli-Lift Services (G-BPCT)	
G-LEFT	Cassutt Racer IIIM	Air Race CC Ltd (G-CGSU)	
G-LEGC	Embraer EMB-135BJ Legacy	London Executive Aviation Ltd	
G-LEGD	Vickers-Armstrong Spitfire IX	G. P. Jones	
G-LEGG	Cessna F.182Q	W. A. L. Mitchell (G-GOOS)	
G-LEGO	Cameron O-77 balloon	P. M. Traviss	
G-LEGY	Flight Design CTLS	T. R. Grief	
G-LEGZ	Rockwell Commander 695	Leg Air Ltd	
G-LELE	Lindstrand LBL-31A balloon	D. S. Wilson	
G-LEMI	Van's RV-8	The Lord Rotherwick	
G-LEMM	Ultramagic Z-90 balloon	I. Vastano/Italy	
G-LEMP	P & M Quik R	E. M. & A. M. Brewis	
G-LENI	AS.355F1 Twin Squirrel	Grid Defence Systems Ltd (G-ZFDB/G-BLEV)	
G-LENN	Cameron V-56 balloon	D. J. Groombridge	
G-LENZ	Cirrus SR20	Renneta Ltd	
G-LEOD	Pietenpol Aircamper	I. D. McCleod	
G-LEOG	Airbus Helicopters AS.350B3 Ecureuil	Leo Group Ltd (G-CIRG)	
G-LEOS	Robin DR.400/120	Exavia Ltd	
G-LEPR	Aeropro Eurofox 3K	G-LEPR Group	
G-LERE	Aerospatiale ATR-72-212A	Aurigny Air Services Ltd	
G-LESZ	Denney Kitfox Mk 5	G. M. Park	
G-LETS	Van's RV-7	M. O'Hearne	
G-LEVI	Aeronca 7AC Champion	G-LEVI Group	
G-LEXS	Agusta A.109E Power	Blade 5 Ltd (G-IVJM/G-MOMO)	
G-LEXX	Van's RV-8	S. Emery	
G-LEXY	Van's RV-8	R. McCarthy	
G-LEZE	Rutan LongEz	Bill Allen's Autos Ltd	
G-LFBD	Cessna 525A Citationjet CJ2	Centreline AV Ltd	
G-LFES	AB Sportine LAK-17B FES	C. J. Tooze	
G-LFEZ	AB Sportine LAK-17B FES	Baltic Sailplanes Ltd	
G-LFIX	VS.509 Spitfire T.IX (ML407/NL-D))	Air Leasing Ltd	
G-LFLF	Autogyro MTOsport	C. J. Adey	
G-LFSA	PA-38-112 Tomahawk	Liverpool Flying School Ltd (G-BSFC)	
G-LFSB	PA-38-112 Tomahawk	J. D. Burford (G-BLYC)	
G-LFSC	PA-28 Cherokee 140	G-LFSC Flying Group (G-BGTR)	
G-LFSG	PA-28 Cherokee 180E	North East Aviation Ltd (G-AYAA)	
G-LFSH	PA-38-112 Tomahawk	Liverpool Flying School Ltd (G-BOZM)	
G-LFSI	PA-28 Cherokee 140	Elliott Holdings Ltd (G-AYKV)	
G-LFSJ	PA-28-161 Warrior II	Scenic Air Tours North East Ltd	
G-LFSL	PA-38-112 Tomahawk II	J. A. Keen (G-BNSL)	
G-LFSM	PA-38-112 Tomahawk	Liverpool Flying School Ltd (G-BWNR)	
G-LFSN	PA-38-112 Tomahawk	Liverpool Flying School Ltd (G-BNYV)	
G-LFSO	PA-38-112 Tomahawk	J. A. Keen (G-BGRM)	
G-LFSR	PA-28RT-201 Arrow IV	D. Sluman	
G-LFSU	PA-38-112 Tomahawk II	J. A. Keen (G-BNNU)	
G-LFSW	PA-28-161 Warrior II	Liverpool Flying School Ltd (G-BSGL)	
G-LFVB	VS.349 Spitfire LF.Vb (EP120)	Patina Ltd	
G-LFVC	VS.349 Spitfire VC (JG891)	Comanche Warbirds Ltd	
G-LGAN	PA-28-181Archer III	Corporate Aviation UK Ltd	
G-LGCA	Robin DR.400/180R	London Gliding Club Proprietary Ltd	
G-LGCB	Robin DR.400/180R	London Gliding Club Proprietary Ltd	
G-LGCC	Robin DR.400/180R	London Gliding Club Proprietary Ltd (G-BNXI)	
G-LGEZ	Rutan Long-EZ	P. C. Elliott	
G-LGIS	Dornier 228-202K	Aurigny Air Services Ltd	
G-LGLG	Cameron Z-210 balloon	Flying Circus SRL/Spain	
G-LGNA	SAAB SF.340B	Loganair Ltd	
G-LGNB	SAAB SF.340B	Loganair Ltd	
G-LGNC	SAAB SF.340B	Loganair Ltd	
G-LGND	SAAB SF.340B	Loganair Ltd (G-GNTH)	
G-LGNE	SAAB SF.340B	Loganair Ltd (G-GNTI)	
G-LGNG	SAAB SF.340B	Loganair Ltd	
G-LGNH	SAAB SF.340B	Loganair Ltd	

Notes	Reg	Type	Owner or Operator
	G-LGNI	SAAB SF.340B	Loganair Ltd
	G-LGNJ	SAAB SF.340B	Loganair Ltd
	G-LGNK	SAAB SF.340B	Loganair Ltd
	G-LGNM	SAAB SF.340B	Loganair Ltd
	G-LGNN	SAAB SF.340B	Loganair Ltd
	G-LGNP	SAAB 2000	Loganair Ltd
	G-LHAB	TAF Sling 2	A. P. Beggin
	G-LHCB	Robinson R22 Beta	Helipower Hire Ltd (G-SIVX)
	G-LHCI	Bell 47G-5	W. K. MacGillivray (G-SOLH/G-AZMB)
	G-LHER	Czech Sport Aircraft Piper Sport	M. P. Lhermette
	G-LHPM	Robinson R44 II	HQ Aviation Ltd
	G-LHXA	Diamond DA.42NG Twin Star	L3 CTS Airline and Academy Training Ltd
	G-LHXB	Diamond DA.42NG Twin Star	L3 CTS Airline and Academy Training Ltd
	G-LHXC	Diamond DA.42NG Twin Star	L3 CTS Airline and Academy Training Ltd
	G-LHXD	Diamond DA.42NG Twin Star	L3 CTS Airline and Academy Training Ltd
	G-LIBB	Cameron V-77 balloon	R. J. Mercer
	G-LIBI	Glasflugel Standard Libelle 201B	O. Spreckley
	G-LIBS	Hughes 369HS	R. J. H. Strong
	G-LIBY	Glasflugel Standard Libelle 201B	R. P. Hardcastle
	G-LICK	Cessna 172N II	Sky Back Ltd (G-BNTL)
	G-LIDA	Hoffmann H36 Dimona	W. D. & S. M. Inglis
	G-LIDE	PA-31-350 Navajo Chieftain	Blue Sky Investments Ltd
	G-LIIZ	Boeing Stearman D75N1 Kaydet (44)	M. L. Blaze (G-DINS/G-RJAH)
	G-LIKE	Europa	N. G. Henry (G-CHAV)
	G-LIKK	Robinson R66 Turbine	G-LIKK Ltd
	G-LIKY	Aviat A-1C-180 Husky	L. W. H. Griffith
	G-LILE	Cessna 525 Citationjet CJ1	Sovereign Business Jets Ltd (G-SOVI)
	G-LILY	Bell 206B JetRanger 3	T. S. Brown (G-NTBI)
	G-LIMO	Bell 206L-1 LongRanger	Aerospeed Ltd
	G-LIMP	Cameron C-80 balloon	Balloons over Yorkshire Ltd
	G-LINE	AS.355N Twin Squirrel	MCF Aviation Ltd
	G-LINJ	Robinson R44 II	Helicentre Ltd (G-ODCR)
	G-LINN	Shaw Europa XS	C. J. Challener
	G-LINY	Robinson R44 II	Helicentre Aviation Ltd
	G-LINZ	Robinson R44 II	Helicentre Aviation Ltd
	G-LIOA	Lockheed 10A ElectraH (NC5171N) ★	Science Museum/South Kensington
	G-LION	PA-18 Super Cub 135 (R-167)	JG Jones Haulage Ltd
	G-LIOT	Cameron O-77 balloon	N. D. Eliot
	G-LIPS	Cameron 90 Lips SS balloon	Reach For The Sky Ltd (G-BZBV)
	G-LISS	AutogGyro UK Calidus	Gyronauts Flying Club Ltd
	G-LITE	Rockwell Commander 112A	B. G. Rhodes
	G-LITO	Agusta A109S Grand	Castle Air Ltd
	G-LITS	P & M Quik R	A. Dixon
	G-LITZ	Pitts S-1E Special	H. J. Morton
	G-LIVH	Piper J-3C-65 Cub (330238:A-24)	B. L. Procter
	G-LIVS	Schleicher ASH-26E	P. O. Sturley
	G-LIZI	PA-28 Cherokee 160	Peterborough Flying School Ltd (G-ARRP)
	G-LIZY	Westland Lysander III (V9673) ★	Imperial War Museum/Duxford
	G-LJCC	Murphy Rebel	P. H. Hyde
	G-LKAM	Sonaca S200	Blueplane Ltd
	G-LKSM	Sonaca S200	Blueplane Ltd
	G-LKVA	Tecnam P2010	K. Yurovskiy
	G-LLBE	Lindstrand LBL-360A balloon	Adventure Balloons Ltd
	G-LLCH	Cessna 172S	Bristol Flying Club Ltd (G-PLBI)
	G-LLEW	Aeromot AMT-200S Super Ximango	M. P. Brockington & K. Richards
	G-LLGE	Lindstrand LBL-360A balloon	Adventure Balloons Ltd
	G-LLIZ	Robinson R44 II	E. Z. Amaira
	G-LLLL	Rolladen-Schneider LS8-18	P. C. Fritche
	G-LLMW	Diamond DA42 Twin Star	Ming W. L.
	G-LLNT	Schleicher ASW-27-18E	N. D. Tillett
	G-LLOY	Alpi Pioneer 300	N. J. A. Tsappis
	G-LLLY	Enstrom 480B	AR-Pats LLP
	G-LLYN	Eurofox 912(IS)	D. M. Griffiths
	G-LMAO	Cessna F.172N	K. Miramar
	G-LMCB	Raj Hamsa X'Air Hawk	B. N. Thresher

Reg	Type	Owner or Operator	Notes
G-LMLV	Dyn'Aéro MCR-01	G-LMLV Flying Group	
G-LMRA	Avions Transport ATR-42-500	Loganair Ltd	
G-LMRB	Avions Transport ATR-42-500	Loganair Ltd	
G-LMRC	Avions Transport ATR-42-500	Loganair Ltd	
G-LMRD	Avions Transport ATR-42-500	Loganair Ltd (G-HUET)	
G-LMRZ	Avions Transport ATR-72-212A	Loganair Ltd	
G-LNAC	Leonardo AW169	Specialist Aviation Services Ltd	
G-LNCT	MDH MD-900 Explorer	Specialist Aviation Services Ltd	
G-LNDA	BRM Bristell NG5 Speed Wing	D. J. Medcraft	
G-LNDN	MDH MD-900 Explorer	London's Air Ambulance Ltd	
G-LNIG	Flylight Dragonfly	P. J. Cheyney	
G-LNKX	Westland Lynx AH Mk.7	A. D. Whitehouse	
G-LOAD	Dan Rihn DR.107 One Design	M. J. Clark	
G-LOAM	Flylight MotorFloater	I. White	
G-LOAN	Cameron N-77 balloon	P. Lawman	
G-LOBO	Cameron O-120 balloon	Solo Aerostatics	
G-LOCH	Piper J-3C-65 Cub	M. C. & M. R. Greenland	
G-LOFM	Maule MX-7-180A	B. R. Alexander	
G-LOFT	Cessna 500 Citation 1	Janez Let D. O . O.	
G-LOGN	PA-28-181 Cherokee Archer III	ICorporate Aviation UK Ltd	
G-LOIS	Avtech Jabiru UL	C. Conidaris	
G-LOKI	Ultramagic M-77C balloon	L. J. M. Muir	
G-LOLI	DG Flugzeugbau DG-1000M	P. Crawley	
G-LOLL	Cameron V-77 balloon	P. Spellward	
G-LOLZ	Robinson R22 Beta	Swift Helicopter Services Ltd	
G-LOMN	Cessna 152	North Weald Flying Group Ltd	
G-LONE	Bell 206L-1 LongRanger	Central Helicopters Ltd	
G-LOOC	Cessna 172S	Goodwood Road Racing Co.Ltd	
G-LOON	Cameron C-60 balloon	T. Lex/Germany	
G-LOOP	Pitts S-1D Special	N. Tomlinson	
G-LORC	PA-28-161 Cadet	Advanced Flight Training Ltd	
G-LORD	PA-34-200T Seneca II	The Flying Griggin GmbH/Germany	
G-LORN	Avions Mudry CAP-10B	R. G. Drury	
G-LORR	PA-28-181 Archer III	Shropshire Aero Club Ltd	
G-LORY	Thunder Ax4-31Z balloon	M. J. Woodcock	
G-LOSM	Gloster Meteor NF.11 (WM167)	D. G. Thomas	
G-LOSY	Aerotechnik EV-97 Eurostar	M. L. Willmington	
G-LOTE	PA-28-161 Cadet	AJW Construction Ltd	
G-LOTI	Bleriot XI (replica) ★	Brooklands Museum Trust Ltd	
G-LOTY	P & M Aviation Pegasus Quik	L. Hewitt	
G-LOUD	Schleicher ASW-27-18E	T. Stuart	
G-LOUS	EV-97 Eurostar SL	S. E. Bettley & M. D. Jealous	
G-LOWE	Monett Sonerai I	P. A. Hall	
G-LOWS	Sky 77-24 balloon	A. J. Byrne & D. J. Bellinger	
G-LOWZ	P & M Quik GT450	R. E. J. Pattenden	
G-LOYA	Cessna FR.172J	R. I. Dawson (G-BLVT)	
G-LOYD	Aérospatiale SA.341G Gazelle 1	S. Athgerton (G-SFTC)	
G-LPAD	Lindstrand LBL-105A balloon	G. R. Down	
G-LPIN	P & M Aviation Quik R	G. P. D. Coan	
G-LRBW	Lindstrand LBL HS-110 Hot-Air Airship	C. J. Sanger-Davies	
G-LREE	Grob G.109B	G-LREE Group	
G-LRNC	PA-28-161 Warrior II	JABM Ltd (G-BOFZ)	
G-LROK	Robinson R66	London Rock Supplies Ltd	
G-LSAA	Boeing 757-236	Jet 2.com (G-BNSF)	
G-LSAB	Boeing 757-27B	Jet 2.com (G-OAHF)	
G-LSAC	Boeing 757-23A	Jet 2.com	
G-LSAD	Boeing 757-236	Jet 2.com (G-OOOS/G-BRJD)	
G-LSAE	Boeing 757-27B	Jet 2.com	
G-LSAH	Boeing 757-21B	Jet 2.com	
G-LSAI	Boeing 757-21B	Jet 2.com	
G-LSAJ	Boeing 757-236	Jet 2.com (G-CDUP/G-OOOT/G-BRJJ)	
G-LSAK	Boeing 757-23N	Jet 2.com	
G-LSAN	Boeing 757-2K2	Jet 2.com	
G-LSCM	Cessna 172S	Pooler-LMT Ltd	
G-LSCP	Rolladen-Schneider LS6-18W	M. F. Collins & L. G. Blows	
G-LSCW	Gulfstream 550	Langley Aviation Ltd	

Notes	Reg	Type	Owner or Operator
	G-LSED	Rolladen-Schneider LS6-c	K. Atkinson & T. Faver
	G-LSFB	Rolladen-Schneider LS7-WL	G. K. Stanford
	G-LSFR	Rolladen-Schneider LS4-a	A. Mulder
	G-LSFT	PA-28-161 Warrior II	Falcon Flying Services Ltd (G-BXTX)
	G-LSGB	Rolladen-Schneider LS6-b	A. Rieder
	G-LSGM	Rolladen-Schneider LS3-17	M. R. W. Crook
	G-LSHI	Colt 77A balloon	J. H. Dobson
	G-LSIF	Rolladen-Schneider LS1-f	G. P. T. White & D. Heslop
	G-LSIO	DG Flugzeugbau LS10-ST	C. Darlow
	G-LSIV	Rolladen-Schneider LS4	G. M. O'Hagan
	G-LSIX	Rolladen-Schneider LS6-18W	D. P. Masson
	G-LSJE	Escapade Jabiru(1)	L. S. J. Webb
	G-LSKS	Robinson R66	Net Blocks Ltd
	G-LSKV	Rolladen-Schneider LS8-18	J. R. W. Luxton, C. E. Garner & P. A. Binnee
	G-LSKY	Mainair Pegasus Quik	M. Gudgeon
	G-LSLS	Rolladen-Schneider LS4	288 Syndicate
	G-LSPH	Van's RV-8	R. S. Partridge-Hicks
	G-LSTA	Stoddard-Hamilton Glastar	I. V. Sharman & R. J. Sheridan
	G-LSTR	Stoddard-Hamilton Glastar	R. J. Wesley
	G-LSVI	Rolladen-Schneider LS6-c18	R. Hanks
	G-LSZA	Diamond DA.42NG Twin Star	J. Molen
	G-LTBR	Courtford DB-3 balloon	A. B. Court
	G-LTFB	PA-28-140 Cherokee	D-L Bostock
	G-LTFC	PA-28-140 Cherokee B	N. M. G. Pearson (G-AXTI)
	G-LTSB	Cameron LTSB-90 balloon	ABC Flights Ltd
	G-LTWA	Robinson R44	L. T. W. Alderman
	G-LTZY	Eurocopter EC 120B Colibri	J. Henshall (G-OTFL/G-IBRI)
	G-LUBB	Cessna 525 Citationjet	Surrey Heli Charters LLP
	G-LUBY	Jabiru J430	K. Luby
	G-LUCK	Cessna F.150M	A. W. C. Knight
	G-LUCL	Colomban MC-30 Luciole	A. McQueen
	G-LUDM	Van's RV-8	A. G. Ransom
	G-LUED	Aero Designs Pulsar	J. C. Anderson
	G-LUEK	Cessna 182T	S. R. Greenall
	G-LUEY	Rans S-7S Courier	S. Garfield
	G-LUGS	Agusta A109S Grand	Myheli Ltd (G-FRZN)
	G-LUKA	Beech G.58 Baron	Bentley O-S Ltd
	G-LUKE	Rutan LongEz	W. S. Allen
	G-LULA	Cameron C-90 balloon	S. D. Davis
	G-LULU	Grob G.109	Itos BV
	G-LULV	Diamond DA-42 Twin Star	B. A. & M. L. M. Langevad
	G-LUNE	Mainair Pegasus Quik	D. Muir
	G-LUNG	Rotorsport UK MT-03	P. Krysiak
	G-LUNY	Pitts S-1S Special	G-LUNY Group
	G-LUON	Schleicher ASW-27-18E	P. C. Naegeli
	G-LUSC	Luscombe 8E Silvaire	M. Fowler
	G-LUSI	Luscombe 8F Silvaire	P. H. Isherwood
	G-LUSK	Luscombe 8F Silvaire	M. A. Lamprell & P. J. Laycock (G-BRGG)
	G-LUSO	Pilatus PC-121/47E	Eurokey Aviation Ltd
	G-LUST	Luscombe 8E Silvaire	C. J. Watson & M. R. Griffiths
	G-LUUP	Pilatus B4-PC11AF	B. L. Coopere (G-ECSW)
	G-LUXE	BAe 146-301	United Kingdom Research & Innovation (G-SSSH)
	G-LVCY	Colomban MC-30 Luciole	C. Wright
	G-LVDC	Bell 206L Long Ranger III	WAG Aviation Ltd (G-OFST/G-BXIB)
	G-LVIE	Robinson R44 II	Luviair Ltd (G-GEST)
	G-LVME	Cessna F.152 II	Superior Air SA/Greece (G-BGHI)
	G-LVPL	Edge XT912 B/Streak III/B	R. G. Mason
	G-LVRS	PA-28-181 Archer II	L. V. Liveras (G-ZMAM/G-BNPN)
	G-LWLW	Diamond DA.40D Star	M. P. Wilkinson (G-CCLV)
	G-LWNG	Aero Designs Pulsar	D. W. Bowman (G-OMKF)
	G-LXUS	Alpi Pioneer 300	A. & J. Oswald
	G-LXVI	Schempp-Hirth Arcus T	Arcus Group
	G-LXWD	Cessna 560XL Citation XLS	Catreus AOC Ltd
	G-LYDA	Hoffmann H-36 Dimona	G-LYDA Flying Group

Reg	Type	Owner or Operator	Notes
G-LYDF	PA-31-350 Navajo Chieftain	Atlantic Bridge Aviation Ltd	
G-LYFA	IDABacau Yakovlev Yak-52	Fox Alpha Group	
G-LYFT	Magni M24C Plus	L. Baring	
G-LYNC	Robinson R22 Beta II	P. M. Phillips	
G-LYND	PA-25 Pawnee 235	York Gliding Centre (Operations) Ltd (G-ASFX/G-BSFZ)	
G-LYNI	Aerotechnik EV-97 Eurostar	G. Clipston	
G-LYNK	CFM Shadow Srs DD	R. R. Till	
G-LYNX	Westland WG.13 Lynx ★	The Helicopter Museum/Weston-super-Mare	
G-LYPG	Avtech Jabiru UL	A. J. Geary	
G-LYPH	Rolladen-Schneider LS8-18-st	S. & S. Barter	
G-LYTE	Thunder Ax7-77 balloon	R. G. Turnbull	
G-LYZA	Guimbal Cabri G2	Lyza Aviation Ltd (G-IZOO)	
G-LZED	AutoGyro MTO Sport	L. Zivanovic	
G-LZII	Laser Z200	K. G. Begley	
G-MAAN	Shaw Europa XS	P. S. Mann	
G-MABE	Cessna F.150L	Aviolease Ltd (G-BLJP)	
G-MABL	Quik GTR	M. Tomlinson	
G-MACA	Robinson R22 Beta	S. J. E. Smith	
G-MACC	Cub Crafters Carbon Cub EX-2	M. W. Albery	
G-MACH	SIAI-Marchetti SF.260	Cheyne Motors Ltd	
G-MACI	Van's RV-7	N. J. F. Campbell	
G-MACR	Cirrus SR22T	J. D. M. Tickell	
G-MADC	Grif 3DC/Eurofly Snake	N. C. Milnes	
G-MADV	P & M Quik GT450	N. C. Michell	
G-MADX	AgustaWestland AW.119 Mk.II	SaxonAir Helicopters	
G-MADZ	Bell 505 Jet Ranger X	Overby Ltd	
G-MAFA	Cessna F.406	Directflight Ltd (G-DFLT)	
G-MAFB	Cessna F.406	Directflight Ltd	
G-MAFF	BN-2T Turbine Islander	Islander Aircraft Ltd (G-BJED)	
G-MAFI	Dornier 228-202K	RUAG Aerospace Services GmbH/Germany	
G-MAGC	Cameron Grand Illusion SS balloon	Magical Adventures Ltd	
G-MAGG	Pitts S-1SE Special	R. G. Gee	
G-MAGK	Schleicher ASW-20L	A. G. K. Mackenzie	
G-MAGN	Magni M-24C	R. Subberwal	
G-MAGZ	Robin DR.400/500	T. J. Thomas	
G-MAHY	Cessna 182T	G. J. Mahoney (G-SKEN)	
G-MAIE	PA-32RT-301T Turbo Saratoga II TC	S. James	
G-MAIN	Mainair Blade 912	J. G. Parkin	
G-MAJA	BAe Jetstream 4102	Eastern Airways	
G-MAJB	BAe Jetstream 4102	Eastern Airways (G-BVKT)	
G-MAJC	BAe Jetstream 4102	Eastern Airways (G-LOGJ)	
G-MAJD	BAe Jetstream 4102	Eastern Airways (G-WAWR)	
G-MAJG	BAe Jetstream 4102	Eastern Airways (G-LOGL)	
G-MAJJ	BAe Jetstream 4102	Eastern Airways (G-WAFT)	
G-MAJK	BAe Jetstream 4102	Eastern Airways	
G-MAJL	BAe Jetstream 4102	Eastern Airways	
G-MAJR	DHC.1 Chipmunk 22 (WP805)	C. Adams	
G-MAJT	BAe Jetstream 4100	Eastern Airways	
G-MAJU	BAe Jetstream 4100	Eastern Airways	
G-MAJW	BAe Jetstream 4100	Eastern Airways	
G-MAJY	BAe Jetstream 4100	Eastern Airways	
G-MAJZ	BAe Jetstream 4100	Eastern Airways	
G-MAKE	Rotorsport UK Calidus	A. R. Hawes	
G-MAKK	Aeroprakt A22-L Foxbat	M. A. McKillop	
G-MAKN	Pilatus PC-12/47E	Ravenair Aircraft Ltd	
G-MAKS	Cirrus SR22	J. P. Briggs	
G-MALC	AA-5 Traveler	M. A. Ray (G-BCPM)	
G-MALE	Balony Kubicek BB-S Skyballs SS balloon	A. M. Holly	
G-MALS	Mooney M.20K-231	P. Mouterde	
G-MALT	Colt Flying Hop SS balloon	P. J. Stapley	
G-MAMM	Ikarus C42 FB80	Mid Anglia Microlights Ltd	
G-MAMZ	Ikarus C42 FB80	Mid Anglia Microlights Ltd	
G-MANH	BAe ATP	Atlantic Airlines Ltd (G-LOGC/G-OLCC)	
G-MANX	FRED Srs 2	S. Styles	
G-MANZ	Robinson R44 II	S. M. Hill	
G-MAOL	Agusta AW109SP Grand New	Sloane Helicopters Ltd	
G-MAPY	PA-31-350 Chieftain	Blue Sky Investments Ltd (G-BXUV)	
G-MARE	Schweizer 269C	The Earl of Caledon	

Notes	Reg	Type	Owner or Operator
	G-MARL	Autogyro Calidus	M. R. Love
	G-MARO	Skyranger J2.2 (2)	Strathaven Airfield Ltd
	G-MARZ	Thruster T.600N 450	A. S. R. Czajka
	G-MASC	Jodel 150A	K. F. & R. Richardson
	G-MASF	PA-28-181 Archer II	Mid-Anglia School of Flying
	G-MASH	Westland-Bell 47G-4A	D. J. Mountain (G-AXKU)
	G-MASS	Cessna 152 II	MK Aero Support Ltd (G-BSHN)
	G-MATB	Robin DR.400-160	J. C. Bacon (G-BAFP)
	G-MATO	Dassault Falcon 7X	SDI Aviation Ltd
	G-MATS	Colt GA-42 airship	P. A. Lindstrand
	G-MATT	Robin R.2160	Swift Flying Group (G-BKRC)
	G-MATZ	PA-28 Cherokee 140	Midland Air Training School (G-BASI)
	G-MAUS	Shaw Europa XS	A. P. Ringrose
	G-MAUX	Raj Hamsa X'Air Hawk	M. A. Urch
	G-MAVK	Pitts S-1S	M. O'Leary
	G-MAXA	PA-32-301FT	L. Bennett & Son Ltd
	G-MAXB	Cameron Z-90 balloon	Discoverthesky SRLS/Italy
	G-MAXD	Robinson R44 1	M. Smith
	G-MAXG	Pitts S-1S Special	The Assets of G-MAXG Group
	G-MAXI	PA-34-200T Seneca II	Draycott Seneca Syndicate Ltd
	G-MAXS	Mainair Pegasus Quik 912S	S. Cooper
	G-MAXT	PA-28RT-201T Turbo Arrow IV	M. Toninelli/Italy
	G-MAXV	Van's RV-4	CRM Aviation Europe Ltd
	G-MAZA	Rotorsport UK MT-03	N. Crownshaw & M. Manson
	G-MAZY†	DH.82A Tiger Moth ★	Newark Air Museum/Newark
	G-MBAA	Hiway Skytrike Mk 2	M. J. Aubrey
	G-MBAB	Hovey Whing-Ding II	M. J. Aubrey
	G-MBAD	Weedhopper JC-24A	M. Stott
	G-MBAF	R. J. Swift 3	C. G. Wrzesien
	G-MBBJ	Hiway Demon	M. J. Aubrey
	G-MBBZ	Volmer VJ-24 ★	Newark Air Museum/Newark
	G-MBCG	Solar Wings Typhoon/Tri-Pacer 250 ★	Lakeland Motor Museum/Ulverston
	G-MBCJ	Mainair Sports Tri-Flyer	R. A. Smith
	G-MBCL	Sky-Trike/Typhoon	P. J. Callis
	G-MBCX	Airwave Nimrod 165	M. Maylor
	G-MBDL	AES Lone Ranger ★	North East Aircraft Museum
	G-MBDM	Southdown Sigma Trike	A. R. Prentice
	G-MBEP	American Aerolights Eagle 215B	M. J. Aubrey
	G-MBFO	Eipper Quicksilver MX	R. A. Szczepanik
	G-MBGF	Twamley Trike	T. B. Woolley
	G-MBHE	American Aerolights Eagle	R. J. Osborne
	G-MBHK	Flexiform Skytrike	A. L. Virgoe
	G-MBIO	American Eagle 215B	D. J. Lewis
	G-MBIT	Hiway Demon Skytrike	K. S. Hodgson
	G-MBJK	American Aerolights Eagle	B. W. Olley
	G-MBKY	American Aerolight Eagle	M. J. Aubrey
	G-MBKZ	Hiway Skytrike	L. Magill
	G-MBLU	Southdown Lightning L.195	C. R. Franklin
	G-MBMG	Rotec Rally 2B	J. R. Pyper
	G-MBOF	Pakes Jackdaw	M. J. Aubrey
	G-MBOH	Microlight Engineering Mistral	T. J. Gayton-Polley
	G-MBPB	Pterodactyl Ptraveller	T. D. Dawson
	G-MBPX	Eurowing Goldwing SP	V. H. Hallam
	G-MBRB	Electraflyer Eagle 1	R. C. Bott
	G-MBRD	American Aerolights Eagle	R. J. Osborne
	G-MBSJ	American Aerolights Eagle 215B	T. J. Gayton-Polley
	G-MBSX	Ultraflight Mirage II	A. D. Russell
	G-MBTJ	Solar Wings Microlight	H. A. Comber
	G-MBUD	Skycraft Scout 2 ★	Norfolk and Suffolk Aviation Museum/Flixton
	G-MBUE	MBA Tiger Cub 440 ★	Newark Air Museum/Newark
	G-MBVE	Hiway Super Scorpion/Sky-Trike ★	Newark Air Museum/Newark
	G-MBWL	Huntair Pathfinder Mk.1	A. D. Russell
	G-MBYK	Huntair Pathfinder Mk.1	S. McGirr
	G-MBZO	Tri-Pacer 330	A. N. Burrows
	G-MBZV	American Aerolights Eagle	M. J. Aubrey
	G-MCAB	Gardan GY-201 Minicab	P. G. Hooper
	G-MCAP	Cameron C-80 balloon	L. D. Pickup
	G-MCAZ	Robinson R44 II	M. C. Allen
	G-MCCF	Thruster T.600N	I. J. Webb

G-AVDF Beagle B.121 Pup *Peter R. March*

G-BPTA Stinson 180-2 *Allan S. Wright*

G-BWSH Jet Provost T.3A *Andrew March*

G-CEYE Piper PA-32R-300 Cherokee Lance *Allan S. Wright*

G-CGCE Magni M16C Tandem Trainer *Peter R. March*

G-CHST Van's RV-9A *Peter R. March*

G-EMSY DH.82A Tiger Moth *Allan S. Wright*

G-ESSL Cessna R.182 Skylane *Allan S. Wright*

G-FFFC Cessna 510 Citation Mustang *Allan S. Wright*

G-HEBO BN-2B-20 Islander *Peter R. March*

G-IACY ATR-72-212A of Eastern Airways *Allan S. Wright*

G-KRFX Embraer EMB-135BJ Legacy 600 *Allan S. Wright*

G-LIKY Aviat A-1C-180 Husky *Peter R. March*

G-PCIZ Pilatus PC-12/47E *Peter R. March*

G-PMIZ Pitts Model 12 *Peter R. March*

G-SAJD Embraer EMB-145EP of Loganair *Allan S. Wright*

G-SIRS Cessna 560XL Citation Excel *Peter R. March*

G-SVAN Cessna 208B Grand Caravan *Peter R. March*

G-UZLA Airbus A.320-251N of Easyjet *Allan S. Wright*

G-WLTS Bell 429 *Peter R. March*

M-BIGG Bombardier BD700-1A11 Global 5000 *Peter R. March*

M-CDMS Beech B.200GT Super King Air *Peter R. March*

WK577/G-BCYM DHC.1 Chipmunk 22 *Peter R. March*

XJ729/G-BVGE WS-55 Whirlwind HAR.10 *Peter R. March*

RB142/G-CEFC Supermarine Spitfire 26 *Peter R. March*

XX537/G-TDOG SA Bulldog Srs.120/121 *Peter R. March*

EC-JZM Airbus A.321-211 of Iberia *Allan S. Wright*

HB-JVO Embraer ERJ190-100LR of Helvetic Airways *Allan S. Wright*

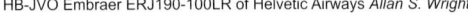

N731AN Boeing 777-323ER of American Airlines *Allan S. Wright*

OO-SND Airbus A.320-214 of Brussels Airlines *Allan S. Wright*

TC-JOU Airbus A.330-243F of Turkish Cargo *Allan S. Wright*

VT-ANY Boeing 787-8 of Air India *Allan S. Wright*

Reg	Type	Owner or Operator	Notes
G-MCCY	IAV Bacau Yak-52	D. P. McCoy	
G-MCDB	VS.361 Spitfire LF.IX	M. Collenette	
G-MCEL	Pegasus Quantum 15-912	F. Hodgson	
G-MCFK	P & M Quik GT450	F. A. A. Kay	
G-MCGB	Sikorsky S-92A	Bristow Helicopters Ltd	
G-MCGC	Sikorsky S-92A	Bristow Helicopters Ltd	
G-MCGD	Sikorsky S-92A	Bristow Helicopters Ltd	
G-MCGE	Sikorsky S-92A	Bristow Helicopters Ltd	
G-MCGF	Sikorsky S-92A	Bristow Helicopters Ltd	
G-MCGG	Sikorsky S-92A	Bristow Helicopters Ltd	
G-MCGH	Sikorsky S-92A	Bristow Helicopters Ltd	
G-MCGI	Sikorsky S-92A	Bristow Helicopters Ltd	
G-MCGJ	Sikorsky S-92A	Bristow Helicopters Ltd	
G-MCGK	Sikorsky S-92A	Bristow Helicopters Ltd	
G-MCGL	Sikorsky S-92A	Bristow Helicopters Ltd	
G-MCGM	Agusta AW189	Bristow Helicopters Ltd	
G-MCGN	Agusta AW189	Bristow Helicopters Ltd (G-CJNV)	
G-MCGO	Agusta AW189	Bristow Helicopters Ltd	
G-MCGP	Agusta AW189	Bristow Helicopters Ltd	
G-MCGR	Agusta AW189	Bristow Helicopters Ltd	
G-MCGS	Agusta AW189	Bristow Helicopters Ltd	
G-MCGT	Agusta AW189	Bristow Helicopters Ltd	
G-MCGU	Leonardo AW189	Bristow Helicopters Ltd	
G-MCGV	Leonardo AW189	Bristow Helicopters Ltd	
G-MCGW	Leonardo AW189	Bristow Helicopters Ltd	
G-MCGX	Leonardo MW189	Bristow Helicopters Ltd	
G-MCGY	Sikorsky S-92A	Bristow Helicopters Ltd	
G-MCGZ	Sikorsky S-92A	Bristow Helicopters Ltd	
G-MCJL	Pegasus Quantum 15-912	RM Aviation Ltd	
G-MCLK	Van's RV-10	M. W. Clarke	
G-MCLY	Cessna 172P	McAully Flying Group Ltd	
G-MCOW	Lindstrand LBL-77A balloon	S. & S. Villiers	
G-MCOX	Fuji FA.200-180AO	A. M. Cox	
G-MCPR	PA-32-301T Turbo Saratoga	M. C. Plomer-Roberts (G-MOLL)	
G-MCRO	Dyn'Aero MCR-01	J. M. Keane	
G-MCSA	Sikorsky S-92A	Macquarie Rotorcraft Leasing Holdings Ltd	
G-MCSB	Sikorsky S-92A	Babcock Mission Critical Services Offshore Ltd	
G-MCSC	Agusta Westland AW139	Babcock Mission Critical Services Offshore Ltd	
G-MCSD	Agusta Westland AW139	Babcock Mission Critical Services Offshore Ltd	
G-MCSF	Airbus Helicopters EC175B	Babcock Mission Critical Services Offshore Ltd	
G-MCSG	Airbus Helicopters EC175B	Babcock Mission Critical Services Offshore Ltd	
G-MCSH	Airbus Helicopters EC175B	Babcock Mission Critical Services Offshore Ltd	
G-MCSI	Sikorsky S-92A	Babcock Mission Critical Services Offshore Ltd	
G-MCSJ	Sikorsky S-92A	Babcock Mission Critical Services Offshore Ltd	
G-MCSK	Sikorsky S-92A	Babcock Mission Critical Services Offshore Ltd	
G-MCSL	Sikorsky S-92A	Babcock Mission Critical Services Offshore Ltd	
G-MCSN	Airbus Helicopters EC175B	Babcock Mission Critical Services Offshore Ltd (G-EMEA)	
G-MCSO	Airbus Helicopters EC175B	Babcock Mission Critical Services Offshore Ltd	
G-MCTO	Flylight Dragon Chaser	B. J. Syson	
G-MCUB	Reality Escapade	M. A. Appleby	
G-MCVE	Ikarus C42 FB80	A. & J. McVey	
G-MCVY	Flight Design CT2K	A. & J. McVey (G-CBNA)	
G-MDAC	PA-28-181 Archer II	S. A. Nicklen	
G-MDAM	Fuji FA.200-180 Aero Subaru	Romeo Whisky Ltd	
G-MDAY	Cessna 170B	M. Day	
G-MDBC	Pegasus Quantum 15-912	J. D. Ryan	
G-MDDE	Hughes 369E	Draper Gain Aviation Ltd	
G-MDMX	Hughes 369E	MH Pilot Services Ltd (G-CHRI)	
G-MDPI	Agusta A109A-II	Castle Air Ltd (G-PERI/G-EXEK/G-SLNE/ G-EEVS/G-OTSL)	
G-MDSI	Pilatus PC-12/47E	Ravenair Aircraft Ltd	
G-MEDF	Airbus A.321-231	British Airways PLC	
G-MEDG	Airbus A.321-231	British Airways PLC	
G-MEDJ	Airbus A.321-232	British Airways PLC	
G-MEDK	Airbus A.320-232	British Airways PLC	
G-MEDL	Airbus A.321-231	British Airways PLC	
G-MEDM	Airbus A.321-231	British Airways PLC	
G-MEDN	Airbus A.321-231	British Airways PLC	

Notes	Reg	Type	Owner or Operator
	G-MEDU	Airbus A.321-231	British Airways PLC
	G-MEEE	Schleicher ASW-20L	T. E. Macfadyen
	G-MEEP	Robinson R44 II	Blue Sky Aviation Ltd (G-PAMY)
	G-MEGG	Shaw Europa XS	R. L. Hitchcock
	G-MEGN	Beech B200 Super King Air	Dragonfly Aviation Services Ltd
	G-MEGZ	Ikarus C42 FB100	My New Flying Club Ltd
	G-MEIS	CASA 1-133 Jungmeister	B. S. Charters
	G-MELL	CZAW Sportcruiser	G. A. & J. A. Mellins
	G-MELS	PA-28-181 Archer III	P. J. Sowood
	G-MELT	Cessna F.172H	Falcon Aviation Ltd (G-AWTI)
	G-MEME	PA-28R-201 Arrow III	R. C. Tye
	G-MEMS	Diamond DA.42	AKM Aviation Ltd
	G-MENU	Robinson R44 II	HQ Aviation Ltd
	G-MEOW	CFM Streak Shadow	G. J. Moor
	G-MEPS	Embraer EMB-500 Phenom 100	Affinity Flying Training Services Ltd
	G-MERB	Dassault Falcon 900	XJC Jets Ltd (G-JSSE)
	G-MERE	Lindstrand LBL-77A balloon	R. D. Baker
	G-MERF	Grob G.115A	G-MERF Group
	G-MERL	PA-28RT-201 Arrow IV	J. Gubbay & D. Brennan
	G-MERR	Cessna 550 Citation Bravo	XJC Jets Ltd (G-XJCI)
	G-MESH	CZAW Sportcruiser	M. E. S. Heaton
	G-METH	Cameron C-90 balloon	A. & D. Methley
	G-MEUP	Cameron A-120 balloon	J. M. Woodhouse
	G-MFAB	PA-46-500TP Malibu Meridian	A. Brakewell
	G-MFAC	Cessna F.172H	Synnova Aviation Ltd (G-AVGZ)
	G-MFEF	Cessna FR.172J	A. Boyes
	G-MFHI	Shaw Europa	Hi Fliers
	G-MFLI	Cameron V-90 balloon	J. M. Percival
	G-MFLJ	P & M Quik GT450	J. A. Davies
	G-MFLM	Cessna F.152 II	Synnova Aviation Ltd (G-BFFC)
	G-MFLT	Eurocopter AS.365N3 Dauphin II	Ven Air ULC
	G-MFLY	Mainair Rapier	J. J. Tierney
	G-MFMF	Bell 206B JetRanger 3	Polo Aviation Ltd (G-BJNJ)
	G-MFMM	Scheibe SF.25C Falke	J. E. Selman
	G-MFOX	Aeropro Eurofox 912(1)	D. W. & M. L. Squire
	G-MFUX	Eurofly Minifox	Airplay Aircraft Ltd
	G-MGAG	Aviasud Mistral	M. J. Houghton
	G-MGBG	Cessna 310Q	Cotswold Aero Maintenance Ltd (G-AYND)
	G-MGCK	Whittaker MW6-S FT	H. A. Kruczek
	G-MGDL	Pegasus Quantum 15	M. J. Buchanan
	G-MGEC	Rans S.6-ESD-XL Coyote II	D. Williams & S. P. Tkaczyk
	G-MGEF	Pegasus Quantum 15	M. A. Steadman
	G-MGFC	Aeropro Eurofox 912(1)	M. G. F. Cawson
	G-MGFK	Pegasus Quantum 15	R. J. Whitmarsh
	G-MGGG	Pegasus Quantum 15	R. A. Beauchamp
	G-MGGT	CFM Streak Shadow SA	C. R. Newport
	G-MGGV	Pegasus Quantum 15-912	I. S. Duffy
	G-MGIC	Ace Magic Cyclone	P. J. Hopkins
	G-MGNI	Magni M.16C Tandem Trainer	Gyromania Ltd
	G-MGOD	Medway Raven	N. R. Andrew, A. Wherrett & D. J. Millward
	G-MGOO	Renegade Spirit UK Ltd	J. Aley
	G-MGPA	Ikarus C42 FB100	S. Ashley
	G-MGPH	CFM Streak Shadow	V. C. Readhead (G-RSPH)
	G-MGPS	Leonardo AW169	Specialist Aviation Services Ltd
	G-MGTG	Pegasus Quantum 15	F. B. Oram (G-MZIO)
	G-MGTV	Thruster T.600N 450	R. Bingham
	G-MGTW	CFM Shadow Srs DD	J. H. H. Turner
	G-MGUN	Cyclone AX2000	M. A. Boffin
	G-MGWH	Thruster T.300	Bluestreak Thruster Group
	G-MGWI	Robinson R44	Hields Aviation (G-BZEF)
	G-MHAN	Just Superstol	A. M. Hanson (G-HONO)
	G-MHCE	Enstrom F-28A	M. P. Larsen (G-BBHD)
	G-MHCM	Enstrom 280FX	Dave Tinsley Ltd (G-IBWF/G-ZZWW/G-BSIE)
	G-MHGS	Stoddard-Hamilton Glastar	D. F. Sutherland
	G-MHMR	Pegasus Quantum 15-912	Hadair
	G-MHPS	Glasair Sportsman	Hardmead Ltd
	G-MHRV	Van's RV-6A	M. R. Harris

Reg	Type	Owner or Operator	Notes
G-MIAN	Skyranger Nynja 912S(1)	I. P. Stubbins	
G-MICH	Robinson R22 Beta	Tiger Helicopters Ltd (G-BNKY)	
G-MICI	Cessna 182S	Magic Carpet Flying Company (G-WARF)	
G-MICK	Cessna F.172N	D. H. G. Penney	
G-MICX	Air Creation Tanarg/Bionix 13 912S(1)	M. J. Moulton	
G-MICY	Everett Srs 1 gyroplane	G. M. V. Richardson	
G-MIDD	PA-28 Cherokee 140	Midland Air Training School (G-BBDD)	
G-MIDO	Airbus A.320-232	British Airways PLC	
G-MIDS	Airbus A.320-232	British Airways PLC	
G-MIDT	Airbus A.320-232	British Airways PLC	
G-MIDX	Airbus A.320-232	British Airways PLC	
G-MIDY	Airbus A.320-232	British Airways PLC	
G-MIFF	Robin DR.400/180	G. E. Snushall	
G-MIGG	WSK-Mielec LiM-5 (1211) ★	D. Miles (G-BWUF)	
G-MIHD	Agusta A109S Grand	Myheli Ltd (G-SAFA/G-PBWR?G-VERU)	
G-MIII	Extra EA.300/L	Angels High Ltd	
G-MIKE	Brookland Hornet	M. H. J. Goldring	
G-MIKI	Rans S.6-ESA Coyote II	S. P. Slade	
G-MILD	Scheibe SF.25C Falke	C. A. & L. J. Bailey	
G-MILE	Cameron N-77 balloon	Miles Air Ltd	
G-MILF	Harmon Rocket II	E. Stinton	
G-MILR	Aeroprakt A22-LS Foxbat	Myrtlegrove Aviation Services	
G-MIMU	CFM Shadow Series CD	N. M. Barriskell (G-MYXY)	
G-MIND	Cessna 404	Reconnaissance Ventures Ltd	
G-MINJ	Diamond DA.42 Twin Star	Barkley Consulting BV/Belgium (G-ITFL)	
G-MINN	Lindstrand LBL-90A balloon	S. M. & D. Johnson (G-SKKC/G-OHUB)	
G-MINS	Nicollier HN.700 Menestrel II	H. Fenion	
G-MINT	Pitts S-1S Special	T. R. G. Barnby	
G-MIOO	M.100 Student ★	Museum of Berkshire Aviation/Woodley (G-APLK)	
G-MIRA	Jabiru SP-340	C. P. L. Helson/Belgium (G-LUMA)	
G-MIRN	Remos GX	M. Kurkic	
G-MIRV	Van's RV-8	E. R. J. Hicks & S. P. Ayres	
G-MISH	Cessna 182R	A. C. Hill & A. A. D. McKerrell (G-RFAB/G-BIXT)	
G-MISJ	CZAW Sportcruiser	B. P. Clarke	
G-MITE	Raj Hamsa X'Air Falcon	W. Parker	
G-MITY	Mole Mite	R. H. Mole	
G-MITZ	Cameron N-77 balloon	Colt Car Co Ltd	
G-MJAD	Eipper Quicksilver MX	J. McCullough	
G-MJAE	American Aerolights Eagle	T. B. Woolley	
G-MJAJ	Eurowing Goldwing	M. J. Aubrey	
G-MJAM	Eipper Quicksilver MX	P. R. Szczepanik	
G-MJAN	Hiway Skytrike	G. M. Sutcliffe	
G-MJBK	Swallow AeroPlane Swallow B	M. A. Newbould	
G-MJBL	American Aerolights Eagle	B. W. Olley	
G-MJCF	Maxair Sports Hummer ★	Newark Air Museum/Newark	
G-MJCU	Tarjani	J. K. Ewing	
G-MJDE	Huntair Pathfinder	P. Rayson	
G-MJDJ	Hiway Skytrike Demon	A. J. Cowan	
G-MJDP	Eurowing Goldwing	A. D. Russell	
G-MJDW	Eipper Quicksilver MX ★	Newark Air Museum/Newark	
G-MJEO	American Aerolights Eagle	A. M. Shaw	
G-MJER	Flexiform Striker	D. S. Simpson	
G-MJFM	Huntair Pathfinder	M. J. Aubrey	
G-MJFX	Skyhook TR-1	M. R. Dean	
G-MJFZ	Hiway Demon/Tri-flyer	A. W. Lowrie	
G-MJHV	Hiway Demon 250	A. G. Griffiths	
G-MJJA	Huntair Pathfinder	D. H. Edwards	
G-MJJK	Eipper Quicksilver MXII	J. McCullough	
G-MJKP	Super Scorpion/Sky-Trike ★	South Yorkshire Aircraft Museum/Doncaster	
G-MJKX	Ultralight Skyrider Phantom	R. J. Turner	
G-MJOC	Huntair Pathfinder	A. J. Glynn	
G-MJOE	Eurowing Goldwing	R. J. Osborne	
G-MJPB	Manuel Ladybird	J. Aubert	
G-MJPE	Hiway Demon Skytrike	T. G. Elmhirst	
G-MJPV	Eipper Quicksilver MX	F. W. Ellis	
G-MJRA	Mainair Tri-Flyer 330 ★	Yorkshire Air Museum/Elvington	
G-MJSE	Skyrider Airsports Phantom	R. P. Tribe	
G-MJSF	Skyrider Airsports Phantom	R. P. Stonor	
G-MJSL	Dragon 200	M. J. Aubrey	

Notes	Reg	Type	Owner or Operator
	G-MJSO	Hiway Skytrike	D. C. Read
	G-MJSP	Romain Tiger Cub 440	A. R. Sunley
	G-MJST	Pterodactyl Ptraveller	T. D. Dawson
	G-MJSU	Flylite Tiger Cub ★	Norfolk and Suffolk Aviation Museum/Flixton
	G-MJSY	Eurowing Goldwing	A. J. Rex
	G-MJSZ	DH Wasp	J. J. Hill
	G-MJTM	Aerostructure Pipistrelle 2B	A. M. Sirant
	G-MJTX	Skyrider Airsports Phantom	P. D. Coppin
	G-MJTY	Huntair Pathfinder Mk.1	A. S. Macdonald
	G-MJTZ	Skyrider Airsports Phantom	B. J. Towers
	G-MJUF	MBA Super Tiger Cub 440	D. G. Palmer
	G-MJUW	MBA Tiger Cub 440	D. G. Palmer
	G-MJUX	Skyrider Airsports Phantom	T. J. Searle
	G-MJVF	CFM Shadow series CD	J. A. Cook
	G-MJVI	Rooster 1 Series 4 ★	Norfolk and Suffolk Aviation Museum/Flixton
	G-MJVN	Ultrasports Puma 440	R. McGookin
	G-MJVP	Eipper Quicksilver MX II	G. J. Ward
	G-MJVU	Eipper Quicksilver MX II	G. Hayes
	G-MJVY	Dragon Srs 150	J. C. Craddock
	G-MJWB	Eurowing Goldwing	D. G. Palmer
	G-MJWF	Tiger Cub 440	R. A. & T. Maycock
	G-MJYV	Mainair Triflyer 2 Seat	H. L. Phillips
	G-MJYW	Wasp Gryphon III	P. D. Lawrence
	G-MJYX	Mainair Tri-Flyer/Hiway Demon	K. G. Grayson & R. D. Leigh
	G-MJZK	Southdown Puma Sprint 440	R. J. Osborne
	G-MJZX	Hummer TX	M. J. Aubrey
	G-MKAK	Colt 77A balloon	M. A. Webb & P. M. Davies
	G-MKAS	PA-28 Cherokee 140	G-Hire Ltd (G-BKVR)
	G-MKER	P & M QuikR	M. C. Kerr
	G-MKEV	EV-96 Eurostar	K. Laud
	G-MKHB	Aeropro Eurofox 912(iS)	Ascent Industries Ltd
	G-MKVB	VS.349 Spitfire LF.VB (BM597)	Historic Aircraft Collection
	G-MKXI	VS.365 Spitfire PR.XI (PL965)	Hangar 11 Collection
	G-MKZG	Super Marine Spitfire Mk.26	D. G. Richardson
	G-MLAL	Jabiru J400	K. Lafferty
	G-MLAP	Agusta Westland AW169	Starspeed Ltd
	G-MLAS	Cessna 182E ★	Parachute jump trainer/St. Merryn
	G-MLAW	P & M Quik GT450	J. R. Payne
	G-MLHI	Maule MX-7-180 Star Rocket	Maulehigh Group (G-BTMJ)
	G-MLKE	P & M Aviation Quik R	G. Oliver
	G-MLLI	PA-32RT-300 Lance II	T. Steward (G-JUPP/G-BNJF)
	G-MLSY	BRM Bristell NG5 Speed Wing	T. E. Mills
	G-MLTA	UltraMagic M-77 balloon	R. Parr
	G-MLWI	Thunder Ax7-77 balloon	C. A. Butter
	G-MLXP	Europa	M. Davies
	G-MLZZ	Best Off Sky Ranger Swift 912S(1)	D. S. T. Harris
	G-MMAG	MBA Tiger Cub 440	M. J. Aubrey
	G-MMAM	MBA Tiger Cub 440	I. Pearson
	G-MMAR	Mainair Gemini/Southdown Puma Sprint	B. A. Fawkes
	G-MMCB	Huntair Pathfinder III ★	Science Musem/Wroughton
	G-MMDJ	Mainair Tri-Flyer 250/Solar Wings Typhoon	A. M. Webb
	G-MMDK	Flexiform Striker/Tri-Flyer ★	South Yorkshire Aircraft Museum/Doncaster
	G-MMDO	Hornet Invader/Southdown Sprint	M. Roberts
	G-MMEK	Medway Hybred 44XL	West Country Wings
	G-MMFV	Flexiform Striker	R. A. Walton
	G-MMGF	MBA Tiger Cub 440	I. J. Webb
	G-MMGL	MBA Tiger Cub 440	H. E. Dunning
	G-MMGS	Solar Wings Panther XL	G. C. Read
	G-MMGT	Solar Wings Typhoon	H. Cook
	G-MMGV	Whittaker MW5 Sorcerer	M. W. J. Whittaker & G. N. Haffey
	G-MMHN	MBA Tiger Cub 440	M. J. Aubrey
	G-MMHS	SMD Viper	C. J. Meadows
	G-MMIE	MBA Tiger Cub 440	B. M. Olliver
	G-MMIH	MBA Tiger Cub 440	S. Sparkey
	G-MMJD	Southdown Puma Sprint	M. P. Robertshaw
	G-MMJV	MBA Tiger Cub 440	D. G. Palmer
	G-MMKA	Ultrasports Panther Dual	R. S. Wood
	G-MMKM	Flexiform Dual Striker	S. W. Hutchinson

Reg	Type	Owner or Operator	Notes
G-MMKP	MBA Tiger Cub 440	J. W. Beaty	
G-MMKR	Southdown Lightning DS/Tri-Flyer 440	C. R. Madden	
G-MMKT	MBA Tiger Cub 440	A. R. Sunley	
G-MMKX	Skyrider Phantom 330	G. J. Lampitt	
G-MMLE	Eurowing Goldwing SP	M. J. Aubrey	
G-MMLK	MBA Tiger Cub 440	M. J. Aubrey	
G-MMLM	MBA Tiger Cub 440 ★	Montrose Air Station Heritage Centre/Montrose	
G-MMMG	Eipper Quicksilver MXL	L. Swift	
G-MMMH	Hadland Willow	M. J. Hadland	
G-MMML	Dragon 150	M. J. Aubrey	
G-MMNA	Eipper Quicksilver MXII	G. A. Marples	
G-MMNB	Eipper Quicksilver MX	M. J. Lindop	
G-MMNC	Eipper Quicksilver MX	W. S. Toulmin	
G-MMOK	Solar Wings Panther XL	R. F. & A. J. Foster	
G-MMPH	Southdown Puma Sprint	J. Siddle	
G-MMPL	Lanashire Micro-Trike 440/Flexiform Dual Striker (modified)	P. D. Lawrence	
G-MMPZ	Teman Mono-Fly	H. Smith	
G-MMRH	Highway Skytrike	A. M. Sirant	
G-MMRL	Solar Wings Panther XL	R. J. Hood	
G-MMRN	Southdown Puma Sprint	D. C. Read	
G-MMRP	Mainair Gemini	J. C. S. Jones	
G-MMSP	Mainair Gemini/Flash	J. Whiteford	
G-MMSS	Lightning/Tri-Pacer	G. A. Hazell	
G-MMSZ	Medway Half Pint/Aerial Arts 130SX	A. M. Sutton	
G-MMTD	Mainair Tri-Flyer 330	W. E. Teare	
G-MMTY	Fisher FP.202U	M. A. Welch	
G-MMUV	Southdown Puma Sprint	D. C. Read	
G-MMUX	Gemini Sprint	D. R. Gregson	
G-MMVI	Southdown Puma Sprint	G. R. Williams	
G-MMVS	Skyhook Pixie	B. W. Olley	
G-MMWG	Greenslade Mono-Trike	G-MMWG Group	
G-MMWL	Eurowing Foldwing ★	Norfolk and Suffolk Aviation Museum/Flixton	
G-MMWX	Southdown Puma Sprint	G. A. Webb	
G-MMXU	Mainair Gemini/Flash	T. J. Franklin	
G-MMXV	Mainair Gemini/Flash	M. A. Boffin	
G-MMZA	Mainair Gemini/Flash	G. T. Johnston	
G-MMZD	Mainair Gemini/Flash	S. McDonnell	
G-MMZW	Southdown Puma Sprint	M. G. Ashbee	
G-MNAE	Mainair Gemini/Flash	G. C. luddington	
G-MNAZ	Solar Wings Pegasus XL-R	R. W. houldsworth	
G-MNBA	Solar Wings Pegasus XL-R	V. C. Chambers	
G-MNBB	Solar Wings Pegasus XL-R	A. A. Sawera	
G-MNBP	Mainair Gemini/Flash	B. J. James	
G-MNBS	Mainair Gemini/Flash	P. A. Comins	
G-MNCA	Hiway Demon 175	M. A. Sirant	
G-MNCF	Mainair Gemini/Flash	C. F. Janes	
G-MNCM	CFM Shadow Srs C	A. Gibson	
G-MNCP	Southdown Puma Sprint	D. A. Payne	
G-MNCS	Skyrider Airsports Phantom	J. A. Harris	
G-MNCU	Medway Hybred 44XL	J. E. Evans	
G-MNDC	Mainair Gemini Flash	M. A. Medlock	
G-MNDE	Medway Half Pint	C. G. Chambers	
G-MNDU	Midland Sirocco 377GB	M. A. Collins	
G-MNDY	Southdown Puma Sprint	A. M. Coupland	
G-MNER	CFM Shadow Srs B	C. Parkinson & P. McDonald	
G-MNEY	Mainair Gemini/Flash	D. A. Spiers	
G-MNFG	Southdown Puma Sprint	M. Ingleton	
G-MNFL	AMF Chevvron	J. Pool	
G-MNFM	Mainair Gemini/Flash	P. M. Fidell	
G-MNGK	Mainair Gemini/Flash	A. R. Hawes	
G-MNHI	Solar Wings Pegasus XL-R	B. R. Claughton	
G-MNHJ	Solar Wings Pegasus XL-R	C. Council	
G-MNHK	Solar Wings Pegasus XL-R	M. J. Searle	
G-MNHR	Solar Wings Pegasus XL-R	B. D. Jackson	
G-MNHZ	Mainair Gemini/Flash	I. O. S. Ross	
G-MNIA	Mainair Gemini/Flash	W. R. Furness	
G-MNIF	Mainair Gemini/Flash	W. Montgomery	
G-MNIG	Mainair Gemini/Flash	M. Grimes	

Notes	Reg	Type	Owner or Operator
	G-MNII	Mainair Gemini/Flash	R. F. Finnis
	G-MNIK	Pegasus Photon	M. Belemet
	G-MNJD	Southdown Puma Sprint	S. D. Smith
	G-MNJJ	Solar Wings Pegasus Flash	P. A. Shelley
	G-MNJR	Solar Wings Pegasus Flash	M. G. Ashbee
	G-MNJS	Southdown Puma Sprint	E. A. Frost
	G-MNJX	Medway Hybred 44XL	H. A. Stewart
	G-MNKC	Solar Wings Pegasus Photon	K. B. Woods
	G-MNKD	Solar Wings Pegasus Photon	A. M. Sirant
	G-MNKE	Solar Wings Pegasus Photon	H. C. Lowther
	G-MNKK	Solar Wings Pegasus Photon	M. E. Gilbert
	G-MNKM	MBA Tiger Cub 440	A. R. Sunley
	G-MNKN	Skycraft Scout Mk.3-3R	M. A. Aubrey
	G-MNKP	Solar Wings Pegasus Flash	I. N. Miller
	G-MNLT	Southdown Raven	J. L. Stachini
	G-MNMC	Mainair Gemini Sprint	J. C. Peat
	G-MNMG	Mainair Gemini/Flash	N. A. M. Beyer-Kay
	G-MNMK	Solar Wings Pegasus XL-R	A. F. Smallacombe
	G-MNMM	Aerotech MW5 Sorcerer	S. F. N. Warnell
	G-MNMU	Southdown Raven	M. J. Curley
	G-MNMV	Mainair Gemini/Flash	E. J. Reilly
	G-MNMW	Aerotech MW6 Merlin	E. F. Clapham
	G-MNMY	Cyclone 70	N. R. Beale
	G-MNNA	Southdown Raven	D. & G. D. Palfrey
	G-MNNF	Mainair Gemini/Flash	W. J. Gunn
	G-MNNG	Solar Wings Photon	K. B. Woods
	G-MNNJ	Mainair Gemini/Flash II	L. J. Nelson
	G-MNNL	Mainair Gemini/Flash II	C. L. Rumney
	G-MNNM	Mainair Scorcher Solo	S. R. Leeper
	G-MNNO	Southdown Raven	M. J. Robbins
	G-MNNS	Eurowing Goldwing	N. K. Geddes
	G-MNPY	Mainair Scorcher Solo	R. J. Turner
	G-MNPZ	Mainair Scorcher Solo	S. Stevens
	G-MNRD	Ultraflight Lazair IIIE	Sywell Lazair Group
	G-MNRE	Mainair Scorcher Solo	I. B. Currer
	G-MNRT	Sirocco 377GB ★	Newark Air Museum/Newark
	G-MNRZ	Mainair Scorcher Solo	R. D. Leigh
	G-MNSJ	Mainair Gemini/Flash	P. Cooney
	G-MNSL	Southdown Raven X	P. B. Robinson
	G-MNSY	Southdown Raven X	L. A. Hosegood
	G-MNTD	Aerial Arts Chaser 110SX	B. Richardson
	G-MNTK	CFM Shadow Srs B	K. Davies
	G-MNTP	CFM Shadow Srs B	A. C. Leak
	G-MNTV	Mainair Gemini/Flash II	A.M. Sirant
	G-MNUI	Skyhook Cutlass Dual	M. Holling
	G-MNVE	Solar Wings Pegasus XL-R	M. P. Aris
	G-MNVG	Solar Wings Pegasus Flash II	D. J. Ward
	G-MNVI	CFM Shadow Srs B	D. R. C. Pugh
	G-MNVJ	CFM Shadow Srs CD	R. Delaney
	G-MNVK	CFM Shadow Srs B	E. C. & P. King
	G-MNVO	Hovey Whing-Ding II	C. Wilson
	G-MNVW	Mainair Gemini/Flash II	J. C. Munro-Hunt
	G-MNVZ	Solar Wings Pegasus Photon	J. J. Russ
	G-MNWG	Southdown Raven X	D. Murray
	G-MNWI	Mainair Gemini/Flash II	P. Dickinson
	G-MNWL	Aerial Arts 130SX	E. H. Snook
	G-MNWW	Solar Wings Pegasus XL-R	G-MNWW Group
	G-MNWY	CFM Shadow Srs C	S. R. Potts
	G-MNXE	Southdown Raven X	A. E. Silvey
	G-MNXX	CFM Shadow Srs BD	R. Sinclair-Brown
	G-MNYD	Aerial Arts 110SX Chaser	B. Richardson
	G-MNYF	Aerial Arts 110SX Chaser	R. W. Twamley
	G-MNYP	Southdown Raven X	A. G. Davies
	G-MNYU	Pegasus XL-R	G. L. Turner
	G-MNZD	Mainair Gemini/Flash II	N. D. Carter
	G-MNZJ	CFM Shadow Srs BD	W. Hepburn
	G-MNZP	CFM Shadow Series BD	G. C. White
	G-MNZU	Eurowing Goldwing	P. D. Coppin & P. R. Millen
	G-MNZW	Southdown Raven X	T. A. Willcox
	G-MOAC	Beech F33A Bonanza	R. M. Camrass

Reg	Type	Owner or Operator	Notes
G-MOAL	Agusta Westland AW109SP Grand New	SDI Aviation Ltd	
G-MOAN	Aeromot AMT-200S Super Ximango	T. Boin/Switzerland	
G-MOCL	Bombardier CL600-2B16 Challenger 604	London Executive Aviation Ltd	
G-MODE	Eurocopter EC 120B	P. G. Barker	
G-MOEL	Schempp-Hirth Arcus M	R. B. Witter & J. P. Roland	
G-MOFB	Cameron O-120 balloon	D. M. Moffat	
G-MOGN	BRM Bristell NG5 Speedwing	Morgan Land Sea and Air LLP	
G-MOGS	CZAW Sportcruiser	J. M. Oliver	
G-MOJI	Lindstrand LTL Series SS balloon	L. P. Cooper	
G-MOKE	Cameron V-77 balloon	G-MOKE ASBC/Luxembourg	
G-MOLA	Evektor EV-97 TeamEurostar UK	A. Szczepanek	
G-MOMA	Thruster T.600N 450	Compton Abbas Microlight Group (G-CCIB)	
G-MONI	Monnett Moni	T. McKinley	
G-MOOD	Ikarus C42 FB100	R. Moody (G-HARL)	
G-MOOR	SOCATA TB10 Tobago	P. D. Kirkham (G-MILK)	
G-MOOS	P.56 Provost T.1 (XF690)	Yeo Pro Group (G-BGKA)	
G-MOOV	CZAW Sportcruiser	G-MOOV Syndicate	
G-MOPS	Best Off Sky Ranger Swift 912S	M. Gates	
G-MOSH	PA-28R-201 Arrow	S. J. Griggs	
G-MOSJ	Beech C90 GTI King Air	Moss Aviation LLP	
G-MOSY	Cameron O-84 balloon	P. L. Mossman	
G-MOTA	Bell 206B JetRanger 3	J. W. Sandle	
G-MOTH	DH.82A Tiger Moth (K2567)	P. T. Szluha	
G-MOTI	Robin DR.400/500	Tango India Flying Group	
G-MOTO	PA-24 Comanche 180	B. Spiralke (G-EDHE/G-ASFH)	
G-MOTW	Meyers OTW-145	J. K. Padden	
G-MOUR	HS. Gnat T.1 (XR992)	Heritage Aircraft Ltd	
G-MOUT	Cessna 182T	C. Mountain	
G-MOUZ	Cameron O-26 balloon	T. J. Orchard & M. E. Banks	
G-MOVI	PA-32R-301 Saratoga SP	J. E. Bray (G-MARI)	
G-MOWG	Aeroprakt A22-L Foxbat	J. Smith	
G-MOYR	Aeropro Eurofox 912(S)	The Northumbria Gliding Club Ltd	
G-MOZE	P & M Quik GTR	M. R. Mosley	
G-MOZI	Glasflugel Mosquito	P. Smith	
G-MOZZ	Avions Mudry CAP-10B	N. Skipworth	
G-MPAA	PA-28-181 Archer III	Shropshire Aero Club Ltd	
G-MPAT	EV-97 TeamEurostar UK	P. J. Dale	
G-MPFC	Grumman AA-5B	Shipping & Airlines Ltd (G-ZARI/G-BHVY)	
G-MPHY	Ikarus C42 FB100	P. Murphy	
G-MPLA	Cessna 182T	Gazelle Properties Ltd	
G-MPLB	Cessna 182T	A. Walker	
G-MPLC	Cessna 182T	Oxford Aviation Academy (Oxford) Ltd	
G-MPLD	Cessna 182T	Cropspray Ltd	
G-MPLE	Cessna 182T	Oxford Aviation Academy (Oxford) Ltd	
G-MPLF	Cessna 182T	Oxford Aviation Academy (Oxford) Ltd	
G-MPRL	Cessna 210M	Mike Stapleton & Co.Ltd	
G-MPSA	Eurocopter MBB BK-117C-2	Police & Crime Commissioner for West Yorkshire	
G-MPSB	Eurocopter MBB BK-117C-2	Police & Crime Commissioner for West Yorkshire	
G-MPSC	Eurocopter MBB BK-117C-2	Police & Crime Commissioner for West Yorkshire	
G-MRAG	Cessna 182T	C. M. Alonso	
G-MRAJ	Hughes 369E	A. Jardine	
G-MRAM	Mignet HM.1000 Balerit	R. A. Marven	
G-MRDS	CZAW Sportcruiser	P. Wood	
G-MRED	Christavia Mk 1	Mister Ed Group	
G-MRFX	Embraer EMB-550 Legacy 500	Flexjet Ltd	
G-MRGT	Skyranger Swift 912S(1)	G. I. Taylor	
G-MRJC	AutoGyro Cavalon	T. Woodcock	
G-MRJJ	Mainair Pegasus Quik	J.H. Sparks	
G-MRJP	Silence Twister	J. P. Marriott	
G-MRKM	Carbon Cub EX-2	R. C. Loveland	
G-MRKS	Robinson R44	TJD Trade Ltd (G-RAYC)	
G-MRKT	Lindstrand LBL-90A balloon	R. M. Stanley	
G-MRLB	Dassault Falcon 900	XJC Jets Ltd (G-FLCN)	
G-MRLI	Sikorsky S-92A	Bristow Helicopters Ltd (G-CKGZ)	
G-MRLN	Sky 240-24 balloon	M. Wady	
G-MRLS	AutoGyro Calidus	C. N. Fleming	
G-MRLX	Gulfstream 550	Concierge U Ltd	
G-MRLZ	Robinson R44 II	Catedra Services XXI SRL/Spain	
G-MRMA	Cessna 182S	TWC Facilities Ltd	

231

Notes	Reg	Type	Owner or Operator
	G-MRME	Gefa-Flug AS 105 GD airship	Airship Over Atlanta Ltd
	G-MROC	Pegasus Quantum 15-912	P. Hill
	G-MROD	Van's RV-7A	K. R. Emery
	G-MROS	Pipistrel Alpha BCAR-S 164	MKR Aviation Ltd
	G-MRPH	Murphy Rebel	P. & B. S. Metson
	G-MRSS	Ikarus C42 FB80	P. D. Alford
	G-MRST	PA-28 RT-201 Arrow IV	D. C. L. Pluche/France
	G-MRSW	Lindstrand LBL-90A balloon	D. S. Wilson (G-CHWU)
	G-MRTN	SOCATA TB10 Tobago	G. C. Jarvis (G-BHET)
	G-MRTY	Cameron N-77 balloon	R. A. Vale & ptnrs
	G-MRVK	Czech Sport Aircraft Pipersport	M. Farrugia
	G-MRVL	Van's RV-7	T. W. Wielkopolski
	G-MRVN	PZL-Bielsko SZD-50-3	The Bath, Wilts and North Dorset Gliding Club Ltd
	G-MRVP	Van's RV-6	M. R. Parker
	G-MSAL	MS.733 Alcyon (143)	M. Isbister t/a Alcyon Flying Group
	G-MSAV	ICP MXP-740 Savannah VG Camit (1)	J. G. Miller
	G-MSCB	Skyranger Nynja	C. Bannerman & S. M. Spencer
	G-MSCL	AutoGyro Cavalon	Power Management Engineering Ltd
	G-MSES	Cessna 150L	D. Petrauskab
	G-MSFT	PA-28-161 Warrior II	Reborn Leasing (UK) Ltd (G-MUMS)
	G-MSFX	Embraer EMB-550 Legacy 500	Flexjet Ltd
	G-MSGI	Magni M-24C Orion	Orion Cotswolds Aviation Ltd
	G-MSIX	Glaser-Dirks DG.800B	G-MSIX Group
	G-MSKY	Ikarus C.42 FB100 VLA	G-MSKY Group
	G-MSOF	Cessna 172N	Excelis Ltd
	G-MSON	Cameron Z-90 balloon	Regional Property Services Ltd
	G-MSOO	Revolution Mini 500 helicopter	R. H. Ryan
	G-MSPR	Robinson R66	MSPR Aviation LLP
	G-MSPY	Pegasus Quantum 15-912	B. E. Wagenhauser
	G-MSVI	Agusta A.109S Grand	JPM Ltd (G-ETOU)
	G-MTAB	Mainair Gemini/Flash II	M. J. Thompson
	G-MTAC	Mainair Gemini/Flash II	B. T. Bradshaw
	G-MTAF	Mainair Gemini/Flash II	P. J. Byrne
	G-MTAH	Mainair Gemini/Flash II	A. J. Rowe
	G-MTAL	Solar Wings Pegasus Photon	I. T. Callaghan
	G-MTAV	Solar Wings Pegasus XL-R	S. Fairweather
	G-MTAW	Solar Wings Pegasus XL-R	M. G. Ralph
	G-MTAZ	Solar Wings Pegasus XL-R	M. O'Connell
	G-MTBB	Southdown Raven X	A. Miller
	G-MTBD	Mainair Gemini/Flash II	L. J. Tomlinson
	G-MTBE	CFM Shadow Srs BD	A. P. Jones
	G-MTBH	Mainair Gemini Flash II	M. Sheehy
	G-MTBN	Southdown Raven X	A. J. & S. E. Crosby-Jones
	G-MTBO	Southdown Raven X	J. Liversuch
	G-MTBP	Aerotech MW5B Sorcerer	C. G. Chambers
	G-MTBR	Aerotech MW5B Sorcerer	R. Poulter
	G-MTBS	Aerotech MW5B Sorcerer	D. J. Pike
	G-MTCM	Southdown Raven X	J. C. Rose
	G-MTCP	Aerial Arts Chaser 110SX	B. Richardson
	G-MTCU	Mainair Gemini/Flash II	T. J. Philip
	G-MTDD	Aerial Arts Chaser 110SX	B. Richardson
	G-MTDE	American Aerolights 110SX	R. J. Turner
	G-MTDF	Mainair Gemini/Flash II	P. G. Barnes
	G-MTDK	Aerotech MW5B Sorcerer	C. C. Wright
	G-MTDR	Mainair Gemini/Flash II	D. J. Morriss
	G-MTDU	CFM Shadow Srs CD	P. S. Sweet
	G-MTDW	Mainair Gemini/Flash II	S. R. Leeper
	G-MTEK	Mainair Gemini/Flash II	M. O'Hearne
	G-MTER	Solar Wings Pegasus XL-R	S. J. Nix
	G-MTES	Solar Wings Pegasus XL-R	N. P. Read
	G-MTEU	Solar Wings Pegasus XL-R	T. E. Thomas
	G-MTEY	Mainair Gemini/Flash II	B. H. L. Prior
	G-MTFC	Medway Hybred 44XLR	J. K. Masters
	G-MTFG	AMF Chevvron 232	J. Pool
	G-MTFK	Flexiform Striker/Moult Trike ★	Norfolk and Suffolk Aviation Museum/Flixton
	G-MTFN	Aerotech MW5 Sorcerer	S. M. King
	G-MTFU	CFM Shadow Srs CD	J. E. Course
	G-MTGB	Thruster TST Mk 1	M. J. Aubrey

Reg	Type	Owner or Operator	Notes
G-MTGD	Thruster TST Mk 1	B. A. Janaway	
G-MTGL	Solar Wings Pegasus XL-R	R. & P. J. Openshaw	
G-MTGO	Mainair Gemini/Flash	J. Ouru	
G-MTGR	Thruster TST Mk 1	W. H. J. Knowles	
G-MTGS	Thruster TST Mk 1	R. J. Nelson	
G-MTGV	CFM Shadow Srs BD	D. J. Flanagan	
G-MTGW	CFM Shadow Srs CD	A. G. Wright	
G-MTHH	Solar Wings Pegasus XL-R	J. Palmer	
G-MTHN	Solar Wings Pegasus XL-R	G. E. Murphy	
G-MTHT	CFM Shadow Srs BD	A. P. Jones	
G-MTHV	CFM Shadow Srs CD	P. W. Margetson	
G-MTIE	Solar Wings Pegasus XL-R	P. Wibberley	
G-MTIJ	Solar Wings Pegasus XL-R	M. J. F. Gilbody	
G-MTIL	Mainair Gemini/Flash IIA	D. J. Robinson	
G-MTIW	Solar Wings Pegasus XL-R	S. G. Hutchinson	
G-MTIZ	Solar Wings Pegasus XL-R	S. L. Blount	
G-MTJC	Mainair Gemini/Flash IIA	T. A. Dockrell	
G-MTJE	Mainair Gemini/Flash IIA	C. I. Hemingway	
G-MTJH	SW Pegasus Flash	C. G. Ludgate	
G-MTJL	Mainair Gemini/Flash IIA	R. Thompson	
G-MTJN	Midland Ultralights Sirocco 377GB	A. R. Hawes	
G-MTJT	Mainair Gemini/Flash IIA	P. J. Barratt	
G-MTJV	Mainair Gemini/Flash IIA	D. C. Dunn	
G-MTKA	Thruster TST Mk 1	M. J. Coles & S. R. Williams	
G-MTKI	Solar Wings Pegasus XL-R	M. Wady	
G-MTKR	CFM Shadow Srs CD	Shadow Group	
G-MTKW	Mainair Gemini/Flash IIA	J. H. McIvor	
G-MTKX	Mainair Gemini/Flash IIA	S. P. Disney	
G-MTLB	Mainair Gemini/Flash IIA	C. R. Partington	
G-MTLC	Mainair Gemini/Flash IIA	R. J. Alston	
G-MTLG	Solar Wings Pegasus XL-R	D. Young	
G-MTLL	Mainair Gemini/Flash IIA	M. S. Lawrence	
G-MTLM	Thruster TST Mk 1	R.J. Nelson	
G-MTLN	Thruster TST Mk 1	P. W. Taylor	
G-MTLT	Solar Wings Pegasus XL-R	K. M. Mayling	
G-MTLX	Medway Hybred 44XLR	D. A. Coupland	
G-MTLY	Solar Wings Pegasus XL-R	G. J. Prisk	
G-MTMA	Mainair Gemini/Flash IIA	S. Cunningham	
G-MTMC	Mainair Gemini/Flash IIA	M. A. Thomas	
G-MTMF	Solar Wings Pegasus XL-R	H. T. M. Smith	
G-MTMG	Solar Wings Pegasus XL-R	C. W. & P. E. F. Suckling	
G-MTML	Mainair Gemini/Flash IIA	J. F. Ashton	
G-MTMR	Hornet Dual Trainer/Raven	D. J. Smith	
G-MTMW	Mainair Gemini/Flash IIA	M. D. Payne	
G-MTMX	CFM Shadow Srs BD	D. R. White	
G-MTNC	Mainair Gemini/Flash IIA	K. R. Emery	
G-MTND	Medway Hybred 44XLR	Butty Boys Flying Group	
G-MTNE	Medway Hybred 44XLR	A. G. Rodenburg	
G-MTNF	Medway Hybred 44XLR	P. A. Bedford	
G-MTNI	Mainair Gemini/Flash IIA	D. R. McDougall	
G-MTNK	Weedhopper JC-24B	S. D. Hutchinson	
G-MTNR	Thruster TST Mk 1	A. M. Sirant	
G-MTNU	Thruster TST Mk 1	T. H. Brearley	
G-MTNV	Thruster TST Mk 1	J. B. Russell	
G-MTOA	Solar Wings Pegasus XL-R	R. A. Bird	
G-MTOH	Solar Wings Pegasus XL-R	H. Cook	
G-MTOJ	Solar Wings Pegasus XL-R	J. Hennessy	
G-MTON	Solar Wings Pegasus XL-R	D. J. Willett	
G-MTOY	Solar Wings Pegasus XL-R	XL2 Group	
G-MTPB	Mainair Gemini/Flash IIA	G. von Wilcken	
G-MTPF	Solar Wings Pegasus XL-R	G-MTPF Group	
G-MTPH	Solar Wings Pegasus XL-R	D. Bannister	
G-MTPL	Solar Wings Pegasus XL-R	C. J. Jones	
G-MTPM	Solar Wings Pegasus XL-R	V. K. Snell	
G-MTPU	Thruster TST Mk 1	N. Hay	
G-MTPX	Thruster TST Mk 1	T. Snook	
G-MTRC	Midlands Ultralights Sirocco 377G	D. Thorpe	
G-MTRM	Solar Wings Pegasus XL-R	C. H. Edwards	
G-MTRS	Solar Wings Pegasus XL-R	W. R. Edwards	
G-MTRX	Whittaker MW5 Sorceror	W. Turner	
G-MTSC	Mainair Gemini/Flash IIA	J. Kilpatrick	

Notes	Reg	Type	Owner or Operator
	G-MTSH	Thruster TST Mk 1	R. R. Orr
	G-MTSJ	Thruster TST Mk 1	J. D. Buchanan
	G-MTSM	Thruster TST Mk 1	M. A. Horton
	G-MTSS	Solar Wings Pegasus XL-R	V. Marchant
	G-MTSZ	Solar Wings Pegasus XL-R	D. L. Pickover
	G-MTTA	Solar Wings Pegasus XL-R	M. Devlin
	G-MTTF	Aerotech MW6 Merlin	P. Cotton
	G-MTTI	Mainair Gemini/Flash IIA	G-MTTI Flying Group
	G-MTTN	Ultralight Flight Phantom	F. P. Welsh
	G-MTTP	Mainair Gemini/Flash IIA	A. Ormson
	G-MTTU	Solar Wings Pegasus XL-R	A. Friend
	G-MTTZ	Solar Wings Pegasus XL-Q	M. O. Bloy
	G-MTUA	Solar Wings Pegasus XL-R	J. & S. Bunyan
	G-MTUC	Thruster TST Mk 1	N. S. Chittenden
	G-MTUN	Solar Wings Pegasus XL-Q	M. J. O'Connor
	G-MTUR	Solar Wings Pegasus XL-Q	G. Ball
	G-MTUS	Solar Wings Pegasus XL-Q	P. W. Davidson
	G-MTUT	Solar Wings Pegasus XL-Q (modified)	R. E. Bull
	G-MTUV	Mainair Gemini/Flash IIA	J. Norton
	G-MTUY	Solar Wings Pegasus XL-Q	H. C. Lowther
	G-MTVC	Solar Wings Pegasus XL-R	A. Duffy
	G-MTVH	Mainair Gemini/Flash IIA	P. H. Statham
	G-MTVP	Thruster TST Mk 1	J. M. Evans
	G-MTVT	Thruster TST Mk.1	W. H. J. Knowles
	G-MTVX	Solar Wings Pegasus XL-Q	D. A. Foster
	G-MTWK	CFM Shadow Srs BD	M. Cooper
	G-MTWR	Mainair Gemini/Flash IIA	J. B. Hodson
	G-MTWS	Mainair Gemini/Flash IIA	A. Robins
	G-MTWX	Mainair Gemini/Flash IIA	K. Walsh
	G-MTWZ	Thruster TST Mk 1	M. J. Aubrey
	G-MTXA	Thruster TST Mk 1	M. A. Franklin
	G-MTXD	Thruster TST Mk 1	D. Newton
	G-MTXK	Solar Wings Pegasus XL-Q	D. R. G. Whitelaw
	G-MTXM	Mainair Gemini/Flash IIA	H. J. Vinning
	G-MTXO	Whittaker MW6	C. A. Harper & R. E. Arnold
	G-MTXR	CFM Shadow Srs BD	G. E. Arnott
	G-MTXZ	Mainair Gemini/Flash IIA	J. S. Hawkins
	G-MTYC	Solar Wings Pegasus XL-Q	C. I. D. H. Garrison
	G-MTYI	Solar Wings Pegasus XL-Q	Q Group
	G-MTYL	Solar Wings Pegasus XL-Q	S. Cooper
	G-MTYS	Solar Wings Pegasus XL-Q	R. G. Wall
	G-MTYV	Southdown Raven X	S. R. Jones
	G-MTYW	Raven X	R. Solomons
	G-MTYY	Solar Wings Pegasus XL-R	L. A. Hosegood
	G-MTZA	Thruster TST Mk 1	J. F. Gallagher
	G-MTZB	Thruster TST Mk 1	J. E. Davies
	G-MTZC	Thruster TST Mk 1	D. J. L. Scott
	G-MTZE	Thruster TST Mk 1	B. S. P. Finch
	G-MTZF	Thruster TST Mk 1	J. D. Buchanan
	G-MTZG	Mainair Gemini/Flash IIA	A. P. Fenn
	G-MTZL	Mainair Gemini/Flash IIA	N. S. Brayn
	G-MTZM	Mainair Gemini/Flash IIA	G. Burns
	G-MTZS	Solar Wings Pegasus XL-Q	T. M. Evans & T. A. Spencer
	G-MTZX	Mainair Gemini/Flash IIA	N. Musgrave
	G-MTZY	Mainair Gemini/Flash IIA	M. D. Leslie
	G-MTZZ	Mainair Gemini/Flash IIA	G. J. Cadden
	G-MUCK	Lindstrand LBL 77A	C. J. Wootton
	G-MUDD	Hughes 369E	Derwen Aggregates Ltd
	G-MUDX	AutoGyro Cavalon	P. R. Biggs (G-CJVT)
	G-MUDY	PA-18-150 Super Cub	C. J. de Sousa e Morgado (G-OTUG)
	G-MUIR	Cameron V-65 balloon	Border Ballooning Ltd
	G-MUJD	Van's RV-12	M. F. El-Deen
	G-MUKY	Van's RV-8	I. E. K. Mackay
	G-MULE	Zenair CH.701UL	H. S. Urquhart (G-ZENA)
	G-MUMY	Vans RV-4	S. D. Howes
	G-MUNI	Mooney M.20J	P. R. Williams
	G-MUPP	Lindstrand LBL-90A balloon	J. A. Viner
	G-MURG	Van's RV-6	D. S. Lawer
	G-MUSH	Robinson R44 II	Topgrade Propertry Management Ltd
	G-MUSM	Colt 77A balloon	The British Balloon Museum and Library Ltd

Reg	Type	Owner or Operator	Notes
G-MUSO	Rutan LongEz	D. J. Gay	
G-MUTE	Colt 31A balloon	M. A. Stelling	
G-MUTS	Jurca MJ.100 Spitfire (X4683:EB-N)	S. M. Johnston & M. S. Rogerson (G-CDPM)	
G-MUTT	CZAW Sportcruiser	R. S. O'Carroll & R. J. Johnstone	
G-MUTZ	Avtech Jabiru J430	N. C. Dean	
G-MUZY	Titan T-51 Mustang (472218:WZ-I)	A. D. Bales	
G-MUZZ	Agusta AW.109SP Grand New	Newshore Holdings Ltd	
G-MVAC	CFM Shadow Srs BD	R. G. Place	
G-MVAH	Thruster TST Mk 1	M. W. H. Henton	
G-MVAI	Thruster TST Mk 1	P. J. Houtman	
G-MVAJ	Thruster TST Mk 1	D. Watson	
G-MVAM	CFM Shadow Srs BD	C. P. Barber	
G-MVAN	CFM Shadow Srs BD	R. W. Frost	
G-MVAR	Solar Wings Pegasus XL-R	A. J. Thomas	
G-MVAY	Solar Wings Pegasus XL-Q	V. O. Morris	
G-MVBC	Aerial Arts Tri-Flyer 130SX	D. Beer	
G-MVBJ	Solar Wings Pegasus XL-R	M. Sims	
G-MVBN	Mainair Gemini/Flash IIA	S. R. Potts	
G-MVBO	Mainair Gemini/Flash IIA	M. Bailey	
G-MVBZ	Solar Wings Pegasus XL-R	J. Greatwood	
G-MVCA	Solar Wings Pegasus XL-R	R. Walker	
G-MVCC	CFM Shadow Srs BD	Walpole Shadow Group	
G-MVCL	Solar Wings Pegasus XL-Q	T. E. Robinson	
G-MVCT	Solar Wings Pegasus XL-Q	G. S. Lampitt	
G-MVCW	CFM Shadow Srs BD	D. A. Coupland	
G-MVCZ	Mainair Gemini/Flash IIA	S. G. Roberts	
G-MVDA	Mainair Gemini/Flash IIA	C. Tweedley	
G-MVDE	Thruster TST Mk 1	M. N. Watson	
G-MVDH	Thruster TST Mk 1	R. J. Whettem	
G-MVDJ	Medway Hybred 44XLR	W. D. Hutchins	
G-MVDK	Aerial Arts Chaser S	P. D. Curtis	
G-MVDL	Aerial Arts Chaser S	N. P. Lloyd	
G-MVDP	Aerial Arts Chaser S	G. J. Slater	
G-MVEG	Solar Wings Pegasus XL-R	A. M. Shaw	
G-MVEH	Mainair Gemini/Flash IIA	D. Evans	
G-MVEI	CFM Shadow Srs BD	R. L. Morgan	
G-MVEL	Mainair Gemini/Flash IIA	M. R. Starling	
G-MVEN	CFM Shadow Srs BD	M. R. Garwood	
G-MVER	Mainair Gemini/Flash IIA	J. R. Davis	
G-MVES	Mainair Gemini/Flash IIA	R. M. Rose	
G-MVET	Mainair Gemini/Flash IIA	J. R. Kendall	
G-MVEV	Mainair Gemini/Flash IIA	K. Davies	
G-MVFB	Solar Wings Pegasus XL-Q	M. O. Bloy	
G-MVFD	Solar Wings Pegasus XL-Q	C. D. Humphries	
G-MVFE	Solar Wings Pegasus XL-Q	S. J. Weeks	
G-MVFF	Solar Wings Pegasus XL-Q	A. Makepiece	
G-MVFH	CFM Shadow Srs BD	T. E. Twyman	
G-MVFJ	Thruster TST Mk 1	B. E. Reneham	
G-MVFL	Thruster TST Mk 1	E. J. Wallington	
G-MVFM	Thruster TST Mk 1	G. J. Boyer	
G-MVFO	Thruster TST Mk 1	A. Whittaker	
G-MVFT	Solar Wings Pegasus XL-R	R. E. Parker	
G-MVFX	Thruster TST Mk 1	A. M. Dalgetty	
G-MVGA	Aerial Arts Chaser S	Golf Alpha Group	
G-MVGC	AMF Chevvron 2-32	W. Fletcher	
G-MVGD	AMF Chevvron 2-32	D. H. Lewis	
G-MVGF	Aerial Arts Chaser S	P. J. Higgins	
G-MVGG	Aerial Arts Chaser S	J. A. Horn	
G-MVGI	Aerial Arts Chaser S	J. R. Kendall	
G-MVGK	Aerial Arts Chaser S	D. J. Smith	
G-MVGO	Solar Wings Pegasus XL-R	J. B. Peacock	
G-MVGP	Solar Wings Pegasus XL-R	J. W. Norman	
G-MVGZ	Ultraflight Lazair IIIE	D. M. Broom	
G-MVHB	Powerchute Raider	G. A. Marples	
G-MVHE	Mainair Gemini/Flash IIA	T. J. McMenamin	
G-MVHH	Mainair Gemini/Flash IIA	D. Rowland	
G-MVHI	Thruster TST Mk 1	G. L. Roberts	
G-MVHJ	Thruster TST Mk 1	T. Welch	
G-MVHK	Thruster TST Mk 1	D. J. Gordon	
G-MVHP	Solar Wings Pegasus XL-Q	J. B. Gasson	

BRITISH CIVIL AIRCRAFT MARKINGS

Notes	Reg	Type	Owner or Operator
	G-MVHR	Solar Wings Pegasus XL-Q	J. M. Hucker
	G-MVIB	Mainair Gemini/Flash IIA	LSA Systems
	G-MVIE	Aerial Arts Chaser S	C. J. Meadows
	G-MVIG	CFM Shadow Srs BD	M. Roberts
	G-MVIH	Mainair Gemini/Flash IIA	T. M. Gilesnan
	G-MVIN	Noble Hardman Snowbird Mk.IV	C. P. Dawes
	G-MVIP	AMF Chevvron 232	J. Pool
	G-MVIR	Thruster TST Mk 1	T. Dziadkiewicz
	G-MVIU	Thruster TST Mk 1	N. Musgrave
	G-MVIX	Mainair Gemini/Flash IIA	A. J. Howard
	G-MVJF	Aerial Arts Chaser S	V. S. Vellacott
	G-MVJG	Aerial Arts Chaser S	T. H. Scott
	G-MVJJ	Aerial Arts Chaser S	C. W. Potts
	G-MVJK	Aerial Arts Chaser S	M. P. Lomax
	G-MVJN	Solar Wings Pegasus XL-Q	E. R. Termini
	G-MVJP	Solar Wings Pegasus XL-Q	S. H. Bakowski
	G-MVJU	Solar Wings Pegasus XL-Q	J. C. Sutton
	G-MVKH	Solar Wings Pegasus XL-R	D. J. Higham
	G-MVKK	Solar Wings Pegasus XL-R	G. P. Burns
	G-MVKL	Solar Wings Pegasus XL-R	B. J. Morton
	G-MVKN	Solar Wings Pegasus XL-Q	D. Bilan
	G-MVKO	Solar Wings Pegasus XL-Q	A. P. Gunston
	G-MVKU	Solar Wings Pegasus XL-Q	I. K. Priestley
	G-MVLA	Aerial Arts Chaser S	K. R. Emery
	G-MVLB	Aerial Arts Chaser S	R. P. Wilkinson
	G-MVLC	Aerial Arts Chaser S	B. R. Barnes
	G-MVLE	Aerial Arts Chaser S	J. M. Hucker
	G-MVLF	Chaser S 508	A. Matheu/Spain
	G-MVLJ	CFM Shadow Srs CD	D. R. C. Pugh
	G-MVLL	Mainair Gemeni/Flash IIA	A. A. Sawera
	G-MVLS	Aerial Arts Chaser S	P. K. Dale
	G-MVLT	Aerial Arts Chaser S	P. H. Newson
	G-MVLX	Solar Wings Pegasus XL-Q	D. J. Harber
	G-MVLY	Solar Wings Pegasus XL-Q	I. B. Osborn
	G-MVMA	Solar Wings Pegasus XL-Q	M. Peters
	G-MVMC	Solar Wings Pegasus XL-Q	M. W. Holmes
	G-MVMI	Thruster TST Mk 1	I. J. Webb
	G-MVML	Aerial Arts Chaser S	G. C. Luddington
	G-MVMR	Mainair Gemini/Flash IIA	P. W. Ramage
	G-MVMT	Mainair Gemini/Flash IIA	R. F. Sanders
	G-MVMX	Mainair Gemini/Flash IIA	E. A. Dygutowicz
	G-MVNC	Powerchute Raider	S. T. P. Askew
	G-MVNE	Powerchute Raider	A. E. Askew
	G-MVNK	Powerchute Raider	A. E. Askew
	G-MVNM	Gemini/Flash IIA	C. D. Phillips
	G-MVNP	Aerotech MW5 (K) Sorcerer	A. M. Edwards
	G-MVNR	Aerotech MW5 (K) Sorcerer	E. I. Rowlands-Jones
	G-MVNS	Aerotech MW5 (K) Sorcerer	A. M. Sirant
	G-MVNT	Aerotech MW5 (K) Sorcerer ★	South Yorkshire Aircraft Museum/Doncaster
	G-MVNX	Mainair Gemini/Flash IIA ◦	A. R. Lynn
	G-MVNY	Mainair Gemini/Flash IIA	M. K. Buckland
	G-MVNZ	Mainair Gemini/Flash IIA	D. A. Ballard
	G-MVOA	Aerial Arts Chaser S 447	W. A. Emmerson
	G-MVOD	Aerial Arts Chaser 110SX	N. R. Beale
	G-MVOJ	Noble Hardman Snowbird Mk IV	C. D. Beetham
	G-MVON	Mainair Gemini/Flash IIA	D. S. Lally
	G-MVOO	AMF Chevvron 2-32	M. K. Field
	G-MVOP	Aerial Arts Chaser S	D. Thorpe
	G-MVOR	Mainair Gemini/Flash IIA	P. T. & R. M. Jenkins
	G-MVOT	Thruster TST Mk 1	D. R. Hoy
	G-MVOV	Thruster TST Mk 1	I. Garforth
	G-MVPA	Mainair Gemini/Flash IIA	D. Hume
	G-MVPC	Mainair Gemini/Flash IIA	W. O. Flannery
	G-MVPD	Mainair Gemini/Flash IIA	P. Thelwel
	G-MVPF	Medway Hybred 44XLR	G. H. Crick
	G-MVPK	CFM Shadow Srs B	B. R. Swindon
	G-MVPM	Whittaker MW6 Merlin	K. W. Curry
	G-MVPR	Solar Wings Pegasus XL-Q	M. G. J. Bridges
	G-MVPS	Solar Wings Pegasus XL-Q	J. Hough
	G-MVPW	Solar Wings Pegasus XL-R	C. A. Mitchell
	G-MVPX	Solar Wings Pegasus XL-Q	J. R. Appleton

Reg	Type	Owner or Operator	Notes
G-MVRD	Mainair Gemini/Flash IIA	J. D. Pearce	
G-MVRG	Aerial Arts Chaser S	T. M. Stiles	
G-MVRH	Solar Wings Pegasus XL-Q	K. Farr	
G-MVRI	Solar Wings Pegasus XL-Q	R. J. Pattinson	
G-MVRM	Mainair Gemini/Flash IIA	M. Davidson	
G-MVRO	CFM Shadow Srs CD	M. G. Read	
G-MVRR	CFM Shadow Srs BD ★	S. P. Christian	
G-MVRS	CFM Shadow Srs BD ★	Aero Venture	
G-MVRT	CFM Shadow Srs CD	C. M. Webb	
G-MVRW	Solar Wings Pegasus XL-Q	C. A. Hamps	
G-MVRZ	Medway Hybred 44XLR	P. J. Higgins	
G-MVSE	Solar Wings Pegasus XL-Q	T. Wilbor	
G-MVSG	Aerial Arts Chaser S	M. Roberts	
G-MVSI	Medway Hybred 44XLR	R. J. Hood	
G-MVSJ	Aviasud Mistral 532	D. Price & C. J. Barnes	
G-MVSL	Aerial Arts Chaser 5	D. M. Pearson	
G-MVSO	Mainair Gemini/Flash IIA	M. Larrad	
G-MVSP	Mainair Gemini/Flash IIA	D. R. Buchanan	
G-MVTD	Whittaker MW6 Merlin	G. R. Reynolds	
G-MVTJ	Solar Wings Pegasus XL-Q	M. P. & R. A. Wells	
G-MVTL	Aerial Arts Chaser S	N. D. Meer	
G-MVTM	Aerial Arts Chaser S	O. G. Johns	
G-MVUA	Mainair Gemini/Flash IIA	K. D. Sinclair-Russell	
G-MVUB	Thruster T.300	A. K. Grayson	
G-MVUC	Medway Hybred 44XLR	B. Pounder	
G-MVUF	Solar Wings Pegasus XL-Q	G. P. Blakemore	
G-MVUG	Solar Wings Pegasus XL-Q	R. A. Allen	
G-MVUI	Solar Wings Pegasus XL-Q	P. E. Hadley & K. Casserley	
G-MVUJ	Solar Wings Pegasus XL-Q	S. J. Huxtable	
G-MVUO	AMF Chevvron 2-32	W. D. M. Turtle	
G-MVUP	Aviasud Mistral 532GB	M. J. Houghton	
G-MVUS	Aerial Arts Chaser S	H. Poyzer	
G-MVUU	Hornet ZA	K. W. Warn	
G-MVVK	Solar Wings Pegasus XL-R	A. J. Weir	
G-MVVO	Solar Wings Pegasus XL-Q	A. L. Scarlett	
G-MVVT	CFM Shadow Srs CD	S. J. Huxtable	
G-MVVV	AMF Chevvron 2-32	J. S. Firth	
G-MVVZ	Powerchute Raider	G. A. Marples	
G-MVWJ	Powerchute Raider	N. J. Doubek	
G-MVWN	Thruster T.300	R. D. Leigh	
G-MVWS	Thruster T.300	P. P. Tame	
G-MVWW	Aviasud Mistral	S. Wood & S. G. A. Milburn	
G-MVXA	Brewster I MW6 (modified SS)	J. C. Gates	
G-MVXN	Aviasud Mistral	P. W. Cade	
G-MVXP	Aerial Arts Chaser S	J. C. Longmore	
G-MVXR	Mainair Gemini/Flash IIA	D. M. Bayne	
G-MVXV	Aviasud Mistral	D. L. Chalk & G. S. Jefferies	
G-MVXX	AMF Chevvron 232	T. R. James	
G-MVYC	Solar Wings Pegasus XL-Q	P. E. L. Street	
G-MVYD	Solar Wings Pegasus XL-Q	J. S. Hawkins	
G-MVYE	Thruster TST Mk 1	M. J. Aubrey	
G-MVYI	Hornet R-ZA	K. W. Warn	
G-MVYU	Snowbird MV.IV (modified)	R. P. Tribe	
G-MVYV	Noble Hardman Snowbird Mk IV	D. W. Hayden	
G-MVYW	Noble Hardman Snowbird Mk IV	T. J. Harrison	
G-MVYX	Noble Hardman Snowbird Mk IV	R. McBlain	
G-MVYY	Aerial Arts Chaser S508	G. H. Crick	
G-MVYZ	CFM Shadow Series BD	D. H. Lewis	
G-MVZA	Thruster T.300	A. I. Milne	
G-MVZC	Thruster T.300	S. Dougan	
G-MVZD	Thruster T.300	P. Heckles	
G-MVZE	Thruster T.300	J. R. Davis	
G-MVZI	Thruster T.300	G. R. Moore	
G-MVZL	Solar Wings Pegasus XL-Q	P. R. Dobson	
G-MVZM	Aerial Arts Chaser S	P. Leigh	
G-MVZO	Medway Hybred 44XLR	S. J. Taft	
G-MVZP	Murphy Renegade Spirit UK	The North American Syndicate	
G-MVZS	Mainair Gemini/Flash IIA	N. McMaster	
G-MVZT	Solar Wings Pegasus XL-Q	C. J. Meadows	
G-MVZU	Solar Wings Pegasus XL-Q	Burlom Aviation	
G-MVZV	Solar Wings Pegasus XL-Q	K. Mudra	

BRITISH CIVIL AIRCRAFT MARKINGS

Notes	Reg	Type	Owner or Operator
	G-MVZX	Renegade Spirit UK	G. Holmes
	G-MVZZ	AMF Chevvron 232	W. A. L. Mitchell
	G-MWAB	Mainair Gemini/Flash IIA	J. E. Buckley
	G-MWAC	Solar Wings Pegasus XL-Q	H. Lloyd-Hughes & D. Jones
	G-MWAE	CFM Shadow Srs BD	S. J. Robson
	G-MWAJ	Murphy Renegade Spirit UK	L. D. Blair
	G-MWAN	Thruster T.300	M. Jady
	G-MWAT	Solar Wings Pegasus XL-Q	C. A. Reid
	G-MWBI	Medway Hybred 44XLR	G. E. Coates
	G-MWBJ	Medway Sprint	C. C. Strong
	G-MWBP	Hornet R-ZA	Foston Hornet Group
	G-MWBS	Hornet RS-ZA	P. D. Jaques
	G-MWBT	Hornet R-ZA	W. Finley & K. W. Warn
	G-MWCC	Solar Wings Pegasus XL-R	I. K. Priestley
	G-MWCE	Mainair Gemini/Flash IIA	B. A. Tooze
	G-MWCF	Solar Wings Pegasus XL-R	S. P. Tkaczyk
	G-MWCG	Microflight Spectrum (modified)	R. J. Hood
	G-MWCH	Rans S.6 Coyote	J. H. Pfaff
	G-MWCK	Powerchute Kestrel	A. E. Askew
	G-MWCM	Powerchute Kestrel	A. E. Askew
	G-MWCN	Powerchute Kestrel	A. E. Askew
	G-MWCO	Powerchute Kestrel	J. R. E. Gladstone
	G-MWCP	Powerchute Kestrel	A. E. Askew
	G-MWCS	Powerchute Kestrel	S. T. P. Askew
	G-MWCY	Medway Hybred 44XLR	J. K. Masters
	G-MWCZ	Medway Hybed 44XLR	D. Botha
	G-MWDB	CFM Shadow Srs BD	T. D. Dawson
	G-MWDI	Hornet RS-ZA	P. D. Curtis
	G-MWDK	Solar Wings Pegasus XL-R	F. J. Windeth
	G-MWDN	CFM Shadow Srs BD	J. J. J. Roberts
	G-MWDS	Thruster T.300	A. W. Nancarrow
	G-MWDZ	Eipper Quicksilver MXL II	R. G. Cook
	G-MWEG	Solar Wings Pegasus XL-Q	E. R. Muneta
	G-MWEH	Solar Wings Pegasus XL-Q	K. A. Davidson
	G-MWEK	Whittaker MW5 Sorcerer	D. W. & M. L. Squire
	G-MWEL	Mainair Gemini/Flash IIA	D. R. Spencer
	G-MWEN	CFM Shadow Srs BD	C. Dawn
	G-MWEO	Whittaker MW5 Sorcerer	P. M. Quinn
	G-MWEP	Rans S.4 Coyote	E. J. Wallington
	G-MWER	Solar Wings Pegasus XL-Q	N. C. Luciano
	G-MWEZ	CFM Shadow Srs CD	G-MWEZ Group
	G-MWFD	TEAM mini-MAX	C. O'Mahoney
	G-MWFF	Rans S.4 Coyote	P. J. Greenrod
	G-MWFL	Powerchute Kestrel	G. A. Marples
	G-MWFS	Solar Wings Pegasus XL-Q	D. R. Williams
	G-MWFT	MBA Tiger Cub 440	J. R. Ravenhill
	G-MWFU	Quad City Challenger II UK	C. J. Whittaker
	G-MWFV	Quad City Challenger II UK	M. Liptrot
	G-MWFW	Rans S.4 Coyote	C. Dewhurst
	G-MWFX	Quad City Challenger II UK	I. M. Walton
	G-MWGI	Whittaker MW5 (K) Sorcerer	J. Aley
	G-MWGJ	Whittaker MW5 (K) Sorcerer	I. Pearson
	G-MWGK	Whittaker MW5 (K) Sorcerer	D. S. Coutts
	G-MWGM	Solar Wings Pegasus XL-Q	I. Davis
	G-MWGR	Solar Wings Pegasus XL-Q	D. Bilan
	G-MWHF	Solar Wings Pegasus XL-Q	N. J. Troke
	G-MWHG	Solar Wings Pegasus XL-Q	M. D. Morris
	G-MWHH	TEAM mini-MAX	R. J. Hood
	G-MWHP	Rans S.6-ESD Coyote	C. P. Barber
	G-MWHR	Mainair Gemini/Flash IIA	J. E. S. Harter
	G-MWHX	Solar Wings Pegasus XL-Q	N. P. Kelly
	G-MWIB	Aviasud Mistral	P. Brady
	G-MWIC	Whittaker MW5-C Sorcerer	P. J. Cheyney
	G-MWIF	Rans S.6-ESD Coyote II	W. J. Boyd
	G-MWIP	Whittaker MW6 Merlin	B. J. Merret & D. Beer
	G-MWIS	Solar Wings Pegasus XL-Q	Burlom Aviation
	G-MWIU	Pegasus Quasar TC	W. Hepburn
	G-MWIZ	CFM Shadow Srs BD	T. A. England
	G-MWJF	CFM Shadow Srs BD	A. J. Briars
	G-MWJH	Solar Wings Pegasus Quasar	L. A. Hosegood

Reg	Type	Owner or Operator	Notes
G-MWJI	Solar Wings Pegasus Quasar	M. G. J. Bridges	
G-MWJJ	Solar Wings Pegasus Quasar	P. Darcy	
G-MWJN	Solar Wings Pegasus XL-Q	J. C. Corrall	
G-MWJT	Solar Wings Pegasus Quasar	F. McGlynn	
G-MWKE	Hornet R-ZA	D. R. Stapleton	
G-MWKX	Microflight Spectrum	C. R. Ions	
G-MWLD	CFM Shadow Srs BD	M. P. Holdstock	
G-MWLE	Solar Wings Pegasus XL-R	D. Stevenson	
G-MWLG	Solar Wings Pegasus XL-R	C. Cohen	
G-MWLL	Solar Wings Pegasus XL-Q	A. J. Bacon	
G-MWLN	Whittaker MW6-S Fatboy Flyer	S. J. Field	
G-MWLP	Mainair Gemini/Flash IIA	K. M. Husecken	
G-MWLS	Medway Hybred 44XLR	M. D. Morris	
G-MWLU	Solar Wings Pegasus XL-R	T. P. G. Ward	
G-MWLW	TEAM mini-MAX	R. J. Ripley	
G-MWLZ	Rans S.4 Coyote	Hedge Hopper Flying Group	
G-MWMB	Powerchute Kestrel	S. T. P. Askew	
G-MWMC	Powerchute Kestrel	S. T. P. Askew	
G-MWMD	Powerchute Kestrel	S. T. P. Askew	
G-MWMF	Powerchute Kestrel	P. J. Blundell	
G-MWMH	Powerchute Kestrel	E. W. Potts	
G-MWMI	SolarWings Pegasus Quasar	R. A. Khosravi	
G-MWML	SolarWings Pegasus Quasar	F. A. Collar	
G-MWMN	Solar Wings Pegasus XL-Q	P. A. Arnold & N. A. Rathbone	
G-MWMO	Solar Wings Pegasus XL-Q	D. S. F. McNair	
G-MWMV	Solar Wings Pegasus XL-R	M. Nutting	
G-MWMW	Renegade Spirit UK	D. M. Casey	
G-MWMX	Mainair Gemini/Flash IIA	P. G. Hughes/Ireland	
G-MWMY	Mainair Gemini/Flash IIA	G. R. Walker	
G-MWNB	Solar Wings Pegasus XL-Q	G. W. F. J. Dear	
G-MWND	Tiger Cub Developments RL.5A	P. J. Houtman	
G-MWNE	Mainair Gemini/Flash IIA	D. N. Brocklesby & S. D. P. Bridge	
G-MWNF	Renegade Spirit UK	R. Haslam	
G-MWNK	Solar Wings Pegasus Quasar	N. Brigginshaw	
G-MWNL	Solar Wings Pegasus Quasar	N. H. S. Install	
G-MWNO	AMF Chevvron 232	J. Pool	
G-MWNP	AMF Chevvron 232	M. K. Field	
G-MWNR	Renegade Spirit UK	RJR Flying Group	
G-MWOC	Powerchute Kestrel	A. Evans	
G-MWOD	Powerchute Kestrel	T. Morgan	
G-MWOI	Solar Wings Pegasus XL-R	B. T. Geoghegan	
G-MWOJ	Mainair Gemini/Flash IIA	C. Nicholson	
G-MWON	CFM Shadow Series CD	D. A. Crosbie	
G-MWOO	Renegade Spirit UK	R. C. Wood	
G-MWOV	Whittaker MW6 Merlin	T. J. Gayton-Polley	
G-MWPH	Microflight Spectrum	C. G. Chambers	
G-MWPN	CFM Shadow Srs CD	W. R. H. Thomas	
G-MWPP	CFM Streak Shadow	R. B. J. Gordon	
G-MWPR	Whittaker MW6 Merlin	S. F. N. Warnell	
G-MWPU	Solar Wings Pegasus Quasar TC	P. R. Murdock	
G-MWPZ	Renegade Spirit UK	G. V. Crowe	
G-MWRC	Mainair Gemini/Flash IIA	C. J. Eddies	
G-MWRE	Mainair Gemini/Flash IIA	M. R. Gaylor	
G-MWRF	Mainair Gemini/Flash IIA	N. Hay	
G-MWRH	Mainair Gemini/Flash IIA	K. J. Hughes	
G-MWRJ	Mainair Gemini/Flash IIA	P. Mansfield	
G-MWRL	CFM Shadow Srs.CD	G-MWRL Group	
G-MWRN	Solar Wings Pegasus XL-R	Malvern Aerotow Club	
G-MWRS	Ultravia Super Pelican	T. B. Woolley	
G-MWRT	Solar Wings Pegasus XL-R	G. L. Gunnell	
G-MWSA	TEAM mini-MAX	A. R. Stratton	
G-MWSC	Rans S.6-ESD Coyote II	E. J. D. Heathfield	
G-MWSD	Solar Wings Pegasus XL-Q	A. M. Harley	
G-MWSF	Solar Wings Pegasus XL-R	J. J. Freeman	
G-MWSI	Solar Wings Pegasus Quasar TC	S. Chambers	
G-MWSJ	Solar Wings Pegasus XL-Q	R. J. Collison	
G-MWSK	Solar Wings Pegasus XL-Q	J. Doogan	
G-MWSM	Mainair Gemini/Flash IIA	D. Isherwood	
G-MWSO	Solar Wings Pegasus XL-R	M. A. Clayton	
G-MWST	Medway Hybred 44XLR	A. Ferguson	
G-MWSX	Whittaker MW5 Sorcerer	A. T. Armstrong	

Notes	Reg	Type	Owner or Operator
	G-MWSY	Whittaker MW5 Sorcerer	J. E. Holloway
	G-MWSZ	CFM Shadow Srs CD	M. W. W. Clotworthy
	G-MWTC	Solar Wings Pegasus XL-Q	M. M. Chittenden
	G-MWTJ	CFM Shadow Srs CS	Shadow Tango Juliet Group
	G-MWTL	Solar Wings Pegasus XL-R	B. Lindsay
	G-MWTN	CFM Shadow Srs CD	M. J. Broom
	G-MWTO	Mainair Gemini/Flash IIA	M. B. Ryder-Jarvis
	G-MWTP	CFM Shadow Srs CD	P. J. F. Spedding
	G-MWTT	Rans S.6-ESD Coyote II	L. E. Duffin
	G-MWUA	CFM Shadow Srs CD	P. A. James
	G-MWUD	Solar Wings Pegasus XL-R	A. J. Weir
	G-MWUI	AMF Chevvron 2-32C	Group G-MWUI
	G-MWUK	Rans S.6-ESD Coyote II	G. K. Hoult
	G-MWUL	Rans S.6-ESD Coyote II	D. M. Bayne
	G-MWUN	Rans S.6-ESD Coyote II	J. Parke
	G-MWUR	Solar Wings Pegasus XL-R	Scottish Hang Gliding Club
	G-MWUU	Solar Wings Pegasus XL-R	B. R. Underwood
	G-MWUV	Solar Wings Pegasus XL-R	XL Group
	G-MWUW	Solar Wings Pegasus XL-R	Ultraflight Microlights Ltd
	G-MWUX	Solar Wings Pegasus XL-Q	B. D. Attwell
	G-MWVA	Solar Wings Pegasus XL-Q	W. Frosina
	G-MWVE	Solar Wings Pegasus XL-R	W. A. Keel-Stocker
	G-MWVF	Solar Wings Pegasus XL-R	J. B. Wright
	G-MWVG	CFM Shadow Srs CD	Shadow Aviation Ltd
	G-MWVH	CFM Shadow Srs CD	M. McKenzie
	G-MWVL	Rans S.6-ESD Coyote II	J. C. Gates
	G-MWVM	Solar Wings Pegasus Quasar II	A. A. Edmonds
	G-MWVO	Mainair Gemini/Flash IIA	P. J. Bishop
	G-MWVP	Renegade Spirit UK	P. D. Mickleburgh
	G-MWVT	Mainair Gemini/Flash IIA	P. J. Newman
	G-MWVZ	Mainair Gemini/Flash IIA	R. W. Twamley
	G-MWWB	Mainair Gemini/Flash IIA	W. P. Seward
	G-MWWD	Renegade Spirit	R. M. Hughes
	G-MWWH	Solar Wings Pegasus XL-Q	R. G. Wall
	G-MWWI	Mainair Gemini/Flash IIA	M. A. S. Nesbitt
	G-MWWN	Mainair Gemini/Flash IIA	M. M. Pope
	G-MWWO	Solar Wings Pegasus XL-R	M. D.Morris
	G-MWWS	Thruster T.300	J. H. Milne
	G-MWWV	Solar Wings Pegasus XL-Q	R. W. Livingstone
	G-MWWZ	Cyclone Chaser S	P. K. Dale
	G-MWXF	Mainair Mercury	C. Dunford
	G-MWXG	Solar Wings Pegasus Quasar TC	I. A. Macadam
	G-MWXH	Solar Wings Pegasus Quasar IITC	R. P. Wilkinson
	G-MWXJ	Mainair Mercury	P. J. Taylor
	G-MWXK	Mainair Mercury	M. P. Wilkinson
	G-MWXP	Solar Wings Pegasus XL-Q	A. P. Attfield
	G-MWXV	Mainair Gemini/Flash IIA	T. A. Daniel
	G-MWXX	Cyclone Chaser S 447	P. I. Frost
	G-MWXY	Cyclone Chaser S 447	P. D. Curtis
	G-MWXZ	Cyclone Chaser S 508	D. L. Hadley
	G-MWYA	Mainair Gemini/Flash IIA	R. F. Hunt
	G-MWYC	Solar Wings Pegasus XL-Q (modified)	M. Sims
	G-MWYD	CFM Shadow Srs C	W. J. I. Robb
	G-MWYE	Rans S.6-ESD Coyote II	S. J. Ward
	G-MWYG	Mainair Gemini/Flash IIA	J. H. McIvor
	G-MWYI	Solar Wings Pegasus Quasar II	C. R. Dunford
	G-MWYJ	Solar Wings Pegasus Quasar IITC	A. S. Wason
	G-MWYL	Mainair Gemini/Flash IIA	A. J. Hinks
	G-MWYM	Cyclone Chaser S 1000	C. J. Meadows
	G-MWYS	CGS Hawk 1 Arrow	Ulster Seaplane Association Ltd
	G-MWYT	Mainair Gemini/Flash IIA	I. Stanulet
	G-MWYU	Solar Wings Pegasus XL-Q	J. S. Hawkins
	G-MWYV	Mainair Gemini/Flash IIA	C. Balazs
	G-MWYY	Mainair Gemini/Flash IIA	R. D. Allard
	G-MWZA	Mainair Mercury	M. Willan
	G-MWZB	AMF Microlight Chevvron 2-32C	E. Ratcliffe
	G-MWZF	Solar Wings Pegasus Quasar IITC	I. A. Macadam
	G-MWZL	Mainair Gemini/Flash IIA	D. Renton
	G-MWZO	Solar Wings Pegasus Quasar IITC	A. Robinson
	G-MWZP	Solar Wings Pegasus Quasar IITC	C. Garton
	G-MWZR	Solar Wings Pegasus Quasar IITC	N. Dyczko

Reg	Type	Owner or Operator	Notes
G-MWZS	Solar Wings Pegasus Quasar IITC	A. M. Charlton	
G-MWZU	Solar Wings Pegasus XL-R	K. J. Slater	
G-MWZY	Solar Wings Pegasus XL-R	Darley Moor Airsports Club Ltd	
G-MWZZ	Solar Wings Pegasus XL-R	The Microlight School Ltd	
G-MXII	Pitts Model 12	P. T. Borchert	
G-MXMX	PA-46R-350T Malibu Matrix	Feabrex Ltd	
G-MXPH	BAC.167 Strikemaster Mk 84 (311)	Voodooair Ltd (G-SARK)	
G-MXPI	Robinson R44 II	MG Group Ltd (G-CAGE)	
G-MXVI	VS.361 Spitfire LF.XVIe (TE184:9N-B)	S. R. Stead	
G-MYAB	Solar Wings Pegasus XL-R	A. N. F. Stewart	
G-MYAC	Solar Wings Pegasus XL-Q	M. E. Gilman	
G-MYAF	Solar Wings Pegasus XL-Q	J. H. S. Booth	
G-MYAH	Whittaker MW5 Sorcerer	A. R. Hawes	
G-MYAN	Whittaker MW5 (K) Sorcerer	A. F. Reid	
G-MYAR	Thruster T.300	G. Hawkins	
G-MYAS	Mainair Gemini/Flash IIA	J. R. Davis	
G-MYAT	TEAM mini-MAX	C. J. Gillam	
G-MYAZ	Renegade Spirit UK	R. Smith	
G-MYBA	Rans S.6-ESD Coyote II	A. M. Hughes	
G-MYBB	Maxair UK Drifter	M. Ingleton	
G-MYBC	CFM Shadow Srs CD	D. A. Crosbie	
G-MYBF	Solar Wings Pegasus XL-Q	S. J. Hillyard	
G-MYBJ	Mainair Gemini/Flash IIA	I. P. Maltas	
G-MYBM	TEAM mini-MAX	B. Hunter	
G-MYBR	Solar Wings Pegasus XL-Q	M. J. Larbey & G. T. Hunt	
G-MYBT	Solar Wings Pegasus Quasar IITC	G. A. Rainbow-Ockwell	
G-MYBU	Cyclone Chaser S 447	P. B. J. Eveleigh	
G-MYBW	Solar Wings Pegasus XL-Q	P. K. Dale	
G-MYCA	Whittaker MW6 Merlin	C. M. Byford	
G-MYCB	Cyclone Chaser S 447	S. D. Voysey	
G-MYCE	Solar Wings Pegasus Quasar IITC	S. W. Barker	
G-MYCL	Mainair Mercury	P. B. Cole	
G-MYCM	CFM Shadow Srs CD	A. K. Robinson	
G-MYCO	Renegade Spirit UK	T. P. Williams	
G-MYCP	Whittaker MW6 Merlin	K. R. Emery	
G-MYCS	Mainair Gemini/Flash IIA	M. J. Rankin	
G-MYCT	Team Minimax 91	T. B. Livermore	
G-MYCX	Powerchute Kestrel	S. J. Pugh-Jones	
G-MYDA	Powerchute Kestrel	A. E. Askew	
G-MYDC	Mainair Mercury	D. Moore	
G-MYDE	CFM Shadow Srs CD	D. N. L. Howell	
G-MYDF	TEAM mini-MAX	J. L. Barker	
G-MYDK	Rans S.6-ESD Coyote II	J. W. Caush & K. Southam	
G-MYDN	Quad City Challenger II	J. E. Barlow	
G-MYDT	Thruster T.300	A. J. L. Eves	
G-MYDU	Thruster T.300	S. Collins	
G-MYDV	Mainair Gemini /Flash IIA	S. J. Mazilis	
G-MYDX	Rans S.6-ESD Coyote II	A. Tucker	
G-MYDZ	Mignet HM.1000 Balerit	D. S. Simpson	
G-MYEA	Solar Wings Pegasus XL-Q	A. M. Taylor	
G-MYEI	Cyclone Chaser S503	D. J. Hyatt	
G-MYEJ	Cyclone Chaser S447	A. W. Lowrie	
G-MYEK	Solar Wings Pegasus Quasar IITC	The Microlight School Ltd	
G-MYEM	Solar Wings Pegasus Quasar IITC	D. J. Moore	
G-MYEN	Solar Wings Pegasus Quasar IITC	T. J. Feeney	
G-MYEO	Solar Wings Pegasus Quasar IITC	A. R. Young	
G-MYEP	CFM Shadow Srs. CD	S. T. Dixon	
G-MYER	Cyclone AX3/503	T. F. Horrocks	
G-MYFA	Powerchute Kestrel	M. Phillips	
G-MYFL	Solar Wings Pegasus Quasar IITC	C. C. Wright	
G-MYFO	Cyclone Airsports Chaser S	M. H. Broadbent	
G-MYFP	Mainair Gemini/Flash IIA	A. O'Connor	
G-MYFV	Cyclone AX3/503	I. J. Webb	
G-MYGD	Cyclone AX3/503	G. M. R. Keenan	
G-MYGF	TEAM mini-MAX	A. S. R. Galley	
G-MYGK	Cyclone Chaser S 508	P. C. Collins	
G-MYGM	Quad City Challenger II	S. J. Luck	
G-MYGO	CFM Shadow Series CD	D. B. Bullard	
G-MYGP	Rans S.6-ESD Coyote II	The Spirit of Goole	

Notes	Reg	Type	Owner or Operator
	G-MYGR	Rans S.6-ESD Coyote II	S-J. Huxtable
	G-MYGT	Solar Wings Pegasus XL-R	Condors Aerotow Syndicate
	G-MYGU	Solar Wings Pegasus XL-R	J. A. Sims
	G-MYGV	Solar Wings Pegasus XL-R	J. A. Crofts & G. M. Birkett
	G-MYHG	Cyclone AX/503	N. P. Thomson
	G-MYHJ	Cyclone AX3/503	D. H. Edwards
	G-MYHK	Rans S.6-ESD Coyote II	R. A. Durance
	G-MYHL	Mainair Gemini/Flash IIA	O. G. Houghton
	G-MYHM	Cyclone AX3/503	G-MYHM Group
	G-MYHN	Mainair Gemini/Flash IIA	S. N. Pryor
	G-MYHP	Rans S.6-ESD Coyote II	D. M. Smith
	G-MYIA	Quad City Challenger II	I. Pearson
	G-MYIF	CFM Shadow Srs CD	P. J. Edwards
	G-MYII	TEAM mini-MAX	G. H. Crick
	G-MYIK	Kolb Twinstar Mk 3	M. Khalid
	G-MYIL	Cyclone Chaser S 508	R. A. Rawes
	G-MYIP	CFM Shadow Srs CD	D. R. G. Whitelaw
	G-MYIR	Rans S.6-ESD Coyote II	M. L. Foden
	G-MYIS	Rans S.6-ESD Coyote II	I. S. Everett & M. Stott
	G-MYIT	Cyclone Chaser S 508	M. P. Hadden
	G-MYIU	Cyclone AX3/503	Ulster Seaplane Association Ltd
	G-MYIV	Mainair Gemini/Flash IIA	P. Norton & T. Williams
	G-MYIY	Mainair Gemini/Flash IIA	D. Jackson
	G-MYIZ	TEAM mini-MAX 2	J. C. Longmore
	G-MYJC	Mainair Gemini/Flash IIA	M. N. Irven
	G-MYJD	Rans S.6-ESD Coyote II	U. Chakravorty
	G-MYJF	Thruster T.300	P. F. McConville
	G-MYJG	Thruster T.300	J. W. Rice
	G-MYJJ	Solar Wings Pegasus Quasar IITC	G. Stewart
	G-MYJM	Mainair Gemini/Flash IIA	J. G. Treanor
	G-MYJU	Solar Wings Pegasus Quasar IITC	C. Lamb
	G-MYJX	Whittaker MW8 ★	South Yorkshire Aircraft Museum/Doncaster
	G-MYJZ	Whittaker MW5D Sorcerer	P. A. Aston
	G-MYKB	Kolb Twinstar Mk 3	T. Antell
	G-MYKD	Cyclone Chaser S 508	S. D. Pain
	G-MYKE	CFM Shadow Srs BD	MKH Engineering
	G-MYKF	Cyclone AX3/503	M. A. Collins
	G-MYKG	Mainair Gemini/Flash IIA	B. D. Walker
	G-MYKH	Mainair Gemini/Flash IIA	A. W. Leadley
	G-MYKJ	TEAM mini-MAX	J. P. Pullin
	G-MYKO	Whittaker MW6-S Fat Boy Flyer	J. A. Weston
	G-MYKR	Solar Wings Pegasus Quasar IITC	C. Stallard
	G-MYKS	Solar Wings Pegasus Quasar IITC	Hire & Higher Ltd
	G-MYKV	Mainair Gemini/Flash IIA	P. J. Gulliver
	G-MYKX	Mainair Mercury	K. Medd
	G-MYKY	Mainair Mercury	P. M. Kelsey
	G-MYKZ	TEAM mini-MAX	C. H. Smith
	G-MYLC	Solar Wings Pegasus Quantum 15	M. D. Morris
	G-MYLD	Rans S.6-ESD Coyote II	A. W. Nancarrow
	G-MYLE	Solar Wings Pegasus Quantum 15	Quantum Quartet
	G-MYLF	Rans S.6-ESD Coyote II	A. J. Spencer
	G-MYLG	Mainair Gemini/Flash IIA	N. J. Axworthy
	G-MYLH	Solar Wings Pegasus Quantum 15	D. Parsons
	G-MYLI	Solar Wings Pegasus Quantum 15	A. M. Keyte
	G-MYLM	Solar Wings Pegasus Quasar IITC	R. G. Hearsey
	G-MYLN	Kolb Twinstar Mk 3	J. F. Joyes
	G-MYLR	Mainair Gemini/Flash IIA	A. L. Lyall
	G-MYLS	Mainair Mercury	W. K. C. Davies
	G-MYLT	Mainair Blade	T. D. Hall
	G-MYLV	CFM Shadow Srs CD	Aviation for Paraplegics and Tetraplegics Trust
	G-MYLW	Rans S6-ESD Coyote II	T. E. Kiy
	G-MYMC	Solar Wings Pegasus Quantum 15	I. A. Macadam
	G-MYMH	Rans S.6-ESD Coyote II	W. R. Laing
	G-MYMI	Kolb Twinstar Mk.3	F. J. Brown
	G-MYMJ	Medway Raven	N. Brigginshaw
	G-MYMK	Mainair Gemini/Flash IIA	C. L. M. Haywood
	G-MYMM	Ultraflight Fun 18S	N. P. Power
	G-MYMN	Whittaker MW6 Merlin	R. E. Arnold
	G-MYMS	Rans S.6-ESD Coyote II	G. R. Wilson & S. Gibson
	G-MYMW	Cyclone AX3/503	D. I. Lee
	G-MYMZ	Cyclone AX3/503	M. A. Cox

Reg	Type	Owner or Operator	Notes
G-MYNB	Solar Wings Pegasus Quantum 15	N. Robinson	
G-MYNE	Rans S.6-ESD Coyote II	J. L. Smoker	
G-MYNF	Mainair Mercury	S. Carter	
G-MYNI	TEAM mini-MAX	I. Pearson	
G-MYNK	Solar Wings Pegasus Quantum 15	M. T. Cain	
G-MYNL	Solar Wings Pegasus Quantum 15	I. J. Rawlingson	
G-MYNN	Solar Wings Pegasus Quantum 15	V. Loy	
G-MYNP	Solar Wings Pegasus Quantum 15	K. A. Davidson	
G-MYNR	Solar Wings Pegasus Quantum 15	M. R. Mosley	
G-MYNS	Solar Wings Pegasus Quantum 15	W. R. Furness	
G-MYNT	Solar Wings Pegasus Quantum 15	N. Ionita	
G-MYNX	CFM Streak Shadow SA	S. P. Fletcher	
G-MYNY	Kolb Twinstar Mk 3	A. Vaughan	
G-MYNZ	Solar Wings Pegasus Quantum 15	P. W. Rogers	
G-MYOA	Rans S6-ESD Coyote II	P-M. Cavallucci	
G-MYOG	Kolb Twinstar Mk 3	T. A. Womersley	
G-MYOH	CFM Shadow Srs CD	S. E. Lyden	
G-MYOL	Air Creation Fun 18S GTBIS	Condors Aerotow	
G-MYON	CFM Shadow Srs CD	D. J. Shaw	
G-MYOS	CFM Shadow Srs CD	C. A. & E. J. Bowles	
G-MYOU	Solar Wings Pegasus Quantum 15	D. J. Tasker	
G-MYOX	Mainair Mercury	K. Driver	
G-MYPA	Rans S.6-ESD Coyote II	J. D. Avey	
G-MYPE	Mainair Gemini/Flash IIA	A. Matthews	
G-MYPH	Solar Wings Pegasus Quantum 15	I. E. Chapman	
G-MYPI	Solar Wings Pegasus Quantum 15	P. L. Jarvis & D. S. Ross	
G-MYPJ	Rans S.6-ESD Coyote II	K. A. Eden	
G-MYPL	CFM Shadow Srs CD	G. I. Madden	
G-MYPM	Cyclone AX3/503	A. A. Ahmed	
G-MYPN	Solar Wings Pegasus Quantum 15	C. M. Boswell	
G-MYPR	Cyclone AX3/503	W. J. I. Robb	
G-MYPS	Whittaker MW6 Merlin	I. S. Bishop	
G-MYPT	CFM Shadow Srs CD	R. Gray	
G-MYPV	Mainair Mercury	R. Whitworth	
G-MYPW	Mainair Gemini/Flash IIA	P. Lacon & K. Tunnicliff	
G-MYPZ	BFC Challenger II	J. I. Gledhill & J. Harvard	
G-MYRD	Mainair Blade	G. Kirsch	
G-MYRE	Cyclone Chaser S	S. W. Barker	
G-MYRF	Solar Wings Pegasus Quantum 15	K. N. Mosby	
G-MYRG	TEAM mini-MAX	A. R. Hawes	
G-MYRK	Renegade Spirit UK	B. J. Palfreyman	
G-MYRL	TEAM mini-MAX	J. N. Hanson	
G-MYRP	Letov LK-2M Sluka	R. M. C. Hunter	
G-MYRS	Solar Wings Pegasus Quantum 15	N. H. Kirk	
G-MYRT	Solar Wings Pegasus Quantum 15	G. P. Preston	
G-MYRW	Mainair Mercury	G. C. Hobson	
G-MYRZ	Solar Wings Pegasus Quantum 15	R. E. Forbes	
G-MYSA	Cyclone Chaser S508	P. W. Dunn & A. R. Vincent	
G-MYSB	Solar Wings Pegasus Quantum 15	The Microlight School Ltd	
G-MYSC	Solar Wings Pegasus Quantum 15	K. R. White	
G-MYSD	BFC Challlenger II	C. W. Udale	
G-MYSJ	Mainair Gemini/Flash IIA	N. J. Wray	
G-MYSK	Team Minimax 91	T. D. Wolstenholme	
G-MYSL	Aviasud Mistral	R. D. Ainley	
G-MYSR	Solar Wings Pegasus Quantum 15	M. P. Bawden	
G-MYSU	Rans S.6-ESD Coyote II	W. Matthews	
G-MYSV	Aerial Arts Chaser	G. S. Highley	
G-MYSW	Solar Wings Pegasus Quantum 1	M. Richardson	
G-MYSY	Solar Wings Pegasus Quantum 15	G. E. Murphy	
G-MYSZ	Mainair Mercury	W. Fletcher	
G-MYTB	Mainair Mercury	P. J. Higgins	
G-MYTD	Mainair Blade	D. B. Meades	
G-MYTE	Rans S.6-ESD Coyote II	M. F. Hadley	
G-MYTH	CFM Shadow Srs CD	W. J. I. Robb	
G-MYTI	Solar Wings Pegasus Quantum 15	K. M. Gaffney	
G-MYTJ	Solar Wings Pegasus Quantum 15	L. Blight	
G-MYTK	Mainair Mercury	D. A. Holroyd	
G-MYTL	Mainair Blade	C. Richards	
G-MYTN	Solar Wings Pegasus Quantum 15	D. J. T. Reckitt	
G-MYTO	Quad City Challenger II	A. Studley	
G-MYTP	Arrowflight Hawk II	R. J. Turner	

Notes	Reg	Type	Owner or Operator
	G-MYTT	Quad City Challenger II	P. W. Brush
	G-MYTU	Mainair Blade	A. P. Pearce
	G-MYTY	CFM Streak Shadow Srs M	Adventurer's SSDR Group
	G-MYUA	Air Creation Fun 18S GTBIS	A. Shaw
	G-MYUC	Mainair Blade	R. Moss
	G-MYUF	Renegade Spirit	B. W. Webb & S. R. Greasley
	G-MYUH	Solar Wings Pegasus XL-Q	K. S. Daniels
	G-MYUI	Cyclone AX3/503	G. J. Hanlon
	G-MYUJ	Murphy Maverick 430	P. J. Porter (G-ONFL)
	G-MYUN	Mainair Blade	G. A. Barratt
	G-MYUO	Solar Wings Pegasus Quantum 15	E. J. Hughes
	G-MYUP	Letov LK-2M Sluka	G. N. Holland
	G-MYUV	Pegasus Quantum 15	I. Tulkan
	G-MYUW	Mainair Mercury	G. C. Hobson
	G-MYVA	Kolb Twinstar Mk 3	E. Bayliss
	G-MYVB	Mainair Blade	S. Gaskell
	G-MYVC	Pegasus Quantum 15	M. A. Cox
	G-MYVG	Letov LK-2M Sluka	A. Evans
	G-MYVI	Air Creation Fun 18S GTBIS	D. Rowland
	G-MYVJ	Pegasus Quantum 15	A. I. McPherson & P. W. Davidson
	G-MYVK	Pegasus Quantum 15	T. P. C. Hague
	G-MYVM	Pegasus Quantum 15	G. J. Gibson
	G-MYVN	Cyclone AX3/503	F. Watt
	G-MYVO	Mainair Blade	Victor Oscar Group
	G-MYVP	Rans S.6-ESD Coyote II	M. Jady
	G-MYVV	Medway Hybred 44XLR	S. Perity
	G-MYVZ	Mainair Blade	W. C. Hyner
	G-MYWE	Thruster T.600	R. J. Adams
	G-MYWF	CFM Shadow Srs CD	J. Preller
	G-MYWG	Pegasus Quantum 15	S. L. Greene
	G-MYWI	Pegasus Quantum 15	M. S. Ahmadu
	G-MYWJ	Pegasus Quantum 15	L. M. Sams & I. Clarkson
	G-MYWK	Pegasus Quantum 15	S. N. Pryor
	G-MYWL	Pegasus Quantum 15	R. P. McGuffie
	G-MYWM	CFM Shadow Srs CD	N. McKinley
	G-MYWO	Pegasus Quantum 15	K. Grimley
	G-MYWR	Pegasus Quantum 15	The Microlight School Ltd
	G-MYWS	Cyclone Chaser S 447	M. H. Broadbent
	G-MYWU	Pegasus Quantum 15	P. L. Owen
	G-MYWV	Rans S.4C Coyote	G. J. Simon
	G-MYWW	Pegasus Quantum 15	T. A. Dockrell
	G-MYWY	Pegasus Quantum 15	J. P. Rooms
	G-MYXA	TEAM mini-MAX 91	D. C. Marsh
	G-MYXB	Rans S.6-ESD Coyote II	M. Gaffney
	G-MYXD	Pegasus Quasar IITC	A. Knight
	G-MYXE	Pegasus Quantum 15	A. A. Bolton
	G-MYXH	Cyclone AX3/503	T. de Breffe Gardner
	G-MYXI	Aries 1	H. Cook
	G-MYXJ	Mainair Blade	S. N. Robson
	G-MYXL	Mignet HM.1000 Baleri	R. W. Hollamby
	G-MYXM	Mainair Blade	C. Johnson
	G-MYXN	Mainair Blade	J. C. Birkbeck
	G-MYXO	Letov LK-2M Sluka	J. R. Surbey & A. Furness
	G-MYXT	Pegasus Quantum 15	L. A. Washer
	G-MYXU	Thruster T.300	D. W. Wilson
	G-MYXV	Quad City Challenger II	T. S. Savage
	G-MYXW	Pegasus Quantum 15	J. Uttley
	G-MYXX	Pegasus Quantum 15	K. A. Davidson
	G-MYXZ	Pegasus Quantum 15	Opes Independent Financial Advisers Ltd
	G-MYYA	Mainair Blade	D. J. Harrison
	G-MYYB	Pegasus Quantum 15	A. L. Johnson & D. S. Ross
	G-MYYC	Pegasus Quantum 15	T. R. E. Goldfield
	G-MYYF	Quad City Challenger II	L. E. J. Wojciechowski
	G-MYYH	Mainair Blade	D. J. Dodd
	G-MYYI	Pegasus Quantum 15	C. M. Day
	G-MYYK	Pegasus Quantum 15	N. Ionita
	G-MYYL	Cyclone AX3/503	D. Roach
	G-MYYR	TEAM mini-MAX 91	A. Munn
	G-MYYS	TEAM mini-MAX	D. Brunton
	G-MYYV	Rans S.6-ESD XL Coyote II	R. C. Parsons
	G-MYYY	Mainair Blade	R. T. Kirby

Reg	Type	Owner or Operator	Notes
G-MYYZ	Medway Raven X	J. W. Leaper	
G-MYZB	Pegasus Quantum 15	I. K. Priestley	
G-MYZC	Cyclone AX3/503	P. F. J. Rogers	
G-MYZF	Cyclone AX3/503	Ulster Seaplane Association Ltd	
G-MYZG	Cyclone AX3/503	C. J. Browne	
G-MYZH	Chargus Titan 38	T. J. Gayton-Polley	
G-MYZJ	Pegasus Quantum 15	K. Foyen	
G-MYZL	Pegasus Quantum 15	R. F. Greaves	
G-MYZP	CFM Shadow Srs DD	I. G. Poutney	
G-MYZR	Rans S.6-ESD XL Coyote II	N. R. Beale	
G-MYZV	Rans S.6-ESD XL Coyote II	I. M. Charlwood	
G-MYZY	Pegasus Quantum 15	L. Hurman	
G-MZAB	Mainair Blade	D. Brennan	
G-MZAC	Quad City Challenger II	T. R. Gregory	
G-MZAE	Mainair Blade	A. P. Finn	
G-MZAF	Mainair Blade	P. F. Mayes	
G-MZAG	Mainair Blade	M. J. P. Sanderson	
G-MZAK	Mainair Mercury	I. Rawson	
G-MZAM	Mainair Blade	R. J. Coppin	
G-MZAN	Pegasus Quantum 15	P. M. Leahy	
G-MZAR	Mainair Blade	T. H. Beales	
G-MZAS	Mainair Blade	T. Carter	
G-MZAT	Mainair Blade	S. Elmazouri	
G-MZAU	Mainair Blade	A. F. Glover	
G-MZAW	Pegasus Quantum 15	O. O'Donnell	
G-MZAZ	Mainair Blade	A. W. Gunn	
G-MZBC	Pegasus Quantum 15	B. M. Quinn	
G-MZBD	Rans S-6-ESD-XL Coyote II	W. E. Tinsley	
G-MZBF	Letov LK-2M Sluka	V. Simpson	
G-MZBG	Hodder MW6-A	E. I. Rowlands-Jons & M. W. Kilvert	
G-MZBH	Rans S.6-ESD Coyote II	G. L. Campbell	
G-MZBK	Letov LK-2M Sluka	R. M. C. Hunter	
G-MZBL	Mainair Blade	C. J. Rubery	
G-MZBN	CFM Shadow Srs B	W. J. Buskell	
G-MZBS	CFM Shadow Srs D	T. P. Ryan	
G-MZBT	Pegasus Quantum 15	M. L. Saunders	
G-MZBU	Rans S.6-ESD Coyote II	R. S. Marriott	
G-MZBW	Quad City Challenger II UK	R. M. C. Hunter	
G-MZBY	Pegasus Quantum 15	P. L. Wilkinson	
G-MZBZ	Quad City Challenger II UK	T. R. Gregory	
G-MZCB	Cyclone Chaser S 447	A. R. Vincent & P. W. Dunn	
G-MZCC	Mainair Blade 912	K. S. Rissmann	
G-MZCE	Mainair Blade	I. C. Hindle	
G-MZCF	Mainair Blade	C. Hannanby	
G-MZCI	Pegasus Quantum 15	R. J. Hemmings	
G-MZCK	AMF Chevvron 2-32C	S. Mebarki	
G-MZCM	Pegasus Quantum 15	J. M. Reed & L. Smith	
G-MCZR	Pegasus Quantum 15	I. A. Macadam	
G-MZCS	TEAM mini-MAX	J. Aley	
G-MZCT	CFM Shadow Srs CD	W. G. Gill	
G-MZCU	Mainair Blade	C. E. Pearce	
G-MZCV	Pegasus Quantum 15	D. R. Langton	
G-MZCW	Pegasus Quantum 15	K. L. Baldwin	
G-MZCX	Huntwing Avon Skytrike	A. I. Sutherland	
G-MZCY	Pegasus Quantum 15	G. Murphy	
G-MZDA	Rans S.6-ESD Coyote IIXL	R. Plummer	
G-MZDB	Pegasus Quantum 15	M. Heron	
G-MZDC	Pegasus Quantum 15	C. Garton	
G-MZDD	Pegasus Quantum 15	S. D. P. Bridge	
G-MZDF	Mainair Blade	M. Liptrot	
G-MZDG	Rans S.6-ESD Coyote IIXL	P. Coates	
G-MZDH	Pegasus Quantum 15	G-MZDH Flying Group	
G-MZDI	Whittaker MW6-S Fat Boy Flyer	C. M. Byford (G-BUNN)	
G-MZDJ	Medway Raven X	R. Bryan & S. Digby	
G-MZDK	Mainair Blade	R. H. de Castro Ribeiro	
G-MZDM	Rans S.6-ESD Coyote II	M. E. Nicholas	
G-MZDN	Pegasus Quantum 15	N. Cross	
G-MZDS	Cyclone AX3/503	M. J. Cooper	
G-MZDT	Mainair Blade	R. L. Beese	
G-MZDU	Pegasus Quantum 15	J. J. D. Firmino do Carmo	

Notes	Reg	Type	Owner or Operator
	G-MZDV	Pegasus Quantum 15	Griffin Toomes Consulting Engineers Ltd
	G-MZDX	Letov LK-2M Sluka	J. L. Barker
	G-MZDY	Pegasus Quantum 15	D. T. Moeller
	G-MZDZ	Hunt Wing	E. W. Laidlaw
	G-MZEA	BFC Challenger II	G. S. Cridland
	G-MZEB	Mainair Blade	R. A. Campbell
	G-MZEC	Pegasus Quantum 15	A. B. Godber
	G-MZEE	Pegasus Quantum 15	I. W. & J. R. King
	G-MZEG	Mainair Blade	E. D. R. Hill
	G-MZEH	Pegasus Quantum 15	P. S. Hall
	G-MZEK	Mainair Mercury	G. Crane
	G-MZEM	Pegasus Quantum 15	L. H. Black
	G-MZEN	Rans S.6-ESD Coyote II	R. Mills
	G-MZES	Letov LK-2M Sluka	A. P. Love
	G-MZEU	Rans S-6-ESD XL Coyote II	P. Wilcox
	G-MZEV	Mainair Rapier	W. T. Gardner
	G-MZEW	Mainair Blade	D. J. Harrison
	G-MZEX	Pegasus Quantum 15	D. A. Eastough
	G-MZEZ	Pegasus Quantum 15	M. J. Hunt
	G-MZFA	Cyclone AX2000	G. S. Highley
	G-MZFB	Mainair Blade	A. J. Plant
	G-MZFC	Letov LK-2M Sluka	D. W. Bayliss
	G-MZFD	Mainair Rapier	J. Williams
	G-MZFE	Hunt Wing	G. J. Latham
	G-MZFF	Hunt Wing	B. J. Adamson
	G-MZFH	AMF Chevvron 2-32C	Eagle Flying Group
	G-MZFL	Rans S.6-ESD Coyote IIXL	J. J. Lynch
	G-MZFM	Pegasus Quantum 15	N. Musgrave
	G-MZFO	Thruster T.600N	D. A. Noble
	G-MZFS	Mainair Blade	P. L. E. Zelakowski
	G-MZFU	Thruster T.600N	M. I. Garner
	G-MZFX	Cyclone AX2000	AX Group
	G-MZFY	Rans S.6-ESD Coyote IIXL	L. G. Tserkezos
	G-MZFZ	Mainair Blade	D. J. Bateman
	G-MZGA	Cyclone AX2000	R. D. Leigh
	G-MZGC	Cyclone AX2000	T. J. McMenamin
	G-MZGD	Rans S.5 Coyote II	P. J. Greenrod
	G-MZGF	Letov LK-2M Sluka	T. W. Thiele
	G-MZGG	Pegasus Quantum 15	J. M. Chapman
	G-MZGH	Hunt Wing/Avon 462(3)	J. H. Cole
	G-MZGI	Mainair Blade 912	H. M. Roberts
	G-MZGL	Mainair Rapier	A. Robins
	G-MZGM	Cyclone AX2000	A. F. Smallacombe
	G-MZGN	Pegasus Quantum 15	J. B. Peacock
	G-MZGO	Pegasus Quantum 15	S. F. G. Allen
	G-MZGP	Cyclone AX2000	Buchan Light Aeroplane Club
	G-MZGR	TEAM mini-MAX	K. G. Seeley
	G-MZGU	Arrowflight Hawk II (UK)	M. C. Holmes
	G-MZGW	Mainair Blade	R. C. Ford
	G-MZGY	Thruster T.600N 450	C. F. Janes
	G-MZHA	Thruster T.600N	C. Green
	G-MZHB	Mainair Blade	J. F. Davies
	G-MZHD	Thruster T.600N	J. Walsh & A. R. Sunley
	G-MZHF	Thruster T.600N	C. Carmichael
	G-MZHG	Whittaker MW6-S Merlin	J. L. Jordan
	G-MZHI	Pegasus Quantum 15	M. A. Gardiner
	G-MZHJ	Mainair Rapier	G. Standish
	G-MZHM	Team Himax 1700R	M. H. McKeown
	G-MZHN	Pegasus Quantum 15	F. W. Ferichs
	G-MZHO	Quad City Challenger II	J. Pavelin
	G-MZHP	Pegasus Quantum 15	W. J. Flood
	G-MZHR	Cyclone AX2000	T. P. Williams
	G-MZHS	Thruster T.600T	G-MZHS Group
	G-MZHV	Thruster T.600T	H. G. Denton
	G-MZHW	Thruster T.600N	A. J. Glynn
	G-MZHY	Thruster T.600N	B. W. Webster
	G-MZIB	Pegasus Quantum 15	S. Murphy
	G-MZID	Whittaker MW6 Merlin	C. P. F. Sheppard
	G-MZIH	Mainair Blade 912	N. J. Waller
	G-MZIJ	Pegasus Quantum 15	D. L. Wright
	G-MZIK	Pegasus Quantum 15	J. H. Cole

Reg	Type	Owner or Operator	Notes
G-MZIL	Mainair Rapier	B. L. Cook	
G-MZIS	Mainair Blade	M. K. Richings	
G-MZIT	Mainair Blade 912	M. A. Robinson	
G-MZIU	Pegasus Quantum 15-912	E. A. McCabe	
G-MZIV	Cyclone AX2000	B. Burrows	
G-MZIW	Mainair Blade	E. McCallum	
G-MZIZ	Renegade Spirit UK (G-MWGP)	C. B. Hopkins	
G-MZJA	Mainair Blade	D. M. Whelan	
G-MZJE	Mainair Rapier	N. E. Smith	
G-MZJF	Cyclone AX2000	D. J. Lewis	
G-MZJG	Pegasus Quantum 15	J. D. Moon	
G-MZJH	Pegasus Quantum 15	P. Copping	
G-MZJI	Rans S-6-ESD-XL Coyote II	J. P. Hunsdale	
G-MZJJ	Murphy Maverick	M. F. Farrer	
G-MZJK	Mainair Blade	P. G. Angus	
G-MZJL	Cyclone AX2000	M. H. Owen	
G-MZJM	Rans S.6-ESD Coyote IIXL	B. Lorriane	
G-MZJO	Pegasus Quantum 15	P. S. Hall	
G-MZJP	Whittaker MW6-S Fatboy Flyer	R. C. Funnell & D. J. Burton	
G-MZJT	Pegasus Quantum 15	N. Hammerton	
G-MZJV	Mainair Blade 912	M. A. Roberts	
G-MZJW	Pegasus Quantum 15	G. A. & G. E. Blackstone	
G-MZJY	Pegasus Quantum 15	R. G. Wyatt	
G-MZJZ	Mainair Blade	Lima Zulu Owner Syndicate	
G-MZKA	Pegasus Quantum 15	S. P. Tkaczyk	
G-MZKC	Cyclone AX2000	D. J. Pike	
G-MZKD	Pegasus Quantum 15	T. M. Frost	
G-MZKE	Rans S.6-ESD Coyote IIXL	P. A. Flaherty	
G-MZKF	Pegasus Quantum 15	A. H., D. P. & V. J. Tidmas	
G-MZKG	Mainair Blade	N. S. Rigby	
G-MZKH	CFM Shadow Srs DD	S. P. H. Calvert	
G-MZKI	Mainair Rapier	D. L. Aspinall	
G-MZKJ	Mainair Blade	The G-MZKJ Group	
G-MZKL	Pegasus Quantum 15	G-MZKL Group	
G-MZKN	Mainair Rapier	O. P. Farrell	
G-MZKS	Thruster T.600N	J. R. Gardiner	
G-MZKU	Thruster T.600N	A. S. Day	
G-MZKW	Quad City Challenger II	R. A. Allen	
G-MZKY	Pegasus Quantum 15	P. S. Constable	
G-MZLA	Pegasus Quantum 15	A. C. Hodges	
G-MZLD	Pegasus Quantum 15	L. Sokoli	
G-MZLE	Maverick (G-BXSZ)	M. W. Hands	
G-MZLF	Pegasus Quantum 15	S. Seymour	
G-MZLG	Rans S.6-ESD Coyote IIXL	J. Passfield	
G-MZLI	Mignet HM.1000 Balerit	A. G. Barr	
G-MZLJ	Pegasus Quantum 15	M. J. Hyde	
G-MZLL	Rans S.6-ESD Coyote II	D. W. Adams	
G-MZLM	Cyclone AX2000	P. E. Hadley	
G-MZLN	Pegasus Quantum 15	P. A. Greening	
G-MZLP	CFM Shadow Srs D	D. J. Gordon	
G-MZLT	Pegasus Quantum 15	B. Jackson	
G-MZLU	Cyclone AX2000	E. Pashley	
G-MZLV	Pegasus Quantum 15	R. R. Till	
G-MZLW	Pegasus Quantum 15	R. W. R. Crevel	
G-MZLX	Micro Aviation B.22S Bantam	V. J. Vaughan	
G-MZLY	Letov LK-2M Sluka	W. McCarthy	
G-MZMA	Solar Wings Pegasus Quasar IITC	V. Donskovas	
G-MZMC	Pegasus Quantum 15	J. J. Baker	
G-MZME	Medway Eclipser	T. A. Dobbins	
G-MZMF	Pegasus Quantum 15	A. J. Tranter	
G-MZMG	Pegasus Quantum 15	C. J. Meadows	
G-MZMH	Pegasus Quantum 15	A. K. Hole	
G-MZMJ	Mainair Blade	D. Wilson	
G-MZMK	Chevvron 2-32C	R. W. Appleby	
G-MZML	Mainair Blade 912	C. J. Meadows	
G-MZMN	Pegasus Quantum 912	S. Perkins	
G-MZMO	TEAM mini-MAX 91	North East Flight Training Ltd	
G-MZMT	Pegasus Quantum 15	T. Hemsley	
G-MZMU	Rans S.6-ESD Coyote II	WEZ Group	
G-MZMV	Mainair Blade	S. P. Allen & C. J. Tomlin	
G-MZMW	Mignet HM.1000 Balerit	M. E. Whapham	

BRITISH CIVIL AIRCRAFT MARKINGS

Notes	Reg	Type	Owner or Operator
	G-MZMY	Mainair Blade	N. A. Janes
	G-MZMZ	Mainair Blade	D. T. Page
	G-MZNA	Quad City Challenger II UK	S. Hennessy
	G-MZNB	Pegasus Quantum 15	S. J. Metters
	G-MZNC	Mainair Blade 912	A. J. Harrison
	G-MZND	Mainair Rapier	D. W. Stamp
	G-MZNG	Pegasus Quantum 15	The Scottish Flying Club
	G-MZNH	CFM Shadow Srs DD	M. L. Twynham
	G-MZNJ	Mainair Blade	R. A. Hardy
	G-MZNO	Mainair Blade 912	E. McCallum
	G-MZNR	Pegasus Quantum 15	N. J. Clemens
	G-MZNS	Pegasus Quantum 15	T. Eaton & E. A. Brown
	G-MZNT	Pegasus Quantum 15-912	N. W. Barnett
	G-MZNV	Rans S.6-ESD Coyote II	A. P. Thomas
	G-MZNY	Thruster T.600N	Cheshire Flying School Ltd
	G-MZOC	Mainair Blade	A. S. Davies
	G-MZOD	Pegasus Quantum 15	G. P. Burns
	G-MZOE	Cyclone AX2000	B. E. Wagenhauser
	G-MZOF	Mainair Blade	R. M. Ellis
	G-MZOG	Pegasus Quantum 15-912	E. & M. McCallum & G. Jardine
	G-MZOH	Whittaker MW5D Sorcerer	I. Pearson
	G-MZOI	Letov LK-2M Sluka	G. Lafferty
	G-MZOK	Whittaker MW6 Merlin	G-MZOK Syndicate
	G-MZOS	Pegasus Quantum 15-912	T. G. Ryan
	G-MZOV	Pegasus Quantum 15	B. E. Wagenhauser
	G-MZOW	Pegasus Quantum 15-912	G. P. Burns
	G-MZOX	Letov LK-2M Sluka	N. R. Beale
	G-MZOY	TEAM Mini-MAX 91	P. R. & S. E. Whitehouse
	G-MZOZ	Rans S.6-ESA Coyote II	G. L. Daniels
	G-MZPH	Mainair Blade	W. W. Hammond
	G-MZPJ	TEAM mini-MAX	J. Aubert
	G-MZRC	Pegasus Quantum 15	M. Hopkins
	G-MZRM	Pegasus Quantum 15	R. Milwain
	G-MZRS	CFM Shadow Srs CD	C. A. Larkins
	G-MZSP	Spacek SD-1 Minisport	A. M. Hughes
	G-MZTG	Titan T-51 Mustang	A. R. Evans
	G-MZZT	Kolb Twinstar Mk 3	F. Omaraie-Hamdanie
	G-MZZY	Mainair Blade 912	A. Mucznik
	G-NACA	Norman NAC-2 Freelance 180	P. J. L. Caruth
	G-NACI	Norman NAC-1 Srs 100	R. E. Griffiths (G-AXFB)
	G-NACL	Norman NAC-6 Fieldmaster	EPA Aircraft Co Ltd (G-BNEG)
	G-NACO	Norman NAC-6 Fieldmaster	EPA Aircraft Co Ltd
	G-NACP	Norman NAC-6 Fieldmaster	EPA Aircraft Co Ltd
	G-NADN	PA-23-250 Aztec F	N. M. T. Sparks (G-XSFT/G-CPPC/G-BGBH)
	G-NADS	TEAM mini-MAX 91	N. P. St.J Ramsay
	G-NAGG	Rotorsport UK MT-03	C. A. Clements
	G-NALA	Cessna 172S	Atlantic Flight Training Ltd (G-GFEA/G-CEDY)
	G-NALD	Aeroprakt A.32 Vixxen	D. J. Medcraft
	G-NANO	Avid Speed Wing	A. M. Wyndham
	G-NAPO	Pegasus Quantum 15-912	J. K. Kerr & K. S. Henderson
	G-NAPP	Van's RV-7	R. C. Meek
	G-NARG	Tanarg/Ixess 15 912S (1)	K. Kirby
	G-NARL	Zlin Savage Shock Cub	P. F. Rothwell
	G-NATI	Corby CJ-1 Starlet	S. P. Evans
	G-NATT	Rockwell Commander 114A	Northgleam Ltd
	G-NBCA	Pilatus PC-12/47E	Narm Aviation Ltd
	G-NBDD	Robin DR.400/180	The Delta Delta Group
	G-NBOX	Ikarus C42 FB100 Bravo	N. Hammerton
	G-NBPL	Aerospatiale AS.355F2 Ecureuil 2	Nigel Brunt Properties Ltd
	G-NBSI	Cameron N-77 balloon	Nottingham Hot-Air Balloon Club
	G-NCDC	Best Off Skyranger Nynja 912S(1)	C. D. Church
	G-NCFC	PA-38-112 Tomahawk II	N. J. Butler (G-BNOA)
	G-NCKS	Westland WG.13 Lynx AH.Mk.7	G. P. Hinkley
	G-NCUB	Piper J-3C-65 Cub	R. J. Willies (G-BGXV)
	G-NDAD	Medway SLA100 Executive	R. D. Pyne
	G-NDIA	Robinson R22	EBG (Helicopters) Ltd & Altitude Consultants Ltd (G-CCGE)

Reg	Type	Owner or Operator	Notes
G-NDJS	Jonker JS1-C Revelation	A. J. Davis	
G-NDOT	Thruster T.600N	P. C. Bailey	
G-NDPA	Ikarus C42 FB UK	Grandpa's Flying Group	
G-NEAL	PA-32-260 Cherokee Six	S. G. Watson (G-BFPY)	
G-NEAT	Europa	P. F. D. Foden	
G-NEDS	Skyranger Nynja 912S(1)	J. Hunter	
G-NEEE	Cessna F.172M	G-NEEE Group (G-BCZM)	
G-NEEL	Rotorway Executive 90	I. C. Bedford	
G-NEII	Montgomerie-Bensen B8MR	Dept of Doing Ltd (G-BVJF)	
G-NEIL	Thunder Ax3 balloon	R. M. Powell	
G-NEIO	Diamond DA.40NG Star	N. R. Scarles	
G-NELI	PA-28R Cherokee Arrow 180	MK Aero Support Ltd	
G-NELS	Robinson R44	Heliwarns Aviation Ltd	
G-NEMO	Raj Hamsa X'Air Jabiru (4)	C. D. Swift	
G-NEON	PA-32 Cherokee Six 300B	T. F. Rowley	
G-NEOP	Airbus A.321-251NX	British Airways PLC	
G-NEOR	Airbus A.321-251NX	British Airways PLC	
G-NEOS	Airbus A.321-251NX	British Airways PLC	
G-NEOT	Airbus A.321-251NX	British Airways PLC	
G-NEOU	Airbus A.321-251NX	British Airways PLC	
G-NEOV	Airbus A.321-251NX	British Airways PLC	
G-NEOW	Airbus A.321-251NX	British Airways PLC	
G-NEOX	Airbus A.321-251NX	Briitish Airways PLC	
G-NEOY	Airbus A.321-251NX	British Airways PLC	
G-NEOZ	Airbus A.321-251NX	Briitish Airways PLC	
G-NESA	Shaw Europa XS	A. M. Kay	
G-NESE	Tecnam P2002-JF	N. & S. Easton	
G-NESH	Robinson R44 II	Helicentre Aviation Ltd	
G-NESW	PA-34-220T Seneca III	G. C. U. Guida	
G-NESY	PA-18 Super Cub 95	V. Featherstone	
G-NETR	AS.355F1 Twin Squirrel	PLM Dollar Group Ltd (G-JARV/G-OGHL)	
G-NETY	PA-18 Super Cub 150	S. de Sutter	
G-NEUS	Brugger MB.2 Colibri	S. B. Robson	
G-NEVE	Ikarus C42 FB100	M. Neve	
G-NEWA	Rans S-6-ES Coyote II	J. Cook	
G-NEWT	Beech 35 Bonanza	J. S. Allison (G-APVW)	
G-NEWV	Schempp-Hirth Ventus-3T	D. P. Francis	
G-NEWZ	Bell 206B JetRanger 3	H. P. L. Frost	
G-NFLA	BAe Jetstream 3102	Cranfield University (G-BRGN/G-BLHC)	
G-NFLB	SAAB 340B	Cranfield University	
G-NFLC	HP.137 Jetstream 1H (G-AXUI) ★	Instructional airframe/Perth	
G-NFLY	Tecnam P2002-EA Sierra	C. N. Hodgson	
G-NFNF	Robin DR.400/180	M. Child, W. Cobb & J. Archer	
G-NFON	Van's RV-8	N. F. O'Neill	
G-NFOX	Aeropro Eurofox 912(S)	A. E. Mayhew	
G-NFVB	Cameron Z-105 balloon	Ballooning Network Ltd	
G-NGAA	Bristell NG5 Speed Wing	Jet Applications Ltd	
G-NGBB	Bristell NG5 Speed Wing	F. Sayyah & A. J. Palmer	
G-NGCC	Bristell NG5 Speed Wing	G. C. Coull	
G-NGII	Bristell NG5 Speed Wing	F. Sayyah & A. J. Palmer	
G-NHAA	AS.365N-2 Dauphin 2	The Great North Air Ambulance Service (G-MLTY)	
G-NHAB	AS.365N-2 Dauphin 2	The Great North Air Ambulance Service (G-DAUF)	
G-NHAC	AS.365N-2 Dauphin 2	The Great North Air Ambulance Service	
G-NHAD	AS.365N-2 Dauphin 2	The Great North Air Ambulance Service (G-SSKP/G-CIUC)	
G-NHAE	AS.365N-3 Dauphin 2	Multiflight Ltd (G-DOLF)	
G-NHEM	Eurocopter EC.135T2	Babcock Mission Critical Services Onshore Ltd (G-KRNW)	
G-NHRJ	Shaw Europa XS	R. J. Dawson	
G-NHVA	Airbus EC.175B	NHV Helicopters Ltd	
G-NHVB	Agusta Westland AW139	NHV Helicopters Ltd (G-SNSK)	
G-NHVC	Agusta Westland AW139	NHV Helicopters Ltd	
G-NHVD	Agusta Westland AW169	NHV Helicopters Ltd	
G-NHVE	Airbus EC175B	NHV Helicopters Ltd	
G-NHVF	Airbus EC.175B	NHV Helicopters Ltd	

Notes	Reg	Type	Owner or Operator
	G-NHVG	Airbus EC.175B	NHV Helicopters Ltd
	G-NHVI	Airbus EC.175B	NHV Helicopters Ltd
	G-NHVJ	Airbus EC.175B	NHV Helicopters Ltd
	G-NHVN	Agusta Westland AW139	NHV Helicopters Ltd
	G-NHVP	Agusta Westland AW139	NHV Helicopters Ltd
	G-NHVR	Airbus EC175B	NHV Helicopters Ltd
	G-NHVU	Airbus EC175B	NHV Helicopters Ltd
	G-NHVV	Airbus EC175B	NHV Helicopters Ltd
	G-NIAA	Beech B.200 Super King Air	Blue Sky Investments Ltd
	G-NIAB	Beech B.200 Super King Air	Blue Sky Investments Ltd
	G-NIAC	TL2000UK Sting Carbon S4	Royal Air Force Sport Aircraft RAF Flying Schools & Clubs Org
	G-NICB	Beech B200GT King Air	Comis Air Ltd
	G-NICC	Aerotechnik EV-97 Team Eurostar UK	C. Wileman
	G-NICI	Robinson R44	David Fishwick Vehicles Sales Ltd
	G-NICS	Best Off Sky Ranger Swift 912S(1)	I. A. Forrest
	G-NICX	Europa XS	N. Kenney
	G-NIDG	Aerotechnik EV-97 Eurostar	Skydrive Ltd
	G-NIEN	Van's RV-9A	K. N. P. Higgs
	G-NIFE	SNCAN Stampe SV.4A (156)	Training & Leisure Consultants Ltd
	G-NIGC	Avtech Jabiru UL-450	C. K. Fry
	G-NIGE	Luscombe 8E Silvaire	Garden Party Ltd (G-BSHG)
	G-NIGL	Shaw Europa	N. M. Graham
	G-NIHK	Eurocopter EC135 T2+	Babcock Mission Critical Services Onshore Ltd (G-SASA)
	G-NIKE	PA-28-181 Archer II	MET Aviation Ltd
	G-NIKK	Diamond Katana DA20-C1	Cubair Flight Training Ltd
	G-NIKL	Robinson R22	HQ Aviation Ltd (G-BTNA)
	G-NIKO	Airbus A.321-211	SAP Meridian Aviation 25 Ltd
	G-NIKS	Aeropro Eurofox 912(1)	Gosk Ltd
	G-NILT	EV-97 Eurostar SL Microlight	G. I. Nelson
	G-NIMA	Balóny Kubíček BB30Z balloon	C. Williamson
	G-NIMB	Schempp-Hirth Nimbus 2C	W. J. Winthrop & W. P. Stephen
	G-NIME	Cessna T.206H Turbo Stationair	Whitby Seafoods Ltd
	G-NINC	PA-28-180 Cherokee	North Wales Flight Academy Ltd
	G-NIND	PA-28-180 Cherokee	Aquarelle Investments Ltd
	G-NINJ	Best Off Skyranger Nynja 912S(1)	G-NINJ Group
	G-NIOG	Robinson R44 II	Helicopter Sharing Ltd
	G-NIOS	PA-32R-301 Saratoga SP	Plant Aviation
	G-NIPA	Slingsby T.66 Nipper 3	R. J. O. Walker (G-AWDD)
	G-NIPL	Eurocopter AS.350B3 Ecureuil	Pacific Helicopters Ltd
	G-NIPP	Slingsby T.66 Nipper 3	North East Flight Training Ltd (G-AVKJ)
	G-NIPR	Slingsby T.66 Nipper 3	P. A. Gibbs (G-AVXC)
	G-NIPS	Tipsy T.66 Nipper 2	M. D. Gorlov
	G-NISA	Robinson R44 II	Antinori Agricola SRL/Italy (G-HTMT)
	G-NISH	Van's RV-8	N. H. F. Hampton & S. R. Whitling
	G-NIXX	Best Off Skyranger 912(1)	E. W. Barnett (G-CDYJ)
	G-NJAA	Cessna 560XL Citation XLS	Netjets Europe Sociedade Unipessoal Lda/Portugal
	G-NJAB	Cessna 560XL Citation XLS	Netjets Europe Sociedade Unipessoal Lda/Portugal
	G-NJAC	Cessna 560XL Citation XLS	Netjets Europe Sociedade Unipessoal Lda/Portugal
	G-NJBA	Rotorway Executive 162F	A. J. Thomas
	G-NJCZ	Czech Sport Pipersport	Aerocruz Ltd
	G-NJET	Schempp-Hirth Ventus cT	P. S. Carder
	G-NJNH	Robinson R66	Hawesbates LLP
	G-NJOY	PA-28-181 Archer III	M. J. Groves
	G-NJPG	Best Off Skyranger Nynja 912S(1)	P. Gibbs
	G-NJPW	P & M Quik GT450	Golf Papa Whiskey Group
	G-NJSH	Robinson R22 Beta	Hawesbates LLP
	G-NJSP	Jabiru J430	N. J. S. Pitman
	G-NJTC	Aeroprakt A22-L Foxbat	I. R. Russell & P. A. Henretty
	G-NLCH	Lindstrand LBL-35A balloon	S. A. Lacey
	G-NLDR	AS.355F2 Ecureuil 2	PDG Helicopters (G-PDGS)
	G-NLEE	Cessna 182Q	R. J. Houghton
	G-NLMB	Zenair CH.601UL Zodiac	N. Lamb

Reg	Type	Owner or Operator	Notes
G-NLSE	AS.355F2 Ecureuil 2	PLM Dollar Group Ltd (G-ULES/G-OBHL/ G-HARO/G-DAFT/G-BNNN)	
G-NMBS	Schempp-Hirth Nimbus-3/24.5	D. S. Bramwell (G-DFBM)	
G-NMCC	Aviat A-1C-180 Husky	N. W. McConachie	
G-NMCL	Eurofox 912(S)	N. R. McLeod	
G-NMMB	Van's RV-10	M. S. Bamber & N. R. MacLennan	
G-NMMC	Robinson R44 II	BBR Leasing Ltd (G-GIBB)	
G-NMOS	Cameron C-80 balloon	C. J. Thomas & M. C. East	
G-NMRV	Van's RV-6	G. W. Street	
G-NMUS	Steen Skybolt	N. Musgrave	
G-NNAC	PA-18 Super Cub 135	PAW Flying Services Ltd	
G-NNON	Mainair Blade	D. R. Kennedy	
G-NOCK	Cessna FR.182RG II	Just Plane Trading Ltd (G-BGTK)	
G-NOCM	Cessna 525A Citationjet CJ2	Air Charter Scotland Ltd (G-SOVZ)	
G-NODE	AA-5B Tiger	Ultranomad Sro	
G-NOIL	BN-2A-26 Islander	Aerospace Resources Ltd (G-BJWO/G-BAXC)	
G-NONE	Dyn'Aéro MCR-01 ULC	M. A. Collins	
G-NORA	Ikarus C.42 FB UK	N. A. Rathbone	
G-NORB	Saturne S110K hang glider	R. N. Pearce	
G-NORD	SNCAN NC.854	A. D. Pearce	
G-NORG	Gefa-Flug AS105GD airship	Creative Capital Group Ltd (G-BZUR)	
G-NORK	Bell 206B-3 JetRanger III	R. S. Forsyth	
G-NOSE	Cessna 402B	Reconnaissance Ventures Ltd (G-MPCU)	
G-NOTE	PA-28-181 Archer III	J. Beach	
G-NOTS	Skyranger 912S(1)	S. F. N. Warnell	
G-NOWW	Mainair Blade 912	R. S. Sanby	
G-NOXY	Robinson R44	T A Knox Shopfitters Ltd (G-VALV)	
G-NPKJ	Van's RV-6	P. Jamison	
G-NPPL	Comco Ikarus C.42 FB.100	Papa Lima Group	
G-NPTA	Boeing 737-86N(BCF)	West Atlantic UK Ltd	
G-NPTV	AS.355NP Ecureuil II	Arena Aviation Ltd	
G-NPTX	Boeing 737-4C9(F)	West Atlantic UK Ltd	
G-NRFK	Van's RV-8	C. N. Harper & P. G. Peal	
G-NRMA	Dan Rihn DR.107 One Design	A. W. Brown	
G-NRRA	SIAI-Marchetti SF.260 (BF8431)	G. Boot	
G-NSBB	Ikarus C.42 FB-100 VLA	Bravo Bravo Flying Group	
G-NSEY	Embraer ERJ190-200STD	Aurigny Air Services Ltd	
G-NSFS	VS.361 Spitfire IX	Norwegian Spitfire Foundation	
G-NSKB	Aeroprakt A22-L Foxbat	N. F. Smith	
G-NSKY	Alpi Pioneer 400	W. T. D. Gillam	
G-NSSA	TLAC Sherwood Ranger XP	A. R. Stanley	
G-NSTG	Cessna F.150F	Westair Flying Services Ltd (G-ATNI)	
G-NSUK	PA-34-220T Seneca V	Tees Aircraft Leasing LLP	
G-NSYS	Eurocopter EC135 T1	Novas Aerospace Ltd (G-CEYF/G-HARP)	
G-NTPS	BRM Aero Bristell NG5	N. D. H. Stokes	
G-NTWK	AS.355F2 Twin Squirrel	PLM Dollar Group Ltd (G-FTWO/G-OJOR/ G-BMUS)	
G-NUFC	Best Off Skyranger 912S(1)	J. F. Garbutt	
G-NUGC	Grob G.103A Twin II Acro	The University of Nottingham Students Union	
G-NUKA	PA-28-181 Archer II	N. Ibrahim	
G-NULA	Flight Design CT2K	R. Irving & S. L. Cogger	
G-NUNI	Lindstrand LBL-77A balloon	The University of Nottingham	
G-NUTA	Christen Eagle II	A. R. Whincup	
G-NUTT	Mainair Pegasus Quik	M. Jones	
G-NVBF	Lindstrand LBL-210A balloon	Virgin Balloon Flights	
G-NVWV	Agusta A.109E Power	Surge Air Ltd (G-SRGE)	
G-NWAA	Eurocopter EC.135T2	Babcock Mission Critical Services Onshore Ltd	
G-NWAE	Eurocopter EC.135T2	Babcock Mission Critical Services Onshore Ltd (G-DAAT)	
G-NWEM	Eurocopter EC.135T2	Babcock Mission Critical Services Onshore Ltd (G-SSXX/G-SSSX)	

Notes	Reg	Type	Owner or Operator
	G-NWFA	Cessna 150M	North Weald Flying Group Ltd (G-CFBD)
	G-NWFC	Cessna 172P	North Weald Flying Group Ltd
	G-NWFG	Cessna 172P	North Weald Flying Group Ltd
	G-NWFS	Cessna 172P	North Weald Flying Group Ltd (G-TYMS)
	G-NWFT	Cessna F.172N	North Weald Flying Training Ltd (G-BURD)
	G-NWOI	Eurocopter EC135 P2+	Police & Crime Commissioner for West Yorkshire
	G-NWPR	Cameron N-77 balloon	D. B. Court
	G-NXOE	Cessna 172S	Goodwood Road Racing Co.Ltd
	G-NXTE	Electroflight NXTE	Rolls-Royce PLC
	G-NYKS	Cessna 182T	M. Lapidus
	G-NYMB	Schempp-Hirth Nimbus 3	Nimbus Syndicate
	G-NYMF	PA-25 Pawnee 235D	Bristol Gliding Club Pty Ltd
	G-NYNA	Van's RV-9A	B. Greathead & S. Hiscox
	G-NYNE	Schleicher ASW-27-18E	J. Eccles
	G-NYNJ	Best Off Skyranger Nynja 912S)1)	N. J. Sutherland
	G-NZGL	Cameron O-105 balloon	R. A. Vale & ptnrs
	G-NZIC	LeVier Cosmic Wind	J. C. Tempest
	G-NZSS	Boeing Stearman N2S-5 (43517:227)	R. W. Davies
	G-OAAA	PA-28-161 Warrior II	Red Hill Air Services Ltd
	G-OAAM	Cameron C-90 balloon	D. Simoen
	G-OABB	Jodel D.150	K. Manley
	G-OABC	Colt 69A balloon	P. A. C. Stuart-Kregor
	G-OABO	Enstrom F-28A	C. R. Taylor (G-BAIB)
	G-OABR	AG-5B Tiger	F. Hopper & A. Corcoran
	G-OACE	Valentin Taifun 17E	I. F. Wells
	G-OACI	MS.893E Rallye 180GT	J. M. & S. Bain
	G-OADY	Beech 76 Duchess	S. Uerguen
	G-OAFG	Pipistrel Alpha BCAR-S 164	A. F. Greenhalgh
	G-OAGA	Eurocopter EC.225LP Super Puma	CHC Scotia Ltd
	G-OAFA	Cessna F.172M	The Army Flying Association (G-BFZV)
	G-OAGA	Eurocopter EC.225LP Super Puma	Element Capital Corp
	G-OAGI	FLS Aerospace Sprint 160	A. L. Breckell (G-FLSI)
	G-OAHC	Beech F33C Bonanza	SI Aviation Services Ltd (G-BTTF)
	G-OAJL	Ikarus C.42 FB100	J. M. Donnelly
	G-OAJS	PA-39 Twin Comanche 160 C/R	M. C. Bellamy (G-BCIO)
	G-OALC	AS.355F2 Ecureuil II	Alcaline UK Ltd (G-VONG)
	G-OALD	SOCATA TB20 Trinidad	Gold Aviation
	G-OALE	Balony Kubicek BB22XR balloon	Belvoir Brewery Ltd
	G-OALH	Tecnam P92-EA Echo	D. G. I. Wheldon
	G-OALI	AS.355F1 Ecureuil II	Atlas Helicopters Ltd (G-WDKR/G-NEXT/ G-OMAV)
	G-OALP	Alpi Pioneer 300 Hawk	Cavendish Aviation UK Ltd
	G-OAMF	Pegasus Quantum 15-912	J. C. Birkbeck
	G-OAML	Cameron AML-105 balloon	Stratton Motor Co (Norfolk) Ltd
	G-OANI	PA-28-161 Warrior II	Falcon Flying Services
	G-OANN	Zenair CH.601HD	Insch 601 Group
	G-OAPR	Brantly B.2B ★	The Helicopter Museum/Weston-super-Mare
	G-OARA	PA-28R-201 Arrow III	Synergy Aircraft Leasing Ltd
	G-OARC	PA-28RT-201 Arrow IV	Xytal Health Management Ltd (G-BMVE)
	G-OARS	Cessna 172S	De Hertog Juweeldesign GCV/Belgium
	G-OART	PA-23 Aztec 250D	Prescribing Services Ltd (G-AXKD)
	G-OARU	PA-28R-201 Arrow III	Hardman Aviation Ltd
	G-OASA	Flight Design CTSW	O. E. W. & S. M. Achurch (G-CGHE)
	G-OASH	Robinson R22 Beta	J. C. Lane
	G-OASI	Lindstrand LTL Series 1-90 balloon	A. M. Holly
	G-OASK	Aeropro Eurofox 912(S)	Aero Space Scientific Educational Trust
	G-OASL	Avions Transport ATR-72-202F	ASL Airlines UK Ltd
	G-OASM	HpH Glasflugel 304 ES Shark	A. S. Miller
	G-OASP	AS.355F2 Twin Squirrel	Helicopter & Pilot Services Ltd
	G-OASW	Schleicher ASW-27	M. P. W. Mee
	G-OATE	Mainair Pegasus Quantum 15-912	A. Roberts
	G-OATL	Agusta Westland AW109SP Grand New	Helicompany Ltd (G-EMHJ)
	G-OATR	Avions Transport ATR-72-212A	Aurigny Air Services Ltd
	G-OATV	Cameron V-77 balloon	A. W. & E. P. Braund-Smith
	G-OATY	Pipistrel Alpha BCAR-S 164	MGAP London LLP
	G-OATZ	Van's RV-12	J. W. Armstrong
	G-OAUD	Robinson R44	Pinpoint 3D Ltd (G-CDHV)

Reg	Type	Owner or Operator	Notes
G-OAUR	Dornier 228-212	Aurigny Air Services Ltd	
G-OAVC	Cessna F.177RG	Avionicare Ltd (G-BBJV)	
G-OAWM	Cirrus SR20	Cambridge Flying Company Ltd (G-GCDD)	
G-OAWS	Colt 77A balloon	P. Lawman	
G-OBAB	Lindstrand LBL-35A Cloudhopper balloon	M. A. Green	
G-OBAD	EV-97 Eurostar SL	M. J. Robbins	
G-OBAK	PA-28R-201T Turbo Arrow III	G-OBAK Group	
G-OBAL	Mooney M.20J	G-OBAL Group	
G-OBAN	Jodel D.140B	L. P. Keegan (G-ATSU)	
G-OBAS	Hughes 369E	Eastern Atlantic Helicopters Ltd (G-KAYS/ G-CIMJ/G-RISK)	
G-OBAZ	Best Off Skyranger 912(2)	K. A. O'Neill	
G-OBBO	Cessna 182S	A. E. Kedros	
G-OBDA	Diamond Katana DA20-A1	Oscar Papa Ltd	
G-OBDN	PA-28-161 Warrior II	R. M. Bennett	
G-OBEE	Boeing Stearman A75N-1 (3397:174)	R. H. Mackay	
G-OBEN	Cessna 152 II	A. F. M. Guterres (G-NALI/G-BHVM)	
G-OBET	Sky 77-24 balloon	P. M. Watkins & S. M. Carden	
G-OBFE	Sky 120-24 balloon	J. Sonnabend	
G-OBHE	Robinson R44	The BHE Hub Ltd (G-PRET)	
G-OBIC	Robin DR.400/180R	The Windrushers Gliding Club Ltd (G-OTIB)	
G-OBIL	Robinson R22 Beta	Helicopter & Pilot Services Ltd	
G-OBIO	Robinson R22 Beta	Go Exclusive Ltd	
G-OBJB	Lindstrand LBL-90A balloon	B. J. Bower	
G-OBJM	Taylor JT.1 Monoplane	R. K. Thomas	
G-OBJP	Pegasus Quantum 15-912	G. I. Somers	
G-OBJT	Shaw Europa	A. Burill (G-MUZO)	
G-OBLC	Beech 76 Duchess	Air Navigation & Trading Company Ltd	
G-OBLN	DH.115 Vampire T.Mk.11	J. M. Vivash	
G-OBMI	Mainair Blade	A. F. Glover	
G-OBMS	Cessna F.172N	Mike Sierra Group	
G-OBNC	BN-2B-20 Islander	Britten-Norman Aircraft Ltd	
G-OBOF	Remos GX	D. Hawkins	
G-OBPP	Schleicher ASG-29E	R. A. F. King	
G-OBRO	Alpi Pioneer 200M	A. Brown	
G-OBRY	Cameron N-180 balloon	A. C. K. Rawson & J. J. Rudoni	
G-OBSM	Robinson R44 Raven	J. G. Heselden (G-CDSE)	
G-OBSR	Partenavia P68	Ravenair Aircraft Ltd	
G-OBTO	Cub Crafters CC19-180 XCub	STOL Ventures Ltd	
G-OBTS	Cameron C-90 balloon	Skydive Chatteris Club Ltd	
G-OBUC	PA-34-220T Seneca III	Tamara Trading SL	
G-OBUP	DG Flugzeugbau DG-808C	C. J. Lowrie	
G-OBUU	Replica Comper CLA Swift	J. A. Pothecary & R. H. Hunt	
G-OBUY	Colt 69A balloon	E. K. Read	
G-OBUZ	Van's RV-6	A. F. Hall	
G-OBYG	Boeing 767-304ER	TUI Airways Ltd	
G-OBYH	Boeing 767-304ER	TUI Airways Ltd	
G-OBYT	Agusta-Bell 206A JetRanger	J. S. Everett (G-BNRC)	
G-OBZR	Aerostyle Breezer LSA	P. Coomber	
G-OCAC	Robin R-2112	The Cotswold Aero Club Ltd (G-EWHT)	
G-OCAD	Sequoia F.8L Falco	D. R. Vale	
G-OCAF	Robinson R44	Becketts Aviation LLP	
G-OCAK	Bombardier BD700-1A10 Global Express	Gama Aviation (UK) Ltd	
G-OCAM	AA-5A Cheetah	J. Khambatta & G. Fenton (G-BLHO)	
G-OCBI	Schweizer 269C-1	Alpha Properties (London) Ltd	
G-OCCF	Diamond DA40D Star	Flying Time Ltd	
G-OCCG	Diamond DA40D Star	Flying Time Ltd	
G-OCCH	Diamond DA40D Star	Innovative Aviation (Leeds) Ltd	
G-OCCN	Diamond DA40D Star	Flying Time Ltd	
G-OCCX	Diamond DA42 Twin Star	Aeros Global Ltd	
G-OCDC	Best Off Sky Ranger Nynja 912S(1)	C. D. Church	
G-OCDP	Flight Design CTSW	M. A. Beadman	
G-OCDW	Jabiru UL-450	R. J. Grant	
G-OCFD	Bell 206B JetRanger 3	Rushmere Helicopters LLP (G-WGAL/G-OICS)	
G-OCGC	Robin DR.400-180R	Cambridge Gliding Club Ltd	
G-OCGD	Cameron O-26 balloon	C. G. Dobson	
G-OCHM	Robinson R44	C. M. Beighton	
G-OCLC	Aviat A-1B Husky	Aero Club Bolzano/Italy	
G-OCLV	Robinson R44 II	CR Flight Hire Ltd	

Notes	Reg	Type	Owner or Operator
	G-OCMM	Agusta A109A II	Castle Air Ltd (G-BXCB/G-ISEB/G-IADT/ G-HBCA)
	G-OCMS	EV-97 TeamEurostar UK	C. M. Saysell
	G-OCMT	EV-97 TeamEurostar UK	P. Crowhurst
	G-OCOK	American Champion 8KCAB Super Decathlon	Virtual Jet Centre Ltd
	G-OCON	Robinson R44	P. Kelly
	G-OCOV	Robinson R22 Beta	Central Helicopters Ltd
	G-OCPC	Cessna FA.152	Devon & Somerset Flight Training Ltd
	G-OCRI	Colomban MC.15 Cri-Cri	K. A. Beetson & L. A. Fowler
	G-OCRL	Europa	R. J. Lewis (G-OBEV)
	G-OCRM	Slingsby T.67M Firefly II	CRM Aviation Europe Ltd (G-BUUB)
	G-OCRZ	CZAW Sportcruiser	P. Marsden
	G-OCTI	PA-32 Cherokee Six 260	M. B. Dyos (G-BGZX)
	G-OCTO	Van's RV-8	A. P. S. Maynard & A. Stokes
	G-OCTS	Cameron Z-90 balloon	A. Collett
	G-OCTU	PA-28-161 Cadet	Glenn Aviation Ltd
	G-OCUB	Piper J-3C-90 Cub	Zebedee Flying Group
	G-OCXI	Van's RV-8	P. S. Gilmour
	G-OCZA	CZAW Sportcruiser	S. M. Dawson
	G-ODAC	Cessna F.152 II	T. M. Jones (G-BITG)
	G-ODAF	Lindstrand LBL-105A balloon	T. J. Horne
	G-ODAK	PA-28-236 Dakota	Flydak LLP
	G-ODAY	Cameron N-56 balloon	British Balloon Museum & Library
	G-ODBN	Lindstrand LBL Flowers SS balloon	Magical Adventures Ltd
	G-ODCH	Schleicher ASW-20L	T. R. Freeland
	G-ODDF	Siren PIK-30	G. F. Bailey, J. D. Sorrell & D. M. Thomas
	G-ODDZ	Schempp-Hirth Duo Discus T	P. A. King
	G-ODEE	Van's RV-6	J. Redfearn
	G-ODEL	Falconar F-11-3	G. F. Brummell
	G-ODGC	Aeropro Eurofox 912(iS)	Dorset Gliding Club Ltd
	G-ODGS	Avtech Jabiru UL-450	W. K. Evans
	G-ODHB	Robinson R44	RSM Maintenance Ltd
	G-ODHC	DHC.1B-2-S5 Chipmunk	P. M. Wells
	G-ODIN	Avions Mudry CAP-10B	CAP Ten
	G-ODIP	Aviat A-1C-180 Husky	A. J. White
	G-ODIZ	AutoGyro Cavalon	P. Williams
	G-ODJD	Raj Hamsa X'Air 582 (7)	N. M. Toulson
	G-ODJF	Lindstrand LBL-90B balloon	Helena Dos Santos SA/Portugal
	G-ODJG	Shaw Europa	K. R. Challis & C. S. Andersson
	G-ODJH	Mooney M.20C	R. M. Schweitzer/Netherlands (G-BMLH)
	G-ODOG	PA-28R Cherokee Arrow 200-II	M. Brancart (G-BAAR)
	G-ODRT	Cameron Z-105 balloon	N. W. N. Townshend
	G-ODSA	Bell 429	Starspeed Ltd
	G-ODTW	Shaw Europa	D. T. Walters
	G-ODUD	PA-28-181 Archer II	S. Barlow, R. N. Ingle & R. J. Murray (G-IBBO)
	G-ODUO	Schempp-Hirth Duo Discus	3D Syndicate
	G-ODVB	CFM Shadow Srs DD	L. J. E. Moss
	G-ODWS	Silence SA.180 Twister	T. R. Dews
	G-OEAC	Mooney M.20J	S. Lovatt
	G-OECO	Flylight Dragonfly	P. A. & M. W. Aston
	G-OEDP	Cameron N-77 balloon	M. J. Betts
	G-OEFT	PA-38-112 Tomahawk	M. Lee
	G-OEGG	Cameron Egg-65 SS balloon	D. M. Wade
	G-OEGL	Christen Eagle II	E. Mason
	G-OEGO	E-Go	Cambridge Business Travel
	G-OEKS	Ikarus C42 FB80	J. D. Smith
	G-OELZ	Wassmer WA.52 Europa	D. F. Hurn
	G-OEMZ	Pietenpol Air Camper	C. Brockis (G-IMBY)
	G-OENC	Agusta Westland AW.189	Bristow Helicopters Ltd
	G-OERR	Lindstrand LBL-60A balloon	C. Davis
	G-OERS	Cessna 172N	N. J. Smith & A. Stevens (G-SSRS)
	G-OESC	Aquila AT01	Osterreichischer Sportflieger/Austria (G-OZIO)
	G-OESP	Robinson R44 II	Scariff Plant Hire Ltd (G-CGND)
	G-OESY	Easy Raider J2.2 (1)	J. Gray
	G-OETI	Bell 206B JetRanger 3	Jaspa (G-RMIE/G-BPIE)
	G-OETS	Ultramagic M-105 balloon	ETS (SW) Ltd
	G-OETV	PA-31-350 Navajo Chieftain	Atlantic Bridge Aviation Ltd
	G-OEVA	PA-32-260 Cherokee Six	Enterprise Purchasing Ltd (G-FLJA/G-AVTJ)
	G-OEWD	Raytheon 390 Premier 1	Avidus Jet Management Ltd
	G-OEWE	Cameron Sport 80	N. Edmunds

Reg	Type	Owner or Operator	Notes
G-OEZI	Easy Raider J2.2(2)	S. E. J. M. McDonald	
G-OEZY	Shaw Europa	A. W. Wakefield	
G-OFAA	Cameron Z-105 balloon	R. A. Schwab	
G-OFAL	Ozone Roadster/Bailey Quattro	Malcolm Roberts Heating, Plumbing and Electrical Ltd	
G-OFAS	Robinson R22 Beta	Advance Helicopters Ltd	
G-OFBT	Cameron O-84 balloon	A. A. & W. S. Calvert	
G-OFBU	Ikarus C.42 FB UK	Old Sarum C42 Group	
G-OFCM	Cessna F.172L	Advanced Field Solutions Ltd (G-AZUN)	
G-OFDR	PA-28-161 Cadet	Electric Scribe 2000 Ltd	
G-OFDT	Mainair Pegasus Quik	C. Lomas	
G-OFER	PA-18 Super Cub 150	White Watham Airfield Ltd	
G-OFES	Alisport Silent 2 Electro	N. D. A. Graham	
G-OFFA	Pietenpol Air Camper	D. & G. A. Shepherd	
G-OFFO	Extra EA.300/L	2 Excel Aviation Ltd	
G-OFFS	PA-38-112 Tomahawk	NWMAS Leasing Ltd (G-BMSF)	
G-OFGC	Aeroprakt A22-L Foxbat	J. M. Fearn	
G-OFIT	SOCATA TB10 Tobago	GFI Aviation Group (G-BRIU)	
G-OFIX	Grob G.109B	T. R. Dews	
G-OFJC	Eiriavion PIK-20E	G. Bailey, J. D. Sorrell & D. Thomas	
G-OFLI	Colt 105A balloon	Virgin Airship & Balloon Co Ltd	
G-OFLT	EMB-110P1 Bandeirante ★	Rescue trainer/Aveley, Essex (G-MOBL/ G-BGCS)	
G-OFLX	Embraer EMB-145LR	BAE Systems (Corporate Travel) Ltd	
G-OFLY	Cessna 210M	A. P. Mothew	
G-OFNC	Balony Kubicek BB17XR balloon	M. R. Jeynes	
G-OFOM	BAe 146-100	Formula One Management Ltd (G-BSLP/ G-BRLM)	
G-OFRB	Everett gyroplane	J. P. Comerford	
G-OFRY	Cessna 152	Devon and Somerset Flight Training Ltd	
G-OFSP	CZAW Sportcruiser	L. Dempsey	
G-OFTI	PA-28 Cherokee 140	J. L. Sparks	
G-OFZY	Eurocopter AS.355N Ecureuil II	Atlas Helicopters Ltd (G-ORDH)	
G-OGAL	Van's RV-14	M. A. Wyer (G-CLMP)	
G-OGAN	Europa	R. K. W. Moss	
G-OGAR	PZL SZD-45A Ogar	J. F. C. Sergeant	
G-OGAS	Westland WG.30 Srs 100 ★	(stored)/Yeovil (G-BKNW)	
G-OGEM	PA-28-181 Archer II	GEM Integrated Solutions Ltd	
G-OGEO	Aérospatiale SA.341G Gazelle 1	G. Steel (G-BXJK)	
G-OGEZ	Robinson R44 II	G. K. Jewson	
G-OGFC	Aerospatiale ATR-72-600	Aurigny Air Services Ltd	
G-OGGB	Grob G.102 Astir CS	M. P. Webb	
G-OGGM	Cirrus SR22	Datascope Systems Ltd	
G-OGGS	Thunder Ax8-84 balloon	G. Gamble & Sons (Quorn) Ltd	
G-OGGY	Aviat A.1B	J. H. Garrett-Cox	
G-OGIL	Short SD3-30 Variant 100 ★	North East Land Sea and Air Museum/Sunderland (G-BITV)	
G-OGIN	Kubicek BB40Z	A. B. Court	
G-OGJC	Robinson R44 II	Telecom Advertising & Promotions Ltd	
G-OGJM	Cameron C-80 balloon	G. F. Madelin	
G-OGLY	Cameron Z-105 balloon	H. M. Ogston	
G-OGOD	P & M Quik GT450	L. McIlwaine	
G-OGOL	Tecnam P2006T	Cucumber Cow Ltd	
G-OGOS	Everett gyroplane	N. A. Seymour	
G-OGPN	Cassutt Special	S. Alexander (G-OMFI/G-BKCH)	
G-OGRL	Van's RV-7	Attitude Aerobatics Ltd	
G-OGRN	Pipistrel Virus SW128	Ifly Electric UK Ltd	
G-OGSA	Avtech Jabiru SPL-450	G-OGSA Group	
G-OGSE	Gulfstream V-SP	TAG Aviation (UK) Ltd	
G-OGTC	Guimbal Cabri G2	G. A. Richardson (G-VVBH)	
G-OGTR	P & M Quik GTR	K. J. Bowles	
G-OGUN	Eurocopter AS.350B2 Ecureuil	Go Exclusive Ltd (G-SMDJ)	
G-OGZZ	Van's RV-8	E. D. Fern	
G-OHAC	Cessna F.182Q	MaguireIzatt LLP	
G-OHAL	Pietenpol Air Camper	A. Ryan-Fecitt	
G-OHAM	Robinson R44 II	Hamsters Wheel Productions Ltd (G-GBEN/ G-CDJZ)	
G-OHAS	Robinson R66	Heli Air Scotland Ltd	

Notes	Reg	Type	Owner or Operator
	G-OHCP	AS.355F1 Twin Squirrel	Staske Construction Ltd (G-BTVS/G-STVE/ G-TOFF/G-BKJX)
	G-OHDC	Colt Film Cassette SS balloon ★	Balloon Preservation Group
	G-OHDK	Glasflugel 304S Shark	The Shark Syndicate
	G-OHGA	Hughes O-6A (69-16011)	MSS Holdings (UK) Ltd
	G-OHGC	Scheibe SF.25C Falke	Heron Gliding Club
	G-OHIG	EMB-110P1 Bandeirante ★	Air Salvage International/Alton (G-OPPP)
	G-OHIO	Dyn'Aero MCR-01	J. M. Keane
	G-OHJE	Alpi Pioneer 300 Hawk	Abergavenny Flying Group
	G-OHJV	Robinson R44	I. Taylor
	G-OHKS	Pegasus Quantum 15-912	L. J. Nelson
	G-OHLI	Robinson R44 II	NCS Partnership
	G-OHLV	Sackville BM-65 balloon	H. & L. D. Vaughan
	G-OHMS	AS.355F1 Twin Squirrel	HFS (Aviation) Ltd
	G-OHOV	Rotorway Executive 162F	M. G. Bird
	G-OHRA	Jabiru J430	H. R. Apps
	G-OHST	Rotorway A600 Talon	I. C. Bedford
	G-OHUR	Hurricane 315	M. Ingleton
	G-OHWK	Bell 206L-1 LongRanger	Eze Air Ltd (G-PWIT/G-DWMI)
	G-OHZO	Aviat A-1A Husky	Neil's Seaplanes Ltd
	G-OIBO	PA-28 Cherokee 180	M. Kraemer & J. G. C. Schneider (G-AVAZ)
	G-OICU	Learjet 45	Patriot Aviation Ltd (G-GMAA)
	G-OIFM	Cameron 90 Dude SS balloon	Magical Adventures Ltd
	G-OIHC	PA-32R-301 Saratoga IIHP	N. J. Lipczynski (G-PUSK)
	G-OIIO	Robinson R22 Beta	Whizzard Helicopters (G-ULAB)
	G-OIIY	Ultramagic S-70 balloon	M. Cowling
	G-OIMC	Cessna 152 II	East Midlands Flying School Ltd
	G-OINN	UltraMagic H-31 balloon	G. Everett
	G-OINT	Balony Kubicek BB20XR balloon	M. A. Green
	G-OIOB	Mudry CAP.10B	Rolls-Royce PLC
	G-OIOZ	Thunder Ax9-120 S2 balloon	D. Venegoni
	G-OITV	Enstrom 280C-UK-2	C. W. Brierley Jones (G-HRVY/G-DUGY/ G-BEEL)
	G-OIVN	Liberty XL-2	A. P. Christie
	G-OJAB	Avtech Jabiru SK	J. D. Winder
	G-OJAC	Mooney M.20J	Hornet Engineering Ltd
	G-OJAG	Cessna 172S	Valhalla Aviation LLP
	G-OJAN	Robinson R22 Beta	J. C. Lane (G-SANS/G-BUHX)
	G-OJAS	Auster J/1U Workmaster	D. S. Hunt
	G-OJBB	Enstrom 280FX	M. Jones
	G-OJBM	Cameron N-90 balloon	B. J. Bettin
	G-OJBS	Cameron N-105A balloon	J. Bennett & Son (Insurance Brokers) Ltd
	G-OJBW	Lindstrand LBL J & B Bottle SS balloon	G. Gray
	G-OJCL	Robinson R22	JCL Aviation (G-HRHE/G-BTWP)
	G-OJCW	PA-32RT-300 Lance II	P. G. Dobson
	G-OJDA	EAA Acrosport II	D. B. Almey
	G-OJDC	Thunder Ax7-77 balloon	A. Heginbottom
	G-OJEH	PA-28-181 Archer II	P. C. Lilley
	G-OJEN	Cameron V-77 balloon	S. D. Wrighton
	G-OJER	Cessna 560XL Citation XLS	Aviation Beauport
	G-OJGC	Van's RV-4	J. G. Claridge
	G-OJGT	Maule M.5-235C	Newnham Joint Flying Syndicate
	G-OJHC	Cessna 182P	N. Foster
	G-OJHL	Shaw Europa	M. D. Burns & G. Rainey
	G-OJIM	PA-28R-201T Turbo Arrow III	Black Star Aviation Ltd
	G-OJJV	P & M Pegasus Quik	J. J. Valentine
	G-OJKM	Rans S.7 Courier	A. J. Owen
	G-OJLD	Van's RV-7	J. L. Dixon
	G-OJLH	TEAM mini-MAX 91	P. D. Parry (G-MYAW)
	G-OJMP	Cessna 208B Grand Caravan	Parachuting Aircraft Ltd
	G-OJMS	Cameron Z-90 balloon	Joinerysoft Ltd
	G-OJNE	Schempp-Hirth Nimbus 3T	M. R. Garwood
	G-OJON	Taylor JT.2 Titch	Freelance Aviation Ltd
	G-OJPS	Bell 206B JetRanger 2	Aikmo Aviation & Marine Ltd (G-UEST/G-ROYB/ G-BLWU)
	G-OJRM	Cessna T.182T	Romeo Mike Group
	G-OJSD	Aeropro Eurofox 912(S)	J. D. Sinclair-Day
	G-OJSH	Thruster T.600N 450 JAB	G-OJSH Group
	G-OJVA	Van's RV-6	J. A. Village

Reg	Type	Owner or Operator	Notes
G-OJVL	Van's RV-6	S. E. Tomlinson	
G-OJWB	Hawker 800XP	Langford Lane Ltd	
G-OJWS	PA-28-161 Warrior II	MET Aviation Ltd	
G-OKAY	Pitts S-1E Special	S. R. S. Evans	
G-OKCP	Lindstrand LBL Battery SS balloon	Flintnine Fasteners Ltd (G-MAXX)	
G-OKED	Cessna 150L	CM Aviation Ltd	
G-OKEN	PA-28R-201T Turbo Arrow III	L. James & J. D. Hood	
G-OKER	Van's RV-7	W. J. Harrison	
G-OKEV	Shaw Europa	K. A. Kedward	
G-OKEW	UltraMagic M-65C balloon	Hampshire Balloons Ltd	
G-OKID	Reality Escapade Kid	V. H. Hallam	
G-OKIM	Best Off Sykyranger 912 (2)	P. J. Callis	
G-OKIS	Tri-R Kis	T. E. Reeder	
G-OKLY	Cessna F.150K	J. L. Sparks (G-ECBH)	
G-OKMA	Tri-R Kis	K. Miller	
G-OKPS	Best Off Skyranger Nynja 912S(1)	G-OKPS Group	
G-OKTA	Ikarus C42 FB80	Avion Training & Consultancy Ltd	
G-OKTI	Aquila AT01	P. H. Ferdinand	
G-OKUB	TLAC Sherwood Kub	The Light Aircraft Company Ltd	
G-OKYA	Cameron V-77 balloon	R. J. Pearce	
G-OLAA	Alpi Pioneer 300 Hawk	G. G. Hammond	
G-OLAD	Extra EA.300/L	A. P. Walsh	
G-OLAU	Robinson R22 Beta	Whizzard Helicopters	
G-OLAW	Lindstrand LBL-25A balloon	George Law Plant Ltd	
G-OLCP	AS.355N Twin Squirrel	Cheshire Helicopters Ltd (G-CLIP)	
G-OLCY	Lindstrand LTL Series 1-105 balloon	I. Chadwick & S. Richards-Chadwick	
G-OLDG	Cessna T.182T	H. W. Palmer (G-CBTJ)	
G-OLDM	Pegasus Quantum 15-912	J. W. Holme	
G-OLDP	Mainair Pegasus Quik	G. J. Gibson	
G-OLEA	PA-28-151 Cherokee Warrior	London School of Flying Ltd	
G-OLEC	Alisport Silent 2 Electro	N. Parry	
G-OLED	Aeropro Eurofox 912(S)	J. J. & S. J. M. Ledingham	
G-OLEE	Cessna F.152	Redhill Air Services Ltd	
G-OLEG	Yakovlev Yak-3UA	Cirrus Aircraft UK Ltd	
G-OLEM	Jodel D.18	G. E. Roe (G-BSBP)	
G-OLEW	Vans RV-7A	Better Aerobatics Ltd	
G-OLFB	Pegasus Quantum 15-912	M. S. McGimpsey	
G-OLFE	Dassault Falcon 20-E5	Green Go Aircraft KFT	
G-OLFT	Rockwell Commander 114	D. A. Tubby (G-WJMN)	
G-OLFZ	P & M Quik GT450	A. J. Boyd	
G-OLGA	Starstreak Shadow SA-II	G. L. Turner	
G-OLHR	Cassutt Racer IIIM	P. A. Hall & A. R. Lewis (G-BNJZ)	
G-OLIC	Tecnam P2008-JC	Stapleford Flying Club Ltd	
G-OLIV	Beech B.200 Super King Air	Dragonfly Aviation Services Ltd (G-RAFN)	
G-OLNT	SA.365N1 Dauphin 2	LNT Aviation Ltd (G-POAV/G-BOPI)	
G-OLOU	Bell 206B-3 Jet Ranger III	Helitrip Charter LLP	
G-OLPM	P & M Quik R	M. D. Freeman	
G-OLSF	PA-28-161 Cadet	Flew LLP (G-OTYJ)	
G-OLUD	Extra EA.300/200	GFG Aerobatics SRL/Italy	
G-OMAA	Eurocopter EC.135 T2+	Babcock Mission Critical Services Onshore Ltd	
G-OMAF	Dornier 228-200	RUAG Aerospace Services GmbH/Germany	
G-OMAG	Cessna 182B	J. W. N. Sharpe	
G-OMAL	Thruster T.600N 450	M. I. Gardner	
G-OMAO	SOCATA TB-20 Trinidad	Alpha Oscar Group (G-GDGR)	
G-OMAS	Cessna A.150M	A. C. & A. M. McLaird (G-BTFS)	
G-OMAT	PA-28 Cherokee 140	Midland Air Training School (G-JIMY/G-AYUG)	
G-OMCB	TL2000UK Sting Carbon S4	M. C. Bayley	
G-OMCC	AS.350B Ecureuil	Airbourne Solutions Ltd (G-JTCM/G-HLEN/ G-LOLY)	
G-OMCH	PA-28-161 Warrior III	Chalrey Ltd	
G-OMCM	Airbus Helicopters AS.350B3 Ecureuil	T. J. Morris Ltd (G-CKYE)	
G-OMDD	Thunder Ax8-90 S2 balloon	M. D. Dickinson	
G-OMDH	Hughes 369E	Stilgate Ltd	
G-OMDR	Agusta-Bell 206B JetRanger II	Castle Air Ltd (G-HRAY/G-VANG/G-BIZA)	
G-OMEN	Cameron Z-90 balloon	M. G. Howard	
G-OMER	Avtech Jabiru UL-450	B. P. Bradley (G-GPAS)	
G-OMEX	Zenair CH.701 UL	J. W. Johns	
G-OMEZ	Zenair CH.601HDS	A. D. Sutton	

Notes	Reg	Type	Owner or Operator
	G-OMGR	Cameron Z-105 balloon	J. F. A. Strickland
	G-OMHC	PA-28RT-201 Arrow IV	W. J. Bieniasz
	G-OMHD	EE Canberra PR.Mk.9 (XH134)	Kemble Airfield Estates Ltd
	G-OMHI	Mills MH-1	J. P. Mills
	G-OMHP	Avtech Jabiru UL	J. Livingstone
	G-OMIA	MS.893A Rallye Commodore 180	S. R. Winter
	G-OMIK	Shaw Europa	Mikite Flying Group
	G-OMIW	Pegasus Quik	A. J. Ladell
	G-OMJA	PA-28-181 Archer II	J. D. Garton
	G-OMJT	Rutan LongEz	D. A. Daniel
	G-OMMM	Colt 90A balloon	A. & M. Frayling
	G-OMNI	PA-28R Cherokee Arrow 200D	Cotswold Aviation Services Ltd (G-BAWA)
	G-OMPH	Van's RV-7	R. J. Luke
	G-OMPW	Mainair Pegasus Quik	M. P. Wimsey
	G-OMRB	Cameron V-77 balloon	I. J. Jevons
	G-OMRC	Van's RV-10	A. W. Collett
	G-OMRP	Flight Design CTSW	M. E. Parker
	G-OMSA	Flight Design CTSW	Microlight Sport Aviation Ltd
	G-OMSL	Pilatus PC-12/47E	Pink Time Ltd
	G-OMST	PA-28-161 Warrior III	Mid-Sussex Timber Co Ltd (G-BZUA)
	G-OMTX	Bombardier BD700-1A11 Global 5000	OMTX Aviation LP Inc
	G-OMUD	Cessna A.185E	P. A. Greenhalgh
	G-OMUM	Rockwell Commander 114	M. J. P. Lynch
	G-ONAA	North American Rockwell OV-10B Bronco (99+18)	Liberty Aviation Ltd
	G-ONAF	Naval Aircraft Factory N3N-3 (4406:12)	J. P. Birnie
	G-ONAN	Bensen B.8MV	Department of Doing Ltd (G-BKBS)
	G-ONAT	Grob G.102 Astir CS77	N. A. Toogood
	G-ONAV	PA-31-310 Turbo Navajo C	Panther Aviation Ltd (G-IGAR)
	G-ONCB	Lindstrand LBL-31A balloon	B. J. Alford
	G-ONCS	Slingsby T.66 Nipper 3	C. Swann & M. G. Walker (G-AZBA)
	G-ONET	PA-28-180 Cherokee E	Bristol Aero Club (G-AYAU)
	G-ONEZ	Glaser-Dirks DG-200/17	One Zulu Group
	G-ONGC	Robin DR.400/180R	Norfolk Gliding Club Ltd
	G-ONHH	Forney F-1A Aircoupe	R. D. I. Tarry (G-ARHA)
	G-ONHL	SZD-54-2 Perkoz	Devon and Somerset Gliding Club Ltd
	G-ONIC	Evektor EV-97 Sportstar Max	D. M. Jack
	G-ONIG	Murphy Elite	N. S. Smith
	G-ONKA	Aeronca K	N. J. R. Minchin
	G-ONNE	Westland Gazelle HT.3 (XW858:C)	A. M. Parkes (G-DMSS)
	G-ONSW	Skyranger Swift 912S(1)	N. S. Wells
	G-ONTV	Agusta-Bell 206B-3 JetRanger III	Adventure 001 Ltd (G-GOUL)
	G-ONUN	Van's RV-6A	D. Atkinson
	G-ONVG	Guimbal Cabri G2	Vantage Aviation Ltd
	G-ONYX	Bell 206B-3 JetRanger III	Orchid Homes Ltd (G-BXPN)
	G-OOAK	Jabiru J430	R. W. Swift
	G-OOBA	Boeing 757-26N	TUI Airways Ltd
	G-OOBB	Boeing 757-28A	TUI Airways Ltd
	G-OOBN	Boeing 757-2G5	TUI Airways Ltd
	G-OOBP	Boeing 757-2G5	TUI Airways Ltd
	G-OOCP	SOCATA TB-10 Tobago	R. M. Briggs (G-BZRL)
	G-OODD	Robinson R44 II	S. K. Miles
	G-OODE	SNCAN Stampe SV.4C (modified)	G-OODE Flying Group (G-AZNN)
	G-OODI	Pitts S-1D Special	C. Hutson & M. J. McCulloch (G-BBBU)
	G-OODW	PA-28-181 Archer II	Redhill Air Services Ltd
	G-OOEG	Bombardier BD100-1A10 Challenger 350	Catreus Ltd
	G-OOEY	Balony Kubicek BB-222 balloon	A. W. Holly
	G-OOFE	Thruster T.600N 450	D. Dance
	G-OOGO	GA-7 Cougar	Servicos Aereos Scalabitanos Lda/Portugal
	G-OOGY	P & M Quik R	Cambridge Road Professional Services Ltd
	G-OOIO	AS.350B3 Ecureuil	Hovering Ltd
	G-OOLD	Funk B85C	A. D. Pearce & P. King
	G-OOLE	Cessna 172M	J. Edmondson (G-BOSI)
	G-OOMA	PA-28-161 Warrior II	JABM Ltd (G-BRBB)
	G-OOMF	PA-18-150 Super Cub	C. G. Bell
	G-OONE	Mooney M.20J	M. Kalyuzhny, C. Hollis & D. Newton
	G-OONY	PA-28-161 Warrior II	J. R. Golding
	G-OONZ	P & M Aviation Quik	G-OONZ Group
	G-OOON	PA-34-220T Seneca III	R. Paris

Reg	Type	Owner or Operator	Notes
G-OOPY	CSA PS-28 Cruiser	V. Barnes	
G-OORB	Diamond DA.40D Star	Gemstone Aviation Ltd	
G-OORV	Van's RV-6	C. Sharples	
G-OOSH	Zenair CH.601UL Zodiac	J. R. C. Brightman & J. P. Batty	
G-OOSY	DH.82A Tiger Moth (DE971)	S. Philpott & C. Stopher	
G-OOTC	PA-28R-201T Turbo Arrow III	G-OOTC Group (G-CLIV)	
G-OOTT	Eurocopter AS.350B3 Ecureuil	R. J. Green	
G-OOUK	Cirrus SR22	P. R. D. Smith	
G-OOWS	Eurocopter AS.350B3 Ecureuil	Millburn World Travel Services Ltd	
G-OOXP	Aero Designs Pulsar XP	P. C. Avery	
G-OPAG	PA-34-200 Seneca II	A. H. Lavender (G-BNGB)	
G-OPAM	Cessna F.152 II (tailwheel)	PJC Leasing Ltd (G-BFZS)	
G-OPAR	Van's RV-6	L. V. Adams (G-CGNR)	
G-OPAT	Beech 76 Duchess	Golf Alpha Tango Ltd	
G-OPAW	Cameron Z-105 balloon	Lighter Than Air Ltd	
G-OPAZ	Pazmany PL.2	A. D. Wood	
G-OPBW	Cameron nZ-150 balloon	Polar Bear Windows Ltd	
G-OPCB	Van's RV-7	P. C. Burgess	
G-OPCG	Cessna 182T	S. K. Pomfret	
G-OPDG	Robinson R44 II	R. R. Orr (G-DROL)	
G-OPEJ	TEAM Minimax 91A	A. W. McBlain	
G-OPER	Lindstrand LTL Series 1-70 balloon	Lindstrand Balloons Ltd	
G-OPET	PA-28-181 Archer II	Cambrian Flying Group Ltd	
G-OPFA	Pioneer 300	S. Eddison & R. Minett	
G-OPFR	Diamond DA.42 Twin Star	P. F. Rothwell	
G-OPHT	Schleicher ASH-26E	J. S. Wand	
G-OPIC	Cessna FRA.150L	A. V. Harmer (G-BGNZ)	
G-OPIK	Eiri PIK-20E	G-OPIK Syndicate	
G-OPIT	CFM Streak Shadow Srs SA	I. J. Guy	
G-OPJD	PA-28RT-201T Turbo Arrow IV	J. M. McMillan	
G-OPJK	Shaw Europa	P. J. Kember	
G-OPJS	Pietenpol Air Camper	P. J. Shenton	
G-OPKF	Cameron 90 Bowler SS balloon	D. K. Fish	
G-OPLC	DH.104 Dove 8	Columba Aviation Ltd (G-BLRB)	
G-OPME	PA-23 Aztec 250D	R. G. Pardo (G-ODIR/G-AZGB)	
G-OPMJ	Cessna F.172M	Jefferson Air Photography (G-BIIB)	
G-OPMT	Lindstrand LBL-105A balloon	K. R. Karlstrom	
G-OPOT	Agusta A.109S Grand	Sundorne Properties (Llanidloes) Ltd (G-EMHD/G-STGR)	
G-OPPO	Groppo Trail	A. C. Hampson	
G-OPRC	Shaw Europa XS	M. J. Ashby-Arnold & D. Lee	
G-OPSF	PA-38-112 Tomahawk	P. I. Higham (G-BGZI)	
G-OPSG	Aeropro Eurofox 912(S)	P. S. Gregory	
G-OPSL	PA-32R-301 Saratoga SP	P. R. Tomkins (G-IMPW)	
G-OPSS	Cirrus SR20	Clifton Aviation Ltd	
G-OPST	Cessna 182R	Sierra Tango Flying Group Ltd	
G-OPTI	PA-28-161 Warrior II	Rio Leon Services Ltd	
G-OPTZ	Pitts S-2A Special	J. L. Dixon (G—SKNT/G-PEAL)	
G-OPUB	Slingsby T.67M Firefly 160	A. L. Barker (G-DLTA/G-SFTX)	
G-OPUG	Czech Sport PS-28 Cruiser	Pentaction Ltd	
G-OPUK	PA-28-161 Warrior III	D. J. King	
G-OPUP	Beagle B.121 Pup 2	F. A. Zubiel (G-AXEU)	
G-OPVM	Van's RV-9A	R. M. Cochran	
G-OPWR	Cameron Z-90 balloon	Flying Enterprises	
G-OPWS	Mooney M.20K	J. M. Carter	
G-OPYE	Cessna 172S	M. J. Casey	
G-OPYO	Alpi Pioneer 300 Hawk	S. C. Ord	
G-ORAE	Van's RV-7	R. W. Eaton	
G-ORAF	CFM Streak Shadow	G. A. Carter	
G-ORAI	Avions ATR-72-212A	Aurigny Air Services Ltd	
G-ORAM	Thruster T600N 450	D. W. Wilson	
G-ORAR	PA-28-181 Archer III	P. N. & S. M. Thornton	
G-ORAS	Clutton FRED Srs 2	A. I. Sutherland	
G-ORAU	Evektor EV-97 Eurostar	W. R. C. Williams-Wynne	
G-ORAW	Cessna 525 Citation M2	Catreus AOC Ltd	
G-ORAY	Cessna F.182Q II	M. Parrinder (G-BHDN)	
G-ORBK	Robinson R44 II	T2 Technology Ltd (G-CCNO)	
G-ORBS	Mainair Blade	J. W. Dodson	
G-ORBT	BRM Bristell NG5 Speed Wing	R. B. Thomas	

Notes	Reg	Type	Owner or Operator
	G-ORCA	Van's RV-4	I. A. Harding
	G-ORCB	AutoGyro Calidus	J. Marshall
	G-ORCD	Agusta A.109S Grand	Castle Air Ltd (G-GBMM/G-GRND)
	G-ORCV	Cameron Z-120 balloon	A. Collett
	G-ORCW	Schempp-Hirth Ventus 2cT	J. C. A. Garland
	G-ORDA	Cessna F.172N	D. G. Martinez
	G-ORDM	Cessna 182T	The Cambridge Aero Club Ltd (G-KEMY)
	G-ORDS	Thruster T.600N 450	S. R. Pike
	G-ORED	BN-2T Turbine Islander	Britten-Norman Ltd (G-BJYW)
	G-OREZ	Cessna 525 Citation M2	Helitrip Charter LLP
	G-ORIB	Aeropro Eurofox 912(IS)	J. McAlpine
	G-ORIG	Glaser-Dirks DG.800A	M. Bond & R. Kalin
	G-ORIX	ARV K1 Super 2	T. M. Lyons (G-BUXH/G-BNVK)
	G-ORKY	AS.350B2 Ecureuil	PLM Dollar Group Ltd
	G-ORLA	P & M Pegasus Quik	J. Summers
	G-ORLY	AA-5B Tiger	Boker Layla Aviation Ltd (G-DONI/G-BLLT)
	G-ORMB	Robinson R22 Beta	Heli Air Scotland Ltd
	G-ORMW	Ikarus C.42 FB100	A. J. Dixon & J. W. D. Blythe
	G-ORNH	Lindstrand LTL Series 2-50 balloon	A. M. Holly
	G-OROD	PA-18 Super Cub 150	B. W. Faulkner
	G-OROS	Ikarus C.42 FB80	R. I. Simpson
	G-ORPC	Shaw Europa XS	P. W. Churms
	G-ORPR	Cameron O-77 balloon	A. O. H. Harvey
	G-ORRG	Robin DR.400-180 Regent	Radley Robin Group
	G-ORSE	Ikarus C42 FB100 Bravo	D. S. Murrell
	G-ORST	Airbus EC.135 T3	Babcock Mission Critical Services Onshore Ltd (G-DEWF)
	G-ORUG	Thruster T.600N 450	R. D. McKellar
	G-ORUN	Reality Escapade	M. J. Clark
	G-ORVB	McCulloch J-2 ★	The Helicopter Museum/Weston-super-Mare (G-HEKY)
	G-ORVE	Van's RV-6	R. J. F. Swain & F. M. Sperryn
	G-ORVG	Van's RV-6	RV6 Group
	G-ORVI	Van's RV-6	B. O. Harvey
	G-ORVR	Partenavia P.68B	Ravenair Aircraft Ltd (G-BFBD)
	G-ORVS	Van's RV-9	C. J. Marsh
	G-ORVX	Van's RV-10	C. D. Meek (G-OHIY)
	G-ORVZ	Van's RV-7	C. Taylor
	G-ORWS	Van's RV-14	R. W. Sweetnam
	G-ORYG	Rotorsport UK Cavalon	M. P. L. Dowie
	G-OSAI	PA-28-181 Archer II	Falcon Flying Services Ltd (G-BYKL)
	G-OSAR	Bell 206L-1 LongRanger	Vantage Aviation Ltd
	G-OSAT	Cameron Z-105 balloon	A. V. & M. R. Noyce
	G-OSCC	PA-32 Cherokee Six 300	BG & G Airlines Ltd (G-BGFD)
	G-OSCO	TEAM mini-MAX 91	S. H. Slade
	G-OSDF	Schempp-Hirth Ventus a	S. D. Foster
	G-OSEA	BN-2B-26 Islander	W. T. Johnson & Sons (Huddersfield) Ltd (G-BKOL)
	G-OSEM	Robinson R44 II	Sloane Charter
	G-OSEP	Mainair Blade 912	J. D. Smith
	G-OSFB	Diamond HK.36TTC Super Dimona	Oxfordshire Sportflying Ltd
	G-OSFS	Cessan F.177RG	D. G. Wright
	G-OSGC	Aeropro Eurofox 912(S)	Scottish Gliding Union Ltd
	G-OSGU	Aeropro Eurofox 912(S)	Scottish Gliding Union Ltd
	G-OSHK	Schempp-Hirth SHK-1	P. B. Hibbard
	G-OSHL	Robinson R22 Beta	Sloane Helicopters Ltd
	G-OSIC	Pitts S-1C Special	P. J. Hebdon (G-BUAW)
	G-OSII	Cessna 172N	G-OSII Group (G-BIVY)
	G-OSIS	Pitts S-1S Special	D. S. T. Eggleton
	G-OSIT	Pitts S-1T Special	Smart People UK Ltd
	G-OSJC	PA-32R-301 Saratoga IIHP	S-J Clegg (G-GOBD/G-OARW)
	G-OSKR	Skyranger 912 (2)	H. D. Colliver
	G-OSKY	Cessna 172M	Skyhawk Leasing Ltd
	G-OSLD	Shaw Europa XS	S. Percy & C. Davies
	G-OSLO	Schweizer 269C	A. H. Helicopter Services Ltd
	G-OSMD	Bell 206B JetRanger 2	TR Aviation Services Ltd (G-LTEK/G-BMIB)
	G-OSND	Cessna FRA.150M	Group G-OSND (G-BDOU)
	G-OSNX	Grob G.109B	R. J. Barsby
	G-OSOD	P & M Quik GTR	R. Gellert
	G-OSON	P & M QuikR	R. Parr

Reg	Type	Owner or Operator	Notes
G-OSOR	DG Flugzeugbau DG-1000M	Lleweni Parc Ltd	
G-OSOX	Grob G.109B	Aerosparx Ltd	
G-OSPD	Aerotechnik EV-97 TeamEurostar UK	R. A. Stewart-Jones	
G-OSPH	Ikarus C42 FB100	Progress Vehicle Management Ltd	
G-OSPP	Robinson R44	Danelander Ltd	
G-OSPS	PA-18 Super Cub 95 (51-15555)	B. G. Colvin	
G-OSPX	Grob G.109B	Aerosparx (G-BMHR)	
G-OSRA	Boeing 727-2S2F	T2 Aviation Ltd	
G-OSRB	Boeing 727-2S2F	T2 Aviation Ltd	
G-OSRL	Learjet 45	S. R. Lloyd	
G-OSRS	Cameron A-375 balloon	Wickers World Ltd	
G-OSSA	Cessna Tu.206B	Skydive St.Andrews Ltd	
G-OSST	Colt 77A balloon	A. A. Brown	
G-OSTC	AA-5A Cheetah	C. J. Aucken	
G-OSTL	Ikarus C.42 FB 100	G. P. Curtis	
G-OSTX	Grob G.109B	Aerosparx Ltd (G-CKXB)	
G-OSUS	Mooney M.20K	LTV Express Ltd	
G-OSUT	Scheibe SF-25C Rotax-Falke	Yorkshire Gliding Club (Pty.) Ltd	
G-OSVN	AutoGyro Cavalon	Engetel Ltd	
G-OSZB	Christen Pitts S-2B Special	K. A. Fitton & A. M. Gent (G-OGEE)	
G-OSZS	Pitts S-2S Special	G-OSZS Group	
G-OTAL	ARV Super 2	P. Robichaud (G-BNGZ)	
G-OTAM	Cessna 172M	G. V. White	
G-OTAN	PA-18 Super Cub 135 (54-2445)	A. & J. D. Owen	
G-OTAW	BRM Bristell NG5 Speed Wing	Guernsey Aviation & Marine Ltd	
G-OTAY	Tecnam P2006T	Nyuki Ltd (G-ZOOG)	
G-OTCH	Streak Shadow	R. M. M. & A. G. Moura	
G-OTCT	Cameron Z-105 balloon	Lighter Than Air Ltd	
G-OTCV	Skyranger 912S (1)	Charlie Victor Flying Group	
G-OTCZ	Schempp-Hirth Ventus 2cT	A. J. Rees	
G-OTEA	Balony Kubicek BB17XR balloon	A. M. Holly	
G-OTEC	Tecnam P2002 Sierra Deluxe	D. P. Budworth	
G-OTED	Robinson R22 ★	The Helicopter Museum/Weston-super-Mare (G-BMYR)	
G-OTEL	Thunder Ax8-90 balloon	J. W. Adkins	
G-OTFT	PA-38-112 Tomahawk	P. Tribble (G-BNKW)	
G-OTGA	PA-28R-201 Arrow III	TG Aviation Ltd	
G-OTHE	Enstrom 280C-UK Shark	K. P. Groves (G-OPJT/G-BKCO)	
G-OTIG	AA-5B Tiger	L. Burke (G-PENN)	
G-OTIM	Bensen B.8MV	T. J. Deane	
G-OTIV	Aerospool Dynamic WT9 UK	D. P. Pactor & P. O'Donohue	
G-OTJH	Pegasus Quantum 15-912	L. R. Gartside	
G-OTJT	Glasflugel 304SJ Shark	N. J. L. Busvine	
G-OTLC	Grumman AA-5 Traveller	L. P. Keegan & S. R. Cameron (G-BBUF)	
G-OTME	SNCAN Nord 1002 Pingouin	S. H. O'Connell	
G-OTNA	Robinson R44 Raven II	A. N. Abel	
G-OTNM	Tecnam P2008-LC	C. S. Nahhas	
G-OTOE	Aeronca 7AC Champion	M. J. Searle (G-BRWW)	
G-OTOO	Stolp SA.300 Starduster Too	I. M. Castle	
G-OTOP	P & M Quik R	M. I. White	
G-OTOW	Cessna 175BX	C. J. P. Wilkes (G-AROC)	
G-OTRT	Robinson R44 II	Ian Hutchinson Enterprises Ltd (G-CFEC)	
G-OTRV	Van's RV-6	E. Andersen	
G-OTRY	Schleicher ASW-24	A. H. Beckingham	
G-OTSP	AS.355F1 Twin Squirrel	Excel Charter Ltd (G-XPOL/G-BPRF)	
G-OTTI	Cameron Otti-34 balloon	P. Spellward	
G-OTTS	Ikarus C42 FB100 Bravo	B. C. Gotts	
G-OTTY	Rotorsport UK Calidus	GS Aviation (Europe) Ltd	
G-OTUI	SOCATA TB20 Trinidad	H. Graff (G-KKDL/G-BSHU)	
G-OTUM	Skyranger Nynja LS 912S(1)	D. W. Wallington	
G-OTUN	EV-97A Eurostar	L. R. Morris & K. R. Annett	
G-OTVR	PA-34-220T Seneca V	M. Barr	
G-OTWS	Schempp-Hirth Duo Discus XLT	T. W. Slater	
G-OTYE	Aerotechnik EV-97 Eurostar	A. B. Godber	
G-OTYP	PA-28 Cherokee 180	T. C. Lewis	
G-OTZZ	AutoGyro Cavalon	J. C. Collingwood	
G-OUAV	TLAC Sherwood Scout	University of Southampton Aviation Society	
G-OUCP	PA-31 Navajo C	2 Excel Aviation Ltd (G-GURN/G-BHGA)	
G-OUDA	Aeroprakt A22-L Foxbat	A. R. Cattell	

Notes	Reg	Type	Owner or Operator
	G-OUEG	Bombardier BD700-1A10 Global 6000	Catreus AOC Ltd
	G-OUGH	Yakovlev Yak-52	Optimum Promotions Ltd (G-LAOK)
	G-OUHI	Shaw Europa XS	N. M. Graham
	G-OUIK	Mainair Pegasus Quik	M. D. Evans
	G-OURO	Shaw Europa	S. J. Westley
	G-OURT	Lindstrand LTL Series Racer 56 balloon	A. B. Court
	G-OUVI	Cameron O-105 balloon	Bristol University Hot Air Ballooning Society
	G-OVAL	Ikarus C.42 FB100	N. G. Tomes
	G-OVBF	Cameron A-250 balloon	Virgin Balloon Flights
	G-OVBL	Lindstrand LBL-150A balloon	R. J. Henderson
	G-OVEG	Diamond DA.20-C1 Katana	International Flight Referral BVBA/Belgium
	G-OVEY	Van's RV-7	M. Covey
	G-OVFM	Cessna 120	P. A. Harvie
	G-OVFR	Cessna F.172N	Marine and Aviation Ltd
	G-OVII	Van's RV-7	T. J. Richardson
	G-OVIN	Rockwell Commander 112TC	C. S. Higgins
	G-OVIR	Pipistrel Virus SW 121	Ifly Electric UK Ltd
	G-OVIV	Aerostyle Breezer LSA	Chiltern Flying Group
	G-OVLA	Ikarus C.42 FB	Propeller Owners Ltd
	G-OVMC	Cessna F.152 II	Swiftair Maintenance Ltd
	G-OVNE	Cessna 401A H ★	City of Norwich Aviation Museum/Norwich
	G-OVNR	Robinson R22 Beta	HQ Aviation Ltd
	G-OVOL	Skyranger 912S(1)	K. B. Woods
	G-OVON	PA-18-95 Super Cub	V. F. A. Stanley
	G-OVPM	Europa NG	P. Munford
	G-OVSI	Pipistrel Virus SW121	Ifly Electric UK Ltd
	G-OWAG	Cameron TR-70 balloon	M. G. Howard
	G-OWAI	Schleicher ASK-21	Scottish Gliding Union
	G-OWAL	PA-34-220T Seneca III	Corp Straznice SRO/Czech Republic
	G-OWAP	PA-28-161 Cherokee Warrior II	Tayside Aviation Ltd (G-BXNH)
	G-OWAR	PA-28-161 Warrior II	Bickertons Aerodromes Ltd
	G-OWAZ	Pitts S-1C Special	P. E. S. Latham (G-BRPI)
	G-OWBA	Alpi Pioneer 300 Hawk	B. M. & J. O. Davis
	G-OWEN	K & S Jungster	R. C. Owen
	G-OWGC	Slingsby T.61F Venture T.2	Wolds Gliding Club Ltd
	G-OWLL	Ultramagic M-105 balloon	J. A. Lawton
	G-OWLS	Magni M.24C Orion	K. D. Woods
	G-OWLY	Cameron C-70 balloon	M. E. Banks
	G-OWMC	Thruster T.600N	Wilts Microlight Centre
	G-OWOW	Cessna 152 II	T. W. Gilbert (G-BMSZ)
	G-OWPS	Ikarus C42 FB100	Webb Plant Sales
	G-OWRC	Cessna F.152 II	Unimat SA/France
	G-OWRT	Cessna 182G	Tripacer Group
	G-OWST	Cessna 172S	Westair Flying Services Ltd (G-WABH)
	G-OWTF	Pitts S-2B Special	D. P. Curtis (G-BRVT)
	G-OWTN	Embraer EMB-145EP	BAE Systems (Corporate Air Travel) Ltd
	G-OWWW	Shaw Europa	R. F. W. Holder
	G-OXBA	Cameron Z-160 balloon	J. E. Rose
	G-OXBC	Cameron A-140 balloon	J. E. Rose
	G-OXBY	Cameron N-90 balloon	C. A. Oxby
	G-OXFA	PA-34-220T Seneca V	Oxford Aviation Academy (Oxford) Ltd
	G-OXFB	PA-34-220T Seneca V	Oxford Aviation Academy (Oxford) Ltd
	G-OXFC	PA-34-220T Seneca V	Oxford Aviation Academy (Oxford) Ltd
	G-OXFD	PA-34-220T Seneca V	Oxford Aviation Academy (Oxford) Ltd
	G-OXFE	PA-34-220T Seneca V	Oxford Aviation Academy (Oxford) Ltd
	G-OXFF	PA-34-220T Seneca V	Oxford Aviation Academy (Oxford) Ltd
	G-OXFG	PA-34-220T Seneca V	Oxford Aviation Academy (Oxford) Ltd
	G-OXII	Van's RV-12	J. A. King
	G-OXIV	Van's RV-14	M. Browning
	G-OXOM	PA-28-161 Cadet	Aeros Leasing Ltd (G-BRSG)
	G-OXPS	Falcon XPS	J. C. Greenslade (G-BUXP)
	G-OXVI	VS.361 Spitfire LF.XVIe (TD248:CR-S)	Spitfire Ltd
	G-OYAK	Yakovlev C-11 (9 white)	M. G. Jefferies
	G-OYES	Mainair Blade 912	C. R. Chapman
	G-OYGC	Aeropro Eurofox 912(iS)	York Gliding Centre (Operations) Ltd
	G-OYIO	Robin DR.400/120	Exeter Aviation Ltd
	G-OYTE	Rans S.6ES Coyote II	K. C. Noakes

Reg	Type	Owner or Operator	Notes
G-OZEE	Light Aero Avid Speedwing Mk 4	G. D. Bailey	
G-OZIE	Jabiru J400	S. A. Bowkett	
G-OZIP	Christen Eagle II	M. R. C. Sims	
G-OZOE	Lindstrand LBL Cornetto	Flintnine Fasteners Ltd	
G-OZOI	Cessna R.182	J. R. G. & F. L. G. Fleming (G-ROBK)	
G-OZON	PA-32R-301T Saratoga II TC	W. P. Best	
IG-OZOZ	Schempp-Hirth Nimbus 3DT	G-OZOZ Flying Group	
G-OZSB	Geta-Flug AS.105GD airship	Cheers Airships Ltd	
G-OZZE	Lambert Mission M108	Lambert Aircraft Engineering BVBA/Belgium	
G-OZZI	Jabiru SK	A. H. Godfrey	
G-OZZT	Cirrus SR-22T	C. C. Aitkenhead	
G-PACE	Robin R.1180T	C. A. C. Bontet/France	
G-PACO	Sikorsky S-76C	Cardinal Helicopter Services	
G-PACT	PA-28-181 Archer III	A. Parsons	
G-PADE	Escapade 912 (2)	F. Overall	
G-PAFF	AutoGyro MTO Sport	S. R. Paffett	
G-PAIB	PA-18-135 Super Cub	G. Cormack (G-LIBC/G-KAMP)	
G-PAIG	Grob G.109B	M. E. Baker	
G-PAIZ	PA-12 Super Cruiser	B. R. Pearson	
G-PAJU	Rans S-4 Coyote	A. R. Dobrowolski (G-MWES)	
G-PALI	Czech Sport Aircraft Piper Sport	MPG Aviation Ltd	
G-PALT	AutoGyro MTO Sport	D. A. Jordan	
G-PAPE	Diamond DA42 Twin Star	DEA Aviation Ltd	
G-PAPI	Ikarus C42 FB80	Avon Training and Consultancy Ltd	
G-PAPJ	Van's RV-8	P. G. Jenkins	
G-PARG	Pitts S-1C Special	R. J. Dolby	
G-PASA	MBB Bolkow Bo.105D ★	The Helicopter Museum/Weston-super-Mare (G-BGWP)	
G-PASB	MBB Bolkow Bo.105D ★	The Helicopter Museum/Weston-super-Mare (G-BDMC)	
G-PASH	AS.355F1 Twin Squirrel	Excel Charter Ltd	
G-PASL	AS.355F2 Ecureuil 2	C-E. Giblain/France	
G-PASN	Enstrom F-28F	N. Pasha (G-BSHZ)	
G-PATF	Shaw Europa	Condor Aviation International Ltd	
G-PATG	Cameron O-90 balloon	N. & S. Symonds	
G-PATJ	Ikarus C42 FB80	P. J. Oakey	
G-PATN	SOCATA TB10 Tobago	R. W. Sharp (G-LUAR)	
G-PATO	Zenair CH.601UL Zodiac	R. Duckett	
G-PATP	Lindstrand LBL-77A balloon	P. Pruchnickyj	
G-PATS	Shaw Europa	R. A. Harrison	
G-PATX	Lindstrand LBL-90A balloon	M. R. Noyce & R. P. E. Phillips	
G-PATZ	Shaw Europa	C. W. & S. R. Potts	
G-PAWA	PA-28-180 Cherokee C	Lanpro Group (G-AVRU)	
G-PAWS	AA-5A Cheetah	Close Encounters	
G-PAWW	Ultramagic M-90 balloon	S. J. Thomas	
G-PAWZ	Best Off Sky Ranger Swift 912S(1)	G-PAWZ Syndicate	
G-PAXX	PA-20 Pacer 135 (modified)	C. W. Monsell	
G-PAYD	Robin DR.400/180	P. Bigland	
G-PAZY	Pazmany PL.4A	M. Richardson (G-BLAJ)	
G-PBAL	Autogyro MTOsport	P. S. Ball	
G-PBAT	Czech Sport Aircraft Sportcruiser	P. M. W. Bath	
G-PBDG	Glaser-Dirks DG-300	B. G. & P. W. McDermid (G-DJAB)	
G-PBEC	Van's RV-7	P. G. Reid	
G-PBEE	Robinson R44	Echo Echo Syndicate	
G-PBEL	CFM Shadow Srs DD	S. Fairweather	
G-PBII	DR.107 One Design	P. D. Baisden	
G-PBIX	VS.361 Spitfire LF XVI E (RW382)	Downlock Ltd (G-XVIA)	
G-PBWS	Schleicher ASH-31MI	P. B. Walker	
G-PBYA	Consolidated PBY-5A Catalina (433915)	Catalina Aircraft Ltd	
G-PCAT	SOCATA TB10 Tobago	G-PCAT Group (G-BHER)	
G-PCCC	Alpi Pioneer 300	P. F. D. Waltham	
G-PCCM	Alpi Pioneer 200M	M. G. Freeman	
G-PCDP	Zlin Z.526F Trener Master	G. Takacs	
G-PCGC	Allstar PZL SZD-54-2 Perkoz	Cambridge Gliding Club Ltd	
G-PCIZ	Pilatus PC-12/47E	Limbourne Ltd	
G-PCJS	Diamond DA.42NG Twin Star	P. J. Cooper & G. E. J. Sealey	
G-PCMC	P & M Quik R	G. Charman	
G-PCOP	Beech B200 Super King Air	Albert Batlett and Sons (Airdrie) Ltd	

BRITISH CIVIL AIRCRAFT MARKINGS

Notes	Reg	Type	Owner or Operator
	G-PCPC	AutoGyro Calidus	P. E. Churchill
	G-PCTW	Pilatus PC-12/47E	Yellow Skies LLP
	G-PDGF	AS.350B2 Ecureuil	PLM Dollar Group Ltd (G-FROH)
	G-PDGG	Aeromere F.8L Falco Srs 3	T. W. Gilbert
	G-PDGI	AS.350B2 Ecureuil	PLM Dollar Group Ltd (G-BVJE)
	G-PDGN	SA.365N Dauphin 2	PLM Dollar Group Ltd (G-TRAF/G-BLDR)
	G-PDGO	AS.365N2 Dauphin II	PLM Dollar Group Ltd
	G-PDGP	AS.355F2 Ecureuil 2	PLM Dollar Group Ltd (G-ZITZ)
	G-PDGR	AS.350B2 Ecureuil	PLM Dollar Group Ltd (G-RICC/G-BTXA)
	G-PDGT	AS.355F2 Ecureuil 2	PLM Dollar Group Ltd (G-BOOV)
	G-PDGV	Vulcanair P.68C-TC	PLM Dollar Group Ltd
	G-PDGX	Vulcanair P.68C-TC	PLM Dollar Group Ltd
	G-PDOC	PA-44-180 Seminole	Medicare (G-PVAF)
	G-PDOG	Cessna O-1E Bird Dog (24550)	R. J. Dalley
	G-PDRO	Schleicher ASH-31 Mi	P. Crawley
	G-PDSI	Cessna 172N	DA Flying Group
	G-PEAR	P &M Pegasus Quik	N. D. Major
	G-PECK	PA-32-300 Cherokee Six D	K. H. McCune (G-ETAV/G-MCAR/G-LADA/ G-AYWK)
	G-PECX	Eurofox 912S(2)	SAE Systems Ltd
	G-PEGE	Skyranger 912	A. N. Hughes
	G-PEGI	PA-34-200T Seneca II	Go Fly Oxford Ltd
	G-PEGY	Shaw Europa	A. Carter
	G-PEJM	PA-28-181 Archer III	S. J. Clark
	G-PEKT	SOCATA TB20 Trinidad	The WERY Flying Group
	G-PERC	Cameron N-90 balloon	I. R. Warrington
	G-PERD	Agusta Westland AW.139	Babcock Mission Critical Services Offshore Ltd
	G-PERR	Cameron 60 Bottle SS balloon ★	British Balloon Museum/Newbury
	G-PEST	Hawker Tempest II (MW401)	Anglia Aircraft Restorations Ltd
	G-PETH	PA-24-260C Comanche	J. V. Hutchinson & W. T. G. Ponnet
	G-PETO	Hughes 369HM	P. E. Tornberg (G-HAUS/G-KBOT/G-RAMM)
	G-PETR	PA-28-140 Cherokee	D. Prusik (G-BCJL)
	G-PFAA	EAA Biplane Model P	T. A. Fulcher
	G-PFAF	FRED Srs 2	M. S. Perkins
	G-PFAH	Evans VP-1	J. A. Scott
	G-PFAP	Currie Wot/SE-5A (C1904:Z)	J. H. Seed
	G-PFAR	Isaacs Fury II (K2059)	T. Jarvis
	G-PFAT	Monnett Sonerai II	H. B. Carter
	G-PFAW	Evans VP-1	R. F. Shingler
	G-PFKD	Yakovlev Yak-12M	R. D. Bade
	G-PFSL	Cessna F.152	P. A. Simon
	G-PGAC	MCR-01	G. A. Coatesworth
	G-PGEE	PA-18 Super Cub 95	P. S. Gilmour (G-BIYJ)
	G-PGFG	Tecnam P92-EM Echo	T. Farncombe
	G-PGGY	Robinson R44	EBG (Helicopters) Ltd
	G-PGHM	Air Creation 582(2)/Kiss 450	R. J. Turner
	G-PGSA	Thruster T.600N	M. Atkinson
	G-PGSI	Pierre Robin R2160	M. A. Spencer
	G-PHAA	Cessna F.150M	W. B. Bateson (G-BCPE)
	G-PHAB	Cirrus SR22	G3 Aviation Ltd (G-MACL)
	G-PHAT	Cirrus SR20	T. W. Wielkopolski
	G-PHIZ	PA-30 Twin Comanche	T. J. & G. M. Laundy
	G-PHNX	Schempp-Hirth Duo Discus Xt	72 Syndicate
	G-PHOR	Cessna FRA.150L Aerobat	M. Bonsall (G-BACC)
	G-PHOX	Aeroprakt A22-L Foxbat	J. D. Webb
	G-PHSE	Balony Kubicek BB26Z balloon	The Packhouse Ltd
	G-PHSI	Colt 90A balloon	P. H. Strickland
	G-PHTG	SOCATA TB10 Tobago	A. J. Baggarley
	G-PHUN	Cessna FRA.150L Aerobat	M. Bonsall (G-BAIN)
	G-PHVM	Van's RV-8	G. P. Howes & A. Leviston
	G-PHYL	Denney Kitfox Mk 4	R. C. Horan
	G-PHYS	Jabiru SP-470	A. J. Black
	G-PIAF	Thunder Ax7-65 balloon	L. Battersley
	G-PICO	Cameron O-31 balloon	J. F. Trehern

Reg	Type	Owner or Operator	Notes
G-PICU	Leonardo AW169	Specialist Aviation Services Ltd	
G-PICX	P & M Aviation QuikR	C. Phillips	
G-PIEL	CP.301A Emeraude	E. B. Atalay (G-BARY)	
G-PIES	Thunder Ax7-77Z balloon	M. K. Bellamy	
G-PIET	Pietenpol Air Camper	P. Batchelor & J. Granell	
G-PIFZ	Agusta Westland AW109SP Grand New	Thunder Aviation Limited Partnership	
G-PIGI	Aerotechnik EV-97 Eurostar	Pigs Might Fly Group	
G-PIGS	SOCATA Rallye 150ST	Boonhill Flying Group (G-BDWB)	
G-PIGZ	Cameron Z-315 balloon	Wickers World Ltd	
G-PIII	Pitts S-1D Special	M. O'Leary (G-BETI)	
G-PIIT	Pitts S-2 Special	J. Law	
G-PIKD	Eiriavion PIK-20D-78	A. J. Hulme	
G-PIKE	Robinson R22 Mariner	Sloane Helicopters Ltd	
G-PILE	Rotorway Executive 90	J. B. Russell	
G-PILL	Light Aero Avid Flyer Mk 4	D. R. Meston	
G-PILY	Pilatus B4 PC-11	J. Hunt	
G-PILZ	AutoGyro MT-03	D. J. Gavan	
G-PIMM	Ultramagic M-77 balloon	G. Everett	
G-PING	AA-5A Cheetah	AKKI Aviation Services Ltd	
G-PINO	AutoGyro MTO Sport	D. Eaton	
G-PINT	Cameron 65 Barrel SS balloon	D. K. Fish	
G-PINX	Lindstrand Pink Panther SS balloon	Magical Adventures Ltd/USA	
G-PION	Alpi Pioneer 300	A. A. Mortimer	
G-PIPB	AS.355F1 Ecureuil 2	Heli Air Ltd (G-NBEL/G-SKYW/G-BTIS/G-TALI)	
G-PIPI	Mainair Pegasus Quik	R. E. Forbes	
G-PIPR	PA-18 Super Cub 95	R. & T. Kellett (G-BCDC)	
G-PIPS	Van's RV-4	N. S. Lomax	
G-PIPZ	BRM Aero Bristell NG5 Speed Wing	T. W. Lorimer	
G-PITS	Pitts S-2AE Special	P. N. A. & S. N. Whitehead	
G-PITZ	Pitts S-2A Special	M. J. Wood	
G-PIVI	Pipistrel Virus SW127 912S(1)	Pipistrel Virus UK Group	
G-PIXE	Colt 31A balloon	A. D. McCutcheon	
G-PIXI	Pegasus Quantum 15-912	M. R. H. Lewis & K. A. Longshaw	
G-PIXL	Robinson R44 II	Flying TV Ltd	
G-PIXX	Robinson R44 II	Flying TV Ltd	
G-PIXY	Supermarine Aircraft Spitfire Mk.26 (RK855)	R. Collenette	
G-PJMT	Lancair 320	K. A. & P. P. Gilroy	
G-PJSY	Van's RV-6	P. J. York	
G-PJTM	Cessna FR.172K II	J. R. Emery (G-BFIF)	
G-PKHA	Pilatus PC-12/47E	Pilatus Beheer BV/Netherlands	
G-PKPK	Schweizer 269C	C. H. Dobson & M. R. Golden	
G-PLAD	Kolb Twinstar Mk.111 Xtra	A. R. Smith	
G-PLAN	Cessna F.150L	S. J. Brenchley	
G-PLAR	Vans RV-9A	M. P. Board	
G-PLAY	Robin R.2112	Pure Aviation Support Services Ltd	
G-PLAZ	Rockwell Commander 112	I. Hunt (G-RDCI/G-BFWG)	
G-PLEE	Cessna 182Q	A. P. Thomson	
G-PLIP	Diamond DA.40D Star	AJW Construction Ltd	
G-PLJR	Pietenpol Air Camper	P. E. Taylor	
G-PLOP	Magni M-24C	R. F. Tuthill	
G-PLOW	Hughes 269B	D. W. Walton (G-AVUM)	
G-PLPC	Schweizer Hughes 269C	A. R. Baker	
G-PLPM	Shaw Europa XS	P. L. P. Mansfield	
G-PMAM	Cameron V-65 balloon	P. A. Meecham	
G-PMCM	PA-46-600TP M600	Executive Light Aircraft Leasing LLP	
G-PMGG	Agusta-Bell 206A JetRanger	P. M. Gallagher & S. Perry (G-EEGO/G-PELS/G-DNCN)	
G-PMIZ	Pitts Model 12	I. S. Smith (G-DEWD/G-CGRP)	
G-PMNF	VS.361 Spitfire HF.IX (TA805:FX-M)	P. R. Monk	
G-PNAD	Lindstrand LBL Box SS balloon	Gone with the Wind Ltd (G-PLLT)	
G-PNEU	Colt 110 Bibendum SS balloon	P. A. Rowley	
G-PNGB	Partenavia P-68B	P. Morton	
G-PNGC	Schleicher ASK-21	Portsmouth Naval Gliding Centre	
G-PODD	Robinson R66	Jamiroquai Ltd	

Notes	Reg	Type	Owner or Operator
	G-POET	Robinson R44 II	Steptoe & Son Properties Ltd
	G-POGO	Flight Design CT2K	L. I. Bailey
	G-POLA	Eurocopter EC 135 P2+	Police & Crime Commissioner for West Yorkshire
	G-POLB	Eurocopter EC 135 T2+	Police & Crime Commissioner for West Yorkshire
	G-POLC	Eurocopter EC 135 T2+	Police & Crime Commissioner for West Yorkshire (G-CPSH)
	G-POLD	Eurocopter EC 135 T2+	Police & Crime Commissioner for West Yorkshire (G-NMID)
	G-POLF	Eurocopter EC 135 T2+	Police & Crime Commissioner for West Yorkshire (G-ESEX)
	G-POLG	Eurocopter EC 135 T2+	Police & Crime Commissioner for West Yorkshire (G-LASU)
	G-POLH	Eurocopter EC 135 T2+	Police & Crime Commissioner for West Yorkshire (G-WCAO)
	G-POLJ	Eurocopter EC 135 T2+	Police & Crime Commissioner for West Yorkshire (G-NEAU)
	G-POLL	Skyranger 912 (1)	S. Spence
	G-POLR	P & M Quik R	D. Sykes
	G-POLS	Airbus Helicopters EC 135 T3	Babcock Mission Critical Services Onshore Ltd
	G-POLU	Eurocopter EC135 T2+	Police & Crime Commissioner for West Yorkshire (G-XMII)
	G-POLV	Vulcanair P-68R	Police & Crime Commissioner for West Yorkshire
	G-POLW	Vulcanair P-68R	Police & Crime Commissioner for West Yorkshire
	G-POLX	Vulcanair P-68R	Police & Crime Commissioner for West Yorkshire
	G-POLY	Cameron N-77 balloon	S. Church & S. Jenkins
	G-POLZ	Vulcanair P-68R	Police & Crime Commissioner for West Yorkshire
	G-POMP	Cameron Bearskin 100 balloon	Lighter Than Air Ltd
	G-POND	Oldfield Baby Lakes	J. Maehringer/Germany
	G-POOH	Piper J-3C-65 Cub	P. L. Beckwith
	G-POOL	ARV Super 2	A. R. Hawes
	G-POPA	Beech A36 Bonanza	S. F. Payne
	G-POPE	Eiri PIK-20E-1	G-POPE Syndicate
	G-POPG	Aeropro Eurofox 2K	C. M. Hoyle
	G-POPW	Cessna 182S	M. S. Archer
	G-POPY	Best Off Sky Ranger Swift 912S(1)	J. Young
	G-POPZ	Druine D.31A Turbulent	S. A. Blanchard
	G-PORG	AB Sportine LAK-17AT	R. M. Garden
	G-PORK	AA-5B Tiger	S. D. Pryke (G-BFHS)
	G-POSH	Colt 56A balloon	B. K. Rippon (G-BMPT)
	G-POTA	Extra EA.300/LT	M. Frizza & L. Franceschetti
	G-POTR	Agusta 109E Power	Castle Air Ltd (G-OFTC)
	G-POUX	Pou du Ciel-Bifly	G. D. Priest
	G-POWH	Boeing 757-256	Titan Airways Ltd
	G-POWK	Airbus A.320-233	Titan Airways Ltd
	G-POWL	Cessna 182R	Oxford Aeroplane Company Ltd
	G-POWM	Airbus A.320-232	Titan Airways Ltd
	G-POWN	Airbus A.321-211	Titan Airways Ltd
	G-POWP	Boeing 737-436	Titan Airways Ltd (G-DOCY/G-BVBY)
	G-POWS	Boeing 737-436	Titan Airways Ltd (G-DOCT)
	G-POWU	Airbus A.321-211	Titan Airways Ltd
	G-POWV	Airbus A.321-211	Titan Airways Ltd
	G-POWW	Airbus A.321-211	Titan Airways Ltd (G-TCDA/G-JOEE)
	G-POZA	Escapade Jabiru ULP (2)	M. R. Jones
	G-PPBZ	Autogyro Calidus	Dept of Doing Ltd
	G-PPFS	Cessna FRA.150L	M. Bonsall (G-AZJY)
	G-PPIO	Cameron C-90 balloon	A. G. Martin
	G-PPLG	Rotorsport UK MT-03	Gyro Syndicate PPLG
	G-PPLL	Van's RV-7A	D. Bull
	G-PPLS	Cessna F.152	Devon & Somerset Flight Training Ltd
	G-PPOD	Europa Aviation Europa XS	S. Easom
	G-PPPP	Denney Kitfox Mk 3	P. J. Gardner
	G-PRAG	Brügger MB.2 Colibri	Colibri Flying Group
	G-PRAH	Flight Design CT2K	G. P. Blakemore
	G-PRAY	Lindstrand LTL Series 2-60 balloon	M. Warne for Share Jesus International
	G-PRBB	HpH Glasflugel 304ES	P. J. Belcher & R. I. Brickwood
	G-PRDH	AS.355F2 Ecureuil 2	Claremont Air Services
	G-PRDY	Van's RV-8	I. Smith
	G-PREY	Pereira Osprey II	Condor Aviation International Ltd (G-BEPB)
	G-PRFX	Embraer EMB-135BJ Legacy 600	Flexjet Ltd

Reg	Type	Owner or Operator	Notes
G-PRID	Supermarine 353 Spitfire PR.IV (AA810)	Spitfire AA810 Restoration Ltd	
G-PRIV	VS.353 Spitfire PR.IV	P. R. Arnold	
G-PRKZ	Allstar PZL SZD-54-2 Perkoz	Buckminster Gliding Club Ltd	
G-PRLY	Avtech Jabiru SK	J. McVey (G-BYKY)	
G-PROS	Van's RV-7A	A. J. & S. A. Sutcliffe	
G-PROV	P.84 Jet Provost T.52A (T.4)	Provost Group	
G-PROW	EV-97A Eurostar	Quantum Syndicate	
G-PRPA	DHC.8-402Q Dash Eight	Nordeutsche Landesbank Girozentrale	
G-PRPB	DHC.8-402Q Dash Eight	Nordeutsche Landesbank Girozentrale	
G-PRPC	DHC.8-402Q Dash Eight	Nordeutsche Landesbank Girozentrale	
G-PRPD	DHC.8-402Q Dash Eight	Nordeutsche Landesbank Girozentrale	
G-PRPE	DHC.8-402Q Dash Eight	Nordeutsche Landesbank Girozentrale	
G-PRPF	DHC.8-402Q Dash Eight	Nordeutsche Landesbank Girozentrale	
G-PRPG	DHC.8-402Q Dash Eight	Nordeutsche Landesbank Girozentrale	
G-PRPH	DHC.8-402Q Dash Eight	Nordeutsche Landesbank Girozentrale	
G-PRPI	DHC.8-402Q Dash Eight	Nordeutsche Landesbank Girozentrale (G-CJFN)	
G-PRPJ	DHC.8-402Q Dash Eight	NAC Aviation 23 Ltd	
G-PRPK	DHC.8-402Q Dash Eight	NAC Aviation 23 Ltd	
G-PRPL	DHC.8-402Q Dash Eight	Nordeutsche Landesbank Girozentrale	
G-PRPM	DHC.8-402Q Dash Eight	NAC Aviation 23 Ltd	
G-PRPN	DHC.8-402Q Dash Eight	NAC Aviation 23 Ltd	
G-PRPO	DHC.8-402Q Dash Eight	NAC Aviation 23 Ltd	
G-PRXI	VS.365 Spitfire PR.XI (PL983)	Propshop Ltd	
G-PRZI	Cameron A-375 balloon	Bailey Balloons Ltd	
G-PSAX	Lindstrand LBL-77B balloon	M. V. Farrant & I. Risbridger	
G-PSFG	Robin R.21601	Mardenair Ltd (G-COVD/G-BYOF)	
G-PSGC	PA-25 Pawnee 260C (modified)	Peterborough & Spalding Gliding Club Ltd (G-BDDT)	
G-PSHK	Schempp-Hirth SHK-1	P. Gentil	
G-PSHU	Eurocopter EC135 T2+	Babock Mission Critical Services Onshore Ltd (G-WONN)	
G-PSIR	Jurca MJ.77 Gnatsum (474008 'VF-R')	P. W. Carlton & D. F. P. Finan	
G-PSJS	Robinson R22 ll	G. E. J. Sealey (G-PBRL)	
G-PSKY	Skyranger 912S(1)	P. W. Curnock & J. W. Wilcox	
G-PSMS	Aeropro Eurofox 912(S)	I. Archer	
G-PSNI	Eurocopter EC 135T2	Police Service of Northern Ireland	
G-PSNO	Eurocopter MBB BK-117C-2	Police Service of Northern Ireland	
G-PSNR	MBB-BK 117 C-2	Police Service of Northern Ireland (G-LFRS)	
G-PSON	Colt Cylinder One SS balloon	A. G. A. Barclay-Faulkner	
G-PSRT	PA-28-151 Warrior	R. W. Nash (G-BSGN)	
G-PSUE	CFM Shadow Srs CD	D. A. Crosbie (G-MYAA)	
G-PSUK	Thruster T.600N 450	K. Edwards	
G-PSZB	Pitts S-2B	SEAFS Group	
G-PTAG	Shaw Europa	M. A. Coffin	
G-PTAR	Best Off Skyranger 912S(1)	P. Vergette	
G-PTBA	Boeing Stearman A-75	Mach Eight 3 Ltd	
G-PTCC	PA-28RT-201 ArrowIV	B. O'Donnchu (G-BXYS)	
G-PTEK	Van's RV-9A	P. K. Eckersley	
G-PTFE	Bristell NG5 Speed Wing	P. R. Thody	
G-PTIX	VS.361 Spitfire IX (PT879)	Hangar 11 Collection (G-AYDE)	
G-PTOO	Bell 206L-4 LongRanger 4	Helicompany Ltd	
G-PTPA	Pipistrel Virus SW 115	Cold Air Flying Machines Ltd	
G-PTRE	SOCATA TB20 Trinidad	W. M. Chesson (G-BNKU)	
G-PTTA	Cessna F.152	North Weald Flight Training Ltd (G-BJVT)	
G-PTTE	Cessna 152	Synnova Aviation Ltd (G-BXTB)	
G-PTTS	Aerotek Pitts S-2A	P. & J. Voce	
G-PTXC	SOCATA TBM-700C2	Coelus Flight Services Ltd	
G-PUDL	PA-18 Super Cub 150	C. M. Edwards	
G-PUDS	Shaw Europa	C. R. A. Spirit	
G-PUFF	Thunder Ax7-77A balloon	Intervarsity Balloon Club	
G-PUGS	Cessna 182H	D. Waterhouse	
G-PUGZ	P & M Aviation Quik GT450	I. M. Spence	
G-PUKA	Jabiru Aircraft Jabiru J400	D. P. Harris	
G-PULR	Pitts S-2AE	Ayre to Air	
G-PUMM	AS.332L Super Puma	Element Capital Corp	
G-PUMN	AS.332L Super Puma	CHC Scotia Ltd	
G-PUMO	AS.332L-2 Super Puma	Element Capital Corp	

Notes	Reg	Type	Owner or Operator
	G-PUMS	AS.332L-2 Super Puma	Element Capital Corp
	G-PUNK	Thunder Ax8-105 balloon	S. C. Kinsey
	G-PUNT	Robinson R44 II	R. D. Cameron
	G-PUPP	Beagle B.121 Pup 2	M. G. Evans (G-BASD)
	G-PUPY	Shaw Europa XS	D. A. Cameron
	G-PURE	Cameron can 70 SS balloon	Mobberley Balloon Collection
	G-PURL	PA-32R-301 Saratoga II	A. P.H. & E. Hay
	G-PURP	Lindstrand LBL-90 balloon	C. & P. Mackley
	G-PURR	AA-5A Cheetah	G-PURR Owners Group (G-BJDN)
	G-PURS	Rotorway Executive	J. & D. Parke
	G-PUSA	Gefa-Flug AS105GD Hot Air Airship	Skyking Aviation Ltd
	G-PUSH	Rutan Long-Ez	J. P. Watts
	G-PUSI	Cessna T.303	C. Smith & S. Devin
	G-PUSS	Cameron N-77 balloon	B. D. Close
	G-PUTT	Cameron Golfball 76 SS balloon	David P Hopkins
	G-PVBF	Lindstrand LBL-260S balloon	Virgin Balloon Flights
	G-PVCV	Robin DR400/140	Bustard Flying Club Ltd
	G-PVET	DHC.1 Chipmunk 22 (WB565)	Connect Properties Ltd
	G-PVIP	Cessna 421C	Passion 4 Autos Ltd
	G-PVSS	P & M Quik GT450	A. D. Lockwood
	G-PWAL	Aeropro Eurofox 912(1)	M. I. White & B. W. Webb
	G-PWBE	DH.82A Tiger Moth	K. M. Perkins
	G-PWEF	Magni M.24C Orion	P. W. D. Walshe
	G-PWFW	Tecnam P2010	F. C. & P. A. Winters
	G-PWUL	Van's RV-6	The G-PWUL Group
	G-PXMI	Agusta A109C	Brentwood Aviation Services Ltd (G-BWNZ)
	G-PYAK	Yakovlev Yak-18T	P. S. Beardsell
	G-PYNE	Thruster T.600N 450	R. Dereham
	G-PYPE	Van's RV-7	R. & L. Pyper
	G-PYRO	Cameron N-65 balloon	A. C. Booth
	G-PZAS	Schleicher ASW-27-18	A. P. C. Sampson
	G-PZPZ	P & M Aviation Pegasus Quantum 15-912	J. R. Leese
	G-RAAF	VS.359 Spitfire VIII	Composite Mast Engineering and Technology Ltd
	G-RAAM	PA-28-161 Warrior II	A. S. Bamrah (G-BRSE)
	G-RAAY	Taylor JT.1 Monoplane	R. Bowden (G-BEHM)
	G-RABS	Alpi Pioneer 300	J. Mullen
	G-RACA	P.57 Sea Prince T.1 (571/CU) ★	(stored)/Long Marston
	G-RACK	Ikarus C42 FB80	G. P. Burns (G-CFIY)
	G-RACO	PA-28R Cherokee Arrow 200-II	M. J. Sweeney
	G-RACR	Ultramagic M-65C balloon	R. A. Vale
	G-RACY	Cessna 182S	C. M. Bishop & N. K. Wright
	G-RADA	Soko P-2 Kraguj	Airfield Aviation Ltd
	G-RADI	PA-28-181 Archer II	The Sherwood Flying Club Ltd
	G-RADR	Douglas AD-4NA Skyraider (126922:503)	Orion Enterprises Ltd (G-RAID)
	G-RAEF	Schempp-Hirth SHK-1	R. A. Earnshaw-Fretwell
	G-RAES	Boeing 777-236	British Airways
	G-RAFA	Grob G.115	K. J. Peacock & S. F. Turner
	G-RAFB	Grob G.115	RAF College Flying Club Ltd
	G-RAFC	Robin R.2112	RAF Charlie Group
	G-RAFE	Thunder Ax7-77 balloon	Giraffe Balloon Syndicate
	G-RAFG	Slingsby T.67C Firefly	R. C. P. Brookhouse
	G-RAFH	Thruster T.600N 450	G. Loughran, J. McCarrison & J. Nicholls
	G-RAFK	Beech B.200 Super King Air	Serco Ltd
	G-RAFL	Beech B.200 Super King Air	Serco Ltd
	G-RAFR	Skyranger 912S(1)	M. Ellis
	G-RAFS	Thruster T.600N 450	Hoveton Flying Group
	G-RAFT	Rutan LongEz	H. M. & S. Roberts
	G-RAFV	Avid Speedwing	Fox Victor Group (G-MOTT)
	G-RAFW	Mooney M.20E	Warwickshire Aviation Ltd (G-ATHW)
	G-RAFY	Best Off Sky Ranger Swift 912S(1)	A. P. Portsmouth
	G-RAFZ	RAF 2000 GTX-SE	V. G. Freke
	G-RAGE	Wilson Cassutt IIIM	R. S. Grace (G-BEUN)
	G-RAGS	Pietenpol Air Camper	S. H. Leonard
	G-RAGT	PA-32-301FT Cherokee Six	Oxhill Aviation

Reg	Type	Owner or Operator	Notes
G-RAHA	Schempp-Hirth Standard Cirrus	G. C. Stallard	
G-RAIR	Schleicher ASH-25	ASH25 G-RAIR Group	
G-RAJA	Raj Hamsa X'Air 582 (2)	C. Roadnight	
G-RAMI	Bell 206B JetRanger 3	Yorkshire Helicopters	
G-RAML	PA-34-220T Seneca III	P. d'Costa (G-BWDT/G-BKHS)	
G-RAMP	Piper J-3C-65 Cub	M. F. D. Bartley	
G-RAMS	PA-32R-301 Saratoga SP	Mike Sierra LLP	
G-RANE	Bombardier CL600-2B16 Challenger 605	Catreus AOC Ltd (G-LCDH)	
G-RANN	Beech B.300 Super King Air 350	Flycorp Aviation LLP	
G-RAPH	Cameron O-77 balloon	P. A. Sweatman	
G-RAPL	Schempp-Hirth Duo Discus T	G-RAPL Duo XLT Syndicate	
G-RARA	AutoGyro MTO Sport	Gyro School Pro Ltd	
G-RARB	Cessna 172N	H. C. R. Page	
G-RARE	Thunder Ax5-42 SS balloon ★	Balloon Preservation Group	
G-RASA	Diamond DA42 Twin Star	Southern Sailplanes Ltd	
G-RASH	Grob G.109E	G-RASH Syndicate	
G-RASL	Beech 76 Duchess	A. J. Gomes (G-GCCL)	
G-RATC	Van's RV-4	P. Johnson	
G-RATD	Van's RV-8	J. R. Pike	
G-RATE	AA-5A Cheetah	G-RATE Flying Group (G-BIFF)	
G-RATH	Rotorway Executive 162F	W. H. Cole	
G-RATI	Cessna F.172M	N. F. Collins (G-PATI/G-WACZ/G-BCUK)	
G-RATT	Aeropro Eurofox 912(S)	Rattlesden Gliding Club Ltd	
G-RATV	PA-28RT-201T Turbo Arrow IV	Tango Victor Ltd (G-WILS)	
G-RATZ	Shaw Europa	B. Hulme	
G-RAVE	Southdown Raven X	M. J. Robbins (G-MNZV)	
G-RAVN	Robinson R44	Flying Lobster Aviation Ltd	
G-RAWS	Rotorway Executive 162F	R. P. Robinson & P. J. Wood	
G-RAYB	P & M Quik GT450	R. Blatchford	
G-RAYH	Zenair CH.701UL	R. Horner	
G-RAYM	SOCATA TB-20 Trinidad GT	J. Weisz	
G-RAYN	Leonardo AW.109SP Grand New	East Midlands Helicopters	
G-RAYO	Lindstrand LBL-90A balloon	R. Owen	
G-RAYY	Cirrus SR22	Alquiler de Veleros SL/Spain	
G-RAYZ	Tecnam P2002-EA Sierra	R. Wells	
G-RAZE	Bell 407GXi	H C Services Ltd	
G-RAZI	SIAI-Marchetti SF.260	P. A. Freeland	
G-RAZY	PA-28-181 Archer II	T. H. Pemberton (G-REXS)	
G-RAZZ	Maule MX-7-180	R. Giles	
G-RBBB	Shaw Europa	T. J. Hartwell	
G-RBCT	Schempp-Hirth Ventus 2Ct	M. J. Weston & J. D. Huband	
G-RBFX	Aeropro Eurofox 912(iS)	R. Balen	
G-RBHF	Leonardo AW139	RBHF Services Ltd	
G-RBIL	SA.341D Gazelle HT Mk.3	R. B. Illingworth (G-CGJY)	
G-RBLU	PA-28RT-201 Arrow IV	M. & C. Busoni	
G-RBMV	Cameron O-31 balloon	P. D. Griffiths	
G-RBOS	Colt AS-105 airship ★	Science Museum/Wroughton	
G-RBOW	Thunder Ax-7-65 balloon	R. S. McDonald	
G-RBRI	Robinson R44 II	Helicentre Aviation Ltd (G-RWGS)	
G-RBSN	Ikarus C.42 FB80	P. B. & M. Robinson	
G-RBWW	BRM Aero Bristell NG5 Speed Wing	W. Woods & R. J. Baker	
G-RCED	Rockwell Commander 114	D. J. and D. Pitman	
G-RCFC	Hawker 900XP	Voluxis Ltd	
G-RCHE	Cessna 182T	R. S. Bentley (G-PTRI)	
G-RCHL	P & M Quik GT450	A. C. Richards	
G-RCHY	Aerotechnik EV-97 Eurostar	N. McKenzie	
G-RCIE	J-3C-65 Cub	R. P. Marks (G-CCOX)	
G-RCKT	Harmon Rocket II	K. E. Armstrong	
G-RCMC	Murphy Renegade 912	The Renegades	
G-RCMF	Cameron V-77 balloon	J. M. Percival	
G-RCMP	PA-28RT-201T Turbo Arrow IV	Southeast Air Ltd	
G-RCOH	Cameron Cube 105 SS balloon	A. M. Holly	
G-RCRC	P & M Quik	R. M. Brown	
G-RCSR	Replica de Havilland DH.88 Comet	K. Fern	
G-RCST	Jabiru J430	P. M. Jones	
G-RCUB	PA-18-95 Super Cub	D. Bennett (G-BPJH)	
G-RCUS	Schempp-Hirth Arcus T	Arcus G-RCUS Syndicate	
G-RDAD	Reality Escapade ULP(1)	F. Overall	

Notes	Reg	Type	Owner or Operator
	G-RDAR	Van's RV-7	R. P. Marks
	G-RDAS	Cessna 172M	J. Martin
	G-RDAY	Van's RV-9	R. M. Day
	G-RDCO	Avtech Jabiru J430	A. H. & F. A. Macaskill
	G-RDDM	Cessna 182T	Optum Global Ltd
	G-RDEN	Cameron Z-105 balloon	Hillmount Bangor Ltd
	G-RDFX	Aero AT-3	M. W. Richardson
	G-RDHS	Shaw Europa XS	R. D. H. Spencer
	G-RDNS	Rans S.6-S Super Coyote	S. R. Green
	G-RDNY	AutoGyro Cavalon	C. Rodney
	G-RDPH	P & M Quik R	R. S. Partidge-Hicks
	G-RDRL	Reaction Drive Rotorcraft	Genesis Aerotech Ltd
	G-READ	Colt 77A balloon	Intervarsity Balloon Club
	G-REAF	Jabiru J400	S. J. Carr
	G-REAS	Van's RV-6A	T. J. Smith
	G-REBB	Murphy Rebel	K. A. Daniels
	G-RECL	Cameron Z-105 balloon	A. J. Thompson
	G-RECW	PA-28-181 Archer II	R. E. C. Washington (G-BOBZ)
	G-REDC	Pegasus Quantum 15-912	S. Houghton
	G-REDF	Eurocopter AS.365N3 Dauphin 2	Babcock Mission Critical Services Offshore Ltd
	G-REDJ	Eurocopter AS.332L-2 Super Puma	Babcock Mission Critical Services Leasing Ltd
	G-REDN	Eurocopter AS.332L-2 Super Puma	Babcock Mission Critical Services Leasing Ltd
	G-REDO	Eurocopter AS.332L-2 Super Puma	Babcock Mission Critical Services Leasing Ltd
	G-REDP	Eurocopter AS.332L-2 Super Puma	Babcock Mission Critical Services Leasing Ltd
	G-REDR	Eurocopter AS.225LP Super Puma	Babcock Mission Critical Services Leasing Ltd
	G-REDT	Eurocopter EC.225LP Super Puma	Babcock Mission Critical Services Leasing Ltd
	G-REDX	Experimental Aviation Berkut	G. V. Waters
	G-REDZ	Thruster T.600T 450	B. S. W. & T. W. Davis
	G-REEC	Sequoia F.8L Falco	K. J. E. Augustinus/Belgium
	G-REED	Mainair Blade 912S	D. J. Kaye
	G-REEF	Mainair Blade 912S	B. Skidmore
	G-REER	Centrair 101A Pegase	R. L. Howorth & G. C. Stinchcombe
	G-REES	Jodel D.140C	G-REES Flying Group
	G-REEV	Robinson R44 II	SNG Yachting and Aviation Ltd
	G-REGC	Zenair CH.601XL Zodiac	Golf Golf Charlie Group
	G-REGL	Robinson R44 II	HFM Consulting Ltd (G-REGJ/G-OPTF)
	G-REGZ	Aeroprakt A-22L Foxbat	L. Campbell
	G-REJP	Europa XS	A. Milner
	G-RELL	D.62B Condor	M. J. Golder (G-OPJH/G-AVDW)
	G-REMH	Bell 206B-3 JetRanger III	Flightpath Ltd
	G-RENI	Balony Kubicek BB-30Z balloon	A. M. Holly
	G-RENT	Robinson R22 ★	Ulster Aviation Society/Long Kesh
	G-RESG	Dyn'Aéro MCR-01 Club	R. E. S. Greenwood
	G-RESG	Beech P35 Bonanza	C. R. Taylor (G-ASFJ)
	G-RESU	Airbus Helicopters MBB BK-117D-2	Babcock Mission Critical Services Onshore Ltd
	G-RETA	CASA 1.131 Jungmann 2000	A. N. R. Houghton (G-BGZC)
	G-RETH	Rutan Cozy	G. T. Bowker (G-OGJS)
	G-REVE	Van's RV-6	S. D. Foster
	G-REVO	Skyranger 912(2)	D. A. Wilson
	G-REVV	Van's RV-7	T. J. Franklin & P. J. Roy
	G-REXA	Beech B.200GT Super King Air	RVL Aviation Ltd
	G-REYE	Robinson R44 I	Redeye.com Ltd
	G-REYS	Canadair CL600-2B16 Challenger 604	Locally Applied Solutions Ltd
	G-RFAD	Sportavia-Putzer Fournier RF4D	M. P. Dentith
	G-RFCA	Tecnam P2008-JC	The Waddington Flying Club
	G-RFCB	Tecnam P2008-JC	The Waddington Flying Club
	G-RFGB	Fournier RF-6B-100 replica	R. J. Grimstead
	G-RFIO	Aeromot AMT-200 Super Ximango	M. D. Evans
	G-RFLO	Ultramagic M-105 balloon	Flying Enterprises
	G-RFLY	Extra EA.300/L	H. B. Sauer
	G-RFOX	Denney Kitfox Mk 3	D. A. Jackson
	G-RFSB	Sportavia RF-5B	G-RFSB Group
	G-RGTS	Schempp-Hirth Discus b	G. R. & L. R. Green
	G-RGUS	Fairchild 24A-46A Argus III (KK527)	A. R. Willis
	G-RGWY	Bell 206B-3 Jet Ranger III	Ridgway Aviation Ltd (G-OAGL/G-CORN/ G-BHTR)
	G-RGZT	Cirrus SR20	H. Jedermann

Reg	Type	Owner or Operator	Notes
G-RHAM	Skyranger 582(1)	L. Smart & P. Gibson	
G-RHCB	Schweizer 269C-1	P. R. Butler	
G-RHOD	Just Superstol	C. S. & K. D. Rhodes	
G-RHOS	ICP MXP-740 Savannah VG Jabiru(1)	J. C. Munro-Hunt	
G-RHYM	PA-31-310 Turbo Navajo B	2 Excel Aviation Ltd (G-BJLO)	
G-RHYS	Rotorway Executive 90	A. K. Voase	
G-RIBA	P & M Quik GT450	R. J. Murphy	
G-RICO	AG-5B Tiger	Delta Lima Flying Group	
G-RIDA	Eurocopter AS.355NP Ecureuil 2	National Grid Electricity Transmission PLC	
G-RIDB	Bell 429	National Grid Electricity Transmission PLC	
G-RIDE	Stephens Akro	R. Mitchell	
G-RIDG	Van's RV-7	C. Heathcote	
G-RIEF	DG Flugzeugbau DG-1000T	EF Gliding Group	
G-RIET	Hoffmann H.36 Dimona	Dimona Syndicate	
G-RIEV	Rolladen-Schneider LS8-18	R. D. Grieve	
G-RIFD	HpH Glasflugel 304ES	D. Griffiths	
G-RIFN	Avion Mudry CAP-10B	D. E. Starkey & R. A. J. Spurrell	
G-RIGB	Thunder Ax7-77 balloon	N. J. Bettin	
G-RIGH	PA-32R-301 Saratoga IIHP	A. Brinkley	
G-RIGS	PA-60 Aerostar 601P	W. Reinstaller/Italy	
G-RIHN	Dan Rihn DR.107 One Design	P. J. Burgess	
G-RIII	Vans RV-3B	J. F. Dowe	
G-RIIV	Van's RV-4	M. R. Overall	
G-RIKI	Mainair Blade 912	A. Warnock	
G-RIKS	Shaw Europa XS	H. Foster	
G-RIKY	Mainair Pegasus Quik	S. Clarke	
G-RILA	Flight Design CTSW	P. A. Mahony	
G-RIMB	Lindstrand LBL-105A balloon	D. Grimshaw	
G-RIME	Lindstrand LBL-25A balloon	N. Ivison	
G-RIMM	Westland Wasp HAS.1 (XT435:430)	J. M. Heath	
G-RIMR	Cessna F.177RG	B. C. Faulkner (G-SYLM/G-AZTW)	
G-RINN	Mainair Blade	R. A. Swift	
G-RINS	Rans S.6-ESA Coyote II	P. A. Harvie	
G-RINT	CFM Streak Shadow	D. Grint	
G-RINZ	Van's RV-7	R. C. May (G-UZZL)	
G-RIOT	Silence SA.180 Twister	Zulu Glasstek Ltd (G-SWIP)	
G-RIPA	Partenavia P.68 Observer 2	K. Hendry	
G-RIPH	VS.384 Seafire F.XVII	Seafire Displays Ltd (G-CDTM)	
G-RISA	PA-28-180 Cherokee C	Vu JV4 Ltd (G-ATZK)	
G-RISH	Rotorway Exeecutive 162F	K. B. Moore	
G-RISY	Van's RV-7	D. I. Scott	
G-RITS	Pitts S-1C	J. H. D. Newman	
G-RITT	P & M Quik	T. H. Parr	
G-RIVA	SOCATA TBM-700N	MSV GmbH & Co KG/Germany	
G-RIVE	Jodel D.153	M. J. Applewhite	
G-RIVR	Thruster T.600N 450	S. W. Turley	
G-RIVT	Van's RV-6	R. Howard	
G-RIXA	J-3C-65 Cub	J. J. Rix	
G-RIXS	Shaw Europa XS	T. J. Houlihan	
G-RIXY	Cameron Z-77 balloon	Rix Petroleum (Hull) Ltd	
G-RIZI	Cameron N-90 balloon	Asociata Sportiva Nyaradballoon Sky Team	
G-RIZK	Schleicher ASW-27-18E	P. Lund	
G-RIZZ	PA-28-161 Warrior II	W. Ali	
G-RJAM	Sequoia F.8L Falco	D. G. Drew	
G-RJRC	Commander114B	R. M. Jowitt	
G-RJRJ	Evektor EV-97A Eurostar	D. P. Myatt	
G-RJVH	Guimbal Cabri G2	RJV Holdings Ltd	
G-RJWW	Maule M5-235C Lunar Rocket	D. E. Priest (G-BRWG)	
G-RJWX	Shaw Europa XS	D. S. P. Disney	
G-RJXH	Embraer EMB145EP	Loganair Ltd	
G-RKEL	Agusta-Bell 206B JetRanger 3	Nunkeeling Ltd	
G-RKID	Van's RV-6A	I. Shaw	
G-RKKT	Cessna FR.172G	K. L. Irvine (G-AYJW)	
G-RKUS	Arcus T	Arcus Syndicate	
G-RLDS	Cameron A-315 balloon	Bailey Balloons Ltd	
G-RLDX	Cameron A-375 balloon	Bailey Balloons Ltd	
G-RLDZ	Cameron A-315 balloon	Bailey Balloons Ltd	

Notes	Reg	Type	Owner or Operator
	G-RLMW	Tecnam P2002-EA Sierra	S. P. Hoskins
	G-RLON	BN-2A Mk III-2 Trislander ★	Solent Sky Museum/Southampton (G-ITEX/ G-OCTA/G-BCXW)
	G-RLWG	Ryan ST3KR	R. A. Fleming
	G-RMAA	Airbus MBB BK117 D-2	Babcock Mission Critical Services Onshore Ltd
	G-RMAC	Shaw Europa	P. J. Lawless
	G-RMAN	Aero Designs Pulsar	J. M. Angiolini
	G-RMAR	Robinson R66	Marfleet Civil Engineering Ltd (G-NSEV)
	G-RMAV	Ikarus C42 FB80	RM Aviation Ltd
	G-RMAX	Cameron C-80 balloon	J. Kenny
	G-RMBH	Leonardo A109S Trekker	Harpalion Flight Assets Ltd
	G-RMCS	Cessna 182R	R. W. C. Sears
	G-RMHE	Aerospool Dynamic WT9 UK	D. R. Lewis
	G-RMIT	Van's RV-4	J. P. Kloos
	G-RMMT	Europa XS	N. Schmitt
	G-RMPI	Whittaker MW5D Sorcerer	R. W. Twamley
	G-RMPS	Van's RV-12	K. D. Boardman
	G-RMPY	Aerotechnik EV-97 Eurostar	N. R. Beale
	G-RMRV	Van's RV-7A	R. Morris
	G-RMUG	Cameron Nescafe Mug 90 SS balloon	The British Balloon Museum & Library Ltd
	G-RMYD	Robinson R44 II	Kaizen Motorsport and Aviation Ltd
	G-RNAC	IDA Bacau Yakovlev Yak-52	Chewton Glen Aviation
	G-RNAS	DH.104 Sea Devon C.20 (XK896) ★	Airport Fire Service/Filton
	G-RNDD	Robin DR.400/500	Witham (Specialist Vehicles) Ltd
	G-RNDE	Kubicek BB-S/Grenade balloon	A. G. A. Barclay-Faulkner
	G-RNER	Cessna 510 Citation Mustang	S. J. Davies
	G-RNFA	BAe. Sea Harrier FA.Mk.2	Fly Harrier Ltd
	G-RNGD	Murphy Renegade Spirit UK	Spirit Flying Group
	G-RNGS	Airbus MBB BK117 D-2	QinetiQ Ltd
	G-RNHF	Hawker Sea Fury T.Mk.20 (VX281)	Naval Aviation Ltd (G-BCOW)
	G-RNIE	Cameron 70 Ball SS balloon	N. J. Bland
	G-RNMZ	Fairey Swordfish Mk.II	White Waltham Airfield Ltd
	G-RNRM	Cessna A.185F	Skydive St. Andrews Ltd
	G-RNTB	BAe. Harrier T.Mk.8	Fly Harrier Ltd
	G-ROAD	Robinson R44 II	MLJ Heli Ltd
	G-ROAT	Robinson R44 II	R. D. Jordan
	G-ROBA	Grob G.115D-2 Heron	Adastral Flying Displays Ltd (G-BVHF)
	G-ROBD	Shaw Europa	Condor Aviation International Ltd
	G-ROBG	P & M Quik GT450	Exodus Airsports Ltd
	G-ROBJ	Robin DR.500/200i	D. R. L. Jones
	G-ROBN	Pierre Robin R1180T	E. R. Hall
	G-ROBT	Hawker Hurricane I (P2902:DX-X)	Anglia Aircraft Restorations Ltd
	G-ROBX	Cameron Sport-80 balloon	R. P. Cross
	G-ROBZ	Grob G109B	Bravo Zulu Group
	G-ROCH	Cessna T.303	R. S. Bentley
	G-ROCK	Thunder Ax7-77 balloon	M. A. Green
	G-ROCR	Schweizer 269C	A. Harvey & M. Wilkinson
	G-ROCT	Robinson R44 II	A. von Liechtenstein
	G-RODC	Steen Skybolt	D. G. Girling
	G-RODD	Cessna 310R II	Alpha Properties (London) Ltd (G-TEDD/ G-MADI)
	G-RODG	Avtech Jabiru UL	A. I. Freeman
	G-RODI	Isaacs Fury (K3731)	C. F. Pote
	G-RODJ	Ikarus C42 FB80	Medaviate Ltd
	G-RODO	Shaw Europa XS	R. M. Carson (G-ROWI)
	G-RODZ	Van's RV-3A	C. C. Cooper
	G-ROEI	Avro Roe 1 Replica	Brooklands Museum Trust Ltd
	G-ROEN	Cameron C-70 balloon	R. M. W. Romans
	G-ROFS	Groppo Trail	J. S. Evans
	G-ROGY	Cameron 60 Concept balloon	S. A. Laing
	G-ROKO	Roko-Aero NG-4HD	C. D. Sidoli
	G-ROKS	Robinson R44 II	Swift Helicopter Services Ltd (G-WEGO)
	G-ROKT	Cessna FR.172E	P. Donohoe
	G-ROKY	Groppo Trail	J. Webb
	G-ROLL	Pitts S-2A Special	P. H. Meeson
	G-ROLY	Cessna F.172N	Hields Aviation (G-BHIH)
	G-ROME	I.I.I. Sky Arrow 650TC	B. P. S. Pieterse

Reg	Type	Owner or Operator	Notes
G-ROMK	Magni M16C Tandem Trainer	G. B. Porter	
G-ROMP	Extra 230H	D. G. Cowden & S. C. Hipwell	
G-ROMT	Robinson R44 II	DYDB Marketing Ltd (G-RALA)	
G-RONA	Shaw Europa	C. M. Noakes	
G-RONI	Cameron V-77 balloon	R. E. Simpson	
G-RONK	Aeropro Eurofox	P. Knowles	
G-RONS	Robin DR.400/180	Robin Flying Club Ltd	
G-RONW	FRED Srs 2	RONW Syndicate	
G-RONZ	Ikarus C42 FB80 Bravo	R. F. Dean	
G-ROOG	Extra EA.300/LT	M. J. Coward	
G-ROOK	Cessna F.172P	Rolim Ltd	
G-ROON	Sikorsky S-76C	Rooney Air Ltd	
G-ROOO	Jabiru J430	H. S. A. Brewis (G-HJZN)	
G-ROOV	Shaw Europa XS	P. W. Hawkins	
G-ROPO	Groppo Trail	W. Wennington	
G-ROPP	Groppo Trail	D. A. Small	
G-RORA	Embraer EMB-550 Legacy 500	Centreline	
G-RORB	Spitfire Mk.26	Bertha Property LLP	
G-RORI	Folland Gnat T.1 (XR538)	Heritage Aircraft Ltd	
G-RORY	Piaggio FWP.149D	M. Edwards (G-TOWN)	
G-ROSI	Thunder Ax7-77 balloon	J. E. Rose	
G-ROSK	Ultramagic M-90 balloon	N. Roskell	
G-ROSS	Practavia Pilot Sprite	A. N. Barley	
G-ROTI	Luscombe 8A Silvaire	R. Ludgate & L. Prebble	
G-ROTS	CFM Streak Shadow Srs SA	J. Edwards	
G-ROUS	PA-34-200T Seneca II	R. Pedersen	
G-ROVA	Aviat A-1B Husky Pup	Jigsaw Aviation Ltd	
G-ROVE	PA-18 Super Cub 135 (R-156)	S. J. Gaveston	
G-ROVY	Robinson R22 Beta	East Midlands Helicopters Engineering Ltd	
G-ROWA	Aquila AT01	R. Simpson	
G-ROWL	AA-5B Tiger	Box MR Ltd	
G-ROWS	PA-28-151 Warrior	Air Academy	
G-ROXI	Cameron C-90 balloon	D. Marshall	
G-ROYC	Avtech Jabiru UL450	G-ROYC Flying Group	
G-ROYM	Robinson R44 II	HQ Aviation Ltd	
G-ROYP	Robinson R22	R. M. Price	
G-ROZE	Magni M-24C	R. I. Simpson	
G-ROZZ	Ikarus C.42 FB 80	M. S. Foster & D. J. Brookfield	
G-RPAF	Europa XS	G-RPAF Group	
G-RPAX	CASA 1-133 Jungmeister	A. J. E. Smith	
G-RPCC	Europa XS	R. P. Churchill-Coleman	
G-RPEZ	Rutan LongEz	M. P. Dunlop	
G-RPPO	Groppo Trail	D. R. Baker	
G-RPRP	P & M Quik R	R. M. Brown	
G-RPRV	Van's RV-9A	T. A. Willcox	
G-RRAK	Enstrom 480B	P. J. Began (G-RIBZ)	
G-RRAT	CZAW Sportcruiser	G. Sipson	
G-RRCU	CEA DR.221B Dauphin	Merlin Flying Club Ltd	
G-RRED	PA-28-181 Archer II	J. P. Reddington	
G-RRFF	VS.329 Spitfire Mk.IIB	Retro Track & Air (UK) Ltd	
G-RRGN	VS.390 Spitfire PR.XIX (PS853)	Rolls-Royce PLC (G-MXIX)	
G-RROB	Robinson R44 II	R. S. Rai	
G-RROK	Cessna FR.172E	H. W. Palmer (G-AWDR)	
G-RRRV	Van's RV-6	C. St. J. Hall	
G-RRRZ	Van's RV-8	S. Whatmough	
G-RRSR	Piper J-3C-65 Cub (480173:57-H)	R. W. Roberts	
G-RRVX	Van's RV-10	T. Booth	
G-RSAF	BAC.167 Strikemaster 80A	NWMAS Leasing Ltd	
G-RSAM	P & M Quik GTR	J. W. Foster	
G-RSCU	Agusta A.109E	Sloane Helicopters Ltd	
G-RSFX	Learjet 75	Flexjet Ltd	
G-RSHI	PA-34-220T Seneca V	R. S. Hill and Sons	
G-RSKR	PA-28-161 Warrior II	JABM Ltd (G-BOJY)	
G-RSKY	Skyranger 912(2)	P. Lister	
G-RSSF	Denney Kitfox Mk 2	M. E. Lockett	
G-RSXP	Cessna 560 Citation XLS	Fly Vectra Ltd	
G-RTFM	Jabiru J400	A. H. Hamilton	

Notes	Reg	Type	Owner or Operator
	G-RTHS	Rans S-6-ES Coyote II	R. G. Hughes
	G-RTMS	Rans S.6 ES Coyote II	C. J. Arthur
	G-RTMY	Ikarus C.42 FB 100	Mike Yankee Group
	G-RTNA	Beech B.300C King Air 350C	Raytheon Systems Ltd
	G-RTRV	V an's RV-9A	R. Taylor
	G-RUBB	AA-5B Tiger	D. E. Gee
	G-RUBY	PA-28RT-201T Turbo Arrow IV	Arrow Aircraft Group (G-BROU)
	G-RUCK	Bell 206B-3 JetRanger III	J. A. Ruck
	G-RUES	Robin HR.100/210	R. H. R. Rue
	G-RUFF	Mainair Blade 912	P. Mulvey
	G-RUFS	Avtech Jabiru UL	M. Bastin
	G-RUGS	Campbell Cricket Mk 4 gyroplane	J. L. G. McLane
	G-RUIA	Cessna F.172N	D. R. Clyde
	G-RUKA	Boeing 737-8AS	Ryanair UK Ltd
	G-RULE	Robinson R44 Raven II	Huckair
	G-RUMI	Noble Harman Snowbird Mk.IV	G. Crossley (G-MVOI)
	G-RUMM	Grumman F8F-2P Bearcat (121714:201B)	Patina Ltd
	G-RUMN	AA-1A Trainer	A. M. Leahy
	G-RUMW	Grumman FM-2 Wildcat (JV579:F)	Patina Ltd
	G-RUNS	P & M Quik GT450	S. Nicol
	G-RUNT	Cassutt Racer IIIM	D. P. Lightfoot
	G-RUPS	Cameron TR-70 balloon	R. M. Stanley
	G-RUSL	Van's RV-6A	G. R. Russell
	G-RUSO	Robinson R22 Beta	R. M. Barnes-Gorell
	G-RUSS	Cessna 172N ★	Leisure Lease (stored)/Southend
	G-RUVE	Van's RV-8	J. P. Brady & D. J. Taylor
	G-RUVI	Zenair CH.601UL	P. G. Depper
	G-RUVY	Van's RV-9A	R. D. Taylor
	G-RVAA	Van's RV-7	A. J. Almosawi
	G-RVAB	Van's RV-7	I. M. Belmore & A. T. Banks
	G-RVAC	Van's RV-7	A. F. S. & B. Caldecourt
	G-RVAH	Van's RV-7	Regent Group
	G-RVAL	Van's RV-8	P. D. Scandrett
	G-RVAN	Van's RV-6	C. Richards
	G-RVAR	Van's RV-8	B. A. Ridgway
	G-RVAT	Van's RV-8	T. R. Grief
	G-RVAW	Van's RV-6	M. E. & R. E. Lee
	G-RVBA	Van's RV-8A	D. P. Richard
	G-RVBC	Van's RV-6A	B. J. Clifford
	G-RVBF	Cameron A-340 balloon	Virgin Balloon Flights
	G-RVBH	Van's RV-8	J. L. & M. R. Hunter
	G-RVBI	Van's RV-8	R. J. Lea
	G-RVBJ	Van's RV-8A	K. R. H. Wingate
	G-RVBP	Van's RV-7	B. J. A. Polwin
	G-RVBZ	Van's RV-7	R. A. Broad
	G-RVCE	Van's RV-6A	C. & M. D. Barnard
	G-RVCH	Van's RV-8A	JB Aviation Ltd
	G-RVCL	Van's RV-6	I. C. Mills
	G-RVDB	Van's RV-7	D. Broom
	G-RVDC	Van's RV-8	D. P. Catt
	G-RVDD	Van's RV-14	D. M. Dash
	G-RVDG	Van's RV-9	D. M. Gill
	G-RVDH	Van's RV-8	R. D. Masters (G-ONER)
	G-RVDJ	Van's RV-6	C. S. & P. S. Foster
	G-RVDR	Van's RV-6A	P. R. Redfern
	G-RVDX	Van's RV-4	P. Musso (G-FTUO)
	G-RVEA	BRM Aero Bristell NG5 Speed Wing	R. V. Emerson
	G-RVEE	Van's RV-6	J. C. A. Wheeler
	G-RVEI	Van's RV-8	M. R. Turner
	G-RVEM	Van's RV-7A	D. A. Cowan (G-CBJU)
	G-RVER	Van's RV-4	G-RVER Flying Group
	G-RVET	Van's RV-6	D. R. Coleman
	G-RVFT	Van's RV-8	R. H. W. A. Westerhuis
	G-RVGA	Van's RV-6A	R. Emery
	G-RVGB	SAAB SF.340B	RVL Aviation Ltd (G-LGNF/G-GNTJ)
	G-RVGO	Van's RV-10	Tapeformers Ltd
	G-RVHD	Van's RV-7	N. Lamb
	G-RVIA	Van's RV-6A	K. R. W. Scull & J. Watkins
	G-RVIB	Van's RV-6	R. D. Myles

Reg	Type	Owner or Operator	Notes
G-RVIC	Van's RV-6A	I. T. Corse	
G-RVII	Van's RV-7	P. H. C. Hall	
G-RVIL	Van's RV-4	S. C. Hipwell	
G-RVIN	Van's RV-6	M. Lawton	
G-RVIO	Van's RV-10	G-RVIO Group	
G-RVIS	Van's RV-8	M. W. Edwards	
G-RVIT	Van's RV-8	P. J. Shotbolt	
G-RVIV	Van's RV-4	S. B. Robson	
G-RVIW	Van's RV-9	C. R. James	
G-RVIX	Van's RV-9A	J. R. Holt & C. S. Simmons	
G-RVIZ	Van's RV-12	Chelwood Flying Group	
G-RVJG	Van's RV-7	J. W. Ellis (G-JTEM)	
G-RVJL	Van's RV-6	A. R. Williams	
G-RVJM	Van's RV-6	M. D. Challoner	
G-RVJO	Van's RV-9A	P. D. Chandler	
G-RVJP	Van's RV-9A	R. M. Palmer	
G-RVJS	Van's RV-8	J. Stringer	
G-RVJW	Van's RV-4	J. M. Williams	
G-RVLC	Van's RV-9A	M. C. Wilksch	
G-RVLG	Cessna F.406	RVL Aviation Ltd	
G-RVLL	Van's RV-6	S. C. Hipwell	
G-RVLW	Cessna F.406 Caravan II	RVL Aviation Ltd	
G-RVLX	Cessna F.406 Caravan II	RVL Aviation Ltd	
G-RVLY	Cessna F.406 Caravan II	RVL Aviation Ltd (G-BPSX)	
G-RVMB	Van's RV-9A	M. James	
G-RVMM	Van's RV-7	M. Malone	
G-RVMS	Van's RV-7	M. P. C. Sweeney	
G-RVMT	Van's RV-6	R. Thomas & J. Hearn	
G-RVMZ	Van's RV-8	A. E. Kay	
G-RVNA	PA-38-112 Tomahawk	Ravenair Aircraft Ltd (G-DFLY)	
G-RVNC	PA-38-112 Tomahawk	Ravenair Aircraft Ltd (G-BTJK)	
G-RVND	PA-38-112 Tomahawk	E. L. Fox (G-BTAS)	
G-RVNE	Partenavia P.68B	Ravenair Aircraft Ltd (G-SAMJ)	
G-RVNG	Partenavia P.68B	Ravenair Aircraft Ltd (G-BMOI)	
G-RVNH	Van's RV-9A	Brimpton Flying Group Ltd	
G-RVNI	Van's RV-6A	G-RVNI Group	
G-RVNJ	Partenavia P.68B	Ravenair Aircraft Ltd	
G-RVNK	Partenavia P.68B	Ravenair Aircraft Ltd (G-BHBZ)	
G-RVNM	Partenavia P.68B	Ravenair Aircraft Ltd (G-BFBU)	
G-RVNO	PA-34-200T Seneca II	Ravenair Aircraft Ltd (G-VVBK/G-SBHS/ G-BDRI)	
G-RVNP	Partenavia P.68B	Ravenair Aircraft Ltd	
G-RVNR	Partenavia P.68B	Ravenair Aircraft Ltd	
G-RVNS	Van's RV-4	G. D. Connolly (G-CBGN)	
G-RVNV	Van's RV-9	M. Owen & N. D. McAllister (G-IRAR)	
G-RVOM	Van's RV-8	C. Watson	
G-RVPH	Van's RV-8	J. C. P. Herbert	
G-RVPL	Van's RV-8	B. J. Summers	
G-RVPM	Van's RV-4	D. P. Lightfoot (G-RVDS)	
G-RVPW	Van's RV-6A	C. G. Deeley	
G-RVRA	PA-28 Cherokee 140	J. D. C. Lea (G-OWVA)	
G-RVRB	PA-34-200T Seneca II	Ravenair Aircraft Ltd (G-BTAJ)	
G-RVRE	Partenavia P.68B	Ravenair Aircraft Ltd	
G-RVRJ	PA-E23 Aztec 250E	Ravenair Aircraft Ltd (G-BBGB)	
G-RVRK	PA-38-112 Tomahawk	Ravenair Aircraft Ltd (G-BGZW)	
G-RVRL	PA-38-112 Tomahawk	Aviation South West Ltd (G-BGZW/G-BGBY)	
G-RVRM	PA-38-112 Tomahawk	Ravenair Aircraft Ltd (G-BGEK)	
G-RVRN	PA-28-161 Warrior II	Ravenair Aircraft Ltd (G-BPID)	
G-RVRO	PA-38-112 Tomahawk II	Ravenair Aircraft Ltd (G-BOUD)	
G-RVRP	Van's RV-7	R. C. Parris	
G-RVRT	PA-28-140 Cherokee C	Full Sutton Flying Centre Ltd (G-AYKX)	
G-RVRU	PA-38-112 Tomahawk	Ravenair Aircraft Ltd (G-NCFE/G-BKMK)	
G-RVRV	Van's RV-4	P. Jenkins	
G-RVRW	PA-23 Aztec 250E	Ravenair Aircraft Ltd (G-BAVZ)	
G-RVRX	Partenavia P.68B	Ravenair Aircraft Ltd (G-PART)	
G-RVRY	PA-38-112 Tomahawk	Ravenair Aircraft Ltd (G-BTND)	
G-RVRZ	PA-23-250 Aztec E	Ravenair Aircraft Ltd (G-NRSC/G-BSFL)	
G-RVSA	Van's RV-6A	N. Grantham	
G-RVSB	Van's RV-6	S. Beard	
G-RVSD	Van's RV-9A	S. W. Damarell	
G-RVSE	Van's RV-6	T. J. Miller & R. P. Marks (G-USRV)	

Notes	Reg	Type	Owner or Operator
	G-RVSG	Van's RV-9A	S. Gerrish
	G-RVSH	Van's RV-6A	S. F. A. Madi
	G-RVSK	Van's RV-9A	D. A. Kenworthy
	G-RVSR	Van's RV-8	R. K. & S. W. Elders
	G-RVST	Van's RV-6	A. F. Vizoso (G-BXYX)
	G-RVSX	Van's RV-6	M. J. Benham
	G-RVTA	Van's RV-7	A. G. Andrew
	G-RVTB	Van's RV-7	T. M. Bootyman (G-CIWM)
	G-RVTE	Van's RV-6	E. McShane & T. Feeny
	G-RVTN	Van's RV-10	C. I. Law
	G-RVTT	Van's RV-7	R. L. Mitcham
	G-RVTW	Van's RV-12	A. P. Watkins
	G-RVTX	Van's RV-8	M. J. Tetlow
	G-RVUK	Van's RV-7	P. D. G. Grist
	G-RVVE	Saab 340B	RVL Aviation Ltd (G-LGNU)
	G-RVVI	Van's RV-6	P. J. Pengilly
	G-RVWJ	Van's RV-9A	N. J. Williams-Jones
	G-RVXP	Van's RV-3B	A. N. Buchan
	G-RVZZ	Van's RV-7	D. L. Stabbert & D. R. Gilbert
	G-RWAY	Rotorway Executive 162F	C. R. Johnson (G-URCH)
	G-RWCA	PA-18-150 Super Cub	R. J. Williamson
	G-RWIA	Robinson R22 Beta	S. A. Wolski (G-BOEZ)
	G-RWIN	Rearwin 175	P. A. Bourne
	G-RWOD	Dan Rihn DR.107 One Design	R. S. Wood
	G-RWSS	Denney Kitfox Mk 2	D. Reilly
	G-RWWW	WS-55 Whirlwind HCC.12 (XR486)★	IHM/Weston-super-Mare
	G-RXTV	Agusta A.109E Power	Arena Aviation Ltd (G-GCMM)
	G-RXUK	Lindstrand LBL-105A balloon	C. C. & R. K. Scott
	G-RYDR	Rotorsport UK MT-03	H. W. Parsons & U. Junger
	G-RYFF	Agusta A. 109S Grand	Bandersnatch Ltd Partnership Inc (G-DEUP/ G-FUFU)
	G-RYNS	PA-32-301FT Cherokee Six	D. A. Earle
	G-RYON	Mudry CAP-231	Ryan Lincoln Jetson (RLJ) Aviation (G-CPII)
	G-RYPE	DG Flugzeugbau DG-1000T	DG-1000T Partners
	G-RYPH	Mainair Blade 912	P. J. Kirkpatrick
	G-RYZZ	Robinson R44 II	Rivermead Aviation Ltd
	G-RZEE	Schleicher ASW-19B	R. Christopherson
	G-RZLY	Flight Design CTSW	J. D. Macnamara
	G-SAAA	Flight Design CTSW	Comunica Industries International Ltd
	G-SAAR	Agusta Westland AW-189	British International Helicopter Services Ltd
	G-SABA	PA-28R-201T Turbo Arrow III	Saba Flying Group (G-BFEN)
	G-SACH	Stoddard-Hamilton Glastar	R. S. Holt
	G-SACI	PA-28-161 Warrior II	PJC (Leasing) Ltd
	G-SACL	Tecnam P2006T	Surrey Aero LLP
	G-SACM	TL2000UK Sting Carbon	M. Clare
	G-SACN	Scheibe SF-25C Falke	The RAF Gliding and Soaring Association
	G-SACO	PA-28-161 Warrior II	Stapleford Flying Club Ltd
	G-SACP	Aero AT-3 R100	Sherburn Aero Club Ltd
	G-SACR	PA-28-161 Cadet	Sherburn Aero Club Ltd
	G-SACS	PA-28-161 Cadet	Sherburn Aero Club Ltd
	G-SACT	PA-28-161 Cadet	Sherburn Aero Club Ltd
	G-SACW	Aero AT-3 R100	Sherburn Aero Club Ltd
	G-SACX	Aero AT-3 R100	Sherburn Aero Club Ltd
	G-SADB	Diamond DA.42M Twin Star	Skyborne Aviation Ltd
	G-SADK	Diamond DA.40D Star	Skyborne Aviation Ltd
	G-SAEA	Vickers Armstrongs Spitfire LF XVI E	M. Harris
	G-SAEB	Supermarine Spitfire LF XVI E	M. Harris
	G-SAFE	Cameron N-77 balloon	P. J. Waller
	G-SAFI	CP.1320 Super Emeraude	C. S. Carleton-Smith
	G-SAGA	Grob G.109B	M. C. Downey
	G-SAGE	Luscombe 8A Silvaire	C. Howell (G-AKTL)
	G-SAHI	Trago Mills SAH-1	Aerial Vocations Ltd
	G-SAIG	Robinson R44 II	Thurston Helicopters Ltd
	G-SAJA	Schempp-Hirth Discus 2	J. G. Arnold
	G-SAJB	Embraer EMB 135LR	Loganair Ltd (G-RJXJ)
	G-SAJC	Embraer EMB 145EP	Loganair Ltd (G-RJXF)

Reg	Type	Owner or Operator	Notes
G-SAJD	Embraer EMB 145EP	Loganair Ltd (G-RJXI)	
G-SAJF	Embraer EMB-145EP	Loganair Ltd (G-RJXE)	
G-SAJG	Embraer EMB 145EP	Loganair Ltd (G-EMBI)	
G-SAJH	Embraer EMB 145EP	Loganair Ltd (G-EMBJ)	
G-SAJI	Embraer EMB 145EP	Loganair Ltd (G-EMBN)	
G-SAJJ	Embraer EMB 145EP	Loganair Ltd (G-RJXB)	
G-SAJK	Embraer EMB 145EP	Loganair Ltd (G-RJXC)	
G-SAJL	Embraer EMB 145EP	Loganair Ltd (G-RJXA)	
G-SAJM	Diamond DA.42 Twin Star	Skyborne Aviation Ltd (G-CJFO)	
G-SAJN	Embraer EMB 145EP	Loganair Ltd (G-RJXD)	
G-SAJO	Embraer EMB 145MP	Loganair Ltd (G-RJXM)	
G-SAJR	Embraer EMB 135ER	Loganair Ltd (G-RJXP/G-CDFS)	
G-SAJS	Embraer EMB 145EP	Loganair Ltd (G-RJXG)	
G-SAJT	Embraer EMB 135ER	Loganair Ltd (G-RJXL)	
G-SAJU	Embraer EMB 135ER	Loganair Ltd (G-RJXK)	
G-SALD	Bombardier BD700-1A10 Global 6000	Gama Aviation (UK) Ltd	
G-SALE	Cameron Z-90 balloon	R. D. Baker	
G-SAMC	Ikarus C42 FB80	C. A. & C. D. Spence	
G-SAMG	Grob G.109B	The Royal Air Force Gliding and Soaring Association	
G-SAMY	Shaw Europa	K. R. Tallent	
G-SAMZ	Cessna 150D	A. J. Taylor (G-ASSO)	
G-SANJ	Guimbal Cabri G2	Wizzjet Aviation Ltd	
G-SANT	Schempp-Hirth Discus bT	S. Cervantes (G-JPIP)	
G-SAOC	Schempp-Hirth Discus 2cT	The Royal Air Force Gliding and Soaring Association	
G-SAPA	Robinson R66	S. Chenevix-Trench & P. Wills	
G-SAPI	PA-28-181 Archer II	Biggleswade Flying Group Ltd	
G-SAPM	SOCATA TB20 Trinidad	G-SAPM Ltd (G-EWFN)	
G-SARA	PA-28-181 Archer II	Clifton Aviation Ltd	
G-SARJ	P & M Quik GT450	A. R. Jones	
G-SARM	Ikarus C.42 FB80	G-SARM Group	
G-SARP	Cessna R182RG	Top Gun Indomitable Aces, Unipessoal LDA/Portugal	
G-SARV	Van's RV-4	Hinton Flying Group	
G-SASC	Beech B200C Super King Air	Gama Aviation (UK) Ltd	
G-SASD	Beech B200C Super King Air	Gama Aviation (UK) Ltd	
G-SASF	Scheibe SF-25C Rotor-Falke	The RAF Gliding and Soaring Association	
G-SASG	Schleicher ASW-27-18E	C. Jackson	
G-SASI	CZAW Sportcruiser	K. W. Allan	
G-SASK	PA-31P Pressurised Navajo	Middle East Business Club Ltd (G-BFAM)	
G-SASM	Westland Scout AH.Mk.1 (XV138)	C. J. Marsden	
G-SASN	MBB-BK 117D-2	Babcock Mission Critical Services Onshore Ltd	
G-SASO	MD Helicopters MD.900 Explorer	Specialist Aviation Services Ltd	
G-SASR	MDH MD-900 Explorer	Specialist Aviation Services Ltd (G-LNAA)	
G-SASS	MBB-BK 117D-2	Babcock Mission Critical Services Onshore Ltd	
G-SASX	Leonardo AW.169	Specialist Aviation Services Ltd	
G-SATI	Cameron Sphere 105 SS balloon	M. A. Sterling	
G-SATL	Cameron Sphere 105 SS balloon	M. A. Sterling	
G-SATM	Diamond DA.42M Twin Star	Skyborne Aviation Ltd	
G-SATN	PA-25-260 Pawnee C	The Royal Gliding and Soaring Association	
G-SAUK	Rans S6-ES Coyote II	J. M. A. Juanos	
G-SAUL	Robin HR.200-160	J. C. Wignall	
G-SAUO	Cessna A.185F	T. G. Lloyd	
G-SAUP	Slingsby T.67M-200 Firefly	Skyborne Aviation Ltd (G-ONES)	
G-SAVY	Savannah VG Jabiru(1)	S. P. Yardley	
G-SAWG	Scheibe SF.25C Falke	The RAF Gliding and Soaring Association Ltd	
G-SAWI	PA-32RT-300T Turbo Lance II	Easyfly SRLS/Italy	
G-SAXL	Schempp-Hirth Duo Discus T	The Royal Air Force Gliding and Soaring Association	
G-SAXT	Schempp-Hirth Duo Discus Xt	The Royal Air Force Gliding and Soaring Association	
G-SAYE	Dornier 228-200	Aurigny Air Services Ltd	
G-SAYS	RAF 2000 GTX-SE gyroplane	G. D. Prebble	
G-SAYX	Cessna 152	Aero Club de Portugal/Portugal	
G-SAZM	Piper J-3C-65 Cub	I. E. M. J. Van Vuuren	
G-SAZY	Avtech Jabiru J400	S.M. Pink	
G-SAZZ	CP.328 Super Emeraude	D. J. Long	
G-SBAG	Phoenix Currie Wot	R. W. Clarke (G-BFAH)	
G-SBDB	Remos GX	M. J. Woollard	

Notes	Reg	Type	Owner or Operator
	G-SBII	Steen Skybolt	K. G., P. D. & P. J. Begley
	G-SBIZ	Cameron Z-90 balloon	Snow Business International Ltd
	G-SBLT	Steen Skybolt	Skybolt Group
	G-SBOL	Steen Skybolt	C. M. Evans & J. W. Blaylock
	G-SBOY	PA-28-181 Archer III	Phoenix Flight Training Ltd (G-LACD/G-BYBG)
	G-SBRK	Aero AT-3 R100	Sywell Aerodrome Ltd
	G-SBSB	Diamond DA.40NG Star	Diamond Aviation Training Ltd
	G-SBUS	BN-2A-26 Islander	Isles of Scilly Skybus Ltd (G-BMMH)
	G-SBVT	Schempp-Hirth Ventus-3T	S. Barter
	G-SCAA	Eurocopter EC135 T2	Babcock Mission Critical Services Onshore Ltd (G-SASB)
	G-SCAP	Leonardo AW109SP Grand New	Apollo Air Services Ltd
	G-SCCA	Cessna 510 Citation Mustang	SCCA Ltd
	G-SCCZ	CZAW Sportcruiser	J. Metcalfe & P. McCusker
	G-SCFC	Ultramagic S-90 balloon	J. S. Russon
	G-SCHI	AS.350B2 Ecureuil	Patriot Aviation Ltd
	G-SCHW	Schweizer 269C	I. D. Jones
	G-SCHZ	Eurocopter AS.355N Ecureuil 2	TSL Contractors Ltd (G-STON)
	G-SCIP	SOCATA TB20 Trinidad GT	The Studio People Ltd
	G-SCIR	PA-31 Navajo C	2 Excel Aviation Ltd
	G-SCLX	FLS Aerospace Sprint 160	Aero Sprint Group (G-PLYM)
	G-SCMG	Ikarus C42 FB80	C. J. Bishop & B. N. Thresher
	G-SCMR	PA-31 Navajo	2 Excel Aviation Ltd
	G-SCNN	Schempp-Hirth Standard Cirrus	G. C. Short
	G-SCOL	Gippsland GA-8 Airvan	Parachuting Aircraft Ltd
	G-SCOR	Eurocopter EC.155 B1	Starspeed Ltd
	G-SCPD	Escapade 912 (1)	C. W. Potts
	G-SCPI	CZAW Sportcruiser	M. R. Foreman
	G-SCPL	PA-28 Cherokee 140	Aeros Training Ltd (G-BPVL)
	G-SCRZ	CZAW Sportcruiser	R. Vora
	G-SCSC	CZAW Sportcruiser	R. Powers
	G-SCTA	Westland Scout AH.1	T. L. Hobbs
	G-SCTR	PA-31 Navajo C	2 Excel Aviation Ltd
	G-SCUB	PA-18 Super Cub 135 (542447)	R. A. Stephens
	G-SCUL	Rutan Cozy	K. R. W. Scull
	G-SCZR	CZAW Sportcruiser	K. D. Taylor
	G-SDAT	Flight Design CTSW	S. P. Pearson
	G-SDFM	Aerotechnik EV-97 Eurostar	G-SDFM Eurostar Group
	G-SDII	Eurocopter AS.350B2 Ecureuil	KC Aviation LLP
	G-SDNI	VS.361 Spitfire LF.IX E	P. M. Andrews
	G-SDOA	Aeropro Eurofox 912(S)	S. P. S. Dornan
	G-SDOB	Tecnam P2002-EA Sierra	A. B. Dean
	G-SDOI	Aeroprakt A.22 Foxbat	S. A. Owen
	G-SDOZ	Tecnam P92-EA Echo Super	Cumbernauld Flyers G-SDOZ
	G-SDRV	Van's RV-8	S. M. Dawson
	G-SDRY	Cessna 525C CitationJet CJ4	Dowdeswell Aviation LLP
	G-SDTL	Guimbal Cabri G2	Advanced Aviation Services Ltd
	G-SDTO	Stolp SA.300 Starduster Too	M. J. Golder
	G-SEAF	Hawker Sea Fury FB.11	Patina Ltd (G-BWOL)
	G-SEAI	Cessna U.206G (amphibian)	K. O'Conner
	G-SEAK	Westland Sea King HAR.3	Lift West (Helicopters) Ltd
	G-SEAT	Colt 42A balloon	T. G. Read
	G-SEBN	Skyranger 912S(1)	C. M. James
	G-SEBS	Ultramagic M-77 balloon	C. Collins
	G-SEDC	Fairchild 24W-46 Argus	G. E. J. Spooner
	G-SEDO	Cameron N-105 balloon	I. M. Ashpole
	G-SEED	Piper J-3C-65 Cub	J. H. Seed
	G-SEEE	Pegasus Quik GT450	I. M. Spence
	G-SEEK	Cessna T.210N	A. Hopper
	G-SEHK	Cessna 182T	Golf HK Ltd
	G-SEJW	PA-28-161 Warrior II	Tor Financial Consulting Ltd
	G-SEKR	ISA 180 Seeker	Northern Aircraft Company Ltd
	G-SELA	Cessna 152	Cloud Global Ltd (G-FLOP)
	G-SELB	PA-28-161 Warrior II	POM Flight Training Ltd (G-LFSK)
	G-SELC	Diamond DA42 Twin Star	Stapleford Flying Club Ltd
	G-SELF	Shaw Europa	N. D. Crisp & ptnrs
	G-SELL	Robin DR.400/180	C. R. Beard Farmers Ltd
	G-SELY	Agusta-Bell 206B JetRanger 3	M. D. Tracey

Reg	Type	Owner or Operator	Notes
G-SEMI	PA-44-180 Seminole	J. Benfell & M. Djukic (G-DENW)	
G-SEMR	Cessna T206H Turbo Stationair	Semer LLP	
G-SENA	Rutan LongEz	G. Bennett	
G-SENE	PA-34-200T Seneca II	Orion Coil Coating Ltd	
G-SENS	Eurocopter EC.135T2+	Saville Air Services	
G-SENX	PA-34-200T Seneca II	First Air Ltd (G-DARE/G-WOTS/G-SEVL)	
G-SEPT	Cameron N-105 balloon	A. G. Merry	
G-SERE	Diamond DA42 Twin Star	Atlantic Flight Training Ltd	
G-SERL	SOCATA TB10 Tobago	G. C. Jarvis (G-LANA)	
G-SERV	Cameron N-105 balloon	Servo & Electronic Sales Ltd	
G-SETI	Cameron Sky 80-16 balloon	R. P. Allan	
G-SEUK	Cameron TV-80 ss balloon	Mobberley Balloon Collection	
G-SEVA	SE-5A (replica) (F141:G)	G-SEVA Trust	
G-SEVN	Van's RV-7	N. Reddish	
G-SEXE	Scheibe SF.25C Falke	SF25C G-SESE Syndicate	
G-SEXX	PA-28-161 Warrior II	Weald Air Services Ltd	
G-SEXY	AA-1 Yankee ★	Jetstream Club, Liverpool Marriott Hotel South, Speke (G-AYLM)	
G-SEZA	Schleicher ASW-20C	J. F. Paterson	
G-SFAR	Ikarus C42 FB100	R. Moore	
G-SFCM	P & M PulsR	J. D. Harrison	
G-SFLA	Ikarus C42 FB80	Solent Flight Ltd	
G-SFLB	Ikarus C42 FB80	Solent Flight Ltd	
G-SFLY	Diamond DA40 Star	L. & N. P. L. Turner	
G-SFOX	Rotorway Executive 90	J. G. Vissers (G-BUAH)	
G-SFSA	American Champion 8KCAB Super Decathlon	S. R. Evans	
G-SFSL	Cameron Z-105 balloon	A. J. Gregory	
G-SFTZ	Slingsby T.67M Firefly 160	Slingsby T.67M Group	
G-SGEN	Ikarus C.42 FB 80	G. A. Arturi	
G-SGFE	Liberty XL-2	I. Fidler (G-OLAR)	
G-SGNT	Skylark	N. H. Townsend	
G-SGRP	Agusta AW.109SP Grand New	Apollo Air Services Ltd	
G-SGSE	PA-28-181 Archer II	U. Patel (G-BOJX)	
G-SGSG	Bombardier BD700-1A11 Global 5000	TAG Aviation (UK) Ltd	
G-SGTS	Viking DHC.6-400 Twin Otter	Loganair Ltd	
G-SGWA	Ikarus C42 FB100	A. & C. Williams	
G-SHAA	Enstrom 280-UK	D. McCann	
G-SHAK	Cameron Cabin SS balloon	Magical Adventures Ltd (G-ODIS)	
G-SHAR	Cessna 182T Skylane	G. N. Clarkson	
G-SHAY	PA-28R-201T Turbo Arrow III	Alpha Yankee Flying Group (G-BFDG/G-JEFS)	
G-SHAZ	Guimbal Cabri G2	Elite Helicopters	
G-SHBA	Cessna F.152	Paul's Planes Ltd	
G-SHCK	Ikarus C42 FB80	CK Group	
G-SHED	PA-28-181 Archer II	G-SHED Flying Group (G-BRAU)	
G-SHEE	P & M Quik GT450	C. J. Millership	
G-SHEZ	Mainair Pegasus Quik	R. & S. Wells	
G-SHHH	Glaser-Dirks DG-100G	G-SHHH Group	
G-SHIM	CFM Streak Shadow	P. D. Babin	
G-SHIP	PA-23 Aztec 250F ★	Midland Air Museum/Coventry	
G-SHKI	Ikarus C42 FB80	K. S. Daniels & G. R. Barker	
G-SHLS	Agusta A109E Power	Sloane Helicopters Ltd	
G-SHMB	Aero L-39ZA Albatross	L39 Aviation Ltd	
G-SHMI	Evektor EV-97 Team EuroStar UK	Mike India Flying Group	
G-SHMN	Alpi Pioneer 300 Hawk	E. G. Shimmin (G-GKEV)	
G-SHOG	Colomban MC.15 Cri-Cri	K. D. & C. S. Rhodes (G-PFAB)	
G-SHOW	MS.733 Alycon	P. Cartwright & F. A. Forster	
G-SHRD	Eurocopter AS.350B2 Ecureuil	Jet Helicopters Ltd (G-LHTB)	
G-SHRK	Enstrom 280C-UK	Shark Helicopters Ltd (G-BGMX)	
G-SHRT	Robinson R44 II	Hingley Aviation Ltd	
G-SHSH	Shaw Europa	S. G. Hayman & J. Price	
G-SHSP	Cessna 172S	Shropshire Aero Club Ltd	
G-SHUC	Rans S-6-ESA Coyote II	E. W. Calvin (G-MYKN)	
G-SHUF	Mainair Blade	G. Holdcroft	
G-SHUG	PA-28R-201T Turbo Arrow III	G-SHUG Ltd	
G-SHUI	Cessna 680A Citation Latitude	Air Charter Scotland Ltd	
G-SHUU	Enstrom 280C-UK-2	Tinles DOO/Slovenia (G-OMCP/G-KENY/G-BJFG)	

Notes	Reg	Type	Owner or Operator
	G-SHUV	Aerosport Woody Pusher	J. R. Wraigh
	G-SHWK	Cessna 172S	Cambridge Aero Club Ltd
	G-SHWN	P-51D Mustang (413779/WD-C)	Sharkmouth Ltd
	G-SIBK	Raytheon Beech A36 Bonanza	W. Robson
	G-SICA	BN-2B-20 Islander	Shetland Leasing and Property Development Ltd (G-SLAP)
	G-SICB	BN-2B-20 Islander	Shetlands Islands Council (G-NESU/G-BTVN)
	G-SIGN	PA-39 Twin Comanche 160 C/R	D. Buttle
	G-SIIE	Christen Pitts S-2B Special	Wild Thing (G-SKYD)
	G-SIII	Extra EA.300	Owners of G-SIII
	G-SIIO	Schempp-Hirth Ventus 3T	P. J. Harvey
	G-SIIX	PA-32-260 NCherokee Six	UK Flying Clubs Ltd (G-CHFK)
	G-SIJJ	North American P-51D-NA Mustang (472035)	Hangar II Collection
	G-SIJW	SA Bulldog Srs 120/121 (XX630:5)	M. Miles
	G-SILS	Pietenpol Skyscout	D. Silsbury
	G-SILY	Pegasus Quantum 15	S. D. Sparrow
	G-SIMM	Ikarus C.42 FB 100 VLA	D. Simmons
	G-SIMY	PA-32-300 Cherokee Six	I. Simpson (G-OCPF/G-BOCH)
	G-SINK	Schleicher ASH-25	K. Atkinson
	G-SINN	EV-97 Eurostar SL microlight	J. C. Miller
	G-SIPA	SIPA 903	A. C. Leak & G. S. Dilland (G-BGBM)
	G-SIPP	Lindstrand lbl-35a Cloudhopper balloon	A. R. Rich
	G-SIRD	Robinson R44 II	Peglington Productions Ltd
	G-SIRE	Best Off Sky Ranger Swift 912S(1)	P. W. F. Coleman
	G-SIRO	Dassault Falcon 900EX	Condor Aviation LLP
	G-SIRS	Cessna 560XL Citation Excel	London Executive Aviation Ltd
	G-SISI	Schempp-Hirth Duo Discus	Glider Sierra India
	G-SISU	P & M Quik GT450	M. W. Abbott
	G-SISX	Pitts S-1S Special	A. J. & C. A. J. Millson
	G-SITA	Pegasus Quantum 15-912	P. N. Thompson
	G-SIVJ	Westland Gazelle HT.2	Skytrace (UK) Ltd (G-CBSG)
	G-SIXC	Douglas DC-6B★	The DC-6 Diner/Coventry
	G-SIXD	PA-32 Cherokee Six 300D	M. B. Paine & I. Gordon
	G-SIXP	Cameron Sport-90 balloon	Sarnia Balloon Group
	G-SIXT	PA-28-161 Warrior II	Airways Aero Associations Ltd (G-BSSX)
	G-SIXX	Colt 77A balloon	S. Drawbridge
	G-SIXY	Van's RV-6	C. J. Hall & C. R. P. Hamlett
	G-SIZZ	Jabiru J400	K. J. Betteley
	G-SJBB	Robin DR400/140B	SJ Aircraft
	G-SJBI	Pitts S-2C Special	S. L. Walton
	G-SJEF	AutoGyro Cavalon	J. Smith
	G-SJEN	Ikarus C42 FB80 ★	Museum of Flight/East Fortune
	G-SJKR	Lindstrand LBL-90A balloon	P. Richardson
	G-SJMW	SD-1 Minisport	M. A. Wood
	G-SJPC	Van's RV-8	J. T. Garrett
	G-SJPI	Dynamic WT9 UK	S. R. Wilkinson
	G-SKAL	Cessna 560XL Citation XLS+	Volar Ltd
	G-SKAN	Cessna F.172M	M. Richardson & J. Williams (G-BFKT)
	G-SKAZ	Aero AT-3 R100	G-SKAZ Flying Group
	G-SKBD	Raytheon Beech 400A	Sky Border Logistics Ltd
	G-SKCI	Rutan Vari-Eze	C. Boyd
	G-SKFY	Robinson R44 II	Skyfly Air Ltd (G-GRGE)
	G-SKIE	Steen Skybolt	G-SKIE Group
	G-SKKY	Cessna 172S Skyhawk	J. Herbert & G. P. Turner
	G-SKLR	Eurocopter EC.120B Colibri	C. R. Tilley (G-VIPR)
	G-SKNG	Westlasnd Sea King HAR Mk.3	Lift West (Helicopters) Ltd
	G-SKOT	Cameron V-42 balloon	S. A. Laing
	G-SKPG	Best Off Skyranger 912 (2)	T. Farncombe
	G-SKPH	Yakovlev Yak-50	R. S. Partridge-Hicks & I. C. Austin (G-BWWH)
	G-SKPP	Eurocopter EC.120B Colbri	Bliss Aviation Ltd (G-MKII)
	G-SKRA	Best Off Skyranger 912S (1)	J. S. Peer
	G-SKRG	Best Off Skyranger 912 (2)	M. J. Kingsley & D. J. Liddle
	G-SKSW	Best Off Sky Ranger Swift 912S	J. & J. A. Pegram
	G-SKTN	Avro 696 Shackleton MR.Mk.2 (WR963)	Shackleton Aviation Group CIC
	G-SKUA	Stoddard-Hamilton Glastar	F. P. Smiddy (G-LEZZ/G-BYCR)
	G-SKUB	TLAC Sherwood Cub	M. J. A. Yates
	G-SKYC	Slingsby T.67M Firefly	K. Taylor (G-BLDP)

Reg	Type	Owner or Operator	Notes
G-SKYF	SOCATA TB10 Tobago	W. L. McNeil	
G-SKYL	Cessna 182S	G. A. Gee	
G-SKYN	AS.355F1 Twin Squirrel	RCR Aviation Limited (G-OGRK/G-BWZC/ G-MODZ)	
G-SKYO	Slingsby T.67M-200	VG Flight Ltd	
G-SKYT	I.I.I. Sky Arrow 650TC	W. M. Bell & S. J. Brooks	
G-SKYV	PA-28RT-201T Turbo Arrow IV	Pek Aviation BV/Netherlands (G-BNZG)	
G-SLAR	Agusta A109C	Excel Charter Ltd (G-OWRD/G-USTC/G-LAXO)	
G-SLCC	EV-97 Eurostar SL	G-SLCC Group	
G-SLCE	Cameron C-80 balloon	A. M. Holly	
G-SLCT	Diamond DA42NG Twin Star	Stapleford Flying Club Ltd	
G-SLEA	Mudry/CAARP CAP-10B	M. J. M. Jenkins, N. R. Thorburn & R. Harris	
G-SLIP	Reality Easy Raider J2.2(3)	R. G. Hicks	
G-SLIV	TAF Sling 4	D. J. Pilkington	
G-SLNG	TAF Sling 4	R. S. D. Wheeler & R. J. H. Davis	
G-SLNT	Flight Design CTSW	K. Kirby	
G-SLNW	Robinson R22 Beta	Sky Helicopters Ltd (G-LNIC)	
G-SLYR	Gnat Mk.1	Heritage Aircraft Ltd	
G-SLYY	Ultramagic M-105 balloon	J. A. Lawton	
G-SLZT	TAF Sling 2	D. J. Pilkington	
G-SMAJ	DG Flugzeugbau DG-808C	S. Marriott (G-TRTM)	
G-SMAR	Schempp-Hirth Arcus M	AR Syndicate	
G-SMAT	SA Bulldog Srs.120/121 (XX658:07)	Skysmart MRO Ltd (G-BZPS)	
G-SMBA	Cessna P.210N Pressurized Centurion	NAL Engineering Ltd	
G-SMBM	Pegasus Quantum 15-912	B. Cook	
G-SMDH	Shaw Europa XS	S. W. Pitt	
G-SMEG	Cessna 172S	Air-Unlimited Sweden AB/Sweden	
G-SMHA	Dassault Falcon 7X	Concierge U Ltd	
G-SMIG	Cameron O-65 balloon	R. D. Parry	
G-SMIL	Lindstrand LBL-105A balloon	A. L. Wade	
G-SMKR	Eurofox 912(S)	S. M. Kenyon-Roberts	
G-SMLA	BAe.146-200	Jota Aviation Ltd (G-OZRH)	
G-SMLE	Robinson R44 II	English Braids Ltd	
G-SMLI	Groppo Trail	A. M. Wilson	
G-SMLZ	Groppo Trail Mk.2	A. M. Wilson	
G-SMMA	Cessna F.406 Caravan II	Secretary of State for Scotland per Environmental and Rural Affairs Department	
G-SMMB	Cessna F.406 Caravan II	Secretary of State for Scotland per Environmental and Rural Affairs Department	
G-SMMF	Lindstrand LBL-77A balloon	M. & S. Mitchell	
G-SMON	Cessna A.152	North Weald Flying Group Ltd (G-BNJE/ G-OWFS/G-DESY)	
G-SMRS	Cessna 172F	M. R. Sarling	
G-SMSM	Dassault Falcon 2000LX	London Executive Aviation Ltd	
G-SMSP	Super Marine Spitfire Mk.26B (JG241:ZX-J)	S. J. D. Hall	
G-SMYK	PZL-Swidnik PW-5 Smyk	PW-5 Syndicate	
G-SNAL	Cessna 182T	N. S. Lyndhurst	
G-SNCA	PA-34-200T Seneca II	Social Infrastructure Ltd	
G-SNDR	Supermarine S5 Replica	W. B. Hosie	
G-SNDS	Cirrus SR20	Sands Wealth Management Ltd	
G-SNEV	CFM Streak Shadow SA	A. Child	
G-SNOG	Kiss 400-582 (1)	C. R. Sanders	
G-SNOP	Shaw Europa	M. Stow (G-DESL/G-WWWG)	
G-SNOW	Cameron V-77 balloon	I. Welsford	
G-SNOZ	Shaw Europa	P. O. Bayliss (G-DONZ)	
G-SNSA	Agusta Westland AW139	CHC Scotia Ltd	
G-SNSE	Agusta Westland AW139	CHC Scotia Ltd	
G-SNSG	Agusta Westland AW139	Waypoint Asset Co.3 Ltd	
G-SNSI	Agusta Westland AW139	CHC Scotia Ltd (G-FTOM)	
G-SNUG	Best Off Skyranger 912S(1)	J. C. Mundy & J. D. Fielding	
G-SNUZ	PA-28-161 Warrior II	Freedom Aviation Ltd	
G-SNXA	Sonex	S. J. Moody	
G-SOAF	BAC.167 Strikemaster Mk. 82A (425)	Strikemaster Flying Club	
G-SOBI	PA-28-181 Archer II	G-SOBI Flying Group	
G-SOCK	Mainair Pegasus Quik	K. R. McCartney	
G-SOCT	Yakovlev Yak-50 (AR-B)	M. J. Gadsby & M. P. Blokland	
G-SODA	Balony Kubicek BB-22Z balloon	C. T. E. Wetters (G-CIWE)	

BRITISH CIVIL AIRCRAFT MARKINGS

Notes	Reg	Type	Owner or Operator
	G-SOKO	Soko P-2 Kraguj (30149)	P. C. Avery (G-BRXK)
	G-SOLA	Aero Designs Star-Lite SL.1	G. P. Thomas
	G-SONA	SOCATA TB10 Tobago	G-SONA Group (G-BIBI)
	G-SONE	Cessna 525A Citationjet	Centreline AV Ltd
	G-SONX	Sonex	A. J. L. Eves
	G-SOOC	Hughes 369HS	R.J.H. Strong (G-BRRX)
	G-SOOH	Hughes 369E	Flitwick Helicopters Ltd (G-BRTL)
	G-SOOS	Colt 21A balloon	P. J. Stapley
	G-SOOT	PA-28 Cherokee 180	R. J. Hunter (G-AVNM)
	G-SOOZ	Rans S-6-ES Coyote II	S. R. Davis
	G-SOPC	Replica Sopwith Camel	C. I. Law & P. Hoeft
	G-SORA	Glaser-Dirks DG.500/22	DG Syndicate
	G-SOUT	Van's RV-8	J. M. Southern (G-CDPJ)
	G-SOVB	Learjet 45	Zenith Aviation Ltd (G-OLDJ)
	G-SPAM	Avid Aerobat (modified)	M. Durcan
	G-SPAT	Aero AT-3 R100	S2T Aero Ltd
	G-SPCI	Cessna 182P	K. Brady (G-GUMS/G-CBMN)
	G-SPCY	Embraer EMB-135BJ Legacy 650	London Executive Aviation Ltd (G-OTGL)
	G-SPCZ	CZAW Sportcruiser	R. J. Robinson
	G-SPDY	Raj Hamsa X'Air Hawk	A. A. Rowson
	G-SPED	Alpi Pioneer 300	R. B. Shaw
	G-SPEL	Sky 220-24 balloon	T. G. Church
	G-SPEY	Agusta-Bell 206B JetRanger 3	Castle Air Ltd (G-BIGO)
	G-SPFX	Rutan Cozy	B. D. Tutty
	G-SPHU	Eurocopter EC 135T2+	Babcock Mission Critical Services Onshore Ltd
	G-SPID	Ultramagic S-90 balloon	A. Fawcett
	G-SPIN	Pitts S-2A Special	P. Avery
	G-SPIP	SNCAN Stampe SV.4C	A. G. & P. M. Solleveld (G-BTIO)
	G-SPIT	VS.379 Spitfire FR.XIV (MV268)	Anglia Aircraft Restorations Ltd (G-BGHB)
	G-SPMM	Best Off Sky Ranger Swift 912S(1)	A. W. Paterson
	G-SPOG	Jodel DR.1050	G-SPOG Group (G-AXVS)
	G-SPRC	Van's RV-8	A. P. & C. Durston & J. C. Gowdy
	G-SPRE	Cessna 550 Citation Bravo	Synergy Aviation Ltd
	G-SPRI	Agusta A109E Power	Arnhem Aviation Ltd (G-EMHC)
	G-SPRK	Van's RV-4	Jack Aviation Ltd
	G-SPRX	Van's RV-4	Jack Aviation Ltd
	G-SPTR	Robinson R44 II	Heli Air Ltd
	G-SPTT	Diamond DA.40D Star	Acrobat Ltd (G-OCCS)
	G-SPTX	Dassault Falcon 7X	Concierge U Ltd
	G-SPUR	Cessna 550 Citation II	London Executive Aviation Ltd
	G-SPUT	Yakovlev Yak-52	D. J. Hopkinson (G-BXAV)
	G-SPVI	SOCATA TB.20 Trinidad	Teegee Group
	G-SPVK	AS.350B3 Ecureuil	Squirrel Hire LLP (G-CERU)
	G-SPWP	Cirrus SR22	S. Pope
	G-SPXX	VS.356 Spitfire F.22	P. R. Arnold
	G-SRAH	Schempp-Hirth Mini-Nimbus C	R. A. Hall
	G-SRBM	Beech B350 Super King Air	Skyhopper LLP
	G-SRCB	Van's RV-12	C. Burgess
	G-SRII	Easy Raider 503	K. Myles
	G-SRNE	Eurocopter MBB BK-117C-2	Starspeed Ltd
	G-SROE	Westland Scout AH.1 (XP907)	Saunders-Roe Helicopter Ltd
	G-SROY	PA-28-180 Cherokee E	R. L. West (G-DLTR/G-AYAV)
	G-SRRA	Tecnam P2002-EA Sierra	J. Dunn
	G-SRWN	PA-28-161 Warrior II	A. J. Bell (G-MAND/G-BRKT)
	G-SRYY	Shaw Europa XS	I. O'Brien
	G-SRZZ	Cirrus SR22	A. Bodaghi
	G-SSCL	MDH Hughes 369E	Shaun Stevens Contractors Ltd
	G-SSDI	SD-1 Minisport	P. C. Piggott & B. A. Fairston
	G-SSDR	Scooter	J. Attard
	G-SSIX	Rans S.6-116 Coyote II	R. I. & D. M. Kelly
	G-SSKY	BN-2B-26 Islander	Isles of Scilly Skybus Ltd (G-BSWT)
	G-SSRD	Balony Kubicek BB17XR balloon	G. Hoefler
	G-SSTI	Cameron N-105 balloon	A. A. Brown
	G-SSTL	Just Superstol	Avalanche Aviation Ltd
	G-SSVB	VS.349 Spitfire LF.Vb	T. W. Gilbert (G-CGBI)
	G-SSWV	Sportavia Fournier RF-5B	Fournier Flying Group
	G-SSXL	Just Superstol XL	P. T. Price

Reg	Type	Owner or Operator	Notes
G-STAC	Lindstrand LTL Series 1-105 balloon	S. M. Heard	
G-STAV	Cameron O-84 balloon	A. Pollock	
G-STAY	Cessna FR.172K	J. M. Wilkins	
G-STBA	Boeing 777-336ER	British Airways PLC	
G-STBB	Boeing 777-36NER	British Airways PLC	
G-STBC	Boeing 777-36NER	British Airways PLC	
G-STBD	Boeing 777-36NER	British Airways PLC	
G-STBE	Boeing 777-36NER	British Airways PLC	
G-STBF	Boeing 777-336ER	British Airways PLC	
G-STBG	Boeing 777-336ER	British Airways PLC	
G-STBH	Boeing 777-336ER	British Airways PLC	
G-STBI	Boeing 777-336ER	British Airways PLC	
G-STBJ	Boeing 777-336ER	British Airways PLC	
G-STBK	Boeing 777-336ER	British Airways PLC	
G-STBL	Boeing 777-336ER	British Airways PLC	
G-STBM	Boeing 777-300ER	British Airways PLC	
G-STBN	Boeing 777-300ER	British Airways PLC	
G-STBO	Boeing 777-300ER	British Airways PLC	
G-STBP	Boeing 777-300ER	British Airways PLC	
G-STBT	Cameron N-42 balloon	M. D. A. Billing (G-BVLC)	
G-STBY	Flylight MotorFloater	B. C. C. Middleton	
G-STDO	BRM Aero Bristell NG Speed Wing	S. M. Wade & J. A. Strong	
G-STEA	PA-28R Cherokee Arrow 200	D. W. Breden	
G-STEE	EV-97 Eurostar	S. G. Beeson	
G-STEL	BRM Aero Bristell NG5	J. M. Naylor & L. C. Rowson	
G-STEM	Stemme S.10V	A. M. Booth	
G-STEN	Stemme S.10 (4)	G-STEN Syndicate	
G-STES	Europa XS	S. K. Ridge & S. A. Ivell	
G-STEU	Rolladen-Schneider LS6-18W	F. K. Russell	
G-STFO	TL.2000UK Sting Carbon S4	G. P. D. Clover	
G-STIN	TL 2000UK Sting Carbon	R. J. Field	
G-STIX	Van's RV-7	R. D. S. Jackson	
G-STMT	Dassault Falcon 7X	TAG Aviation (UK) Ltd	
G-STNG	TL2000UK Sting Carbon	P. S. Ganczakowski	
G-STNS	Agusta A109A-II	Eurotech SRL/Italy	
G-STOD	ICP MXP-740 Savannah VG Jabiru(1)	M. P. Avison & L. J. Boardman	
G-STOK	Colt 77B balloon	A. C. Booth	
G-STOO	Stolp Starduster Too	A. K. Robinson	
G-STOP	Robinson R44 Raven II	HLQ Services Ltd/Ireland	
G-STOW	Cameron 90 Wine Box SS balloon	Flying Enterprises	
G-STPK	Lambert Mission M108	S. T. P. Kember	
G-STRG	Cyclone AX2000	D. R. Thompson	
G-STRK	CFM Streak Shadow SA	E. McCall	
G-STRV	Van's RV-14	S. D. Hicks	
G-STSN	Stinson 108-3 Voyager	M. S. Colebrook (G-BHMR)	
G-STUA	Aerotek Pitts S-2A Special (modified)	G-STUA Group	
G-STUE	Europa	F. Xuereb	
G-STUI	Pitts S-2AE	S. L. Goldspink & J-M. M. Munn	
G-STUN	TL2000UK Sting Carbon	D. Russell (G-KEVT)	
G-STUU	Bristell NG5 Speed Wing	S. M. Spencer	
G-STUY	Robinson R44 II	Central Helicopters Ltd	
G-STUZ	Lambert Mission M108	C. J. Finnigan	
G-STVL	Lindstrand LBL-77A balloon	S. J. Donkin	
G-STVT	CZAW Sportcruiser	S. Taylor	
G-STVZ	Bell 206B Jet Ranger 3	Mediatech Consulting Ltd (G-XBCI)	
G-STWB	Hawker 750	Voluxis Ltd	
G-STWO	ARV Super 2	R. E. Griffiths	
G-STZZ	TL2000UK Sting Carbon	M. Salt	
G-SUAU	Cameron C-90 balloon	A. Heginbottom	
G-SUCT	Robinson R22	Irwin Plant Sales	
G-SUED	Thunder Ax8-90 balloon	E. C. Lubbock & S. A. Kidd (G-PINE)	
G-SUEI	Diamond DA.42 Twin Star	Sue Air	
G-SUEL	P & M Quik GT450	D. A. Ellis	
G-SUEM	Diamond DA.42 Twin Star	Sue Air	
G-SUEO	Diamond DA.40NG Star	Sue Air	
G-SUER	Bell 206B JetRanger	Aerospeed Ltd (G-CBYX)	
G-SUET	Bell 206B JetRanger	Aerospeed Ltd (G-BLZN)	
G-SUEY	Bell 206L-1 Long Ranger	Aerospeed Ltd	
G-SUEZ	Agusta-Bell 206B JetRanger 2	Aerospeed Ltd	

Notes	Reg	Type	Owner or Operator
	G-SUFK	Eurocopter EC 135P2+	Police & Crime Commissioner for West Yorkshire
	G-SUGR	Embraer EMB-135BJ Legacy 650	Air Charter Scotland Ltd
	G-SUKI	PA-38-112 Tomahawk	Merseyflight Ltd (G-RVNB/G-BPNV)
	G-SUKK	Sukhoi Su-29	M. Benshemesh
	G-SULU	Best Off Skyranger 912(2)	S. Marathe (G-SOPH)
	G-SUMM	Best Off Skyranger Nynja 912S(1)	A. Summers
	G-SUMO	Best Off Skyranger Nynja LS 912S(1)	J. A. Hunt
	G-SUMX	Robinson R22 Beta	Bickerstaffe Aviation Ltd
	G-SUNN	Robinson R44	Phoenix Helicopter Academy Ltd
	G-SUPA	PA-18 Super Cub 150	S. E. Leach
	G-SURY	Eurocopter EC 135T2+	Police & Crime Commissioner for West Yorkshire
	G-SUSE	Shaw Europa XS	P. R. Tunney
	G-SUSH	Schleicher ASK-21Mi	S. M. Chapman
	G-SUSI	Cameron V-77 balloon	J. H. Dryden
	G-SUTD	Jabiru UL-D	W. J. Lister & R. F. G. Bermudez
	G-SUTE	Van's RV-8	C. R. Robert
	G-SUTY	Robinson R44 II	Heli Air Ltd (G-HOCA)
	G-SUUK	Sukhoi Su-29	D. J. Barke
	G-SUZN	PA-28-161 Warrior II	A. J. Gomes
	G-SVAN	Cessna 208B Grand Caravan	Parachuting Caravan Leasing Ltd
	G-SVAS	PA-18-150 Super Cub	Richard Shuttleworth Trustees
	G-SVDG	Jabiru SK	R. Tellegen
	G-SVEN	Centrair 101A Pegase	G7 Group
	G-SVET	Yakovlev Yak-50	The Assets of the Svetlana Group
	G-SVGL	SNCAN Stampe SV-4A	G. W. Lynch
	G-SVIP	Cessna 421B Golden Eagle II	R. P. Bateman
	G-SVIV	SNCAN Stampe SV.4C	J. E. Keighley
	G-SVNH	Savannah VG Jabiru(1)	K. Harmston (G-CFKV)
	G-SVNP	Bell 429 Global Ranger	Seven Up Aviation Ltd
	G-SVNX	Dassault Falcon 7X	Executive Jet Charter Ltd
	G-SVPN	PA-32R-301T Turbo Saratoga	Stratton Motor Company (Norfolk) Ltd
	G-SWAB	Tiger Cub RL5A Sherwood Ranger XP	D. S. Brown
	G-SWAI	Swift SWO1A	Swift Aircraft Ltd
	G-SWAK	Oldfield Baby Lakes	B. Bryan
	G-SWAT	Robinson R44 II	Unique Helicopters (NI) Ltd
	G-SWAY	PA-18-150 Super Cub	S. J. Gaveston & R. L. Brinklow
	G-SWCT	Flight Design CTSW	J. A. Shufflebotham
	G-SWEE	Beech 95-B55 Baron	T. Slotover (G-AZDK)
	G-SWEL	Hughes 369HS	M. A. Crook & A. E. Wright (G-RBUT)
	G-SWIF	VS.541 Swift F.7 (XF114) ★	Solent Sky, Southampton
	G-SWIG	Robinson R44	S. Goddard
	G-SWLL	Aero AT-3 R100	Sywell Aerodrome Ltd
	G-SWNS	Robinson R44 II	Swan Staff Recruitment Ltd (G-PROJ)
	G-SWON	Pitts S-1S Special	S. L. Goldspink
	G-SWOT	Currie Wot (C3011:S)	P. N. Davis
	G-SWRD	Boeing 737-3L9	21T Ltd (G-OGBE)
	G-SWRE	Tecnam P2002-EA Sierra	W. Swire
	G-SWSW	Schempp-Hirth Ventus bT	R. Kalin
	G-SWYF	Best Off Skyranger Swift 912(1)	C. Moore & K. J. Bradley
	G-SWYM	CZAW Sportcruiser	R. W. Beal
	G-SXIX	Rans S.19	R. J. Almey
	G-SXSX	Robinson R66	M. Struth
	G-SYDH	Bell 206B-3 Jet Ranger III	SJH North West Ltd (G-BXNT)
	G-SYEL	Aero AT-3 R100	Sywell Aerodrome Ltd
	G-SYFW	Focke-Wulf Fw.190 replica (2+1)	D. J. Howell
	G-SYLJ	Embraer RJ135BJ	Blue Wings Ltd
	G-SYLL	PA-31-350 Navajo Chieftain	Sywell Aerodrome Ltd (G-BVYF/G-SAVE)
	G-SYLV	Cessna 208B Grand Caravan	WAS Aircraft Leasing Ltd
	G-SYWL	Aero AT-3 R100	Sywell Aerodrome Ltd
	G-SZDA	PZL SZD-59 Acro	P. C. Sharphouse
	G-TAAB	Cirrus SR22	Alpha Bravo Aviation Ltd
	G-TAAC	Cirrus SR20	S. Tweedie
	G-TAAS	Agusta AW.109SP Grand New	Sloane Helicopters Ltd

Reg	Type	Owner or Operator	Notes
G-TAAT	PA-32-301FT	A. D. Trotter	
G-TACC	SOCATA TB-20 Trinidad	F. Taccogna (G-GVFR/G-CEPT/G-BTEK)	
G-TACK	Grob G.109B	A. P. Mayne	
G-TACN	Diamond DA.62	Flight Calibration Services Ltd	
G-TADI	Magni M.24C Orion	REB Ltd	
G-TADS	Mead BM-77 balloon	D. J. Stagg	
G-TAFF	CASA 1.131E Jungmann 1000	A. J. E. Smith (G-BFNE)	
G-TAJB	Airbus MBB BK-117 D-2	Blythe HCI Ltd	
G-TAJF	Lindstrand LBL-77A balloon	T. A. J. Fowles	
G-TAKE	AS.355F1 Ecureuil II	Arena Aviation Ltd (G-OITN)	
G-TALA	Cessna 152 II	Tatenhill Aviation Ltd (G-BNPZ)	
G-TALB	Cessna 152 II	Tatenhill Aviation Ltd (G-BORO)	
G-TALC	Cessna 152	Tatenhill Aviation Ltd (G-BPBG)	
G-TALD	Cessna F.152	Tatenhill Aviation Ltd (G-BHRM)	
G-TALE	PA-28-181 Archer II	Tatenhill Aviation Ltd (G-BJOA)	
G-TALF	PA-24-250 Comanche	Tatenhill Aviation Ltd (G-APUZ)	
G-TALG	PA-28-151 Warrior	Tatenhill Aviation Ltd (G-BELP)	
G-TALH	PA-28-181 Archer II	Tatenhill Aviation Ltd (G-CIFR)	
G-TALJ	Grumman AA-5 Traveler	The Lima Juliet Group (G-BBUE)	
G-TALN	Rotorway A600 Talon	Southern Helicopters Ltd	
G-TALO	Cessna FA.152	Tatenhill Aviation Ltd (G-BFZU)	
G-TALP	Cessna 172N	Tatenhill Aviation Ltd (G-BOUF)	
G-TALR	Cessna 152	Tatenhill Aviation Ltd (G-FIGA)	
G-TALX	Bellanca 8KCAB Decathlon	Tatenhill Aviation Ltd (G-BTXX)	
G-TAMI	Diamond DA.40 Star	AJW Construction Ltd	
G-TAMR	Cessna 172S	Caledonian Air Surveys Ltd	
G-TAMS	Beech A23-24 Musketeer Super	C. P. Allen	
G-TANA	Tanarg 912S(2)/Ixess 15	S. S. Smy	
G-TANG	Tanarg 912S(2)/Ixess 15	N. L. Stammers	
G-TANJ	Raj Hamsa X'Air 582(5)	K. P. Smith	
G-TANO	Rolladen-Schneider LS3-a	T. Cavattoni	
G-TANY	EAA Acrosport 2	P. J. Tanulak	
G-TAPS	PA-28RT-201T Turbo Arrow IV	R. L. Nunn, T. R. Edwards & T. G. Sarson	
G-TARN	Pietenpol Air Camper	P. J. Heilbron	
G-TARR	P & M Quik	A. Edwards	
G-TART	PA-28-236 Dakota	N. K. G. Prescot	
G-TATR	Replica Travelair R Type	R. A. Seeley	
G-TATS	AS.350BA Ecureuil	Helitrain Ltd	
G-TATT	Gardan GY-20 Minicab	Tatt's Group	
G-TAUT	Pipistrel Alpha BCAR-S 164	M. Tautz	
G-TAWA	Boeing 737-8K5	TUI Airways Ltd	
G-TAWB	Boeing 737-8K5	TUI Airways Ltd	
G-TAWC	Boeing 737-8K5	TUI Airways Ltd	
G-TAWD	Boeing 737-8K5	TUI Airways Ltd	
G-TAWF	Boeing 737-8K5	TUI Airways Ltd	
G-TAWG	Boeing 737-8K5	TUI Airways Ltd	
G-TAWI	Boeing 737-8K5	TUI Airways Ltd	
G-TAWK	Boeing 737-8K5	TUI Airways Ltd	
G-TAWL	Boeing 737-8K5	TUI Airways Ltd	
G-TAWM	Boeing 737-8K5	TUI Airways Ltd	
G-TAWN	Boeing 737-8K5	TUI Airways Ltd	
G-TAWO	Boeing 737-8K5	TUI Airways Ltd	
G-TAWS	Boeing 737-8K5	TUI Airways Ltd	
G-TAWU	Boeing 737-8K5	TUI Airways Ltd	
G-TAWV	Boeing 737-8K5	TUI Airways Ltd	
G-TAWW	Boeing 737-8K5	TUI Airways Ltd	
G-TAWX	Boeing 737-8K5	TUI Airways Ltd	
G-TAXI	PA-23-250 Aztec E	S. Waite	
G-TAYC	Gulfstream G450	Executive Jet Charter Ltd	
G-TAYI	Grob G.115	K. P. Widdowson (G-DODO)	
G-TAYL	Pitts S-1S Special	R. S. Taylor	
G-TAZZ	Dan Rihn DR.107 One Design	N. J. Riddin	
G-TBAG	Murphy Renegade II	M. R. Tetley	
G-TBDI	Ikarus C42 FB100 Bravo	D. Curtis	
G-TBET	Ultramagic M-77 balloon	H. Crawley & P. Dopson	
G-TBHH	AS355F2 Twin Squirrel	Alpha Properties (London) Ltd (G-HOOT/ G-SCOW/ G-POON/G-MCAL)	
G-TBGO	SOCATA TB-10 Tobago	P. P. W. Lowe (G-RIAM)	
G-TBIO	SOCATA TB10 Tobago	O. Fooks	
G-TBJP	Mainair Pegasus Quik	D. J. Bromley	

Notes	Reg	Type	Owner or Operator
	G-TBLB	P & M Quik GT450	S. Speake
	G-TBLC	Rans S-6-ES Coyote II	Royal Aeronautical Society
	G-TBMD	Bell 206L-3 Long Ranger III	T. B. McDermott (G-CIUY)
	G-TBMR	P & M Aviation Quik GT450	G-TBMR Syndicate
	G-TBOK	SOCATA TB10 Tobago	TB10 Ltd
	G-TBSV	SOCATA TB20 Trinidad GT	Condron Concrete Ltd
	G-TBTN	SOCATA TB10 Tobago	O. McLoughlin & S. Edghill (G-BKIA)
	G-TBUC	Airbus Helicopters EC155 B1	Noirmont (EC155) Ltd
	G-TBXX	SOCATA TB20 Trinidad	Aeroplane Ltd
	G-TBYD	Raj Hamsa X'Air Falcon D(1)	T. Collins
	G-TBZO	SOCATA TB20 Trinidad	J. P. Bechu & J. L. Aubergot
	G-TCAA	Leonardo AW169	Specialist Aviation Services Ltd
	G-TCAN	Colt 69A balloon	H. C. J. Williams
	G-TCEE	Hughes 369HS	A. M. E. Castro (G-AZVM)
	G-TCHI	VS.509 Spitfire Tr.9	M. B. Phillips
	G-TCHO	VS Spitfire Mk.IX	B. Phillips
	G-TCHZ	VS.329 Spitfire IIA (P7819)	M. B. Phillips
	G-TCNM	Tecnam P92-EA Echo	P. T. Trivett
	G-TCNY	Mainair Pegasus Quik	B. J. Wardle
	G-TCTC	PA-28RT-200 Arrow IV	P. Salemis
	G-TCUB	Piper J-3C-65 Cub (modified)	C. Kirk
	G-TCUK	Agusta A109S Grand	Castle Air Ltd (G-REXC/G-MCAN)
	G-TDJP	Van's RV-8	D. J. Pearson
	G-TDOG	SA Bulldog Srs 120/121 (XX538:O)	R. F. M. Jones
	G-TDSA	Cessna F.406 Caravan II	Nor Leasing
	G-TDVB	Dyn' Aero MCR-01ULC	D. V. Brunt
	G-TDYN	Aerospool Dynamic WT9 UK	N. Lilley & N. C. Herrington
	G-TEBZ	PA-28R-201 Arrow III	Aeros Leasing Ltd
	G-TECA	Tecnam P2002-JF	Aeros Global Ltd
	G-TECC	Aeronca 7AC Champion	N. J. Orchard-Armitage
	G-TECH	Rockwell Commander 114	A. S. Turner (G-BEDH)
	G-TECI	Tecnam P2002-JF	G-TECI Flying Club Ltd
	G-TECM	Tecnam P92-EA Echo	N. Stamford
	G-TECO	Tecnam P92-EM Echo	A. N. Buchan
	G-TECS	Tecnam P2002-EA Sierra	D. A. Lawrence
	G-TECT	Tecnam P2006T	Cabledraw Ltd
	G-TEDB	Cessna F.150L	R. Nightingale (G-AZLZ)
	G-TEDI	Best Off Skyranger J2.2(1)	P. W. Reid
	G-TEDW	Kiss 450-582 (2)	G. Frost
	G-TEDY	Evans VP-1	N. K. Marston (G-BHGN)
	G-TEFC	PA-28 Cherokee 140	Elliott Holdings
	G-TEGS	Bell 206B JetRanger III	HC Services Ltd
	G-TEHL	CFM Streak Shadow SA-M	R. Wilkinson (G-MYJE)
	G-TEKR	Tekever AR5 Evolution Mk.2	Tekever Ltd
	G-TEKV	Tekever AR5 Evolution Mk.2	Tekever Ltd
	G-TELY	Agusta A109A-II	Castle Air Ltd
	G-TEMB	Tecnam P2000-EA Sierra	M. Howes
	G-TEMP	PA-28 Cherokee 180	A. K. Hulme (G-AYBK)
	G-TEMT	Hawker Tempest II (MW763)	Anglia Aircraft Restorations Ltd
	G-TENG	Extra EA.300/L	D. C. Mowat
	G-TENN	Van's RV-10	RV10 Group
	G-TENT	Auster J/1N Alpha	R. Callaway-Lewis (G-AKJU)
	G-TERN	Shaw Europa	J. Smith
	G-TERO	Van's RV-7	A. Phillips
	G-TERR	Mainair Pegasus Quik	M. Faulkner
	G-TERY	PA-28-181 Archer II	J. R. Bratherton (G-BOXZ)
	G-TESI	Tecnam P2002 EA Sierra	C. C. Burgess
	G-TESR	Tecnam P2002-RG Sierra	Tecnam RG Group
	G-TEWS	PA-28-140 Cherokee	S. G. Brown (G-KEAN/G-AWTM)
	G-TEXN	North American T-6G Texan (KF402:HT-Y)	Boultbee Classic LLP (G-BHTH)
	G-TEZZ	CZAW Sportcruiser	G. Watts & M. D. Cligman
	G-TFAM	PA-46-350T Malibu Matrix	Take Flight Aviation Ltd (G-UDMS)
	G-TFCC	Cub Crafters Carbon Cub SS CC11-160	Patina Ltd
	G-TFIX	Mainair Pegasus Quantum 15-912	T. G. Jones
	G-TFLX	P & M Quik GT450	L. Bligh
	G-TFLY	Air Creation Kiss 450-582 (1)	A. J. Ladell
	G-TFOG	Best Off Skyranger 912(2)	T. J. Fogg

Reg	Type	Owner or Operator	Notes
G-TFRB	Air Command 532 Elite ★	Yorkshire Air Museum/Elvington	
G-TFSI	NA TF-51D Mustang (414251:WZ-I)	Anglia Aircraft Restorations Ltd	
G-TFUN	Valentin Taifun 17E	North West Taifun Group	
G-TGER	AA-5B Tiger	L. Walkden (G-BFZP)	
G-TGGR	Eurocopter EC 120B	Messiah Corporation Ltd	
G-TGJH	Evans VP-1 series 2	Condor Aviation International Ltd	
G-TGLG	AutoGyro Calidus	T. R. Galloway	
G-TGPG	Boeing 737-3YO	21T Ltd	
G-TGRA	Agusta A109A	Tiger Helicopters Ltd	
G-TGRC	Robinson R22 Beta	Tiger Aviation Ltd (G-RSWW)	
G-TGRD	Robinson R22 Beta II	Tiger Aviation Ltd (G-OPTS)	
G-TGRE	Robinson R22 Alpha	Tiger Aviation Ltd (G-SOLD)	
G-TGRS	Robinson R22 Beta	Tiger Aviation Ltd (G-DELL)	
G-TGRZ	Bell 206B JetRanger 3	Tiger Aviation Ltd (G-BXZX)	
G-TGTT	Robinson R44 II	Smart People UK Ltd	
G-TGUK	Ultramagic F-38 Helmet balloon	A. M. Holly	
G-TGUL	Earthstar Thundergull J	P. J. Reilly	
G-TGVP	Cunliffe-Owen Seafire Mk.XV	T. A. V. Percy	
G-THAT	Raj Hamsa X'Air Falcon 912 (1)	M. C. Sawyer	
G-THDR	Leonardo AW109SP Grand New	Thunder Aviation Limited Partnership	
G-THEO	TEAM mini-MAX 91	A. W. Gunn	
G-THFC	Embraer RJ135BJ Legacy	Raz Air Ltd (G-RRAZ/G-RUBN)	
G-THFW	Bell 206B-3 JetRanger III	Fly Heli Wales Ltd	
G-THIN	Cessna FR.172E	T. B. Sumner (G-BXYY)	
G-THOM	Thunder Ax-6-56 balloon	T. H. Wilson	
G-THOT	Avtech Jabiru SK	S. G. Holton	
G-THRE	Cessna 182S	J. P. Monjalet	
G-THSL	PA-28R-201 Arrow III	D. M. Markscheffe	
G-THUN	Republic P-47D-40-RA Thunderbolt (549192)	Fighter Aviation Engineering Ltd	
G-THYB	Cessna 172S	Atlantic Flight Training Ltd	
G-TIAB	Schleicher ASW-27	D. N. Tew (G-CKCN)	
G-TIAC	Tiger Cub RL5A LW Sherwood Ranger	The Light Aircraft Co.Ltd	
G-TIBF	Balony Kubicek BB34Z balloon	G. B.Lescott	
G-TIBS	SOCATA TB.20 Trinidad	C. C. Jewell	
G-TICH	Taylor JT.2 Titch	J. W. Graham-White	
G-TICO	Cameron O-77 balloon	J. F. Trehern	
G-TIDS	Jodel 150	M. R. Parker	
G-TIDY	Sky Ranger Nynja 912S(1)	J. M. Stables	
G-TIFG	Ikarus C42 FB80	B. Thornton	
G-TIFY	Hawker Typhoon IB	Hawker Typhoon Preservation Group	
G-TIGA	DH.82A Tiger Moth	D. E. Leatherland (G-AOEG)	
G-TIGC	AS.332L Super Puma	Airbus Helicopters (G-BJYH)	
G-TIGS	AS.332L Super Puma	Airbus Helicopters	
G-TIII	Aerotek Pitts S-2A Special	D. D. & D. S. Welch	
G-TIJL	Airbus Helicopters AS.355NP Ecureuil II	Wycombe Helicopter Services LLP (G-PERX)	
G-TILE	Robinson R22 Beta	Heli Air Ltd	
G-TIMA	Van's RV-7	T. J. Arnold	
G-TIMC	Robinson R44	T. Clark Aviation LLP (G-CDUR)	
G-TIMI	BRM Aero Bristell NG5	A. J. L. Gordon	
G-TIMK	PA-28-181 Archer II	I. R. Wellesley-Harding	
G-TIMO	Eurocopter EC.120B	T Clark Aviation LLP (G-SWNG)	
G-TIMP	Aeronca 7BCM Champion	R. B. Valler	
G-TIMS	Falconar F-12A	T. Sheridan	
G-TIMX	Head AX8-88B balloon	J. Edwards & S. McMahon	
G-TIMY	Gardan GY-80 Horizon 160	R. G. Whyte	
G-TINK	Robinson R22 Beta	Helimech Ltd	
G-TINT	Aerotechnik EV-97 Team Eurostar UK	I. A. Cunningham	
G-TINY	Z.526F Trener Master	D. Evans	
G-TIPJ	Cameron Z-77 balloon	Servowarm Balloon Syndicate	
G-TIPP	Aeroprakt A22-LS Foxbat	E. Fogarty	
G-TIPR	Eurocopter AS.350B2 Ecureuil	Thames Materials Holdings Ltd (G-PATM)	
G-TIPS	Nipper T.66 Srs.3	F. V. Neefs	
G-TIPY	Czech Sport PS-28 Cruiser	I. C. Tandy	
G-TIVV	Aerotechnik EV-97 Team Eurostar UK	A. W. K. van der Schatt	
G-TIZY	TAF Sling 4 TSI	Connecting Lines Ltd	
G-TJAL	Jabiru SPL-430	M. R. Williamson	
G-TJAV	Mainair Pegasus Quik	Access Anywhere Ltd	

Notes	Reg	Type	Owner or Operator
	G-TJAY	PA-22 Tri-Pacer 135	D. Pegley
	G-TJCL	P &M QuikR	S. D. J. Hagen
	G-TJDM	Van's RV-6A	J. D. Michie
	G-TKAY	Shaw Europa	A. M. Kay
	G-TKEV	P & M Quik R	N. F. Dee
	G-TKHE	PA-28R-201T Turbo Arrow IV	C. H. Smith (G-EPTL)
	G-TKIS	Tri-R Kis	T. J. Bone
	G-TKNO	UltraMagic S-50 balloon	R. A. Durham
	G-TLAC	Sherwood Ranger ST	The Light Aircraft Co.Ltd
	G-TLDK	PA-22-150 Caribbean	M. R. Masters
	G-TLDL	Medway SLA 100 Executive	J. M. Clifford
	G-TLEE	TLAC Sherwood Kub	T. H. Lee
	G-TLET	PA-28-161 Cadet	ADR Aviation (G-GFCF/G-RHBH)
	G-TLMA	Lindstrand LTL 1-105 balloon	A. M. Holly
	G-TLMI	Robinson R66	HQ Aviation Ltd
	G-TLST	TL 2000UK Sting Carbon	W. H. J. Knowles
	G-TLTL	Schempp-Hirth Discus CS	E. K. Armitage
	G-TMAX	Evektor EV-97 Sportstar Max	G-TMAX Group
	G-TMCB	Best Off Skyranger 912 (2)	J. R. Davis
	G-TMCC	Cameron N-90 balloon	M. S. Jennings
	G-TMHK	PA-38-112 Tomahawk	Aeros Leasing Ltd (G-GALL/G-BTEV)
	G-TMPV	Hawker Tempest V	Anglia Aircraft Restorations Ltd
	G-TMRL	Zenair CH.750	A. D. J. Morris
	G-TNGO	Van's RV-6	J. D. M. Willis
	G-TNIK	Dassault Falcon 2000	Blu Halkin Ltd
	G-TNJB	P & M Quik R	J. H. Bradbury
	G-TNRG	Tanarg/Ixess 15 912S(2)	I. M. Lane
	G-TNTN	Thunder Ax6-56 balloon	H. M. Savage & A. A. Leggate
	G-TNUP	Avions Max Holste MH.1521C1 Broussard	M. J. Babbage
	G-TOBI	Cessna F.172K	The TOBI Group (G-AYVB)
	G-TODD	ICA IS-28M2A	C. I. Roberts & C. D. King
	G-TOES	PA-28-161 Warrior II	Freedom Aviation Ltd
	G-TOFT	Colt 90A balloon	C. S. Perceval
	G-TOGO	Van's RV-6	N. A. Onions
	G-TOLL	PA-28R-201 Arrow III	Arrow Aircraft Ltd
	G-TOLS	Robinson R44	K. N. Tolley (G-CBOT)
	G-TOLY	Robinson R22 Beta	Helicopter & Pilot Services Ltd (G-NSHR)
	G-TOMC	NA AT-6D Harvard III (51-14700)	A. A. Marshall
	G-TOMJ	Flight Design CT2K	Avair Ltd
	G-TOML	Cessna F.150M	UK Flying Clubs Ltd (G-CSBM)
	G-TOMX	MCR-01 VLA Sportster	P. T. Knight
	G-TONE	Pazmany PL-4	P. I. Morgans
	G-TONN	Mainair Pegasus Quik	T. D. Evans
	G-TOOB	Schempp-Hirth Discus 2b	M. F. Evans
	G-TOOL	Thunder Ax8-105 balloon	D. V. Howard
	G-TOOO	Guimbal Cabri G2	Helicentre Aviation Ltd
	G-TOPB	Cameron Z-140 balloon	Anana Ltd
	G-TOPC	AS.355F1 Twin Squirrel	Wavendon Social Housing Ltd
	G-TOPK	Shaw Europa XS	P. J. Kember & B. MacKay
	G-TOPM	Agusta-Bell 206B-2 JetRanger 2	A & W Demolition (Bracknell) (G-CCBL)
	G-TOPO	PA-23-250 Turbo Aztec	Ravenair Aircraft Ltd (G-BGWW)
	G-TOPP	Van's RV-10	D. Topp & S. E. Coles
	G-TORC	PA-28R Cherokee Arrow 200)	Aeros Leasing Ltd
	G-TORE	P.84 Jet Provost T.3A ★ (XM405)	Instructional airframe/City University, Islington
	G-TORI	Zenair CH.701SP	R. W. H. Watson (G-CCSK)
	G-TORK	Cameron Z-105 balloon	M. E. Dunstan
	G-TORN	Flight Design CTSW	N. C. Harper
	G-TORO	Skyranger Nynja 912S(1)	L. J. E. Moss & C. Fenwick
	G-TOSH	Robinson R22 Beta	Choicecircle Ltd
	G-TOTN	Cessna 210M	Quay Financial Strategies Ltd (G-BVZM)
	G-TOTO	Cessna F.177RG	Airspeed Aviation Ltd (G-OADE/G-AZKH)
	G-TOUR	Robin R.2112	R. M. Wade
	G-TOWA	Zenair CH.750 Cruzer	T. W. Slater
	G-TOWS	PA-25 Pawnee 260	Lasham Gliding Society Ltd
	G-TOYZ	Bell 206B JetRanger 3	BEMC Corporate Hire Ltd (G-RGER)

Reg	Type	Owner or Operator	Notes
G-TPAL	P & M Aviation Quik GT450	R. Robertson	
G-TPPW	Van's RV-7	R. S. Grace	
G-TPSL	Cessna 182S	A. N. Purslow	
G-TPSY	Champion 8KCAB Super Decathlon	Aerial Advantage Ltd (G-CEOE)	
G-TPTP	Robinson R44	AIT Air Ltd	
G-TPTR	Agusta Bell 206B Jet Ranger II ★	The Helicopter Museum/Weston-super-Mare (G-LOCK)	
G-TPWL	P & M Quik GT450	The G-TPWL Group	
G-TPWX	Heliopolis Gomhouria Mk.6 (TP+WX)	Cirrus Aircraft UK Ltd	
G-TRAC	Robinson R44	C. J. Sharples	
G-TRAM	Pegasus Quantum 15-912	G-TRAM Group	
G-TRAT	Pilatus PC-12/45	Flew LLP	
G-TRBN	HpH Glasflugel 304S Shark	A. Cluskey	
G-TRBO	Schleicher ASW-28-18E	M. P. Weaver	
G-TRCY	Robinson R44	Marman Aviation Ltd	
G-TRDS	Guimbal Cabri G2	W. R. Harford	
G-TREB	Cessna 182T	Camel Aviation Ltd	
G-TREC	Cessna 421C	Sovereign Business Integration PLC (G-TLOL)	
G-TREE	Bell 206B JetRanger 3	Heliflight (UK) Ltd	
G-TREK	Jodel D.18	R. H. Mole	
G-TREX	Alpi Pioneer 300	S. R. Winter	
G-TRIG	Cameron Z-90 balloon	Hedge Hoppers Balloon Group	
G-TRIN	SOCATA TB20 Trinidad	M. J. Porter	
G-TRJB	Beech A36 Bonanza	G. A. J. Bowles	
G-TRLL	Groppo Trail	P. M. Grant	
G-TRNG	Agusta A109E Power	G. Walters (Leasing) Ltd (G-NWOY/G-JMXA)	
G-TRON	Robinson R66	PFR Aviation Ltd	
G-TROW	Ikarus C42 FB80	Blue Socks Aviation Ltd	
G-TROY	NA T-28A Fennec (51-7692)	Air Leasing Ltd	
G-TRTL	Skyranger Nynja LS 912S(1)	J. T. & J. W. Whicher	
G-TRUE	MDH Hughes 369E	N. E. Bailey	
G-TRUK	Stoddard-Hamilton Glasair RG	T. R. Whittome	
G-TRUU	PA-34-220T Seneca III	Omega Sky Taxi Ltd (G-BOJK/G-BRUF)	
G-TRUX	Colt 77A balloon	J. R. Lawson	
G-TRVR	Van's RV-7	The Richard Ormonde Shuttleworth Remembrance Trust	
G-TSAC	Tecnam P2002-EA Sierra	P. E. Riding	
G-TSAS	PA-28-181 Archer II	M. E. McElhinney (G-MALA/G-BIIU)	
G-TSBY	Robinson R44 II	A Woodward Aviation Ltd	
G-TSDA	Aquila AT-01-100A	Tayside Aviation Ltd	
G-TSDB	Aquila AT-01-100A	Tayside Aviation Ltd	
G-TSDC	Aquila AT-01-100A	Tayside Aviation Ltd	
G-TSDE	Aquila AT-01-100A	Tayside Aviation Ltd	
G-TSDI	Spacek SD-1 Minisport	M. Innes	
G-TSDS	PA-32R-301 Saratoga SP	I. R. Jones (G-TRIP/G-HOSK)	
G-TSFC	Tecnam P2008-JC	Stapleford Flying Club Ltd	
G-TSGA	PA-28R-201 Arrow III	I. R. Lockhart & J. N. Bailey (G-ONSF/G-EMAK)	
G-TSGJ	PA-28-181 Archer II	Golf Juliet Flying Club	
G-TSHO	Ikarus C42 FB80	A. McDougall	
G-TSIM	Titan T-51 Mustang	P. T. Claiden	
G-TSIX	AT-6C Harvard IIA (111836:JZ-6)	Bulldog Aviation Ltd	
G-TSKD	Raj Hamsa X'Air Jabiru J.2.2.	T. Sexton & K. B. Dupuy	
G-TSKS	EV-97 TeamEurostar UK	North East Aviation Ltd	
G-TSLC	Schweizer 269C-1	C. J. Cox Ltd	
G-TSOB	Rans S.6-ESA Coyote II	A. A. Sawera	
G-TSOG	TLAC Sherwood Ranger XP	The Spirit of Goole	
G-TSOL	EAA Acrosport 1	D. F. Cumberlidge & H. Stuart (G-BPKI)	
G-TSTR	Westland SA.341D Gazelle HT.Mk.3 (ZB625)	Nova Aerospace Ltd	
G-TSUE	Shaw Europa	H. J. C. Maclean	
G-TSWI	Lindstrand LBL-90A balloon	R. J. Gahan	
G-TSWZ	Cameron Z-77 balloon	Business First Centre	
G-TTAT	ICP MXP-740 Savannah VG Jabiru(1)	D. Varley & D. J. Broughall	
G-TTEA	Cirrus SR20	A9 Leasing LLP	
G-TTEC	PA-32-301FT 6X	Taytech Environmental Ltd	
G-TTFG	Colt 77B balloon	T. J. & M. J. Turner (G-BUZF)	
G-TTGV	Bell 206L-4 LongRanger IV	Langley Aviation Ltd (G-JACI)	
G-TTKP	Enstrom 280FX Shark	K. & M. A. Payne (G-HDIX)	

BRITISH CIVIL AIRCRAFT MARKINGS

Notes	Reg	Type	Owner or Operator
	G-TTNA	Airbus A.320-251N	British Airways PLC
	G-TTNB	Airbus A.320-251N	British Airways PLC
	G-TTNC	Airbus A.320-251N	British Airways PLC
	G-TTND	Airbus A.320-251N	British Airways PLC
	G-TTNE	Airbus A.320-251N	British Airways PLC
	G-TTNF	Airbus A.320-251N	British Airways PLC
	G-TTNG	Airbus A.320-251N	British Airways PLC
	G-TTNH	Airbus A.320-251N	British Airways PLC
	G-TTNI	Airbus A.320-251N	British Airways PLC
	G-TTNJ	Airbus A.320-251N	British Airways PLC
	G-TTNK	Airbus A.320-251N	British Airways PLC
	G-TTNL	Airbus A.320-251N	British Airways PLC
	G-TTNM	Airbus A.320-251N	British Airways PLC
	G-TTOB	Airbus A.320-232	British Airways PLC
	G-TTOE	Airbus A.320-232	British Airways PLC
	G-TTOM	Zenair CH.601HD Zodiac	G-TTOM Group
	G-TTOY	CFM Streak Shadow SA	J. Softley
	G-TTRL	Van's RV-9A	J. E. Gattrell
	G-TTUG	Aeropro Eurofox 912(IS)	Buckminster Gliding Club Ltd (G-WTUG)
	G-TUBB	Avtech Jabiru UL	A. H. Bower
	G-TUCK	Van's RV-8	N. G. R. Moffat
	G-TUGG	PA-18 Super Cub 150	Ulster Gliding Club Ltd
	G-TUGI	CZAW Sportcruiser	T. J. Wilson
	G-TUGY	Robin DR.400/180	GY Group
	G-TUGZ	Robin DR.400/180R	M. J. Aldridge
	G-TUIA	Boeing 787-8	TUI Airways Ltd
	G-TUIB	Boeing 787-8	TUI Airways Ltd
	G-TUIC	Boeing 787-8	TUI Airways Ltd
	G-TUID	Boeing 787-8	TUI Airways Ltd
	G-TUIE	Boeing 787-8	TUI Airways Ltd
	G-TUIF	Boeing 787-8	TUI Airways Ltd
	G-TUIH	Boeing 787-8	TUI Airways Ltd
	G-TUII	Boeing 787-8	TUI Airways Ltd
	G-TUIJ	Boeing 787-9	TUI Airways Ltd
	G-TUIK	Boeing 787-9	TUI Airways Ltd
	G-TUIL	Boeing 787-9	TUI Airways Ltd
	G-TUIM	Boeing 787-9	TUI Airways Ltd
	G-TUIN	Boeing 787-9	TUI Airways Ltd
	G-TUIO	Boeing 787-9	TUI Airways Ltd
	G-TUKC	Boeing 737-8FZ	TUI Airways Ltd
	G-TUKF	Boeing 737-8AS	TUI Airways Ltd
	G-TUKG	Boeing 737-8KN	TUI Airways Ltd
	G-TUKM	Boeing 737-8K5	TUI Airways Ltd
	G-TUKN	Boeing 737-8K5	TUI Airways Ltd
	G-TUKO	Boeing 737-8K5	TUI Airways Ltd
	G-TULI	Embraer EMB550 Legacy 500	Centreline
	G-TUMA	Boeing 737-MAX8	TUI Airways Ltd
	G-TUMB	Boeing 737-MAX8	TUI Airways Ltd
	G-TUMC	Boeing 737-MAX8	TUI Airways Ltd
	G-TUMD	Boeing 737-MAX8	TUI Airways Ltd
	G-TUMF	Boeing 737-MAX8	TUI Airways Ltd
	G-TUMG	Boeing 737-MAX8	TUI Airways Ltd
	G-TUMH	Boeing 737-MAX8	TUI Airways Ltd
	G-TUMJ	Boeing 737-MAX8	TUI Airways Ltd
	G-TUMK	Boeing 737-MAX8	TUI Airways Ltd
	G-TUNE	Robinson R22 Beta	Heli Air Ltd (G-OJVI)
	G-TUNL	Robinson R44 II	Barhale Ltd (G-TCAL)
	G-TUTU	Cameron O-105 balloon	A. C. K. Rawson & J. J. Rudoni
	G-TVAL	Airbus Helicopters EC 135 T3	Babcock Mission Critical Services Onshore Ltd
	G-TVBF	Lindstrand LBL-310A balloon	Virgin Balloons Flights
	G-TVCO	Gippsland GA-8 Airvan	P. Ligertwood
	G-TVGB	Airbus AS.350B3 Ecureuil	GB Helicopters
	G-TVGC	Schempp-Hirth Janus A	Trent Valley Gliding Club Ltd
	G-TVHB	Eurocopter EC 135 P2+	Police & Crime Commissioner for West Yorkshire
	G-TVHD	AS.355F2 Ecureuil 2	Arena Aviation Ltd
	G-TVSI	Campbell Cricket Replica	G. Smith
	G-TVSK	Ultramagic B-50 balloon	M. Warne

Reg	Type	Owner or Operator	Notes
G-TWAL	Rutan Long-Ez	T. Walsh (G-BNCZ)	
G-TWAZ	Rolladen-Schneider LS7-WL	S. Derwin	
G-TWEL	PA-28-181 Archer II	International Aerospace Engineering Ltd	
G-TWIS	Silence Twister	C. S. & K. D. Rhodes	
G-TWIZ	Rockwell Commander 114	M. A. Lorne	
G-TWLV	Van's RV-12	P. R. Thorne	
G-TWNN	Beech 76 Duchess	M. Magrabi	
G-TWOC	Schempp-Hirth Ventus 2cT	G. C. Lewis	
G-TWOO	Extra EA.300/200	North West Aerobatics Ltd (G-MRKI)	
G-TWOP	Cessna 525A Citationjet CJ2	Centreline AV Ltd (G-ODAG)	
G-TWRL	Pitts S-1S Special	M. G. Duffy	
G-TWSR	Silence Twister	J. A. Hallam	
G-TWSS	Silence Twister	T. R. Dews	
G-TWST	Silence Twister	Zulu Glasstek Ltd (G-ZWIP)	
G-TWTR	Robinson R44 II	Volitant Aviation Ltd	
G-TWTW	Denney Kitfox Mk.2	R. M. Bremner	
G-TXAS	Cessna A.150L	T. H. Scott (G-HFCA)	
G-TXTV	AgustaWestland A.109E Power	Arena Aviation Ltd	
G-TYAK	IDA Bacau Yakovlev Yak-52	S. J. Ducker	
G-TYER	Robin DR.400/500	C. A. White	
G-TYGA	AA-5B Tiger	Three Musketeers Flying Group (G-BHNZ)	
G-TYGR	Best Off Skyranger Swift 912S(1)	B. W. G. Stanbridge	
G-TYKE	Avtech Jabiru UL-450	J. & T. Scott	
G-TYNE	SOCATA TB20 Trinidad	N. V. Price	
G-TYRE	Cessna F.172M	J. S. C. English	
G-TZED	SOCATA TB-200 Tobago XL	Zytech Ltd	
G-TZII	Thorp T.211B	M. J. Newton	
G-UACA	Best Off Skyranger Swift 912(1)	Light Flight GUACA Syndicate	
G-UAKE	NA P-51D-5-NA Mustang	P. S. Warner	
G-UANO	DHC.1 Chipmunk 22 (1367)	R. J. Stirk (G-BYYW)	
G-UANT	PA-28 Cherokee 140	Air Navigation & Trading Co Ltd	
G-UAPA	Robin DR.400/140B	Sor Air Sociedade de Aeronautica SA/Portugal	
G-UAPO	Ruschmeyer R.90-230RG	J. Randall	
G-UART	Moravan Zlin Z-242L	Oxford Aviation Academy (Oxford) Ltd (G-EKMN)	
G-UASA	Schiebell Camcopter S-100	Bristow Helicopters Ltd	
G-UASB	Schiebell Camcopter S-100	Bristow Helicopters Ltd	
G-UAVA	PA-30 Twin Comanche	Marhel Management Ltd	
G-UBOO	Schleicher ASW-27-18E	S. G. Hunt	
G-UCAM	PA-31-350 Navajo Chieftain	Blue Sky Investments Ltd (G-NERC/G-BBXX)	
G-UCAN	Tecnam P2002-JF Sierra	Aerobility	
G-UCCC	Cameron 90 Sign SS balloon	Unipart Group of Companies Ltd	
G-UCLU	Schleicher ASK-21	University College London Union	
G-UDET	Replica Fokker E.111 (105/15)	M. J. Clark	
G-UDGE	Thruster T.600N	G-UDGE Syndicate (G-BYPI)	
G-UDIX	Schempp-Hirth Duo Discus T	R. Banks	
G-UFAW	Raj Hamsa X'Air 582 (15)	R. Bricknell	
G-UFCB	Cessna 172S	The Cambridge Aero Club Ltd	
G-UFCG	Cessna 172S	Ulster Flying Club (1961) Ltd	
G-UFCI	Cessna 172S	Ulster Flying Club (1961) Ltd	
G-UFCN	Cessna 152	Ulster Flying Club (1961) Ltd	
G-UFCP	Cessna F.152 II	Ulster Flying Club (1961) Ltd (G-PTTB/G-WACT/ G-BKFT)	
G-UFLY	Cessna F.150H	Westair Flying Services Ltd (G-AVVY)	
G-UFOE	Grob G.115	Swiftair Maintenance Ltd	
G-UFOX	Aeropro Eurofox 912(1)	G-UFOX Group	
G-UHGB	Bell 205A-1	Heli-Lift Services	
G-UHIH	Bell UH-1H Iroquois (21509)	MSS Holdings Ltd	
G-UHOP	UltraMagic H-31 balloon	A. R. Brown	
G-UIII	Extra EA.300/200	M. Thomas	
G-UIKR	P & M Quik R	A. M. Sirant	
G-UILD	Grob G.109B	K. Butterfield	

Notes	Reg	Type	Owner or Operator
	G-UILE	Lancair 320	R. J. Martin
	G-UILT	Cessna T.303	D. L. Tucker (G-EDRY)
	G-UIMB	Guimbal Cabri G2	Helitrain Ltd
	G-UINN	Stolp SA.300 Starduster Too	A. Dunne
	G-UINS	Ultramagic B-70 balloon	A. M. Holly
	G-UINZ	Ultramagic B-70 balloon	A. M. Holly
	G-UIRO	AutoGyro MT-03	S. D. Kellner (G-CFAG)
	G-UISE	Van's RV-8	J. A. Green
	G-UJAB	Avtech Jabiru UL	C. A. Thomas
	G-UJGK	Avtech Jabiru UL	W. G. Upton & J. G. Kosak
	G-UKAL	Cessna F.406 Caravan II	Aero Lease UK
	G-UKAW	Agusta A.109E	Castle Air Ltd
	G-UKCS	PA-31 Navajo	2 Excel Aviation Ltd
	G-UKOZ	Avtech Jabiru SK	D. J. Burnett
	G-UKPA	Cessna 208B Grand Caravan	UK Parachute Services Ltd
	G-UKPB	Cessna 208B Grand Caravan	UK Parachute Services Ltd
	G-UKPS	Cessna 208 Caravan 1	UK Parachute Services Ltd
	G-UKRB	Colt 105A balloon	Virgin Airship & Balloon Co Ltd
	G-UKRO	Evektor Sportstar RTC	Co and Builder Ltd
	G-UKRV	Van's RV-7A	Netwasp.net Ltd
	G-UKTV	AS.355F2 Ecureuil 2	Arena Aviation Ltd (G-JESE/G-EMHH/G-BYKH)
	G-UKUK	Head Ax8-105 balloon	P. A. George
	G-ULAG	PA-34-220T Seneca V	N. Holden
	G-ULAS	DHC.1 Chipmunk 22 (WK517)	M. B. Phillips
	G-ULCC	Schleicher ASH-30 MI	G-ULCC Flying Club
	G-ULFM	Gulfstream 450	Pendley Aviation LLP
	G-ULHI	SA Bulldog Srs.100/101	Kryten Systems Ltd (G-OPOD/G-AZMS)
	G-ULPS	Everett Srs 1 gyroplane	I. Pearson (G-BMNY)
	G-ULRK	Sequoia F.8L Falco	U. K. S. S. N. M. Lawson
	G-ULSY	Ikarus C.42 FB 80	M. L. Cade
	G-ULTR	Cameron A-105 balloon	P. Glydon
	G-ULUL	Rotorsport UK Calidus	R. S. Payne & P. J. Tyler (G-HTBT)
	G-ULZE	Robinson R22	HQ Aviation Ltd (G-BUBW)
	G-UMBL	Guimbal Cabri G2	European Helicopter Importers Ltd
	G-UMBO	Thunder Ax7-77A balloon	Virgin Airship & Balloon Co Ltd
	G-UMBS	Solo Aerostatics DE-12/70 balloon	E. A. Butter
	G-UMBY	Hughes 369E	HQ Aviation Ltd
	G-UMMI	PA-31-310 Turbo Navajo	2 Excel Aviation Ltd (G-BGSO)
	G-UMMS	EV-97 TeamEurostar UK	G. W. Carwardine (G-ODRY)
	G-UMMY	Best Off Skyranger J2.2(2)	D. A. Tibbals
	G-UMPY	Shaw Europa	G. D. Bird
	G-UNAC	PA-32R-301T Saratoga II TC	A. C. Campbell
	G-UNDD	PA-23 Aztec 250E	G. J. & D. P. Deadman (G-BATX)
	G-UNES	Van's RV-6	C. A. Greatrex
	G-UNGE	Lindstrand LBL-90A balloon	Silver Ghost Balloon Club (G-BVPJ)
	G-UNGO	Pietenpol Air Camper	A. R. Wyatt
	G-UNIN	Schempp-Hirth Ventus b	U9 Syndicate
	G-UNIV	Montgomerie JM Gyroplane ★	Museum of Flight/East Fortune
	G-UNIX	VPM M16 Tandem Trainer	A. P. Wilkinson
	G-UNJA	Pipistrel Alpha BCAR-S 164	Fly About Aviation Ltd
	G-UNKY	Ultramagic S-50 balloon	A. M. Holly
	G-UNNA	Jabiru UL-450WW	J. F. Heath
	G-UNNR	Schempp-Hirth Arcus T	C. S. Crocker
	G-UNRL	Lindstrand LBL-RR21 balloon	Lindstrand Media Ltd
	G-UNZZ	Bell 206L Long Ranger	K. Hayes (G-DSTN/G-CYRS)
	G-UORO	Shaw Europa	D. Dufton
	G-UPFS	Waco UPS-7	D. N. Peters & N. R. Finlayson
	G-UPHI	Best Off Skyranger Swift 912S(1)	C. E. Walsh & M. B. Harper
	G-UPID	Bowers Fly Baby 1A	R. D. Taylor
	G-UPIZ	BRM Aero Bristell NG5 Speed Wing	C. P. & K. J. Faint
	G-UPOI	Cameron TR-84 S1 balloon	Cameron Balloons Ltd
	G-UPRT	Slingsby T.67M-260 Firefly	L3 CTS Airline and Academy Training Ltd (G-BWXU)
	G-UPTA	Skyranger 912S (1)	R. A. Buttle
	G-UPUZ	Lindstrand LBL-120A balloon	C.J. Sanger-Davies

Reg	Type	Owner or Operator	Notes
G-URMS	Europa	C. Parkinson (G-DEBR)	
G-UROP	Beech 95-B55 Baron	Wallis Health Consultants Ltd	
G-URRR	Air Command 582 Sport	L. Armes	
G-URUH	Robinson R44	Heli Air Ltd	
G-USAA	Cessna F.150G	Aeros Global Ltd (G-OIDW)	
G-USAI	Agusta-Bell 47J-2A Ranger	Hields Aviation	
G-USAR	Cessna 441 Conquest	I. Annenskiy	
G-USCO	Hughes 269C	N. Sheldrake (G-CECO)	
G-USHA	Learjet 75	Essexjets Ltd	
G-USHI	PA-28-140 Cherokee Cruiser	M. Rajain (G-BZWG)	
G-USIL	Thunder Ax7-77 balloon	Window On The World Ltd	
G-USKY	Aviat A-1B Husky	Axis Technology & Development Ltd	
G-USTH	Agusta A109A-II	Stratton Motor Co.(Norfolk) Ltd	
G-UTRA	Ultramagic M-77 balloon	Ultrait Ltd	
G-UTSI	Rand-Robinson KR-2	K. B. Gutridge	
G-UUPP	Cameron Z-70 balloon	C. W. Clarke	
G-UURO	Aerotechnik EV-97 Eurostar	Romeo Oscar Syndicate	
G-UUUU	Ikarus C42 FB100	R. Engelhard	
G-UVBF	Lindstrand LBL-400A balloon	Virgin Balloon Flights	
G-UWAS	SA Bulldog Srs 120/121 (XX625)	Mid America (UK) Ltd (G-CBAB)	
G-UWEB	Cameron Z-120 balloon	GWE Business West Ltd	
G-UYAK	Yakovlev Yak-18T	C. A. Brightwell	
G-UZHA	Airbus A.320-251N	easyJet Airline Co.Ltd	
G-UZHB	Airbus A.320-251N	easyJet Airline Co.Ltd	
G-UZHC	Airbus A.320-251N	easyJet Airline Co.Ltd	
G-UZHD	Airbus A.320-251N	easyJet Airline Co.Ltd	
G-UZHE	Airbus A.320-251N	easyJet Airline Co.Ltd	
G-UZHF	Airbus A.320-251N	easyJet Airline Co.Ltd	
G-UZHG	Airbus A.320-251N	easyJet Airline Co.Ltd	
G-UZHH	Airbus A.320-251N	easyJet Airline Co.Ltd	
G-UZHI	Airbus A.320-251N	easyJet Airline Co.Ltd	
G-UZHJ	Airbus A.320-251N	easyJet Airline Co.Ltd	
G-UZHK	Airbus A.320-251N	easyJet Airline Co.Ltd	
G-UZHL	Airbus A.320-251N	easyJet Airline Co.Ltd	
G-UZHM	Airbus A.320-251N	easyJet Airline Co.Ltd	
G-UZHN	Airbus A.320-251N	easyJet Airline Co.Ltd	
G-UZHO	Airbus A.320-251N	easyJet Airline Co.Ltd	
G-UZHP	Airbus A.320-251N	easyJet Airline Co.Ltd	
G-UZHR	Airbus A.320-251N	easyJet Airline Co.Ltd	
G-UZHS	Airbus A.320-251N	easyJet Airline Co.Ltd	
G-UZHT	Airbus A.320-251N	easyJet Airline Co.Ltd	
G-UZHU	Airbus A.320-251N	easyJet Airline Co.Ltd	
G-UZHV	Airbus A.320-251N	easyJet Airline Co.Ltd	
G-UZHW	Airbus A.320-251N	easyJet Airline Co.Ltd	
G-UZHX	Airbus A.320-251N	easyJet Airline Co.Ltd	
G-UZHY	Airbus A.320-251N	easyJet Airline Co.Ltd	
G-UZHZ	Airbus A.320-251N	easyJet Airline Co.Ltd	
G-UZLA	Airbus A.320-251N	easyJet Airline Co.Ltd	
G-UZLB	Airbus A.320-251N	easyJet Airline Co.Ltd	
G-UZLC	Airbus A.320-251N	easyJet Airline Co.Ltd	
G-UZLD	Airbus A.320-251N	easyJet Airline Co.Ltd	
G-UZLF	Airbus A.320-251N	easyJet Airline Co.Ltd	
G-UZLG	Airbus A.320-251N	easyJet Airline Co.Ltd	
G-UZLH	Airbus A.320-251N	easyJet Airline Co.Ltd	
G-UZLI	Airbus A.320-251N	easyJet Airline Co.Ltd	
G-UZLJ	Airbus A.320-251N	easyJet Airline Co.Ltd	
G-UZLK	Airbus A.320-251N	easyJet Airline Co.Ltd	
G-UZLL	Airbus A.320-251N	easyJet Airline Co.Ltd	
G-UZLM	Airbus A.320-251N	easyJet Airline Co.Ltd	
G-UZMA	Airbus A.321-251NX	easyJet Airline Co.Ltd	
G-UZMB	Airbus A.321-251NX	easyJet Airline Co.Ltd	
G-UZMC	Airbus A.321-251NX	easyJet Airline Co.Ltd	
G-UZMD	Airbus A.321-251NX	easyJet Airline Co.Ltd	
G-UZME	Airbus A.321-251NX	easyJet Airline Co.Ltd	

Notes	Reg	Type	Owner or Operator
	G-UZMF	Airbus A.321-251NX	easyJet Airline Co.Ltd
	G-UZMG	Airbus A.321-251NX	easyJet Airline Co.Ltd
	G-UZMH	Airbus A.321-251NX	easyJet Airline Co.Ltd
	G-UZMI	Airbus A.321-251NX	easyJet Airline Co.Ltd
	G-UZMJ	Airbus A.321-251NX	easyJet Airline Co.Ltd
	G-UZUP	Aerotechnik EV-97A Eurostar	G-UZUP Flying Group
	G-UZZI	Lancair LC41-550FG Corvalis TT	The Lord Rotherwick
	G-VAAC	PA-28-181 Archer III	G. J. Eijken (G-CCDN)
	G-VAAV	P & M Quik R	M. Kent
	G-VAGA	PA-15 Vagabond	J. P. Walsh (G-CCEE)
	G-VAHH	Boeing 787-9	Virgin Atlantic Airways Ltd
	G-VALG	Evektor EV-97 Eurostar SL	J. A. Ganderton
	G-VALK	Beech 200 Super King Air	Alto Aerospace Ltd (G-ROWN/G-BHLC)
	G-VALS	Pietenpol Air Camper	G-VALS Flying Group
	G-VALY	SOCATA TB21 Trinidad GT Turbo	Richard Thwaites Aviation Ltd
	G-VALZ	Cameron N-120 balloon	J. D. & K. Griffiths
	G-VANA	Gippsland GA-8 Airvan	P. Marsden
	G-VANC	Gippsland GA-8 Airvan	Irish Skydiving Club Ltd
	G-VAND	Gippsland GA-8 Airvan	Irish Skydiving Club Ltd
	G-VANN	Van's RV-7A	G-VANN Flying Group
	G-VANS	Van's RV-4	R. J. Marshall
	G-VANU	PA-28RT-201 Turbo Arrow IV	G. Chandrasekaran
	G-VANX	Gippsland GA-8 Airvan	Airkix Aircraft Ltd
	G-VANZ	Van's RV-6A	M. Wright
	G-VARG	Varga 2150A Kachina	R. A. Denton
	G-VARK	Van's RV-7	W. J. Miazek
	G-VBAA	Cameron A-400 balloon	Virgin Balloon Flights
	G-VBAB	Cameron A-400 balloon	Virgin Balloon Flights
	G-VBAD	Cameron A-300 balloon	Virgin Balloon Flights
	G-VBAE	Cameron A-400 balloon	Virgin Balloon Flights
	G-VBAF	Cameron A-300 balloon	Virgin Balloon Flights
	G-VBAG	Cameron A-400 balloon	Virgin Balloon Flights
	G-VBAH	Cameron A-400 balloon	Virgin Balloon Flights
	G-VBAI	Cameron A-400 balloon	Virgin Balloon Flights
	G-VBAJ	Cameron A-400 balloon	Virgin Balloon Flights
	G-VBAK	Cameron A-400 balloon	Virgin Balloon Flights
	G-VBAL	Cameron A-400 balloon	Virgin Balloon Flights
	G-VBAM	Cameron A-400 balloon	Virgin Balloon Flights
	G-VBAN	Cameron A-400 balloon	Virgin Balloon Flights
	G-VBAO	Cameron A-400 balloon	Virgin Balloon Flights
	G-VBAP	Cameron A-400 balloon	Virgin Balloon Flights
	G-VBAR	Cameron A-400 balloon	Virgin Balloon Flights
	G-VBAS	Cameron A-400 balloon	Virgin Balloon Flights
	G-VBAT	Cameron A-400 balloon	Virgin Balloon Flights
	G-VBAU	Cameron A-400 balloon	Virgin Balloon Flights
	G-VBAV	Cameron A-400 balloon	Virgin Balloon Flights
	G-VBAW	Cameron A-400 balloon	Virgin Balloon Flights
	G-VBAX	Cameron A-400 balloon	Virgin Balloon Flights
	G-VBAY	Cameron A-400 balloon	Virgin Balloon Flights
	G-VBAZ	Cameron A-400 balloon	Virgin Balloon Flights
	G-VBBA	Cameron A-300 balloon	Virgin Balloon Flights
	G-VBCA	Cirrus SR22	C. A. S. Atha
	G-VBEL	Boeing 787-9	Virgin Atlantic Airways Ltd *Show Girl*
	G-VBFA	Ultramagic N-250 balloon	Virgin Balloon Flights
	G-VBFB	Ultramagic N-355 balloon	Virgin Balloon Flights
	G-VBFC	Ultramagic N-250 balloon	Virgin Balloon Flights
	G-VBFD	Ultramagic N-250 balloon	Virgin Balloon Flights
	G-VBFE	Ultramagic N-255 balloon	Virgin Balloon Flights
	G-VBFF	Lindstrand LBL-360A balloon	Virgin Balloon Flights
	G-VBFG	Cameron Z-350 balloon	Virgin Balloon Flights
	G-VBFH	Cameron Z-350 balloon	Virgin Balloon Flights
	G-VBFI	Cameron Z-350 balloon	Virgin Balloon Flights
	G-VBFJ	Cameron Z-350 balloon	Virgin Balloon Flights
	G-VBFK	Cameron Z-350 balloon	Virgin Balloon Flights
	G-VBFL	Cameron Z-400 balloon	Virgin Balloon Flights
	G-VBFM	Cameron Z-375 balloon	Virgin Balloon Flights
	G-VBFN	Cameron Z-375 balloon	Virgin Balloon Flights
	G-VBFO	Cameron Z-375 balloon	Virgin Balloon Flights
	G-VBFP	Ultramagic N-425 balloon	Virgin Balloon Flights

Reg	Type	Owner or Operator	Notes
G-VBFR	Cameron Z-375 balloon	Virgin Balloon Flights	
G-VBFS	Cameron Z-375 balloon	Virgin Balloon Flights	
G-VBFT	Cameron Z-375 balloon	Virgin Balloon Flights	
G-VBFU	Cameron A-400 balloon	Virgin Balloon Flights	
G-VBFV	Cameron Z-400 balloon	Virgin Balloon Flights	
G-VBFW	Cameron Z-77 balloon	Virgin Balloon Flights	
G-VBFX	Cameron Z-400 balloon	Virgin Balloon Flights	
G-VBFY	Cameron Z-400 balloon	Virgin Balloon Flights	
G-VBFZ	Cameron A-300 balloon	Virgin Balloon Flights	
G-VBOW	Boeing 787-9	Virgin Atlantic Airways Ltd *Pearly Queen*	
G-VBPM	Cirrus SR22	S. Perkes	
G-VBZZ	Boeing 787-9	Virgin Atlantic Airways Ltd	
G-VCIO	EAA Acro Sport II	J. W. Graham-White	
G-VCJH	Robinson R22 Beta	Pickup & Son Ltd	
G-VCML	Beech 58 Baron	St. Angelo Aviation Ltd	
G-VCRU	Boeing 787-9	Virgin Atlantic Airways Ltd	
G-VCRZ	Schleicher ASH-31 MI	C. A. & S. C. Noujaim	
G-VCUB	PA-18-150 Super Cub	N. J. Morgan	
G-VCXT	Schempp-Hirth Ventus 2cT	E. Joseph	
G-VDIA	Boeing 787-9	Virgin Atlantic Airways Ltd	
G-VDIR	Cessna T.310R	J. Driver	
G-VDOG	Cessna 305C Bird Dog (24582)	J. A. Watt	
G-VDOT	Airbus A.350-1041	Virgin Atlantic Airways Ltd	
G-VECD	Robin R.1180T	B. Lee	
G-VEGA	Slingsby T.65A Vega	R. A. Rice (G-BFZN)	
G-VELA	SIAI-Marchetti S.205-22R	G-VELA Group	
G-VENC	Schempp-Hirth Ventus 2cT	A. James	
G-VERA	Gardan GY-201 Minicab	D. K. Shipton	
G-VETC	Lambert Mission M108	C. J. Cheetham	
G-VETT	Guimbal Cabri G2	Farm Veterinary Aviation Ltd	
G-VEYE	Robinson R22	K. A. Jones (G-BPTP)	
G-VEZE	Rutan Vari-Eze	J. M. Keane	
G-VFAN	Boeing 787-9	Virgin Atlantic Airways Ltd *Pin Up Girl*	
G-VFAS	PA-28R-200 Cherokee Arrow	P. Wood (G-MEAH/G-BSNM)	
G-VFDS	Van's RV-8	S. B. Shirley	
G-VGAG	Cirrus SR20 GTS	C. M. O'Connell	
G-VGBR	Airbus A.330-343	Virgin Atlantic Airways Ltd	
G-VGEM	Airbus A.330-343	Virgin Atlantic Airways Ltd	
G-VGFS	Cameron Z-90 balloon	Western Commodities Ltd	
G-VGMC	Eurocopter AS.355N Ecureuil II	Cheshire Helicopters Ltd (G-HEMH)	
G-VGMP	Airbus Helicopters AS.350B3 Ecureuil	Airbus Helicopters UK Ltd	
G-VGVG	Savannah VG Jabiru(1)	M. A. Jones	
G-VICC	PA-28-161 Warrior II	Freedom Aviation Ltd (G-JFHL)	
G-VIIA	Boeing 777-236	British Airways	
G-VIIB	Boeing 777-236	British Airways	
G-VIIC	Boeing 777-236	British Airways	
G-VIID	Boeing 777-236	British Airways	
G-VIIE	Boeing 777-236	British Airways	
G-VIIF	Boeing 777-236	British Airways	
G-VIIG	Boeing 777-236	British Airways	
G-VIIH	Boeing 777-236	British Airways	
G-VIIJ	Boeing 777-236	British Airways	
G-VIIK	Boeing 777-236	British Airways	
G-VIIL	Boeing 777-236	British Airways	
G-VIIM	Boeing 777-236	British Airways	
G-VIIN	Boeing 777-236	British Airways	
G-VIIO	Boeing 777-236	British Airways	
G-VIIP	Boeing 777-236	British Airways	
G-VIIR	Boeing 777-236	British Airways	
G-VIIS	Boeing 777-236	British Airways	
G-VIIT	Boeing 777-236	British Airways	
G-VIIU	Boeing 777-236	British Airways	
G-VIIV	Boeing 777-236	British Airways	
G-VIIW	Boeing 777-236	British Airways	
G-VIIX	Boeing 777-236	British Airways	

Notes	Reg	Type	Owner or Operator
	G-VIIY	Boeing 777-236	British Airways
	G-VIIZ	CZAW Sportcruiser	Skyview Systems Ltd
	G-VILL	Lazer Z.200 (modified)	S. A. Youngman (G-BOYZ)
	G-VINA	Aeroprakt A-22L Foxbat	J. M. Davidson
	G-VIND	Sikorsky S-92A	Babcock Mission Critical Services Offshore Ltd
	G-VINE	Airbus A.330-343	Virgin Atlantic Airways Ltd
	G-VINF	Sikorsky S-92A	Babcock Mission Critical Services Offshore Ltd
	G-VING	Sikorsky S-92A	Wilmington Trust SP Services (Dublin) Ltd
	G-VINI	Sikorsky S-92A	Wilmington Trust SP Services (Dublin) Ltd
	G-VINK	Sikorsky S-92A	Macquarie Rotorcraft Leasing Holdings Ltd
	G-VINL	Sikorsky S-92A	Macquarie Rotorcraft Leasing Holdings Ltd
	G-VINP	Sikorsky S-92A	Wilmington Trust SP Services (Dublin) Ltd
	G-VINT	Sikorsky S-92A	Wilmington Trust SP Services (Dublin) Ltd
	G-VIOF	Gulfstream VI (G650)	Executive Jet Charter Ltd
	G-VIPA	Cessna 182S	Stallingborough Aviation Ltd
	G-VIPH	Agusta A109C	Cheqair Ltd(G-BVNH/G-LAXO)
	G-VIPR	Eurocopter EC 120B Colibri	EFL Helicopters Ltd
	G-VIPU	PA-31-350 Navajo Chieftain	Atlantic Bridge Aviation Ltd
	G-VIPW	PA-31-350 Navajo Chieftain	Flight Calibration Services Ltd
	G-VIPY	PA-31-350 Navajo Chieftain	Atlantique Airlines Voyages/France
	G-VITE	Robin R.1180T	The G-VITE Flying Group
	G-VITL	Lindstrand LBL-105A balloon	M. J. Axtell
	G-VIVE	Leonardo AW.109SP Grand New	Oxford Helicopter Services LLP
	G-VIVI	Taylor JT.2 Titch	P. J. Hebdon & C. S. Hales
	G-VIVM	P.84 Jet Provost T.5	Victor Mike Group (G-BVWF)
	G-VIVO	Nicollier HN700 Menestrel II	D. G. Tucker
	G-VIXN	DH.110 Sea Vixen FAW.2 (XS587) ★	P. G. Vallance Ltd/Charlwood
	G-VIXX	Alpi Pioneer 300	N. Harrison (G-CESE/G-CERJ)
	G-VIXY	Aeroprakt A-32 Vixxen	A. Everitt
	G-VIZZ	Sportavia RS.180 Sportsman	The Exeter Fournier Group
	G-VJAM	Airbus A.350-1041	Virgin Atlantic Airways Ltd
	G-VJET	Avro 698 Vulcan B.2 (XL426) ★	Vulcan Restoration Trust
	G-VKRP	PA-32R-301 Saratoga IITC	R. G. Poxon
	G-VKSS	Airbus A.330-343	Virgin Atlantic Airways Ltd *Mademoiselle Rouge*
	G-VKUP	Cameron Z-90 balloon	T. P. E. Y. Eyckerman
	G-VLCN	Avro 698 Vulcan B.2 (XH558) ★	Vulcan to the Sky Trust
	G-VLET	Ikarus C42 FB100	J. W. D. Blythe
	G-VLNM	Airbus A.330-223	Virgin Atlantic Airways Ltd
	G-VLTT	Diamond DA.42 Twin Star	R. H. Butterfield
	G-VLUV	Airbus A.330-343	Virgin Atlantic Airways Ltd
	G-VLUX	Airbus A.350-1041	Virgin Atlantic Airways Ltd
	G-VMAP	Boeing 787-9	Virgin Atlantic Airways Ltd *West End Girl*
	G-VMCG	PA-38-112 Tomahawk	Pure Aviation Support Services Ltd (G-BSVX)
	G-VMIK	Airbus A.330-223	Virgin Atlantic Airways Ltd
	G-VMJM	SOCATA TB10 Tobago	D. J. Bryan (G-BTOK)
	G-VMNK	Airbus A.330-223	B & B Air Acquisition 403 Leasing Ltd
	G-VMOZ	Van's RV-8	V. Millard (G-CIKP)
	G-VMSO	Autogyro Cavalon	P. Setterfield
	G-VMVM	Cessna Z-77 balloon	Ballooning in Tuscany SRL/Italy
	G-VNAM	Cessna 305A Bird Dog	O-1 Aviation Ltd & L. J. Gregoire
	G-VNAV	Diamond DA.62	Flight Calibration Services Ltd
	G-VNEW	Boeing 787-9	Virgin Atlantic Airways Ltd
	G-VNOM	DH.112 Venom FB.50 (J-1632) ★	de Havilland Heritage Museum/London Colney
	G-VNON	Escapade Jabiru (5)	P. A. Vernon
	G-VNTS	Schempp-Hirth Ventus bT	911 Syndicatem
	G-VNYC	Airbus A.330-343	Virgin Atlantic Airways Ltd
	G-VNYL	Boeing 787-9	Virgin Atlantic Airways Ltd
	G-VOAR	PA-28-181 Archer III	Carlisle Flight Training Ltd
	G-VOCA	Extra EA.230	D. Hart (G-IEII/G-CBUA)
	G-VODA	Cameron N-77 balloon	H. Cusden
	G-VOID	PA-28RT-201 Arrow IV	Doublecube Aviation LLP

Reg	Type	Owner or Operator	Notes
G-VOIP	Westland SA.341G Gazelle	C3 Property Consultants Ltd	
G-VOLO	Alpi Pioneer 300	J. Buglass	
G-VONI	PA-32R-301T Saratoga II TC	W. S. Stanley	
G-VONK	AS.355F1 Squirrel	Airbourne Solutions Ltd (G-BLRI/G-NUTZ)	
G-VONS	PA-32R-301T Saratoga IITC	Vox Filemaker Solutions SRL/Romania	
G-VONY	Cessna T182T	J. Heffernan	
G-VOOH	Boeing 787-9	Virgin Atlantic Airways Ltd	
G-VOOM	Pitts S-1S Special	VOOM Syndicate	
G-VORN	Aerotechnik EV-97 Eurostar	J. Parker (G-ODAV)	
G-VOUS	Cessna 172S	Flyglass Ltd	
G-VOWS	Boeing 787-9	Virgin Atlantic Airways Ltd *Maid Marion*	
G-VPAT	Evans VP-1 Srs 2	A. P. Twort	
G-VPOP	Airbus A.350-1041	Virgin Atlantic Airways Ltd	
G-VPPL	SOCATA TB20 Trinidad	J. M. Thorpe (G-BPAS)	
G-VPRD	Airbus A.350-1041	Virgin Atlatic Airways Ltd	
G-VPSJ	Shaw Europa	J. D. Bean	
G-VRAY	Airbus A.330-343	Virgin Atlantic Airways Ltd	
G-VRNB	Airbus A.350-1041	Virgin Atlantic Airways Ltd	
G-VROE	Avro 652A Anson T.21 (WD413)	Fly the Dream Ltd (G-BFIR)	
G-VROM	Boeing 747-443	Celestial Aviation Trading 8 Ltd	
G-VROS	Boeing 747-443	Virgin Atlantic Airways Ltd *English Rose*	
G-VRRV	Van's RV-12	J. F. Edmunds	
G-VRVB	Van's RV-8	R. J. Verrall (G-CETI)	
G-VRVI	Cameron O-90 balloon	Air Events BVBA/Belgium	
G-VSGE	Cameron O-105 balloon	P. M. Oggioni/Italy	
G-VSGG	Schempp-Hirth Ventus 2b	S. G. Gaunt	
G-VSIX	Schempp-Hirth Ventus 2cT	V6 Group	
G-VSOZ	Yakovlev Yak-18T	N. R. Parsons & J. Dodd	
G-VSPY	Boeing 787-9	Virgin Atlantic Airways Ltd *Miss Moneypenny*	
G-VSTR	Stolp SA-900 V-Star	R. H. Mackay	
G-VSXY	Airbus A.330-343	Virgin Atlantic Airways Ltd *Beauty Queen*	
G-VTAL	Beech V35 Bonanza	M. A. Rooney	
G-VTCT	Schempp-Hirth Ventus-2cT	V26 Syndicate	
G-VTEA	Airbus A.350-1041	Virgin Atlantic Airways Ltd *Rosie Lee*	
G-VTGE	Bell 206L LongRanger	Vantage Helicopters Ltd (G-ELIT)	
G-VTII	DH.115 Vampire T.11 (XX507:74)	M. B. Hooton	
G-VTOL	Hawker Siddeley Harrier T.52 ★ (ZA250)	Brooklands Museum of Aviation/Weybridge	
G-VTUS	Schempp-Hirth Ventus 2cT	Ventus 02 Syndicate	
G-VUFO	Airbus A.330-343	Virgin Atlantic Airways Ltd	
G-VULC	Avro 698 Vulcan B.2A (XM655) ★	Radarmoor Ltd/Wellesbourne	
G-VVBF	Colt 315A balloon	Virgin Balloon Flights	
G-VVBO	Bell 206L-3 LongRanger III	Nugent Aviation Ltd	
G-VVBR	Robinson R22	A & M Helicopters Ltd (G-SIMS)	
G-VVRV	Van's RV-9A	I. G. Garban (G-ENTS)	
G-VVTV	Diamond DA42 Twin Star	A. D. R. Northeast	
G-VVVV	Skyranger 912 (2)	J. Thomas	
G-VVWW	Enstrom 280C Shark	P. J. Odendaal	
G-VWAG	Airbus A.330-343	Virgin Atlantic Airways Ltd	
G-VWHO	Boeing 787-9	Virgin Atlantic Airways Ltd	
G-VWND	Airbus A.330-223	Virgin Atlantic Airways Ltd	
G-VWOO	Boeing 787-9	Virgin Atlantic Airways Ltd *Leading Lady*	
G-VXXN	Aeroprakt A-32 Vixxen	P. J. Harle	
G-VXXY	Aeroprakt A-32 Vixxen	A. Everitt	
G-VYAK	Yakovlev Yak-18T	A. I. McRobbie	
G-VYGJ	Airbus A.330-243	Air Tanker Ltd	
G-VYGK	Airbus A.330-243	Air Tanker Ltd	
G-VYGL	Airbus A.330-243	Air Tanker Ltd	
G-VYGM	Airbus A.330-243	Air Tanker Ltd	
G-VYUM	Boeing 787-9	Virgin Atlantic Airways Ltd	
G-VZED	Magni M.16C Tandem Trainer	A. C. S. M. Hart	
G-VZIG	Boeing 787-9	Virgin Atlantic Airways Ltd	

Notes	Reg	Type	Owner or Operator
	G-VZIM	Alpha R2160	I. M. Hollingsworth
	G-VZSF	Hawker Sea Fury T.Mk.20	Patina Ltd
	G-WACB	Cessna F.152 II	Airways Aero Associations Ltd
	G-WACE	Cessna F.152 II	Airways Aero Associations Ltd
	G-WACF	Cessna 152 II	Airways Aero Associations Ltd
	G-WACH	Cessna FA.152 II	Airways Aero Associations Ltd
	G-WACU	Cessna FA.152	Airways Aero Associations Ltd (G-BJZU)
	G-WACW	Cessna 172P	Civil Service Flying Club (Biggin Hill) Ltd
	G-WACY	Cessna F.172P	The Vintage Wings Aviation Co.Ltd
	G-WADD	Airbus Helicopters EC120B Colibri	GGR Group Ltd
	G-WADF	Tanarg/Bionix 13 912S(2)	W. O. Fogden
	G-WADS	Robinson R22 Beta	P. Kelly (G-NICO)
	G-WADZ	Lindstrand LBL-90A balloon	A. K. C., J. E. H., M. H. & Y. K. Wadsworth (G-CGVN)
	G-WAFI	Van's RV-12	M. N. Fotherby & B. M. Lloyd
	G-WAGA	Wag-Aero Wagabond	A. I. Sutherland (G-BNJA)
	G-WAGG	Robinson R22 Beta II	Geoge J Goff Ltd
	G-WAGN	Stinson 108-3 Voyager	S. E. H. Ellcome
	G-WAHT	Albatross D.Va-1 replica (D2263)	O. Wulff
	G-WAIR	PA-32-301 Saratoga	Finningley Aviation
	G-WAIT	Cameron V-77 balloon	C. P. Brown
	G-WAKE	Mainair Blade 912	G. J. Molloy
	G-WAKY	Cyclone AX2000	G. M. R. Keenan
	G-WALI	Robinson R44 II	Incre Investments Ltd
	G-WALZ	Best Off Sky Ranger Nynja 912S(1)	R. J. Thomas
	G-WAMS	PA-28R-201 Arrow	Stapleford Flying Club Ltd
	G-WANA	P & M Quik	A. Lord
	G-WAPA	Robinson R44 II	Aerocorp Ltd
	G-WARB	PA-28-161 Warrior III	D. J. Howell
	G-WARD	Taylor JT.1 Monoplane	R. P. J. Hunter
	G-WARE	PA-28-161 Warrior II	I. D. Wakeling
	G-WARO	PA-28-161 Warrior III	T. G. D. Leasing Ltd
	G-WARP	Cessna 182F Sylane	R. D. Fowden (G-ASHB)
	G-WARR	PA-28-161 Warrior II	R. N. Carnegie
	G-WARS	PA-28-161 Warrior III	London School of Flying Ltd
	G-WARU	PA-28-161 Warrior III	Aeros Leasing Ltd
	G-WARV	PA-28-161 Warrior III	Bickertons Aerodromes Ltd
	G-WARW	PA-28-161 Warrior III	AT Aviation Sales Ltd
	G-WARX	PA-28-161 Warrior III	White Waltham Airfield Ltd
	G-WARY	PA-28-161 Warrior III	Brighton Aviation Ltd
	G-WASC	Eurocopter EC.135 T2+	Babcock Mission Critical Services Onshore Ltd
	G-WASS	Eurocopter EC.135 T2+	Babcock Mission Critical Services Onshore Ltd
	G-WATR	Christen A1 Husky	Clipper Aviation Ltd
	G-WAVA	Robin HR.200/120B	Carlisle Flight Training Ltd
	G-WAVE	Grob G.109B	J. M. Roach
	G-WAVV	Robon HR200/120B	Carlisle Flight Training Ltd (G-GORF)
	G-WAVY	Grob G.109B	G-WAVY Group
	G-WAWW	P & M Quik GT450	R. Waghorn
	G-WAYS	Lindstrand LBL-105A balloon	D. B. Green
	G-WAYY	Maule MX-7-180	Blockworks Group Ltd (G-WALY)
	G-WAZP	Skyranger 912 (2)	M. Gilson & P. C. Terry
	G-WBEV	Cameron N-77 balloon	T. J. & M. Turner (G-PVCU)
	G-WBLY	Mainair Pegasus Quik	A. J. Lindsey
	G-WBRD	Avro Curtiss 1911 Replica	Cooper Aerial Surveys Engineering Ltd & The Lakes Flying Company Ltd
	G-WBTS	Falconar F-11	M. K. Field (G-BDPL)
	G-WCAT	Colt Flying Mitt SS balloon	I. Chadwick
	G-WCCP	Beech B200 Super King Air	GCP Aviation Ltd
	G-WCKM	Best Off Sky Ranger 912(1)	D. R. Hardy
	G-WCME	Grumman FM-2 Wildcat	Wildcat WP Ltd
	G-WCMI	Grumman FM-2 Wildcat	Wildcat WP Ltd
	G-WCMO	Grumman FM-2 Wildcat	Wildcat WP Ltd
	G-WCUB	PA-18 Super Cub 150	P. A. Walley
	G-WDCL	Agusta A.109E Power	Wickford Development Company Ltd (G-WELY)
	G-WDEB	Thunder Ax-7-77 balloon	A. Heginbottom
	G-WDGC	Rolladen-Schneider LS8-18	W. D. G. Chappel (G-CEWJ)

Reg	Type	Owner or Operator	Notes
G-WEAT	Robinson R44 II	R. F. Brook	
G-WEBY	Ace Magic Cyclone	B. W. Webster	
G-WECG	AS.355NP Ecureuil 2	WEC Group Ltd (G-MXCO)	
G-WEEK	Skyranger 912(2)	R. E. Williams	
G-WEEV	Van's RV-8	Double Whisky Flying Group (G-JBTR)	
G-WEFR	Alpi Pioneer 200-M	S. G. Llewelyn	
G-WEFX	Avro RJ100	Airbus Exo Alpha SAS (G-ILLR/G-CFAC)	
G-WEND	PA-28RT-201 Arrow IV	Tayside Aviation Ltd	
G-WENU	Airbus Helicopters MBB-BK117 D-2	Babcock Mission Critical Services Onshore Ltd	
G-WENY	Zenair CH.750 Cruzer	P. W. Porter	
G-WEPW	Skyranger Swift 912S(1)	British Microlight Aircraft Association Ltd	
G-WERY	SOCATA TB20 Trinidad	R-Aviation SARL/France	
G-WESS	Lindstrand LTL Series 1-90 balloon	A. Moore	
G-WESX	CFM Streak Shadow	M. Catania	
G-WETI	Cameron N-31 balloon	C. A. Butter & J. J. T. Cooke	
G-WEWI	Cessna 172	T. J. Wassell (G-BSEP)	
G-WEZZ	Taylor JT.1 Monoplane	W. A. Tierney (G-BDRF)	
G-WFFW	PA-28-161 Warrior II	S. Letheren & D. Jelly	
G-WFIT	Zenair CH.701SP	Pilot Taining Services Ltd (G-OBAP)	
G-WFLY	Mainair Pegasus Quik	S. Turton	
G-WFWA	PA-28-161 Cherokee Warrior II	Wings for Warriors (G-BPMR)	
G-WGCS	PA-18 Super Cub 95	S. C. Thompson	
G-WGSI	Tanarg/Ixess 13 912S(1)	M. Nazm	
G-WHAA	TLAC Sherwood Ranger ST	Progress Vehicle Management Ltd	
G-WHAT	Colt 77A balloon	M. A. Scholes	
G-WHEE	Pegasus Quantum 15-912	G-WHEE Group	
G-WHEN	Tecnam P92-EM Echo	F. G. Walker	
G-WHGA	Robinson R44	A & R Helicopters Ltd (G-EGTC/G-CCNK)	
G-WHIL	Balony Kubicek BB-S Cup SS balloon	A. M. Holly	
G-WHIM	Colt 77A balloon	D. L. Morgan	
G-WHIP	Agusta Westland AW119 Mk.II	SaxonAir Helicopters	
G-WHOG	CFM Streak Shadow	B. R. Cannell	
G-WHOO	Rotorway Executive 162F	J. White	
G-WHPG	Ikarus C42 FB80	T. Penn & C. P. Roche	
G-WHRL	Schweizer 269C	A. Harvey	
G-WHST	AS.350B2 Ecureuil	Toppesfield Ltd (G-BWYA)	
G-WHYS	ICP MXP-740 Savannah VG Jabiru(1)	R. W. Swift	
G-WIBB	Jodel D.18	C. J. Bragg	
G-WIBS	CASA 1-131E Jungmann 2000	C. Willoughby	
G-WICH	Clutton FRED Srs II	D. R. G. Griffith	
G-WIFE	Cessna R.182 RG II	Wife 182 Group (G-BGVT)	
G-WIFI	Cameron Z-90 balloon	A. R. Rich	
G-WIGI	Aeroprakt A22-LS Foxbat	K. E., M. & P. Wigginton	
G-WIGS	Yeoman Dynamic WT9 UK	A. Wiggins (G-DYMC)	
G-WIGY	Pitts S-1S Special	R. E. Welch (G-ITTI)	
G-WIII	Schempp-Hirth Ventus bT	I. G. Carrick	
G-WIIZ	Augusta-Bell 206B JetRanger 2	Bradawl Ltd	
G-WIKD	Van's RV-8	E. P. Morrow	
G-WIKI	Europa XS	A. H. Smith & S. P. Kirton	
G-WILB	Ultramagic M-105 balloon	Nottingham & Derby Hot Air Balloon Club	
G-WILC	Robinson R66	wilc llp	
G-WILD	Pitts S-1T Special	S. L. Goldspink	
G-WILG	PZL-104 Wilga 35	M. H. Bletsoe-Brown (G-AZYJ)	
G-WILI	PA-32R-301 Saratoga SP	R. Herold	
G-WILN	Tecnam P2006T	W Flight Hire Ltd	
G-WILT	Ikarus C42 FB80	V. J. P. R. Denecker	
G-WIMP	Colt 56A balloon	D. M. Wade	
G-WINE	Thunder Ax7-77Z balloon ★	Balloon Preservation Group/Lancing	
G-WINH	EV-97 TeamEurostar UK	J. A. Warters	
G-WINI	SA Bulldog Srs.120/121 (XX546:03)	A. Bole (G-CBCO)	
G-WINK	AA-5B Tiger	B. St. J. Cooke	
G-WINN	Stolp SA300 Starduster Too	R. J. Woodhams	
G-WINO	Aeropro Eurofox 912S(1)	M. A. J. Spiers	
G-WINR	Robinson R22	Heli Air Ltd (G-BTHG)	
G-WINS	PA-32 Cherokee Six 300	Cheyenne Ltd	
G-WINZ	Lindstrand LTL Penguin balloon	A. M. Holly	
G-WIRL	Robinson R22 Beta	Swift Helicopter Services Ltd	

Notes	Reg	Type	Owner or Operator
	G-WISZ	Steen Skybolt	G. S. Reid
	G-WIXI	Avions Mudry CAP-10B	A. R. Harris
	G-WIZG	Agusta A.109E Power	Tycoon Aviation Ltd (G-TYCN/G-VMCO)
	G-WIZI	Enstrom 280FX	Gateway Auctions Ltd
	G-WIZR	Robinson R22 Beta II	Helimech Ltd
	G-WIZS	Mainair Pegasus Quik	L. Hogan
	G-WIZZ	Agusta-Bell 206B JetRanger 2	Rivermead Aviation Ltd
	G-WJAC	Cameron TR-70 balloon	S. J. & J. A. Bellaby
	G-WJCM	CASA 1.131E Jungmann 2000 (S5+B06)	G. W. Lynch (G-BSFB)
	G-WJET	HpH Glasflugel 304 S Shark	P. Thomson
	G-WJSG	P & M Quik GT450	W. J. Hardy
	G-WKDB	Ikarus C42 FB80 Bravo	W. Broadbent
	G-WKNS	Shaw Europa XS	A. L. Wickens
	G-WKTG	Diamond DA.42M-NG Twin Star	DEA Aviation Ltd
	G-WKTH	Diamond DA.62	DEA Aviation Ltd
	G-WKTI	Diamond DA.62	DEA Aviation Ltd
	G-WLAC	PA-18 Super Cub 150	White Waltham Airfield Ltd (G-HAHA/G-BSWE)
	G-WLDN	Robinson R44 Raven	M. R. J. Pearson
	G-WLGC	PA-28-181 Archer III	E. F. Mangion (G-FLUX)
	G-WLKR	Embraer EMB-550 Legacy 500	Air Charter Scotland Ltd
	G-WLKS	Schleicher ASW-20L	S. E. Wilks (G-IUMB)
	G-WLLS	Rolladen-Schneider LS8-18	L & A Wells
	G-WLMS	Mainair Blade 912	N. J. Cowdery
	G-WLRS	Supermarine 236 Walrus Mk.1 (W2718)	T. W. Harris (G-RNLI)
	G-WLSN	Best Off Skyranger 912S (1)	A. R. Wilson
	G-WLTS	Bell 429	Wiltshire Air Ambulance Charitable Trust
	G-WLVE	Cameron Buddy-90 SS balloon	J. C. M. Greatrix
	G-WMBL	P & M Quik R	W M Buchanan Ltd
	G-WMRN	SOCATA TBM-900	Ravenair
	G-WMTM	AA-5B Tiger	R. K. Hyatt
	G-WNCH	Beech B200 Super King Air	Synergy Aircraft Leasing Ltd (G-OMGI)
	G-WNDR	ULTRA-UAS	Windracers Ltd
	G-WNSC	Eurocopter AS.332L2 Super Puma	Airbus Helicopters Ltd
	G-WNSD	Sikorsky S-92A	CHC Scotia Ltd
	G-WNSE	Sikorsky S-92A	CHC Scotia Ltd
	G-WNSF	Sikorsky S-92A	CHC Scotia Ltd
	G-WNSG	Sikorsky S-92A	CHC Scotia Ltd
	G-WNSL	Sikorsky S-92A	CHC Scotia Ltd
	G-WNSP	Eurocopter EC.225LP Super Puma	Lombard North Central PLC
	G-WNST	Sikorsky S-92A	CHC Scotia Ltd
	G-WNSU	Sikorsky S-92A	CHC Scotia Ltd
	G-WNSV	Sikorsky S-92A	CHC Scotia Ltd
	G-WNTR	PA-28-161 Warrior II	Fleetlands Flying Group (G-BFNJ)
	G-WOFM	Agusta A109E Power	Quinnasette Ltd (G-NWRR)
	G-WOLF	PA-28 Cherokee 140	G-WOLF Group
	G-WONE	Schempp-Hirth Ventus 2cT	J. P. Wright
	G-WOOD	Beech 95-B55A Baron	M. S. Choskey (G-AYID)
	G-WOOF	Enstrom 480	Netcopter.co.uk Ltd & Curvature Ltd
	G-WOOL	Colt 77A balloon	D. P. MacGregor
	G-WOOO	CZAW Sportcruiser	J. J. Nicholson
	G-WORM	Thruster T.600N	WORM Group
	G-WOTW	Ultramagic M-77 balloon	Window on the World Ltd
	G-WOWI	Van's RV-7	P. J. Wood
	G-WOWS	Sirrus SR22T	A. M. & R. W. Glaves
	G-WPDA	Eurocopter EC135 P1	WPD Helicopter Unit
	G-WPDB	Eurocopter EC135 P1	WPD Helicopter Unit
	G-WPDC	Eurocopter EC135 P1	WPD Helicopter Unit
	G-WPDD	Eurocopter EC135 P1	WPD Helicopter Unit
	G-WPDE	Eurocopter EC135P2+	WPD Helicopter Unit
	G-WPNS	BN-2T-4S Defender 4000	Britten-Norman Ltd (G-GMPB/G-BWPU)
	G-WREN	Pitts S-2A Special	W. Ali
	G-WRFM	Enstrom 280C-UK Shark	A. J. Clark (G-CTSI/G-BKIO)
	G-WRIT	Colt 77A balloon	G. Pusey
	G-WRLY	Robinson R22 Beta	Burman Aviation Ltd (G-OFJS/G-BNXJ)

Reg	Type	Owner or Operator	Notes
G-WROL	MBB-BK 117 D-2	Babcock Mission Critical Services Onshore Ltd (G-OLWG)	
G-WSEX	Westland Wessex HU.Mk.5 (XT761)	A. D. Whitehouse	
G-WSKY	Enstrom 280C-UK-2 Shark	B. J. Rutterford (G-BEEK)	
G-WSMW	Robinson R44	Chunnel Plant Hire & Contractors Ltd (G-SGPL)	
G-WSSX	Ikarus C42 FB100	J. M. Crane	
G-WSTY	Lindstrand LBL-77A balloon	C. & C. Westwood	
G-WTAV	Robinson R44 II	T. Levitan	
G-WTFH	Van's RV-6	N. M. R. Richards	
G-WTSN	Van's RV-8	S. R. Watson	
G-WTWO	Aquila AT01	J. P. Wright	
G-WUFF	Shaw Europa	G-WUFF Group	
G-WUKC	Airbus A.321-231	Wizz Air UK Ltd	
G-WUKD	Airbus A.320-232	Wizz Air UK Ltd	
G-WUKE	Airbus A.320-232	Wizz Air UK Ltd	
G-WUKF	Airbus A.320-232	Wizz Air UK Ltd	
G-WUKG	Airbus A.321-231	Wizz Air UK Ltd	
G-WUKH	Airbus A.321-231	Wizz Air UK Ltd	
G-WUKI	Airbus A.321-231	Wizz Air UK Ltd	
G-WUKJ	Airbus A.321-231	Wizz Air UK Ltd	
G-WUKK	Airbus A.321-231	Wizz Air UK Ltd	
G-WUKL	Airbus A.321-231	Wizz Air UK Ltd	
G-WUKM	Airbus A.321-271NX	Wizz Air UK Ltd	
G-WULF	Replica WAR Focke-Wulf 190	B. Hunter	
G-WVBF	Lindstrand LBL-210A balloon	Virgin Balloon Flights Ltd	
G-WVEN	Extra EA300/200	R. J. Hunter	
G-WVIP	Beech B.200 Super King Air	Newbery Metals Ltd	
G-WWAL	PA-28R Cherokee Arrow 180	White Waltham Airfield Ltd (G-AZSH)	
G-WWAY	Piper PA-28-181 Archer II	R. A. Witchell	
G-WWLF	Extra EA.300/L	P. Sapignoli	
G-WWLK	Boeing Stearman A75N1 Kaydet	The Wing Walk Company Ltd	
G-WWZZ	CZAW Sportcruiser	L. Hogan	
G-WXYZ	Zenair CH.750	C. A. Bickley	
G-WYAT	CFM Streak Shadow Srs SA	J. L. Wolstenholme	
G-WYKD	Tanarg/Ixess 15 912S(2)	M. R. Thorley	
G-WYLD	Cessna T.210N Turbo Centurion II	R. M. de Roeck (G-EEWS)	
G-WYMM	PA-15 Vagabond	N. G. Busschsau (G-AWOF)	
G-WYND	Wittman W.8 Tailwind	R. S. Marriott	
G-WYNT	Cameron N-56 balloon	P. Richardson	
G-WYSZ	Robin DR.400/100	Exavia Ltd (G-FTIM)	
G-WYVN	DG Flugzeugbau DG-1000S	Army Gliding Association	
G-WZAP	Embraer EMB-505 Phenom 300	Hagondale Ltd/Titan Airways	
G-WZOL	RL.5B LWS Sherwood Ranger	D. Lentell (G-MZOL)	
G-WZOY	Rans S.6-ESA Coyote II	M. J. Laundy	
G-XACS	Airbus A.320-232	ACS Aero 1 Gamma Ltd	
G-XALT	PA-38-112 Tomahawk	D. R. Clyde	
G-XALZ	Rans S6S-116 Super Six	D. W. & S. J. McAllister	
G-XARA	Czech Sport PS-28 Cruiser	C. W. D. Ross	
G-XARV	ARV Super 2	C. M. Rose (G-OPIG/G-BMSJ)	
G-XASH	Schleicher ASH-31 MI	R. C. Wilson	
G-XATV	Bombardier BD100-1A10 Challenger 300	Arena Aviation Ltd	
G-XATW	Airbus A.321-253NX	Titan Airways Ltd	
G-XAVI	PA-28-161 Warrior II	Freedom Aviation Ltd (G-SACZ)	
G-XAVV	Schempp-Hirth Ventus 2c	R. S. Hood	
G-XBAL	Skyringer Nynja 912S(1)	W. G. Gill & N. D. Ewer	
G-XBGA	Glaser-Dirks DG500/22 Elan	N. Kelly	
G-XBJT	Aerotechnik EV-97 Eurostar	C. J. & J. A. Aldous (G-WHOA/G-DATH)	
G-XBLD	MBB Bo.105DB	Recovair Ltd	
G-XBOX	Bell 206B JetRanger 3	Castle Air Ltd (G-OOHO/G-OCHC/G-KLEE/ G-SIZL/G-BOSW)	
G-XBXX	Lindstrand LTL Series 1-90 balloon	A. M. Holly	

Notes	Reg	Type	Owner or Operator
	G-XCAP	Mudry CAP-232	D. M. Britten
	G-XCCC	Extra EA.300/L	P. T. Fellows
	G-XCID	SAAB 91D Safir	J. T. Hunter
	G-XCIT	Alpi Pioneer 300	A. Thomas
	G-XCRI	Colomban MC-15 Cri-Cri	P. A. Harvie
	G-XCRJ	Van's RV-9A	Romeo Juliet Group
	G-XCUB	PA-18 Super Cub 150	White Waltham Airfield Ltd
	G-XDEA	Diamond DA.42 Twin Star	Tesla Aviation Ltd
	G-XDUO	Schempp-Hirth Duo Discus xT	G-XDUO Group
	G-XDWE	P & M Quik GT450	D. Sullivan
	G-XELL	Schleicher ASW-27-18E	S. R. Ell
	G-XENA	PA-28-161 Warrior II	P. Brewer
	G-XERK	Van's RV-7	C. A. Morris
	G-XERO	CZAW Sportcruiser	M. R. Mosley
	G-XFLY	Lambert Mission M212-100	Lambert Aircraft Engineering BVBA
	G-XFOX	Aeropro Eurofox 912(S)	Fox Five Group
	G-XFTF	BRM Aero Bristell NG5	N. G. Parr
	G-XFYF	Guimbal Cabri G2	R. O'Donnell
	G-XGAB	Bristell NG5 Speed Wing	G. A. Beale
	G-XIFR	Lambert Mission M108	Lambert Aircraft Engineering BVBA
	G-XIII	Van's RV-7	Icarus Flying Group
	G-XIIO	Schempp-Hirth Ventus-3T	S. G. Jones
	G-XIIX	Robinson R22 Beta ★	(Static exhibit)/Blackbushe
	G-XILM	TL-3000 Sirius	M. Smith
	G-XINE	PA-28-161 Warrior II	P. Tee (G-BPAC)
	G-XION	Dassault Falcon 8X	Execujet (UK) Ltd
	G-XIOO	Raj Hamsa X'Air 133 (1)	G. M. R. Keenan
	G-XIVA	Van's RV-14A	R. Jones
	G-XIXI	Evektor EV-97 TeamEurostar UK	J. A. C. Cockfield
	G-XIXT	AB Sportine LAK-19T	P. R. Thomas & W. M. Kay
	G-XIXX	Glaser-Dirks DG-300 Elan	S. D. Black
	G-XJCJ	Cessna 550 Citation Bravo	XJC Jets Ltd
	G-XJET	Learjet 45	Patriot Aviation Ltd (G-IZAP/G-OLDK)
	G-XJON	Schempp-Hirth Ventus 2b	J. C. Bastin
	G-XKKA	Diamond KH36 Super Dimona	G-XKKA Group
	G-XKRV	Best Off Skyranger Nynja LS 912S(1)	A. V. Francis
	G-XLAM	Best Off Skyranger 912S	X-LAM Skyranger Syndicate
	G-XLEA	Airbus A.380-841	British Airways
	G-XLEB	Airbus A.380-841	British Airways
	G-XLEC	Airbus A.380-841	British Airways
	G-XLED	Airbus A.380-841	British Airways
	G-XLEE	Airbus A.380-841	British Airways
	G-XLEF	Airbus A.380-841	British Airways
	G-XLEG	Airbus A.380-841	British Airways
	G-XLEH	Airbus A.380-841	British Airways
	G-XLEI	Airbus A.380-841	British Airways
	G-XLEJ	Airbus A.380-841	British Airways
	G-XLEK	Airbus A.380-841	British Airways
	G-XLEL	Airbus A.380-841	British Airways
	G-XLII	Schleicher ASW-27-18E	K. S. McPhee
	G-XLLL	AS.355F1 Twin Squirrel	Excel Charter Ltd (G-PASF/G-SCHU)
	G-XLNT	Zenair CH.601XL	Lampy Investments Ltd
	G-XLTG	Cessna 182S	The G-XLTG Flying Group
	G-XLXL	Robin DR.400/160	L. R. Marchant (G-BAUD)
	G-XMGO	Aeromot AMT-200S Super Ximango	C. & R. P. Beck
	G-XONE	Canadair CL600-2B16	Gama Aviation (UK) Ltd
	G-XPBI	Letov LK-2M Sluka	R. M. C. Hunter
	G-XPDA	Cameron Z-120 balloon	C. D. Monk
	G-XPII	Cessna R.172K	London Denham Aviation Ltd (G-DIVA)
	G-XPWW	Cameron TR-77 balloon	Chalmers Ballong Corps/Sweden

Reg	Type	Owner or Operator	Notes
G-XPXP	Aero Designs Pulsar XP	B. J. Edwards	
G-XRAF	Raj Hamsa X'Air 582 (11)	D. Brunton	
G-XRAY	Rand-Robinson KR-2	R. S. Smith	
G-XRED	Pitts S-1C Special	J. E. Rands (G-SWUN/G-BSXH)	
G-XRLD	Cameron A-250 balloon	Aeolus Aviation GmbH/Germany	
G-XRVB	Van's RV-8	R. E. Kelly	
G-XRVX	Van's RV-10	N. K. Lamping	
G-XRXR	Raj Hamsa X'Air 582 (5)	J. E. Merriman	
G-XSAM	Van's RV-9A	Parachuting Aircraft Ltd	
G-XSCP	PA-46-600TP Meridian M600	British European Aviation Ltd	
G-XSDJ	Europa XS	D. N. Joyce	
G-XSEA	Van's RV-8	H. M. Darlington	
G-XSEL	Silence Twister	Skyview Systems Ltd	
G-XSFT	PA-23-250 Aztec F	M. Lawrynowicz (G-NADN/G-CPPC/G-BGBH)	
G-XSRF	Europa NG	R. L. W. Frank	
G-XTAZ	Van's RV-7	G-XTAZ Group	
G-XTEE	Edge XT912-B/Streak III	Shropshire Bush Pilots	
G-XTNI	AirBorne XT912-B/Streak	A. J. Parry	
G-XTRA	Extra EA.230	C. Butler	
G-XTUG	Lambert Mission M108	Lambert Aircraft Engineering BVBA/Belgium	
G-XTUN	Westland-Bell 47G-3B1 (XT223)	P. A. Rogers (G-BGZK)	
G-XVAT	Schleicher ASW-27	B. Pridgeon	
G-XVAX	Tecnam P2006T	M. A. Baldwin	
G-XVII	Schleicher ASW-17	C. A. & S. C. Noujaim (G-DCTE)	
G-XVIP	Beech 200 Super King Air	Gama Aviation (UK) Ltd (G-OCEG)	
G-XVOM	Van's RV-6	A. Baker-Munton	
G-XWBA	Airbus A.350-1041	British Airways PLC	
G-XWBB	Airbus A.350-1041	British Airways PLC	
G-XWBC	Airbus A.350-1041	British Airways PLC	
G-XWBD	Airbus A.350-1041	British Airways PLC	
G-XWBE	Airbus A.350-1041	British Airways PLC	
G-XWBF	Airbus A.350-1041	British Airways PLC	
G-XWBG	Airbus A.350-1041	British Airways PLC	
G-XWBH	Airbus A.350-1041	British Airways PLC	
G-XWEB	Best Off Skyranger 912 (2)	A. P. Dalgetty & M. Chambers	
G-XWON	Rolladen-Schneider LS8-18	G-XWON Syndicate	
G-XXBH	Agusta-Bell 206B JetRanger 3	Temchu Ltd (G-BYBA/G-BHXV/G-OWJM)	
G-XXEB	Sikorsky S-76C	M. Stevens, Keeper of the Privy Purse	
G-XXEC	Agusta A.109S Grand	Leonardo SPA	
G-XXED	Sikorsky S-76C	M. Stevens, Keeper of the Privy Purse (G-MRRI/G-URSA/G-URSS)	
G-XXHP	Extra EA.300/L	A. R. Willis (G-BZFR)	
G-XXIV	Agusta-Bell 206B JetRanger 3	Adventure 001 Ltd	
G-XXIX	Schleicher ASW-27-18E	P. R. & A. H. Pentecost	
G-XXRS	Bombardier BD-700 Global Express	TAG Aviation (UK) Ltd	
G-XXRV	Van's RV-9	D. R. Gilbert & D. Slabbert	
G-XXSF	Bell 505 Jet Ranger X	Seafresh Group (Holdings) Ltd	
G-XXTR	Extra EA.300/L	The Shoreham Extra Group (G-ECCC)	
G-XXVB	Schempp-Hirth Ventus b	R. Johnson	
G-XYJY	Best Off Skyranger 912(1)	A. V. Francis	
G-XYZT	Aeromot AMT-200S Super Ximango	Betav BV/Netherlands	
G-XZXZ	Robinson R44 II	Ashley Martin Ltd	
G-YAAC	Airbus Helicopters MBB-BK117 D-2	Yorkshire Air Ambulance Ltd	
G-YAAK	Yakovlev Yak-50 (20)	D. J. Hopkinson (G-BWJT)	
G-YACC	Yakovlev Yak-18T	M. J. Babage	
G-YADA	Ikarus C42 FB100	S. G. Weaver	
G-YAKC	Yakovlev Yak-52	Airborne Services Ltd	
G-YAKE	Yakovlev Yak-52	D. J. Hopkinson (G-BVVA)	
G-YAKF	Aerostar Yakovlev Yak-52	R. S. Trives	
G-YAKG	Yakovlev Yak-18T	G. van Eeckhoudt	
G-YAKH	IDA Bacau Yakovlev Yak-52	Plus 7 minus 5 Ltd	
G-YAKI	IDA Bacau Yakovlev Yak-52 (100 blue)	Yak One Ltd	

Notes	Reg	Type	Owner or Operator
	G-YAKJ	Yakovlev Yak-18T	Teshka Aviation Syndicate
	G-YAKM	IDA Bacau Yakovlev Yak-50 (61 red)	Airborne Services Ltd
	G-YAKN	IDA Bacau Yakovlev Yak-52 (66 red)	Airborne Services Ltd
	G-YAKU	IDA Bacau Yakovlev Yak-50 (49 red)	D. J. Hopkinson (G-BXND)
	G-YAKX	IDA Bacau Yakovlev Yak-52 (27 red)	The X-Flyers Ltd
	G-YAKZ	IDA Bacau Yakovlev Yak-50 (33 red)	Airborne Services Ltd
	G-YANK	PA-28-181 Archer II	M. Cason
	G-YARD	Robinson R44 II	Caffco Ltd
	G-YARR	Mainair Rapier	D. Yarr
	G-YARV	ARV Super 2	A. M. Oliver (G-BMDO)
	G-YAWW	PA-28RT-201T Turbo Arrow IV	Barton Aviation Ltd
	G-YBAA	Cessna FR.172J	G-YBAA Flying Group
	G-YBES	Eurocopter EC130 B4	Gybe Ho Air LLP
	G-YCMI	Sonex	D. R. D. H. Mobbs
	G-YCUB	PA-18 Super Cub 150	F. W. Rogers
	G-YDEA	DA-42 Twin Star	DEA Aviation Ltd
	G-YEHA	Schleicher ASW-27	B. L. Cooper
	G-YELA	Van's RV-8	C. D. Meek
	G-YELL	Murphy Rebel	I. N. Scott
	G-YELO	Autogyro MT-03	P. A. Gardner
	G-YELP	RL5A Sherwood Ranger ST	C. Blount
	G-YEOM	PA-31-350 Navajo Chieftain	Strata Aviation Services Ltd
	G-YETI	Europa	C. G. Sutton (G-CILF)
	G-YEWS	Rotorway Executive 152	R. Turrell & P. Mason
	G-YFOX	Dassault Falcon 2000EX	London Executive Aviation Ltd
	G-YIPI	Cessan FR.172K	M. Klies
	G-YIRO	Campbell Cricket Mk.4	M. A. Ward (G-KGED)
	G-YJET	Montgomerie-Bensen B.8MR	P. D. Davis-Ratcliffe (G-BMUH)
	G-YKSO	Yakovlev Yak-50 (23)	A. M. Holman-West
	G-YKSS	Yakovlev Yak-55	T. Ollivier
	G-YMFC	Waco YMF	S. J. Brenchley
	G-YMMA	Boeing 777-236ER	British Airways
	G-YMMB	Boeing 777-236ER	British Airways
	G-YMMC	Boeing 777-236ER	British Airways
	G-YMMD	Boeing 777-236ER	British Airways
	G-YMME	Boeing 777-236ER	British Airways
	G-YMMF	Boeing 777-236ER	British Airways
	G-YMMG	Boeing 777-236ER	British Airways
	G-YMMH	Boeing 777-236ER	British Airways
	G-YMMI	Boeing 777-236ER	British Airways
	G-YMMJ	Boeing 777-236ER	British Airways
	G-YMMK	Boeing 777-236ER	British Airways
	G-YMML	Boeing 777-236ER	British Airways
	G-YMMN	Boeing 777-236ER	British Airways
	G-YMMO	Boeing 777-236ER	British Airways
	G-YMMP	Boeing 777-236ER	British Airways
	G-YMMR	Boeing 777-236ER	British Airways
	G-YMMS	Boeing 777-236ER	British Airways
	G-YMMT	Boeing 777-236ER	British Airways
	G-YMMU	Boeing 777-236ER	British Airways
	G-YNJA	Skyranger Nynja LS 912S(1)	C. A. Green
	G-YNOT	D.62B Condor	T. Littlefair (G-AYFH)
	G-YNYS	Cessna 172S Skyhawk	T. V. Hughes
	G-YOAA	Airbus Helicopters MBB BK117 D-2	Yorkshire Air Ambulance Ltd
	G-YOBI	Schleicher ASH-25	J. Kangurs
	G-YODA	Schempp-Hirth Ventus 2cT	J. W. M. Gijrath
	G-YOGI	Robin DR.400/140B	G-YOGI Flying Group (G-BDME)
	G-YOLK	P & M Aviation Quik GT450	G. J. Wright
	G-YOLO	Aeroprakt A22-L2 Foxbat	J. W. Mann
	G-YORE	CZAW Sportcruiser	R. Yore (G-CFNV)

Reg	Type	Owner or Operator	Notes
G-YORK	Cessna F.172M	EIMH-Flying Group	
G-YOTS	IDA Bacau Yakovlev Yak-52	G-YOTS Group	
G-YOYO	Pitts S-1E Special	P. M. Jarvis (G-OTSW/G-BLHE)	
G-YPDN	Rotorsport UK MT-03	T. M. Jones	
G-YPSY	Andreasson BA-4B	J. P. Burrill	
G-YRAF	RAF 2000 GTX-SE gyroplane	J. R. Cooper	
G-YRAX	Magni M-24C	R. D. Armishaw	
G-YRIL	Luscombe 8E Silvaire	I. de Groot	
G-YROA	Rotorsport UK MTO Sport	S. Smith	
G-YROC	Rotorsport UK MT-03	C. V. Catherall	
G-YROF	Magni M22C Voyager	Clocktower Fund Management Ltd	
G-YROG	Magni M24C Orion	Fairoaks Gyros Ltd	
G-YROH	Rotorsport UK MTO Sport	M. Winship	
G-YROI	Air Command 532 Elite	W. B. Lumb	
G-YROJ	RAF2000 GTX-SE	Condor Aviation International Ltd	
G-YROK	Magni M-16C	K. J. Yeadon	
G-YROL	Rotorsport UK Cavalon	C. G. Gilbert	
G-YROM	Rotorsport UK MT-03	A. Wallace	
G-YRON	Magni M-16C Tandem Trainer	H. E. Simons	
G-YROO	RAF 2000 GTX-SE gyroplane	L. Goodison	
G-YROP	Magni M-16C Tandem Trainer	Clocktower Fund Management Ltd	
G-YROR	Magni M.24C	R. M. Stanley	
G-YROT	Rotorsport UK MTO Sport 2017	R. Wright	
G-YROU	Magni M24C Orion	Fairoaks Gyros Ltd	
G-YROV	Rotorsport UK MT-03	Carnie Aviation Ltd (G-UMAS)	
G-YROX	Rotorsport UK MT-03	Surplus Art	
G-YROY	Montgomerie-Bensen B.8MR	S. S. Wilson	
G-YROZ	Rotorsport UK Calidus	A. M. Mackey	
G-YRRO	Rotorsport UK Calidus	C. M. Leivers	
G-YRTE	Agusta A.109S Grand	Galegrove 2 LBG	
G-YRUS	Jodel D.140E	W. E. Massam (G-YRNS)	
G-YSIR	Van's RV-8	The Lord Rotherwick	
G-YSMO	Mainair Pegasus Quik	T. M. Shaw	
G-YTLY	Rans S-6-ES Coyote II	D. M. Geddes	
G-YUGE	Schempp-Hirth Ventus cT	T. Janikowski (G-CFNN)	
G-YUGO	HS.125 Srs 1B/R-522 ★	Fire Section/Dunsfold (G-ATWH)	
G-YULL	PA-28 Cherokee 180E	G-YULL Flying Group (G-BEAJ)	
G-YUMM	Cameron N-90 balloon	H. Stringer	
G-YUPI	Cameron N-90 balloon	MCVH SA/Belgium	
G-YURO	Shaw Europa ★	Yorkshire Air Museum/Elvington	
G-YVES	Alpi Pioneer 300	A. P. Anderson	
G-YVIP	Beech B200 Super King Air	Gama Aviation (UK) Ltd	
G-YXLX	ISF Mistral C	R. R. Penman	
G-YYAK	Aerostar SA Yak-52	Repxper SARL/France	
G-YYRO	Magni M-16C Tandem Trainer	A. Yin-Tuen Leung	
G-YYYY	MH.1521C-1 Broussard (208)	Aerosuperbatics Ltd	
G-YZYZ	Mainair Blade 912	A. M. Beale	
G-ZAAP	CZAW Sportcruiser	H. Page	
G-ZAAZ	Van's RV-8	P. A. Soper	
G-ZABA	Kubicek BB26E	J. A. Viner	
G-ZABC	Sky 90-24 balloon	P. Donnelly	
G-ZACE	Cessna 172S	Sywell Aerodrome Ltd	
G-ZACH	Robin DR.400/100	A. P. Wellings (G-FTIO)	
G-ZACK	Cirrus SR20	Modern Air (UK) Ltd	
G-ZADA	Best Off Skyranger 912S(1)	C. P. Lincoln	
G-ZAIR	Zenair CH 601HD	A. D. Brown	
G-ZAKA	Diamond DA.40D Star	o. IANLEHIN	
G-ZANY	Diamond DA.40D Star	Altair Aviation Ltd	
G-ZAPX	Boeing 757-256	Titan Airways Ltd	
G-ZAPY	Robinson R22 Beta	HQ Aviation Ltd (G-INGB)	
G-ZARV	ARV Super 2	P. R. Snowden	

BRITISH CIVIL AIRCRAFT MARKINGS

Notes	Reg	Type	Owner or Operator
	G-ZASH	Ikarus C42 FB80	J. W. D. Blythe
	G-ZAST	Christen A-1 Husky	E. Marinoni/Italy
	G-ZATG	Diamond DA.42M Twin Star	Directflight Ltd (G-DOSA)
	G-ZAVI	Ikarus C42 FB100	M. de Cleen & M. J. Hawkins
	G-ZAZA	PA-18 Super Cub 95	G. J. Harry, The Viscount Goschen
	G-ZAZU	Diamond DA.42 Twin Star	Cloud Global Ltd (G-GFDA/G-CEFX)
	G-ZAZZ	Lindstrand LBL-120A balloon	Idea Balloon SAS Di Stefano Travaglia and Co./ Italy
	G-ZBAP	Airbus A.320-214	First Star Speir Aviation 1 Ltd (G-OOPT/ G-OOAT)
	G-ZBED	Robinson R22 Beta	M. J. Wearing
	G-ZBEN	IAV Bacau Yakovlev Yak-52	B. A. Nicholson
	G-ZBJA	Boeing 787-8	British Airways PLC
	G-ZBJB	Boeing 787-8	British Airways PLC
	G-ZBJC	Boeing 787-8	British Airways PLC
	G-ZBJD	Boeing 787-8	British Airways PLC
	G-ZBJE	Boeing 787-8	British Airways PLC
	G-ZBJF	Boeing 787-8	British Airways PLC
	G-ZBJG	Boeing 787-8	British Airways PLC
	G-ZBJH	Boeing 787-8	British Airways PLC
	G-ZBJI	Boeing 787-8	British Airways PLC
	G-ZBJJ	Boeing 787-8	British Airways PLC
	G-ZBJK	Boeing 787-8	British Airways PLC
	G-ZBJM	Boeing 787-8	British Airways PLC
	G-ZBKA	Boeing 787-9	British Airways PLC
	G-ZBKB	Boeing 787-9	British Airways PLC
	G-ZBKC	Boeing 787-9	British Airways PLC
	G-ZBKD	Boeing 787-9	British Airways PLC
	G-ZBKE	Boeing 787-9	British Airways PLC
	G-ZBKF	Boeing 787-9	British Airways PLC
	G-ZBKG	Boeing 787-9	British Airways PLC
	G-ZBKH	Boeing 787-9	British Airways PLC
	G-ZBKI	Boeing 787-9	British Airways PLC
	G-ZBKJ	Boeing 787-9	British Airways PLC
	G-ZBKK	Boeing 787-9	British Airways PLC
	G-ZBKL	Boeing 787-9	British Airways PLC
	G-ZBKM	Boeing 787-9	British Airways PLC
	G-ZBKN	Boeing 787-9	British Airways PLC
	G-ZBKO	Boeing 787-9	British Airways PLC
	G-ZBKP	Boeing 787-9	British Airways PLC
	G-ZBKR	Boeing 787-9	British Airways PLC
	G-ZBKS	Boeing 787-9	British Airways PLC
	G-ZBLA	Boeing 787-10	British Airways PLC
	G-ZBLB	Boeing 787-10	British Airways PLC
	G-ZBLC	Boeing 787-10	British Airways PLC
	G-ZBLD	Boeing 787-10	British Airways PLC
	G-ZBLE	Boeing 787-10	British Airways PLC
	G-ZBLF	Boeing 787-10	British Airways PLC
	G-ZBLT	Cessna 182S Skylane	Cessna 182S Group/Ireland
	G-ZBOP	PZL-Bielsko SZD-36A Cobra 15	S. Bruce
	G-ZDEA	Diamond DA.42 Twin Star	DEA Aviation Ltd
	G-ZEBY	PA-28-140 Cherokee	A. McKie (G-BFBF)
	G-ZECH	CZAW Sportcruiser	Sportcruiser UK015
	G-ZEIN	Slingsby T.67M Firefly 260	James A Mutton Consulting Ltd
	G-ZENJ	Learjet 75	Jet Aircraft Ltd
	G-ZENR	Zenair CH.601HD Zodiac	N. G. Bumford (G-BRJB)
	G-ZENY	Zenair CH.601HD Zodiac	T. R. & B. K. Pugh
	G-ZEPI	Colt GA-42 gas airship	P. A. Lindstrand (G-ISPY/G-BPRB)
	G-ZERO	AA-5B Tiger	N. R. Evans & D. K. Rose
	G-ZEUZ	Cessna 525A Citationjet CJ2	Zenith Aviation Ltd (G-MROO/G-EEBJ)
	G-ZEVS	Cessna F.172H	D. M. White
	G-ZEXL	Extra EA.300/L	2 Excel Aviation Ltd
	G-ZEZE	Cessna 182S	S. Bonham (G-LVES/G-ELIE)
	G-ZFOO	Tucano Replica	A. J. Palmer & D. Sayyah
	G-ZFOX	Denney Kitfox Mk.2	S. M. Hall
	G-ZGAB	BRM Aero Bristell NG5 Speed Wing	W. J. Miazek

Reg	Type	Owner or Operator	Notes
G-ZGZG	Cessna 182T	J. Noble	
G-ZGTK	Schleicher ASH-26E	P. M. Wells (G-BWBY)	
G-ZHKF	Escapade 912(2)	C. D. & C. M. Wills	
G-ZHWH	Rotorway Executive 162F	B. Alexander	
G-ZIGI	Robin DR.400/180	Aeroclub du Bassin D'Arcachon/France	
G-ZIGY	Europa XS	K. D. Weston	
G-ZIII	Pitts S-2B	T. R. Dews (G-CDBH)	
G-ZINC	Cessna 182S	M. Mears (G-VALI)	
G-ZINT	Cameron Z-77 balloon	G. Bogliaccino/Italy	
G-ZION	Cessna 177B	J. Tully	
G-ZIPA	Rockwell Commander 114A	R. Robson (G-BHRA)	
G-ZIPI	Robin DR.400/180	A. J. Cooper	
G-ZIPY	Wittman W.8 Tailwind	A. L. Hamer	
G-ZIRA	Z-1RA Stummelflitzer	P. J. Dale	
G-ZIVA	Cirrus SR22T	C. R. Barr	
G-ZIZY	TL2000UK Sting Carbon S4	C. E. & R. P. Reeves	
G-ZLSK	TLAC Sherwood Scout	P. J. Laycock	
G-ZNTH	Learjet 75	Zenith Aircraft Ltd	
G-ZNTJ	Learjet 75	Zenith Aircraft Ltd	
G-ZODY	Zenair CH.601UL Zodiac	Sarum AX2000 Group	
G-ZOFG	PA-28-181 Cherokee Archer II	The Zero Oktas Flying Group	
G-ZOIZ	Ultramagic M-105 balloon	S. Dyer	
G-ZOMB	Ikarus C42 FB100	The Ikarus Flying Group	
G-ZOOB	Tecnam P2008-JC	Century Aviation Ltd	
G-ZOOL	Cessna FA.152	A. S. C. Rathmell-Davey (G-BGXZ)	
G-ZORO	Shaw Europa	N. T. Read	
G-ZOSA	Champion 7GCAA	R. McQueen	
G-ZOZO	Cameron R-77 balloon	Cameron Balloons Ltd	
G-ZPPY	PA-18-95 Super Cub	R. Sims (G-NICK)	
G-ZSDB	PA-28-236 Dakota	Dakota Air Services LLP (G-BPCX)	
G-ZSIX	Schleicher ASW-27-18E	F. J. Davies & K. W. Payne	
G-ZSKD	Cameron Z-90 balloon	M. J. Gunston	
G-ZSKY	Best Off Sky Ranger Swift 912S(1)	J. E. Lipinski	
G-ZTED	Shaw Europa	J. J. Kennedy	
G-ZTOO	Staaken Z-2 Flitzer	E. B. Toulson	
G-ZTUG	Aeropro Eurofox 914	G. Donnelly (G-CICX)	
G-ZTWO	Staaken Z-2 Flitzer	S. J. Randle	
G-ZUFL	Lindstrand LBL-90A balloon	Zuffle Dog Balloon Team (G-CHLL)	
G-ZUMI	Van's RV-8	D. R. Cairns	
G-ZVIP	Beech 200 Super King Air	Centreline AV Ltd (G-SAXN/G-OMNH)	
G-ZVKO	Edge 360	S. & J. Wood	
G-ZXCL	Extra EA.300/L	2 Excel Aviation Ltd	
G-ZXEL	Extra EA.300/L	2 Excel Aviation Ltd	
G-ZXLL	Extra EA.300/L	2 Excel Aviation Ltd	
G-ZZAC	Aerotechnik EV-97 Eurostar	N. R. Beale	
G-ZZAJ	Schleicher ASH-26E	A.T. Johnstone	
G-ZZDD	Schweizer 269C	D. D. Saint (G-OCJK)	
G-ZZDG	Cirrus SR20 G2	B. Lane & N. Deeks	
G-ZZEL	Westland Gazelle AH.1	The Gazelle Squadron Display Team Ltd	
G-ZZIJ	PA-28-180 Cherokee C	M. Meddle (G-AVGK)	
G-ZZLE	Westland Gazelle AH.2 (XX436)	A. Moorhouse, S. Qardan & P. J. Whitaker	
G-ZZMM	Enstrom 480B	Fly 7 Helicopters LLP (G-TOIL)	
G-ZZOE	Eurocopter EC 120B	J. F. H. James	
G-ZZOT	PA-34-220T Seneca V	Cheshire Aircraft Leasing Ltd	
G-ZZOW	Medway Eclipse	M. Belemet	
G-ZZSI	Eurocopter EC.225LP Super Puma	Verical Aviation No.1 Ltd (G-CGES)	
G-ZZXX	P & M Quik GT450	Mid Anglia Microlights Ltd	
G-ZZZA	Boeing 777-236	British Airways	
G-ZZZB	Boeing 777-236	British Airways	
G-ZZZS	Eurocopter EC.120B Colibri	Rosegate Helicopter Services Ltd	

G-ABLS DH.80A Puss Moth *Andrew March*

G-XWBB Airbus A.350-941 of British Airways *Allan S. Wright*

Reg	Type	Owner or Operator	Notes
M-AAAA	Bombardier CL600-2B16 Challenger	Lee Fai International Ltd	
M-AAAL	Gulfstream 650	ALM New Jet Ltd	
M-AAAM	Bombardier CL600-2B16 Challenger	Durstwell Ltd	
M-AABG	Bombardier BD700-1A11 Global 5000	AB Air Holdings	
M-AAMK	Boeing 737-8 BBJ	AMK Aircraft Ltd	
M-AAKV	Embraer EMB-135BJ Legacy	AAK Company Ltd	
M-AAMM	Gulfstream 45	Al-Sahab G450 Ltd	
M-AATD	Bombardier BD700-1A10 Global 6000	STC Jet Ltd	
M-ABCC	Bombardier BD700-1A10 Global 6000	Global Aviation Partners LP Inc	
M-ABEC	Embraer EMB-135BJ Legacy 600	Carys Investment Group Ltd	
M-ABEU	Learjet 45	Aviation Leasing (IOM) Ltd	
M-ABFD	Aerospatiale ATR-72-212A	KP Aero	
M-ABFE	Aerospatiale ATR-72-212A	KP Aero	
M-ABFI	Aerospatiale ATR-72-212A	Plateau Aviation Ltd	
M-ABFQ	Bombardier BD700-1A10 Global 6000	AGT International GmbH	
M-ABFR	Bombardier BD700-1A10 Global 6000	AGT International GmbH	
M-ABGG	Bombardier CL600-2B16 Challenger	Zarox Holdings Ltd	
M-ABGS	Bombardier CL600-2B16 Challenger 605	Viking Travel Services Ltd	
M-ABGV	Learjet 45	Aviation Leasing (IOM) Ltd	
M-ABIY	Airbus A.320-232	CIT Aerospace International	
M-ABJA	Learjet 45	Aviation Leasing (IOM) Ltd	
M-ABKB	Eurocopter EC.225LP Super Puma	Parilease SAS	
M-ABKF	Eurocopter EC.225LP Super Puma	Parilease SAS	
M-ABKG	Eurocopter EC.225LP Super Puma	Parilease SAS	
M-ABKH	Eurocopter EC.225LP Super Puma	Parilease SAS	
M-ABKI	Eurocopter EC.225LP Super Puma	Parilease SAS	
M-ABKR	Embraer ERJ170-200LR	Celestial Aviation Trading 71 Ltd	
M-ABKT	Embraer ERJ170-200LR	Celestial Aviation Trading 71 Ltd	
M-ABLL	Airbus A.330-343	GHY Aviation Lease 1739 Co.Ltd	
M-ABLV	Airbus A.330-302	Aptree Aviation Trading 5 Co.Ltd	
M-ABLW	Airbus A.330-302	Aptree Aviation Trading 5 Co.Ltd	
M-ABMC	ATR-72-212A	Constellation Aircraft Leasing Ltd	
M-ABMD	ATR-72-212A	Constellation Aircraft Leasing Ltd	
M-ABMF	ATR-72-212A	Constellation Aircraft Leasing Ltd	
M-ABMH	ATR-72-212A	Constellation Aircraft Leasing Ltd	
M-ABMK	ATR-72-212A	Ezen Aviation Pty Ltd	
M-ABMM	Boeing 737-8K5	K2 Aircraft Leasing (Holding) Ltd	
M-ABNF	Avro RJ100	Executive Jet Support Ltd	
M-ABNG	Boeing 737-8K5	Wellington Leasing No.8 Ltd	
M-ABNI	Airbus A.320-214	Osprey Aircraft Leasing Ltd (Fifteen)	
M-ABNK	Embraer ERJ190-100LR	CLC Aircraft Leasing (Shanghai) Co.Ltd	
M-ABNP	Airbus A.320-214	Osprey Aircraft Leasing Ltd (Thirteen)	
M-ABOA	Embraer ERJ190-100LR	E190 MSN354LLC	
M-ABOB	Embraer ERJ190-100LR	E190 MSN420LLC	
M-ABST	Bombardier BD700-1A10 Global 6500	Global Aviation Partners LP Inc	
M-ABNV	Embraer ERJ190-100LR	Aero Power Leasing Company Ltd	
M-ACPT	BAe. 125 Srs.1000	Remo Investments Ltd	
M-ACRO	Eurocopter AS.350B3 Ecureuil	F. Allani	
M-AERO	Dassault Falcon 2000LX	Rirox Ltd	
M-AFAC	Bombardier CL600-2B16 Challenger 604	FAI Asset Management GmbH	
M-AFAJ	Dassault Falcon 900EX	Elan Finance Management SA	
M-AGIC	Dassault Falcon 2000EX	Avtorita Holdings Ltd	
M-AGIK	Dassault Falcon 900LX	Amboy Overseas Ltd	
M-AGMA	Bombardier BD700-1A10 Global Express XRS	Sugar Mama Ltd	
M-AGRI	Bombardier BD700-1A11 Global 5000	Blezir Invest Ltd	
M-AHAA	Bombardier BD700-IA10 Global 6000	AH Aviation Ltd	
M-AJOR	Airbus MBB BK117 D-2	Major Aviation LLP	
M-AKAR	Sikorsky S-76C	Starspeed Ltd	
M-AKKA	Dassaulty Falcon 900EX	REmpterwik Special Services Ltd	
M-ALCB	Pilatus PC-24	Sunseeker Aviation Ltd	
M-ALDI	Embraer ERJ190-100ECJ	Aliforti Ltd	
M-ALEN	Embraer EMB-135BJ Legacy	ATT Aviation Ltd	
M-ALFA	Eurocopter MBB BK-117C-2	ALF Air International Ltd	
M-ALLB	Pilatus PC-12/47E	M. S. Bartlett	
M-ALSH	Bombardier BD700-1A10 Global Express	Mirgab Aviation Ltd	
M-ALTI	Bombardier CL600-2B16 Challenger 605	Hartsage International Ltd	
M-ALUN	BAe 125 Srs.700A	Briarwood Products Ltd	
M-AMAN	Pilatus PC-12	Pilatus PC-12 Centre UK Ltd	
M-AMBA	Gulfstream GVII-G600	Hampshire Aviation LLP	
M-AMRM	ATR-72-212A	Fastjet Air Four Ltd	
M-ANAP	Embraer EMB-505 Phenom	Equiom (Isle of Man) Ltd	

Notes	Reg	Type	Owner or Operator
	M-ANGO	Bombardier BD700-1A11 Global 5000	Waylawn Ltd
	M-ARDI	Gulfstream 650	Comet Limited Partnership Inc
	M-AREA	Hawker 900XP	Area Plus JV Ltd
	M-ARGO	Bombardier BD700-1A10 Global 6000	Sun Burst Invest & Finance Inc
	M-ARIA	Gulfstream V-SP	SDQ Aviation IOM Ltd
	M-ARIE	Hawker 800XP	Surf-Air Ltd
	M-ARKZ	Bombardier CL600-2B16 Challenger	Markz Jet Ltd
	M-ARTY	Pilatus PC-12/47E	Creston (UK) Ltd
	M-ARVA	Bombardier BD700-1A10 Global 6000	Newjourney Trading Ltd
	M-ASER	Embraer EMB-505 Phenom 300	Maser Aviation Ltd
	M-ATAK	Gulfstream 650	STC Airliner Ltd
	M-ATEX	Dassault Falcon 8X	Maritime Investment and Shipping Company Ltd
	M-AVIR	Bombardier BD700-1A10 Global 6000	Anjet Co. Ltd
	M-AXIM	CessnaT.206H Turbo Stationair	C. D. B. Cope
	M-AZIA	Cessna 525C CitationJet CJ4	Hunting Star Ltd
	M-BADU	Gulfstream VI	BH2 Aviation Ltd
	M-BAEP	Bombardier CL600-2B16 Challenger	Swift Cloud Aviation Services Ltd
	M-BELL	Pilatus PC-12/47E	B. L. Bell LP Inc
	M-BETS	Rockwell Commander 695A	Aldersey Aviation Ltd
	M-BETY	Dornier Do.328-310	Funfte XR-GmbH
	M-BHBH	Gulfstream 650	Caldana Holding and Invest Ltd
	M-BIGG	Bombardier BD700-1A11 Global 5000	Harley Airlines Ltd
	M-BIRD	Embraer EMB-135BJ Legacy 600	YH Aviation Ltd
	M-BJEP	Gulfstream 550	M-BJEP Ltd
	M-BLUE	Bombardier BD700-1A10 Global 6000	Bluesky Aviation Group Ltd
	M-BONO	Cessna 172N Skyhawk II	J. McCandless
	M-BRAB	Diamond DA.42M Twin Star	Bravura Group of Companies Ltd
	M-BRAC	Diamond DA.42M Twin Star	Bravura Group of Companies Ltd
	M-CAPE	Gulfstream VII-G600	Highland Aviation CY Ltd
	M-CARA	Cessna 525 Citation M2	Anam Cara Aviation
	M-CCCP	Bombardier BD700-1A11 Global 5000	Heda Airlines Ltd
	M-CDBM	Bell B.200GT Super King Air	BAE Systems Ltd
	M-CDJC	Beech B.200GT Super King Air	BAE Systems Marine Ltd
	M-CDMS	Beech B.200GT Super King Air	BAE Systems Marine Ltd
	M-CDOM	Aerospatiale ATR-72-212A	Fastjet Air Four Ltd
	M-CELT	Dassault Falcon 7X	Cravant Ltd
	M-CESC	Cessna 560XL	Cessna Spanish Citation Service Center SL
	M-CESD	Cessna 560XL	Cessna Spanish Citation Service Center SL
	M-CHEM	Gulfstream V-SP	Hampshire Aviation LLP
	M-CICO	Dassault Falcon 50	BZ Air Ltd
	M-CITI	Bomvbardier BD700-1A11 Global 5000	Global 9683 Ltd
	M-CKAY	Learjet 40	Danish Aircraft Management APS
	M-CKSB	Dassault Falcon 2000	John Mason Aircraft Management Services
	M-CLAB	Bombardier BD100-1A10 Challenger 300	Shamrock Trading Ltd
	M-CLHL	Bombardier CL600-2B16 Challenger 650	H. C. Luffy Inc
	M-CNZI	Bombardier BD700-1A10 Global 6000	Lavenda Services Inc
	M-COOL	Cessna 510 Citation Mustang	E. Keats
	M-CPAY	Dassault Falcon 900LX	Puru Aviation Ltd
	M-CRAO	Beech B.300 Super King Air 350	Dr. A. Oetker
	M-CRDL	Gulfstream 450	Samika Ltd
	M-CSMS	Learjet 45	SMS Aviation Service SA
	M-CVGL	Bombardier BD700-1A11 Global 5000	Aircraft Operations Ltd
	M-DADA	Bombardier BD700-1A10 Global 6000	STC Aviation Services Ltd
	M-DATA	Cessna 525 Citationjet	Myworld Aero Ltd
	M-DAWN	Beech B200GT King Air	Dawn Meats Group UC
	M-DEND	Bombardier BD100-1A10 Challenger 300	Campino Ltd
	M-DKVL	Gulfstream 450	Fiordani Holding Ltd
	M-DLBA	Airbus EC.155 B1	Airborne Marine Ltd
	M-DMBP	Learjet 40	VEN Air
	M-DMUC	Gulfstream GVII-G500	C-Airop Ltd
	M-DODO	Embraer EMB-545 Legacy 450	Navajo
	M-DRIL	Pilatus PC-12/47E	Pilatus Centre (BIS) Ltd
	M-DSKY	SOCATA TBM.930	Sterna Aviation Ltd
	M-DSML	BAe.125-800B	St. Francis Group (Aviation) Ltd
	M-DSTZ	Bombardiewer CL600-2B16 Challenger 650	Cameron Industries Consult Inc
	M-DSUN	Bombardier BD700-1A10 Global 6000	Splendiferous Global Ltd
	M-DUBS	Dassault Falcon 900EX	Six Daughters Ltd
	M-DWWW	Bombardier CL600-2B19 Challenger	Dragon Asset Global Investment Group Ltd
	M-EAGL	Dassault Falcon 900EX	Faycroft Finance
	M-EBOY	Embraer EMB-135BJ Legacy 650	Transeurope Air Ltd
	M-ECJI	Dassault Falcon 10	Fleet International Aviation and Finance Ltd

Reg	Type	Owner or Operator	Notes
M-EDIA	Dassault Falcon 7X	M-EDIA Aviation Ltd	
M-EGGA	Beech B200 Super King Air	Langley Aviation Ltd	
M-EKSL	Airbus A.330-243F	DHL Air Ltd	
M-ELAS	Gulfstream 280	Aventurine Aviation Ltd	
M-ELON	Embraer EMB-505 Phenom 300	Sleepwell Aviation Ltd	
M-ENTA	Dassault Falcon 200	Riviera Invest und Services SA	
M-ETAL	Piaggio P.180 Avanti	GFG Aviation Ltd	
M-EVAN	Bombardier BD100-1A10 Challenger 300	Marcus Evans (Aviation) Ltd	
M-EXPL	Eurocopter AS.355N Ecureuil 2	Select Plant Hire Co.Ltd	
M-FALZ	Dassault Falcon 7X	Pacelli Beteiligungs GmbH & Company KG	
M-FAST	IAI Gulfstream 150	G-150 Aeronautics Ltd	
M-FINE	Bombardier BD700-1A11 Global 5000	Noristevo Investments Ltd	
M-FLCN	Dassault Falcon 2000EX	Omega Aviation Ltd	
M-FLIG	Bombardier BD700-1A11 Global 5000	Faraotis Holdings Ltd	
M-FLYI	Cessna 525 Citationjet CJ4	Avtrade Ltd	
M-FROG	Beech 390 Premier 1	White and Cope Aviation LLP	
M-FRZN	Bombardier CL600-2B16 Challenger	Iceland Foods Ltd	
M-FTHD	Dassault Falcon 2000EX	Eagle Reach Group Ltd	
M-FUAD	Gulfstream VI	Future Aviation (IOM) Ltd	
M-GACB	Dassault Falcon 10	Valiant Aviation Ltd	
M-GAGA	Gulfstream 650ER	Advance Global Development Ltd	
M-GCAP	Piaggio P.180 Avanti	Greensill Capital (IOM) Ltd	
M-GDRS	Hawker 850XP	Surf-Air Ltd	
M-GETS	Pilatus PC-12/47E	3FS Aviation Ltd	
M-GFGC	Piaggio P.180 Avanti	Greensill Capital (IOM) Ltd	
M-GGAL	Dassault Falcon 7X	Charter Air Ltd	
M-GMKM	Dassault Falcon 7X	MKAir7X Pty Ltd	
M-GSIR	Dassault Falcon 900DX	Sublime Holdings Ltd	
M-GSKY	Bombardier BD700-1A10 Global Express	Jerand Holdings Ltd	
M-GZOO	IAI Gulfstram 200	Multiflight Charter Services LLP	
M-HAWK	Bombardier BD700-1A10 Global 6000	Genetechma Finance Ltd	
M-HEAD	Bombardier CL600-2B16 Challenger 650	Step Six International Ltd	
M-HELI	Eurocopter EC.155-B1	Flambards Ltd	
M-HERI	Gulfstream V-SP	Heri Aviation Ltd	
M-HOME	Bombardier BD700-1A10 Global 6000	Symphony Master (IOM) Ltd	
M-HSCZ	Gulfstream 650ER	Shine Wealth Consultants Ltd	
M-IABU	Airbus A.340-313	Klaret Aviation Ltd	
M-IAMI	Falcon 7X	Delane Finance Ltd	
M-IBAD	ATR-72-212A	INV Jet Leasing Ltd	
M-IBAM	ATR-72-212A	Injet Leasing Company Ltd	
M-IBAN	ATR-72-212A	Injet Leasing Company Ltd	
M-IBAO	ATR-72-212A	Injet Leasing Company Ltd	
M-IBAP	ATR-72-212A	Injet Leasing Company Ltd	
M-IBAQ	ATR-72-212A	Injet Leasing Company Ltd	
M-IBAR	ATR-72-212A	Injet Leasing Company Ltd	
M-ICRO	Cessna 525C Citationjet CJ4	Pektron Group Ltd	
M-IFFY	Cessna 510 Citation Mustang	Xead Aviation Ltd	
M-IGHT	Learjet 60	High Wing Aviation Ltd	
M-IGWT	Bombardier BD700-1A10	Business Encore (IOM) Ltd	
M-IKEY	Airbus Helicopters AS.365N3	Whirligig Ltd	
M-ILAN	Embraer EMB-135BJ Legacy 650	Artjet Ltd	
M-ILLA	Beech 400XP	Sunshine Aviation Ltd	
M-ILTA	Dassault Falcon 900LX	Delta Technical Services Ltd	
M-INES	Agusta AW109SP Grand New	GFG 109 Ltd	
M-INNI	Learjet 60	M-INNI Aviation Ltd	
M-INOR	Bell 429	Major Aviation LLP	
M-INSK	GulfstreamVI	Skyfort Aviation Ltd	
M-INTY	IAI Gulfstream 280	Hampshire Aviation LLP	
M-IPHS	Gulfstream 550	Islands Aviation Ltd	
M-IRAS	Bombardier BD700-1A10 Global 6000	STC Jet Ltd	
M-IRTH	Pilatus PC-12/47E	Wingmen Ltd	
M-ISRA	Agusta A109E Power	Perfectway Services Ltd	
M-ISTY	IAI Gulfstream 280	Hampshire Aviation LLP	
M-JACK	Beech B200GT King Air	Jetstream Aviation Ltd	
M-JCBA	Sikorsky S-76C	J C Bamford Excavators Ltd	
M-JCBB	Gulfstream 650	J C Bamford Excavators Ltd	
M-JCBC	Sikorsky S-76C	J C Bamford Excavators Ltd	
M-JCCA	Embraer EMB-135BJ Legacy	Jeju China Castle Ltd	
M-JETT	Dassault Falcon 200	Piraeus Leasing Chrimatodotikes Mishoseis SA	
M-JETZ	Dassault Falcon 2000EX	Avtorita Holdings Ltd	
M-JGVJ	Bombardier BD700-1A11	Aquatics Ventures Holdings Ltd	

ISLE OF MAN REGISTER

Notes	Reg	Type	Owner or Operator
	M-JIMI	Bombardier CL600-2B19 Challenger 850	LSFL Cayman Company Ltd
	M-JJTL	Pilatus PC-12/47E	L. Uggia, J. P. Huth & K. Giannamore
	M-JNJL	Bombardier BD700-1A11 Global Express	Global Thirteen Worldwide Resources Ltd
	M-JPEB	Learjet 75	ADD SARL
	M-JSMN	Bombardier BD700-1A11 Global 5000	Jasmin Aviation Ltd
	M-JSTA	Bombardier CL600-2B16 Challenger	Jetsteff Aviation Ltd
	M-JSTR	Bombardier BD700-1A11 Global 5000	Jetsteff Aviation Ltd
	M-JSWB	Gulfstram 650	Treasure Depot Ltd
	M-KATE	Airbus A.319-133	Sophar Property Holding
	M-KBSD	Bombardier BD700-1A11 Global 5000	Faraotis Holdings Ltd
	M-KELI	Embraer EMB-505 Phenom 300	Kelly Airways Ltd
	M-KELY	Embraer EMB-500 Phenom 100	Kelly Air Ltd
	M-KNOX	Cessna 525C Citationjet CJ4	Cabbane Ltd
	M-KSSN	Gulfstream 650	NS Aviation Ltd
	M-LANG	Dassault Falcon 900LX	Longest Day International Ltd
	M-LCFC	Boeing 737-7EI	Ceilo Del Rey Co.Ltd
	M-LDME	ATR-72-212A	Elix Assets 7 Ltd
	M-LEKT	Robin DR.400/180	T. D. Allan, P. & J. P. Bromley
	M-LENR	Beech B.200GT Super King Air	BAE Systems Marine Ltd
	M-LEOG	Leonardo AW109SP Grand New	Leo Aviation Ltd
	M-LILY	Airbus A.318-112	Lili Jet (Cayman) Ltd
	M-LION	Hawker 900XP	Lion Invest and Trade Ltd
	M-LLIN	Bombardier BD700-1A10 Global 6000	Tian Yi Ltd
	M-LLMW	Beech Super King Air 300	Trosa Ltd
	M-LOOK	Bombardier CL600-2B16 Challenger	Kennington Ltd
	M-LUNA	Eurocopter MBB BK-117C-2	Flambards Ltd
	M-LVIA	Eurocopter AS.365N3 Dauphin 2	Flambards Ltd
	M-LWCW	Bombardier BD700-2A12 Global 7500	Eircraft Ltd
	M-LWSA	Bombardier BD700-1A10 Global Express	Lynx Aviation (Isle of Man) Ltd
	M-LWSG	Bombardier BD700-1A10 Global 6000	Lynx Aircraft Ltd
	M-MAEE	Gulfstream 450	Royston Sky Holdings Ltd
	M-MANX	Cessna 425 Conquest	Suas Investments Ltd
	M-MAVP	Bombardier BD700-1A10 Global 6000	Sentonian Investments Ltd
	M-MAXX	Bombardier BD700-1A10 Global 6000	Max Smart Development Ltd
	M-MDBD	Bombardier BD700-1A10 Global Express	Cozuro Holdings Ltd
	M-MEVA	Cessna 560 Citation Ultra	AVEM'R
	M-MIKE	Cessna 525C Citationjet CJ4	Aviation by Westminster Ltd
	M-MBLY	Bombardier BD700-1A10 Global 6000	Asaj Holdings LLC
	M-MOON	Cessna 750	Bambara Holding SA
	M-OUNT	Dassault Falcon 8X	Abelia Ltd
	M-MRBB	Learjet 45	Boultbee Aviation 3 LLP
	M-MSVI	Cessna 525B Citationjet CJ3	JPM Ltd
	M-MTOO	Bombardier BD100-1A10 Challenger 300	Nadremal Air Holding Ltd
	M-MYNA	Bombardier BD700-1A10 Global 6000	Tibit Ltd
	M-NAME	Bombardier BD700-1A10 Global 6000	Blezir Aircraft Leasing (IOM) Ltd
	M-NELS	Gulfstream 450	Citylink Partners Ltd
	M-NGNG	Gulfstream 650	Infinity Sky Ltd
	M-NGSN	Pilatus PC-12/47E	N. Stolt-Nielson
	M-NICE	Gulfstream 200	M-NICE Ltd
	M-NLYY	PA-42-1000 Cheyenne 400LS	Factory Leasing Ltd
	M-NNNN	Gulfstream 650	Matrix Aviation 650 Ltd
	M-NREN	Embraer EMB-505 Phenom 300	Cross Aviation Ltd
	M-NTOS	Cessna 525B Citationjet CJ4	Selementos Ltd
	M-OBIL	Cessna 525C Citationjet C14	Popken Fashion Services GmbH
	M-OCNY	Bombardier BD100-1A10 Challenger 350	RH-Flugdienst GmbH & Co KG
	M-OCOM	Bombardier CL600-2B16 Challenger 604	Focus Holdings Ltd
	M-ODEL	Gulfstream 450	Hampshire Aviation LLP
	M-ODKZ	Dassault Falcon 900EX	Skylane LP
	M-OEPL	Dassault Falcon 8X	Cloud Services Ltd
	M-OGUL	Agusta A109S Grand	Medway Leasing Ltd
	M-OIWA	Bombardier BD100-1A10 Challenger	Delta A/S
	m-ojom	Gulfstream V-SP	CMP Leasing Ltd
	M-OLEG	Embraer 135BJ Legacy	Hermitage Air Ltd
	M-OLJM	Agusta Westland AW.139	Boutique Aviation Ltd
	M-OLLY	Cessna 525 Citationjet CJ1	MBK Maschinenbau GmbH/Bohnet GmbH
	M-OLOT	Bombardier CL600-2B16 Challenger	Kellie Aviation Ltd
	M-OLTT	Pilatus PC-12/47E	One Luxury Travel LLP
	M-OMAN	Dassault Falcon 7X	RUWI Ltd
	M-ONDE	Eurocopter MBB BK.117C2	Peyton Ltd
	M-ONEM	Gulfstream 550	G550 Ltd
	M-ONEY	Bombardier BD700-1A10 Global Express XRS	Apollo Impact Ltd

Reg	Type	Owner or Operator	Notes
M-ONTE	Piaggio P.180 Avanti II	Scotia Aviation Ltd	
M-ONTY	Sikorsky S-76C	Trustair Ltd	
M-OONL	Bombardier BD700-1A10 Global Express XRS	Parker Holdings Ltd	
M-OPHS	Gulfstream 550	Islands Aviation Ltd	
M-ORAD	Dassault Falcon 7X	Swift New Jet Ltd	
M-ORIS	Embraer EMB-550 Legacy 500	Legacy 500 Ltd	
M-ORZE	Eurocopter EC135 P2+	G650 Management Ltd	
M-OTOR	Beech B200GT Super King Air	Pektron Group Ltd	
M-OUNT	Dassault Falcon 8X	Abelia Ltd	
M-OUSE	Cessna 510 Citation Mustang	Mouse (IOM) Ltd	
M-OVIE	Gulfstream 650	Hampshire Aviation LLP	
M-OWLS	Agusta A109S Grand	Memory Recall (Aviation) Ltd	
M-PACF	Eurocopter EC135 P2+	Starspeed Ltd	
M-PAPA	Airbus EC130 T2	Papa Fly Ltd	
M-PCPC	Pilatus PC-12/45	Treetops Aviation LLP	
M-PDCS	Dassault Falcon 2000EX	Six Daughters Ltd	
M-PECL	Bombardier BD700-1A10 Global 6000	Pacific Energy Company Ltd	
M-PHML	American General AG-5B Tiger	I. J. Ross & J. R. Shannon	
M-PORT	Bombardier BD700-1A11 Global 5000	Sirom Aviation Ltd	
M-POWR	Beech C.90A King Air	Northside Aviation Ltd	
M-PTGG	Dassault Falcon 8X	Prime Galaxy International Ltd	
M-PURE	Airbus MBB BK117 D-2	Nelida Ltd	
M-PVGK	Airbus A.330-343	DHL Air Ltd	
M-PZPZ	Gulfstream IV	A. I. Eze	
M-RBIG	Learjet 45	Volantair LP Inc	
M-RBUS	Airbus A.319-115CJ	Belville Investment Ltd	
M-REEE	Dassault Falcon 7X	B. C. Ecclestone	
M-REEM	AS.355NP Ecureuil 2	Kingdom 5-KR-267 Ltd	
M-RFAP	Dassault Falcon 7X	PPAR Enterprises Ltd	
M-RISE	Boeing 757-23N	Talos Aviation Ltd	
M-RKAY	Raytheon 390 Premier 1A	Sunseeker Corporate Aviation Ltd	
M-RLIV	Bombardier CL600-2B16 Challenger	Mobyhold Ltd	
M-ROCA	Bombardier CL600-2B16 Challenger 605	Alpfa Aeria LP Inc	
M-RONE	Dassault Falcon 2000EX	Ocean Sky Aircraft Management Ltd	
M-RRRR	Bombardier BD700-1A11 Global 6000	Prestige Investments Ltd	
M-RTFS	Dassault Falcon 7X	CIM Corporate Services Ltd	
M-RZDC	Gulfstream 550	KRP Aviation Ltd	
M-SAIL	Pilatus PC-12/47E	G. G. & L. G. Gordon	
M-SAJJ	Gulfstream V-SP	Horizon Aviation Ltd	
M-SALT	Bell 429	Ridler Verwaltungs-Und Vermittlungs GmbH	
M-SAPD	Bombardier BD700-1A10 Global 6000	Sapetro Aviation (BVI) Ltd	
M-SAPT	Bombardier BD700-1A11 Global 5000	Sapetro Aviation Ltd	
M-SASS	IAI Gulfstream 200	Falcon Crest Resources Inc	
M-SAXY	Pilatus PC12/45	Saxon Logistics Ltd	
M-SCMG	Dassault Falcon 7X	BlueSky International Management Ltd	
M-SCOT	Dassault 7X	Arirang Aviation IOM Ltd	
M-SETT	Bombardier BD700-1A11 Global 5000	Lodging 2020 LP Inc	
M-SEVN	Bombardier CL600-2B16 Challenger	Persimmon Trading Ltd	
M-SEXY	Embraer EMB-135BJ Legacy 650	Gerfaut Capital Ltd	
M-SFAM	McDonnell Douglas MD-87	Montavachi Ltd	
M-SFOZ	Dassault Falcon 2000	Alaman for Jets Ltd	
M-SGCR	Cessna 550 Citation Bravo	Labraid Ltd	
M-SHRM	AgustaWestland AW139	Frozendale Ltd	
M-SIYU	Bombardier BD700-1A1A Global Express	Cutlass Ltd	
M-SKAL	Airbus A.330-343	DHL Air Ltd	
M-SKSM	Bombardier BD700-1A11 Global	Tesker Management Ltd	
M-SNER	Dassault Falcon 2000EX	Wincor Aviation Establishment	
M-SOBM	Gulfstream 450	Sobha Aviation Ltd	
M-SOBR	Gulfstream 450	Sobha & BR Aviation Ltd	
M-SOLA	Airbus MBB BK117 D-2	Clear Skies Flights Ltd	
M-SOLO	Airbus MBB BK117 D-2	Clear Skies Flights Ltd	
M-SOZO	Gulfstream VI	Greenshill Capital II (IoM) LTD	
M-SPBM	Bombardier CL600-2B16 Challenger 605	G200 Ltd	
M-SPEC	Beech B300 Super King Air	Specsavers Corporate Aircraft Leasing Ltd	
M-SPEK	Beech B300 Super King Air	Specsavers Corporate Aircraft Leasing Ltd	
M-SPOR	Beech B200 King Air	Select Plant Hire Co.Ltd	
M-SQAR	Gulfstream V-SP	M Square Aviation Ltd	
M-SSYS	Cessna 525C CitationJet CJ4	Fimway Asset Holdings Ltd	
M-STAR	Boeing 727-2X8	Starling Aviation Ltd	
M-STRY	Avro RJ70	B. C. Ecclestone	
M-SUNY	Dassault Falcon 7X	Harmony Flight International Ltd	

Notes	Reg	Type	Owner or Operator
	M-SURE	Dassault Falcon 7X	Arirang Aviation IOM Ltd
	M-SVGN	Cessna 680 Citation Sovereign	Vocalion Ltd
	M-SZSZ	Gulfstream IV	HDL Smart Technology Ltd
	M-TBEA	Cessna 525A Citationjet CJ2	Bealaw (Man) 8 Ltd
	M-TBUC	Dassault Falcon 200LX	Blackthorn Aviation Ltd
	M-TELE	Gulfstream 400	Arena Aviation Ltd
	M-TFFS	Dassault Falcon 900LX	Astira Holdings Ltd
	M-THOR	Gulfstream V	Argus Bahamas Ltd
	M-TINK	Dassault Falcon 8X	Velut Ltd
	M-TOPI	Bombardier CL600-2B16 Challenger	Gladiator Flight Ltd
	M-TRBS	Bombardier CL600-2B16 Challenger	Arrow Management Property Corp
	M-TSRI	Beech C.90GTI King Air	Timpson Ltd
	M-UGIC	Gulfstream 550	Cityville Capital Ltd
	M-ULTI	Bombardier BD700-1A10 Global Express XRS	Multibird Overseas Ltd
	M-UNIS	Bombardier BD700-1A10 Global Express	Lapwing Ltd
	M-URRY	Hawker 800XP	Corporate Sealandair Ltd
	M-URUS	Boeing 737-7GC	Ingram Services Ltd
	M-USBA	Gulfstream V	Shukra Ltd
	M-USIC	Gulfstream 550	Hampshire Aviation Ltd
	M-USIK	Gulfstream 650	OS Aviation Ltd
	M-USTG	Cessna 510 Citation Mustang	OSM Aviation Ltd
	M-VITB	Gulfstream 650	Matrix Aviation 650 III Ltd
	M-VLCC	Cessna 525A Citationjet CJ2	Shiphold Management Services Ltd
	M-VNES	Hawker 800XP	Vivines Ltd
	M-VRNY	Gulfstream 550	Mirtos Ltd
	M-WANG	Dassault Falcon 7X	Keystone International Co.Ltd
	M-WHAT	Eurocopter EC.135T2+	Starspeed Ltd
	M-WIND	Gulfstream 650	Nursam Invest SA
	M-WINT	Pilatus PC-12/43E	Air Winton Ltd
	M-WONE	Gulfstream IV-X	RYT Aviation LP Inc
	M-XHEC	Eurocopter EC155B	Flambards Ltd
	M-YAIC	Embraer EMB-505 Phenom 300	AIC Spolka Akcyjna
	M-YANG	Gulfstream 450	DJM Holding Ltd
	M-YBBJ	Boeing 737-7HE BBJ	Hamilton Jets Ltd
	M-YBLS	Pilatus PC-12/45	B. L. Schroder
	M-YBUS	Airbus A.320-214ACJ	STC Flight Ltd
	M-YFLY	Pilatus PC-12/47E	Fly High Ltd
	M-YGIG	Gulfstream 650	AC Executive Aircraft (2017) Ltd
	M-YGJL	Bombardier BD700-1A10 Global Express	Ansakl Aviation Two Ltd
	M-YGLF	Gulfstream 650	Quantum Air Ltd
	M-YIGO	Raytheon Hawker 850XP	NNG Aviation Ltd
	M-YJET	Dassault Falcon 7	M-EDIA Aviation Ltd
	M-YKBO	Embraer EMB-135BJ Legacy	Transeurope Air Establishment
	M-YMCM	Bell 429	T. J. Morris Ltd
	M-YNNS	Gulfstream VI	Aviation One Ltd
	M-YOIL	Bombardier BD700-1A10 Global 6000	Shelf Support Shiphold Ltd
	M-YRGL	Aerospatiale ATR-72-212A	Turbo 72-500 Leasing Ltd
	M-YSPC	Cessna 525 Citationjet	M-YSPC Ltd
	M-YSSF	Bombardier BD700-1A10 Global 6000	Springtime Ltd
	M-YTAF	Beech B.36TC Bonanza	FBS Aviation Ltd
	M-YULI	Airbus A.319-115CJ	Fourstars Trading Ltd
	M-YWAY	Gulfstream IV	Blue Sky Leasing Ltd
	M-ZELL	Cessna 208 Caravan	Ridler Verwaltungs und Vermittlungs GmbH
	M-ZJBT	Dassault Falcon 7X	Thrive Star Leasing Ltd
	M-ZLAM	Dassault Falcon 2000	District One Ltd
	M-ZMDZ	Bombardier BD700-1A10 Global Express XRS	Zhong Jia Global Ltd

M-ABJA Learjet 45 *Allan S. Wright*

Reg	Type	Owner or Operator	Notes
2-ACED	Boeing 747-4EVERF	Ace Aviation III Ltd	
2-ACSD	Airbus A.320-232	ACS Aero 2 Omega Ltd	
2-ACSE	Airbus A.319-112	ACS Aero 2 Omega Ltd	
2-ACSF	Airbus A.319-112	ACS Aero 2 Omega Ltd	
2-ACSG	Airbus A.319-112	ACS Aero 2 Omega Ltd	
2-ACSH	Airbus A.319-112	ACS Aero 2 Omega Ltd	
2-ACSJ	Airbus A.320-214	ACS Aero 2 Alpha Ltd	
2-ACSL	Airbus A.319-111	ACS Aero 1 Alpha Ltd	
2-ACSM	Boeing 737-76N	ACS Aero 1 Alpha Ltd	
2-ACSN	Airbus A.320-214	ACS Aero 1 Beta Ltd	
2-AERK	Boeing 737-83N	International Lease Finance Corporation	
2-AERL	Boeing 737-8Q8	Wilmington Trust SP Services (Dublin) Ltd	
2-AERM	Boeing 737-86J	Eden Irish Aircraft Leasing MSN 30876 Ltd	
2-AERN	Boeing 737-81M	AerCap Ireland Capital Ltd	
2-AERO	Embraer EMB-135LR	Aero Technologies Inc	
2-AERP	Boeing 737-81M	Dara Aviation Bravo Ltd	
2-AKOP	Commander 114B	M. A. Perry	
2-ALOU	Sud Aviation 3130 Alouette II	S. Atherton	
2-AMGL	Airbus A.330-203	Viking Leasing 882 DAC	
2-ANBA	Airbus A.320-214	Zephyrus Capital Aviation Partners 1C Ltd	
2-ANLD	PA-34-220T Seneca V	D. & L. Medcraft	
2-AOBG	Boeing 737-8FZ	Horizon II Aviation 2 Ltd	
2-AODZ	Airbus A.330-343	QIC Europe Ltd	
2-ATLN	ATR-42-500	Elix Asset 5 Ltd	
2-ATRB	ATR-72-212A	NAC Aviation 29 DAC	
2-ATRF	ATR-72-212A	NAC Aviation 29 DAC	
2-ATRN	ATR-72-212A	NAC Aviation 8 Ltd	
2-AUER	Cirrus Vision SF-50	Euro Aircraft Leasing Ltd	
2-AVCO	Canadair CRJ200	Avionco Ltd	
2-AVLA	Boeing 737-790	Sapphire Leasing I (AOE 1) Ltd	
2-AVLB	Boeing 737-790	CIT Aerospace International	
2-AVLD	Airbus A.320-214	Avolon Aerospace (Ireland) AOE 45 Ltd	
2-AVOM	Airbus A.320-233	Amentum Aircraft Leasing No.Fifteen Ltd	
2-AVRA	Airbus A.340-311	Avro Global Ltd	
2-AVRB	Airbus A.340-313	Avro Global Ltd	
2-AVRC	Airbus A.340-313	Avro Global Ltd	
2-AVRD	Airbus A.340-313	Avro Global Ltd	
2-AWBN	PA-30-160 Twin Comanche	Bravo November Ltd	
2-AZFR	Cessna 401B	R. E. H. Wragg	
2-BBRV	Boeing 737-8GJ	ECAF I 34899 DAC	
2-BELL	Bell 505vJet Ranger X	Mistral Bus and Coach PLC	
2-BEST	Commander 114B	D. W. R. Best	
2-BHXG	Airbus A.340-313	Aerfin Ltd	
2-BOYS	Commander 114B	I. Barker	
2-BREM	MBB Bolkow BO.105 DBS-5	Wessex Aviation Ltd	
2-BTTA	Boeing 737-85R	Fly Aircraft Holdings Seventeen Ltd	
2-BTTB	Boeing 737-85R	Fly Aircraft Holdings Eighteen Ltd	
2-BVSD	Sud Aviation SE.3130 Alouette II	private	
2-CATS	Agusta A.109E Power	My Heli Ltd	
2-CAUL	DHC.8-402 Dash Eight	Aero Century Corp	
2-CCEA	Boeing 757-223	Loftleidir-Icelandic ehf	
2-CCLF	Airbus A.319-112	Wells Fargo Trust Company National Association	
2-CFFX	Canadair CRJ200ER	Regional One Inc	
2-CFFZ	Canadair CRJ200ER	Regional One Inc	
2-CHEZ	PA-28-161 Warrior II	Fletcher Aviation Ltd	
2-CHIU	Gulfstream 300	Business Aviation Services Guernsey Ltd	
2-CIAS	BN-2B-26 Islander	Channel Island Air Search	
2-CINE	Aerospatiale AS.355N Ecureuil 2	Pursuit Aviation UK Ltd	
2-CJIM	Airbus A.330-203	Viking Leasing 901 DAC	
2-CLES	Bombardier CL600-2B16 Challenger 604	C & L Engine Solutions LLC	
2-CLEV	Cessna 525A Citationjet CJ2	Clevewood Aviation Ltd	
2-CLRK	Eclipse 500	Aeris Aviation Ltd	
2-COOK	PA-46-500TP Malibu Meridian	William Cook Aviation	
2-CRGD	PA-34-220T Seneca V	private	
2-CSKL	Airbus A.321-231	ZAL Aviation 1670 Ltd	
2-CYAS	Embraer ERJ190-200IGW	Aldus Portfolio T Ltd	
2-CYFR	Cirrus SR22T	2608AD Ltd	
2-DARE	Pilatus PC-12/47E	Brightling Services Ltd	
2-DBRV	Cirrus Vision SF50	Ferimare Ltd	
2-DCBU	ATR-72-212A	Elix Assets 14 Ltd	

Notes	Reg	Type	Owner or Operator
	2-DEAL	PA-32-301XTC 6XT	private
	2-DEER	Boeing 787-8(BBJ)	Ocean Transportation Facility Investment Ltd
	2-DEWS	Eclipse EA.500	TAK Aviation LLC
	2-DITO	PA-46-500TP Malibu Meridian	Citavia BV
	2-DLOO	Tecnam P2006T MMA	White Arrow Associates Ltd
	2-DOGZ	Diamond DA.62	2DOGZ LLP
	2-DOLS	PA-28-236 Dakota	private
	2-DRDR	Cirrus Vision SF50	private
	2-EALB	Airbus A.340-642	European Aviation Ltd
	2-EALD	Airbus A.340-641	European Aviation Ltd
	2-AELF	Airbus A.340-642	European Aviation Ltd
	2-EALG	Airbus A.340-641	European Aviation Ltd
	2-EALH	Airbus A.340-541	European Aviation Ltd
	2-EALI	Airbus A.340-541	European Aviation Ltd
	2-EALK	Airbus A.340-642	European Skybus Ltd
	2-EGJB	Cirrus SR22	private
	2-ELGE	Bombardier DHC-8-402 Dash Eight	EIC Aircraft Leasing Ltd
	2-ELLY	Cessna T.206H Turbo Stationair	private
	2-EMBR	Embraer EMB-505 Phenom 300	X'Air Ltd
	2-EPIC	Gulfstream 650ER	Business Aviation Services Guernsey Ltd
	2-ESKA	Boeing 737-301	European Aviation Ltd
	2-FALA	Embraer ERJ170-100LR	Rapide Aircraft Leasing 1 Ltd
	2-FALB	Embraer ERJ170-100LR	Rapide Aircraft Leasing 1 Ltd
	2-FALC	Embraer ERJ170-100LR	Rapide Jet Leasing 1 DAC
	2-FALD	Embraer ERJ170-100LR	Rapide Jet Leasing 1 DAC
	2-FAST	Piaggio P.180 Avanti II	Skypark (UK) Ltd
	2-FEEL	Cirrus Vision SF50	Brachert Aviation GbR
	2-FFLY	Cirrus SR22T	private
	2-FIFI	Beech B.200GT King Air	TWOFIFI Ltd
	2-FINA	Embraer ERJ170-200	AerFin Ltd
	2-FINB	Embraer ERJ170-100LR	AerFin Ltd
	2-FINC	Embraer ERJ170-100LR	AerFin Ltd
	2-FIND	Embraer ERJ170-100LR	AerFin Ltd
	2-FINE	Embraer ERJ170-100LR	AerFin Ltd
	2-FLUX	PA-32R-301T Saratoga II TC	Fluxitech Consulting
	2-FLYT	Pilatus PC-12/47	Anatino Aviation Ltd
	2-FOHS	Airbus A.330-202	GA Telesis LLC
	2-FPLF	Beech B.350 Super King Air	Miralty Holdings Ltd
	2-FUNN	PA-32R-301T Saratoga II TC	Gamit Ltd
	2-GAFO	Agusta A.109A II	GFO Capital Ltd
	2-GAZL	Westland SA.341G Gazelle 1	The Gazelle Squadron Display Team Ltd
	2-GECC	Sikorsky S-76C	Wilmington Trust SP Services (Dublin) Ltd
	2-GECE	Bell 412EP	Vertical Aviation 1 Ltd
	2-GGGT	Cessna 560 Citation Encore	Wells Fargo Bank Northwest
	2-GIAR	Bombardier CL600-2B19 CRJ200ER	Sky Swallows Capital Ltd
	2-GIGI	Agusta A.109E Power	private
	2-GNSY	Cammander Aircraft Commander 114B	J. Tostevin
	2-GODS	Cirrus SR22T	Jetworx Ltd
	2-GOLD	PA-28-235 Cherokee F	private
	2-GOOD	PA-32-301T Saratoga II TC	S. R. Miller
	2-GPIB	ATR-212A	GPFC Ireland Ltd
	2-GSYJ	Diamond DA.42 Twin Star	Crosby Aviation (Jersey) Ltd
	2-GULF	Gulfstream IVSP	Travcorp Transportation Ltd
	2-HAWK	SA.318C Alouette Astazou	private
	2-HELO	Agusta A109C	Helicopter (Seychelles) Ltd
	2-HEVE	McD Douglas MD-87	Jet Express Holdings Ltd
	2-HHLL	Airbus A.330-343	AC Finance MSN1779 Ltd
	2-HJCH	Fokker 70	Airline Fleet Support BV
	2-HLLV	Boeing 737-8F2	ECAF I 34406 DAC
	2-HOPL	Avions Transport ATR-72-212A	SAFE Capital 2015-1 LLC
	2-HOPY	Avions Transport ATR-72-212A	SAFE Capital 2015-1 LLC
	2-HVUR	Boeing 737-8FE	Shenton Aircraft Leasing 2 (Ireland) Ltd
	2-HXFJ	Airbus A.330-243	CBA A330 1561 Pty Ltd
	2-HXHU	Airbus A.320-232	CBA A320 6749 Pty Ltd
	2-HZPN	Embraer ERJ190-100 IGW	Ravelin Jet Leasing 3 Designated Activity Company
	2-HZPO	Embraer ERJ190-100 IGW	Ravelin Jet Leasing 3 Designated Activity Company
	2-HZPQ	Embraer ERJ190-100 IGW	Ravelin Jet Leasing 3 Designated Activity Company

Reg	Type	Owner or Operator	Notes
2-HZPR	Embraer ERJ190-100 IGW	Ravelin Jet Leasing 3 Designated Activity Company	
2-ITLG	Boeing 737-8K5	ILFC Ireland Ltd	
2-ITLH	Boeing 737-8K5	ILFC Ireland Ltd	
2-JACK	PA-46-500TP Malibu Meridian	Icaris Ventura SA	
2-JBZI	Boeing 737-96NER	Celestial Aviation Training 49 Ltd	
2-JEFS	PA-32R-301T Turbo Saratoga SP	J. Barnet	
2-JEZA	Eclipse EA500	Eclipse 2018 LLP	
2-JRSY	Embraer EMB-550 Praetor 600	Trustflight (Jersey) Ltd	
2-JSEG	Eclipse EA500	Truly Classic LP Inc	
2-JXAX	Boeing 737-8	Celestial Aviation Trading 11 Ltd	
2-JXBZ	Boeing 737-8	Celestial Aviation Trading 22 Ltd	
2-JXCY	Boeing 737-8	Celestial Aviation Trading 11 Ltd	
2-JXDW	Boeing 737-8	Celestial Aviation Trading 22 Ltd	
2-JXEE	Boeing 737-8	SMBC Aviation Capital Ltd	
2-KNIL	Piper J-3C-65 Cub	private	
2-KNOW	Cirrus SR22	private	
2-KOOL	PA-28-181 Archer II	Charlie Alpha Ltd	
2-KSFR	Bombardier BD700-1A10 Global 6000	Linden Lea Partnership	
2-KSRA	Bombardier CL600-2B19 CRJ200ER	EFTEC (UK) Ltd	
2-KYCM	Gulfstream 650ER	Business Aviation Services Guernsey Ltd	
2-LAND	Rockwell Commander 114B	88 Zulu Ltd	
2-LCXO	BAe Jetstream 3102	J. Ibbotson	
2-LFEA	Aerospatiale ATR-42-500	Phoenix Aircraft Leasing PTE Ltd	
2-LIFT	Agusta A109A II	Lift West Ltd	
2-LIVE	Pilatus PC-12/47E	Stammair Guernsey	
2-LOKI	Eclipse 500	Jaguar Investco SL	
2-LOLA	Beech A.36 Bonanza	Lima Alfa Ltd	
2-LONG	Airbus A.320-232	Wells Fargo Trust Company, National Association	
2-LOUD	Sud SA.318C Alouette Astazou	private	
2-LOVE	Beech A.36 Bonanza	Immuno Biotech Ltd	
2-LVHK	Boeing 737-8AS	Wilmington Trust SP Services (Dublin) Ltd	
2-LYCO	PA-39 Twin Comanche	MMC Aircraft Ltd	
2-MAPP	Cessna 421C	MBA Aviation Ltd	
2-MAPZ	Beech C.90A King Air	Zeusch Aviation BV	
2-MARS	PA-46-500TP Malibu Meridian	Air MC	
2-MATO	Bombardier CL600-2B16 Challenger	Volare Aviation Ltd	
2-MCLN	Cirrus SR22T	private	
2-META	Bombardier DHC-8-311 Dash Eight	Elix 2 Asset 2 Ltd	
2-MIKE	Commander 114B	M. A. Perry	
2-MLBU	PA-46-350P Malibu Mirage	private	
2-MOVE	Boeing 737-382QC	European Aviation Ltd	
2-MRGT	Cirrus SR22T	Gringford Ltd	
2-MSTG	Cessna 510 Citation Mustang	Mustang Sally Aviation Ltd	
2-MUST	Cessna 510 Citation Mustang	W. F. McSweeney	
2-NAOM	Eclipse EA.500	TAK Aviation LLC	
2-NAPA	Hawker 800XP	2NAPA LLC	
2-NGUS	Diamond DA.42NG Twin Star	Twinstar4Hire Ltd	
2-NGUT	Diamond DA.62	Twinstar4Hire Ltd	
2-NJOY	Cessna 335	Morada Merchant Ltd	
2-NNGF	Boeing 737-8JP	Horizon III Aviation 3 Ltd	
2-NNGG	Boeing 737-8JP	Fly Aircraft Holdings Twelve Ltd	
2-NOOR	Commander 114B	As-Al Ltd	
2-NOVA	Beech 95-B55 Baron	Novatrust Agency SRL	
2-NYAW	Dassault Falcon 50	H2M	
2-OCST	Agusta-Bell 206B-3 Jet Ranger 3	Lift West Ltd	
2-ODAY	Bombardier CL600-2B16 Challenger 601	Pixwood Limited Partnership	
2-OFUS	Cirrus SR22	L. J. Murray	
2-OJSE	Airbus A.330-202	Hinode Aviation Investments LLC	
2-OTWO	Hawker 800XP	Inuit Holdings Ltd	
2-OWLC	PA-31 Turbo Navajo	Channel Airways Ltd	
2-PASA	Diamond DA.40D Star	Tesla Aviation Ltd	
2-PASB	Diamond DA.40D Star	Tesla Aviation Ltd	
2-PASC	Diamond DA.40D Star	Tesla Aviation Ltd	
2-PASD	Diamond DA.40D Star	Tesla Aviation Ltd	
2-PNBR	Bombardier CL600-2B16 Challenger 604	Volare Aviation Ltd	
2-PCBS	Bombardier CL600-2B16 Challenger 601-3A	Volare Aviation Ltd	
2-PDPD	Agusta-Bell 206B-3 Jet Ranger III	Pink Time Ltd	
2-PETE	PA-32-300 Cherokee Six	P. Biggins	
2-PJBA	Aerospatiale SA.341G Gazelle	S. Atherton	

Notes	Reg	Type	Owner or Operator
	2-PKCE	Embraer ERJ190-100LR	NAC Aviation 29 Designated Activity Company DAC
	2-PLAY	SOCATA TBM-700C-1	N700 VB Ltd
	2-POOR	Bombardier CL600-2B16 Challenger 605	Global Fleet 695 Inc
	2-PROF	Robinson R66	HT Flight Ltd
	2-PROP	Beech 58 Baron	L. Moore
	2-PSFI	Boeing 737-33A	European Aviation Ltd
	2-QWEB	Boeing 737-8H6	Alip No.37 Co.Ltd
	2-RACE	Commander 114B	M. A. Perry
	2-RASA	ATR-72-212A	NK Aviation Ltd
	2-RAYS	Eclipse EA.500	Evradale Ltd
	2-RBLE	Hawker 800XP	Eskimo Holdings Ltd
	2-REIN	Bombardier CL600-2B16 Challenger 604	Barents Air LLC
	2-RICH	PA-46-500TP Malibu Meridian	M K Homes Ltd
	2-RIDE	SOCATA TBM-850	Gazelle Properties Ltd
	2-RIOH	Navion H Rangemaster	M K Homes Ltd
	2-RLAD	Embraer EMB-145LI	Komiaviatrans
	2-RLAX	Airbus A.330-223	UMB Bank National Association
	2-RLAY	Airbus A.330-223	UMB Bank National Association
	2-RLBC	Airbus A.340-541	Global Airways Ltd
	2-RLBF	Boeing 737-85P	Sasof III (A5) Aviation Ireland DAC
	2-RLBS	Avions Transport ATR-42-500	Knight Aircraft Leasing (2017-A) Ltd
	2-RLBT	Avions Transport ATR-42-500	Knight Aircraft Leasing (2017-A) Ltd
	2-RLBU	Embraer ERJ170-200LR	Flybe Leasing Cayman 1 Ltd
	2-RLBV	Embraer ERJ170-200LR	Flybe Leasing Cayman 1 Ltd
	2-RLBW	Embraer ERJ170-200LR	Flybe Leasing Cayman 1 Ltd
	2-RLBX	Embraer ERJ170-200LR	Flybe Leasing Cayman 1 Ltd
	2-RLBY	Embraer ERJ170-200LR	Flybe Leasing Cayman 1 Ltd
	2-RLBZ	Embraer ERJ170-200LR	Flybe Leasing Cayman 1 Ltd
	2-RNWL	Cessna 525 M2	Norbert Blueskies Two Ltd
	2-ROCK	Cirrus SR22	Fletcher Aviation Ltd
	2-ROKK	Saab 2000	Rockton Aviation AB
	2-RPDA	ATR-72-212A	NAC Aviation 29 Ltd
	2-RPDC	ATR-72-212A	NAC Aviation 29 Ltd
	2-RTNA	Boeing 737-86N	LAF Leasing Ireland 2 Ltd
	2-SAAY	Canadair CRJ701ER	EIC Aircraft Leasing Ltd
	2-SAAZ	Canadair CRJ701ER	EIC Aircraft Leasing Ltd
	2-SAFA	Canadair CRJ900ER	EIC Aircraft Leasing Ltd
	2-SAFB	Canadair CRJ900ER	EIC Aircraft Leasing Ltd
	2-SAIL	Agusta-Bell 206B Jet Ranger II	L. E. V. Knifton
	2-SALA	PA-32-300 Cherokee Six	R. M. Harrison & J. W. A. Portch
	2-SALE	Diamond DA.62	Morson Group Ltd
	2-SCSG	Boeing 737-7H6	Kuwait International Company for Leasing Sale & Ownership of Aircraft WLL
	2-SING	Cirrus SR22 GTS	private
	2-SKYZ	Cirrus SR22 GTS	NRS Aviation
	2-SLOW	Bombardier CL600-2B16 Challenger 604	Volare Aviation GST Ltd
	2-SMKM	Cirrus SR20	K. Mallet
	2-SMTD	Airbus A.320-233	Skylink 3-Aircraft Ltd
	2-SNOW	PA-46-350P Malibu Mirage	Jetprop Aviation LLP
	2-SOAR	Sud SA.318C Alouette Astazou	private
	2-SSCA	Airbus A.330-343	HCC Reinsurance Company Ltd
	2-STEV	SNCASE SE.3130 Alouette II	private
	2-STFK	Cessna 525 Citation M2	Ortac (AOC) Ltd
	2-TABS	Eclipse EA.500	TAK Aviation LLC
	2-TAKA	Eclipse EA.500	TAK Aviation LLC
	2-TBMI	SOCATA TBM-930	TBM Aviation Ltd
	2-TECH	Commander 114B	private
	2-TGHA	Embraer EMB-145LR	Airbus SAS
	2-TGHB	Embraer EMB-145LR	Airbus SAS
	2-TGHC	Embraer EMB-145LR	Airbus SAS
	2-TGHD	Embraer EMB-145LR	Airbus SAS
	2-TGHE	Embraer EMB-145LI	Airbus SAS
	2-TGHF	Embraer EMB-145LR	Airbus SAS
	2-TGHG	Embraer EMB-145LR	Airbus SAS
	2-TGHH	Embraer EMB-145LR	Alphastream Ltd
	2-TGHI	Embraer EMB-145LR	Alphastream Ltd
	2-TJEH	Boeing 777-35RER	JIHB DAC
	2-TJEX	Boeing 777-35RER	JIHB DAC
	2-TJFM	Boeing 737-8AL	Carlow Aircraft Leasing Ltd
	2-TRAV	Gulfstream 550	Travcorp Air Transportation 2 (IOM) Ltd

Reg	Type	Owner or Operator	Notes
2-TRVL	Bombardier CL600-2B16 Challenger 650	Volare Aviation Guernsey Ltd	
2-TSSA	Boeing 767-239ER	Weststar Ltd	
2-UPCL	Bombardier CL600-2C10 CRJ700	EIC Aircraft Leasing Ltd	
2-VJWR	Airbus A.330-302	Celestial Aviation Trading 4 Ltd	
2-VJWU	Airbus A.330-302	Celestial Aviation Trading 52 Ltd	
2-VSLO	Airbus A.320-233	Viking 5050 Pte Ltd	
2-VSLQ	Airbus A.320-233	Viking 5050 Pte Ltd	
2-VSLS	Airbus A.320-233	Viking 5794 Pte Ltd	
2-VSYF	Boeing 737-85R	Crolly Aviation Ltd	
2-VSYG	Boeing 737-85R	Mardal Aviation Ltd	
2-VSYM	Boeing 737-8BK	CIT Group Finance (Ireland)	
2-VSYO	Boeing 737-7BK	Wells Fargo Trust Company NA	
2-VSYP	Boeing 737-7BK	Sapphire Leasing (AOE6) Ltd	
2-VYFG	Boeing 737-8FE	Wilmington Trust Company	
2-VYFI	Boeing 737-8FE	Wilmington Trust Company	
2-VYFN	Boeing 737-8FE	Wilmington Trust Company	
2-VYFP	Boeing 737-8FE	Wilmington Trust Company	
2-VYFQ	Boeing 737-8FE	Wilmington Trust Company	
2-WARD	SOCATA TBM-700	private	
2-WESX	Westland Wessex HC Mk.2	private	
2-WILD	Aerospatiale SA.342J Gazelle	X. de Tracy	
2-WKTJ	Beech B.300 King Air 350	DEA Aviation Ltd	
2-WMAN	Aerospatiale SA.341G Gazelle	J. Wightman	
2-WOOD	Cessna 550 Citation Bravo	Horizon Air LLP	
2-WZIE	Airbus A.320-214	SMBC Aviation Capital Ltd	
2-XAJV	ATR-72-212A	Billund Leasing XI Ltd	
2-XAPA	Boeing 737-752	Wells Fargo Trust Company, National Association	
2-XAVT	ATR-72-212A	KA1 P/S	
2-XEAR	Boeing 767-352ER	Aercap Ireland Capital Designated Activity Company	
2-XEME	Embraer ERJ190-100 IGW	NAC Aviation 19 Ltd	
2-YAYA	Gulfstream IV	Weststar Ltd	
2-YELL	PA-28R-201 Arrow III	private	
2-YOLO	Cirrus SF50	private	
2-YULL	Cirrus SR20	private	
2-ZIVA	Cirrus SR22T	private	
2-ZOOM	Commander 114B	Bagair (Guernsey) Ltd	

2-SKYZ Cirrus SR22 *Peter R. March*

JERSEY REGISTER

Reg	Type	Owner or Operator	Notes
ZJ-CER	Beech 58P	Aero Acquitaine	
ZJ-DAN	Pilatus Britten-Norman BN-2T Islander	K. D. R. T. Brem-Wilson	
ZJ-THC	Cessna 525c Citationjet CJ4	Tower House Consultants	

Serial Carried	Civil Identity	Serial Carried	Civil Identity
1	G-BPVE	687	G-AWYI
1 (Soviet AF)	G-BZMY	699 (USAAC)	G-CCXB
6	G-CAMM	781-32 (Spanish AF)	G-BPDM
6G+ED (Lutwaffe)	G-BZOB	854 (USAAC)	G-BTBH
7 (yellow)	G-AWHM	897:E (USN)	G-BJEV
9 (white)	G-AWHH	99+18 (Luftwaffe)	G-ONAA
9 (Soviet AF)	G-OYAK	99+26 (Luftwaffe)	G-BZGL
03 (Soviet AF)	G-CEIB	99+32 (Luftwaffe)	G-BZGK
07 (Soviet AF)	G-BMJY	1018 (Polish AF)	G-ISKA
10 (DOSAAF)	G-BTZB	1102:102 (USN)	G-AZLE
10 (yellow)	G-AWHK	1130 (Royal Saudi AF)	G-VPER
11 (red)	G-AWHC	1164:64 (USAAC)	G-BKGL
14 (USAAC)	G-ISDN	1211(North Korean AF)	G-MIGG
20 (Soviet AF)	G-YAAK	1264	G-FDHB
21 (Soviet AF)	G-CDBJ	1342 (Soviet AF)	G-BTZD
23 (Soviet AF)	G-YKSO	1350 (Portuguese AF)	G-CGAO
26 (USAAC)	G-BAVO	1365 (Portuguese AF)	G-DHPM
26 (DOSAAF)	G-BVXK	1367 (Portuguese AF)	G-UANO
27 (Soviet AF)	G-YAKX	1373 (Portuguese AF)	G-CBJG
27 (USN)	G-BRVG	1377 (Portuguese AF)	G-BARS
27 (USAAC)	G-AGYY	1747 (Portuguese AF)	G-BGPB
27 (Soviet AF)	G-YAKX	1801/18 (Luftwaffe)	G-BNPV
28 (Soviet AF)	G-BSSY	1803/18 (Luftwaffe)	G-BUYU
33 (grey) (Soviet AF)	G-YAKH	2345 (RFC)	G-ATVP
33 (red) (Soviet AF)	G-YAKZ	3066	G-AETA
43 (Soviet AF)	G-BWSV	3072:72 (USN)	G-TEXN
43:SC (USAF)	G-AZSC	3091 (RCAF)	G-CPPM
44 (USAAC)	G-LIIZ	3303 (Portuguese AF)	G-CBGL
44 (DOSAAF)	G-BXAK	3349 (RCAF)	G-BYNF
49 (Soviet AF)	G-YAKU	3397:174 (USN)	G-OBEE
50 (DOSAAF)	G-CBPM	3681 (USAAC)	G-AXGP
50 (DOSAAF)	G-CBRW	4034 (Luftwaffe)	G-CDTI
50 (DOSAAF)	G-EYAK	4406:12 (USN)	G-ONAF
52 (DOSAAF)	G-BWVR	4513:1 (French AF)	G-BFYO
52 (Soviet AF)	G-CCJK	5084: (RCAF)	G-FCTK
52 (Soviet AF)	G-YAKY	51970(USN)	G-TXAN
54 (French Army)	G-CGWR	5964 (RFC)	G-BFVH
61 (Soviet AF)	G-YAKM	6136:205 (USN)	G-BRUJ
66 (Soviet AF)	G-YAKN	7198/18 (Luftwaffe)	G-AANJ
68 (Chinese AF)	G-BVVG	7797 (USAAF)	G-BFAF
78 (French Army)	G-BIZK	8084 (USAAF)	G-KAMY
82:8 (French AF)	G-CCVH	8449M (RAF)	G-ASWJ
100 (DOSAAF)	G-YAKI	9917	G-EBKY
104 (South Arabian AF)	G-PROV	01420 (Polish AF but in Korean colours)	G-BMZF
105/15 (Luftwaffe)	G-UDET	14863 (USAAF)	G-BGOR
112 (USAAC)	G-BSWC	16037 (USAAC)	G-BSFD
113 (Kuwait AF)	G-CFBK	16693:693 (RCAF)	G-BLPG
118 (USAAC)	G-BSDS	18393:393 (RCAF)	G-BCYK
124 (French Army)	G-BOSJ	18671:671 (RCAF)	G-BNZC
143 (French AF)	G-MSAL	20310:310 (RCAF)	G-BSBG
152/17 (Luftwaffe)	G-BVGZ	21261:261 (RCAF)	G-TBRD
156 (French AF)	G-NIFE	21509 (US Army)	G-UHIH
161 (Irish Air Corps)	G-CCCA	24541:BMG (French Army)	G-JDOG
168 (RFC)	G-BFDE	24550 (US Army)	G-PDOG
174 (Royal Netherlands Navy)	G-BEPV	24582 (US Army)	G-VDOG
208 (French Army)	G-YYYY	30146 (Yugoslav Army)	G-BSXD
255 (French Army)	G-CIGH	30149 (Yugoslav Army)	G-SOKO
309 (USAAC)	G-IIIG	31145:G-26 (USAAF)	G-BBLH
311 (Singapore AF)	G-MXPH	3-1923 (USAAF)	G-BRHP
317 (USAAC)	G-CIJN	31952 (USAAF)	G-BRPR
354	G-BZNK	39-160:160 10AB (USAAF)	G-CIIO
379 (USAAC)	G-ILLE	43517:227 (USN)	G-NZSS
403/17 (Luftwaffe)	G-CDXR	43583	G-FINT
416/15 (Luftwaffe)	G-GSAL	56321:U-AB (Royal Norwegian AF)	G-BKPY
422/15 (Luftwaffe)	G-AVJO	61367	G-CGHB
422/15 (Luftwaffe)	G-FOKR	66-374:EO (USAAF)	G-BAGT
425 (Oman AF)	G-SOAF	80105 (US Air Service)	G-CCBN
441 (USN)	G-BTFG	80425:WT-4 (USN)	G-RUMT
477/17 (Luftwaffe)	G-FOKK	85061:7F-061 (USN)	G-CHIA
503 (Hungarian AF)	G-BRAM	111836:JZ-6 (USN)	G-TSIX
540 (USAAF)	G-BCNX	115042:TA-042 (USAF)	G-BGHU
556/17 (Luftwaffe)	G-CFHY	115227 (USN)	G-BKRA
669 (USAAC)	G-CCXA	115302:TP (USMC)	G-BJTP
671 (USAAC)	G-CGPY	115373 (USAAF)	G-AYPM

Serial Carried	Civil Identity	Serial Carried	Civil Identity
115684 (USAAF)	G-BKVM	108-1601 (USAAF)	G-CFGE
121714:201-B (USN)	G-RUMM	A-10 (Swiss AF)	G-BECW
124485:DF-A (USAAF)	G-BEDF	A11-301 (RAN)	G-ARKG
126922:503 (USN)	G-RADR	A16-199:SF-R (RAAF)	G-BEOX
150225:123 (USMC)	G-AWOX	A17-48 (RAAF)	G-BPHR
18-2001 (USAAF)	G-BIZV	A-57 (Swiss AF)	G-BECT
18-5395:CDG (French Army)	G-CUBJ	A58-606:ZP-W (RAAF)	G-AWGB
2106638:E9-R (USAAF)	G-CIFD	A-806 (Swiss AF)	G-BTLL
236657:D-72 (USAAF)	G-BGSJ	A126	G-CILI
238410:A-44 (USAAF)	G-BHPK	A2767	G-CJZP
314887 (USAAF)	G-AJPI	A2943	G-CJZO
315509:W7-S (USAAF)	G-BHUB	A8226	G-BIDW
329405:A-23 (USAAF)	G-BCOB	B595:W	G-BUOD
329417 (USAAF)	G-BDHK	B1807	G-EAVX
329471:F-44 (USAAF)	G-BGXA	B6401	G-AWYY
329601:D-44 (USAAF)	G-AXHR	B7270	G-BFCZ
329707:S-44 (USAAF)	G-BFBY	C1096	G-ERFC
329854:R-44 (USAAF)	G-BMKC	C1904:Z	G-PFAP
329934:B-72 (USAAF)	G-BCPH	C3009	G-BFWD
330238:A-24 (USAAF)	G-LIVH	C3011:S	G-SWOT
330244:C-46 (USAAF)	G-CGIY	C4918	G-BWJM
330314 (USAAF)	G-BAET	C4994	G-BLWM
330372 (USAAF)	G-AISX	C5430	G-CCXG
330485:C-44 (USAAF)	G-AJES	C9533:M	G-BUWE
379994:J-52 (USAAF)	G-BPUR	D-692	G-BVAW
413779:WD-C (USAAF)	G-SHWN	D1851	G-BZSC
414251:WZ-I (USAAF)	G-TFSI	D2263 (Luftwaffe)	G-WAHT
414673:LH-I (USAAF)	G-BDWM	D5397/17 (Luftwaffe)	G-BFXL
414907:CY-S (USAAF)	G-DHYS	D8084	G-ACAA
433915 (USAAF)	G-PBYA	D8096:D	G-AEPH
436021 (USAAF)	G-BWEZ	E-15 (Royal Netherlands AF)	G-BIYU
454467:J-44 (USAAF)	G-BILI	E3B-143 (Spanish AF)	G-JUNG
454537:J-04 (USAAF)	G-BFDL	E3B-153:781-75 (Spanish AF)	G-BPTS
454630 (USAAF)	G-BDOL	E3B-350:05-97 (Spanish AF)	G-BHPL
461748:Y (USAF)	G-BHDK	E449	G-EBJE
472035 (USAAF)	G-SIJJ	E2977	G-EBHB
472216:HO-M (USAAF)	G-BIXL	E3273	G-ADEV
472218:WZ-I (USAAF)	G-MUZY	E8894	G-CDLI
474008:VF-R (USAAF)	G-PSIR	F141:G	G-SEVA
479712:8-R (USAAF)	G-AHIP	F235:B	G-BMDB
479744:M-49 (USAAF)	G-BGPD	F904	G-EBIA
479766:D-63 (USAAF)	G-BKHG	F938	G-EBIC
479878 (USAAF)	G-BEUI	F943	G-BIHF
479897:JD(USAAF)	G-BOXJ	F2367	G-CKBB
480015:M-44 (USAAF)	G-AKIB	F5447:N	G-BKER
480133:B-44 (USAAF)	G-BDCD	F5459:Y	G-INNY
480173:57-H (USAAF)	G-RRSR	F5621:K	G-CLOY
480321:H-44 (USAAF)	G-FRAN	F8010:Z	G-BDWJ
480480:E-44 (USAAF)	G-BECN	F8614	G-AWAU
480636:A-58 (USAAF)	G-AXHP	G-48-1 (Class B)	G-ALSX
480723:E5-J (USAAF)	G-BFZB	J-1605 (Swiss AF)	G-BLID
480752:E-39 (USAAF)	G-BCXJ	J-1632 (Swiss AF)	G-VNOM
493209 (US ANG)	G-DDMV	J-1758 (Swiss AF)	G-BLSD
542447 (USAF)	G-SCUB	J-1790 (Swiss AF)	G-BLKA
549192 (USAAF)	G-THUN	J-4021 (Swiss AF)	G-HHAC
2632019 (Chinese AF)	G-BXZB	J7326	G-EBQP
41-19841:X-17	G-CGZP	J9941:57	G-ABMR
41-33275:CE (USAAF)	G-BICE	K1786	G-AFTA
42-35870:129 (USN)	G-BWLJ	K2048	G-BZNW
42-38384(USMC)	G-BHVV	K2050	G-ASCM
42-58678:IY (USAAF)	G-BRIY	K2059	G-PFAR
42-78044 (USAAF)	G-BRXL	K2065	G-AYJY
42-84555:EP-H (USAAF)	G-ELMH	K2075	G-BEER
43-35943 (USN)	G-BKRN	K2227	G-ABBB
44-79609:44-S (USAAF)	G-BHXY	K2567	G-MOTH
44-79790 (USAAF)	G-BJAY	K2572	G-AOZH
44-80594 (USAAF)	G-BEDJ	K2585	G-ANKT
51-7692 (French AF)	G-TROY	K2587	G-BJAP
51-14700	G-TOMC	K3241	G-AHSA
51-15319 (USAAF)	G-FUZZ	K3661	G-BURZ
51-15527 (USN)	G-BKRA	K3731	G-RODI
51-15555 (US Army)	G-OSPS	K4259:71	G-ANMO
54-2445 (USAF)	G-OTAN	K5054	G-BRDV
69-16011 (USAAF)	G-OHGA	K5414:XV	G-AENP

Serial Carried	Civil Identity	Serial Carried	Civil Identity
K5600	G-BVVI	T7909	G-ANON
K5673	G-BZAS	T7997	G-AHUF
K5674	G-CBZP	T8191	G-BWMK
K5682	G-BBVO	T9707	G-AKKR
K7271	G-CCKV	T9738	G-AKAT
K7985	G-AMRK	T9768	G-AIUA
K8203	G-BTVE	U-0247 (Class B identity)	G-AGOY
K8303:D	G-BWWN	U-80 (Swiss AF)	G-BUKK
L2301	G-AIZG	U-95 (Swiss AF)	G-BVGP
L6739:YP-Q	G-BPIV	U-99 (Swiss AF)	G-AXMT
L6906	G-AKKY	U-108 (Swiss AF)	G-BJAX
N-294 (RNeth AF)	G-KAXF	V3388	G-AHTW
N-321 (RNethAF)	G-BWGL	V7497	G-HRLI
N500	G-BWRA	V9312	G-CCOM
N856 (French AF)	G-CDWE	V9367:MA-B	G-AZWT
N1854	G-AIBE	V9673:MA-J	G-LIZY
N1977:8 (French AF)	G-BWMJ	W2718	G-WLRS
N3200	G-CFGJ	W5856:A2A	G-BMGC
N3788	G-AKPF	W9385:YG-L	G-ADND
N4877:MK-V	G-AMDA	X4276	G-CDGU
N5182	G-APUP	X4496	G-CCJY
N5195	G-ABOX	X4650	G-CGUK
N5719	G-CBHO	X4683:EB-N	G-MUTS
N5903:H	G-GLAD	Z2033:N/275	G-ASTL
N6161	G-ELRT	Z5207	G-BYDL
N6290	G-BOCK	Z5252:GO-B	G-BWHA
N6377	G-BPOB	Z7015:7-L	G-BKTH
N6452	G-BIAU	Z7197	G-AKZN
N6466	G-ANKZ	AA810	G-PRID
N6537	G-AOHY	AB196	G-CCGH
N6720:VX	G-BYTN	AD370 : PJ-C	G-CHBW
N6797	G-ANEH	AG244	G-CBOE
N6847	G-APAL	AJ841	G-BJST
N6965:FL-J	G-AJTW	AP506	G-ACWM
N9191	G-ALND	AP507:KX-P	G-ACWP
N9192:RCO-N	G-DHZF	AR501:DU-E	G-AWII
N9328	G-ALWS	BB697	G-ADGT
N9389	G-ANJA	BB803	G-ADWJ
N9503	G-ANFP	BB807	G-ADWO
P2902:DX-X	G-ROBT	BE505:XP-L	G-HHII
P2921:GZ-L	G-CHTK	BF8431 (Burkina Faso)	G-NRRA
P3700:RF-E	G-HURI	BL735 (BT-A)	G-HABT
P3717:SW-P	G-HITT	BL927 (JH-I)	G-CGWI
P6382:C	G-AJRS	BM597:JH-C	G-MKVB
P7308:XR-D	G-AIST	CW-BG (Luftwaffe)	G-BXBD
P7819	G-TCHZ	DE208	G-AGYU
P8331:RF-M	G-KOSC	DE470	G-ANMY
P9398	G-CEPL	DE623	G-ANFI
R-55 (RNethAF)	G-BLMI	DE673	G-ADNZ
R-151 (RNethAF)	G-BIYR	DE971	G-OOSY
R-156 (RNethAF)	G-ROVE	DE974	G-ANZZ
R-167 (RNethAF)	G-LION	DE992	G-AXXV
R1914	G-AHUJ	DF112	G-ANRM
R4118:UP-W	G-HUPW	DF128:RCO-U	G-AOJJ
R4922	G-APAO	DF198	G-BBRB
R4959:59	G-ARAZ	DG590	G-ADMW
R5136	G-APAP	EE602:DV-V	G-IBSY
R5172:FIJ-E	G-AOIS	EM720	G-AXAN
R5246	G-AMIV	EM726	G-ANDE
R5250	G-AODT	EM973	G-ALNA
S1287	G-BEYB	EN130 : FN-A	G-ENAA
S1581:573	G-BWWK	EN224	G-FXII
T5854	G-ANKK	EN961:SD-X	G-CGIK
T5879:RUC-W	G-AXBW	EP120:AE-A	G-LFVB
T6562	G-ANTE	ES.1-4 (Spanish AF)	G-BUTX
T6830	G-ANJI	EX490	G-CLCJ
T6953	G-ANNI	FE511	G-CIUW
T7109	G-AOIM	FE695:94	G-BTXI
T7281	G-ARTL	FE788	G-CTKL
T7290	G-ANNK	FE992 :ER-992 (CAF)	G-BDAM
T7793	G-ANKV	FH153	G-BBHK
T7794	G-ASPV	FJ777 (RCAF)	G-BIXN
T7798	G-ANZT	FK338	G-AJOZ
T7842	G-AMTF	FR886	G-BDMS

Serial Carried	Civil Identity	Serial Carried	Civil Identity
FS628	G-AIZE	PV303:ON-B	G-CCJL
FT391	G-AZBN	RB142:DW-B	G-CEFC
FZ626:YS-DH	G-AMPO	RG333	G-AIEK
HB275	G-BKGM	RG333	G-AKEZ
HB612	G-AJSN	RH377	G-ALAH
HB737	G-BCBH	RK855	G-PIXY
HB751	G-BCBL	RL962	G-AHED
HD-75 (R Belgian AF)	G-AFDX	RM221	G-ANXR
HG691	G-AIYR	RN201	G-BSKP
HM580	G-ACUU	RN218:N	G-BBJI
JG241 (ZX-J)	G-SMSP	RR232	G-BRSF
JG891	G-LFVC	RT486:PF-A	G-AJGJ
JV579:F	G-RUMW	RT520	G-ALYB
KB889:NA-I	G-LANC	RT610	G-AKWS
KD345:130-A	G-FGID	RW382:3W-P	G-PBIX
KF183	G-CORS	RX168	G-BWEM
KF402 (HT-Y)	G-TEXN	SM520:KJ-1	G-ILDA
KG651	G-AMHJ	SM845:R	G-BUOS
KK116	G-AMPY	SM969:D-A	G-BRAF
KK527	G-RGUS	SX336:105-VL	G-KASX
KN353	G-AMYJ	SR661	G-CBEL
KP220	G-ANAF	TA634:8K-K	G-AWJV
LB264	G-AIXA	TA719:6T	G-ASKC
LB323	G-AHSD	TA805:FX-M	G-PMNF
LB367	G-AHGZ	TD248:CR-S	G-OXVI
LB375	G-AHGW	TD314:FX-P	G-CGYJ
LF858	G-BLUZ	TE184:9N-B	G-MXVI
LZ766	G-ALCK	TE517	G-JGCA
LZ842:EF-F	G-CGZU	TJ343	G-AJXC
MH434:ZD-B	G-ASJV	TJ518	G-AJIH
MH526:LO-D	G-CJWW	TJ534	G-AKSY
MJ627:9G-Q	G-BMSB	TJ565	G-AMVD
MJ755 (Hellenic Air Force)	G-CLGS	TJ569	G-AKOW
MJ772:GW-A	G-AVAV	TJ672:TS-D	G-ANIJ
MK912:SH-L	G-BRRA	TJ704:JA	G-ASCD
ML407:NL-D	G-LFIX	TS798	G-AGNV
MM51-15302:EI-51 (Italian Army)	G-BITP	TW439	G-ANRP
MM52-2392:EI-69 (Italian Army)	G-HELN	TW467	G-ANIE
MP425	G-AITB	TW501	G-ALBJ
MS824 (French AF)	G-AWBU	TW511	G-APAF
MT166	G-BICD	TW519	G-ANHX
MT182	G-AJDY	TW536:TS-V	G-BNGE
MT197	G-ANHS	TW641	G-ATDN
MT438	G-AREI	TX176	G-AHKX
MT818	G-AIDN	TX213	G-AWRS
MT928	G-BKMI	TX310	G-AIDL
MV268:JE-J	G-SPIT	TZ164:OI-A	G-ISAC
MW401	G-PEST	VF512:PF-M	G-ARRX
MW763:HF-A	G-TEMT	VF516	G-ASMZ
NH341	G-CICK	VF526:T	G-ARXU
NJ633	G-AKXP	VF557:H	G-ARHM
NJ673	G-AOCR	VL348	G-AVVO
NJ689	G-ALXZ	VL349	G-AWSA
NJ695	G-AJXV	VM360	G-APHV
NJ703	G-AKPI	VN799	G-CDSX
NJ719	G-ANFU	VP955	G-DVON
NJ728	G-AIKE	VP967	G-KOOL
NJ889	G-AHLK	VP981	G-DHDV
NL750	G-AOBH	VR192	G-APIT
NL985	G-DHBZ	VR249:FA-EL	G-APIY
NM138	G-ANEW	VR259:M	G-APJB
NM181	G-AZGZ	VR930	G-CLNJ
NX534	G-BUDL	VS356	G-AOLU
NX611:LE-C/DX-C	G-ASXX	VS610:K-L	G-AOKL
PG657	G-AGPK	VS623	G-AOKZ
PL788	G-CIEN	VX113	G-ARNO
PL793	G-CIXM	VX118	G-ASNB
PL965	G-MKXI	VX147	G-AVIL
PL983	G-PRXI	VX281	G-RNHF
PP972 : II-5	G-BUAR	VX653	G-BUCM
PS853:C	G-RRGN	VX927	G-ASYG
PT462:SW-A	G-CTIX	VZ638:HF	G-JETM
PT879	G-PTIX	VZ728	G-AGOS
PV202	G-CCCA	WA576	G-ALSS

Serial Carried	Civil Identity	Serial Carried	Civil Identity
WA577	G-ALST	WP800:2	G-BCXN
WA638	G-JWMA	WP803	G-HAPY
WB549:7	G-BAPB	WP805:D	G-MAJR
WB565:X	G-PVET	WP809:78 RN	G-BVTX
WB569:R	G-BYSJ	WP811	G-BCKN
WB585:M	G-AOSY	WP831	G-BBMT
WB588:D	G-AOTD	WP848	G-BFAW
WB615:E	G-BXIA	WP860:6	G-BXDA
WB652:V	G-CHPY	WP870:12	G-BCOI
WB654:U	G-BXGO	WP896	G-BWVY
WB671:910	G-BWTG	WP901:B	G-BWNT
WB697:95	G-BXCT	WP903	G-BCGC
WB702	G-AOFE	WP925:C	G-BXHA
WB703	G-ARMC	WP928:D	G-BXGM
WB711	G-APPM	WP929:F	G-BXCV
WB726:E	G-AOSK	WP930:J	G-BXHF
WB763:14	G-BBMR	WP964	G-HDAE
WD286	G-BBND	WP971	G-ATHD
WD292	G-BCRX	WP973	G-BCPU
WD310:B	G-BWUN	WP983:B	G-BXNN
WD327	G-ATVF	WP984:H	G-BWTO
WD331:J	G-BXDH	WR963	G-SKTN
WD363:5	G-BCIH	WT333	G-BVXC
WD373:12	G-BXDI	WT933	G-ALSW
WD379:K	G-APLO	WV198:K	G-BJWY
WD390:68	G-BWNK	WV322:VL	G-BZSE
WD413	G-VROE	WV493:29	G-BDYG
WE569	G-ASAJ	WV514	G-BLIW
WE724:062	G-BUCM	WV740	G-BNPH
WF118	G-DACA	WV783	G-ALSP
WF877	G-BPOA	WZ507:74	G-VTII
WG308:8	G-BYHL	WZ662	G-BKVK
WG316	G-BCAH	WZ679	G-CIUX
WG321:G	G-DHCC	WZ706	G-BURR
WG348	G-BBMV	WZ847:F	G-CPMK
WG350	G-BPAL	WZ868:H	G-ARMF
WG407:67	G-BWMX	WZ879	G-BWUT
WG422:16	G-BFAX	WZ882:K	G-BXGP
WG465	G-BCEY	XD693:Z-Q	G-AOBU
WG472	G-AOTY	XE489	G-JETH
WG655	G-INVN	XE685:861/VL	G-GAII
WG719	G-BRMA	XE856	G-DUSK
WJ358	G-ARYD	XE956	G-OBLN
WJ368	G-ASZX	XF114	G-SWIF
WJ404	G-ASOI	XF597:AH	G-BKFW
WJ945:21	G-BEDV	XF603	G-KAPW
WK163	G-CTTS	XF690	G-MOOS
WK512:A	G-BXIM	XF785	G-ALBN
WK514	G-BBMO	XF836:J-G	G-AWRY
WK517	G-ULAS	XG160:U	G-BWAF
WK522	G-BCOU	XG452	G-BRMB
WK558:DH	G-ARMG	XH134	G-OMHD
WK577	G-BCYM	XH558	G-VLCN
WK585	G-BZGA	XJ389	G-AJJP
WK586:V	G-BXGX	XJ398	G-BDBZ
WK590:69	G-BWVZ	XJ729	G-BVGE
WK608	G-CLNI	XK417	G-AVXY
WK609:93	G-BXDN	XK896	G-RNAS
WK611	G-ARWB	XK940:911	G-AYXT
WK624	G-BWHI	XL426	G-VJET
WK628	G-BBMW	XL500	G-KAEW
WK630	G-BXDG	XL502	G-BMYP
WK633:A	G-BXEC	XL571:V	G-HNTR
WK634:902	G-CIGE	XL573	G-BVGH
WK635	G-HFRH	XL577	G-BXKF
WK640:C	G-BWUV	XL587	G-HPUX
WL419	G-JSMA	XL621	G-BNCX
WL626:P	G-BHDD	XL714	G-AOGR
WM167	G-LOSM	XL809	G-BLIX
WP308:572CU	G-GACA	XL929	G-BNPU
WP321	G-BRFC	XL954	G-BXES
WP788	G-BCHL	XM405	G-TORE
WP790:T	G-BBNC	XM424	G-BWDS
WP795:901	G-BVZZ	XM479:54	G-BVEZ

Serial Carried	Civil Identity	Serial Carried	Civil Identity
XM497	G-AOVF	XX538:O	G-TDOG
XM553	G-AWSV	XX546:03	G-WINI
XM575	G-BLMC	XX549:6	G-CBID
XM655	G-VULC	XX550:Z	G-CBBL
XM685:513/PO	G-AYZJ	XX551:E	G-BZDP
XM819	G-APXW	XX561:7	G-BZEP
XN351	G-BKSC	XX611:7	G-CBDK
XN437	G-AXWA	XX612:A, 03	G-BZXC
XN441	G-BGKT	XX614:V	G-GGRR
XN459	G-BWOT	XX619:T	G-CBBW
XN498	G-BWSH	XX621:H	G-CBEF
XN637:03	G-BKOU	XX622:B	G-CBGZ
XP241	G-CEHR	XX624:E	G-KDOG
XP254	G-ASCC	XX625	G-UWAS
XP282	G-BGTC	XX626:02, W	G-CDVV
XP355	G-BEBC	XX628:9	G-CBFU
XP820	G-CICP	XX629:V	G-BZXZ
XP907	G-SROE	XX630:5	G-SIJW
XP924	G-CVIX	XX631:W	G-BZXS
XR240	G-BDFH	XX636:Y	G-CBFP
XR241	G-AXRR	XX638	G-DOGG
XR244	G-CICR	XX658:07	G-SMAT
XR246	G-AZBU	XX667:16	G-BZFN
XR267	G-BJXR	XX668:1	G-CBAN
XR486	G-RWWW	XX692:A	G-BZMH
XR538:01	G-RORI	XX693:07	G-BZML
XR595	G-BWHU	XX694:E	G-CBBS
XR673:L	G-BXLO	XX695:3	G-CBBT
XR724	G-BTSY	XX698:9	G-BZME
XR944	G-ATTB	XX699:F	G-IDID
XR992	G-MOUR	XX700:17	G-CBEK
XS104	G-FRCE	XX702:P	G-CBCR
XS235	G-CPDA	XX704	G-BCUV
XS587	G-VIXN	XX885	G-HHAA
XS765	G-BSET	XZ329	G-BZYD
XT131	G-CICN	XZ933	G-CGJZ
XT223	G-XTUN	XZ934:U	G-CBSI
XT420:606	G-CBUI	XZ937:Y	G-CBKA
XT435:430	G-RIMM	ZA250	G-VTOL
XT626	G-CIBW	ZA634:C	G-BUHA
XT634	G-BYRX	ZA652	G-BUDC
XT671	G-BYRC	ZA656	G-BTWC
XT761	G-WSEX	ZA730	G-FUKM
XT787	G-KAXT	ZB625	G-TSTR
XT788:316	G-BMIR	ZB627:A	G-CBSK
XV134:P	G-BWLX	ZB646:59/CU	G-CBGZ
XV137	G-CRUM	HKG-5 (Royal Hong Kong AAF)	G-BULL
XV138	G-SASM	HKG-6 (Royal Hong Kong AAF)	G-BPCL
XV268	G-BVER	HKG-11 (Royal Hong Kong AAF)	G-BYRY
XW283	G-CIMX	HKG-13 (Royal Hong Kong AAF)	G-BXKW
XW324:K	G-BWSG	2+1:7334 Luftwaffe)	G-SYFW
XW325:E	G-BWGF	3+ (Luftwaffe)	G-BAYV
XW333:79	G-BVTC	4+ (Luftwaffe)	G-BSLX
XW354	G-JPTV	07 (Russian AF)	G-BMJY
XW422:3	G-BWEB	F+IS (Luftwaffe)	G-BIRW
XW423:14	G-BWUW	BG+KM (Luftwaffe)	G-ASTG
XW433	G-JPRO	BU+CC (Luftwaffe)	G-BUCC
XW612	G-KAXW	BU+CK (Luftwaffe)	G-BUCK
XW613	G-BXRS	DM+BK (Luftwaffe)	G-BPHZ
XW635	G-AWSW	LG+01 (Luftwaffe)	G-CIJV
XW784:VL	G-BBRN	LG+03 (Luftwaffe)	G-AEZX
XW853	G-IBNH	KG+EM (Luftwaffe)	G-ETME
XW854:46/CU	G-TIZZ	NJ+C11 (Luftwaffe)	G-ATBG
XW858:C	G-ONNE	S4+A07 (Luftwaffe)	G-BWHP
XX432	G-CDNO	S5+B06 (Luftwaffe)	G-WJCM
XX436	G-ZZLE	TP+WX (Luftwaffe)	G-TPWX
XX513:10	G-KKKK	6J+PR (Luftwaffe)	G-AWHB
XX515:4	G-CBBC	57-H (USAAC)	G-AKAZ
XX521:H	G-CBEH	+14 (Luftwaffe)	G-BSMD
XX522:06	G-DAWG	146-11083 (5)	G-BNAI
XX524:04	G-DDOG		
XX528:D	G-BZON		
XX534:B	G-EDAV		
XX537:C	G-CBCB		

Notes	Reg	Type († False registration)	Owner or Operator
	EI-ABI	DH.84 Dragon	Aer Lingus Charitable Foundation (EI-FBK)
	EI-ABS	Boeing B75N1 Stearman	S. Bennett
	EI-AED	Cessna 120	A. Brophy
	EI-AEE	Auster 3/1 Autocrat	O. & N. A. O'Sullivan
	EI-AEF	Cessna 120	J. Halligan
	EI-AEH	Luscombe 8F	D. Kelly
	EI-AEI	Aeronca 65-TACS	F. J. McMorrow
	EI-AEL	PA-16	G. Dolan
	EI-AEM	Cessna 140	Cessna 140 Flying Group
	EI-AET	Piper J3C-65 Cub	S. T. Scully
	EI-AFE	Piper J3C-65 Cub	4 of Cubs Flying Group
	EI-AFZ	DHC.1 Chipmunk 22	Gipsy Captains Group
	EI-AGJ	Auster J/1 Autocrat	T. G. Rafter
	EI-AHI	DH.82A Tiger Moth	High Fidelity Flyers
	EI-AII	Cessna 150F	L. Bagnell
	EI-AIR	PA-18-135 Super Cub	The Vintage Aircraft Flying Group
	EI-AKM	Piper J-3C-65 Cub	J. A. Kent
	EI-ALP	Avro 643 Cadet	J. C. O'Loughlin
	EI-AMK	Auster J/1 Autocrat	Iona National Airways
	EI-ANT	Champion 7ECA Citabria	T. Croke & ptnrs
	EI-ANY	PA-18 Super Cub 95	Bogavia Group
	EI-AOB	PA-28 Cherokee 140	Knock Flying Group
	EI-AOO	Cessna 150E	C. Sheridan
	EI-ARW	Jodel D.R.1050	J. Davy
	EI-ATJ	B.121 Pup Srs 2	C. Barrett & N. James
	EI-AUM	Auster J/1 Autocrat	T. G. Rafter
	EI-AUO	Cessna FA.150K Aerobat	Aerobat Aviation Ltd
	EI-AVE	PA-18-95 Super Cub	A. R. Hassett & P. Morgan
	EI-AVM	Cessna F.150L	J. Nugent
	EI-AWP	DH.82A Tiger Moth	O. E. P. O'Sullivan
	EI-AWR	Malmö MFI-9 Junior	L. P. Murray
	EI-AYB	GY-80 Horizon 180	J. B. Smith
	EI-AYI	MS.880B Rallye Club	J. McNamara
	EI-AYN	BN-2A-8 Islander	Aer Arann
	EI-AYR	Schleicher ASK-16	B. O'Broin & ptnrs
	EI-AYT	MS.894A Rallye Minerva	K. A. O'Connor
	EI-AYY	Evans VP-1	Ballyboughal VP-1 Flying Group
	EI-BAJ	Stampe SV.4C	W. Rafter & Partners
	EI-BAV	PA-22 Colt 108	E. Finnamore
	EI-BBE	Champion 7FC Tri-Traveler	J. E. Coughlan
	EI-BBV	Piper J-3C-65 Cub	A. N. Johnston
	EI-BCE	BN-2A-26 Islander	Aer Arann
	EI-BCF	Bensen B.8M	P. Flanagan
	EI-BCJ	Aeromere F.8L Falco 1 Srs 3	M. P. McLoughlin
	EI-BCK	Cessna F.172N II	National Flight Centre Ltd
	EI-BCM	Piper J-3C-65 Cub	M. Bergin & Partners
	EI-BCN	Piper J-3C-65 Cub	H. Diver
	EI-BCP	D.62B Condor	T. Delaney
	EI-BDL	Evans VP-2	P. Buggle
	EI-BDR	PA-28 Cherokee 180	Cherokee Group
	EI-BDX	D.62B Condor	The Brian Douglas Trust BDX Group
	EI-BEN	Piper J-3C-65 Cub	Ballyboughal L4 Flying Group
	EI-BFR	MS.880B Rallye	J. M. Fingleton
	EI-BHV	Champion 7EC Traveler	P. O'Donnell & ptnrs
	EI-BIB	Cessna F.152	Sligo Aeronautical Club Ltd
	EI-BID	PA-18 Super Cub 95	A. Connaire & Partners
	EI-BIK	PA-18 Super Cub 180	Dublin Gliding Club
	EI-BIO	Piper J-3C-65 Cub	H. Duggan & Partners
	EI-BIR	Cessna F.172M	Figile Flying Group
	EI-BIV	Bellanca 8KCAB	Atlantic Flight Training Ltd
	EI-BJB	Aeronca 7AC Champion	A. W. Kennedy
	EI-BJC	Aeronca 7AC Champion	A. E. Griffin
	EI-BJK	MS.880B Rallye 110ST	M. Keenen
	EI-BJM	Cessna A.152	National Flight Centre Ltd
	EI-BJO	Cessna R.172K	The XP Group
	EI-BKC	Aeronca 15AC Sedan	G. Hendrick & M. Farrell
	EI-BKK	Taylor JT.1 Monoplane	D. Doyle
	EI-BMI	SOCATA TB9 Tampico	A. Breslin
	EI-BMN	Cessna F.152 II	National Flight Centre Ltd
	EI-BMU	Monnet Sonerai IIL	N. O'Donnell
	EI-BNL	Rand-Robinson KR-2	K. Hayes

Reg	Type († False registration)	Owner or Operator	Notes
EI-BNU	MS.880B Rallye Club	J. Cooke	
EI-BOV	Rand-Robinson KR-2	G. O'Hara & G. Callan	
EI-BPL	Cessna F.172K	Phoenix Flying	
EI-BPP	Quicksilver MX	J. A. Smith	
EI-BRU	Evans VP-1	C. O'Shea	
EI-BSB	Wassmer Jodel D.112	T. Darmody	
EI-BSG	Bensen B.80	J. Todd	
EI-BSK	SOCATA TB9 Tampico	J. Byrne	
EI-BSL	PA-34-220T Seneca III	P. Sreenan	
EI-BSN	Cameron O-65 balloon	L. Duncan	
EI-BSO	PA-28 Cherokee 140B	S. Brazil	
EI-BSW	Solar Wings Pegasus XL-R	E. Fitzgerald	
EI-BSX	J-3C-65 Cub	J. O'Dwyer	
EI-BUC	Jodel D.9 Bébé	M. Blake	
EI-BUF	Cessna 210N	210 Group	
EI-BUG	SOCATA ST.10 Diplomate	J. Cooke	
EI-BUL	Whittaker MW5 Sorcerer	J. Culleton	
EI-BUN	Beech 76 Duchess	National Flight Centre Ltd	
EI-BUT	MS.893A Commodore 180	T. Keating	
EI-BVJ	AMF Chevvron 232	A. Dunn	
EI-BVK	PA-38-112 Tomahawk	B. Lowe	
EI-BVT	Evans VP-2	P. Morrison	
EI-BVY	Zenith 200AA-RW	J. Matthews & M. Skelly	
EI-BYL	Zenith CH.250	I. Calton	
EI-BYX	Champion 7GCAA	P. J. Gallagher	
EI-BYY	Piper J-3C-85 Cub	8 Ball Cub Club	
EI-CAC	Grob G.115A	C. Phillips	
EI-CAD	Grob G.115A	C. Phillips	
EI-CAE	Grob G.115A	R. M. Davies	
EI-CAN	Aerotech MW5 Sorcerer	V. A. Vaughan	
EI-CAU	AMF Chevvron 232	J. Tarrant	
EI-CAX	Cessna P.210N	K. A. O'Connor	
EI-CBK	Aérospatiale ATR-42-310	Stobart Air/Aer Lingus Regional	
EI-CCF	Aeronca 11AC Chief	G. McGuinness	
EI-CCM	Cessna 152 II	E. Hopkins	
EI-CDP	Cessna 182L	Irish Parachute Club	
EI-CDV	Cessna 150G	K. A. O'Connor	
EI-CEG	MS.893A Rallye 180GT	M. Jarrett	
EI-CES	Taylorcraft BC-65	G. Higgins	
EI-CFF	PA-12 Super Cruiser	J. & T. O'Dwyer	
EI-CFG	CP.301B Emeraude	F. Doyle	
EI-CFH	PA-12 Super Cruiser	G. Treacy	
EI-CFO	Piper J-3C-65 Cub	J. Brouder	
EI-CFY	Cessna 172N	National Flight Centre Ltd	
EI-CGF	Luton LA-5 Major	P. Jones	
EI-CGH	Cessna 210N	J. Greif-Wustenbecker	
EI-CGP	PA-28 Cherokee 140C	L. A. Tattan	
EI-CHR	CFM Shadow Srs BD	B. Kelly	
EI-CIF	PA-28 Cherokee 180C	AA Flying Group	
EI-CIG	PA-18 Super Cub 150	8 Ball Cub Club	
EI-CIM	Avid Flyer Mk IV	P. Swan	
EI-CIN	Cessna 150K	K. A. O'Connor	
EI-CJJ	Slingsby T-31M	J. J. Sullivan	
EI-CJS	Jodel D.120A	A. Flood	
EI-CJT	Slingsby Motor Cadet III	J. Tarrant	
EI-CKH	PA-18 Super Cub 95	G. Brady	
EI-CKI	Thruster TST Mk 1	S. Woodgates	
EI-CKJ	Cameron N-77 balloon	A. F. Meldon	
EI-CKZ	Jodel D.18	J. O'Brien	
EI-CLQ	Cessna F.172N	E. Finnamore	
EI-CML	Cessna 150M	L. Kapser	
EI-CMN	PA-12 Super Cruiser	A. McNamee & ptnrs	
EI-CMR	Rutan LongEz	F. & C. O'Caoimh	
EI-CMT	PA-34-200T Seneca II	Atlantic Flight Training	
EI-CMU	Mainair Mercury	Bill O'Neill	
EI-CMW	Rotorway Executive	B. McNamee	
EI-CNG	Air & Space 18A gyroplane	P. Joyce	
EI-CNU	Pegasus Quantum 15-912	M. Ffrench	
EI-COT	Cessna F.172N	Tojo Air Leasing	
EI-COW	ICP Savannah S	L. Kennard & K. Kerrian	

REPUBLIC OF IRELAND CIVIL REGISTRATIONS

Notes	Reg	Type († False registration)	Owner or Operator
	EI-COY	Piper J-3C-65 Cub	The Real Seaplane Flying Group
	EI-CPE	Airbus A.321-211	Aer Lingus St Enda
	EI-CPG	Airbus A.321-211	Aer Lingus St Aidan
	EI-CPH	Airbus A.321-211	Aer Lingus St Dervilla
	EI-CPI	Rutan LongEz	D. J. Ryan
	EI-CPP	Piper J-3C-65 Cub	W. Kennedy
	EI-CPX	I.I.I. Sky Arrow 650T	M. Tormey
	EI-CRB	Lindstrand LBL-90A balloon	J. & C. Concannon
	EI-CRG	Robin DR.400/180R	D. & B. Lodge
	EI-CRX	SOCATA TB-9 Tampico	J. W. Leonard
	EI-CSI	Boeing 737-8AS	Sapphire Leasing 1 (AOE 4) Ltd
	EI-CTL	Aerotech MW-5B Sorcerer	M. Wade
	EI-CUJ	Cessna 172N	The Hotel Bravo Flying Club
	EI-CUS	AB-206B JetRanger 3	H. Hassard
	EI-CUW	BN-2B-20 Islander	Aer Arann
	EI-CVA	Airbus A.320-214	Aer Lingus St Schira
	EI-CVB	Airbus A.320-214	Aer Lingus St Mobhi
	EI-CVC	Airbus A.320-214	Aer Lingus St Kealin
	EI-CVL	Ercoupe 415CD	V. O'Rourke
	EI-CVW	Bensen B.8M	F. Kavanagh
	EI-CXC	Raj Hamsa X'Air 502T	D.White
	EI-CXN	Boeing 737-329	Transalpine Leasing Ltd
	EI-CXR	Boeing 737-329	Transalpine Leasing Ltd
	EI-CXV	Boeing 737-8CX	MASL Ireland(14)Ltd/MIAT Mongolian Airlines
	EI-CXY	Evektor EV-97 Eurostar	G. Doody & ptnrs
	EI-CXZ	Boeing 767-216ER	Transalpine Leasing Ltd
	EI-CZA	ATEC Zephyr 2000	D. Cassidy
	EI-CZP	Schweizer 269C-1	T. Ng Kam
	EI-DAA	Airbus A.330-202	Aer Lingus St Keeva
	EI-DAC	Boeing 737-8AS	ASL Airlines (Ireland) Ltd
	EI-DAD	Boeing 737-8AS	ASL Airlines (Ireland) Ltd
	EI-DAJ	Boeing 737-8AS	Celestial Aviation Trading 23 Ltd
	EI-DAK	Boeing 737-8AS	Ryanair
	EI-DAM	Boeing 737-8AS	Ryanair
	EI-DAN	Boeing 737-8AS	Ryanair
	EI-DAO	Boeing 737-8AS	Ryanair
	EI-DAP	Boeing 737-8AS	Ryanair
	EI-DAR	Boeing 737-8AS	Ryanair
	EI-DAS	Boeing 737-8AS	Ryanair
	EI-DBI	Raj Hamsa X'Air Mk.2 Falcon	D. Cornally
	EI-DBJ	Huntwing Pegasus XL Classic	P. A. McMahon
	EI-DBK	Boeing 777-243ER	Alitalia
	EI-DBL	Boeing 777-243ER	Alitalia
	EI-DBM	Boeing 777-243ER	Alitalia
	EI-DBO	Air Creation Kiss 400	E. Spain
	EI-DBV	Rand Kar X' Air 602T	S. Scanlon
	EI-DCA	Raj Hamsa X'Air	S. Cahill
	EI-DCF	Boeing 737-8AS	Ryanair
	EI-DCG	Boeing 737-8AS	Ryanair
	EI-DCH	Boeing 737-8AS	Ryanair
	EI-DCI	Boeing 737-8AS	Ryanair
	EI-DCJ	Boeing 737-8AS	Ryanair
	EI-DCK	Boeing 737-8AS	Ryanair
	EI-DCL	Boeing 737-8AS	Ryanair
	EI-DCM	Boeing 737-8AS	Ryanair
	EI-DCN	Boeing 737-8AS	Ryanair
	EI-DCO	Boeing 737-8AS	Ryanair
	EI-DCP	Boeing 737-8AS	Ryanair
	EI-DCR	Boeing 737-8AS	Ryanair
	EI-DCW	Boeing 737-8AS	Ryanair
	EI-DCX	Boeing 737-8AS	Ryanair
	EI-DCY	Boeing 737-8AS	Ryanair
	EI-DCZ	Boeing 737-8AS	Ryanair
	EI-DDC	Cessna F.172M	P. Murphy & J. Sullivan
	EI-DDD	Aeronca 7AC	J. Sullivan & M. Quinn
	EI-DDH	Boeing 777-243ER	Alitalia
	EI-DDJ	Raj Hamsa X'Air 582	I. Talt
	EI-DDP	Southdown International microlight	M. Mannion
	EI-DDR	Bensen B8V	P. MacCabe & Partners
	EI-DDX	Cessna 172S	Atlantic Flight Training
	EI-DEB	Airbus A.320-214	Aer Lingus St Nathy

328

Reg	Type († False registration)	Owner or Operator	Notes
EI-DEC	Airbus A.320-214	Wilmington Trust SP Services (Dublin) Ltd	
EI-DEE	Airbus A.320-214	Aer Lingus St Fintan	
EI-DEF	Airbus A.320-214	Aer Lingus St Declan	
EI-DEG	Airbus A.320-214	Aer Lingus St Fachtna	
EI-DEH	Airbus A.320-214	Aer Lingus St Malachy	
EI-DEI	Airbus A.320-214	Aer Lingus St Kilian	
EI-DEJ	Airbus A.320-214	Aer Lingus St Oliver Plunkett	
EI-DEK	Airbus A.320-214	Aer Lingus St Eunan	
EI-DEL	Airbus A.320-214	Aer Lingus St Ibar	
EI-DEM	Airbus A.320-214	Aer Lingus St Canice	
EI-DEN	Airbus A.320-214	Aer Lingus St Kieran	
EI-DEO	Airbus A.320-214	Aer Lingus St Senan	
EI-DEP	Airbus A.320-214	Aer Lingus St Eugene	
EI-DER	Airbus A.320-214	Aer Lingus St Mel	
EI-DES	Airbus A.320-214	Aer Lingus St Pappin	
EI-DFM	Evektor EV-97 Eurostar	J. Gibbons	
EI-DFO	Airbus A.320-211	Windjet	
EI-DFS	Boeing 767-33AER	Transalpine Leasing Ltd	
EI-DFX	Air Creation Kiss 400	L. Daly	
EI-DFY	Raj Hamsa R100 (2)	P. McGirr & R Gillespie	
EI-DGA	Urban Air UFM-11UK Lambada	Dr. P. & D. Durkin	
EI-DGG	Raj Hamsa X'Air 582	P. A. Weldon	
EI-DGH	Raj Hamsa X'Air 582	C. D. & W. Baker	
EI-DGJ	Raj Hamsa X'Air 582	N. Brereton	
EI-DGK	Raj Hamsa X'Air 133	B. Chambers	
EI-DGP	Urban Air UFM-11 Lambada	R. Linehan	
EI-DGT	Urban Air UFM-11UK Lambada	P. Walsh & Partners	
EI-DGU	Airbus A.300-622R	ASL Airlines (Ireland) Ltd	
EI-DGV	ATEC Zephyr 2000	K. Higgins	
EI-DGW	Cameron Z-90 balloon	J. Leahy	
EI-DGX	Cessna 152 II	National Flight Centre Ltd	
EI-DGY	Urban Air UFM-11 Lambada	D. McMorrow	
EI-DHA	Boeing 737-8AS	Ryanair	
EI-DHB	Boeing 737-8AS	Ryanair	
EI-DHC	Boeing 737-8AS	Ryanair	
EI-DHD	Boeing 737-8AS	Ryanair	
EI-DHE	Boeing 737-8AS	Ryanair	
EI-DHF	Boeing 737-8AS	Ryanair	
EI-DHG	Boeing 737-8AS	Ryanair	
EI-DHH	Boeing 737-8AS	Ryanair	
EI-DHK	Boeing 737-8AS	STLC Europe Seventeen Leasing Ltd	
EI-DHN	Boeing 737-8AS	Ryanair	
EI-DHO	Boeing 737-8AS	Ryanair	
EI-DHP	Boeing 737-8AS	Ryanair	
EI-DHR	Boeing 737-8AS	Ryanair	
EI-DHS	Boeing 737-8AS	Ryanair	
EI-DHT	Boeing 737-8AS	Ryanair	
EI-DHV	Boeing 737-8AS	Ryanair	
EI-DHW	Boeing 737-8AS	Ryanair	
EI-DHX	Boeing 737-8AS	Ryanair	
EI-DHY	Boeing 737-8AS	Ryanair	
EI-DHZ	Boeing 737-8AS	Ryanair	
EI-DIA	Solar Wings Pegasus XL-Q	P. Byrne	
EI-DIP	Airbus A.330-202	Alitalia	
EI-DIR	Airbus A.330-202	Alitalia	
EI-DIY	Van's RV-4	J. A. Kent	
EI-DJF	Luscombe 8F	S. Forde	
EI-DKE	Air Creation Kiss 450-582	S. Smith & A. Duffy	
EI-DKJ	Thruster T.600N	C. Brogan	
EI-DKK	Raj Hamsa X'Air Jabiru	M. Tolan	
EI-DKT	Raj Hamsa X'Air 582 (11)	P. & D. Darcy	
EI-DKU	Air Creation Kiss 450-582 (1)	P. Kirwan	
EI-DKW	Evektor EV-97 Eurostar	Ormand Flying Club	
EI-DKY	Raj Hamsa X'Air 582	M. Clarke	
EI-DKZ	Reality Aircraft Escapade 912 (1)	J. Deegan	
EI-DLB	Boeing 737-8AS	Ryanair	
EI-DLC	Boeing 737-8AS	Ryanair	
EI-DLD	Boeing 737-8AS	Ryanair	
EI-DLE	Boeing 737-8AS	Ryanair	
EI-DLF	Boeing 737-8AS	Ryanair	
EI-DLG	Boeing 737-8AS	Ryanair	

REPUBLIC OF IRELAND CIVIL REGISTRATIONS

Notes	Reg	Type († False registration)	Owner or Operator
	EI-DLH	Boeing 737-8AS	Ryanair
	EI-DLI	Boeing 737-8AS	Ryanair
	EI-DLJ	Boeing 737-8AS	Ryanair
	EI-DLK	Boeing 737-8AS	Ryanair
	EI-DLN	Boeing 737-8AS	Ryanair
	EI-DLO	Boeing 737-8AS	ASL Aviation Holdings DAC
	EI-DLR	Boeing 737-8AS	ASL Aviation Holdings DAC
	EI-DLV	Boeing 737-8AS	Ryanair
	EI-DLW	Boeing 737-8AS	Ryanair
	EI-DLX	Boeing 737-8AS	Ryanair
	EI-DLY	Boeing 737-8AS	Ryanair
	EI-DMA	MS.892E Rallye 150	J. Lynn & Partners
	EI-DMB	Best Off Skyranger 912S (1)	E. Spain
	EI-DMG	Cessna 441	Dawn Meats Group
	EI-DMU	Whittaker MW6S Merlin	M. Heaton
	EI-DNM	Boeing 737-4S3	Transaero
	EI-DNR	Raj Hamsa X'Air 582 (5)	N. Furlong & J. Grattan
	EI-DNV	Urban Air UFM-11UK Lambada	F. Maughan
	EI-DOB	Zenair CH-701	D. O'Brien
	EI-DOW	Mainair Blade 912	G. D. Fortune
	EI-DOY	PZL Koliber 150A	T. J. Britton
	EI-DPB	Boeing 737-8AS	ASL Aviation Holdings DAC
	EI-DPC	Boeing 737-8AS	KV Aircraft No.16 DAC
	EI-DPF	Boeing 737-8AS	Ryanair
	EI-DPG	Boeing 737-8AS	Ryanair
	EI-DPH	Boeing 737-8AS	Ryanair
	EI-DPI	Boeing 737-8AS	Ryanair
	EI-DPJ	Boeing 737-8AS	Ryanair
	EI-DPK	Boeing 737-8AS	Ryanair
	EI-DPL	Boeing 737-8AS	Ryanair
	EI-DPM	Boeing 737-8AS	Ryanair
	EI-DPN	Boeing 737-8AS	Ryanair
	EI-DPO	Boeing 737-8AS	Ryanair
	EI-DPP	Boeing 737-8AS	Ryanair
	EI-DPR	Boeing 737-8AS	Ryanair
	EI-DPT	Boeing 737-8AS	Ryanair
	EI-DPV	Boeing 737-8AS	Ryanair
	EI-DPW	Boeing 737-8AS	Ryanair
	EI-DPX	Boeing 737-8AS	Ryanair
	EI-DPY	Boeing 737-8AS	Ryanair
	EI-DPZ	Boeing 737-8AS	Ryanair
	EI-DRH	Mainair Blade	J. McErlain
	EI-DRL	Raj Hamsa X'Air Jabiru	N. Brunton
	EI-DRM	Urban Air UFM-10 Samba	K. Haslett
	EI-DRT	Air Creation Tanarg 912	P. McMahon
	EI-DRU	Tecnam P92/EM Echo	P. Gallogly
	EI-DRW	Evektor EV-97R Eurostar	Eurostar Flying Club
	EI-DRX	Raj Hamsa X'Air 582 (5)	M. Sheelan & D. McShane
	EI-DSA	Airbus A.320-216	Alitalia
	EI-DSG	Airbus A.320-216	Alitalia
	EI-DSL	Airbus A.320-216	Alitalia
	EI-DSU	Airbus A.320-216	Alitalia
	EI-DSV	Airbus A.320-216	Alitalia
	EI-DSW	Airbus A.320-216	Alitalia
	EI-DSX	Airbus A.320-216	Alitalia
	EI-DSY	Airbus A.320-216	Alitalia
	EI-DSZ	Airbus A.320-216	Alitalia
	EI-DTA	Airbus A.320-216	Alitalia
	EI-DTB	Airbus A.320-216	Alitalia
	EI-DTD	Airbus A.320-216	Alitalia
	EI-DTE	Airbus A.320-216	Alitalia
	EI-DTF	Airbus A.320-216	Alitalia
	EI-DTG	Airbus A.320-216	Alitalia
	EI-DTH	Airbus A.320-216	Alitalia
	EI-DTI	Airbus A.320-216	Alitalia
	EI-DTJ	Airbus A.320-216	Alitalia
	EI-DTK	Airbus A.320-216	Alitalia
	EI-DTL	Airbus A.320-216	Alitalia
	EI-DTM	Airbus A.320-216	Alitalia
	EI-DTN	Airbus A.320-216	Alitalia
	EI-DTO	Airbus A.320-216	Alitalia

Reg	Type († False registration)	Owner or Operator	Notes
EI-DTS	PA-18 Super Cub	M. D. Murphy	
EI-DTT	ELA-07 R-100 Gyrocopter	N. Steele	
EI-DUH	Scintex CP.1310C3 Emeraude	W. Kennedy	
EI-DUJ	Evektor EV-97 Eurostar	E. Fitzpatrick	
EI-DUL	Alpi Aviation Pioneer	Alpi Pioneer Group	
EI-DUO	Airbus A.330-203	Aer Lingus	
EI-DUZ	Airbus A.330-203	Aer Lingus	
EI-DVE	Airbus A.320-214	Aer Lingus	
EI-DVG	Airbus A.320-214	Aer Lingus	
EI-DVH	Airbus A.320-214	Aer Lingus	
EI-DVI	Airbus A.320-214	Aer Lingus	
EI-DVJ	Airbus A.320-214	Aer Lingus	
EI-DVK	Airbus A.320-214	Aer Lingus	
EI-DVL	Airbus A.320-214	Aer Lingus	
EI-DVM	Airbus A.320-214	Aer Lingus	
EI-DVN	Airbus A.320-214	Aer Lingus	
EI-DVO	Barnett J4B2	T. Brennan	
EI-DVZ	Robinson R44 II	M. O'Donovan	
EI-DWA	Boeing 737-8AS	Ryanair	
EI-DWB	Boeing 737-8AS	Ryanair	
EI-DWC	Boeing 737-8AS	Ryanair	
EI-DWD	Boeing 737-8AS	Ryanair	
EI-DWE	Boeing 737-8AS	Ryanair	
EI-DWF	Boeing 737-8AS	Ryanair	
EI-DWG	Boeing 737-8AS	Ryanair	
EI-DWH	Boeing 737-8AS	Ryanair	
EI-DWI	Boeing 737-8AS	Ryanair	
EI-DWJ	Boeing 737-8AS	Ryanair	
EI-DWK	Boeing 737-8AS	Ryanair	
EI-DWL	Boeing 737-8AS	Ryanair	
EI-DWM	Boeing 737-8AS	Ryanair	
EI-DWO	Boeing 737-8AS	Ryanair	
EI-DWP	Boeing 737-8AS	Ryanair	
EI-DWR	Boeing 737-8AS	Ryanair	
EI-DWS	Boeing 737-8AS	Ryanair	
EI-DWT	Boeing 737-8AS	Ryanair	
EI-DWV	Boeing 737-8AS	Ryanair	
EI-DWW	Boeing 737-8AS	Ryanair	
EI-DWX	Boeing 737-8AS	Ryanair	
EI-DWY	Boeing 737-8AS	Ryanair	
EI-DWZ	Boeing 737-8AS	Ryanair	
EI-DXA	Ikarus C42	S. Ryan	*
EI-DXL	CFM Shadow	F. Lynch	
EI-DXM	Raj Hamsa X'Air 582	B. Nugent	
EI-DXP	Cyclone AX3/503	J. Hennessey	
EI-DXS	CFM Shadow	R. W. Frost	
EI-DXT	UrbanAir UFM-10 Samba	N. Irwin	
EI-DXV	Thruster T.600N	P. Higgins	
EI-DXX	Raj Hamsa X'AIR 582(5)	E. D. Hanly & S. Macsweeney	
EI-DXZ	UrbanAir UFM-10 Samba	D. O'Leary	
EI-DYA	Boeing 737-8AS	Ryanair	
EI-DYB	Boeing 737-8AS	Ryanair	
EI-DYC	Boeing 737-8AS	Ryanair	
EI-DYD	Boeing 737-8AS	Ryanair	
EI-DYE	Boeing 737-8AS	Ryanair	
EI-DYF	Boeing 737-8AS	Ryanair	
EI-DYL	Boeing 737-8AS	Ryanair	
EI-DYM	Boeing 737-8AS	Ryanair	
EI-DYN	Boeing 737-8AS	Ryanair	
EI-DYO	Boeing 737-8AS	Ryanair	
EI-DYP	Boeing 737-8AS	Ryanair	
EI-DYR	Boeing 737-8AS	Ryanair	
EI-DYV	Boeing 737-8AS	Ryanair	
EI-DYW	Boeing 737-8AS	Ryanair	
EI-DYX	Boeing 737-8AS	Ryanair	
EI-DYY	Boeing 737-8AS	Ryanair	
EI-DYZ	Boeing 737-8AS	Ryanair	
EI-DZA	Colt 21A balloon	P. Baker	
EI-DZB	Colt 21A balloon	P. Baker	
EI-DZE	UrbanAir UFM-10 Samba	J. P. Gilroy	
EI-DZF	Pipistrel Sinus 912	Light Sport Aviation Ltd	

Notes	Reg	Type († False registration)	Owner or Operator
	EI-DZK	Robinson R22B2 Beta	Skywest Aviation Ltd
	EI-DZL	Urban Air Samba XXL	M. Tormey
	EI-DZM	Robinson R44 II	E1-SUB Ltd
	EI-DZN	Bell 222	B. McCarty & A. Dalton
	EI-DZO	Dominator Gyroplane Ultrawhite	P. O'Reilly
	EI-DZS	BRM Land Africa	M. Whyte
	EI-EAJ	RAF-2000GTX-SE	J. P. Henry
	EI-EAK	Airborne Windsports Edge XT	M. O'Brien
	EI-EAM	Cessna 172R	Atlantic Flight Training Ltd
	EI-EAV	Airbus A.330-302	Aer Lingus
	EI-EAW	Airborne Windsports Edge XT582	F. Heary
	EI-EAY	Raj Hamsa X'Air 582 (5)	West-Tech Aviation Ltd
	EI-EAZ	Cessna 172R	Atlantic Flight Training Ltd
	EI-EBA	Boeing 737-8AS	Ryanair
	EI-EBC	Boeing 737-8AS	Ryanair
	EI-EBD	Boeing 737-8AS	Ryanair
	EI-EBE	Boeing 737-8AS	Ryanair
	EI-EBF	Boeing 737-8AS	Ryanair
	EI-EBG	Boeing 737-8AS	Ryanair
	EI-EBH	Boeing 737-8AS	Ryanair
	EI-EBI	Boeing 737-8AS	Ryanair
	EI-EBK	Boeing 737-8AS	Ryanair
	EI-EBL	Boeing 737-8AS	Ryanair
	EI-EBM	Boeing 737-8AS	Ryanair
	EI-EBN	Boeing 737-8AS	Ryanair
	EI-EBO	Boeing 737-8AS	Ryanair
	EI-EBP	Boeing 737-8AS	Ryanair
	EI-EBR	Boeing 737-8AS	Ryanair
	EI-EBS	Boeing 737-8AS	Ryanair
	EI-EBV	Boeing 737-8AS	Ryanair
	EI-EBW	Boeing 737-8AS	Ryanair
	EI-EBX	Boeing 737-8AS	Ryanair
	EI-EBY	Boeing 737-8AS	Ryanair
	EI-EBZ	Boeing 737-8AS	Ryanair
	EI-ECC	Cameron Z-90 balloon	J. J. Daly
	EI-ECG	BRM Land Africa	J. McGuinness
	EI-ECK	Raj Hamsa X'Air Hawk	N. Geh
	EI-ECL	Boeing 737-86N	Rise Aviation 1 (Ireland) Ltd
	EI-ECM	Boeing 737-86N	Celestial Aviation Trading 26 Ltd
	EI-ECP	Raj Hamsa X'Air Hawk	S. P. McGirr & J. McDaid
	EI-ECZ	Raj Hamsa X'Air Hawk	M. Tolan
	EI-EDB	Cessna 152	National Flight Centre Ltd
	EI-EDC	Cessna FA.152	National Flight Centre Ltd
	EI-EDI	Ikarus C42	M. Owens
	EI-EDJ	CZAW Sportcruiser	Croftal Ltd
	EI-EDP	Airbus A.320-214	Aer Lingus
	EI-EDR	PA-28R Cherokee Arrow 200	Dublin Flyers
	EI-EDS	Airbus A.320-214	Aer Lingus
	EI-EDY	Airbus A.330-302	Aer Lingus
	EI-EEH	BRM Land Africa	R. Duffy
	EI-EEO	Van's RV-7	A. Butler
	EI-EES	ELA-07R	D. Doyle & Partners
	EI-EEU	Osprey II	P. Forde & S. Coughlan
	EI-EFC	Boeing 737-8AS	Ryanair
	EI-EFD	Boeing 737-8AS	Ryanair
	EI-EFE	Boeing 737-8AS	Ryanair
	EI-EFF	Boeing 737-8AS	Ryanair
	EI-EFG	Boeing 737-8AS	Ryanair
	EI-EFH	Boeing 737-8AS	Ryanair
	EI-EFI	Boeing 737-8AS	Ryanair
	EI-EFJ	Boeing 737-8AS	Ryanair
	EI-EFK	Boeing 737-8AS	Ryanair
	EI-EFN	Boeing 737-8AS	Ryanair
	EI-EFO	Boeing 737-8AS	Ryanair
	EI-EFX	Boeing 737-8AS	Ryanair
	EI-EFY	Boeing 737-8AS	Ryanair
	EI-EFZ	Boeing 737-8AS	Ryanair
	EI-EGA	Boeing 737-8AS	Ryanair
	EI-EGB	Boeing 737-8AS	Ryanair
	EI-EGC	Boeing 737-8AS	Ryanair
	EI-EGD	Boeing 737-8AS	Ryanair

Reg	Type († False registration)	Owner or Operator	Notes
EI-EGO	Gulfstream V-SP	Vipjet Ltd	
EI-EHF	Aeroprakt A22 Foxbat	K. Glynn	
EI-EHG	Robinson R22 Beta	G. Jordan	
EI-EHK	Magni Gyro M-22 Voyager	M. Concannon	
EI-EHL	Air Creation Tanarg/Ixess 15 912S	S. Woods	
EI-EHM	Rand KR-2T	A. Lagun	
EI-EHY	Urban Air Samba XXL	C. N. Murphy & R. White	
EI-EIA	Airbus A.320-216	Alitalia	
EI-EIB	Airbus A.320-216	Alitalia	
EI-EIC	Airbus A.320-216	Alitalia	
EI-EID	Airbus A.320-216	Alitalia	
EI-EIE	Airbus A.320-216	Alitalia	
EI-EIK	Airbus A.330-302	Aer Lingus	
EI-EIM	Airbus A.330-302	Aer Lingus	
EI-EIN	Airbus A.330-302	Aer Lingus	
EI-EJG	Airbus A.330-202	Alitalia	
EI-EJH	Airbus A.330-202	Alitalia	
EI-EJI	Airbus A.330-202	Alitalia	
EI-EJJ	Airbus A.330-202	Alitalia	
EI-EJK	Airbus A.330-202	Alitalia	
EI-EJL	Airbus A.330-202	Alitalia	
EI-EJM	Airbus A.330-202	Alitalia	
EI-EJN	Airbus A.330-202	Alitalia	
EI-EJO	Airbus A.330-202	Alitalia	
EI-EJP	Airbus A.330-202	Alitalia	
EI-EKA	Boeing 737-8AS	Constitution Aircraft Leasing (Ireland) 9 Ltd	
EI-EKB	Boeing 737-8AS	Constitution Aircraft Leasing (Ireland) 9 Ltd	
EI-EKC	Boeing 737-8AS	Ryanair	
EI-EKD	Boeing 737-8AS	Ryanair	
EI-EKE	Boeing 737-8AS	Ryanair	
EI-EKF	Boeing 737-8AS	Ryanair	
EI-EKG	Boeing 737-8AS	Ryanair	
EI-EKH	Boeing 737-8AS	Ryanair	
EI-EKI	Boeing 737-8AS	Ryanair	
EI-EKJ	Boeing 737-8AS	Ryanair	
EI-EKK	Boeing 737-8AS	Ryanair	
EI-EKL	Boeing 737-8AS	Ryanair	
EI-EKM	Boeing 737-8AS	Ryanair	
EI-EKN	Boeing 737-8AS	Ryanair	
EI-EKO	Boeing 737-8AS	Ryanair	
EI-EKP	Boeing 737-8AS	Ryanair	
EI-EKR	Boeing 737-8AS	Ryanair	
EI-EKS	Boeing 737-8AS	Ryanair	
EI-EKT	Boeing 737-8AS	Ryanair	
EI-EKV	Boeing 737-8AS	Ryanair	
EI-EKW	Boeing 737-8AS	Ryanair	
EI-EKX	Boeing 737-8AS	Ryanair	
EI-EKY	Boeing 737-8AS	Ryanair	
EI-EKZ	Boeing 737-8AS	Ryanair	
EI-ELA	Airbus A.330-302	Aer Lingus	
EI-ELB	Raj Hamsa X'Air 582 (1)	G. McLaughlin	
EI-ELC	Ikarus C42B	A. Kilpatrick & M. Mullin	
EI-ELL	Medway Eclipser	P. McMahon	
EI-ELM	PA-18-95 Super Cub	O. D. Fitzgibbon	
EI-EMA	Boeing 737-8AS	Ryanair	
EI-EMB	Boeing 737-8AS	Ryanair	
EI-EMC	Boeing 737-8AS	Ryanair	
EI-EMD	Boeing 737-8AS	Ryanair	
EI-EME	Boeing 737-8AS	Ryanair	
EI-EMF	Boeing 737-8AS	Ryanair	
EI-EMH	Boeing 737-8AS	Ryanair	
EI-EMI	Boeing 737-8AS	Ryanair	
EI-EMJ	Boeing 737-8AS	Ryanair	
EI-EMK	Boeing 737-8AS	Ryanair	
EI-EML	Boeing 737-8AS	Ryanair	
EI-EMM	Boeing 737-8AS	Ryanair	
EI-EMN	Boeing 737-8AS	Ryanair	
EI-EMO	Boeing 737-8AS	Ryanair	
EI-EMP	Boeing 737-8AS	Ryanair	
EI-EMR	Boeing 737-8AS	Ryanair	
EI-EMT	PA-16 Clipper	G. Dolan	

Notes	Reg	Type († False registration)	Owner or Operator
	EI-EMU	Cessna F.152	National Flight Centre Ltd
	EI-EMV	CZAW Sportcruiser	L. Doherty & partners
	EI-ENA	Boeing 737-8AS	Ryanair
	EI-ENB	Boeing 737-8AS	Ryanair
	EI-ENC	Boeing 737-8AS	Ryanair
	EI-ENE	Boeing 737-8AS	Ryanair
	EI-ENF	Boeing 737-8AS	Ryanair
	EI-ENG	Boeing 737-8AS	Ryanair
	EI-ENH	Boeing 737-8AS	Ryanair
	EI-ENI	Boeing 737-8AS	Ryanair
	EI-ENJ	Boeing 737-8AS	Ryanair
	EI-ENK	Boeing 737-8AS	Ryanair
	EI-ENL	Boeing 737-8AS	Ryanair
	EI-ENM	Boeing 737-8AS	Ryanair
	EI-ENN	Boeing 737-8AS	Ryanair
	EI-ENO	Boeing 737-8AS	Ryanair
	EI-ENP	Boeing 737-8AS	Ryanair
	EI-ENR	Boeing 737-8AS	Ryanair
	EI-ENS	Boeing 737-8AS	Ryanair
	EI-ENT	Boeing 737-8AS	Ryanair
	EI-ENV	Boeing 737-8AS	Ryanair
	EI-ENW	Boeing 737-8AS	Ryanair
	EI-ENX	Boeing 737-8AS	Ryanair
	EI-ENY	Boeing 737-8AS	FGL Aircraft Ireland Ltd
	EI-EOA	Raj Hamsa X'Air Jabiru	B. Lynch Jnr
	EI-EOB	Cameron Z-69 balloon	J. Leahy
	EI-EOC	Van's RV-6	V. P. & N. O'Brien
	EI-EOF	Jabiru SP430	J. Bermingham
	EI-EOH	BRM Land Africa	M. McCarrick
	EI-EOI	Take Off Merlin 1100	N. Fitzmaurice
	EI-EOU	Evektor EV-97 Eurostar SL	S. Kearney
	EI-EOW	Flight Design CTSW	J. Moriarty
	EI-EPA	Boeing 737-8AS	Ryanair
	EI-EPB	Boeing 737-8AS	Ryanair
	EI-EPC	Boeing 737-8AS	Ryanair
	EI-EPD	Boeing 737-8AS	Ryanair
	EI-EPF	Boeing 737-8AS	SMBC Aviation Capital Ireland Leasing 3 Ltd
	EI-EPH	Boeing 737-8AS	Ryanair
	EI-EPI	Medway Hybred 44XLR	H. J. Long
	EI-EPJ	Mainair/Gemini Flash IIA	L. Flannery
	EI-EPK	Pegasus Quantum 15-912	H. J. Long
	EI-EPP	PA-22-160	P. McCabe
	EI-EPW	MXP-740 Savannah Jabiru(5)	L. Reilly
	EI-EPY	UFM-11 Lambada	P. Kearney
	EI-EPZ	Jodel DR.1050M1	A. Dunne & Partners
	EI-ERE	Pegasus Quantum 15-912	M. Carter
	EI-ERH	Airbus A.320-232	CRA Aircraft No.1 Ltd
	EI-ERI	Air Creation Clipper/Kiss 400-582(1)	E. Thompson
	EI-ERJ	Southdown Raven X	M. Hanley
	EI-ERL	Best Off Sky Ranger 912	B. Chambers
	EI-ERM	Ikarus C42B	C42 Club
	EI-ERO	Pegasus XL-R	M. Doyle
	EI-ERZ	Flight Design CT-2K	T. McHolmes
	EI-ESB	Urban Air Samba XXL	G. Creegan
	EI-ESC	BRM Land Africa	D. Killian
	EI-ESE	Zenair CH.601XL Zodiac	C. O'Connell
	EI-ESF	PA-22-160	G. Dolan
	EI-ESN	Boeing 737-8AS	Wilmington Trust SP Services (Dublin) Ltd
	EI-ESS	Boeing 737-8AS	Ryanair
	EI-EST	Boeing 737-8AS	Ryanair
	EI-ESV	Boeing 737-8AS	Ryanair
	EI-ESY	Boeing 737-8AS	Bank of America Leasing Ireland Ltd
	EI-ESZ	Boeing 737-8AS	Bank of America Leasing Ireland Ltd
	EI-ETB	Ikarus C42B	P. Connolly
	EI-ETD	Raj Hamsa X'Air Hawk	T. McDevitt
	EI-ETE	MS.880B Rallye	Wicklow Wings Ltd
	EI-ETF	Samba XXL	V. Vaughan
	EI-ETV	Raj Hamsa X'Air Hawk	P. Higgins & Partners
	EI-EUA	Airbus A.320-232	GASL Leasing Ireland No.1 Ltd
	EI-EUE	Airbus A.320-232	Wilmington Trust SP Services (Dublin) Ltd
	EI-EUK	Airbus A.320-232	Aercap Ireland Capital DAC

Reg	Type († False registration)	Owner or Operator	Notes
EI-EVA	Boeing 737-8AS	Ryanair	
EI-EVB	Boeing 737-8AS	Ryanair	
EI-EVC	Boeing 737-8AS	Ryanair	
EI-EVE	Boeing 737-8AS	Ryanair	
EI-EVF	Boeing 737-8AS	Ryanair	
EI-EVG	Boeing 737-8AS	Ryanair	
EI-EVH	Boeing 737-8AS	Ryanair	
EI-EVI	Boeing 737-8AS	Ryanair	
EI-EVJ	Boeing 737-8AS	Ryanair	
EI-EVK	Boeing 737-8AS	Ryanair	
EI-EVL	Boeing 737-8AS	Ryanair	
EI-EVM	Boeing 737-8AS	Ryanair	
EI-EVN	Boeing 737-8AS	Ryanair	
EI-EVO	Boeing 737-8AS	Ryanair	
EI-EVP	Boeing 737-8AS	Ryanair	
EI-EVR	Boeing 737-8AS	Ryanair	
EI-EVS	Boeing 737-8AS	Ryanair	
EI-EVT	Boeing 737-8AS	Ryanair	
EI-EVV	Boeing 737-8AS	Ryanair	
EI-EVW	Boeing 737-8AS	Ryanair	
EI-EVX	Boeing 737-8AS	Ryanair	
EI-EVY	Boeing 737-8AS	Wilmington Trust SP Services (Dublin) Ltd	
EI-EVZ	Boeing 737-8AS	Wilmington Trust SP Services (Dublin) Ltd	
EI-EWB	Ikarus C42B	P. O'Reilly	
EI-EWC	Beech 76	National Flight Centre Ltd	
EI-EWG	Airbus A.330-223	Nightjar Ltd	
EI-EWH	Airbus A.330-223	Skua Ltd	
EI-EWI	Boeing 717-2BL	Ruby Leasing (Ireland) Ltd	
EI-EWR	Airbus A.330-202	Aercap Ireland Ltd	
EI-EWV	Ikarus C42 FB100 VLA	D. Parke	
EI-EWX	Aeropro Eurofox 912	R. E. Barrington	
EI-EWZ	MB-2 Colibri	Colibri Group	
EI-EXB	Boeing 717-2BL	Ruby Leasing (Ireland) Ltd	
EI-EXD	Boeing 737-8AS	Ryanair	
EI-EXE	Boeing 737-8AS	Ryanair	
EI-EXF	Boeing 737-8AS	Ryanair	
EI-EXI	Boeing 717-2BL	Ruby Leasing (Ireland) Ltd	
EI-EXR	Airbus A.300-B4622RF	Air Contractors (Ireland) Ltd	
EI-EXY	Urban Air Samba XXL	R. G. Linehan & S. P. Sarsfield	
EI-EYI	PA-28-181	C. Rooney	
EI-EYJ	Cessna F.172N	Trim Flying Club Ltd	
EI-EYK	Airbus A.300B4-622R	Air Contractors (Ireland) Ltd	
EI-EYT	Ikarus C42B	Croom C42 Club	
EI-EYW	Thruster T600N 450	M. O'Carroll & B. Corrigan	
EI-EYY	Aerospatiale ATR-72-212A	Lighthouse Alpha Ltd	
EI-EZK	Aerospatiale ATR-72-212A	Lighthouse Alpha Ltd	
EI-EZU	Cessna FR.172K	The Hawk Group	
EI-EZX	PA-22-108 Colt	A. Fenton	
EI-EZY	Dominator Ultrawhite	J. Dowling	
EI-FAB	Eurocopter EC.120B	Billy Jet Ltd	
EI-FAD	Van's RV-7A	J. Lynch & Partners	
EI-FAM	Rans S-6ES Coyote II	N. Blair	
EI-FAN	Aerospatiale ATR-72-212A	Lighthouse Alpha Ltd	
EI-FAS	Aerospatiale ATR-72-212A	Stobart Air	
EI-FAT	Aerospatiale ATR-72-600	Stobart Air	
EI-FAU	Aerospatiale ATR-72-600	Stobart Air	
EI-FAV	Aerospatiale ATR-72-600	Stobart Air	
EI-FAW	Aerospatiale ATR-72-600	Stobart Air	
EI-FAX	Aerospatiale ATR-72-600	Stobart Air	
EI-FAZ	Urban Air UFM-10 Samba	J. Halpin	
EI-FBC	Cessna 172N	National Flight Centre Ltd	
EI-FBM	Boeing 717-2BL	Ruby Leasing (Ireland) Ltd	
EI-FBW	BRM Land Africa	J. O'Connor	
EI-FBX	BRM Land Africa Citius	P. Higgins	
EI-FBY	BRM Land Africa Citius	S. Smith	
EI-FBZ	Thruster T.600N	V. Vaughan	
EI-FCA	Urban Air UFM-11 Lambada	S. Walshe	
EI-FCB	Boeing 717-200	Ruby Leasing (Ireland) Ltd	
EI-FCH	Boeing 737-83N	Alrosa Airlines	
EI-FCI	Zenair CH-601HD	J. Kenny	
EI-FCU	Boeing 717-2BL	Ruby Leasing (Ireland) Ltd	

Notes	Reg	Type († False registration)	Owner or Operator
	EI-FCY	Aerospatiale ATR-72-600	Aer Arran
	EI-FCZ	Aerospatiale ATR-72-600	Aer Arran
	EI-FDC	PZL-110 Koliber 150	Ardfert Quarry Products ULC
	EI-FDD	Cameron Z-105 balloon	The Travel Department
	EI-FDF	Urban Air Samba XXL	K. Dardis
	EI-FDO	Jabiru UL-D	O. Matthews
	EI-FDR	Bombardier CL600-2B16 Challenger	P. Collins
	EI-FDS	Boeing 737-86N	ECAF I 28595 Designated Activity Company
	EI-FDY	Ikarus C42	N. Dockery
	EI-FEJ	Pipistrel Virus 912	R. Armstrong
	EI-FEO	ELA-07S	H. Graham
	EI-FEP	Aviatika MAI-890	H. A. Humphreys
	EI-FET	Raj Hamsa X'Air 502T	A. Cunningham
	EI-FEU	Aviatika MAI-890	P. O'Donnell
	EI-FEV	Raj Hamsa X'Air 582	M. Garvey
	EI-FEW	Van's RV-7	P. Hayes
	EI-FFM	Boeing 737-73S	Airopco II ME Ireland Designated Activity Company
	EI-FFN	Raj Hamsa X'Air 582	P. J. Gleeson
	EI-FFV	AA-5 Traveler	K. A. J. O'Doherty
	EI-FFZ	Magni M16	S. Brennan
	EI-FGB	BRM Land Africa	P J Piling Contracts Ltd
	EI-FGF	Ikarus C42	Tibohine Flying Club
	EI-FGG	Ikarus C42	M. Murphy
	EI-FGI	Boeing 717-2BL	Ruby Leasing (Ireland) Ltd
	EI-FGN	Boeing 767-3BGER	WWTAI AirOpco II DAC
	EI-FGU	Sky Ranger 912S(1)	A. Ryan
	EI-FGW	PA-22-108	T. Byrne
	EI-FHA	Boeing 737-8JP	Norwegian Air International Ltd
	EI-FHD	Boeing 737-8JP	Norwegian Air International Ltd
	EI-FHE	Boeing 737-8JP	Norwegian Air International Ltd
	EI-FHJ	Boeing 737-8JP	Norwegian Air International Ltd
	EI-FHK	Boeing 737-8JP	Norwegian Air International Ltd
	EI-FHN	Boeing 737-8JP	Norwegian Air International Ltd
	EI-FHP	Boeing 737-8JP	Norwegian Air International Ltd
	EI-FHR	Boeing 737-8JP	Norwegian Air International Ltd
	EI-FHT	Boeing 737-8JP	SMBC Aviation Capital Ireland Leasing 3 Ltd
	EI-FHV	Boeing 737-8JP	Norwegian Air International Ltd
	EI-FHW	Boeing 737-8JP	Norwegian Air International Ltd
	EI-FHX	Boeing 737-8JP	Bank of America Leasing Ireland Ltd
	EI-FHZ	Boeing 737-8JP	Norwegian Air International Ltd
	EI-FII	Cessna 172RG	National Flight Centre Ltd
	EI-FJH	Boeing 737-8JP	Norwegian Air International Ltd
	EI-FJJ	Boeing 737-8JP	Norwegian Air International Ltd
	EI-FJY	Boeing 737-8JP	Norwegian Air International Ltd
	EI-FJZ	Boeing 737-8JP	Norwegian Air International Ltd
	EI-FLA	Rotor Flight Dominator	P. Flanagan
	EI-FLF	Rans S-6ES Coyote II	E. Tougher
	EI-FLH	BRM Land Africa	S. O'Neill
	EI-FLI	Urban Air Samba XXL	M. Tormey
	EI-FLK	BRM Land Africa	P. O'Dowd
	EI-FLL	Ikarus C42	A. Clarke
	EI-FLM	Boeing 737-85F	Meridiana
	EI-FLO	Kitfox Mk.IV	M. Nee
	EI-FLS	Ikarus C42	J. & O. Houlihan
	EI-FLU	PA-22-108	M. Bergin
	EI-FLW	Ikarus C42	D. Browne
	EI-FLX	Raj Hamsa X'Air 582(5)	P. M. Noons, I. Bennett & P. J. Keating
	EI-FMA	Aeropro Eurofox 912 3K	P. Reilly
	EI-FMF	Bellanca 7GCAA	Citabria Flying Group
	EI-FMG	Solar Wings Pegasus XL-R	T. Noonan
	EI-FMJ	Aerospatiale ATR-72-212A	Stobart Air
	EI-FMO	BRM Land Africa	J. Minogue
	EI-FMP	Agusta AW.169	LCI Helicopters Eleven Ltd
	EI-FNA	Aerospatiale ATR-72-600	Stobart Air
	EI-FNC	BRM Land Africa Citius	FNC Group
	EI-FNE	Javron PA-18	P. J. McKenna
	EI-FNG	Airbus A.330-302	Aer Lingus Ltd
	EI-FNH	Airbus A.330-302	Aer Lingus Ltd
	EI-FNI	Boeing 777-2Q8ER	Alitalia
	EI-FNJ	Airbus A.320-214	Aer Lingus Ltd

Reg	Type († False registration)	Owner or Operator	Notes
EI-FNO	Aeropro Eurofox	M. P. Breen & D. Carr	
EI-FNS	Ikarus C42	M. J. Brady	
EI-FNT	Agusta AW.169	Como Aviation Ltd	
EI-FNW	Boeing 737-86N	Genesis Ireland Aviation Trading 3 Ltd	
EI-FNX	Airbus A.330-243	DAE Leasing (Ireland) Ltd	
EI-FPA	Canadair CRJ900LR	Truenoord Ramor Ltd	
EI-FPB	Canadair CRJ900LR	Cityjet/SAS	
EI-FPC	Canadair CRJ900LR	Truenoord Ramor Ltd	
EI-FPD	Canadair CRJ900LR	Cityjet/SAS	
EI-FPE	Canadair CRJ900LR	Cityjet/SAS	
EI-FPF	Canadair CRJ900LR	Cityjet/SAS	
EI-FPG	Canadair CRJ900LR	Cityjet/SAS	
EI-FPH	Canadair CRJ900LR	Cityjet/SAS	
EI-FPI	Canadair CRJ900LR	Cityjet/SAS	
EI-FPJ	Canadair CRJ900LR	Cityjet/SAS	
EI-FPK	Canadair CRJ900LR	Cityjet/SAS	
EI-FPM	Canadair CRJ900LR	Cityjet/SAS	
EI-FPN	Canadair CRJ900LR	Cityjet/SAS	
EI-FPO	Canadair CRJ900LR	Cityjet/SAS	
EI-FPP	Canadair CRJ900LR	Cityjet/SAS	
EI-FPR	Canadair CRJ900LR	Cityjet/SAS	
EI-FPS	Canadair CRJ900LR	Cityjet/SAS	
EI-FPT	Canadair CRJ900LR	Cityjet/SAS	
EI-FPU	Canadair CRJ900LR	Cityjet/SAS	
EI-FPV	Canadair CRJ900LR	Cityjet/SAS	
EI-FPW	Canadair CRJ900LR	Cityjet/SAS	
EI-FPX	Canadair CRJ900LR	Cityjet/SAS	
EI-FSA	TL3000 Sirius	M. J. Kirrane	
EI-FSE	Airbus A.330-243	DAE Leasing (Ireland) Ltd	
EI-FSF	Airbus A.330-243	DAE Leasing (Ireland) 16 Ltd	
EI-FSK	Aerospatiale ATR-72-600	Stobart Air	
EI-FSL	Aerospatiale ATR-72-600	Stobart Air	
EI-FSR	ELA Aviacion ELA-07S	J. Heffernan	
EI-FSS	Boeing 777-2Q8ER	MASL Ireland (11) Ltd	
EI-FST	Ikarus C42	Ikarus Aviation Ireland Ltd	
EI-FSU	Airbus A.321-231	ACG Acquisition 2004-1 Ireland Ltd	
EI-FSW	Rans S-6 ESD	A. J., A. & J. Cunningham	
EI-FSX	Pegasus Quantum 15	G. Hanna	
EI-FSZ	Pipistrel Virus 912	J. Tierney	
EI-FTX	Rans S-6ES Coyote II	N. Blair	
EI-FVF	Raj Hamsa X'Air 582(1)	D. Greziner	
EI-FVJ	Boeing 737-800	Norwegian Air International Ltd	
EI-FVK	Boeing 737-800	Wilmington Trust SP Services (Dublin) Ltd	
EI-FVM	Boeing 737-800	Norwegian Air International Ltd	
EI-FVN	Boeing 737-800	Norwegian Air International Ltd	
EI-FVR	Boeing 737-800	Norwegian Air International Ltd	
EI-FVT	Boeing 737-800	Norwegian Air International Ltd	
EI-FVU	Boeing 737-800	Wilmington Trust SP Services (Dublin) Ltd	
EI-FVV	Boeing 737-800	Norwegian Air International Ltd	
EI-FVW	Boeing 737-800	Norwegian Air International Ltd	
EI-FVX	Boeing 737-800	Norwegian Air International Ltd	
EI-FVY	Boeing 737-800	Norwegian Air International Ltd	
EI-FVZ	Boeing 737-800	Norwegian Air International Ltd	
EI-FXA	Aérospatiale ATR-42-300	Air Contractors (Ireland) Ltd	
EI-FXB	Aérospatiale ATR-42-300	Air Contractors (Ireland) Ltd	
EI-FXC	Aérospatiale ATR-42-300	Air Contractors (Ireland) Ltd	
EI-FXD	Aérospatiale ATR-42-300	Air Contractors (Ireland) Ltd	
EI-FXE	Aérospatiale ATR-42-300	Air Contractors (Ireland) Ltd	
EI-FXI	Aérospatiale ATR-72-202	Air Contractors (Ireland) Ltd	
EI-FXJ	Aérospatiale ATR-72-202	Air Contractors (Ireland) Ltd	
EI-FXK	Aérospatiale ATR-72-202	Air Contractors (Ireland) Ltd	
EI-FXL	Robinson R44	National Flight Centre Ltd	
EI-FXU	Aerospatiale ATR-72-212A	Aircraft International Renting (A.I.R.) Ltd	
EI-FXW	Best Off Sky Ranger Swift 912(2)	P. Marnane	
EI-FXZ	Roko Aero NG 4UL	Fly Hubair Ltd	
EI-FYD	Boeing 737-MAX8	Norwegian Air International Ltd	
EI-FYE	Boeing 737-MAX8	Norwegian Air International Ltd	
EI-GAH	Ikarus C42B	Tibohine Flying Club Ltd	
EI-GAJ	Airbus A.330-302	Aer Lingus	
EI-GAL	Airbus A.320-214	Aer Lingus	
EI-GAM	Airbus A.320-214	Aer Lingus	

Notes	Reg	Type († False registration)	Owner or Operator
	EI-GBB	Boeing 737-86N	AWAS Aviation Leasing (36809) Ltd
	EI-GCC	Airbus A.320-233	Macquarie Aerospace AF (Ireland) Ltd
	EI-GCF	Airbus A.330-302	Aer Lingus
	EI-GCG	BRM Land Africa Citius	D. Bolger
	EI-GCJ	CSA Sportcruiser	S. Meagher, N. Mulligan, D. O'Reilly & M. D. Ryan
	EI-GCP	Sky Ranger 912(2)	J. Marbach
	EI-GCT	ATEC Zephyr 2000	C. S. Kilpatrick & S. R. McGirr
	EI-GCU	Airbus A.330-223	DAE Leasing (Ireland) 31 Ltd
	EI-GCV	Boeing 737-7CT	Wilmington Trust SP Services (Dublin) Ltd/Alrosa Air
	EI-GCZ	Airbus A.330-223	SASOF III (A3) Aviation Ireland
	EI-GDJ	Piper J-4E	Ballyboughal J4 Flying Group
	EI-GEA	Canadair CRJ900ER	Cityjet/SAS
	EI-GEB	Canadair CRJ900ER	Cityjet/SAS
	EI-GEC	Canadair CRJ900ER	Cityjet/SAS
	EI-GED	Canadair CRJ900ER	Cityjet/SAS
	EI-GEF	Canadair CRJ900ER	Cityjet/SAS
	EI-GEH	Canadair CRJ900ER	Cityjet/SAS
	EI-GEN	Skyranger 912(2)	Skybound Air Sports Ltd
	EI-GEO	ICP MXP-740 Savannah S	Funfly Aerosports Ltd
	EI-GEP	Boeing 767-323	Spectre Overseas Aircraft Ltd
	EI-GER	Maule MX7-180A	R. Lanigan & J.Patrick
	EI-GES	Boeing 777-31HER	Aercap Ireland Ltd/Rossiya
	EI-GET	Boeing 777-31HER	Aercap Ireland Ltd
	EI-GEU	Boeing 777-31HER	Altair Aviation No.3 Ltd
	EI-GEV	Aerospatiale ATR-42-600	Aer Lingus Regional
	EI-GEY	Airbus A.330-202	Aer Lingus
	EI-GFA	Boeing 777-31HER	Rossiya
	EI-GFB	Boeing 777-31HER	Rossiya
	EI-GFN	Airbus A.319-112	I-Fly
	EI-GFR	Boeing 737-7CT	Wilmington Trust SP Services (Dublin) Ltd
	EI-GFV	Jodel D.112	J. B. Bolger
	EI-GFX	Airbus A.330-202	Wilmington Trust SP Services (Dublin) Ltd
	EI-GFY	Boeing 737-MAX8	Pembroke Aircraft Leasing 8 Ltd
	EI-GGE	BRM Land Africa Citius	P. M. Finlay
	EI-GGH	Agusta AW.169	LCI Helicopters Eighteen Ltd
	EI-GGK	Boeing 737-MAX8	Pembroke Aircraft Leasing 8 Ltd
	EI-GGL	Boeing 737-MAX8	Pembroke Aircraft Leasing 8 Ltd
	EI-GGO	Airbus A.330-202	Wilmington Trust SPO Services (Dublin) Ltd
	EI-GGP	Airbus A.330-202	Wilmington Trust SPO Services (Dublin) Ltd
	EI-GGV	Thruster TST Mk.1	S. Newlands
	EI-GGX	Zenair CH.601UL	N. Farrell
	EI-GGY	P & M Quik GT450	J. Doran
	EI-GGS	Agusta AW.139	LCI Helicopters (Labuan) Ltd
	EI-GHA	Boeing 737-490	Mistral Air
	EI-GHB	Boeing 737-490	Mistral Air
	EI-GHC	Boeing 737-490F	Mistral Air
	EI-GHH	Europa	Lee Aero Club
	EI-GHI	PA-22-150	H. Taggart
	EI-GHJ	Embraer ERJ190-100IGW	Stobart Air
	EI-GHK	Embraer ERJ190-100IGW	Stobart Air
	EI-GHR	ICP MXP-740 Savannah S	Funfly Aerosports Flying Club Ltd
	EI-GHS	ICP Ventura	R. F. Gibney
	EI-GHU	Agusta AW.119 Mk.II	Perspect Aviation DAC
	EI-GHW	Bell 505	Yoyo Capital Unlimited Company
	EI-GIH	Boeing 737-86N	Rise Aviation 1 (Ireland) Ltd
	EI-GIJ	Van's RV-9	D. Horan
	EI-GIM	Boeing 737-86Q	ALC Blarney Aircraft Ltd
	EI-GIO	Magni VPM M-16	P. M. Flanagan
	EI-GIR	Sky Ranger 912S	P. O'Reilly
	EI-GIU	Cessna F.172N	National Flight Centre Ltd
	EI-GJL	AS.365N3	Anglo Beef Processors Ireland
	EI-GJS	Boeing 737-800	Ryanair
	EI-GJT	Boeing 737-800	Ryanair
	EI-GKN	Cessna 172S	Atlantic Flight Training Ltd
	EI-GKZ	Mainair Gemeni/Flash II	A. Ryan
	EI-GLA	Schleicher ASK-21	Dublin Gliding Club Ltd
	EI-GLB	Schleicher ASK-21	Dublin Gliding Club Ltd
	EI-GLC	Centrair 101A Pegase	Dublin Gliding Club Ltd
	EI-GLD	Schleicher ASK-13	Dublin Gliding Club Ltd

Reg	Type († False registration)	Owner or Operator	Notes
EI-GLF	Schleicher K-8B	Dublin Gliding Club Ltd	
EI-GLG	Schleicher Ka 6CR	C. Sinclair	
EI-GLH	AB Sportine LAK-17A	S. Kinnear & B. O'Neill	
EI-GLL	Glaser-Dirks DG-200	P. Denman & C. Craig	
EI-GLM	Schleicher Ka-6CR	P. Denman, C. Craig & J. Finnan	
EI-GLO	Scheibe Zugvogel IIIB	J. Walsh, J. Murphy & N. Short	
EI-GLP	Olympia 2B	J. Cashin	
EI-GLT	Schempp-Hirth Discus b	D. Thomas	
EI-GLU	Schleicher Ka-6CR	K. Cullen & Partners	
EI-GLV	Schleicher ASW-19B	A. McDermott	
EI-GLZ	ASK-21	Dublin Gliding Club Ltd	
EI-GMB	Schleicher ASW-17	ASW-17 Group	
EI-GMC	Schleicher ASK-18	The Eighteen Group	
EI-GMD	Phoebus C	F. McDonnell & Partners	
EI-GMF	Schleicher ASK-13	Dublin Gliding Club Ltd	
EI-GMG	H201B Standard Libelle	The Dragonfliers	
EI-GMH	WAG-Aero Sport Trainer	J. Matthews	
EI-GMI	PZL PW-5 Smyk	P. Walsh, S. Meagher, M. D. Ryan & J. Whelan	
EI-GMJ	Schleicher ASW-19B	L. Keegan	
EI-GMK	Glasflugel H.201B Standard Libelle	P. Moran	
EI-GMM	Schleicher ASW-22	The 22 Group	
EI-GMO	Schleicher Ka 6E	C. Ainclair & W. Kilroy	
EI-GMP	Rolladen-Schneider LS1-D	O. Grogan	
EI-GMR	Rolladen-Schneider LS1-O	R. Staeps-Morgenstern	
EI-GOD	PA-28-180 Cherokee	M. & P. M. Corrigan	
EI-GOE	Thruster T600N 450	J. Hennessy	
EI-GOT	Airbus A.330-323	ALC Blarney Aircraft Ltd	
EI-GOU	Agusta AW.139	LCI Helicopters Eight Ltd	
EI-GPF	Ikarus C42C	Tibohine Flying Club Ltd	
EI-GPH	Bell 206L-4 Long Ranger	National Helicopter Flight Centre Ltd	
EI-GPJ	Airbus A.330-343	I-Fly	
EI-GPM	Magni Gyro M24 Orion	B. McCafferty	
EI-GPN	Aerospatiale ATR-72-600	Stobart Air Ltd	
EI-GPO	Aerospatiale ATR-72-600	Commuter Aircraft Leasing 2017 I Ltd	
EI-GPP	Aerospatiale ATR-72-600	Commuter Aircraft Leasing 2017 I Ltd	
EI-GPR	Noble Hardman Snowbird Mk.IV	P. Cattigan & J. Selman	
EI-GPS	Grob G.120TP-A	Grob Power Service Ltd	
EI-GPT	Robinson R22 Beta	Treaty Plant & Tool (Hire & Sales)	
EI-GPV	Ikarus C42B	Tibohine Flying Club	
EI-GRA	Urban Air UFM-13 Lambada	J. Selman	
EI-GRB	J-3F-65 Cub	A. Power & C. Hennesey	
EI-GRF	Raj Hamsa X'Air 582(6)	M. Duffy	
EI-GRG	Super J300 Joker	F. Lynch	
EI-GRH	Ikarus C42B	Tibohine Flying Club Ltd	
EI-GRI	ICP MXP-740 Savannah S	Funfly Aerosports Ltd	
EI-GRJ	Boeing 737-8Q8	Neos	
EI-GRV	Van's RV-7	M. D. Murphy, D. Donoghue & C. Keane	
EI-GRX	Cessna 172S	Waterford Aero Club Ltd	
EI-GRY	Mooney M.20R	DK Innovation Ltd	
EI-GRZ	Airbus A.320-216	Macquarie Airfinance Acquisitions (Ireland) Ltd	
EI-GSG	Boeing 737-800	Ryanair	
EI-GSH	Boeing 737-800	Ryanair	
EI-GSI	Boeing 737-800	Ryanair	
EI-GSJ	Boeing 737-800	Ryanair	
EI-GSK	Boeing 737-800	Ryanair	
EI-GSL	Boeing 737-85R	KLAATU Aircraft Leasing (Ireland) Ltd	
EI-GSM	Cessna 182S	Westpoint Flying Group	
EI-GSN	Boeing 737-85R	KLAATU Aircraft Leasing (Ireland) Ltd	
EI-GSP	Airbus A.321-231	Merx Aviation Ireland 1 Ltd	
EI-GST	Littlewing Autogyros Inc LW3	J. Todd	
EI-GSU	P & M Quik GT450	J. Ryan	
EI-GSV	Airbus A.320-232	ECAF I 2587 DAC	
EI-GSY	Airbus A.320-214	JPA Leasing Libra Ltd	
EI-GSZ	Airbus A.320-214	JPA Leasing Libra Ltd	
EI-GTB	ICP MXP-740 Savannah S	K. P. Walsh & G. McGuinness	
EI-GTC	Robin HR.200/120B	Nogaro Ltd	
EI-GTE	Airbus A.330-203	Aptree Aviation Trading 2 Co.Ltd	
EI-GTI	Embraer ERJ190-100LR	GY Aviation Lease 1707 Co.Ltd	
EI-GTJ	Airbus A.320-232	KLAATU Aircraft Leasing (Ireland) Ltd	
EI-GTN	Boeing 737-85F	Macquarie Aerospace Ireland Ltd	

Notes	Reg	Type († False registration)	Owner or Operator
	EI-GTO	Airbus A.320-232	Pembroke Aircraft Leasing 6 Ltd
	EI-GTP	Boeing 737-86Q	KLAATU Aircraft Leasing (Ireland) Ltd
	EI-GTR	Airbus A.320-214	KLAATU Aircraft Leasing (Ireland) Ltd
	EI-GTS	Airbus A.320-232	KLAATU Aircraft Leasing (Ireland) Ltd
	EI-GTT	Airbus A.330-343	JLPS Leasing Virgo Ltd
	EI-GTV	Boeing 737-800	Silver Aircraft Leasing (Ireland) 2 Ltd
	EI-GTW	Boeing 757-2GS	AS Air Lease XVII (Ireland) Ltd
	EI-GTX	Skyranger 912(2)	K. Roche
	EI-GUA	Boeing 737-490F	Aircraft 23810 QC Holdings Ltd
	EI-GUB	Boeing 737-490F	Aircraft 23810 QC Holdings Ltd
	EI-GUC	Airbus A.320-214	Macquarir Aerospace AF (Ireland) Ltd
	EI-GUH	Airbus A.320-232	Klaatu Aircraft Leasing (Ireland) Ltd
	EI-GUL	Aerospatiale ATR-72-600F	ASL Airlines Ireland Ltd
	EI-GUY	Beech 1900D	ACIA Aero Leasing (Ireland) Ltd
	EI-GUZ	ICP MXP-740 Savannah S	Funfly Aerosports Flying Club Company Ltd
	EI-GVA	Airbus A.320-232	Pembroke Aircraft Leasing 13 Ltd
	EI-GVB	PA-28-140	Sun Mingxia
	EI-GVC	Aerospool WT-9 Dynamic LSA	D. Conway
	EI-GVG	Rockwell Commander 112A	Iomys Ltd
	EI-GVH	Airbus A.330-243	Thunderbolt Leasing Ltd
	EI-GVI	Airbus A.320-232	JLPS Leasing Stella Ltd
	EI-GVM	Robinson R22 Beta	J. Porter
	EI-GVT	Beagle A.61 Terrier 3	N. O'Brien & F. Hopkins
	EI-GWY	Cessna 172R	Waterford Aero Club Ltd
	EI-GXG	Boeing 737-800	Ryanair
	EI-GXH	Boeing 737-800	Ryanair
	EI-GXI	Boeing 737-800	Ryanair
	EI-GXJ	Boeing 737-800	Ryanair
	EI-GXK	Boeing 737-800	Ryanair
	EI-GXL	Boeing 737-800	Ryanair
	EI-GXM	Boeing 737-800	Ryanair
	EI-GXN	Boeing 737-800	Ryanair
	EI-HAA	Boeing 737-4YOF	ASL Airlines (Ireland) Ltd
	EI-HAT	Boeing 737-MAX8-200	Ryanair
	EI-HBA	Canadair CRJ1000	Hibernian Airlines Ltd
	EI-HBB	Canadair CRJ1000	Hibernian Airlines Ltd
	EI-HEA	Airbus A.330-322F	ASL Airlines (Ireland) Ltd
	EI-HEB	Airbus A.330-322F	ASL Airlines (Ireland) Ltd
	EI-HEC	Airbus A.330-322	ASL Airlines (Ireland) Ltd
	EI-HFA	DHC-1 Chipmunk 22	Irish Historic Flight Foundation Ltd
	EI-HFB	DHC-1 Chipmunk 22	Irish Historic Flight Foundation Ltd
	EI-HFC	DHC-1 Chipmunk 22	Irish Historic Flight Foundation Ltd
	EI-HFD	Boeing E75 Stearman	Irish Historic Flight Foundation Ltd
	EI-HOP	Van's RV-7	F. Hopkins
	EI-HUM	Van's RV-7	G. Humphreys
	EI-IAL	Agusta AW.109SP	Ion Aviation Ltd
	EI-ICA	Sikorsky S-92A	CHC Ireland Ltd
	EI-ICD	Sikorsky S-92A	CHC Ireland Ltd
	EI-ICG	Sikorsky S-92A	CHC Ireland Ltd
	EI-ICP	ICP MXP-740 Savannah S	Funfly Aerosports Ltd
	EI-ICR	Sikorsky S-92A	CHC Ireland Ltd
	EI-ICS	Sikorsky S-92A	CHC Ireland Ltd
	EI-ICU	Sikorsky S-92A	CHC Ireland Ltd
	EI-IIN	Bombardier BD700-1A11	Airlink Airways Ltd
	EI-IKB	Airbus A.320-214	Alitalia
	EI-IKF	Airbus A.320-214	Alitalia
	EI-IKG	Airbus A.320-214	Alitalia
	EI-IKL	Airbus A.320-214	Alitalia
	EI-IKU	Airbus A.320-214	Alitalia
	EI-IMB	Airbus A.319-112	Alitalia
	EI-IMC	Airbus A.319-112	Alitalia
	EI-IMD	Airbus A.319-112	Alitalia
	EI-IME	Airbus A.319-112	Alitalia
	EI-IMF	Airbus A.319-112	Alitalia
	EI-IMG	Airbus A.319-112	Alitalia
	EI-IMH	Airbus A.319-112	Alitalia
	EI-IMI	Airbus A.319-112	Alitalia
	EI-IMJ	Airbus A.319-112	Alitalia
	EI-IML	Airbus A.319-112	Alitalia
	EI-IMM	Airbus A.319-112	Alitalia
	EI-IMN	Airbus A.319-111	Alitalia

Reg	Type († False registration)	Owner or Operator	Notes
EI-IMO	Airbus A.319-112	Alitalia	
EI-IMP	Airbus A.319-111	Alitalia	
EI-IMR	Airbus A.319-111	Alitalia	
EI-IMS	Airbus A.319-111	Alitalia	
EI-IMT	Airbus A.319-111	Alitalia	
EI-IMU	Airbus A.319-111	Alitalia	
EI-IMV	Airbus A.319-111	Alitalia	
EI-IMW	Airbus A.319-111	Alitalia	
EI-IMX	Airbus A.319-111	Alitalia	
EI-ISA	Boeing 777-243ER	Alitalia	
EI-ISB	Boeing 777-243ER	Alitalia	
EI-ISD	Boeing 777-243ER	Alitalia	
EI-ISE	Boeing 777-243ER	Alitalia	
EI-ISO	Boeing 777-243ER	Alitalia	
EI-ITN	Bombardier BD700-1A10	Airlink Airways	
EI-IXH	Airbus A.321-112	Alitalia	
EI-IXJ	Airbus A.321-112	Alitalia	
EI-IXV	Airbus A.321-112	Alitalia	
EI-IXZ	Airbus A.321-112	Alitalia	
EI-JAM	Cessna 172RG	Mannion Automation Ltd	
EI-JIA	Beech 200 Super King Air	Jobec Aviation Ltd	
EI-JIM	Urban Air Samba XLA	J. Smith	
EI-JPK	Tecnam P2002-JF	Limerick Flying Club (Coonagh) Ltd	
EI-JSK	Gulfstream VI	Westair Aviation	
EI-KEL	Eurocopter EC.135T2+	Bond Air Services (Ireland) Ltd	
EI-KEV	Raj Hamsa X'Air Jabiru(3)	P. Kearney	
EI-LAD	Robinson R44 II	Helicopter Support Ireland Ltd	
EI-LAX	Airbus A.330-202	Aer Lingus St Mella	
EI-LCM	TBM-700N	G. Power	
EI-LFC	Tecnam P.2002-JF	Limerick Flying Club (Coonagh) Ltd	
EI-LID	Agusta AW.169	Vertical Aviation No.1 Ltd	
EI-LIM	Agusta AW.139	Westair Aviation	
EI-LOW	AS.355N	Executive Helicopter Maintenance Ltd	
EI-LRA	Airbus A.321-253NX	Aer Lingus	
EI-LRB	Airbus A.321-253NX	Aer Lingus	
EI-LRC	Airbus A.321-253NX	Aer Lingus	
EI-LRD	Airbus A.321-253NX	Aer Lingus	
EI-LRE	Airbus A.321-253NX	Aer Lingus	
EI-LSA	Cub Crafters CC11-160	Directsky Aviation Ltd	
EI-LSN	Gulfstream VI	Gain Jet Ireland Ltd	
EI-LSY	Gulfstream V-SP	Gain Jet (Ireland) Ltd	
EI-MCF	Cessna 172R	National Flight Centre Ltd	
EI-MCG	Cessna 172R	Galway Flying Club	
EI-MIK	Eurocopter EC.120B	Executive Helicopter Maintenance Ltd	
EI-MIR	Roko Aero NG 4HD	A. Fegan	
EI-MNG	Boeing 737-MAX8	MIAT Mongolian Airlines	
EI-MPC	Agusta AW.109SP	Quarry and Mining Equipment Ltd	
EI-MPW	Robinson R44	Connacht Helicopters	
EI-MRB	Denney Kitfox Mk.2	D. Doyle	
EI-MTZ	Urban Air Samba XXL	M. Motz	
EI-NEO	Boeing 787-9	Neos	
EI-NEU	Boeing 787-9	Neos	
EI-NEW	Boeing 787-9	Neos	
EI-NFW	Cessna 172S	Galway Flying Club	
EI-NJA	Robinson R44 II	Nojo Aviation Ltd	
EI-NUA	Boeing 787-9	Neos	
EI-NVL	Jora spol S. R. O. Jora	S. Farrell	
EI-NYE	Boeing 787-9	Celtago II Leasing Ltd	
EI-ODD	Bell 206B JetRanger	Newcastle Logistics Ltd	
EI-OFM	Cessna F.172N	National Flight Centre Ltd	
EI-OOR	Cessna 172S	M. Casey	
EI-OZL	Airbus A.300B4-622R	ASL Airlines (Ireland) Ltd	
EI-OZM	Airbus A.300B4-622R	ASL Airlines (Ireland) Ltd	
EI-PCI	Bell 206B	Marketside Ltd	
EI-PGA	Dudek Hadron XX	F. Taylor	
EI-PGB	Dudek Hadron 28	C. Fowler	
EI-PGD	Paramania Reflex Wings Revolution 2	D. Keoghegan	
EI-PGI	Dudek Hadron 28	J. McGovern	
EI-PGJ	Swing Sting 2	A. Auffret	
EI-PGK	Ozone Power Spyder 26	O. Creagh	
EI-PGM	Dudek Nucleon XX	L. Graham	

Notes	Reg	Type († False registration)	Owner or Operator
	EI-PGN	ITV Boxer	N. Burke
	EI-PGO	Fly Market Relax 25	M. N. Bendon
	EI-PGP	Paramania Reflex Wings Fusion 26	E. DeKhors
	EI-PGS	Dudek Universal 25.5	M. Markowicz
	EI-PGT	ITV Boxer	M. Hastings
	EI-PGV	Ozone Power Spyder 26	R. Tobin
	EI-PGW	Dudek Universal 1.1	C. Finn
	EI-PGX	ITV Boxer 2	R. Leslie
	EI-PMI	Agusta-Bell 206B JetRanger III	Eirland Ltd
	EI-POK	Robinson R44	Zeus Packaging Ltd
	EI-POP	Cameron Z-90 balloon	The Travel Department
	EI-PRO	Airbus Helicopters AS.365N2	Executive Helicopter Maintenance Ltd
	EI-PWC	Magni M-24 Orion	R. Macnioclais
	EI-RCA	Roko Aero NG4UL	A. Breslin
	EI-RDA	Embraer ERJ170-200LR	Alitalia Cityliner
	EI-RDB	Embraer ERJ170-200LR	Alitalia Cityliner
	EI-RDC	Embraer ERJ170-200LR	Alitalia Cityliner
	EI-RDD	Embraer ERJ170-200LR	Alitalia Cityliner
	EI-RDE	Embraer ERJ170-200LR	Alitalia Cityliner
	EI-RDF	Embraer ERJ170-200LR	Alitalia Cityliner
	EI-RDG	Embraer ERJ170-200LR	Alitalia Cityliner
	EI-RDH	Embraer ERJ170-200LR	Alitalia Cityliner
	EI-RDI	Embraer ERJ170-200LR	Alitalia Cityliner
	EI-RDN	Embraer ERJ170-200LR	Alitalia Cityliner
	EI-RDO	Embraer ERJ170-200LR	Alitalia Cityliner
	EI-RNA	Embraer ERJ190-100STD	Alitalia Cityliner
	EI-RNB	Embraer ERJ190-100STD	Alitalia Cityliner
	EI-RNC	Embraer ERJ190-100STD	Alitalia Cityliner
	EI-RND	Embraer ERJ190-100STD	Alitalia Cityliner
	EI-RNE	Embraer ERJ190-100STD	Alitalia Cityliner
	EI-ROK	Roko Aero NG 4UL	K. Harley
	EI-SAC	Cessna 172P	Sligo Aero Club
	EI-SEA	SeaRey	J. Brennan
	EI-SEV	Boeing 737-73S	Ryanair
	EI-SID	Airbus A.320-251N	Scandinavian Airlines Ireland Ltd
	EI-SIE	Airbus A.320-251N	Scandinavian Airlines Ireland Ltd
	EI-SIF	Airbus A.320-251N	Scandinavian Airlines Ireland Ltd
	EI-SIG	Airbus A.320-251N	Scandinavian Airlines Ireland Ltd
	EI-SIH	Airbus A.320-251N	Scandinavian Airlines Ireland Ltd
	EI-SII	Airbus A.320-251N	Scandinavian Airlines Ireland Ltd
	EI-SKP	Cessna F.172P	National Flight Centre Ltd
	EI-SKS	Robin R.2160	Shemburn Ltd
	EI-SKV	Robin R.2160	Shemburn Ltd
	EI-SKW	PA-28-161 Warrior II	Shemburn Ltd
	EI-SLF	Aérospatiale ATR-72-201	ASL Airlines (Ireland) Ltd
	EI-SLP	Aerospatiale ATR-72-212	ASL Airlines (Ireland) Ltd
	EI-SLS	Aerospatiale ATR-72-201	ASL Airlines (Ireland) Ltd
	EI-SLU	Aerospatiale ATR-72-202	ASL Airlines (Ireland) Ltd
	EI-SLV	Aerospatiale ATR-72-202	ASL Airlines (Ireland) Ltd
	EI-SLW	Aerospatiale ATR-72-202	ASL Airlines (Ireland) Ltd
	EI-SLY	Aerospatiale ATR-72-202	ASL Airlines (Ireland) Ltd
	EI-SLZ	Aerospatiale ATR-72-202	ASL Airlines (Ireland) Ltd
	EI-SMK	Zenair CH701	S. King
	EI-SNG	ICP Ventura	S. Grehan
	EI-SOO	Aerospatiale ATR-72-212A	ASL Airlines (Ireland) Ltd
	EI-SOP	Aerospatiale ATR-72-212A	ASL Airlines (Ireland) Ltd
	EI-SRV	Van's RV-7	T. M. Doddy & K. Keigher
	EI-STJ	Boeing 737-490F	ASL Airlines (Ireland) Ltd
	EI-STK	Boeing 737-448	ASL Airlines (Ireland) Ltd
	EI-STL	Boeing 737-42C	ASL Airlines (Ireland) Ltd
	EI-STM	Boeing 737-4Z9F	ASL Airlines (Ireland) Ltd
	EI-STN	Boeing 737-4Q8	ASL Airlines (Ireland) Ltd
	EI-STO	Boeing 737-43Q	ASL Airlines (Ireland) Ltd
	EI-STP	Boeing 737-4Q8F	ASL Airlines (Ireland) Ltd
	EI-STS	Boeing 737-48E	ASL Airlines (Ireland) Ltd
	EI-STU	Boeing 737-4MOF	ASL Airlines (Ireland) Ltd
	EI-SYM	Van's RV-7	E. Symes
	EI-TAT	Bombardier CL600-2B16	Bandon Aircraft Leasing Ltd
	EI-TIM	Piper J-5A	N. & C. Murphy
	EI-TKI	Robinson R22 Beta	J. McDaid
	EI-TON	M. B. Cooke 582 (5)	T. Merrigan

Reg	Type († False registration)	Owner or Operator	Notes
EI-TVG	Boeing 737-7ZF	Hansel Jet Ireland Ltd	
EI-UFO	PA-22 Tri-Pacer 150 (tailwheel)	W. Treacy	
EI-ULN	Boeing 737-73V	SASOF II (G) Aviation Ireland Ltd	
EI-UNL	Boeing 777-312	Stecker Ltd	
EI-UNM	Boeing 777-312	VEBL-767-300 Ltd	
EI-UNN	Boeing 777-312	Stecker Ltd	
EI-UNP	Boeing 777-312	VEBL-767-300 Ltd	
EI-VII	Vans RV-7	B. Sheane	
EI-VLN	PA-18A-150	D. O'Mahony	
EI-WAC	PA-23 Aztec 250E	Westair Aviation	
EI-WFD	Tecnam P.2002-JF	Limerick Flying Club (Coonagh) Co.Ltd	
EI-WFI	Bombardier CL600-2B16 Challenger	Midwest Atlantic/Westair	
EI-WIG	Sky Ranger 912	K. Lannery	
EI-WLA	Boeing 777-3Q8ER	Alitalia	
EI-WMN	PA-23 Aztec 250F	Westair Aviation	
EI-WOT	Currie Wot	D. Doyle & Partners	
EI-WWI	Robinson R44 II	Ourville Ltd	
EI-WXP	Hawker 800XP	Westair Aviation Ltd	
EI-XHI	Airbus Helicopters EC.155B	Executive Helicopter Maintenance Ltd	
EI-XIN	Boeing 787-9	Neos	
EI-XLC	Boeing 747-446	SB Leasing Ireland Ltd	
EI-XLD	Boeing 747-446	VEBL-767-300 Ltd	
EI-XLE	Boeing 747-446	SB Leasing Ireland Ltd	
EI-XLF	Boeing 747-446	SB Leasing Ireland Ltd	
EI-XLG	Boeing 747-446	SB Leasing Ireland Ltd	
EI-XLH	Boeing 747-446	Pembroke Exchanges Ltd	
EI-XLI	Boeing 747-446	Pembroke Exchanges Ltd	
EI-XLJ	Boeing 747-446	Richdale Investments Ltd	
EI-XLL	Boeing 747-412	VEBL-767-300 Ltd	
EI-XLM	Boeing 747-412	Richdale Investments Ltd	
EI-XLN	Boeing 747-412	VEBL-767-300 Ltd	
EI-XLO	Boeing 747-412	VEBL-767-300 Ltd	
EI-XLP	Boeing 777-312	VEBL-767-300 Ltd	
EI-YLG	Robin HR.200/120B	Leinster Aero Club	
EI-ZZZ	Bell222	Executive Helicopter Maintenance Ltd	
EJ-ADMI	Gulfstream VI	Gain Jet Ireland Ltd	
EJ-AWES	Bombardier CL600-2B16	Sonas Aviation Ltd	
EJ-CORE	Embraer EMB-135BJ	Gain Jet Ireland Ltd	
EJ-KGRP	Gulfstream V-SP	KGP Aviation Ltd	
EJ-ROXY	Bombardier CL600-2B16	ACASS Ireland Ltd	
EJ-SAID	Bombardier BD700-1A10	Gain Jet Ireland Ltd	

EI-AED Cessna 120 *Peter R. March*

Notes	Reg	Type	Owner or Operator

A6 (United Arab Emirates)

A6-APA	Airbus A.380-861	Etihad Airways
A6-APB	Airbus A.380-861	Etihad Airways
A6-APC	Airbus A.380-861	Etihad Airways
A6-APD	Airbus A.380-861	Etihad Airways
A6-APE	Airbus A.380-861	Etihad Airways
A6-APF	Airbus A.380-861	Etihad Airways
A6-APG	Airbus A.380-861	Etihad Airways
A6-APH	Airbus A.380-861	Etihad Airways
A6-API	Airbus A.380-861	Etihad Airways
A6-APJ	Airbus A.380-861	Etihad Airways
A6-BLA	Boeing 787-9	Etihad Airways
A6-BLB	Boeing 787-9	Etihad Airways
A6-BLC	Boeing 787-9	Etihad Airways
A6-BLD	Boeing 787-9	Etihad Airways
A6-BLE	Boeing 787-9	Etihad Airways
A6-BLF	Boeing 787-9	Etihad Airways
A6-BLG	Boeing 787-9	Etihad Airways
A6-BLH	Boeing 787-9	Etihad Airways
A6-BLI	Boeing 787-9	Etihad Airways
A6-BLJ	Boeing 787-9	Etihad Airways
A6-BLK	Boeing 787-9	Etihad Airways
A6-BLL	Boeing 787-9	Etihad Airways
A6-BLM	Boeing 787-9	Etihad Airways
A6-BLN	Boeing 787-9	Etihad Airways
A6-BLO	Boeing 787-9	Etihad Airways
A6-BLP	Boeing 787-9	Etihad Airways
A6-BLQ	Boeing 787-9	Etihad Airways
A6-BLR	Boeing 787-9	Etihad Airways
A6-BLS	Boeing 787-9	Etihad Airways
A6-BLT	Boeing 787-9	Etihad Airways
A6-BLU	Boeing 787-9	Etihad Airways
A6-BLV	Boeing 787-9	Etihad Airways
A6-BLW	Boeing 787-9	Etihad Airways
A6-BLX	Boeing 787-9	Etihad Airways
A6-BLY	Boeing 787-9	Etihad Airways
A6-BLZ	Boeing 787-9	Etihad Airways
A6-BMA	Boeing 787-10	Etihad Airways
A6-BMB	Boeing 787-10	Etihad Airways
A6-BMC	Boeing 787-10	Etihad Airways
A6-BMD	Boeing 787-10	Etihad Airways
A6-BME	Boeing 787-10	Etihad Airways
A6-BMF	Boeing 787-10	Etihad Airways
A6-BMG	Boeing 787-10	Etihad Airways
A6-BMH	Boeing 787-10	Etihad Airways
A6-BMI	Boeing 787-10	Etihad Airways
A6-BMJ	Boeing 787-10	Etihad Airways
A6-BNA	Boeing 787-9	Etihad Airways
A6-BNB	Boeing 787-9	Etihad Airways
A6-BNC	Boeing 787-9	Etihad Airways
A6-BND	Boeing 787-9	Etihad Airways
A6-DDB	Boeing 777-FFX	Etihad Airways Cargo
A6-DDC	Boeing 777-FFX	Etihad Airways Cargo
A6-DDD	Boeing 777-FFX	Etihad Airways Cargo
A6-DDE	Boeing 777-FFX	Etihad Airways Cargo
A6-DDF	Boeing 777-FFX	Etihad Airways Cargo
A6-EBJ	Boeing 777-36NER	Emirates Airlines
A6-EBK	Boeing 777-36NER	Emirates Airlines
A6-EBM	Boeing 777-31HER	Emirates Airlines
A6-EBN	Boeing 777-36NER	Emirates Airlines
A6-EBO	Boeing 777-36NER	Emirates Airlines
A6-EBR	Boeing 777-36NER	Emirates Airlines
A6-EBQ	Boeing 777-36NER	Emirates Airlines
A6-EBU	Boeing 777-31HER	Emirates Airlines
A6-EBW	Boeing 777-36NER	Emirates Airlines
A6-EBY	Boeing 777-36NER	Emirates Airlines
A6-ECA	Boeing 777-36NER	Emirates Airlines
A6-ECC	Boeing 777-36NER	Emirates Airlines

Reg	Type	Owner or Operator	Notes
A6-ECD	Boeing 777-36NER	Emirates Airlines	
A6-ECE	Boeing 777-31HER	Emirates Airlines	
A6-ECF	Boeing 777-31HER	Emirates Airlines	
A6-ECG	Boeing 777-31HER	Emirates Airlines	
A6-ECH	Boeing 777-31HER	Emirates Airlines	
A6-ECI	Boeing 777-31HER	Emirates Airlines	
A6-ECJ	Boeing 777-31HER	Emirates Airlines	
A6-ECK	Boeing 777-31HER	Emirates Airlines	
A6-ECM	Boeing 777-36NER	Emirates Airlines	
A6-ECN	Boeing 777-36NER	Emirates Airlines	
A6-ECO	Boeinb 777-36NER	Emirates Airlines	
A6-ECP	Boeing 777-36HER	Emirates Airlines	
A6-ECQ	Boeing 777-31HER	Emirates Airlines	
A6-ECR	Boeing 777-31HER	Emirates Airlines	
A6-ECS	Boeing 777-31HER	Emirates Airlines	
A6-ECT	Boeing 777-31HER	Emirates Airlines	
A6-ECU	Boeing 777-31HER	Emirates Airlines	
A6-ECV	Boeing 777-31HER	Emirates Airlines	
A6-ECW	Boeing 777-31HER	Emirates Airlines	
A6-ECX	Boeing 777-31HER	Emirates Airlines	
A6-ECY	Boeing 777-31HER	Emirates Airlines	
A6-ECZ	Boeing 777-31HER	Emirates Airlines	
A6-EDA	Airbus A.380-861	Emirates Airlines	
A6-EDB	Airbus A.380-861	Emirates Airlines	
A6-EDC	Airbus A.380-861	Emirates Airlines	
A6-EDD	Airbus A.380-861	Emirates Airlines	
A6-EDE	Airbus A.380-861	Emirates Airlines	
A6-EDF	Airbus A.380-861	Emirates Airlines	
A6-EDG	Airbus A.380-861	Emirates Airlines	
A6-EDH	Airbus A.380-861	Emirates Airlines	
A6-EDI	Airbus A.380-861	Emirates Airlines	
A6-EDJ	Airbus A.380-861	Emirates Airlines	
A6-EDK	Airbus A.380-861	Emirates Airlines	
A6-EDL	Airbus A.380-861	Emirates Airlines	
A6-EDM	Airbus A.380-861	Emirates Airlines	
A6-EDN	Airbus A.380-861	Emirates Airlines	
A6-EDO	Airbus A.380-861	Emirates Airlines	
A6-EDP	Airbus A.380-861	Emirates Airlines	
A6-EDQ	Airbus A.380-861	Emirates Airlines	
A6-EDR	Airbus A.380-861	Emirates Airlines	
A6-EDS	Airbus A.380-861	Emirates Airlines	
A6-EDT	Airbus A.380-861	Emirates Airlines	
A6-EDU	Airbus A.380-861	Emirates Airlines	
A6-EDV	Airbus A.380-861	Emirates Airlines	
A6-EDW	Airbus A.380-861	Emirates Airlines	
A6-EDX	Airbus A.380-861	Emirates Airlines	
A6-EDY	Airbus A.380-861	Emirates Airlines	
A6-EDZ	Airbus A.380-861	Emirates Airlines	
A6-EEA	Airbus A.380-861	Emirates Airlines	
A6-EEB	Airbus A.380-861	Emirates Airlines	
A6-EEC	Airbus A.380-861	Emirates Airlines	
A6-EED	Airbus A.380-861	Emirates Airlines	
A6-EEE	Airbus A.380-861	Emirates Airlines	
A6-EEF	Airbus A.380-861	Emirates Airlines	
A6-EEG	Airbus A.380-861	Emirates Airlines	
A6-EEH	Airbus A.380-861	Emirates Airlines	
A6-EEI	Airbus A.380-861	Emirates Airlines	
A6-EEJ	Airbus A.380-861	Emirates Airlines	
A6-EEK	Airbus A,380-861	Emirates Airlines	
A6-EEL	Airbus A.380-861	Emirates Airlines	
A6-EEM	Airbus A.380-861	Emirates Airlines	
A6-EEN	Airbus A.380-861	Emirates Airlines	
A6-EEO	Airbus A.380-861	Emirates Airlines	
A6-EEP	Airbus A.380-861	Emirates Airlines	
A6-EEQ	Airbus A.380-861	Emirates Airlines	
A6-EER	Airbus A.380-861	Emirates Airlines	
A6-EES	Airbus A.380-861	Emirates Airlines	
A6-EET	Airbus A.380-861	Emirates Airlines	
A6-EEU	Airbus A.380-861	Emirates Airlines	
A6-EEV	Airbus A.380-861	Emirates Airlines	
A6-EEW	Airbus A.380-861	Emirates Airlines	

Notes	Reg	Type	Owner or Operator
	A6-EEX	Airbus A.380-861	Emirates Airlines
	A6-EEY	Airbus A.380-861	Emirates Airlines
	A6-EEZ	Airbus A.380-861	Emirates Airlines
	A6-EGA	Boeing 777-31HER	Emirates Airlines
	A6-EGB	Boeing 777-31HER	Emirates Airlines
	A6-EGC	Boeing 777-31HER	Emirates Airlines
	A6-EGD	Boeing 777-31HER	Emirates Airlines
	A6-EGE	Boeing 777-31HER	Emirates Airlines
	A6-EGF	Boeing 777-31HER	Emirates Airlines
	A6-EGG	Boeing 777-31HER	Emirates Airlines
	A6-EGH	Boeing 777-31HER	Emirates Airlines
	A6-EGI	Boeing 777-31HER	Emirates Airlines
	A6-EGJ	Boeing 777-31HER	Emirates Airlines
	A6-EGK	Boeing 777-31HER	Emirates Airlines
	A6-EGL	Boeing 777-31HER	Emirates Airlines
	A6-EGM	Boeing 777-31HER	Emirates Airlines
	A6-EGN	Boeing 777-31HER	Emirates Airlines
	A6-EGO	Boeing 777-31HER	Emirates Airlines
	A6-EGP	Boeing 777-31HER	Emirates Airlines
	A6-EGQ	Boeing 777-31HER	Emirates Airlines
	A6-EGR	Boeing 777-31HER	Emirates Airlines
	A6-EGS	Boeing 777-31HER	Emirates Airlines
	A6-EGT	Boeing 777-31HER	Emirates Airlines
	A6-EGU	Boeing 777-31HER	Emirates Airlines
	A6-EGV	Boeing 777-31HER	Emirates Airlines
	A6-EGW	Boeing 777-31HER	Emirates Airlines
	A6-EGX	Boeing 777-31HER	Emirates Airlines
	A6-EGY	Boeing 777-31HER	Emirates Airlines
	A6-EGZ	Boeing 777-31HER	Emirates Airlines
	A6-ENA	Boeing 777-31HER	Emirates Airlines
	A6-ENB	Boeing 777-31HER	Emirates Airlines
	A6-ENC	Boeing 777-31HER	Emirates Airlines
	A6-END	Boeing 777-31HER	Emirates Airlines
	A6-ENE	Boeing 777-31HER	Emirates Airlines
	A6-ENF	Boeing 777-31HER	Emirates Airlines
	A6-ENG	Boeing 777-31HER	Emirates Airlines
	A6-ENH	Boeing 777-31HER	Emirates Airlines
	A6-ENI	Boeing 777-31HER	Emirates Airlines
	A6-ENJ	Boeing 777-31HER	Emirates Airlines
	A6-ENK	Boeing 777-31HER	Emirates Airlines
	A6-ENL	Boeing 777-31HER	Emirates Airlines
	A6-ENM	Boeing 777-31HER	Emirates Airlines
	A6-ENN	Boeing 777-31HER	Emirates Airlines
	A6-ENO	Boeing 777-31HER	Emirates Airlines
	A6-ENP	Boeing 777-31HER	Emirates Airlines
	A6-ENQ	Boeing 777-31HER	Emirates Airlines
	A6-ENR	Boeing 777-31HER	Emirates Airlines
	A6-ENS	Boeing 777-31HER	Emirates Airlines
	A6-ENT	Boeing 777-31HER	Emirates Airlines
	A6-ENU	Boeing 777-31HER	Emirates Airlines
	A6-ENV	Boeing 777-31HER	Emirates Airlines
	A6-ENW	Boeing 777-31HER	Emirates Airlines
	A6-ENX	Boeing 777-31HER	Emirates Airlines
	A6-ENY	Boeing 777-31HER	Emirates Airlines
	A6-ENZ	Boeing 777-31HER	Emirates Airlines
	A6-EOA	Airbus A.380-861	Emirates Airlines
	A6-EOB	Airbus A.380-861	Emirates Airlines
	A6-EOC	Airbus A.380-861	Emirates Airlines
	A6-EOD	Airbus A.380-861	Emirates Airlines
	A6-EOE	Airbus A.380-861	Emirates Airlines
	A6-EOF	Airbus A.380-861	Emirates Airlines
	A6-EOG	Airbus A.380-861	Emirates Airlines
	A6-EOH	Airbus A.380-861	Emirates Airlines
	A6-EOI	Airbus A.380-861	Emirates Airlines
	A6-EOJ	Airbus A.380-861	Emirates Airlines
	A6-EOK	Airbus A.380-861	Emirates Airlines
	A6-EOL	Airbus A.380-861	Emirates Airlines
	A6-EOM	Airbus A.380-861	Emirates Airlines
	A6-EON	Airbus A.380-861	Emirates Airlines
	A6-EOO	Airbus A.380-861	Emirates Airlines
	A6-EOP	Airbus A.380-861	Emirates Airlines

Reg	Type	Owner or Operator	Notes
A6-EOQ	Airbus A.380-861	Emirates Airlines	
A6-EOR	Airbus A.380-861	Emirates Airlines	
A6-EOS	Airbus A.380-861	Emirates Airlines	
A6-EOT	Airbus A.380-861	Emirates Airlines	
A6-EOU	Airbus A.380-861	Emirates Airlines	
A6-EOV	Airbus A.380-861	Emirates Airlines	
A6-EOW	Airbus A.380-861	Emirates Airlines	
A6-EOX	Airbus A.380-861	Emirates Airlines	
A6-EOY	Airbus A.380-861	Emirates Airlines	
A6-EOZ	Airbus A.380-861	Emirates Airlines	
A6-EPA	Boeing 777-31HER	Emirates Airlines	
A6-EPB	Boeing 777-31HER	Emirates Airlines	
A6-EPC	Boeing 777-31HER	Emirates Airlines	
A6-EPD	Boeing 777-31HER	Emirates Airlines	
A6-EPE	Boeing 777-31HER	Emirates Airlines	
A6-EPF	Boeing 777-31HER	Emirates Airlines	
A6-EPG	Boeing 777-31HER	Emirates Airlines	
A6-EPH	Boeing 777-31HER	Emirates Airlines	
A6-EPI	Boeing 777-31HER	Emirates Airlines	
A6-EPJ	Boeing 777-31HER	Emirates Airlines	
A6-EPK	Boeing 777-31HER	Emirates Airlines	
A6-EPL	Boeing 777-31HER	Emirates Airlines	
A6-EPM	Boeing 777-31HER	Emirates Airlines	
A6-EPN	Boeing 777-31HER	Emirates Airlines	
A6-EPO	Boeing 777-31HER	Emirates Airlines	
A6-EPP	Boeing 777-31HER	Emirates Airlines	
A6-EPQ	Boeing 777-31HER	Emirates Airlines	
A6-EPR	Boeing 777-31HER	Emirates Airlines	
A6-EPS	Boeing 777-31HER	Emirates Airlines	
A6-EPT	Boeing 777-31HER	Emirates Airlines	
A6-EPU	Boeing 777-31HER	Emirates Airlines	
A6-EPV	Boeing 777-31HER	Emirates Airlines	
A6-EPW	Boeing 777-31HER	Emirates Airlines	
A6-EPX	Boeing 777-31HER	Emirates Airlines	
A6-EPY	Boeing 777-31HER	Emirates Airlines	
A6-EPZ	Boeing 777-31HER	Emirates Airlines	
A6-EQA	Boeing 777-31HER	Emirates Airlines	
A6-EQB	Boeing 777-31HER	Emirates Airlines	
A6-EQC	Boeing 777-31HER	Emirates Airlines	
A6-EQD	Boeing 777-31HER	Emirates Airlines	
A6-EQE	Boeing 777-31HER	Emirates Airlines	
A6-EQF	Boeing 777-31HER	Emirates Airlines	
A6-EQG	Boeing 777-31HER	Emirates Airlines	
A6-EQH	Boeing 777-31HER	Emirates Airlines	
A6-EQI	Boeing 777-31HER	Emirates Airlines	
A6-EQJ	Boeing 777-31HER	Emirates Airlines	
A6-EQK	Boeing 777-31HER	Emirates Airlines	
A6-EQL	Boeing 777-31HER	Emirates Airlines	
A6-EQM	Boeing 777-31HER	Emirates Airlines	
A6-EQN	Boeing 777-31HER	Emirates Airlines	
A6-EQO	Boeing 777-31HER	Emirates Airlines	
A6-EQP	Boeing 777-31HER	Emirates Airlines	
A6-EUA	Airbus A.380-861	Emirates Airlines	
A6-EUB	Airbus A.380-861	Emirates Airlines	
A6-EUC	Airbus A.380-861	Emirates Airlines	
A6-EUD	Airbus A.380-861	Emirates Airlines	
A6-EUE	Airbus A.380-861	Emirates Airlines	
A6-EUF	Airbus A.380-861	Emirates Airlines	
A6-EUG	Airbus A.380-861	Emirates Airlines	
A6-EUH	Airbus A.380-861	Emirates Airlines	
A6-EUI	Airbus A.380-861	Emirates Airlines	
A6-EUJ	Airbus A.380-861	Emirates Airlines	
A6-EUK	Airbus A.380-861	Emirates Airlines	
A6-EUL	Airbus A.380-861	Emirates Airlines	
A6-EUM	Airbus A.380-861	Emirates Airlines	
A6-EUN	Airbus A.380-861	Emirates Airlines	
A6-EUO	Airbus A.380-861	Emirates Airlines	
A6-EUP	Airbus A.380-861	Emirates Airlines	
A6-EUQ	Airbus A.380-861	Emirates Airlines	
A6-EUR	Airbus A.380-861	Emirates Airlines	
A6-EUS	Airbus A.380-861	Emirates Airlines	

Notes	Reg	Type	Owner or Operator
	A6-EUT	Airbus A.380-861	Emirates Airlines
	A6-EUU	Airbus A.380-861	Emirates Airlines
	A6-EUV	Airbus A.380-861	Emirates Airlines
	A6-EUW	Airbus A.380-861	Emirates Airlines
	A6-EUX	Airbus A.380-861	Emirates Airlines
	A6-EUY	Airbus A.380-861	Emirates Airlines
	A6-EUZ	Airbus A.380-861	Emirates Airlines
	A6-EVA	Airbus A.380-842	Emirates Airlines
	A6-EVB	Airbus A.380-842	Emirates Airlines
	A6-EVC	Airbus A.380-842	Emirates Airlines
	A6-EVD	Airbus A.380-842	Emirates Airlines
	A6-EVE	Airbus A.380-842	Emirates Airlines
	A6-EVF	Airbus A.380-842	Emirates Airlines
	A6-EVG	Airbus A.380-842	Emirates Airlines
	A6-EVH	Airbus A.380-842	Emirates Airlines
	A6-EVI	Airbus A.380-842	Emirates Airlines
	A6-EVJ	Airbus A.380-842	Emirates Airlines
	A6-EVK	Airbus A.380-842	Emirates Airlines
	A6-EVL	Airbus A.380-842	Emirates Airlines
	A6-EVM	Airbus A.380-842	Emirates Airlines
	A6-EVN	Airbus A.380-842	Emirates Airlines
	A6-EVO	Airbus A.380-842	Emirates Airlines
	A6-EVP	Airbus A.380-842	Emirates Airlines
	A6-EVQ	Airbus A.380-842	Emirates Airlines

A7 (Qatar)

Notes	Reg	Type	Owner or Operator
	A7-ALA	Airbus A.350-941	Qatar Airways
	A7-ALB	Airbus A.350-941	Qatar Airways
	A7-ALC	Airbus A.350-941	Qatar Airways
	A7-ALD	Airbus A.350-941	Qatar Airways
	A7-ALE	Airbus A.350-941	Qatar Airways
	A7-ALF	Airbus A.350-941	Qatar Airways
	A7-ALG	Airbus A.350-941	Qatar Airways
	A7-ALH	Airbus A.350-941	Qatar Airways
	A7-ALI	Airbus A.350-941	Qatar Airways
	A7-ALJ	Airbus A.350-941	Qatar Airways
	A7-ALK	Airbus A.350-941	Qatar Airways
	A7-ALL	Airbus A.350-941	Qatar Airways
	A7-ALM	Airbus A.350-941	Qatar Airways
	A7-ALN	Airbus A.350-941	Qatar Airways
	A7-ALO	Airbus A.350-941	Qatar Airways
	A7-ALP	Airbus A.350-941	Qatar Airways
	A7-ALQ	Airbus A.350-941	Qatar Airways
	A7-ALR	Airbus A.350-941	Qatar Airways
	A7-ALS	Airbus A.350-941	Qatar Airways
	A7-ALT	Airbus A.350-941	Qatar Airways
	A7-ALU	Airbus A.350-941	Qatar Airways
	A7-ALV	Airbus A.350-941	Qatar Airways
	A7-ALW	Airbus A.350-941	Qatar Airways
	A7-ALX	Airbus A.350-941	Qatar Airways
	A7-ALY	Airbus A.350-941	Qatar Airways
	A7-ALZ	Airbus A.350-941	Qatar Airways
	A7-AME	Airbus A.350-941	Qatar Airways
	A7-AMF	Airbus A.350-941	Qatar Airways
	A7-AMG	Airbus A.350-941	Qatar Airways
	A7-AMH	Airbus A.350-941	Qatar Airways
	A7-AMI	Airbus A.350-941	Qatar Airways
	A7-AMJ	Airbus A.350-941	Qatar Airways
	A7-AMK	Airbus A.350-941	Qatar Airways
	A7-AML	Airbus A.350-941	Qatar Airways
	A7-ANA	Airbus A.350-1041	Qatar Airways
	A7-ANB	Airbus A.350-1041	Qatar Airways
	A7-ANC	Airbus A.350-1041	Qatar Airways
	A7-AND	Airbus A.350-1041	Qatar Airways
	A7-ANE	Airbus A.350-1041	Qatar Airways
	A7-ANF	Airbus A.350-1041	Qatar Airways
	A7-ANG	Airbus A.350-1041	Qatar Airways
	A7-ANH	Airbus A.350-1041	Qatar Airways
	A7-ANI	Airbus A.350-1041	Qatar Airways
	A7-ANJ	Airbus A.350-1041	Qatar Airways

Reg	Type	Owner or Operator	Notes
A7-ANK	Airbus A.350-1041	Qatar Airways	
A7-ANL	Airbus A.350-1041	Qatar Airways	
A7-ANM	Airbus A.350-1041	Qatar Airways	
A7-ANN	Airbus A.350-1041	Qatar Airways	
A7-ANO	Airbus A.350-1041	Qatar Airways	
A7-ANP	Airbus A.350-1041	Qatar Airways	
A7-ANQ	Airbus A.350-1041	Qatar Airways	
A7-ANR	Airbus A.350-1041	Qatar Airways	
A7-ANS	Airbus A.350-1041	Qatar Airways	
A7-ANT	Airbus A.350-1041	Qatar Airways	
A7-AOB	Airbus A.350-1041	Qatar Airways	
A7-APA	Airbus A.380-861	Qatar Airways	
A7-APB	Airbus A.380-861	Qatar Airways	
A7-APC	Airbus A.380-861	Qatar Airways	
A7-APD	Airbus A.380-861	Qatar Airways	
A7-APE	Airbus A.380-861	Qatar Airways	
A7-APF	Airbus A.380-861	Qatar Airways	
A7-APG	Airbus A.380-861	Qatar Airways	
A7-APH	Airbus A.380-861	Qatar Airways	
A7-API	Airbus A.380-861	Qatar Airways	
A7-APJ	Airbus A.380-861	Qatar Airways	
A7-BAA	Boeing 777-3DZ ER	Qatar Airways	
A7-BAB	Boeing 777-3DZ ER	Qatar Airways	
A7-BAC	Boeing 777-3DZ ER	Qatar Airways	
A7-BAE	Boeing 777-3DZ ER	Qatar Airways	
A7-BAF	Boeing 777-3DZ ER	Qatar Airways	
A7-BAG	Boeing 777-3DZ ER	Qatar Airways	
A7-BAH	Boeing 777-3DZ ER	Qatar Airways	
A7-BAI	Boeing 777-3DZ ER	Qatar Airways	
A7-BAJ	Boeing 777-3DZ ER	Qatar Airways	
A7-BAK	Boeing 777-3DZ ER	Qatar Airways	
A7-BAL	Boeing 777-3DZ ER	Qatar Airways	
A7-BAM	Boeing 777-3DZ ER	Qatar Airways	
A7-BAN	Boeing 777-3DZ ER	Qatar Airways	
A7-BAO	Boeing 777-3DZ ER	Qatar Airways	
A7-BAP	Boeing 777-3DZ ER	Qatar Airways *Al Qattard*	
A7-BAQ	Boeing 777-3DZ ER	Qatar Airways	
A7-BAS	Boeing 777-3DZ ER	Qatar Airways	
A7-BAT	Boeing 777-3DZ ER	Qatar Airways	
A7-BAU	Boeing 777-3DZ ER	Qatar Airways	
A7-BAV	Boeing 777-3DZ ER	Qatar Airways	
A7-BAW	Boeing 777-3DZ ER	Qatar Airways	
A7-BAX	Boeing 777-3DZ ER	Qatar Airways	
A7-BAY	Boeing 777-3DZ ER	Qatar Airways	
A7-BAZ	Boeing 777-3DZ ER	Qatar Airways	
A7-BCA	Boeing 787-8	Qatar Airways	
A7-BCB	Boeing 787-8	Qatar Airways	
A7-BCC	Boeing 787-8	Qatar Airways	
A7-BCD	Boeing 787-8	Qatar Airways	
A7-BCE	Boeing 787-8	Qatar Airways	
A7-BCF	Boeing 787-8	Qatar Airways	
A7-BCG	Boeing 787-8	Qatar Airways	
A7-BCH	Boeing 787-8	Qatar Airways	
A7-BCI	Boeing 787-8	Qatar Airways	
A7-BCJ	Boeing 787-8	Qatar Airways	
A7-BCK	Boeing 787-8	Qatar Airways	
A7-BCL	Boeing 787-8	Qatar Airways	
A7-BCM	Boeing 787-8	Qatar Airways	
A7-BCN	Boeing 787-8	Qatar Airways	
A7-BCO	Boeing 787-8	Qatar Airways	
A7-BCP	Boeing 787-8	Qatar Airways	
A7-BCQ	Boeing 787-8	Qatar Airways	
A7-BCR	Boeing 787-8	Qatar Airways	
A7-BCS	Boeing 787-8	Qatar Airways	
A7-BCT	Boeing 787-8	Qatar Airways	
A7-BCU	Boeing 787-8	Qatar Airways	
A7-BCV	Boeing 787-8	Qatar Airways	
A7-BCW	Boeing 787-8	Qatar Airways	
A7-BCX	Boeing 787-8	Qatar Airways	
A7-BCY	Boeing 787-8	Qatar Airways	
A7-BCZ	Boeing 787-8	Qatar Airways	

Notes	Reg	Type	Owner or Operator
	A7-BDA	Boeing 787-8	Qatar Airways
	A7-BDB	Boeing 787-8	Qatar Airways
	A7-BDC	Boeing 787-8	Qatar Airways
	A7-BDD	Boeing 787-8	Qatar Airways
	A7-BEA	Boeing 777-3DZER	Qatar Airways
	A7-BEB	Boeing 777-3DZER	Qatar Airways
	A7-BEC	Boeing 777-3DZER	Qatar Airways
	A7-BED	Boeing 777-3DZER	Qatar Airways
	A7-BEE	Boeing 777-3DZER	Qatar Airways
	A7-BEF	Boeing 777-3DZER	Qatar Airways
	A7-BEG	Boeing 777-3DZER	Qatar Airways
	A7-BEH	Boeing 777-3DZER	Qatar Airways
	A7-BEI	Boeing 777-3DZER	Qatar Airways
	A7-BEJ	Boeing 777-3DZER	Qatar Airways
	A7-BEK	Boeing 777-3DZER	Qatar Airways
	A7-BEL	Boeing 777-3DZER	Qatar Airways
	A7-BEM	Boeing 777-3DZER	Qatar Airways
	A7-BEN	Boeing 777-3DZER	Qatar Airways
	A7-BEO	Boeing 777-3DZER	Qatar Airways
	A7-BEP	Boeing 777-3DZER	Qatar Airways
	A7-BEQ	Boeing 777-3DZER	Qatar Airways
	A7-BER	Boeing 777-3DZER	Qatar Airways
	A7-BES	Boeing 777-3DZER	Qatar Airways
	A7-BET	Boeing 777-3DZER	Qatar Airways
	A7-BEU	Boeing 777-3DZER	Qatar Airways
	A7-BEV	Boeing 777-3DZER	Qatar Airways
	A7-BEW	Boeing 777-3DZER	Qatar Airways
	A7-BEX	Boeing 777-3DZER	Qatar Airways
	A7-BFA	Boeing 777-FDZ	Qatar Airways Cargo
	A7-BFB	Boeing 777-FDZ	Qatar Airways Cargo
	A7-BFC	Boeing 777-FDZ	Qatar Airways Cargo
	A7-BFD	Boeing 777-FDZ	Qatar Airways Cargo
	A7-BFE	Boeing 777-FDZ	Qatar Airways Cargo
	A7-BFF	Boeing 777-FDZ	Qatar Airways Cargo
	A7-BFG	Boeing 777-FDZ	Qatar Airways Cargo
	A7-BFH	Boeing 777-FDZ	Qatar Airways Cargo
	A7-BFI	Boeing 777-FDZ	Qatar Airways Cargo
	A7-BFJ	Boeing 777-FDZ	Qatar Airways Cargo
	A7-BFK	Boeing 777-FDZ	Qatar Airways Cargo
	A7-BFL	Boeing 777-FDZ	Qatar Airways Cargo
	A7-BFM	Boeing 777-FDZ	Qatar Airways Cargo
	A7-BFN	Boeing 777-FDZ	Qatar Airways Cargo
	A7-BFO	Boeing 777-FDZ	Qatar Airways Cargo
	A7-BFP	Boeing 777-FDZ	Qatar Airways Cargo
	A7-BFQ	Boeing 777-FDZ	Qatar Airways Cargo
	A7-BFR	Boeing 777-200F	Qatar Airways Cargo
	A7-BFS	Boeing 777-200F	Qatar Airways Cargo
	A7-BFT	Boeing 777-200F	Qatar Airways Cargo
	A7-BFU	Boeing 777-200F	Qatar Airways Cargo
	A7-BFV	Boeing 777-200F	Qatar Airways Cargo
	A7-BFW	Boeing 777-200F	Qatar Airways Cargo
	A7-BFX	Boeing 777-200F	Qatar Airways Cargo
	A7-BHA	Boeing 787-9	Qatar Airways
	A7-BHB	Boeing 787-9	Qatar Airways
	A7-BHC	Boeing 787-9	Qatar Airways
	A7-BHD	Boeing 787-9	Qatar Airways
	A7-BHE	Boeing 787-9	Qatar Airways
	A7-BHF	Boeing 787-9	Qatar Airways
	A7-BHG	Boeing 787-9	Qatar Airways
	A7-BHH	Boeing 787-9	Qatar Airways
	A7-BHI	Boeing 787-9	Qatar Airways
	A7-BHJ	Boeing 787-9	Qatar Airways
	A7-BHK	Boeing 787-9	Qatar Airways
	A7-BHL	Boeing 787-9	Qatar Airways
	A7-BHM	Boeing 787-9	Qatar Airways

A9C (Bahrain)

	A9C-FA	Boeing 787-9	Gulf Air
	A9C-FB	Boeing 787-9	Gulf Air
	A9C-FC	Boeing 787-9	Gulf Air

Reg	Type	Owner or Operator	Notes
A9C-FD	Boeing 787-9	Gulf Air	
A9C-FE	Boeing 787-9	Gulf Air	
A9C-FF	Boeing 787-9	Gulf Air	
A9C-FG	Boeing 787-9	Gulf Air	
A9C-FH	Boeing 787-9	Gulf Air	
A9C-FI	Boeing 787-9	Gulf Air	
A9C-FJ	Boeing 787-9	Gulf Air	

A4O (Oman)

Reg	Type	Owner or Operator	Notes
A4O-SA	Boeing 787-8	Oman Air	
A4O-SB	Boeing 787-8	Oman Air	
A4O-SC	Boeing 787-9	Oman Air	
A4O-SD	Boeing 787-9	Oman Air	
A4O-SE	Boeing 787-9	Oman Air	
A4O-SF	Boeing 787-9	Oman Air	
A4O-SG	Boeing 787-9	Oman Air	
A4O-SH	Boeing 787-9	Oman Air	
A4O-SI	Boeing 787-9	Oman Air	
A4O-SJ	Boeing 787-9	Oman Air	

AP (Pakistan)

Reg	Type	Owner or Operator	Notes
AP-BGJ	Boeing 777-240ER	Pakistan International Airlines	
AP-BGK	Boeing 777-240ER	Pakistan International Airlines	
AP-BGL	Boeing 777-240ER	Pakistan International Airlines	
AP-BGY	Boeing 777-240LR	Pakistan International Airlines	
AP-BGZ	Boeing 777-240LR	Pakistan International Airlines	
AP-BHV	Boeing 777-340ER	Pakistan International Airlines	
AP-BHW	Boeing 777-340ER	Pakistan International Airlines	
AP-BHX	Boeing 777-240ER	Pakistan International Airlines	
AP-BID	Boeing 777-340ER	Pakistan International Airlines	
AP-BMG	Boeing 777-2Q8ER	Pakistan International Airlines	
AP-BMH	Boeing 777-2Q8ER	Pakistan International Airlines	
AP-BMS	Boeing 777-3Q8ER	Pakistan International Airlines	

B (China/Taiwan/Hong Kong)

Reg	Type	Owner or Operator	Notes
B-HNR	Boeing 777-367ER	Cathay Pacific Airways	
B-KPA	Boeing 777-367ER	Cathay Pacific Airways	
B-KPC	Boeing 777-367ER	Cathay Pacific Airways	
B-KPD	Boeing 777-367ER	Cathay Pacific Airways	
B-KPE	Boeing 777-367ER	Cathay Pacific Airways	
B-KPF	Boeing 777-367ER	Cathay Pacific Airways	
B-KPH	Boeing 777-367ER	Cathay Pacific Airways	
B-KPI	Boeing 777-367ER	Cathay Pacific Airways	
B-KPJ	Boeing 777-367ER	Cathay Pacific Airways	
B-KPK	Boeing 777-367ER	Cathay Pacific Airways	
B-KPL	Boeing 777-367ER	Cathay Pacific Airways	
B-KPM	Boeing 777-367ER	Cathay Pacific Airways	
B-KPN	Boeing 777-367ER	Cathay Pacific Airways	
B-KPO	Boeing 777-367ER	Cathay Pacific Airways	
B-KPP	Boeing 777-367ER	Cathay Pacific Airways	
B-KPQ	Boeing 777-367ER	Cathay Pacific Airways	
B-KPR	Boeing 777-367ER	Cathay Pacific Airways	
B-KPS	Boeing 777-367ER	Cathay Pacific Airways	
B-KPT	Boeing 777-367ER	Cathay Pacific Airways	
B-KPU	Boeing 777-367ER	Cathay Pacific Airways	
B-KPV	Boeing 777-367ER	Cathay Pacific Airways	
B-KPW	Boeing 777-367ER	Cathay Pacific Airways	
B-KPX	Boeing 777-367ER	Cathay Pacific Airways	
B-KPY	Boeing 777-367ER	Cathay Pacific Airways	
B-KPZ	Boeing 777-367ER	Cathay Pacific Airways	
B-KQA	Boeing 777-367ER	Cathay Pacific Airways	
B-KQB	Boeing 777-367ER	Cathay Pacific Airways	
B-KQC	Boeing 777-367ER	Cathay Pacific Airways	
B-KQD	Boeing 777-367ER	Cathay Pacific Airways	
B-KQE	Boeing 777-367ER	Cathay Pacific Airways	
B-KQF	Boeing 777-367ER	Cathay Pacific Airways	
B-KQG	Boeing 777-367ER	Cathay Pacific Airways	

Notes	Reg	Type	Owner or Operator
	B-KQH	Boeing 777-367ER	Cathay Pacific Airways
	B-KQI	Boeing 777-367ER	Cathay Pacific Airways
	B-KQJ	Boeing 777-367ER	Cathay Pacific Airways
	B-KQK	Boeing 777-367ER	Cathay Pacific Airways
	B-KQL	Boeing 777-367ER	Cathay Pacific Airways
	B-KQM	Boeing 777-367ER	Cathay Pacific Airways
	B-KQN	Boeing 777-367ER	Cathay Pacific Airways
	B-KQO	Boeing 777-367ER	Cathay Pacific Airways
	B-KQP	Boeing 777-367ER	Cathay Pacific Airways
	B-KQQ	Boeing 777-367ER	Cathay Pacific Airways
	B-KQR	Boeing 777-367ER	Cathay Pacific Airways
	B-KQS	Boeing 777-367ER	Cathay Pacific Airways
	B-KQT	Boeing 777-367ER	Cathay Pacific Airways
	B-KQU	Boeing 777-367ER	Cathay Pacific Airways
	B-KQV	Boeing 777-367ER	Cathay Pacific Airways
	B-KQW	Boeing 777-367ER	Cathay Pacific Airways
	B-KQX	Boeing 777-367ER	Cathay Pacific Airways
	B-KQY	Boeing 777-367ER	Cathay Pacific Airways
	B-KQZ	Boeing 777-367ER	Cathay Pacific Airways
	B-LIA	Boeing 747-467ERF	Cathay Pacific Airways
	B-LIB	Boeing 747-467ERF	Cathay Pacific Airways
	B-LIC	Boeing 747-467ERF	Cathay Pacific Airways
	B-LID	Boeing 747-467ERF	Cathay Pacific Airways
	B-LIE	Boeing 747-467ERF	Cathay Pacific Airways
	B-LIF	Boeing 747-467ERF	Cathay Pacific Airways
	B-LJA	Boeing 747-867F	Cathay Pacific Airways
	B-LJB	Boeing 747-867F	Cathay Pacific Airways
	B-LJC	Boeing 747-867F	Cathay Pacific Airways
	B-LJD	Boeing 747-867F	Cathay Pacific Airways
	B-LJE	Boeing 747-867F	Cathay Pacific Airways
	B-LJF	Boeing 747-867F	Cathay Pacific Airways
	B-LJG	Boeing 747-867F	Cathay Pacific Airways
	B-LJH	Boeing 747-867F	Cathay Pacific Airways
	B-LJI	Boeing 747-867F	Cathay Pacific Airways
	B-LJJ	Boeing 747-867F	Cathay Pacific Airways
	B-LJK	Boeing 747-867F	Cathay Pacific Airways
	B-LJL	Boeing 747-867F	Cathay Pacific Airways
	B-LJM	Boeing 747-867F	Cathay Pacific Airways
	B-LJN	Boeing 747-867F	Cathay Pacific Airways
	B-LQA	Airbus A.350-941	Cathay Pacific Airways
	B-LQB	Airbus A.350-941	Cathay Pacific Airways
	B-LQC	Airbus A.350-941	Cathay Pacific Airways
	B-LQD	Airbus A.350-941	Cathay Pacific Airways
	B-LQE	Airbus A.350-941	Cathay Pacific Airways
	B-LQF	Airbus A.350-941	Cathay Pacific Airways
	B-LRA	Airbus A.350-941	Cathay Pacific Airways
	B-LRB	Airbus A.350-941	Cathay Pacific Airways
	B-LRC	Airbus A.350-941	Cathay Pacific Airways
	B-LRD	Airbus A.350-941	Cathay Pacific Airways
	B-LRE	Airbus A.350-941	Cathay Pacific Airways
	B-LRF	Airbus A.350-941	Cathay Pacific Airways
	B-LRG	Airbus A.350-941	Cathay Pacific Airways
	B-LRI	Airbus A.350-941	Cathay Pacific Airways
	B-LRJ	Airbus A.350-941	Cathay Pacific Airways
	B-LRK	Airbus A.350-941	Cathay Pacific Airways
	B-LRL	Airbus A.350-941	Cathay Pacific Airways
	B-LRM	Airbus A.350-941	Cathay Pacific Airways
	B-LRN	Airbus A.350-941	Cathay Pacific Airways
	B-LRO	Airbus A.350-941	Cathay Pacific Airways
	B-LRP	Airbus A.350-941	Cathay Pacific Airways
	B-LRQ	Airbus A.350-941	Cathay Pacific Airways
	B-LRR	Airbus A.350-941	Cathay Pacific Airways
	B-LRS	Airbus A.350-941	Cathay Pacific Airways
	B-LRT	Airbus A.350-941	Cathay Pacific Airways
	B-LRU	Airbus A.350-941	Cathay Pacific Airways
	B-LRV	Airbus A.350-941	Cathay Pacific Airways
	B-LRX	Airbus A.350-941	Cathay Pacific Airways
	B-LXA	Airbus A.350-1041	Cathay Pacific Airways
	B-LXB	Airbus A.350-1041	Cathay Pacific Airways
	B-LXC	Airbus A.350-1041	Cathay Pacific Airways
	B-LXD	Airbus A.350-1041	Cathay Pacific Airways

Reg	Type	Owner or Operator	Notes
B-LXE	Airbus A.350-1041	Cathay Pacific Airways	
B-LXF	Airbus A.350-1041	Cathay Pacific Airways	
B-LXG	Airbus A.350-1041	Cathay Pacific Airways	
B-LXH	Airbus A.350-1041	Cathay Pacific Airways	
B-LXI	Airbus A.350-1041	Cathay Pacific Airways	
B-LXJ	Airbus A.350-1041	Cathay Pacific Airways	
B-LXK	Airbus A.350-1041	Cathay Pacific Airways	
B-LXL	Airbus A.350-1041	Cathay Pacific Airways	
B-LXM	Airbus A.350-1041	Cathay Pacific Airways	
B-LXN	Airbus A.350-1041	Cathay Pacific Airways	
B-LXO	Airbus A.350-1041	Cathay Pacific Airways	
B-20AA	Boeing 787-9	China Southern Airlines	
B-20C6	Boeing 787-9	China Southern Airlines	
B-20CJ	Boeing 787-9	China Southern Airlines	
B-20D1	Boeing 787-9	Juneyao Airlines	
B-20D7	Boeing 787-9	China Southern Airlines	
B-20DT	Boeing 787-9	Juneyao Airlines	
B-20E8	Boeing 787-9	China Southern Airlines	
B-20EC	Boeing 787-9	Juneyao Airlines	
B-20EH	Boeing 787-9	China Southern Airlines	
B-20EL	Boeing 787-9	China Southern Airlines	
B-20EM	Boeing 777-F	China Southern Airlines Cargo	
B-20EN	Boeing 777- F	China Southern Airlines Cargo	
B-20EP	Boeing 787-9	China Southern Airlines	
B-20EQ	Boeing 787-9	Juneyao Airlines	
B-20EW	Boeing 787-9	China Southern Airlines	
B-207N	Boeing 787-9	Juneyao Airlines	
B-208A	Boeing 787-9	Juneyao Airlines	
B-209D	Boeing 787-9	China Southern Airlines	
B-209E	Boeing 787-9	China Southern Airlines	
B-209R	Boeing 787-9	Juneyao Airlines	
B-209X	Boeing 787-9	China Southern Airlines	
B-302E	Airbus A.330-343	Shenzhen Airlines	
B-303C	Airbus A.330-343	Hainan Airlines	
B-303N	Airbus A.330-343	Shenzhen Airlines	
B-303Z	Airbus A.330-343	Hainan Airlines	
B-304K	Airbus A.330-343	Hainan Airlines	
B-304L	Airbus A.330-343	Hainan Airlines	
B-307A	Airbus A.350-941	Air China	
B-307C	Airbus A.350-941	Air China	
B-308C	Airbus A.350-941	Air China	
B-308M	Airbus A.350-941	Air China	
B-321M	Airbus A.350-941	Air China	
B-321N	Airbus A.350-941	Air China	
B-1017	Airbus A.330-343	Shenzhen Airlines	
B-1020	Airbus A.330-343	Hainan Airlines	
B-1021	Airbus A.330-343	Hainan Airlines	
B-1022	Airbus A.330-343	Hainan Airlines	
B-1036	Airbus A.330-343	Shenzhen Airlines	
B-1048	Airbus A.330-343	Hainan Airlines	
B-1072	Airbus A.330-343	Shenzhen Airlines	
B-1080	Airbus A.350-941	Air China	
B-1081	Airbus A.350-941	Air China	
B-1082	Airbus A.350-941	Air China	
B-1083	Airbus A.350-941	Air China	
B-1085	Airbus A.350-941	Air China	
B-1086	Airbus A.350-941	Air China	
B-1096	Airbus A.330-343	Hainan Airlines	
B-1097	Airbus A.330-343	Hainan Airlines	
B-1098	Airbus A.330-343	Hainan Airlines	
B-1115	Boeing 787-9	Juneyao Airlines	
B-1119	Boeing 787-9	Hainan Airlines	
B-1128	Boeing 787-9	China Southern Airlines	
B-1132	Boeing 787-9	Hainan Airlines	
B-1133	Boeing 787-9	Hainan Airlines	
B-1135	Boeing 787-9	Hainan Airlines	
B-1138	Boeing 787-9	Hainan Airlines	
B-1167	Boeing 787-9	China Southern Airlines	
B-1168	Boeing 787-9	China Southern Airlines	
B-1169	Boeing 787-9	China Southern Airlines	
B-1242	Boeing 787-9	China Southern Airlines	

Notes	Reg	Type	Owner or Operator
	B-1243	Boeing 787-9	China Southern Airlines
	B-1293	Boeing 787-9	China Southern Airlines
	B-1297	Boeing 787-9	China Southern Airlines
	B-1323	Boeing 787-9	Hainan Airlines
	B-1341	Boeing 787-9	Hainan Airlines
	B-1342	Boeing 787-9	Hainan Airlines
	B-1343	Boeing 787-9	Hainan Airlines
	B-1345	Boeing 787-9	Hainan Airlines
	B-1356	Boeing 787-9	Xiamen Airlines
	B-1357	Boeing 787-9	Xiamen Airlines
	B-1499	Boeing 787-9	Hainan Airlines
	B-1539	Boeing 787-9	Hainan Airlines
	B-1540	Boeing 787-9	Hainan Airlines
	B-1543	Boeing 787-9	Hainan Airlines
	B-1546	Boeing 787-9	Hainan Airlines
	B-1566	Boeing 787-9	Xiamen Airlines
	B-1567	Boeing 787-9	Xiamen Airlines
	B-2001	Boeing 777-39PER	China Eastern Airlines
	B-2002	Boeing 777-39PER	China Eastern Airlines
	B-2003	Boeing 777-39PER	China Eastern Airlines
	B-2005	Boeing 777-2PER	China Eastern Airlines
	B-2006	Boeing 777-39LER	Air China
	B-2010	Boeing 777-F1B	China Southern Airlines Cargo
	B-2020	Boeing 777-39PER	China Eastern Airlines
	B-2021	Boeing 777-39PER	China Eastern Airlines
	B-2022	Boeing 777-39PER	China Eastern Airlines
	B-2023	Boeing 777-39PER	China Eastern Airlines
	B-2025	Boeing 777-39PER	China Eastern Airlines
	B-2026	Boeing 777-F1B	China Southern Airlines Cargo
	B-2027	Boeing 777-F1B	China Southern Airlines Cargo
	B-2028	Boeing 777-F1B	China Southern Airlines Cargo
	B-2031	Boeing 777-39LER	Air China
	B-2032	Boeing 777-39LER	Air China
	B-2033	Boeing 777-39LER	Air China
	B-2035	Boeing 777-39LER	Air China
	B-2036	Boeing 777-39LER	Air China
	B-2037	Boeing 777-39LER	Air China
	B-2038	Boeing 777-39LER	Air China
	B-2039	Boeing 777-39LER	Air China
	B-2040	Boeing 777-39LER	Air China
	B-2041	Boeing 777-F1B	China Southern Airlines Cargo
	B-2042	Boeing 777-F1B	China Southern Airlines Cargo
	B-2043	Boeing 777-39LER	Air China
	B-2045	Boeing 777-39LER	Air China
	B-2046	Boeing 777-39LER	Air China
	B-2047	Boeing 777-39LER	Air China
	B-2071	Boeing 777-F1B	China Southern Airlines Cargo
	B-2072	Boeing 777-F1B	China Southern Airlines Cargo
	B-2073	Boeing 777-F1B	China Southern Airlines Cargo
	B-2075	Boeing 777-F1B	China Southern Airlines Cargo
	B-2080	Boeing 777-F1B	China Southern Airlines Cargo
	B-2081	Boeing 777-F1B	China Southern Airlines Cargo
	B-2085	Boeing 777-39LER	Air China
	B-2086	Boeing 777-39LER	Air China
	B-2087	Boeing 777-39LER	Air China
	B-2088	Boeing 777-39LER	Air China
	B-2089	Boeing 777-39LER	Air China
	B-2090	Boeing 777-39LER	Air China
	B-2722	Boeing 787-8	Hainan Airlines
	B-2723	Boeing 787-8	Hainan Airlines
	B-2725	Boeing 787-8	China Southern Airlines
	B-2726	Boeing 787-8	China Southern Airlines
	B-2727	Boeing 787-8	China Southern Airlines
	B-2728	Boeing 787-8	Hainan Airlines
	B-2729	Boeing 787-8	Hainan Airlines
	B-2730	Boeing 787-8	Hainan Airlines
	B-2731	Boeing 787-8	Hainan Airlines
	B-2732	Boeing 787-8	China Southern Airlines
	B-2733	Boeing 787-8	China Southern Airlines
	B-2735	Boeing 787-8	China Southern Airlines
	B-2736	Boeing 787-8	China Southern Airlines

Reg	Type	Owner or Operator	Notes
B-2737	Boeing 787-8	China Southern Airlines	
B-2738	Boeing 787-8	Hainan Airlines	
B-2739	Boeing 787-8	Hainan Airlines	
B-2750	Boeing 787-8	Hainan Airlines	
B-2759	Boeing 787-8	Hainan Airlines	
B-2760	Boeing 787-8	Xiamen Airlines	
B-2761	Boeing 787-8	Xiamen Airlines	
B-2762	Boeing 787-8	Xiamen Airlines	
B-2763	Boeing 787-8	Xiamen Airlines	
B-2768	Boeing 787-8	Xiamen Airlines	
B-2769	Boeing 787-8	Xiamen Airlines	
B-2787	Boeing 787-8	China Southern Airlines	
B-2788	Boeing 787-8	China Southern Airlines	
B-5901	Airbus A.330-343	Air China	
B-5902	Airbus A.330-243	China Eastern Airlines	
B-5903	Airbus A.330-243	China Eastern Airlines	
B-5905	Airbus A.330-343	Hainan Airlines	
B-5906	Airbus A.330-343	Air China	
B-5908	Airbus A.330-243	China Eastern Airlines	
B-5912	Airbus A.330-343	Air China	
B-5913	Airbus A.330-343	Air China	
B-5916	Airbus A.330-343	Air China	
B-5918	Airbus A.330-243	Air China	
B-5919	Airbus A.330-343	Air China	
B-5920	Airbus A.330-243	China Eastern Airlines	
B-5921	Airbus A.330-243	China Eastern Airlines	
B-5925	Airbus A.330-243	Air China	
B-5926	Airbus A.330-243	China Eastern Airlines	
B-5927	Airbus A.330-243	Air China	
B-5930	Airbus A.330-243	China Eastern Airlines	
B-5931	Airbus A.330-243	China Eastern Airlines	
B-5932	Airbus A.330-243	Air China	
B-5933	Airbus A.330-243	Air China	
B-5935	Airbus A.330-343	Hainan Airlines	
B-5936	Airbus A.330-243	China Eastern Airlines	
B-5937	Airbus A.330-243	China Eastern Airlines	
B-5938	Airbus A.330-243	China Eastern Airlines	
B-5941	Airbus A.330-243	China Eastern Airlines	
B-5942	Airbus A.330-243	China Eastern Airlines	
B-5943	Airbus A.330-243	China Eastern Airlines	
B-5946	Airbus A.330-343	Air China	
B-5947	Airbus A.330-343	Air China	
B-5948	Airbus A.330-343	Air China	
B-5949	Airbus A.330-243	China Eastern Airlines	
B-5950	Airbus A.330-343	Hainan Airlines	
B-5952	Airbus A.330-243	China Eastern Airlines	
B-5956	Airbus A.330-343	Air China	
B-5957	Airbus A.330-343	Air China	
B-5961	Airbus A.330-243	China Eastern Airlines	
B-5962	Airbus A.330-243	China Eastern Airlines	
B-5968	Airbus A.330-243	China Eastern Airlines	
B-5971	Airbus A.330-343	Hainan Airlines	
B-5972	Airbus A.330-343	Hainan Airlines	
B-5973	Airbus A.330-243	China Eastern Airlines	
B-5975	Airbus A.330-243	China Eastern Airlines	
B-5977	Airbus A.330-343	Air China	
B-5978	Airbus A.330-343	Air China	
B-6070	Airbus A.330-243	Air China	
B-6071	Airbus A.330-243	Air China	
B-6072	Airbus A.330-243	Air China	
B-6073	Airbus A.330-243	Air China	
B-6075	Airbus A.330-243	Air China	
B-6076	Airbus A.330-243	Air China	
B-6079	Airbus A.330-243	Air China	
B-6080	Airbus A.330-243	Air China	
B-6081	Airbus A.330-243	Air China	
B-6082	Airbus A.330-243	China Eastern Airlines	
B-6090	Airbus A.330-243	Air China	
B-6091	Airbus A.330-243	Air China	
B-6092	Airbus A.330-243	Air China	
B-6093	Airbus A.330-243	Air China	

Notes	Reg	Type	Owner or Operator
	B-6099	Airbus A.330-243	China Eastern Airlines
	B-6101	Airbus A.330-343	Air China
	B-6102	Airbus A.330-343	Air China
	B-6113	Airbus A.330-243	Air China
	B-6115	Airbus A.330-243	Air China
	B-6117	Airbus A.330-243	Air China
	B-6130	Airbus A.330-243	Air China
	B-6131	Airbus A.330-243	Air China
	B-6132	Airbus A.330-243	Air China
	B-6135	Airbus A.330-223	China Southern Airlines
	B-6136	Airbus A.380-841	China Southern Airlines
	B-6137	Airbus A.380-841	China Southern Airlines
	B-6138	Airbus A.380-841	China Southern Airlines
	B-6139	Airbus A.380-841	China Southern Airlines
	B-6140	Airbus A.380-841	China Southern Airlines
	B-6503	Airbus A.330-343	Air China
	B-6505	Airbus A.330-243	Air China
	B-6515	Airbus A.330-223	China Southern Airlines
	B-6516	Airbus A.330-223	China Southern Airlines
	B-6520	Airbus A.330-343	Hainan Airlines
	B-6526	Airbus A.330-223	China Southern Airlines
	B-6527	Airbus A.330-343	Hainan Airlines
	B-6528	Airbus A.330-223	China Southern Airlines
	B-6529	Airbus A.330-343	Hainan Airlines
	B-6531	Airbus A.330-223	China Southern Airlines
	B-6532	Airbus A.330-223	China Southern Airlines
	B-6533	Airbus A.330-243	Air China
	B-6536	Airbus A.330-243	Air China
	B-6537	Airbus A.330-243	China Eastern Airlines
	B-6538	Airbus A.330-243	China Eastern Airlines
	B-6539	Airbus A.330-343	Hainan Airlines
	B-6540	Airbus A.330-243	Air China
	B-6541	Airbus A.330-243	Air China
	B-6542	Airbus A.330-223	China Southern Airlines
	B-6543	Airbus A.330-243	China Eastern Airlines
	B-6547	Airbus A.330-223	China Southern Airlines
	B-6548	Airbus A.330-223	China Southern Airlines
	B-6549	Airbus A.330-243	Air China
	B-6969	Boeing 787-9	Hainan Airlines
	B-6998	Boeing 787-9	Hainan Airlines
	B-7302	Boeing 787-9	Hainan Airlines
	B-7343	Boeing 777-39PER	China Eastern Airlines
	B-7347	Boeing 777-39PER	China Eastern Airlines
	B-7349	Boeing 777-39PER	China Eastern Airlines
	B-7365	Boeing 777-39PER	China Eastern Airlines
	B-7367	Boeing 777-39PER	China Eastern Airlines
	B-7368	Boeing 777-39PER	China Eastern Airlines
	B-7369	Boeing 777-39PER	China Eastern Airlines
	B-7667	Boeing 787-9	Hainan Airlines
	B-7835	Boeing 787-9	Hainan Airlines
	B-7836	Boeing 787-9	Xiamen Airlines
	B-7837	Boeing 787-9	Hainan Airlines
	B-7838	Boeing 787-9	Xiamen Airlines
	B-7839	Boeing 787-9	Hainan Airlines
	B-7868	Boeing 777-39PER	China Eastern Airlines
	B-7880	Boeing 787-9	Hainan Airlines
	B-7881	Boeing 777-39PER	China Eastern Airlines
	B-7882	Boeing 777-39PER	China Eastern Airlines
	B-7883	Boeing 777-39PER	China Eastern Airlines
	B-8015	Airbus A.330-343	Hainan Airlines
	B-8016	Airbus A.330-343	Hainan Airlines
	B-8019	Airbus A.330-243	Capital Airlines
	B-8117	Airbus A.330-343	Hainan Airlines
	B-8118	Airbus A.330-343	Hainan Airlines
	B-8221	Airbus A.330-243	Capital Airlines
	B-8226	Airbus A.330-243	China Eastern Airlines
	B-8231	Airbus A.330-243	China Eastern Airlines
	B-8287	Airbus A.330-343	Hainan Airlines
	B-8383	Airbus A.330-343	Air China
	B-8385	Airbus A.330-343	Air China
	B-8386	Airbus A.330-343	Air China

Reg	Type	Owner or Operator	Notes
B-8549	Airbus A.330-243	Capital Airlines	
B-8550	Airbus A.330-243	Capital Airlines	
B-8577	Airbus A.330-343	Air China	
B-8579	Airbus A.330-343	Air China	
B-8596	Airbus A.330-243	Tianjin Airlines	
B-8659	Airbus A.330-243	Tianjin Airlines	
B-8689	Airbus A.330-343	Air China	
B-8776	Airbus A.330-243	Tianjin Airlines	
B-8865	Airbus A.330-343	Shenzhen Airlines	
B-8959	Airbus A.330-243	Tianjin Airlines	
B-8981	Airbus A.330-243	Capital Airlines	
B-8982	Airbus A.330-243	Capital Airlines	
B-16703	Boeing 777-35EER	EVA Airways	
B-16705	Boeing 777-35EER	EVA Airways	
B-16706	Boeing 777-35EER	EVA Airways	
B-16707	Boeing 777-35EER	EVA Airways	
B-16708	Boeing 777-35EER	EVA Airways	
B-16709	Boeing 777-35EER	EVA Airways	
B-16710	Boeing 777-35EER	EVA Airways	
B-16711	Boeing 777-35EER	EVA Airways	
B-16712	Boeing 777-35EER	EVA Airways	
B-16713	Boeing 777-35EER	EVA Airways	
B-16715	Boeing 777-35EER	EVA Airways	
B-16716	Boeing 777-35EER	EVA Airways	
B-16717	Boeing 777-35EER	EVA Airways	
B-16718	Boeing 777-35EER	EVA Airways	
B-16719	Boeing 777-35EER	EVA Airways	
B-16720	Boeing 777-35EER	EVA Airways	
B-16721	Boeing 777-35EER	EVA Airways	
B-16722	Boeing 777-36NER	EVA Airways	
B-16723	Boeing 777-36NER	EVA Airways	
B-16725	Boeing 777-35EER	EVA Airways	
B-16726	Boeing 777-35EER	EVA Airways	
B-16727	Boeing 777-35EER	EVA Airways	
B-16728	Boeing 777-36NER	EVA Airways	
B-16729	Boeing 777-36NER	EVA Airways	
B-16730	Boeing 777-36NER	EVA Airways	
B-16731	Boeing 777-36NER	EVA Airways	
B-16732	Boeing 777-36NER	EVA Airways	
B-16733	Boeing 777-36NER	EVA Airways	
B-16735	Boeing 777-36NER	EVA Airways	
B-16736	Boeing 777-36NER	EVA Airways	
B-16737	Boeing 777-36NER	EVA Airways	
B-16738	Boeing 777-36NER	EVA Airways	
B-16739	Boeing 777-36NER	EVA Airways	
B-16740	Boeing 777-36NER	EVA Airways	
B-18901	Airbus A.350-941	China Airlines	
B-18902	Airbus A.350-941	China Airlines	
B-18903	Airbus A.350-941	China Airlines	
B-18905	Airbus A.350-941	China Airlines	
B-18906	Airbus A.350-941	China Airlines	
B-18907	Airbus A.350-941	China Airlines	
B-18908	Airbus A.350-941	China Airlines	
B-18909	Airbus A.350-941	China Airlines	
B-18910	Airbus A.350-941	China Airlines	
B-18912	Airbus A.350-941	China Airlines	
B-18915	Airbus A.350-941	China Airlines	
B-18916	Airbus A.350-941	China Airlines	
B-18917	Airbus A.350-941	China Airlines	
B-18918	Airbus A.350-941	China Airlines	

C (Canada)

Reg	Type	Owner or Operator	Notes
C-FCAE	Boeing 767-375ERBDSF	Cargojet Airways	
C-FCCJ	Boeing 767-323ERBDSF	Cargojet Airways	
C-FCTK	Boeing 737-MAX8	Westjet	
C-FDIJ	Boeing 767-39HERBDSF	Cargojet Airways	
C-FGDT	Boeing 787-9	Air Canada	
C-FGDX	Boeing 787-9	Air Canada	
C-FGDZ	Boeing 787-9	Air Canada	
C-FGEI	Boeing 787-9 (838)	Air Canada	

Notes	Reg	Type	Owner or Operator
	C-FGEO	Boeing 787-9 (839)	Air Canada
	C-FGFZ	Boeing 787-9 (840)	Air Canada
	C-FGHZ	Boeing 787-9	Air Canada
	C-FGSJ	Boeing 767-39HERBCF	Cargojet Airways
	C-FHCM	Boeing 737-MAX8	Westjet
	C-FITL	Boeing 777-333ER (731)	Air Canada
	C-FITU	Boeing 777-333ER (732)	Air Canada
	C-FITW	Boeing 777-3Q8ER (733)	Air Canada
	C-FIUA	Boeing 777-233LR (701)	Air Canada
	C-FIUF	Boeing 777-233LR (702)	Air Canada
	C-FIUJ	Boeing 777-233LR (703)	Air Canada
	C-FIUL	Boeing 777-333ER (734)	Air Canada
	C-FIUR	Boeing 777-333ER (735)	Air Canada
	C-FIUV	Boeing 777-333ER (736)	Air Canada
	C-FIUW	Boeing 777-333ER (737)	Air Canada
	C-FIVK	Boeing 777-233LR (704)	Air Canada
	C-FIVM	Boeing 777-333ER (738)	Air Canada
	C-FIVQ	Boeing 777-333ER (740)	Air Canada
	C-FIVR	Boeing 777-333ER (741)	Air Canada
	C-FIVS	Boeing 777-333ER (742)	Air Canada
	C-FIVW	Boeing 777-333ER (743)	Air Canada
	C-FIVX	Boeing 777-333ER (744)	Air Canada
	C-FJZS	Boeing 777-333ER (748)	Air Canada
	C-FKAU	Boeing 777-333ER (749)	Air Canada
	C-FKSV	Boeing 787-9 (843)	Air Canada
	C-FMIJ	Boeing 767-328ERBDSF	Cargojet Airways
	C-FNAX	Boeing 737-MAX8	Westjet
	C-FNND	Boeing 777-233LR (705)	Air Canada
	C-FNNH	Boeing 777-233LR (706)	Air Canada
	C-FNNQ	Boeing 777-333ER (745)	Air Canada
	C-FNNU	Boeing 777-333ER (746)	Air Canada
	C-FNNW	Boeing 777-333ER (747)	Air Canada
	C-FNOE	Boeing 787-9 (831)	Air Canada
	C-FNOG	Boeing 787-9 (832)	Air Canada
	C-FNOH	Boeing 787-9 (833)	Air Canada
	C-FNOI	Boeing 787-9 (834)	Air Canada
	C-FNWD	Boeing 737-MAX8	Westjet
	C-FPIJ	Boeing 767-33AERBDSF	Cargojet Airways
	C-FPQB	Boeing 787-9 (841)	Air Canada
	C-FRAM	Boeing 777-333ER (739)	Air Canada
	C-FRAX	Boeing 737-MAX8	Westjet
	C-FRSA	Boeing 787-9 (844)	Air Canada
	C-FRSE	Boeing 787-9 (845)	Air Canada
	C-FRSI	Boeing 787-9 (846)	Air Canada
	C-FRSO	Boeing 787-9 (847)	Air Canada
	C-FRSR	Boeing 787-9 (848)	Air Canada
	C-FRTG	Boeing 787-9 (849)	Air Canada
	C-FRTU	Boeing 787-9 (850)	Air Canada
	C-FRTW	Boeing 787-9(851)	Air Canada
	C-FRYV	Boeing 737-MAX8	Westjet
	C-FSBV	Boeing 787-9 (852)	Air Canada
	C-FSCY	Boeing 737-MAX8 (502)	Air Canada
	C-FSDB	Boeing 737-MAX8 (503)	Air Canada
	C-FSDQ	Boeing 737-MAX8 (504)	Air Canada
	C-FSDW	Boeing 737-MAX8 (505)	Air Canada
	C-FSEQ	Boeing 737-MAX8 (506)	Air Canada
	C-FSES	Boeing 737-MAX8 (507)	Air Canada
	C-FSIL	Boeing 737-MAX8 (508)	Air Canada
	C-FSIP	Boeing 737-MAX8 (509)	Air Canada
	C-FSIQ	Boeing 737-MAX8 (510)	Air Canada
	C-FSJH	Boeing 737-MAX8 (511)	Air Canada
	C-FSJJ	Boeing 737-MAX8 (512)	Air Canada
	C-FSKZ	Boeing 737-MAX8 (513)	Air Canada
	C-FSLU	Boeing 737-MAX8 (514)	Air Canada
	C-FSNQ	Boeing 737-MAX8 (515)	Air Canada
	C-FSNU	Boeing 737-MAX8 (516)	Air Canada
	C-FSOC	Boeing 737-MAX8 (517)	Air Canada
	C-FSOI	Boeing 737-MAX8 (518)	Air Canada
	C-FTJV	Boeing 737-MAX8 (501)	Air Canada
	C-FVLQ	Boeing 787-9 (853)	Air Canada
	C-FVLU	Boeing 787-9 (854)	Air Canada

Reg	Type	Owner or Operator	Notes
C-FVLX	Boeing 787-9 (855)	Air Canada	.
C-FVLZ	Boeing 787-9 (856)	Air Canada	
C-FVNB	Boeing 787-9 (857)	Air Canada	
C-FVND	Boeing 787-9 (858)	Air Canada	
C-FVNF	Boeing 787-9 (859)	Air Canada	
C-GAAJ	Boeing 767-323ERBDSF	Cargojet Airways	
C-GAJG	Boeing 767-323ERBDSF	Cargojet Airways	
C-GAMQ	Boeing 737-MAX8	Westjet	
C-GCAM	Boeing 737-MAX8	Westjet	
C-GCIJ	Boeing 767-306ERBDSF	Cargojet Airways	
C-GCTS	Airbus A.330-342	Air Transat	
C-GDDR	Boeing 737-MAX8	Westjet	
C-GEFA	Airbus A.330-343 (939)	Air Canada	
C-GEGC	Airbus A.330-343 (940)	Air Canada	
C-GEGI	Airbus A.330-343 (941)	Air Canada	
C-GEGP	Airbus A.330-343 (942)	Air Canada	
C-GEHF	Boeing 737-MAX8	Westjet	
C-GEHI	Boeing 737-MAX8 (519)	Air Canada	
C-GEHQ	Boeing 737-MAX8 (520)	Air Canada	
C-GEHV	Boeing 737-MAX8 (521)	Air Canada	
C-GEHY	Boeing 737-MAX8 (522)	Air Canada	
C-GEIV	Boeing 737-MAX8 (523)	Air Canada	
C-GEJL	Boeing 737-MAX8 (524)	Air Canada	
C-GEJN	Boeing 737-MAX8	Air Canada	
C-GEKH	Boeing 737-MAX8	Air Canada	
C-GEKX	Boeing 737-MAX8	Air Canada	
C-GEKZ	Boeing 737-MAX8	Air Canada	
C-GELJ	Boeing 737-MAX8	Air Canada	
C-GELQ	Boeing 737-MAX8	Air Canada	
C-GELU	Boeing 737-MAX8	Air Canada	
C-GEMV	Boeing 737-MAX8	Air Canada	
C-GEOJ	Boeing 737-MAX8	Air Canada	
G-GEPB	Boeing 737-MAX8	Air Canada	
C-GEPF	Boeing 737-MAX8	Air Canada	
C-GEPG	Boeing 737-MAX8	Air Canada	
C-GFAF	Airbus A.330-343X (931)	Air Canada	
C-GFAH	Airbus A.330-343X (932)	Air Canada	
C-GFAJ	Airbus A.330-343X (933)	Air Canada	
C-GFUR	Airbus A.330-343X (934)	Air Canada	
C-GGTS	Airbus A.330-243	Air Transat	
C-GHKC	Airbus A.330-343X	Air Canada	
C-GHKR	Airbus A.330-343X (935)	Air Canada	
C-GHKW	Airbus A.330-343X (936)	Air Canada	
C-GHKX	Airbus A.330-343X (937)	Air Canada	
C-GHLM	Airbus A.330-343X (938)	Air Canada	
C-GHPQ	Boeing 787-8 (801)	Air Canada	
C-GHPT	Boeing 787-8 (802)	Air Canada	
C-GHPU	Boeing 787-8 (803)	Air Canada	
C-GHPV	Boeing 787-8 (804)	Air Canada	
C-GHPX	Boeing 787-8 (805)	Air Canada	
C-GHPY	Boeing 787-8 (806)	Air Canada	
C-GHQQ	Boeing 787-8 (807)	Air Canada	
C-GHQY	Boeing 787-8 (808)	Air Canada	
C-GITS	Airbus A.330-243	Air Transat	
C-GJDA	Airbus A.330-243	Air Transat	
C-GKKN	Boeing 787-9	Westjet	
C-GKTS	Airbus A.330-342	Air Transat	
C-GKUG	Airbus A.330-343	Air Canada	
C-GMKS	Boeing 787-9	Westjet	
G-GOCJ	Boeing 767-316ERBDSF	Cargojet Airways	
C-GOFV	Airbus A.330-343E	Air Canada	
C-GOFW	Airbus A.330-343E	Air Canada	
C-GOIE	Airbus A.321-271NX	Air Transat	
C-GOIF	Airbus A.321-271NX	Air Transat	
C-GOIH	Airbus A.321-271NX	Air Transat	
C-GOIJ	Airbus A.321-271NX	Air Transat	
C-GOIK	Airbus A.321-271NX	Air Transat	
C-GOIM	Airbus A.321-271NX	Air Transat	
C-GOIO	Airbus A.321-271NX	Air Transat	
C-GPTS	Airbus A.330-243	Air Transat	
C-GRAX	Boeing 737-MAX8	Westjet	

Notes	Reg	Type	Owner or Operator
	C-GTSD	Airbus A.330-343	Air Transat
	C-GTSI	Airbus A.330-243	Air Transat
	C-GTSJ	Airbus A.330-243	Air Transat
	C-GTSN	Airbus A.330-243	Air Transat
	C-GTSO	Airbus A.330-342	Air Transat
	C-GTSR	Airbus A.330-243	Air Transat
	C-GTSZ	Airbus A.330-243	Air Transat
	C-GUAJ	Boeing 767-35EERBCF	Cargojet Airways
	C-GUBC	Airbus A.330-243	Air Transat
	C-GUBD	Airbus A.330-243	Air Transat
	C-GUBF	Airbus A.330-243	Air Transat
	C-GUBH	Airbus A.330-243	Air Transat
	C-GUBL	Airbus A.330-243	Air Transat
	C-GUBT	Airbus A.330-243	Air Transat
	C-GUDH	Boeing 787-9	Westjet
	C-GUDO	Boeing 787-9	Westjet
	C-GUFR	Airbus A.330-243	Air Transat
	C-GVIJ	Boeing 767-328ERBDSF	Cargojet Airways
	C-GURP	Boeing 787-9	Westjet
	C-GWLK	Boeing 737-MAX8	Westjet
	C-GXAJ	Boeing 767-323ERBDSF	Cargojet Airways
	C-GXAX	Boeing 737-MAX8	Westjet
	C-GYAJ	Boeing 767-35EERBCF	Cargojet Airways
	C-GYRS	Boeing 787-9	Westjet
	C-GZSG	Boeing 737-MAX8	Westjet

Note: Airline fleet number when carried on aircraft is shown in parentheses.

CN (Morocco)

	CN-MAW	Boeing 737-MAX8	Royal Air Maroc
	CN-MAX	Boeing 737-MAX8	Royal Air Maroc
	CN-MAY	Boeing 737-MAX8	Royal Air Maroc
	CN-MAZ	Boeing 737-MAX8	Royal Air Maroc
	CN-NMF	Airbus A.320-214	Air Arabia Maroc
	CN-NMG	Airbus A.320-214	Air Arabia Maroc
	CN-NMH	Airbus A.320-214	Air Arabia Maroc
	CN-NMI	Airbus A.320-214	Air Arabia Maroc
	CN-NMJ	Airbus A.320-214	Air Arabia Maroc
	CN-NMK	Airbus A.320-214	Air Arabia Maroc
	CN-NML	Airbus A.320-214	Air Arabia Maroc
	CN-NMN	Airbus A.320-214	Air Arabia Maroc
	CN-NMO	Airbus A.320-214	Air Arabia Maroc
	CN-RGE	Boeing 737-86N	Royal Air Maroc
	CN-RGF	Boeing 737-86N	Royal Air Maroc
	CN-RGG	Boeing 737-86N	Royal Air Maroc
	CN-RGH	Boeing 737-86N	Royal Air Maroc
	CN-RGI	Boeing 737-86N	Royal Air Maroc
	CN-RGJ	Boeing 737-8B6	Royal Air Maroc
	CN-RGK	Boeing 737-8B6	Royal Air Maroc
	CN-RGM	Boeing 737-8B6	Royal Air Maroc
	CN-RGN	Boeing 737-8B6	Royal Air Maroc
	CN-RGO	Embraer ERJ190-100AR	Royal Air Maroc
	CN-RGP	Embraer ERJ190-100AR	Royal Air Maroc
	CN-RGQ	Embraer ERJ190-100AR	Royal Air Maroc
	CN-RGR	Embraer ERJ190-100AR	Royal Air Maroc
	CN-RGV	Boeing 737-85P	Royal Air Maroc
	CN-RNJ	Boeing 737-8B6	Royal Air Maroc
	CN-RNK	Boeing 737-8B6	Royal Air Maroc
	CN-RNL	Boeing 737-7B6	Royal Air Maroc
	CN-RNM	Boeing 737-7B6	Royal Air Maroc
	CN-RNP	Boeing 737-8B6	Royal Air Maroc
	CN-RNQ	Boeing 737-7B6	Royal Air Maroc
	CN-RNR	Boeing 737-7B6	Royal Air Maroc
	CN-RNU	Boeing 737-8B6	Royal Air Maroc
	CN-RNV	Boeing 737-7B6	Royal Air Maroc
	CN-RNW	Boeing 737-8B6	Royal Air Maroc
	CN-RNZ	Boeing 737-8B6	Royal Air Maroc
	CN-ROA	Boeing 737-8B6	Royal Air Maroc
	CN-ROB	Boeing 737-8B6	Royal Air Maroc
	CN-ROC	Boeing 737-8B6	Royal Air Maroc

Reg	Type	Owner or Operator	Notes
CN-ROD	Boeing 737-7B6	Royal Air Maroc	
CN-ROE	Boeing 737-8B6	Royal Air Maroc	
CN-ROH	Boeing 737-8B6	Royal Air Maroc	
CN-ROJ	Boeing 737-8B6	Royal Air Maroc	
CN-ROK	Boeing 737-8B6	Royal Air Maroc	
CN-ROL	Boeing 737-8B6	Royal Air Maroc	
CN-ROP	Boeing 737-8B6	Royal Air Maroc	
CN-ROR	Boeing 737-8B6	Royal Air Maroc	
CN-ROS	Boeing 737-8B6	Royal Air Maroc	
CN-ROT	Boeing 737-8B6	Royal Air Maroc	
CN-ROU	Boeing 737-8B6	Royal Air Maroc	
CN-ROY	Boeing 737-8B6	Royal Air Maroc	
CN-ROZ	Boeing 737-8B6	Royal Air Maroc	

CS (Portugal)

Reg	Type	Owner or Operator	Notes
CS-TFM	Boeing 777-212ER	Euro Atlantic Airways	
CS-TFU	Airbus A.319-115	White Airways	
CS-TJE	Airbus A.321-211	TAP Air Portugal *Pero Vaz de Caminha*	
CS-TJF	Airbus A.321-211	TAP Air Portugal *Luis Vaz de Cameos*	
CS-TJH	Airbus A.321-211	TAP Air Portugal *Manuel de Oliveira*	
CS-TJI	Airbus A.321-251N	TAP Air Portugal *Julio Pomar*	
CS-TJJ	Airbus A.321-251N	TAP Air Portugal *Goncalo Velho Cabral*	
CS-TJK	Airbus A.321-251N	TAP Air Portugal *Eugenio de Andrade*	
CS-TJL	Airbus A.321-251N	TAP Air Portugal *Ze Pedro*	
CS-TJM	Airbus A.321-251N	TAP Air Portugal *Raul Solnado*	
CS-TJN	Airbus A.321-251N	TAP Air Portugal *Nadir Afonso*	
CS-TJO	Airbus A.321-251N	TAP Air Portugal *Viera Da Silva*	
CS-TJP	Airbus A.321-251N	TAP Air Portugal *Gago Coutinho*	
CS-TJQ	Airbus A.321-251N	TAP Air Portugal	
CS-TJR	Airbus A.321-251N	TAP Air Portugal *Portugal*	
CS-TKK	Airbus A.320-214	Azores Airlines	
CS-TKP	Airbus A.320-214	Azores Airlines	
CS-TKQ	Airbus A.320-214	Azores Airlines	
CS-TKR	Boeing 767-36NER	Euro Atlantic Airways	
CS-TKS	Boeing 767-36NER	Euro Atlantic Airways	
CS-TKT	Boeing 767-36NER	Euro Atlantic Airways	
CS-TKX	Airbus A.340-313X	Hi-Fly	
CS-TKY	Airbus A.330-941	Hi Fly	
CS-TMW	Airbus A.320-214	TAP Air Portugal *Luisa Todi*	
CS-TNH	Airbus A.320-214	TAP Air Portugal *Almada Negreiros*	
CS-TNJ	Airbus A.320-214	TAP Air Portugal *Florbela Espanca*	
CS-TNK	Airbus A.320-214	TAP Air Portugal *Teofilo Braga*	
CS-TNL	Airbus A.320-214	TAP Air Portugal *Vitorino Nermesio*	
CS-TNM	Airbus A.320-214	TAP Air Portugal *Natalia Correia*	
CS-TNN	Airbus A.320-214	TAP Air Portugal *Gil Vicente*	
CS-TNQ	Airbus A.320-214	TAP Air Portugal *Jose Regio*	
CS-TNR	Airbus A.320-214	TAP Air Portugal *Luis de Freitas Branco*	
CS-TNS	Airbus A.320-214	TAP Air Portugal *D.Alfonso Henriques*	
CS-TNT	Airbus A.320-214	TAP Air Portugal *Rafael Bordaio Pinheiro*	
CS-TNU	Airbus A.320-214	TAP Air Portugal *Columbano Bordalo Pinheiro*	
CS-TNV	Airbus A.320-214	TAP Air Portugal *Grao Vasco*	
CS-TNW	Airbus A.320-214	TAP Air Portugal *Jose Saramago*	
CS-TNX	Airbus A.320-214	TAP Air Portugal *Malangatana*	
CS-TNY	Airbus A.320-214	TAP Air Portugal *Dominigos Sequeira*	
CS-TOL	Airbus A.330-202	TAP Air Portugal *Joao Goncalves Zarco*	
CS-TOM	Airbus A.330-202	TAP Air Portugal *Vasco da Gama*	
CS-TON	Airbus A.330-202	TAP Air Portugal *Ja-o XXI*	
CS-TOO	Airbus A.330-202	TAP Air Portugal *Fernao de Magalhaes*	
CS-TOP	Airbus A.330-202	TAP Air Portugal *Pedro Nunes*	
CS-TPO	Embraer ERJ190-100LR	TAP Express	
CS-TPP	Embraer ERJ190-100LR	TAP Express	
CS-TPQ	Embraer ERJ190-100LR	TAP Express	
CS-TPR	Embraer ERJ190-100LR	TAP Express	
CS-TPS	Embraer ERJ190-100LR	TAP Express	
CS-TPT	Embraer ERJ190-100LR	TAP Express	
CS-TPU	Embraer ERJ190-100LR	TAP Express	
CS-TPV	Embraer ERJ190-100LR	TAP Express	
CS-TPW	Embraer ERJ190-100LR	TAP Express	
CS-TQP	Airbus A.330-202	Hi Fly	
CS-TQU	Boeing 737-8K2	Euro Atlantic Airways	

Notes	Reg	Type	Owner or Operator
	CS-TQY	Airbus A.340-313X	Hi Fly
	CS-TRJ	Airbusd A.321-231	Hi Fly
	CS-TRO	Airbus A.320-214	White Airways
	CS-TSF	Airbus A.321-253N	Azores Airlines
	CS-TSG	Airbus A.321-253N	Azores Airlines
	CS-TSH	Airbus A.321-253NX	Azores Airlines
	CS-TSI	Airbus A.321-253NX	Azores Airlines
	CS-TST	Boeing 767-34PER	Euro Atlantic Airways
	CS-TSU	Boeing 767-34PER	Euro Atlantic Airways
	CS-TSV	Boeing 767-34PER	Euro Atlantic Airways
	CS-TTG	Airbus A.319-111	TAP Air Portugal *Humberto Delgado*
	CS-TTK	Airbus A.319-111	TAP Air Portugal *Miguel Torga*
	CS-TTL	Airbus A.319-111	TAP Air Portugal *Almeida Garrett*
	CS-TTM	Airbus A.319-111	TAP Air Portugal *Alexandre Herculano*
	CS-TTN	Airbus A.319-111	TAP Air Portugal *Camilo Castelo Branco*
	CS-TTO	Airbus A.319-111	TAP Air Portugal *Antero de Quental*
	CS-TTP	Airbus A.319-111	TAP Air Portugal *Josefa d'Obidos*
	CS-TTR	Airbus A.319-112	TAP Air Portugal *Soares dos Reis*
	CS-TTS	Airbus A.319-112	TAP Air Portugal *Guilhermina Suggia*
	CS-TTW	Embraer ERJ190-200IGW	TAP Express
	CS-TTX	Embraer ERJ190-200IGW	TAP Express
	CS-TTY	Embraer ERJ190-200IGW	TAP Express
	CS-TTZ	Embraer ERJ190-200IGW	TAP Express
	CS-TUA	Airbus A.330-941	TAP Air Portugal *D. Maria I*
	CS-TUB	Airbus A.330-941	TAP Air Portugal *d joao ii o pricipe perfeito*
	CS-TUC	Airbus A.330-941	TAP Air Portugal *Nuno Goncalves*
	CS-TUD	Airbus A.330-941	TAP Air Portugal *John Dos Passos*
	CS-TUE	Airbus A.330-941	TAP Air Portugal *Marques de Pombal*
	CS-TUF	Airbus A.330-941	TAP Air Portugal *Bartolomeu Presetrelo*
	CS-TUG	Airbus A.330-941	TAP Air Portugal *Pedro Alvares Cabral*
	CS-TUH	Airbus A.330-941	TAP Air Portugal *D. Dinis*
	CS-TUI	Airbus A.330-941	TAP Air Portugal *D. Afonso Henriques*
	CS-TUJ	Airbus A.330-941	TAP Air Portugal *D. Maria II*
	CS-TUK	Airbus A.330-941	TAP Air Portugal *D. Francisco De Almeida*
	CS-TUL	Airbus A.330-941	TAP Air Portugal *Joao Vaz Corte-Real*
	CS-TUM	Airbus A.330-941	TAP Air Portugal *Nuno Alvares Pereira*
	CS-TUN	Airbus A.330-941	TAP Air Portugal *D. Fuas Roupinho*
	CS-TUO	Airbus A.330-941	TAP Air Portugal *Fernao Mendes Pinto*
	CS-TUP	Airbus A.330-941	TAP Air Portugal *D. Joao De Castro*
	CS-TUQ	Airbus A.330-941	TAP Air Portugal
	CS-TUR	Airbus A.330-941	TAP Air Portugal
	CS-TUS	Airbus A.330-941	TAP Air Portugal
	CS-TVA	Airbus A.320-251N	TAP Air Portugal *Padre Americo*
	CS-TVB	Airbus A.320-251N	TAP Air Portugal *Agustina Bessa-luis*
	CS-TVC	Airbus A.320-251N	TAP Air Portugal *Nicolau Breyner*
	CS-TVD	Airbus A.320-251N	TAP Air Portugal *Carlos Paredes*
	CS-TVE	Airbus A.320-251N	TAP Air Portugal *Amelia Rey Colaco*
	CS-TVF	Airbus A.320-251N	TAP Air Portugal *Jose Carlos Ary Dos Santos*
	CS-TVG	Airbus A.320-251N	TAP Air Portugal *Amadeo De Souza Cardozo*
	CS-TVH	Airbus A.320-251N	TAP Air Portugal
	CS-TXA	Airbus A.321-251NX	TAP Air Portugal *Agostinho da Silva*
	CS-TXB	Airbus A.321-251NX	TAP Air Portugal *Jorge de Sina*
	CS-TXC	Airbus A.321-251NX	TAP Air Portugal *Pero da Covilha*
	CS-TXD	Airbus A.321-251NX	TAP Air Portugal *Roberto Ivens*
	CS-TXE	Airbus A.321-251NX	TAP Air Portugal
	CS-TXF	Airbus A.321-251NX	TAP Air Portugal

D (Germany)

Notes	Reg	Type	Owner or Operator
	D-AALA	Boeing 777-FZN	AeroLogic
	D-AALB	Boeing 777-FZN	AeroLogic
	D-AALC	Boeing 777-FZN	AeroLogic
	D-AALD	Boeing 777-FZN	AeroLogic
	D-AALE	Boeing 777-FZN	AeroLogic
	D-AALF	Boeing 777-FZN	AeroLogic
	D-AALG	Boeing 777-FZN	AeroLogic
	D-AALH	Boeing 777-FZN	AeroLogic
	D-AALI	Boeing 777-FZN	AeroLogic
	D-AALJ	Boeing 777-FZN	AeroLogic
	D-AALK	Boeing 777-FZN	AeroLogic
	D-AALL	Boeing 777-200F	AeroLogic

Reg	Type	Owner or Operator	Notes
D-AALM	Boeing 777-200F	AeroLogic	
D-AALN	Boeing 777-200F	AeroLogic	
D-AALO	Boeing 777-200F	AeroLogic	
D-AALP	Boeing 777-200F	AeroLogic	
D-AALQ	Boeing 777-200F	AeroLogic	
D-AALR	Boeing 777-200F	AeroLogic	
D-ABAF	Boeing 737-86J	TUIfly	
D-ABAG	Boeing 737-86J	TUIfly	
D-ABBD	Boeing 737-86J	TUIfly	
D-ABDP	Airbus A.320-214	Eurowings	
D-ABDQ	Airbus A.320-214	Eurowings	
D-ABDT	Airbus A.320-214	Eurowings	
D-ABDU	Airbus A.320-214	Eurowings	
D-ABFP	Airbus A.320-214	Eurowings	
D-ABFR	Airbus A.320-214	Eurowings	
D-ABGH	Airbus A.319-112	Eurowings	
D-ABGJ	Airbus A.319-112	Eurowings	
D-ABGK	Airbus A.319-112	Eurowings	
D-ABGN	Airbus A.319-112	Eurowings	
D-ABGP	Airbus A.319-112	Eurowings	
D-ABGQ	Airbus A.319-112	Eurowings	
D-ABGR	Airbus A.319-112	Eurowings	
D-ABHA	Airbus A.320-214	Eurowings	
D-ABHC	Airbus A.320-214	Eurowings	
D-ABHF	Airbus A.320-214	Eurowings	
D-ABHG	Airbus A.320-214	Eurowings	
D-ABHN	Airbus A.320-214	Eurowings	
D-ABKI	Boeing 737-86J	TUIfly	
D-ABKJ	Boeing 737-86J	TUIfly	
D-ABKM	Boeing 737-86J	TUIfly	
D-ABKN	Boeing 737-86J	TUIfly	
D-ABMQ	Boeing 737-86J	TUIfly	
D-ABMV	Boeing 737-86J	TUIfly	
D-ABNI	Airbus A.320-214	Eurowings	
D-ABNK	Airbus A.320-214	Eurowings	
D-ABNL	Airbus A.320-214	Eurowings	
D-ABNN	Airbus A.320-214	Eurowings	
D-ABNT	Airbus A.320-214	Eurowings	
D-ABNU	Airbus A.320-214	Eurowings	
D-ABOA	Boeing 757-330	Condor	
D-ABOB	Boeing 757-330	Condor	
D-ABOC	Boeing 757-330	Condor	
D-ABOE	Boeing 757-330	Condor	
D-ABOF	Boeing 757-330	Condor	
D-ABOG	Boeing 757-330	Condor	
D-ABOH	Boeing 757-330	Condor	
D-ABOI	Boeing 757-330	Condor	
D-ABOJ	Boeing 757-330	Condor	
D-ABOK	Boeing 757-330	Condor	
D-ABOL	Boeing 757-330	Condor	
D-ABOM	Boeing 757-330	Condor	
D-ABON	Boeing 757-330	Condor	
D-ABTA	Boeing 777-9	Lufthansa	
D-ABTB	Boeing 777-9	Lufthansa	
D-ABTC	Boeing 777-9	Lufthansa	
D-ABUA	Boeing 767-330ER	Condor	
D-ABUB	Boeing 767-330ER	Condor	
D-ABUC	Boeing 767-330ER	Condor	
D-ABUD	Boeing 767-330ER	Condor	
D-ABUE	Boeing 767-330ER	Condor	
D-ABUF	Boeing 767-330ER	Condor	
D-ABUH	Boeing 767-330ER	Condor	
D-ABUI	Boeing 767-330ER	Condor	
D-ABUK	Boeing 767-343ER	Condor	
D-ABUL	Boeing 767-31BER	Condor	
D-ABUM	Boeing 767-31BER	Condor	
D-ABUO	Boeing 767-3Q8ER	Condor	
D-ABUP	Boeing 767-3Q8ER	Condor	
D-ABUS	Boeing 767-38EER	Condor	
D-ABUT	Boeing 767-3Q8ER	Condor	
D-ABUZ	Boeing 767-330ER	Condor	

Notes	Reg	Type	Owner or Operator
	D-ABVM	Boeing 747-430	Lufthansa
	D-ABVT	Boeing 747-430	Lufthansa
	D-ABVU	Boeing 747-430	Lufthansa
	D-ABVW	Boeing 747-430	Lufthansa
	D-ABVX	Boeing 747-430	Lufthansa
	D-ABVY	Boeing 747-430	Lufthansa
	D-ABVZ	Boeing 747-430	Lufthansa
	D-ABYA	Boeing 747-830	Lufthansa
	D-ABYC	Boeing 747-830	Lufthansa
	D-ABYD	Boeing 747-830	Lufthansa
	D-ABYF	Boeing 747-830	Lufthansa
	D-ABYG	Boeing 747-830	Lufthansa
	D-ABYH	Boeing 747-830	Lufthansa
	D-ABYI	Boeing 747-830	Lufthansa
	D-ABYJ	Boeing 747-830	Lufthansa
	D-ABYK	Boeing 747-830	Lufthansa
	D-ABYL	Boeing 747-830	Lufthansa
	D-ABYM	Boeing 747-830	Lufthansa
	D-ABYN	Boeing 747-830	Lufthansa
	D-ABYO	Boeing 747-830	Lufthansa
	D-ABYP	Boeing 747-830	Lufthansa
	D-ABYQ	Boeing 747-830	Lufthansa
	D-ABYR	Boeing 747-830	Lufthansa
	D-ABYS	Boeing 747-830	Lufthansa
	D-ABYT	Boeing 747-830	Lufthansa
	D-ABYU	Boeing 747-830	Lufthansa
	D-ABZE	Airbus A.320-216	Eurowings
	D-ABZI	Airbus A.320-216	Eurowings
	D-ABZK	Airbus A.320-216	Eurowings
	D-ABZL	Airbus A.320-216	Eurowings
	D-ABZN	Airbus A.320-216	Eurowings
	D-ACKA	Canadair CRJ900ER	Lufthansa CityLine
	D-ACKB	Canadair CRJ900ER	Lufthansa CityLine
	D-ACKC	Canadair CRJ900ER	Lufthansa CityLine
	D-ACKD	Canadair CRJ900ER	Lufthansa CityLine
	D-ACKE	Canadair CRJ900ER	Lufthansa CityLine
	D-ACKF	Canadair CRJ900ER	Lufthansa CityLine
	D-ACKG	Canadair CRJ900ER	Lufthansa CityLine
	D-ACKH	Canadair CRJ900ER	Lufthansa CityLine
	D-ACKI	Canadair CRJ900ER	Lufthansa CityLine
	D-ACKJ	Canadair CRJ900ER	Lufthansa CityLine
	D-ACKK	Canadair CRJ900ER	Lufthansa CityLine
	D-ACKL	Canadair CRJ900ER	Lufthansa CityLine
	D-ACLG	Boeing 737-46JSF	CargoLogic Germany
	D-ACLO	Boeing 737-4H6SF	CargoLogic Germany
	D-ACLW	Boeing 737-48EF	CargoLogic Germany
	D-ACNA	Canadair CRJ900ER	Lufthansa CityLine
	D-ACNB	Canadair CRJ900ER	Lufthansa CityLine
	D-ACNC	Canadair CRJ900ER	Lufthansa CityLine
	D-ACND	Canadair CRJ900ER	Lufthansa CityLine
	D-ACNE	Canadair CRJ900ER	Lufthansa CityLine
	D-ACNF	Canadair CRJ900ER	Lufthansa CityLine
	D-ACNG	Canadair CRJ900ER	Lufthansa CityLine
	D-ACNH	Canadair CRJ900ER	Lufthansa CityLine
	D-ACNI	Canadair CRJ900ER	Lufthansa CityLine
	D-ACNJ	Canadair CRJ900ER	Lufthansa CityLine
	D-ACNK	Canadair CRJ900ER	Lufthansa CityLine
	D-ACNL	Canadair CRJ900ER	Lufthansa CityLine
	D-ACNM	Canadair CRJ900ER	Lufthansa CityLine
	D-ACNN	Canadair CRJ900ER	Lufthansa CityLine
	D-ACNO	Canadair CRJ900ER	Lufthansa CityLine
	D-ACNP	Canadair CRJ900ER	Lufthansa CityLine
	D-ACNQ	Canadair CRJ900ER	Lufthansa CityLine
	D-ACNR	Canadair CRJ900ER	Lufthansa CityLine
	D-ACNT	Canadair CRJ900ER	Lufthansa CityLine
	D-ACNU	Canadair CRJ900ER	Lufthansa CityLine
	D-ACNV	Canadair CRJ900ER	Lufthansa CityLine
	D-ACNW	Canadair CRJ900ER	Lufthansa CityLine
	D-ACNX	Canadair CRJ900ER	Lufthansa CityLine
	D-AEAA	Airbus A.300B4-622R	EAT Leipzig/DHL
	D-AEAB	Airbus A.300B4-622R	EAT Leipzig/DHL

Reg	Type	Owner or Operator	Notes
D-AEAC	Airbus A.300B4-622R	EAT Leipzig/DHL	
D-AEAD	Airbus A.300B4-622R	EAT Leipzig/DHL	
D-AEAE	Airbus A.300B4-622R	EAT Leipzig/DHL	
D-AEAF	Airbus A.300B4-622R	EAT Leipzig/DHL	
D-AEAG	Airbus A.300B4-622R	EAT Leipzig/DHL	
D-AEAH	Airbus A.300B4-622R	EAT Leipzig/DHL	
D-AEAI	Airbus A.300B4-622R	EAT Leipzig/DHL	
D-AEAJ	Airbus A.300B4-622R	EAT Leipzig/DHL	
D-AEAK	Airbus A.300B4-622R	EAT Leipzig/DHL	
D-AEAL	Airbus A.300B4-622R	EAT Leipzig/DHL	
D-AEAM	Airbus A.300B4-622R	EAT Leipzig/DHL	
D-AEAN	Airbus A.300B4-622R	EAT Leipzig/DHL	
D-AEAO	Airbus A.300B4-622R	EAT Leipzig/DHL	
D-AEAP	Airbus A.300B4-622R	EAT Leipzig/DHL	
D-AEAQ	Airbus A.300B4-622R	EAT Leipzig/DHL	
D-AEAR	Airbus A.300B4-622R	EAT Leipzig/DHL	
D-AEAS	Airbus A.300B4-622R	EAT Leipzig/DHL	
D-AEAT	Airbus A.300B4-622R	EAT Leipzig/DHL	
D-AEBB	Embraer ERJ190-200LR	Lufthansa CityLine	
D-AEBC	Embraer ERJ190-200LR	Lufthansa CityLine	
D-AECA	Embraer ERJ190-100LR	Lufthansa CityLine	
D-AECB	Embraer ERJ190-100LR	Lufthansa CityLine	
D-AECC	Embraer ERJ190-100LR	Lufthansa CityLine	
D-AECD	Embraer ERJ190-100LR	Lufthansa CityLine	
D-AECE	Embraer ERJ190-100LR	Lufthansa CityLine	
D-AECF	Embraer ERJ190-100LR	Lufthansa CityLine	
D-AECG	Embraer ERJ190-100LR	Lufthansa CityLine	
D-AECH	Embraer ERJ190-100LR	Lufthansa CityLine	
D-AECI	Embraer ERJ190-100LR	Lufthansa CityLine	
D-AEUA	Airbus A.321-211	Eurowings	
D-AEUB	Airbus A.321-211	Eurowings	
D-AEUC	Airbus A.321-211	Eurowings	
D-AEUD	Airbus A.320-214	Eurowings	
D-AEUE	Airbus A.320-214	Eurowings	
D-AEUH	Airbus A.320-214	Eurowings	
D-AEUI	Airbus A.321-211	Eurowings	
D-AEUJ	Airbus A.321-211	Eurowings	
D-AEWF	Airbus A.320-214	Eurowings	
D-AEWG	Airbus A.320-214	Eurowings	
D-AEWI	Airbus A.320-214	Eurowings	
D-AEWJ	Airbus A.320-214	Eurowings	
D-AEWK	Airbus A.320-214	Eurowings	
D-AEWL	Airbus A.320-214	Eurowings	
D-AEWM	Airbus A.320-214	Eurowings	
D-AEWN	Airbus A.320-214	Eurowings	
D-AEWO	Airbus A.320-214	Eurowings	
D-AEWP	Airbus A.320-214	Eurowings	
D-AEWQ	Airbus A.320-214	Eurowings	
D-AEWR	Airbus A.320-214	Eurowings	
D-AEWS	Airbus A.320-214	Eurowings	
D-AEWT	Airbus A.320-214	Eurowings	
D-AEWU	Airbus A.320-214	Eurowings	
D-AEWV	Airbus A.320-214	Eurowings	
D-AEWW	Airbus A.320-214	Eurowings	
D-AGWA	Airbus A.319-132	Eurowings	
D-AGWB	Airbus A.319-132	Eurowings	
D-AGWC	Airbus A.319-132	Eurowings	
D-AGWD	Airbus A.319-132	Eurowings	
D-AGWE	Airbus A.319-132	Eurowings	
D-AGWF	Airbus A.319-132	Eurowings	
D-AGWG	Airbus A.319-132	Eurowings	
D-AGWH	Airbus A.319-132	Eurowings	
D-AGWI	Airbus A.319-132	Eurowings	
D-AGWK	Airbus A.319-132	Eurowings	
D-AGWL	Airbus A.319-132	Eurowings	
D-AGWM	Airbus A.319-132	Eurowings	
D-AGWN	Airbus A.319-132	Eurowings	
D-AGWO	Airbus A.319-132	Eurowings	
D-AGWU	Airbus A.319-132	Eurowings	
D-AGWV	Airbus A.319-132	Eurowings	
D-AGWX	Airbus A.319-132	Eurowings	

Notes	Reg	Type	Owner or Operator
	D-AGWY	Airbus A.319-132	Eurowings
	D-AGWZ	Airbus A.319-132	Eurowings
	D-AHFT	Boeing 737-8K5	TUIfly
	D-AHFV	Boeing 737-8K5	TUIfly
	D-AHLK	Boeing 737-8K5	TUIfly
	D-AHXG	Boeing 737-7K5	TUIfly
	D-AIAC	Airbus A.321-211	Condor
	D-AIAD	Airbus A.321-211	Condor
	D-AIAF	Airbus A.321-211	Condor
	D-AIAG	Airbus A.321-211	Condor
	D-AIAI	Airbus A.321-211	Condor
	D-AIBA	Airbus A.319-114	Lufthansa
	D-AIBB	Airbus A.319-114	Lufthansa
	D-AIBC	Airbus A.319-114	Lufthansa
	D-AIBD	Airbus A.319-114	Lufthansa
	D-AIBE	Airbus A.319-114	Lufthansa
	D-AIBF	Airbus A.319-112	Lufthansa
	D-AIBG	Airbus A.319-112	Lufthansa
	D-AIBH	Airbus A.319-112	Lufthansa
	D-AIBI	Airbus A.319-112	Lufthansa
	D-AIBJ	Airbus A.319-112	Lufthansa
	D-AICA	Airbus A.320-212	Condor
	D-AICC	Airbus A.320-212	Condor
	D-AICD	Airbus A.320-212	Condor
	D-AICE	Airbus A.320-212	Condor
	D-AICF	Airbus A.320-212	Condor
	D-AICG	Airbus A.320-212	Condor
	D-AICH	Airbus A.320-212	Condor
	D-AICI	Airbus A.320-212	Condor
	D-AICJ	Airbus A.320-212	Condor
	D-AICK	Airbus A.320-212	Condor
	D-AICP	Airbus A.320-214	Condor
	D-AICR	Airbus A.320-214	Condor
	D-AICS	Airbus A.320-214	Condor
	D-AIDA	Airbus A.321-231	Lufthansa
	D-AIDB	Airbus A.321-231	Lufthansa
	D-AIDC	Airbus A.321-231	Lufthansa
	D-AIDD	Airbus A.321-231	Lufthansa
	D-AIDE	Airbus A.321-231	Lufthansa
	D-AIDF	Airbus A.321-231	Lufthansa
	D-AIDG	Airbus A.321-231	Lufthansa
	D-AIDH	Airbus A.321-231	Lufthansa
	D-AIDI	Airbus A.321-231	Lufthansa
	D-AIDJ	Airbus A.321-231	Lufthansa
	D-AIDK	Airbus A.321-231	Lufthansa
	D-AIDL	Airbus A.321-231	Lufthansa
	D-AIDM	Airbus A.321-231	Lufthansa
	D-AIDN	Airbus A.321-231	Lufthansa
	D-AIDO	Airbus A.321-231	Lufthansa
	D-AIDP	Airbus A.321-231	Lufthansa
	D-AIDQ	Airbus A.321-231	Lufthansa
	D-AIDT	Airbus A.321-231	Lufthansa
	D-AIDU	Airbus A.321-231	Lufthansa
	D-AIDV	Airbus A.321-231	Lufthansa
	D-AIDW	Airbus A.321-231	Lufthansa
	D-AIDX	Airbus A.321-231	Lufthansa
	D-AIEA	Airbus A.321-271NX	Lufthansa
	D-AIEB	Airbus A.321-271NX	Lufthansa
	D-AIEC	Airbus A.321-271NX	Lufthansa
	D-AIED	Airbus A.321-271NX	Lufthansa
	D-AIEE	Airbus A.321-271NX	Lufthansa
	D-AIEF	Airbus A.321-271NX	Lufthansa
	D-AIEG	Airbus A.321-271NX	Lufthansa
	D-AIEI	Airbus A.321-271NX	Lufthansa
	D-AIEJ	Airbus A.321-271NX	Lufthansa
	D-AIFC	Airbus A.340-313X	Lufthansa
	D-AIFD	Airbus A.340-313X	Lufthansa
	D-AIFE	Airbus A.340-313X	Lufthansa
	D-AIFF	Airbus A.340-313X	Lufthansa
	D-AIGL	Airbus A.340-313X	Lufthansa
	D-AIGM	Airbus A.340-313X	Lufthansa

Reg	Type	Owner or Operator	Notes
D-AIGN	Airbus A.340-313X	Lufthansa	
D-AIGO	Airbus A.340-313X	Lufthansa	
D-AIGP	Airbus A.340-313X	Lufthansa	
D-AIGS	Airbus A.340-313X	Lufthansa	
D-AIGT	Airbus A.340-313X	Lufthansa	
D-AIGU	Airbus A.340-313X	Lufthansa	
D-AIGV	Airbus A.340-313X	Lufthansa	
D-AIGW	Airbus A.340-313X	Lufthansa	
D-AIGX	Airbus A.340-313X	Lufthansa	
D-AIGY	Airbus A.340-313X	Lufthansa	
D-AIGZ	Airbus A.340-313X	Lufthansa	
D-AIHB	Airbus A.340-642	Lufthansa	
D-AIHC	Airbus A.340-642	Lufthansa	
D-AIHD	Airbus A.340-642	Lufthansa	
D-AIHE	Airbus A.340-642	Lufthansa	
D-AIHF	Airbus A.340-642	Lufthansa	
D-AIHH	Airbus A.340-642	Lufthansa	
D-AIHI	Airbus A.340-642	Lufthansa	
D-AIHK	Airbus A.340-642	Lufthansa	
D-AIHL	Airbus A.340-642	Lufthansa	
D-AIHP	Airbus A.340-642	Lufthansa	
D-AIHT	Airbus A.340-642	Lufthansa	
D-AIHU	Airbus A.340-642	Lufthansa	
D-AIHV	Airbus A.340-642	Lufthansa	
D-AIHW	Airbus A.340-642	Lufthansa	
D-AIHX	Airbus A.340-642	Lufthansa	
D-AIHY	Airbus A.340-642	Lufthansa	
D-AIHZ	Airbus A.340-642	Lufthansa	
D-AIJA	Airbus A.320-271N	Lufthansa	
D-AIJB	Airbus A.320-271N	Lufthansa	
D-AIJC	Airbus A.320-271N	Lufthansa	
D-AIJD	Airbus A.320-271N	Lufthansa	
D-AIJE	Airbus A.320-271N	Lufthansa	
D-AIKB	Airbus A.330-343X	Lufthansa	
D-AIKD	Airbus A.330-343X	Lufthansa	
D-AIKE	Airbus A.330-343X	Lufthansa	
D-AIKF	Airbus A.330-343X	Lufthansa	
D-AIKH	Airbus A.330-343X	Lufthansa	
D-AIKI	Airbus A.330-343X	Lufthansa	
D-AIKK	Airbus A.330-343X	Lufthansa	
D-AIKL	Airbus A.330-343X	Lufthansa	
D-AIKM	Airbus A.330-343X	Lufthansa	
D-AIKN	Airbus A.330-343X	Lufthansa	
D-AIKO	Airbus A.330-343X	Lufthansa	
D-AIKP	Airbus A.330-343X	Lufthansa	
D-AIKQ	Airbus A.330-343X	Lufthansa	
D-AIKR	Airbus A.330-343X	Lufthansa	
D-AIKS	Airbus A.330-343X	Lufthansa	
D-AILA	Airbus A.319-114	Lufthansa	
D-AILB	Airbus A.319-114	Lufthansa CityLine	
D-AILC	Airbus A.319-114	Lufthansa	
D-AILD	Airbus A.319-114	Lufthansa	
D-AILE	Airbus A.319-114	Lufthansa	
D-AILF	Airbus A.319-114	Lufthansa	
D-AILH	Airbus A.319-114	Lufthansa	
D-AILI	Airbus A.319-114	Lufthansa	
D-AILK	Airbus A.319-114	Lufthansa	
D-AILL	Airbus A.319-114	Lufthansa	
D-AILM	Airbus A.319-114	Lufthansa	
D-AILN	Airbus A.319-114	Lufthansa	
D-AILP	Airbus A.319-114	Lufthansa CityLine	
D-AILS	Airbus A.319-114	Lufthansa CityLine	
D-AILT	Airbus A.319-114	Lufthansa CityLine	
D-AILU	Airbus A.319-114	Lufthansa	
D-AILW	Airbus A.319-114	Lufthansa CityLine	
D-AILX	Airbus A.319-114	Lufthansa CityLine	
D-AILY	Airbus A.319-114	Lufthansa	
D-AIMA	Airbus A.380-841	Lufthansa	
D-AIMB	Airbus A.380-841	Lufthansa	
D-AIMC	Airbus A.380-841	Lufthansa	
D-AIMD	Airbus A.380-841	Lufthansa	

Notes	Reg	Type	Owner or Operator
	D-AIME	Airbus A.380-841	Lufthansa
	D-AIMF	Airbus A.380-841	Lufthansa
	D-AIMG	Airbus A.380-841	Lufthansa
	D-AIMH	Airbus A.380-841	Lufthansa
	D-AIMI	Airbus A.380-841	Lufthansa
	D-AIMJ	Airbus A.380-841	Lufthansa
	D-AIMK	Airbus A.380-841	Lufthansa
	D-AIML	Airbus A.380-841	Lufthansa
	D-AIMM	Airbus A.380-841	Lufthansa
	D-AIMN	Airbus A.380-841	Lufthansa
	D-AINA	Airbus A.320-271N	Lufthansa
	D-AINB	Airbus A.320-271N	Lufthansa
	D-AINC	Airbus A.320-271N	Lufthansa
	D-AIND	Airbus A.320-271N	Lufthansa
	D-AINE	Airbus A.320-271N	Lufthansa
	D-AINF	Airbus A.320-271N	Lufthansa
	D-AING	Airbus A.320-271N	Lufthansa
	D-AINH	Airbus A.320-271N	Lufthansa
	D-AINI	Airbus A.320-271N	Lufthansa
	D-AINJ	Airbus A.320-271N	Lufthansa
	D-AINK	Airbus A.320-271N	Lufthansa
	D-AINL	Airbus A.320-271N	Lufthansa
	D-AINM	Airbus A.320-271N	Lufthansa
	D-AINN	Airbus A.320-271N	Lufthansa
	D-AINO	Airbus A.320-271N	Lufthansa
	D-AINP	Airbus A.320-271N	Lufthansa
	D-AINQ	Airbus A.320-271N	Lufthansa
	D-AINR	Airbus A.320-271N	Lufthansa
	D-AINT	Airbus A.320-271N	Lufthansa
	D-AINU	Airbus A.320-271N	Lufthansa
	D-AINV	Airbus A.320-271N	Lufthansa
	D-AINW	Airbus A.320-271N	Lufthansa
	D-AINX	Airbus A.320-271N	Lufthansa
	D-AINY	Airbus A.320-271N	Lufthansa
	D-AINZ	Airbus A.320-271N	Lufthansa
	D-AIPF	Airbus A.320-211	Lufthansa
	D-AIPH	Airbus A.320-211	Lufthansa
	D-AIPL	Airbus A.320-211	Lufthansa
	D-AIPM	Airbus A.320-211	Lufthansa
	D-AIPP	Airbus A.320-211	Lufthansa
	D-AIPR	Airbus A.320-211	Lufthansa
	D-AIPS	Airbus A.320-211	Lufthansa
	D-AIPT	Airbus A.320-211	Lufthansa
	D-AIPY	Airbus A.320-211	Lufthansa
	D-AIPZ	Airbus A.320-211	Lufthansa
	D-AIQA	Airbus A.320-211	Lufthansa
	D-AIQD	Airbus A.320-211	Lufthansa
	D-AIQF	Airbus A.320-211	Lufthansa
	D-AIQH	Airbus A.320-211	Lufthansa
	D-AIQS	Airbus A.320-211	Lufthansa
	D-AIQT	Airbus A.320-211	Lufthansa
	D-AIQU	Airbus A.320-211	Lufthansa
	D-AIQW	Airbus A.320-211	Lufthansa
	D-AIRA	Airbus A.321-131	Lufthansa
	D-AIRB	Airbus A.321-131	Lufthansa
	D-AIRC	Airbus A.321-131	Lufthansa
	D-AIRD	Airbus A.321-131	Lufthansa
	D-AIRE	Airbus A.321-131	Lufthansa
	D-AIRF	Airbus A.321-131	Lufthansa
	D-AIRH	Airbus A.321-131	Lufthansa
	D-AIRK	Airbus A.321-131	Lufthansa
	D-AIRL	Airbus A.321-131	Lufthansa
	D-AIRM	Airbus A.321-131	Lufthansa
	D-AIRN	Airbus A.321-131	Lufthansa
	D-AIRO	Airbus A.321-131	Lufthansa
	D-AIRP	Airbus A.321-131	Lufthansa
	D-AIRR	Airbus A.321-131	Lufthansa
	D-AIRS	Airbus A.321-131	Lufthansa
	D-AIRT	Airbus A.321-131	Lufthansa
	D-AIRU	Airbus A.321-131	Lufthansa
	D-AIRW	Airbus A.321-131	Lufthansa

Reg	Type	Owner or Operator	Notes
D-AIRX	Airbus A.321-131	Lufthansa	
D-AIRY	Airbus A.321-131	Lufthansa	
D-AISB	Airbus A.321-231	Lufthansa	
D-AISC	Airbus A.321-231	Lufthansa	
D-AISD	Airbus A.321-231	Lufthansa	
D-AISF	Airbus A.321-231	Lufthansa	
D-AISG	Airbus A.321-231	Lufthansa	
D-AISH	Airbus A.321-231	Lufthansa	
D-AISI	Airbus A.321-231	Lufthansa	
D-AISJ	Airbus A.321-231	Lufthansa	
D-AISK	Airbus A.321-231	Lufthansa	
D-AISL	Airbus A.321-231	Lufthansa	
D-AISN	Airbus A.321-231	Lufthansa	
D-AISO	Airbus A.321-231	Lufthansa	
D-AISP	Airbus A.321-231	Lufthansa	
D-AISQ	Airbus A.321-231	Lufthansa	
D-AISR	Airbus A.321-231	Lufthansa	
D-AIST	Airbus A.321-231	Lufthansa	
D-AISU	Airbus A.321-231	Lufthansa	
D-AISV	Airbus A.321-231	Lufthansa	
D-AISW	Airbus A.321-231	Lufthansa	
D-AISX	Airbus A.321-231	Lufthansa	
D-AISZ	Airbus A.321-231	Lufthansa	
D-AIUA	Airbus A.320-214	Lufthansa	
D-AIUB	Airbus A.320-214	Lufthansa	
D-AIUC	Airbus A.320-214	Lufthansa	
D-AIUD	Airbus A.320-214	Lufthansa	
D-AIUE	Airbus A.320-214	Lufthansa	
D-AIUF	Airbus A.320-214	Lufthansa	
D-AIUG	Airbus A.320-214	Lufthansa	
D-AIUH	Airbus A.320-214	Lufthansa	
D-AIUI	Airbus A.320-214	Lufthansa	
D-AIUJ	Airbus A.320-214	Lufthansa	
D-AIUK	Airbus A.320-214	Lufthansa	
D-AIUL	Airbus A.320-214	Lufthansa	
D-AIUM	Airbus A.320-214	Lufthansa	
D-AIUN	Airbus A.320-214	Lufthansa	
D-AIUO	Airbus A.320-214	Lufthansa	
D-AIUP	Airbus A.320-214	Lufthansa	
D-AIUQ	Airbus A.320-214	Lufthansa	
D-AIUR	Airbus A.320-214	Lufthansa	
D-AIUS	Airbus A.320-214	Lufthansa	
D-AIUT	Airbus A.320-214	Lufthansa	
D-AIUU	Airbus A.320-214	Lufthansa	
D-AIUV	Airbus A.320-214	Lufthansa	
D-AIUW	Airbus A.320-214	Lufthansa	
D-AIUX	Airbus A.320-214	Lufthansa	
D-AIUY	Airbus A.320-214	Lufthansa	
D-AIUZ	Airbus A.320-214	Lufthansa	
D-AIWA	Airbus A.320-214	Lufthansa	
D-AIWB	Airbus A.320-214	Lufthansa	
D-AIWC	Airbus A.320-214	Lufthansa	
D-AIWD	Airbus A.320-214	Lufthansa	
D-AIWE	Airbus A.320-214	Lufthansa	
D-AIWF	Airbus A.320-214	Lufthansa	
D-AIWG	Airbus A.320-214	Lufthansa	
D-AIWH	Airbus A.320-214	Lufthansa	
D-AIWI	Airbus A.320-214	Lufthansa	
D-AIWJ	Airbus A.320-214	Lufthansa	
D-AIWK	Airbus A.320-214	Lufthansa	
D-AIXA	Airbus A.350-941	Lufthansa	
D-AIXB	Airbus A.350-941	Lufthansa	
D-AIXC	Airbus A.350-941	Lufthansa	
D-AIXD	Airbus A.350-941	Lufthansa	
D-AIXE	Airbus A.350-941	Lufthansa	
D-AIXF	Airbus A.350-941	Lufthansa	
D-AIXG	Airbus A.350-941	Lufthansa	
D-AIXH	Airbus A.350-941	Lufthansa	
D-AIXI	Airbus A.350-941	Lufthansa	
D-AIXJ	Airbus A.350-941	Lufthansa	
D-AIXK	Airbus A.350-941	Lufthansa	

OVERSEAS AIRLINERS

Notes	Reg	Type	Owner or Operator
	D-AIXL	Airbus A.350-941	Lufthansa
	D-AIXM	Airbus A.350-941	Lufthansa
	D-AIXN	Airbus A.350-941	Lufthansa
	D-AIXO	Airbus A.350-941	Lufthansa
	D-AIXP	Airbus A.350-941	Lufthansa
	D-AIXQ	Airbus A.350-941	Lufthansa
	D-AIZA	Airbus A.320-214	Lufthansa
	D-AIZB	Airbus A.320-214	Lufthansa
	D-AIZC	Airbus A.320-214	Lufthansa
	D-AIZD	Airbus A.320-214	Lufthansa
	D-AIZE	Airbus A.320-214	Lufthansa
	D-AIZF	Airbus A.320-214	Lufthansa
	D-AIZG	Airbus A.320-214	Lufthansa
	D-AIZH	Airbus A.320-214	Lufthansa
	D-AIZI	Airbus A.320-214	Lufthansa
	D-AIZJ	Airbus A.320-214	Lufthansa
	D-AIZM	Airbus A.320-214	Lufthansa
	D-AIZN	Airbus A.320-214	Lufthansa
	D-AIZO	Airbus A.320-214	Lufthansa
	D-AIZP	Airbus A.320-214	Lufthansa
	D-AIZQ	Airbus A.320-214	Eurowings
	D-AIZR	Airbus A.320-214	Eurowings
	D-AIZS	Airbus A.320-214	Eurowings
	D-AIZT	Airbus A.320-214	Eurowings
	D-AIZU	Airbus A.320-214	Eurowings
	D-AIZV	Airbus A.320-214	Eurowings
	D-AIZW	Airbus A.320-214	Lufthansa
	D-AIZX	Airbus A.320-214	Lufthansa
	D-AIZY	Airbus A.320-214	Lufthansa
	D-AIZZ	Airbus A.320-214	Lufthansa
	D-AKNK	Airbus A.319-112	Eurowings
	D-AKNL	Airbus A.319-112	Eurowings
	D-AKNM	Airbus A.319-112	Eurowings
	D-AKNN	Airbus A.319-112	Eurowings
	D-AKNO	Airbus A.319-112	Eurowings
	D-AKNP	Airbus A.319-112	Eurowings
	D-AKNQ	Airbus A.319-112	Eurowings
	D-AKNR	Airbus A.319-112	Eurowings
	D-AKNS	Airbus A.319-112	Eurowings
	D-AKNT	Airbus A.319-112	Eurowings
	D-AKNU	Airbus A.319-112	Eurowings
	D-AKNV	Airbus A.319-112	Eurowings
	D-ALCA	McD Douglas MD-11F	Lufthansa Cargo
	D-ALCC	McD Douglas MD-11F	Lufthansa Cargo
	D-ALCD	McD Douglas MD-11F	Lufthansa Cargo
	D-ALEN	Boeing 757-2Q8F	EAT Leipzig/DHL
	D-ALEO	Boeing 757-2Q8F	EAT Leipzig/DHL
	D-ALEP	Boeing 757-2Q8F	EAT Leipzig/DHL
	D-ALEQ	Boeing 757-2Q8F	EAT Leipzig/DHL
	D-ALER	Boeing 757-2Q8F	EAT Leipzig/DHL
	D-ALES	Boeing 757-2Q8F	EAT Leipzig/DHL
	D-ALET	Boeing 757-28AF	EAT Leipzig/DHL
	D-ALEU	Boeing 757-23NF	EAT Leipzig/DHL
	D-ALEV	Boeing 757-28ASF	EAT Leipzig/DHL
	D-ALFA	Boeing 777FBT	Lufthansa Cargo
	D-ALFB	Boeing 777FBT	Lufthansa Cargo
	D-ALFC	Boeing 777FBT	Lufthansa Cargo
	D-ALFD	Boeing 777FBT	Lufthansa Cargo
	D-ALFE	Boeing 777FBT	Lufthansa Cargo
	D-ALFF	Boeing 777FBT	Lufthansa Cargo
	D-ALFG	Boeing 777FBT	Lufthansa Cargo
	D-ALFH	Boeing 777FBT	Lufthansa Cargo
	D-ALFI	Boeing 777FBT	Lufthansa Cargo
	D-AMAA	Boeing 737-MAX8	TUIfly
	D-AMAB	Boeing 737-MAX8	TUIfly
	D-AMAC	Boeing 737-MAX8	TUIfly
	D-AMAX	Boeing 737-MAX8	TUIfly
	D-ASTX	Airbus A.319-112	Eurowings
	D-ASUN	Boeing 737-8BK	TUIfly
	D-ATCA	Airbus A.321-211	Condor
	D-ATCB	Airbus A.321-211	Condor

Reg	Type	Owner or Operator	Notes
D-ATCC	Airbus A.321-211	Condor	
D-ATCF	Airbus A.321-211	Condor	
D-ATCG	Airbus A.321-211	Condor	
D-ATCH	Airbus A.320-214	Condor	
D-ATUA	Boeing 737-8K5	TUIfly	
D-ATUC	Boeing 737-8K5	TUIfly	
D-ATUD	Boeing 737-8K5	TUIfly	
D-ATUE	Boeing 737-8K5	TUIfly	
D-ATUF	Boeing 737-8K5	TUIfly	
D-ATUI	Boeing 737-8K5	TUIfly	
D-ATUJ	Boeing 737-8K5	TUIfly	
D-ATUK	Boeing 737-8K5	TUIfly	
D-ATUM	Boeing 737-8K5	TUIfly	
D-ATUN	Boeing 737-8K5	TUIfly	
D-ATUO	Boeing 737-8K5	TUIfly	
D-ATUR	Boeing 737-8K5	TUIfly	
D-ATUZ	Boeing 737-8K5	TUIfly	
D-ATYA	Boeing 737-8K5	TUIfly	
D-ATYB	Boeing 737-8K5	TUIfly	
D-ATYI	Boeing 737-8K5	TUIfly	
D-ATYJ	Boeing 737-8K5	TUIfly	
D-AZMK	Airbus A.300F4-622R	EAT Leipzig/DHL	
D-AZMO	Airbus A.300F4-622R	EAT Leipzig/DHL	

EC (Spain)

Reg	Type	Owner or Operator	Notes
EC-HDS	Boeing 757-256	Privilege Style	
EC-HUH	Airbus A.321-211	Iberia *Benidorm*	
EC-HUI	Airbus A.321-211	Iberia *Comunidad Autonoma de la Rioja*	
EC-IDA	Boeing 737-86Q	Air Europa	
EC-IDT	Boeing 737-86Q	Air Europa	
EC-IEF	Airbus A.320-214	Iberia *Castillo de Loarre*	
EC-IEG	Airbus A.320-214	Iberia *Costa Brava*	
EC-IGK	Airbus A.321-213	Iberia *Costa Calida*	
EC-IJN	Airbus A.321-212	Iberia *Merida*	
EC-ILO	Airbus A.321-211	Iberia *Cueva de Nerja*	
EC-ILP	Airbus A.321-211	Iberia *Peniscola*	
EC-ILQ	Airbus A.320-214	Iberia Express	
EC-ILR	Airbus A.320-214	Iberia *San Juan de la Pena*	
EC-ILS	Airbus A.320-214	Iberia *Sierra de Cameros*	
EC-ISN	Boeing 737-86Q	Air Europa	
EC-ISY	Boeing 757-256	Privilege Style	
EC-IXD	Airbus A.321-212	Iberia *Vall d'Aran*	
EC-IZH	Airbus A.320-214	Iberia *San Pere de Roda*	
EC-IZR	Airbus A.320-214	Iberia *Urkiola*	
EC-JAZ	Airbus A.319-111	Iberia *Las Medulas*	
EC-JDL	Airbus A.319-111	Iberia *Los Llanos de Aridane*	
EC-JDM	Airbus A.321-213	Iberia Express	
EC-JDR	Airbus A.321-213	Iberia Express	
EC-JEI	Airbus A.319-111	Iberia *Xátiva*	
EC-JEJ	Airbus A.321-231	Iberia Express	
EC-JFG	Airbus A.320-214	Iberia Express	
EC-JFH	Airbus A.320-214	Iberia Express	
EC-JFN	Airbus A.320-214	Iberia *Sirrea de las Nieves*	
EC-JGM	Airbus A.320-214	Vueling Airlines *The joy of vueling*	
EC-JGS	Airbus A.321-213	Iberia *Guadelupe*	
EC-JLI	Airbus A.321-211	Iberia Express	
EC-JQZ	Airbus A.321-211	Iberia *Generalife*	
EC-JRE	Airbus A.321-211	Iberia *Villa de Uncastillo*	
EC-JSY	Airbus A.320-214	Vueling Airlines	
EC-JTQ	Airbus A.320-214	Vueling Airlines *Vueling, que es gerundio*	
EC-JTR	Airbus A.320-214	Vueling Airlines *No Vueling no party*	
EC-JYX	Airbus A.320-214	Vueling Airlines *Elisenda Masana*	
EC-JZI	Airbus A.320-214	Vueling Airlines *Vueling in love*	
EC-JZM	Airbus A.321-211	Iberia *Águila Imperial Ibérica*	
EC-KCU	Airbus A.320-216	Vueling Airlines	
EC-KDG	Airbus A.320-214	Vueling Airlines	
EC-KDH	Airbus A.320-214	Vueling Airlines *Ain't no Vueling high enough*	
EC-KDT	Airbus A.320-216	Vueling Airlines	
EC-KDX	Airbus A.320-216	Vueling Airlines *Francisco Jose Ruiz Cortizo*	
EC-KHM	Airbus A.319-111	Iberia *Buho Real*	

Notes	Reg	Type	Owner or Operator
	EC-KHN	Airbus A.320-216	Vueling Airlines
	EC-KJD	Airbus A.320-216	Vueling Airlines
	EC-KKS	Airbus A.319-111	Iberia *Halcon Peregrino*
	EC-KLB	Airbus A.320-214	Vueling Airlines *Vuela Punto*
	EC-KLT	Airbus A.320-214	Vueling Airlines
	EC-KMI	Airbus A.320-216	Vueling Airlines *How are you? I'm Vueling!*
	EC-KOH	Airbus A.320-214	Iberia *Fontibre*
	EC-KOY	Airbus A.319-111	Iberia *Vencejo*
	EC-KRH	Airbus A.320-214	Vueling Airlines *Vueling me softly*
	EC-KUB	Airbus A.319-111	Iberia *Flamenco*
	EC-KXN	Boeing 747-4H6	Wamos Air
	EC-LAA	Airbus A.320-214	Vueling Airlines
	EC-LAB	Airbus A.320-214	Vueling Airlines
	EC-LEA	Airbus A.320-214	Iberia Express
	EC-LKH	Airbus A.320-214	Iberia Express
	EC-LLE	Airbus A.320-214	Iberia Express
	EC-LLJ	Airbus A.320-214	Vueling Airlines
	EC-LLM	Airbus A.320-216	Vueling Airlines *Be happy, be Vueling*
	EC-LNH	Airbus A.330-243	Wamos Air
	EC-LOB	Airbus A.320-232	Vueling Airlines
	EC-LOC	Airbus A.320-232	Vueling Airlines *Vueling on heaven's door*
	EC-LOP	Airbus A.320-214	Vueling Airlines
	EC-LPQ	Boeing 737-85P	Air Europa
	EC-LPR	Boeing 737-85P	Air Europa
	EC-LQK	Airbus A.320-232	Vueling Airlines
	EC-LQX	Boeing 737-85P	Air Europa
	EC-LRG	Airbus A.320-214	Iberia
	EC-LRY	Airbus A.320-232	Vueling Airlines
	EC-LTM	Boeing 737-85P	Air Europa
	EC-LUB	Airbus A.330-302	Iberia *Tikal*
	EC-LUC	Airbus A.320-214	Iberia Express
	EC-LUD	Airbus A.320-214	Iberia Express
	EC-LUK	Airbus A.330-302E	Iberia *Costa Rica*
	EC-LUL	Airbus A.320-216	Iberia *Cangas de Onis*
	EC-LUN	Airbus A.320-232	Vueling Airlines
	EC-LUO	Airbus A.320-232	Vueling Airlines
	EC-LUS	Airbus A.320-216	Iberia Express
	EC-LUT	Boeing 737-85P	Air Europa
	EC-LUX	Airbus A.330-302	Iberia *Panama*
	EC-LVD	Airbus A.320-216	Iberia *Valle de Mena*
	EC-LVO	Airbus A.320-214	Vueling Airlines
	EC-LVP	Airbus A.320-214	Vueling Airlines
	EC-LVQ	Airbus A.320-216	Iberia Express
	EC-LVR	Boeing 737-85P	Air Europa
	EC-LVS	Airbus A.320-214	Vueling Airlines
	EC-LVT	Airbus A.320-214	Vueling Airlines
	EC-LVU	Airbus A.320-214	Vueling Airlines
	EC-LVV	Airbus A.320-214	Vueling Airlines
	EC-LXK	Airbus A.330-302E	Iberia *El Salvador*
	EC-LXQ	Airbus A.320-216	Iberia *Penon de Ifach*
	EC-LXV	Boeing 737-86N	Air Europa
	EC-LYE	Airbus A.320-216	Iberia Express
	EC-LYF	Airbus A.330-302E	Iberia *Juan Carlos I*
	EC-LYM	Airbus A.320-216	Iberia Express
	EC-LYR	Boeing 737-85P	Air Europa
	EC-LZJ	Airbus A.330-302E	Iberia *Miami*
	EC-LZN	Airbus A.320-214	Vueling Airlines
	EC-LZO	Boeing 767-35DER	Privilege Style
	EC-LZX	Airbus A.330-302E	Iberia *Madrid*
	EC-LZZ	Airbus A.320-214	Vueling Airlines
	EC-MAA	Airbus A.330-302	Iberia *Rio de Janeiro*
	EC-MAD	Boeing 737-4YOF	Swiftair
	EC-MAH	Airbus A.320-214	Vueling Airlines
	EC-MAI	Airbus A.320-214	Vueling Airlines
	EC-MAN	Airbus A.320-214	Vueling Airlines
	EC-MAO	Airbus A.320-214	Vueling Airlines
	EC-MBD	Airbus A.320-214	Vueling Airlines
	EC-MBE	Airbus A.320-214	Vueling Airlines
	EC-MBF	Airbus A.320-214	Vueling Airlines
	EC-MBK	Airbus A.320-214	Volotea Airlines
	EC-MBS	Airbus A.320-214	Vueling Airlines

Reg	Type	Owner or Operator	Notes
EC-MBT	Airbus A.320-214	Vueling Airlines	
EC-MBY	Airbus A.320-214	Vueling Airlines	
EC-MCI	Boeing 737-4Q8F	Swiftair	
EC-MCS	Airbus A.320-216	Iberia *Playa de Los Lances*	
EC-MCU	Airbus A.320-214	Vueling Airlines	
EC-MDK	Airbus A.320-214	Iberia *P.N.Picas de Europa*	
EC-MDZ	Airbus A.320-232	Vueling Airlines	
EC-MEA	Airbus A.320-232	Vueling Airlines	
EC-MEG	Airbus A.320-214	Iberia Express	
EC-MEH	Airbus A.320-214	Iberia Express	
EC-MEL	Airbus A.320-232	Vueling Airlines	
EC-MEQ	Airbus A.320-232	Vueling Airlines	
EC-MER	Airbus A.320-232	Vueling Airlines	
EC-MES	Airbus A.320-232	Vueling Airlines	
EC-MEY	Boeing 737-476F	Swiftair	
EC-MFE	Boeing 737-476F	Swiftair	
EC-MFK	Airbus A.320-232	Vueling Airlines	
EC-MFL	Airbus A.320-232	Vueling Airlines	
EC-MFM	Airbus A.320-232	Vueling Airlines	
EC-MFN	Airbus A.320-232	Vueling Airlines	
EC-MFP	Airbus A.319-111	Iberia	
EC-MFS	Boeing 737-4YO	AlbaStar	
EC-MGE	Airbus A.320-232	Vueling Airlines	
EC-MGF	Airbus A.319-111	Vueling Airlines	
EC-MGY	Airbus A.321-231	Vueling Airlines	
EC-MGZ	Airbus A.321-231	Vueling Airlines	
EC-MHA	Airbus A.321-231	Vueling Airlines *Good Sense and Rebelliousness*	
EC-MHB	Airbus A.321-231	Vueling Airlines	
EC-MHS	Airbus A.321-231	Vueling Airlines *Vuelissimo*	
EC-MIE	Boeing 737-4YOF	Swiftair	
EC-MIL	Airbus A.330-202	Iberia *Oaxaca*	
EC-MIQ	Airbus A.319-112	Vueling Airlines	
EC-MIR	Airbus A.319-112	Vueling Airlines	
EC-MJA	Airbus A.330-202	Iberia *Buenos Aires*	
EC-MJB	Airbus A.320-232	Vueling Airlines *Alex Cruz 5.0*	
EC-MJC	Airbus A.320-232	Vueling Airlines	
EC-MJR	Airbus A.321-231	Vueling Airlines	
EC-MJT	Airbus A.330-202	Iberia *La Habana*	
EC-MJU	Boeing 737-85P	Air Europa	
EC-MKI	Airbus A.330-202	Iberia *Buenos Aires*	
EC-MKJ	Airbus A.330-202	Iberia *Montevideo*	
EC-MKL	Boeing 737-85P	Air Europa	
EC-MKM	Airbus A.320-232	Vueling Airlines *Miguel Angel Galan*	
EC-MKN	Airbus A.320-232	Vueling Airlines *Arelis & Carlos*	
EC-MKO	Airbus A.320-232	Vueling Airlines *The Tutu Project*	
EC-MKV	Airbus A.319-112	Vueling Airlines	
EC-MKX	Airbus A.319-112	Vueling Airlines	
EC-MLB	Airbus A.330-202	Iberia *Iberoamerica*	
EC-MLD	Airbus A.321-231	Vueling Airlines	
EC-MLE	Airbus A.320-232	Vueling Airlines *Amrani-Bus*	
EC-MLM	Airbus A.321-231	Vueling Airlines	
EC-MLP	Airbus A.330-202	Iberia *Lima*	
EC-MMG	Airbus A.330-202	Iberia *Santiago de Chile*	
EC-MMH	Airbus A.321-231	Vueling Airlines *Ryan's Well*	
EC-MMU	Airbus A.321-231	Vueling Airlines *Mason Wartman*	
EC-MNK	Airbus A.330-202	Iberia *Bogota*	
EC-MNL	Airbus A.330-202	Iberia *Tokio*	
EC-MNM	Boeing 737-4YOF	Swiftair	
EC-MNZ	Airbus A.320-232	Vueling Airlines	
EC-MOG	Airbus A.320-232	Vueling Airlines	
EC-MOO	Airbus A.321-231	Vueling Airlines	
EC-MPG	Boeing 737-85P	Air Europa	
EC-MPS	Boeing 737-85P	Air Europa	
EC-MPV	Airbus A.321-231	Vueling Airlines	
EC-MQB	Airbus A.321-231	Vueling Airlines *Biciclown*	
EC-MQE	Airbus A.320-232	Vueling Airlines	
EC-MQL	Airbus A.321-231	Vueling Airlines *Klaus' Angels*	
EC-MQP	Boeing 737-85P	Air Europa	
EC-MRF	Airbus A.321-231	Vueling Airlines *Flavia Carvalho*	
EC-MSY	Airbus A.330-202	Iberia *Santo Domingo*	
EC-MTB	Airbus A.319-111	Volotea Airlines	

OVERSEAS AIRLINERS

Notes	Reg	Type	Owner or Operator
	EC-MTC	Airbus A.319-111	Volotea Airlines
	EC-MTD	Airbus A.319-111	Volotea Airlines
	EC-MTE	Airbus A.319-112	Volotea Airlines
	EC-MTF	Airbus A.319-112	Volotea Airlines
	EC-MTL	Airbus A.319-111	Volotea Airlines
	EC-MTM	Airbus A.319-111	Volotea Airlines
	EC-MTN	Airbus A.319-111	Volotea Airlines
	EC-MTT	Airbus A.330-223	Wamos Air
	EC-MTU	Airbus A.330-223	Wamos Air
	EC-MTV	Boeing 737-86J	AlbaStar
	EC-MUB	Boeing 737-86J	AlbaStar
	EC-MUC	Airbus A.319-112	Volotea Airlines
	EC-MUD	Airbus A.330-302	Iberia *Johannesburgo*
	EC-MUF	Airbus A.320-214	Iberia Express
	EC-MUK	Airbus A.320-214	Iberia Express
	EC-MUM	Airbus A.320-214	Vueling Airlines
	EC-MUT	Airbus A.319-111	Volotea Airlines
	EC-MUU	Airbus A.319-111	Volotea Airlines
	EC-MUX	Airbus A.319-111	Volotea Airlines
	EC-MUY	Airbus A.319-111	Volotea Airlines
	EC-MUZ	Boeing 737-85P	Air Europa
	EC-MVD	Airbus A.320-214	Vueling Airlines
	EC-MVE	Airbus A.320-214	Vueling Airlines
	EC-MVM	Airbus A.320-232	Vueling Airlines
	EC-MVN	Airbus A.320-232	Vueling Airlines
	EC-MVO	Airbus A.320-232	Vueling Airlines
	EC-MVY	Boeing 737-800	Air Europa
	EC-MXG	Airbus A.320-232	Vueling Airlines
	EC-MXM	Boeing 737-800	Air Europa
	EC-MXP	Airbus A.320-232	Vueling Airlines
	EC-MXU	Airbus A.320-251N	Iberia *Patrulla Aguila*
	EC-MXV	Airbus A.350-941	Iberia *Pacido Domingo*
	EC-MXY	Airbus A.320-251N	Iberia *Getafe*
	EC-MYB	Airbus A.320-214	Vueling Airlines
	EC-MYC	Airbus A.320-232	Vueling Airlines
	EC-MYX	Airbus A.350-941	Iberia *Paco de Lucia*
	EC-MZT	Airbus A.320-271N	Vueling Airlines
	EC-NAB	Boeing 737-81Q	AlbaStar
	EC-NAE	Airbus A.320-271N	Vueling Airlines
	EC-NAF	Airbus A.320-271N	Vueling Airlines
	EC-NAJ	Airbus A.320-271N	Vueling Airlines
	EC-NAV	Airbus A.320-271N	Vueling Airlines
	EC-NAX	Airbus A.320-271N	Vueling Airlines
	EC-NAY	Airbus A.320-271N	Vueling Airlines
	EC-NAZ	Airbus A.320-271N	Vueling Airlines
	EC-NBA	Airbus A.320-271N	Vueling Airlines
	EC-NBC	Airbus A.319-112	Volotea Airlines
	EC-NBD	Airbus A.319-112	Volotea Airlines
	EC-NBE	Airbus A.350-941	Iberia *Museo del Prado*
	EC-NBL	Boeing 737-MAX8	Air Europa
	EC-NBN	Airbus A.330-243	Wamos Air
	EC-NBV	Boeing 737-MAX8	Air Europa
	EC-NCB	Airbus A.319-111	Volotea Airlines
	EC-NCF	Airbus A.320-271N	Vueling Airlines
	EC-NCG	Airbus A.320-271N	Vueling Airlines
	EC-NCK	Airbus A.330-243	Wamos Air
	EC-NCM	Airbus A.320-251N	Iberia *Amelia Earhart*
	EC-NCS	Airbus A.320-271N	Vueling Airlines
	EC-NCT	Airbus A.320-271N	Vueling Airlines
	EC-NCU	Airbus A.320-271N	Vueling Airlines
	EC-NCX	Airbus A.350-941	Iberia *Seleccion Espanola de Futbol*
	EC-NDA	Airbus A.320-271N	Vueling Airlines
	EC-NDB	Airbus A.320-271N	Vueling Airlines
	EC-NDC	Airbus A.320-271N	Vueling Airlines
	EC-NDG	Airbus A.319-112	Volotea Airlines
	EC-NDH	Airbus A.319-112	Volotea Airlines
	EC-NDN	Airbus A.320-251N	Iberia *Cuatro Vientos*
	EC-NDR	Airbus A.350-941	Iberia *Juan Sebastian Elcano*
	EC-NEA	Airbus A.320-271N	Vueling Airlines
	EC-NEN	Airbus A.330-202	Iberia
	EC-NER	Airbus A.320-251N	Iberia *Barajas*

Reg	Type	Owner or Operator	Notes
EC-NFH	Airbus A.320-271N	Vueling Airlines	
EC-NFI	Airbus A.320-271N	Vueling Airlines	
EC-NFJ	Airbus A.320-271N	Vueling Airlines	
EC-NFK	Airbus A.320-271N	Vueling Airlines	
EC-NFZ	Airbus A.320-251N	Iberia *Virgen de Loreto*	
EC-NGB	Airbus A.319-111	Vueling Airlines	
EC-NGC	Boeing 737-809	AlbaStar	
EC-NGL	Airbus A.319-112	Volotea Airlines	
EC-NGP	Airbus A.321-251NX	Iberia Express	
EC-NGT	Airbus A.350-941	Iberia *Equipo Olimpico Espanol*	
EC-NHM	Airbus A.330-343	Wamos Air	
EC-NHP	Airbus A.319-111	Volotea Airlines	
EC-NHQ	Airbus A.319-132	Volotea Airlines	
EC-NIA	Airbus A.321-251NX	Iberia Express	
EC-NIF	Airbus A.321-251NX	Iberia Express	
EC-NIG	Airbus A.350-941	Iberia *Seleccion Espanola de Baloncesto*	
EC-NIJ	Airbus A.320-271N	Vueling Airlines	
EC-NIS	Airbus A.350-941	Iberia *Talento a Bordo*	
EC-NIX	Airbus A.320-271N	Vueling Airlines	
EC-NIY	Airbus A.320-271N	Vueling Airlines	
EC-NJI	Airbus A.321-251NX	Iberia Express	
EC-NJM	Airbus A.350-941	Iberia *Flamenco*	
EC-NJP	Airbus A.319-111	Volotea Airlines	
EC-NJQ	Airbus A.319-111	Volotea Airlines	
EC-NJU	Airbus A.320-251N	Iberia *Maria Bernaldo de Quiros*	
EC-NJY	Airbus A.320-251N	Iberia *graciasheroes*	
EC-NLJ	Airbus A.321-231	Privilege Style	
EC-NLK	Boeing 737-81M	AlbaStar	
EC-NLP	Airbus A.350-941	Iberia	
EC-NLS	Boeing 737-436F	Swiftair	
EC-NLU	Boeing 737-4Q8F	Swiftair	
EC-NLV	Airbus A.321-211	Vueling Airlines	
EC-NLX	Airbus A.321-211	Vueling Airlines	
EC-NLY	Airbus A.321-211	Vueling Airlines	
EC-NLZ	Airbus A.321-211	Vueling Airlines	
EC-NMJ	Boeing 737-4K5F	Swiftair	
EC-NMK	Boeing 737-406F	Swiftair	
EC-NML	Boeing 737-436F	Swiftair	
EC-NMZ	Airbus A.350-941	Iberia *Volando*	
EC-NNL	Airbus A.320-214	Volotea Airlines	
EC-NNM	Airbus A.320-214	Volotea Airlines	
EC-NNN	Airbus A.320-214	Volotea Airlines	
EC-NNY	Airbus A.320-214	Volotea Airlines	
EC-NNZ	Airbus A.320-214	Volotea Airlines	

EP (Iran)

Reg	Type	Owner or Operator	Notes
EP-IBA	Airbus A.300B4-605R	Iran Air	
EP-IBB	Airbus A.300B4-605R	Iran Air	
EP-IBC	Airbus A.300B4-605R	Iran Air	
EP-IBD	Airbus A.300B4-605R	Iran Air	
EP-IBK	Airbus A.310-304	Iran Air	
EP-IBL	Airbus A.310-304	Iran Air	
EP-IJA	Airbus A.330-243	Iran Air	
EP-IJB	Airbus A.330-243	Iran Air	

ER (Moldova)

Reg	Type	Owner or Operator	Notes
ER-00002	Airbus A.319-112	Fly One	
ER-00004	Airbus A.320-232	Fly One	
ER-00005	Airbus A.320-232	Fly One	
ER-AXL	Airbus A.319-115	Air Moldova	
ER-AXM	Airbus A.319-112	Air Moldova	
ER-AXP	Airbus A.320-233	Air Moldova	
ER-AXR	Airbus A.321-211	Air Moldova	

ES (Estonia)

Reg	Type	Owner or Operator	Notes
ES-SAM	Airbus A.320-232	Smart Lynx Airlines Estonia	
ES-SAQ	Airbus A.320-214	Smart Lynx Airlines Estonia	

Notes	Reg	Type	Owner or Operator
	ES-SAS	Airbus A.320-214	Smart Lynx Airlines Estonia

ET (Ethiopia)

Notes	Reg	Type	Owner or Operator
	ET-AOO	Boeing 787-8	Ethiopian Airlines
	ET-AOP	Boeing 787-8	Ethiopian Airlines
	ET-AOQ	Boeing 787-8	Ethiopian Airlines
	ET-AOR	Boeing 787-8	Ethiopian Airlines
	ET-AOS	Boeing 787-8	Ethiopian Airlines
	ET-AOT	Boeing 787-8	Ethiopian Airlines
	ET-AOU	Boeing 787-8	Ethiopian Airlines
	ET-AOV	Boeing 787-8	Ethiopian Airlines
	ET-APX	Boeing 777-36NER	Ethiopian Airlines
	ET-APY	Boeing 777-36NER	Ethiopian Airlines
	ET-ARE	Boeing 787-8	Ethiopian Airlines
	ET-ARF	Boeing 787-8	Ethiopian Airlines
	ET-ASG	Boeing 787-8	Ethiopian Airlines
	ET-ASH	Boeing 787-8	Ethiopian Airlines
	ET-ASI	Boeing 787-8	Ethiopian Airlines
	ET-ASK	Boeing 777-360ER	Ethiopian Airlines
	ET-ASL	Boeing 777-360ER	Ethiopian Airlines
	ET-ATG	Boeing 787-8	Ethiopian Airlines
	ET-ATH	Boeing 787-8	Ethiopian Airlines
	ET-ATI	Boeing 787-8	Ethiopian Airlines
	ET-ATJ	Boeing 787-8	Ethiopian Airlines
	ET-ATK	Boeing 787-8	Ethiopian Airlines
	ET-ATL	Boeing 787-8	Ethiopian Airlines
	ET-ATQ	Airbus A.350-941	Ethiopian Airlines
	ET-ATR	Airbus A.350-941	Ethiopian Airlines
	ET-ATY	Airbus A.350-941	Ethiopian Airlines
	ET-AUA	Airbus A.350-941	Ethiopian Airlines
	ET-AUB	Airbus A.350-941	Ethiopian Airlines
	ET-AUC	Airbus A.350-941	Ethiopian Airlines
	ET-AUO	Boeing 787-9	Ethiopian Airlines
	ET-AUP	Boeing 787-9	Ethiopian Airlines
	ET-AUQ	Boeing 787-9	Ethiopian Airlines
	ET-AUR	Boeing 787-9	Ethiopian Airlines
	ET-AVB	Airbus A.350-941	Ethiopian Airlines
	ET-AVC	Airbus A.350-941	Ethiopian Airlines
	ET-AVD	Airbus A.350-941	Ethiopian Airlines
	ET-AVE	Airbus A.350-941	Ethiopian Airlines
	ET-AWM	Airbus A.350-941	Ethiopian Airlines
	ET-AWN	Airbus A.350-941	Ethiopian Airlines
	ET-AWO	Airbus A.350-941	Ethiopian Airlines
	ET-AWP	Airbus A.350-941	Ethiopian Airlines
	ET-AXK	Boeing 787-9	Ethiopian Airlines
	ET-AXL	Boeing 787-9	Ethiopian Airlines
	ET-AXS	Boeing 787-9	Ethiopian Airlines
	ET-AYA	Airbus A.350-941	Ethiopian Airlines
	ET-AYB	Airbus A.350-941	Ethiopian Airlines
	ET-AYC	Boeing 787-9	Ethiopian Airlines

EW (Belarus)

Notes	Reg	Type	Owner or Operator
	EW-250PA	Boeing 737-524	Belavia
	EW-254PA	Boeing 737-3Q8	Belavia
	EW-290PA	Boeing 737-5Q8	Belavia
	EW-340PO	Embraer ERJ170-200LR	Belavia
	EW-341PO	Embraer ERJ170-200LR	Belavia
	EW-366PA	Boeing 737-31S	Belavia
	EW-399PO	Embraer ERJ190-200LR	Belavia
	EW-400PO	Embraer ERJ190-200LR	Belavia
	EW-407PA	Boeing 737-36M	Belavia
	EW-437PA	Boeing 737-8K5	Belavia
	EW-438PA	Boeing 737-86Q	Belavia
	EW-455PA	Boeing 737-8ZM	Belavia
	EW-456PA	Boeing 737-8ZM	Belavia
	EW-457PA	Boeing 737-8ZM	Belavia
	EW-512PO	Embraer ERJ170-200LR	Belavia
	EW-513PO	Embraer ERJ190-200LR	Belavia

Reg	Type	Owner or Operator	Notes
EW-514PO	Embraer ERJ190-200LR	Belavia	
EW-526PA	Boeing 737-86N	Belavia	
EW-527PA	Boeing 737-82R	Belavia	
EW-528PA	Boeing 737-MAX8	Belavia	
EW-529PA	Boeing 737-MAX8	Belavia	
EW-531PO	Embraer ERJ170-200LR	Belavia	
EW-532PO	Embraer ERJ190-200LR	Belavia	
EW-533PO	Embraer ERJ190-200LR	Belavia	
EW-543PA	Boeing 737-8K5	Belavia	
EW-544PA	Boeing 737-8K5	Belavia	
EW-545PO	Embraer ERJ190-200LR	Belavia	
EW-554PO	Embraer ERJ170-200LR	Belavia	
EW-555PO	Embraer ERJ190-400STD	Belavia	

EZ (Turkmenistan)

Reg	Type	Owner or Operator	Notes
EZ-A004	Boeing 737-82K	Turkmenistan Airlines	
EZ-A015	Boeing 737-82K	Turkmenistan Airlines	
EZ-A016	Boeing 737-82K	Turkmenistan Airlines	
EZ-A017	Boeing 737-82K	Turkmenistan Airlines	
EZ-A018	Boeing 737-82K	Turkmenistan Airlines	
EZ-A019	Boeing 737-82K	Turkmenistan Airlines	
EZ-A020	Boeing 737-82K	Turkmenistan Airlines	

F (France)

Reg	Type	Owner or Operator	Notes
F-GIXC	Boeing 737-38B	ASL Airlines France	
F-GIXN	Boeing 737-4YOF	ASL Airlines France	
F-GIXT	Boeing 737-39M	ASL Airlines France	
F-GIXU	Boeing 737-4YO	ASL Airlines France	
F-GKXC	Airbus A.320-214	Air France	
F-GKXE	Airbus A.320-214	Air France	
F-GKXG	Airbus A.320-214	Air France	
F-GKXH	Airbus A.320-214	Air France	
F-GKXI	Airbus A.320-214	Air France	
F-GKXJ	Airbus A.320-214	Air France	
F-GKXK	Airbus A.320-214	Air France	
F-GKXL	Airbus A.320-214	Air France	
F-GKXM	Airbus A.320-214	Air France	
F-GKXN	Airbus A.320-214	Air France	
F-GKXO	Airbus A.320-214	Air France	
F-GKXP	Airbus A.320-214	Air France	
F-GKXQ	Airbus A.320-214	Air France	
F-GKXR	Airbus A.320-214	Air France	
F-GKXS	Airbus A.320-214	Air France	
F-GKXT	Airbus A.320-214	Air France	
F-GKXU	Airbus A.320-214	Air France	
F-GKXV	Airbus A.320-214	Air France	
F-GKXY	Airbus A.320-214	Air France	
F-GKXZ	Airbus A.320-214	Air France	
F-GMZA	Airbus A.321-111	Air France	
F-GMZB	Airbus A.321-111	Air France	
F-GMZC	Airbus A.321-111	Air France	
F-GMZD	Airbus A.321-111	Air France	
F-GMZE	Airbus A.321-111	Air France	
F-GRGC	Embraer ERJ145EU	Air France HOP	
F-GRGD	Embraer ERJ145EU	Air France HOP	
F-GRGF	Embraer ERJ145EU	Air France HOP	
F-GRGG	Embraer ERJ145EU	Air France HOP	
F-GRGH	Embraer ERJ145EU	Air France HOP	
F-GRGI	Embraer ERJ145EU	Air France HOP	
F-GRGJ	Embraer ERJ145EU	Air France HOP	
F-GRGK	Embraer ERJ145EU	Air France HOP	
F-GRGL	Embraer ERJ145EU	Air France HOP	
F-GRHB	Airbus A.319-111	Air France	
F-GRHE	Airbus A.319-111	Air France	
F-GRHF	Airbus A.319-111	Air France	
F-GRHG	Airbus A.319-111	Air France	
F-GRHH	Airbus A.319-111	Air France	
F-GRHI	Airbus A.319-111	Air France	

Notes	Reg	Type	Owner or Operator
	F-GRHJ	Airbus A.319-111	Air France
	F-GRHK	Airbus A.319-111	Air France
	F-GRHL	Airbus A.319-111	Air France
	F-GRHM	Airbus A.319-111	Air France
	F-GRHN	Airbus A.319-111	Air France
	F-GRHO	Airbus A.319-111	Air France
	F-GRHP	Airbus A.319-111	Air France
	F-GRHQ	Airbus A.319-111	Air France
	F-GRHR	Airbus A.319-111	Air France
	F-GRHS	Airbus A.319-111	Air France
	F-GRHT	Airbus A.319-111	Air France
	F-GRHU	Airbus A.319-111	Air France
	F-GRHV	Airbus A.319-111	Air France
	F-GRHX	Airbus A.319-111	Air France
	F-GRHY	Airbus A.319-111	Air France
	F-GRHZ	Airbus A.319-111	Air France
	F-GRXA	Airbus A.319-111	Air France
	F-GRXB	Airbus A.319-111	Air France
	F-GRXC	Airbus A.319-111	Air France
	F-GRXD	Airbus A.319-111	Air France
	F-GRXE	Airbus A.319-111	Air France
	F-GRXF	Airbus A.319-111	Air France
	F-GRXJ	Airbus A.319-111LR	Air France
	F-GRXK	Airbus A.319-111LR	Air France
	F-GRXL	Airbus A.319-111	Air France
	F-GRXM	Airbus A.319-111	Air France
	F-GRZE	Canadair CRJ700	Air France HOP
	F-GRZH	Canadair CRJ700	Air France HOP
	F-GRZI	Canadair CRJ700	Air France HOP
	F-GRZJ	Canadair CRJ700	Air France HOP
	F-GRZK	Canadair CRJ700	Air France HOP
	F-GRZL	Canadair CRJ700	Air France HOP
	F-GRZM	Canadair CRJ700	Air France HOP
	F-GRZN	Canadair CRJ700	Air France HOP
	F-GRZO	Canadair CRJ700	Air France HOP
	F-GSPA	Boeing 777-228ER	Air France
	F-GSPB	Boeing 777-228ER	Air France
	F-GSPC	Boeing 777-228ER	Air France
	F-GSPD	Boeing 777-228ER	Air France
	F-GSPE	Boeing 777-228ER	Air France
	F-GSPF	Boeing 777-228ER	Air France
	F-GSPG	Boeing 777-228ER	Air France
	F-GSPH	Boeing 777-228ER	Air France
	F-GSPI	Boeing 777-228ER	Air France
	F-GSPJ	Boeing 777-228ER	Air France
	F-GSPK	Boeing 777-228ER	Air France
	F-GSPL	Boeing 777-228ER	Air France
	F-GSPM	Boeing 777-228ER	Air France
	F-GSPN	Boeing 777-228ER	Air France
	F-GSPO	Boeing 777-228ER	Air France
	F-GSPP	Boeing 777-228ER	Air France
	F-GSPQ	Boeing 777-228ER	Air France
	F-GSPR	Boeing 777-228ER	Air France
	F-GSPS	Boeing 777-228ER	Air France
	F-GSPT	Boeing 777-228ER	Air France
	F-GSPU	Boeing 777-228ER	Air France
	F-GSPV	Boeing 777-228ER	Air France
	F-GSPX	Boeing 777-228ER	Air France
	F-GSPY	Boeing 777-228ER	Air France
	F-GSPZ	Boeing 777-228ER	Air France
	F-GSQA	Boeing 777-328ER	Air France
	F-GSQB	Boeing 777-328ER	Air France
	F-GSQC	Boeing 777-328ER	Air France
	F-GSQD	Boeing 777-328ER	Air France
	F-GSQE	Boeing 777-328ER	Air France
	F-GSQF	Boeing 777-328ER	Air France
	F-GSQG	Boeing 777-328ER	Air France
	F-GSQH	Boeing 777-328ER	Air France
	F-GSQI	Boeing 777-328ER	Air France
	F-GSQJ	Boeing 777-328ER	Air France
	F-GSQK	Boeing 777-328ER	Air France

Reg	Type	Owner or Operator	Notes
F-GSQL	Boeing 777-328ER	Air France	
F-GSQM	Boeing 777-328ER	Air France	
F-GSQN	Boeing 777-328ER	Air France	
F-GSQO	Boeing 777-328ER	Air France	
F-GSQP	Boeing 777-328ER	Air France	
F-GSQR	Boeing 777-328ER	Air France	
F-GSQS	Boeing 777-328ER	Air France	
F-GSQT	Boeing 777-328ER	Air France	
F-GSQU	Boeing 777-328ER	Air France	
F-GSQV	Boeing 777-328ER	Air France	
F-GSQX	Boeing 777-328ER	Air France	
F-GSQY	Boeing 777-328ER	Air France	
F-GSTA	Airbus A.300-608ST Beluga (1)	Airbus Transport International	
F-GSTB	Airbus A.300-608ST Beluga (2)	Airbus Transport International	
F-GSTC	Airbus A.300-608ST Beluga (3)	Airbus Transport International	
F-GSTD	Airbus A.300-608ST Beluga (4)	Airbus Transport International	
F-GSTF	Airbus A.300-608ST Beluga (5)	Airbus Transport International	
F-GTAD	Airbus A.321-211	Air France	
F-GTAE	Airbus A.321-211	Air France	
F-GTAH	Airbus A.321-211	Air France	
F-GTAJ	Airbus A.321-211	Air France	
F-GTAK	Airbus A.321-211	Air France	
F-GTAM	Airbus A.321-211	Air France	
F-GTAO	Airbus A.321-211	Air France	
F-GTAP	Airbus A.321-212	Air France	
F-GTAQ	Airbus A.321-211	Air France	
F-GTAS	Airbus A.321-211	Air France	
F-GTAT	Airbus A.321-211	Air France	
F-GTAU	Airbus A.321-211	Air France	
F-GTAX	Airbus A.321-211	Air France	
F-GTAY	Airbus A.321-211	Air France	
F-GTAZ	Airbus A.321-211	Air France	
F-GUBC	Embraer ERJ145MP	Air France HOP	
F-GUBE	Embraer ERJ145MP	Air France HOP	
F-GUBF	Embraer ERJ145MP	Air France HOP	
F-GUBG	Embraer ERJ145MP	Air France HOP	
F-GUEA	Embraer ERJ145MP	Air France HOP	
F-GUGA	Airbus A.318-111	Air France	
F-GUGB	Airbus A.318-111	Air France	
F-GUGC	Airbus A.318-111	Air France	
F-GUGD	Airbus A.318-111	Air France	
F-GUGE	Airbus A.318-111	Air France	
F-GUGF	Airbus A.318-111	Air France	
F-GUGG	Airbus A.318-111	Air France	
F-GUGH	Airbus A.318-111	Air France	
F-GUGI	Airbus A.318-111	Air France	
F-GUGJ	Airbus A.318-111	Air France	
F-GUGK	Airbus A.318-111	Air France	
F-GUGL	Airbus A.318-111	Air France	
F-GUGM	Airbus A.318-111	Air France	
F-GUGN	Airbus A.318-111	Air France	
F-GUGO	Airbus A.318-111	Air France	
F-GUGP	Airbus A.318-111	Air France	
F-GUGQ	Airbus A.318-111	Air France	
F-GUGR	Airbus A.318-111	Air France	
F-GUOB	Boeing 777-F28	Air France Cargo	
F-GUOC	Boeing 777-F28	Air France Cargo	
F-GVHD	Embraer RJ145MP	Air France HOP	
F-GZCA	Airbus A.330-203	Air France	
F-GZCB	Airbus A.330-203	Air France	
F-GZCC	Airbus A.330-203	Air France	
F-GZCD	Airbus A.330-203	Air France	
F-GZCE	Airbus A.330-203	Air France	
F-GZCF	Airbus A.330-203	Air France	
F-GZCG	Airbus A.330-203	Air France	
F-GZCH	Airbus A.330-203	Air France	
F-GZCI	Airbus A.330-203	Air France	
F-GZCJ	Airbus A.330-203	Air France	
F-GZCK	Airbus A.330-203	Air France	
F-GZCL	Airbus A.330-203	Air France	
F-GZCM	Airbus A.330-203	Air France	

OVERSEAS AIRLINERS

Notes	Reg	Type	Owner or Operator
	F-GZCN	Airbus A.330-203	Air France
	F-GZCO	Airbus A.330-203	Air France
	F-GZHA	Boeing 737-8GJ	Transavia France
	F-GZHB	Boeing 737-8GJ	Transavia France
	F-GZHC	Boeing 737-8GJ	Transavia France
	F-GZHD	Boeing 737-8K2	Transavia France
	F-GZHE	Boeing 737-8K2	Transavia France
	F-GZHF	Boeing 737-8HX	Transavia France
	F-GZHI	Boeing 737-8K2	Transavia France
	F-GZHJ	Boeing 737-8K2	Transavia France
	F-GZHK	Boeing 737-8K2	Transavia France
	F-GZHL	Boeing 737-8K2	Transavia France
	F-GZHM	Boeing 737-8K2	Transavia France
	F-GZHN	Boeing 737-8K2	Transavia France
	F-GZHO	Boeing 737-8K2	Transavia France
	F-GZHP	Boeing 737-8K2	Transavia France
	F-GZHQ	Boeing 737-8K2	Transavia France
	F-GZHR	Boeing 737-8K2	Transavia France
	F-GZHS	Boeing 737-84P	Transavia France
	F-GZHT	Boeing 737-8K2	Transavia France
	F-GZHU	Boeing 737-8K2	Transavia France
	F-GZHV	Boeing 737-85H	Transavia France
	F-GZHX	Boeing 737-8K2	Transavia France
	F-GZHY	Boeing 737-8K2	Transavia France
	F-GZHZ	Boeing 737-85P	Transavia France
	F-GZNA	Boeing 777-328ER	Air France
	F-GZNB	Boeing 777-328ER	Air France
	F-GZNC	Boeing 777-328ER	Air France
	F-GZND	Boeing 777-328ER	Air France
	F-GZNE	Boeing 777-328ER	Air France
	F-GZNF	Boeing 777-328ER	Air France
	F-GZNG	Boeing 777-328ER	Air France
	F-GZNH	Boeing 777-328ER	Air France
	F-GZNI	Boeing 777-328ER	Air France
	F-GZNJ	Boeing 777-328ER	Air France
	F-GZNK	Boeing 777-328ER	Air France
	F-GZNL	Boeing 777-328ER	Air France
	F-GZNN	Boeing 777-328ER	Air France
	F-GZNO	Boeing 777-328ER	Air France
	F-GZNP	Boeing 777-328ER	Air France
	F-GZNQ	Boeing 777-328ER	Air France
	F-GZNR	Boeing 777-328ER	Air France
	F-GZNS	Boeing 777-328ER	Air France
	F-GZNT	Boeing 777-328ER	Air France
	F-GZNU	Boeing 777-328ER	Air France
	F-GZTB	Boeing 737-33V	ASL Airlines France
	F-GZTD	Boeing 737-73V	ASL Airlines France
	F-GZTI	Boeing 737-408F	ASL Airlines France
	F-GZTJ	Boeing 737-4S3F	ASL Airlines France
	F-GZTK	Boeing 737-4Q8F	ASL Airlines France
	F-GZTN	Boeing 737-73S	ASL Airlines France
	F-GZTO	Boeing 737-73S	ASL Airlines France
	F-GZTP	Boeing 737-71B	ASL Airlines France
	F-GZTQ	Boeing 737-73S	ASL Airlines France
	F-GZTS	Boeing 737-73V	ASL Airlines France
	F-GZTT	Boeing 737-48EF	ASL Airlines France
	F-GZTU	Boeing 737-73V	ASL Airlines France
	F-GZTV	Boeing 737-8K5	ASL Airlines France
	F-GZTX	Boeing 737-4YO	ASL Airlines France
	F-GZTZ	Boeing 737-8K5	ASL Airlines France
	F-HBEV	Airbus A.320-216	Air Corsica
	F-HBLA	Embraer ERJ190-100LR	Air France HOP
	F-HBLB	Embraer ERJ190-100LR	Air France HOP
	F-HBLC	Embraer ERJ190-100LR	Air France HOP
	F-HBLD	Embraer ERJ190-100LR	Air France HOP
	F-HBLE	Embraer ERJ190-100LR	Air France HOP
	F-HBLF	Embraer ERJ190-100LR	Air France HOP
	F-HBLG	Embraer ERJ190-100LR	Air France HOP
	F-HBLH	Embraer ERJ190-100LR	Air France HOP
	F-HBLI	Embraer ERJ190-100LR	Air France HOP!
	F-HBLJ	Embraer ERJ190-100LR	Air France HOP

Reg	Type	Owner or Operator	Notes
F-HBLK	Embraer ERJ190-100STD	Air France HOP	
F-HBLL	Embraer ERJ190-100STD	Air France HOP	
F-HBLM	Embraer ERJ190-100STD	Air France HOP	
F-HBLN	Embraer ERJ190-100STD	Air France HOP	
F-HBLO	Embraer ERJ190-100STD	Air France HOP	
F-HBLP	Embraer ERJ190-100STD	Air France HOP	
F-HBLQ	Embraer ERJ190-100STD	Air France HOP	
F-HBNA	Airbus A.320-214	Air France	
F-HBNB	Airbus A.320-214	Air France	
F-HBNC	Airbus A.320-214	Air France	
F-HBND	Airbus A.320-214	Air France	
F-HBNE	Airbus A.320-214	Air France	
F-HBNF	Airbus A.320-214	Air France	
F-HBNG	Airbus A.320-214	Air France	
F-HBNH	Airbus A.320-214	Air France	
F-HBNI	Airbus A.320-214	Air France	
F-HBNJ	Airbus A.320-214	Air France	
F-HBNK	Airbus A.320-214	Air France	
F-HBNL	Airbus A.320-214	Air France	
F-HBSA	Airbus A.320-216	Air Corsica	
F-HBXA	Embraer RJ170-100LR	Air France HOP	
F-HBXB	Embraer RJ170-100LR	Air France HOP	
F-HBXC	Embraer RJ170-100LR	Air France HOP	
F-HBXD	Embraer RJ170-100LR	Air France HOP	
F-HBXE	Embraer RJ170-100LR	Air France HOP	
F-HBXF	Embraer RJ170-100LR	Air France HOP	
F-HBXG	Embraer RJ170-100LR	Air France HOP	
F-HBXH	Embraer RJ170-100LR	Air France HOP	
F-HBXI	Embraer RJ170-100LR	Air France HOP	
F-HBXJ	Embraer RJ170-100LR	Air France HOP	
F-HBXK	Embraer RJ170-100LR	Air France HOP	
F-HBXL	Embraer RJ170-100LR	Air France HOP	
F-HBXM	Embraer RJ170-100LR	Air France HOP	
F-HBXN	Embraer RJ170-100LR	Air France HOP	
F-HBXO	Embraer RJ170-100LR	Air France HOP	
F-HEPA	Airbus A.320-214	Air France	
F-HEPB	Airbus A.320-214	Air France	
F-HEPC	Airbus A.320-214	Air France	
F-HEPD	Airbus A.320-214	Air France	
F-HEPE	Airbus A.320-214	Air France	
F-HEPF	Airbus A.320-214	Air France	
F-HEPG	Airbus A.320-214	Air France	
F-HEPH	Airbus A.320-214	Air France	
F-HEPI	Airbus A.320-214	Air France	
F-HEPJ	Airbus A.320-214	Air France	
F-HEPK	Airbus A.320-214	Air France	
F-HIQB	Boeing 737-8AS	ASL Airlines France	
F-HMLA	Canadair CRJ1000	Air France HOP	
F-HMLC	Canadair CRJ1000	Air France HOP	
F-HMLD	Canadair CRJ1000	Air France HOP	
F-HMLE	Canadair CRJ1000	Air France HOP	
F-HMLF	Canadair CRJ1000	Air France HOP	
F-HMLG	Canadair CRJ1000	Air France HOP	
F-HMLH	Canadair CRJ1000	Air France HOP	
F-HMLI	Canadair CRJ1000	Air France HOP	
F-HMLJ	Canadair CRJ1000	Air France HOP	
F-HMLK	Canadair CRJ1000	Air France HOP	
F-HMLL	Canadair CRJ1000	Air France HOP	
F-HMLM	Canadair CRJ1000	Air France HOP	
F-HMLN	Canadair CRJ1000	Air France HOP	
F-HMLO	Canadair CRJ1000	Air France HOP	
F-HRBA	Boeing 787-9	Air France	
F-HRBB	Boeing 787-9	Air France	
F-HRBC	Boeing 787-9	Air France	
F-HRBD	Boeing 787-9	Air France	
F-HRBE	Boeing 787-9	Air France	
F-HRBF	Boeing 787-9	Air France	
F-HRBG	Boeing 787-9	Air France	
F-HRBH	Boeing 787-9	Air France	
F-HRBI	Boeing 787-9	Air France	
F-HRBJ	Boeing 787-9	Air France	

OVERSEAS AIRLINERS

Notes	Reg	Type	Owner or Operator
	F-HTVA	Boeing 737-8K2	Transavia France
	F-HTVB	Boeing 737-8K2	Transavia France
	F-HTVC	Boeing 737-8K2	Transavia France
	F-HTVD	Boeing 737-8K2	Transavia France
	F-HTVE	Boeing 737-8K2	Transavia France
	F-HTVF	Boeing 737-8K2	Transavia France
	F-HTVG	Boeing 737-8K2	Transavia France
	F-HTVH	Boeing 737-8K2	Transavia France
	F-HTVI	Boeing 737-8K2	Transavia France
	F-HTVJ	Boeing 737-8K2	Transavia France
	F-HTVK	Boeing 737-8K2	Transavia France
	F-HTVL	Boeing 737-84P	Transavia France
	F-HTVM	Boeing 737-8K2	Transavia France
	F-HTVN	Boeing 737-8GJ	Transavia France
	F-HTVO	Boeing 737-8GJ	Transavia France
	F-HTVP	Boeing 737-8AL	Transavia France
	F-HTVR	Boeing 737-86J	Transavia France
	F-GTVS	Boeing 737-86J	Transavia France
	F-HTVQ	Boeing 737-8AL	Transavia France
	F-HTVV	Boeing 737-8JP	Transavia France
	F-HTVY	Boeing 737-8JP	Transavia France
	F-HTYA	Airbus A.350-941	Air France
	F-HTYB	Airbus A.350-941	Air France
	F-HTYC	Airbus A.350-941	Air France
	F-HTYD	Airbus A.350-941	Air France
	F-HTYE	Airbus A.350-941	Air France
	F-HTYF	Airbus A.350-941	Air France
	F-HTYG	Airbus A.350-941	Air France
	F-HXKB	Airbus A.320-251N	Air Corsica
	F-HXKJ	Airbus A.320-251N	Air Corsica
	F-HZDP	Airbus A.320-214	Air Corsica
	F-HZFM	Airbus A.320-214	Air France
	F-HZGS	Airbus A.320-214	Air Corsica

HA (Hungary)

Notes	Reg	Type	Owner or Operator
	HA-FAU	Boeing 737-43QF	ASL Airlines Hungary
	HA-FAW	Boeing 737-476SF	ASL Airlines Hungary
	HA-FAY	Boeing 737-429F	ASL Airlines Hungary
	HA-FAZ	Boeing 737-476SF	ASL Airlines Hungary
	HA-LJA	Airbus A.320-271N	Wizz Air
	HA-LJB	Airbus A.320-271N	Wizz Air
	HA-LJC	Airbus A.320-271N	Wizz Air
	HA-LJD	Airbus A.320-271N	Wizz Air
	HA-LJE	Airbus A.320-271N	Wizz Air
	HA-LJF	Airbus A.320-271N	Wizz Air
	HA-KAD	Boeing 737-4YOSF	ASL Airlines Hungary
	HA-LKG	Boeing 737-8CX	Smart Wings
	HA-LPJ	Airbus A.320-232	Wizz Air
	HA-LPK	Airbus A.320-231	Wizz Air
	HA-LPL	Airbus A.320-232	Wizz Air
	HA-LPM	Airbus A.320-232	Wizz Air
	HA-LPN	Airbus A.320-232	Wizz Air
	HA-LPO	Airbus A.320-232	Wizz Air
	HA-LPQ	Airbus A.320-232	Wizz Air
	HA-LPR	Airbus A.320-232	Wizz Air
	HA-LPS	Airbus A.320-232	Wizz Air
	HA-LPT	Airbus A.320-232	Wizz Air
	HA-LPU	Airbus A.320-232	Wizz Air
	HA-LPW	Airbus A.320-232	Wizz Air
	HA-LPX	Airbus A.320-232	Wizz Air
	HA-LPY	Airbus A.320-232	Wizz Air
	HA-LSA	Airbus A.320-232	Wizz Air
	HA-LSB	Airbus A.320-232	Wizz Air
	HA-LSC	Airbus A.320-232	Wizz Air
	HA-LTA	Airbus A.321-231	Wizz Air
	HA-LTB	Airbus A.321-231	Wizz Air
	HA-LTC	Airbus A.321-231	Wizz Air
	HA-LTD	Airbus A.321-231	Wizz Air
	HA-LTE	Airbus A.321-231	Wizz Air
	HA-LTF	Airbus A.321-231	Wizz Air

Reg	Type	Owner or Operator	Notes
HA-LTG	Airbus A.321-231	Wizz Air	
HA-LTH	Airbus A.321-231	Wizz Air	
HA-LTI	Airbus A.321-231	Wizz Air	
HA-LVA	Airbus A.321-271NX	Wizz Air	
HA-LVB	Airbus A.321-271NX	Wizz Air	
HA-LVC	Airbus A.321-271NX	Wizz Air	
HA-LVD	Airbus A.321-271NX	Wizz Air	
HA-LVE	Airbus A.321-271NX	Wizz Air	
HA-LVF	Airbus A.321-271NX	Wizz Air	
HA-LVG	Airbus A.321-271NX	Wizz Air	
HA-LVH	Airbus A.321-271NX	Wizz Air	
HA-LVI	Airbus A.321-271NX	Wizz Air	
HA-LVJ	Airbus A.321-271NX	Wizz Air	
HA-LVK	Airbus A.321-271NX	Wizz Air	
HA-LVM	Airbus A.321-271NX	Wizz Air	
HA-LVN	Airbus A.321-271NX	Wizz Air	
HA-LVO	Airbus A.321-271NX	Wizz Air	
HA-LWA	Airbus A.320-232	Wizz Air	
HA-LWB	Airbus A.320-232	Wizz Air	
HA-LWC	Airbus A.320-232	Wizz Air	
HA-LWD	Airbus A.320-232	Wizz Air	
HA-LWE	Airbus A.320-232	Wizz Air	
HA-LWF	Airbus A.320-232	Wizz Air	
HA-LWG	Airbus A.320-232	Wizz Air	
HA-LWH	Airbus A.320-232	Wizz Air	
HA-LWI	Airbus A.320-214	Wizz Air	
HA-LWJ	Airbus A.320-214	Wizz Air	
HA-LWK	Airbus A.320-232	Wizz Air	
HA-LWL	Airbus A.320-232	Wizz Air	
HA-LWM	Airbus A.320-232	Wizz Air	
HA-LWN	Airbus A.320-232	Wizz Air	
HA-LWO	Airbus A.320-232	Wizz Air	
HA-LWP	Airbus A.320-232	Wizz Air	
HA-LWQ	Airbus A.320-232	Wizz Air	
HA-LWR	Airbus A.320-232	Wizz Air	
HA-LWS	Airbus A.320-232	Wizz Air	
HA-LWT	Airbus A.320-232	Wizz Air	
HA-LWU	Airbus A.320-232	Wizz Air	
HA-LWV	Airbus A.320-232	Wizz Air	
HA-LWX	Airbus A.320-232	Wizz Air	
HA-LWY	Airbus A.320-232	Wizz Air	
HA-LWZ	Airbus A.320-232	Wizz Air	
HA-LXA	Airbus A.321-231	Wizz Air	
HA-LXB	Airbus A.321-231	Wizz Air	
HA-LXC	Airbus A.321-231	Wizz Air	
HA-LXD	Airbus A.321-231	Wizz Air	
HA-LXE	Airbus A.321-231	Wizz Air	
HA-LXF	Airbus A.321-231	Wizz Air	
HA-LXG	Airbus A.321-231	Wizz Air	
HA-LXH	Airbus A.321-231	Wizz Air	
HA-LXI	Airbus A.321-231	Wizz Air	
HA-LXJ	Airbus A.321-231	Wizz Air	
HA-LXK	Airbus A.321-231	Wizz Air	
HA-LXL	Airbus A.321-231	Wizz Air	
HA-LXM	Airbus A.321-231	Wizz Air	
HA-LXN	Airbus A.321-231	Wizz Air	
HA-LXO	Airbus A.321-231	Wizz Air	
HA-LXP	Airbus A.321-231	Wizz Air	
HA-LXQ	Airbus A.321-231	Wizz Air	
HA-LXR	Airbus A.321-231	Wizz Air	
HA-LXS	Airbus A.321-231	Wizz Air	
HA-LXT	Airbus A.321-211	Wizz Air	
HA-LXU	Airbus A.321-231	Wizz Air	
HA-LXV	Airbus A.321-231	Wizz Air	
HA-LXW	Airbus A.321-231	Wizz Air	
HA-LXY	Airbus A.321-231	Wizz Air	
HA-LXZ	Airbus A.321-231	Wizz Air	
HA-LYA	Airbus A.320-232	Wizz Air	
HA-LYB	Airbus A.320-232	Wizz Air	
HA-LYC	Airbus A.320-232	Wizz Air	
HA-LYD	Airbus A.320-232	Wizz Air	

Notes	Reg	Type	Owner or Operator
	HA-LYE	Airbus A.320-232	Wizz Air
	HA-LYF	Airbus A.320-232	Wizz Air
	HA-LYG	Airbus A.320-232	Wizz Air
	HA-LYH	Airbus A.320-232	Wizz Air
	HA-LYI	Airbus A.320-232	Wizz Air
	HA-LYJ	Airbus A.320-232	Wizz Air
	HA-LYK	Airbus A.320-232	Wizz Air
	HA-LYL	Airbus A.320-232	Wizz Air
	HA-LYM	Airbus A.320-232	Wizz Air
	HA-LYN	Airbus A.320-232	Wizz Air
	HA-LYO	Airbus A.320-232	Wizz Air
	HA-LYP	Airbus A.320-232	Wizz Air
	HA-LYQ	Airbus A.320-232	Wizz Air
	HA-LYR	Airbus A.320-232	Wizz Air
	HA-LYS	Airbus A.320-232	Wizz Air
	HA-LYT	Airbus A.320-232	Wizz Air
	HA-LYU	Airbus A.320-232	Wizz Air
	HA-LYV	Airbus A.320-232	Wizz Air
	HA-LYW	Airbus A.320-232	Wizz Air
	HA-LYX	Airbus A.320-232	Wizz Air
	HA-LYZ	Airbus A.320-232	Wizz Air

HB (Switzerland)

Notes	Reg	Type	Owner or Operator
	HB-AFL	Aerospatiale ATR-72-202F	Zimex Aviation
	HB-ALL	Aerospatiale ATR-72-202F	Zimex Aviation
	HB-ALM	Aerospatiale ATR-72-202F	Zimex Aviation
	HB-ALQ	Aerospatiale ATR-72-202F	Zimex Aviation
	HB-ALR	Aerospatiale ATR-72-212AF	Zimex Aviation
	HB-AZA	Embraer ERJ190-300STD	Helvetic Airways
	HB-AZB	Embraer ERJ190-300STD	Helvetic Airways
	HB-AZC	Embraer ERJ190-300STD	Helvetic Airways
	HB-AZD	Embraer ERJ190-300STD	Helvetic Airways
	HB-AZE	Embraer ERJ190-300STD	Helvetic Airways
	HB-AZF	Embraer ERJ190-300STD	Helvetic Airways
	HB-AZG	Embraer ERJ190-300STD	Helvetic Airways
	HB-IHX	Airbus A.320-214	Edelweiss Air
	HB-IHY	Airbus A.320-214	Edelweiss Air
	HB-IHZ	Airbus A.320-214	Edelweiss Air
	HB-IJD	Airbus A.320-214	Swiss International
	HB-IJE	Airbus A.320-214	Swiss International *Arosa*
	HB-IJH	Airbus A.320-214	Swiss International *Dubendorf*
	HB-IJI	Airbus A.320-214	Swiss International *Basodino*
	HB-IJJ	Airbus A.320-214	Swiss International *Les Diablerets*
	HB-IJK	Airbus A.320-214	Swiss International *Wissigstock*
	HB-IJL	Airbus A.320-214	Swiss International *Pizol*
	HB-IJM	Airbus A.320-214	Swiss International *Schilthorn*
	HB-IJN	Airbus A.320-214	Swiss International *Vanil Noir*
	HB-IJO	Airbus A.320-214	Swiss International *Lissengrat*
	HB-IJP	Airbus A.320-214	Swiss International *Nollen*
	HB-IJQ	Airbus A.320-214	Swiss International *Agassizhorn*
	HB-IJR	Airbus A.320-214	Swiss International *Dammastock*
	HB-IJS	Airbus A.320-214	Swiss International *Creux du Van*
	HB-IJU	Airbus A.320-214	Edelweiss Air
	HB-IJV	Airbus A.320-214	Edelweiss Air
	HB-IJW	Airbus A.320-214	Edelweiss Air
	HB-IOC	Airbus A.321-111	Swiss International *Eiger*
	HB-IOD	Airbus A.321-111	Swiss International *Zermatt*
	HB-IOF	Airbus A.321-111	Swiss International Winterthur
	HB-IOH	Airbus A.321-111	Swiss International *Wengen*
	HB-IOK	Airbus A.321-111	Swiss International *Biefertenstock*
	HB-IOL	Airbus A.321-111	Swiss International *Kaiseregg*
	HB-IOM	Airbus A.321-212	Swiss International *Biel/Bienne*
	HB-ION	Airbus A.321-212	Swiss International *Lugano*
	HB-IOO	Airbus A.321-212	Swiss International
	HB-JBA	Airbus A.220-100	Swiss International
	HB-JBB	Airbus A.220-100	Swiss International
	HB-JBC	Airbus A.220-100	Swiss International
	HB-JBD	Airbus A.220-100	Swiss International
	HB-JBE	Airbus A.220-100	Swiss International
	HB-JBF	Airbus A.220-100	Swiss International

Reg	Type	Owner or Operator	Notes
HB-JBG	Airbus A.220-100	Swiss International	
HB-JBH	Airbus A.220-100	Swiss International	
HB-JBI	Airbus A.220-100	Swiss International	
HB-JCA	Airbus A.220-300	Swiss International	
HB-JCB	Airbus A.220-300	Swiss International	
HB-JCC	Airbus A.220-300	Swiss International	
HB-JCD	Airbus A.220-300	Swiss International	
HB-JCE	Airbus A.220-300	Swiss International	
HB-JCF	Airbus A.220-300	Swiss International	
HB-JCG	Airbus A.220-300	Swiss International	
HB-JCH	Airbus A.220-300	Swiss International	
HB-JCI	Airbus A.220-300	Swiss International	
HB-JCJ	Airbus A.220-300	Swiss International	
HB-JCK	Airbus A.220-300	Swiss International	
HB-JCL	Airbus A.220-300	Swiss International	
HB-JCM	Airbus A.220-300	Swiss International	
HB-JCN	Airbus A.220-300	Swiss International	
HB-JCO	Airbus A.220-300	Swiss International	
HB-JCP	Airbus A.220-300	Swiss International	
HB-JCQ	Airbus A.220-300	Swiss International	
HB-JCR	Airbus A.220-300	Swiss International	
HB-JCS	Airbus A.220-300	Swiss International	
HB-JCT	Airbus A.220-300	Swiss International	
HB-JDA	Airbus A.320-271N	Swiss International	
HB-JDB	Airbus A.320-271N	Swiss International	
HB-JDC	Airbus A.320-271N	Swiss International	
HB-JHA	Airbus A.330-343	Swiss International	
HB-JHB	Airbus A.330-343	Swiss International *Sion*	
HB-JHC	Airbus A.330-343	Swiss International *Bellinzona*	
HB-JHD	Airbus A.330-343	Swiss International *St.Gallen*	
HB-JHE	Airbus A.330-343	Swiss International *Fribourg*	
HB-JHF	Airbus A.330-343	Swiss International *Bern*	
HB-JHG	Airbus A.330-343	Swiss International *Glarus*	
HB-JHH	Airbus A.330-343	Swiss International *Neuchatel*	
HB-JHI	Airbus A.330-343	Swiss International *Geneve*	
HB-JHJ	Airbus A.330-343	Swiss International *Appenzell*	
HB-JHK	Airbus A.330-343	Swiss International *Herisau*	
HB-JHL	Airbus A.330-343	Swiss International *Sarnen*	
HB-JHM	Airbus A.330-343	Swiss International	
HB-JHN	Airbus A.330-343	Swiss International	
HB-JJK	Airbus A.320-214	Edelweiss Air	
HB-JJL	Airbus A.320-214	Edelweiss Air	
HB-JJM	Airbus A.320-214	Edelweiss Air	
HB-JJN	Airbus A.320-214	Edelweiss Air	
HB-JLP	Airbus A.320-214	Swiss International *Allschwil*	
HB-JLQ	Airbus A.320-214	Swiss International *Bllach*	
HB-JLR	Airbus A.320-214	Swiss International *Bassersdorf*	
HB-JLS	Airbus A.320-214	Swiss International *Niederhasli*	
HB-JLT	Airbus A.320-214	Swiss International *Grenchen*	
HB-JMA	Airbus A.340-313X	Swiss International *Matterhorn*	
HB-JMB	Airbus A.340-313X	Swiss International *Zurich*	
HB-JMC	Airbus A.340-313X	Swiss International *Basel*	
HB-JMH	Airbus A.340-313X	Swiss International *Chur*	
HB-JMI	Airbus A.340-313X	Swiss International *Schaffhausen*	
HB-JNA	Boeing 777-3DEER	Swiss International	
HB-JNB	Boeing 777-3DEER	Swiss International	
HB-JNC	Boeing 777-3DEER	Swiss International	
HB-JNE	Boeing 777-3DEER	Swiss International	
HB-JNF	Boeing 777-3DEER	Swiss International	
HB-JNG	Boeing 777-3DEER	Swiss International	
HB-JNH	Boeing 777-3DEER	Swiss International	
HB-JNI	Boeing 777-3DEER	Swiss International	
HB-JNJ	Boeing 777-3DEER	Swiss International	
HB-JNK	Boeing 777-300ER	Swiss International	
HB-JNL	Boeing 777-300ER	Swiss International	
HB-JPA	Airbus A.321-271NX	Swiss International	
HB-JPB	Airbus A.321-271NX	Swiss International	
HB-JVM	Embraer ERJ190-100LR	Helvetic Airways	
HB-JVN	Embraer ERJ190-100LR	Helvetic Airways	
HB-JVO	Embraer ERJ190-100LR	Helvetic Airways	
HB-JVP	Embraer ERJ190-100LR	Helvetic Airways	

Notes	Reg	Type	Owner or Operator
	HB-JVS	Embraer ERJ190-100LR	Helvetic Airways
	HB-JVT	Embraer ERJ190-100LR	Helvetic Airways
	HB-JVU	Embraer ERJ190-100LR	Helvetic Airways
	HB-JVV	Embraer ERJ190-100LR	Helvetic Airways
	HB-JXA	Airbus A.320-214	easyJet Switzerland
	HB-JXB	Airbus A.320-214	easyJet Switzerland
	HB-JXC	Airbus A.320-214	easyJet Switzerland
	HB-JXD	Airbus A.320-214	easyJet Switzerland
	HB-JXE	Airbus A.320-214	easyJet Switzerland
	HB-JXF	Airbus A.320-214	easyJet Switzerland
	HB-JXI	Airbus A.320-214	easyJet Switzerland
	HB-JXJ	Airbus A.320-214	easyJet Switzerland
	HB-JXK	Airbus A.320-214	easyJet Switzerland
	HB-JXL	Airbus A.320-214	easyJet Switzerland
	HB-JXM	Airbus A.320-214	easyJet Switzerland
	HB-JXN	Airbus A.320-214	easyJet Switzerland
	HB-JXO	Airbus A.320-214	easyJet Switzerland
	HB-JXP	Airbus A.320-214	easyJet Switzerland
	HB-JXQ	Airbus A.320-214	easyJet Switzerland
	HB-JXR	Airbus A.320-214	easyJet Switzerland
	HB-JYA	Airbus A.320-214	easyJet Switzerland
	HB-JYD	Airbus A.320-214	easyJet Switzerland
	HB-JYF	Airbus A.319-111	easyJet Switzerland
	HB-JYH	Airbus A.319-111	easyJet Switzerland
	HB-JYI	Airbus A.319-111	easyJet Switzerland
	HB-JYJ	Airbus A.319-111	easyJet Switzerland
	HB-JYK	Airbus A.319-111	easyJet Switzerland
	HB-JZR	Airbus A.320-214	easyJet Switzerland
	HB-JZX	Airbus A.320-214	easyJet Switzerland
	HB-JZY	Airbus A.320-214	easyJet Switzerland
	HB-JZZ	Airbus A.320-214	easyJet Switzerland

HL (Korea)

Notes	Reg	Type	Owner or Operator
	HL7202	Boeing 777-3B5EER	Korean Air
	HL7203	Boeing 777-3B5EER	Korean Air
	HL7204	Boeing 777-3B5EER	Korean Air
	HL7205	Boeing 777-3B5EER	Korean Air
	HL7413	Boeing 747-48EBCF	Asiana Airlines Cargo
	HL7415	Boeing 747-48EBCF	Asiana Airlines Cargo
	HL7417	Boeing 747-48EBCF	Asiana Airlines Cargo
	HL7419	Boeing 747-48EF (SCD)	Asiana Airlines Cargo
	HL7420	Boeing 747-48EF (SCD)	Asiana Airlines Cargo
	HL7421	Boeing 747-48EBSF	Asiana Airlines Cargo
	HL7423	Boeing 747-48EBSF	Asiana Airlines Cargo
	HL7436	Boeing 747-48EF (SCD)	Asiana Airlines Cargo
	HL7578	Airbus A.350-941	Asiana Airlines
	HL7579	Airbus A.350-941	Asiana Airlines
	HL7611	Airbus A.380-861	Korean Air
	HL7612	Airbus A.380-861	Korean Air
	HL7613	Airbus A.380-861	Korean Air
	HL7614	Airbus A.380-861	Korean Air
	HL7615	Airbus A.380-861	Korean Air
	HL7616	Boeing 747-446F	Asiana Airlines Cargo
	HL7618	Boeing 747-446F	Asiana Airlines Cargo
	HL7619	Airbus A.380-861	Korean Air
	HL7620	Boeing 747-419F	Asiana Airlines Cargo
	HL7621	Airbus A.380-861	Korean Air
	HL7622	Airbus A.380-861	Korean Air
	HL7627	Airbus A.380-861	Korean Air
	HL7628	Airbus A.380-861	Korean Air
	HL7630	Boeing 747-8	Korean Air
	HL7631	Boeing 747-8	Korean Air
	HL7632	Boeing 747-8	Korean Air
	HL7633	Boeing 747-8	Korean Air
	HL7636	Boeing 747-8	Korean Air
	HL7637	Boeing 747-8	Korean Air
	HL7638	Boeing 747-8	Korean Air
	HL7639	Boeing 747-8	Korean Air
	HL7642	Boeing 747-8	Korean Air
	HL7643	Boeing 747-8	Korean Air

Reg	Type	Owner or Operator	Notes
HL7644	Boeing 747-8	Korean Air	
HL7771	Airbus A.350-941	Asiana Airlines	
HL7782	Boeing 777-3B5ER	Korean Air	
HL7783	Boeing 777-3B5ER	Korean Air	
HL7784	Boeing 777-3B5ER	Korean Air	
HL8005	Boeing 777-FB5	Korean Air Cargo	
HL8006	Boeing 777-3B5ER	Korean Air	
HL8007	Boeing 777-3B5ER	Korean Air	
HL8008	Boeing 777-3B5ER	Korean Air	
HL8009	Boeing 777-3B5ER	Korean Air	
HL8010	Boeing 777-3B5ER	Korean Air	
HL8011	Boeing 777-3B5ER	Korean Air	
HL8041	Boeing 777-3B5ER	Korean Air	
HL8042	Boeing 777-3B5ER	Korean Air	
HL8043	Boeing 777-FB5	Korean Air Cargo	
HL8044	Boeing 777-FB5	Korean Air Cargo	
HL8045	Boeing 777-FB5	Korean Air Cargo	
HL8046	Boeing 777-FB5	Korean Air Cargo	
HL8075	Boeing 777-FB5	Korean Air Cargo	
HL8076	Boeing 777-FB5	Korean Air Cargo	
HL8077	Boeing 777-FB5	Korean Air Cargo	
HL8078	Airbus A.350-941	Asiana Airlines	
HL8079	Airbus A.350-941	Asiana Airlines	
HL8208	Boeing 777-3B5ER	Korean Air	
HL8209	Boeing 777-3B5ER	Korean Air	
HL8210	Boeing 777-3B5ER	Korean Air	
HL8216	Boeing 777-3B5ER	Korean Air	
HL8217	Boeing 777-3B5ER	Korean Air	
HL8218	Boeing 777-3B5ER	Korean Air	
HL8226	Boeing 777-FB5	Korean Air Cargo	
HL8250	Boeing 777-3B5ER	Korean Air	
HL8251	Boeing 777-FB5	Korean Air Cargo	
HL8252	Boeing 777-FB5	Korean Air Cargo	
HL8274	Boeing 777-3B5ER	Korean Air	
HL8275	Boeing 777-3B5ER	Korean Air	
HL8285	Boeing 777-FB5	Korean Air Cargo	
HL8308	Airbus A.350-941	Asiana Airlines	
HL8346	Boeing 777-300ER	Korean Air	
HL8347	Boeing 777-300ER	Korean Air	
HL8359	Airbus A.350-941	Asiana Airlines	
HL8360	Airbus A.350-941	Asiana Airlines	
HL8361	Airbus A.350-941	Asiana Airlines	
HL8362	Airbus A.350-941	Asiana Airlines	
HL8381	Airbus A.350-941	Asiana Airlines	
HL8382	Airbus A.350-941	Asiana Airlines	
HL8383	Airbus A.350-941	Asiana Airlines	

HS (Thailand)

Reg	Type	Owner or Operator	Notes
HS-TKK	Boeing 777-3ALER	Thai Airways International	
HS-TKL	Boeing 777-3ALER	Thai Airways International	
HS-TKM	Boeing 777-3ALER	Thai Airways International	
HS-TKN	Boeing 777-3ALER	Thai Airways International	
HS-TKO	Boeing 777-3ALER	Thai Airways International	
HS-TKP	Boeing 777-3ALER	Thai Airways International	
HS-TKQ	Boeing 777-3ALER	Thai Airways International	
HS-TKR	Boeing 777-3ALER	Thai Airways International	
HS-TKU	Boeing 777-3D7ER	Thai Airways International	
HS-TKV	Boeing 777-3D7ER	Thai Airways International	
HS-TKW	Boeing 777-3D7ER	Thai Airways International	
HS-TKX	Boeing 777-3D7ER	Thai Airways International	
HS-TKY	Boeing 777-3D7ER	Thai Airways International	
HS-TKZ	Boeing 777-3D7ER	Thai Airways International	
HS-TTA	Boeing 777-300ER	Thai Airways International	
HS-TTB	Boeing 777-300ER	Thai Airways International	
HS-TTC	Boeing 777-300ER	Thai Airways International	
HS-TUA	Airbus A.380-841	Thai Airways International	
HS-TUB	Airbus A.380-841	Thai Airways International	
HS-TUC	Airbus A.380-841	Thai Airways International	
HS-TUD	Airbus A.380-861	Thai Airways International	
HS-TUE	Airbus A.380-861	Thai Airways International	

Reg	Type	Owner or Operator
HS-TUF	Airbus A.380-861	Thai Airways International

HZ (Saudi Arabia)

Reg	Type	Owner or Operator
HZ-AK11	Boeing 777-368ER	Saudi Arabian Airlines
HZ-AK12	Boeing 777-368ER	Saudi Arabian Airlines
HZ-AK13	Boeing 777-368ER	Saudi Arabian Airlines
HZ-AK14	Boeing 777-368ER	Saudi Arabian Airlines
HZ-AK15	Boeing 777-368ER	Saudi Arabian Airlines
HZ-AK16	Boeing 777-368ER	Saudi Arabian Airlines
HZ-AK17	Boeing 777-368ER	Saudi Arabian Airlines
HZ-AK18	Boeing 777-368ER	Saudi Arabian Airlines
HZ-AK19	Boeing 777-368ER	Saudi Arabian Airlines
HZ-AK20	Boeing 777-368ER	Saudi Arabian Airlines
HZ-AK21	Boeing 777-368ER	Saudi Arabian Airlines
HZ-AK22	Boeing 777-368ER	Saudi Arabian Airlines
HZ-AK23	Boeing 777-368ER	Saudi Arabian Airlines
HZ-AK24	Boeing 777-368ER	Saudi Arabian Airlines
HZ-AK25	Boeing 777-368ER	Saudi Arabian Airlines
HZ-AK26	Boeing 777-368ER	Saudi Arabian Airlines
HZ-AK27	Boeing 777-368ER	Saudi Arabian Airlines
HZ-AK28	Boeing 777-368ER	Saudi Arabian Airlines
HZ-AK29	Boeing 777-368ER	Saudi Arabian Airlines
HZ-AK30	Boeing 777-368ER	Saudi Arabian Airlines
HZ-AK31	Boeing 777-3FGER	Saudi Arabian Airlines
HZ-AK32	Boeing 777-3FGER	Saudi Arabian Airlines
HZ-AK33	Boeing 777-3FGER	Saudi Arabian Airlines
HZ-AK34	Boeing 777-3FGER	Saudi Arabian Airlines
HZ-AK35	Boeing 777-3FGER	Saudi Arabian Airlines
HZ-AK36	Boeing 777-3FGER	Saudi Arabian Airlines
HZ-AK37	Boeing 777-3FGER	Saudi Arabian Airlines
HZ-AK38	Boeing 777-3FGER	Saudi Arabian Airlines
HZ-AK39	Boeing 777-3FGER	Saudi Arabian Airlines
HZ-AK40	Boeing 777-3FGER	Saudi Arabian Airlines
HZ-AK41	Boeing 777-3FGER	Saudi Arabian Airlines
HZ-AK42	Boeing 777-3FGER	Saudi Arabian Airlines
HZ-AK43	Boeing 777-3FGER	Saudi Arabian Airlines
HZ-AK44	Boeing 777-3FGER	Saudi Arabian Airlines
HZ-AK45	Boeing 777-3FGER	Saudi Arabian Airlines
HZ-AR11	Boeing 787-9	Saudi Arabian Airlines
HZ-AR12	Boeing 787-9	Saudi Arabian Airlines
HZ-AR13	Boeing 787-9	Saudi Arabian Airlines
HZ-AR22	Boeing 787-9	Saudi Arabian Airlines
HZ-AR23	Boeing 787-9	Saudi Arabian Airlines
HZ-AR24	Boeing 787-10	Saudi Arabian Airlines
HZ-AR25	Boeing 787-10	Saudi Arabian Airlines
HZ-AR26	Boeing 787-10	Saudi Arabian Airlines
HZ-AR27	Boeing 787-10	Saudi Arabian Airlines
HZ-AR28	Boeing 787-10	Saudi Arabian Airlines
HZ-AR29	Boeing 787-10	Saudi Arabian Airlines
HZ-ARA	Boeing 787-9	Saudi Arabian Airlines
HZ-ARB	Boeing 787-9	Saudi Arabian Airlines
HZ-ARC	Boeing 787-9	Saudi Arabian Airlines
HZ-ARD	Boeing 787-9	Saudi Arabian Airlines
HZ-ARE	Boeing 787-9	Saudi Arabian Airlines
HZ-ARF	Boeing 787-9	Saudi Arabian Airlines
HZ-ARG	Boeing 787-9	Saudi Arabian Airlines
HZ-ARH	Boeing 787-9	Saudi Arabian Airlines

I (Italy)

Reg	Type	Owner or Operator
I-BIKA	Airbus A.320-214	Alitalia *Johann Sebastian Bach*
I-BIKC	Airbus A.320-214	Alitalia *Zefiro*
I-BIKD	Airbus A.320-214	Alitalia *Maestrale*
I-BIKI	Airbus A.320-214	Alitalia *Girolamo Frescobaldi*
I-BIKO	Airbus A.320-214	Alitalia *George Bizet*
I-BIMA	Airbus A.319-112	Alitalia *Isola d'Elba*
I-BIXK	Airbus A.321-112	Alitalia *Piazza Ducale Vigevano*
I-DISU	Boeing 777-243ER	Alitalia *Madonna di Campiglio*
I-EJGA	Airbus A.330-202	Alitalia

Reg	Type	Owner or Operator	Notes
I-NEOT	Boeing 737-86N	Neos	
I-NEOU	Boeing 737-86N	Neos	
I-NEOW	Boeing 737-86N	Neos	
I-NEOZ	Boeing 737-86N	Neos *Monte Rosa*	

JA (Japan)

Reg	Type	Owner or Operator	Notes
JA731A	Boeing 777-381ER	All Nippon Airways	
JA731J	Boeing 777-346ER	Japan Airlines	
JA732A	Boeing 777-381ER	All Nippon Airways	
JA732J	Boeing 777-346ER	Japan Airlines	
JA733J	Boeing 777-346ER	Japan Airlines	
JA734A	Boeing 777-381ER	All Nippon Airways	
JA734J	Boeing 777-346ER	Japan Airlines	
JA735A	Boeing 777-381ER	All Nippon Airways	
JA735J	Boeing 777-346ER	Japan Airlines	
JA736A	Boeing 777-381ER	All Nippon Airways	
JA736J	Boeing 777-346ER	Japan Airlines	
JA737J	Boeing 777-346ER	Japan Airlines	
JA738J	Boeing 777-346ER	Japan Airlines	
JA739J	Boeing 777-346ER	Japan Airlines	
JA740J	Boeing 777-346ER	Japan Airlines	
JA741J	Boeing 777-346ER	Japan Airlines	
JA742J	Boeing 777-346ER	Japan Airlines	
JA743J	Boeing 777-346ER	Japan Airlines	
JA777A	Boeing 777-381ER	All Nippon Airways	
JA778A	Boeing 777-381ER	All Nippon Airways	
JA779A	Boeing 777-381ER	All Nippon Airways	
JA780A	Boeing 777-381ER	All Nippon Airways	
JA781A	Boeing 777-381ER	All Nippon Airways	
JA782A	Boeing 777-381ER	All Nippon Airways	
JA783A	Boeing 777-381ER	All Nippon Airways	
JA784A	Boeing 777-381ER	All Nippon Airways	
JA785A	Boeing 777-381ER	All Nippon Airways	
JA786A	Boeing 777-381ER	All Nippon Airways	
JA787A	Boeing 777-381ER	All Nippon Airways	
JA788A	Boeing 777-381ER	All Nippon Airways	
JA789A	Boeing 777-381ER	All Nippon Airways	
JA790A	Boeing 777-381ER	All Nippon Airways	
JA791A	Boeing 777-381ER	All Nippon Airways	
JA792A	Boeing 777-381ER	All Nippon Airways	
JA793A	Boeing 777-381ER	All Nippon Airways	
JA794A	Boeing 777-381ER	All Nippon Airways	
JA795A	Boeing 777-381ER	All Nippon Airways	
JA796A	Boeing 777-381ER	All Nippon Airways	
JA797A	Boeing 777-381ER	All Nippon Airways	
JA798A	Boeing 777-381ER	All Nippon Airways	
JA821J	Boeing 787-8	Japan Airlines	
JA823J	Boeing 787-8	Japan Airlines	
JA824J	Boeing 787-8	Japan Airlines	
JA826J	Boeing 787-8	Japan Airlines	
JA827J	Boeing 787-8	Japan Airlines	
JA828J	Boeing 787-8	Japan Airlines	
JA829J	Boeing 787-8	Japan Airlines	
JA830J	Boeing 787-8	Japan Airlines	
JA831J	Boeing 787-8	Japan Airlines	
JA832J	Boeing 787-8	Japan Airlines	
JA833J	Boeing 787-8	Japan Airlines	
JA834J	Boeing 787-8	Japan Airlines	
JA835J	Boeing 787-8	Japan Airlines	
JA836J	Boeing 787-8	Japan Airlines	
JA837J	Boeing 787-8	Japan Airlines	
JA838J	Boeing 787-8	Japan Airlines	
JA839J	Boeing 787-8	Japan Airlines	
JA840J	Boeing 787-8	Japan Airlines	
JA841J	Boeing 787-8	Japan Airlines	
JA842J	Boeing 787-8	Japan Airlines	
JA843J	Boeing 787-8	Japan Airlines	
JA844J	Boeing 787-8	Japan Airlines	
JA845J	Boeing 787-8	Japan Airlines	
JA846J	Boeing 787-8	Japan Airlines	

Notes	Reg	Type	Owner or Operator
	JA847J	Boeing 787-8	Japan Airlines
	JA848J	Boeing 787-8	Japan Airlines
	JA849J	Boeing 787-8	Japan Airlines
	JA861J	Boeing 787-9	Japan Airlines
	JA862J	Boeing 787-9	Japan Airlines
	JA863J	Boeing 787-9	Japan Airlines
	JA864J	Boeing 787-9	Japan Airlines
	JA865J	Boeing 787-9	Japan Airlines
	JA866J	Boeing 787-9	Japan Airlines
	JA867J	Boeing 787-9	Japan Airlines
	JA868J	Boeing 787-9	Japan Airlines
	JA869J	Boeing 787-9	Japan Airlines
	JA870J	Boeing 787-9	Japan Airlines
	JA871J	Boeing 787-9	Japan Airlines
	JA872J	Boeing 787-9	Japan Airlines
	JA873J	Boeing 787-9	Japan Airlines
	JA874J	Boeing 787-9	Japan Airlines
	JA875J	Boeing 787-9	Japan Airlines
	JA876J	Boeing 787-9	Japan Airlines
	JA877J	Boeing 787-9	Japan Airlines
	JA878J	Boeing 787-9	Japan Airlines
	JA879J	Boeing 787-9	Japan Airlines
	JA880J	Boeing 787-9	Japan Airlines
	JA881J	Boeing 787-9	Japan Airlines
	JA882J	Boeing 787-9	Japan Airlines

JY (Jordan)

Notes	Reg	Type	Owner or Operator
	JY-AYC	Airbus A.319-112	Royal Jordanian
	JY-AYN	Airbus A.319-132	Royal Jordanian
	JY-AYP	Airbus A.319-132	Royal Jordanian
	JY-AYQ	Airbus A.320-232	Royal Jordanian
	JY-AYR	Airbus A.320-232	Royal Jordanian
	JY-AYS	Airbus A.320-232	Royal Jordanian
	JY-AYT	Aitbus A.321-231	Royal Jordanian
	JY-AYU	Airbus A.320-232	Royal Jordanian
	JY-AYV	Airbus A.321-231	Royal Jordanian
	JY-AYW	Airbus A.320-232	Royal Jordanian
	JY-AYX	Airbus A.320-232	Royal Jordanian
	JY-AYY	Airbus A.319-112	Royal Jordanian
	JY-AYZ	Airbus A.319-111	Royal Jordanian
	JY-BAA	Boeing 787-8	Royal Jordanian
	JY-BAB	Boeing 787-8	Royal Jordanian
	JY-BAC	Boeing 787-8	Royal Jordanian
	JY-BAE	Boeing 787-8	Royal Jordanian
	JY-BAF	Boeing 787-8	Royal Jordanian
	JY-BAG	Boeing 787-8	Royal Jordanian
	JY-BAH	Boeing 787-8	Royal Jordanian

LN (Norway)

Notes	Reg	Type	Owner or Operator
	LN-BKA	Boeing 737-MAX8	Norwegian Air International
	LN-BKB	Boeing 737-MAX8	Norwegian Air International
	LN-BKC	Boeing 737-MAX8	Norwegian Air International
	LN-BKG	Boeing 737-MAX8	Norwegian Air International
	LN-DYT	Boeing 737-8JP	Norwegian Air Shuttle *Kirsten Flagstad*
	LN-DYU	Boeing 737-8JP	Norwegian Air Shuttle *Jorn Utzon*
	LN-NGD	Boeing 737-8JP	Norwegian Air Shuttle *Ivo Caprino*
	LN-NGM	Boeing 737-8JP	Norwegian Air Shuttle
	LN-NGN	Boeing 737-8JP	Norwegian Air Shuttle *Georg Sverdrup*
	LN-NGP	Boeing 737-8JP	Norwegian Air Shuttle *Ivar Aasen*
	LN-NGS	Boeing 737-8JP	Norwegian Air Shuttle
	LN-NHC	Boeing 737-8JP	Norwegian Air Shuttle
	LN-NHD	Boeing 737-8JP	Norwegian Air Shuttle
	LN-NIB	Boeing 737-8JP	Norwegian Air Shuttle *Helmer Hanssen*
	LN-NIC	Boeing 737-8JP	Norwegian Air Shuttle *Fredrikke Marie Qvam*
	LN-NID	Boeing 737-8JP	Norwegian Air Shuttle
	LN-NIE	Boeing 737-8JP	Norwegian Air Shuttle *Asta Nielsen*
	LN-NIG	Boeing 737-8JP	Norwegian Air Shuttle *Juan Sebastian Elcano*
	LN-NIH	Boeing 737-8JP	Norwegian Air Shuttle *Cristopher Columbus*

Reg	Type	Owner or Operator	Notes
LN-NII	Boeing 737-8JP	Norwegian Air Shuttle *Jacob Ellehammer*	
LN-RCN	Boeing 737-883	SAS *Hedrun Viking*	
LN-RDV	DHC.8-402 Dash Eight	Wideroe's Flyveselskap	
LN-RDY	DHC.8-402 Dash Eight	Wideroe's Flyveselskap	
LN-RDZ	DHC.8-402 Dash Eight	Wideroe's Flyveselskap	
LN-RGD	Boeing 737-883	SAS *Dygve Viking*	
LN-RGE	Boeing 737-883	SAS *Egil Viking*	
LN-RGF	Boeing 737-883	SAS *Torolf Viking*	
LN-RGG	Boeing 737-883	SAS *Asgerd Viking*	
LN-RGH	Boeing 737-883	SAS *Odvar Viking*	
LN-RGI	Boeing 737-883	SAS *Turid Viking*	
LN-RGL	Airbus A.320-251N	SAS *Sol Viking*	
LN-RGM	Airbus A.320-251N	SAS *Silje Viking*	
LN-RGN	Airbus A.320-251N	SAS *Ulrik Viking*	
LN-RGO	Airbus A.320-251N	SAS *Brage Viking*	
LN-RKH	Airbus A.330-343X	SAS *Emund Viking*	
LN-RKI	Airbus A.321-231	SAS *Gunnhild Viking*	
LN-RKK	Airbus A.321-231	SAS *Svipdag Viking*	
LN-RKM	Airbus A.330-343	SAS *Eystein Viking*	
LN-RKN	Airbus A.330-343	SAS *Erik Viking*	
LN-RKO	Airbus A.330-343	SAS *Sigrid Viking*	
LN-RKR	Airbus A.330-343	SAS *Tore Viking*	
LN-RKS	Airbus A.330-343	SAS *Frithiof Viking*	
LN-RKT	Airbus A.330-343	SAS *Bele Viking*	
LN-RKU	Airbus A.330-343	SAS *Helge Viking*	
LN-RNU	Boeing 737-783	SAS *Hans Viking*	
LN-RNW	Boeing 737-783	SAS *Granmar Viking*	
LN-RPJ	Boeing 737-783	SAS *Grimhild Viking*	
LN-RRA	Boeing 737-783	SAS *Steinar Viking*	
LN-RRB	Boeing 737-783	SAS *Cecilia Viking*	
LN-RRE	Boeing 737-883	SAS *Knut Viking*	
LN-RRF	Boeing 737-883	SAS *Froydis Viking*	
LN-RRG	Boeing 737-883	SAS *Einar Viking*	
LN-RRH	Boeing 737-883	SAS *Freja Viking*	
LN-RRJ	Boeing 737-883	SAS *Frida Viking*	
LN-RRK	Boeing 737-883	SAS *Gerud Viking*	
LN-RRL	Boeing 737-883	SAS *Jarlabanke Viking*	
LN-RRM	Boeing 737-783	SAS *Erland Viking*	
LN-RRS	Boeing 737-883	SAS *Ymir Viking*	
LN-RRT	Boeing 737-883	SAS *Lodyn Viking*	
LN-RRU	Boeing 737-883	SAS *Vingolf Viking*	
LN-RRW	Boeing 737-883	SAS *Saga Viking*	
LN-TUJ	Boeing 737-705	SAS *Eirik Blodoks*	
LN-TUK	Boeing 737-705	SAS *Inge Bardsson*	
LN-TUL	Boeing 737-705	SAS *Haakon IV Haakonson*	
LN-TUM	Boeing 737-705	SAS	
LN-WDF	DHC.8-402 Dash Eight	Wideroe's Flyveselskap	
LN-WDG	DHC.8-402 Dash Eight	Wideroe's Flyveselskap	
LN-WDH	DHC.8-402 Dash Eight	Wideroe's Flyveselskap	
LN-WDI	DHC.8-402 Dash Eight	Wideroe's Flyveselskap	
LN-WDJ	DHC.8-402 Dash Eight	Wideroe's Flyveselskap	
LN-WDK	DHC.8-402 Dash Eight	Wideroe's Flyveselskap	
LN-WDL	DHC.8-402 Dash Eight	Wideroe's Flyveselskap	
LN-WEA	Embraer ERJ190-300STD	Wideroe's Flyveselskap	
LN-WEB	Embraer ERJ190-300STD	Wideroe's Flyveselskap	
LN-WEC	Embraer ERJ190-300STD	Wideroe's Flyveselskap	
LN-WFO	DHC.8Q-311 Dash Eight	Wideroe's Flyveselskap	
LN-WFP	DHC.8Q-311 Dash Eight	Wideroe's Flyveselskap	
LN-WFS	DHC.8Q-311 Dash Eight	Wideroe's Flyveselskap	
LN-WFT	DHC.8Q-311 Dash Eight	Wideroe's Flyveselskap	
LN-WFU	DHC.8Q-311 Dash Eight	Wideroe's Flyveselskap	

LX (Luxembourg)

Reg	Type	Owner or Operator	Notes
LX-ECV	Boeing 747-4HQERF	Cargolux	
LX-GCL	Boeing 747-467F	Cargolux	
LX-ICL	Boeing 747-467f	Cargolux	
LX-JCV	Boeing 747-4EVERF	Cargolux	
LX-KCL	Boeing 747-4HAERF	Cargolux	
LX-LBA	Boeing 737-8C9	Luxair	
LX-LBB	Boeing 737-86J	Luxair	

Notes	Reg	Type	Owner or Operator
	LX-LBR	Boeing 737-7K2	Luxair
	LX-LBT	Boeing 737-706	Luxair
	LX-LCL	Boeing 747-4HAF	Cargolux
	LX-LGE	DHC.8Q-402 Dash Eight	Luxair
	LX-LGF	DHC.8Q-402 Dash Eight	Luxair
	LX-LGG	DHC.8Q-402 Dash Eight	Luxair
	LX-LGM	DHC.8Q-402 Dash Eight	Luxair
	LX-LGN	DHC.8Q-402 Dash Eight	Luxair
	LX-LGQ	Boeing 737-7C9	Luxair
	LX-LGS	Boeing 737-7C9	Luxair
	LX-LGU	Boeing 737-8C9	Luxair
	LX-LGV	Boeing 737-8C9	Luxair
	LX-LQA	DHC.8Q-402 Dash Eight	Luxair
	LX-LQB	DHC.8Q-402 Dash Eight	Luxair
	LX-LQC	DHC.8Q-402 Dash Eight	Luxair
	LX-LQD	DHC.8Q-402 Dash Eight	Luxair
	LX-LQI	DHC.8Q-402 Dash Eight	Luxair
	LX-LQJ	DHC.8Q-402 Dash Eight	Luxair
	LX-MCL	Boeing 747-4HAF	Cargolux
	LX-NCL	Boeing 747-4EVF	Cargolux
	LX-OCV	Boeing 747-4R7F (SCD)	Cargolux
	LX-RCV	Boeing 747-4R7F (SCD)	Cargolux
	LX-SCV	Boeing 747-4R7F (SCD)	Cargolux Italia
	LX-TCV	Boeing 747-4R7F (SCD)	Cargolux Italia
	LX-UCV	Boeing 747-4R7F (SCD)	Cargolux *City of Bertragne*
	LX-VCA	Boeing 747-8R7F	Cargolux *City of Vianden*
	LX-VCB	Boeing 747-8R7F	Cargolux *City of Esch-sur-Aizette*
	LX-VCC	Boeing 747-8R7F	Cargolux *City of Ettelbruck*
	LX-VCD	Boeing 747-8R7F	Cargolux *City of Luxembourg*
	LX-VCE	Boeing 747-8R7F	Cargolux *City of Echternach*
	LX-VCF	Boeing 747-8R7F	Cargolux *City of Grevenmacher*
	LX-VCG	Boeing 747-8R7F	Cargolux *City of Diekirch*
	LX-VCH	Boeing 747-8R7F	Cargolux *City of Dudelange*
	LX-VCI	Boeing 747-8R7F	Cargolux *City of Troisvierges*
	LX-VCJ	Boeing 747-8R7F	Cargolux *City of Zhengzhou*
	LX-VCK	Boeing 747-8R7F	Cargolux *City of Contern*
	LX-VCL	Boeing 747-8R7F	Cargolux *Joe Sutter-Father of the Boeing 747*
	LX-VCM	Boeing 747-8R7F	Cargolux*City of Redange-sur-Attert*
	LX-VCN	Boeing 747-8R7F	Cargolux *Spirit of Schengen*
	LX-VCV	Boeing 747-4R7F (SCD)	Cargolux Italia
	LX-WCV	Boeing 747-4R7F (SCD)	Cargolux *City of Petange*
	LX-YCV	Boeing 747-4R7F	Cargolux Italia

LY (Lithuania)

Notes	Reg	Type	Owner or Operator
	LY-NVV	Airbus A.320-232	Avion Express
	LY-NVW	Airbus A.320-232	Avion Express
	LY-NVZ	Airbus A.320-214	Avion Express
	LY-VEA	Airbus A.321-231	Avion Express
	LY-VEB	Airbus A.320-214	Avion Express
	LY-VEC	Airbus A.321-211	Avion Express
	LY-VED	Airbus A.321-211	Avion Express
	LY-VEG	Airbus A.321-211	Avion Express
	LY-VEH	Airbus A.321-231	Avion Express
	LY-VEL	Airbus A.320-232	Avion Express
	LY-VEN	Airbus A.320-233	Avion Express
	LY-VEW	Airbus A.320-214	Avion Express

LZ (Bulgaria)

Notes	Reg	Type	Owner or Operator
	LZ-BHI	Airbus A.320-232	BH Air
	LZ-BHL	Airbus A.320-232	BH Air
	LZ-BHM	Airbus A.320-232	BH Air
	LZ-BUR	Embraer ERJ190-100IGW	Bulgaria Air
	LZ-CGO	Boeing 737-301SF	Cargo Air
	LZ-CGP	Boeing 737-35BSF	Cargo Air
	LZ-CGQ	Boeing 737-3Y5SF	Cargo Air
	LZ-CGR	Boeing 737-448SF	Cargo Air
	LZ-CGS	Boeing 737-4Q8SF	Cargo Air
	LZ-CGT	Boeing 737-4YOSF	Cargo Air
	LZ-CGU	Boeing 737-448SF	Cargo Air

Reg	Type	Owner or Operator	Notes
LZ-CGV	Boeing 737-405SF	Cargo Air	
LZ-CGW	Boeing 737-46JSF	Cargo Air	
LZ-CGX	Boeing 737-43QSF	Cargo Air	
LZ-CGY	Boeing 737-49RSF	Cargo Air	
LZ-FBA	Airbus A.319-112	Bulgaria Air	
LZ-FBB	Airbus A.319-112	Bulgaria Air	
LZ-FBC	Airbus A.320-214	Bulgaria Air	
LZ-FBD	Airbus A.320-214	Bulgaria Air	
LZ-FBE	Airbus A.320-214	Bulgaria Air	
LZ-FBG	Airbus A.320-214	Bulgaria Air	
LZ-PLO	Embraer ERJ190-100STD	Bulgaria Air	
LZ-SOF	Embraer ERJ190-100IGW	Bulgaria Air	
LZ-VAR	Embraer ERJ190-100IGW	Bulgaria Air	

N (USA)

Reg	Type	Owner or Operator	Notes
N128AM	Boeing 787-9	Aeromexico	
N152DL	Boeing 767-3P6ER	Delta Air Lines	
N154DL	Boeing 767-3P6ER	Delta Air Lines	
N155DL	Boeing 767-3P6ER	Delta Air Lines	
N156DL	Boeing 767-3P6ER	Delta Air Lines	
N169DZ	Boeing 767-332ER	Delta Air Lines	
N171DZ	Boeing 767-332ER	Delta Air Lines	
N172DZ	Boeing 767-332ER	Delta Air Lines	
N173DZ	Boeing 767-332ER	Delta Air Lines	
N174DN	Boeing 767-332ER	Delta Air Lines	
N174DZ	Boeing 767-332ER	Delta Air Lines	
N175DN	Boeing 767-332ER	Delta Air Lines	
N175DZ	Boeing 767-332ER	Delta Air Lines	
N176DZ	Boeing 767-332ER	Delta Air Lines	
N177DZ	Boeing 767-332ER	Delta Air Lines	
N178DZ	Boeing 767-332ER	Delta Air Lines	
N179DN	Boeing 767-332ER	Delta Air Lines	
N180DN	Boeing 767-332ER	Delta Air Lines	
N181DN	Boeing 767-332ER	Delta Air Lines	
N182DN	Boeing 767-332ER	Delta Air Lines	
N183AM	Boeing 787-9	Aeromexico	
N183DN	Boeing 767-332ER	Delta Air Lines	
N184DN	Boeing 767-332ER	Delta Air Lines	
N185DN	Boeing 767-332ER	Delta Air Lines	
N186DN	Boeing 767-332ER	Delta Air Lines	
N187DN	Boeing 767-332ER	Delta Air Lines	
N188DN	Boeing 767-332ER	Delta Air Lines	
N189DN	Boeing 767-332ER	Delta Air Lines	
N190DN	Boeing 767-332ER	Delta Air Lines	
N191DN	Boeing 767-332ER	Delta Air Lines	
N192DN	Boeing 767-332ER	Delta Air Lines	
N193DN	Boeing 767-332ER	Delta Air Lines	
N194DN	Boeing 767-332ER	Delta Air Lines	
N195DN	Boeing 767-332ER	Delta Air Lines	
N196DN	Boeing 767-332ER	Delta Air Lines	
N197DN	Boeing 767-332ER	Delta Air Lines	
N198DN	Boeing 767-332ER	Delta Air Lines	
N199DN	Boeing 767-332ER	Delta Air Lines	
N204UA	Boeing 777-222ER	United Airlines	
N206UA	Boeing 777-222ER	United Airlines	
N209UA	Boeing 777-222ER	United Airlines	
N216UA	Boeing 777-222ER	United Airlines	
N217UA	Boeing 777-222ER	United Airlines	
N218UA	Boeing 777-222ER	United Airlines	
N219CY	Boeing 767-383ERBDSF	ABX Air	
N219UA	Boeing 777-222ER	United Airlines	
N220CY	Boeing 767-383ERBDSF	ABX Air	
N220UA	Boeing 777-222ER	United Airlines	
N221UA	Boeing 777-222ER	United Airlines	
N222UA	Boeing 777-222ER	United Airlines	
N224UA	Boeing 777-222ER	United Airlines	
N225UA	Boeing 777-222ER	United Airlines	
N226CY	Boeing 767-383ERBDSF	ABX Air	
N226UA	Boeing 777-222ER	United Airlines	
N227UA	Boeing 777-222ER	United Airlines	

Notes	Reg	Type	Owner or Operator
	N228UA	Boeing 777-222ER	United Airlines
	N229UA	Boeing 777-222ER	United Airlines
	N301UP	Boeing 767-34AFER	United Parcel Service
	N302UP	Boeing 767-34AFER	United Parcel Service
	N303UP	Boeing 767-34AFER	United Parcel Service
	N304UP	Boeing 767-34AFER	United Parcel Service
	N305UP	Boeing 767-34AFER	United Parcel Service
	N306UP	Boeing 767-34AFER	United Parcel Service
	N307UP	Boeing 767-34AFER	United Parcel Service
	N308UP	Boeing 767-34AFER	United Parcel Service
	N309UP	Boeing 767-34AFER	United Parcel Service
	N310UP	Boeing 767-34AFER	United Parcel Service
	N311UP	Boeing 767-34AFER	United Parcel Service
	N312UP	Boeing 767-34AFER	United Parcel Service
	N313UP	Boeing 767-34AFER	United Parcel Service
	N314UP	Boeing 767-34AFER	United Parcel Service
	N315UP	Boeing 767-34AFER	United Parcel Service
	N316CM	Boeing 767-338ERBDSF	Amerijet International
	N316UP	Boeing 767-34AFER	United Parcel Service
	N317CM	Boeing 767-338ERBDSF	ABX Air
	N317UP	Boeing 767-34AFER	United Parcel Service
	N318UP	Boeing 767-34AFER	United Parcel Service
	N319CM	Boeing 767-338ERBDSF	Amerijet International
	N319UP	Boeing 767-34AFER	United Parcel Service
	N320UP	Boeing 767-34AFER	United Parcel Service
	N322UP	Boeing 767-34AFER	United Parcel Service
	N323UP	Boeing 767-34AFER	United Parcel Service
	N324UP	Boeing 767-34AFER	United Parcel Service
	N325UP	Boeing 767-34AFER	United Parcel Service
	N326UP	Boeing 767-34AFER	United Parcel Service
	N327UP	Boeing 767-34AFER	United Parcel Service
	N328UP	Boeing 767-34AFER	United Parcel Service
	N329UP	Boeing 767-34AER	United Parcel Service
	N330UP	Boeing 767-34AER	United Parcel Service
	N331UP	Boeing 767-34AER	United Parcel Service
	N332UP	Boeing 767-34AER	United Parcel Service
	N334UP	Boeing 767-34AER	United Parcel Service
	N335UP	Boeing 767-34AF	United Parcel Service
	N336UP	Boeing 767-34AF	United Parcel Service
	N337UP	Boeing 767-34AF	United Parcel Service
	N338UP	Boeing 767-34AF	United Parcel Service
	N339UP	Boeing 767-34AF	United Parcel Service
	N340UP	Boeing 767-34AF	United Parcel Service
	N341UP	Boeing 767-34AF	United Parcel Service
	N342UP	Boeing 767-34AF	United Parcel Service
	N343UP	Boeing 767-34AF	United Parcel Service
	N344UP	Boeing 767-34AF	United Parcel Service
	N345UP	Boeing 767-34AF	United Parcel Service
	N346UP	Boeing 767-34AF	United Parcel Service
	N347CM	Boeing 767-323ERBDSF	Amerijet International
	N347UP	Boeing 767-34AF	United Parcel Service
	N348UP	Boeing 767-34AF	United Parcel Service
	N349CM	Boeing 767-323ERBDSF	Amerijet International
	N349UP	Boeing 767-34AF	United Parcel Service
	N350UP	Boeing 767-34AF	United Parcel Service
	N351UP	Boeing 767-34AF	United Parcel Service
	N352UP	Boeing 767-34AF	United Parcel Service
	N353UP	Boeing 767-34AF	United Parcel Service
	N354UP	Boeing 767-34AF	United Parcel Service
	N355UP	Boeing 767-34AF	United Parcel Service
	N356UP	Boeing 767-34AF	United Parcel Service
	N357UP	Boeing 767-34AF	United Parcel Service
	N358UP	Boeing 767-34AF	United Parcel Service
	N359UP	Boeing 767-34AF	United Parcel Service
	N360UP	Boeing 767-34AF	United Parcel Service
	N361UP	Boeing 767-34AF	United Parcel Service
	N362CY	Boeing 767-338ERBDSF	ABX Air
	N362UP	Boeing 767-346ER	United Parcel Service
	N363UP	Boeing 767-346ER	United Parcel Service
	N364CM	Boeing 767-338ERBDSF	ABX Air
	N364UP	Boeing 767-346ER	United Parcel Service

Reg	Type	Owner or Operator	Notes
N365UP	Boeing 767-300F	United Parcel Service	
N366UP	Boeing 767-300F	United Parcel Service	
N367UP	Boeing 767-300F	United Parcel Service	
N368UP	Boeing 767-300F	United Parcel Service	
N369UP	Boeing 767-300F	United Parcel Service	
N370UP	Boeing 767-300F	United Parcel Service	
N371CM	Boeing 767-338ERBDSF	ABX Air	
N371UP	Boeing 767-300F	United Parcel Service	
N372CM	Boeing 767-338ERBDSF	ABX Air	
N372UP	Boeing 767-300F	United Parcel Service	
N373CM	Boeing 767-338ERBDSF	Amerijet International	
N373UP	Boeing 767-300F	United Parcel Service	
N374UP	Boeing 767-300F	United Parcel Service	
N375UP	Boeing 767-300F	United Parcel Service	
N378CM	Boeing 767-323ERBDSF	Amerijet International	
N391UP	Boeing 767-304ERF	United Parcel Service	
N392UP	Boeing 767-304ERF	United Parcel Service	
N393UP	Boeing 767-316ER	United Parcel Service	
N394DL	Boeing 767-324ER	Delta Air Lines	
N394UP	Boeing 767-381ERF	United Parcel Service	
N395UP	Boeing 767-316ER	United Parcel Aervice	
N396CM	Boeing 767-323ERBDSF	Amerijet International	
N401KZ	Boeing 747-481F	Kalitta Air	
N402KZ	Boeing 747-481F	Kalitta Air	
N403KZ	Boeing 747-481F	Kalitta Air	
N404KZ	Boeing 747-4KZF	Atlas Air	
N405KZ	Boeing 747-4KZF	Atlas Air	
N406KZ	Boeing 747-4KZF	Atlas Air	
N407KZ	Boeing 747-4KZF	Atlas Air	
N408MC	Boeing 747-47UF	Atlas Air	
N409MC	Boeing 747-47UF	Atlas Air	
N412MC	Boeing 747-47UF	Atlas Air	
N415MC	Boeing 747-47UF	Atlas Air	
N416MC	Boeing 747-47UF	Atlas Air	
N418MC	Boeing 747-47UF	Atlas Air	
N419MC	Boeing 747-48EF	Atlas Air	
N429MC	Boeing 747-481	Atlas Air	
N438AM	Boeing 787-9	Aeromexico	
N446AM	Boeing 787-9	Aeromexico	
N445MC	Boeing 747-4B5ERF	Atlas Air	
N446MC	Boeing 747-4B5ERF	Atlas Air	
N471MC	Boeing 747-412BCF	Atlas Air	
N472MC	Boeing 747-45EF	Atlas Air	
N473MC	Boeing 747-45EF	Atlas Air	
N475MC	Boeing 747-47U	Atlas Air	
N476MC	Boeing 747-47U	Atlas Air	
N477MC	Boeing 747-47U	Atlas Air	
N485MC	Boeing 747-45EF	Atlas Air	
N486MC	Boeing 747-45EF	Atlas Air	
N487MC	Boeing 747-45EF	Atlas Air	
N489MC	Boeing 747-412F	Atlas Air	
N492MC	Boeing 747-47UF	Atlas Air	
N493MC	Boeing 747-47UF	Atlas Air	
N496MC	Boeing 747-47UF	Atlas Air	
N498MC	Boeing 747-47UF	Atlas Air	
N499MC	Boeing 747-47UF	Atlas Air	
N508KZ	Boeing 747-4ZKF	Atlas Air	
N523FE	McD Douglas MD-11F	Federal Express	
N525FE	McD Douglas MD-11F	Federal Express	
N528FE	McD Douglas MD-11F	Federal Express	
N529FE	McD Douglas MD-11F	Federal Express	
N572FE	McD Douglas MD-11F	Federal Express	
N573FE	McD Douglas MD-11F	Federal Express	
N574FE	McD Douglas MD-11F	Federal Express	
N575FE	McD Douglas MD-11F	Federal Express	
N576FE	McD Douglas MD-11F	Federal Express	
N582FE	McD Douglas MD-11F	Federal Express *Jamie*	
N583FE	McD Douglas MD-11F	Federal Express *Nancy*	
N584FE	McD Douglas MD-11F	Federal Express *Jeffrey Wellington*	
N585FE	McD Douglas MD-11F	Federal Express *Katherine*	
N586FE	McD Douglas MD-11F	Federal Express *Dylan*	

Notes	Reg	Type	Owner or Operator
	N587FE	McD Douglas MD-11F	Federal Express *Jeanna*
	N588FE	McD Douglas MD-11F	Federal Express *Kendra*
	N589FE	McD Douglas MD-11F	Federal Express *Shaun*
	N590FE	McD Douglas MD-11F	Federal Express
	N591FE	McD Douglas MD-11F	Federal Express *Giovanni*
	N592FE	McD Douglas MD-11F	Federal Express *Joshua*
	N593FE	McD Douglas MD-11F	Federal Express *Harrison*
	N594FE	McD Douglas MD-11F	Federal Express
	N595FE	McD Douglas MD-11F	Federal Express *Avery*
	N596FE	McD Douglas MD-11F	Federal Express
	N597FE	McD Douglas MD-11F	Federal Express
	N598FE	McD Douglas MD-11F	Federal Express
	N599FE	McD Douglas MD-11F	Federal Express *Mariana*
	N601FE	McD Douglas MD-11F	Federal Express *Jim Riedmeyer*
	N602FE	McD Douglas MD-11F	Federal Express *Malcolm Baldridge 1990*
	N603FE	McD Douglas MD-11F	Federal Express
	N604FE	McD Douglas MD-11F	Federal Express *Hollis*
	N605FE	McD Douglas MD-11F	Federal Express *April Star*
	N605UP	Boeing 747-8F	United Parcel Service
	N606FE	McD Douglas MD-11F	Federal Express *Charles & Theresa*
	N606UP	Boeing 747-8F	United Parcel Service
	N607FE	McD Douglas MD-11F	Federal Express
	N607UP	Boeing 747-8F	United Parcel Service
	N608FE	McD Douglas MD-11F	Federal Express *Karen*
	N608UP	Boeing 747-8F	United Parcel Service
	N609FE	McD Douglas MD-11F	Federal Express *Scott*
	N609UP	Boeing 747-8F	United Parcel Service
	N610FE	McD Douglas MD-11F	Federal Express *Marisa*
	N610UP	Boeing 747-8F	United Parcel Service
	N611UP	Boeing 747-8F	United Parcel Service
	N612FE	McD Douglas MD-11F	Federal Express *Alyssa*
	N612UP	Boeing 747-8F	United Parcel Service
	N613FE	McD Douglas MD-11F	Federal Express *Krista*
	N613UP	Boeing 747-8F	United Parcel Service
	N614FE	McD Douglas MD-11F	Federal Express *Christy Allison*
	N614UP	Boeing 747-8F	United Parcel Service
	N615FE	McD Douglas MD-11F	Federal Express *Max*
	N615UP	Boeing 747-8F	United Parcel Service
	N616FE	McD Douglas MD-11F	Federal Express *Shanita*
	N616UP	Boeing 747-8F	United Parcel Service
	N617FE	McD Douglas MD-11F	Federal Express *Travis*
	N617UP	Boeing 747-8F	United Parcel Service
	N618FE	McD Douglas MD-11F	Federal Express *Justin*
	N618UP	Boeing 747-8F	United Parcel Service
	N619FE	McD Douglas MD-11F	Federal Express *Lyndon*
	N620FE	McD Douglas MD-11F	Federal Express
	N620UP	Boeing 747-8F	United Parcel Service
	N621FE	McD Douglas MD-11F	Federal Express *Connor*
	N621UP	Boeing 747-8F	United Parcel Service
	N622UP	Boeing 747-8F	United Parcel Service
	N623FE	McD Douglas MD-11F	Federal Express *Meghan*
	N623UP	Boeing 747-8F	United Parcel Service
	N624AG	Boeing 757-2Q8	Delta Air Lines
	N624FE	McD Douglas MD-11F	Federal Express
	N624UP	Boeing 747-8F	United Parcel Service
	N625FE	McD Douglas MD-11F	Federal Express
	N625UP	Boeing 747-8F	United Parcel Service
	N626UP	Boeing 747-8F	United Parcel Service
	N628FE	McD Douglas MD-11F	Federal Express
	N631FE	McD Douglas MD-11F	Federal Express
	N641UA	Boeing 767-322ER	United Airlines
	N642FE	McD Douglas MD-11F	Federal Express
	N642UA	Boeing 767-322ER	United Airlines
	N643FE	McD Douglas MD-11F	Federal Express
	N643UA	Boeing 767-322ER	United Airlines
	N644UA	Boeing 767-322ER	United Airlines
	N646UA	Boeing 767-322ER	United Airlines
	N647UA	Boeing 767-322ER	United Airlines
	N648UA	Boeing 767-322ER	United Airlines
	N649UA	Boeing 767-322ER	United Airlines
	N651UA	Boeing 767-322ER	United Airlines

Reg	Type	Owner or Operator	Notes
N652UA	Boeing 767-322ER	United Airlines	
N653UA	Boeing 767-322ER	United Airlines	
N654UA	Boeing 767-322ER	United Airlines	
N655UA	Boeing 767-322ER	United Airlines	
N656UA	Boeing 767-322ER	United Airlines	
N657UA	Boeing 767-322ER	United Airlines	
N658UA	Boeing 767-322ER	United Airlines	
N659UA	Boeing 767-322ER	United Airlines	
N660UA	Boeing 767-322ER	United Airlines	
N661UA	Boeing 767-322ER	United Airlines	
N662UA	Boeing 767-322ER	United Airlines	
N663UA	Boeing 767-322ER	United Airlines	
N664UA	Boeing 767-322ER	United Airlines	
N665UA	Boeing 767-322ER	United Airlines	
N666UA	Boeing 767-322ER	United Airlines	
N667UA	Boeing 767-322ER	United Airlines	
N668UA	Boeing 767-322ER	United Airlines	
N669UA	Boeing 767-322ER	United Airlines	
N670UA	Boeing 767-322ER	United Airlines	
N671UA	Boeing 767-322ER	United Airlines	
N672UA	Boeing 767-322ER	United Airlines	
N673UA	Boeing 767-322ER	United Airlines	
N674UA	Boeing 767-322ER	United Airlines	
N675UA	Boeing 767-322ER	United Airlines	
N676UA	Boeing 767-322ER	United Airlines	
N677UA	Boeing 767-322ER	United Airlines	
N684UA	Boeing 767-3CBER	United Airlines	
N685UA	Boeing 767-3CBER	United Airlines	
N686UA	Boeing 767-3CBER	United Airlines	
N702CA	Boeing 747-412BCF	National Airlines	
N700CK	Boeing 747-4R7F	Kalitta Air	
N701CK	Boeing 747-4B5F	Kalitta Air	
N702CK	Boeing 747-4B5F	Kalitta Air	
N702GT	Boeing 777-F16	Southern Air	
N702TW	Boeing 757-2Q8	Delta Air Lines	
N703CK	Boeing 747-412BCF	Kalitta Air	
N703GT	Boeing 777-F16	Southern Air	
N703TW	Boeing 757-2Q8	Delta Air Lines	
N704GT	Boeing 777-F16	Southern Air	
N704X	Boeing 757-2Q8	Delta Air Lines	
N705CK	Boeing 747-4B5F	Kalitta Air	
N705GT	Boeing 777-FZB	Southern Air	
N705TW	Boeing 757-231	Delta Air Lines	
N706CK	Boeing 747-4B5F	Kalitta Air	
N706GT	Boeing 777-FZB	Southern Air	
N706TW	Boeing 757-2Q8	Delta Air Lines	
N707CK	Boeing 747-4B5F	Kalitta Air	
N707TW	Boeing 757-2Q8	Delta Air Lines	
N708CK	Boeing 747-4B5F	Kalitta Air	
N709CA	Boeing 747-412BCF	National Airlines	
N709CK	Boeing 747-4B5F	Kalitta Air	
N709TW	Boeing 757-2Q8	Delta Air Lines	
N710CK	Boeing 747-4B5F	Kalitta Air	
N710TW	Boeing 757-2Q8	Delta Air Lines	
N711ZX	Boeing 757-231	Delta Air Lines	
N712CK	Boeing 747-4B5F	Kalitta Air	
N712TW	Boeing 757-2Q8	Delta Air Lines	
N713CK	Boeing 747-4B5F	Kalitta Air	
N713TW	Boeing 757-2Q8	Delta Air Lines	
N714SA	Boeing 777-FZB	Southern Air	
N715CK	Boeing 747-4B5F	Kalitta Air	
N716CK	Boeing 747-4B5F	Kalitta Air	
N717AN	Boeing 777-323ER	American Airlines	
N717TW	Boeing 757-231	Delta Air Lines	
N718AN	Boeing 777-323ER	American Airlines	
N718TW	Boeing 757-231	Delta Air Lines	
N719AN	Boeing 777-323ER	American Airlines	
N720AN	Boeing 777-323ER	American Airlines	
N721AN	Boeing 777-323ER	American Airlines	
N721TW	Boeing 757-231	Delta Air Lines	
N722AN	Boeing 777-323ER	American Airlines	

Notes	Reg	Type	Owner or Operator
	N722FD	Airbus A.300B4-622RF	Federal Express
	N722TW	Boeing 757-231	Delta Air Lines
	N723AN	Boeing 777-323ER	American Airlines
	N723TW	Boeing 757-231	Delta Air Lines
	N724AN	Boeing 777-323ER	American Airlines
	N724FD	Airbus A.300B4-622RF	Federal Express
	N725AN	Boeing 777-323ER	American Airlines
	N726AN	Boeing 777-323ER	American Airlines
	N727AN	Boeing 777-323ER	American Airlines
	N727TW	Boeing 757-231	Delta Air Lines
	N728AN	Boeing 777-323ER	American Airlines
	N729AN	Boeing 777-323ER	American Airlines
	N730AN	Boeing 777-323ER	American Airlines
	N731AN	Boeing 777-323ER	American Airlines
	N732AN	Boeing 777-323ER	American Airlines
	N733AR	Boeing 777-323ER	American Airlines
	N734AR	Boeing 777-323ER	American Airlines
	N735AT	Boeing 777-323ER	American Airlines
	N736AT	Boeing 777-323ER	American Airlines
	N740CK	Boeing 747-4H6BCF	Kalitta Air
	N741CK	Boeing 747-4H6F	Kalitta Air
	N742CK	Boeing 747-446BCF	Kalitta Air
	N740FD	Airbus A.300B4-622RF	Federal Express
	N743CK	Boeing 747-446BCF	Kalitta Air
	N743FD	Airbus A.300B4-622RF	Federal Express
	N744CK	Boeing 747-446BCF	Kalitta Air
	N745CK	Boeing 747-446BCF	Kalitta Air
	N750AN	Boeing 777-223ER	American Airlines
	N751AN	Boeing 777-223ER	American Airlines
	N752AN	Boeing 777-223ER	American Airlines
	N753AN	Boeing 777-223ER	American Airlines
	N754AN	Boeing 777-223ER	American Airlines
	N755AN	Boeing 777-223ER	American Airlines
	N756AM	Boeing 777-223ER	American Airlines
	N756CA	Boeing 747-412BCF	National Airlines
	N757AN	Boeing 777-223ER	American Airlines
	N758AN	Boeing 777-223ER	American Airlines
	N759AN	Boeing 777-223ER	American Airlines
	N760AN	Boeing 777-223ER	American Airlines
	N761AJ	Boeing 777-223ER	American Airlines
	N762AN	Boeing 777-223ER	American Airlines
	N765AN	Boeing 777-223ER	American Airlines
	N766AN	Boeing 777-223ER	American Airlines
	N767AJ	Boeing 777-223ER	American Airlines
	N768AA	Boeing 777-223ER	American Airlines
	N770AN	Boeing 777-223ER	American Airlines
	N771AN	Boeing 777-223ER	American Airlines
	N772AN	Boeing 777-223ER	American Airlines
	N773AN	Boeing 777-223ER	American Airlines
	N774AN	Boeing 777-223ER	American Airlines
	N774SA	Boeing 777-FZB	Southern Air
	N775AN	Boeing 777-223ER	American Airlines
	N775SA	Boeing 777-FZB	Southern Air
	N776AN	Boeing 777-223ER	American Airlines
	N777AN	Boeing 777-223ER	American Airlines
	N777SA	Boeing 777-FZB	Southern Air
	N778AN	Boeing 777-223ER	American Airlines
	N778LA	Boeing 777-F16	Southern Air
	N779AN	Boeing 777-223ER	American Airlines
	N780AN	Boeing 777-223ER	American Airlines
	N780AV	Boeing 787-8	AVIANCA
	N781AN	Boeing 777-223ER	American Airlines
	N781AV	Boeing 787-8	AVIANCA
	N782AM	Boeing 787-8	Aeromexico
	N782AN	Boeing 777-223ER	American Airlines
	N782AV	Boeing 787-8	AVIANCA
	N782CK	Boeing 747-4HQF	Kalitta Air
	N782UA	Boeing 777-222ER	United Airlines
	N783AM	Boeing 787-8	Aeromexico
	N783AN	Boeing 777-223ER	American Airlines
	N783AV	Boeing 787-8	AVIANCA

Reg	Type	Owner or Operator	Notes
N783UA	Boeing 777-222ER	United Airlines	
N784AN	Boeing 777-223ER	American Airlines	
N784AV	Boeing 787-8	AVIANCA	
N784UA	Boeing 777-222ER	United Airlines	
N785AN	Boeing 777-223ER	American Airlines	
N785AV	Boeing 787-8	AVIANCA	
N785CK	Boeing 747-4BF	Kalitta Air	
N785UA	Boeing 777-222ER	United Airlines	
N786AN	Boeing 777-223ER	American Airlines	
N786AV	Boeing 787-8	AVIANCA	
N786UA	Boeing 777-222ER	United Airlines	
N787AL	Boeing 777-223ER	American Airlines	
N787UA	Boeing 777-222ER	United Airlines	
N788AN	Boeing 777-223ER	American Airlines	
N788UA	Boeing 777-222ER	United Airlines	
N789AN	Boeing 777-223ER	American Airlines	
N790AN	Boeing 777-223ER	American Airlines	
N791AN	Boeing 777-223ER	American Airlines	
N791AV	Boeing 787-8	AVIANCA	
N791UA	Boeing 777-222ER	United Airlines	
N792AN	Boeing 777-223ER	American Airlines	
N792AV	Boeing 787-8	AVIANCA	
N792UA	Boeing 777-222ER	United Airlines	
N793AN	Boeing 777-223ER	American Airlines	
N793AV	Boeing 787-8	AVIANCA	
N793UA	Boeing 777-222ER	United Airlines	
N794AN	Boeing 777-223ER	American Airlines	
N794AV	Boeing 787-8	AVIANCA	
N794UA	Boeing 777-222ER	United Airlines	
N795AN	Boeing 777-223ER	American Airlines	
N795AV	Boeing 787-8	AVIANCA	
N795UA	Boeing 777-222ER	United Airlines	
N796AN	Boeing 777-223ER	American Airlines	
N796AV	Boeing 787-8	AVIANCA	
N796UA	Boeing 777-222ER	United Airlines	
N797AN	Boeing 777-223ER	American Airlines	
N797AV	Boeing 787-9	AVIANCA	
N797UA	Boeing 777-222ER	United Airlines	
N798AN	Boeing 777-223ER	American Airlines	
N798UA	Boeing 777-222ER	United Airlines	
N799AN	Boeing 777-223ER	American Airlines	
N799UA	Boeing 777-222ER	United Airlines	
N800AN	Boeing 787-8	American Airlines	
N801AC	Boeing 787-8	American Airlines	
N801NW	Airbus A.330-323X	Delta Airlines	
N802AN	Boeing 787-8	American Airlines	
N802NW	Airbus A.330-323X	Delta Airlines	
N803AL	Boeing 787-8	American Airlines	
N803NW	Airbus A.330-323X	Delta Air Lines	
N804AN	Boeing 787-8	American Airlines	
N804NW	Airbus A.330-323X	Delta Air Lines	
N805AN	Boeing 787-8	American Airlines	
N805NW	Airbus A.330-323X	Delta Air Lines	
N806AA	Boeing 787-8	American Airlines	
N806NW	Airbus A.330-323X	Delta Air Lines	
N807AA	Boeing 787-8	American Airlines	
N807NW	Airbus A.330-323X	Delta Air Lines	
N808AN	Boeing 787-8	American Airlines	
N808NW	Airbus A.330-323X	Delta Air Lines	
N809AA	Boeing 787-8	American Airlines	
N809NW	Airbus A.330-323E	Delta Air Lines	
N810AN	Boeing 787-8	American Airlines	
N810NW	Airbus A.330-323E	Delta Air Lines	
N811AB	Boeing 787-8	American Airlines	
N811NW	Airbus A.330-323E	Delta Air Lines	
N812AA	Boeing 787-8	American Airlines	
N812NW	Airbus A.330-323E	Delta Air Lines	
N813AN	Boeing 787-8	American Airlines	
N813NW	Airbus A.330-323E	Delta Air Lines	
N814AA	Boeing 787-8	American Airlines	
N814NW	Airbus A.330-323E	Delta Air Lines	

Notes	Reg	Type	Owner or Operator
	N815AA	Boeing 787-8	American Airlines
	N815NW	Airbus A.330-323E	Delta Air Lines
	N816AA	Boeing 787-8	American Airlines
	N816NW	Airbus A.330-323E	Delta Air Lines
	N817AN	Boeing 787-8	American Airlines
	N817NW	Airbus A.330-323E	Delta Air Lines
	N818AL	Boeing 787-8	American Airlines
	N818NW	Airbus A.330-323E	Delta Air Lines
	N819AN	Boeing 787-8	American Airlines
	N819NW	Airbus A.330-323E	Delta Air Lines
	N820AL	Boeing 787-9	American Airlines
	N820NW	Airbus A.330-323E	Delta Air Lines
	N821AN	Boeing 787-9	American Airlines
	N821NW	Airbus A.330-323E	Delta Air Lines
	N822AN	Boeing 787-9	American Airlines
	N822NW	Airbus A.330-323E	Delta Air Lines
	N823AN	Boeing 787-9	American Airlines
	N823NW	Airbus A.330-302	Delta Air Lines
	N824AN	Boeing 787-9	American Airlines
	N824NW	Airbus A.330-302	Delta Air Lines
	N825AA	Boeing 787-9	American Airlines
	N825MH	Boeing 767-432ER (1801)	Delta Air Lines
	N825NW	Airbus A.330-302	Delta Air Lines
	N826AN	Boeing 787-9	American Airlines
	N826MH	Boeing 767-432ER (1802)	Delta Air Lines
	N826NW	Airbus A.330-302	Delta Air Lines
	N827AN	Boeing 787-9	American Airlines
	N827MH	Boeing 767-432ER (1803)	Delta Air Lines
	N827NW	Airbus A.330-302	Delta Air Lines
	N828AA	Boeing 787-9	American Airlines
	N828MH	Boeing 767-432ER (1804)	Delta Air Lines
	N828NW	Airbus A.330-302	Delta Air Lines
	N829AN	Boeing 787-9	American Airlines
	N829MH	Boeing 767-432ER (1805)	Delta Air Lines
	N829NW	Airbus A.330-302	Delta Air Lines
	N830AN	Boeing 787-9	American Airlines
	N830MH	Boeing 767-432ER (1806)	Delta Air Lines
	N830NW	Airbus A.330-302	Delta Air Lines
	N831AA	Boeing 787-9	American Airlines
	N831MH	Boeing 767-432ER (1807)	Delta Air Lines
	N831NW	Airbus A.330-302	Delta Air Lines
	N832AA	Boeing 787-9	American Airlines
	N832MH	Boeing 767-432ER (1808)	Delta Air Lines
	N833AA	Boeing 787-9	American Airlines
	N833MH	Boeing 767-432ER (1809)	Delta Air Lines
	N834AA	Boeing 787-9	American Airlines
	N834MH	Boeing 767-432ER (1810)	Delta Air Lines
	N835AN	Boeing 787-9	American Airlines
	N835MH	Boeing 767-432ER (1811)	Delta Air Lines
	N836AA	Boeing 787-9	American Airlines
	N836MH	Boeing 767-432ER (1812)	Delta Air Lines
	N837AN	Boeing 787-9	American Airlines
	N837MH	Boeing 767-432ER (1813)	Delta Air Lines
	N838AA	Boeing 787-9	American Airlines
	N838MH	Boeing 767-432ER (1814)	Delta Air Lines
	N839AA	Boeing 787-9	American Airlines
	N839MH	Boeing 767-432ER (1815)	Delta Air Lines
	N840AN	Boeing 787-9	American Airlines
	N840FD	Boeing 777-FHT	Federal Express
	N840MH	Boeing 767-432ER (1816)	Delta Air Lines
	N841AN	Boeing 787-9	American Airlines
	N841MH	Boeing 767-432ER (1817)	Delta Air Lines
	N842FD	Boeing 777-FHT	Federal Express
	N842MH	Boeing 767-432ER (1818)	Delta Air Lines
	N843FD	Boeing 777-FHT	Federal Express
	N843MH	Boeing 767-432ER (1819)	Delta Air Lines
	N844FD	Boeing 777-FHT	Federal Express
	N844MH	Boeing 767-432ER (1820)	Delta Air Lines
	N845FD	Boeing 777-FHT	Federal Express
	N845MH	Boeing 767-432ER (1821)	Delta Air Lines
	N846FD	Boeing 777-200F	Federal Express

Reg	Type	Owner or Operator	Notes
N850FD	Boeing 777-2S2LRF	Federal Express	
N850GT	Boeing 747-87UF	Atlas Air	
N851FD	Boeing 777-2S2LRF	Federal Express	
N851NW	Airbus A.330-223	Delta Air Lines	
N852FD	Boeing 777-2S2LRF	Federal Express	
N852NW	Airbus A.330-223	Delta Air Lines	
N853FD	Boeing 777-2S2LRF	Federal Express	
N853NW	Airbus A.330-223	Delta Air Lines	
N854FD	Boeing 777-2S2LRF	Federal Express	
N854GT	Boeing 747-87UF	Atlas Air	
N854NW	Airbus A.330-223	Delta Air Lines	
N855FD	Boeing 777-2S2LRF	Federal Express	
N855NW	Airbus A.330-223	Delta Air Lines	
N856FD	Boeing 777-2S2LRF	Federal Express	
N856GT	Boeing 747-87UF	Atlas Air	
N856NW	Airbus A.330-223	Delta Air Lines	
N857FD	Boeing 777-2S2LRF	Federal Express	
N857NW	Airbus A.330-223	Delta Air Lines	
N858FD	Boeing 777-2S2LRF	Federal Express	
N858NW	Airbus A.330-223	Delta Air Lines	
N859FD	Boeing 777-2S2LRF	Federal Express	
N859GT	Boeing 747-87UF	Atlas Air	
N859NW	Airbus A.330-223	Delta Air Lines	
N860FD	Boeing 777-2S2LRF	Federal Express	
N860NW	Airbus A.330-223	Delta Air Lines	
N861FD	Boeing 777-2S2LRF	Federal Express	
N861NW	Airbus A.330-223	Delta Air Lines	
N862FD	Boeing 777-2S2LRF	Federal Express	
N863FD	Boeing 777-2S2LRF	Federal Express	
N864FD	Boeing 777-2S2LRF	Federal Express	
N865FD	Boeing 777-2S2LRF	Federal Express	
N866FD	Boeing 777-2S2LRF	Federal Express	
N868FD	Boeing 777-2S2LRF	Federal Express	
N869FD	Boeing 777-2S2LRF	Federal Express	
N870AX	Boeing 787-8	American Airlines	
N871AY	Boeing 787-8	American Airlines	
N872AN	Boeing 787-8	American Airlines	
N873BB	Boeing 787-8	American Airlines	
N874AN	Boeing 787-8	American Airlines	
N875BD	Boeing 787-8	American Airlines	
N876AL	Boeing 787-8	American Airlines	
N876FD	Boeing 777-2S2LRF	Federal Express	
N877BF	Boeing 787-8	American Airlines	
N877FD	Boeing 777-2S2LRF	Federal Express	
N878BG	Boeing 787-8	American Airlines	
N878FD	Boeing 777-2S2LRF	Federal Express	
N879FD	Boeing 777-2S2LRF	Federal Express	
N880FD	Boeing 777-2S2LRF	Federal Express	
N882FD	Boeing 777-2S2LRF	Federal Express	
N883FD	Boeing 777-2S2LRF	Federal Express	
N884FD	Boeing 777-2S2LRF	Federal Express	
N885FD	Boeing 777-2S2LRF	Federal Express	
N886FD	Boeing 777-2S2LRF	Federal Express	
N887FD	Boeing 777-2S2LRF	Federal Express	
N888FD	Boeing 777-2S2LRF	Federal Express	
N889FD	Boeing 777-2S2LRF	Federal Express	
N890FD	Boeing 777-2S2LRF	Federal Express	
N891FD	Boeing 777-2S2LRF	Federal Express	
N892FD	Boeing 777-2S2LRF	Federal Express	
N893FD	Boeing 777-2S2LRF	Federal Express	
N894FD	Boeing 777-2S2LRF	Federal Express	
N895FD	Boeing 777-2S2LRF	Federal Express	
N896FD	Boeing 777-2S2LRF	Federal Express	
N897FD	Boeing 777-2S2LRF	Federal Express	
N901FD	Boeing 757-2B7	Federal Express	
N903FD	Boeing 757-2B7	Federal Express	
N910FD	Boeing 757-28A	Federal Express	
N912FD	Boeing 757-28A	Federal Express	
N913FD	Boeing 757-28A	Federal Express	
N915FD	Boeing 757-236	Federal Express	
N916FD	Boeing 757-27B	Federal Express	

Notes	Reg	Type	Owner or Operator
	N917FD	Boeing 757-23A	Federal Express
	N918FD	Boeing 757-23A	Federal Express
	N919CA	Boeing 747-428BCF	National Airlines
	N920FD	Boeing 757-23A	Federal Express
	N922FD	Boeing 757-23A	Federal Express
	N923FD	Boeing 757-204	Federal Express
	N927FD	Boeing 757-204	Federal Express
	N939FD	Boeing 757-23A	Federal Express
	N952CA	Boeing 747-428BCF	National Airlines
	N964AM	Boeing 787-8	Aeromexico
	N965AM	Boeing 787-8	Aeromexico
	N966AM	Boeing 787-8	Aeromexico
	N967AM	Boeing 787-8	Aeromexico
	N968FD	Boeing 757-28A	Federal Express
	N972FD	Boeing 757-28A	Federal Express
	N974FD	Boeing 757-2YOSF	Federal Express
	N976BA	Boeing 747-4B5CF	Kalitta Air
	N1200K	Boeing 767-332ER (200)	Delta Air Lines
	N1201P	Boeing 767-332ER (201)	Delta Air Lines
	N1602	Boeing 767-332ER (1602)	Delta Air Lines
	N1603	Boeing 767-332ER (1603)	Delta Air Lines
	N1604R	Boeing 767-332ER (1604)	Delta Air Lines
	N1605	Boeing 767-332ER (1605)	Delta Air Lines
	N1607B	Boeing 767-332ER (1607)	Delta Air Lines
	N1608	Boeing 767-332ER (1608)	Delta Air Lines
	N1609	Boeing 767-332ER (1609)	Delta Air Lines
	N1610D	Boeing 767-332ER (1610)	Delta Air Lines
	N1613B	Boeing 767-332ER (1613)	Delta Air Lines
	N2135U	Boeing 777-322ER	United Airlines
	N2136U	Boeing 777-322ER	United Airlines
	N2138U	Boeing 777-322ER	United Airlines
	N2140U	Boeing 777-322ER	United Airlines
	N2142U	Boeing 777-322ER	United Airlines
	N2243U	Boeing 777-322ER	United Airlines
	N2250U	Boeing 777-300ER	United Airlines
	N2251U	Boeing 777-300ER	United Airlines
	N2331U	Boeing 777-322ER	United Airlines
	N2332U	Boeing 777-322ER	United Airlines
	N2333U	Boeing 777-322ER	United Airlines
	N2341U	Boeing 777-322ER	United Airlines
	N2352U	Boeing 777-300ER	United Airlines
	N2534U	Boeing 777-322ER	United Airlines
	N2639U	Boeing 777-322ER	United Airlines
	N2644U	Boeing 777-322ER	United Airlines
	N2645U	Boeing 777-322ER	United Airlines
	N2737U	Boeing 777-322ER	United Airlines
	N2747U	Boeing 777-322ER	United Airlines
	N2748U	Boeing 777-322ER	United Airlines
	N2749U	Boeing 777-300ER	United Airlines
	N2846U	Boeing 777-322ER	United Airlines
	N12003	Boeing 787-10	United Airlines
	N12004	Boeing 787-10	United Airlines
	N12005	Boeing 787-10	United Airlines
	N12006	Boeing 787-10	United Airlines
	N12010	Boeing 787-10	United Airlines
	N12012	Boeing 787-10	United Airlines
	N12109	Boeing 757-224	United Airlines
	N12114	Boeing 757-224	United Airlines
	N12116	Boeing 757-224	United Airlines
	N12125	Boeing 757-224	United Airlines
	N13013	Boeing 787-10	United Airlines
	N13110	Boeing 757-224	United Airlines
	N13113	Boeing 757-224	United Airlines
	N13138	Boeing 757-224	United Airlines
	N13954	Boeing 787-9	United Airlines
	N14001	Boeing 787-10	United Airlines
	N14011	Boeing 787-10	United Airlines
	N14102	Boeing 757-224	United Airlines
	N14106	Boeing 757-224	United Airlines
	N14107	Boeing 757-224	United Airlines
	N14115	Boeing 757-224	United Airlines

Reg	Type	Owner or Operator	Notes
N14118	Boeing 757-224	United Airlines	
N14120	Boeing 757-224	United Airlines	
N14121	Boeing 757-224	United Airlines	
N15969	Boeing 787-9	United Airlines	
N16008	Boeing 787-10	United Airlines	
N16009	Boeing 787-10	United Airlines	
N16065	Boeing 767-332ER (1606)	Delta Air Lines	
N17002	Boeing 787-10	United Airlines	
N17104	Boeing 757-224	United Airlines	
N17105	Boeing 757-224	United Airlines	
N17122	Boeing 757-224	United Airlines	
N17126	Boeing 757-224	United Airlines	
N17128	Boeing 757-224	United Airlines	
N17133	Boeing 757-224	United Airlines	
N17139	Boeing 757-224	United Airlines	
N17963	Boeing 787-9	United Airlines	
N18112	Boeing 757-224	United Airlines	
N18119	Boeing 757-224	United Airlines	
N19117	Boeing 757-224	United Airlines	
N19130	Boeing 757-224	United Airlines	
N19136	Boeing 757-224	United Airlines	
N19141	Boeing 757-224	United Airlines	
N19951	Boeing 787-9	United Airlines	
N19986	Boeing 787-9	United Airlines	
N20904	Boeing 787-8	United Airlines	
N21108	Boeing 757-224	United Airlines	
N23983	Boeing 787-9	United Airlines	
N24972	Boeing 787-9	United Airlines	
N24973	Boeing 787-9	United Airlines	
N24974	Boeing 787-9	United Airlines	
N24976	Boeing 787-9	United Airlines	
N24979	Boeing 787-9	United Airlines	
N24980	Boeing 787-9	United Airlines	
N25982	Boeing 787-9	United Airlines	
N26902	Boeing 787-8	United Airlines	
N26906	Boeing 787-8	United Airlines	
N26909	Boeing 787-8	United Airlines	
N26910	Boeing 787-8	United Airlines	
N26952	Boeing 787-9	United Airlines	
N26960	Boeing 787-9	United Airlines	
N26966	Boeing 787-9	United Airlines	
N26967	Boeing 787-9	United Airlines	
N26970	Boeing 787-9	United Airlines	
N27015	Boeing 777-224ER	United Airlines	
N27901	Boeing 787-8	United Airlines	
N27903	Boeing 787-8	United Airlines	
N27908	Boeing 787-8	United Airlines	
N27957	Boeing 787-9	United Airlines	
N27958	Boeing 787-9	United Airlines	
N27959	Boeing 787-9	United Airlines	
N27964	Boeing 787-9	United Airlines	
N27965	Boeing 787-9	United Airlines	
N28912	Boeing 787-8	United Airlines	
N28987	Boeing 787-9	United Airlines	
N29124	Boeing 757-224	United Airlines	
N29129	Boeing 757-224	United Airlines	
N29907	Boeing 787-8	United Airlines	
N29961	Boeing 787-9	United Airlines	
N29968	Boeing 787-9	United Airlines	
N29971	Boeing 787-9	United Airlines	
N29975	Boeing 787-9	United Airlines	
N29977	Boeing 787-9	United Airlines	
N29978	Boeing 787-9	United Airlines	
N29981	Boeing 787-9	United Airlines	
N29984	Boeing 787-9	United Airlines	
N29985	Boeing 787-9	United Airlines	
N30913	Boeing 787-8	United Airlines	
N33103	Boeing 757-224	United Airlines	
N33132	Boeing 757-224	United Airlines	
N34131	Boeing 757-224	United Airlines	
N34137	Boeing 757-224	United Airlines	

Notes	Reg	Type	Owner or Operator
	N35953	Boeing 787-9	United Airlines
	N36962	Boeing 787-9	United Airlines
	N37018	Boeing 777-224ER	United Airlines
	N38950	Boeing 787-9	United Airlines
	N38955	Boeing 787-9	United Airlines
	N41135	Boeing 757-224	United Airlines
	N41140	Boeing 757-224	United Airlines
	N45905	Boeing 787-8	United Airlines
	N45956	Boeing 787-9	United Airlines
	N48127	Boeing 757-224	United Airlines
	N57016	Boeing 777-224ER	United Airlines
	N57111	Boeing 757-224	United Airlines
	N58101	Boeing 757-224	United Airlines
	N59053	Boeing 767-424ER	United Airlines
	N66051	Boeing 767-424ER	United Airlines
	N66056	Boeing 767-424ER	United Airlines
	N66057	Boeing 767-424ER	United Airlines
	N67052	Boeing 767-424ER	United Airlines
	N67058	Boeing 767-424ER	United Airlines
	N67134	Boeing 757-224	United Airlines
	N68061	Boeing 767-424ER	United Airlines
	N69020	Boeing 777-224ER	United Airlines
	N69059	Boeing 767-424ER	United Airlines
	N69063	Boeing 767-424ER	United Airlines
	N74007	Boeing 777-224ER	United Airlines
	N76010	Boeing 777-224ER	United Airlines
	N76021	Boeing 777-224ER	United Airlines
	N76054	Boeing 767-424ER	United Airlines
	N76055	Boeing 767-424ER	United Airlines
	N76062	Boeing 767-424ER	United Airlines
	N76064	Boeing 767-424ER	United Airlines
	N76065	Boeing 767-424ER	United Airlines
	N77006	Boeing 777-224ER	United Airlines
	N77012	Boeing 777-224ER	United Airlines
	N77014	Boeing 777-224ER	United Airlines
	N77019	Boeing 777-224ER	United Airlines
	N77022	Boeing 777-224ER	United Airlines
	N77066	Boeing 767-424ER	United Airlines
	N78001	Boeing 777-224ER	United Airlines
	N78002	Boeing 777-224ER	United Airlines
	N78003	Boeing 777-224ER	United Airlines
	N78004	Boeing 777-224ER	United Airlines
	N78005	Boeing 777-224ER	United Airlines
	N78008	Boeing 777-224ER	United Airlines
	N78009	Boeing 777-224ER	United Airlines
	N78013	Boeing 777-224ER	United Airlines
	N78017	Boeing 777-224ER	United Airlines
	N78060	Boeing 767-424ER	United Airlines
	N79011	Boeing 777-224ER	United Airlines
	N91007	Boeing 787-10	United Airlines

OD (Lebanon)

	OD-MEA	Airbus A.330-243	Middle East Airlines
	OD-MEB	Airbus A.330-243	Middle East Airlines
	OD-MEC	Airbus A.330-243	Middle East Airlines
	OD-MED	Airbus A.330-243	Middle East Airlines
	OD-MEE	Airbus A.330-243	Middle East Airlines
	OD-MRL	Airbus A.320-232	Middle East Airlines
	OD-MRM	Airbus A.320-232	Middle East Airlines
	OD-MRN	Airbus A.320-232	Middle East Airlines
	OD-MRO	Airbus A.320-232	Middle East Airlines
	OD-MRR	Airbus A.320-232	Middle East Airlines
	OD-MRS	Airbus A.320-232	Middle East Airlines
	OD-MRT	Airbus A.320-232	Middle East Airlines

OE (Austria)

	OE-IAB	Boeing 737-4Z9	ASL Airlines Belgium
	OE-IAC	Boeing 737-4MO	ASL Airlines Belgium

Reg	Type	Owner or Operator	Notes
OE-IAD	Boeing 737-4MOF	ASL Airlines Belgium	
OE-IAE	Boeing 737-4Q8	ASL Airlines Belgium	
OE-IAG	Boeing 737-4Q8	ASL Airlines Belgium	
OE-IAJ	Boeing 737-476F	ASL Airlines Belgium	
OE-IAK	Boeing 737-4Q8	ASL Airlines Belgium	
OE-IAM	Boeing 737-490SF	ASL Airlines Belgium	
OE-IAP	Boeing 737-4MO	ASL Airlines Belgium	
OE-IAQ	Boeing 737-4MO	ASL Airlines Belgium	
OE-IAR	Boeing 737-4MO	ASL Airlines Belgium	
OE-IAT	Boeing 737-4MO	ASL Airlines Belgium	
OE-IAU	Boeing 737-4MO	ASL Airlines Belgium	
OE-IAY	Boeing 737-4Q8	ASL Airlines Belgium	
OE-IAZ	Boeing 737-4Q8F	ASL Airlines Belgium	
OE-IBI	Boeing 737-490SF	ASL Airlines Belgium	
OE-IBL	Boeing 737-490F	ASL Airlines Belgium	
OE-IBO	Boeing 737-490SF	ASL Airlines Belgium	
OE-IBW	Boeing 737-4Q8F	ASL Airlines Belgium	
OE-ICB	Airbus A.320-214	easyJet Europe	
OE-ICD	Airbus A.320-214	easyJet Europe	
OE-ICF	Airbus A.320-214	easyJet Europe	
OE-ICI	Airbus A.320-214	easyJet Europe	
OE-ICJ	Airbus A.320-214	easyJet Europe	
OE-ICK	Airbus A.320-214	easyJet Europe	
OE-ICM	Airbus A.320-214	easyJet Europe	
OE-ICP	Airbus A.320-214	easyJet Europe	
OE-ICR	Airbus A.320-214	easyJet Europe	
OE-ICS	Airbus A.320-214	easyJet Europe	
OE-ICT	Airbus A.320-214	easyJet Europe	
OE-ICU	Airbus A.320-214	easyJet Europe	
OE-ICW	Airbus A.320-214	easyJet Europe	
OE-ICZ	Airbus A.320-214	easyJet Europe	
OE-IEU	Airbus A.320-214	Eurowings Europe	
OE-IEW	Airbus A.320-214	Eurowings Europe	
OE-IJA	Airbus A.320-214	easyJet Europe	
OE-IJB	Airbus A.320-214	easyJet Europe	
OE-IJD	Airbus A.320-214	easyJet Europe	
OE-IJE	Airbus A.320-214	easyJet Europe	
OE-IJF	Airbus A.320-214	easyJet Europe	
OE-IJG	Airbus A.320-214	easyJet Europe	
OE-IJH	Airbus A.320-214	easyJet Europe	
OE-IJI	Airbus A.320-214	easyJet Europe	
OE-IJJ	Airbus A.320-214	easyJet Europe	
OE-IJK	Airbus A.320-214	easyJet Europe	
OE-IJL	Airbus A.320-214	easyJet Europe	
OE-IJN	Airbus A.320-214	easyJet Europe	
OE-IJO	Airbus A.320-214	easyJet Europe	
OE-IJQ	Airbus A.320-214	easyJet Europe	
OE-IJR	Airbus A.320-214	easyJet Europe	
OE-IJS	Airbus A.320-214	easyJet Europe	
OE-IJU	Airbus A.320-214	easyJet Europe	
OE-IJV	Airbus A.320-214	easyJet Europe	
OE-IJW	Airbus A.320-214	easyJet Europe	
OE-IJX	Airbus A.320-214	easyJet Europe	
OE-IJY	Airbus A.320-214	easyJet Europe	
OE-IJZ	Airbus A.320-214	easyJet Europe	
OE-IMC	Boeing 737-83NF	ASL Airlines Belgium	
OE-IMD	Boeing 737-83NF	ASL Airlines Belgium	
OE-INA	Airbus A.320-214	easyJet Europe	
OE-INB	Airbus A.320-214	easyJet Europe	
OE-IND	Airbus A.320-214	easyJet Europe	
OE-INE	Airbus A.320-214	easyJet Europe	
OE-INF	Airbus A.320-214	easyJet Europe	
OE-ING	Airbus A.320-214	easyJet Europe	
OE-INH	Airbus A.320-214	easyJet Europe	
OE-INI	Airbus A.320-214	easyJet Europe	
OE-INM	Airbus A.320-214	easyJet Europe	
OE-INP	Airbus A.320-214	easyJet Europe	
OE-IQA	Airbus A.320-214	Eurowings Europe	
OE-IQB	Airbus A.320-214	Eurowings Europe	
OE-IQC	Airbus A.320-214	Eurowings Europe	
OE-IQD	Airbus A.320-214	Eurowings Europe	

Notes	Reg	Type	Owner or Operator
	OE-ISB	Airbus A.321-251NX	easyJet Europe
	OE-ISC	Airbus A.321-251NX	easyJet Europe
	OE-ISD	Airbus A.321-251NX	easyJet Europe
	OE-ISE	Airbus A.321-251NX	easyJet Europe
	OE-IVA	Airbus A.320-214	easyJet Europe
	OE-IVB	Airbus A.320-214	easyJet Europe
	OE-IVC	Airbus A.320-214	easyJet Europe
	OE-IVD	Airbus A.320-214	easyJet Europe
	OE-IVE	Airbus A.320-214	easyJet Europe
	OE-IVF	Airbus A.320-214	easyJet Europe
	OE-IVI	Airbus A.320-214	easyJet Europe
	OE-IVJ	Airbus A.320-214	easyJet Europe
	OE-IVL	Airbus A.320-214	easyJet Europe
	OE-IVM	Airbus A.320-214	easyJet Europe
	OE-IVN	Airbus A.320-214	easyJet Europe
	OE-IVQ	Airbus A.320-214	easyJet Europe
	OE-IVR	Airbus A.320-214	easyJet Europe
	OE-IVS	Airbus A.320-214	easyJet Europe
	OE-IVT	Airbus A.320-214	easyJet Europe
	OE-IVU	Airbus A.320-214	easyJet Europe
	OE-IVV	Airbus A.320-214	easyJet Europe
	OE-IVW	Airbus A.320-214	easyJet Europe
	OE-IVZ	Airbus A.320-214	easyJet Europe
	OE-IWA	Boeing 737-8AS	ASL Airlines Belgium
	OE-IZB	Airbus A.320-214	easyJet Europe
	OE-IZC	Airbus A.320-214	easyJet Europe
	OE-IZD	Airbus A.320-214	easyJet Europe
	OE-IZE	Airbus A.320-214	easyJet Europe
	OE-IZF	Airbus A.320-214	easyJet Europe
	OE-IZG	Airbus A.320-214	easyJet Europe
	OE-IZH	Airbus A.320-214	easyJet Europe
	OE-IZJ	Airbus A.320-214	easyJet Europe
	OE-IZL	Airbus A.320-214	easyJet Europe
	OE-IZN	Airbus A.320-214	easyJet Europe
	OE-IZO	Airbus A.320-214	easyJet Europe
	OE-IZP	Airbus A.320-214	easyJet Europe
	OE-IZQ	Airbus A.320-214	easyJet Europe
	OE-IZS	Airbus A.320-214	easyJet Europe
	OE-IZT	Airbus A.320-214	easyJet Europe
	OE-IZU	Airbus A.320-214	easyJet Europe
	OE-IZV	Airbus A.320-214	easyJet Europe
	OE-IZW	Airbus A.320-214	easyJet Europe
	OE-LAE	Boeing 767-3Z9ER	Austrian Airlines *Malaysia*
	OE-LAT	Boeing 767-31AER	Austrian Airlines *Enzo Ferrari*
	OE-LAW	Boeing 767-3Z9ER	Austrian Airlines *China*
	OE-LAX	Boeing 767-3Z9ER	Austrian Airlines *Thailand*
	OE-LAY	Boeing 767-3Z9ER	Austrian Airlines *Japan*
	OE-LAZ	Boeing 767-3Z9ER	Austrian Airlines *India*
	OE-LBA	Airbus A.321-111	Austrian Airlines *Salzkammergut*
	OE-LBB	Airbus A.321-111	Austrian Airlines *Pinzgau*
	OE-LBC	Airbus A.321-111	Austrian Airlines *Sudtirol*
	OE-LBD	Airbus A.321-111	Austrian Airlines *Steirisches Weinland*
	OE-LBE	Airbus A.321-111	Austrian Airlines *Wachau*
	OE-LBF	Airbus A.321-111	Austrian Airlines *Wien*
	OE-LBI	Airbus A.320-214	Austrian Airlines *Marchfeld*
	OE-LBJ	Airbus A.320-212	Austrian Airlines *Hohe Tauern*
	OE-LBK	Airbus A.320-214	Austrian Airlines *Sterisches Thermenland*
	OE-LBL	Airbus A.320-214	Austrian Airlines *Ausseerland*
	OE-LBM	Airbus A.320-214	Austrian Airlines *Arlberg*
	OE-LBN	Airbus A.320-214	Austrian Airlines *Osttirol*
	OE-LBO	Airbus A.320-214	Austrian Airlines *Pyhrn-Eisenwurzen*
	OE-LBP	Airbus A.320-214	Austrian Airlines *Neusiedler See*
	OE-LBQ	Airbus A.320-214	Austrian Airlines *Wienerwald*
	OE-LBR	Airbus A.320-214	Austrian Airlines *Frida Kahle*
	OE-LBS	Airbus A.320-214	Austrian Airlines *Waldviertel*
	OE-LBT	Airbus A.320-214	Austrian Airlines *Worthersee*
	OE-LBU	Airbus A.320-214	Austrian Airlines *Muhlviertel*
	OE-LBV	Airbus A.320-214	Austrian Airlines *Weinviertel*
	OE-LBW	Airbus A.320-214	Austrian Airlines *Innviertel*
	OE-LBX	Airbus A.320-214	Austrian Airlines *Mostviertel*
	OE-LBY	Airbus A.320-214	Austrian Airlines *Camuntum*

Reg	Type	Owner or Operator	Notes
OE-LBZ	Airbus A.320-214	Austrian Airlines *Obertauern*	
OE-LDA	Airbus A.319-112	Austrian Airlines *Sofia*	
OE-LDB	Airbus A.319-112	Austrian Airlines *Bucharest*	
OE-LDC	Airbus A.319-112	Austrian Airlines *Kiev*	
OE-LDD	Airbus A.319-112	Austrian Airlines *Moscow*	
OE-LDE	Airbus A.319-112	Austrian Airlines *Baku*	
OE-LDF	Airbus A.319-112	Austrian Airlines *Sarajevo*	
OE-LDG	Airbus A.319-112	Austrian Airlines *Tbilisi*	
OE-LFB	Boeing 757-23APF	ASL Airlines Belgium	
OE-LFE	Boeing 757-28AF	ASL Airlines Belgium	
OE-LGI	DHC.8Q-402 Dash Eight	Austrian Airlines *Eisenstadt*	
OE-LGJ	DHC.8Q-402 Dash Eight	Austrian Airlines *St Pölten*	
OE-LGK	DHC.8Q-402 Dash Eight	Austrian Airlines *Burgenland*	
OE-LGL	DHC.8Q-402 Dash Eight	Austrian Airlines *Altenrhein*	
OE-LGM	DHC.8Q-402 Dash Eight	Austrian Airlines *Villach*	
OE-LGN	DHC.8Q-402 Dash Eight	Austrian Airlines *Gmunden*	
OE-LGO	DHC.8Q-402 Dash Eight	Austrian Airlines *Innsbruck*	
OE-LGQ	DHC.8Q-402 Dash Eight	Austrian Airlines *Wilder Kaiser*	
OE-LKC	Airbus A.319-111	easyJet Europe	
OE-LKD	Airbus A.319-111	easyJet Europe	
OE-LKF	Airbus A.319-111	easyJet Europe	
OE-LKI	Airbus A.319-111	easyJet Europe	
OE-LKJ	Airbus A.319-111	easyJet Europe	
OE-LKK	Airbus A.319-111	easyJet Europe	
OE-LKL	Airbus A.319-111	easyJet Europe	
OE-LKM	Airbus A.319-111	easyJet Europe	
OE-LKO	Airbus A.319-111	easyJet Europe	
OE-LKP	Airbus A.319-111	easyJet Europe	
OE-LKQ	Airbus A.319-111	easyJet Europe	
OE-LME	Airbus A.320-214	Laudamotion	
OE-LMM	Airbus A.320-214	Laudamotion	
OE-LMN	Airbus A.320-214	Laudamotion	
OE-LMO	Airbus A.320-214	Laudamotion	
OE-LMS	Airbus A.320-214	Laudamotion	
OE-LPA	Boeing 777-2Z9	Austrian Airlines *Melbourne*	
OE-LPB	Boeing 777-2Z9	Austrian Airlines *Sydney*	
OE-LPC	Boeing 777-2Z9ER	Austrian Airlines *Donald Bradman*	
OE-LPD	Boeing 777-2Z9ER	Austrian Airlines *America*	
OE-LPE	Boeing 777-2Q8ER	Austrian Airlines *Blue Danube*	
OE-LPF	Boeing 777-2Q8ER	Austrian Airlines	
OE-LQA	Airbus A.319-111	easyJet Europe	
OE-LQB	Airbus A.319-111	easyJet Europe	
OE-LQC	Airbus A.319-111	easyJet Europe	
OE-LQD	Airbus A.319-111	easyJet Europe	
OE-LQE	Airbus A.319-111	easyJet Europe	
OE-LQF	Airbus A.319-111	easyJet Europe	
OE-LQG	Airbus A.319-111	easyJet Europe	
OE-LQI	Airbus A.319-111	easyJet Europe	
OE-LQJ	Airbus A.319-111	easyJet Europe	
OE-LQL	Airbus A.319-111	easyJet Europe	
OE-LQM	Airbus A.319-111	easyJet Europe	
OE-LQN	Airbus A.319-111	easyJet Europe	
OE-LQP	Airbus A.319-111	easyJet Europe	
OE-LQQ	Airbus A.319-111	easyJet Europe	
OE-LQR	Airbus A.319-111	easyJet Europe	
OE-LQS	Airbus A.319-111	easyJet Europe	
OE-LQT	Airbus A.319-111	easyJet Europe	
OE-LQU	Airbus A.319-111	easyJet Europe	
OE-LQW	Airbus A.319-111	easyJet Europe	
OE-LQX	Airbus A.319-111	easyJet Europe	
OE-LQZ	Airbus A.319-111	easyJet Europe	
OE-LWA	Embraer ERJ190-200LR	Austrian Airlines	
OE-LWB	Embraer ERJ190-200LR	Austrian Airlines	
OE-LWC	Embraer ERJ190-200LR	Austrian Airlines	
OE-LWD	Embraer ERJ190-200LR	Austrian Airlines	
OE-LWE	Embraer ERJ190-200LR	Austrian Airlines	
OE-LWF	Embraer ERJ190-200LR	Austrian Airlines	
OE-LWG	Embraer ERJ190-200LR	Austrian Airlines	
OE-LWH	Embraer ERJ190-200LR	Austrian Airlines	
OE-LWI	Embraer ERJ190-200LR	Austrian Airlines	
OE-LWJ	Embraer ERJ190-200LR	Austrian Airlines	

Notes	Reg	Type	Owner or Operator
	OE-LWK	Embraer ERJ190-200LR	Austrian Airlines
	OE-LWL	Embraer ERJ190-200LR	Austrian Airlines
	OE-LWM	Embraer ERJ190-200LR	Austrian Airlines
	OE-LWN	Embraer ERJ190-200LR	Austrian Airlines
	OE-LWO	Embraer ERJ190-200LR	Austrian Airlines
	OE-LWP	Embraer ERJ190-200LR	Austrian Airlines
	OE-LWQ	Embraer ERJ190-200LR	Austrian Airlines
	OE-LXA	Airbus A.320-216	Austrian Airlines
	OE-LXB	Airbus A.320-216	Austrian Airlines
	OE-LXC	Airbus A.320-216	Austrian Airlines
	OE-LXD	Airbus A.320-216	Austrian Airlines
	OE-LXE	Airbus A.320-216	Austrian Airlines
	OE-LYU	Airbus A.319-132	Eurowings Europe
	OE-LYV	Airbus A.319-132	Eurowings Europe
	OE-LYW	Airbus A.319-132	Eurowings Europe
	OE-LYX	Airbus A.319-132	Eurowings Europe
	OE-LYY	Airbus A.319-132	Eurowings Europe
	OE-LYZ	Airbus A.319-132	Eurowings Europe
	OE-LZA	Airbus A.320-214	Austrian Airlines
	OE-LZB	Airbus A.320-214	Austrian Airlines
	OE-LZC	Airbus A.320-214	Austrian Airlines
	OE-LZD	Airbus A.320-214	Austrian Airlines
	OE-LZE	Airbus A.320-214	Austrian Airlines
	OE-LZF	Airbus A.320-214	Austrian Airlines

OH (Finland)

Notes	Reg	Type	Owner or Operator
	OH-LKE	Embraer RJ190-100LR	Nordic Regional Airlines/Finnair
	OH-LKF	Embraer RJ190-100LR	Nordic Regional Airlines/Finnair
	OH-LKG	Embraer RJ190-100LR	Nordic Regional Airlines/Finnair
	OH-LKH	Embraer RJ190-100LR	Nordic Regional Airlines/Finnair
	OH-LKI	Embraer RJ190-100LR	Nordic Regional Airlines/Finnair
	OH-LKK	Embraer RJ190-100LR	Nordic Regional Airlines/Finnair
	OH-LKL	Embraer RJ190-100LR	Nordic Regional Airlines/Finnair
	OH-LKM	Embraer RJ190-100LR	Nordic Regional Airlines/Finnair
	OH-LKN	Embraer RJ190-100LR	Nordic Regional Airlines/Finnair
	OH-LKO	Embraer RJ190-100LR	Nordic Regional Airlines/Finnair
	OH-LKP	Embraer RJ190-100LR	Nordic Regional Airlines/Finnair
	OH-LKR	Embraer RJ190-100LR	Nordic Regional Airlines/Finnair
	OH-LTM	Airbus A.330-302	Finnair
	OH-LTN	Airbus A.330-302	Finnair
	OH-LTO	Airbus A.330-302	Finnair
	OH-LTP	Airbus A.330-302	Finnair
	OH-LTR	Airbus A.330-302	Finnair
	OH-LTS	Airbus A.330-302	Finnair
	OH-LTT	Airbus A.330-302	Finnair
	OH-LTU	Airbus A.330-302	Finnair
	OH-LVB	Airbus A.319-112	Finnair
	OH-LVC	Airbus A.319-112	Finnair
	OH-LVD	Airbus A.319-112	Finnair
	OH-LVH	Airbus A.319-112	Finnair
	OH-LVI	Airbus A.319-112	Finnair
	OH-LVK	Airbus A.319-112	Finnair
	OH-LVL	Airbus A.319-112	Finnair
	OH-LWA	Airbus A.350-941	Finnair
	OH-LWB	Airbus A.350-941	Finnair
	OH-LWC	Airbus A.350-941	Finnair
	OH-LWD	Airbus A.350-941	Finnair
	OH-LWE	Airbus A.350-941	Finnair
	OH-LWF	Airbus A.350-941	Finnair
	OH-LWG	Airbus A.350-941	Finnair
	OH-LWH	Airbus A.350-941	Finnair
	OH-LWI	Airbus A.350-941	Finnair
	OH-LWK	Airbus A.350-941	Finnair
	OH-LWL	Airbus A.350-941	Finnair
	OH-LWM	Airbus A.350-941	Finnair
	OH-LWN	Airbus A.350-941	Finnair
	OH-LWO	Airbus A.350-941	Finnair
	OH-LWP	Airbus A.350-941	Finnair
	OH-LWR	Airbus A.350-941	Finnair
	OH-LXA	Airbus A.320-214	Finnair

Reg	Type	Owner or Operator	Notes
OH-LXB	Airbus A.320-214	Finnair	
OH-LXC	Airbus A.320-214	Finnair	
OH-LXD	Airbus A.320-214	Finnair	
OH-LXF	Airbus A.320-214	Finnair	
OH-LXH	Airbus A.320-214	Finnair	
OH-LXI	Airbus A.320-214	Finnair	
OH-LXK	Airbus A.320-214	Finnair	
OH-LXL	Airbus A.320-214	Finnair	
OH-LXM	Airbus A.320-214	Finnair	
OH-LZA	Airbus A.321-211	Finnair	
OH-LZB	Airbus A.321-211	Finnair	
OH-LZC	Airbus A.321-211	Finnair	
OH-LZD	Airbus A.321-211	Finnair	
OH-LZE	Airbus A.321-211	Finnair	
OH-LZF	Airbus A.321-211	Finnair	
OH-LZG	Airbus A.321-231	Finnair	
OH-LZH	Airbus A.321-231	Finnair	
OH-LZI	Airbus A.321-231	Finnair	
OH-LZK	Airbus A.321-231	Finnair	
OH-LZL	Airbus A.321-231	Finnair	
OH-LZM	Airbus A.321-231	Finnair	
OH-LZN	Airbus A.321-231	Finnair	
OH-LZO	Airbus A.321-231	Finnair	
OH-LZP	Airbus A.321-231	Finnair	
OH-LZR	Airbus A.321-231	Finnair	
OH-LZS	Airbus A.321-231	Finnair	
OH-LZT	Airbus A.321-231	Finnair	
OH-LZU	Airbus A.321-231	Finnair	

OK (Czech Republic)

Reg	Type	Owner or Operator	Notes
OK-HEU	Airbus A.320-214	CSA Czech Airlines	
OK-REQ	Airbus A.319-112	CSA Czech Airlines	
OK-SWA	Boeing 737-MAX8	Smart Wings	
OK-SWB	Boeing 737-MAX8	Smart Wings	
OK-SWC	Boeing 737-MAX8	Smart Wings	
OK-SWD	Boeing 737-MAX8	Smart Wings	
OK-SWE	Boeing 737-MAX8	Smart Wings	
OK-SWF	Boeing 737-MAX8	Smart Wings	
OK-SWH	Boeing 737-MAX8	Smart Wings	
OK-SWI	Boeing 737-MAX8	Smart Wings	
OK-SWJ	Boeing 737-MAX8	Smart Wings	
OK-SWK	Boeing 737-MAX8	Smart Wings	
OK-SWL	Boeing 737-MAX8	Smart Wings	
OK-SWM	Boeing 737-MAX8	Smart Wings	
OK-SWN	Boeing 737-MAX8	Smart Wings	
OK-SWO	Boeing 737-MAX8	Smart Wings	
OK-SWP	Boeing 737-MAX8	Smart Wings	
OK-SWQ	Boeing 737-MAX8	Smart Wings	
OK-SWR	Boeing 737-MAX8	Smart Wings	
OK-SWS	Boeing 737-MAX8	Smart Wings	
OK-SWT	Boeing 737-7Q8	Smart Wings	
OK-SWU	Boeing 737-MAX8	Smart Wings	
OK-SWV	Boeing 737-MAX8	Smart Wings	
OK-SWW	Boeing 737-7Q8	Smart Wings	
OK-SWX	Boeing 737-MAX8	Smart Wings	
OK-TSE	Boeing 737-81D	Smart Wings	
OK-TSF	Boeing 737-8GJ	Smart Wings	
OK-TSI	Boeing 737-9GJ	Smart Wings	
OK-TSM	Boeing 737-9GJ	Smart Wings	
OK-TSO	Boeing 737-8GQ	Smart Wings	
OK-TSR	Boeing 737-82R	Smart Wings	
OK-TSS	Boeing 737-8Q8	Smart Wings	
OK-TST	Boeing 737-86N	Smart Wings	
OK-TSU	Boeing 737-8FZ	Smart Wings	
OK-TVF	Boeing 737-8FH	Smart Wings	
OK-TVG	Boeing 737-8Q8	Smart Wings	
OK-TVH	Boeing 737-8Q8	Smart Wings	
OK-TVJ	Boeing 737-8Q8	Smart Wings	
OK-TVL	Boeing 737-8FN	Smart Wings	
OK-TVM	Boeing 737-8FN	Smart Wings	

Notes	Reg	Type	Owner or Operator
	OK-TVO	Boeing 737-8CX	Smart Wings
	OK-TVP	Boeing 737-8K5	Smart Wings
	OK-TVR	Boeing 737-86N	Smart Wings
	OK-TVS	Boeing 737-86N	Smart Wings
	OK-TVT	Boeing 737-86N	Smart Wings
	OK-TVU	Boeing 737-86N	Smart Wings
	OK-TVV	Boeing 737-86N	Smart Wings
	OK-TVW	Boeing 737-86Q	Smart Wings
	OK-TVX	Boeing 737-8Z9	Smart Wings
	OK-TVY	Boeing 737-8Q8	Smart Wings

OM (Slovakia)

	OM-FEX	Boeing 737-8Q8	AirExplore
	OM-GEX	Boeing 737-8AS	AirExplore
	OM-HEX	Boeing 737-81Q	AirExplore
	OM-IEX	Boeing 737-8BK	AirExplore
	OM-JEX	Boeing 737-8AS	AirExplore
	OM-KEX	Boeing 737-8BK	AirExplore
	OM-LEX	Boeing 737-8BK	AirExplore
	OM-TSG	Boeing 737-82R	Smart Wings

OO (Belgium)

	OO-JAA	Boeing 737-8BK	TUI Airlines Belgium
	OO-JAF	Boeing 737-8K5	TUI Airlines Belgium
	OO-JAL	Boeing 737-7K2	TUI Airlines Belgium
	OO-JAO	Boeing 737-7K5	TUI Airlines Belgium
	OO-JAQ	Boeing 737-8K5	TUI Airlines Belgium
	OO-JAR	Boeing 737-7K5	TUI Airlines Belgium
	OO-JAS	Boeing 737-7K5	TUI Airlines Belgium
	OO-JAU	Boeing 737-8K5	TUI Airlines Belgium
	OO-JAV	Boeing 737-8K5	TUI Airlines Belgium
	OO-JAX	Boeing 737-8K5	TUI Airlines Belgium
	OO-JAY	Boeing 737-8K5	TUI Airlines Belgium
	OO-JBG	Boeing 737-8K5	TUI Airlines Belgium
	OO-JDL	Boeing 787-8K5	TUI Airlines Belgium
	OO-JEB	Embraer ERJ190-100STD	TUI Airlines Belgium
	OO-JEF	Boeing 737-8K5	TUI Airlines Belgium
	OO-JEM	Embraer ERJ190-100STD	TUI Airlines Belgium
	OO-JLO	Boeing 737-8K5	TUI Airlines Belgium
	OO-JNL	Boeing 767-304ER	TUI Airlines Belgium
	OO-JVA	Embraer ERJ190-100STD	TUI Airlines Belgium
	OO-LOE	Boeing 787-8	TUI Airlines Belgium
	OO-MAX	Boeing 737-8MAX	TUI Airlines Belgium
	OO-SNA	Airbus A.320-214	Brussels Airlines
	OO-SNB	Airbus A.320-214	Brussels Airlines
	OO-SNC	Airbus A.320-214	Brussels Airlines
	OO-SND	Airbus A.320-214	Brussels Airlines
	OO-SNE	Airbus A.320-214	Brussels Airlines
	OO-SNF	Airbus A.320-214	Brussels Airlines
	OO-SNH	Airbus A.320-214	Brussels Airlines
	OO-SNI	Airbus A.320-214	Brussels Airlines
	OO-SNJ	Airbus A.320-214	Brussels Airlines
	OO-SNK	Airbus A.320-214	Brussels Airlines
	OO-SNL	Airbus A.320-214	Brussels Airlines
	OO-SNM	Airbus A.320-214	Brussels Airlines
	OO-SNN	Airbus A.320-214	Brussels Airlines
	OO-SRO	Boeing 737-86N	TUI Airlines Belgium
	OO-SSA	Airbus A.319-111	Brussels Airlines
	OO-SSB	Airbus A.319-111	Brussels Airlines
	OO-SSE	Airbus A.319-111	Brussels Airlines
	OO-SSF	Airbus A.319-111	Brussels Airlines
	OO-SSH	Airbus A.319-112	Brussels Airlines
	OO-SSI	Airbus A.319-112	Brussels Airlines
	OO-SSJ	Airbus A.319-111	Brussels Airlines
	OO-SSK	Airbus A.319-112	Brussels Airlines
	OO-SSL	Airbus A.319-112	Brussels Airlines
	OO-SSM	Airbus A.319-112	Brussels Airlines
	OO-SSN	Airbus A.319-112	Brussels Airlines

Reg	Type	Owner or Operator	Notes
OO-SSO	Airbus A.319-111	Brussels Airlines	
OO-SSQ	Airbus A.319-112	Brussels Airlines	
OO-SSR	Airbus A.319-112	Brussels Airlines	
OO-SSS	Airbus A.319-111	Brussels Airlines	
OO-SSU	Airbus A.319-111	Brussels Airlines	
OO-SSV	Airbus A.319-111	Brussels Airlines	
OO-SSW	Airbus A.319-111	Brussels Airlines	
OO-SSX	Airbus A.319-111	Brussels Airlines	
OO-TCH	Airbus A.320-214	Brussels Airlines	
OO-TCQ	Airbus A.320-214	Brussels Airlines	
OO-TCV	Airbus A.320-212	Brussels Airlines	
OO-TEA	Embraer ERJ190-100LR	TUI Airlines Belgium	
OO-TFC	Boeing 757-222	ASL Airlines Belgium	
OO-TMA	Boeing 737-MAX8	TUI Airlines Belgium	
OO-TMB	Boeing 737-MAX8	TUI Airlines Belgium	
OO-TMY	Boeing 737-MAX8	TUI Airlines Belgium	
OO-TNB	Boeing 737-8K5	TUI Airlines Belgium	
OO-TNC	Boeing 737-8K5	TUI Airlines Belgium	
OO-TNN	Boeing 737-45D	ASL Airlines Belgium/Federal Express	
OO-TNO	Boeing 737-49RF	ASL Airlines Belgium	
OO-TNP	Boeing 737-45D	ASL Airlines Belgium/Federal Express	
OO-TNQ	Boeing 737-4MOF	ASL Airlines Belgium	
OO-TUK	Boeing 737-86J	TUI Airlines Belgium	
OO-TUP	Boeing 737-85P	TUI Airlines Belgium	
OO-TUV	Boeing 737-86J	TUI Airlines Belgium	
OO-TUX	Boeing 737-86N	TUI Airlines Belgium	
OO-VLS	Fokker 50	Air Antwerp	

OY (Denmark)

Reg	Type	Owner or Operator	Notes
OY-JRK	Airbus A.320-231	Danish Air Transport	
OY-KAL	Airbus A.320-232	SAS *Jon Viking*	
OY-KAM	Airbus A.320-232	SAS *Randver Viking*	
OY-KAN	Airbus A.320-232	SAS *Refil Viking*	
OY-KAO	Airbus A.320-232	SAS *Amled Viking*	
OY-KAP	Airbus A.320-232	SAS *Viglek Viking*	
OY-KAR	Airbus A.320-232	SAS *Vermund Viking*	
OY-KAS	Airbus A.320-232	SAS *Igulfsast Viking*	
OY-KAT	Airbus A.320-232	SAS *Hildegun Viking*	
OY-KAU	Airbus A.320-232	SAS *Hjorvard Viking*	
OY-KAW	Airbus A.320-232	SAS *Tyke Viking*	
OY-KAY	Airbus A.320-232	SAS *Runar Viking*	
OY-KBB	Airbus A.321-231	SAS *Hjorulf Viking*	
OY-KBE	Airbus A.321-231	SAS *Emma Viking*	
OY-KBF	Airbus A.321-231	SAS *Skapti Viking*	
OY-KBH	Airbus A.321-231	SAS *Sulke Viking*	
OY-KBK	Airbus A.321-231	SAS *Arne Viking*	
OY-KBL	Airbus A.321-231	SAS *Gynnbjorn Viking*	
OY-KBO	Airbus A.319-132	SAS *Christian Valdemar Viking*	
OY-KBP	Airbus A.319-132	SAS *Viger Viking*	
OY-KBR	Airbus A.319-132	SAS *Finnboge Viking*	
OY-KBT	Airbus A.319-132	SAS *Ragnvald Viking*	
OY-NCI	Dornier 328-300 JET	Sun-Air/British Airways	
OY-NCL	Dornier 328-300 JET	Sun-Air/British Airways	
OY-NCM	Dornier 328-300 JET	Sun-Air/British Airways	
OY-NCN	Dornier 328-300 JET	Sun-Air/British Airways	
OY-NCO	Dornier 328-300 JET	Sun-Air/British Airways	
OY-NCP	Dornier 328-300 JET	Sun-Air/British Airways	
OY-NCU	Dornier 328-300 JET	Sun-Air/British Airways	
OY-NCW	Dornier 328-300 JET	Sun-Air/British Airways	
OY-RCG	Airbus A.319-112	Atlantic Airways	
OY-RCJ	Airbus A.320-214	Atlantic Airways	
OY-RCK	Airbus A.320-251N	Atlantic Airways	
OY-RCL	Airbus A.320-251N	Atlantic Airways	
OY-RUE	McD Douglas MD-83	Danish Air Transport	
OY-RUT	McD Douglas MD-82	Danish Air Transport	
OY-RUU	Airbus A.321-231	Danish Air Transport	
OY-RUZ	Airbus A.320-232	Danish Air Transport	
OY-SRF	Boeing 767-219 (SF)	Star Air	
OY-SRG	Boeing 767-219 (SF)	Star Air	
OY-SRH	Boeing 767-204 (SF)	Star Air	

Notes	Reg	Type	Owner or Operator
	OY-SRI	Boeing 767-25E (SF)	Star Air
	OY-SRJ	Boeing 767-25E (SF)	Star Air
	OY-SRK	Boeing 767-204 (SF)	Star Air
	OY-SRL	Boeing 767-232 (SF)	Star Air
	OY-SRM	Boeing 767-25E (SF)	Star Air
	OY-SRN	Boeing 767-219 (SF)	Star Air
	OY-SRO	Boeing 767-25E (SF)	Star Air
	OY-SRP	Boeing 767-232 (SF)	Star Air
	OY-SRU	Boeing 767-36NER	Star Air
	OY-SRV	Boeing 767-346ERF	Star Air
	OY-SRW	Boeing 767-346ERF	Star Air

P4 (Aruba)

Notes	Reg	Type	Owner or Operator
	P4-KGA	Airbus A.321-271NX	Air Astana
	P4-KGB	Airbus A.321-271NX	Air Astana
	P4-KGC	Airbus A.321-271NX	Air Astana
	P4-KGD	Airbus A.321-271NX	Air Astana
	P4-KGE	Airbus A.321-271NX	Air Astana

PH (Netherlands)

Notes	Reg	Type	Owner or Operator
	PH-AKA	Airbus A.330-303	KLM *Times Square – New York*
	PH-AKB	Airbus A.330-303	KLM *Piazza Navona-Roma*
	PH-AKD	Airbus A.330-303	KLM *Plaza de la Catedral-La Habana*
	PH-AKE	Airbus A.330-303	KLM *Pracia de Rossio-Lisboa*
	PH-AKF	Airbus A.330-303	KLM *Hofplein-Rotterdam*
	PH-AOA	Airbus A.330-203	KLM *Dam – Amsterdam*
	PH-AOB	Airbus A.330-203	KLM *Potsdamer Platz - Berlin*
	PH-AOC	Airbus A.330-203	KLM *Place de la Concorde – Paris*
	PH-AOD	Airbus A.330-203	KLM *Plazza del Duomo – Milano*
	PH-AOE	Airbus A.330-203	KLM *Parliament Square - Edinburgh*
	PH-AOF	Airbus A.330-203	KLM *Federation Square – Melbourne*
	PH-AOM	Airbus A.330-203	KLM *Piazza San Marco-Venezia*
	PH-AON	Airbus A.330-203	KLM *Museumplein-Amsterdam*
	PH-BCA	Boeing 737-8K2	KLM *Flamingo*
	PH-BCB	Boeing 737-8BK	KLM *Grote Pijlstormvogel/Great Shearwater*
	PH-BCD	Boeing 737-8BK	KLM
	PH-BCE	Boeing 737-8CK	KLM *Blauwborst/Bluethroat*
	PH-BCG	Boeing 737-8K2	KLM *Ivoormeeuw/Ivory Gull*
	PH-BCH	Boeing 737-8K2	KLM *Nightjar/Nachtzwaluw*
	PH-BCK	Boeing 737-8K2	KLM *Amsterdamalbatros/Amsterdam Albatross*
	PH-BCL	Boeing 737-8K2	KLM *Krooneend/Red-Crested Pochard*
	PH-BGA	Boeing 737-8K2	KLM *Tureluur/Redshank*
	PH-BGB	Boeing 737-8K2	KLM *Whimbrel/Regenwulg*
	PH-BGC	Boeing 737-8K2	KLM *Pijlstaart/Pintail*
	PH-BGF	Boeing 737-7K2	KLM *Great White Heron/Grote Ziverreiger*
	PH-BGG	Boeing 737-706	KLM *King Eider/Koening Seider*
	PH-BGH	Boeing 737-7K2	KLM *Grutto/Godwit*
	PH-BGI	Boeing 737-7K2	KLM *Vink/Finch*
	PH-BGK	Boeing 737-7K2	KLM *Noordse Stormvogel/Fulmar*
	PH-BGL	Boeing 737-7K2	KLM *Rietzangler/Warbler*
	PH-BGM	Boeing 737-7K2	KLM *Aabscholver/Cormorant*
	PH-BGN	Boeing 737-7K2	KLM *Jan van Gent/Gannet*
	PH-BGO	Boeing 737-7K2	KLM *Paradijsvogel/Bird of Paradise*
	PH-BGP	Boeing 737-7K2	KLM *Pelikaan/Pelican*
	PH-BGQ	Boeing 737-7K2	KLM *Wielewaal/Golden Oriole*
	PH-BGR	Boeing 737-7K2	KLM *Zwarte Wouw/Black Kite*
	PH-BGT	Boeing 737-7K2	KLM *Zanglijster/Song Thrush*
	PH-BGU	Boeing 737-7K2	KLM *Koekoek/Cuckoo*
	PH-BGW	Boeing 737-7K2	KLM *Zanglijster/Song Thrush*
	PH-BGX	Boeing 737-7K2	KLM *Scholekster/Oystercatcher*
	PH-BHA	Boeing 787-9	KLM *Anjer/Crnation*
	PH-BHC	Boeing 787-9	KLM *Zonnebloem/Sunflower*
	PH-BHD	Boeing 787-9	KLM *Bougainville*
	PH-BHE	Boeing 787-9	KLM *Dahlia*
	PH-BHF	Boeing 787-9	KLM *Hisbiscus*
	PH-BHG	Boeing 787-9	KLM *Mimosa*
	PH-BHH	Boeing 787-9	KLM *Jasmine*

Reg	Type	Owner or Operator	Notes
PH-BHI	Boeing 787-9	KLM *Lavender*	
PH-BHL	Boeing 787-9	KLM *Lily*	
PH-BHM	Boeing 787-9	KLM *Marguerite*	
PH-BHN	Boeing 787-9	KLM *Morning Star*	
PH-BHO	Boeing 787-9	KLM *Orchid*	
PH-BHP	Boeing 787-9	KLM *Tulip*	
PH-BKA	Boeing 787-10	KLM *Orange Blossom*	
PH-BKC	Boeing 787-10	KLM *Busy Lizzie*	
PH-BKD	Boeing 787-10	KLM *Heavenly Blue*	
PH-BKF	Boeing 787-10	KLM *Snowdrop*	
PH-BKG	Boeing 787-10	KLM *Hyacinth*	
PH-BKH	Boeing 787-10	KLM *White Lotus*	
PH-BKI	Boeing 787-10	KLM	
PH-BKK	Boeing 787-10	KLM	
PH-BQA	Boeing 777-206ER	KLM *Albert Plesman*	
PH-BQB	Boeing 777-206ER	KLM *Borobudur*	
PH-BQC	Boeing 777-206ER	KLM *Chichen-Itza*	
PH-BQD	Boeing 777-206ER	KLM *Darjeeling Highway*	
PH-BQE	Boeing 777-206ER	KLM *Epidaurus*	
PH-BQF	Boeing 777-206ER	KLM *Ferrara City*	
PH-BQG	Boeing 777-206ER	KLM *Galapagos Islands*	
PH-BQH	Boeing 777-206ER	KLM *Hadrian's Wall*	
PH-BQI	Boeing 777-206ER	KLM *Iguazu Falls*	
PH-BQK	Boeing 777-206ER	KLM *Mount Kilimanjaro*	
PH-BQL	Boeing 777-206ER	KLM *Litomysl Castle*	
PH-BQM	Boeing 777-206ER	KLM *Macchu Picchu*	
PH-BQN	Boeing 777-206ER	KLM *Nahanni National Park*	
PH-BQO	Boeing 777-206ER	KLM *Old Rauma*	
PH-BQP	Boeing 777-206ER	KLM *Pont du Gard*	
PH-BVA	Boeing 777-306ER	KLM *National Park De Hoge Veluwe*	
PH-BVB	Boeing 777-306ER	KLM *Fulufjallet National Park*	
PH-BVC	Boeing 777-306ER	KLM *National ParkSian Ka'an*	
PH-BVD	Boeing 777-306ER	KLM *Amboseli National Park*	
PH-BVF	Boeing 777-306ER	KLM *Yakushima*	
PH-BVG	Boeing 777-306ER	KLM *National Park Wolong*	
PH-BVI	Boeing 777-306ER	KLM *Nationaal Park Vuurland*	
PH-BVK	Boeing 777-306ER	KLM *Yellowstone National Park*	
PH-BVN	Boeing 777-306ER	KLM *Tijuca National Park*	
PH-BVO	Boeing 777-306ER	KLM *Kaziranga National Park*	
PH-BVP	Boeing 777-306ER	KLM *Jasper National Park*	
PH-BVR	Boeing 777-306ER	KLM *Gunung Mulu National Park*	
PH-BVS	Boeing 777-306ER	KLM *Darien National Park*	
PH-BVU	Boeing 777-300ER	KLM *Grand Canyon National Park*	
PH-BVV	Boeing 777-300ER	KLM *Cocos Island National Park*	
PH-BVW	Boeing 777-300ER	KLM	
PH-BXA	Boeing 737-8K2	KLM *Zwaan/Swan*	
PH-BXB	Boeing 737-8K2	KLM *Valk/Falcon*	
PH-BXC	Boeing 737-8K2	KLM *Korhoen/Grouse*	
PH-BXD	Boeing 737-8K2	KLM *Arend/Eagle*	
PH-BXE	Boeing 737-8K2	KLM *Harvik/Hawk*	
PH-BXF	Boeing 737-8K2	KLM *Zwallou/Swallow*	
PH-BXG	Boeing 737-8K2	KLM *Kraanvogel/Crane*	
PH-BXH	Boeing 737-8K2	KLM *Gans/Goose*	
PH-BXI	Boeing 737-8K2	KLM *Zilvermeeuw*	
PH-BXK	Boeing 737-8K2	KLM *Gierzwallou/Swift*	
PH-BXL	Boeing 737-8K2	KLM *Sperwer/Sparrow*	
PH-BXM	Boeing 737-8K2	KLM *Kluut/Avocet*	
PH-BXN	Boeing 737-8K2	KLM *Merel/Blackbird*	
PH-BXO	Boeing 737-9K2	KLM *Plevier/Plover*	
PH-BXP	Boeing 737-9K2	KLM *Meerkoet/Crested Coot*	
PH-BXR	Boeing 737-9K2	KLM *Nachtegaal/Nightingale*	
PH-BXS	Boeing 737-9K2	KLM *Buizerd/Buzzard*	
PH-BXT	Boeing 737-9K2	KLM *Zeestern/Sea Tern*	
PH-BXU	Boeing 737-8BK	KLM *Albatros/Albatross*	
PH-BXV	Boeing 737-8K2	KLM *Roodborstje*	
PH-BXW	Boeing 737-8K2	KLM *Patrijs/Partridge*	
PH-BXY	Boeing 737-8K2	KLM *Fuut/Grebe*	
PH-BXZ	Boeing 737-8K2	KLM *Uil/Owl*	
PH-CKA	Boeing 747-406ERF	KLM Cargo *Eendracht*	
PH-CKB	Boeing 747-406ERF	KLM Cargo *Leeuwin*	
PH-CKC	Boeing 747-406ERF	KLM Cargo *Oranje*	

Notes	Reg	Type	Owner or Operator
	PH-EXA	Embraer ERJ190-100STD	KLM Cityhopper
	PH-EXB	Embraer ERJ190-100STD	KLM Cityhopper
	PH-EXC	Embraer ERJ190-100STD	KLM Cityhopper
	PH-EXD	Embraer ERJ190-100STD	KLM Cityhopper
	PH-EXE	Embraer ERJ190-100STD	KLM Cityhopper
	PH-EXF	Embraer ERJ190-100STD	KLM Cityhopper
	PH-EXG	Embraer ERJ170-200STD	KLM Cityhopper
	PH-EXH	Embraer ERJ170-200STD	KLM Cityhopper
	PH-EXI	Embraer ERJ170-200STD	KLM Cityhopper
	PH-EXJ	Embraer ERJ170-200STD	KLM Cityhopper
	PH-EXK	Embraer ERJ170-200STD	KLM Cityhopper
	PH-EXL	Embraer ERJ170-200STD	KLM Cityhopper
	PH-EXM	Embraer ERJ170-200STD	KLM Cityhopper
	PH-EXN	Embraer ERJ170-200STD	KLM Cityhopper
	PH-EXO	Embraer ERJ170-200STD	KLM Cityhopper
	PH-EXP	Embraer ERJ170-200STD	KLM Cityhopper
	PH-EXR	Embraer ERJ170-200STD	KLM Cityhopper
	PH-EXS	Embraer ERJ170-200STD	KLM Cityhopper
	PH-EXT	Embraer ERJ170-200STD	KLM Cityhopper
	PH-EXU	Embraer ERJ170-200STD	KLM Cityhopper
	PH-EXV	Embraer ERJ190-100STD	KLM Cityhopper
	PH-EXW	Embraer ERJ170-200STD	KLM Cityhopper
	PH-EXX	Embraer ERJ170-200STD	KLM Cityhopper
	PH-EXY	Embraer ERJ190-100STD	KLM Cityhopper
	PH-EXZ	Embraer ERJ170-200STD	KLM Cityhopper
	PH-EZA	Embraer ERJ190-100STD	KLM Cityhopper
	PH-EZB	Embraer ERJ190-100STD	KLM Cityhopper
	PH-EZC	Embraer ERJ190-100STD	KLM Cityhopper
	PH-EZD	Embraer ERJ190-100STD	KLM Cityhopper
	PH-EZE	Embraer ERJ190-100STD	KLM Cityhopper
	PH-EZF	Embraer ERJ190-100STD	KLM Cityhopper
	PH-EZG	Embraer ERJ190-100STD	KLM Cityhopper
	PH-EZH	Embraer ERJ190-100STD	KLM Cityhopper
	PH-EZI	Embraer ERJ190-100STD	KLM Cityhopper
	PH-EZK	Embraer ERJ190-100STD	KLM Cityhopper
	PH-EZL	Embraer ERJ190-100STD	KLM Cityhopper
	PH-EZM	Embraer ERJ190-100STD	KLM Cityhopper
	PH-EZN	Embraer ERJ190-100STD	KLM Cityhopper
	PH-EZO	Embraer ERJ190-100STD	KLM Cityhopper
	PH-EZP	Embraer ERJ190-100STD	KLM Cityhopper
	PH-EZR	Embraer ERJ190-100STD	KLM Cityhopper
	PH-EZS	Embraer ERJ190-100STD	KLM Cityhopper
	PH-EZT	Embraer ERJ190-100STD	KLM Cityhopper
	PH-EZU	Embraer ERJ190-100STD	KLM Cityhopper
	PH-EZV	Embraer ERJ190-100STD	KLM Cityhopper
	PH-EZW	Embraer ERJ190-100STD	KLM Cityhopper
	PH-EZX	Embraer ERJ190-100STD	KLM Cityhopper
	PH-EZY	Embraer ERJ190-100STD	KLM Cityhopper
	PH-EZZ	Embraer ERJ190-100STD	KLM Cityhopper
	PH-HSA	Boeing 737-8K2	Transavia
	PH-HSB	Boeing 737-8K2	Transavia
	PH-HSC	Boeing 737-8K2	Transavia
	PH-HSD	Boeing 737-8K2	KLM *Groene Specht*
	PH-HSE	Boeing 737-8K2	KLM *Blauwstaart*
	PH-HSF	Boeing 737-8K2	Transavia
	PH-HSG	Boeing 737-8K2	Transavia
	PH-HSI	Boeing 737-8K2	Transavia
	PH-HSJ	Boeing 737-8K2	Transavia
	PH-HSK	Boeing 737-8K2	Transavia
	PH-HSM	Boeing 737-8K2	Transavia
	PH-HSW	Boeing 737-8K2	Transavia
	PH-HXA	Boeing 737-8K2	Transavia
	PH-HXB	Boeing 737-8K2	Transavia
	PH-HXC	Boeing 737-8K2	Transavia
	PH-HXD	Boeing 737-8K2	Transavia
	PH-HXE	Boeing 737-8K2	Transavia
	PH-HXF	Boeing 737-8K2	Transavia
	PH-HXG	Boeing 737-8K2	Transavia
	PH-HXI	Boeing 737-8K2	Transavia
	PH-HXJ	Boeing 737-8K2	Transavia
	PH-HXK	Boeing 737-8K2	Transavia

Reg	Type	Owner or Operator	Notes
PH-HXL	Boeing 737-8K2	Transavia	
PH-HXM	Boeing 737-8K2	Transavia	
PH-HXN	Boeing 737-8K2	Transavia	
PH-HXO	Boeing 737-8K2	Transavia	
PH-HZD	Boeing 737-8K2	Transavia	
PH-HZE	Boeing 737-8K2	Transavia	
PH-HZG	Boeing 737-8K2	Transavia	
PH-HZI	Boeing 737-8K2	Transavia	
PH-HZJ	Boeing 737-8K2	Transavia	
PH-HZL	Boeing 737-8K2	Transavia	
PH-HZN	Boeing 737-8K2	Transavia	
PH-HZO	Boeing 737-8K2	Transavia	
PH-HZV	Boeing 737-8K2	Transavia	
PH-HZW	Boeing 737-8K2	Transavia	
PH-HZX	Boeing 737-8K2	Transavia	
PH-MPS	Boeing 747-412BCF	Martinair Cargo	
PH-OYI	Boeing 767-304ER	TUI Airlines Nederland	
PH-TFA	Boeing 737-8FH	TUI Airlines Nederland	
PH-TFK	Boeing 787-8	TUI Airlines Nederland	
PH-TFL	Boeing 787-8	TUI Airlines Nederland	
PH-TFM	Boeing 787-8	TUI Airlines Nederland	
PH-TFN	Boeing 737-MAX8	TUI Airlines Nederland	
PH-TFO	Boeing 737-MAX8	TUI Airlines Nederland	
PH-TFP	Boeing 737-MAX8	TUI Airlines Nederland	
PH-TFR	Boeing 737-MAX8	TUI Airlines Nederland	
PH-TFT	Boeing 737-MAX8	TUI Airlines Nederland	
PH-TFU	Boeing 737-MAX8	TUI Airlines Nederland	
PH-XRB	Boeing 737-7K2	Transavia	
PH-XRC	Boeing 737-7K2	Transavia	
PH-XRD	Boeing 737-7K2	Transavia	
PH-XRX	Boeing 737-7K2	Transavia	
PH-XRY	Boeing 737-7K2	Transavia	

PP/PR/PT (Brazil)

Reg	Type	Owner or Operator	Notes
PR-XTC	Airbus A.350-941	LATAM Airlines	
PR-XTD	Airbus A.350-941	LATAM Airlines	
PR-XTE	Airbus A.350-941	LATAM Airlines	
PR-XTH	Airbus A.350-941	LATAM Airlines	
PR-XTI	Airbus A.350-941	LATAM Airlines	
PR-XTJ	Airbus A.350-941	LATAM Airlines	
PR-XTK	Airbus A.350-941	LATAM Airlines	
PR-XTL	Airbus A.350-941	LATAM Airlines	
PR-XTM	Airbus A.350-941	LATAM Airlines	
PT-MUA	Boeing 777-32WER	LATAM Airlines	
PT-MUB	Boeing 777-32WER	LATAM Airlines	
PT-MUC	Boeing 777-32WER	LATAM Airlines	
PT-MUD	Boeing 777-32WER	LATAM Airlines	
PT-MUE	Boeing 777-32WER	LATAM Airlines	
PT-MUF	Boeing 777-32WER	LATAM Airlines	
PT-MUG	Boeing 777-32WER	LATAM Airlines	
PT-MUH	Boeing 777-32WER	LATAM Airlines	
PT-MUI	Boeing 777-32WER	LATAM Airlines	
PT-MUJ	Boeing 777-32WER	LATAM Airlines	

RA (Russia)

Reg	Type	Owner or Operator	Notes
RA-82042	An-124	Volga-Dnepr	
RA-82043	An-124	Volga-Dnepr	
RA-82044	An-124	Volga-Dnepr	
RA-82045	An-124	Volga-Dnepr	
RA-82046	An-124	Volga-Dnepr	
RA-82047	An-124	Volga-Dnepr	
RA-82068	An-124	Volga-Dnepr	
RA-82074	An-124	Volga-Dnepr	
RA-82077	An-124	Volga-Dnepr	
RA-82078	An-124	Volga-Dnepr	
RA-82079	An-124	Volga-Dnepr	
RA-82081	An-124	Volga-Dnepr	
RA-76503	Ilyushin Il-76TD	Volga-Dnepr	

Notes	Reg	Type	Owner or Operator
	RA-76511	Ilyushin Il-76TD	Volga-Dnepr
	RA-76950	Ilyushin Il-76TD	Volga-Dnepr
	RA-76951	Ilyushin Il-76TD	Volga-Dnepr
	RA-76952	Ilyushin Il-76TD	Volga-Dnepr

RP (Philippines)

	RP-C3501	Airbus A.350-941	Philippine Airlines
	RP-C3503	Airbus A.350-941	Philippine Airlines
	RP-C3504	Airbus A.350-941	Philippine Airlines
	RP-C3506	Airbus A.350-941	Philippine Airlines
	RP-C3507	Airbus A.350-941	Philippine Airlines
	RP-C3508	Airbus A.350-941	Philippine Airlines
	RP-C7772	Boeing 777-3F6ER	Philippine Airlines
	RP-C7773	Boeing 777-3F6ER	Philippine Airlines
	RP-C7774	Boeing 777-3F6ER	Philippine Airlines
	RP-C7775	Boeing 777-3F6ER	Philippine Airlines
	RP-C7776	Boeing 777-36NER	Philippine Airlines
	RP-C7777	Boeing 777-36NER	Philippine Airlines
	RP-C7778	Boeing 777-3F6ER	Philippine Airlines
	RP-C7779	Boeing 777-3F6ER	Philippine Airlines
	RP-C7781	Boeing 777-3F6ER	Philippine Airlines
	RP-C7782	Boeing 777-3F6ER	Philippine Airlines

S2 (Bangladesh)

	S2-AFO	Boeing 777-3E9ER	Bangladesh Biman
	S2-AFP	Boeing 777-3E9ER	Bangladesh Biman
	S2-AHM	Boeing 777-3E9ER	Bangladesh Biman
	S2-AHN	Boeing 777-3E9ER	Bangladesh Biman
	S2-AJS	Boeing 787-8	Bangladesh Biman
	S2-AJT	Boeing 787-8	Bangladesh Biman
	S2-AJU	Boeing 787-8	Bangladesh Biman
	S2-AJV	Boeing 787-8	Bangladesh Biman
	S2-AJX	Boeing 787-9	Bangladesh Biman
	S2-AJY	Boeing 787-9	Bangladesh Biman

SE (Sweden)

	SE-DMO	Airbus A.321-253NX	SAS *Jarl Viking*
	SE-DOX	Airbus A.320-251N	SAS *Torarve Viking*
	SE-DOY	Airbus A.320-251N	SAS *Markus Viking*
	SE-DOZ	Airbus A.320-251N	SAS *Jarngerd Viking*
	SE-DYC	Airbus A.320-251N	SAS *Ulv Viking*
	SE-DYD	Airbus A.320-251N	SAS
	SE-DYM	Airbus A.320-251N	SAS
	SE-KXP	BAe ATP	West Air Sweden
	SE-LGX	BAe ATP	West Air Sweden
	SE-LGZ	BAe ATP	West Air Sweden
	SE-LPS	BAe ATP	West Air Sweden
	SE-MAI	BAe ATP	West Air Sweden
	SE-MAJ	BAe ATP	West Air Sweden
	SE-MAM	BAe ATP	West Air Sweden
	SE-MAN	BAe ATP	West Air Sweden
	SE-MAO	BAe ATP	West Air Sweden
	SE-MAP	BAe ATP	West Air Sweden
	SE-MHD	BAe ATP	West Air Sweden
	SE-MHK	BAe ATP	West Air Sweden
	SE-REH	Airbus A.330-343E	SAS *Birk Viking*
	SE-RES	Boeing 737-7BX	SAS *Rut Viking*
	SE-RET	Boeing 737-76N	SAS *Katarina Viking*
	SE-REU	Boeing 737-76N	SAS *Folke Viking*
	SE-REX	Boeing 737-76N	SAS *Lodin Viking*
	SE-RFM	Boeing 737-8K5	TUIfly Nordic
	SE-RFN	Boeing 737-8K5	TUIfly Nordic
	SE-RFR	Boeing 767-38AER	TUIfly Nordic
	SE-RFX	Boeing 737-8K5	TUIfly Nordic
	SE-RJT	Boeing 737-76N	SAS *Tora Viking*
	SE-RJU	Boeing 737-76N	SAS *Ubbe Viking*
	SE-RJX	Boeing 737-76N	SAS *Vagn Viking*

Reg	Type	Owner or Operator	Notes
SE-RKA	Airbus A.321-251N	Novair	
SE-RKB	Airbus A.321-251N	Novair	
SE-RLK	Boeing 737-83NF	West Air Sweden	
SE-RLL	Boeing 737-83NF	West Air Sweden	
SE-RLM	Boeing 737-83NF	West Air Sweden	
SE-RNA	Boeing 737-MAX8	TUIfly Nordic	
SE-RNB	Boeing 737-MAX8	TUIfly Nordic	
SE-RNC	Boeing 767-304ER	TUIfly Nordic	
SE-ROA	Airbus A.320-251N	SAS	
SE-ROB	Airbus A.320-251N	SAS	
SE-ROC	Airbus A.320-251N	SAS	
SE-ROD	Airbus A.320-251N	SAS	
SE-ROE	Airbus A.320-251N	SAS	
SE-ROF	Airbus A.320-251N	SAS	
SE-ROG	Airbus A.320-251N	SAS	
SE-ROH	Airbus A.320-251N	SAS	
SE-ROI	Airbus A.320-251N	SAS	
SE-ROJ	Airbus A.320-251N	SAS	
SE-ROK	Airbus A.320-251N	SAS	
SE-ROL	Airbus A.320-251N	SAS	
SE-ROM	Airbus A.320-251N	SAS	
SE-RON	Airbus A.320-251N	SAS	
SE-ROO	Airbus A.320-251N	SAS	
SE-ROP	Airbus A.320-251N	SAS	
SE-ROR	Airbus A.320-251N	SAS	
SE-ROS	Airbus A.320-251N	SAS	
SE-ROT	Airbus A.320-251N	SAS	
SE-ROU	Airbus A.320-251N	SAS	
SE-ROX	Airbus A.320-251N	SAS	
SE-ROY	Airbus A.320-251N	SAS	
SE-ROZ	Airbus A.320-251N	SAS	
SE-RPA	Boeing 737-8JP	Norwegian Air Sweden AB	
SE-RPD	Boeing 737-8JP	Norwegian Air Sweden AB	
SE-RPE	Boeing 737-8JP	Norwegian Air Sweden AB	
SE-RPF	Boeing 737-8JP	Norwegian Air Sweden AB	
SE-RPG	Boeing 737-8JP	Norwegian Air Sweden AB	
SE-RPH	Boeing 737-8JP	Norwegian Air Sweden AB	
SE-RPI	Boeing 737-8JP	Norwegian Air Sweden AB	
SE-RPJ	Boeing 737-8JP	Norwegian Air Sweden AB	
SE-RPK	Boeing 737-8JP	Norwegian Air Sweden AB	
SE-RPL	Boeing 737-8JP	Norwegian Air Sweden AB	
SE-RPM	Boeing 737-8JP	Norwegian Air Sweden AB	
SE-RPR	Boeing 737-8JP	Norwegian Air Sweden AB	
SE-RPS	Boeing 737-8JP	Norwegian Air Sweden AB	
SE-RPT	Boeing 737-8JP	Norwegian Air Sweden AB	
SE-RPU	Boeing 737-8JP	Norwegian Air Sweden AB	
SE-RPX	Boeing 737-8JP	Norwegian Air Sweden AB	
SE-RRA	Boeing 737-8JP	Norwegian Air Sweden AB	
SE-RRB	Boeing 737-8JP	Norwegian Air Sweden AB	
SE-RRC	Boeing 737-8JP	Norwegian Air Sweden AB	
SE-RRD	Boeing 737-8JP	Norwegian Air Sweden AB	
SE-RRE	Boeing 737-8JP	Norwegian Air Sweden AB	
SE-RRF	Boeing 737-8JP	Norwegian Air Sweden AB	
SE-RRG	Boeing 737-8JP	Norwegian Air Sweden AB	
SE-RRH	Boeing 737-8JP	Norwegian Air Sweden AB	
SE-RRI	Boeing 737-8JP	Norwegian Air Sweden AB	
SE-RRJ	Boeing 737-8JP	Norwegian Air Sweden AB	
SE-RRN	Boeing 737-8JP	Norwegian Air Sweden AB	
SE-RRO	Boeing 737-8JP	Norwegian Air Sweden AB	
SE-RRP	Boeing 737-8JP	Norwegian Air Sweden AB	
SE-RRS	Boeing 737-8JP	Norwegian Air Sweden AB	
SE-RRY	Boeing 737-8JP	Norwegian Air Sweden AB	
SE-RRZ	Boeing 737-8JP	Norwegian Air Sweden AB	
SE-RSA	Airbus A.350-941	SAS	
SE-RSB	Airbus A.350-941	SAS	
SE-RSC	Airbus A.350-941	SAS	
SE-RSD	Airbus A.350-941	SAS	
SE-RTA	Boeing 737-MAX8	Norwegian Air Sweden AB	
SE-RTB	Boeing 737-MAX8	Norwegian Air Sweden AB	
SE-RTC	Boeing 737-MAX8	Norwegian Air Sweden AB	
SE-RTD	Boeing 737-MAX8	Norwegian Air Sweden AB	

Notes	Reg	Type	Owner or Operator
	SE-RTE	Boeing 737-MAX8	Norwegian Air Sweden AB
	SE-RTF	Boeing 737-MAX8	Norwegian Air Sweden AB
	SE-RTG	Boeing 737-MAX8	Norwegian Air Sweden AB
	SE-RTH	Boeing 737-MAX8	Norwegian Air Sweden AB
	SE-RTI	Boeing 737-MAX8	Norwegian Air Sweden AB
	SE-RTJ	Boeing 737-MAX8	Norwegian Air Sweden AB
	SE-RTK	Boeing 737-MAX8	Norwegian Air Sweden AB
	SE-RTL	Boeing 737-MAX8	Norwegian Air Sweden AB
	SE-RTM	Boeing 737-MAX8	Norwegian Air Sweden AB
	SE-RTN	Boeing 737-MAX8	Norwegian Air Sweden AB
	SE-RTO	Boeing 737-MAX8	Norwegian Air Sweden AB
	SE-RTP	Boeing 737-MAX8	Norwegian Air Sweden AB
	SE-RUA	Airbus A.320-251N	SAS
	SE-RUB	Airbus A.320-251N	SAS
	SE-RUC	Airbus A.320-251N	SAS
	SE-RUD	Airbus A.320-251N	SAS
	SE-RUE	Airbus A.320-251N	SAS
	SE-RUF	Airbus A.320-251N	SAS
	SE-RYA	Boeing 737-MAX8	Norwegian Air Sweden AB
	SE-RYB	Boeing 737-MAX8	Norwegian Air Sweden AB
	SE-RYC	Boeing 737-MAX8	Norwegian Air Sweden AB
	SE-RYF	Boeing 737-MAX8	Norwegian Air Sweden AB
	SE-RYG	Boeing 737-MAX8	Norwegian Air Sweden AB
	SE-RYH	Boeing 737-MAX8	Norwegian Air Sweden AB
	SE-RYI	Boeing 737-MAX8	Norwegian Air Sweden AB
	SE-RYJ	Boeing 737-MAX8	Norwegian Air Sweden AB
	SE-RYK	Boeing 737-MAX8	Norwegian Air Sweden AB
	SE-RYL	Boeing 737-MAX8	Norwegian Air Sweden AB

SP (Poland)

Notes	Reg	Type	Owner or Operator
	SP-ENG	Boeing 737-8CX	Enter Air
	SP-ENL	Boeing 737-8CX	Enter Air
	SP-ENM	Boeing 737-8CX	Enter Air
	SP-ENN	Boeing 737-8CX	Enter Air
	SP-ENO	Boeing 737-8AS	Enter Air
	SP-ENP	Boeing 737-8AS	Enter Air
	SP-ENQ	Boeing 737-85R	Enter Air
	SP-ENR	Boeing 737-8Q8	Enter Air
	SP-ENT	Boeing 737-8AS	Enter Air
	SP-ENU	Boeing 737-83N	Enter Air
	SP-ENV	Boeing 737-8BK	Enter Air
	SP-ENW	Boeing 737-86J	Enter Air
	SP-ENX	Boeing 737-8Q8	Enter Air
	SP-ENZ	Boeing 737-85F	Enter Air
	SP-ESA	Boeing 737-8AL	Enter Air
	SP-ESB	Boeing 737-86N	Enter Air
	SP-ESC	Boeing 737-8AS	Enter Air
	SP-ESD	Boeing 737-8AS	Enter Air
	SP-ESE	Boeing 737-8Q8	Enter Air
	SP-ESF	Boeing 737-8AS	Enter Air
	SP-ESG	Boeing 737-8Q8	Enter Air
	SP-ESH	Boeing 737-81M	Enter Air
	SP-EXA	Boeing 737-MAX8	Enter Air
	SP-EXB	Boeing 737-MAX8	Enter Air
	SP-LDE	Embraer ERJ170 100LR	LOT
	SP-LDF	Embraer ERJ170 100LR	LOT
	SP-LDG	Embraer ERJ170 100LR	LOT
	SP-LDH	Embraer ERJ170 100LR	LOT
	SP-LDI	Embraer ERJ170 100LR	LOT
	SP-LDK	Embraer ERJ170 100LR	LOT
	SP-LIA	Embraer ERJ170-200STD	LOT
	SP-LIB	Embraer ERJ170-200STD	LOT
	SP-LIC	Embraer ERJ170-200STD	LOT
	SP-LID	Embraer ERJ170-200STD	LOT
	SP-LII	Embraer ERJ170-200STD	LOT
	SP-LIK	Embraer ERJ170-200STD	LOT
	SP-LIL	Embraer ERJ170-200STD	LOT
	SP-LIM	Embraer ERJ170-200STD	LOT
	SP-LIN	Embraer ERJ170-200STD	LOT
	SP-LIO	Embraer ERJ170-200STD	LOT

Reg	Type	Owner or Operator	Notes
SP-LMA	Embraer ERJ190-100STD	LOT	
SP-LMB	Embraer ERJ190-100STD	LOT	
SP-LMC	Embraer ERJ190-100STD	LOT	
SP-LMD	Embraer ERJ190-100STD	LOT	
SP-LNA	Embraer ERJ190-200LR	LOT	
SP-LNB	Embraer ERJ190-200LR	LOT	
SP-LNC	Embraer ERJ190-200LR	LOT	
SP-LND	Embraer ERJ190-200LR	LOT	
SP-LNE	Embraer ERJ190-200LR	LOT	
SP-LNF	Embraer ERJ190-200LR	LOT	
SP-LNG	Embraer ERJ190-200LR	LOT	
SP-LNH	Embraer ERJ190-200LR	LOT	
SP-LNI	Embraer ERJ190-200LR	LOT	
SP-LNK	Embraer ERJ190-200LR	LOT	
SP-LNL	Embraer ERJ190-200LR	LOT	
SP-LNM	Embraer ERJ190-200LR	LOT	
SP-LNN	Embraer ERJ190-200LR	LOT	
SP-LNO	Embraer ERJ190-200LR	LOT	
SP-LNP	Embraer ERJ190-200LR	LOT	
SP-LRA	Boeing 787-8	LOT	
SP-LRB	Boeing 787-8	LOT	
SP-LRC	Boeing 787-8	LOT	
SP-LRD	Boeing 787-8	LOT	
SP-LRE	Boeing 787-8	LOT	
SP-LRF	Boeing 787-8	LOT	
SP-LRG	Boeing 787-8	LOT	
SP-LRH	Boeing 787-8	LOT	
SP-LSA	Boeing 787-9	LOT	
SP-LSB	Boeing 787-9	LOT	
SP-LSC	Boeing 787-9	LOT	
SP-LSD	Boeing 787-9	LOT	
SP-LSE	Boeing 787-9	LOT	
SP-LSF	Boeing 787-9	LOT	
SP-LSG	Boeing 787-9	LOT	
SP-LSH	Boeing 787-9	LOT	
SP-LSI	Boeing 787-9	LOT	
SP-LVA	Boeing 737-MAX8	LOT	
SP-LVB	Boeing 737-MAX8	LOT	
SP-LVC	Boeing 737-MAX8	LOT	
SP-LVD	Boeing 737-MAX8	LOT	
SP-LVE	Boeing 737-MAX8	LOT	
SP-LVF	Boeing 737-MAX8	LOT	
SP-LVG	Boeing 737-MAX8	LOT	
SP-LVH	Boeing 737-MAX8	LOT	
SP-LVI	Boeing 737-MAX8	LOT	
SP-LVN	Boeing 737-MAX8	LOT	
SP-LVO	Boeing 737-MAX8	LOT	
SP-LVP	Boeing 737-MAX8	LOT	
SP-LWA	Boeing 737-89P	LOT	
SP-LWB	Boeing 737-89P	LOT	
SP-LWC	Boeing 737-89P	LOT	
SP-LWD	Boeing 737-89P	LOT	
SP-LWE	Boeing 737-8Q8	LOT	
SP-LWF	Boeing 737-86N	LOT	
SP-LWG	Boeing 737-86N	LOT	
SP-RKA	Boeing 737-8AS	Ryanair Sun	
SP-RKB	Boeing 737-8AS	Ryanair Sun	
SP-RKC	Boeing 737-8AS	Ryanair Sun	
SP-RKD	Boeing 737-8AS	Ryanair Sun	
SP-RKE	Boeing 737-8AS	Ryanair Sun	
SP-RKF	Boeing 737-8AS	Ryanair Sun	
SP-RKG	Boeing 737-8AS	Ryanair Sun	
SP-RKH	Boeing 737-8AS	Ryanair Sun	
SP-RKI	Boeing 737-8AS	Ryanair Sun	
SP-RKK	Boeing 737-8AS	Ryanair Sun	
SP-RKL	Boeing 737-8AS	Ryanair Sun	
SP-RKM	Boeing 737-8AS	Ryanair Sun	
SP-RKN	Boeing 737-8AS	Ryanair Sun	
SP-RKO	Boeing 737-8AS	Ryanair Sun	
SP-RKP	Boeing 737-8AS	Ryanair Sun	
SP-RKQ	Boeing 737-8AS	Ryanair Sun	

OVERSEAS AIRLINERS

Notes	Reg	Type	Owner or Operator
	SP-RKR	Boeing 737-8AS	Ryanair Sun
	SP-RKS	Boeing 737-8AS	Ryanair Sun
	SP-RKT	Boeing 737-8AS	Ryanair Sun
	SP-RKU	Boeing 737-8AS	Ryanair Sun
	SP-RKV	Boeing 737-8AS	Ryanair Sun
	SP-RKW	Boeing 737-8AS	Ryanair Sun
	SP-RSA	Boeing 737-8AS	Ryanair Sun
	SP-RSB	Boeing 737-8AS	Ryanair Sun
	SP-RSC	Boeing 737-8AS	Ryanair Sun
	SP-RSD	Boeing 737-8AS	Ryanair Sun
	SP-RSE	Boeing 737-8AS	Ryanair Sun
	SP-RSF	Boeing 737-8AS	Ryanair Sun
	SP-RSG	Boeing 737-8AS	Ryanair Sun
	SP-RSH	Boeing 737-8AS	Ryanair Sun
	SP-RSI	Boeing 737-8AS	Ryanair Sun
	SP-RSK	Boeing 737-8AS	Ryanair Sun
	SP-RSL	Boeing 737-8AS	Ryanair Sun
	SP-RSM	Boeing 737-8AS	Ryanair Sun
	SP-RSN	Boeing 737-8AS	Ryanair Sun
	SP-RSO	Boeing 737-8AS	Ryanair Sun
	SP-RSP	Boeing 737-8AS	Ryanair Sun
	SP-RSQ	Boeing 737-8AS	Ryanair Sun
	SP-RSR	Boeing 737-8AS	Ryanair Sun
	SP-RSS	Boeing 737-8AS	Ryanair Sun
	SP-RST	Boeing 737-8AS	Ryanair Sun
	SP-RSU	Boeing 737-8AS	Ryanair Sun
	SP-RSV	Boeing 737-8AS	Ryanair Sun
	SP-RSW	Boeing 737-8AS	Ryanair Sun
	SP-RSX	Boeing 737-8AS	Ryanair Sun
	SP-RSY	Boeing 737-8AS	Ryanair Sun
	SP-RSZ	Boeing 737-8AS	Ryanair Sun
	SP-RZA	Boeing 737-8-200	Ryanair Sun
	SP-RZB	Boeing 737-8-200	Ryanair Sun
	SP-RZC	Boeing 737-8-200	Ryanair Sun
	SP-RZD	Boeing 737-8-200	Ryanair Sun
	SP-RZE	Boeing 737-8-200	Ryanair Sun
	SP-RZF	Boeing 737-8-200	Ryanair Sun
	SE-RZG	Boeing 737-8-200	Ryanair Sun
	SP-RZH	Boeing 737-8-200	Ryanair Sun

SU (Egypt)

Notes	Reg	Type	Owner or Operator
	SU-GCM	Boeing 737-866WIN	EgyptAir
	SU-GCN	Boeing 737-866WIN	EgyptAir
	SU-GCO	Boeing 737-866WIN	EgyptAir
	SU-GCP	Boeing 737-866WIN	EgyptAir
	SU-GCR	Boeing 737-866WIN	EgyptAir
	SU-GCS	Boeing 737-866WIN	EgyptAir
	SU-GCZ	Boeing 737-866WIN	EgyptAir
	SU-GDA	Boeing 737-866WIN	EgyptAir
	SU-GDB	Boeing 737-866WIN	EgyptAir
	SU-GDC	Boeing 737-866WIN	EgyptAir
	SU-GDD	Boeing 737-866WIN	EgyptAir
	SU-GDE	Boeing 737-866WIN	EgyptAir
	SU-GDL	Boeing 777-36NER	EgyptAir
	SU-GDM	Boeing 777-36NER	EgyptAir
	SU-GDN	Boeing 777-36NER	EgyptAir
	SU-GDO	Boeing 777-36NER	EgyptAir
	SU-GDP	Boeing 777-36NER	EgyptAir
	SU-GDR	Boeing 777-36NER	EgyptAir
	SU-GDX	Boeing 737-866WIN	EgyptAir
	SU-GDY	Boeing 737-866WIN	EgyptAir
	SU-GDZ	Boeing 737-866WIN	EgyptAir
	SU-GEA	Boeing 737-866WIN	EgyptAir
	SU-GEB	Boeing 737-866WIN	EgyptAir
	SU-GEC	Boeing 737-866WIN	EgyptAir
	SU-GED	Boeing 737-866WIN	EgyptAir
	SU-GEE	Boeing 737-866WIN	EgyptAir
	SU-GEF	Boeing 737-866WIN	EgyptAir
	SU-GEG	Boeing 737-866WIN	EgyptAir
	SU-GEH	Boeing 737-866WIN	EgyptAir

Reg	Type	Owner or Operator	Notes
SU-GEI	Boeing 737-866WIN	EgyptAir	
SU-GEJ	Boeing 737-866WIN	EgyptAir	
SU-GEK	Boeing 737-866WIN	EgyptAir	
SU-GEL	Boeing 737-866WIN	EgyptAir	
SU-GEM	Boeing 737-866WIN	EgyptAir	
SU-GEN	Boeing 737-866WIN	EgyptAir	
SU-GER	Boeing 787-9	EgyptAir	
SU-GES	Boeing 787-9	EgyptAir	
SU-GET	Boeing 787-9	EgyptAir	
SU-GEU	Boeing 787-9	EgyptAir	
SU-GEV	Boeing 787-9	EgyptAir	
SU-GEW	Boeing 787-9	EgyptAir	

SX (Greece)

Reg	Type	Owner or Operator	Notes
SX-DGA	Airbus A.321-231	Aegean Airlines	
SX-DGB	Airbus A.320-232	Aegean Airlines	
SX-DGC	Airbus A.320-232	Aegean Airlines	
SX-DGD	Airbus A.320-232	Aegean Airlines	
SX-DGE	Airbus A.320-232	Aegean Airlines	
SX-DGF	Airbus A.319-132	Aegean Airlines	
SX-DGJ	Airbus A.320-232	Aegean Airlines	
SX-DGK	Airbus A.320-232	Aegean Airlines	
SX-DGL	Airbus A.320-232	Aegean Airlines	
SX-DGN	Airbus A.320-232	Aegean Airlines	
SX-DGO	Airbus A.320-232	Aegean Airlines	
SX-DGP	Airbus A.321-232	Aegean Airlines	
SX-DGQ	Airbus A.321-232	Aegean Airlines	
SX-DGR	Airbus A.320-232	Aegean Airlines	
SX-DGT	Airbus A.321-231	Aegean Airlines	
SX-DGX	Airbus A.320-232	Aegean Airlines	
SX-DGY	Airbus A.320-232	Aegean Airlines	
SX-DGZ	Airbus A.320-232	Aegean Airlines	
SX-DNA	Airbus A.320-232	Aegean Airlines	
SX-DNB	Airbus A.320-232	Aegean Airlines	
SX-DNC	Airbus A.320-232	Aegean Airlines	
SX-DND	Airbus A.320-232	Aegean Airlines	
SX-DNE	Airbus A.320-232	Aegean Airlines	
SX-DNF	Airbus A.321-231	Aegean Airlines	
SX-DNG	Airbus A.321-231	Aegean Airlines	
SX-DNH	Airbus A.321-231	Aegean Airlines	
SX-DVG	Airbus A.320-232	Aegean Airlines	
SX-DVH	Airbus A.320-232	Aegean Airlines	
SX-DVI	Airbus A.320-232	Aegean Airlines	
SX-DVJ	Airbus A.320-232	Aegean Airlines	
SX-DVK	Airbus A.320-232	Aegean Airlines	
SX-DVL	Airbus A.320-232	Aegean Airlines	
SX-DVM	Airbus A.320-232	Aegean Airlines	
SX-DVN	Airbus A.320-232	Aegean Airlines	
SX-DVO	Airbus A.321-232	Aegean Airlines	
SX-DVP	Airbus A.321-232	Aegean Airlines	
SX-DVQ	Airbus A.320-232	Aegean Airlines	
SX-DVR	Airbus A.320-232	Aegean Airlines	
SX-DVS	Airbus A.320-232	Aegean Airlines	
SX-DVT	Airbus A.320-232	Aegean Airlines	
SX-DVU	Airbus A.320-232	Aegean Airlines	
SX-DVV	Airbus A.320-232	Aegean Airlines	
SX-DVW	Airbus A.320-232	Aegean Airlines	
SX-DVX	Airbus A.320-232	Aegean Airlines	
SX-DVY	Airbus A.320-232	Aegean Airlines	
SX-DVZ	Airbus A.321-232	Aegean Airlines	
SX-NAA	Airbus A.321-271NX	Aegean Airlines	
SX-NAB	Airbus A.321-271NX	Aegean Airlines	
SX-NAC	Airbus A.321-271NX	Aegean Airlines	
SX-NEA	Airbus A.320-271N	Aegean Airlines	
SX-NEB	Airbus A.320-271N	Aegean Airlines	
SX-NEC	Airbus A.320-271N	Aegean Airlines	
SX-NED	Airbus A.320-271N	Aegean Airlines	
SX-NEO	Airbus A.320-271N	Aegean Airlines	

Notes	Reg	Type	Owner or Operator
	T7 (San Marino)		
	T7-ME1	Airbus A.321-271NX	Middle East Airlines
	T7-ME2	Airbus A.321-271NX	Middle East Airlines
	T7-ME3	Airbus A.321-271NX	Middle East Airlines
	T7-ME4	Airbus A.321-271NX	Middle East Airlines
	T7-ME5	Airbus A.321-271NX	Middle East Airlines
	T7-ME6	Airbus A.321-271NX	Middle East Airlines
	T7-ME7	Airbus A.321-271NX	Middle East Airlines
	T7-ME8	Airbus A.321-271NX	Middle East Airlines
	T7-MRD	Airbus A.320-214	Middle East Airlines
	T7-MRE	Airbus A.320-214	Middle East Airlines
	T7-MRF	Airbus A.320-214	Middle East Airlines
	TC (Turkey)		
	TC-AAU	Boeing 737-82R	Pegasus Airlines
	TC-ACF	Boeing 747-481F	AirACT Cargo
	TC-ACG	Boeing 747-481F	AirACT Cargo
	TC-ACM	Boeing 747-428F	AirACT Cargo
	TC-ACR	Boeing 747-428F	AirACT Cargo
	TC-ADP	Boeing 737-82R	Pegasus Airlines
	TC-AEP	Boeing 737-82R	Pegasus Airlines
	TC-AIS	Boeing 737-82R	Pegasus Airlines
	TC-ANP	Boeing 737-82R	Pegasus Airlines
	TC-AVP	Boeing 737-82R	Pegasus Airlines
	TC-AZP	Boeing 737-82R	Pegasus Airlines
	TC-CCJ	Boeing 737-82R	Pegasus Airlines
	TC-COE	Boeing 737-86J	Corendon Air
	TC-COH	Boeing 737-8EH	Corendon Air
	TC-CON	Boeing 737-8JP	Corendon Air
	TC-COR	Boeing 737-800	Corendon Air
	TC-CPA	Boeing 737-82R	Pegasus Airlines
	TC-CPB	Boeing 737-82R	Pegasus Airlines
	TC-CPC	Boeing 737-82R	Pegasus Airlines
	TC-CPD	Boeing 737-82R	Pegasus Airlines
	TC-CPE	Boeing 737-82R	Pegasus Airlines
	TC-CPI	Boeing 737-82R	Pegasus Airlines
	TC-CPJ	Boeing 737-82R	Pegasus Airlines
	TC-CPK	Boeing 737-82R	Pegasus Airlines
	TC-CPL	Boeing 737-82R	Pegasus Airlines
	TC-CPM	Boeing 737-82R	Pegasus Airlines
	TC-CPN	Boeing 737-82R	Pegasus Airlines
	TC-CPS	Boeing 737-8GJ	Pegasus Airlines
	TC-CPU	Boeing 737-86N	Pegasus Airlines
	TC-CPV	Boeing 737-86J	Pegasus Airlines
	TC-CPY	Boeing 737-8H6	Pegasus Airlines
	TC-CPZ	Boeing 737-8H6	Pegasus Airlines
	TC-CRA	Boeing 737-8H6	Pegasus Airlines
	TC-CRB	Boeing 737-8H6	Pegasus Airlines
	TC-CRE	Boeing 737-800	Pegasus Airlines
	TC-CRF	Boeing 737-800	Pegasus Airlines
	TC-CRG	Boeing 737-800	Pegasus Airlines
	TC-DCA	Airbus A.320-214	Pegasus Airlines
	TC-DCB	Airbus A.320-214	Pegasus Airlines
	TC-DCC	Airbus A.320-214	Pegasus Airlines
	TC-DCD	Airbus A.320-214	Pegasus Airlines
	TC-DCE	Airbus A.320-216	Pegasus Airlines
	TC-DCF	Airbus A.320-216	Pegasus Airlines
	TC-DCG	Airbus A.320-216	Pegasus Airlines
	TC-DCH	Airbus A.320-216	Pegasus Airlines
	TC-DCI	Airbus A.320-216	Pegasus Airlines
	TC-DCJ	Airbus A.320-214	Pegasus Airlines
	TC-DCL	Airbus A.320-214	Pegasus Airlines
	TC-DCM	Airbus A.320-214	Pegasus Airlines
	TC-FBO	Airbus A.320-214	Freebird Airlines
	TC-FBR	Airbus A.320-232	Freebird Airlines
	TC-FBV	Airbus A.320-214	Freebird Airlines
	TC-FHC	Airbus A.320-214	Freebird Airlines
	TC-FHG	Airbus A.320-214	Freebird Airlines
	TC-FHM	Airbus A.320-232	Freebird Airlines

Reg	Type	Owner or Operator	Notes
TC-FHN	Airbus A.320-214	Freebird Airlines	
TC-FHY	Airbus A.320-214	Freebird Airlines	
TC-IZI	Boeing 737-8GJ	Pegasus Airlines	
TC-IZJ	Boeing 737-82R	Pegasus Airlines	
TC-JCI	Airbus A.330-223F	Turkish Cargo	
TC-JDO	Airbus A.330-243F	Turkish Cargo	
TC-JDP	Airbus A.330-243F	Turkish Cargo	
TC-JDR	Airbus A.330-243F	Turkish Cargo	
TC-JDS	Airbus A.330-243F	Turkish Cargo	
TC-JFC	Boeing 737-8F2	AnadoluJet	
TC-JFD	Boeing 737-8F2	AnadoluJet	
TC-JFE	Boeing 737-8F2	AnadoluJet	
TC-JFF	Boeing 737-8F2	AnadoluJet	
TC-JFG	Boeing 737-8F2	AnadoluJet	
TC-JFH	Boeing 737-8F2	AnadoluJet	
TC-JFI	Boeing 737-8F2	AnadoluJet	
TC-JFJ	Boeing 737-8F2	AnadoluJet	
TC-JFK	Boeing 737-8F2	AnadoluJet	
TC-JFL	Boeing 737-8F2	Turkish Airlines	
TC-JFM	Boeing 737-8F2	Turkish Airlines	
TC-JFN	Boeing 737-8F2	AnadoluJet	
TC-JFO	Boeing 737-8F2	AnadoluJet	
TC-JFP	Boeing 737-8F2	AnadoluJet	
TC-JFR	Boeing 737-8F2	AnadoluJet	
TC-JFT	Boeing 737-8F2	AnadoluJet	
TC-JFU	Boeing 737-8F2	Turkish Airlines	
TC-JFV	Boeing 737-8F2	Turkish Airlines	
TC-JFY	Boeing 737-8F2	AnadoluJet	
TC-JFZ	Boeing 737-8F2	AnadoluJet	
TC-JGA	Boeing 737-8F2	Turkish Airlines	
TC-JGB	Boeing 737-8F2	AnadoluJet	
TC-JGC	Boeing 737-8F2	Turkish Airlines	
TC-JGD	Boeing 737-8F2	Turkish Airlines	
TC-JGF	Boeing 737-8F2	AnadoluJet	
TC-JGR	Boeing 737-8F2	Turkish Airlines	
TC-JGS	Boeing 737-8F2	Turkish Airlines	
TC-JGT	Boeing 737-8F2	Turkish Airlines	
TC-JGU	Boeing 737-8F2	Turkish Airlines	
TC-JGV	Boeing 737-8F2	Turkish Airlines	
TC-JGY	Boeing 737-8F2	Turkish Airlines	
TC-JHA	Boeing 737-8F2	Turkish Airlines	
TC-JHB	Boeing 737-8F2	Turkish Airlines	
TC-JHC	Boeing 737-8F2	Turkish Airlines	
TC-JHD	Boeing 737-8F2	Turkish Airlines	
TC-JHE	Boeing 737-8F2	Turkish Airlines	
TC-JHF	Boeing 737-8F2	Turkish Airlines	
TC-JHK	Boeing 737-8F2	Turkish Airlines	
TC-JHL	Boeing 737-8F2	Turkish Airlines	
TC-JHM	Boeing 737-8F2	Turkish Airlines	
TC-JHN	Boeing 737-8F2	Turkish Airlines	
TC-JHO	Boeing 737-8F2	Turkish Airlines	
TC-JHP	Boeing 737-8F2	Turkish Airlines	
TC-JHR	Boeing 737-8F2	Turkish Airlines	
TC-JHS	Boeing 737-8F2	Turkish Airlines	
TC-JHT	Boeing 737-8F2	Turkish Airlines	
TC-JHU	Boeing 737-8F2	Turkish Airlines	
TC-JHV	Boeing 737-8F2	Turkish Airlines	
TC-JHY	Boeing 737-8F2	Turkish Airlines	
TC-JHZ	Boeing 737-8F2	Turkish Airlines	
TC-JIO	Airbus A.330-223	Turkish Airlines	
TC-JIP	Airbus A.330-223	Turkish Airlines	
TC-JIR	Airbus A.330-223	Turkish Airlines	
TC-JIS	Airbus A.330-223	Turkish Airlines	
TC-JIT	Airbus A.330-223	Turkish Airlines	
TC-JIZ	Airbus A.330-223	Turkish Airlines	
TC-JJE	Boeing 777-3F2ER	Turkish Airlines	
TC-JJF	Boeing 777-3F2ER	Turkish Airlines	
TC-JJG	Boeing 777-3F2ER	Turkish Airlines	
TC-JJH	Boeing 777-3F2ER	Turkish Airlines	
TC-JJI	Boeing 777-3F2ER	Turkish Airlines	
TC-JJJ	Boeing 777-3F2ER	Turkish Airlines	

Notes	Reg	Type	Owner or Operator
	TC-JJK	Boeing 777-3F2ER	Turkish Airlines
	TC-JJL	Boeing 777-3F2ER	Turkish Airlines
	TC-JJM	Boeing 777-3F2ER	Turkish Airlines
	TC-JJN	Boeing 777-3F2ER	Turkish Airlines
	TC-JJO	Boeing 777-3F2ER	Turkish Airlines
	TC-JJP	Boeing 777-3F2ER	Turkish Airlines
	TC-JJR	Boeing 777-3F2ER	Turkish Airlines
	TC-JJS	Boeing 777-3F2ER	Turkish Airlines
	TC-JJT	Boeing 777-3F2ER	Turkish Airlines
	TC-JJU	Boeing 777-3F2ER	Turkish Airlines
	TC-JJV	Boeing 777-3F2ER	Turkish Airlines
	TC-JJY	Boeing 777-3F2ER	Turkish Airlines
	TC-JJZ	Boeing 777-3F2ER	Turkish Airlines
	TC-JKU	Boeing 737-8Q8	AnadoluJet
	TC-JKV	Boeing 737-8Q8	AnadoluJet
	TC-JLS	Airbus A.319-132	Turkish Airlines
	TC-JLT	Airbus A.319-132	Turkish Airlines
	TC-JLU	Airbus A.319-132	Turkish Airlines
	TC-JLV	Airbus A.319-132	Turkish Airlines
	TC-JLY	Airbus A.319-132	Turkish Airlines
	TC-JLZ	Airbus A.319-132	Turkish Airlines
	TC-JMH	Airbus A.321-232	Turkish Airlines
	TC-JMI	Airbus A.321-232	Turkish Airlines
	TC-JMJ	Airbus A.321-232	Turkish Airlines
	TC-JMK	Airbus A.321-232	Turkish Airlines
	TC-JML	Airbus A.321-231	Turkish Airlines
	TC-JNA	Airbus A.330-203	Turkish Airlines
	TC-JNB	Airbus A.330-203	Turkish Airlines
	TC-JNC	Airbus A.330-203	Turkish Airlines
	TC-JND	Airbus A.330-203	Turkish Airlines
	TC-JNE	Airbus A.330-203	Turkish Airlines
	TC-JNH	Airbus A.330-343	Turkish Airlines
	TC-JNI	Airbus A.330-343	Turkish Airlines
	TC-JNJ	Airbus A.330-343	Turkish Airlines
	TC-JNK	Airbus A.330-343	Turkish Airlines
	TC-JNL	Airbus A.330-343	Turkish Airlines
	TC-JNM	Airbus A.330-343	Turkish Airlines
	TC-JNN	Airbus A.330-343	Turkish Airlines
	TC-JNO	Airbus A.330-343	Turkish Airlines
	TC-JNP	Airbus A.330-343	Turkish Airlines
	TC-JNR	Airbus A.330-343	Turkish Airlines
	TC-JNS	Airbus A.330-303	Turkish Airlines
	TC-JNT	Airbus A.330-303	Turkish Airlines
	TC-JNZ	Airbus A.330-303	Turkish Airlines
	TC-JOA	Airbus A.330-303	Turkish Airlines
	TC-JOB	Airbus A.330-303	Turkish Airlines
	TC-JOD	Airbus A.330-303	Turkish Airlines
	TC-JOE	Airbus A.330-303	Turkish Airlines
	TC-JOF	Airbus A.330-303	Turkish Airlines
	TC-JOG	Airbus A.330-303	Turkish Airlines
	TC-JOH	Airbus A.330-303	Turkish Airlines
	TC-JOI	Airbus A.330-303	Turkish Airlines
	TC-JOJ	Airbus A.330-303	Turkish Airlines
	TC-JOK	Airbus A.330-303	Turkish Airlines
	TC-JOL	Airbus A.330-303	Turkish Airlines
	TC-JOM	Airbus A.330-302	Turkish Airlines
	TC-JOO	Airbus A.330-223F	Turkish Cargo
	TC-JOU	Airbus A.330-243F	Turkish Cargo
	TC-JOV	Airbus A.330-243F	Turkish Cargo
	TC-JOY	Airbus A.330-243F	Turkish Cargo
	TC-JOZ	Airbus A.330-243F	Turkish Cargo
	TC-JPH	Airbus A.320-232	Turkish Airlines
	TC-JPI	Airbus A.320-232	Turkish Airlines
	TC-JPJ	Airbus A.320-232	Turkish Airlines
	TC-JPK	Airbus A.320-232	Turkish Airlines
	TC-JPL	Airbus A.320-232	Turkish Airlines
	TC-JPM	Airbus A.320-232	Turkish Airlines
	TC-JPN	Airbus A.320-232	Turkish Airlines
	TC-JPO	Airbus A.320-232	Turkish Airlines
	TC-JPP	Airbus A.320-232	Turkish Airlines
	TC-JPR	Airbus A.320-232	Turkish Airlines

Reg	Type	Owner or Operator	Notes
TC-JPS	Airbus A.320-232	Turkish Airlines	
TC-JPT	Airbus A.320-232	Turkish Airlines	
TC-JRA	Airbus A.321-231	Turkish Airlines	
TC-JRB	Airbus A.321-231	Turkish Airlines	
TC-JRC	Airbus A.321-231	Turkish Airlines	
TC-JRD	Airbus A.321-231	Turkish Airlines	
TC-JRE	Airbus A.321-231	Turkish Airlines	
TC-JRF	Airbus A.321-231	Turkish Airlines	
TC-JRG	Airbus A.321-231	Turkish Airlines	
TC-JRH	Airbus A.321-231	Turkish Airlines	
TC-JRI	Airbus A.321-232	Turkish Airlines	
TC-JRJ	Airbus A.321-232	Turkish Airlines	
TC-JRK	Airbus A.321-231	Turkish Airlines	
TC-JRL	Airbus A.321-231	Turkish Airlines	
TC-JRM	Airbus A.321-232	Turkish Airlines	
TC-JRN	Airbus A.321-232	Turkish Airlines	
TC-JRO	Airbus A.321-231	Turkish Airlines	
TC-JRP	Airbus A.321-231	Turkish Airlines	
TC-JRR	Airbus A.321-231	Turkish Airlines	
TC-JRS	Airbus A.321-231	Turkish Airlines	
TC-JRT	Airbus A.321-231	Turkish Airlines	
TC-JRU	Airbus A.321-231	Turkish Airlines	
TC-JRV	Airbus A.321-232	Turkish Airlines	
TC-JRY	Airbus A.321-232	Turkish Airlines	
TC-JRZ	Airbus A.321-232	Turkish Airlines	
TC-JSA	Airbus A.321-232	Turkish Airlines	
TC-JSB	Airbus A.321-231	Turkish Airlines	
TC-JSC	Airbus A.321-231	Turkish Airlines	
TC-JSD	Airbus A.321-231	Turkish Airlines	
TC-JSE	Airbus A.321-231	Turkish Airlines	
TC-JSF	Airbus A.321-231	Turkish Airlines	
TC-JSG	Airbus A.321-231	Turkish Airlines	
TC-JSH	Airbus A.321-231	Turkish Airlines	
TC-JSI	Airbus A.321-231	Turkish Airlines	
TC-JSJ	Airbus A.321-232	Turkish Airlines	
TC-JSK	Airbus A.321-232	Turkish Airlines	
TC-JSL	Airbus A.321-232	Turkish Airlines	
TC-JSM	Airbus A.321-231	Turkish Airlines	
TC-JSN	Airbus A.321-231	Turkish Airlines	
TC-JSO	Airbus A.321-231	Turkish Airlines	
TC-JSP	Airbus A.321-231	Turkish Airlines	
TC-JSR	Airbus A.321-231	Turkish Airlines	
TC-JSS	Airbus A.321-231	Turkish Airlines	
TC-JST	Airbus A.321-231	Turkish Airlines	
TC-JSU	Airbus A.321-231	Turkish Airlines	
TC-JSV	Airbus A.321-231	Turkish Airlines	
TC-JSY	Airbus A.321-231	Turkish Airlines	
TC-JSZ	Airbus A.321-231	Turkish Airlines	
TC-JTA	Airbus A.321-231	Turkish Airlines	
TC-JTD	Airbus A.321-231	Turkish Airlines	
TC-JTE	Airbus A.321-231	Turkish Airlines	
TC-JTF	Airbus A.321-231	Turkish Airlines	
TC-JTG	Airbus A.321-231	Turkish Airlines	
TC-JTH	Airbus A.321-231	Turkish Airlines	
TC-JTI	Airbus A.321-231	Turkish Airlines	
TC-JTJ	Airbus A.321-231	Turkish Airlines	
TC-JTK	Airbus A.321-231	Turkish Airlines	
TC-JTL	Airbus A.321-231	Turkish Airlines	
TC-JTM	Airbus A.321-231	Turkish Airlines	
TC-JTN	Airbus A.321-231	Turkish Airlines	
TC-JTO	Airbus A.321-231	Turkish Airlines	
TC-JTP	Airbus A.321-231	Turkish Airlines	
TC-JTR	Airbus A.321-231	Turkish Airlines	
TC-JUK	Airbus A.320-232	Turkish Airlines	
TC-JVA	Boeing 737-8F2	Turkish Airlines	
TC-JVB	Boeing 737-8F2	Turkish Airlines	
TC-JVC	Boeing 737-8F2	Turkish Airlines	
TC-JVD	Boeing 737-8F2	Turkish Airlines	
TC-JVE	Boeing 737-8F2	Turkish Airlines	
TC-JVF	Boeing 737-8F2	Turkish Airlines	
TC-JVG	Boeing 737-8F2	Turkish Airlines	

Notes	Reg	Type	Owner or Operator
	TC-JVH	Boeing 737-8F2	Turkish Airlines
	TC-JVI	Boeing 737-8F2	Turkish Airlines
	TC-JVJ	Boeing 737-8F2	Turkish Airlines
	TC-JVK	Boeing 737-8F2	Turkish Airlines
	TC-JVL	Boeing 737-8F2	Turkish Airlines
	TC-JVM	Boeing 737-8F2	Turkish Airlines
	TC-JVN	Boeing 737-8F2	Turkish Airlines
	TC-JVO	Boeing 737-8F2	Turkish Airlines
	TC-JVP	Boeing 737-8F2	Turkish Airlines
	TC-JVR	Boeing 737-8F2	Turkish Airlines
	TC-JVS	Boeing 737-8F2	Turkish Airlines
	TC-JVT	Boeing 737-8F2	Turkish Airlines
	TC-JVU	Boeing 737-8F2	Turkish Airlines
	TC-JVV	Boeing 737-8F2	Turkish Airlines
	TC-JVY	Boeing 737-8F2	Turkish Airlines
	TC-JVZ	Boeing 737-8F2	Turkish Airlines
	TC-JYA	Boeing 737-9F2ER	Turkish Airlines
	TC-JYB	Boeing 737-9F2ER	Turkish Airlines
	TC-JYC	Boeing 737-9F2ER	Turkish Airlines
	TC-JYD	Boeing 737-9F2ER	Turkish Airlines
	TC-JYE	Boeing 737-9F2ER	Turkish Airlines
	TC-JYF	Boeing 737-9F2ER	Turkish Airlines
	TC-JYG	Boeing 737-9F2ER	Turkish Airlines
	TC-JYH	Boeing 737-9F2ER	Turkish Airlines
	TC-JYI	Boeing 737-9F2ER	Turkish Airlines
	TC-JYJ	Boeing 737-9F2ER	Turkish Airlines
	TC-JYL	Boeing 737-9F2ER	Turkish Airlines
	TC-JYM	Boeing 737-9F2ER	Turkish Airlines
	TC-JYN	Boeing 737-9F2ER	Turkish Airlines
	TC-JYO	Boeing 737-9F2ER	Turkish Airlines
	TC-JYP	Boeing 737-9F2ER	Turkish Airlines
	TC-JZE	Boeing 737-8F2	Turkish Airlines
	TC-JZF	Boeing 737-8F2	Turkish Airlines
	TC-JZG	Boeing 737-8F2	Air Albania
	TC-JZH	Boeing 737-8F2	Turkish Airlines
	TC-JZJ	Boeing 737-8AS	AndoluJet
	TC-JZK	Boeing 737-8AS	AndoluJet
	TC-JZL	Boeing 737-8AS	AndoluJet
	TC-JZN	Boeing 737-8JP	Turkish Airlines
	TC-JZO	Boeing 737-8JP	AndoluJet
	TC-JZR	Boeing 737-8JP	AndoluJet
	TC-JZS	Boeing 737-8JP	AndoluJet
	TC-JZT	Boeing 737-8JP	AndoluJet
	TC-JZU	Boeing 737-8AS	AndoluJet
	TC-JZV	Boeing 737-8AS	AndoluJet
	TC-LCA	Boeing 737-MAX8	Turkish Airlines
	TC-LCB	Boeing 737-MAX8	Turkish Airlines
	TC-LCC	Boeing 737-MAX8	Turkish Airlines
	TC-LCD	Boeing 737-MAX8	Turkish Airlines
	TC-LCE	Boeing 737-MAX8	Turkish Airlines
	TC-LCF	Boeing 737-MAX8	Turkish Airlines
	TC-LCG	Boeing 737-MAX8	Turkish Airlines
	TC-LCH	Boeing 737-MAX8	Turkish Airlines
	TC-LCI	Boeing 737-MAX8	Turkish Airlines
	TC-LCJ	Boeing 737-MAX8	Turkish Airlines
	TC-LCK	Boeing 737-MAX8	Turkish Airlines
	TC-LCL	Boeing 737-MAX8	Turkish Airlines
	TC-LCM	Boeing 737-MAX8	Turkish Airlines
	TC-LCN	Boeing 737-MAX8	Turkish Airlines
	TC-LCO	Boeing 737-MAX8	Turkish Airlines
	TC-LCP	Boeing 737-MAX8	Turkish Airlines
	TC-LCR	Boeing 737-MAX8	Turkish Airlines
	TC-LCS	Boeing 737-MAX8	Turkish Airlines
	TC-LCT	Boeing 737-MAX8	Turkish Airlines
	TC-LGA	Airbus A.350-941	Turkish Airlines
	TC-LGB	Airbus A.350-941	Turkish Airlines
	TC-LGC	Airbus A.350-941	Turkish Airlines
	TC-LGD	Airbus A.350-941	Turkish Airlines
	TC-LGE	Airbus A.350-941	Turkish Airlines
	TC-LJA	Boeing 777-3F2ER	Turkish Airlines
	TC-LJB	Boeing 777-3F2ER	Turkish Airlines

Reg	Type	Owner or Operator	Notes
TC-LJC	Boeing 777-3F2ER	Turkish Airlines	
TC-LJD	Boeing 777-3F2ER	Turkish Airlines	
TC-LJE	Boeing 777-3F2ER	Turkish Airlines	
TC-LJF	Boeing 777-3F2ER	Turkish Airlines	
TC-LJG	Boeing 777-3F2ER	Turkish Airlines	
TC-LJH	Boeing 777-3F2ER	Turkish Airlines	
TC-LJI	Boeing 777-3F2ER	Turkish Airlines	
TC-LJJ	Boeing 777-3F2ER	Turkish Airlines	
TC-LJK	Boeing 777-3F2ER	Turkish Airlines	
TC-LJL	Boeing 777-FF2	Turkish Cargo	
TC-LJM	Boeing 777-FF2	Turkish Cargo	
TC-LJN	Boeing 777-FF2	Turkish Cargo	
TC-LJO	Boeing 777-FF2	Turkish Cargo	
TC-LJP	Boeing 777-FF2	Turkish Cargo	
TC-LJR	Boeing 777-FF2	Turkish Cargo	
TC-LJS	Boeing 777-200F	Turkish Cargo	
TC-LJT	Boeing 777-200F	Turkish Cargo	
TC-LKA	Boeing 777-36NER	Turkish Airlines	
TC-LKB	Boeing 777-36NER	Turkish Airlines	
TC-LKC	Boeing 777-3U8ER	Turkish Airlines	
TC-LNC	Airbus A.330-303	Turkish Airlines	
TC-LND	Airbus A.330-303	Turkish Airlines	
TC-LNE	Airbus A.330-303	Turkish Airlines	
TC-LNF	Airbus A.330-303	Turkish Airlines	
TC-LNG	Airbus A.330-303	Turkish Airlines	
TC-LOA	Airbus A.330-343	Turkish Airlines	
TC-LOD	Airbus A.330-343	Turkish Airlines	
TC-LOE	Airbus A.330-343	Turkish Airlines	
TC-LOF	Airbus A.330-343	Turkish Airlines	
TC-LOG	Airbus A.330-343	Turkish Airlines	
TC-LOH	Airbus A.330-223	Turkish Airlines	
TC-LOI	Airbus A.330-223	Turkish Airlines	
TC-LOJ	Airbus A.330-343	Turkish Airlines	
TC-LOK	Airbus A.330-343	Turkish Airlines	
TC-LOL	Airbus A.330-343	Turkish Airlines	
TC-LPA	Airbus A.350-941	Turkish Airlines	
TC-LSA	Airbus A.321-271NX	Turkish Airlines	
TC-LSB	Airbus A.321-271NX	Turkish Airlines	
TC-LSC	Airbus A.321-271NX	Turkish Airlines	
TC-LSD	Airbus A.321-271NX	Turkish Airlines	
TC-LSE	Airbus A.321-271NX	Turkish Airlines	
TC-LSF	Airbus A.321-271NX	Turkish Airlines	
TC-LSG	Airbus A.321-271NX	Turkish Airlines	
TC-LSH	Airbus A.321-271NX	Turkish Airlines	
TC-LSJ	Airbus A.321-271NX	Turkish Airlines	
TC-LSK	Airbus A.321-271NX	Turkish Airlines	
TC-LSL	Airbus A.321-271NX	Turkish Airlines	
TC-LSM	Airbus A.321-271NX	Turkish Airlines	
TC-LSN	Airbus A.321-271NX	Turkish Airlines	
TC-LSO	Airbus A.321-271NX	Turkish Airlines	
TC-LSP	Airbus A.321-271NX	Turkish Airlines	
TC-LSR	Airbus A.321-271NX	Turkish Airlines	
TC-LSS	Airbus A.321-271NX	Turkish Airlines	
TC-LST	Airbus A.321-271NX	Turkish Airlines	
TC-LSU	Airbus A.321-271NX	Turkish Airlines	
TC-LSV	Airbus A.321-271NX	Turkish Airlines	
TC-LSY	Airbus A.321-271NX	Turkish Airlines	
TC-LSZ	Airbus A.321-271NX	Turkish Airlines	
TC-LTA	Airbus A.321-271NX	Turkish Airlines	
TC-LTB	Airbus A.321-271NX	Turkish Airlines	
TC-LTC	Airbus A.321-271NX	Turkish Airlines	
TC-LYA	Boeing 737-MAX9	Turkish Airlines	
TC-LYB	Boeing 737-MAX9	Turkish Airlines	
TC-LYC	Boeing 737-MAX9	Turkish Airlines	
TC-LYD	Boeing 737-MAX9	Turkish Airlines	
TC-LYE	Boeing 737-MAX9	Turkish Airlines	
TC-MCC	Airbus A.300B4-622RF	MNG Cargo	
TC-MCD	Airbus A.300B4-605RF	MNG Cargo	
TC-MCE	Airbus A.300B4-605R	MNG Cargo	
TC-MCG	Airbus A.300B4-622RF	MNG Cargo	
TC-MCZ	Airbus A.330-243F	MNG Cargo	

Notes	Reg	Type	Owner or Operator
	TC-MKB	Boeing 737-MAX8	Corendon Airlines
	TC-MKE	Boeing 737-MAX8	Corendon Airlines
	TC-MKS	Boeing 737-MAX8	Corendon Airlines
	TC-MKZ	Boeing 737-MAX8	Corendon Airlines
	TC-MNV	Airbus A.300B4-605R	MNG Cargo
	TC-NBA	Airbus A.320-251N	Pegasus Airlines
	TC-NBB	Airbus A.320-251N	Pegasus Airlines
	TC-NBC	Airbus A.320-251N	Pegasus Airlines
	TC-NBD	Airbus A.320-251N	Pegasus Airlines
	TC-NBE	Airbus A.320-251N	Pegasus Airlines
	TC-NBF	Airbus A.320-251N	Pegasus Airlines
	TC-NBG	Airbus A.320-251N	Pegasus Airlines
	TC-NBH	Airbus A.320-251N	Pegasus Airlines
	TC-NBI	Airbus A.320-251N	Pegasus Airlines
	TC-NBJ	Airbus A.320-251N	Pegasus Airlines
	TC-NBK	Airbus A.320-251N	Pegasus Airlines
	TC-NBL	Airbus A.320-251N	Pegasus Airlines
	TC-NBM	Airbus A.320-251N	Pegasus Airlines
	TC-NBN	Airbus A.320-251N	Pegasus Airlines
	TC-NBO	Airbus A.320-251N	Pegasus Airlines
	TC-NBP	Airbus A.320-251N	Pegasus Airlines
	TC-NBR	Airbus A.320-251N	Pegasus Airlines
	TC-NBS	Airbus A.320-251N	Pegasus Airlines
	TC-NBT	Airbus A.320-251N	Pegasus Airlines
	TC-NBU	Airbus A.320-251N	Pegasus Airlines
	TC-NBV	Airbus A.320-251N	Pegasus Airlines
	TC-NBY	Airbus A.320-251N	Pegasus Airlines
	TC-NBZ	Airbus A.320-251N	Pegasus Airlines
	TC-NCA	Airbus A.320-251N	Pegasus Airlines
	TC-NCB	Airbus A.320-251N	Pegasus Airlines
	TC-NCC	Airbus A.320-251N	Pegasus Airlines
	TC-NCD	Airbus A.320-251N	Pegasus Airlines
	TC-NCE	Airbus A.320-251N	Pegasus Airlines
	TC-NCF	Airbus A.320-251N	Pegasus Airlines
	TC-NCG	Airbus A.320-251N	Pegasus Airlines
	TC-NCH	Airbus A.320-251N	Pegasus Airlines
	TC-NCI	Airbus A.320-251N	Pegasus Airlines
	TC-NCJ	Airbus A.320-251N	Pegasus Airlines
	TC-NCK	Airbus A.320-251N	Pegasus Airlines
	TC-NCL	Airbus A.320-251N	Pegasus Airlines
	TC-NCM	Airbus A.320-251N	Pegasus Airlines
	TC-NCN	Airbus A.320-251N	Pegasus Airlines
	TC-NCO	Airbus A.320-251N	Pegasus Airlines
	TC-NCP	Airbus A.320-251N	Pegasus Airlines
	TC-NCR	Airbus A.320-251N	Pegasus Airlines
	TC-NCS	Airbus A.320-251N	Pegasus Airlines
	TC-NCT	Airbus A.320-251N	Pegasus Airlines
	TC-OBG	Airbus A.320-233	Onur Air
	TC-OBK	Airbus A.321-231	Onur Air
	TC-OBS	Airbus A.320-232	Onur Air
	TC-OBU	Airbus A.320-231	Onur Air
	TC-OBY	Airbus A.321-231	Onur Air
	TC-ODA	Airbus A.320-233	Onur Air
	TC-ODB	Airbus A.320-232	Onur Air
	TC-ODC	Airbus A.320-233	Onur Air
	TC-ODD	Airbus A.320-232	Onur Air
	TC-ODE	Airbus A.320-232	Onur Air
	TC-OEA	Airbus A.321-131	Onur Air
	TC-ONJ	Airbus A.321-131	Onur Air
	TC-ONS	Airbus A.321-131	Onur Air
	TC-RBA	Airbus A.321-251NX	Pegasus Airlines
	TC-RBB	Airbus A.321-251NX	Pegasus Airlines
	TC-RBC	Airbus A.321-251NX	Pegasus Airlines
	TC-RBD	Airbus A.321-251NX	Pegasus Airlines
	TC-RBE	Airbus A.321-251NX	Pegasus Airlines
	TC-RBF	Airbus A.321-251NX	Pegasus Airlines
	TC-RBG	Airbus A.321-251NX	Pegasus Airlines
	TC-SBN	Boeing 737-86N	AnadoluJet
	TC-SBP	Boeing 737-86N	AnadoluJet
	TC-SBR	Boeing 737-86N	AnadoluJet
	TC-SBV	Boeing 737-86N	AnadoluJet

Reg	Type	Owner or Operator	Notes
TC-SCF	Boeing 737-8AL	AnadoluJet	
TC-SCG	Boeing 737-8AL	AnadoluJet	
TC-SCK	Boeing 737-8GJ	AnadoluJet	
TC-SCL	Boeing 737-8GJ	AnadoluJet	
TC-SED	Boeing 737-86N	SunExpress	
TC-SEE	Boeing 737-86N	SunExpress	
TC-SEI	Boeing 737-8Q8	SunExpress	
TC-SEJ	Boeing 737-8HC	SunExpress	
TC-SEK	Boeing 737-8HC	SunExpress	
TC-SEM	Boeing 737-8HC	SunExpress	
TC-SEN	Boeing 737-8HC	SunExpress	
TC-SEO	Boeing 737-8HC	SunExpress	
TC-SEP	Boeing 737-8HC	SunExpress	
TC-SEU	Boeing 737-8HC	SunExpress	
TC-SEY	Boeing 737-8HC	SunExpress	
TC-SEZ	Boeing 737-8HC	SunExpress	
TC-SNN	Boeing 737-8HC	SunExpress	
TC-SNR	Boeing 737-8HC	SunExpress	
TC-SNT	Boeing 737-8HC	SunExpress	
TC-SNU	Boeing 737-8HC	SunExpress	
TC-SNV	Boeing 737-86J	SunExpress	
TC-SOA	Boeing 737-86N	SunExpress	
TC-SOB	Boeing 737-8HC	SunExpress	
TC-SOC	Boeing 737-8HC	SunExpress	
TC-SOD	Boeing 737-8HC	SunExpress	
TC-SOE	Boeing 737-8HC	SunExpress	
TC-SOF	Boeing 737-8HC	SunExpress	
TC-SOG	Boeing 737-8HC	SunExpress	
TC-SOH	Boeing 737-8HC	SunExpress	
TC-SOI	Boeing 737-MAX8	SunExpress	
TC-SOJ	Boeing 737-MAX8	SunExpress	
TC-SOK	Boeing 737-MAX8	SunExpress	
TC-SOL	Boeing 737-MAX8	SunExpress	
TC-SOM	Boeing 737-MAX8	SunExpress	
TC-SON	Boeing 737-86J	SunExpress	
TC-SOO	Boeing 737-8AS	SunExpress	
TC-SOP	Boeing 737-8AS	SunExpress	
TC-SOR	Boeing 737-8AS	SunExpress	
TC-SOT	Boeing 737-8Z9	SunExpress	
TC-SOU	Boeing 737-8Z9	SunExpress	
TC-SOV	Boeing 737-8HC	SunExpress	
TC-SOY	Boeing 737-8HC	SunExpress	
TC-SOZ	Boeing 737-8HX	SunExpress	
TC-SPA	Boeing 737-8HX	SunExpress	
TC-SPB	Boeing 737-86Q	SunExpress	
TC-SPC	Boeing 737-8AS	SunExpress	
TC-SPD	Boeing 737-8AS	SunExpress	
TC-SPE	Boeing 737-8HC	SunExpress	
TC-SPF	Boeing 737-8K5	SunExpress	
TC-SPG	Boeing 737-86N	SunExpress	
TC-SUU	Boeing 737-86Q	SunExpress	
TC-TJI	Boeing 737-8S3	Corendon Air	
TC-TJJ	Boeing 737-8S3	Corendon Air	
TC-TJO	Boeing 737-86N	Corendon Air	
TC-TJP	Boeing 737-8BK	Corendon Air	
TC-TJR	Boeing 737-82R	Corendon Air	
TC-TJS	Boeing 737-86N	Corendon Air	
TC-TJT	Boeing 737-8HC	Corendon Air	
TC-TJU	Boeing 737-8HX	Corendon Air	
TC-TLA	Boeing 737-4Q8	Tailwind Airlines	
TC-TLB	Boeing 737-4Q8	Tailwind Airlines	
TC-TLC	Boeing 737-4Q8	Tailwind Airlines	
TC-TLD	Boeing 737-4Q8	Tailwind Airlines	
TC-TLE	Boeing 737-4Q8	Tailwind Airlines	

TF (Iceland)

Reg	Type	Owner or Operator	Notes
TF-AAJ	Boeing 747-428	Air Atlanta Icelandic/Saudi Arabian Airlines	
TF-AAK	Boeing 747-428	Air Atlanta Icelandic/Saudi Arabian Airlines	
TF-AAL	Boeing 747-428	Air Atlanta Icelandic/Saudi Arabian Airlines	
TF-AAM	Boeing 747-4H6	Air Atlanta Icelandic/Saudi Arabian Airlines	

Notes	Reg	Type	Owner or Operator
	TF-AMA	Boeing 747-45ESF	Air Atlanta Icelandic/Astral Aviation
	TF-AMB	Boeing 747-412F	Air Atlanta Icelandic/Saudi Arabian Airlines
	TF-AMC	Boeing 747-412F	Air Atlanta Icelandic/Magma Aviation
	TF-AMI	Boeing 747-412BCF	Air Atlanta Icelandic/Magma Aviation
	TF-AMM	Boeing 747-4H6BCF	Air Atlanta Icelandic/Astral Aviation
	TF-AMN	Boeing 747-4F6SF	Air Atlanta Icelandic/Astral Aviation
	TF-AMP	Boeing 747-481BCF	Air Atlanta Icelandic/Magma Aviation
	TF-AMR	Boeing 747-45E	Air Atlanta Icelandic/Magma Aviation
	TF-AMU	Boeing 747-48EF	Air Atlanta Icelandic/Astral Aviation
	TF-BBH	Boeing 737-4YO	Bluebird Cargo
	TF-BBJ	Boeing 737-476F	Bluebird Cargo
	TF-BBK	Boeing 737-4Q8SF	Bluebird Cargo
	TF-BBL	Boeing 737-490	Bluebird Cargo
	TF-BBM	Boeing 737-4Q8F	Bluebird Cargo
	TF-BBN	Boeing 737-4B3F	Bluebird Cargo
	TF-FIA	Boeing 757-256	Icelandair
	TF-FIC	Boeing 757-23N	Icelandair
	TF-FIG	Boeing 757-23APF	Icelandair Cargo
	TF-FIH	Boeing 757-208PCF	Icelandair Cargo
	TF-FIJ	Boeing 757-208	Icelandair
	TF-FIK	Boeing 757-256	Icelandair
	TF-FIN	Boeing 757-208	Icelandair
	TF-FIO	Boeing 757-208	Icelandair
	TF-FIP	Boeing 757-208	Icelandair
	TF-FIR	Boeing 757-256	Icelandair
	TF-FIS	Boeing 757-256	Icelandair
	TF-FIT	Boeing 757-256	Icelandair
	TF-FIU	Boeing 757-256	Icelandair
	TF-FIV	Boeing 757-208	Icelandair
	TF-FIX	Boeing 757-308	Icelandair
	TF-ICA	Boeing 737-MAX9	Icelandair
	TF-ICB	Boeing 737-MAX9	Icelandair
	TF-ICC	Boeing 737-MAX9	Icelandair
	TF-ICE	Boeing 737-MAX8	Icelandair
	TF-ICN	Boeing 737-MAX8	Icelandair
	TF-ICO	Boeing 737-MAX8	Icelandair
	TF-ICP	Boeing 737-MAX8	Icelandair
	TF-ICU	Boeing 737-MAX8	Icelandair
	TF-ICY	Boeing 737-MAX8	Icelandair
	TF-ISD	Boeing 757-223	Icelandair
	TF-ISF	Boeing 757-223	Icelandair
	TF-ISJ	Boeing 757-256	Icelandair
	TF-ISK	Boeing 757-223	Icelandair
	TF-ISN	Boeing 767-319ER	Icelandair
	TF-ISO	Boeing 767-319ER	Icelandair
	TF-ISP	Boeing 767-319ER	Icelandair
	TF-ISR	Boeing 757-256	Icelandair
	TF-ISS	Boeing 757-223	Icelandair
	TF-ISV	Boeing 757-256	Icelandair
	TF-ISW	Boeing 767-319ER	Icelandair
	TF-ISX	Boeing 757-3E7	Icelandair
	TF-ISY	Boeing 757-223	Icelandair
	TF-LLM	Boeing 737-86N	Icelandair
	TF-LLW	Boeing 757-223	Icelandair

TS (Tunisia)

	TS-IFM	Airbus A.330-243	Tunis Air
	TS-IFN	Airbus A.330-243	Tunis Air
	TS-IMF	Airbus A.320-211	Tunis Air *Djerba*
	TS-IMG	Airbus A.320-211	Tunis Air *Abou el Kacem Chebbi*
	TS-IMH	Airbus A.320-211	Tunis Air *Ali Belhaouane*
	TS-IMI	Airbus A.320-211	Tunis Air *Jughurta*
	TS-IML	Airbus A.320-211	Tunis Air *Gafsa el Ksar*
	TS-IMM	Airbus A.320-211	Tunis Air *Le Bardo*
	TS-IMN	Airbus A.320-211	Tunis Air *Ibn Khaldoun*
	TS-IMO	Airbus A.319-114	Tunis Air *Hannibal*
	TS-IMP	Airbus A.320-211	Tunis Air *La Galite*
	TS-IMQ	Airbus A.319-112	Tunis Air *Alyssa*
	TS-IMR	Airbus A.320-211	Tunis Air *Habib Bourguiba*
	TS-IMS	Airbus A.320-214	Tunis Air *Dougga*

Reg	Type	Owner or Operator	Notes
TS-IMT	Airbus A.320-214	Tunis Air *Aziza Othmana*	
TS-IMU	Airbus A.320-214	Tunis Air *Sousse*	
TS-IMV	Airbus A.320-214	Tunis Air *Ibn Eljazzar*	
TS-IMW	Airbus A.320-214	Tunis Air *Farhat Hached*	
TS-INC	Airbus A.320-214	Nouvelair	
TS-IND	Airbus A.320-214	Nouvelair	
TS-INH	Airbus A.320-214	Nouvelair	
TS-INO	Airbus A.320-214	Nouvelair	
TS-INP	Airbus A.320-214	Nouvelair	
TS-INQ	Airbus A.320-214	Nouvelair	
TS-INR	Airbus A.320-214	Nouvelair	
TS-INT	Airbus A.320-214	Nouvelair	
TS-INU	Airbus A.320-214	Nouvelair	
TS-IOK	Boeing 737-6H3	Tunis Air *Kairouan*	
TS-IOL	Boeing 737-6H3	Tunis Air *Tozeur-Nefta*	
TS-IOM	Boeing 737-6H3	Tunis Air *Carthage*	
TS-ION	Boeing 737-6H3	Tunis Air *Utique*	
TS-IOP	Boeing 737-6H3	Tunis Air *El Jem*	
TS-IOQ	Boeing 737-6H3	Tunis Air *Bizerte*	
TS-IOR	Boeing 737-6H3	Tunis Air *Tahar Haddad*	

UK (Uzbekistan)

UK-67003	Boeing 767-33PER	Uzbekistan Airways	
UK-67004	Boeing 767-33PER	Uzbekistan Airways	
UK-67005	Boeing 767-33PER	Uzbekistan Airways	
UK-67006	Boeing 767-33PER	Uzbekistan Airways	
UK-67007	Boeing 767-3CBER	Uzbekistan Airways	
UK-67008	Boeing 767-3CBER	Uzbekistan Airways	
UK-75701	Boeing 757-23P	Uzbekistan Airways	
UK-75702	Boeing 757-23P	Uzbekistan Airways	
UK-75703	Boeing 757-231	Uzbekistan Airways	
UK-75704	Boeing 757-231	Uzbekistan Airways	
UK-75705	Boeing 757-231	Uzbekistan Airways	

UN (Kazakhstan)

Note: Air Astana operates P4- registered Airbus A.321LRs.

UR (Ukraine)

UR-EMA	Embraer ERJ190LR	Ukraine International	
UR-EMB	Embraer ERJ190LR	Ukraine International	
UR-EMC	Embraer ERJ190LR	Ukraine International	
UR-EMD	Embraer ERJ190LR	Ukraine International	
UR-EME	Embraer ERJ190LR	Ukraine International	
UR-EMF	Embraer ERJ195LR	Ukraine International	
UR-EMG	Embraer ERJ195LR	Ukraine International	
UR-MXA	Boeing 737-MAX8	Ukraine International	
UR-MXB	Boeing 737-MAX8	Ukraine International	
UR-MXC	Boeing 737-MAX8	Ukraine International	
UR-PSE	Boeing 737-84R	Ukraine International	
UR-PSF	Boeing 737-84R	Ukraine International	
UR-PSG	Boeing 737-85R	Ukraine International	
UR-PSI	Boeing 737-9KVER	Ukraine International	
UR-PSJ	Boeing 737-9KVER	Ukraine International	
UR-PSK	Boeing 737-94XER	Ukraine International	
UR-PSL	Boeing 737-94XER	Ukraine International	
UR-PSM	Boeing 737-8FZ	Ukraine International	
UR-PSN	Boeing 737-86N	Ukraine International	
UR-PSO	Boeing 737-8Q8	Ukraine International	
UR-PSP	Boeing 737-8Q8	Ukraine International	
UR-PSQ	Boeing 737-86N	Ukraine International	
UR-PSW	Boeing 737-8AS	Ukraine International	
UR-PSX	Boeing 737-8EH	Ukraine International	
UR-PSY	Boeing 737-8EH	Ukraine International	
UR-PSZ	Boeing 737-86N	Ukraine International	
UR-UBA	Boeing 737-8HX	Ukraine International	
UR-UBB	Boeing 737-8HX	Ukraine International	
UR-UIA	Boeing 737-8KV	Ukraine International	

Notes	Reg	Type	Owner or Operator
	UR-82007	Antonov An-124	Antonov Airlines
	UR-82008	Antonov An-124	Antonov Airlines
	UR-82009	Antonov An-124	Antonov Airlines
	UR-82027	Antonov An-124	Antonov Airlines
	UR-82029	Antonov An-124	Antonov Airlines
	UR-82060	Antonov An-225	Antonov Airlines
	UR-82072	Antonov An-124	Antonov Airlines
	UR-82073	Antonov An-124	Antonov Airlines

V8 (Brunei)

	V8-DLA	Boeing 787-8	Royal Brunei Airlines
	V8-DLB	Boeing 787-8	Royal Brunei Airlines
	V8-DLC	Boeing 787-8	Royal Brunei Airlines
	V8-DLD	Boeing 787-8	Royal Brunei Airlines
	V8-DLE	Boeing 787-8	Royal Brunei Airlines

VH (Australia)

	VH-OQA	Airbus A.380-841	QANTAS
	VH-OQB	Airbus A.380-841	QANTAS
	VH-OQC	Airbus A.380-841	QANTAS
	VH-OQD	Airbus A.380-841	QANTAS
	VH-OQE	Airbus A.380-841	QANTAS
	VH-OQF	Airbus A.380-841	QANTAS
	VH-OQG	Airbus A.380-841	QANTAS
	VH-OQH	Airbus A.380-841	QANTAS
	VH-OQI	Airbus A.380-841	QANTAS
	VH-OQJ	Airbus A.380-841	QANTAS
	VH-OQK	Airbus A.380-841	QANTAS
	VH-OQL	Airbus A.380-841	QANTAS
	VH-ZNA	Boeing 787-9	QANTAS
	VH-ZNB	Boeing 787-9	QANTAS
	VH-ZNC	Boeing 787-9	QANTAS
	VH-ZND	Boeing 787-9	QANTAS
	VH-ZNE	Boeing 787-9	QANTAS
	VH-ZNF	Boeing 787-9	QANTAS
	VH-ZNG	Boeing 787-9	QANTAS
	VH-ZNH	Boeing 787-9	QANTAS
	VH-ZNI	Boeing 787-9	QANTAS
	VH-ZNJ	Boeing 787-9	QANTAS
	VH-ZNK	Boeing 787-9	QANTAS
	VH-ZNL	Boeing 787-9	QANTAS
	VH-ZNM	Boeing 787-9	QANTAS
	VH-ZNN	Boeing 787-9	QANTAS

VN (Vietnam)

	VN-A861	Boeing 787-9	Vietnam Airlines
	VN-A862	Boeing 787-9	Vietnam Airlines
	VN-A863	Boeing 787-9	Vietnam Airlines
	VN-A864	Boeing 787-9	Vietnam Airlines
	VN-A865	Boeing 787-9	Vietnam Airlines
	VN-A866	Boeing 787-9	Vietnam Airlines
	VN-A867	Boeing 787-9	Vietnam Airlines
	VN-A868	Boeing 787-9	Vietnam Airlines
	VN-A869	Boeing 787-9	Vietnam Airlines
	VN-A870	Boeing 787-9	Vietnam Airlines
	VN-A871	Boeing 787-9	Vietnam Airlines

VP-B/VP-Q (Bermuda)

	VP-BAC	Airbus A.320-214	Aeroflot Russian International *L. Tolstoy*
	VP-BAD	Airbus A.320-214	Aeroflot Russian International *A. Ioffe*
	VP-BAE	Airbus A.321-211	Aeroflot Russian International *S. Bondarchuk*
	VP-BAF	Airbus A.321-211	Aeroflot Russian International *A. Tarkovsky*
	VP-BAV	Airbus A.321-211	Aeroflot Russian International *F. Ushakov*
	VP-BAX	Airbus A.321-211	Aeroflot Russian International *S. Richter*
	VP-BAY	Airbus A,321-211	Aeroflot Russian International *V. Shukshin*
	VP-BAZ	Airbus A.321-211	Aeroflot Russian International *Y. Levitan*

Reg	Type	Owner or Operator	Notes
VP-BBG	Airbus A.319-112	Ural Airlines	
VP-BBL	Boeing 747-8F	AirBridge Cargo Airlines	
VP-BBQ	Airbus A.320-214	Ural Airlines	
VP-BBP	Boeing 747-8F	AirBridge Cargo Airlines	
VP-BBR	Boeing 787-8	Azerbaijan Airlines	
VP-BBS	Boeing 787-8	Azerbaijan Airlines	
VP-BBT	Airbus A.319-112	Rossiya	
VP-BBU	Airbus A.319-112	Rossiya	
VP-BBY	Boeing 747-8F	AirBridge Cargo Airlines	
VP-BCA	Airbus A.320-214	Aeroflot Russian International A. German	
VP-BCB	Airbus A.320-214	Aeroflot Russian International S. Gerasimov	
VP-BCD	Boeing 737-8LJ	Aeroflot Russian International N. Karamzin	
VP-BCE	Airbus A.320-214	Aeroflot Russian International F. Dostoevsky	
VP-BCF	Boeing 737-8LJ	Aeroflot Russian International I. Krylov	
VP-BCG	Boeing 737-8LJ	Aeroflot Russian International N. Ieskov	
VP-BDD	Airbus A.330-343	Aeroflot Russian International A. Mozhaysky	
VP-BDE	Airbus A.330-343	Aeroflot Russian International L. Kantorovich	
VP-BDL	Airbus A.320-232	Ural Airlines	
VP-BEA	Airbus A.321-211	Aeroflot Russian International I. Dunayevsky	
VP-BEE	Airbus A.321-211	Aeroflot Russian International Y. Lyubimov	
VP-BEG	Airbus A.321-211	Aeroflot Russian International V. Nemirovich-Danchenko	
VP-BEO	Airbus A.320-214	Aeroflot Russian International A. Fet	
VP-BES	Airbus A.321-211	Aeroflot Russian International I. Dunayevsky	
VP-BET	Airbus A.320-214	Aeroflot Russian International A. Voznesensky	
VP-BEW	Airbus A.321-211	Aeroflot Russian International M. Zoschenko	
VP-BFA	Airbus A.320-214	Aeroflot Russian International F. Chaliapin	
VP-BFB	Boeing 737-800	Aeroflot Russian International M. Balakirev	
VP-BFE	Airbus A.320-214	Aeroflot Russian International I. Levitan	
VP-BFF	Airbus A.321-211	Aeroflot Russian International E. Ryazanov	
VP-BFG	Airbus A.320-214	Aeroflot Russian International G. Flerov	
VP-BFH	Airbus A.320-214	Aeroflot Russian International K. Malevich	
VP-BFK	Airbus A.321-211	Aeroflot Russian International F. Volkov	
VP-BFQ	Airbus A.321-211	Aeroflot Russian International A. Alexandrov	
VP-BFX	Airbus A.321-211	Aeroflot Russian International I. Shishkin	
VP-BFZ	Airbus A.350-941	Aeroflot Russian Interntional	
VP-BGB	Boeing 777-300	Aeroflot Russian International M. Kutuzov	
VP-BGC	Boeing 777-300	Aeroflot Russian International P. Bagration	
VP-BGD	Boeing 777-300	Aeroflot Russian International M. Barclay-de-Tolly	
VP-BGF	Boeing 777-300	Aeroflot Russian International D. Davydov	
VP-BGG	Boeing 737-8LJ	Aeroflot Russian International G. Sviridov	
VP-BGI	Boeing 737-8LJ	Aeroflot Russian International Mikhail Vrubel	
VP-BGN	Boeing 737-8LJ	Aeroflot Russian International L. Utesov	
VP-BHA	Boeing 777-300	Aeroflot Russian International A. Skriabin	
VP-BID	Airbus A.320-214	Aeroflot Russian International I. Tamm	
VP-BIE	Airbus A.320-214	Ural Airlines	
VP-BIF	Airbus A.320-214	Aeroflot Russian International L. Gaidai	
VP-BIG	Boeing 747-46NERF	AirBridge Cargo Airlines	
VP-BII	Airbus A.320-214	Aeroflot Russian International S. Dovlatov	
VP-BIJ	Airbus A.320-214	Aeroflot Russian International M. Liepa	
VP-BIK	Boeing 747-46NERF	AirBridge Cargo Airlines	
VP-BIL	Airbus A.320-214	Aeroflot Russian International I. Poddubny	
VP-BIM	Boeing 747-4HAERF	AirBridge Cargo Airlines	
VP-BIN	Boeing 747-8F	AirBridge Cargo Airlines	
VP-BIP	Airbus A.320-214	Aeroflot Russian International I. Severyanin	
VP-BIQ	Airbus A.319-111	Rossiya	
VP-BIT	Airbus A.319-111	Rossiya	
VP-BIU	Airbus A.319-114	Rossiya	
VP-BIV	Airbus A.319-115	Rossiya	
VP-BIW	Airbus A.320-214	Aeroflot Russian International A. Glazunov	
VP-BIX	Airbus A.320-214	Aeroflot Russian International Y. Gagarin	
VP-BIY	Airbus A.320-214	Aeroflot Russian International V. Bryusov	
VP-BJA	Airbus A.320-214	Aeroflot Russian International L. Mechnikov	
VP-BJS	Boeing 747-8F	AirBridge Cargo Airlines	
VP-BJV	Airbus A.319-112	Ural Airlines	
VP-BJW	Airbus A.320-214	Aeroflot Russian International K. Paustovsky	
VP-BJX	Airbus A.321-211	Aeroflot Russian International I. Goncharov	
VP-BJY	Airbus A.320-214	Aeroflot Russian International S. Marshak	
VP-BKA	Boeing 737-800	Aeroflot Russian International M. Magomaev	
VP-BKB	Airbus A.320-214	Ural Airlines	

Notes	Reg	Type	Owner or Operator
	VP-BKE	Boeing 737-800	Aeroflot Russian International *M. Tariverdiev*
	VP-BKF	Boeing 737-800	Aeroflot Russian International *Y. Nikulin*
	VP-BKI	Airbus A.321-211	Aeroflot Russian International *D. Ryabushinsky*
	VP-BKJ	Airbus A.321-211	Aeroflot Russian International
	VP-BKK	Boeing 737-800	Aeroflot Russian International *M. Botvinnik*
	VP-BKN	Boeing 737-800	Aeroflot Russian International *B. Okudzhava*
	VP-BKP	Airbus A.320-214	Aeroflot Russian International *S. Prokofiev*
	VP-BKQ	Airbus A.321-211	Aeroflot Russian International *D. Mendeleev*
	VP-BKR	Airbus A.321-211	Aeroflot Russian International *S. Rachmaninoff*
	VP-BKX	Airbus A.320-214	Ural Airlines
	VP-BKY	Airbus A.320-214	Aeroflot Russian International *M. Rostropovich*
	VP-BKZ	Airbus A.321-211	Aeroflot Russian International *M. Bernes*
	VP-BLH	Airbus A.320-214	Aeroflot Russian International *P. Cherenkov*
	VP-BLL	Airbus A.320-214	Aeroflot Russian International *N. Basov*
	VP-BLN	Airbus A.320-214	Aeroflot Russian International *A. Tarasov*
	VP-BLO	Airbus A.320-214	Aeroflot Russian International *I. Repin*
	VP-BLP	Airbus A.320-214	Aeroflot Russian International *A. Popov*
	VP-BLR	Airbus A.320-214	Aeroflot Russian International *P. Yablochkov*
	VP-BLX	Airbus A.330-243	Aeroflot Russian International *E. Svetlanov*
	VP-BLY	Airbus A.330-243	Aeroflot Russian International *V. Vysotskiy*
	VP-BMB	Boeing 737-8LJ	Aeroflot Russian International
	VP-BMD	Boeing 737-800	Aeroflot Russian International *Igor Stravinsky*
	VP-BME	Airbus A.320-214	Aeroflot Russian International *N. Mikluho-Maklay*
	VP-BMF	Airbus A.320-214	Aeroflot Russian International *G. Shelihov*
	VP-BMI	Boeing 737-800	Aeroflot Russian International *A. Dargomyzhsky*
	VP-BML	Boeing 737-800	Aeroflot Russian International *A. Khachaturian*
	VP-BMM	Boeing 737-800	Aeroflot Russian International *V. Kandinsky*
	VP-BMO	Boeing 737-800	Aeroflot Russian International *M. Mussorgsky*
	VP-BMT	Airbus A.320-214	Ural Airlines
	VP-BMW	Airbus A.320-214	Ural Airlines
	VP-BNC	Boeing 737-800	Aeroflot Russian International *V. Serov*
	VP-BNJ	Airbus A.319-111	Rossiya
	VP-BNL	Airbus A.320-214	Aeroflot Russian International *A. Suvorov*
	VP-BNP	Boeing 737-800	Aeroflot Russian International *I. Ayvazovsky*
	VP-BNQ	Boeing 737-800	Aeroflot Russian International *S. Taneyev*
	VP-BNT	Airbus A.320-214	Aeroflot Russian International *Dobrolet*
	VP-BOC	Airbus A.321-231	Aeroflot Russian International *S. Mikhalkov*
	VP-BOE	Airbus A.321-211	Aeroflot Russian International *G. Vishnevskaya*
	VP-BON	Boeing 737-8LJ	Aeroflot Russian International *N. Berdyaev*
	VP-BPF	Boeing 737-800	Aeroflot Russian International *N. Rerih*
	VP-BPG	Boeing 777-300	Aeroflot Russian International *A. Babajanyan*
	VP-BPM	Airbus A.320-251N	Aeroflot Russian International
	VP-BPP	Airbus A.321-251NX	Aeroflot Russian International *N. Vavilov*
	VP-BPQ	Airbus A.320-251N	Aeroflot Russian International
	VP-BPR	Airbus A.320-251N	Aeroflot Russian International
	VP-BQK	Airbus A.319-111	Rossiya
	VP-BQW	Airbus A.320-214	Ural Airlines
	VP-BRF	Boeing 737-8LJ	Aeroflot Russian International *Sergey Obraztsov*
	VP-BRG	Airbus A.320-251N	Aeroflot Russian International
	VP-BRH	Boeing 737-8LJ	Aeroflot Russian International *B. Kustodiev*
	VP-BRR	Boeing 737-8LJ	Aeroflot Russian International *Alexander Solzhenitsin*
	VP-BSB	Boeing 737-800	Aeroflot Russian International *A. Koni*
	VP-BSF	Airbus A.320-251N	Aeroflot Russian International
	VP-BTA	Airbus A.320-214	Aeroflot Russian International *A. Borodin*
	VP-BTC	Airbus A.320-214	Aeroflot Russian International *S. Chelyuskin*
	VP-BTG	Airbus A.321-211	Aeroflot Russian International *K. Stanivlaskey*
	VP-BTH	Airbus A.321-211	Aeroflot Russian International *R. Rozhdestvensky*
	VP-BTI	Airbus A.320-214	Aeroflot Russian International *V. Meyerhold*
	VP-BTJ	Airbus A.320-214	Aeroflot Russian International *A. Rublev*
	VP-BTK	Airbus A.321-211	Aeroflot Russian International *A. Vertinsky*
	VP-BTL	Airbus A.321-211	Aeroflot Russian International *E. Vakhtangov*
	VP-BTO	Airbus A.320-214	Aeroflot Russian International *N. Semashko*
	VP-BTR	Airbus A.321-211	Aeroflot Russian International *S. Diaghilev*
	VP-BTZ	Airbus A.320-214	Ural Airlines
	VP-BUS	Boeing 737-8MC	Aeroflot Russian International *R. Gamzatov*
	VP-BWG	Airbus A.319-111	Rossiya
	VP-BWH	Airbus A.320-214	Rossiya
	VP-BWI	Airbus A.320-214	Rossiya

Reg	Type	Owner or Operator	Notes
VP-BWJ	Airbus A.319-111	Rossiya	
VP-BXA	Airbus A.350-941	Aeroflot Russian International	
VP-BXC	Airbus A.350-941	Aeroflot Russian International	
VP-BXD	Airbus A.350-941	Aeroflot Russian International	
VP-BXP	Airbus A.350-941	Aeroflot Russian International	
VP-BXS	Airbus A.350-941	Aeroflot Russian International	
VP-BYE	Airbus A.350-941	Aeroflot Russian International	
VP-BYF	Airbus A.350-941	Aeroflot Russian International	
VP-BYG	Airbus A.350-941	Aeroflot Russian International	
VP-BZA	Boeing 737-8LJ	Aeroflot Russian International *Ch.Aytmatov*	
VP-BZB	Boeing 737-8LJ	Aeroflot Russian International *K. Simonov*	
VP-BZQ	Airbus A.320-214	Rossiya	
VP-BZR	Airbus A.320-214	Rossiya	
VQ-BAG	Airbus A.320-214	Ural Airlines	
VQ-BAQ	Airbus A.319-111	Rossiya	
VQ-BAR	Airbus A.319-111	Rossiya	
VQ-BAS	Airbus A.319-111	Rossiya	
VQ-BAT	Airbus A.319-111	Rossiya	
VQ-BAU	Airbus A.319-111	Rossiya	
VQ-BAV	Airbus A.319-111	Rossiya	
VQ-BAX	Airbus A.320-214	Aeroflot Russian International *G. Nevelskoy*	
VQ-BBA	Airbus A.319-111	Rossiya	
VQ-BBE	Airbus A.330-243	Aeroflot Russian International *I. Brodsky*	
VQ-BBF	Airbus A.330-243	Aeroflot Russian International *A. Griboedov*	
VQ-BBG	Airbus A.330-243	Aeroflot Russian International *N. Gogol*	
VQ-BCG	Airbus A.320-214	Rossiya	
VQ-BCI	Airbus A.320-214	Ural Airlines	
VQ-BCM	Airbus A.320-214	Aeroflot Russian International *G. Titov*	
VQ-BCN	Airbus A.320-214	Aeroflot Russian International *V. Chelomey*	
VQ-BCO	Airbus A.319-112	Rossiya	
VQ-BCP	Airbus A.319-112	Rossiya	
VQ-BCY	Airbus A.320-214	Ural Airlines	
VQ-BCZ	Airbus A.320-214	Ural Airlines	
VQ-BDJ	Airbus A.320-214	Ural Airlines	
VQ-BDM	Airbus A.320-214	Ural Airlines	
VQ-BEA	Airbus A.321-211	Aeroflot Russian International *I. Michurin*	
VQ-BED	Airbus A.321-211	Aeroflot Russian International *N. Pirogov*	
VQ-BEG	Airbus A.321-211	Aeroflot Russian International *K. Tsiolkovsky*	
VQ-BEH	Airbus A.320-214	Aeroflot Russian International *I. Pavlov*	
VQ-BEJ	Airbus A.320-214	Aeroflot Russian International *I. Kurchatov*	
VQ-BFE	Boeing 747-8F	AirBridge Cargo Airlines	
VQ-BFK	Boeing 777-300	Aeroflot Russian International *V. Chuikov*	
VQ-BFL	Boeing 777-300	Aeroflot Russian International *K. Balmont*	
VQ-BFM	Airbus A.320-214	Rossiya	
VQ-BFN	Boeing 777-300ER	Aeroflot Russian International	
VQ-BFO	Boeing 777-300ER	Aeroflot Russian International	
VQ-BFU	Boeing 747-8F	AirBridge Cargo Airlines	
VQ-BFV	Airbus A.320-214	Ural Airlines	
VQ-BFW	Airbus A.320-214	Ural Airlines	
VQ-BFY	Airbus A.350-941	Aeroflot Russian International *P. Tchaikovsky*	
VQ-BFZ	Airbus A.350-941	Aeroflot Russian International	
VQ-BGI	Airbus A.320-232	Ural Airlines	
VQ-BGJ	Airbus A.320-232	Ural Airlines	
VQ-BGZ	Boeing 747-8F	AirBridge Cargo Airlines	
VQ-BHB	Boeing 737-800	Aeroflot Russian International *N. Nekrasov*	
VQ-BHC	Boeing 737-800	Aeroflot Russian International *P. Nakhimov*	
VQ-BHD	Boeing 737-800	Aeroflot Russian International *I. Frolov*	
VQ-BHL	Airbus A.320-214	Aeroflot Russian International *S. Vavilov*	
VQ-BHN	Airbus A.320-214	Aeroflot Russian International *N. Lobachevsky*	
VQ-BHQ	Boeing 737-800	Aeroflot Russian International *D. Khvorostovsky*	
VQ-BHR	Boeing 737-800	Aeroflot Russian International *I. Sikorsky*	
VQ-BHT	Boeing 737-800	Aeroflot Russian International *A. Grin*	
VQ-BHU	Boeing 737-800	Aeroflot Russian International *I. Kobzon*	
VQ-BHV	Boeing 737-800	Aeroflot Russian International *N. Nosov*	
VQ-BHW	Boeing 737-800	Aeroflot Russian International *F. Plevako*	
VQ-BHX	Boeing 737-800	Aeroflot Russian International *V. Kotenochkin*	
VQ-BIL	Boeing 777-300	Aeroflot Russian International *A. Pushkin*	
VQ-BIR	Airbus A.320-214	Aeroflot Russian International *S. Kovalevskaya*	
VQ-BIT	Airbus A.320-214	Aeroflot Russian International *L. Landau*	
VQ-BIU	Airbus A.320-214	Aeroflot Russian International *K. Timiryazev*	
VQ-BIV	Airbus A.320-214	Aeroflot Russian International *A. Kolmogorov*	

Notes	Reg	Type	Owner or Operator
	VQ-BIW	Airbus A.320-214	Aeroflot Russian International *V. Glushko*
	VQ-BKS	Airbus A.320-214	Aeroflot Russian International *A. Chivhevsky*
	VQ-BKT	Airbus A.320-214	Aeroflot Russian International *V. Vernadsky*
	VQ-BKU	Airbus A.320-214	Aeroflot Russian International *A. Nikolaev*
	VQ-BLO	Airbus A.320-214	Ural Airlines
	VQ-BLQ	Boeing 747-8F	AirBridge Cargo Airlines
	VQ-BLR	Boeing 747-8F	AirBridge Cargo Airlines
	VQ-BMV	Airbus A.330-343	Aeroflot Russian International *P. Kapitsa*
	VQ-BMX	Airbus A.330-343	Aeroflot Russian International *A. Sakharov*
	VQ-BMY	Airbus A.330-343	Aeroflot Russian International *Ilya Frank*
	VQ-BNI	Airbus A.320-214	Ural Airlines
	VQ-BNS	Airbus A.330-343	Aeroflot Russian International *A. Bakulev*
	VQ-BOX	Airbus A.319-111	Rossiya
	VQ-BPI	Airbus A.330-343	Aeroflot Russian International *L. Yashin*
	VQ-BPJ	Airbus A.330-343	Aeroflot Russian International *V. Brumel*
	VQ-BPK	Airbus A.330-343	Aeroflot Russian International *L. Kulibin*
	VQ-BPU	Airbus A.320-214	Aeroflot Russian International
	VQ-BPV	Airbus A.320-214	Aeroflot Russian International
	VQ-BPW	Airbus A.320-214	Aeroflot Russian International
	VQ-BQB	Boeing 777-300	Aeroflot Russian International *A. Kuprin*
	VQ-BQC	Boeing 777-300	Aeroflot Russian International *I. Bunin*
	VQ-BQD	Boeing 777-300	Aeroflot Russian International *A. Chekhov*
	VQ-BQE	Boeing 777-300	Aeroflot Russian International *M. Lermontov*
	VQ-BQF	Boeing 777-300	Aeroflot Russian International *A. Blok*
	VQ-BQG	Boeing 777-300	Aeroflot Russian International
	VQ-BQM	Boeing 777-300	Aeroflot Russian International *L. Turgenev*
	VQ-BQN	Airbus A.320-214	Ural Airlines
	VQ-BQX	Airbus A.330-343	Aeroflot Russian International
	VQ-BQY	Airbus A.330-343	Aeroflot Russian International *M. Sholohov*
	VQ-BQZ	Airbus A.330-343	Aeroflot Russian International *N. Burdenko*
	VQ-BRE	Airbus A.320-214	Ural Airlines
	VQ-BRH	Boeing 747-8F	AirBridge Cargo Airlines
	VQ-BRJ	Boeing 747-8F	AirBridge Cargo Airlines
	VQ-BRV	Airbus A.320-214	Rossiya
	VQ-BRW	Airbus A.320-214	Aeroflot Russian International
	VQ-BSE	Airbus A.320-214	Rossiya
	VQ-BSG	Airbus A.320-214	Rossiya
	VQ-BSH	Airbus A.320-214	Rossiya
	VQ-BSI	Airbus A.320-214	Aeroflot Russian International *V. Komarov*
	VQ-BSJ	Airbus A.320-214	Aeroflot Russian International *B. Egorov*
	VQ-BSL	Airbus A.320-214	Aeroflot Russian International *K. Feoktistov*
	VQ-BST	Airbus A.320-214	Aeroflot Russian International *P. Popovich*
	VQ-BSU	Airbus A.320-214	Aeroflot Russian International *G. Zhukov*
	VQ-BTP	Airbus A.319-112	Ural Airlines
	VQ-BTT	Airbus A.321-211	Aeroflot Russian International *A. Gomelsky*
	VQ-BTU	Airbus A.321-211	Aeroflot Russian International *S. Belov*
	VQ-BTW	Airbus A.320-214	Aeroflot Russian International *F. Tolbukhin*
	VQ-BTX	Airbus A.320-214	Aeroflot Russian International *G. Fedotov*
	VQ-BTY	Airbus A.319-112	Ural Airlines
	VQ-BTZ	Airbus A.319-112	Ural Airlines
	VQ-BUA	Boeing 777-300	Aeroflot Russian International *S. Esenin*
	VQ-BUB	Boeing 777-300	Aeroflot Russian International *M. Bulgakov*
	VQ-BUC	Boeing 777-300	Aeroflot Russian International *A. Ostrovsky*
	VQ-BVO	Boeing 737-8LJ	Aeroflot Russian International *V. Belinsky*
	VQ-BVP	Boeing 737-8LJ	Aeroflot Russian International *L. Gumilev*
	VQ-BVR	Boeing 747-8F	AirBridge Cargo Airlines
	VQ-BVU	Boeing 737-8LJ	Aeroflot Russian International *V. Shukhov*
	VQ-BVV	Boeing 737-8LJ	Aeroflot Russian International *A. Gromyko*
	VQ-BWA	Boeing 737-8LJ	Aeroflot Russian International *V. Dahl*
	VQ-BWB	Boeing 737-8LJ	Aeroflot Russian International *S. Ozhegov*
	VQ-BWC	Boeing 737-8LJ	Aeroflot Russian International *S. Soloviev*
	VQ-BWD	Boeing 737-8LJ	Aeroflot Russian International *G. Tovstonogov*
	VQ-BWE	Boeing 737-8LJ	Aeroflot Russian International *M. Shchepkin*
	VQ-BWF	Boeing 737-8LJ	Aeroflot Russian International *S. Eisenstein*
	VQ-BWW	Boeing 747-4EVERF	AirBridge Cargo Airlines

VT (India)

	VT-ALJ	Boeing 777-337ER	Air India
	VT-ALK	Boeing 777-337ER	Air India
	VT-ALL	Boeing 777-337ER	Air-India

Reg	Type	Owner or Operator	Notes
VT-ALM	Boeing 777-337ER	Air India	
VT-ALN	Boeing 777-337ER	Air India	
VT-ALO	Boeing 777-337ER	Air India	
VT-ALP	Boeing 777-337ER	Air India	
VT-ALQ	Boeing 777-337ER	Air India	
VT-ALR	Boeing 777-337ER	Air India	
VT-ALS	Boeing 777-337ER	Air India	
VT-ALT	Boeing 777-337ER	Air India	
VT-ALU	Boeing 777-337ER	Air India	
VT-ALX	Boeing 777-337ER	Air India	
VT-ANA	Boeing 787-8	Air India	
VT-ANB	Boeing 787-8	Air India	
VT-ANC	Boeing 787-8	Air India	
VT-AND	Boeing 787-8	Air India	
VT-ANE	Boeing 787-8	Air India	
VT-ANG	Boeing 787-8	Air India	
VT-ANH	Boeing 787-8	Air India	
VT-ANI	Boeing 787-8	Air India	
VT-ANJ	Boeing 787-8	Air India	
VT-ANK	Boeing 787-8	Air India	
VT-ANL	Boeing 787-8	Air India	
VT-ANM	Boeing 787-8	Air India	
VT-ANN	Boeing 787-8	Air India	
VT-ANO	Boeing 787-8	Air India	
VT-ANP	Boeing 787-8	Air India	
VT-ANQ	Boeing 787-8	Air India	
VT-ANR	Boeing 787-8	Air India	
VT-ANS	Boeing 787-8	Air India	
VT-ANT	Boeing 787-8	Air India	
VT-ANU	Boeing 787-8	Air India	
VT-ANV	Boeing 787-8	Air India	
VT-ANW	Boeing 787-8	Air India	
VT-ANX	Boeing 787-8	Air India	
VT-ANY	Boeing 787-8	Air India	
VT-ANZ	Boeing 787-8	Air India	
VT-NAA	Boeing 787-8	Air India	
VT-NAC	Boeing 787-8	Air India	
VT-TSD	Boeing 787-9	Vistara	
VT-TSE	Boeing 787-9	Vistara	
VT-TSH	Boeing 787-9	Vistara	
VT-TSN	Boeing 787-9	Vistara	

XA (Mexico)

Reg	Type	Owner or Operator	Notes
XA-ADC	Boeing 787-9	Aeromexico	
XA-ADD	Boeing 787-9	Aeromexico	
XA-ADG	Boeing 787-9	Aeromexico	
XA-ADH	Boeing 787-9	Aeromexico	
XA-ADL	Boeing 787-9	Aeromexico	
XA-AMR	Boeing 787-8	Aeromexico	
XA-AMX	Boeing 787-8	Aeromexico	
XA-MFG	Boeing 787-9	Aeromexico	
XA-RRR	Boeing 787-9	Aeromexico	
XA-SSS	Boeing 787-9	Aeromexico	

YI (Iraq)

Reg	Type	Owner or Operator	Notes
YI-ARA	Airbus A.320-214	Iraqi Airways	
YI-ARB	Airbus A.320-214	Iraqi Airways	
YI-ARD	Airbus A.320-214	Iraqi Airways	

YL (Latvia)

Reg	Type	Owner or Operator	Notes
YL-AAO	Airbus A.220-300	Air Baltic	
YL-AAP	Airbus A.220-300	Air Baltic	
YL-AAQ	Airbus A.220-300	Air Baltic	
YL-AAR	Airbus A.220-300	Air Baltic	
YL-AAS	Airbus A.220-300	Air Baltic	
YL-AAT	Airbus A.220-300	Air Baltic	
YL-AAU	Airbus A.220-300	Air Baltic	

Notes	Reg	Type	Owner or Operator
	YL-AAV	Airbus A.220-300	Air Baltic
	YL-AAW	Airbus A.220-300	Air Baltic
	YL-AAX	Airbus A.220-300	Air Baltic
	YL-AAY	Airbus A.220-300	Air Baltic
	YL-CSA	Airbus A.220-300	Air Baltic
	YL-CSB	Airbus A.220-300	Air Baltic
	YL-CSC	Airbus A.220.300	Air Baltic
	YL-CSD	Airbus A.220.300	Air Baltic
	YL-CSE	Airbus A.220.300	Air Baltic
	YL-CSF	Airbus A.220-300	Air Baltic
	YL-CSG	Airbus A.220.300	Air Baltic
	YL-CSH	Airbus A.220.300	Air Baltic
	YL-CSI	Airbus A.220.300	Air Baltic
	YL-CSJ	Airbus A.220.300	Air Baltic
	YL-CSK	Airbus A.220.300	Air Baltic
	YL-CSL	Airbus A.220.300	Air Baltic
	YL-CSM	Airbus A.220.300	Air Baltic
	YL-CSN	Airbus A.220.300	Air Baltic
	YL-LCL	Airbus A.320-214	Smart Lynx Airlines
	YL-LCP	Airbus A.320-232	Smart Lynx Airlines
	YL-LCQ	Airbus A.321-231	Smart Lynx Airlines
	YL-LCS	Airbus A.320-214	Smart Lynx Airlines
	YL-LCU	Airbus A.320-214	Smart Lynx Airlines
	YL-LCV	Airbus A.321-231	Smart Lynx Airlines
	YL-LCX	Airbus A.321-211	Smart Lynx Airlines
	YL-LCY	Airbus A.321-211	Smart Lynx Airlines
	YL-LCZ	Airbus A.321-211	Smart Lynx Airlines
	YL-LDA	Airbus A.321-211	Smart Lynx Airlines
	YL-LDB	Airbus A.321-211	Smart Lynx Airlines
	YL-LDD	Airbus A.321-231	Smart Lynx Airlines
	YL-LDH	Airbus A.321-211	Smart Lynx Airlines

YR (Romania)

Notes	Reg	Type	Owner or Operator
	YR-AMA	Boeing 737-530	Blue Air
	YR-AMB	Boeing 737-530	Blue Air
	YR-AME	Boeing 737-530	Blue Air
	YR-ASA	Airbus A.318-111	Tarom *Aurel Vlaicu*
	YR-ASB	Airbus A.318-111	Tarom *Traian Vuia*
	YR-ASC	Airbus A.318-111	Tarom *Henri Coanda*
	YR-ASD	Airbus A.318-111	Tarom *Smaranda Braescu*
	YR-BAG	Boeing 737-5L9	Blue Air
	YR-BAP	Boeing 737-3YO	Blue Air
	YR-BGA	Boeing 737-38J	Tarom *Alba Iulia*
	YR-BGB	Boeing 737-38J	Tarom *Bucuresti*
	YR-BGD	Boeing 737-38J	Tarom *Deva*
	YR-BGE	Boeing 737-38J	Tarom *Timisoara*
	YR-BGF	Boeing 737-78J	Tarom *Braila*
	YR-BGG	Boeing 737-78J	Tarom *Craiova*
	YR-BGH	Boeing 737-78J	Tarom *Hunedoara*
	YR-BGI	Boeing 737-78J	Tarom *Iasi*
	YR-BGJ	Boeing 737-82R	Tarom *Sarmizegetusa*
	YR-BGK	Boeing 737-82R	Tarom *Marea Unire*
	YR-BGL	Boeing 737-8H6	Tarom *Alexandru Ioan Cuza*
	YR-BGM	Boeing 737-8H6	Tarom *Mihai Vitaezul*
	YR-BMB	Boeing 737-85R	Blue Air
	YR-BMG	Boeing 737-86N	Blue Air
	YR-BMJ	Boeing 737-82R	Blue Air
	YR-BMK	Boeing 737-82R	Blue Air
	YR-BML	Boeing 737-82R	Blue Air
	YR-BMM	Boeing 737-82R	Blue Air
	YR-BMN	Boeing 737-82R	Blue Air
	YR-BMO	Boeing 737-883	Blue Air
	YR-BMP	Boeing 737-883	Blue Air
	YR-BMQ	Boeing 737-8FH	Blue Air
	YR-BMR	Boeing 737-7K2	Blue Air
	YR-BMS	Boeing 737-8Q8	Blue Air
	YR-MXA	Boeing 737-MAX8	Blue Air

Reg	Type	Owner or Operator	Notes
YU (Serbia and Montenegro)			
YU-APA	Airbus A.319-132	Air Serbia	
YU-APB	Airbus A.319-132	Air Serbia	
YU-APC	Airbus A.319-131	Air Serbia	
YU-APD	Airbus A.319-132	Air Serbia	
YU-APE	Airbus A.319-132	Air Serbia	
YU-APF	Airbus A.319-131	Air Serbia	
YU-APH	Airbus A.320-232	Air Serbia	
YU-API	Airbus A.319-132	Air Serbia	
YU-APJ	Airbus A.319-132	Air Serbia	
YU-APK	Airbus A.319-132	Air Serbia	
YU-APL	Airbus A.319-132	Air Serbia	
YU-APM	Airbus A.319-132	Air Serbia	
ZA (Albania)			
ZA-ALB	Boeing 737-46J	Albawings	
ZA-ALC	Boeing 737-4Q8	Albawings	
ZA-AWB	Boeing 737-408	Albawings	
ZS (South Africa)			
ZS-SNC	Airbus A.340-642	South African Airways	
ZS-SND	Airbus A.340-642	South African Airways	
ZS-SNF	Airbus A.340-642	South African Airways	
ZS-SNG	Airbus A.340-642	South African Airways	
ZS-SXE	Airbus A.340-313E	South African Airways	
ZS-SXF	Airbus A.340-313E	South African Airways	
ZS-SXM	Airbus A.330-343E	South African Airways	
3B (Mauritius)			
3B-NBD	Airbus A.340-313X	Air Mauritius *Parakeet*	
3B-NBE	Airbus A.340-313X	Air Mauritius *Paille en Queue*	
3B-NBP	Airbus A.350-941	Air Mauritius *Le Morne Brabant*	
3B-NBQ	Airbus A.350-941	Air Mauritius *Pieter Both*	
3B-NBU	Airbus A.330-941N	Air Mauritius *Aapravasi Ghat*	
3B-NBV	Airbus A.330-941N	Air Mauritius *Chagos Archipelago*	
3B-NCE	Airbus A.350-941	Air Mauritius	
3B-NCF	Airbus A.350-941	Air Mauritius	
4K (Azerbaijan)			
4K-AZ81	Boeing 767-32LER	Azerbaijan Airlines	
4K-AZ82	Boeing 767-32LER	Azerbaijan Airlines	
4L (Georgia)			
4L-MGT	Embraer ERJ190-200LR	Georgian Airways	
4L-TGC	Boeing 737-8FH	Georgian Airways	
4L-TGH	Embraer ERJ190-100AR	Georgian Airways	
4R (Sri Lanka)			
4R-ALL	Airbus A.330-343	SriLankan Airlines	
4R-ALM	Airbus A.330-343	SriLankan Airlines	
4R-ALN	Airbus A.330-343	SriLankan Airlines	
4R-ALO	Airbus A.330-343	SriLankan Airlines	
4R-ALP	Airbus A.330-343	SriLankan Airlines	
4R-ALQ	Airbus A.330-343	SriLankan Airlines	
4R-ALR	Airbus A.330-343	SriLankan Airlines	
4X (Israel)			
4X-ABF	Airbus A.320-232	Israir	
4X-ABG	Airbus A.320-232	Israir	
4X-ABI	Airbus A.320-232	Israir	
4X-ABS	Airbus A.320-232	Israir	

Notes	Reg	Type	Owner or Operator
	4X-AGH	Airbus A.321-251NX	Arkia
	4X-AGK	Airbus A.321-251NX	Arkia
	4X-ECA	Boeing 777-258ER	El Al
	4X-ECB	Boeing 777-258ER	El Al
	4X-ECC	Boeing 777-258ER	El Al
	4X-ECD	Boeing 777-258ER	El Al
	4X-ECE	Boeing 777-258ER	El Al
	4X-ECF	Boeing 777-258ER	El Al
	4X-EDA	Boeing 787-9	El Al
	4X-EDB	Boeing 787-9	El Al
	4X-EDC	Boeing 787-9	El Al
	4X-EDD	Boeing 787-9	El Al
	4X-EDE	Boeing 787-9	El Al
	4X-EDF	Boeing 787-9	El Al
	4X-EDH	Boeing 787-9	El Al
	4X-EDI	Boeing 787-9	El Al
	4X-EDJ	Boeing 787-9	El Al
	4X-EDK	Boeing 787-9	El Al
	4X-EDL	Boeing 787-9	El Al
	4X-EDM	Boeing 787-9	El Al
	4X-EHA	Boeing 737-958ER	El Al
	4X-EHB	Boeing 737-958ER	El Al
	4X-EHC	Boeing 737-958ER	El Al
	4X-EHD	Boeing 737-958ER	El Al
	4X-EHE	Boeing 737-958ER	El Al
	4X-EHF	Boeing 737-958ER	El Al
	4X-EHH	Boeing 737-958ER	El Al
	4X-EHI	Boeing 737-958ER	El Al
	4X-EKA	Boeing 737-858	El Al
	4X-EKB	Boeing 737-858	El Al
	4X-EKC	Boeing 737-858	El Al
	4X-EKF	Boeing 737-858	El Al
	4X-EKH	Boeing 737-85P	El Al
	4X-EKI	Boeing 737-86N	El Al
	4X-EKJ	Boeing 737-85P	El Al
	4X-EKK	Boeing 737-800	El Al
	4X-EKL	Boeing 737-85P	El Al
	4X-EKM	Boeing 737-804	El Al
	4X-EKO	Boeing 737-86Q	El Al
	4X-EKP	Boeing 737-8Q8	El Al
	4X-EKS	Boeing 737-8Q8	El Al
	4X-EKT	Boeing 737-8BK	El Al
	4X-EKU	Boeing 737-8Z9	El Al
	4X-EKV	Boeing 737-85R	El Al
	4X-ERA	Boeing 787-8	El Al
	4X-ERB	Boeing 787-8	El Al
	4X-ERC	Boeing 787-8	El Al
	4X-ERD	Boeing 787-8	El Al

5Y (Kenya)

Notes	Reg	Type	Owner or Operator
	5Y-KZA	Boeing 787-8	Kenya Airways
	5Y-KZB	Boeing 787-8	Kenya Airways
	5Y-KZC	Boeing 787-8	Kenya Airways
	5Y-KZD	Boeing 787-8	Kenya Airlines
	5Y-KZE	Boeing 787-8	Kenya Airways
	5Y-KZF	Boeing 787-8	Kenya Airways
	5Y-KZG	Boeing 787-8	Kenya Airways
	5Y-KZH	Boeing 787-8	Kenya Airways
	5Y-KZJ	Boeing 787-8	Kenya Airways

7T (Algeria)

Notes	Reg	Type	Owner or Operator
	7T-VJA	Airbus A.330-202	Air Algerie
	7T-VJB	Airbus A.330-202	Air Algerie
	7T-VJC	Airbus A.330-202	Air Algerie
	7T-VJK	Boeing 737-8D6	Air Algerie *Mansourah*
	7T-VJL	Boeing 737-8D6	Air Algerie *Illizi*
	7T-VJM	Boeing 737-8D6	Air Algerie
	7T-VJN	Boeing 737-8D6	Air Algerie

Reg	Type	Owner or Operator	Notes
7T-VJO	Boeing 737-8D6	Air Algerie	
7T-VJP	Boeing 737-8D6	Air Algerie	
7T-VJQ	Boeing 737-6D6	Air Algerie *Kasbah d'Alger*	
7T-VJR	Boeing 737-6D6	Air Algerie	
7T-VJS	Boeing 737-6D6	Air Algerie	
7T-VJT	Boeing 737-6D6	Air Algerie	
7T-VJU	Boeing 737-6D6	Air Algerie	
7T-VJV	Airbus A.330-202	Air Algerie *Tinhinan*	
7T-VJW	Airbus A.330-202	Air Algerie *Lalla Setti*	
7T-VJX	Airbus A.330-202	Air Algerie *Mers el Kebir*	
7T-VJY	Airbus A.330-202	Air Algerie *Monts des Beni Chougrane*	
7T-VJZ	Airbus A.330-202	Air Algerie *Teddis*	
7T-VKA	Boeing 737-8D6	Air Algerie	
7T-VKB	Boeing 737-8D6	Air Algerie	
7T-VKC	Boeing 737-8D6	Air Algerie	
7T-VKD	Boeing 737-8D6	Air Algerie	
7T-VKE	Boeing 737-8D6	Air Algerie	
7T-VKF	Boeing 737-8D6	Air Algerie	
7T-VKG	Boeing 737-8D6	Air Algerie	
7T-VKH	Boeing 737-8D6	Air Algerie	
7T-VKI	Boeing 737-8D6	Air Algerie	
7T-VKJ	Boeing 737-8D6	Air Algerie	
7T-VKK	Boeing 737-8D6	Air Algerie	
7T-VKL	Boeing 737-8D6	Air Algerie	
7T-VKM	Boeing 737-8D6	Air Algerie	
7T-VKN	Boeing 737-8D6	Air Algerie	
7T-VKO	Boeing 737-8D6	Air Algerie	
7T-VKP	Boeing 737-8D6	Air Algerie	
7T-VKQ	Boeing 737-8D6	Air Algerie	
7T-VKR	Boeing 737-8D6	Air Algerie	
7T-VKS	Boeing 737-7D6	Air Algerie	
7T-VKT	Boeing 737-7D6	Air Algerie	

9A (Croatia)

Reg	Type	Owner or Operator	Notes
9A-CTG	Airbus A.319-112	Croatia Airlines *Zadar*	
9A-CTH	Airbus A.319-112	Croatia Airlines *Zagreb*	
9A-CTI	Airbus A.319-112	Croatia Airlines *Vukovar*	
9A-CTJ	Airbus A.320-214	Croatia Airlines *Dubrovnik*	
9A-CTK	Airbus A.320-214	Croatia Airlines *Split*	
9A-CTL	Airbus A.319-112	Croatia Airlines *Pula*	
9A-CTN	Airbus A.319-112	Croatia Airlines	

9H (Malta)

Reg	Type	Owner or Operator	Notes
9H-AEN	Airbus A.320-214	Air Malta	
9H-AEO	Airbus A.320-214	Malta Med Air	
9H-AEP	Airbus A.320-214	Air Malta	
9H-AEQ	Airbus A.320-214	Air Malta	
9H-AHS	Airbus A.320-214	Air Malta	
9H-EAC	Airbus A.340-642	Maleth-Aero	
9H-EAD	Airbus A.340-642	Maleth-Aero	
9H-EAL	Airbus A.340-642	Maleth-Aero	
9H-FOX	Airbus A.340-313X	Hi Fly Malta	
9H-HFC	Airbus A.330-343	Hi Fly Malta	
9H-HFE	Airbus A.330-343	Hi Fly Malta	
9H-IBJ	Airbus A.320-232	Lauda Europe	
9H-IHD	Airbus A.320-232	Lauda Europe	
9H-IHH	Airbus A.320-232	Lauda Europe	
9H-IHL	Airbus A.320-232	Lauda Europe	
9H-JAI	Airbus A.340-313X	Hi Fly Malta	
9H-LAJ	Airbus A.320-232	Lauda Europe	
9H-LAX	Airbus A.320-214	Lauda Europe	
9H-LMB	Airbus A.320-232	Lauda Europe	
9H-LMC	Airbus A.320-214	Lauda Europe	
9H-LMG	Airbus A.320-232	Lauda Europe	
9H-LMH	Airbus A.320-232	Lauda Europe	
9H-LMI	Airbus A.320-232	Lauda Europe	
9H-LMJ	Airbus A.320-232	Lauda Europe	
9H-LMP	Airbus A.320-214	Lauda Europe	

OVERSEAS AIRLINERS

Notes	Reg	Type	Owner or Operator
	9H-LMR	Airbus A.320-214	Lauda Europe
	9H-LMT	Airbus A.320-214	Lauda Europe
	9H-LOA	Airbus A.320-214	Lauda Europe
	9H-LOB	Airbus A.320-232	Lauda Europe
	9H-LOI	Airbus A.320-214	Lauda Europe
	9H-LOM	Airbus A.320-232	Lauda Europe
	9H-LON	Airbus A.320-214	Lauda Europe
	9H-LOO	Airbus A.320-214	Lauda Europe
	9H-LOP	Airbus A.320-232	Lauda Europe
	9H-LOQ	Airbus A.320-232	Lauda Europe
	9H-LOR	Airbus A.320-214	Lauda Europe
	9H-LOS	Airbus A.320-214	Lauda Europe
	9H-LOT	Airbus A.320-232	Lauda Europe
	9H-LOU	Airbus A.320-214	Lauda Europe
	9H-LOW	Airbus A.320-214	Lauda Europe
	9H-LOY	Airbus A.320-232	Lauda Europe
	9H-LOZ	Airbus A.320-232	Lauda Europe
	9H-NEB	Airbus A.320-251N	Air Malta
	9H-NEC	Airbus A.320-251N	Air Malta
	9H-NED	Airbus A.320-251N	Air Malta
	9H-NEO	Airbus A-320-251N	Air Malta
	9H-NHS	Airbus A.340-642	Maleth-Aero
	9H-QAA	Boeing 737-8AS	Ryanair/Malta Air
	9H-QAB	Boeing 737-8AS	Ryanair/Malta Air
	9H-QAC	Boeing 737-8AS	Ryanair/Malta Air
	9H-QAD	Boeing 737-8AS	Ryanair/Malta Air
	9H-QAE	Boeing 737-8AS	Ryanair/Malta Air
	9H-QAF	Boeing 737-8AS	Ryanair/Malta Air
	9H-QAG	Boeing 737-8AS	Ryanair/Malta Air
	9H-QAH	Boeing 737-8AS	Ryanair/Malta Air
	9H-QAI	Boeing 737-8AS	Ryanair/Malta Air
	9H-QAJ	Boeing 737-8AS	Ryanair/Malta Air
	9H-QAK	Boeing 737-8AS	Ryanair/Malta Air
	9H-QAL	Boeing 737-8AS	Ryanair/Malta Air
	9H-QAM	Boeing 737-8AS	Ryanair/Malta Air
	9H-QAN	Boeing 737-8AS	Ryanair/Malta Air
	9H-QAO	Boeing 737-8AS	Ryanair/Malta Air
	9H-QAP	Boeing 737-8AS	Ryanair/Malta Air
	9H-OAQ	Boeing 737-8AS	Ryanair/Malta Air
	9H-QAR	Boeing 737-8AS	Ryanair/Malta Air
	9H-QAS	Boeing 737-8AS	Ryanair/Malta Air
	9H-QAT	Boeing 737-8AS	Ryanair/Malta Air
	9H-QAU	Boeing 737-8AS	Ryanair/Malta Air
	9H-QAV	Boeing 737-8AS	Ryanair/Malta Air
	9H-QAW	Boeing 737-8AS	Ryanair/Malta Air
	9H-QAX	Boeing 737-8AS	Ryanair/Malta Air
	9H-QAY	Boeing 737-8AS	Ryanair/Malta Air
	9H-QAZ	Boeing 737-8AS	Ryanair/Malta Air
	9H-QBA	Boeing 737-8AS	Ryanair/Malta Air
	9H-QBB	Boeing 737-8AS	Ryanair/Malta Air
	9H-QBC	Boeing 737-8AS	Ryanair/Malta Air
	9H-QBD	Boeing 737-8AS	Ryanair/Malta Air
	9H-QBE	Boeing 737-8AS	Ryanair/Malta Air
	9H-QBF	Boeing 737-8AS	Ryanair/Malta Air
	9H-QBG	Boeing 737-8AS	Ryanair/Malta Air
	9H-QBH	Boeing 737-8AS	Ryanair/Malta Air
	9H-QBI	Boeing 737-8AS	Ryanair/Malta Air
	9H-QBJ	Boeing 737-8AS	Ryanair/Malta Air
	9H-QBK	Boeing 737-8AS	Ryanair/Malta Air
	9H-QBL	Boeing 737-8AS	Ryanair/Malta Air
	9H-QBM	Boeing 737-8AS	Ryanair/Malta Air
	9H-QBN	Boeing 737-8AS	Ryanair/Malta Air
	9H-QBO	Boeing 737-8AS	Ryanair/Malta Air
	9H-QBP	Boeing 737-8AS	Ryanair/Malta Air
	9H-QBR	Boeing 737-8AS	Ryanair/Malta Air
	9H-QBQ	Boeing 737-8AS	Ryanair/Malta Air
	9H-QBS	Boeing 737-8AS	Ryanair/Malta Air
	9H-QBT	Boeing 737-8AS	Ryanair/Malta Air
	9H-QBU	Boeing 737-8AS	Ryanair/Malta Air
	9H-QBV	Boeing 737-8AS	Ryanair/Malta Air
	9H-QBW	Boeing 737-8AS	Ryanair/Malta Air

Reg	Type	Owner or Operator	Notes
9H-QBX	Boeing 737-8AS	Ryanair/Malta Air	
9H-QBY	Boeing 737-8AS	Ryanair/Malta Air	
9H-QBZ	Boeing 737-8AS	Ryanair/Malta Air	
9H-QCA	Boeing 737-8AS	Ryanair/Malta Air	
9H-QCB	Boeing 737-8AS	Ryanair/Malta Air	
9H-QCC	Boeing 737-8AS	Ryanair/Malta Air	
9H-QCD	Boeing 737-8AS	Ryanair/Malta Air	
9H-QCE	Boeing 737-8AS	Ryanair/Malta Air	
9H-QCF	Boeing 737-8AS	Ryanair/Malta Air	
9H-QCG	Boeing 737-8AS	Ryanair/Malta Air	
9H-QCH	Boeing 737-8AS	Ryanair/Malta Air	
9H-QCI	Boeing 737-8AS	Ryanair/Malta Air	
9H-QCJ	Boeing 737-8AS	Ryanair/Malta Air	
9H-QCK	Boeing 737-8AS	Ryanair/Malta Air	
9H-QCL	Boeing 737-8AS	Ryanair/Malta Air	
9H-QCM	Boeing 737-8AS	Ryanair/Malta Air	
9H-QCN	Boeing 737-8AS	Ryanair/Malta Air	
9H-QCO	Boeing 737-8AS	Ryanair/Malta Air	
9H-QCP	Boeing 737-8AS	Ryanair/Malta Air	
9H-QCQ	Boeing 737-8AS	Ryanair/Malta Air	
9H-QCR	Boeing 737-8AS	Ryanair/Malta Air	
9H-QCS	Boeing 737-8AS	Ryanair/Malta Air	
9H-QCT	Boeing 737-8AS	Ryanair/Malta Air	
9H-QCU	Boeing 737-8AS	Ryanair/Malta Air	
9H-QCV	Boeing 737-8AS	Ryanair/Malta Air	
9H-QCW	Boeing 737-8AS	Ryanair/Malta Air	
9H-QCX	Boeing 737-8AS	Ryanair/Malta Air	
9H-QCY	Boeing 737-8AS	Ryanair/Malta Air	
9H-QCZ	Boeing 737-8AS	Ryanair/Malta Air	
9H-QDA	Boeing 737-8AS	Ryanair/Malta Air	
9H-QDB	Boeing 737-8AS	Ryanair/Malta Air	
9H-QDC	Boeing 737-8AS	Ryanair/Malta Air	
9H-QDD	Boeing 737-8AS	Ryanair/Malta Air	
9H-QDE	Boeing 737-8AS	Ryanair/Malta Air	
9H-QDF	Boeing 737-8AS	Ryanair/Malta Air	
9H-QDG	Boeing 737-8AS	Ryanair/Malta Air	
9H-QDH	Boeing 737-8AS	Ryanair/Malta Air	
9H-QDI	Boeing 737-8AS	Ryanair/Malta Air	
9H-QDJ	Boeing 737-8AS	Ryanair/Malta Air	
9H-QDK	Boeing 737-8AS	Ryanair/Malta Air	
9H-QDL	Boeing 737-8AS	Ryanair/Malta Air	
9H-QDM	Boeing 737-8AS	Ryanair/Malta Air	
9H-QDN	Boeing 737-8AS	Ryanair/Malta Air	
9H-QDO	Boeing 737-8AS	Ryanair/Malta Air	
9H-QDP	Boeing 737-8AS	Ryanair/Malta Air	
9H-QDQ	Boeing 737-8AS	Ryanair/Malta Air	
9H-QDR	Boeing 737-8AS	Ryanair/Malta Air	
9H-QDS	Boeing 737-8AS	Ryanair/Malta Air	
9H-QDT	Boeing 737-8AS	Ryanair/Malta Air	
9H-QDU	Boeing 737-8AS	Ryanair/Malta Air	
9H-QDV	Boeing 737-8AS	Ryanair/Malta Air	
9H-QDW	Boeing 737-8AS	Ryanair/Malta Air	
9H-QDX	Boeing 737-8AS	Ryanair/Malta Air	
9H-QDY	Boeing 737-8AS	Ryanair/Malta Air	
9H-QDZ	Boeing 737-8AS	Ryanair/Malta Air	
9H-QEA	Boeing 737-8AS	Ryanair/Malta Air	
9H-QEB	Boeing 737-8AS	Ryanair/Malta Air	
9H-QEC	Boeing 737-8AS	Ryanair/Malta Air	
9H-QED	Boeing 737-8AS	Ryanair/Malta Air	
9H-QEE	Boeing 737-8AS	Ryanair/Malta Air	
9H-QEF	Boeing 737-8AS	Ryanair/Malta Air	
9H-QEG	Boeing 737-8AS	Ryanair/Malta Air	
9H-QEH	Boeing 737-8AS	Ryanair/Malta Air	
9H-QEI	Boeing 737-8AS	Ryanair/Malta Air	
9H-QEJ	Boeing 737-8AS	Ryanair/Malta Air	
9H-QEK	Boeing 737-8AS	Ryanair/Malta Air	
9H-QEL	Boeing 737-8AS	Ryanair/Malta Air	
9H-QEM	Boeing 737-8AS	Ryanair/Malta Air	
9H-QEN	Boeing 737-8AS	Ryanair/Malta Air	
9H-QEO	Boeing 737-8AS	Ryanair/Malta Air	
9H-QEP	Boeing 737-8AS	Ryanair/Malta Air	

Notes	Reg	Type	Owner or Operator
	9H-QEW	Boeing 737-8AS	Ryanair/Malta Air
	9H-SOL	Airbus A.340-313X	Hi Fly Malta
	9H-SUN	Airbus A.340-313X	Hi Fly Malta
	9H-SZN	Airbus A.330-941	Hi Fly Malta
	9H-TAJ	Airbus A.330-343	Hi Fly Malta

9K (Kuwait)

	9K-AOC	Boeing 777-369ER	Kuwait Airways *Failaka*
	9K-AOD	Boeing 777-369ER	Kuwait Airways *Ul Almaradim*
	9K-AOE	Boeing 777-369ER	Kuwait Airways *Kathma*
	9K-AOF	Boeing 777-369ER	Kuwait Airways *Kubbar*
	9K-AOH	Boeing 777-369ER	Kuwait Airways *Warbah*
	9K-AOI	Boeing 777-369ER	Kuwait Airways *Meskan*
	9K-AOJ	Boeing 777-369ER	Kuwait Airways *Bubiyan*
	9K-AOK	Boeing 777-369ER	Kuwait Airways *Auhah*
	9K-AOL	Boeing 777-369ER	Kuwait Airways *Al Wafrah*
	9K-AOM	Boeing 777-369ER	Kuwait Airways *Garouh*
	9K-APA	Airbus A.330-243	Kuwait Airways
	9K-APB	Airbus A.330-243	Kuwait Airways
	9K-APC	Airbus A.330-243	Kuwait Airways
	9K-APD	Airbus A.330-243	Kuwait Airways
	9K-APE	Airbus A.330-243	Kuwait Airways
	9K-APF	Airbus A.330-841N	Kuwait Airways
	9K-APG	Airbus A.330-841N	Kuwait Airways
	9K-CAQ	Airbus A.320-251N	Jazeera Airways
	9K-CBB	Airbus A.320-251N	Jazeera Airways
	9K-CBC	Airbus A.320-251N	Jazeera Airways
	9K-CBD	Airbus A.320-251N	Jazeera Airways
	9K-CBE	Airbus A.320-251N	Jazeera Airways
	9K-CBF	Airbus A.320-251N	Jazeera Airways

9M (Malaysia)

	9M-MAB	Airbus A.350-941	Malaysian Airlines
	9M-MAC	Airbus A.350-941	Malaysian Airlines
	9M-MAD	Airbus A.350-941	Malaysian Airlines
	9M-MAE	Airbus A.350-941	Malaysian Airlines
	9M-MAF	Airbus A.350-941	Malaysian Airlines
	9M-MAG	Airbus A.350-941	Malaysian Airlines

9V (Singapore)

	9V-SFI	Boeing 747-412F	Singapore Airlines Cargo
	9V-SFK	Boeing 747-412F	Singapore Airlines Cargo
	9V-SFM	Boeing 747-412F	Singapore Airlines Cargo
	9V-SFN	Boeing 747-412F	Singapore Airlines Cargo
	9V-SFO	Boeing 747-412F	Singapore Airlines Cargo
	9V-SFP	Boeing 747-412F	Singapore Airlines Cargo
	9V-SFQ	Boeing 747-412F	Singapore Airlines Cargo
	9V-SJA	Airbus A.350-941	Singapore Airlines
	9V-SKF	Airbus A.380-841	Singapore Airlines
	9V-SKG	Airbus A.380-841	Singapore Airlines
	9V-SKH	Airbus A.380-841	Singapore Airlines
	9V-SKI	Airbus A.380-841	Singapore Airlines
	9V-SKJ	Airbus A.380-841	Singapore Airlines
	9V-SKK	Airbus A.380-841	Singapore Airlines
	9V-SKL	Airbus A.380-841	Singapore Airlines
	9V-SKM	Airbus A.380-841	Singapore Airlines
	9V-SKN	Airbus A.380-841	Singapore Airlines
	9V-SKP	Airbus A.380-841	Singapore Airlines
	9V-SKQ	Airbus A.380-841	Singapore Airlines
	9V-SKR	Airbus A.380-841	Singapore Airlines
	9V-SKS	Airbus A.380-841	Singapore Airlines
	9V-SKT	Airbus A.380-841	Singapore Airlines
	9V-SKU	Airbus A.380-841	Singapore Airlines
	9V-SKV	Airbus A.380-841	Singapore Airlines
	9V-SKW	Airbus A.380-841	Singapore Airlines
	9V-SKY	Airbus A.380-841	Singapore Airlines
	9V-SKZ	Airbus A.380-841	Singapore Airlines

Reg	Type	Owner or Operator	Notes
9V-SMA	Airbus A.350-941	Singapore Airlines	
9V-SMB	Airbus A.350-941	Singapore Airlines	
9V-SMC	Airbus A.350-941	Singapore Airlines	
9V-SMD	Airbus A.350-941	Singapore Airlines	
9V-SME	Airbus A.350-941	Singapore Airlines	
9V-SMF	Airbus A.350-941	Singapore Airlines	
9V-SMG	Airbus A.350-941	Singapore Airlines	
9V-SMH	Airbus A.350-941	Singapore Airlines	
9V-SMI	Airbus A.350-941	Singapore Airlines	
9V-SMJ	Airbus A.350-941	Singapore Airlines	
9V-SMK	Airbus A.350-941	Singapore Airlines	
9V-SML	Airbus A.350-941	Singapore Airlines	
9V-SMM	Airbus A.350-941	Singapore Airlines	
9V-SMN	Airbus A.350-941	Singapore Airlines	
9V-SMO	Airbus A.350-941	Singapore Airlines	
9V-SMP	Airbus A.350-941	Singapore Airlines	
9V-SMQ	Airbus A.350-941	Singapore Airlines	
9V-SMR	Airbus A.350-941	Singapore Airlines	
9V-SMS	Airbus A.350-941	Singapore Airlines	
9V-SMT	Airbus A.350-941	Singapore Airlines	
9V-SMU	Airbus A.350-941	Singapore Airlines	
9V-SMV	Airbus A.350-941	Singapore Airlines	
9V-SMW	Airbus A.350-941	Singapore Airlines	
9V-SMY	Airbus A.350-941	Singapore Airlines	
9V-SMZ	Airbus A.350-941	Singapore Airlines	
9V-SNA	Boeing 777-312ER	Singapore Airlines	
9V-SNB	Boeing 777-312ER	Singapore Airlines	
9V-SNC	Boeing 777-312ER	Singapore Airlines	
9V-SWA	Boeing 777-312ER	Singapore Airlines	
9V-SWB	Boeing 777-312ER	Singapore Airlines	
9V-SWD	Boeing 777-312ER	Singapore Airlines	
9V-SWE	Boeing 777-312ER	Singapore Airlines	
9V-SWF	Boeing 777-312ER	Singapore Airlines	
9V-SWG	Boeing 777-312ER	Singapore Airlines	
9V-SWH	Boeing 777-312ER	Singapore Airlines	
9V-SWI	Boeing 777-312ER	Singapore Airlines	
9V-SWJ	Boeing 777-312ER	Singapore Airlines	
9V-SWK	Boeing 777-312ER	Singapore Airlines	
9V-SWL	Boeing 777-312ER	Singapore Airlines	
9V-SWM	Boeing 777-312ER	Singapore Airlines	
9V-SWN	Boeing 777-312ER	Singapore Airlines	
9V-SWO	Boeing 777-312ER	Singapore Airlines	
9V-SWP	Boeing 777-312ER	Singapore Airlines	
9V-SWQ	Boeing 777-312ER	Singapore Airlines	
9V-SWR	Boeing 777-312ER	Singapore Airlines	
9V-SWS	Boeing 777-312ER	Singapore Airlines	
9V-SWT	Boeing 777-312ER	Singapore Airlines	
9V-SWU	Boeing 777-312ER	Singapore Airlines	
9V-SWV	Boeing 777-312ER	Singapore Airlines	
9V-SWW	Boeing 777-312ER	Singapore Airlines	
9V-SWY	Boeing 777-312ER	Singapore Airlines	
9V-SWZ	Boeing 777-312ER	Singapore Airlines	

9XR (Rwanda)

Reg	Type	Owner or Operator	Notes
9XR-WN	Airbus A.330-343E	Rwand Air	
9XR-WP	Airbus A.330-343E	Rwand Air	
9XR-WS	Airbus A.330-941	Rwand Air	
9XR-WT	Airbus A.330-941	Rwand Air	

9H-QCS Boeing
737-8AS of
Ryanair/Malta Air
Allan S. Wright

Some of the key radio frequencies used by busier airports and airfields are listed below.
TWR = Tower   APP = Approach   A/G = Air Ground or Flight Information Service
Radio frequencies can and do change during the life of this publication; this information should not be used operationally.

	TWR	APP	A/G		TWR	APP	A/G
Aberdeen	118.100	119.050		Jersey	119.450	120.300	
Alderney	125.350	128.650		Kemble			118.900
Andrewsfield			130.550	Land's End	120.250		
Barton			120.250	Lasham			131.030
Barrow		123.200		Leeds Bradford	120.300	123.750	
Beccles			120.380	Leicester			122.125
Belfast International	118.300	128.500		Liverpool	126.350	119.850	
Belfast City	122.825	130.850		London City	118.075	132.700	
Bembridge			123.255	Luton	132.550	129.550	
Biggin Hill	134.800	129.400		Lydd			120.700
Birmingham	118.300	118.050		Manchester	135.000	118.575	
Blackbushe			122.300	Netherthorpe			123.275
Blackpool	118.405	119.955		Newcastle	119.700	124.375	
Bodmin			120.330	Newquay	134.375	133.400	
Bourn		124.350		North Denes			123.400
Bournemouth	125.605	119.480		North Weald			123.530
Breighton			129.805	Norwich	124.250	119.350	
Bristol	133.850	125.650		Nottingham EMA	124.000	134.175	
Caernarfon			122.250	Old Warden			130.700
Cambridge	125.905	120.965		Oxford	133.425	125.325	
Cardiff	133.100	125.850		Penzance			120.060
Carlisle	123.605	120.965		Perth	119.800		
Clacton			118.155	Popham			129.805
Compton Abbas			122.700	Prestwick	118.150	120.550	
Conington			129.725	Redhill	119.600		
Cosford	128.650	135.875		Rochester			122.250
Coventry	124.800	119.250		Ronaldsway IOM	119.005	135.905	
Cranfield	134.925	122.850		Sandown			119.280
Cumbernauld	120.600			Sandtoft			130.425
Denham			130.725	Scilly Isles	123.825		
Doncaster RHA	128.775	126.225		Seething			118.435
Dundee	122.900			Sherburn			122.600
Dunkeswell			123.475	Shipdham			132.255
Durham Tees Valley	119.805	118.855		Shobdon			123.500
Duxford			122.075	Shoreham	125.400	123.150	
Earls Colne			122.425	Sibson			122.330
Edinburgh	118.700	121.200		Sleap			122.450
Elstree			122.400	Southampton	118.200	128.850	
Exeter	119.805	128.980		Southend	127.725	128.950	
Fairoaks			123.425	Stansted	123.800	120.625	
Farnborough	122.500	134.350		Stapleford			122.800
Fenland			122.925	Sumburgh	118.250	131.300	
Fowlmere			135.705	Swansea			119.700
Gamston			130.475	Sywell			122.700
Gatwick	124.225	126.825		Tatenhill			124.075
Glasgow	118.800	119.100		Thruxton			130.450
Gloucester/Staverton	122.900	128.550		Tollerton (Nottingham)			134.875
Goodwood			122.450	Wellesbourne			124.025
Guernsey	119.950	128.650		Welshpool			128.000
Haverfordwest			122.205	White Waltham			122.605
Hawarden	124.950	123.350		Wick			119.700
Henstridge			130.255	Wickenby			122.450
Headcorn			122.210	Wolverhampton			123.300
Heathrow	118.500	119.725		Woodford	120.700	130.750	
Hethel			122.350	Woodvale	119.750	121.000	
Hucknall			130.800	Wycombe Air Park			126.55
Humberside	124.900	119.125		Yeovil	125.400	130.800	
Inverness			122.600				

Those listed below identify many of the UK and overseas carriers appearing in the book

Code	Airline	Reg	Code	Airline	Reg	Code	Airline	Reg
AAL	American Airlines	N	DHK	DHL Air	D/G	NVQ	Nouvelair	TS
AAR	Asiana Airlines	HL	DLA	Air Dolomiti	I	NVR	Novair Airlines	SE
ABO	Air Atlanta Icelandic	TF	DLH	Lufthansa	D	OAE	Omni Air International	N
ABR	ASL Airlines Ireland	EI	DTR	Danish Air Transport	OY	OAW	Helvetic Airways	HB
ABW	AirBridge Cargo	RA	EDW	Edelweiss Air	HB	OHY	Onur Air	TC
ABX	ABX Air	N	EIN	Aer Lingus	EI	OMA	Oman Air	A4O
ACA	Air Canada	C	ELY	El Al	4X	OVA	Air Europa	EC
AEE	Aegean Airlines	SX	ENT	Enter Air	SP	PAC	Polar Air Cargo	N
AFL	Aeroflot	RA	ENZ	Jota Aviation	G	PAL	Philippine Airlines	RP
AFR	Air France	F	ETD	Etihad Airways	A6	PGT	Pegasus Airlines	TC
AHY	Azerbaijan Airlines	4K	ETH	Ethiopian Airlines	ET	PIA	Pakistan International	AP
AIC	Air-India	VT	EVA	EVA Airways	B	PLM	Wamos Air	EC
AIZ	Arkia Israel Airlines	4X	EWG	Eurowings	D	PVG	Privilege Style	EC
AJA	Anadolujet	TC	EXS	Jet2.com	G	QFA	QANTAS	VH
AJT	Amerijet International	N	EZE	Eastern Airways	G	QTR	Qatar Airways	A7
ALK	SriLankan Airlines	4R	EZS	easyJet Switzerland	HB	RAM	Royal Air Maroc	CN
AMC	Air Malta	9H	EZY	easyJet	G	RBA	Royal Brunei Airlines	V8
AMX	Aeromexico	XA	FAH	ASL Airlines Hungary	HA	RJA	Royal Jordanian	JY
ANA	All Nippon Airways	JA	FDX	Federal Express	N	ROT	Tarom	YR
ANE	Air Nostrum	EC	FHY	Freebird Airlines	TC	RWD	RwandAir	9XR
ASL	Air Serbia	YU	FIN	Finnair	OH	RYR	Ryanair	EI
ATW	Air Antwerp	OO	FLI	Atlantic Airways	OY	RZO	Azores Airlines	CS
AUA	Austrian Airlines	OE	FPO	ASL Airlines France	F	SAA	South African Airways	ZS
AUI	Ukraine International	UR	GCR	Tianjin Airlines	B	SAS	SAS	SE/ OY/LN
AUR	Aurigny A/S	G	GEC	Lufthansa Cargo	D	SIA	Singapore Airlines	9V
AVA	AVIANCA	HK	GFA	Gulf Air	A9C	SQC	Singapore Airlines Cargo	9V
AWC	Titan Airways	G	GIA	Garuda Indonesia Airlines	PK	SRR	Star Air	OY
AWT	Albawings	ZA	GTI	Atlas Air	N	STK	Stobart Air	EI
AXE	AirExplore	OM	GWI	Germanwings	D	SUS	Sun-Air	OY
AZA	Alitalia	I	HFY	HiFly	CS	SVA	Saudi Arabian Airlines	HZ
BAW	British Airways	G	HVN	Vietnam Airlines	VN	SWN	West Atlantic Airlines	SE
BBC	Biman Bangladesh	S2	IAW	Iraqi Airways	YI	SWR	Swiss International	HB
BBD	Bluebird Cargo	TF	IBE	Iberia	EC	SXS	SunExpress	TC
BCI	Blue Islands	G	IBS	Iberia Express	EC	TAM	TAM Linhas Aereas	PT
BCS	European A/T	OO	ICE	Icelandair	TF	TAP	TAP Portugal	CS
BCY	CityJet	EI	ICV	Cargolux Italia	I	TAR	Tunis Air	TS
BEL	Brussels Airlines	OO	IOS	Isles of Scilly Skybus	G	TAY	ASL Airlines Belgium	OO
BGA	Airbus Tpt International	F	IRA	Iran Air	EP	TFL	TUIfly	PH
BGH	BH Air	LZ	JAF	TUI Airlines Belgium	OO	TGZ	Georgian Airways	4L
BLC	TAM Linhas Aereas	PT	JAL	Japan Airlines	JA	THA	Thai Airways International	HS
BLX	TUIfly Nordic	SE	JOR	Blue Air	YR	THY	Turkish Airlines	TC
BOX	AeroLogic	D	KAC	Kuwait Airways	9K	TOM	TUIfly	G
BPA	Blue Panorama	I	KAL	Korean Air	HL	TRA	Transavia	PH
BRU	Belavia	EW	KLC	KLM CityHopper	PH	TSC	Air Transat	C
BTI	Air Baltic	YL	KLM	KLM	PH	TUA	Turkmenistan Airlines	EZ
BUC	Bulgarian Air Charter	LZ	KQA	Kenya Airways	5Y	TUI	TUIfly	D,G
CAI	Corendon Airlines	TC	KZR	Air Astana	UN	TVF	Transavia France	F
CAL	China Airlines	B	LAV	Alba Star	EC	TVS	Travel Service/Smart Wings	OK
CCA	Air China	B	LBT	Nouvelair	TS	TWI	Tailwind Airlines	TC
CCM	Air Corsica	F	LGL	Luxair	LX	UAE	Emirates Airlines	A6
CES	China Eastern	B	LOG	Loganair	G	UAL	United Airlines	N
CFE	BA Cityflyer	G	LOT	LOT Polish Airlines	SP	UPS	United Parcel Service	N
CFG	Condor	D	LTC	Smart Lynx Airlines	YL	UZB	Uzbekistan Airways	UK
CGF	Cargo Air	LZ	LZB	Bulgaria Air	LZ	VDA	Volga-Dnepr Airlines	RA
CHH	Hainan Airlines	B	MAC	Air Arabia Maroc	CN	VIR	Virgin Atlantic Airways	G
CJT	Cargojet Airways	C	MAS	Malaysian Airlines	9M	VLG	Vueling Airlines	EC
CKS	Kalitta Air	N	MAU	Air Mauritius	3B	VOE	Volotea Airlines	EC
CLH	Lufthansa CityLine	D	MEA	Middle East Airlines	OD	WHT	White Airways	CS
CLJ	Cello Aviation	G	MLD	Air Moldova	ER	WIF	Wideroe's	LN
CLU	CargoLogicAir	G	MMZ	Euro Atlantic Airways	CS	WJA	Westjet	C
CLX	Cargolux	LX	MNG	MNG Airlines	TC	WZZ	Wizz Air	HA
CPA	Cathay Pacific	B	MPH	Martinair	PH			
CRL	Corsair	F	MSR	EgyptAir	SU			
CSA	CSA Czech Airlines	OK	NAX	Norwegian Air Shuttle	LN			
CSN	China Southern Airlines	B	NCA	Nippon Cargo Airlines	JA			
CSW	Silkway Italia	I	NOS	Neos	I			
CTN	Croatia Airlines	9A	NPT	West Atlantic Airlines	G			
DAH	Air Algerie	7T	NRS	Norwegian Air UK	G			
DAL	Delta Air Lines	N	NVD	Avion Express	LY			

447

The British Aircraft Preservation Council was formed in 1967 to co-ordinate the works of all bodies involved in the preservation, restoration and display of historical aircraft. In October 2017 the organisation celebrated its fiftieth anniversary and changed its name to Aviation Heritage UK. Membership covers the whole spectrum of national, Service, commercial and voluntary groups, and meetings are held regularly at the bases of member organisations. The organisation is able to provide a means of communication, helping to resolve any misunderstandings or duplication of effort. Every effort is taken to encourage the raising of standards of both organisation and technical capacity amongst the member groups to the benefit of everyone interested in aviation. To assist historians, the B.A.P.C. register has been set up and provides an identity for those aircraft which do not qualify for a Service serial or inclusion in the UK Civil Register whether located in the UK or overseas.

Note: Registrations/Serials carried are mostly false identities.
FSM = Full Scale Model, MPA = Man Powered Aircraft, IHM = International Helicopter Museum.
The aircraft, listed as 'models' are generally intended for exhibition purposes and are not airworthy although they are full scale replicas. However, in a few cases the machines have the ability to taxi when used for film work.

Aircraft on the current B.A.P.C. Register are as follows.

Notes	Reg	Type	Owner or Operator
	1	Roe Triplane Type 4 (replica)	Shuttleworth Collection as G-ARSG (not carried)
	2	Bristol Boxkite (replica)	Shuttleworth Collection as G-ASPP (not carried)
	3	Bleriot Type XI	Shuttleworth Collection as G-AANG (not carried)
	4	Deperdussin Monoplane	Shuttleworth Collection as G-AANH (not carried)
	5	Blackburn Monoplasne	Shuttleworth Collection as G-AANI (not carried)
	6	Roe Triplane Type IV (replica)	Manchester Museum of Science & Industry
	7	Southampton University MPA	Solent Sky, Southampton
	8	Dixon ornithopter	Shuttleworth Collection
	9	Humber Monoplane (replica)	Midland Air Museum (Coventry)
	10	Hafner R.11 Revoplane	International Helicopter Museum/Weston-Super-Mare
	11	English Electric Wren Composite	Shuttleworth Collection
	12	Mignet HM.14	Manchester Museum of Science and Industry
	13	Mignet HM.14	Brimpex Metal Treatments
	14	Addyman Standard Training Glider	A. Lindsay & N. H. Ponsford
	15	Addyman Standard Training Glider	The Aeroplane Collection
	16	Addyman ultra-light aircraft	N. H. Ponsford
	17	Woodhams Sprite	BB Aviation/Canterbury
	18	Killick MP gyroplane	A. Lindsay & N. H. Ponsford
	19	Bristol F.2b Fighter	Musee Royal de l'Armee Brussels
	20	Lee-Richards annular biplane (replica)	Visitor Centre Shoreham Airport
	21	D. H. 82A Tiger Moth	Newark Air Museum
	22	Mignet HM.14 (G-AEOF)	Aviodome, Netherlands
	23	SE-5A Scale Model	Newark Air Museum
	24	Currie Wot (replica)	Newark Air Museum
	25	Nyborg TGN-III glider	Warwick
	28	Wright Flyer (replica)	Yorkshire Air Museum Elvington
	29	Mignet HM.14 (G-ADRY)	Brooklands Museum of Aviation/Weybridge
	32	Crossley Tom Thumb	Midland Air Museum
	33	DFS.108-49 Grunau Baby IIb	Denmark
	34	DFS.108-49 Grunau Baby IIb	D. Elsdon
	35	EoN primary glider	–
	36	Fieseler Fi 103 (V-1) (replica)	Kent Battle of Britain Museum/Hawkinge
	37	Blake Bluetit (G-BXIY)	The Shuttleworth Collection/Old Warden
	38	Bristol Scout replica (A1742)	Shuttleworth Trust
	39	Addyman Zephyr sailplane	A. Lindsay & N. H. Ponsford
	40	Bristol Boxkite (replica)	Bristol City Museum
	41	B.E.2C (replica) (6232)	Yorkshire Air Museum/Elvington
	42	Avro 504 (replica) (H1968)	Yorkshire Air Museum/Elvington
	43	Mignet HM.14	Newark Air Museum/Winthorpe
	44	Miles Magister (L6906)	Museum of Berkshire Aviation (G-AKKY)/Woodley
	45	Pilcher Hawk (replica)	Percy Pilcher Museum Rugby
	47	Watkins Monoplane	National Waterfront Museum Swansea
	48	Pilcher Hawk (replica)	Glasgow Museum of Transport
	49	Pilcher Hawk	Royal Scottish Museum/East Fortune
	50	Roe Triplane Type 1	Science Museum/South Kensington
	51	Vickers Vimy IV	Science Museum/South Kensington
	52	Lilienthal glider	National Museum of Science and Industry/Wroughton
	53	Wright Flyer (replica)	Science Museum/South Kensington

Reg	Type	Owner or Operator	Notes
54	JAP-Harding monoplane	Science Museum/South Kensington	
55	Levavasseur Antoinette VII	Science Museum/South Kensington	
56	Fokker E.III (210/16)	Science Museum/South Kensington	
57	Pilcher Hawk (replica)	Duxford	
58	Yokosuka MXY7 Ohka II (15-1585)	F.A.A. Museum/Yeovilton	
59	Sopwith Camel (replica) (D3419)	East Fortune	
60	Murray M.1 helicopter	International Helicopter Museum/Weston-super-Mare	
61	Stewart man-powered ornithopter	Boston Lincolnshire	
62	Cody Biplane (304)	Science Museum/South Kensington	
63	Hurricane (replica) (P3208)	Kent Battle of Britain Museum/Hawkinge	
64	Hurricane (replica) (P3059)	Kent Battle of Britain Museum/Hawkinge	
65	Spitfire (replica) (N3289)	Kent Battle of Britain Museum/Hawkinge	
66	Bf 109 (replica) (1480)	Kent Battle of Britain Museum/Hawkinge	
67	Bf 109 (replica) (14)	Kent Battle of Britain Museum/Hawkinge	
68	Hurricane (replica) (H3426)	–	
69	Spitfire (replica) (N3313)	Kent Battle of Britain Museum/Hawkinge	
70	Auster AOP.5 (TJ398)	North East Aircraft Museum/Usworth	
71	Spitfire (replica) (P8140)	Norfolk & Suffolk Aviation Museum	
72	Hurricane (model) (V6779)	Gloucestershire Aviation Collection	
73	Hurricane (replica)	New Zealand	
74	Bf 109 (replica) (6357)	Kent Battle of Britain Museum/Hawkinge	
75	Mignet HM.14 (G-AEFG)	N. H. Ponsford	
76	Mignet HM.14 (G-AFFI)	Yorkshire Air Museum/Elvington	
77	Mignet HM.14 (replica) (G-ADRG)	Lower Stondon Transport Museum	
78	Hawker Hind (K5414) (G-AENP)	The Shuttleworth Collection/Old Warden	
79	Fiat G.46-4B (MM53211)	Norfolk	
80	Airspeed Horsa (KJ351)	Museum of Army Flying/Middle Wallop	
81	Hawkridge Dagling	stored Bedford	
82	Hawker Hind (Afghan)	RAF Museum/Cosford	
83	Kawasaki Ki-100-1b (24)	RAF Museum/Hendon	
84	Nakajima Ki-46 (Dinah III)(5439)	RAF Museum/Cosford	
85	Weir W-2 autogyro	Museum of Flight/East Fortune	
86	de Havilland Tiger Moth (replica)	Yorkshire Aircraft Preservation Society	
87	Bristol Babe (replica) (G-EASQ)	Bristol Aero Collection/Kemble	
88	Fokker Dr 1 (replica) (102/17)	F.A.A. Museum/Yeovilton	
89	Cayley glider (replica)	Yorkshire Air Museum/Elvington	
90	Colditz Cock (replica)	Imperial War Museum/South Lambeth	
91	Fieseler Fi 103 (V-1)	Germany	
92	Fieseler Fi 103 (V-1)	RAF Museum/Hendon	
93	Fieseler Fi 103 (V-1)	Imperial War Museum/Duxford	
94	Fieseler Fi 103 (V-1)	RAF Museum/Cosford	
95	Gizmer autogyro	F. Fewsdale	
96	Brown helicopter	North East Aircraft Museum	
97	Luton L.A.4A Minor	North East Aircraft Museum	
98	Yokosuka MXY7 Ohka II (997)	Manchester Museum of Science & Industry	
99	Yokosuka MXY7 Ohka II (8486M)	RAF Museum/Cosford	
100	Clarke Chanute biplane gliderr	RAF Museum/Hendon	
101	Mignet HM.14	Newark Air Museum/Winthorpe	
102	Mignet HM.14	Not completed	
103	Hulton hang glider (replica)	Personal Plane Services Ltd	
105	Blériot XI (replica)	San Diego Aerospace Museum	
106	Blériot XI (164)	RAF Museum/Hendon	
107	Blériot XXVII	RAF Museum/Hendon	
108	Fairey Swordfish IV (HS503)	Stafford	
109	Slingsby Kirby Cadet TX.1	–	
110	Fokker D.VII replica (static) (5125)	USA	
111	Sopwith Triplane replica (static) (N5492)	F.A.A. Museum/Yeovilton	
112	DH.2 replica (static) (5964)	Museum of Army Flying/Middle Wallop	
113	S.E.5A replica (static) (B4863)	Orlando Florida	
114	Vickers Type 60 Viking (static) (G-EBED)	Brooklands Museum of Aviation/Weybridge	
115	Mignet HM.14	Norfolk & Suffolk Aviation Museum/Flixton	
116	Santos-Dumont Demoiselle (replica)	–	
117	B.E.2C (replica)(1701)	Stored Hawkinge	
119	Bensen B.7	North East Aircraft Museum	
120	Mignet HM.14 (G-AEJZ)	South Yorkshire Aviation Museum/Doncaster	

Notes	Reg	Type	Owner or Operator
	121	Mignet HM.14 (G-AEKR)	South Yorkshire Aviation Society
	122	Avro 504 (replica) (1881)	Stored
	123	Vickers FB.5 Gunbus (replica)	A. Topen (stored)/Cranfield
	124	Lilienthal Glider Type XI (replica)	Science Museum/South Kensington
	126	D.31 Turbulent (static)	Midland Air Museum/Coventry
	127	Halton Jupiter MPA	Wannock Eastbourne
	128	Watkinson Cyclogyroplane Mk IV	IHM/Weston-super-Mare
	129	Blackburn 1911 Monoplane (replica)	–
	130	Blackburn 1912 Monoplane (replica)	Yorkshire Air Museum/Elvington
	131	Pilcher Hawk (replica)	C. Paton
	132	Blériot XI (G-BLXI)	Montelimar France
	133	Fokker Dr 1 (replica) (425/17)	Kent Battle of Britain Museum/Hawkinge
	134	Pitts S-2A static (G-AXNZ)	Istanbul Turkey
	135	Bristol M.1C (replica) (C4912)	Stored
	136	Deperdussin Seaplane (replica)	Planes of Fame Musem Chino/USA
	137	Sopwith Baby Floatplane (replica) (8151)	Stored
	138	Hansa Brandenburg W.29 Floatplane (replica) (2292)	Stored
	139	Fokker Dr 1 (replica) 150/17	Orlando Florida
	140	Curtiss 42A (replica)	Planes of Fame Museum Chino USA
	141	Macchi M39 (replica)	Planes of Fame Museum Chino USA
	142	SE-5A (replica) (F5459)	Switzerland
	143	Paxton MPA	–
	144	Weybridge Mercury MPA	–
	145	Oliver MPA	Stored
	146	Pedal Aeronauts Toucan MPA	Stored
	147	Bensen B.7	Norfolk & Suffolk Aviation Museum/Flixton
	148	Hawker Fury II (replica) (K7271)	High Ercall Aviation Museum
	149	Short S.27 (replica)	F.A.A. Museum (stored)/Yeovilton
	150	SEPECAT Jaguar GR.1 (replica) (XX728)	Oman
	151	SEPECAT Jaguar GR.1 (replica) (XZ363)	RAF M & R Unit/St. Athan
	152	BAe Hawk T.1 (replica) (XX227)	RAF M & R Unit/Bottesford
	153	Westland WG.33	IHM/Weston-super-Mare
	154	D.31 Turbulent	Lincolnshire Aviation Museum/E. Kirkby
	155	Panavia Tornado GR.1 (model) (ZA556)	RAF M & R Unit/St. Athan
	156	Supermarine S-6B (replica)	Planes of Fame Museum Chino/USA
	157	Waco CG-4A(237123)	Yorkshire Air Museum/Elvington
	158	Fieseler Fi 103 (V-1)	Defence Ordnance Disposal School/Chattenden
	159	Yokosuka MXY7 Ohka II	Imperial War Museum/Duxford
	160	Chargus 18/50 hang glider	Museum of Flight/East Fortune
	161	Stewart Ornithopter Coppelia	stored Louth
	162	Goodhart MPA	Science Museum/Wroughton
	163	AFEE 10/42 Rotabuggy (replica)	Museum of Army Flying/Middle Wallop
	164	Wight Quadruplane Type 1 (replica)	Solent Sky, Southampton
	165	Bristol F.2b (E2466)	RAF Museum/Hendon
	166	Bristol F.2b (D7889)	Canada
	167	Bristol SE-5A	USA
	168	DH.60G Moth (static replica)	Stored Hawkinge (G-AAAH)
	169	BAC/Sepecat Jaguar GR.1 (XX110)	RAF Training School/Cosford
	170	Pilcher Hawk (replica)	–
	171	BAe Hawk T.1 (model) (XX308)	RAF Marketing & Recruitment Unit/Bottesford
	172	Chargus Midas Super 8 hang glider	Science Museum/Wroughton
	173	Birdman Promotions Grasshopper	Science Museum/Wroughton
	174	Bensen B.7	Science Museum/Wroughton
	175	Volmer VJ-23 Swingwing	Manchester Museum of Science & Industry
	176	SE-5A (replica) (A4850)	Bygone Times Antiques Warehouse/Eccleston
	177	Avro 504K (replica) (G-AACA)	Brooklands Museum of Aviation/Weybridge
	178	Avro 504K (replica) (E373)	–
	179	Sopwith Pup (replica) (A7317)	Sywell
	180	McCurdy Silver Dart (replica)	Reynolds Pioneer Museum/Canada
	181	RAF B.E.2b (replica) (687)	RAF Museum/Hendon
	182	Wood Ornithopter	Manchester Museum of Science & Industry
	183	Zurowski ZP.1 helicopter	Newark Air Museum/Winthorpe
	184	Spitfire IX (replica) (EN398)	Sleap

Reg	Type	Owner or Operator	Notes
185	Waco CG-4A (243809)	Museum of Army Flying/Middle Wallop	
186	DH.82B Queen Bee (LF789)	de Havilland Aircraft Heritage Museum/London Colney	
187	Roe Type 1 biplane (replica)	Brooklands Museum of Aviation/Weybridge	
188	McBroom Cobra 88	Science Museum/Wroughton	
189	Bleriot XI (replica)	Stored	
190	Spitfire (replica) (K5054)	P. Smith/Hawkinge	
191	BAe Harrier GR.7 (model) (ZH139)	RAF M & R Unit/St. Athan	
192	Weedhopper JC-24	The Aeroplane Collection	
193	Hovey WD-11 Whing Ding	The Aeroplane Collection	
194	Santos Dumont Demoiselle (replica)	Deutches Technikmuseum/Berlin	
195	Moonraker 77 hang glider	Museum of Flight/East Fortune	
196	Sigma 2M hang glider	Museum of Flight/East Fortune	
197	Scotkites Cirrus III hang glider	Museum of Flight/East Fortune	
198	Fieseler Fi 103 (V-1)	Imperial War Museum/Duxford	
199	Fieseler Fi 103 (V-1)	Science Museum/South Kensington	
200	Bensen B.7	stored Leeds	
201	Mignet HM.14	stored Hooton Park	
202	Spitfire V (model) (MAV467)	–	
203	Chrislea LC.1 Airguard (G-AFIN)	stored Dunkeswell	
204	McBroom hang glider	stored Hooton Park	
205	Hurricane (replica) (Z3427)	RAF Museum/Hendon	
206	Spitfire (replica) (MH486)	RAF Museum/Hendon	
207	Austin Whippet (replica) (K.158)	South Yorkshire Aviation Museum/Doncaster	
208	SE-5A (replica) (D276)	Prince's Mead Shopping Precinct/Farnborough	
209	Spitfire IX (replica) (MJ751)	Niagara Falls Canada	
210	Avro 504J (replica) (C4451)	Solent Sky, Southampton	
211	Mignet HM.14 (replica) (G-ADVU)	North East Aircraft Museum	
212	Bensen B.8	IHM/Weston-super-Mare	
213	Vertigo MPA	IHM/Weston-super-Mare	
214	Spitfire prototype (replica) (K5054)	Tangmere Military Aviation Museum	
215	Airwave hang-glider prototype	Solent Sky, Southampton	
216	DH.88 Comet (replica) (G-ACSS)	de Havilland Heritage Museum/London Colney	
217	Spitfire (replica) (K9926)	RAF Museum/Bentley Priory	
218	Hurricane (replica) (P3386)	RAF Museum/Bentley Priory	
219	Hurricane (replica) (L1710)	Northolt	
220	Spitfire 1 (replica) (N3194)	Shirleywich	
221	Spitfire LF.IX (replica) (MH777)	RAF Museum/Northolt	
222	Spitfire IX (replica) (BR600)	RAF Museum/Uxbridge	
223	Hurricane 1 (replica) (V7467)	RAF High Wycombe	
224	Spitfire V (replica) (BR600)	National Air Force Museum Trenton Canada	
225	Spitfire IX (replica) (P8448)	RAF Museum/Cranwell	
226	Spitfire XI (replica) (EN343)	RAF Museum/Benson	
227	Spitfire 1A (replica) (L1070)	RAF Museum/Turnhouse	
228	Olympus hang-glider	North East Aircraft Museum/Usworth	
229	Spitfire IX (replica) (MJ832)	RAF Museum/Digby	
230	Spitfire (replica) (AA550)	Eden Camp/Malton	
231	Mignet HM.14 (G-ADRX)	South Copeland Aviation Group	
232	AS.58 Horsa I/II	de Havilland Heritage Museum/London Colney	
233	Broburn Wanderlust sailplane	Museum of Berkshire Aviation/Woodley	
234	Vickers FB.5 Gunbus (replica)	Sywell	
235	Fieseler Fi 103 (V-1) (replica)	Eden Camp Wartime Museum	
237	Fieseler Fi 103 (V-1)	Netherlands	
238	Waxflatter ornithopter	Wycombe Air Park	
239	Fokker D.VIII 5/8 scale replica	Norfolk & Suffolk Aviation Museum/Flixton	
240	Messerschmitt Bf.109G replica	Yorkshire Air Museum/Elvington	
241	Hurricane 1 (replica) (L1679)	Tangmere Military Aviation Museum	
242	Spitfire Vb (replica) (BL924)	Tangmere Military Aviation Museum	
243	Mignet HM.14 (replica) (G-ADYV)	stored Malvern Wells	
244	Solar Wings Typhoon	Museum of Flight/East Fortune	
245	Electraflyer Floater hang glider	Museum of Flight/East Fortune	
246	Hiway Cloudbase hang glider	Museum of Flight/East Fortune	
247	Albatross ASG.21 hang glider	Museum of Flight/East Fortune	
248	McBroom hang glider	Museum of Berkshire Aviation/Woodley	

Notes	Reg	Type	Owner or Operator
	249	Hawker Fury 1 (replica) (K5673)	Brooklands Museum of Aviation/Weybridge
	250	RAF SE-5A (replica) (F5475)	Brooklands Museum of Aviation/Weybridge
	251	Hiway Spectrum hang glider (replica)	Manchester Museum of Science & Industry
	252	Flexiform Wing hang glider	Manchester Museum of Science & Industry
	253	Mignet HM.14 (G-ADZW)	Solent Sky/Southampton
	254	Hawker Hurricane (P3873)	Yorkshire Air Museum/Elvington
	255	NA P-51D Mustang (replica) (463209)	American Air Museum/Duxford
	256	Santos Dumont Type 20 (replica)	Brooklands Museum of Aviation/Weybridge
	257	DH.88 Comet (G-ACSS)	Sywell
	258	Adams balloon	British Balloon Museum
	259	Gloster Gamecock (replica)	Jet Age Museum Gloucestershire
	260	Mignet HM280	–
	261	GAL Hotspur (replica)	Museum of Army Flying/ Middle Wallop
	262	Catto CP-16	Museum of Flight/East Fortune
	263	Chargus Cyclone	Ulster Aviation Heritage/Langford Lodge
	264	Bensen B.8M	IHM/Weston-super-Mare
	265	Spitfire 1 (P3873)	Yorkshire Air Museum/Elvington
	266	Rogallo hang glider	Ulster Aviation Heritage
	267	Hurricane (model)	Imperial War Museum/Duxford
	268	Spifire (model)	stored St.Mawgan
	269	Spitfire (model) USAF	RAF Lakenheath
	270	DH.60 Moth (model)	Yorkshire Air Museum/Elvington
	271	Messerschmitt Me 163B	Shuttleworth Collection/Old Warden
	272	Hurricane (model)	Kent Battle of Britain Museum/Hawkinge
	273	Hurricane (model)	Kent Battle of Britain Museum/Hawkinge
	274	Boulton & Paul P.6 (model)	Pendeford Wolverhampton
	275	Bensen B.7 gyroglider	Doncaster Museum
	276	Hartman Ornithopter	Science Museum/Wroughton
	277	Mignet HM.14	Visitor Centre Shoreham Airport
	278	Hurricane (model)	Kent Battle of Britain Museum/Hawkinge
	279	Airspeed Horsa	RAF Shawbury
	280	DH.89A Dragon Rapide (model)	Crowne Plaza Hotel Speke
	281	Boulton & Paul Defiant (model)	Pendeford
	282	Manx Elder Duck	Isle of Man Airport Terminal
	283	Spitfire (model	Jurby, Isle of Man
	284	Gloster E.28/39 (model)	Lutterworth Leics
	285	Gloster E.28/39 (model)	Farnborough
	286	Mignet HM.14	Caernarfon Air Museum
	287	Blackburn F.2 Lincock (model)	Street Life Museum/Hull
	288	Hurricane (model)	Wonderland Pleasure Park, Mansfield
	289	Gyro Boat	IHM Weston-super-Mare
	290	Fieseler Fi 103 (V1) (model)	Dover Museum
	291	Hurricane (model)	National Battle of Britain Memorial, Capel-le-Ferne, Kent
	292	Eurofighter Typhoon (model)	RAF Museum/Hendon
	293	Spitfire (model)	RAF Museum/Hendon
	294	Fairchild Argus (model)	Visitor Centre, Thorpe Camp, Woodhall Spa
	295	Da Vinci hang glider (replica)	Skysport Engineering
	296	Army Balloon Factory NulII (replica)	RAF Museum, Hendon
	297	Spitfire (replica)	Kent Battle of Britain Museum/Hawkinge
	298	Spitfire IX (Model)	RAF Cosford Parade Ground
	299	Spitfire 1 (model).	National Battle of Britain Memorial, Capel-le-Ferne, Kent
	300	Hummingbird (replica)	Shoreham Airport Historical Association
	301	Spitfire V FSM (replica)	Thornaby Aerodrome Memorial, Thornaby-on-Tees
	302	Mignet HM.14 reproduction	Shoreham Airport Historical Association
	303	Goldfinch 161 Amphibian	Norfolk and Suffolk Aviation Museum, Flixton
	304	Supermaine Spitfire FSM	
	305	Mersnier pedal powered airship Reproduction	British Balloon Museum and Library
	306	Lovegrove Autogyro trainer	Norfolk and Suffolk Aviation Museum, Flixton
	307	Bleriot XI (replica)	
	308	Supermarine Spitfire 1 FSM	
	309	Fairey Gannet T.2 cockpit	The Aeroplane Collection, Hooton Park

Reg	Type	Owner or Operator	Notes
310	Miles Wings (Engineers) Ltd Gulp 100A Hang Glider	The Aeroplane Collection, Hooton Park	
311	GEC-Ferranti Phoenix UAV	National Museum of Flight, East Fortune	
312	Airwave Magic Kiss Hang Glider	National Museum of Flight, East Fortune	
313	Firebird Sierra Hang Glider	National Museum of Flight, East Fortune	
314	Gold Marque Gyr Hang Glider	National Museum of Flight, East Fortune	
315	Bensen B.8 Gyroglider	APSS/National Museum of Flight (Store), East Fortune	
316	Pilcher Bat Replica	Riverside Museum, Glasgow	
317	WACO CG-4A Hadrian cockpit	National Museum of Flight, East Fortune	
318	Supermarine Spitfire FSM (PT462)	H. Macleod, Moffatt, Dumfries and Galloway	
319	Supermarine Spitfire FSM (X4859)	No.1333 Sqn. Air Training Corps, Grangemouth	
320	Supermarine Spitfire FSM (EP121)	Air Station Heritage Centre, Montrose	
321	Royal Aircraft Factory BE.2c FSM	Air Station Heritage Centre, Montrose	
322	Handley Page Halifax III cockpit replica	Dumfries & Galloway Aviation Museum, Tinwald Downs	
323	Supermarine Spitfire Vb FSM (W3644)	Fairhaven Lake, Lytham St. Annes	
324	Supermarine Spitfire IX FSM (BS435)	Lytham Spitfire Display Team, Blackpool	
325	Supermarine Spitfire FSM (PL256)	Lytham Spitfire Display Team, Blackpool	
326	Supermaine Spitfire II FSM (X4253)	Lytham Spitfire Display Team, Blackpool	
327	Fiesler Fi.103 (FZG-76) FSM	Simon Pulford	
328	Avro F Type cabin reproduction	Museum of Science and Industry, Manchester	
329	Mignet HM.14 Pou-du-Ciel	Breighton	
330	Ward Gnome	Newark Air Museum, Winthorpe	
331	Gloster E28/39 FSM (W4041)		
332	Royal Aircraft Factory BE.2b reproduction (2783)	Boscombe Down Aviation Collection, Old Sarum	
333	Supermarine Spitfire II FSM (RG904)	Royal Air Force Museum, RAF Cosford	
334	Hawker Hurricane FSM (R4229)	Alexandra Park, Windsor	
335	Supermarine Spitfire IIa FSM (P7666)	RAF High Wycombe	
336	Northrop F-5E Tiger II FSM (01532)	RAF Alconbury	
337	Pilcher Bat Mk.3 reproduction	The Shuttleworth Collection, Old Warden	
338	Halton Aero Club Mayfly reproduction	Trenchard Museum, RAF Halton	
339	Husband Modac 500 Hornet Gyroplane	The Helicopter Museum, Weston-Super-Mare	
340	Dickson Primary Glider	Nigel Ponsford Collection	
341	Lockheed-Martin F-35 Lightning II FSM	Royal Air Force Museum, Hendon	
342	Lockheed-Martin F-35 Lightning II FSM	Royal Air Force	
343	Lockheed-Martin F-35 Lightning II FSM	Royal Air Force	
344	Fiesler Fi.103 (FZG-76/V-1)	Cornwall Aviation Heritage Centre, Newquay	
345	Fiesler Fi.103 (FZG-76/V-1)	Cornwall At War Museum, Davidstow Moor	
346	Hawker Hurricane (V7313)	Gate Guard, North Weald	
347	Colditz Cock reproduction	Gliding Heritage Centre, Lasham	
348	Sopwith 7F.1 Snipe reproduction	Royal Air Force Museum, Hendon	
349	de Havilland DH.103 Hornet F.1 cockpit composite	DH Hornet Project, Chelmsford	
350	TEAM Minimax Hi-MAX	LAA Build-A-Plane Project mobile exhibit	
351	Airspeed Horsa replica	Cobbaton Combat Collection, Chittlehampton	
352	Hawker Sea Hawk cockpit	Graham Sparkes/Fort Perch Museum, stored Hooton Park	
353	Sopwith 5F1 Dolphin composite (C3988)	Royal Air Force Museum, Hendon	
354	Sopwith Tabloid Floatplane reproduction	Brooklands Museum, Weybridge	
355	Slingsby T.7 Cadet (PD685)	Tettenhall Transport Heritage Centre, Wolverhampton	
356	BAe Systems Phoenix UAV composite	Medway Aircraft Preservation Society, Rochester	
357	BAC Lightning	BAe Systems, Salmesbury	
358	Boulton-Paul Overstrand cockpit reproduction (K4556)	Norfolk & Suffolk Aviation Museum, Flixton	
359	Cody Army Aeroplane No.1A reproduction	Farnborough Air Sciences Trust, Farnborough	
360	Eurofighter Typhoon FGR.4 FSM (IR106)	RAF Exhibition Unit	
361	Boeing-Vertol CH-47 Chinook HC.2 FSM (IR108)	RAF Exhibition Unit	
362	Hawker Fury reproduction (L1639)	Cambridge Bomber and Fighter Society, Cambridge	
363	Hawker Typhoon cockpit	Jet Age Museum, Staverton	

Notes	Reg	Type	Owner or Operator
	364	Kiceniuk Icsarus II	Norfolk & Suffolk Aviation Museum, Flixton
	365	Northrop MQM-36 Shelduck D.1 UAV (XT005)	Medway Aircraft Preservation Society, Rochester
	366	Percival E.2H Mew Gull reproduction (G-AEXF)	Royal Air Force Museum, Hendon
	367	Percival E.2H Mew Gull reproduction (G-AEXF)	Thorpe Camp Visitor Centre, Woodhall Spa
	368	Supermarine 361 Spitfire LF.XVIe (TD248)	Norfolk & Suffolk Aviation Museum, Flixton
	369	Supermarine Spitfire FSM (P7895)	Ulster Aviation Collection, Long Kesh
	370	WACO CG-4A reproduction (241079)	Royal Air Force Museum, RAF Cosford
	371	Westland Lysander FSM (V9875)	
	372	Wasp Falcon 4 Hang Glider	Norfolk & Suffolk Aviation Museum, Flixton
	373	Westland Whirlwind Mk.1 reproduction	Whirlwind Fighter Project
	374	Antonov C.12 Hang Glider	Norfolk & Suffolk Aviation Museum, Flixton
	375	Boeing Stearman PT-27 composite	Norfolk & Suffolk Aviation Museum, Flixton
	376	Messerschmidt Bf.109 FSM	Northern Forties Re-enactment Group
	377	Supermarine Spitfire IX FSM (EN398)	Northern Forties Re-enactment Group
	378	Hawker Hurricane IIc FSM (V7467)	Gate Guard, RAF High Wycombe
	379	Supermarine Spitfire FSM	Formerly with Dumfries & Galloway Aviation Museum, Tinwald Downs
	380	Vlackburn Triplane reproduction	Fort Paull Museum
	381	Westland Wallace reproduction	
	382	BAe 125 forward fuselage	Deeside College, Connah's Quay
	383	Airspeed Horsa cockpit reproduction	Jet Age Museum, Staverton
	384	Flight Refuelling Ltd Falconet UAV	Mark Oliver, Knutsford
	385	Sopwith F.1 Camel reproduction (D6447)	Mark Oliver, Knutsford
	386	Bristol F.28 Fighter replica (A7228)	Bristol Aero Collection, Filton
	387	Bristol F.2B Fighter replica	Bristol Aero Collection, Filton
	388	Short Stirling B.III composite	The Stirling Project, Alconbury
	389	Heinkel He.111 Recreation	Lincolnshire Aviation Heritage Centre, East Kirkby
	390	Felixstowe F.5 cockpit	Norfolk and Suffolk Aviation Museum, Flixton
	391	Cody Type V Bi-Plane reproduction	Farnborough Air Sciences Trust, Farnborough
	392	Avro RJX100	Bristol Aero Collection, Filton
	393	Supermarine Spitfire FSM (N3310/N3320)	Lodge Hill Garage, Abingdon
	394	Supermarine Spitfire 1 FSM (X4178)	Imperial War Museum, Duxford
	395	Pilatus P2-05 replica	Personal Plane Services, Booker
	396	Airspeed AS.51 Horsa II cockpit	Imperial War Museum, Duxford
	397	General Aircraft GAL.48 Hotspur II cockpit	Imperial War Museum, Duxford
	398	Bristol 156 Beaufighter VI cockpit	Midland Air Museum, Coventry
	399	Hawker Hurricane FSM (P2793)	Eden Camp Wartime Museum, Old Malton
	400	RAF FE.2b reproduction (A6526)	Royal Air Force Museum, Hendon
	401	Mignet HM.14 Pou-du-Ciel	Catford Independent Air Force
	402	Hawker Hurricane I composite (L1639)	Cambridge Bomber and Fighter Society, Cambridge
	403	Fieseler Fi.103 FSM (FZG-76/V-1)	Ulster Aviation Museum, Long Kesh
	404	Civilian Aircraft Company Coupe (incomplete)	Shipping and Airlines Ltd, Biggin Hill
	405	BGA.178 Manuel Crested Wing	Gliding Heritage Centre, Lasham
	406	Electro Flight Lightning P.1E FSM	Stroud
	407	DH.2 7/8 scale model	Great War Aerodrome, Stow Maries
	408	BAe Systems Phoenix UAV composite	Larkhill
	409	DH.82A Tiger Moth composite	Thorpe Camp Visitor Centre, Woodhall Spa
	410	Supermarine Spitfire FSM (P7370)	War and Peace, Ash
	411	Hawker Hurricane FSM (V6555)	War and Peace, Ash
	412	Gotha G.V. cockpit reproduction	Great War Aerodrome, Stow Maries
	413	Sopwith Strutter reproduction (A8274)	Great War Aerodrome, Stow Maries
	414	Sopwith F.1 Camel reproduction	Great War Aerodrome, Stow Maries
	415	ML Aviation Sprite UAV	Museum of Berkshire Aviation, Woodley
	416	ML Aviation Sprite UAV	Museum of Army Flying, Middle Wallop
	417	Airspeed Horsa replica	Museum of Army Flying, Middle Wallop
	418	Airspeed Horsa cockpit replica	Museum of Army Flying, Middle Wallop
	419	Fieseler Fi.103 (FZG-76/V-1) FSM	North East Land Sea and Air Museum, Usworth
	420	Vickers FB.27A Vimy cockpit	Brooklands Museum, Weybridge
	421	Vickers Wellington forward fuselage	Brooklands Museum, Weybridge

Reg	Type	Owner or Operator	Notes
422	Avro 683 Lancaster Composite cockpit	Avro Heritage Trust, Woodford	
423	EoN AP.5 Primary	Aircraft Restoration Group, Fishburn-Morgansfield	
424	Manchester University BAe. JAVA UAV	Museum of Science and Industry, Manchester	
425	Avro 683 Lancaster cockpit	Pitstone Museum	
426	Supermarine Spitfire IX FSM (MK805)	Simply Spitfires, Lowestoft	
427	Skyhook Safari powered hang glider	The Science Museum, Wroughton	
428	Cody man-lifting kite reproduction	Museum of Science and Industry, Manchester	
429	Bleriot XI cockpit	The Science Museum, South Kensington	
430	Army Balloon Factory Airship Beta II	The Science Museum, South Kensington	
431	Supermarine Spitfire FSM (K9998)	RAF Chapel, Biggin Hill	
432	Breen hang glider	Tettenhall Transport Heritage Collection, Wolverhampton	
433	Westland Whirlwind Mk.1 cockpit	City of Norwich Aviation Museum	
434	DH.98 Mosquito recreation (HJ711)	Yorkshire Air Museum, Elvington	
435	WACO CG-4A Hadrian cockpit	Museum of Military Life, Carlisle	
436	Bristol 152 Beaufort composite (DD931)	Royal Air Force Museum, Hendon	
437	Lilienthal Kleiner Doppeldecker reproduction	Shuttleworth Collection	
438	Lilienthal Normal Apparatus reproduction	Shuttleworth Collection	
439	Lilienthal Type XI glider reproduction	Shuttleworth Collection	
440	Lovegrove Rota-Glida Gyro-Glider	The Gyrocopter Experience, Rufforth	
441	Pilcher Triplane reproduction	Shuttleworth Collection	
442	Sopwith Baby Composite (N2078)	Fleet Air Arm Museum, Yeovilton	
443	WACO CG-4A Hadrian cockpit reproduction	South Yorkshire Aviation Museum, Doncaster	
444	Westland WG-25 Mote remotely piloted helicopter	The Helicopter Museum, Weston-Super-Mare	
445	Westland WG-25 Wideye remotely piloted helicopter	The Helicopter Museum, Weston-Super-Mare	
446	Westland WG-25 Wisp remotely piloted helicopter	The Helicopter Museum, Weston-Super-Mare	
447	Yamaha Motors remotely piloted helicopter	The Helicopter Museum, Weston-Super-Mare	
448	Bleriot XI reproduction	Caernafon Airworld Museum	
449	HP.61 Halifax B.III composite(LV907/NP763)	Yorkshire Air Museum, Elvington	
450	Hawker Siddeley Harrier composite	The Helicopter Museum, Weston-Super-Mare	
451	Westland WG-25 Sharpeye remotely piloted helicopter	The Helicopter Museum, Weston-Super-Mare	
452	Sopwith Strutter replica (N5177/B9708)	In store, Mersham, Surrey	
453	F-35B Lightning II ground training aid	Fleet Air Arm, RNAS Culdrose	
454	F-35B Lightning II ground training aid	Fleet Air Arm, RNAS Culsrose	
455	F-35B Lightning FSM	Fleet Air Arm, RNAS Culdrose	
456	Supermarine Spitfire FSM	Seymour-Johnson AFB, USA	
457	Supermarine Spitfire Mk.VIII FSM (A58-492)	RAAF Museum, Point Cook, Victoria	
458	P-51D Mustang FSM	Business Park, Auckland, New Zealand	
459	Levasseur PL.8 biplane 7/8 scale FSM	Peninsular Hotel, Paris	
460	Supermarine Spitfire V FSM	Oxfordshire	
461	Supermarine Spitfire cockpit FSM		
462	Supermarine Spitfire cockpit FSM		
463	Bristol 156 Beaufighter IIF cockpit	Royal Air Force Museum, Hendon	
464	P-51D Mustang FSM 'Duchess Arlene'	Tuskegee, Alabama, USA	
465	Fieseler Fi.103 FSM (FZG-76/V-1)	RAF Manston Museum	
466	Huntair Pathfinder 2	RAF Manston Museum	
467	Nieuport 17 reproduction (A213)	RAF Manston Museum	
468	Sopwith Strutter reproduction (B619)	RAF Manston Museum	
469	Nieuport 17 reproduction	RAF Manston Museum	
470	DH.60G Gipsy Moth FSM (G-AAAH)	Paragon Station, Hull	
471	Avro 683 Lancaster cockpit reproduction	Mobile exhibit, Lincolnshire	
472	Morane-Saulnier N reproduction	North-East Land Sea Air Museum, Usworth	
473	Messerschmitt Bf.109 FSM	War and Peace, Ash, Kent	
474	Philips British Matchless Flying Machine	Shuttleworth Collection	
475	Hawker Hurricane 1 FSM	The Battle of Britain Bunker, Uxbridge	
476	Supermarine Spitfire cockpit reproduction (TB885)	Biggin Hill Heritage Limited	
477	Hawker Hurricane FSM	St. George's Chapel of Remembrance, Biggin Hill	
478	Supermarine Spitfire cockpit reproduction	RAF Elsham Wolds Memorial Garden	
479	Bleriot XI reproduction	Under construction, Ipswich	

Notes	Reg	Type	Owner or Operator
	480	Ferranti/Slingsby T.68 Phoenix UAV	National Museum of Flight Scotland, East Fortune
	481	Mignet HM.14 Pou-du-Ciel ('G-ADRZ')	Aircraft Restoration Group, Masham
	482	Avro Lancaster cockpit reproduction	Staffordshire
	483	Supermarine Spitfire II cockpit reproduction	Staffordshire
	484	British Aerospace Harrier Composite (XV281)	South Yorkshire Aviation Museum, Doncaster
	485	GAF Jindivik Mk.103A (A-92-466 RAAF)	Boscombe Down Aviation Collection
	486	Curtiss P-40N Warhawk FSM	GateGuards UK Ltd
	487	Curtiss P-40N Warhawk FSM	GateGuards UK Ltd
	488	Curtiss P-40N Warhawk FSM	GateGuards UK Ltd
	489	North American P-51D Mustang FSM	GateGuards UK Ltd
	490	North American P-51D Mustang FSM	GateGuards UK Ltd
	491	North American P-51D Mustang FSM	GateGuards UK Ltd
	492	Supermarine Spitfire FSM	GateGuards UK Ltd
	493	Supermarine Spitfire FSM	Planes of Fame Air Museum, Chino, USA
	494	Supermarine Spitfire Cockpit Reproduction	Cornwall Aviation
	495	Supermarine Spitfire V FSM (L2016)	Makoanyane Square, Kingsway, Maseru, Lesotho
	496	Bristol F.2b Fighter Reconstruction	Bristol Aero Collection, Filton
	497	Comper/Cranwell Light Aeroplane Club CLA.4	Alberta Aviation Museum, Edmonton, Canada
	498	Avro 616 Avian IVA Reproduction (G-ABCF)	Guy Menzies Memorial, Hari Hari, New Zealand
	499	DH.82A Tiger Moth Reproduction	Hokitika Airport, New Zealand
	500	Supermarine Spitfire FSM (L1035)	Battle of Britain Bunker & Visitor Centre, Uxbridge
	501	Northrop Shelduck D.1 Composite	Muckleburgh Collection, Weybourne
	502	Short 184 Reproduction (N9190)	Estonian Maritime Museum, Tallinn
	503	Airspeed AS Horsa Fuselage	Dumfries and Galloway Aviation Museum
	504	deHavilland DH.9	Royal Saudi Air Force Musem, Riyadh
	505	Westland Wapiti Reproduction	Royal Saudi Air Force Musem, Riyadh
	506	Vickers Type 60 Viking 7/8 scale model (G-CAEB)	Alberta Aviation Museum, Canada
	507	Bristol 86A Tourer Reproduction (G-AUDK)	Aviation Heritage Museum of Western Australia, Perth
	508	Sopwith F.1 Camel Reproduction (M6394)	Aviation Heritage Museum of Western Australia, Perth
	509	Hinkler Ibis Reproduction	Hinkler House Memorial Museum, Bundaberg
	510	Sopwith Triplane Reproduction (N500)	Aerospace Museum, Calgary, Canada
	511	D.H.83 Fox Moth reproduction (ZK-ADI)	Max Dowell, Hokitika Airport, Westland District, New Zealand
	512	P-51D Mustang cockpit reproduction (44-14134)	Gary Dean, Wiltshire
	513	Supermarine Spitfire FSM	Essex Memorial Spitfire Monument, Essex, Ontario, Canada
	514	Miles M.25 Martinet Cockpit composite (RG907)	Transport Heritage Centre, West Midlands
	515	TASUMA Observer Concept UAV	Newark Air Museum
	516	TASUMA Navigator CSV30 UAV	Newark Air Museum
	517	TASUMA Navigator CSV30 UAV	Newark Air Museum
	518	EE Canberra PR.9 Cockpit	Newark Air Museum
	519	Supermarine Spitfire IX FSM (JK769)	South African Air Force Museum
	520	BAC Concorde scale model (F-WTSA)	Flugausstellung Hermeskeil, Rheinland-Palatinate, Germany
	521	Hawker Hurricane I FSM composite	North East Land, Sea and Air Museum, Usworth
	522	Supermarine Spitfire FSM	Andy Harper, Blackpool
	523	Supermarine Spitfire cockpit reproduction	Lytham Spitfire Display Team
	524	Morane-Saulnier MS.406 cockpit repro.	Lytham Spitfire Display Team
	525	Messerschmitt Bf.109 cockpit reproduction	Lytham Spitfire Display Team
	526	Hawker Typhoon reproduction (JP656)	Le Memorial de Caen, France
	527	Supermarine Spitfire Vc FSM (JK715)	The Classic Flyers Museum, Tauranga, New Zealand
	528	Fairey Swordfish reproduction (DK791)	The Classic Flyers Museum, Tauranga, New Zealand
	529	BAe Systems Tempest Concept Model	BAe Systems travelling exhibit
	530	Supermarine Spitfire IX two third scale model (BS306)	Greenwood Military Aviation Museum, Nova Scotia

Reg	Type	Owner or Operator	Notes
531	QinetiQ Zephyr 6 (6-1)	Farnborough Air Sciences Trust, Farnborough	
532	QinetiQ Zephyr 6 (6-2)	The Winchester Science Centre	
533	Bensen B.8 Gyrocopter	The South Yorkshire Aircraft Museum, Doncaster	
534	Hawker Typhoon IB Cockpit	The South Yorkshire Aircraft Museum, Doncaster	
535	Hawker Typhoon IB Cockpit	The South Yorkshire Aircraft Museum, Doncaster	
536	Hawker Tempest II Cockpit	The South Yorkshire Aircraft Museum, Doncaster	
537	Ford Flivver Reproduction	The South Yorkshire Aircraft Museum, Doncaster	
538	Supermarine Spitfire FSM (ML296)	The Czech Spitfire Club	
539	Supermarine Spitfire FSM (R6599)	Romney Marsh Wartime Collection, Brenzett	
540	Supermarine Spitfire I FSM	Fenland and West Norfolk Aviation Museum, Bambers Garden Centre	
541	Supermarine Spitfite IX FSM (EN398)	GB Replicas, RAF Coningsby	
542	Supermarine Spitfire IX FSM (542)	The Aviodrome Museum, Lelystad	
543	Avro 594 Avian Reproduction (G-CAVB)	Fort Edmonton Park, Edmonton, Alberta	
544	Handley Page Halifax cockpit reproduction	Lincolnshire Aviation Heritage Centre, East Kirkby	
545	Bae SysteMS Demon UAV	Aerospace Brisol, Filton	
546	Grumman AA-5B Tiger cockpit	Great War Museum, Stoke Maries	
547	Eastbourne Monoplane replica	Cornwall Aviation Heritage Centre, Newquay	
548	Hawker Hunter composite	The Aeropark, East Midlands Airport	
549	Sopwith Triplane reproduction (N5902)	Hangar Flight Museum, Calgary	
550	Fieseler Fi.103 FSM	Muckleburgh Collection, Weybourne, Norfolk	
551	Hawker Hurricane FSM (LK-A)	Shoot Aviation, White Waltham	
552	Supermarine Spitfire IX FSM (EN398)	Aircraft Maintenance Support Services, Pyle	
553	Avro 683 Lancaster cockpit reproduction	Lincolnshire Aviation Collection, East Kirkby	
554	Supermarine Spitfire V reproduction	Airframe Assemblies Ltd	
555	Supermarine Spitfire FSM (EN398)	Spitfire Spares, Graham Adlam, Taunton	
556	Hawker Typhoon FSM	Spitfire Spares, Graham Adlam, Taunton	
557	Royal Aircraft Factory SE.5A reproduction (E1294)	The Warbird and Wheels Museum, Wanaka	
558	Airspeed AS.5 Horsa reproduction (PF800)	Pegasus Bridge Museum, Benouville	
559	Flight Refuelling Falconet UAV	The Museum of Army Flying, Middle Wallop	
560	TASUMA MMT-100 UAV	The Museum of Army Flying, Middle Wallop	
561	Westland WG-25/WR-06 Wisp	The Museum of Army Flying, Middle Wallop	
562	Westland WG-25/WR-07 Wideye	The Museum of Army Flying, Middle Wallop	
563	Aerospatiale AS.365 Dauphin composite	Survivex, Kirkhill Commercial Park, Aberdeen	
564	Gotha VI reproduction	Kent Battle of Britain Museum, Hawkinge	
565	Fokker Dr.1 Triplane reproduction	Kent Battle of Britain Museum, Hawkinge	
566	Messerschmitt Bf.110 reproduction	Kent Battle of Britain Museum, Hawkinge	
567	Sopwith F.1 Camel reproduction (D8118)	Graham Holmes, Chalfont	
568	Adams-Wilson Hobbycopter		
569	Fieseler Fi.103 FSM	Le Val Ygot, Ardouval, Normandy	
570	Fieseler Fi.103 FSM	Avesnes-Chaussoy, Sum, Hauts-de-France	
571	Horvath No.3 reproduction	Atrium of the Budapest Sofitrl Hotel	
572	Junkers Ju-87 FSM	Omaka Aviation Heritage Centre, Blenheim, New Zealand	
573	Goodwin-Kent GK3 Racer	David Kent, Turweston	
574	Percival P.56 Provost T.1 cockpit recreation	Leicester Aviation Restoration Workshop	
575	Supermarine Spitfire XVIe FSM (TB592)	Aviation Heritage Museum of Western Australia	
576	Junkers Ju.87 reproduction	The Museum on the Demarcation Line, Rokycany	
577	Avro 683 Lancaster cockpit reproduction	Malcolm Goosey	
578	Vickers Type 22 Monoplane reproduction	Southward Car Museum, Papaparaumu, New Zealand	
579	Passat Ornithopter	In store, Old Rhinebeck, New York	

Reg	Type	Owner or Operator
Reg	Type	Owner or Operator

Reg	Type	Owner or Operator

Reg	Type	Owner or Operator

Reg	Type	Owner or Operator

Reg	Type	Owner or Operator

Reg	Type	Owner or Operator

OVERSEAS AIRLINER REGISTRATIONS

D (Germany)

| D-AIEH | Airbus A.321-271NX | Lufthansa |